ELECTRONIC ENGINE CONTROLS MANUAL 1978 to 1985

Managing Editor John H. Weise, S.A.E. □ **Assistant Managing Editor** David H. Lee, A.S.E., S.A.E.
Technical Editor Tony Molla, S.A.E.

Service Editors Nick D'Andrea, Martin Gunther, Robert McAnally,
Michael D. Powers, Jack T. Kaufmann, Lawrence C. Braun
Editorial Consultants Edward K. Shea, S.A.E., Stan Stephenson

Production Manager John Cantwell
Manager Editing & Design Dean F. Morgantini
Art & Production Coordinator Robin S. Miller
Supervisor Mechanical Paste Up Margaret Stoner
Mechanical Artists Cynthia Fiore, Bill Gaskins

National Sales Manager Albert M. Kushnerick □ **Assistant** Jacquelyn T. Powers
Regional Managers Joseph Andrews, Jr., James O. Callahan, David Flaherty

OFFICERS
President Lawrence A. Fornasieri
Vice President & General Manager John P. Kushnerick

CHILTON BOOK COMPANY Chilton Way, Radnor, Pa. 19089

Manufactured in USA © 1985 Chilton Book Company ISBN 0-8019-7545-X
Library of Congress Catalog Card No. 83-45291

2345678901 4321098765

HOW TO USE THIS MANUAL

For ease of use, this manual is divided into sections:

The **CONTENTS,** inside the front cover, summarize the subjects covered in each section.

To quickly locate the proper service section, use the chart on the following pages. It references applicable **CAR MODELS** and **SERVICE SECTIONS** for major engine performance control systems.

It is recommended that the service technician be familiar with the applicable **GENERAL INFORMATION** and **SERVICE PRE-CAUTIONS** (if any) before testing or servicing the system.

Major service sections are grouped by individual vehicle or component manufacturers. Each manufacturer's sub-section contains:

☐ **GENERAL INFORMATION** Information pertaining to the operation of the system, individual components and the overall logic by which components work together.

☐ **SERVICE PRECAUTIONS (if any)** Precautions of which the service technician should be aware to prevent injury or damage to the vehicle or components.

☐ **TESTS, ADJUSTMENTS, AND COMPONENT R & R** Performance tests and specifications, adjustments and component replacement procedures.

☐ **FAULT DIAGNOSIS** Complete troubleshooting for the entire system.

SAFETY NOTICE

Proper service and repair procedures are vital to the safe, reliable operation of all motor vehicles, as well as the personal safety of those performing repairs. This manual outlines procedures for servicing and repairing vehicles using safe effective methods. The procedures contain many NOTES, CAUTIONS and WARNINGS which should be followed along with standard safety procedures to eliminate the possibility of personal injury or improper service which could damage the vehicle or compromise its safety.

It is important to note that repair procedures and techniques, tools and parts for servicing motor vehicles, as well as the skill and experience of the individual performing the work vary widely. It is not possible to anticipate all of the conceivable ways or conditions under which vehicles may be serviced, or to provide cautions as to all of the possible hazards that may result. Standard and accepted safety precautions and equipment should be used when handling toxic or flammable fluids, and safety goggles or other protection should be used during cutting, grinding chiseling, prying, or any other process that can cause material removal or projectiles.

Some procedures require the use of tools specially designed for a specific purpose. Before substituting another tool or procedure, you must be completely satisfied that neither your personal safety, nor the performance of the vehicle will be endangered.

PART NUMBERS

Part numbers listed in this reference are not recommendations by Chilton for any product by brand name. They are references that can be used with interchange manuals and aftermarket supplier catalogs to locate each brand supplier's discrete part number.

Although information in this manual is based on industry sources and is as complete as possible at the time of publication, the possibility exists that some car manufacturers made later changes which could not be included here. While striving for total accuracy, Chilton Book Company cannot assume responsibility for any errors, changes, or omissions that may occur in the compilation of this data.

QUICK LOCATOR INDEX

310-A

COMPUTERIZED ENGINE CONTROL APPLICATIONS

Manufacturer	Year	Engine	SECTION 4 Electronic Ignition System	SECTION 5 Computer Control System	SECTION 6 Feedback Carburetor	SECTION 7 Fuel Injection System
Ford	1983–85	1.6L	DuraSpark III	EEC IV	—	EFI
		2.3L	DuraSpark II	MCU	C-YFA	—
		2.3L HSC	DuraSpark III	EEC IV	H-6149	—
		5.0L	DuraSpark III	EEC IV	—	CFI
		5.0L	DuraSpark II	MCU	H-4180C	
General Motors	1978–79	4 cyl	HEI	EFC	R-E2SE	—
		6 cyl	HEI	C4	R-E2SE	—
		8 cyl	HEI	C4	R-E2SE, E4SE	—
		8 cyl⑱	HEI	EFI	—	AFC
	1980	4 cyl	HEI	C4	R-E2SE	—
		6 cyl	HEI	C4	R-E2SE	—
		8 cyl	HEI	⑲	R-E2SE, E4SE	—
	1981	all	HEI	CCC	R-E2SE, E4SE, R-M4ME, M2ME	⑪
	1982	all (carb)	HEI	CCC	R-E2SE, E4SE, R-M4ME, M2ME	—
		all (fuel inj)	HEI	CCC	—	TBI⑪
	1983	all (carb)	HEI	CCC	R-E2SE, E4SE, R-M2ME, M4ME	—
		4 cyl (fuel inj)	HEI	CCC	—	MFI
		8 cyl (fuel inj)	HEI	CCC	—	TBI
	1984–85	4 cyl	HEI	CCC	—	MFI
		6 cyl	HEI⑳	CCC	—	㉑
		8 cyl	HEI	CCC	㉒	㉓

AFC—Air Flow Controlled
CIS—Constant Injection System
TBI—Throttle Body Injection
C—Carter carburetor
R—Rochester carburetor
H—Holley carburetor
M—Motorcraft carburetor
EGI—Electronic Gasoline Injection
ECCS—Electronic Concentrated Engine Control
MCU—Microprocessor Control Unit
EEC—Electronic Engine Controls
C4—Computer Controlled Catalytic Converter
CCC—Computer Command Control
EFC—Electronic Fuel Control
EIS—Electronic Ignition System
EFI—Electronic Fuel Injection
CFI—Central Fuel Injection
① CEC system on some models

② Carter BBD used on engine with CEC system
③ Bosch impulse generator or Hall effect distributor
④ Mikuni carburetor on some models
⑤ CIS on 320i models
⑥ Bosch L-Jetronic up to 1982. Motronic on 1983 and later (except 320i)
⑦ Combustion control computer used on Imperial models with fuel injection
⑧ EFC on carbureted engines
⑨ Holley 6500 on California models
⑩ EFI on Lincoln and Mark IV. Carter thermo quad (TQ) on 4 bbl models
⑪ Digital Fuel Injection on Cadillac models
⑫ Bosch K-Jetronic (KE-Jetronic on 1984 and later models)

⑬ 1984 models use Bosch Constant Idle Speed system in addition to fuel inj.
⑭ Schlumberger ignition system on 505 models
⑮ 1984 and later 911 uses Bosch Motronic System
⑯ CIS on 1979 240 Federal models
⑰ AFC on California; TBI on Federal
⑱ Cadillac only
⑲ CCC system used on some 1980 1/2 models
⑳ Computer Controlled Coil Ignition (C31) used on Buick V6 engines
㉑ MFI, SFI fuel injection systems on Buick models
㉒ E2SE, E4SE, M2SE or M4SE on carbureted engines
㉓ TBI or MFI on fuel injected engines
㉔ DITC or DME system on some models

Manufacturer	Year	Engine	SECTION 4 Electronic Ignition System	SECTION 5 Computer Control System	SECTION 6 Feedback Carburetor	SECTION 7 Fuel Injection System
Isuzu	1983–85	Impulse	EIS	I-TEC	—	AFC
Mazda	1984–85	13B	Nippondenso	EGI	—	AFC
Mercedes-Benz	1978–85	all	Bosch ③	Bosch ⑬	—	CIS ⑫
Mitsubishi	1983–85	1.8L	EIS	ECI	—	TBI
	85	2.6L	EIS	ECI	—	TBI
Nissan (Datsun)	1982–85	2.8L	Hitachi	ECCS	—	AFC
	85	3.0L	Hitachi	ECCS	—	AFC
Oldsmobile			See General Motors			
Peugeot	1980–85	1.9L	Ducellier ⑭	Bosch K-Jet	—	CIS
Pontiac			See General Motors			
Porsche	1979	all	Bosch ③	Bosch	—	CIS
	1980–85	924, 944	Bosch ㉔	Bosch	—	AFC
	1980–85	911, 928 ⑮	Bosch ㉔	Bosch	—	CIS
Renault	1981–85	18i, Fuego	Ducellier	Bosch	—	AFC
	1983–85	Alliance, Encore	Ducellier	Bosch	—	⑰

AFC—Air Flow Controlled
CIS—Constant Injection System
TBI—Throttle Body Injection
C—Carter carburetor
R—Rochester carburetor
H—Holley carburetor
M—Motorcraft carburetor
EGI—Electronic Gasoline Injection
ECCS—Electronic Concentrated Engine Control
MCU—Microprocessor Control Unit
EEC—Electronic Engine Controls
C4—Computer Controlled Catalytic Converter
CCC—Computer Command Control
EFC—Electronic Fuel Control
EIS—Electronic Ignition System
EFI—Electronic Fuel Injection
CFI—Central Fuel Injection
① CEC system on some models
② Carter BBD used on engine with CEC system

③ Bosch impulse generator or Hall effect distributor
④ Mikuni carburetor on some models
⑤ CIS on 320i models
⑥ Bosch L-Jetronic up to 1982. Motronic on 1983 and later (except 320i)
⑦ Combustion control computer used on Imperial models with fuel injection
⑧ EFC on carbureted engines
⑨ Holley 6500 on California models
⑩ EFI on Lincoln and Mark IV. Carter thermo quad (TQ) on 4 bbl models
⑪ Digital Fuel Injection on Cadillac models
⑫ Bosch K-Jetronic (KE-Jetronic on 1984 and later models)
⑬ 1984 models use Bosch Constant Idle Speed system in addition to fuel inj.
⑭ Schlumberger ignition system on 505 models

⑮ 1984 and later 911 uses Bosch Motronic System
⑯ CIS on 1979 240 Federal models
⑰ AFC on California; TBI on Federal
⑱ Cadillac only
⑲ CCC system used on some 1980 1/2 models
⑳ Computer Controlled Coil Ignition (C31) used on Buick V6 engines
㉑ MFI, SFI fuel injection systems on Buick models
㉒ E2SE, E4SE, M2SE or M4SE on carbureted engines
㉓ TBI or MFI on fuel injected engines
㉔ DITC or DME system on some models

Continued

COMPUTERIZED ENGINE CONTROL APPLICATIONS

Manufacturer	Year	Engine	SECTION 4 Electronic Ignition System	SECTION 5 Computer Control System	SECTION 6 Feedback Carburetor	SECTION 7 Fuel Injection System
American Motors	1980	4 cyl	HEI	C4	R-E2SE	—
		6 cyl	HEI	CEC	C-BBD	—
	1981	4 cyl	HEI	C4	R-E2SE	—
		6 cyl	SSI	CEC	C-BBD	—
	1982	4 cyl	HEI	C4①	R-E2SE②	—
		6 cyl	SSI	CEC	C-BBD	—
	1983–85	4 cyl	SSI	C4	E2SE	—
		6 cyl	SSI	CEC	BBD	—
Audi	1978–84	all	Bosch③	Bosch K-Jet	—	CIS
	1984–85	all	Bosch③	Bosch KE-Jet	—	CIS
BMW	1978–82	all	Bosch③	Bosch K-Jet	—	AFC⑤
	1983–85	all	Bosch③	Motronic	—	AFC⑤
Buick	——————————————— See General Motors ———————————————					
Cadillac	——————————————— See General Motors ———————————————					
Chevrolet	——————————————— See General Motors ———————————————					
Chrysler	1979–80	4 cyl	Hall	EFC	H-5220	—
		6 cyl	EIS	EFC	C-BBD	—
		8 cyl	EIS	EFC	C-TQ	—
	1981–82	4 cyl	EIS	EFC	H-6520④	—
		6 cyl	EIS	EFC	H-6145	—
		8 cyl	EIS	EFC	C-BBD	—
		8 cyl	EIS	CCC⑦	—	EFI

AFC—Air Flow Controlled
CIS—Constant Injection System
TBI—Throttle Body Injection
C—Carter carburetor
R—Rochester carburetor
H—Holley carburetor
M—Motorcraft carburetor
EGI—Electronic Gasoline Injection
ECCS—Electronic Concentrated Engine Control
MCU—Microprocessor Control Unit
EEC—Electronic Engine Controls
C4—Computer Controlled Catalytic Converter
CCC—Computer Command Control
EFC—Electronic Fuel Control
EIS—Electronic Ignition System
EFI—Electronic Fuel Injection
CFI—Central Fuel Injection
① CEC system on some models
② Carter BBD used on engine with CEC system

③ Bosch impulse generator or Hall effect distributor
④ Mikuni carburetor on some models
⑤ CIS on 320i models
⑥ Bosch L-Jetronic up to 1982. Motronic on 1983 and later (except 320i)
⑦ Combustion control computer used on Imperial models with fuel injection
⑧ EFC on carbureted engines
⑨ Holley 6500 on California models
⑩ EFI on Lincoln and Mark IV. Carter thermo quad (TQ) on 4 bbl models
⑪ Digital Fuel Injection on Cadillac models
⑫ Bosch K-Jetronic (KE-Jetronic on 1984 and later models)
⑬ 1984 models use Bosch Constant Idle Speed system in addition to fuel inj.

⑭ Schlumberger ignition system on 505 models
⑮ 1984 and later 911 uses Bosch Motronic System
⑯ CIS on 1979 240 Federal models
⑰ AFC on California; TBI on Federal
⑱ Cadillac only
⑲ CCC system used on some 1980 1/2 models
⑳ Computer Controlled Coil Ignition (C3I) used on Buick V6 engines
㉑ MFI, SFI fuel injection systems on Buick models
㉒ E2SE, E4SE, M2SE or M4SE on carbureted engines
㉓ TBI or MFI on fuel injected engines
㉔ DITC or DME system on some models

Manufacturer	Year	Engine	SECTION 4 Electronic Ignition System	SECTION 5 Computer Control System	SECTION 6 Feedback Carburetor	SECTION 7 Fuel Injection System
Chrysler	1983–85	1.6L	EIS	EFC	H-6520	—
		1.7L	EIS	EFC	H-6520	—
		2.2L	EIS	EFI⑧	—	AFC
		2.6L	EIS	EFI⑧	—	TBI
		3.7L	EIS	EFC	H-6145	—
		5.2L	EIS	EFC⑦	C-TQ	—
Datsun			See Nissan			
Fiat	1980–85	1.7L	Marelli	Bosch L-Jet	—	AFC
		2.0L	Bosch	Bosch L-Jet	—	AFC
Ford	1978–79	2.3L	DuraSpark	EEC I	H-5200⑨	—
		2.8L	DuraSpark	EEC I	M-2700VV	—
		5.0L	DuraSpark	EEC I	M-2700VV	—
		5.8L	DuraSpark	EEC II	H-2150	—
	1980	4 cyl	DuraSpark	EEC II	H-5200	—
		6 cyl	DuraSpark	EEC II	C-YFA	—
		8 cyl	DuraSpark II	MCU	C-BBD⑩	—
		8 cyl	DuraSpark II	EEC III	M-7200VV	—
	1981	4 cyl	DuraSpark II	MCU	H-6500	—
		6 cyl	DuraSpark II	MCU	H-1946	—
		8 cyl	DuraSpark II	MCU	—	CFI
		8 cyl	DuraSpark II	EEC III	M-7200VV	—
	1982	4 cyl	TFI	MCU	H-6500	—
		6 cyl	DuraSpark II	MCU	C-YFA	—
		8 cyl	DuraSpark II	MCU	H-4180C	—
		8 cyl	DuraSpark II	EEC III	—	CFI

AFC—Air Flow Controlled
CIS—Constant Injection System
TBI—Throttle Body Injection
C—Carter carburetor
R—Rochester carburetor
H—Holley carburetor
M—Motorcraft carburetor
EGI—Electronic Gasoline Injection
ECCS—Electronic Concentrated Engine Control
MCU—Microprocessor Control Unit
EEC—Electronic Engine Controls
C4—Computer Controlled Catalytic Converter
CCC—Computer Command Control
EFC—Electronic Fuel Control
EIS—Electronic Ignition System
EFI—Electronic Fuel Injection
CFI—Central Fuel Injection
① CEC system on some models

② Carter BBD used on engine with CEC system
③ Bosch impulse generator or Hall effect distributor
④ Mikuni carburetor on some models
⑤ CIS on 320i models
⑥ Bosch L-Jetronic up to 1982. Motronic on 1983 and later (except 320i)
⑦ Combustion control computer used on Imperial models with fuel injection
⑧ EFC on carbureted engines
⑨ Holley 6500 on California models
⑩ EFI on Lincoln and Mark IV. Carter thermo quad (TQ) on 4 bbl models
⑪ Digital Fuel Injection on Cadillac models
⑫ Bosch K-Jetronic (KE-Jetronic on 1984 and later models)

⑬ 1984 models use Bosch Constant Idle Speed system in addition to fuel inj.
⑭ Schlumberger ignition system on 505 models
⑮ 1984 and later 911 uses Bosch Motronic System
⑯ CIS on 1979 240 Federal models
⑰ AFC on California; TBI on Federal
⑱ Cadillac only
⑲ CCC system used on some 1980 1/2 models
⑳ Computer Controlled Coil Ignition (C3I) used on Buick V6 engines
㉑ MFI, SFI fuel injection systems on Buick models
㉒ E2SE, E4SE, M2SE or M4SE on carbureted engines
㉓ TBI or MFI on fuel injected engines
㉔ DITC or DME system on some models

Continued

COMPUTERIZED ENGINE CONTROL APPLICATIONS

Manufacturer	Year	Engine	SECTION 4 Electronic Ignition System	SECTION 5 Computer Control System	SECTION 6 Feedback Carburetor	SECTION 7 Fuel Injection System
Saab	1979–80	99, 900	Bosch ③	Bosch	—	CIS
	1981–85	900, Turbo	Bosch ③	Bosch Lambda	—	CIS
Subaru	1983–85	1.8L Turbo	Nippondenso	Bosch	—	AFC
Toyota	1980–85	all (fuel inj)	Nippondenso	Bosch	—	AFC
Triumph	1980–81	TR7, TR8	Lucas	Bosch-Lucas	—	AFC
Volkswagen	1979	Type 1, 2	Bosch③	Bosch	—	AFC
	1980–85	Vanagon	Bosch③	Bosch	—	AFC
	1980–85	all 4 cyl exc. Vanagon	Bosch ③	Bosch Lambda	—	CIS
Volvo	1978–85	all (fuel inj)	Bosch	Bosch Lambda ⑯	—	CIS

NOTE: Always check the underhood emission sticker to determine exactly which engine control system is used on the vehicle

AFC—Air Flow Controlled
CIS—Constant Injection System
TBI—Throttle Body Injection
C—Carter carburetor
R—Rochester carburetor
H—Holley carburetor
M—Motorcraft carburetor
EGI—Electronic Gasoline Injection
ECCS—Electronic Concentrated Engine Control
MCU—Microprocessor Control Unit
EEC—Electronic Engine Controls
C4—Computer Controlled Catalytic Converter
CCC—Computer Command Control
EFC—Electronic Fuel Control
EIS—Electronic Ignition System
EFI—Electronic Fuel Injection
CFI—Central Fuel Injection
① CEC system on some models
② Carter BBD used on engine with CEC system

③ Bosch impulse generator or Hall effect distributor
④ Mikuni carburetor on some models
⑤ CIS on 320i models
⑥ Bosch L-Jetronic up to 1982. Motronic on 1983 and later (except 320i)
⑦ Combustion control computer used on Imperial models with fuel injection
⑧ EFC on carbureted engines
⑨ Holley 6500 on California models
⑩ EFI on Lincoln and Mark IV. Carter thermo quad (TQ) on 4 bbl models
⑪ Digital Fuel Injection on Cadillac models
⑫ Bosch K-Jetronic (KE-Jetronic on 1984 and later models)
⑬ 1984 models use Bosch Constant Idle Speed system in addition to fuel inj.

⑭ Schlumberger ignition system on 505 models
⑮ 1984 and later 911 uses Bosch Motronic System
⑯ CIS on 1979 240 Federal models
⑰ AFC on California; TBI on Federal
⑱ Cadillac only
⑲ CCC system used on some 1980 1/2 models
⑳ Computer Controlled Coil Ignition (C31) used on Buick V6 engines
㉑ MFI, SFI fuel injection systems on Buick models
㉒ E2SE, E4SE, M2SE or M4SE on carbureted engines
㉓ TBI or MFI on fuel injected engines
㉔ DITC or DME system on some models

Electronics and Automotive Computers

INDEX

FUNDAMENTALS OF ELECTRICITY

All matter is made up of tiny particles called molecules. Each molecule is made up of two or more atoms. Atoms may be divided into even smaller particles called protons, neutrons and electrons. These particles are the same in all matter and differences in materials (hard or soft, conductive or nonconductive) occur only because of the number and arrangement of these particles. Protons and neutrons form the nucleus of the atom, while electrons orbit around the nucleus much the same way as the planets of the solar system orbit around the sun.

The proton is a small positive natural charge of electricity, while the neutron has no electrical charge. The electron carries a negative charge equal to the positive charge of the proton. Every electrically neutral atom contains the same number of protons and electrons, the exact number of which determines the element. The only difference between a conductor and an insulator is that a conductor possesses free electrons in large quantities, while an insulator has only a few. A material must have very few free electrons to be a good insulator, and vice-versa. When we speak of electricity, we're talking about these electrons.

Typical atoms of copper (A), hydrogen (B) and helium (C), showing electron flow through a battery (D)

Electircal resistance can be compared to water flow through a pipe. The smaller the wire (pipe), the more resistance to the flow of electrons (water)

In a conductor, the movement of the free electrons is hindered by collisions with the adjoining atoms of the material (matter). This hindrance to movement is called RESISTANCE and it varies with different materials and temperatures. As temperature increases, the movement of the free electrons increases, causing more frequent collisions and therefore increasing resistance to the movement of the electrons. The number of collisions (resistance) also increases with the number of electrons flowing (current). Current is defined as the movement of electrons through a conductor such as a wire. In a conductor (such as copper) electrons can be caused to leave their atoms and move to other atoms. This flow is continuous in that every time an atom gives up an electron, it collects another one to take its place. This movement of electrons is called electric current and is measured in amperes. When 6.28 billion, billion electrons pass a certain point in the circuit in one second, the amount of current flow is called one ampere.

The force or pressure which causes electrons to flow in any conductor (such as a wire) is called voltage. It is measured in volts and is similar to the pressure that causes water to flow in a pipe. Voltage is the difference in electrical pressure measured between two different points in a circuit. In a 12 volt system, for example, the force measured between the two battery posts is 12 volts. Two important concepts are voltage potential and polarity. Voltage potential is the amount of voltage or electrical pressure at a certain point in the circuit with respect to another point. For example, if the voltage potential at one post of the 12 volt battery is zero, the voltage potential at the other post is 12 volts with respect to the first post. One post of the battery is said to be positive (+); the other post is negative (−) and the conventional direction of current flow is from positive to negative in an electrical circuit. It should be noted that the electron flow in the wire is opposite the current flow. In other words, when the circuit is energized, the current flows from positive to negative, but the electrons actually flow from negative to positive. The voltage or pressure needed to produce a current flow in a circuit must be greater than the resistance present in the circuit. In other words, if the voltage drop across the resistance is greater than or equal to the voltage input, the voltage potential will be zero—no voltage will flow through the circuit. Resistance to the flow of electrons is measured in ohms. One volt will cause one ampere to flow through a resistance of one ohm.

Magnetism and Electromagnets

Electricity and magnetism are very closely associated because when electric current passes through a wire, a magnetic field is created around the wire. When a wire, carrying electric current, is wound into a coil, a magnetic field with North and South poles is created

The left hand rule determines magnetic polarity.

just like in a bar magnet. If an iron core is placed within the coil, the magnetic field becomes stronger because iron conducts magnetic lines much easier than air. This arrangement is called an electromagnet.

The direction of current flow is determined by the direction of the magnetic lines of force and the direction of motion of the magnetic field with respect to the conductor. The direction of current flow can be determined by using the "right hand rule". Grasp the conductor with the right hand with the fingers on the leading side of the conductor and pointed in the direction of the magnetic lines of force. The thumb will then point in the direction of current flow.

UNITS OF ELECTRICAL MEASUREMENT

There are three fundamental characteristics of a direct-current electrical circuit: volts, amperes and ohms.

VOLTAGE is the difference of potential between the positive and negative terminals of a battery or generator. Voltage is the pressure or electromotive force required to produce a current of one ampere through a resistance of one ohm.

AMPERE is the unit of measurement of current in an electrical circuit. One ampere is the quantity of current that will flow through a resistance of one ohm at a pressure of one volt.

OHM is the unit of measurement of resistance. One ohm is the resistance of a conductor through which a current of one ampere will flow at a pressure of one volt.

Ohms Law

Ohms law is a statement of the relationship between the three fundamental characteristics of an electrical circuit. These rules apply to direct current only.

$$AMPERES = \frac{VOLTS}{OHMS} \quad or \quad \frac{E}{R} I = \frac{3}{M}$$

$$OHMS = \frac{VOLTS}{AMPERES} \quad or \quad R = \frac{E}{I}$$

$$VOLTS = AMPERES \times OHMS \quad or \quad E = I \times R$$

Ohms law provides a means to make an accurate circuit analysis without actually seeing the circuit. If, for example, one wanted to check the condition of the rotor winding in an alternator whose specifications indicate that the field (rotor) current draw is normally 2.5 amperes at 12 volts, simply connect the rotor to a 12 volt battery and measure the current with an ammeter. If it measures about 2.5 amperes, the rotor winding can be assumed good.

An ohmmeter can be used to test components that have been removed from the vehicle in much the same manner as an ammeter. Since the voltage and the current of the rotor windings used as an earlier example are known, the resistance can be calculated using Ohms law. The formula would be:

$$R = \frac{E}{I} \quad Where: \begin{aligned} E &= 12 \text{ volts} \\ I &= 2.5 \text{ amperes} \end{aligned}$$

If the rotor resistance measures about 4.8 ohms when checked with an ohmmeter, the winding can be assumed good. By plugging in different specifications, additional circuit information can be determined such as current draw, etc.

Electrical Circuits

An electrical circuit must start from a source of electrical supply and return to that source through a continuous path. There are two basic types of circuit; series and parallel. In a series circuit, all of the elements are connected in chain fashion with the same amount of current passing through each element or load. No matter where

MAGNETISM & PERMANENT MAGNETS

MAGNETIC FILED

OPPOSITE POLES ATTRACT

LIKE POLES REPEL

Magnetic field surrounding a bar magnet

ELECTRO-MAGNETS

FORCE FIELD SURROUNDING A CURRENT CARRYING COIL
ALL FORCE LINES ARE COMPLETE LOOPS

FORCE FIELD WITH SOFT IRON CORE
NOTE CONCENTRATION OF LINES IN IRON CORE

Magnetic field surrounding an electromagnet

an ammeter is connected in a series circuit, it will always read the same. The most important fact to remember about a series circuit is that the sum of the voltages across each element equals the source voltage. The total resistance of a series circuit is equal to the sum of the individual resistances within each element of the circuit. Using ohms law, one can determine the voltage drop across each element in the circuit. If the total resistance and source voltage is known, the amount of current can be calculated. Once the amount of current (amperes) is known, values can be substituted in the Ohms law formula to calculate the voltage drop across each individual element in the series circuit. The individual voltage drops must add up to the same value as the source voltage.

Example of a series circuit

Example of a parallel circuit

Voltage drop in a parallel circuit. Voltage drop across each lamp is 12 volts

Example of a series-parallel circuit

By measuring the voltage drops, you are in effect measuring the resistance of each element within the circuit. The greater the voltage drop, the greater the resistance. Voltage drop measurements are a common way of checking circuit resistances in automotive electrical systems. When part of a circuit develops excessive resistance (due to a bad connection) the element will show a higher than normal voltage drop. Normally, automotive wiring is selected to limit voltage drops to a few tenths of a volt.

A parallel circuit, unlike a series circuit, contains two or more branches, each branch a separate path independent of the others. The total current draw from the voltage source is the sum of all the currents drawn by each branch. Each branch of a parallel circuit can be analyzed separately. The individual branches can be either simple circuits, series circuits or combinations of series-parallel circuits. Ohms law applies to parallel circuits just as it applies to series circuits, by considering each branch independently of the others. The most important thing to remember is that the voltage across each branch is the same as the source voltage. The current in any branch is that voltage divided by the resistance of the branch.

A practical method of determining the resistance of a parallel circuit is to divide the product of the two resistances by the sum of two resistances at a time. Amperes through a parallel circuit is the sum of the amperes through the separate branches. Voltage across a parallel circuit is the same as the voltage across each branch.

BASIC SOLID STATE

The term "solid state" refers to devices utilizing transistors, diodes and other components which are made from materials known as semiconductors. A semiconductor is a material that is neither a good insulator or a good conductor; principally silicon and germanium. The semiconductor material is specially treated to give it certain qualities that enhance its function, therefore becoming either p-type (positive) or n-type (negative) material. Most modern

Total current (amps) in a parallel circuit. 4 + 6 + 12 = 22 amps

semiconductors are constructed of silicon and can be made to change their characteristics depending on whether its function calls for an insulator or conductor.

The simplest semiconductor function is that of the diode or rectifier (the two terms mean the same thing). A diode will pass current in one direction only, like a one-way valve, because it has low resistance in one direction and high resistance on the other. Whether the diode conducts or not depends on the polarity of the voltage applied to it. A diode has two electrodes, an anode and a cathode. When the anode receives positive (+) voltage and the cathode receives negative (−) voltage, current can flow easily through the diode. When the voltage is reversed, the diode becomes non-conducting and only allows a very slight amount of current to flow in the circuit. Because the semiconductor is not a perfect insulator, a small amount of reverse current leakage will occur, but the amount is usually too small to consider.

Like any other electrical device, diodes have certain ratings that must be observed and should not be exceeded. The forward current rating indicates how much current can safely pass through the diode without causing damage or destroying it. Forward current rating is usually given in either amperes or milliamperes. The voltage drop across a diode remains constant regardless of the current flowing through it. Small diodes designed to carry low amounts of current need no special provision for dissipating the heat generated in any electrical device, but large current carrying diodes are usually mounted on heat sinks to keep the internal temperature from rising to the point where the silicon will melt and destroy the diode. When diodes are operated in a high ambient temperature environment, they must be de-rated to prevent failure.

Diode with foreward bias

Diode with reverse bias

Another diode specification is its peak inverse voltage rating. This value is the maximum amount of voltage the diode can safely handle when operating in the blocking mode. This value can be anywhere from 50–1000 volts, depending on the diode, and if exceeded can damage the diode just as too much forward current will. Most semiconductor failures are caused by excessive voltage or internal heat.

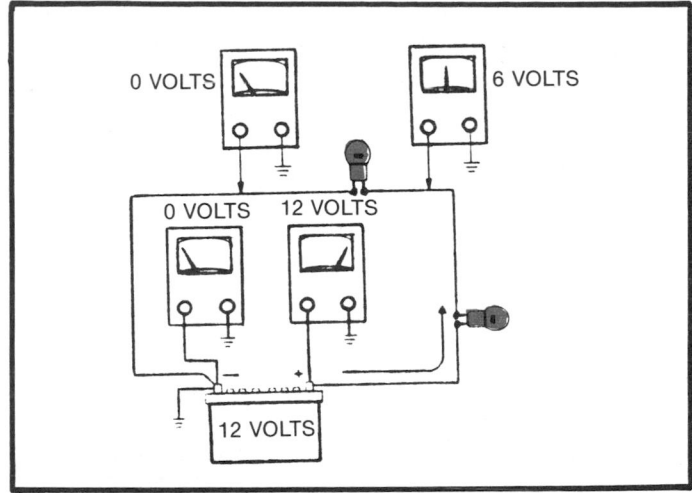

Voltage drop in a series circuit

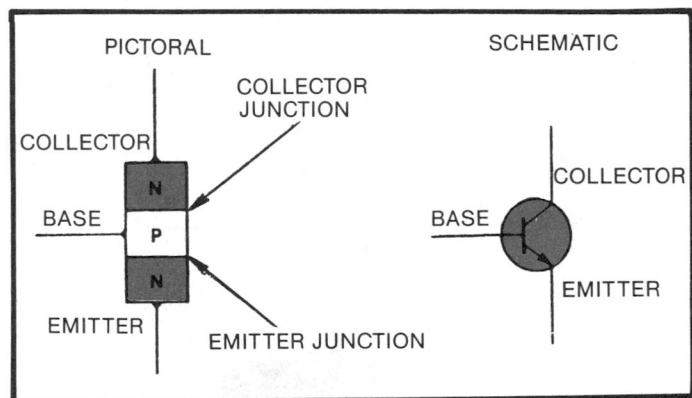

NPN transistor showing both pictoral and schematic illustrations

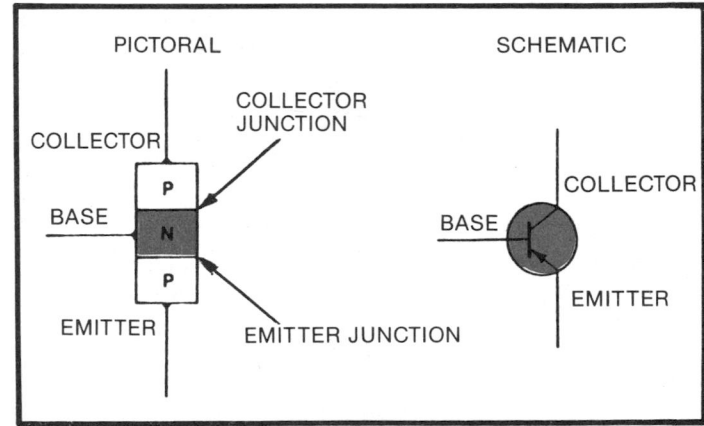

PNP transistor showing both pictoral and schematic illustrations

One can test a diode with a small battery and a lamp with the same voltage rating. With this arrangement one can find a bad diode and determine the polarity of a good one. A diode can fail and cause either a short or open circuit, but in either case it fails to function as a diode. Testing is simply a matter of connecting the test bulb first in one direction and then the other and making sure that current flows in one direction only. If the diode is shorted, the test bulb will remain on no matter how the light is connected.

ZENER DIODES

Normally, exceeding the reverse voltage rating of a conventional diode will cause it to fail; the Zener diode is an exception to this rule. Because of this characteristic, it can perform the important function of regulation and become the essential ingredient in the solid state voltage regulator. A Zener diode behaves like any other silicon diode in the forward direction and, up to a point, in the reverse direction also. As the reverse voltage increases, very little reverse current flows since this is normally the non-conducting direction; but when the reverse voltage reaches a certain point, the reverse current suddenly begins to increase. In a conventional

diode, this is known as breakdown and the heat caused by the resulting high leakage current would melt the semiconductor junction. In a Zener diode, due to its particular junction construction, the resulting heat is spread out and damage does not occur. Instead the reverse current (called Zener current) begins to increase very rapidly with only a very slight increase in the reverse (or Zener) voltage. This characteristic permits the Zener diode to function as a voltage regulator. The specific reverse voltage at which the Zener diode becomes conductive is controlled by the diode manufacturing process. Almost any Zener voltage rating can be obtained, from a few volts up to several hundred volts.

TRANSISTORS

The transistor is an electrical device used to control voltage within a circuit. A transistor can be considered a "controllable diode" in that, in addition to passing or blocking current, the transistor can control the amount of current passing through it. Simple transistors are composed of three pieces of semiconductor material, P and N type, joined together and enclosed in a container. If two sections of P material and one section of N material are used, it is known as the PNP transistor; if the reverse is true, then it is known as an NPN transistor. The two types cannot be interchanged. Most modern transistors are made from silicon (earlier transistors were made from germanium) and contain three elements; the emitter, the collector and the base. In addition to passing or blocking current, the transistor can control the amount of current passing through it and because of this can function as an amplifier or a switch.

The collector and emitter form the main current-carrying circuit

Cross section of typical alternator diode

PNP transistor with base switch open (no current flow)

Hydraulic analogy to transistor function with the base circuit energized

PNP transistor with base switch closed (base emitter and collector emitter current flow)

Hydraulic analogy to transistor function with the base circuit shut off

of the transistor. The amount of current that flows through the collector-emitter junction is controlled by the amount of current in the base circuit. Only a small amount of base-emitter current is necessary to control a large amount of collector-emitter current (the amplifier effect). In automotive applications, however, the transistor is used primarily as a switch.

When no current flows in the base-emitter junction, the collector-emitter circuit has a high resistance, like to open contacts of a relay. Almost no current flows through the circuit and transistor is considered OFF. By bypassing a small amount of current into the base circuit, the resistance is low, allowing current to flow through the circuit and turning the resistor ON. This condition is known as "saturation" and is reached when the base current reaches the maximum value designed into the transistor that allows current to flow. Depending on various factors, the transistor can turn on and off (go from cutoff to saturation) in less than one millionth of a second.

Much of what was said about ratings for diodes applies to transistors, since they are constructed of the same materials. When transistors are required to handle relatively high currents, such as in voltage regulators or ignition systems, they are generally mounted on heat sinks in the same manner as diodes. They can be damaged or destroyed in the same manner if their voltage ratings are exceeded. A transistor can be checked for proper operation by measuring the resistance with an ohmmeter between the base-emitter terminals and then between the base-collector terminals. The forward resistance should be small, while the reverse resistance should be large. Compare the readings with those from a known good transistor. As a final check, measure the forward and reverse resistance between the collector and emitter terminals.

MICROPROCESSORS, COMPUTERS AND LOGIC SYSTEMS

Mechanical or electromechanical control devices lack the precision necessary to meet the requirements of modern Federal emission control standards, and the ability to respond to a variety of input conditions common to normal engine operation. To meet these requirements, manufacturers have gone to solid state logic systems and microprocessors to control the basic functions of fuel mixture, spark timing and emission control.

One of the more vital roles of solid state systems is their ability to perform logic functions and make decisions. Logic designers use a shorthand notation to indicate whether a voltage is present in a circuit (the number 1) or not present (the number 0), and their systems are designed to respond in different ways depending on the output signal (or the lack of it) from various control devices.

Schematic of an AND circuit and how it responds to various input signals

Multiple input AND operation in a typical automotive starting circuit

Typical two-input OR circuit operation

There are three basic logic functions or "gates" used to construct a control system: the AND gate, the OR gate or the NOT gate. Stated simply, the AND gate works when voltage is present in two or more circuits which then energize a third (A and B energize C). The OR gate works when voltage is present at either circuit A or circuit B which then energizes circuit C. The NOT function is performed by a solid state device called an "inverter" which reverses the input from a circuit so that, if voltage is going in, no voltage comes out and vice versa. With these three basic building blocks, a logic designer can create complex systems easily. In actual use, a logic or decision making system may employ many logic gates and receive inputs from a number of sources (sensors), but for the most part, all utilize the basic logic gates discussed above.

TRUTH TABLE FOR EXCLUSIVE "OR" OPERATION

Inputs		Output
B	A	Q
0	0	0
0	1	1
1	0	1
1	1	0

Exclusive OR (EOR) circuit operation

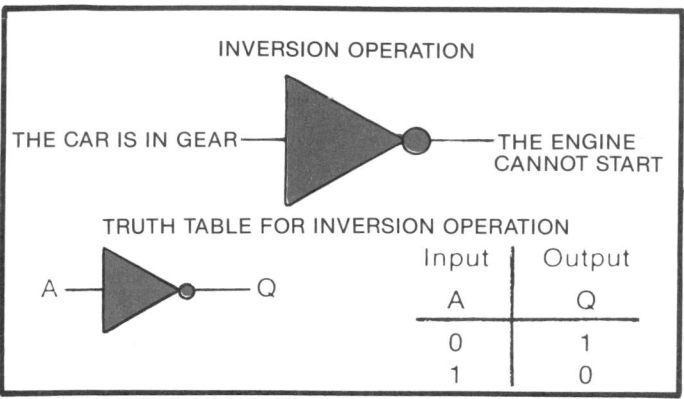

Inversion operation characteristics

NOTE: There is one more basic logic gate, called the Exclusive OR Gate (EOR) that is commonly used where arithmetical calculations (addition and subtraction) must be performed.

Stripped to its bare essentials, a decision making system is made up of three subsystems:

a. Input devices (sensors)
b. Logic circuits (computer control unit)
c. Output devices (actuators or controls)

The input devices are usually nothing more than switches or sensors that provide a voltage signal to the control unit logic circuits that is read as a 1 or 0 (on or off) by the logic circuits. The output devices are anything from a warning light to solenoid operated valves, motors, etc. In most cases, the logic circuits themselves lack sufficient output power to operate these devices directly. Instead, they operate some intermediate device such as a relay or power transistor which in turn operates the appropriate device or control. Many problems diagnosed as computer failures are really the result of a malfunctioning intermediate device like a relay and this must be kept in mind whenever troubleshooting any computer based control system.

The logic systems discussed above are called "hardware" systems, because they consist only of the physical electronic components (gates, resistors, transistors, etc.). Hardware systems do not contain a program and are designed to perform specific or "dedicated" functions which cannot readily be changed. For many simple automotive control requirements, such dedicated logic systems are perfectly adequate. When more complex logic functions are required, or where it may be desirable to alter these functions (e.g. from one model car to another) a true computer system is used. A computer can be programmed through its software to perform many different functions and, if that program is stored on a separate chip called a ROM (Read Only Memory), it can be easily changed simply by plugging in a different ROM with the desired program. Most on-board automotive computers are designed with this capability. The on-board computer method of engine control offers the manufacturer a flexible method of responding to data from a variety of input devices and of controlling an equally large variety of output controls. The computer response can be changed quickly and easily by simply modifying its software program.

Microprocessors

The microprocessor is the heart of the microcomputer. It is the thinking part of the computer system through which all the data from the various sensors passes. Within the microprocessor, data is acted upon, compared, manipulated or stored for future use. A microprocessor is not necessarily a microcomputer, but the differences between the two are becoming very minor. Originally, a microprocessor was a major part of a microcomputer, but nowadays microprocessors are being called "single-chip microcomputers". They contain all the essential elements to make them behave as a computer, including the most important ingredient—the program.

All computers require a program. In a general purpose computer, the program can be easily changed to allow different tasks to be performed. In a "dedicated" computer, such as most on-board automotive computers, the program isn't quite so easily altered.

Typical PROM showing carrier and reference markings for installation

Schematic of typical microprocessor based on-board computer showing essential components

These automotive computers are designed to perform one or several specific tasks, such as maintaining an engine's air/fuel ratio at a specific, predetermined level. A program is what makes a computer smart; without a program a computer can do absolutely nothing. The term "software" refers to the program that makes the hardware do what you want it to do. The software program is simply a listing in sequential order of the steps or commands necessary to make a computer perform the desired task.

Before the computer can do anything at all, the program must be fed into it by one of several possible methods. A computer can never be "smarter" than the person programming it, but it is a lot faster.

Although it cannot perform any calculation or operation that the programmer himself cannot perform, its processing time is measured in millionths of a second.

Because a computer is limited to performing only those operations (instructions) programmed into its memory, the program must be broken down into a large number of very simple steps. Two different programmers can come up with two different programs, since there is usually more than one way to perform any task or solve a problem. In any computer, however, there is only so much memory space available, so an overly long or inefficient program may not fit into the memory. In addition to performing arithmetic functions (such as with a trip computer), a computer can also store data, look up data in a table and perform the logic functions previously discussed. A Random Access Memory (RAM) allows the computer to store bits of data temporarily while waiting to be acted upon by the program. It may also be used to store output data that is to be sent to an output device. Whatever data is stored in a RAM is lost when power is removed from the system by turning off the ignition key, for example.

Computers have another type of memory called a Read Only Memory (ROM) which is permanent. This memory is not lost when the power is removed from the system.

Most programs for automotive computers are stored on a ROM memory chip. Data is usually in the form of a look-up table that saves computing time and program steps. For example, a computer designed to control the amount of distributor advance can have this information stored in a table. The information that determines distributor advance (engine rpm, manifold vacuum and temperature) is coded to produce the correct amount of distributor advance over a wide range of engine operating conditions. Instead of the computer computing the required advance, it simply looks it up in a pre-programmed table.

However, not all engine control functions can be handled in this manner; some must be computed.

There are several ways of programming a ROM, but once programmed, the ROM cannot be changed. If the ROM is made on the same chip that contains the microprocessor, the whole computer must be altered if a program change is needed. For this reason, a ROM is usually placed on a separate chip. Another type of memory is the Programmable Read Only Memory (PROM) that has the program "burned in" with the appropriate programming machine.

Like the ROM, once a PROM has been programmed, it cannot be changed. The advantage of the PROM is that it can be produced in small quantities economically, since it is manufactured with a blank memory. Program changes for various vehicles can be made readily. There is still another type of memory called an EPROM (Erasable PROM) which can be erased and programmed many times, but they are used only in research and development work, not on production vehicles.

The primary function of the on-board computer is to achieve the necessary emission control while maintaining the maximum fuel economy. It should be remembered that all on-board computers perform all the functions described; some perform only one function, such as spark control or idle speed control. Others handle practically all engine functions. As computers increase in complexity and memory capacity, more engine and non-engine (e.g. suspension control, climate control, etc.) functions will be controlled by them.

Installation of PROM unit in GM on-board computer

Feedback carburetor system components

Electronic control assembly (© Ford Motor Co.)

AIR CHARGE TEMPERATURE
(ACT) SENSOR

EGR VALVE

THROTTLE
KICKER
SOLENOID

EGR VENT
EGR CONTROL
(EGRC EGRV)
SOLENOID VALVES
ASSEMBLY

EGR VALVE
POSITION (EVP)
SENSOR

THROTTLE
KICKER
ACTUATOR

IGNITION
MODULE
(IM)

THROTTLE
POSITION
(TP) SENSOR

ENGINE
COOLANT
TEMPERATURE
(ECT) SENSOR

EXHAUST GAS
OXYGEN (EGO)
SENSOR

THERMACTOR AIR
BYPASS AND
DIVERTER (TAB/TAD)
SOLENOID VALVES
ASSEMBLY

THROTTLE
BODY

BAROMETRIC/MANIFOLD
ABSOLUTE PRESSURE
(B/MAP) SENSOR

CANISTER PURGE
(CANP) SOLENOID
VALVE

CRANKSHAFT
POSITION
(CP) SENSOR

Ford fuel injection system components

Diagnostic Equipment and Special Tools

INDEX

SPECIAL TOOLS AND DIAGNOSTIC EQUIPMENT

General Information

At the rate which both import and domestic manufacturers are incorporating electronic engine control systems into their production lines, it won't be long before every new vehicle is equipped with one or more on-board computers. These computers and their electronic components (with no moving parts) should theoretically last the life of the car, provided nothing external happens to damage the circuits or memory chips. While it is true that electronic components should last longer than a similar, mechanical system, it is also true that any computer-based system is extremely sensitive to electrical voltages and cannot tolerate careless or haphazard testing or service procedures. An inexperienced individual can literally do major electronic circuit damage looking for a minor problem by using the wrong kind of test equipment or connecting test leads or connectors with the ignition switch ON in any computerized control system. When selecting test equipment, make sure the manufacturers instructions state that the tester is compatible with whatever manufacturer or type of electronic control system is being serviced. Read all instructions and system operation information carefully and double check all test points before installing probes or making any equipment connections.

The following outlines basic diagnosis techniques for dealing with most computerized engine control systems. Along with a general explanation of the various types of test equipment available to aid in servicing modern electronic automotive systems, basic electrical repair techniques for wiring harnesses and weatherproof connectors is given. Read this basic information before attempting any repairs or testing on any computerized system to provide the background of information necessary to avoid the most common and obvious mistakes that can cost both time and money. Although the actual test and replacement procedures are simple, a few different rules apply when dealing with microprocessor-based, on-board computer control systems. Read all service precautions carefully before attempting anything. Likewise, the individual system sections for electronic engine controls, fuel injection and feedback carburetors (both import and domestic) should be read from the beginnning to the end before any repairs or diagnosis is attempted. Although the component replacement and testing procedures are basically simple in themselves, the systems are not, and unless one has a thorough understanding of all particular components and their function within a particular system (fuel injection, for example), the logical test sequence that must be followed to isolate the problem becomes impossible. Minor component malfunctions can make a big difference, so it is important to know how different components interact and how each component affects the operation of the overall computer control system to find the ultimate cause of a problem without replacing electronic components unnecessarily.

GENERAL SAFETY PRECAUTIONS

CAUTION

Whenever working on or around any computer-based microprocessor control system such as if found on most electronic fuel injection, feedback carburetor or emission control systems, always observe these general precautions to prevent the possibility of personal injury or damage to electronic components. Additional precautions (not covered here) may be found in the individual system sections.

• Never install or remove battery cables with the key ON or the engine running. Jumper cables should be connected and disconnected with the key OFF to avoid possible power surges that can damage electronic control units. Engines equipped with computer controlled systems should avoid both giving and getting jump starts due to the possibility of serious damage to computer compo-

nents from arcing in the engine compartment when connections are made with the ignition ON.

• Always remove the battery cables before charging the battery in the car. Never use a high-output charger on an installed battery or attempt to use any type of "hot shot" (24 volt) starting aid.

• Never remove or attach wiring harness connectors with the ignition switch ON, especially to the electronic control unit.

• When checking compression on engines with AFC injection systems, unplug the cable from the battery to the main power or fuel pump relays before cranking the engine to prevent fuel delivery and possible engine starting during tests. Always look for uniform compression readings between cylinders, rather than specific values.

• Always depressurize fuel injection systems before attempting to disconnect any fuel lines. Although only fuel injection-equipped vehicles use a pressurized fuel system, it's a good idea to exercise caution whenever disconnecting any fuel line or hose during any test procedures. Take adequate precautions to avoid a fire hazard.

• Always use clean rags and tools when working on any open fuel system and take care to prevent any dirt from entering the fuel lines. Wipe all components clean before installation and prepare a clean work area for disassembly and inspection of components. Use lint-free towels to wipe components and avoid using any caustic cleaning solvents.

• Do not drop any components (especially the on-board computer unit) during service procedures and never apply 12 volts directly to any component (like a fuel injector) unless instructed specifically to do so. Some component electrical windings are designed to safely handle only 4 or 5 volts in operation and can be destroyed in approximately 1½ seconds if 12 volts are applied directly to the connector.

• Remove the electronic control unit(s) if the vehicle is to be placed in an environment where temperatures exceed approximately 176 degrees F (80 degrees C), such as a paint spray booth or when arc or gas welding near the control unit location in the car. Control units can be damaged by heat and sudden impact (like a fall from about waist height onto a concrete floor).

UNDERHOOD EMISSION STICKER

The Vehicle Emission Control Information Label is located somewhere in the engine compartment (fan shroud, valve cover, radiator support, hood underside, etc.) of every vehicle produced for sale in the USA or Canada. The label contains important emission specifications and setting procedures, as well as a vacuum hose schematic with emission components identified. This label is permanently attached and cannot be removed without destroying. The specifications shown on the label are correct for the vehicle the label is mounted on. If any difference exists between the specifications shown on the label and those shown in any service manual, those shown on the label should be used.

NOTE: When servicing the engine or emission control systems, the vehicle emission control information label should be checked for up-to-date information, vacuum schematics, etc. Some manufacturers also list the type of engine control system installed.

An additional information label may also be used for any applicable engine calibration numbers. There are several styles and types of calibration labels, but they all carry basically the same information. Finally, a color coded schematic of the vacuum hoses is included on most emission labels. Although the color coding on the schematic represents the actual color of the vacuum hose tracer, there may be instances where an individual hose color may be different.

The emission control decal contains information on the engine normal and fast idle speeds, enriched idle speed, exhaust emission information (model year standards the engine meets), initial timing, spark plug type and gap, vacuum hose routing, and special

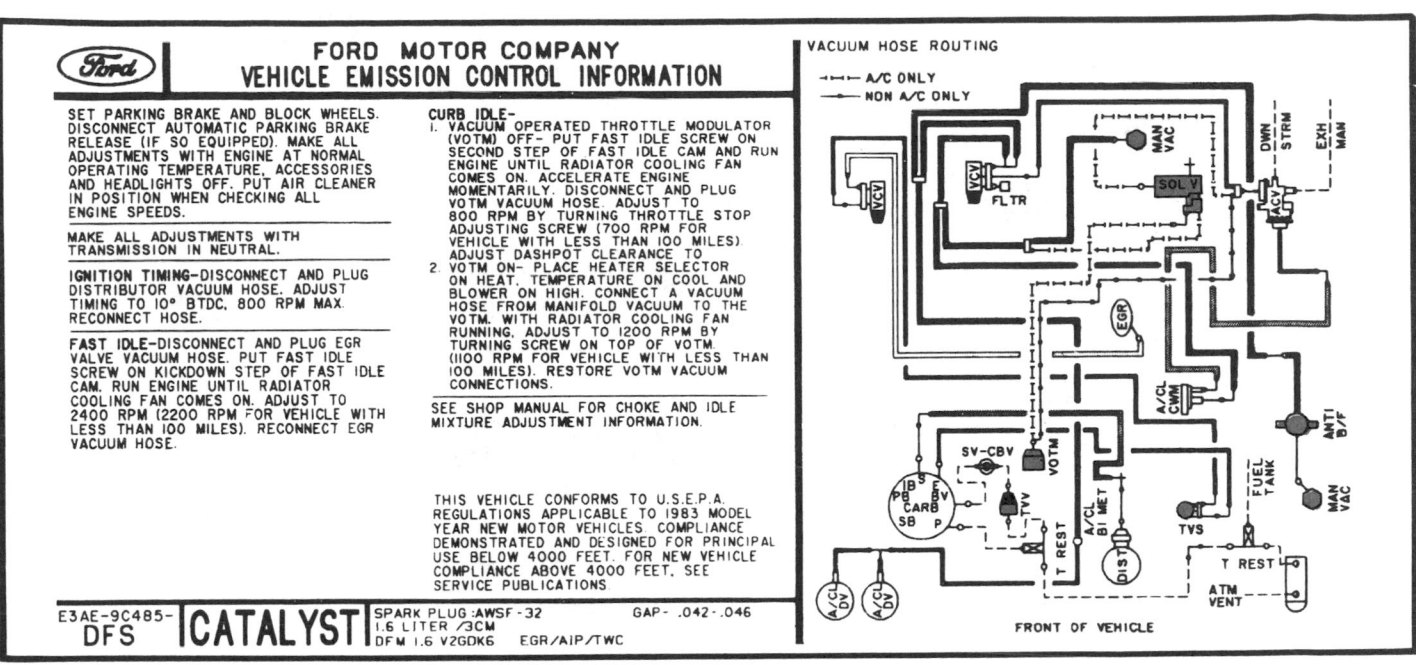

FORD MOTOR COMPANY
VEHICLE EMISSION CONTROL INFORMATION

SET PARKING BRAKE AND BLOCK WHEELS. DISCONNECT AUTOMATIC PARKING BRAKE RELEASE (IF SO EQUIPPED). MAKE ALL ADJUSTMENTS WITH ENGINE AT NORMAL OPERATING TEMPERATURE, ACCESSORIES AND HEADLIGHTS OFF. PUT AIR CLEANER IN POSITION WHEN CHECKING ALL ENGINE SPEEDS.

MAKE ALL ADJUSTMENTS WITH TRANSMISSION IN NEUTRAL.

IGNITION TIMING-DISCONNECT AND PLUG DISTRIBUTOR VACUUM HOSE. ADJUST TIMING TO 10° BTDC, 800 RPM MAX. RECONNECT HOSE.

FAST IDLE-DISCONNECT AND PLUG EGR VALVE VACUUM HOSE. PUT FAST IDLE SCREW ON KICKDOWN STEP OF FAST IDLE CAM. RUN ENGINE UNTIL RADIATOR COOLING FAN COMES ON. ADJUST TO 2400 RPM (2200 RPM FOR VEHICLE WITH LESS THAN 100 MILES). RECONNECT EGR VACUUM HOSE.

CURB IDLE-
1. VACUUM OPERATED THROTTLE MODULATOR (VOTM) OFF- PUT FAST IDLE SCREW ON SECOND STEP OF FAST IDLE CAM AND RUN ENGINE UNTIL RADIATOR COOLING FAN COMES ON. ACCELERATE ENGINE MOMENTARILY. DISCONNECT AND PLUG VOTM VACUUM HOSE. ADJUST TO 800 RPM BY TURNING THROTTLE STOP ADJUSTING SCREW (700 RPM FOR VEHICLE WITH LESS THAN 100 MILES). ADJUST DASHPOT CLEARANCE TO
2. VOTM ON - PLACE HEATER SELECTOR ON HEAT, TEMPERATURE ON COOL AND BLOWER ON HIGH. CONNECT A VACUUM HOSE FROM MANIFOLD VACUUM TO THE VOTM. WITH RADIATOR COOLING FAN RUNNING, ADJUST TO 1200 RPM BY TURNING SCREW ON TOP OF VOTM. (1100 RPM FOR VEHICLE WITH LESS THAN 100 MILES). RESTORE VOTM VACUUM CONNECTIONS.

SEE SHOP MANUAL FOR CHOKE AND IDLE MIXTURE ADJUSTMENT INFORMATION.

THIS VEHICLE CONFORMS TO U.S.E.P.A. REGULATIONS APPLICABLE TO 1983 MODEL YEAR NEW MOTOR VEHICLES. COMPLIANCE DEMONSTRATED AND DESIGNED FOR PRINCIPAL USE BELOW 4000 FEET. FOR NEW VEHICLE COMPLIANCE ABOVE 4000 FEET. SEE SERVICE PUBLICATIONS.

E3AE-9C485-DFS | **CATALYST** | SPARK PLUG :AWSF-32 | GAP- .042-.046
1.6 LITER /3CM
DFM 1.6 V2GDK6 | EGR/AIP/TWC

VACUUM HOSE ROUTING
--•-- A/C ONLY
— NON A/C ONLY

FRONT OF VEHICLE

Typical underhood emission control label found on Ford models.

ADJUSTMENT PROCEDURE

ENGINE ADJUSTMENT SPECIFICATIONS

LABEL CODE
ENGINE SIZE
EXHAUST EMISSION FAMILY
EVAPORATIVE EMISSION FAMILY

CARBURETOR FITTINGS

PDK
2.5 LITER
12X2NN
1B6-2

VEHICLE EMISSION CONTROL INFORMATION GM **CATALYST** | PDK

VACUUM HOSE ROUTING

FRONT OF VEHICLE

GENERAL MOTORS CORPORATION

AIR/BPERG/ORC/OC LOW ALTITUDE CERTIFICATION	AUTOMATIC TRANSMISSION
TIMING (°BTC @ RPM)	4° @ 672
SPARK PLUG GAP (IN)	0 060
FAST IDLE SCREW (P.N)	2600
NOMINAL IDLE RPM (D)	672 · 32

1. SET PARKING BRAKE AND BLOCK DRIVE WHEELS.
2. REMOVE AIR CLEANER AND PLUG AIR CLEANER VACUUM SOURCE. REMOVE PURGE HOSE AT CARBURETOR AND DO NOT PLUG. START ENGINE AND MAKE ALL CHECKS AND ADJUSTMENTS WITH ENGINE OPERATING AT NORMAL OPERATING TEMPERATURE, CHOKE OPEN, ELECTRIC COOLING FAN NOT RUNNING A/C OFF, AUTOMATIC TRANSMISSION IN DRIVE — UNLESS OTHERWISE NOTED.
3. VERIFY NO CHECK ENGINE LIGHT.
4. DISCONNECT FOUR WIRE DISTRIBUTOR CONNECTOR FROM WIRE HARNESS, CHECK ENGINE LIGHT WILL COME ON.
5. SET TIMING TO SPECIFIED ADVANCE WITH ENGINE RUNNING AT/OR BELOW RECOMMENDED IDLE SPEED SETTING.
6. RECONNECT FOUR WIRE DISTRIBUTOR CONNECTOR. VERIFY NO CHECK ENGINE LIGHT.
7. PLACE AUTOMATIC TRANSMISSION IN PARK.
8. DISCONNECT EGR VACUUM HOSE FROM CARBURETOR AND PLUG CARBURETOR FITTING.
9. WITH ENGINE RUNNING ON TOE STOP OF FAST IDLE CAM, ADJUST FAST IDLE SCREW TO OBTAIN SPECIFIED RPM.
10. STOP ENGINE, REINSTALL AIR CLEANER, RECONNECT AIR CLEANER VACUUM SOURCE, RECONNECT EGR VACUUM HOSE AND CANISTER PURGE HOSE. MOMENTARILY DISCONNECT BATTERY TO CANCEL ANY STORED CODES.
11. WITH ENGINE RUNNING IN DRIVE VERIFY IDLE IS WITHIN SPECIFIED LIMITS. IF RPM IS NOT WITHIN SPECIFICATION, REFER TO SERVICE MANUAL FOR ADJUSTMENT PROCEDURE.

HOT IDLE SPEED IS CONTROLLED ELECTRONICALLY; DO NOT ADJUST IDLE MOTOR RAM OR CARBURETOR SPEED SCREW.

IDLE MIXTURE SCREWS, CHOKE INDEX, AND VACUUM BREAK ARE PRESET AND SEALED AT THE FACTORY PROVISION FOR ADJUSTMENT IS NOT PROVIDED DURING THE TUNE UP PROCEDURE

VIEW A

SEE SERVICE MANUAL FOR CLOSED LOOP TEST. AND MAINTENANCE SCHEDULE FOR ADDITIONAL INFORMATION

PRINTED IN U.S.A. THIS VEHICLE CONFORMS TO U.S. EPA AND CALIFORNIA REGULATIONS APPLICABLE TO 1981 MODEL YEAR NEW PASSENGER CARS. P/ 10018254

SAMPLE

LABEL PART NUMBER

EMISSION COMPONENT AND VACUUM HOSE SCHEMATIC

Typical underhood emission control label found on GM models.

13

Examples of various types of calibration stickers found on Ford models.

instructions on carburetor and ignition timing adjustment procedures. Some manufacturers use more than one label or decal per car, but all contain important information tailored to that specific vehicle and engine. Any late changes made during the model year will be printed on the emission control label and any required changes made to the vehicle (such as adjustments for high altitude operation) should be marked on the decal for future reference.

WIRING DIAGRAMS

Wiring diagrams are used to show, on paper, how the electrical system of a car is constructed. These diagrams use color coding and symbols that identify different circuits. If an electrical system is at fault, an electrical diagram will show:
• Where the circuit receives battery voltage
• What switches control current flow
• What devices use current flow to do a job
• Where the circuit is grounded

When testing the problem system, look for this pattern of source, flow controls, and work done by the devices. Similar patterns can be seen in fuel and air delivery systems.

VACUUM DIAGRAMS

Vacuum-controlled systems are used to regulate an engine's operation for better emission control. Vacuum systems also are used to control air conditioners, headlamp doors, power brakes, and other devices. Several of these systems are often used on the same engine.

They have become quite complex, and are often connected to each other to change their own operation, as well as engine operation. The engine compartment of many late-model cars is crisscrossed with vacuum lines and hoses, each of which does a specific job. When disconnecting these lines to test or service engine parts, be sure to reinstall them correctly. To help properly route and connect vacuum lines, manufacturers provide vacuum diagrams for each engine and vehicle combination.

NOTE: Vacuum hoses, like electrical wires, can be color coded for easier identification. The vacuum diagram can be printed in color or the color name can be printed near the line in the drawing.

A vacuum diagram is especially needed with late-model engines. The routing and connection pattern of vacuum lines can vary a great deal on a given engine during a single model year. One diagram may apply to an engine sold in California but a different diagram is used when the same engine is sold in a high-altitude area. The problem is compounded when carmakers make running changes in emission systems during a model year. This can result in two identical engines in the same geographical region having slightly different devices and systems. In this case, trying to route and connect vacuum lines properly without the help of a factory vacuum diagram can be next to impossible.

After establishing what area is to be tested, you can study that area in detail. If it is a vacuum system, a vacuum diagram will show:
• The source of vacuum
• Where specific hoses should be connected
• What switches and solenoids control vacuum flow
• What devices are affected by the presence or absence of vacuum.

Fuse	Single filament light
Fusible link	Double filament light
Switch	Motor
Grounding	Buzzer
Condenser	Diode
Resistor	Contact wiring
Variable resistance	
Coil	

Examples of various electrical symbols found on wiring diagrams

Troubleshooting

BASIC DIAGNOSIS TECHNIQUES

When diagnosing engine performance because of a specific condition, such as poor idling or stalling, it used to be possible to fix most common problems by adjusting timing or idle mixture. However, on today's vehicles, there are many emission–related engine controls that could be responsible for poor performance. The sensitivity of electronic control systems makes organized troubleshooting a must; since almost any component malfunction will affect performance, it's important that you approach the problem in a logical, organized manner. There are some basic troubleshooting techniques that are standard for diagnosing any problem:

1. **Establish when the problem occurs.** Does the problem appear only under certain conditions such as cold start, hot idle or hard acceleration? Were there any noises, odors, or other unusual symptoms? Make notes on any symptoms found, including warning lights and trouble codes, if applicable.

2. **Isolate the problem area.** To do this, make some simple tests and visual under-hood observations; then eliminate the systems that are working properly. For example, a rough idle could be caused by an electrical or a vacuum problem. Check for the obvious problems such as broken wires or split or disconnected vacuum hoses. Always check the obvious before assuming something complicated is the cause. Most of the time, it's NOT the computer.

3. **Test for problems systematically** to determine the cause once the problem area is isolated. Are all the components functioning properly? Is there power going to electrical switches and motors? Is there vacuum at vacuum switches and/or actuators? Is there a mechanical problem such as bent linkage or loose mounting screws? Doing careful, systematic checks will often turn up most causes on the first inspection without wasting time checking components that have little or no relationship to the problem. A no-start or rough running condition on a fuel injected engine (for example) could be caused by a loose air cleaner cover, clogged filter, or a blown fuse. Always start with the easy checks first, before going ahead with any diagnostic routines.

4. **Test all repairs after the work is done.** Make sure that the problem is fixed. Some causes can be traced to more than one component, so a careful verification of repair work is important to pick up additional malfunctions that may cause a problem to reap-

pear or a different problem to arise. A blown fuse, for example, is a simple problem that may require more than another fuse to repair. If you don't look for a problem that caused a fuse to blow, a shorted wire may go undetected and cause another problem.

DIAGNOSIS CHARTS

The diagnostic tree charts are designed to help solve problems on fuel injected vehicles by leading the user through closely defined conditions and tests so that only the most likely components, vacuum and electrical circuits are checked for proper operation when troubleshooting a particular malfunction. By using the trouble trees to eliminate those systems and components which normally

Typical vacuum schematic for a tubrocharged four cylinder engine.

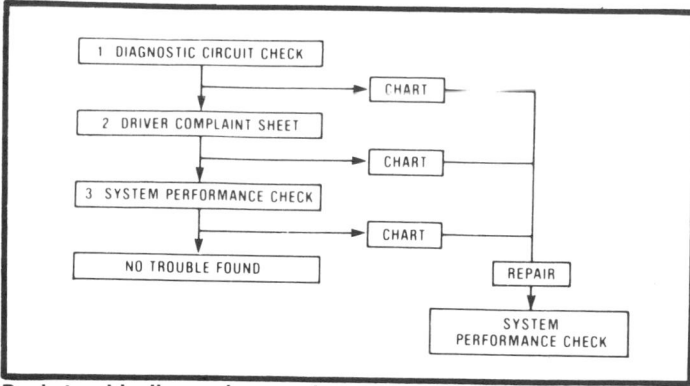

Basic trouble diagnosis procedure

will not cause the condition described, a problem can be isolated within one or more systems or circuits without wasting time on unnecessary testing. Experience has shown that most problems tend to be the result of a fairly simple and obvious cause, such as loose or corroded connectors or air leaks in the intake system; making a careful inspection of components during testing is essential to quick and accurate troubleshooting. Frequent references to the various system testers for fuel injection, feedback carburetors and computerized engine controls will be found in the text and in the diagnosis charts. These devices or their compatible equivalents are necessary to perform some of the more complicated test procedures listed, but many of the electronic fuel injection components can be functionally tested with the quick checks outlined in the "On-Car Service" procedures. Aftermarket electronic system testers are available from a variety of sources, as well as from the manufacturer, but care should be taken that the test equipment being used is designed to diagnose the particular engine control system accurately without damaging the electronic control unit (ECU) or components being tested. You should understand the basic theory of electricity, and know the meaning of voltage, amps, and ohms. You should understand what happens in a circuit with an open or a shorted wire. You should be able to read and understand a wiring diagram. You should know how to use a test light, how to connect and use a tachometer, and how to use jumper wires to by-pass components to test circuits. These techniques are all covered later in this section.

You should also be familiar with the digital volt-ohm meter, a particularly essential tool. You should be able to measure voltage, resistance, and current, and should be familiar with the controls of the meter and how to use it correctly. Without this basic knowledge, the diagnosis trees are impossible to use.

NOTE: Some test procedures incorporate other engine systems in diagnosis routines, since many conditions are the result of something other than the fuel, air, or ignition systems alone. Electrical and vacuum circuits are included wherever possible to help identify small changes incorporated into later models that may affect the diagnosis results. Circuit numbers are OEM designations and should only be used for reference purposes.

Because of the specific nature of the conditions listed in the individual diagnosis procedures, it's important to understand exactly what the definitions of various engine operating conditions are:
• STALLS—engine stops running at idle or when driving. Determine if the stalling condition is only present when the engine is either hot or cold, or if it happens consistently regardless of operating temperature.
• LOADS UP—engine misses due to excessively rich mixture. This usually occurs during cold engine operation and is characterized by black smoke from the tailpipe.
• ROUGH IDLE—engine runs unevenly at idle. This condition can range from a slight stumble or miss up to a severe shake.
• TIP IN STUMBLE—a delay or hesitation in engine response when accelerating from idle with the car at a standstill. Some slight

hesitation conditions are considered normal when they only occur during cold operation and gradually vanish as the engine warms up.
• MISFIRE—rough engine operation due to a lack of combustion in one or more cylinders. Fouled spark plugs or loose ignition wires are the most common cause.
• HESITATION—a delay in engine response when accelerating from cruise or steady throttle operation at road speed. Not to be confused with the tip in stumble described above.
• SAG—engine responds initially, then flattens out or slows down before recovering. Severe sags can cause the engine to stall.
• SURGE—engine power variation under steady throttle or cruise. Engine will speed up or slow down with no change in the throttle position. Can happen at a variety of speeds.
• SLUGGISH—engine delivers limited power under load or at high speeds. Engine loses speed going up hills, doesn't accelerate as fast as normal, or has less top speed than was noted previously.
• CUTS OUT—temporary complete loss of power at sharp, irregular intervals. May occur repeatedly or intermittently, but is usually worse under heavy acceleration.
• POOR FUEL ECONOMY—significantly lower gas mileage than is considered normal for the model and drivetrain in question. Always perform a careful mileage test under a variety of road conditions to determine the severity of the problem before attempting corrective measures. Fuel economy is influenced more by external conditions, such as driving habits and terrain, than by a minor malfunction in the fuel delivery system (carburetor or injector) that doesn't cause another problem (like rough operation).

BATTERY TESTING

A variety of battery testing methods and instruments are available, from simple hydrometer checks to specialized load testers. Each method has its features and limitations. Most manufacturers specify a particular type of battery test. Since these vary, check the particular manufacturer's requirements. On models with computerized engine controls, all tests should be done with the battery removed.

Battery Load Test

This is frequently called a high-rate discharge test, since it approximates the current drawn by the starter. These testers may have either a fixed load or an adjustable load controlled by a *carbon pile*. The latter provides greater flexibility in testing because the test load can be adjusted to match the rating of the battery. The basic test procedure is to draw current out of the battery equal to three times the battery's ampere-hour rating (e.g. If amp-hour rating = 60, load current equals 3 x 60 or 180 amperes). While this load is being applied, the voltage of the battery is measured and then compared to specified load voltage.

If this voltage is above the specified minimum, the battery is considered to be in a serviceable state. However, if the voltage is below the minimum, the battery may be either defective or merely in a discharged state. The specific gravity should be checked. If it is below a certain level, typically 1.225, it is necessary to recharge the battery and then retest. A discharged battery should not be replaced on the basis of a load test alone. However, if the battery is sufficiently charged and still fails the load test, it may be considered defective and should be replaced.

Battery Cell Test

The battery cell test measures individual cell voltages which are then compared for variations. If the cell-to-cell variation exceeds a certain amount, for example, 0.05 volt, the battery is considered defective. The test is made with only a small load on the battery, such as that of the headlights. Cell voltages must be measured through the electrolyte between two adjacent cells. Special, immersion-type test prods connected to a suitable voltmeter are required for this. The cell prods are transferred to each cell pair, in turn, noting the voltage readings of each.

BATTERY CHARGING

If a battery is not at full charge, it should be recharged before being put back into service. This is especially important for computer-equipped and electronic ignition models that require a fully charged battery for proper operation. If a battery installed in an operating vehicle is found to be partly discharged, it too should be recharged. The cause for its discharged condition should also be investigated and corrected. It may be a malfunctioning charging system. A number of battery chargers are available and each type is designed for a particular charging requirement.

Constant Current Chargers

The constant current method of charging is one of the oldest methods in use. It is principally used where a number of batteries must be charged at the same time. With this method, all the batteries being charged are connected in series, using short connector straps between each. The string of batteries is then connected to the charger which is adjusted to produce a fixed charging current, typically about 6 or 7 amperes, and all batteries receive the same charge rate.

NOTE: The batteries under charge must be frequently checked for specific gravity and removed when they reach full charge. Since the charge rate remains constant and does not taper off as for other types of chargers, there is danger of overcharging.

Fast Chargers

The fast charger was developed to enable a severely discharged battery to be quickly brought up to a serviceable state of charge. It is based on the principle that a discharged, but otherwise healthy, battery can readily absorb a moderately high charge rate for a short period. Because of their high output, fast chargers must be used with care. Not all batteries can or should be charged at the maximum rate available from the charger. Charging at too high a rate will simply overheat the battery and cause excessive gassing.

---CAUTION---

A fast charge should never be used to bring a battery up to full charge. This should be accomplished by slow charging. Some chargers automatically switch from fast to slow charge at the end of the preset fast-charge period. Never use a fast charger on an installed batter or damage to the on-board computer can result.

Slow Chargers

A slow charger has a much lower output current than a fast charger. Generally, they do not produce more than about ten amperes. Because their mode of operation is known as the *constant potential* method of charging, they can bring a battery to full charge. The constant potential method simulates the charging system of a vehicle by holding the voltage at a fixed level. As the battery comes up on charge, its counter voltage increases, causing the charge rate to gradually decrease. This is why slow chargers are said to give a tapering charge; when the battery charge is low, the charge current is high, but it tapers to a low value as the battery reaches full charge.

Although the charge rate of a slow charger does taper off, it never drops to zero. It is possible to overcharge a battery with a slow charger if it is left on too long. About 15 hours is the recommended maximum charging period with a slow charger. Many batteries reach full charge in much less time. To prevent accidental overcharging, the automatic battery charger was developed. Basically, this is a slow charger containing an electronic circuit that automatically switches off the charging current when battery voltage reaches a predetermined level. It works on the principle that the voltage of a semi-charged battery will remain low during charge

Typical battery load tester with separate voltmeter and ammeter

but will become high when full charge is reached. This increase in voltage is sensed by a zener-controlled circuit that electronically turns the charger off. When battery voltage drops below a certain level, due to the normal self-discharge of the battery, this circuit automatically turns the charger on. Because of this feature, an automatic charger can be left connected to a battery for long periods of time without danger of overcharging.

Trickle Chargers

Trickle chargers are effectively used for keeping batteries freshly charged and ready for use. Avoid continuous overcharge for long periods of time. Whenever such chargers are used which have an output of less than one ampere, it is very important that such "trickle" chargers be used in strict accordance with directions. Continuous overcharging for an indefinite time, even though at a very low rate, can be very destructive to the grids of the positive plates, causing them to disintegrate.

NOTE: Pinpointing trouble in the ignition, electrical, or fuel system can sometimes only be detected by the use of special test equipment. In fact, test equipment and the wiring diagrams are your best tools. The following describes commonly used test equipment and explains how to put it to best use in diagnosis.

Electrical Test Equipment
JUMPER WIRES

Jumper wires are simple, yet extremely valuable, pieces of test equipment. Jumper wires are merely short pieces of 16, 18 or 20 gauge wire that are used to bypass sections of an electrical circuit. The simplest type of jumper is merely a length of multistrand wire with an alligator clip at each end. Jumper wires are usually fabricated from standard automotive wire and whatever type of connector (alligator clip, spade connector or pin connector) that is required for the particular system being tested. The well-equipped tool box will have several different styles of jumper wires in several different lengths. Some jumper wires are made with three or more terminals coming from a common splice for special-purpose testing. In cramped, hard-to-reach areas it is advisable to have insulated boots over the jumper wire terminals in order to prevent accidental grounding, sparks, and possible fire, especially when testing fuel system components.

Typical jumper wires with various terminal ends

—————————————CAUTION—————————————

On-board computers are especially sensitive to arcing anywhere in the system with the ignition switch ON. Circuit damage is possible during testing.

Jumper wires are used primarily to locate open electrical circuits, on either the ground (−) side of the circuit or on the hot (+) side. If an electrical component fails to operate, connect the jumper wire between the component and a good ground. If the component operates only with the jumper installed, the ground circuit is open. If the ground circuit is good, but the component does not operate, the circuit between the power feed and component is open. You can sometimes connect the jumper wire directly from the battery to the hot terminal of the component, but first make sure the component uses 12 volts in operation. Some electrical components, such as fuel injectors, are designed to operate on about 4 volts and running 12 volts directly to the injector terminals can burn out the windings. When in doubt, check the voltage input to the component and measure how much voltage is being applied normally. See the information under "voltmeter." By moving the jumper wire successively back from the lamp toward the power source, you can isolate the

area of the circuit where the open circuit is located. When the component stops functioning, or the power is cut off, the open is in the segment of wire between the jumper and the point previously tested.

—————————————CAUTION—————————————

Never use jumpers made from wire that is of lighter gauge than used in the circuit under test. If the jumper wire is of too small gauge, it may overheat and possibly melt. Never use jumpers to bypass high-resistance loads (such as motors) in a circuit. Bypassing resistances, in effect, creates a short circuit which may, in turn, cause damage and fire. Never use a jumper for anything other than temporary bypassing of components in a circuit.

12-VOLT TEST LIGHT

The 12 volt (unpowered) test light is used to check circuits and components while electrical current is flowing through them. It is used for voltage and ground tests. Twelve volt test lights come in different styles but all have three main parts—a ground clip, a sharp probe, and a light. The most commonly used test lights have pick-type probes. To use a test light, connect the ground clip to a good ground and probe the wires or connectors wherever necessary with the pick. The pick should be sharp so that it can penetrate wire insulation to make contact with the wire without making a large hole in the insulation. The wrap-around light is handy in hard-to-reach areas or where it is difficult to support a wire to push a probe pick into it. To use the wrap around light, hook the wire to probed with the hook and pull the trigger. A small pick will be forced through the wire insulation into the wire core. After testing, the wire can be resealed with a dab of silicone or electrical tape.

—————————————CAUTION—————————————

Do not use a test light to probe electronic ignition spark plug or secondary coil wires. Never use a pick-type test light to pierce wiring on computer controlled systems unless specifically instructed to do so.

Like the jumper wire, a 12-volt test light is used to isolate opens (breaks or shorts) in circuits. But, whereas the jumper wire is used to bypass the open to operate the load, the 12-volt test light is used to locate the presence or absence of voltage in a circuit. If the test light glows, you know that there is power up to that point; if the

Typical 12 volt test lights

test light does not glow when its probe is inserted into the wire or connector, you know that there is an open circuit (no power). Move the test light in successive steps back along the wire harness, toward the power source, until the light in the handle does glow. When it does glow, the open circuit is between the probe and point previously probed.

NOTE: The test light does not detect that 12 volts (or any particular amount of voltage) is present in a circuit; it only detects that some voltage is present. It is advisable before using the test light to touch its terminals across the battery posts to make sure the light is operating properly. The light should glow brightly.

SELF-POWERED TEST LIGHT (CONTINUITY TESTER)

The typical continuity tester is powered by a 1.5 volt penlight battery. One type of self-powered test light is similar in design to the 12–volt test light; this type has both the battery and the light in the handle and pick-type probe tip. The second type has the light toward the open tip, so that the light illuminates the contact point. The self-powered test light is a dual-purpose piece of test equipment. It can be used to test for either open or short circuits when power is disconnected from the circuit (continuity test). A powered test light should not be used on any computer controlled system or component unless specifically instructed to do so. Many engine sensors (like the oxygen sensor) can be destroyed by even this small amount of voltage applied directly to the terminals.

NOTE: The following procedures are meant to be general in nature and apply to most electrical systems. See the individual system sections for specific circuit testing procedures.

Open Circuit Testing

To use the self-powered test light to check for open circuits, first isolate the circuit from the vehicle's 12 volt power source by disconnecting the battery positive (+) terminal or the wiring harness connector. Connect the test light ground clip to a good ground and probe sections of the circuit sequentially with the test light (start from either end of the circuit). If the light is out, the open wire or connection is between the probe and the circuit ground. If the light is on, the open is between the probe and end of the circuit toward the power source.

Short Circuit Testing

By isolating the circuit both from power and from ground, and using a self-powered test light, you can check for shorts to ground in the circuit. Isolate the circuit from power and ground. Connect the test light ground clip to a good ground and probe any easy-to-

reach test point in the circuit. If the light comes on, there is a short somewhere in the circuit. To isolate the short, probe a test point at either end of the isolated circuit (the light should be on). Leave the test light probe connected and open connectors, switches, remove parts, etc., sequentially, until the light goes out. When the light goes out, the short is between the last circuit component opened and the previous circuit opened.

NOTE: The 1.5 volt battery in the test light does not provide much current. A weak battery may not provide enough power to illuminate the test light even when a complete circuit is made (especially if there are high resistances in the circuit). Always make sure that the test battery is strong. To check the battery, briefly touch the ground clip to the probe; if the light glows brightly the battery is strong enough for testing. Never use a self-powered test light to perform checks for opens or shorts when power is applied to the electrical system under test. The 12–volt vehicle power will burn out the 1.5 volt light bulb in the test light.

VOLTMETER

A voltmeter is used to measure electrical voltage at any point in a circuit, or to measure the voltage drop across any part of a circuit. It can also be used to check continuity in a wire or circuit by indicating current flow from one end to the other. Analog voltmeters usually have various scales on the meter dial, while digital models only have a four or more digit readout. Both will have a selector switch to allow the selection of different voltage ranges. The voltmeter has a positive and a negative lead; to avoid damage to the meter, always connect the negative lead to the negative (−) side of circuit (to ground or nearest the ground side of the circuit) and always connect the positive lead to the positive (+) side of the circuit (to the power source or the nearest power source). Note that the negative voltmeter lead will always be black and that the positive voltmeter will always be some color other than black (usually red). Depending on how the voltmeter is connected into the electrical circuit, it has several uses.

NOTE: Some engine control systems (like the GM CCC or C4) require the use of a voltmeter with a high impedence rating of 20 megohms or higher. A standard, 9-volt powered analog voltmeter can damage computer components if used improperly.

A voltmeter can be connected either in parallel or in series with a circuit and it has a very high resistance to current flow. When connected in parallel, only a small amount of current will flow through the voltmeter current path; the rest will flow through the normal circuit current path and the circuit will work normally. When the

Typical analog-type voltmeter

voltmeter is connected in series with a circuit, only a small amount of current can pass through the voltmeter and flow through the circuit. The circuit will not work properly, but the voltmeter reading will show if the circuit is complete and being energized through the wiring harness and/or electronic control unit.

Available Voltage Measurement

Set the voltmeter selector switch to the 20V position and connect the meter negative lead to the negative post of the battery. Connect the positive meter lead to the positive post of the battery and turn the ignition switch ON to provide a load. Read the voltage level measured on the meter or digital display. A well-charged battery should register over 12 volts. If the meter reads below 11.5 volts, the battery power may be insufficient to operate the electrical system properly. This test determines the amount of voltage available from the battery and should be the first step in any electrical trouble diagnosis procedure. Many electrical problems, especially on computer controlled systems, can be caused by a low state of charge in the battery. Excessive corrosion at the battery cable terminals at the battery, ground or starter can cause a poor contact that will prevent proper charging and full battery current flow.

Normal battery voltage is 12 volts when fully charged. When the battery is supplying current to one or more circuits it is said to be "under load". When everything is off the electrical system is under a "no-load" condition. A fully charged battery may show about 12.5 volts at no load; will drop to 12 volts under medium load; and will drop even lower under heavy load. If the battery is partially discharged the voltage decrease under heavy load may be excessive, even though the battery shows 12 volts or more at no load. When allowed to discharge further, the battery's available voltage under load will decrease more severely. For this reason, it is important that the battery be fully charged during all testing procedures to avoid errors in diagnosis and incorrect test results. See the general battery charging precautions outlined earlier.

Voltage Drop

When current flows through a resistance, the voltage beyond the resistance is reduced (the larger the current, the greater the reduction in voltage). When no current is flowing, there is no voltage drop because there is no current flow. All points in the circuit which are connected to the power source are at the same voltage as the power source. The total voltage drop always equals the total source voltage. In a long circuit with many connectors, a series of small, unwanted voltage drops due to corrosion at the connectors can add up to a total loss of voltage which impairs the operation of the normal loads in the circuit.

A high impedence digital multimeter (volt-ohmmeter) is necessary for testing computerized engine control systems

INDIRECT COMPUTATION OF VOLTAGE DROPS

1. Set the voltmeter selector switch to the 20 volt position.
2. Connect the meter negative lead to a good ground.
3. Probe all resistances in the circuit with the positive meter lead.
4. Operate the circuit in all modes and observe the voltage readings. Record the voltage values for later reference.

DIRECT MEASUREMENT OF VOLTAGE DROPS

1. Set the voltmeter switch to the 20 volt position.
2. Connect the voltmeter negative lead to the ground side of the resistance load to be measured.
3. Connect the positive lead to the positive side of the resistance or load to be measured.
4. Read the voltage drop directly on the 20 volt scale and record the results for later reference.

Too high a voltage indicates too high a resistance. If, for example, a blower motor runs too slowly, you can determine if there is too high a resistance in the resistor pack. By taking voltage drop readings in all parts of the circuit, you can isolate the problem. Too low a voltage drop indicates too low a resistance. If, for example, a blower motor runs too fast in the MED and/or LOW position, the problem can be isolated in the resistor pack by taking voltage drop readings in all parts of the circuit to locate a possibly shorted resistor. The maximum allowable voltage drop under load is critical, especially if there is more than one high resistance problem in a circuit because all voltage drops are cumulative. A small drop is normal due to the resistance of the conductors.

High Resistance Testing

1. Set the voltmeter selector switch to the 4 volt position.
2. Connect the voltmeter positive lead to the positive post of the battery.
3. Turn on the headlights and heater blower to provide a load for proper circuit operation.
4. Probe various points in the circuit with the negative voltmeter lead.
5. Read the voltage drop on the 4 volt scale. Some average maximum allowable voltage drops are:

FUSE PANEL . . . . .0.7 volt
IGNITION SWITCH . . . . .0.5 volt
HEADLIGHT SWITCH. . . . . .0.7 volt
IGNITION COIL (+) . . . . .0.5 volt
ANY OTHER LOAD. . . . . .1.3 volt

NOTE: Voltage drops are all measured while a load is operating; without current flow, there will be no voltage drop.

OHMMETER

The ohmmeter is designed to read resistance (ohms) in a circuit or component. Although there are several different styles of ohmmeters, all will have a selector switch or a number of buttons which permits the measurement of different ranges of resistance (usually the selector switch allows the multiplication of the meter reading by 10, 100, 1000, and 10,000). A calibration knob allows the analog type meter to be set at zero for accurate measurement. Digital type ohmmeters are usually self-calibrating. Since all ohmmeters are powered by an internal battery (usually 9 volts), the ohmmeter can be used as a self-powered test light or continuity tester. When the ohmmeter is connected, current from the ohmmeter flows through the circuit or component being tested. Since the ohmmeter's internal resistance and voltage are known values, the amount of current flow through the meter depends on the resistance of the circuit or component being tested.

The ohmmeter can be used to perform continuity test for open or short circuits (either by observation of the meter needle or as a self-powered test light), and to read actual resistance in a circuit. It should be noted that the ohmmeter is used to check the resistance of a component or wire while there is no voltage applied to the circuit (wire harness disconnected). Current flow from an outside voltage source (such as the vehicle battery) can damage the ohmmeter, so the circuit or component should be isolated from the vehicle 12 volt electrical system before any testing is done. Since the ohmmeter uses its own voltage source, either test lead can be connected to any test point.

NOTE: When checking diodes or other solid state components, the ohmmeter leads can only be connected one way in order to measure current flow in a single direction. Make sure the positive (+) and negative (−) terminal connections are as described in the test procedures to verify the one-way diode operation.

In using the ohmmeter for making continuity checks, do not be too concerned with the actual resistance readings. Zero resistance, or any resistance readings, indicate continuity in the circuit. Infinite resistance indicates an open in the circuit. A high resistance reading where there should be none indicates a problem in the circuit. Checks for short circuits are made in the same manner as checks for open circuits except that the circuit must be isolated from both power and normal ground. Infinite resistance indicates no continuity to ground, while zero resistance indicates a dead short to ground. This test is useful for testing temperature sensors.

Measuring Resistance

The batteries in an analog ohmmeter will weaken with age and temperature, so the ohmmeter must be calibrated or "zeroed", before taking measurements, to insure accurate readings. To zero the meter, place the selector switch in its lowest range and touch the two ohmmeter leads together. Turn the calibration knob until the meter needle is exactly on zero.

NOTE: All analog (needle) type ohmmeters must be zeroed before use, but some digital ohmmeter models are automatically calibrated when the switch is turned on. Self-calibrating digital ohmmeters do not have an adjusting knob, but it's a good idea to check for a zero readout before use by touching the leads together. Some computer controlled systems require the use of a digital ohmmeter with at least 10 megohms impedance for testing. Before any test procedures are attempted, make sure the ohmmeter used is compatible with the electrical system or damage to the on-board computer could result.

To measure the resistance of a circuit, first isolate the circuit from the vehicle power source by disconnecting the battery cables or the harness connector. Make sure the key is OFF when disconnecting any components or the battery. Where necessary, also isolate at least one side of the circuit to be checked to avoid reading parallel resistances. Parallel circuit resistances will always give a lower reading than the actual resistance of either of the branches. When measuring the resistance of parallel circuits, the total resistance will always be lower than the smallest resistance in the circuit. Connect the meter leads to both sides of the circuit (wire or component) and read the actual measured ohms on the meter scale. Make sure the selector switch is set to the proper ohm scale for the circuit being tested to avoid misreading the ohmmeter test value. Specific component tests are outlined in the individual system sections.

─────CAUTION─────

Never use an ohmmeter for testing with power applied to the circuit. Like the self-powered test light, the ohmmeter is designed to operate on its own power supply. The normal 12 volt automotive electrical system current could damage the meter.

AMMETERS

An ammeter measures the amount of current flowing through a circuit in units called amperes or amps. Amperes are units of electron flow which indicate how fast the electrons are flowing through the circuit. Since Ohms Law dictates that current flow in a circuit is equal to the circuit voltage divided by the total circuit resistance, increasing voltage also increases the current level (amps). Likewise, any decrease in resistance will increase the amount of amps in a circuit. At normal operating voltage, most circuits have a characteristic amount of amperes, called "current

Analog ohmmeters must be calibrated before use by touching the probes together and turning the adjustment knob

draw" which can be measured using an ammeter. By referring to a specified current draw rating, measuring the amperes, and comparing the two values, one can determine what is happening within the circuit to aid in diagnosis. An open circuit, for example, will not allow any current to flow so the ammeter reading will be zero. More current flows through a heavily loaded circuit or when the charging system is operating.

An ammeter is always connected in series with the circuit being tested. All of the current that normally flows through the circuit must also flow through the ammeter; if there is any other path for the current to follow, the ammeter reading will not be accurate. The ammeter itself has very little resistance to current flow and therefore will not affect the circuit, but it will measure current draw only when the circuit is closed and electricity is flowing. Excessive current draw can blow fuses and drain the battery, while

An ammeter must be connected in series with the circuit being tested

Analog tach-dwell meter with insulated spring clip test leads

Analog tachometer with inductive pick-up test lead

DIGITAL VOLT/OHMMETER

Digital Volt-ohmmeter

Tach-dwell combination meter

a reduced current draw can cause motors to run slowly, lights to dim and other components to not operate properly. The ammeter can help diagnose these conditions by locating the cause of the high or low reading.

TACHOMETER

The function of the tachometer is to measure engine speed, and it is primarily used for adjusting idle rpm and setting engine speed for other test purposes, such as analyzing the charging system or ignition system. Tachometers are basic instruments for all tuneup work. A wide variety of automotive tachometers are available, from single-range "idle" tachometers to multi-range "universal" instruments. The most common test tachs are dual-range, primary operated units. This means the instrument is connected to the ignition primary circuit, usually at the coil positive (+) terminal. Some have a cylinder selector switch to match the instrument to the number of cylinders in the engine being tested. Others dispense with this switch and provide a separate scale range for each number of cylinders.

NOTE: Some tachometers are designed to use a crankshaft harmonic balancer pickup for the rpm signal.

The "universal" or "secondary" type tachometer is connected to a spark plug wire. This eliminates the need for a cylinder selector switch, although these instruments usually incorporate a 2-cycle/4-cycle switch. This allows them to function accurately on either four-cycle engines (standard automotive), two-cycle engines (outboards) or four-cycle engines with two-cycle or magnetotype ignition systems which produce a spark for every revolution of the crankshaft (outboards, some motorcycles, other small engines). Secondary tachs are useful for servicing electronic ignition systems, but not all primary tachs operate properly on electronic ignition systems.

Single-range tachometers usually measure up to 2000 or 2500 rpm and are used for idle adjustments and other low-speed testing. Dual-range tachs usually measure from 0–1000 rpm and 0–5000 rpm, although ranges up to 10,000 rpm are also available. The higher ranges are primarily for road testing or dynamometer use. The low range is principally used for accurate idle and timing-speed adjustments, since it is commonly scaled in 20-rpm increments. To provide even closer low-speed readings, some low-range tachometers are expanded. That is, the low end of the range is eliminated, thus stretching out or magnifying the range from about 400 rpm to 1000 rpm. The higher speed ranges are primarily for other purposes, such as checking alternator output at certain speeds or noting the setting of the fast-idle adjustment. Some of the various uses of a tachometer include idle speed resets and adjustments, checking ignition timing advance, ignition system tests, mixture adjustments (if applicable) and emissions testing.

MULTIMETERS

Different combinations of test meters can be built into a single unit designed for specific tests. Some of the more common combination test devices are known as Volt-Amp testers, Tach-Dwell meters, or Digital Multimeters. The Volt-Amp tester is used for charging system, starting system or battery tests and consists of a voltmeter, an ammeter and a variable resistance carbon pile. The voltmeter will usually have at least two ranges for use with 6, 12 and 24 volt systems. The ammeter also has more than one range for testing various levels of battery loads and starter current draw and the carbon pile can be adjusted to offer different amount of resistance. The Volt-Amp tester has heavy leads to carry large amounts of current and many later models have an inductive ammeter pickup that clamps around the wire to simplify test connections. On some models, the ammeter also has a zero-center scale to allow testing of charging and starting systems without switching leads or polarity. A digital multimeter is a voltmeter, ammeter and ohmmeter combined in an instrument which gives a digital readout. These are often used when testing solid state circuits because of their high input impedance (usually 10 megohms or more).

The tach-dwell meter combines a tachometer and a dwell (cam angle) meter and is a specialized kind of voltmeter. The tachometer scale is marked to show engine speed in rpm and the dwell scale is marked to show degrees of distributor shaft rotation. In most electronic ignition systems, dwell is determined by the control unit, but the dwell meter can also be used to check the duty cycle (operation) of some electronic engine control systems. Some tach-dwell meters are powered by an internal battery, while others take their power from the car battery in use. The battery powered testers usually required calibration much like an ohmmeter before testing.

TIMING LIGHT

A timing light is basically a hand-held stroboscope that, when connected to the No. 1 spark plug wire, will flash on and off every time the plug fires. This flashing strobe light will "freeze" the timing marks to allow a check of the ignition timing during service. The timing light may be powered by the car battery, or it can be designed to run off of house current (120 volts), but most of them are designed to operate on a 12 volt current. Some timing lights have an adapter to allow connection to the No. 1 spark plug wire and others use an inductive pickup that simply clamps around the plug wire, but under no circumstances should a spark plug wire be punctured with a sharp probe to make a connection. Simple timing lights do nothing more than flash when the plug fires, but there are other types called adjustable timing lights that contain circuitry which delays the flashing of the light. This delay feature is adjustable and the amount of deadly in degrees is measured by a meter built into the timing light. The adjustable timing light can be used to test advance mechanisms and timing control systems.

OSCILLOSCOPE

An oscilloscope is a sophisticated electronic test device that shows the changing voltage levels in a electrical circuit over a period of time. The scope has a display screen much like the picture tube of a television set and displays a line of light called a trace which indicates the voltage levels. The screen is usually marked with voltage and time scales. The ignition waveform pattern on the oscilloscope screen indicates the point of ignition, spark duration, voltage level, coil/condenser operation, dwell angle and the condition of the spark plugs and wires.

The oscilloscope patterns formed by electronic systems vary slightly from one manufacturer to another, but generally the firing section of a trace can be interpreted the same way for all models because the same basic thing is happening to all systems. The length of the dwell section, for example, is not important to an electronic ignition system, although some systems are designed to lengthen the dwell at higher engine rpm. The dwell reading that indicates the duty cycle of a fuel mixture control device, on the other hand, is very important and in fact may go a long way toward indicating a problem or verifying that everything is functioning normally.

NOTE: Follow the manufacturer's instructions for all oscilloscope connections and test procedures. Make sure the scope being used is compatible with the system being tested before any diagnosis is attempted.

SOLDERING GUN

Soldering is a quick, efficient method of joining metals permanently. Everyone who has the occasion to make electrical repairs should know how to solder. Electrical connections that are soldered are far less likely to come apart and will conduct electricity far better than connections that are only "pig-tailed" together. The most popular (and preferred) method of soldering is with an electric soldering gun. Soldering irons are available in many sizes and wattage ratings. Irons with high wattage ratings deliver higher temperatures and recover lost heat faster. A small soldering iron rated for no more than 50 watts is recommended for home use, especially

Typical timing light with inductive pick-up

on electrical projects where excess heat can damage the components being soldered.

There are three ingredients necessary for successful soldering—proper flux, good solder and sufficient heat. A soldering flux is necessary to clean the metal of tarnish, prepare it for soldering and to enable the solder to spread into tiny crevices. When soldering electrical work, always use a resin flux or resin core solder, which is non-corrosive and will not attract moisture once the job is finished. Other types of flux (acid-core) will leave a residue that will attract moisture, causing the wires to corrode. Tin is a unique metal with a low melting point. In a molten state, it dissolves and alloys easily with many metals. Solder is made by mixing tin (which is very expensive) with lead (which is very inexpensive). The most common proportions are 40/60, 50/50 and 60/40, the percentage of tin always being listed first. Low-priced solders often contain less tin, making them very difficult for a beginner to use because more heat is required to melt the solder. A common solder is 40/60 which is well suited for all-around general use, but 60/40 melts easier, has more tin for a better joint and is preferred for electrical work.

Various types of soldering guns

Soldering Techniques

Successful soldering requires that the metals to be joined be heated to a temperature that will melt the solder, usually somewhere around 360–460°F., depending on the tin content of the solder. Contrary to popular belief, the purpose of the soldering iron is not to melt the solder itself, but to heat the parts being soldered to a temperature high enough to melt solder when it is touched to the work. Melting flux-cored solder on the soldering iron will usually destroy the effectiveness of the flux.

NOTE: Soldering tips are made of copper for good heat conductance, but must be "tinned" regularly for quick transference of heat to the project and to prevent the solder from sticking to the iron. To "tin" the iron, simply heat it and touch flux-cored solder to the tip; the solder will flow over the tip. Wipe the excess off with a rag. Be careful; soldering iron will be hot.

Tinning the soldering iron before use

Proper soldering method. Allow the soldering iron to heat the wire first, then apply solder as shown

After some use, the tip may become pitted. If so, simply dress the tip smooth with a smooth file and "tin" the tip again. An old saying holds that "metals well-cleaned are half soldered." Flux-cored solder will remove oxides, but rust, bits of insulation and oil or grease must be removed with a wire brush or emery cloth. For maximum strength in soldered parts, the joint must start off clean and tight. Weak joints will result in gaps too wide for the solder to bridge.

If a separate soldering flux is used, it should be brushed or swabbed on only those areas that are to be soldered. Most solders contain a core of flux and separate fluxing is unnecessary. Hold the work to be soldered firmly. It is best to solder on a wooden board, because a metal vise will only rob the piece to be soldered of heat and make it difficult to melt solder. Hold the soldering tip with the broadest face against the work to be soldered. Apply solder under the tip close to the work; using enough solder to give a heavy film between the iron and piece being soldered, while moving slowly and making sure the solder melts properly. Keep the work level or the solder will run to the lowest part, and favor the thicker parts, because these require more heat to melt the solder. If the soldering tip overheats (the solder coating on the face of the tip burns up), it should be retinned. Once the soldering is completed, let the soldered joint stand until cool. Tape and seal all soldered wire splices after the repair has cooled.

WIRE HARNESS REPAIR PROCEDURES

Condition	Location	Correction
Non-continuity	Using the electric wiring diagram and the wiring harness diagram as a guideline, check the continuity of the circuit in question by using a tester, and check for breaks, loose connector couplings, or loose terminal crimp contacts.	**Breaks**—Reconnect the point of the break by using solder. If the wire is too short and the connection is impossible, extend it by using a wire of the same or larger size.

Solder

Be careful concerning the size of wire used for the extension

Loose couplings—Hold the connector securely, and insert it until there is a definite joining of the coupling. If the connector is equipped with a locking mechanism, insert the connector until it is locked securely.

Crimp by using pliers

Solder

Loose terminal crimp contacts—Remove approximately 2 in. (5mm) of the insulation covering from the end of the wire, crimp the terminal contact by using a pair of pliers, and then, in addition, complete the repair by soldering.

Condition	Location	Correction
Short-circuit	Using the electric wiring diagram and the wiring harness diagram as a guideline, check the entire circuit for pinched wires.	Remove the pinched portion, and then repair any breaks in the insulation covering with tape. Repair breaks of the wire by soldering.
Loose terminal	Pull the wiring lightly from the connector. A special terminal removal tool may be necessary for complete removal.	Raise the terminal catch pin, and then insert it until a definite clicking sound is heard.

Catch pin

Note: There is the chance of short circuits being caused by insulation damage at soldered points. To avoid this possibility, wrap all splices with electrical tape and use a layer of silicone to seal the connection against moisture. Incorrect repairs can cause malfunctions by creating excessive resistance in a circuit.

WIRE HARNESS AND CONNECTORS

Repairs and Replacement

The on-board computer (ECM) wire harness electrically connects the control unit to the various solenoids, switches, and sensors in the engine compartment. Most connectors in the engine compartment are protected against moisture and dirt which could create oxidation and deposits on the terminals. This protection is important because of the very low voltage and current levels used by the computer and engine sensors. All connectors have a lock which secures the male and female terminals together; a secondary lock holds the seal and terminal into the connector. Both terminal locks must be released when disconnecting ECM connectors.

These special connectors are weather-proof and all repairs require the use of a special terminal and the tool required to service it. This tool is used to remove the pin and sleeve terminals. If removal is attempted with an ordinary pick, there is a good chance that the terminal will be bent or deformed. Unlike standard blade type terminals, these terminals cannot be straightened once they are bent. Make certain that the connectors are properly seated and all of the sealing rings in place when connecting leads. On some models, a hinge–type flap provides a backup, or secondary locking feature for the terminals. Most secondary locks are used to improve the connector reliability by retaining the terminals if the small terminal lock tangs are not positioned properly.

Molded-on connectors require complete replacement of the connection. This means splicing a new connector assembly into the harness. All splices in on-board computer systems should be soldered to insure proper contact. Use care when probing the connections or replacing terminals in them; it is possible to short between opposite terminals. If this happens to the wrong terminal pair, it is possible to damage certain components. Always use jumper wires between connectors for circuit checking. NEVER probe through the weather-proof seals.

Open circuits are often difficult to locate by sight because corrosion or terminal misalignment are hidden by the connectors. Merely wiggling a connector on a sensor or in the wiring harness may correct the open circuit condition. This should always be considered when an open circuit or failed sensor is indicated. Intermittent problems may also be caused by oxidized or loose connections. When using a circuit tester for diagnosis, always probe connectors from the wire side. Be careful not to damage sealed connectors with test probes.

All wiring harnesses should be replaced with identical parts, using the same gauge wire and connectors. When signal wires are spliced into a harness, use wire with high temperature insulation only. With the low current and voltage levels found in the system, it is important that the best possible connection at all wire splices be made by soldering the splices together. It is seldom necessary to replace a complete harness. If replacement is necessary, pay close attention to insure proper harness routing. Secure the harness with suitable plastic wire clamps to prevent vibrations from causing the harness to wear in spots or contact hot engine components.

NOTE: Weather-proof connections cannot be replaced with standard connections. Instructions are provided with replacement connector and terminal packages. Some wire harnesses have mounting indicators (usually pieces of colored tape) to mark where the harness is to be secured.

Replacement of Open or Shorted Wires

In making wiring repairs, it's important that you always replace broken or shorted wires with the same gauge wire. The heavier the wire, the smaller the gauge number. Wires are usually color-coded to aid in identification and, whenever possible, the same color coded wire should be used for replacement. A wire stripping and crimping tool is necessary to install solderless terminal connectors properly. Test all crimps by pulling on the wires; it should not be possible to pull the wires out of a good crimp.

NOTE: Some late model on-board computer control systems require that all wiring be soldered to insure proper contact

Some electrical connectors use a lock spring instead of the molded locking tabs

Secure the wiring harness at the indication marks, if used, to prevent vibrations from causing wear and a possible short

Various types of locking harness connectors. Depress the locks at the arrows to separate the connector

Probe all connectors from the wire side when testing

Slide back the weatherproof seals or boots on sealed terminals for testing, if necessary

Correct method of testing weatherproof connectors—do not pierce connector seals with test probes

Special purpose testing connectors for use on fuel injected engines

NOTE: Most of the problems caused in the wiring harness are usually due to bad ground connections. Always check all vehicle ground connections for corrosion or looseness before performing any power feed checks to eliminate the chance of a bad ground affecting the circuit. Electrical wiring connectors can be classified according to the type of terminals (such as pin terminals or flat terminals), the number of poles (terminals), whether they are male or female, whether they have a locking device or not, etc.

Repairing Hard Shell Connectors

Unlike molded connectors, the terminal contacts in hard shell connectors can be replaced. Weatherproof hard-shell connectors (like solid state ignition module connectors) with the leads molded into the shell have non-replaceable terminal ends. Replacement usually involves the use of a special terminal removal tool that depress the locking tangs (barbs) on the connector terminal and allow the connector to be removed from the rear of the shell. The connector shell should be replaced if it shows any evidence of burning, melting, cracks, or breaks. Replace individual terminals that are burnt, corroded, distorted or loose.

The insulation crimp must be tight to prevent the insulation from sliding back on the wire when the wire is pulled. The insulation must be visibly compressed under the crimp tabs, and the ends of the crimp should be turned in for a firm grip on the insulation. The wire crimp must be made with all wire strands inside the crimp. The terminal must be fully compressed on the wire strands with the ends of the crimp tabs turned in to make a firm grip on the wire. Check all connections with an ohmmeter to insure a good contact. There should be no measurable resistance between the wire and the terminal when connected.

Diagnostic Connectors

Some cars have diagnostic connectors mounted on the firewall or fender panel. Each terminal is connected in parallel with a voltage test point in the electrical system. Many test equipment companies make special testers that plug into the connector. These have the advantage of fast hookup and test time, but in most cases the same tests can be done with a suitable voltmeter. By connecting the voltmeter negative (−) lead to the diagnostic ground terminal and the positive (+) lead to the other terminals in turn, one can make seven or eight voltage tests from a single point on the car. Jumper wires may be necessary to connect some voltmeters to the connector.

On GM models, later model diagnostic connector has a variety of information available. Called Serial Data, there are several tools on the market for reading this information. These tools do not make the use of diagnostic charts unnecessary. They do not tell exactly where a problem is in a given circuit. However, with an understanding of what each position on the equipment measures, and knowledge of the circuit involved, the tools can be very useful in getting information which would be more time consuming to get with other equipment. In some cases, it will provide information that is either extremely difficult or impossible to get with other equipment. When a chart calls for a sensor reading, the diagnostic

Wires which are open, exposed or otherwise damaged are repaired by simple splicing. Where possible, if the wiring harness is accessible and the damaged place in the wire can be located, it is best to open the harness and check for all possible damage. In an inaccessible harness, the wire must be bypassed with a new insert, usually taped to the outside of the old harness.

Fusible Links

When replacing fusible links, be sure to use fusible link wire, NOT ordinary automotive wire. Make sure the fusible wire segment is of the same gauge and construction as the one being replaced and double the stripped end when crimping the terminal connector for a good contact. The melted (open) fusible link segment of the wiring harness should be cut off as close to the harness as possible, then a new segment spliced in as described. In the case of a damaged fusible link that feeds two harness wires, the harness connections should be replaced with two fusible link wires so that each circuit will have its own separate protection.

AMP CONNECTOR

SHOULDER
LOCKING TAB
PIN CONTACT
LOCKING TAB
LATCHING LEG
SOCKET CONTACT
BRIDGE

BLADE CONNECTOR

LATCHING TONGUE
LOCKING FINGER
SOCKET CONTACT
T-SHAPED SLOTS
BLADE CONTACT
LOCKING FINGER

TANG CONNECTOR

PLASTIC SPRING
SHOULDER
LOCKING TANG
LATCHING TONGUE

LOCKING WEDGE CONNECTOR

GROOVE
WEDGE
RETAINING FINGER GROOVE
LATCHING TONGUE
WEDGE

PRINTED CIRCUIT CONNECTOR

FINGER NOTCH
LOCKING FINGER
CONTACT FINGER

INTERNAL LOCKING FINGER CONNECTOR

SOCKET CONTACT
LOCKING FINGER
PIN CONTACT
CUT-OUT NOTCH
CUT-OUT NOTCH
LATCHING LEG
LOCKING FINGER

SUPER CHAMP FT

AMP INCORPORATED

CRIMPING TOOL AMP-29564

CRIMPING TOOL
C4AZ 17018-A
OR
AMPC-90124-2

BEFORE CRIMP

INSULATION
WIRE
INSULATION TABS
WIRE TABS
TERMINAL

AFTER CRIMP

FINAL CRIMP

FLATTENED
TURNED IN
COMPRESSED

UPPER JAW
ANVIL
TERMINAL TABS
WIRE

Correct method of crimping terminals with special tool

WEATHER PACK CONNECTORS
REPAIR PROCEDURE

FEMALE
CONNECTOR
BODY

MALE
CONNECTOR
BODY

1. OPEN SECONDARY LOCK HINGE ON CONNECTOR

2. REMOVE TERMINALS USING SPECIAL TOOL

J-28742

TERMINAL REMOVAL
TOOL

3. CUT WIRE IMMEDIATELY BEHIND CABLE SEAL

WIRE

SEAL

4.
A. SLIP NEW SEAL ONTO WIRE
B. STRIP 5.0 mm (0.2'') OF
   INSULATION FROM WIRE
C. CRIMP TERMINAL OVER
   WIRE AND SEAL

SEAL

Repairing GM Weatherpak connectors. Note special terminal removal tools

MCU TESTER

STAR TESTER WITH
EFI/EEC-IV ADAPTER
HARNESS

Self-Test and Automatic Readout (STAR) tester used for obtaining trouble codes from Ford MCU and EEC IV systems

TORQUE
CONVERTER
CLUTCH
SOLENOID

"CHECK
ENGINE"
LIGHT

AIR SELECT/EARLY
FUEL EVAPORATION
SOLENOID

TEST
TERMINAL

GROUND

ASSEMBLY LINE
DIAGNOSTIC LINK (ALDL)
CONNECTOR

UNDER LEFT HAND SIDE
OF INSTRUMENT PANEL

UNDER RIGHT HAND SIDE
OF INSTRUMENT PANEL
AT KICK PANEL

ALDL
CONNECTOR

ASHTRAY
MOUNTING
BRACKET

UNDER INSTRUMENT PANEL
TO LEFT OF ASHTRAY

ALDL CONNECTOR

INSTRUMENT PANEL
BELOW STEERING COLUMN

Typical diagnostic terminal locations on GM models. The diagnosis terminals are usually mounted under the dash or in the engine compartment

connector tool can be used to read the following voltage signals directly:
• Park/Neutral
• Throttle Position Sensor
• Manifold Absolute Pressure Sensor
• Coolant Temperature Sensor
• Vehicle Speed Sensor

Typical adapter wiring harness for connecting tester to diagnostic terminal

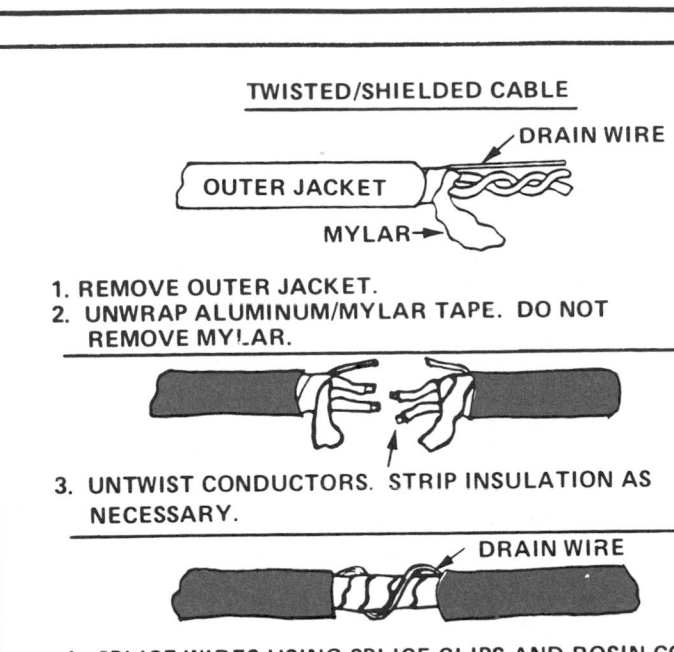

TWISTED/SHIELDED CABLE

1. REMOVE OUTER JACKET.
2. UNWRAP ALUMINUM/MYLAR TAPE. DO NOT REMOVE MYLAR.

3. UNTWIST CONDUCTORS. STRIP INSULATION AS NECESSARY.

4. SPLICE WIRES USING SPLICE CLIPS AND ROSIN CORE SOLDER. WRAP EACH SPLICE TO INSULATE.
5. WRAP WITH MYLAR AND DRAIN (UNINSULATED) WIRE.

6. TAPE OVER WHOLE BUNDLE TO SECURE AS BEFORE

TWISTED LEADS

1. LOCATE DAMAGED WIRE.
2. REMOVE INSULATION AS REQUIRED.

3. SPLICE TWO WIRES TOGETHER USING SPLICE CLIPS AND ROSIN CORE SOLDER.

4. COVER SPLICE WITH TAPE TO INSULATE FROM OTHER WIRES.
5. RETWIST AS BEFORE AND TAPE WITH ELECTRICAL TAPE AND HOLD IN PLACE.

Typical wire harness repair methods

When the diagnosis tool is plugged in on GM models, it takes out the timer that keeps the fuel injection system in open loop for a certain period of time. Therefore, it will go closed loop as soon as the car is started, if all other closed loop conditions are met. This means that if, for example, the air management operation were checked with the diagnosis tool plugged in, the air managment system would not function normally.

More elaborate electronic engine control testers are necessary for testing Ford's EEC II and EEC III systems

The diagnosis tester is helpful in cases of intermittent operation. The tool can be plugged in and observed while driving the car under the condition where the light comes ON momentarily, or the engine driveability is poor momentarily. If the problem seems to be related to certain areas that can be checked on the diagnosis tool, then those are the positions that should be checked while driving the car. If there does not seem to be any correlation between the problem and any specific circuit, the diagnosis tool can be checked on each position, watching for a period of time to see if there is any change in the readings that indicates intermittent operation.

Mechanical Test Equipment

VACUUM GAUGE

How much vacuum an engine produces depends on efficiency; a badly worn engine cannot produce as much vacuum as one in good condition. Piston rings, valves, carburetion, ignition timing and exhaust all have a predictable effect on engine vacuum, making it possible to diagnose engine condition and performance by measuring the amount of vacuum. There are two types of vacuum produced by an engine-manifold and ported vacuum.

Manifold vacuum is drawn directly from a tap on the intake manifold and is greatest at idle and decreases as the throttle is opened. At wide-open throttle, there is very little vacuum in the intake manifold. Ported vacuum is drawn from an opening in the carburetor just above the throttle valve. When the throttle valve is closed during idle or deceleration, ported vacuum is low or non-existent. As the throttle is opened, it uncovers the port and the vacuum level becomes essentially the same as manifold vacuum. Ported vacuum is used to operate vacuum switches and diaphragms; it is not used to diagnose engine problems.

Many late model engines have two other vacuum sources at the carburetor, used to control EGR and other emission control devices. EGR ported vacuum is taken from a tap in the carburetor barrel slightly above the ported vacuum tap. The EGR ported vacuum tap often has two openings in the barrel so that vacuum is applied to the EGR control valve in two stages. Another vacuum source on late model carburetors is venturi vacuum, usually used with a vacuum amplifier to control EGR during and slightly above cruising speed.

Most vacuum readings are taken at engine idle speed with a vacuum gauge that measures the difference between atmospheric and intake manifold pressure. Most gauges are graduated in inches of mercury (in. Hg), although a device called a manometer reads vacuum in inches of water (in. H2O). The normal vacuum reading usually varies between 18 and 22 in. Hg at sea level. To test engine vacuum, the vacuum gauge must be connected to a source of manifold vacuum. Many engines have a plug in the intake manifold which can be removed and replaced with an adapter fitting. Connect the vacuum gauge to the fitting with a suitable rubber hose or, if no manifold plug is available, connect the vacuum gauge to any device using manifold vacuum, such as EGR valves, etc.

Typical hand vacuum pumps

HAND VACUUM PUMP

Small, hand-held vacuum pumps come in a variety of designs. Most have a built-in vacuum gauge and allow the component to be tested without removing it from the vehicle. Operate the pump lever or plunger to apply the correct amount of vacuum required for the test specified in the diagnosis routines. The level of vacuum in inches of Mercury (in. Hg) is indicated on the pump gauge. For some testing, an additional vacuum gauge may be necessary.

Testing Vacuum Components

Intake manifold vacuum is used to operate various systems and devices on late model cars. To correctly diagnose and solve problems in vacuum control systems, a vacuum source is necessary for testing. In some cases, vacuum can be taken from the intake manifold when the engine is running, but vacuum is normally provided by a hand vacuum pump. These hand vacuum pumps have a built-in vacuum gauge that allow testing while the device is still attached to the car. For some tests, an additional vacuum gauge may be necessary.

MANOMETER

A manometer measures vacuum in inches of water and is required for synchronizing minimum idle speed on some throttle body fuel injection systems.

COMPRESSION GAUGE

A compression gauge is designed to measure the amount of air pressure in psi that a cylinder is capable of producing. Some gauges have a hose that screws into the spark plug hole while others have a tapered rubber tip which is held in the spark plug hole. Engine compression depends on the sealing ability of the rings, valves,

Typical compression tester

head gasket and spark plug gaskets. If any of these parts are not sealing well, compression will be lost and the power output of the engine will be reduced. The compression in each cylinder should be measured and the variation between cylinders noted. The engine should be cranked through five or six compression strokes while it is warm, with all the spark plugs removed.

FUEL PRESSURE GAUGE

A fuel pressure gauge is required to test the operation of any fuel injection system. Some systems also need a three way valve to check the fuel pressure in various modes of operation, or special adapters for making fuel connections. Always observe the cautions outlined in the individual fuel system sections when working around any pressurized fuel system.

USING A VACUUM GAUGE

White needle = steady needle   *Dark needle = drifting needle*

The vacuum gauge is one of the most useful and easy-to-use diagnostic tools. It is inexpensive, easy to hook up, and provides valuable information about the condition of your engine.

Indication: Normal engine in good condition

Gauge reading: Steady, from 17–22 in./Hg.

Indication: Sticking valve or ignition miss

Gauge reading: Needle fluctuates from 15–20 in./Hg. at idle

Indication: Late ignition or valve timing, low compression, stuck throttle valve, leaking carburetor or manifold gasket.

Gauge reading: Low (15–20 in./Hg.) but steady

Indication: Improper carburetor adjustment, or minor intake leak at carburetor or manifold

Gauge reading: Drifting needle

Indication: Weak valve springs, worn valve stem guides, or leaky cylinder head gasket (vibrating excessively at all speeds).

Gauge reading: Needle fluctuates as engine speed increases

Indication: Burnt valve or improper valve clearance. The needle will drop when the defective valve operates.

Gauge reading: Steady needle, but drops regularly

Indication: Choked muffler or obstruction in system. Speed up the engine. Choked muffler will exhibit a slow drop of vacuum to zero.

Gauge reading: Gradual drop in reading at idle

Indication: Worn valve guides

Gauge reading: Needle vibrates excessively at idle, but steadies as engine speed increases

Fuel pressure gauge with tee adapter

Repairing Fuel Lines

---CAUTION---

Fuel supply lines on vehicles equipped with fuel injected engines will remain pressurized for long periods of time after engine shutdown. The pressure must be relieved before servicing the fuel system.

Vehicles equipped with nylon fuel tubes and push connect fittings have three types of service that can be performed to the fuel lines; replacing nylon tubing (splicing nylon to nylon), replacing push connector retainer clip, and replacing damaged push connect tube end. These nylon lines replace the conventional steel tubing. The individual tubes are taped together by the manufacturer and are supplied as an assembly. The plastic fuel tube assembly is secured to the body rails with nylon wrap-around clips and push-in pins. To make hand insertion of the barbed connectors into the nylon easier, the tube end must be soaked in a cup of boiling water for one minute immediately before pushing the barbs into the nylon. Damaged push connectors must be discarded and replaced with new push connectors. If only the retaining clip is damaged, replace the clip.

---CAUTION---

The plastic fuel lines can be damaged by torches, welding sparks, grinding and other operations which involve heat and high temperatures. If any repair or service operation will be used which involves heat and high temperatures locate all fuel system components, especially the plastic fuel lines to be certain they will not be damaged.

Fuel pressure gauge with three-way valve adapter. Some fuel systems use test points with quick disconnect fittings

On-Board Diagnostic Systems

INDEX

NOTE: Please refer to the Application Chart at the front of this Manual.

SELF-DIAGNOSING ELECTRONIC ENGINE CONTROL

General Information

Some on-board computer systems are equipped with a self-diagnosis capability to allow retrieval of stored trouble codes from the ECU memory. The number of codes stored and the meaning of the code numbers varies from one manufacturer to another. By activating the diagnostic mode and counting the number of flashes on the CHECK ENGINE or ECU lights, it is possible to ask the computer where the problem is (which circuit) and narrow down the number of pin connectors tested when diagnosing an AFC fuel injection problem. It should be noted that the trouble codes are only an indication of a circuit malfunction, not a component analysis. A trouble code that indicates a specific component has failed may be caused by a loose connection, rather than some mechanical problem. Use the trouble codes as a guide for further diagnosis or you may replace expensive electronic devices unnecessarily.

NOTE: Remember to clear the trouble codes as outlined in the various sections whenever all diagnosis procedures are complete, or the same trouble code may remain stored in the computer memory even though repairs have been made.

On-Board Diagnosis Procedures

The following information describes how to activate the self-diagnosis mode on several of the most popular engine control systems. Do not attempt to enter the diagnostic mode on any electronic computer based system unless all indicated special tools are available. Follow the instructions carefully to avoid misdiagnosis or possible circuit damage from improper connections or procedures. It is very important to cancel the diagnosis mode when all service codes have been recorded in order to restore the computer to its normal operating mode. Some systems may be self-canceling, but most require specific steps to be taken or the computer may be damaged or fail to operate properly when the ignition is switched ON.

Chrysler ESA System

The electronic Spark Advance (ESA) on-board computer is programmed to monitor several different component systems simultaneously. If a problem is detected in a monitored circuit often enough to indicate a malfunction, a fault code is stored in the computer memory for eventual display on a diagnostic readout tool (Part No. C-4805 or equivalent). If the problem is repaired or disappears, the computer cancels the fault code after 30 ignition ON/OFF cycles. If a fault code appears on the diagnostic readout tool, perform a careful visual check of all wiring and vacuum connections. Many problems are the result of loose, disconnected, or cracked vacuum hoses or wiring connectors.

The readout tool can be used to test the engine control system in three different modes; the diagnostic test mode, the circuit actuation test (ATM) mode, and the switch test mode. The diagnostic test mode is used to retrieve fault codes that are stored in the computer memory. The circuit actuation test mode is used to test specific component circuits and systems. The switch test mode is used to test switch circuits and operation. When a fault code appears on the display screen, it indicates that the spark control computer has detected an abnormal signal in the system. Fault codes indicate a problem in a circuit, but do not necessarily identify the failed component.

Diagnostic read out tool used to obtain trouble codes from Chrysler ESA system

CHRYSLER ESA SYSTEM TROUBLE CODES

Code Number	Circuit
00	Diagnostic readout tool connected properly
11	02 solenoid control circuit
13	Canister purge solenoid circuit ①
14	Battery has been disconnected
16	Radiator fan control relay ②
17	Electronic throttle control vacuum solenoid ①
18	Vacuum operated secondary control solenoid system ①

CHRYSLER ESA SYSTEM TROUBLE CODES

Code Number	Circuit
21	Distributor pick-up system
22	02 system full rich or full lean
24	Computer (ECU) failure
25	Radiator fan coolant sensor ①
26	Engine temperature sensor
28	Odometer sensor (mileage counter) ③
31	Engine has not been started since battery disconnection
32	Computer (ECU) failure
33	Computer (ECU) failure
55	End of message (trouble codes)
88	Start of message (trouble codes)

① 2.2L engines only
② 2.2L engines only. Disregard if air conditioned
③ Manual transmission only

Tester used to diagnose Chrysler EFI system

Analog voltmeter and STAR tester

Activating Circuit Actuation Test (ATM) Mode

Place the system into the diagnostic test mode as previously described and wait for code 55 to appear on the diagnostic readout tool display screen. Press the ATM button down until the desired test code appears. The computer will continue to turn the selected circuit on and off for as long as five minutes or until the ATM button is pressed again or the ignition switch is turned OFF. If the ATM button is not pressed a second time, the computer will continue cycling the selected circuit for five minutes and then shut the system off.

TROUBLE CODES

91 Oxygen sensor feedback solenoid activated
92 Shift indicator light activated (manual transmission only)
93 Canister purge solenoid activated
96 Fan relay activated
97 Electronic throttle control solenoid activated
98 Vacuum operated secondary control solenoid activated

Activating Switch Test Mode

Place the system into the diagnostic test mode as previously described and wait for code 55 to appear on the diagnostic readout tool display screen. Check that both the air conditioning and heated rear window switches are in the OFF position. Press the ATM button and immediately move the read/hold switch to the read position; wait for code 00 to appear on the display screen. Turn the air conditioning switch to the ON position. If the computer is receiving information (switch input) the display will change to 88 when the switch is turned ON and switch back to 00 when the switch is turned OFF. Repeat the test for the heated rear window

switch. Code 00 indicates the switch is OFF and code 88 indicates that the switch is ON.

Ford EEC IV System

The 2.3L system is similar to the 1.6L, with the addition of a "keep alive" memory in the ECA that retains any intermittent trouble codes stored within the last 20 engine starts. With this system, the memory is not erased when the ignition is switched OFF. A self-diagnosis capability is built into the EEC IV system to aid in troubleshotting. The primary tool necessary to read the trouble codes stored in the system is an analog voltmeter or special Self Test Automatic Readout (STAR) tester (Motorcraft No. 007-0M004, or equivalent). While the self-test is not conclusive by itself, when activated it checks the EFC IV system by testing its memory integrity and processing capability. The self-test also verifies that all sensors and actuators are connected and working properly.

When a service code is displayed on an analog voltmeter, each code number is represented by pulses or sweeps of the meter needle. A code 3, for example, will be read as three needle pulses followed by a six-second delay. If a two digit code is stored, there will be a two second delay between the pulses for each digit of the number. Code 23, for example, will be displayed as two needle pulses, a two second pause, then three more pulses followed by a four second pause. All testing is complete when the codes have been repeated once. The pulse format is ½ second ON-time for each digit, 2 seconds OFF-time between digits, 4 seconds OFF-time between codes and either 6 seconds (1.6L) or or 10 seconds (2.3L) OFF-time before and after the half-second separator pulse.

NOTE: If using the STAR tester, or equivalent, consult the manufacturers instructions included with the unit for correct hookup and trouble code interpretation.

In addition to the service codes, two other types of coded information are outputted during the self-test; engine identification and fast codes. Engine ID codes are one digit numbers equal to one-half the number of engine cylinders (e.g. 4 cylinder is code 2, 8 cylinder is code 4, etc.). Fast codes are simply the service codes transmitted at 100 times the normal rate in a short burst of information. Some meters may detect these codes and register a slight meter deflection just before the trouble codes are flashed. Both the ID and fast codes serve no purpose in the field and this meter deflection should be ignored.

Typical digital volt/ohmmeter used to test electronic engine control systems

Ford EEC tester connector harness showing computer hookup

Activating Self-Test Mode on EEC IV

Turn the ignition key OFF. On the 2.3L engine, connect a jumper wire from the self-test input (STI) to pin 2 (signal return) on the self-test connector. On the 1.6L engine, connect a jumper wire from pin 5 self-test input to pin 2 (signal return) on the self-test connector. Set the analog voltmeter on a DC voltage range to read from 0–15 volts, then connect the voltmeter from the battery positive (+) terminal to pin 4 self-test output in the self-test connector. Turn the ignition switch ON (engine off) and read the trouble codes on the meter needle as previously described. A code 11 means that the EEC IV system is operating properly and no faults are detected by the computer.

NOTE: This test will only detect "hard" failures that are present when the self-test is activated. For intermittent problems, remove the voltmeter clip from the self-test trigger terminal and wiggle the wiring harness. With the voltmeter still attached to the self-test output, watch for a needle deflection that signals an intermittent condition has occurred. The meter will deflect each time the fault is induced and a trouble code will be stored. Reconnect the self-test trigger terminal to the voltmeter to retrieve the code.

EEC IV TROUBLE CODES (2.3L)

Code	Diagnosis
11	Normal operation (no codes stored)
12	Incorrect high idle rpm value
13	Incorrect curb idle rpm value
14	Erratic Profile Ignition Pickup (PIP) signal
15	Read Only Memory (ROM) failure
21	Incorrect engine coolant temperature (ECT) sensor signal
22	Incorrect barometric pressure (BAP) sensor signal
23	Incorrect throttle position sensor (TPS) signal
24	Incorrect vane air temperature (VAT) sensor signal
26	Incorrect vane air flow (VAF) sensor signal
41	System always lean
42	System always rich
51	Engine coolant temperature (ECT) sensor signal too high
53	Throttle position sensor (TPS) signal too high
54	Vane air temperature (VAT) sensor signal too high
56	Vane air flow (VAF) sensor signal too high
61	Engine coolant temperature (ECT) signal too low

EEC IV TROUBLE CODES (2.3L)

Code	Diagnosis
63	Throttle position sensor (TPS) signal too low
64	Vane air temperature (VAT) signal too low
66	Vane air flow (VAF) sensor signal too low
67	A/C compressor clutch ON
73	No vane air temperature (VAT) signal change when engine speed is increased
76	No vane air flow (VAF) signal change when engine speed is increased
77	Engine speed not increased to check VAT and VAF signal change

NOTE: Incorrect sensor signals could be out of range or not being received by the control unit. Perform wiring harness and sensor checks to determine the cause, or check for additional codes to indicate high or low reading

EEC IV TROUBLE CODES (1.6L)

Code	Diagnosis
11	Normal operation (no codes stored)
12	Incorrect high idle rpm value
13	Incorrect curb idle rpm value
15	Read Only Memory (ROM) failure
21	Incorrect engine coolant temperature (ECT) sensor signal
23	Incorrect throttle position sensor (TPS) signal
24	Incorrect vane air temperature (VAT) sensor signal
26	Incorrect vane air flow (VAF) sensor signal
41	System always lean
42	System always rich
67	Neutral/Drive switch in Neutral

NOTE: Incorrect rpm values could be high or low and an incorrect sensor signal could be caused by a defective sensor or a wiring harness problem. Use the trouble codes to isolate the circuit, then continue diagnosis to determine the exact cause of the problem

General Motors C4 and CCC Systems

When an electrical or electronic malfunction is detected, the CHECK ENGINE light will illuminate on the dash. When any input circuit (such as the engine temperature sensor) is supplying unreasonable information, the computer will substitute a fixed value from its programmed memory so the vehicle can be driven. If such a substitution occurs, the CHECK ENGINE light will come on and a numerical trouble code will be stored in the on-board computer memory to indicate that a malfunction has occurred. If the problem is intermittent, the light will go out but the trouble code will remain stored until the battery is disconnected or the system fuse is removed from the fuse panel. To eliminate the trouble codes stored for an occasional stray voltage or other non-malfunction reason, the computer is programmed to erase the trouble code memory after a certain number of ignition switch ON/OFF cycles.

The CHECK ENGINE light on the instrument panel is used as a warning lamp to tell the driver that a problem has occurred in the electronic engine control system. When the self-diagnosis mode is activated by grounding the test terminal of the diagnostic connec-tor, the check engine light will flash stored trouble codes to help isolate system problems. The electronic control module (ECM) has a memory that knows what certain engine sensors should be under certain conditions. If a sensor reading is not what the ECM thinks it should be, the control unit will illuminate the check engine light and store a trouble code in its memory. The trouble code indicates what circuit the problem is in, each circuit consisting of a sensor, the wiring harness and connectors to it and the ECM.

NOTE: Some models have a "Service Engine Soon" light instead of a "Check Engine" display

Activating Diagnosis Mode

To retrieve any stored trouble codes, an under dash diagnosis connector is provided. On the C4 system, the test lead can be identified by a green plastic connector with an integral clip. The test lead is usually located under the instrument panel at the extreme right (passenger) side, usually above the right hand kick panel. Grounding the test terminal while the ignition is ON will cause the system to display any stored trouble codes by flashing the CHECK ENGINE light in two-digit code sequences. For example, a code 12 is displayed as one flash followed by a pause and two more flashes. After a longer pause, the pattern will repeat itself two more times and the cycle will continue to repeat itself unless the engine is started, the test lead is disconnected or the ignition power is interrupted by turning the switch OFF or disconnecting the battery.

The Assembly Line Communications Link (ALCL) is a diagnostic connector located in the passenger compartment, usually under the left side of the instrument panel. It has terminals which are used in the assembly plant to check that the engine is operating properly before shipment. One of the terminals is the diagnostic test terminal and another is the ground. By connecting the two terminals together with a jumper wire, the diagnostic mode is activated and the control unit will begin to flash trouble codes using the check engine light. When the test terminal is grounded with the key ON and the engine stopped, the ECM will display code 12 until the test terminal is disconnected. Each trouble code will be flashed three times, then code 12 will display again. The ECM will also energize all controlled relays and solenoids when in the diagnostic mode to check function.

When the test terminal is grounded with the engine running, it will cause the ECM to enter the Field Service Mode. In this mode, the SERVICE ENGINE SOON light will indicate whether the system is in Open or Closed Loop operation. In open loop, the light will flash 2½ times per second; in closed loop, the light will flash once per second. In closed loop, the light will stay out most of the time if the system is too lean and will stay on most of the time if the system is too rich.

NOTE: The vehicle may be driven in the Field Service mode and system evaluated at any steady road speed. This mode is useful in diagnosing driveability problems where the system is rich or lean too long.

Typical ALCL connector

1	JUMPER "B" TO "A" TO DISPLAY DIAGNOSTIC CODES
2	TEST TERMINAL
3	GROUND TERMINAL

Trouble codes should be cleared after service is completed. To clear the trouble code memory, disconnect the battery for at least 10 seconds. This may be accomplished by disconnecting the ECM harness from the positive battery pigtail or by removing the ECM fuse. The vehicle should be driven after the ECM memory is cleared to allow the system to readjust itself. The vehicle should be driven at part throttle under moderate acceleration with the engine at normal operating temperature. A change in performance should be noted initially, but normal performance should return quickly.

———————————CAUTION———————————
The ignition switch must be OFF when disconnecting or reconnecting power to the ECM.

EXPLANATION OF TROUBLE CODES
GM C-4 AND CCC SYSTEMS
(Ground test lead or terminal AFTER engine is running.)

Trouble Code	Applicable System	Notes	Possible Problem Area
12	C-4, CCC		No tachometer or reference signal to computer (ECM). This code will only be present while a fault exists, and will not be stored if the problem is intermittent.
13	C-4, CCC		Oxygen sensor circuit. The engine must run for about five minutes (eighteen on C-4 equipped 231 cu in. V6) at part throttle (and under road load—CCC equipped cars) before this code will show.
13 & 14 (at same time)	C-4	Except Cadillac and 171 cu in. V6	See code 43.
13 & 43 (at same time)	C-4	Cadillac and 171 cu in. V6	See code 43.
14	C-4, CCC		Shorted coolant sensor circuit. The engine has to run 2 minutes before this code will show.
15	C-4, CCC		Open coolant sensor circuit. The engine has to operate for about five minutes (18 minutes for C-4 equipped 231 cu in. V6) at part throttle (some models) before this code will show.
21	C-4		Shorted wide open throttle switch and/or open closed-throttle switch circuit (when used).
	C-4, CCC		Throttle position sensor circuit. The engine must be run up to 10 seconds (25 seconds—CCC System) below 800 rpm before this code will show.

EXPLANATION OF TROUBLE CODES
GM C-4 AND CCC SYSTEMS
(Ground test lead or terminal AFTER engine is running.)

Trouble Code	Applicable System	Notes	Possible Problem Area
21 & 22 (at same time)	C-4		Grounded wide open throttle switch circuit (231 cu in. V6, 151 cu in. 4 cylinder).
22	C-4		Grounded closed throttle or wide open throttle switch circuit (231 cu in. V6, 151 cu in. 4 cylinder).
23	C-4, CCC		Open or grounded carburetor mixture control (M/C) solenoid circuit.
24	CCC		Vehicle speed sensor (VSS) circuit. The car must operate up to five minutes at road speed before this code will show.
32	C-4, CCC		Barometric pressure sensor (BARO) circuit output low.
32 & 55 (at same time)	C-4		Grounded + 8V terminal or V(REF) terminal for barometric pressure sensor (BARO), or faulty ECM computer.
34	C-4	Except 1980 260 cu in. Cutlass	Manifold absolute pressure (MAP) sensor output high (after ten seconds and below 800 rpm).
34	CCC	Including 1980 260 cu in. Cutlass	Manifold absolute pressure (MAP) sensor circuit or vacuum sensor circuit. The engine must run up to five minutes below 800 RPM before this code will set.
35	CCC		Idle speed control (ISC) switch circuit shorted (over ½ throttle for over two seconds).
41	CCC		No distributor reference pulses to the ECM at specified engine vacuum. This code will store in memory.
42	CCC		Electronic spark timing (EST) bypass circuit grounded.
43	C-4		Throttle position sensor adjustment (on some models, engine must run at part throttle up to ten seconds before this code will set).
44	C-4, CCC		Lean oxygen sensor indication. The engine must run up to five minutes in closed loop (oxygen sensor adjusting carburetor mixture), at part throttle and under road load (drive car) before this code will set.
44 & 55 (at same time)	C-4, CCC		Faulty oxygen sensor circuit.
45	C-4, CCC	Restricted air cleaner can cause code 45	Rich oxygen sensor system indication. The engine must run up to five minutes in closed loop (oxygen sensor adjusting carburetor mixture), at part throttle under road load before this code will set.
51	C-4, CCC		Faulty calibration unit (PROM) or improper PROM installation in electronic control module (ECM). It takes up to thirty seconds for this code to set.
52 & 53	C-4		"Check Engine" light off: Intermittent ECM computer problem. "Check Engine" light on: Faulty ECM computer (replace).
52	C-4, CCC		Faulty ECM computer.
53	CCC	Including 1980 260 cu in. Cutlass	Faulty ECM computer.
54	C-4, CCC		Faulty mixture control solenoid circuit and/or faulty ECM computer.

EXPLANATION OF TROUBLE CODES
GM C-4 AND CCC SYSTEMS
(Ground test lead or terminal AFTER engine is running.)

Trouble Code	Applicable System	Notes	Possible Problem Area
55	C-4	Except 1980 260 cu. in. Cutlass	Faulty oxygen sensor, open manifold absolute pressure sensor or faulty ECM computer (231 cu in. V6). Faulty throttle position sensor or ECM computer (except 231 cu. in. V6). Faulty ECM computer (151 cu in. 4 cylinder)
55	CCC	Including 1980 260 cu in. Cutlass	Grounded + 8 volt supply (terminal 19 of ECM computer connector), grounded 5 volt reference (terminal 21 of ECM computer connector), faulty oxygen sensor circuit or faulty ECM computer.

GM PORT INJECTION TROUBLE CODES

Trouble Code	Circuit
12	Normal operation
13	Oxygen sensor
14	Coolant sensor (low voltage)
15	Coolant sensor (high voltage)
21	Throttle position sensor (high voltage)
22	Throttle position sensor (low voltage)
24	Speed sensor
32	EGR vacuum control
33	Mass air flow sensor
34	Mass air flow sensor
42	Electronic spark timing
43	Electronic spark control
44	Lean exhaust
45	Rich exhaust
51	PROM failure
52	CALPAK
55	ECM failure

Isuzu I-Tec System

The self-diagnosis system is designed to monitor the input and output signals of the sensors and actuators and to store any malfunctions in its memory as a trouble code. When the electronic control unit detects a problem, it will activate a CHECK ENGINE light on the dash board. To activate the trouble code readout, locate the diagnosis connector near the control unit and connect the two leads with the ignition ON. The trouble codes stored in the memory will be displayed as flashes of the CHECK ENGINE light, the flashes corresponding to the first and second digit of a two digit number. The Isuzu I-TEC system is capable of storing three trouble codes which are displayed in numerical sequence no matter what order the faults occur in. Each trouble code will be displayed three times, then the next code is displayed. The control unit will display all trouble codes stored in its memory as long as the diagnostic lead is connected with the key ON. A code 12 indicates that the I-TEC system is functioning normally and that no further testing is necessary. After service, clear the trouble codes by disconnecting the No.

4 fuse from the fuse holder. All codes stored will be automatically cleared whenever the main harness connector is disconnected from the control unit.

NOTE: For further trouble diagnosis procedures, see the Isuzu I-TEC section.

Isuzu trouble code connector

ISUZU I-TEC SYSTEM TROUBLE CODE CHART

Trouble Code	ECU Circuit	Possible Cause
12	Normal operation	No testing required
13	Oxygen sensor	Open or short circuit, failed sensor
44	Oxygen sensor	Low voltage signal
45	Oxygen sensor	High voltage signal
14	Coolant temperature sensor	Shorted with ground (no signal)
15	Coolant temperature sensor	Incorrect signal
16	Coolant temperture sensor	Excessive signal (harness open)
21	Throttle valve switch	Idle and WOT contacts closed at the same time
43	Throttle valve switch ①	Idle contact shorted
65	Throttle valve switch	Full throttle contact shorted
22	Starter signal	No signal
41	Crank angle sensor	No signal or wrong signal
61	Air flow sensor	Weak signal (harness shorted or open hot wire)
62	Air flow sensor	Excessive signal (open cold wire)
63	Speed sensor ①	No signal
66	Detonation sensor	Harness open or shorted to ground
51, 52, 55	ECU malfunction	Incorrect injection pulse or fixed timing

Mazda EGI System

The Mazda System Checker 83 (49 G040 920) is necessary to troubleshoot the EGI electronic control system with the test connector located next to the ECU harness connectors at the control unit.

Mazda EGI tester used to read trouble codes

With the tester, the on-board diagnosis system will read out trouble codes (1 through 6) to indicate problems in different circuits within the fuel injection system. Follow the manufacturer's instructions included with the tester for all wiring and sensor checks using the special tester.

—CAUTION—

Do not attempt to disconnect or reconnect the control unit main harness connector with the ignition switch ON, or the ECU can be damaged or destroyed.

MAZDA TROUBLE CODES

Code Number	Circuit
1	Engine speed (rpm) signal
2	Air flow meter
3	Coolant temperature sensor
4	Oxygen sensor
5	Throttle position sensor
6	Atmospheric pressure sensor

Mitsubishi ECI System

The Mitsubishi self-diagnosis system monitors the various input signals from the engine sensors and enters a trouble code in the on-board computer memory if a problem is detected. There are nine monitored items, including the "normal operation" code which can be read by using a special ECI tester (MD9984 06 or equivalent) and adapter. The adapter connects the ECI tester to the diagnosis connector located on the right cowl, next to the control unit. Because the computer memory draws its power directly from the battery, the trouble codes are not erased when the ignition is switched OFF. The memory can only be cleared (trouble codes erased) if a battery cable is disconnected or the main ECU wiring harness connector is disconnected from the computer module. The trouble codes will not be erased if the battery cable or harness connector is reconnected within 10 seconds.

---CAUTION---

Before any ECU harness connectors are removed or installed, make sure the ignition is switched OFF or the control unit may be damaged. Make sure the connector is seated properly and the lock is in its correct position.

If two or more trouble codes are stored in the memory, the computer will read out the codes in order beginning with the lowest number. The needle of the ECI tester will swing back and forth between 0 and 12 volts to indicate the trouble code stored. There is no memory for code No. 1 (oxygen sensor) once the ignition is switched OFF, so it is necessary to perform this diagnosis with the engine running. The oxygen sensor should be allowed to warm up for testing (engine at normal operating temperature) and the trouble code should be read before the ignition is switched OFF. All other codes will be read out with the engine ON or OFF. If there are no trouble codes stored in the computer (system is operating normally), the ECI tester will indicate a constant 12 volts on the meter. Consult the instructions supplied with the test equipment to insure proper connections for diagnosis and testing of all components.

If there is a problem stored, the meter needle will swing back and forth every 0.4 seconds. Trouble codes are read by counting the pulses, with a two second pause between different codes. If the battery voltage is low, the self-diagnosis system will not operate properly, so the battery condition and state of charge should be checked before attempting any self-diagnosis inspection procedures. After completing service procedures, the computer trouble code memory should be erased; by disconnecting the battery cable or main harness connectors to the control unit for at least 10 seconds. See the Mitsubishi ECI section for details on further trouble diagnosis procedures.

MITSUBISHI ECI TROUBLE CODES

Trouble Code	ECU Circuit	Possible Cause
1	Oxygen sensor	Open circuit in wire harness, faulty oxygen sensor or connector
2	Ignition signal	Open or shorted wire harness, faulty igniter
3	Air flow sensor	Open or shorted wire harness, loose connector, defective air flow sensor
4	Boost pressure sensor	Defective boost sensor, open or shorted wire harness or connector
5	Throttle position sensor	Sensor contacts shorted, open or shorted wire harness or connector
6	ISC motor position sensor	Defective throttle sensor open or shorted wire harness or connector, defective ISC servo
7	Coolant temperature sensor	Defective sensor, open or shorted wire harness or connector
8	Speed sensor	Malfunction in speed sensor circuit, open or shorted wire harness or connector

Nissan E.C.C.S. System

The self-diagnostic system determines the malfunctions of signal systems such as sensors, actuators and wire harness connectors based on the status of the input signals received by the E.C.C.S. control unit. Malfunction codes are displayed by two LED's (red and green) mounted on the side of the control unit. The self-diagnosis results are retained in the memory clip of the ECU and displayed only when the diagnosis mode selector (located on the

left side of the ECU) is turned fully clockwise. The self-diagnosis system on the E.C.C.S. control unit is capable of displaying malfunctions being checked, as well as trouble codes stored in the memory. In this manner, an intermittent malfunction can be detected during service procedures.

---CAUTION---

Turn the diagnostic mode selector carefully with a small screwdriver. Do not press hard to turn or the selector may be damaged.

Activating Diagnosis Mode

Service codes are displayed as flashes of both the red and green LED. The red LED blinks first, followed by the green LED, and the two together indicate a code number. The red LED is the tenth digit, and the green LED is the unit digit. For example; when the red light blinks three times and the green light blinks twice, the code displayed is 32. All malfunctions are classified by code numbers. When all service procedures are complete, erase the memory by disconnecting the battery cable or the ECU harness connector. Removing the power to the control unit automatically erases all trouble codes from the memory. Never erase the stored memory before performing self diagnosis tests.

NISSAN E.C.C.S. TROUBLE CODES

Code Number	ECU Circuit	Test Point Pin Numbers	Normal Test Results
11	Crank Angle Sensor	Check harness for open circuit	Continuity
12	Air Flow Meter	Ground terminal 26① connect VOM @ 26–31	IGN ON—1.5–1.7 volts
		Apply 12v @ E–D② connect VOM @ B–D	1.5–1.7 volts
		VOM @ 12–GND③	Continuity
		VOM @ C–F②	Continuity
13	Cylinder Head Temperature Sensor	VOM @ 23–26①	Above 68 deg F–2.9 kΩ / Below 68 deg F–2.1 kΩ
14	Speed Sensor	VOM @ 29–GND④	Continuity
21	Ignition Signal	VOM @ 3–GND / VOM @ 5–GND / Check power transistor terminals to base plate	Continuity / Continuity / Continuity
22	Fuel Pump	VOM @ 108–GND⑤ / Pump connectors / Pump relay: VOM @ 1–2 / VOM @ 3–4 / 12v @ 1–2, VOM @ 3–4	IGN ON–12 volts / Continuity / Continuity / [if] / Continuity
23	Throttle Valve Switch	VOM @ 18–25⑥ / VOM @ 18–GND / VOM @ 25–GND	Continuity / [if] / [if]
24	Neutral/Park Switch	VOM @ Switch terminals	Neutral–0Ω / Drive–∞Ω
31	Air Conditioner	VOM @ 22–GND①	IGN ON–12 volts
32	Start Signal	VOM @ 9–GND③	12 volts with starter S terminal disconnected
34	Detonation Sensor	Disconnect sensor and check timing with engine running	Timing should retard 5 degrees above 2000 rpm
41	Fuel Temperature Sensor	VOM @ 15–GND③	Above 68 deg. F–2.9 kΩ / Below 68 deg.F–2.1 kΩ
		VOM @ Sensor terminals	Resistance (ohms) should decrease as temperature rises
44	Normal Operation—no further testing required		

NOTE: Make sure test equipment will not damage the control unit before testing
VOM—Volt/ohm meter
GND—Ground
Ω—Ohms (kΩ = kilo-ohms)
∞—Infinite resistance
①16-pin harness connector
②6-pin air flow meter connection
③20-pin harness connector
④16-pin connector at ECU
⑤Throttle valve switch connector

Renault TBI System

On 1983 and later Renault models, the on-board self-diagnosis system will illuminate a test bulb if a malfunction exists. When the trouble code terminal at the diagnostic connector in the engine compartment is connected to a test bulb, the system will flash a trouble code if a malfunction has been detected.

───CAUTION───

Be extremely careful when making test connections. Never apply more than 12 volts to any point or component in the TBI system.

The self-diagnosis feature of the electronic control unit (ECU) provides support for diagnosing system problems by recording six possible failures should they be encountered during normal engine operation. Additional tests should allow specific tracing of a failure to a single circuit or component. Multiple failures of different circuits or components must be diagnosed separately. It is possible that the test procedures can cause false failure codes to be set.

NOTE: In the following procedures, no specialized service equipment is necessary. It is necessary to have available a volt/ohmmeter (with at least 10 megohms impedence), a 12 volt test light and an assortment of jumper wires and probes.

Trouble Code Test Lamp

If the ECU is functional, service diagnosis codes can be obtained by connecting a No. 158 test bulb to pins D2-2 and D2-4 of the large diagnostic connector. With the test bulb installed, push the wide open throttle (WOT) switch lever on the throttle body and, with the idle speed control (ISC) motor plunger also closed, have an assistant turn the ignition switch ON while observing the test bulb. If the ECU is functioning normally, the test bulb should light for a moment and then go out. This will always occur regardless of the failure condition and serves as an indication that the ECU is functional.

After the initial illumination, the ECU will cycle through and flash a single digit code if any system malfunctions have been detected by the ECU during normal engine operation. The ECU is capable of storing various trouble codes in its memory. The initial trouble detected will be flashed first and then a short pause will separate the second trouble code stored. There will be a somewhat longer pause between the second code and the repeat cycle of the first code again to provide distinction between codes like 3-6 and 6-3. Although the two codes indicate the same two failures, the last code stored indicates the most recent failure.

If further testing fails to indicate the cause of the trouble code, an intermittent problem exists and marginal components should be suspected. The most common cause of an intermittent problem is corrosion or loose connections. If the trouble code is erased and

CONNECTOR D2   CONNECTOR D1

1. Battery (memory)
2. Trouble code
3. Park Neutral Switch
4. B+ (power relay)
5. AC on
6. WOT switch
7. Sensor ground
8. Air temp. sensor
9. EGR solenoid
10. Canister purge solenoid
11. ISC motor forward
12. Coolant temp. sensor
13. Closed throttle switch
14. ISC motor reverse
15. Auto trans potentiometer

1. Tach (rpm) voltage
2. Ignition
3. Ground
4. Starter motor relay
5. Battery
6. Fuel pump

Diagnostic connector terminals on Renault TBI system

CONNECTOR D2   CONNECTOR D1   FRONT OF CAR

FENDER

Trouble code test lamp connections

quickly returns with no other symptoms, the ECU should be suspected. If the ECU is determined to be malfunctioning, it must be replaced. No repairs should be attempted. It is important to note that the trouble memory is erased if the ECU power is interrupted by disconnecting the wire harness from the ECU, disconnecting either battery terminal, or allowing the engine to remain unstarted in excess of five days. It is equally important to erase the trouble memory when a defective component is replaced.

TBI TROUBLE DIAGNOSIS

Condition or Trouble Code	Possible Cause	Correction
CODE 1 (poor low air temp. engine performance).	Manifold air/fuel temperature (MAT) sensor resistance is not less than 1000 ohms (HOT) or more than 100 kohms (VERY COLD).	Replace MAT sensor if not within specifications. Refer to MAT sensor test procedure.
CODE 2 (poor warm temp. engine performance-engine lacks power).	Coolant temperature sensor resistance is less than 300 ohms or more than 300 kohms (10 kohms at room temp.).	Replace coolant temperature sensor. Test MAT sensor. Refer to coolant temp. sensor test and MAT sensor test procedures.

TBI TROUBLE DIAGNOSIS

Condition or Trouble Code	Possible Cause	Correction
CODE 3 (poor fuel economy, hard cold engine starting, stalling, and rough idle).	Defective wide open throttle (WOT) switch or closed (idle) throttle switch or both, and/or associated wire harness.	Test WOT switch operation and associated circuit. Refer to WOT switch test procedure. Test closed throttle switch operation and associated circuit. Refer to closed throttle switch test procedure.
CODE 4 (poor engine acceleration, sluggish performance, poor fuel economy).	Simultaneous closed throttle switch and manifold absolute pressure (MAP) sensor failure.	Test closed throttle switch and repair/replace as necessary. Refer to closed throttle switch test procedure. Test MAP sensor and associated hoses and wire harness. Repair or replace as necessary. Refer to MAP sensor test procedure.
CODE 5 (poor acceleration, sluggish performance).	Simultaneous WOT switch and manifold absolute pressure (MAP) sensor failure.	Test WOT switch and repair or replace as necessary. Refer to WOT switch test procedure. Test MAP sensor and associated hoses and wire harness. Repair or replace as necessary. Refer to MAP sensor test procedure.
CODE 6 (poor fuel economy, bad driveability, poor idle, black smoke from tailpipe).	Inoperative oxygen sensor.	Test oxygen sensor operation and replace if necessary. Test the fuel system for correct pressure. Test the EGR solenoid control. Test canister purge. Test secondary ignition circuit. Test PCV circuit. Refer to individual component test procedure.
No test bulb flash.	No battery voltage at ECU (J1-A with key on). No ground at ECU (J1-F). Simultaneous WOT and CTS switch contact (Ground at both D2 Pin 6 and D2 Pin 13). No battery voltage at test bulb (D2 Pin 4). Defective test bulb. Battery voltage low (less than 11.5V).	Repair or replace wire harness, connectors or relays. Repair or replace WOT switch, CTS switch, harness or connectors. Repair wire harness or connector. Replace test bulb. Charge or replace battery, repair vehicle wire harness.

Toyota EFI System

The Toyota electronic control unit uses a dash-mounted CHECK ENGINE light that illuminates when the control unit detects a malfunction. The memory will store the trouble codes until the system is cleared by removing the EFI fuse with the ignition OFF. To activate the trouble code readout and obtain the diagnostic codes stored in the memory, first check that the battery voltage is at least 11 volts, the throttle valve is fully closed, transmission is in neutral, the engine is at normal operating temperature and all accessories are turned OFF.

Activating Diagnosis Mode
Turn the ignition switch ON, but do not start the engine. Locate the Check Engine Connector under the hood near the ignition coil and use a short jumper wire to connect the terminals together.

Read the diagnostic code as indicated by the number of flashes of the CHECK ENGINE light. If normal system operation is occurring, the light will blink once every three seconds to indicate a code 1 (no malfunctions). The light will blink once every three seconds to indicate a trouble code stored in the memory, with three second pauses between each code number. The diagnostic code series will be repeated as long as the CHECK ENGINE terminals are connected together. After all trouble codes are recorded, remove the jumper wire and replace the rubber cap on the connector. Cancel the trouble codes in the memory by removing the STOP fuse for about 30 seconds. If the diagnostic codes are not erased, they will be reported as new problems the next time the diagnosis mode is activated. Verify all repairs by clearing the memory, road testing the car, then entering the diagnosis mode again to check that a code 1 (no malfunctions) is stored. For more information on trouble diagnosis procedures, see the Toyota Fuel Injection section.

Electronic Ignition Systems 4 SECTION

INDEX

NOTE: Please refer to the Application Chart at the front of this Manual.

ELECTRONIC IGNITION SYSTEMS

General Information

The solid state electronic ignition system has replaced the breaker point distributor on all current production automotive gasoline engines. By eliminating the breaker points, electronic ignition systems have become almost maintenance-free and performance doesn't deteriorate with mileage. In a typical system, the distributor contains an electronic control unit or module which replaces the breaker plate. Within the distributor body is a permanent magnet and a variable reluctance pick-up (or Hall Effect pick-up and rotating shutter). The electronic control module receives signals from the pick-up coil and in turn charges and fires the secondary ignition coil. A rotor then distributes the high voltage current to the proper spark plug through the distributor cap and wires. The only exception to this general description is the new GM Computer Controlled Coil Ignition (C3I) system which eliminates the distributor altogether.

All solid state ignition systems can be checked for proper operation by performing simple resistance tests, however some computer-based electronic ignition systems can be damaged by the use of incorrect test equipment. Before testing any primary ignition components, a secondary system inspection should be done to eliminate obvious problems such as loose or corroded connections, broken or shorted wires and damaged components.

---CAUTION---

Due to the dangerously high voltage levels present in any electronic ignition system, DO NOT touch any secondary ignition system components while the engine is running or the starter is being cranked. Use insulated tools to hold coil or spark plug wires when testing.

Intermittent problems can be caused by extremely high or low temperature operating conditions and any damage to the trigger wheel or Hall Effect pick-up (cracks, chips, etc.) will degrade ignition system performance. Service of solid state ignition systems involves testing and fault diagnosis of electronic components and circuits, using a voltohmmeter or digital multimeter. The control units, magnetic pick-ups and other solid state components are replaced as a unit so accurate troubleshooting is essential to avoid the needless replacement of expensive parts.

General Service Precautions

• Always turn the ignition switch OFF when disconnecting or connecting any electrical connectors or components.
• Never reverse the battery polarity or disconnect the battery with the engine running.
• Do not pierce spark plug or wiring harness wires with test probes for any reason. Due to their more pliable construction, it is important to route spark plug wires properly to avoid chafing or cutting.
• Disconnect the ignition switch feed wire at the distributor when making compression tests to avoid arcing that may damage components, especially on computer-based ignition systems.
• Do not remove grease or dielectric compound from components or connectors when installing. Some manufacturers use grease to prevent corrosion and dielectric compound to dissipate heat generated during normal module operation.
• Check all replacement part numbers carefully. Installing the wrong component for a specific application can damage the system.
• All manufacturers instructions included with any testing equipment must be read carefully to insure proper capability and test results. Inaccurate readings and/or damage to ignition system components may result due to the use of improper test equipment.

ELECTRONIC IGNITION QUICK CHECK CHART
(Non-computer controlled systems only)

Condition	Possible Cause	Correction
Abrupt backfire	Control unit or ignition module malfunction. Incorrect timing. Bad cap or rotor	Check ignition timing. Replace control unit or module. Replace cap or rotor
Intermittent running	Magnetic pick-up or stator malfunction. Bad trigger wheel, reluctor or armature. Control unit or ignition module failure	Replace defective components after testing as described under appropriate system in this unit repair section
Does not fire on one or more cylinders	Defective pick-up, stator, trigger wheel, reluctor or armature. Bad spark plugs or ignition wires	Replace components as necessary
Cuts off suddenly	Malfunction in control unit of module. Damaged pick-up or stator	Check operation of pick-up and stator. Replace control unit or module
Won't start	Control unit or module failure. Defective cap, rotor, pick-up or stator ①	Replace control unit or module after testing. Replace distributor components as necessary
Poor performance, no power under load	Defective pick-up, stator, or ignition coil. Worn or fouled spark plugs. Bad plug wires	Check distributor components for signs of wear or damage. Replace spark plugs and wires
Arcing or excessive burning on rotor or distributor cap	Worn or fouled spark plugs. Bad plug wires	Replace spark plugs and wires

NOTE: This chart assumes the described conditions are problems in the electronic ignition system and not the result of another malfunction. Always perform basic checks for fuel, spark and compression first. See the individual system sections for all test procedures

① Check ballast resistor on Chrysler models

AMC BREAKERLESS INDUCTIVE DISCHARGE (BID) IGNITION SYSTEM

General Information

COMPONENTS

First introduced in 1975, the American Motors BID Ignition System consists of five major components: an electronic ignition control unit, an ignition coil, a distributor, high tension wires, and spark plugs.

Control Unit

The electronic control unit is a solid-state, moisture-resistant module. The component parts are permanently sealed in a potting material to resist vibration and environmental conditions. All connections are waterproof. The unit has built-in current regulation, reverse polarity protection and transient voltage protection.

Schematic of AMC Breakerless Inductive Discharge (BID) ignition system

Because the control unit has built-in current regulation, there is no resistance wire or ballast resistor used in the primary circuit. Battery voltage is present at the ignition coil positive terminal whenever the ignition key is in the ON or START position; therefore, there is no need for an ignition system bypass during cranking. The primary (low voltage) coil current is electronically regulated by the control unit. The control unit is not repairable and must be serviced as a unit.

Ignition Coil

The ignition coil is an oil-filled, hermetically-sealed unit (standard constuction). Ignition coils do not require special service other than keeping terminals and connections clean and tight. For correct polarity, the coil positive terminal should be connected to the battery ignition feed. The function of the ignition coil in the BID ignition system is to transform battery voltage in the primary winding to a high voltage for the secondary system. When an ignition coil is suspected of being defective, it should be checked on the car. A coil may break down after it has reached operating temperature; it is important that the coil be at operating temperature when tests are made. Perform the test following the instructions of the test equipment manufacturer.

Distributor

The distributor is conventional except that a sensor and trigger wheel replace the usual contact points, condenser, and distributor cam. The distributor uses two spark advance systems (mechanical and vacuum) to establish the spark timing setting required for various engine speed and load conditions. The two systems operate independently, yet work together to provide proper spark advance.

The mechanical (centrifugal) advance system is built internally into the distributor and consists of two flyweights which pivot on long-life, low-friction bearings and are controlled by calibrated springs which tend to hold the weights in the no-advance position. The flyweights respond to changes in engine (distributor shaft) speed, and rotate the trigger wheel with respect to the distributor shaft to advance the spark as engine speed increases and retard the spark as engine speed decreases. Mechanical advance characteristics can be adjusted by bending the hardened spring tabs to alter the spring tension. The vacuum advance system incorporates a vacuum diaphragm unit which moves the distributor sensor in response to the changes in carburetor throttle bore vacuum.

Sensor/Trigger Wheel

The sensor (a component of the distributor) is a small coil, wound

1. DISTRIBUTOR CAP
2. ROTOR
3. DUST SHIELD
4. TRIGGER WHEEL
5. FELT
6. SENSOR ASSEMBLY
7. HOUSING
8. VACUUM CONTROL SCREW
9. VACUUM CONTROL
10. SHIM
11. DRIVE GEAR
12. PIN

Exploded view of BID distributor components

of fine wire, which receives an alternating current signal from the electronic control unit. The sensor develops an electromagnetic field which is used to detect the presence of metal. The sensor detects the edges of the metal in the teeth of trigger wheel. When a leading edge of a trigger wheel tooth aligns with the center of the sensor coil, a signal is sent to the control unit to open the coil primary circuit. There are no wearing surfaces between the trigger wheel and sensor, dwell angle remains constant and requires no adjustment. The swell angle is determined by the control unit and the angle between the trigger wheel teeth.

OPERATION

With the ignition switch in the START or RUN position, the control unit is activated. At this time, an oscillator, contained in the control unit, excites the sensor which is contained in the distributor. When the sensor is excited, it develops an electromagnetic field. As the leading edge of a tooth of the trigger wheel enters the sensor field, the tooth reduces the strength of oscillation in the sensor. As the oscillator strength is reduced to a predetermined level, the demodulator circuit switches. The demodulator switching signal controls a power transistor which is in series with the coil

primary circuit. The power transistor switches the coil primary circuit off, thereby inducing the high voltage in the coil secondary winding. High voltage is then distributed to the spark plugs by the distributor cap, rotor, and ignition wires.

The following procedures can be used to check operation of the components of the BID ignition system. Electrical components of the ignition system (sensor, coil, and electronic ignition control unit) are not repairable. If the operation test indicates that they are faulty, replace them. The following equipment is required to make this test: ohmmeter, DC voltmeter, jumper wire (12 to 18 inches long) with clip at each end, Tester (distributor sensor substitute) J-25331, insulated pliers (grippers) for handling high tension cables.

NOTE: Always inspect the primary circuit wiring and connectors. Disconnect the connectors and examine them for corrosion and proper fit. Also inspect the secondary cables for cracks and deterioration. Repair or replace any defective wires or connectors. Always use a twisting motion to remove the secondary (spark plug) wires from the spark plugs to prevent damaging them. Use insulated pliers to hold the secondary wires when performing an ignition system check.

TROUBLESHOOTING AMC PRESTOLITE IGNITION

Condition	Possible Cause	Correction
Engine Fails to Start (No Spark at Plugs).	No voltage to ignition system.	Check battery, ignition switch and wiring. Repair as needed.
	Electronic ignition control ground lead open, loose or corroded.	Clean, tighten, or repair as needed.
	Primary wiring connectors not fully engaged.	Make sure connectors are clean and firmly seated.
	Coil open or shorted.	Test coil. Replace if faulty.
	Damaged trigger wheel or sensor	Replace damaged part.
	Electronic ignition control faulty.	Replace electronic ignition control.
Engine Backfires but Fails to Start.	Incorrect ignition timing.	Check timing. Adjust as needed.
	Moisture in distributor cap.	Dry cap and rotor.
	Distributor cap faulty (shorting out).	Check cap for loose terminals, cracks and dirt. Clean or replace as needed.
	Wires not in correct firing order.	Reconnect in proper firing order.
Engine Does Not Operate Smoothly and/or Engine Misfires at High Speed.	Spark plugs fouled or faulty.	Clean and regap plugs. Replace if needed.
	Spark plug cables faulty.	Check cables. Replace if needed.
	Spark advance system(s) faulty.	Check operation of advance system(s). Repair as needed.
Excessive Fuel Consumption.	Incorrect ignition timing.	Check timing. Adjust as needed.
	Spark advance system(s) faulty.	Check operation of advance system(s). Repair as needed.
Erratic Timing Advance.	Faulty vacuum advance assembly.	Check operation of advance diaphragm and replace if needed.
Basic Timing Not Affected by Vacuum. (Disconnected)	Misadjusted, weak or damaged mechanical advance springs.	Readjust or replace springs as needed.
	Worn distributor shaft bushings.	Check for worn bushings. Replace distributor.

TROUBLESHOOTING
AMC PRESTOLITE IGNITION

CHECK ALL CONNECTIONS BEFORE BEGINNING TEST

1 ESTABLISH ½" GAP COIL WIRE TO GROUND—CRANK ENGINE

NO SPARK	SPARK

TROUBLE OTHER THAN IGNITION

TO IGNITION SWITCH
① ½" GAP
TO DISTRIBUTOR
IGNITION COIL
ELECTRONIC CONTROL

2 #57 BULB FROM COIL POSITIVE TO GROUND. IGNITION SWITCH TO "ON" AND "START"

BULB LIGHTS IN BOTH POSITIONS	BULB DOESN'T LIGHT IN BOTH POSITIONS

TROBLE LIES IN CIRCUIT BETWEEN BATTERY AND COIL— CHECK SWITCH AND WIRING

TO IGNITION SWITCH
②
TO DISTRIBUTOR
IGNITION COIL
ELECTRONIC CONTROL

3 #57 BULB ACROSS COIL TERMINALS·UNPLUG DISTRIBUTOR LEADS – IGNITION SWITCH "ON"

BULB LIGHTS	BULB DOESN'T LIGHT

CHECK ELECTRONIC CONTROL GROUND LEAD. IF OK– REPLACE ELECTRONIC CONTROL

TO IGNITION SWITCH
③
TO DISTRIBUTOR
IGNITION COIL
ELECTRONIC CONTROL

4 SHORT ACROSS ELECTRONIC CONTROL LEAD TERMINALS WITH JUMPER LEAD

BULB SWITCHES OFF	BULB STAYS ON

REPLACE ELECTRONIC CONTROL

TO IGNITION SWITCH
④ JUMPER LEAD
④
TO DISTRIBUTOR
IGNITION COIL
ELECTRONIC CONTROL

5 REMOVE BULB – CHECK FOR SPARK AT ½" GAP EACH TIME TERMINALS ARE SHORTED WITH JUMPER LEAD

SPARK	NO SPARK

REPLACE SENSOR | REPLACE COIL

TO IGNITION SWITCH JUMPER LEAD
⑤ ½" GAP
⑤
TO DISTRIBUTOR
IGNITION COIL
ELECTRONIC CONTROL

ELECTRONIC IGNITION SYSTEMS

Performance Tests

Primary and Secondary Circuit Tests

1. Test battery using a DC voltmeter; the voltage should be 12–13 volts for a fully charged battery. If necessary charge or replace the battery.

2. Inspect the ignition primary (low voltage) circuit for loose or damaged wiring. Inspect connectors for proper fit. Spread male connector with punch or awl and crimp female connectors to ensure proper fit. Reconnect connectors, making sure everything is tight.

3. Inspect secondary (high voltage) cables for cracks and deterioration. Replace any defective wiring. Be sure ignition cables are routed correctly, not in contact with any hot manifolds or pinched.

4. Disconnect high tension cable from one spark plug. (Always grasp the spark plug boot and use a twisting motion when removing plug cables so as not to destroy the resistance wire termination.) Using insulated pliers, hold plug cable to create approximately 1/2—3/4-inch gap between cable terminal and engine. Crank engine and observe spark. If a spark jumps the gap, ignition system is satisfactory. If no spark occurs, reinstall spark plug cable and proceed to the next step.

CAUTION

Dangerously high voltages are produced in ANY electronic ignition system. Always use insulated pliers and wear a heavy rubber glove when testing secondary systems.

5. Disconnect high tension cable from center tower terminal of distributor cap. Set up a spark gap of approximately 1/2-3/4 inch by clipping end of jumper wire over the high tension cable 1/2-3/4 inch away from the metal tip at distributor end of cable. Ground other end of jumper wire to engine. Crank engine and observe for spark between jumper wire clip and ignition cable terminal. If spark now occurs, distributor cap or rotor is faulty. Replace faulty part and recheck for spark at spark plug. If no spark occurs between jumper wire clip and cable terminal, check coil secondary wire with the ohmmeter for 5,000–10,000 ohms resistance. If coil wire checks satisfactory, proceed to the next step. If coil wire is faulty, replace wire, then proceed to the next step.

6. Disconnect the distributor primary wires (black and dark green) from the control unit connector (blue and white).

7. Visually inspect the distributor primary wire connectors for proper fit. Spread male connector with a punch or awl and slightly crimp the female connector to ensure proper fit.

8. Connect distributor primary wires to control unit connector and crank engine. Observe for spark between jumper wire clip and ignition cable terminal. If spark now jumps the gap, the ignition system is satisfactory. If no spark occurs between jumper wire clip and cable terminal, proceed to the next step.

9. Disconnect the distributor primary wires (black and dark green) and plug Tester J-25331, or equivalent, into wire harness. Turn ignition switch ON. Cycle test button and observe for spark between jumper wire clip and ignition cable terminal. If spark occurs, distributor sensor unit is faulty and must be replaced. If no spark occurs, proceed to the next step.

10. Connect voltmeter between coil positive (+) terminal and ground. With ignition switch ON, voltmeter should read battery voltage. If voltage at coil positive terminal is noticeably lower than battery (through ignition switch) and the coil. Before proceeding, the resistance must be corrected. If voltage at coil positive terminal equals battery voltage, proceed to the next step.

11. Connect voltmeter between coil negative (–) terminal and ground. With ignition switch ON, voltage should read 5–8 volts. A reading under 5 volts or over 8 volts indicates a bad coil which must be replaced. If voltage is satisfactory, press button on tester and observe voltmeter. Voltage reading should increase to battery voltage (12 to 13 volts). Release button on tester. Voltage should drop to 5 to 8 volts. If voltage does not switch up and down, the electronic ignition control is faulty and must be replaced. If voltage switches up and down but there is no spark between jumper wire clip and ignition cable terminal, proceed to the next step.

12. Disconnect tester from control unit.

13. Turn off ignition switch. Remove wire from the negative terminal of the ignition coil.

14. Connect one clip lead from tester to negative terminal of ignition coil and the other clip lead to an engine ground.

15. Turn on ignition switch. Cycle test button.

16. Spark should jump the gap. If spark does not, test the ignition coil. The coil can be tested on any conventional coil tester or

Secondary circuit test on BID ignition system

Tester connected to coil negative terminal

Voltmeter connections to coil positive terminal

with an ohmmeter. (A coil tester is preferable as it will detect faults that an ohmmeter will not.) The coil primary resistance should be 1–2 ohms. Coil secondary resistance should be 8,000–12,000 ohms. Coil open-circuit output should exceed 20 kv. If the coil does not pass these tests, it must be replaced.

BID SYSTEM TEST SPECIFICATIONS

Coil Resistance
```
1978
    Primary ....................... 1.25–1.4 ohms
    Secondary ................. 9,000–15,000 ohms
```
Sensor Resistance .... 1.6–2.4 ohms
Coil Output Voltage .... 20,000 volts minimum

Control Unit Ground Test

With the ignition switch OFF, connect an ohmmeter (R x 1 scale) to the battery negative (–) terminal. Disconnect the control unit black ground connector and connect the other ohmmeter lead to

Voltmeter connections to coil negative terminal

BID system tester showing connection to ignition control unit

the connector leading to the coil bracket. Continuity should be present. If continuity is not present, repair the ground wire or clean the contact.

Sensor Resistance Test

To measure the sensor resistance, disconnect the sensor connector and connect an ohmmeter (R x 1 scale) to the sensor terminals. The

Removing trigger wheel with puller

Sensor assembly mounting in distributor

resistance should be between 1.6–2.4 ohms. If the reading is not within specifications, replace the sensor.

Trigger Wheel Removal and Installation

To remove the trigger wheel, use a small gear puller. Grip the inner shoulder of the trigger wheel with the puller jaws. Use a thick flat washer or nut as a spacer to protect the distributor shaft. To install the trigger wheel, support the distributor shaft and press the trigger wheel onto yoke. Use a 0.050 in. gauge to measure the distance between the trigger wheel legs and the sensor base. Install the trigger wheel until it just touches the gauge.

Sensor positioning details on BID distributor

Measuring the distance between the trigger wheel legs and sensor base

DISTRIBUTOR OVERHAUL

NOTE: If you must remove the sensor from the distributor for any reason, it will be necessary to have the special sensor positioning gauge in order to align it properly during installation. Scribe matchmarks on the distributor housing, rotor, and engine block. Disconnect the leads and vacuum lines from the distributor. Remove the distributor. Unless the cap is to be replaced, leave it connected to the spark plug cables and position it out of the way.

1. Place distributor in suitable holding device, such as a soft-jawed vise. DO NOT overtighten.
2. Remove rotor and dust shield.
3. Remove trigger wheel using a small gear puller. Be sure the puller jaws are gripping the inner shoulder of the trigger wheel or the trigger wheel may be damaged during removal. Use a thick flat washer or nut as a spacer. Do not press against the small center shaft.
4. Loosen sensor locking screw about three turns. The sensor locking screw has a tamper proof head design which requires a Special Driver Bit Tool J-25097 or equivalent. If a driver bit is not available, use a small needlenose pliers to remove screw. The service sensor has a standard slotted head screw.
5. Lift the sensor lead grommet out of the distributor bowl. Pull sensor leads out of the slot around sensor spring pivot pin. Lift and release sensor spring, making sure it clears the leads, then slide the sensor off bracket.
6. If the vacuum chamber is to be replaced, remove the retaining screw and slide the vacuum changer out of the distributor. DO NOT remove the vacuum chamber unless replacement is required.
7. Clean dirt or grease off of the vacuum chamber bracket. Clean and dry sensor and bracket. The material used for sensor and vacuum chamber requires no lubrication.
8. With the vacuum chamber installed, assemble sensor, sensor guide, flat washer, and retaining screw. Install retaining screw only far enough to hold assembly together and be sure it does not project beyond the bottom of sensor.

NOTE: Replacement sensors come with a slotted-head screw to aid in assembly. If the original sensor is being used, replace the tamper-proof screw with a conventional one. Use the original washer.

9. If the vacuum chamber has been replaced and the original sensor is being used, substitute new screw for original special head screw to facilitate sensor positioning. Use existing flat washer.
10. Install sensor assembly on vacuum chamber bracket, making

certain that the tip of the sensor is located properly in summing bar. Place sensor spring in its proper position on sensor, then route sensor leads around spring pivot pin. Install sensor lead grommet in distributor bowl, then make certain the leads are positioned so they cannot be caught by the trigger wheel.

11. Place sensor positioning gauge over yoke (be sure gauge is against flat of shaft) and move sensor sideways until the gauge can be positioned. With the gauge in place, use small blade screwdriver to snug down retaining screw. Check sensor position by removing and installing gauge. When properly positioned, it should be possible to remove and replace gauge without any sensor side movement. Tighten the retaining screw, then recheck the sensor position as before.

12. Remove gauge and set trigger wheel in place on yoke. Visually check to make certain the sensor core is positioned approximately in the center of trigger wheel legs and that trigger wheel legs cannot touch sensor core.

13. Support distributor shaft and press trigger wheel onto yoke. Using .050 gauge wire, bend wire gauge to the dimension shown. Use gauge to measure the distance between trigger wheel legs and the sensor base. Install trigger wheel until it just touches the gauge.

14. Add about 3–5 drops of SAE 20 oil to the felt wick in the top of the yoke. Install dust shield and rotor.

15. Install the distributor on the engine using the matchmarks made during removal and adjust the timing. Use a new distributor mounting gasket.

AMC SOLID STATE IGNITION (SSI) SYSTEM

General Information

COMPONENTS AND OPERATION

AMC introduced Solid State Ignition (SSI) as a running change on some 1977 Canadian models. It is standard equipment on all 1978–82 six and eight cylinder engines. 1980 and later four cylinder engines use the Delco HEI system, covered later in this section.

The system consists of a sensor and toothed trigger wheel inside the distributor, and a permanently sealed electronic control unit which determines dwell, in addition to the coil, ignition wires, and spark plugs.

The trigger wheel rotates on the distributor shaft. As one of its teeth nears the sensor magnet, the magnetic field shifts toward the tooth. When the tooth and sensor are aligned, the magnetic field is shifted to its maximum, signaling the electronic control unit to

Schematic of AMC Solid State Ignition (SSI) system

switch off the coil primary current. This starts an electronic timer inside the control unit, which allows the primary current to remain off only long enough for the spark plug to fire. The timer adjusts the amount of time primary current is off according to conditions, thus automatically adjusting dwell. There is also a special circuit within the control unit to detect and ignore spurious signals. Spark timing is adjusted by both mechanical (centrifugal) and vacuum advance.

A wire of 1.35 ohms resistance is spliced into the ignition feed to reduce voltage to the coil during running conditions. The resistance wire is by-passed when the engine is being started so that full battery voltage may be supplied to the coil. Bypass is accomplished by the I-terminal on the solenoid. The system uses a Ford Dura-Spark II electronic control unit mounted on the fender apron. The remainder of the system includes a pointless distributor, standard construction ignition coil, ignition switch, resistance wire and bypass, secondary spark plug wires, and spark plugs. The electronic control unit (module) is a solid-state, nonserviceable, sealed unit. This unit has reverse polarity and voltage surge circuit protection built in. Two weatherproof connectors attach the control unit to the ignition circuit.

Exploded view of six cylinder SSI distributor—V8 similar

NOTE: All system electrical connectors use lock tabs that must be released to disconnect components.

Performance Tests

NOTE: To check and diagnose the system, a voltmeter, ohmmeter, and ammeter are required. When disconnecting spark plug wires from the plug or distributor cap, twist the rubber boots slightly to break them loose. Grasp the boot, not the wire. To remove the coil connector, grasp the connector at both sides and slide it from the coil.

Secondary Circuit Test

1. Disconnect the coil wire from the center of the distributor cap. Twist the rubber boot slightly in either direction, then grasp the boot and pull straight up. Do not pull on the wire, and do not use pliers. Hold the wire 1/2 in. from a ground with a pair of insulated pliers and a heavy glove. As the engine is cranked, watch for a spark.

2. If a spark appears, reconnect the coil wire. Remove the wire from one spark plug, and test for a spark as above.

—CAUTION—

Do not remove the spark plug wires from cylinders 3 or 5 (1978–79) or 1 or 5 (1980 and later) on a 6 cylinder engine, or cylinders 3 or 4 of a V8 when performing this test, as sensor damage could occur.

If a spark occurs, the problem is in the fuel system or ignition timing. If no spark occurs, check for a defective rotor, cap, or spark plug wires.

3. If no spark occurs from the coil wire in Step 2, test the coil wire resistance with an ohmmeter. It must not exceed 10,000 ohms.

Coil Primary Circuit Test

1. Turn the ignition ON. Connect a voltmeter to the coil positive + terminal and a ground. If the voltage is 5.5–6.5 volts, go to Step 2. If above 7 volts, go to Step 4. If below 5.5 volts, disconnect the condenser lead and measure. If the voltage is now 5.5–6.5 volts, replace the condenser. If not, go to Step 6.

2. With the voltmeter connected as in Step 1, read the voltage with the engine cranking. If battery voltage is indicated, the circuit is okay. If not, go to Step 3.

3. Check for a short or open in the starter solenoid I-terminal wire. Check the solenoid for proper operation.

Coil primary voltage test

4. Disconnect the wire from the starter solenoid I-terminal, with the ignition ON and the voltmeter connected as in Step 1. If the voltage drops to 5.5–6.5 volts, replace the solenoid. If not, connect a jumper between the coil negative − terminal and a ground. If the voltage drops to 5.5–6.5 volts, go to Step 5. If not, repair the resistance wire.

5. Check for continuity between the coil (−) terminal and D4, and D1 to ground. If the continuity is okay, replace the control unit. If not, check for an open wire and go back to Step 2.

6. Turn ignition OFF. Connect an ohmmeter between the (+) coil terminal and dash connector AV. If above 1.40 ohms, repair the resistance wire.

7. With the ignition OFF, connect the ohmmeter between connector AV and ignition switch terminal 11. If less than 0.1 ohm, replace the ignition switch or repair the wire, whichever is the cause. If above 0.1 ohm, check connections, and check for defective wiring.

Coil Test

1. Check the coil for cracks, carbon tracks, etc., and replace as necessary.

2. Connect an ohmmeter across the coil (+) and (−) terminals, with the coil connector removed. If 1.13–1.23 ohms/75°F, go to Step 3. If not, replace the coil.

3. Measure the resistance across the coil center tower and either the (+) or (−) terminal. If 7700–9300 ohms at 75°F, the coil is okay. If not, replace.

1. With the ignition ON, remove the coil high tension wire from the distributor cap and hold 1/2 in. from ground with insulated pliers. Disconnect the 4 wire connector at the control unit. If a spark occurs (normal), go to Step 2. If not, go to Step 5.

2. Connect an ohmmeter to D2 and D3. If the resistance is 400–800 ohms (normal), go to Step 6. If not, go to Step 3.

3. Disconnect and reconnect the 3 wire connector at distributor. If the reading is now 400–800 ohms, go to Step 6. If not, disconnect the 3 wire connector and go to Step 4.

4. Connect the ohmmeter across B2 and B3. If 400–800 ohms, repair the harness between the 3 wire and 4 wire connectors. If not, replace the sensor.

5. Connect the ohmmeter between D1 and the battery negative terminal. If the reading is 0 (0.002 or less), go to Step 2. If above 0.002 ohms, there is a bad ground in the cable or at the distributor. Repair the ground and retest.

6. Connect a voltmeter across D2 and D3. Crank the engine. If the needle fluctuates, the system is okay. If not, either the trigger wheel is defective, or the distributor is not turning. Repair or replace as required.

SSI SYSTEM TEST SPECIFICATIONS

Coil Resistance

Primary	1.13-1.23 ohms @ 75°F (24°C)
	1.5 ohms @ 200°F (93°C)
Secondary	7,000-9,300 ohms @ 75°F (93°C)
12,000 ohms	@ 200°F (93°C)
Ballast Resistance	1.3-1.4 ohms
Sensor Resistance	400-800 ohms
Coil Output Voltage	24,000 volts @ 1,000 RPM

Ignition Feed to Control Unit Test

NOTE: Do not perform this test without first performing the Coil Primary Circuit Test.

With the ignition ON, unplug the 2 wire connector at the module. Connect a voltmeter between F2 and ground. If the reading is battery voltage, replace the control unit. If not, repair the cause of the voltage reduction: either the ignition switch or a corroded dash connector. Check for a spark at the coil wire. If okay, stop. If not, replace the control unit and check for proper operation. Reconnect the 2 wire connector at the control unit, and unplug the 4 wire connector at the control unit. Connect an ammeter between C1 and ground. If it reads 0.9–1.1 amps, the system is okay. If not, replace the module.

Sensor and Control Unit Test

With the coil wire disconnected from the center tower of the distributor and held 1/4 in. from the engine, disconnect the 4-wire connector at the control unit with the ignition ON. If a spark is produced, it indicates a problem in the sensor circuit. Further testing will be required to locate the problem. If no spark was pro-

Coil primary resistance test

Testing control unit grund at connector teminal

Ignition feed to control unit test

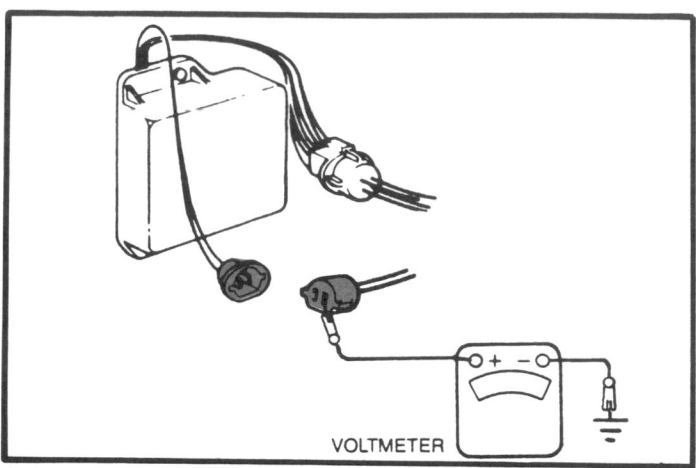

Control unit voltage test

duced, check the control unit ground by turning OFF the ignition switch and disconecting the 4-wire connector at the control unit. Connect an ohmmeter (R x 1 scale) between D1 terminal and battery negative (−) terminal. If the resistance is above 0.002 ohms, locate and repair the source of high resistance ground cable, which could be located at the distributor to block or the ground screw in the distributor to block or the ground screw in the distributor to D1. If the resistance is zero, check the Sensor Resistance, voltage to electronic control unit, and the coil.

Control Unit Current Draw Test

If 11 volts or more were present at the connector's F2 terminal, measure the current draw of control unit with an ammeter. Disconnect 4-wire connector and connect ammeter between the connector

Apply silicone dielectric compound to rotor as shown

terminal C1 and ground. With the ignition ON, current draw should be 0.9–1.1 amps; if it is not, replace the control unit.

Control Unit Voltage Test

Disconnect the 2-wire connector at the control unit and measure the voltage between the connector terminal F2 and ground, with the ignition ON. The voltage should be above 11 volts. If it is not, check the ignition switch and the wiring for an open circuit, or a loose or corroded connector. If, after obtaining the proper voltage at F2 terminal, a spark is not produced at the coil wire when the engine is cranked and the coil and sensor check are OK, replace the control unit.

Sensor Tests

1. Connect an ohmmeter (R x 100 scale) to D2 and D3 connector terminals. The resistance should be 400–800 ohms.
2. If the resistance is not within 400–800 ohms, check the voltage output of the sensor. Connect a voltmeter, 2–3 volt scale, to D2 and D3 connector terminals. Crank the engine and observe the voltmeter. A fluctuating voltmeter indicates proper sensor and trigger wheel operation. If no fluctuations are noted, check for a defective trigger wheel, distributor not turning, or a missing trigger wheel pin.
3. If the resistance in Step 1 was not 400–800 ohms, disconnect and reconnect 3-wire connector at the distributor. If the resistance is now 400–800 ohms, check sensor voltage output, Step 2.
4. If the sensor circuit resistance is still not within specification, disconnect 3-wire connector at the distributor and connect an ohmmeter to B2 and B3 terminals. If the resistance is 400–800 ohms, repair or replace the harness between 3-wire and 4-wire connector. If the resistance is still incorrect, replace the sensor.

Rotor Test

The rotor has silicone dielectric compound applied to the blade to reduce the radio interference. After a few thousand miles, the dielectric compound will become charred by the high voltage, which is normal. Do not scrape the residue off. When installing a new rotor, apply a thin coat (0.03–0.12) in. of Silicone Dielectric Compound to the rotor blade.

Sensor resistance test

AMC—HIGH ENERGY IGNITION (HEI)

General Information

COMPONENTS AND OPERATION

Beginning in 1980 all 4 cylinder engines have used the General Motors High Energy Ignition System (HEI). The operation, diagnosis, and testing is the same as for the GM HEI System. The Delco-Remy High Energy Ignition (HEI) System is a breakerless, pulse triggered, transistor controlled, inductive discharge ignition system used on all 4–151 engines as standard equipment. The ignition coil is located externally on the engine block or is integral with the cap.

The magnetic pick-up assembly located inside the distributor contains a permanent magnet, a pole piece with internal teeth, and a pick-up coil. When the teeth of the rotating timer core and pole piece align, an induced voltage in the pick-up coil signals the electronic module to open the coil primary circuit. As the primary current decreases, a high voltage is induced in the secondary windings

DISTRIBUTOR

IGNITION COIL

TACH OUTPUT

TO IGNITION SWITCH

3   4

TO SPARK PLUGS

1   2

SEC   PRI

TRIGGER WHEEL

PICK-UP COIL

AMPLIFIER

ELECTRONIC SWITCH

ELECTRONIC MODULE

RADIO NOISE CAPACITOR

Schematic of AMC High Energy Ignition (HEI) system

of the ignition coil, directing a spark through the rotor and high voltage leads to fire the spark plugs. The dwell period is automatically controlled by the electronic module and is increased with increasing engine rpm. The HEI System features a longer spark duration which is instrumental in firing lean and EGR (Exhaust Gas Recirculation) diluted fuel/air mixtures. The condenser (capacitor) located within the HEI distributor is provided for noise (static) suppression purposes only and is not a regularly replaced ignition system component.

Beginning in 1980, three different modules are used. The original four terminal module is continued in use for most applications in 1980. Some 1980 models and most 1981 and later models are equipped with an Electronic Spark Timing (EST) distributor, which

is part of the C-4 or CCC System. On these, the ignition timing is determined by the C-4 or CCC Electronic Control Module (ECM). The EST module has seven terminals. The EST distributor can be quickly identified: it has no vacuum advance diagphragm. The EST distributor can be equipped with an additional spark control, the Electronic Spark Control (ESC) system. This is a closed loop system that controls engine detonation by retarding the spark timing. The ESC is usually used on turbocharged engines. Some models are equipped with Electronic Module Retard (EMR). This system uses a five terminal module which retards ignition timing a calibrated number of crankshaft degrees. Distributors with this system are equipped with vacuum advance. When replacing modules on these three systems, be certain to obtain the correct part: the modules are not interchangeable.

Component Replacement (Distributor in Engine)

INTERNAL IGNITION COIL

Removal and Installation

1. Disconnect the feed and module wire terminal connectors from the distributor cap.
2. Remove the ignition wire set retainer.
3. Remove the 4 coil cover-to-distributor cap screws and the coil cover.
4. Remove the 4 coil-to-distributor cap screws.
5. Using a blunt drift, press the coil wire spade terminals up out of distributor cap.
6. Lift the coil up out of the distributor cap.
7. Remove and clean the coil spring, rubber seal washer and coil cavity of the distributor cap.
8. Reverse the above procedures to install.

HIGH VOLTAGE TERMINAL

IGNITION SWITCH AND DISTRIBUTOR TERMINAL (+)

IGNITION COIL

TACH AND DISTRIBUTOR (−) TERMINAL

HEI ignition coil showing terminal locations

Internal components of HEI distributor

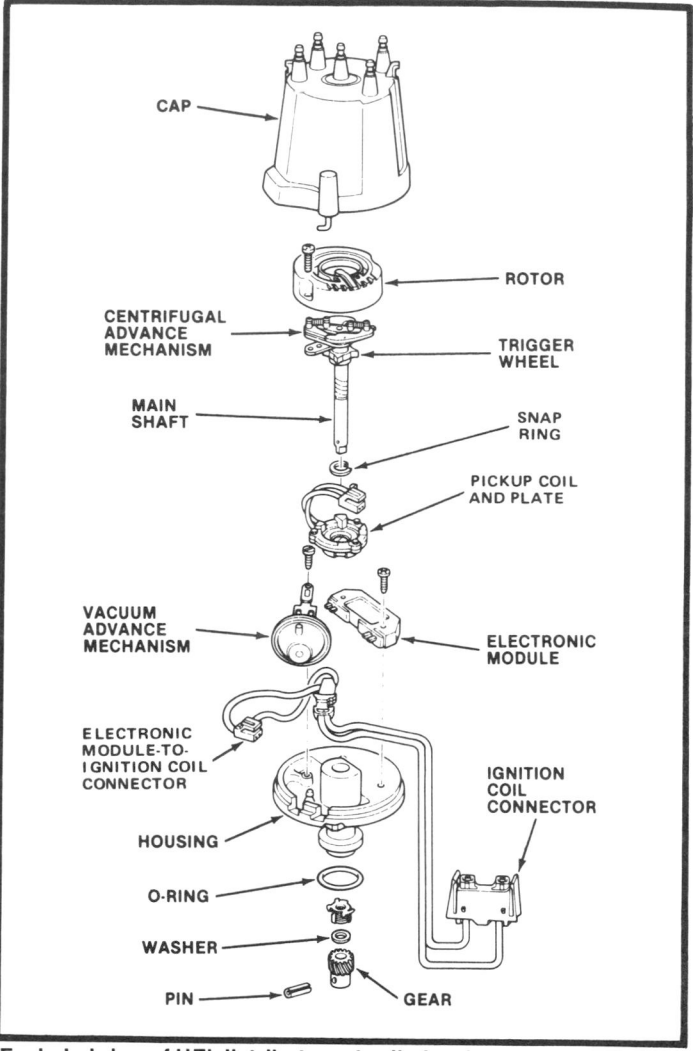

Exploded view of HEI distributor—4 cylinder shown

EXTERNAL IGNITION COIL

Removal and Installation

1. Remove the ignition switch-to-coil lead from the coil.
2. Unfasten the distributor leads from the coil.
3. Remove the screws which secure the coil to the engine and lift it off.
4. Installation is the reverse of removal.

DISTRIBUTOR CAP

Removal and Installation

1. Remove the feed and module wire terminal connectors from the distributor cap.
2. Remove the retainer and spark plug wires from the cap.
3. Depress and release the 4 distributor cap-to-housing retainers and lift off the cap assembly.
4. If the cap has an internal coil, remove the coil from the old cap and install into the new cap.
5. Using a new distributor cap, reverse the above procedures to assemble.

ROTOR

Removal and Installation

1. Disconnect the feed and module wire connectors from the distributor.
2. Depress and release the 4 distributor cap to housing retainers and lift off the cap assembly.
3. Remove the two rotor attaching screws and rotor.
4. Reverse the above procedure to install.

VACUUM ADVANCE UNIT

Removal and Installation

1. Remove the distributor cap and rotor as previously described.
2. Disconnect the vacuum hose from the vacuum advance unit. Remove the module.
3. Remove the two vacuum advance retaining screws, pull the advance unit outward, rotate and disengage the operating rod from its tang.
4. Reverse the above procedure to install.

CONTROL MODULE

Removal and Installation

1. Remove the distributor cap and rotor as previously described.
2. Disconnect the harness connector and pick-up coil spade connectors from the module (note their positions):
3. Remove the two screws and module from the distributor housing.
4. Coat the bottom of the new module with silicone lubricant.
5. Reverse the above procedure to install. Be sure that the leads are installed correctly.

NOTE: If a five terminal or seven terminal module is replaced, the ignition timing must be checked and reset as necessary. The lubricant is necessary for proper cooling of the module in operation.

Distributor Overhaul

DRIVEN GEAR

Removal and Installation

1. Mark the distributor shaft and gear so they can be reassembled in the same position. With the distributor removed, use a 1/8 in. pin punch and tap out the driven gear roll pin.
2. Hold the rotor end of shaft and rotate the driven gear to shear any burrs in the roll pin hole.
3. Remove the driven gear from the shaft.
4. Reverse the above procedure to install.

MAINSHAFT

Removal and Installation

1. With the driven gear and rotor removed, gently pull the mainshaft out of the housing.
2. Remove the advance springs, weights and slide the weight base plate off the mainshaft.
3. Reverse the above procedure to install.

POLE PIECE, MAGNET OR PICK-UP COIL

Removal and Installation

The pole piece, magnet, and pickup coil are serviced as an assembly. With the mainshaft out of its housing, remove the three screws and the magnetic shield (1982 and later), remove the thin "C" washer on top of the pickup coil assembly, remove the pickup coil leads from the module, and remove the pickup coil as an assembly. Do not remove the three screws and attempt to service the parts individually on models through 1980. They are aligned at the factory. Reverse the removal procedure to install. Note the alignment marks when the drive gear is reinstalled.

Performance Tests

An accurate diagnosis is the first step to problem solution and repair. For several of the following steps, a modified spark plug (side electrode removed) is needed. GM makes a modified plug

HEI troubleshooting connections

(tool ST 125) which also has a spring clip to attach it to ground. Use of this tool is recommended, as there is less chance of being shocked. If a tachometer is connected to the TACH terminal on the distributor, disconnect it before proceeding with this test.

Engine Cranks But Will Not Run

1. Check for spark at the spark plugs by attaching the modified spark plug to tone of the plug wires, grounding the modified plug shell on the engine and cranking the starter. Wear heavy gloves, use insulated pliers and make sure the ground is good. If no spark on one wire, check a second. If spark is present, HEI system is good. Check fuel system, plug wires, and spark plugs. If no spark (except EST), proceed to next step. If no spark on EST distributor, disconnect the 4 terminal EST connector and recheck for spark. If spark is present, EST system service check should be performed by qualified service department. If no spark, proceed to Step 2.
2. Check voltage at the BAT terminal of the distributor while cranking the engine. If under 7V, repair the primary circuit to the ignition switch. If over 7V, proceed to Step 3.

AMC HEI system spark plug wire routing

3. With the ignition switch on, check voltage at the TACH terminal of the distributor or coil (external). If under 1V, coil connection or coil are faulty. If over 10V, proceed to Step 4. If 1 to 10V, replace module and check for spark from coil. See Step 4.

4. On external coil models, disconnect coil wire from distributor and connect to grounded modified spark plug. On integral coils, remove distributor cap from distributor without removing its electrical connectors, remove the rotor, then modify a plug boot so that the modified plug can be connected directly to the center terminal of the distributor cap. Ground the shell of the modified plug to the engine block with a jumper wire. Make sure no wires, clothing, etc., are in the way of moving parts and crank the engine. On external coils, if no spark, check secondary coil wire continuity and repair. On both external and integral coils, if spark is present, inspect distributor cap for moisture, cracks, etc. If cap is OK, install new rotor. If no spark, proceed to Step 5.

5. Remove the pick-up coil leads from the module and check TACH terminal voltage with the ignition on. Watch the voltmeter and momentarily (not more than 5 seconds) connect a test light from the positive battery terminal to the appropriate module terminal: 4 terminal module, terminal "G" (small terminal); 5 termi-nal module (ESS or ESC), terminal "D"; 5 terminal module (EMR) terminal "H"; 7 terminal module, terminal "P". If no drop in voltage, check module ground, and check for open in wires from cap to distributor. If OK, replace module. If voltage drops, proceed to next step.

6. Reconnect modified plug to ignition coil as instructed in Step 4, and check for spark as the test light is removed from the appropriate module terminal (see Step 5 for appropriate terminal). Do not connect test light for more than 5 seconds. If spark is present, problem is with pick-up coil or connections. Pick-up coil resistance should be 500–1500 ohms and not grounded. If no spark, proceed to next step.

7. On integral coil distributors, check the coil ground by attaching a test light from the BAT terminal of the cap to the coil ground wire. If the light lights when the ignition is on, replace the ignition coil and repeat Step 6. If the light does not light, repair the ground. On external coil models, replace the ignition coil and repeat Step 6. On both the integral and external coil distributors, if no spark is present, replace the module and reinstall the original coil. Repeat Step 6 again. If no spark is present, replace the original ignition coil with a good one.

BOSCH HALL EFFECT IGNITION SYSTEM

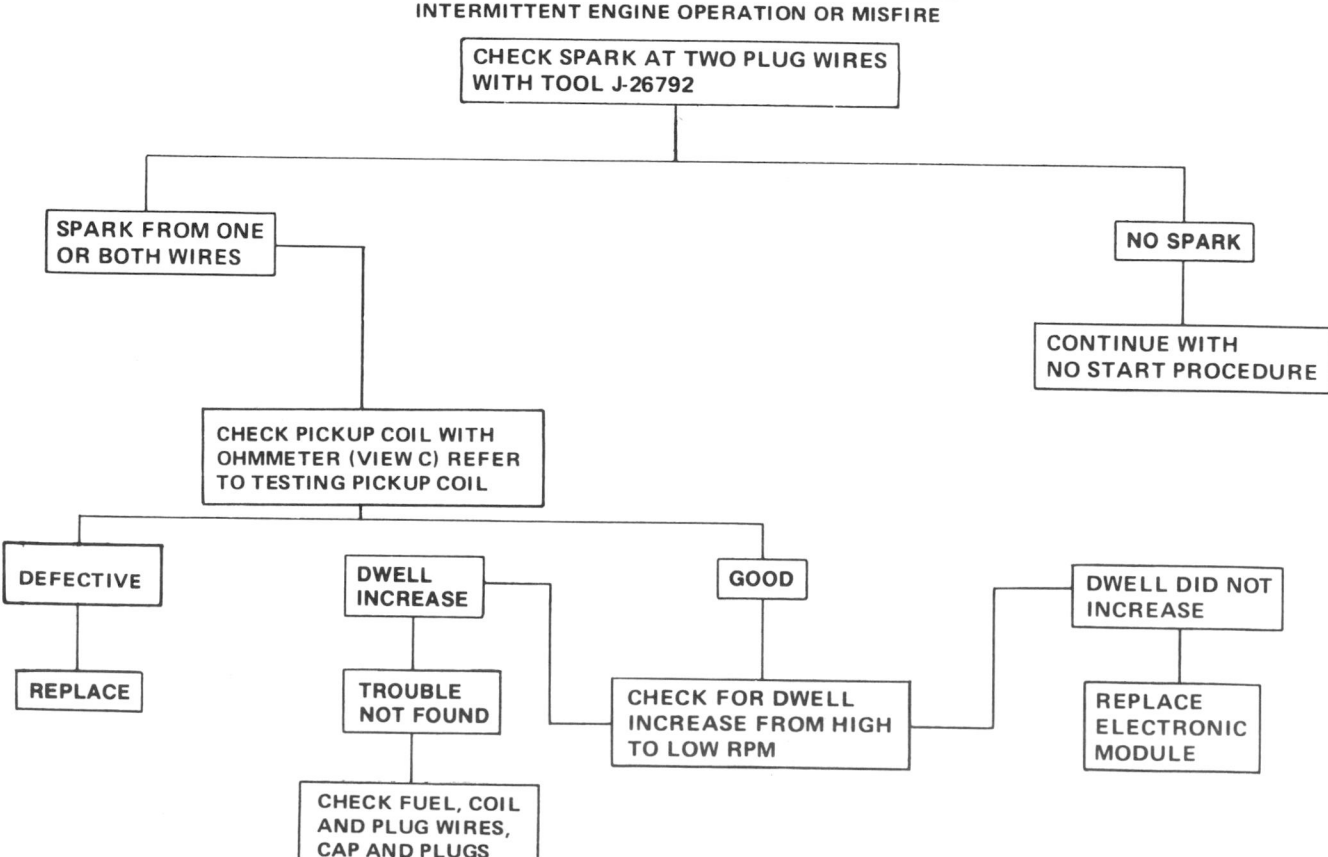

Ignition System Troubleshooting Chart

ENGINE WILL NOT START

NOTE: IF A TACHOMETER IS CONNECTED TO THE TACHOMETER TERMINAL, DISCONNECT IT BEFORE PROCEEDING WITH THE TEST.

1. CHECK SPARK AT PLUG WITH TOOL J-26792 WHILE CRANKING ENGINE (IF NO SPARK FROM FIRST WIRE, CHECK SECOND WIRE).

SPARK

CHECK FUEL, SPARK PLUGS, ETC.

NO SPARK

2. CHECK VOLTAGE AT IGNITION COIL B+ TERMINAL WHILE CRANKING ENGINE.

7 VOLTS OR MORE

3. WITH IGNITION "ON, "CHECK "TACH" TERMINAL VOLTAGE.

UNDER 7 VOLTS

REPAIR PRIMARY WIRE CIRCUIT TO IGNITION SWITCH.

LESS THAN 1 VOLT

REPLACE IGNITION COIL

MORE THAN 10 VOLTS

4. CHECK FOR SPARK AT COIL OUTPUT TERMINAL WITH TOOL J-26792 WHILE CRANKING ENGINE (VIEW A).

1 TO 10 VOLTS

REPLACE MODULE AND CHECK FOR SPARK AS IN STEP 1 ABOVE.

SPARK

SYSTEM OK

NO SPARK

REPLACE IGN. COIL. IT IS ALSO DEFECTIVE.

SPARK

INSPECT CAP FOR WATER, CRACK, ETC. IF OK, REPLACE ROTOR.

NO SPARK

5. REMOVE PICKUP COIL CONNECTOR FROM MODULE. TURN IGNITION SWITCH "ON". WITH HIGH INPUT IMPEDANCE VOLTMETER, OBSERVE VOLTAGE AT "TACH" (—) TERMINAL WHILE TEST LAMP IS MOMENTARILY CONNECTED TO MODULE "P" TERMINAL (NOT MORE THAN 5 SECONDS). VIEW B

NO DROP IN VOLTAGE

CHECK MODULE GROUND AND FOR OPEN IN WIRES FROM COIL TO DISTRIBUTOR. IF OK, REPLACE MODULE.

VOLTAGE DROPS

6. CHECK FOR SPARK FROM COIL WITH TOOL J-26792 AS TEST LAMP IS REMOVED FROM MODULE "P" TERMINAL

NO SPARK

SPARK

REPLACE PICKUP COIL.

IF MODULE TESTER IS AVAILABLE, TEST MODULE.

IF NO MODULE TESTER IS AVAILABLE.

7. CHECK IGN. COIL GROUND CIRCUIT. IF OK, REPLACE IGN. COIL AND REPEAT STEP 6.

OK

DEFECTIVE

REPLACE MODULE

CHECK IGN. COIL GROUND. IF OK, REPLACE IGN. COIL.

SPARK

SYSTEM OK

NO SPARK

COIL REMOVED IS OK, INSTALL ORIGINAL COIL AND REPLACE MODULE.

NOTE: REFER TO VIEWS A, B AND C.

TACH (−) TERMINAL

J-26792 CONNECTED TO COIL

0-20 IN. Hg

TOP VIEW

VACUUM PUMP

TO IGNITION SWITCH

MODULE

CONNECT VOLTMETER BETWEEN (TACH) TERMINAL AND GROUND

PICKUP COIL CONNECTOR DISCONNECTED FROM MODULE

PICKUP COIL

ATTACH GROUND WIRE

B+ TERMINAL

INFINITE RESISTANCE

VIEW A

MODULE

"P" TERMINAL

500 TO 1500 OHMS

TEST LAMP

TO BATTERY (+)

J-26792 CONNECTED TO COIL

OHMMETER

ATTACH GROUND WIRE

REMOVE PICKUP COIL CONNECTOR (GREEN AND WHITE WIRES) FROM MODULE

VIEW B

VIEW C

AMC ignition troubleshooting hookups

Ignition Control Unit

Ignition Coil

7 6 5 4 3 2 1

Ignition Distributor with Hall generator

Idle Stabilizer

Schematic of Bosch Hall Effect electronic ignition system

General Information

COMPONENTS AND OPERATION

The Bosch Electronic Ignition system uses a Hall generator (pick-up coil), ignition control unit (module), and ignition coil. Most Volkswagens equipped with the Hall generator use an electronic idle stabilization system to improve the idle quality. The system consists of an electronic control unit installed between the Hall generator and ignition control unit. If the engine speed drops below a predetermined value, the idle stabilizer begins triggering the ignition control unit sooner causing the ignition timing to advance increasing idle speed. Conventional centrifugal and vacuum advance mechanisms are utilized. No ballast resistor is used in the primary circuit.

The Hall generator consists of a trigger wheel which rotates with the distributor shaft and a Hall sender unit mounted inside the distributor. The Hall sender unit consists of a Hall Effect transistor and IC circuit on a magnetic conducting element. Separated by an air-gap from the Hall Effect transistor and IC circuit permanent magnet. When the trigger wheel shutter enters the air-gap and blocks the magnetic field, the Hall sender will not generate the Hall voltage. As long as the Hall sender is switched off, the electronic control unit will complete the primary ignition circuit. The width of the shutters determines the dwell, which is non-adjustable. When the shutter is no longer blocking the air-gap, the magnetic field will cause Hall sender to generate a voltage. With the Hall sender ON, the signal causes the electronic control unit to interrupt the primary ignition circuit, releasing the secondary high voltage surge through the coil wire, rotor, distributor cap, spark plug wires, and on to the spark plugs.

Performance Tests

Secondary Circuit Test

To check the ignition system operation, remove the coil wire from the distributor cap and hold it 1/4 in. away from ground with insulated pliers or use the tester on page iv and crank the engine. A spark should be present. If no spark is produced, it will be necessary to diagnose the ignition system. If a spark is present at the ignition coil wire, reconnect it and remove a spark plug wire from a spark plug. Hold the spark plug wire 1/4 in. from ground and crank the engine while watching for a spark. If no spark is produced, check the distributor cap and rotor, and spark plug wires. Should a spark be produced, check the fuel system and engine mechanical systems for the malfunction.

Voltage Tests

To check the voltage supply to the distributor, remove the connec-

Control unit voltage test

Exploded view of Hall distributor

tor from the distributor and connect a voltmeter to the outer terminals. With the ignition ON, the voltage should be more than 11 volts. If the voltage is less, check the wire harness from the distributor to the control unit. If there is no voltage at the distributor connector, check for voltage at the control unit. Remove the connector from the control unit and connect the voltmeter between terminals 2 and 4. With the ignition ON the voltage should be above 11 volts. If the voltage is OK, then the control unit is defective. If the voltage was less than 11 volts, locate the open or the high resistance between the control unit and the ignition switch. Also check the ground connection.

Hall Generator Test

Pull back the rubber boot on control unit connector and connect voltmeter between terminals 6 and 3. Make sure the connector is fastened securely to the control unit. With the ignition switch ON and the trigger wheel shutter outside of the air-gap, the voltage should be less than 0.4 volt. Place a steel feeler gauge in the air-gap, the voltmeter reading should increase to about 9 volts. Connect a voltmeter between terminals 5 and 3. With the ignition ON, the voltage should be 7.5 volts minimum. If any of the voltage readings are incorrect, replace the Hall generator.

Hall generator voltage test with the shutter outside the air gap

Hall generator voltage test with the shutter inside the air gap

Control unit to coil voltage test

Ignition Coil Tests

Remove all the wires from the coil and connect an ohmmeter (R x 1 scale) between the positive (+) and negative (–) terminals to measure primary resistance. The resistance should be 0.52–0.76 ohm. To check the coil secondary resistance, connect the ohmmeter (R x 1000 scale) to terminal 4 (coil tower) and coil terminal 1. Resistance should be 2,400–3,500 ohms. If either the coil primary or secondary resistance is not within the specification, replace the ignition coil.

BOSCH HALL EFFECT TEST SPECIFICATIONS

Air-Gap . . . . Nonadjustable
Coil Resistance
   Primary . . . . 0.52–0.76 ohm
   Secondary . . . . 2400–3500 ohms

Ignition Control Unit Test

Remove connector from distributor. Connect positive lead of voltmeter to coil (+). Connect voltmeter negative lead to the coil negative (–) terminal and turn the ignition switch ON. The voltmeter should read 6 volts and drop to 0 volts within 1–2 seconds. If the voltage does not drop, replace the control unit.

NOTE: Check the idle stabilizer when diagnosing a no-start problem on the Bosch system. Remove both connectors from the idle stabilizer and connect them together. If the engine starts, the idle stabilizer is defective.

Hall generator voltage test connections

Idle stabilizer and control unit assembly—typical

BOSCH IMPULSE GENERATOR ELECTRONIC IGNITION

General Information

COMPONENTS AND OPERATION

The Bosch Electronic Ignition System with the Impulse generator consists of a distributor with an impulse generator (pick-up coil), electronic control unit (module), ignition coil, spark plug wires, and spark plugs. The electronic ignition system offers many advantages over the conventional ignition system. By eliminating the breaker points, point replacement is eliminated, and higher voltages are produced firing the spark plugs for a longer period of time. This aids starting, reduces spark plug fouling and provides better emission control. The distributor incorporates conventional centrifugal and vacuum advance mechanisms. The impulse generator (pick-up coil) is used to activate the electronic control unit (module). The components of the impulse generator are the impulse rotor (reluctor), induction coil and permanent magnet.

The impulse rotor rotates with the distributor shaft, and the induction coil and permanent magnet are stationary. The voltage pulses produced as the impulse rotor aligns with the teeth of the permanent magnet are used to trigger the electronic control unit. The electronic control unit switches the primary coil current off which induces the secondary high voltage as the primary magnetic field collapses across the secondary windings. The dwell angle or amount of time current flows in the coil primary is changed by the control unit depending on engine rpm.

Performance Tests

Secondary Circuit Test

Remove coil wire from distributor cap and hold the wire about 1/4 in. (6.35mm) away from ground with insulated pliers or use the Bosch tester, if available. When the engine is cranked a spark should be produced. If there is a spark produced, check the distributor cap and rotor, spark plug wires, spark plugs, fuel system, and engine mechanical system. If there is no spark, make sure the battery is fully charged before beginning a check of the electronic ignition system.

Exploded view of Bosch Impulse Generator distributor

Schematic of Bosch Impulse Generator electronic ignition system

Voltage test at coil positive terminal

Cranking voltage test

Coil Voltage Test

Connect a voltmeter to terminal 15 (+ side) of the ignition coil. With the ignition ON the voltage should be above 5 volts. Connect the voltmeter between the two resistors on the dual resistor systems or ahead of the resistor on a single resistor system and crank the engine. The voltage should be above 9 volts. If either voltage reading is not correct, repair the wiring or resistors between the coil and ignition switch. Also check the ignition switch itself.

Impulse generator resistance test

Impulse Generator (Sensor) Test

Remove the connector from the control unit and connect an ohmmeter between the impulse generator terminals. The resistance should be 890–1285 ohms and 540–660 ohms on 6-cylinder Volvos. If the resistance is incorrect, check the wires between the control unit and the distributor, before replacing the impulse generator.

Ignition Coil Tests

Check the voltage at terminal 1, (−) coil terminal, with the ignition ON. The voltage present should be no greater than 2 volts. If 12 volts is present at the coil's terminal 15 and no voltage is present at terminal 1, replace the coil. If the voltage present at terminal 1 is more than 2 volts, perform the control unit tests. Remove all wires from the coil and measure the coil's primary and secondary resistances. To measure the coil primary resistance, connect an ohmmeter (R x 1 scale) between terminals 15 and 1. The resistance should be 0.95–1.4 ohms, and 1.1–1.7 ohms on Fiats.

Coil voltage drop test

Control unit test

To measure the coil secondary resistance, connect an ohmmeter (R x 1000 scale) between terminals 1 and 4. The resistance should be 5,500–8,000 ohms, and 6,000–10,000 ohms on Fiats. If either the primary or secondary resistance is not within the specifications, replace the coil.

Control Unit Voltage Test

With the connector disconnected from the control unit, check the voltage between terminals 4 and 5 with the ignition ON. The voltage should be more than 11 volts. If the voltage is less, check the wiring and the ignition switch. Also check the ground connection.

Control Unit Test

Check the voltage at terminal 1 with the ignition ON. The voltage present should be no greater than 2 volts. With the coil high tension wire grounded, crank the engine. The voltage should vary between 1 and 12 volts. If it does not, replace the control unit and recheck.

Control unit voltage test

CHRYSLER ELECTRONIC IGNITION SYSTEM

General Information

COMPONENTS AND OPERATION

NOTE: This system is used on all engines except the 1.6L, 2.2L and 2.6L 4 cylinder engines.

This system consists of a special pulse-sending distributor, an electronic control unit, a two-element ballast resistor, and a special ignition coil. The distributor does not contain breaker points or a condenser, these parts being replaced by a distributor reluctor and a pick-up unit. For better timing control and fuel economy, some 1981 and later models use a dual pick-up system. Vehicles with this system use a START pick-up, a RUN pick-up and a dual pick-up start-run delay. In the RUN mode, the operation of the dual pick-up system is the same as that of the single pick-up system. During cranking, the dual pick-up start-run relay is energized (through the starter solenoid circuit), which allows the start pick-up to adjust the timing for starting purposes only. As soon as the starter solenoid is de-energized, the start-run relay switches the sensing function back to the RUN pick-up.

NOTE: Prior to the 1981 model year, the dual pick-up system was used only with the Lean Burn/Electronic Spark Control systems.

The ignition primary circuit is connected from the battery, through the ignition switch, through the primary side of the ignition coil, to the control unit where it is grounded. The secondary circuit is the same as in conventional ignition systems: the secondary side of the

Chrysler electronic distributor

Electronic ignition spark tester

1980-1981 ELECTRONIC IGNITION SYSTEM WIRING DIAGRAM

Schematic of Chrysler electronic ignition system

coil, the coil wire to the distributor, the rotor, the spark plug wires, and the spark plugs. The magnetic pulse distributor is also connected to the control unit. As the distributor shaft rotates, the distributor reluctor turns past the pick-up unit. As the reluctor turns past the pick-up unit, each of the eight (or six) teeth on the reluctor pass near the pickup unit once during each distributor revolution (two crankshaft revolutions since the distributor runs at one-half crankshaft speed). As the reluctor teeth move close to the pick-up unit, the magnetic rotating reluctor induces voltage into the magnetic pick-up unit. This voltage pulse is sent to the ignition control unit from the magnetic pick-up unit. When the pulse enters the control unit, it signals the control unit to interrupt the ignition primary circuit. This causes the primary circuit to collapse and begins the induction of the magnetic lines of force from the pri-

mary side of the coil into the secondary side of the coil. This induction provides the required voltage to fire the spark plugs.

The quicker switching time of this system allows longer coil primary circuit saturation time and longer induction time when the primary circuit collapses. This increased time allows the primary circuit to build up more current and the secondary circuit to discharge more current.

Performance Tests

To properly test the Electronic Ignition system, special testors should be used. But in the event they are not available, the system may be tested using a voltmeter with a 20,000 ohm/volt rating and an ohmmeter which uses a 11/2 volt battery for its operation. Both meters should be in calibration. When Ignition System problems are suspected, the following procedure should be followed:

1. Visually inspect all secondary cables at the coil, distributor and spark plugs for cracks and tightness.

2. To check wiring harness and connections, check primary wire at the ignition coil and ballast resistor for tightness. If the above checks do not determine the problem, the following steps will determine if a component is faulty.

3. Check and note battery voltage reading using voltmeter. Battery voltage should be at least 12 volts.

4. Remove the multi-wiring connector from the control unit.

—————————————CAUTION—————————————
Whenever removing or installing the wiring harness connector to the control unit, the ignition switch must be in the "OFF" position.

5. Turn the ignition switch ON.

6. Connect the negative lead of a voltmeter to a good ground.

7. Connect the positive lead of the voltmeter to the wiring harness connector cavity No. 1. Available voltage at cavity No. 1 should be within 1 volt of battery voltage with all accessories off. If there is more than a 1 volt difference, the circuit must be checked between the battery and the connector.

8. Connect the positive lead of the voltmeter to the wiring harness connector cavity No. 2. Available voltage at cavity No. 2 should be within 1 volt of battery voltage with all accessories off. If there is more than a 1 volt difference, the circuit must be checked back to the battery.

9. Connect the positive lead of the voltmeter to the wiring harness connector cavity No. 3. Available voltage at cavity No. 3 should be within 1 volt of battery voltage with all accessories off. If there is more than a 1 volt difference, the circuit that must be checked back to the battery.

Voltage test at cavity No. 1

10. Turn ignition switch OFF.

11. To check distributor pickup coil connect an ohmmeter to wiring harness connector cavity No. 4 and No. 5. The ohmmeter resistance should be between 150 and 900 ohms.

If the readings are higher or lower than specified, disconnect the dual lead connector coming from the distributor. Using the ohmmeter, check the resistance at the dual lead connector. If the reading is not between the prementioned resistance values, replace the pickup coil assembly in the distributor.

12. Connect one ohmmeter lead to a good ground and the other lead to either connector of the distributor. Ohmmeter should show an open circuit (infinity). If the ohmmeter does show a reading less than infinity the pickup coil in the distributor must be replaced.

13. To check electronic control unit ground circuit connect one ohmmeter lead to a good ground and the other lead to the control unit connector pin No. 5. The ohmmeter should show continuity between the ground and the connector pin. If continuity does not exist, tighten the bolts holding the control unit to the fire wall. Then recheck. If continuity does still not exist, control unit must be replaced.

14. Reconnect wiring harness at control unit and distributor.

NOTE: Whenever removing or installing the wiring harness connector to the control unit, the ignition switch must be in the OFF position.

15. Check air gap between reluctor tooth and pickup coil. To set the gap refer to "Air Gap Adjustment."

Voltage test at cavity No. 2

Pick-up coil resistance test at the wiring harness connector

Voltage test cavity No. 3

Pick-up coil resistance test at the distributor lead connector

Control unit ground test

16. Check ignition secondary; remove the high voltage cable from the center tower of the distributor. Hold the cable approximately 3/16 inch from engine. Crank engine. If arcing does not occur, replace the control unit.

—————————CAUTION—————————

Dangerously high voltages are produced in ANY electronic ignition system. Always use insulated pliers and wear a heavy rubber glove when testing secondary systems.

17. Crank the engine again. If arcing still does not occur, replace the ignition coil.

18. If a problem does not show up when making the voltage checks, coil resistance checks, or ground continuity checks it is likely the control unit or coil is faulty. It is unlikely that both units would fail simultaneously. However, before replacing the control unit make sure no foreign matter is lodged in or blocking the female terminal cavities in the harness connector. If clear, try replacing control unit or coil to see which one restores secondary ignition voltage.

PICK-UP COIL

Removal and Installation

1. Remove the distributor.
2. Remove the two screws and lockwashers attaching the vacuum control unit to the distributor housing. Disconnect the arm and remove the vacuum unit.
3. Remove the reluctor by pulling it off with your fingers, or use two small screwdrivers to pry it off. Be careful not to distort or damage the teeth on the reluctor.
4. Remove the two screws and lockwashers attaching the lower plate to the housing and lift out the lower plate, upper plate, and pick-up coil as an assembly.
5. Remove the upper plate and pick-up coil assembly from the lower plate by depressing the retaining clip and moving it away from the mounting stud.
6. Remove the upper plate and pick-up coil assembly. The pick-up coil is not removable from the upper plate, and is serviced as an assembly. On early models, the coil was removable from the plate.
7. To install the pick-up coil assembly, put a little distributor cam lube on the upper plate pivot pin and lower plate support pins.

HOLD DOWN SCREW

RELUCTOR

PICK-UP

AIR GAP 0.006"

Air gap adjustment

8. Position the upper plate pivot pin through the smallest hole in the lower plate.
9. Install the retaining clip. The upper plate must ride on the three support pins on the lower plate.
10. Install the lower plate, upper plate, and pickup coil assembly into the distributor and install screws.
11. Attach the vacuum advance arm to the pick-up plate, then install the vacuum unit attaching screws and washers.
12. Position the reluctor keeper pin in place on the reluctor sleeve, then slide the reluctor down the sleeve and press firmly into place.

Air Gap Adjustment

1. Align one reluctor tooth with the pick-up coil tooth.
2. Loosen the pick-up coil hold-down screw.
3. Insert a 0.008 in. nonmagnetic feeler gauge between the reluctor tooth and the pick-up coil tooth.
4. Adjust the air gap so that contact is made between the reluctor tooth, the feeler gauge, and the pick-up coil tooth.
5. Tighten the hold-down screw.
6. Remove the feeler gauge.

NOTE: No force should be required in removing the feeler gauge.

7. A 0.010 in. feeler gauge should not fit into the air gap. Do not force the feeler gauge.

—————————CAUTION—————————

Support hub of gear when installing roll-pin so that gear teeth will not be damaged.

8. Apply vacuum to the vacuum unit and rotate the governor shaft. The pick-up pole should not hit the reluctor teeth. The gap is not properly adjusted if any hitting occurs. If hitting occurs on only one side of the reluctor, the distributor shaft is probably bent, and the governor and shaft assembly should be replaced.

Shaft and Bushing Wear Test

1. Remove distributor and rotor.
2. Clamp distributor in a vise equipped with soft jaws and apply only enough pressure to restrict any movement of the distributor during the test.
3. Attach a dial indicator to distributor housing so indicator plunger arm rests against reluctor.
4. Wiggle the shaft and read the total movement of the dial indicator plunger. If the movement exceeds .006 in. replace the housing or shaft.

DISTRIBUTOR OVERHAUL

1. Remove distributor rotor.
2. Remove the two screws and lockwashers attaching the vacuum control unit to distributor housing, disconnect the vacuum control arm from upper plate, and remove control.
3. Remove reluctor by prying up from the bottom of the reluctor with two screwdrivers. Be careful not to distort or damage the teeth on the reluctor.
4. Remove two screws and lockwashers attaching the lower plate to the housing and lift out the lower plate, upper plate, and pick-up coil as an assembly. Distributor cap clamp springs are held in place by peened metal around the openings and should not be removed.
5. If the side play exceeds .006 inch in "Shaft and Bushing Wear Test", replace distributor housing assembly or shaft and governor assembly as follows: Remove distributor drive gear retaining pin and slide gear off end of shaft.

—————————CAUTION—————————

A 0.010 in. feeler gauge can be forced into the air gap. DO NOT FORCE THE FEELER GAUGE INTO THE AIR GAP.

Use a file to clean burrs, from around pin hole in the shaft and remove the lower thrust washer. Push shaft up and remove shaft through top of distributor body.

6. If gear is worn or damaged, replace as follows: Install lower thrust washer and old gear on lower end of shaft and temporarily install rollpin. Scribe a line on the end of the shaft from center to edge, so line is centered between two gear teeth as shown in. **Do not Scribe completely across the shaft.** Remove rollpin and gear. Use a fine file to clean burrs from around pin hole. Install new gear with thrust washer in place. Drill hole in gear and shaft approximately 90 degrees from old hole in shaft and with scribed line centered between the two gear teeth as shown. Before drilling through shaft and gear, place a .007 feeler gauge betweeen gear and thrust washer and after again observing that the centerline between two of the gear teeth is in line with centerline of rotor electrode drill a .124–.129 in. hole and install the rollpin.

———————CAUTION———————
Support hub of gear in a manner that pin can be driven out of gear and shaft without damaging gear teeth.

7. Test operation of governor weights and inspect weight springs for distortion.

8. Lubricate governor weights.

9. Inspect all bearing surfaces and pivot pins for roughness, binding or excessive looseness.

10. Lubricate and install upper thrust washer (or washers) on the shaft and slide the shaft into the distributor body.

11. Install lower plate, upper plate and pick-up coil assembly and install attaching screws.

12. Slide shaft into distributor body, then align scribe marks and install gear and rollpin.

13. Attach vacuum advance unit arm to the pick-up plate.

14. Install vacuum unit attaching screws and washers.

15. Position reluctor keeper pin into place on reluctor sleeve.

16. Slide reluctor down reluctor sleeve and press firmly into place.

17. Lubricate the felt pad in top of reluctor sleeve with 1 drop of light engine oil and install the rotor.

CHRYSLER CORPORATION LEAN BURN/ELECTRONIC SPARK CONTROL SYSTEM

General Information

COMPONENTS

This system was introduced in 1976 as the Lean Burn system; it was renamed Electronic Spark Control in 1979. It is based on the principle that lower NOx emissions would occur if the air/fuel ratio inside the cylinder area was raised from its current point (15.5:1) to a much leaner point (18:1). In order to make the engine workable, a solution to the problems of carburetion and timing had to be found, since a lean running engine is not the most efficient in terms of driveability. Chrysler adapted a conventional Thermo-Quad carburetor, and later a two barrel unit, to handle the added air coming in, but the real advance of the system is the Spark Control Computer. Since a lean burning engine demands precise ignition timing, additional spark control was needed for the distributor. The computer supplies this control by providing an infinitely variable advance curve. Input data is fed instantaneously to the computer by a series of sensors located in the engine compartment which monitor timing, water temperature, air temperature, throttle position, idle/off-idle operation, and intake manifold vacuum. The program schedule module of the Spark Control Computer receives the information from the sensors, processes it, and then directs the ignition control module to advance or retard the timing as necessary. This whole process is going on continuously as the engine is running, taking only a thousandth of a second to complete a circuit from sensor to distributor. The components of the system are as follows: Modified carburetor; Spark Control Computer, consisting of two interacting modules, the Program Schedule Module which is responsible for translating input data, and the Ignition Control Module which transmits data to the distributor to advance or retard the timing.

The start pick-up sensor, located inside the distributor, supplies a signal to the computer providing a fixed timing point that is only used for starting the car. It also has a back-up function of taking over engine timing in case the run pick-up fails. Since the timing in this pick-up is fixed at one point, the car will be able to run but not very well. The run pick-up sensor, also located in the distributor, provides timing data to the computer once the engine is running. It also monitors engine speed, and helps the computer decide when the piston is reaching the top of its compression stroke. Starting 1978, the system is simplified to use only one distributor pick-up.

This pick-up provides the basic timing signal to the computer for both the start and the run modes. However, 1980–82 models with Micro-processor Electonic Spark Advance (a digital system, instead of an analog system) use two pick-ups in the distributor, which function in the same manner as the two pick-ups used previously.

Schematic of Chrysler single pick-up electronic ignition system

Schematic of Chrysler dual pick-up electronic ignition system

NOTE: The two systems will not operate at the same time.

The coolant temperature sensor, located in the thermostat housing (4 cyl.), in the head (6 cyl) or in the intake manifold (V8), informs the computer when the coolant temperature reaches normal operating levels.

The throttle position transducer, located on the carburetor, monitors the position and rate of change of the throttle plates. When the throttle plates start to open and as they continue to open toward full throttle, more and more spark advance is called for by the computer. If the throttle plates are opened quickly, even more spark advance is given for about one second. The throttle position transducer is not used on the 1979 Omni and Horizon and is eliminated altogether starting in 1980.

Electronic Spark Control (ESC) component locations-six cylinder shown

The carburetor switch sensor, located on the end of the idle stop solenoid, tells the computer if the engine is at idle or off-idle.

The vacuum transducer, located on the computer, monitors the amount of intake manifold vacuum; the more vacuum, the more spark advance to the distributor. In order to obtain this spark advance in the distributor, the carburetor switch sensor has to

Typical Chrysler combustion computer assembly showing air cleaner mounting

DISTRIBUTOR

CHARGE
TEMPERATURE
SWITCH

CARBURETOR

FRONT

ROCKER
COVER

DETONATION
SENSOR

WIRING
HARNESS

CHOKE
HEATER

CARBURETOR
SWITCH

COOLANT
SENSOR

ROCKER
COVER

ENGINE
TEMPERATURE
SWITCH

IDLE STOP
SOLENOID

COMPUTER

AIR CLEANER

CHOKE
HEATER

ROCKER
COVER

VACUUM
TRANSDUCER

12 WAY
CONNECTOR

DISTRIBUTOR
RUN
CONNECTOR

DISTRIBUTOR

LOW OIL
PRESSURE
SWITCH

ROCKER
COVER

EXHAUST
MANIFOLD

OXYGEN
SENSOR

FRONT

DISTRIBUTOR
START
CONNECTOR

Electronic Spark Control (ESC) component locations—V8 shown

remain open for a specified amount of time, during which time the advance will slowly build up to the amount indicated as necessary by the vacuum transducer. If the carburetor switch should close during that time, the advance to the distributor will be cancelled. From here the computer will start with an advance countdown if the carburetor switch is reopened within a certain amount of time. The advance will continue from a point decided by the computer. If the switch is reopened after the computer has counted down to "no advance," the vacuum advance process must start over again.

Some 1980 and later models have a detonation sensor mounted on the intake manifold. The sensor is tuned to the frequency characteristic of engine knocking. When detonation (knocking) occurs, the sensor sends a low voltage signal to the computer, which retards ignition timing in proportion to the strength and frequency of the signal. The maximum amount of retard is 11°. When the detonation has ceased, the computer advances timing to the oiginal value.

Many 1981 and later models (except Omni/Horizon and Aries/Reliant) are equipped with an Electronic Throttle Control (ETC) system which is incorporated within the spark control computer. A solenoid mounted on the carburetor is energized whenever the air conditioning (A/C) or electronic timers (some models) are activated. The solenoid acts to control idle under varying engine loads.

On many 1981 and later models, the EGR value is controlled by the spark control computer.

OPERATION

When you turn the ignition key on, the start pick-up sends its signal to the computer, which relays back information for more spark advance during cranking. As soon as the engine starts, the run pick-up takes over, and receives more advance for about one minute. This advance is slowly eliminated during the one minute warm up period. Whole the engine is cold, (coolant temperature below 150° as monitored by the coolant temperature sensor), no more advance will be given to the distributor until it reaches normal operation temperature. At this point, normal operation of the system will begin.

In most 1978 through 1980 models, there is only one pick-up coil. The computer functions on two modes: the start mode and the run mode. These modes are equivalent in function to the two pick-up coils used earlier. 1981 and later 6 and 8 cylinder models are equipped with dual pick:up coils, much the same as 1977 and earlier models.

In normal operation, the basic timing information is related by the run pick-up to the computer along with input signals from all the other sensors. From this data, the computer determines the

Testing for battery voltage at the positive coil terminal

maximum allowable advance or retard to be sent to the distributor for any situation.

If either the run pick-up or the computer should fail, the back up system of the start pick-up takes over. This supplies a fixed timing signal to the distributor which allows the car to be driven until it can be repaired. In this mode, very poor fuel economy and performance will be experienced. If the start pick-up or the ignition control module section of the computer should fail, the car will not start or run. Since most 1978 through 1980 models, including most Omni/Horizon and Aries/Reliant models, have only pick-up, if that pick-up coil or the start mode of the computer should fail, the engine will not start or run.

NOTE: Some of the procedures in this section refer to an adjustable timing light. This is also known as a spark advance tester, i.e., a device that will measure how much spark advance is present going from one point, a base figure, to another. Since precise timing is very important to the system, do not attempt to perform any of the tests calling for an adjustable timing light without one.

Performance Tests

Secondary Circuit Test

Remove the coil wire from the distributor cap and hold it with insulated pliers cautiously about 1/4 in. away from an engine ground, then have someone crank the engine while you check for spark. If you have a good spark, slowly move the coil wire away from the engine and check for arcing at the coil while cranking. If you have good spark and it is not arcing at the coil, check the rest of the parts of the ignition system.

Primary Circuit Tests

ALL EXCEPT 4 CYLINDER ENGINES

This test is for the start pick-up in dual pick-up models, and the entire pick-up assembly in all single pick-up models except the Omni/Horizon and the Aries/Reliant.

1. Check the battery specific gravity; it must be at least 1.220 to deliver the necessary voltage to fire the plugs.

2. Remove the terminal connector from the coolant switch (1978–79), and put a piece of paper or plastic between the curb idle adjusting screw and the carburetor switch (all).

3. Connect the negative lead of a voltmeter to a good engine ground, turn the ignition switch to the "run" position and measure the voltage at the carburetor switch terminal. On 1978–79 models,

Secondary circuit test, Use insulated pliers to hold the coil wire

Testing continuity between cavity No. 1 and ignition switch

Testing resistance at both pick-up coils

if a reading of more than 5 but less than 10 volts is received, go on to Step 7. On 1978–79 models, if the voltage is more than 10 volts, check for continuity between terminal 2 and ground or terminal 10 and ground (1978–79 models). On 1980 and later models, if voltage is approximately 5 volts, proceed to Step 8.

4. If the voltage was less than 5, turn the ignition switch "off" and disconnect the double terminal connector from the bottom of the Spark Control Computer. Turn the ignition switch back to the "run" position and measure the voltage at terminal 2 for 1978 and later models. If the voltage is not within 1 volt of the voltage you received in Step 1, check the wiring between the terminal and the ignition switch. If the voltage is correct, proceed to Step 5.

5. Turn the ignition switch "off" and disconnect the double connector on 1978 and later models. Using an ohmmeter, check for continuity between terminal 7 and the carburetor switch for 1978 and later models. There should be continuity. If not, check the wiring.

6. For 1978 and later models, if there is continuity in Step 5, next check for continuity between terminal 10 and a ground. If continuity exists, replace the computer. If not, check the wire for open or poor connections, and only proceed to Step 7 if the engine still won't start.

7. For all 1978 and later models, turn the ignition switch to the "run" position and touch the positive voltmeter lead to terminal 1 and the negative lead to ground. Voltage should be within one volt of battery voltage measured in Step 1. If so, go to Step 8. If not, check the wiring and connections between the connector and the ignition switch.

8. Turn the ignition switch "off" and with an ohmmeter, measure resistance between 5 and 9. On 1980 and later dual pick-up coil models, test between terminals 5 and 9 for the run pick-up coil, and between terminals 3 and 9 for the start pick-up coil. If you do not receive a reading of 150–900 ohms disconnect the pick-up leads at the distributor.

9. Connector one lead of an ohmmeter to a good engine ground and with the other lead, check the continuity of both pick-up leads going into the distributor. If there is not continuity, go on to the next step. If you do get a reading, replace the pickup.

10. Remove the distributor cap and check the air gap of the pick-up coil(s). Adjust if necessary and proceed to the next step.

11. Replace the distributor cap, and start the engine. If it still will not start, replace the Spark Control Computer. If the engine still does not work, put the old one back and retrace your steps paying close attention to any wiring which may be shorted.

OMNI/HORIZON THROUGH 1980

1. Before performing this test, be sure the basic connector and wire checks are performed. Measure the battery specific gravity; it must be at least 1.220, temperature corrected. Measure the battery voltage and make a note of it.

2. Disconnect the thin wire from the negative coil terminal.

3. Remove the coil high tension lead at the distributor cap.

4. Turn the ignition On. While holding the coil high tension lead 1/4 in. from a ground, connect a jumper wire from the negative coil terminal to a ground. A spark should be obtained from the high tension lead.

---CAUTION---
Hold the lead with insulated pliers and wear a heavy rubber glove.

---

5. If there is no spark, use a voltmeter to test for at least 9 volts at the positive coil terminal (ignition On). If so, the coil must be replaced. If less than 9 volts is obtained, check the ballast resistor

Testing for voltage at cavity No. 2

Testing continuity between cavity No. 2 and negative coil terminal

Testing for short circuits at each pick-up coil terminal

Testing resistance between cavities No. 4 and 5

(through 1979), wiring, and connection. If the car still won't start, proceed to Step 6.

6. If there was a spark in Step 4, turn the ignition Off, reconnect the wire to the negative coil terminal, and disconnect the distributor pick-up coil connector.

7. Turn the ignition On, and measure voltage between pin B of the pick-up coil connector on the spark control computer side, and a good engine ground. Voltage should be the same as the battery voltage measured in Step 1. If so, go to Step 11. If not, go to the next Step.

8. Turn the ignition Off and disconnect the 10 terminal connector at the spark control computer. Do not remove the grease from the connector or the connector terminal in the computer.

9. Check for continuity between pin B of the pick-up coil connector on the computer side, and terminal 3 of the computer connector. If there is no continuity, the wire must be replaced. If continuity exists, go to the next step.

10. With the ignition On, connect a voltmeter between terminals 2 and 10 of the connector. Voltage should be the same as measured in Step 1. If so, the computer is defective and must be replaced.

11. Reconnect the 10 wire computer connector. Turn the ignition On. Hold the coil high tension lead (disconnected at the distributor cap) about 1/4 in. from a ground. Connect a jumper wire between pins A and C of the distributor pick-up coil connector. If a spark is obtained, the distributor pick-up is defective and must be replaced. If not, go to the next step.

12. Turn the ignition Off. Disconnect the 10 wire computer connector.

13. Check for continuity between pin C of the distributor connector and terminal 9 of the computer connector. Also check for continuity between pin A of the distributor connector and terminal 5 of the computer connector. If continuity exists, the computer is defective and must be replaced. If not, the wires are damaged. Repair them and recheck, starting at Step 11.

OMNI/HORIZON AND ARIES/RELIANT 1981 AND LATER

1. Perform the basic connector and wire checks before proceeding with the following. Make sure the battery is fully charged, then measure and record the battery voltage.

2. Remove the coil secondary wire from the distributor cap.

3. With the key on, use the special jumper wire and momentarily

Testing electronic control unit pin No. 5 for ground

connect the negative terminal of the ignition coil to ground while holding the coil secondary wire (using insulated pliers and heavy gloves) about 1/4 in. from a good ground. A spark should fire.

4. If spark was obtained, go to Step 9.

5. If no spark was obtained, turn off the ignition and disconnect the 10-wire harness going into the Spark Control Computer. Do not remove the grease from the connector.

6. With the ignition key on, use the special jumper wire and momentarily connect the negative terminal of the ignition coil to ground while holding the coil wire 1/4 in. from a good engine ground. A spark should fire.

7. If a spark is present, the computer output is shorted; replace the computer.

8. If no spark is obtained, measure the voltage at the coil positive terminal. It should be within 1 volt of battery voltage. If voltage is present but no spark is available when shorting negative terminal, replace the coil. If no voltage is present, replace the coil or check the primary wiring.

9. If voltage was obtained but the engine will not start, hold the carburetor switch open with a thin cardboard insulator and measure the voltage at the switch. It should be at least 5 volts. If voltage is present, go to Step 16.

10. If no voltage is present, turn the ignition switch off and disconnect the 10 wire harness going into the computer.

11. Turn the ignition switch on and measure the voltage at terminal 2 of the harness. It should be within 1 volt of battery voltage.

12. If no battery voltage is present, check for continuity between the battery and terminal 2 of the harness. If no continuity, repair fault and repeat Step 11.

13. If voltage is present turn ignition switch off and check for continuity between the carburetor switch and terminal 7 on connector. If no continuity is present, check for open wire between terminal 7 and the carburetor switch.

14. If continuity is present, check continuity between terminal 10

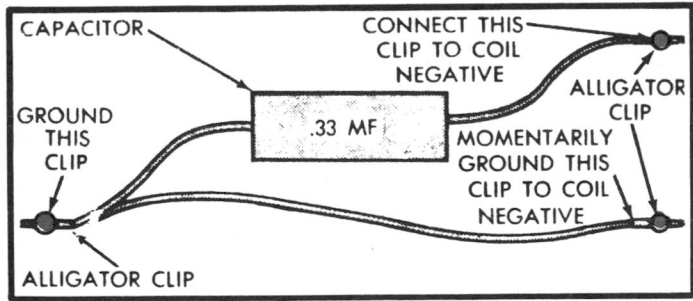

Special jumper wire from coil negative terminal to ground—FWD models

Testing voltage at cavity No. 2—FWD models

Testing continuity at cavity No. 7—FWD models

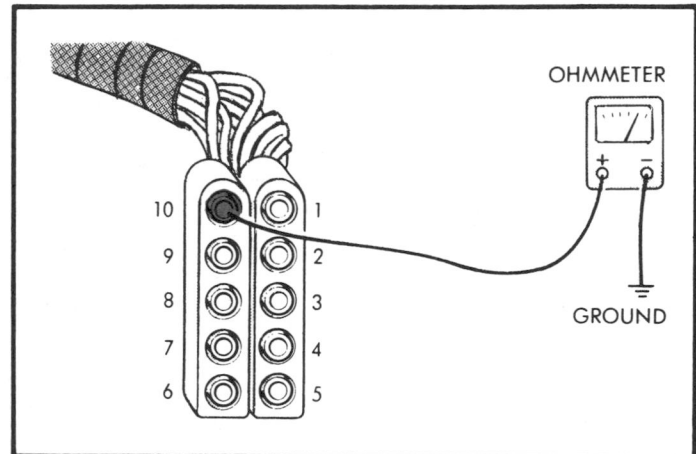

Testing continuity at cavity No. 10—FWD models

Install jumper wire as shown on FWD models

and ground. If continuity is present here, replace the computer. Repeat Step 9.

15. If no continuity is present, check for an open wire. If wiring is OK, but the engine still won't start, go to next step.

16. Plug the 10 terminal dual connector back into the computer and turn the ignition switch on, hold the secondary coil wire near a good ground and disconnect the distributor harness connector. Using a regular jumper wire (not the special one mentioned earlier), jump terminal 2 to terminal 3 of the connector: a spark should fire at the coil wire.

17. If spark is present at the coil wire but the engine won't start,

Testing voltage at distributor harness cavity No 1—FWD models

Voltage tests between cavities No. 2 and 10—FWD models

Continuity tests on FWD models. Connect ohmmeter as shown

Positive locking secondary ignition wire terminal. To remove, press the lock together and push the wire out of the distributor cap.

Continuity test between cavities No. 1 and 3—FWD models

replace the Hall Effect pick-up and check the rotor for cracks or burning. Replace as necessary.

NOTE: When replacing a pick-up, always make sure rotor blades are grounded using a ohmmeter.

18. If no spark is present at the coil wire, measure the voltage at terminal 1 of the distributor harness connector: it should be within 1 volt of battery voltage.

19. If correct, disconnect the dual connector from the computer and check for continuity between terminal 2 of distributor harness and terminal 9 of the dual connector. Repeat test on terminal 3 of distributor harness and terminal 5 of dual connector. If no continuity, repair the harness. If continuity is present, replace the computer and repeat Step 16.

20. If no battery voltage is present in Step 18, turn off the ignition switch, disconnect the 10 terminal dual connector from the computer and check for continuity between terminal 1 of distributor harness and terminal 3 of dual connector. If no continuity, repair wire and repeat Step 16.

21. If continuity is present, turn the ignition switch on and check for battery voltage between terminal 2 and terminal 10 of the dual connector. If voltage is present, replace the computer and repeat Step 16. If no battery voltage is present, the computer is not grounded. Check and repair the ground wire and repeat Step 16.

Start Timer Advance Test

1978 AND LATER

1. Connect an adjustable timing light.
2. Connect a jumper wire from the carburetor switch to a ground.
3. Start the engine and immediately adjust the timing light so that the basic timing light is seen on the timing plate of the engine. The meter (on the timing light) should show an 8° advance on all engines through 1979. For 1980 and later models, refer to the emission control decal in the engine compartment for the proper specification. Continue to observe the mark for 90 seconds, adjusting the light as necessary. The additional advance will slowly decrease to the basic timing signal over a period of about one minute. If not, replace the Spark Control Computer and recheck. If it is ok, go on to the next test.

Throttle Advance Test

Before performing this test, the throttle position transducer must be adjusted. (This test does not apply to 1978 Omnis and Horizons with automatic transmissions, or to any 1979 and later Omnis or Horizons or any 1980 and later models.) The adjustments are as follows:

1978-79 ALL MODELS

1. Disconnect the throttle position transducer wiring.
2. Loosen the locknut.
3. Place the Chrysler special tool #C-4522 between the outer body of the transducer and its mounting bracket.
4. Adjust the transducer for a clearance fit by rotating the body.
5. Retighten the locknut. Go on to Step 6 of this procedure.
6. Turn the ignition switch off and disconnect the single connector computer.
7. With an ohmmeter, measure the resistance between terminals 8 and 9. The measured resistance should be between 50–90 ohms. If it is, reconnect it and go on to the next step. If not, remove the connector from the throttle position transducer and measure the resistance at the transducer terminals. If you now get a reading of 50–90 ohms, check the wiring between the connector terminals and the transducer terminals. If you do not get the 50–90 reading, replace the transducer and proceed to the next step.
8. Position the throttle linkage on the fast idle cam and ground the carb switch with a jumper wire. Disconnect the wiring connector from the transducer and connect it to a transducer that you know is good.
9. Move the core of the transducer all the way in, start the engine, wait about 90 seconds and then move the core out about an inch.
10. Adjust the timing light so that it registers the basic timing. The timing light meter should show the additional amount of advance as given on the tune-up sticker in the engine compartment. If it is within the specifications, move the core back into the transducer, and the timing should go back to the original position. If it did not advance and/or return, replace the Spark Control Computer and try this test over again. If it still fails, replace the transducer.
11. Remove the test transducer (from Step 9) and reconnect all wiring.

Vacuum Advance Test (Vacuum Transducer)

1978 MODELS

1. Hook up an adjustable timing light.
2. Start the engine and let it warm up; make sure the transmission is in Neutral and the parking brake is on.
3. Place a small piece of plastic or paper between the carburetor switch and the curb idle adjusting screw (on the Omni/Horizon, between the carburetor switch and throttle lever); if the screw is not touching the switch make sure the fast idle cam is not on or binding; the linkage is not binding, or the throttle stop screw is not overadjusted. Adjust the timing light for the basic timing figure. On all 1978 models, let the engine run for at least 9 minutes, and check for at least 16 in. Hg. vacuum at the transducer. After this period, the meter on the light should show the additional advance indicated on the tune-up sticker in the engine compartment. If not, replace the Spark Control Computer. On the Omni/Horizon, stop here. On all other 1978 models, go on to Step 5.
4. After the 9 minute waiting period, adjust the timing light so that it registers the basic timing figure. The timing light meter should now register 32–35° of additional engine advance. If the advance is not shown, replace the Spark Control Computer and repeat the test; if it is shown, proceed to Step 5.
5. Remove the insulator (paper or plastic) that was installed in Step 3; the timing should return to its base setting. If it does not, make sure the curb idle adjusting screw is not touching the carburetor switch. If that is alright, turn the engine off and check the wire between terminal 7 on all 1978 cars, and the carburetor switch terminal for a bad connection. If it turns out alright, and the timing still will not return to its base setting, replace the Spark Control Computer.

1979-80 MODELS

A number of different computer programs are used on 1979 and later cars. Refer to the emission control sticker in the engine compartment for the correct timing settings; no timing figures will be given in the following procedure.

1. Connect an adjustable timing light and a tachometer to the engine.
2. Start the engine and allow it to reach normal operating temperature. If the engine is already hot, allow it to idle for at least one minute before beginning tests. The transmission should be in Neutral; apply the parking brake.
3. Check the basic timing (see the emission sticker for the correct figure); adjust if necessary.
4. Disconnect and plug the vacuum line at the vacuum transducer; be careful not to split the hose. The vacuum transducer is located on the Spark Control Computer.
5. Ground the carburetor switch on 1979 models. On 1980 models, remove the carburetor ground switch. If the engine has a throttle position transducer, remove its electrical connector.
6. Increase the engine speed to 1,100 rpm.
7. Check the "Speed Advance Timing" against the figure given on the emission sticker.
8. On the Omni/Horizon raise the engine speed to 2,000 rpm; leave it at 1,100 rpm on all other cars. On all 1979 models, remove the carburetor switch ground and connect the vacuum hose to the transducer. On 1980 models, connect the vacuum hose to the transducer.
9. Check the "Zero Time Offset" against the timing figure given on the emission sticker (1979 models only).
10. Allow the engine to run for 8 minutes; this allows the accumulator in the computer to "clock up." After the time has elapsed, check the "Vacuum Advance" timing against the sticker figure. The engine should be running at 1,100 rpm (2,000 rpm Omni/Horizon) on all models when checking this figure.
11. Disconnect and plug the vacuum hose at the vacuum transducer again. Increase the engine speed to 1,500 rpm (2,500 rpm, 1980) on all cars except the Omni/Horizon, increase the engine speed to 3,000 rpm on those cars. Check the "Speed Advance" timing against the sticker figure.
12. Reconnect the transducer hose. Check the "Vacuum Advance" timing against the sticker figure. Return the engine to curb idle and connect the wire to the carburetor and throttle position transducer as applicable. If the Spark Control Computer fails to meet the specified settings, it must be replaced.

1981 AND LATER MODELS

1. Run the engine to normal operating temperature. Disconnect or unground the carburetor switch. The temperature sensor should remain connected.
2. Remove the plug vacuum hose at the vacuum transducer on the spark control computer.
3. Connect an auxiliary vacuum supply to the vacuum transducer and apply 16 in. of vacuum.
4. Raise the engine speed to 2,000 rpm, wait one minute and (or specified accumulator clock-up time) and check the specifications (see underhood sticker). Advance specifications are in addition to basic advance specifications.

If the spark control computer fails to obtain specified settings, replace the computer.

Coolant Switch Test

1. Connect one lead of the ohmmeter to a good engine ground, the other to the center terminal of the coolant switch.
2. If the engine is cold (below 150°) there should be continuity in the switch. With the thermostat open, and the engine warmed up, there should be no continuity. If either of the conditions in this step are not met, replace the switch.

NOTE: On models so equipped, the charge temperature switch must be cooler than 60°F to achieve cold engine reading.

Air gap adjustment on dual pick-up distributor.

Detonation Sensor Test

1980 AND LATER

1. Connect an adjustable timing light to the engine.
2. Place the fast idle screw on the second highest step of the fast idle cam. Start the engine and allow it to idle. The engine should be running at 1,200 rpm or more.
3. Use an open end wrench or the like to tap lightly on the intake manifold next to the detonation sensor. As you do this, watch the timing marks; a decrease in timing advance should be seen. The amount of decrease should be directly proportional to the strength and frequency of tapping. Maximum retard is 11°.

4. If the sensor is not working correctly, install a new sensor and retest.

PICK-UP GAP SPECIFICATIONS

1978 and Later Single Pick-Up Models	
Pick-up Coil to Reluctor	0.006
1980 and Later Dual Pick-Up Models	
Start Pick-up (set to)	0.006
(check)	0.008
Run Pick-up (set to)	0.012
(check)	0.014

OVERHAUL PROCEDURES

NOTE: None of the components of the Lean Burn System (except the carburetor) may be taken apart and repaired. When a part is known to be bad, it should be replaced.

The Spark Control Computer is held on by mounting screws in the air cleaner on all models except the Omni/Horizon and Aries/Reliant. On those models only, first remove the battery, then disconnect the 10 terminal connector and the air duct from the computer. Next remove the vacuum line from the transducer. Remove the three screws securing the computer to the left front fender, and remove the computer. To remove the Throttle Position Transducer, loosen the locknut and unscrew it from the mounting bracket, then unsnap the core from the carburetor linkage.

Electronic Lean Burn System

HAS SPARK BUT ENGINE WON'T START

STEP 1: TURN IGNITION SWITCH "OFF," PULL E.C.U. HARNESS CONNECTOR AND TURN IGNITION SWITCH ON

CHECK FOR BATTERY VOLTAGE AT CAVITY 2 OF E.C.U. HARNESS IT SHOULD BE WITHIN 1 VOLT OF BATTERY VOLTAGE

IF VOLTAGE IS OK CHECK VOLTAGE AT CAVITY 1 OF ECU CONNECTOR. IT SHOULD BE WITHIN 1 VOLT OF BATTERY VOLTAGE

IF VOLTAGE IS NOT OK CHECK FOR CONTINUITY BETWEEN CAVITY 2 AND COIL NEGATIVE. FIND FAULT AND REPAIR. REPEAT STEP 1

IF VOLTAGE IS ON GO TO STEP 2

IF VOLTAGE IS NOT OK, CHECK FOR CONTINUITY BETWEEN CAVITY 1 AND IGNITION SWITCH, FIND FAULT AND REPAIR

STEP 2: TURN IGNITION SWITCH "OFF" AND CHECK RESISTANCE BETWEEN CAVITIES 4 AND 5 OF E.C.U. CONNECTOR. IT SHOULD BE 150 TO 900 OHMS

IF IT IS, GO TO STEP 3

IF IT IS NOT, TURN IGNITION SWITCH "OFF", DISCONNECT DUAL PICK-UP LEADS AND CHECK RESISTANCE. IT SHOULD BE 150 TO 900 OHMS

IF IT IS, PICK-UPS ARE OK BUT WIRE BETWEEN CAVITIES 4 AND 5 AND DUAL CONNECTOR IS OPEN OR SHORTED— REPAIR CIRCUIT

IF IT IS NOT, REPLACE PICK-UP COIL AND GO TO STEP 3

STEP 4: CHECK FOR GROUND AT PIN 5 OF E.C.U.

SHOWS GROUND, GO TO STEP 5

NO GROUND, CHECK THAT E.C.U. UNIT CONNECTIONS ARE CLEAN AND MOUNTING SCREWS ARE TIGHT REPEAT STEP 4

STEP 5: REINSTALL ALL CONNECTORS AND CHECK FOR A SPARK

HAS SPARK, SYSTEM OK

HAS NO SPARK, REPLACE E.C.U.

MEASURE AND RECORD BATTERY VOLTAGE WITH VOLTMETER MEASURE SPECIFIC GRAVITY IT SHOULD BE AT LEAST 12.20 IF NOT, CHARGE BATTERY TO SPECIFICATION

TURN IGNITION SWITCH TO ON POSITION

HOLD COIL SECONDARY WIRE NEAR GROUND

INTERMITTENTLY SHORT COIL NEGATIVE TO GROUND

STEP A: MEASURE VOLTAGE AT COIL POSITIVE. IT SHOULD BE WITHIN 1 VOLT OF BATTERY VOLTAGE

IF VOLTAGE IS OK, CHECK VOLTAGE AT COIL NEGATIVE. IT SHOULD BE WITHIN 1 VOLT OF BATTERY VOLTAGE.

IF YOU GET BATTERY VOLTAGE BUT NO SPARK WHEN SHORTING NEGATIVE TERMINAL, REPLACE COIL

REPLACE STARTER RELAY AND CHECK WIRING BETWEEN BATTERY AND COIL POSITIVE

CIRCUIT NOT CONTINUOUS BETWEEN BATTERY AND COIL POSITIVE, REPLACE IGNITION RESISTOR AND REPEAT STEP A

STEP 3: CHECK FOR A GROUND OR SHORT AT EACH LEAD OF PICK-UP COILS WITH AN OHMMETER, GROUND ONE SIDE OF OHMMETER

IF THERE IS NO SHORT GO TO STEP 4

IF SHORTED, REPLACE PICK-UP COILS AND SET AIR GAP TO .006 WITH A NON-MAGNETIC FEELER GAUGE. A .008 GAUGE SHOULD NOT GO THROUGH GAP REPEAT STEP 3

HAS NO SPARK UNPLUG E.C.U.

INTERMITTENTLY SHORT COIL NEGATIVE TO GROUND

STILL HAS NO SPARK

NOW HAS SPARK REPLACE E.C.U. CONTROL UNIT

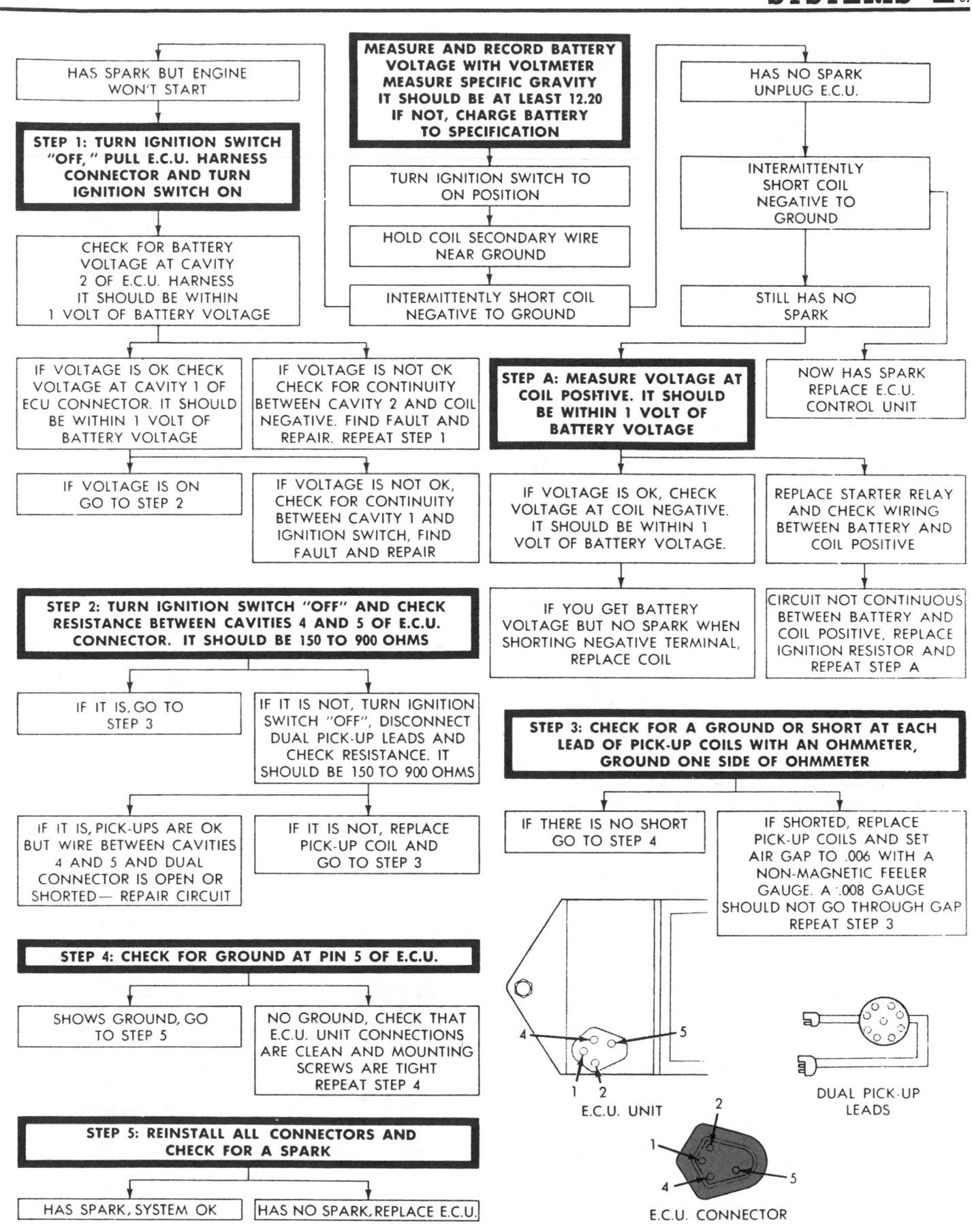

E.C.U. UNIT

DUAL PICK-UP LEADS

E.C.U. CONNECTOR

HAS SPARK BUT ENGINE WON'T START

STEP 1: TURN IGNITION SWITCH OFF, UNPLUG COMPUTER 10 WAY CONNECTOR, TURN IGNITION SWITCH ON

MEASURE VOLTAGE AT CAVITY 1 OF 10 WAY CONNECTOR. IT SHOULD BE WITHIN 1 VOLT OF BATTERY VOLTAGE

IF VOLTAGE IS CORRECT GO TO STEP 3

REPAIR HARNESS AND REPEAT STEP 1

STEP 3: PLACE A THIN INSULATOR BETWEEN CARB IDLE ADJUSTING SCREW AND CARB SWITCH. MEASURE VOLTAGE AT CARB SWITCH. IT SHOULD BE AT LEAST 5 VOLTS

IF VOLTAGE IS OK GO TO STEP 5

TURN IGNITION SWITCH ON, MEASURE VOLTAGE AT CAVITY 2 OF THE 10 WAY CONNECTOR. IT SHOULD BE WITHIN 1 VOLT OF BATTERY VOLTAGE

IF IT IS GO TO STEP 4

IF IT IS NOT, REPAIR WIRING BETWEEN CAVITY 2 AND BATTERY REPEAT STEP 3

STEP 5: TURN IGNITION SWITCH OFF. MEASURE RESISTANCE BETWEEN CAVITIES 3 AND 9 THEN 5 AND 9 OF THE 10 WAY CONNECTOR. RESISTANCE SHOULD BE 150-900 OHMS

IF IT IS GO TO STEP 6

DISCONNECT PICK-UP LEADS MEASURE RESISTANCE, IT SHOULD BE 150 TO 900 OHMS

IF RESISTANCE IS 150 TO 900 OHMS, REPAIR HARNESS OPEN OR SHORT AND REPEAT STEP 5

IF RESISTANCE IS NOT 150 TO 900 OHMS, PICK-UP COIL IS BAD. REPLACE PICK-UP AND SET AIR GAP, STEP 7, THEN REPEAT STEP 5

STEP 6: CHECK FOR GROUND OR SHORT AT EACH PICK-UP LEAD WITH OHMMETER. GROUND ONE LEAD OF OHMMETER

NO SHORT, GO TO STEP 8

SHORTED, REPLACE PICK-UP COIL AND GO TO STEP 7

MEASURE AND RECORD BATTERY VOLTAGE WITH VOLTMETER MEASURE SPECIFIC GRAVITY. IT SHOULD BE AT LEAST 12:20. IF NOT CHARGE BATTERY TO SPECIFICATION

TURN IGNITION SWITCH TO ON POSITION

HOLD SECONDARY COIL WIRE NEAR GROUND

INTERMITTENTLY SHORT COIL NEGATIVE TO GROUND

HAS NO SPARK. UNPLUG COMPUTER 10 WAY CONNECTOR

INTERMITTENTLY SHORT COIL NEGATIVE TO GROUND

NOW HAS SPARK REPLACE MODULE

STEP 2: NO SPARK. CHECK BATTERY VOLTAGE AT COIL POSITIVE IT SHOULD BE WITHIN 1 VOLT OF BATTERY VOLTAGE

HAS VOLTAGE: CHECK FOR VOLTAGE AT COIL NEGATIVE. IT SHOULD BE WITHIN 1 VOLT OF BATTERY VOLTAGE

NO VOLTAGE: WIRING BETWEEN BATTERY AND COIL POSITIVE, REPAIR AND REPEAT STEP 2

HAS VOLTAGE BUT NO SPARK. REPLACE COIL

NO VOLTAGE REPLACE COIL

STEP 4: TURN IGNITION SWITCH OFF AND WITH AN OHMMETER CHECK FOR CONTINUITY BETWEEN CARB SWITCH AND CAVITY OF 10 WAY CONNECTOR

CIRCUIT SHOULD BE CONTINUOUS

IF IT IS, CHECK FOR CONTINUITY BETWEEN CAVITY 10 AND GROUND

IF IT IS NOT, FIND OPEN AND REPAIR

IF THERE IS CONTINUITY REPLACE COMPUTER

IF THERE IS NOT, FIND OPEN AND REPAIR AND REPEAT STEP 4

10 WAY CONNECTOR

10 1
9   2
8   3
7   4
6   5

STEP 7: ADJUST PICK-UP COIL AIR GAP TO SPECIFICATION. START PICK-UP .006 WITH NON MAGNETIC FEELER GAUGE AN .008 SHOULD NOT PASS THROUGH GAP RUN PICK-UP .012. A .014 SHOULD NOT PASS THROUGH GAP

STEP 8: ATTACH ALL CONNECTORS AND TRY TO START ENGINE

ENGINE STARTS SYSTEM OK

ENGINE WILL NOT START REPLACE COMPUTER AND START ENGINE

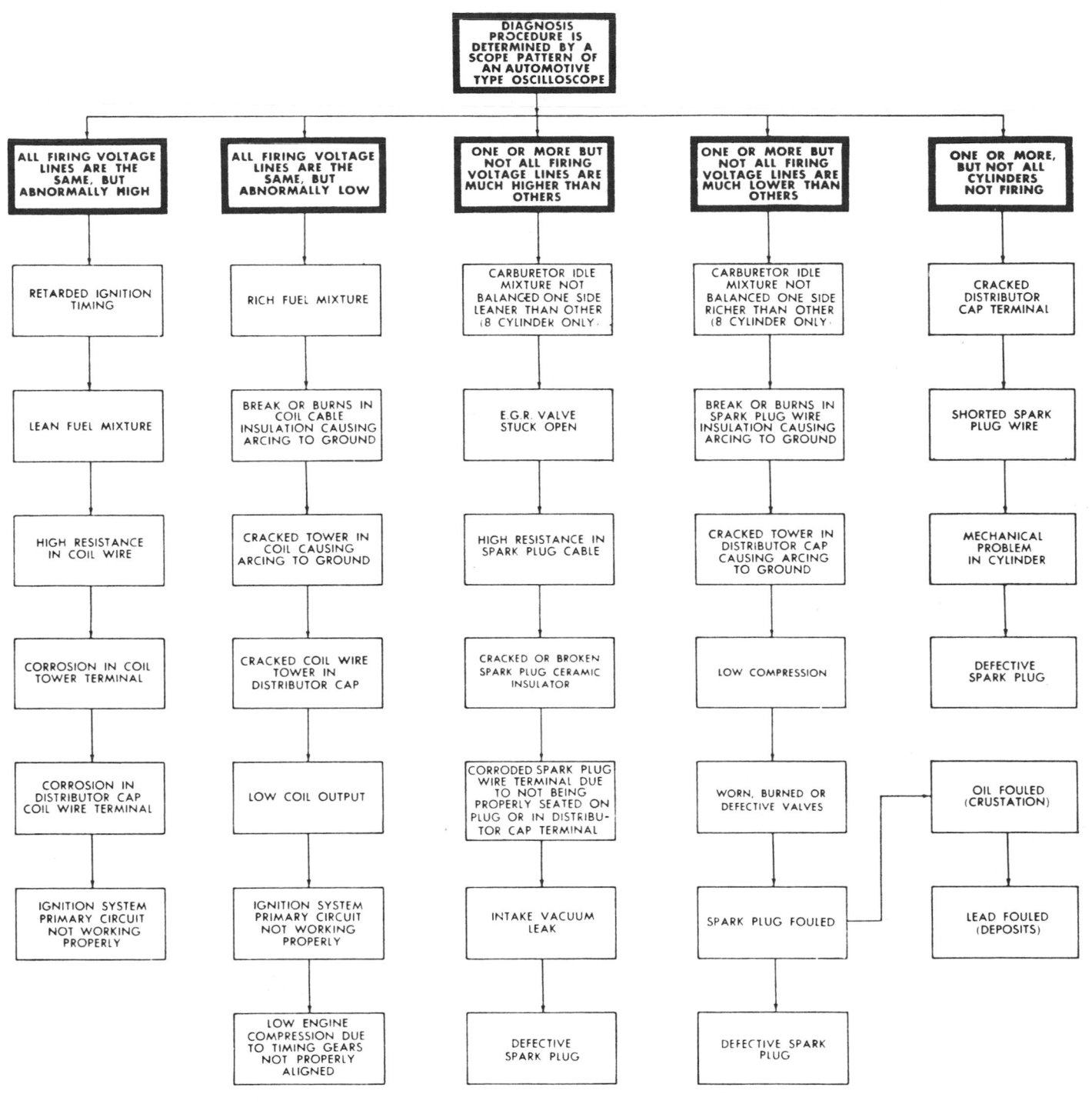

DIAGNOSIS PROCEDURE IS DETERMINED BY A SCOPE PATTERN OF AN AUTOMOTIVE TYPE OSCILLOSCOPE

ALL FIRING VOLTAGE LINES ARE THE SAME, BUT ABNORMALLY HIGH
- RETARDED IGNITION TIMING
- LEAN FUEL MIXTURE
- HIGH RESISTANCE IN COIL WIRE
- CORROSION IN COIL TOWER TERMINAL
- CORROSION IN DISTRIBUTOR CAP COIL WIRE TERMINAL
- IGNITION SYSTEM PRIMARY CIRCUIT NOT WORKING PROPERLY

ALL FIRING VOLTAGE LINES ARE THE SAME, BUT ABNORMALLY LOW
- RICH FUEL MIXTURE
- BREAK OR BURNS IN COIL CABLE INSULATION CAUSING ARCING TO GROUND
- CRACKED TOWER IN COIL CAUSING ARCING TO GROUND
- CRACKED COIL WIRE TOWER IN DISTRIBUTOR CAP
- LOW COIL OUTPUT
- IGNITION SYSTEM PRIMARY CIRCUIT NOT WORKING PROPERLY
- LOW ENGINE COMPRESSION DUE TO TIMING GEARS NOT PROPERLY ALIGNED

ONE OR MORE BUT NOT ALL FIRING VOLTAGE LINES ARE MUCH HIGHER THAN OTHERS
- CARBURETOR IDLE MIXTURE NOT BALANCED ONE SIDE LEANER THAN OTHER (8 CYLINDER ONLY)
- E.G.R. VALVE STUCK OPEN
- HIGH RESISTANCE IN SPARK PLUG CABLE
- CRACKED OR BROKEN SPARK PLUG CERAMIC INSULATOR
- CORRODED SPARK PLUG WIRE TERMINAL DUE TO NOT BEING PROPERLY SEATED ON PLUG OR IN DISTRIBUTOR CAP TERMINAL
- INTAKE VACUUM LEAK
- DEFECTIVE SPARK PLUG

ONE OR MORE BUT NOT ALL FIRING VOLTAGE LINES ARE MUCH LOWER THAN OTHERS
- CARBURETOR IDLE MIXTURE NOT BALANCED ONE SIDE RICHER THAN OTHER (8 CYLINDER ONLY)
- BREAK OR BURNS IN SPARK PLUG WIRE INSULATION CAUSING ARCING TO GROUND
- CRACKED TOWER IN DISTRIBUTOR CAP CAUSING ARCING TO GROUND
- LOW COMPRESSION
- WORN, BURNED OR DEFECTIVE VALVES
- SPARK PLUG FOULED
- DEFECTIVE SPARK PLUG

ONE OR MORE, BUT NOT ALL CYLINDERS NOT FIRING
- CRACKED DISTRIBUTOR CAP TERMINAL
- SHORTED SPARK PLUG WIRE
- MECHANICAL PROBLEM IN CYLINDER
- DEFECTIVE SPARK PLUG
- OIL FOULED (CRUSTATION)
- LEAD FOULED (DEPOSITS)

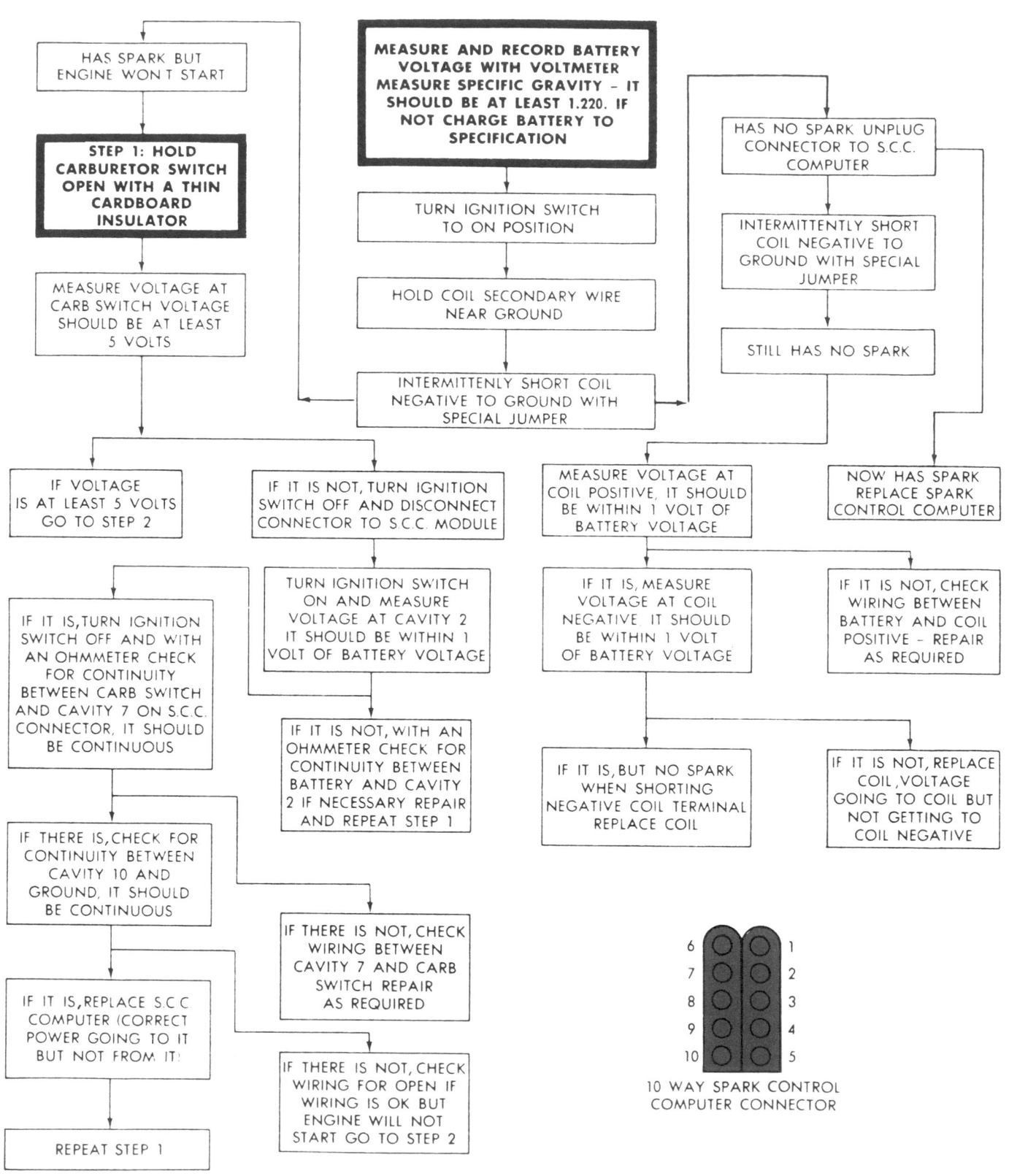

HAS SPARK BUT ENGINE WON'T START

STEP 1: HOLD CARBURETOR SWITCH OPEN WITH A THIN CARDBOARD INSULATOR

MEASURE VOLTAGE AT CARB SWITCH VOLTAGE SHOULD BE AT LEAST 5 VOLTS

MEASURE AND RECORD BATTERY VOLTAGE WITH VOLTMETER MEASURE SPECIFIC GRAVITY – IT SHOULD BE AT LEAST 1.220. IF NOT CHARGE BATTERY TO SPECIFICATION

TURN IGNITION SWITCH TO ON POSITION

HOLD COIL SECONDARY WIRE NEAR GROUND

INTERMITTENLY SHORT COIL NEGATIVE TO GROUND WITH SPECIAL JUMPER

HAS NO SPARK UNPLUG CONNECTOR TO S.C.C. COMPUTER

INTERMITTENTLY SHORT COIL NEGATIVE TO GROUND WITH SPECIAL JUMPER

STILL HAS NO SPARK

IF VOLTAGE IS AT LEAST 5 VOLTS GO TO STEP 2

IF IT IS NOT, TURN IGNITION SWITCH OFF AND DISCONNECT CONNECTOR TO S.C.C. MODULE

MEASURE VOLTAGE AT COIL POSITIVE, IT SHOULD BE WITHIN 1 VOLT OF BATTERY VOLTAGE

NOW HAS SPARK REPLACE SPARK CONTROL COMPUTER

IF IT IS, TURN IGNITION SWITCH OFF AND WITH AN OHMMETER CHECK FOR CONTINUITY BETWEEN CARB SWITCH AND CAVITY 7 ON S.C.C. CONNECTOR, IT SHOULD BE CONTINUOUS

TURN IGNITION SWITCH ON AND MEASURE VOLTAGE AT CAVITY 2 IT SHOULD BE WITHIN 1 VOLT OF BATTERY VOLTAGE

IF IT IS, MEASURE VOLTAGE AT COIL NEGATIVE. IT SHOULD BE WITHIN 1 VOLT OF BATTERY VOLTAGE

IF IT IS NOT, CHECK WIRING BETWEEN BATTERY AND COIL POSITIVE – REPAIR AS REQUIRED

IF IT IS NOT, WITH AN OHMMETER CHECK FOR CONTINUITY BETWEEN BATTERY AND CAVITY 2 IF NECESSARY REPAIR AND REPEAT STEP 1

IF THERE IS, CHECK FOR CONTINUITY BETWEEN CAVITY 10 AND GROUND, IT SHOULD BE CONTINUOUS

IF IT IS, BUT NO SPARK WHEN SHORTING NEGATIVE COIL TERMINAL REPLACE COIL

IF IT IS NOT, REPLACE COIL, VOLTAGE GOING TO COIL BUT NOT GETTING TO COIL NEGATIVE

IF THERE IS NOT, CHECK WIRING BETWEEN CAVITY 7 AND CARB SWITCH REPAIR AS REQUIRED

IF IT IS, REPLACE S.C.C. COMPUTER (CORRECT POWER GOING TO IT BUT NOT FROM IT)

IF THERE IS NOT, CHECK WIRING FOR OPEN IF WIRING IS OK BUT ENGINE WILL NOT START GO TO STEP 2

REPEAT STEP 1

6 1
7 2
8 3
9 4
10 5

10 WAY SPARK CONTROL COMPUTER CONNECTOR

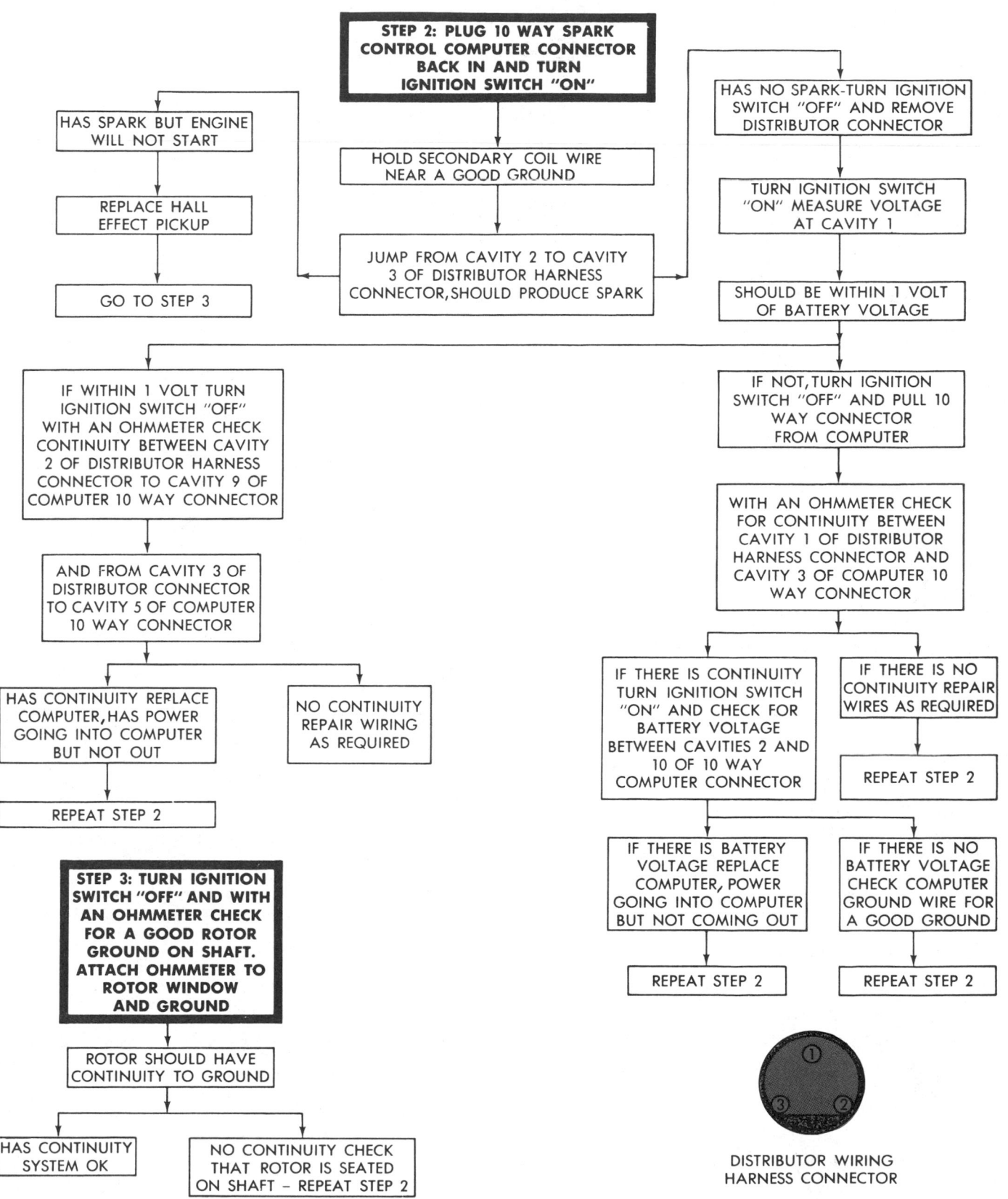

STEP 2: PLUG 10 WAY SPARK CONTROL COMPUTER CONNECTOR BACK IN AND TURN IGNITION SWITCH "ON"

HAS SPARK BUT ENGINE WILL NOT START

REPLACE HALL EFFECT PICKUP

GO TO STEP 3

HOLD SECONDARY COIL WIRE NEAR A GOOD GROUND

JUMP FROM CAVITY 2 TO CAVITY 3 OF DISTRIBUTOR HARNESS CONNECTOR, SHOULD PRODUCE SPARK

HAS NO SPARK-TURN IGNITION SWITCH "OFF" AND REMOVE DISTRIBUTOR CONNECTOR

TURN IGNITION SWITCH "ON" MEASURE VOLTAGE AT CAVITY 1

SHOULD BE WITHIN 1 VOLT OF BATTERY VOLTAGE

IF WITHIN 1 VOLT TURN IGNITION SWITCH "OFF" WITH AN OHMMETER CHECK CONTINUITY BETWEEN CAVITY 2 OF DISTRIBUTOR HARNESS CONNECTOR TO CAVITY 9 OF COMPUTER 10 WAY CONNECTOR

AND FROM CAVITY 3 OF DISTRIBUTOR CONNECTOR TO CAVITY 5 OF COMPUTER 10 WAY CONNECTOR

HAS CONTINUITY REPLACE COMPUTER, HAS POWER GOING INTO COMPUTER BUT NOT OUT

NO CONTINUITY REPAIR WIRING AS REQUIRED

REPEAT STEP 2

IF NOT, TURN IGNITION SWITCH "OFF" AND PULL 10 WAY CONNECTOR FROM COMPUTER

WITH AN OHMMETER CHECK FOR CONTINUITY BETWEEN CAVITY 1 OF DISTRIBUTOR HARNESS CONNECTOR AND CAVITY 3 OF COMPUTER 10 WAY CONNECTOR

IF THERE IS CONTINUITY TURN IGNITION SWITCH "ON" AND CHECK FOR BATTERY VOLTAGE BETWEEN CAVITIES 2 AND 10 OF 10 WAY COMPUTER CONNECTOR

IF THERE IS NO CONTINUITY REPAIR WIRES AS REQUIRED

REPEAT STEP 2

IF THERE IS BATTERY VOLTAGE REPLACE COMPUTER, POWER GOING INTO COMPUTER BUT NOT COMING OUT

REPEAT STEP 2

IF THERE IS NO BATTERY VOLTAGE CHECK COMPUTER GROUND WIRE FOR A GOOD GROUND

REPEAT STEP 2

STEP 3: TURN IGNITION SWITCH "OFF" AND WITH AN OHMMETER CHECK FOR A GOOD ROTOR GROUND ON SHAFT. ATTACH OHMMETER TO ROTOR WINDOW AND GROUND

ROTOR SHOULD HAVE CONTINUITY TO GROUND

HAS CONTINUITY SYSTEM OK

NO CONTINUITY CHECK THAT ROTOR IS SEATED ON SHAFT – REPEAT STEP 2

① ③ ②

DISTRIBUTOR WIRING HARNESS CONNECTOR

CHRYSLER HALL EFFECT IGNITION SYSTEM

General Information

COMPONENTS AND OPERATION

NOTE: This system is not used on 2.6L 4 cylinder engines

The Hall Effect electronic ignition is used in conjunction with the Chrysler Lean Burn/Electronic Spark Control System. It consists of a sealed Spark Control Computer, five engine sensors (vacuum transducer, coolant switch, Hall Effect pickup assembly, throttle position transducer, and carburetor switch), coil, spark plugs, ballast resistor, and the various wires needed to connect the compo-

Chrysler Hall Effect distributor components

nents. Only four of the five engine sensors are used on all 1979–80 models and on 1981 and later models not equipped with the Feed Back carburetor; the throttle position transducer is no longer used. On 1981 and later models with Feed Back carburetor, an oxygen sensor in the exhaust manifold is included.

The distributor contains the Hall Effect pickup assembly which replaces the breaker points assembly in conventional systems. The pickup assembly supplies the computer with information on engine speed and crankshaft position, and is only one of signals which the computer uses as input to determine ignition timing. The Hall Effect is a shift in magnetic field, caused, in this installation, when one of the rotor blades passes between the two arms of the sensor.

There are essentially two modes of operation of the Spark Control Computer: the start mode and the run mode. The start mode is only used during engine cranking. During cranking only the Hall Effect pickup signals the computer. These signals are interpreted to provide a fixed number of degrees of spark advance. The computer shuts off coil primary current in accordance with the pickup signals. As in conventional ignition systems, primary current shutdown causes secondary field collapse, and the high voltage is sent from the coil to the distributor, which then sends it to the spark plug.

After the engine starts, and during normal engine operation, the computer functions in the run mode. In this mode the Hall Effect pickup serves as only one of the signals to the computer. It is a reference signal of maximum possible spark advance. The computer then determines, from information provided by the other engine sensors, how much of this advance is necessary, and shuts down the primary current accordingly to fire the spark plug at the exact moment when this advance (crankshaft position) is reached.

There is a third mode of operation which only becomes functional when the computer fails. This is the limp-in mode. This mode functions on signals from the pickup only, and results in very poor engine performance. However, it does allow the car to be driven to a repair shop. If a failure occurs in the pickup assembly or the start mode of the computer, the engine will neither start nor run.

Schematic of Chrysler Hall Effect ignition system

Typical Hall Effect rotor

Performance Tests

Secondary Circuit Tests

For all system testing not covered here, see the "Chrysler Corporation System" section.

The ignition coil can be tested on a conventional coil tester. The ballast resistor, mounted on the firewall, must be included in all tests (through 1980). Primary resistance at 70°F should be 1.60–1.79 ohms for the Chrysler Prestolite coil, and 1.41–1.62 ohms for the Chrysler Essex coil. Secondary resistance should be 9400–11,700.

Remove the coil secondary wire from the distributor cap. Hold end of wire about 1/4 in. from an engine ground. Crank engine and watch for a spark at the coil wire. If no spark is produced, go on to voltage checks. While cranking engine slowly move the coil wire away from the ground and look for arcing at the coil tower. If arcing occurs, replace coil. If a spark is present at coil wire, reconnect coil wire and remove one spark plug wire and hold it 1/4″ from a ground or use tester on page iv, and crank engine. If no spark is present, check the rotor, distributor, or spark plug wires. If a spark is produced, check the fuel and engine mechanical systems to locate the source of the malfunction.

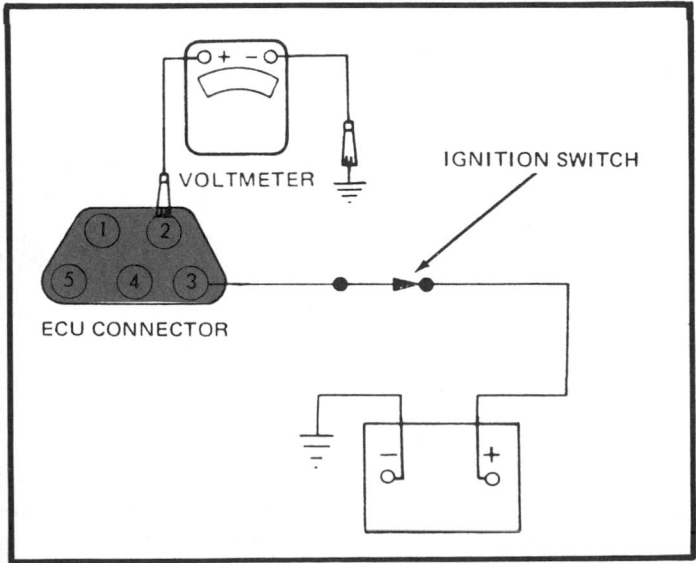

Testing voltage at cavity No. 2

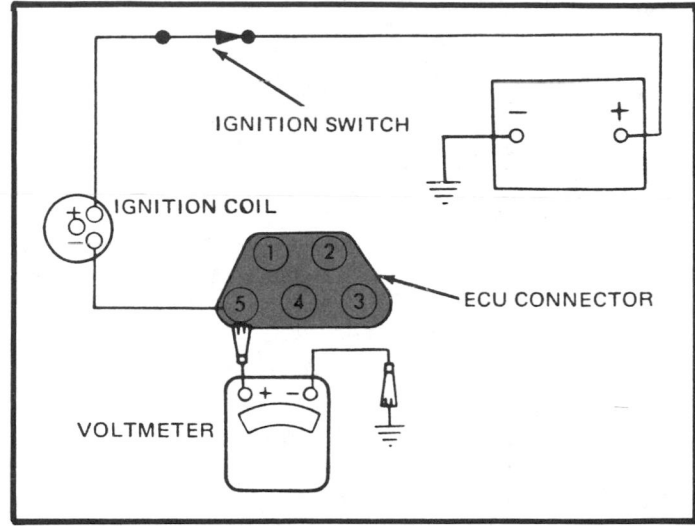

Testing voltage at cavity NO. 5

Cavity 2 Voltage Test

Turn the ignition switch OFF and remove the connector from control unit. With the positive lead of the voltmeter connected to the number 2 terminal of the wiring harness connector and the negative lead connected to ground, check the voltage present with ignition switch ON. The voltage should be more than 11 volts. If the voltage is not correct, check the ignition switch and the wiring from the ignition switch.

Cavity 5 Voltage Test

Connect the positive lead of voltmeter to cavity 5 of the harness connector. The voltage should be over 11 volts. If the voltage is less, check the wire from the connector to the (−) side of coil, coil, and the wire from coil (+) side to the ignition switch.

Hall Effect Pick-up Test

Reconnect the electronic control unit connector and disconnect the distributor 3-pin connector. With the ignition switch ON, momentarily jump between cavity 2 and 3 while holding the coil wire about 1/4 in. from an engine ground. If a spark is produced, replace the Hall Effect distributor plate assembly. If no spark is produced, check the voltage at cavity 1 of the female end of distributor 3-pin connector. If the voltage is less than 11 volts, turn the ignition switch OFF and disconnect the wiring harness from electronic control unit. Use an ohmmeter to check the continuity between number 1 cavity in the electronic control unit harness connector and the

Jumping cavities No. 2 and 3 at the distributor harness connector

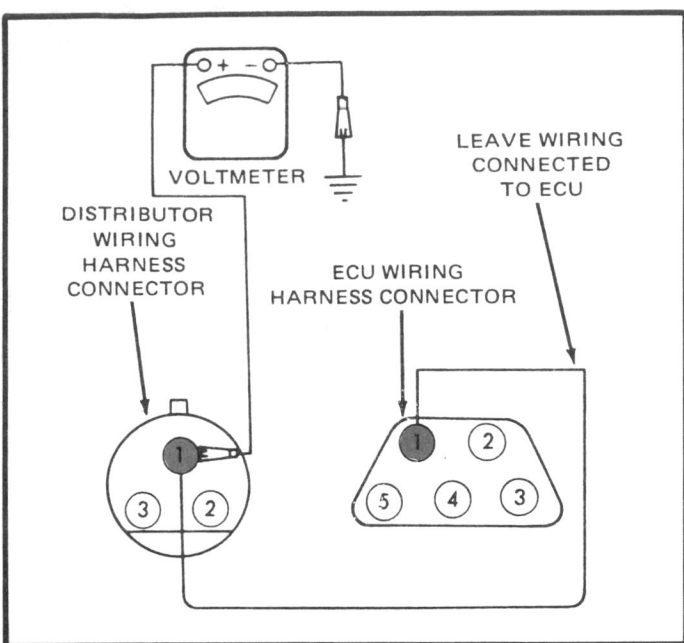

Testing voltage at cavity No. 1 on the distributor connector

Testing continuity at cavity No. 1

continuity is present, remove the electronic control unit and make sure the mounting surfaces are clean. Reinstall the electronic control unit and tighten screws. Recheck for continuity. If continuity still is not present, replace the control unit.

Rotor Ground Test

Whenever the rotor is removed and reinstalled it should be seated so that the rotor shutters are grounded. This can be checked by connecting the ohmmeter lead to the shutter and ground. Continuity should be present. If no continuity is present, push down to properly seat the rotor and recheck. Also, check for excessive plastic material on rotor grounding blade. If excessive plastic is present, replace rotor.

distributor female end cavity 1. If continuity is not present, replace the wiring harness. If continuity is indicated, check the control unit ground.

Electronic Control Unit Ground Test

With the ignition switch OFF, reconnect the wiring harness to electronic control unit. With an ohmmeter, check for continuity between cavity 2 of the distributor harness female connector and ground. If continuity is present, replace the electronic control unit. If no continuity is present, remove the wiring harness connector from the electronic control unit. Check between pin 4 of the control unit and ground with an ohmmeter. If continuity is present, check the connector and wire for an open between the control unit harness connector pin 4 and the distributor connector pin 2. If no

Distributor connector ground test

Carburetor Switch Test

Grounding the carburetor switch controls governor and vacuum advance on some systems, and on most systems with feedback carburetor gives a fixed fuel to air ratio. With key off disconnect 10 way duel connector from Computer. With throttle completely closed, check continuity between pin 7 of disconnected 10-way dual connector and a good ground. If no continuity, check wire and carburetor switch. With throttle opened, check continuity between pin 7 of disconnected 10 way dual connector and a good ground. There should be no continuity. If replacement becomes necessary, replace the bracket and switch as an assembly.

─────CAUTION─────

Do not remove grease from 10 way dual connector or connector cavity in Spark Control Computer. The grease is used in order to prevent moisture from corroding the terminals. If there isn't at least 1/8 inch of grease on bottom of computer connector cavity, apply multi-purpose grease over the entire end of connector plug before reinstalling.

Control unit ground test

Coolant Sensor Test

With key off disconnect wire connector from coolant sensor. Connect one lead of ohmmeter to one terminal of coolant sensor. Connect the other lead of ohmmeter to remaining connector of coolant sensor. The ohmmeter should read 5000–6000 ohms with the engine and sensor both at room temperature (70°F).

Electronic Throttle Control System Test

Incorporated within the spark control computer is the electronic throttle system. A solenoid which regulates a vacuum dashpot is energized when the air conditioner (A/C), heater, or electronic timers are activated. The two timers which are incorporated in the ignition electronics operate when the throttle is closed, plus a time delay (2 seconds) or after an engine start condition.

1. Connect a tachometer to engine.
2. Start engine and run until normal operating temperature is reached.
3. Depress accelerator and let up. A higher than curb idle speed should be seen for a specified time.
4. On vehicles equipped with/and turning on the A/C, a slight decrease in idle speed should be observed. Turning A/C off will produce the normal idle speed.

NOTE: The A/C clutch will cycle on and off as it is running. This should not be mistaken as part of the electronic control.

5. As the A/C compressor clutch cycles on and off, the sole-kicker plunger should extend and retract.
6. If the plunger does not move with clutch cycling or after a start check the kicker system for vacuum leaks.
7. If speed increases do not occur, disconnect the three way connector at the carburetor.
8. Check the solenoid with an ohmmeter by measuring the resistance across the terminal that contained the black wire to ground. The resistance should be between 20—100 ohms. If it is not replace the solenoid.
9. Start the vehicle and before the time delay has timed out, measure the voltage across the vacuum solenoid terminals. The voltmeter should read within 2 volts of charging system voltage, if it does not replace the computer.
10. Turning the A/C on should also produce charging system voltage after the time delay has timed out. If not check the wiring back to the instrument panel for an open circuit.

Spark Control Computer Test

Incorporated in the digital microprocessor electronics are some unique spark advance schedule which will occur during cold engine operation. They have been added to reduce engine emission and improve driveability. Because they will be changing at different engine operating temperatures during warmup, all spark advance testing should be done with the engine fully warmed.

1. Set basic timing. (See "Ignition Timing" procedure).
2. Engine at operating temperature. The temperature sensor must be connected and working properly.
3. Remove and plug vacuum hose at vacuum transducer.
4. Connect an auxiliary vacuum supply to vacuum transducer and set at 16 in. Hg (54 kPa) of vacuum.
5. Raise engine speed to 2000 rpm, wait one minute and check specifications. Advance specifications are in addition to basic advance. If the computer fails to obtain specified settings, replace the computer.

Overhaul Procedures

HALL EFFECT PICKUP

Removal and Installation

1. Loosen the distributor cap retaining screws and remove the cap.
2. Pull straight up on the rotor and remove it from the shaft.

Removing Hall Effect pick-up

3. Disconnect the pickup assembly lead.
4. Remove the pickup lead hold down screw.
5. Remove the pickup assembly lock springs and lift off the pickup.
6. Install the new pickup assembly onto the distributor housing and fasten it into place with the lock springs.
7. Fasten the pickup lead to the housing with the hold down screw.
8. Reconnect the lead to the harness.

Removing Hall Effect rotor

Exploded view of Hall Effect distributor

9. Press the rotor back into place on the shaft. Do not wipe off the silicone grease on the metal portion of the rotor.

10. Replace the distributor cap and tighten the retaining screws.

Ignition Timing Adjustment

---CAUTION---

Do not puncture cables, boots or nipples with test probes. Always use proper adapters. Puncturing the spark plug cables with a probe will damage the cables. The probe can separate the conductor and cause high resistance. In addition breaking the rubber insulation may permit secondary current to arc to ground.

---

1. Connect a suitable timing light according to manufacturer's instructions.

2. Connect red lead of the test tachometer unit to the negative primary terminal of the coil and the black lead to a good ground.

3. Turn selector switch to the appropriate cylinder position.

4. Start engine and run until operating temperature is obtained.

5. With engine at normal operating temperature (off fast idle), momentarily open the throttle and release to make sure there is no bind in the linkage and that idle speed screw is against its stop.

6. On vehicles equipped with a carburetor switch, connect a jumper wire between the carburetor switch and ground. Disconnect and plug the vacuum line at the Spark Control Computer.

7. Read engine rpm on 1000 rpm scale. If the engine rpm is at or below the curb idle specified on the label, proceed to the next step. If it is higher, turn the idle speed screw (on top of solenoid) until the specified curb idle rpm is reached.

8. Aim Power Timing Lamp at timing hole in bell housing or read magnetic timing unit. If flash occurs when timing mark is before specified degree mark, timing is advanced. To adjust, turn distributor housing in direction of rotor rotation.

9. If flash occurs when timing mark is after specified degree mark, timing is retarded. To adjust, turn distributor housing against direction of rotor rotation.

NOTE: If timing is within ±2° of value specified on the emission label, proceed to step 11. If outside specified tolerance proceed to next step.

10. Loosen distributor hold-down arm screw just enough so the distributor housing can be rotated in its mounting. Turn distributor housing until specified label value is reached. Tighten the hold-down arm screw and recheck timing. When timing is acceptable, recheck curb idle rpm. If engine rpm is not at or below the curb idle rpm shown on the label, reset engine rpm and recheck timing. Repeat above until both engine rpm and timing are acceptable.

11. Remove timing lamp. Unplug and reconnect the vacuum host to the SCC unit. Raise the engine speed, then allow the engine to idle again. Check the idle speed with a suitable tachometer.

12. If curb idle speed is not within ± 50 rpm of value shown on label, readjust curb idle rpm. DO NOT reset timing. Turn the engine off. Remove the jumper wire, and tachometer.

DISTRIBUTOR

Removal and Installation

1. Disconnect the distributor pickup lead wire at the wiring harness connector and remove splash shield.

2. Loosen the distributor cap retaining screws and lift off distributor cap.

3. Rotate engine crankshaft until the distributor rotor is pointing toward the cylinder block, scribe a mark on block at this point to indicate position of the rotor as reference when reinstalling distributor.

4. Remove distributor hold down screw and carefully lift the distributor from the engine.

5. Position the distributor in engine. Make certain that the gasket is properly seated on the distributor.

6. Carefully engage distributor drive with distributor drive offset tang drive so that when distributor is installed properly, rotor will be in line with previously scribed line on cylinder block. If engine has been cranked while distributor is removed, it will be necessary to establish proper relationship between the distributor shaft and No. 1 piston position as follows:

a. Rotate the crankshaft until number one piston is at top of compression stroke. Pointer on clutch housing should be in line with the "O" (TDC) mark on flywheel.

b. Rotate rotor to a position just ahead of the number one distributor cap terminal.

c. Lower the distributor into the opening, engaging distributor drive with drive offset drive tang. With distributor fully seated on engine, rotor should be under the cap number 1 tower.

7. Make sure all high tension wires are snapped firmly in the cap towers.

8. Install the distributor cap.

9. Tighten distributor cap retaining screws.

10. Install hold-down arm screw and tighten finger tight.

11. Install splash shield.

12. Connect distributor Hall Effect pickup lead wire at wiring harness connector and set ignition timing.

---CAUTION---

Hall effect pickup assembly leads may be damaged if not properly reinstalled. Make sure lead retainer is in locating hole properly before attaching distributor cap.

CHRYSLER ELECTRONIC IGNITION (EIS) SYSTEM

General Information

COMPONENTS AND OPERATION

2.6L ENGINE ONLY

This system consists of the battery, ignition switch, ignition coil, IC igniter (electronic control unit), built into distributor, spark plugs and intercomponent wiring. Primary current is switched by the IC igniter in response to timing signals produced by a distributor magnetic pickup. The distributor consists of a power distributing section, signal generator, IC igniter, advance mechanism and drive section. The signal generator is a small-size magneto generator which produces signal for driving the IC igniter. The signal is produced in exact synchronism with the rotation of the distributor shaft four times per rotation at equal intervals. The distributor operates by using this signal as an ignition timing signal. The distributor is equipped with both centrifugal and vacuum advance mechanisms.

A centrifugal advance mechanism located below the rotor assembly, has governor weights that move inward or outward with changes in engine speed. As engine speed increases, the weights move outward and cause the reluctor to rotate ahead of the distributor shaft, thus advancing the ignition timing. The vacuum advance has a spring loaded diaphragm connected to the breaker assembly. The diaphragm is actuated against the spring pressure by carburetor vacuum pressure. When the vacuum increases, the diaphragm causes the movable breaker assembly to pivot in a direction opposite to distributor rotation, advancing the ignition timing.

Performance Tests

Secondary Circuit Tests

1. Remove the coil wire from the center of the distributor cap.
2. Using heavy gloves and insulated pliers, hold the end of the wire 3/16–3/8 in. away from a good engine ground and crank the engine.

NOTE: Make sure there are no fuel leaks before performing this test.

3. If there is a spark at the coil wire, it must be bright blue in color and fire consistently. If it is, continue to crank the engine while slowly moving the coil wire away from ground. Look for arcing at the coil tower. If arcing occurs, replace coil. If there is no spark, or spark is weak or not consistent, proceed to the next step.

If a good spark is present, check the condition of the distributor cap, rotor, plug wires and spark plugs. If these check out, the ignition system is working: check the fuel system and engine mechanical systems.

4. With the ignition on, measure the voltage at the negative coil terminal. It should be the same as battery voltage. If it is 3V or less, the IC distributor is defective. If there is no voltage, check for an open circuit in the coil or wiring.

5. With the ignition on, hold the coil wire as instructed in step 2 and, using a jumper wire, momentarily connect the negative coil terminal to ground. There should be a spark at the coil wire.

6. If there is no spark, check for voltage at the positive coil ter-

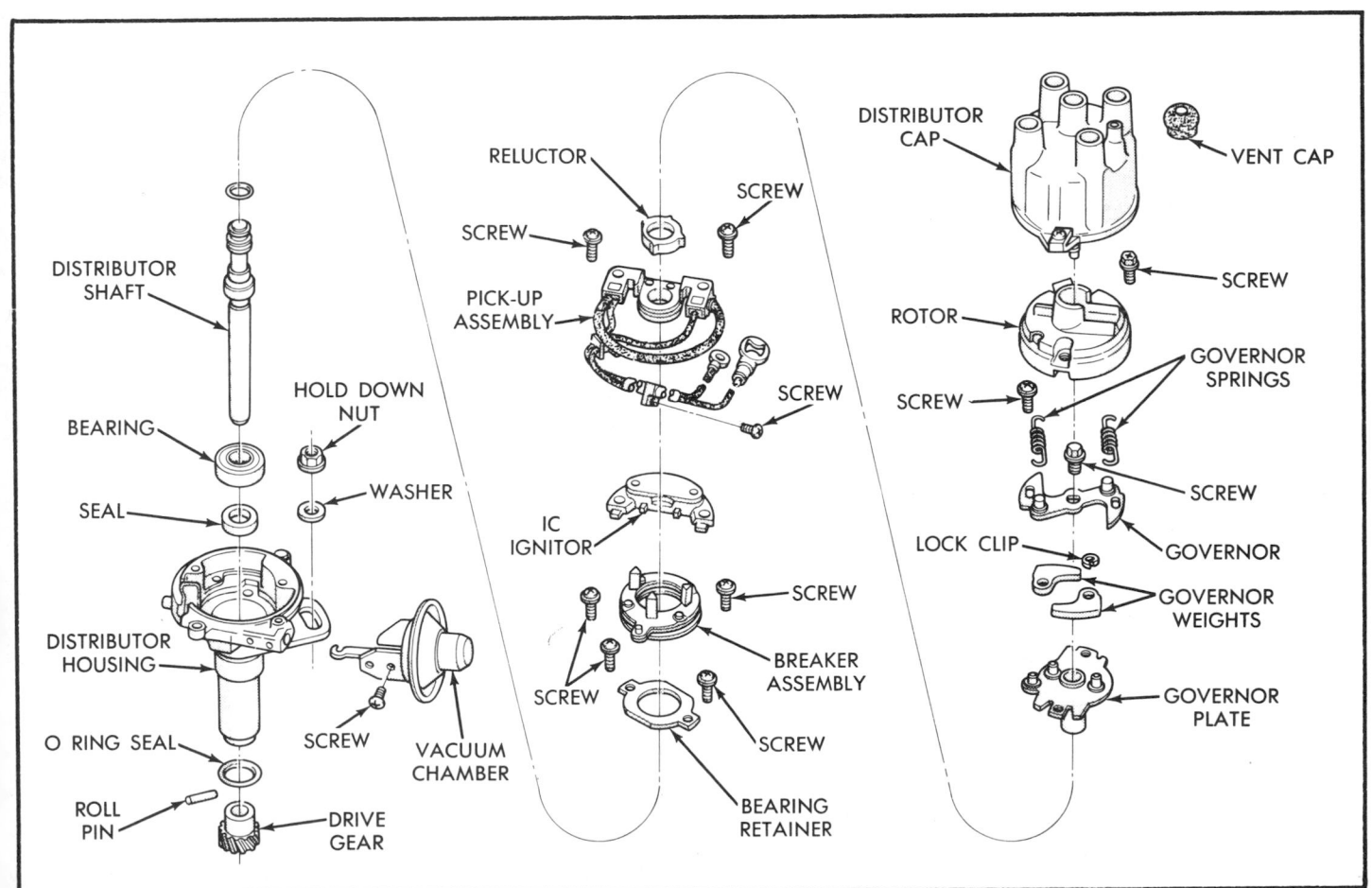

Exploded view of distributor used on 2.6L engines

Testing coil primary resistance—typical

Testing coil secondary resistance—typical

VACUUM CHAMBER

SCREWDRIVER

PICK-UP AND I.C. IGNITER SCREWS

Removing pick-up and IC igniter

minal with the key on. Voltage should be at least 9V. If proper voltage is obtained, the coil is defective and should be replaced. If proper voltage is not obtained, check the wiring and connections.

Centrifugal Advance Test

Run the engine at idle and remove the vacuum hose (non-striped hose) from the vacuum controller. Slowly accelerate the engine to check for advance. Excessive advance indicates a deteriorated governor spring (A broken governor spring will cause abrupt advance.) Insufficient advance is usually caused by a broken governor weight or some malfunction in cam operation.

Vacuum Advance Test

Set engine speed at 2,500 rpm. Check for advance by disconnecting and then reconnecting the vacuum hose at the distributor. For a more precise determination of whether the vacuum advance mechanism is operating properly, remove the vacuum hose from the distributor and connect a hand vacuum pump. Run the engine at idle and slowly apply vacuum pressure to check for advance. Excessive advance; look for a deteriorated (or sagging) vacuum controller spring (A broken spring will cause abrupt advance.) Insufficient advance or no advance may be caused by linkage problems or a ruptured vacuum diaphragm.

Ignition Coil Test

Clean ignition coil. Check coil terminals for cleanliness, and exterior of body for cracks. Replace if necessary. Check for carbon deposit or corrosion in the high tension cable inserting hole. Repair or replace if necessary. Measure the resistance of the primary coil, secondary coil and external resistor. If the reading is not within 1.3–1.8 ohms on the primary coil and 8000–12000 ohms on the secondary coil windings, replace the coil.

Ignition Wire Resistance Test

—————————CAUTION—————————

When removing high tension cable, grasp cable rubber cap. Twist and pull slowly.
  Do not bend the cable. The conductor might break if bent.

Check the cable terminals. A corroded terminal should be cleaned. A broken or distorted cable should be replaced. Check the resistance of each cable between both ends. If it exceeds 22 kilo-ohms, replace the wire. Use silicone lubricant when installing wires on spark plugs.

DISTRIBUTOR

Removal and Installation

1. Disconnect the battery negative cable.
2. Disconnect the wiring harness from the distributor and the wires from the distributor cap.
3. Disconnect the vacuum hose from the vacuum advance unit.
4. Remove the distributor mounting nut and lift the distributor assembly clear from the engine.
5. Remove the distributor cap mounting screws, then remove the distributor cap.
6. Remove the rotor screws and remove the rotor.
7. Remove the governor assembly bolt and remove the governor.

NOTE: Since the bolt is very tight, it is recommended that a box or socket wrench be used to loosen the governor mounting bolt. The two springs on the governor are built to different specifications, so each must be installed in its original position. Mark the springs accordingly if the governor flyweights are being disassembled.

8. Remove the wire clamp screw and remove the clamp.
9. Remove the pickup coil and IC igniter mounting screws.
10. Remove the pickup coil and IC igniter as an assembly.
11. Remove the vacuum advance diaphragm screws and remove the vacuum advance assembly.

Removing breaker assembly

12. Remove the breaker assembly mounting screws and remove the breaker assembly. Do not allow iron filings or other metallic debris to contaminate the breaker assembly while removed.

13. Remove the bearing retainer plate screws and remove the bearing retainer.

14. Scribe alignment marks on the drive gear and distributor shaft for reassembly, then drive out the gear roll pin using a suitable punch and remove the drive gear.

Removing centrifugal governor assembly

15. Remove the distributor shaft and bearing assembly, then remove the housing seal.

16. Reassemble the distributor in the reverse order of disassembly.

DUCELLIER ELECTRONIC IGNITION SYSTEM

General Information

The Ducellier Electronic Ignition System consists of an impulse generator (pick-up coil), electronic control unit (module), coil, and distributor assembly. The system uses a Delco-Remy HEI module and coil which are mounted together in a support that acts like a heat sink to help cool the module in operation. Silicone grease is applied between the module and support to aid heat transfer. The

Support assembly and related components

Schematic of Ducellier electronic ignition system

95

mounting bolts for the support provide the system ground. When the system is energized through the ignition switch, the impulse generator (pick-up coil) transmits a voltage signal every time a trigger plate tooth (reluctor) aligns with the impulse coil. When the control unit (module) receives this signal, it opens the primary circuit, collapsing the magnetic field and inducing a high voltage in the coil secondary windings which is transferred to the distributor cap by the coil wire. The high voltage is distributed to the spark plugs by the rotor and spark plug wires.

The module limits primary current flow, so no ballast resistor is used in the system, and the mechanical and vacuum advance mechanisms are conventional in design and operation. On the Renault 18i, a dual impulse sender is used to advance ignition timing several degrees when the oil temperature is lower than 59 degrees F (15 degrees C). The distributor uses an additional impulse sender which is offset. When the oil temperature is below the predetermined temperature a relay activates the offset impulse sender.

SERVICE PRECAUTIONS

• Do not use a test lamp to check the distributor coil; it cannot withstand current flow.
• Do not disconnect a spark plug wire with the engine running. The high voltage could be grounded through the distributor damaging the distributor.
• When grounding the coil or spark plug wire during a Performance Test do not ground it near the coil or module.
• Turn the ignition OFF when installing or removing test connections or components.

Energize the sensor coil with a magnet as shown

NOTE: Check the oil thermoswitch on Renault LeCar models before replacing any components. If the thermoswitch or its relay fails, the power will be cut off to the ignition system.

Performance Test

Secondary Circuit Test

The ignition system can be checked for proper operation by removing the coil wire from the distributor cap and holding it 1/4 in. from a ground, using insulated pliers. Pick a ground point that is as far away from the coil and control module as possible. Cranking

Wiring schematic of dual impulse senders used on Renault models the engine should produce a spark. On Renault models, the system can also be checked by removing the distributor cap and energizing the sensor coil with a magnet. With the ignition ON, move the magnet in and out above the sensor coil. On dual sensor models, move the magnet above the sensor which is controlling the ignition based on the oil temperature; if the oil temperature is below 59 degrees F, use the secondary pick-up coil. If the oil temperature is above 59 degrees F, use the primary pick-up coil for testing. On Peugeot models, pass the blade of a screwdriver back and forth over the pick-up piece with the ignition ON. A spark should occur every time the screwdriver passes the pole piece. If no spark is produced during the secondary circuit test, it will be necessary to diagnose the primary ignition system malfunction.

If a spark is produced, reinstall the coil wire and remove a spark plug wire from a spark plug. Hold the plug wire 1/4 in. away from a ground and crank the engine. Use insulated pliers or heavy rubber glove to avoid the danger of shock from the high voltages produced during operation. If a spark is produced, check the spark plugs, engine fuel and mechanical systems. If no spark is produced, check the rotor, distributor cap, and the spark plug wire resistance. Check all ignition system connections for loose or broken wires and corrosion on the terminals of the connectors.

Ignition Coil Test

Remove the connectors from the coil terminals and use an ohmmeter to check the primary windings by connecting the test leads to the coil positive (+) and negative (−) terminals. Primary circuit resistance should be 0.48–0.61 ohms. Connect the ohmmeter leads between the coil tower and the positive (+) terminal to measure the secondary circuit resistance. It should be 9–11 kilo-ohms. Check the leads from the control module to the ignition coil for continuity (0 ohms) to make sure there are no open circuits or shorted wires. If any of the test results differ from those described, replace the ignition coil or repair the wiring from the coil to the module.

Module Tests

Remove the pick-up coil leads from the module. Connect a voltmeter between the negative (−) coil terminal and ground. With the ignition ON, watch the voltmeter as a test light is momentarily connected from the battery to module terminal G. If there is no voltage drop, check the module ground and test for an open circuit in the wires from the distributor to the coil. If OK, replace the control module and retest. If the voltage drops, check for spark from the coil with the coil wire held 1/4 in. away from ground as the test light is removed from the module terminal. If a spark is produced, it indicates a sensor (pick-up coil) or sensor connector problem. Check the sensor resistance and make sure it's not grounded. Check the connectors for looseness or corrosion. If no spark is produced, check the ignition coil ground circuit. If it is OK, replace the ignition coil and retest. If a spark is not produced, reinstall the original coil and replace the module.

Sensor test connections

Pick-Up Coil Tests
RENAULT MODELS

Connect an ohmmeter across the terminals of the pick-up coil. It should read 900–1100 ohms. If the ohmmeter indicates infinite resistance, replace the pick-up coil. Connect the ohmmeter to one of the sensor terminals and the other lead to the distributor ground. The resistance should be infinite. If not, replace the sensor. Remove the vacuum line from the vacuum advance unit and attach a hand vacuum pump to the vacuum port. Reconnect the ohmmeter across the terminals of the pick-up coil and slowly apply 20 inches of vacuum to the advance diaphragm with the hand pump while watching the ohmmeter reading. If the normal resistance of 900–1000 ohms changes by more than 50 ohms in either direction while applying vacuum to the advance unit, replace the pick-up coil.

Air Gap Adjustment

Any time the sensor coil is replaced the air gap must be set. The gap should be set to 0.12–0.024 in. (0.3–0.6mm). Use a non-magnetic feeler gauge to check the clearance between the reluctor and pick-up coil. If the clearance is not within specifications, loosen the pick-up coil mounting screws and adjust until the proper clearance is obtained. Tighten the mounting screws and recheck the clearance.

NOTE: **The air gap is not adjustable on Peugeot models. The reluctor is a stationary piece and the only serviceable part in the distributor is the pick-up coil.**

Measuring air gap—typical

Loosen sensor screws to adjust the air gap

DUCELLIER COMPUTERIZED ELECTRONIC IGNITION

General Information

The Ducellier computerized electronic ignition system consists of a distributor, ignition coil, ignition control module, flywheel position sensor, knock sensor (turbo models), manifold absolute pressure (MAP) sensor and related wiring. Some models also use an altitude jumper wire to alter timing according to local elevation for operation in high altitude areas. A vacuum capsule is attached to the computer unit to provide for vacuum advance. Vehicles equipped with throttle body injection have a calibrated orifice in the vacuum line leading to the capsule. A very fine wire connects the vacuum capsule to the computer and this wire will break if

removal is attempted. The flywheel has 44 evenly spaced teeth, but four of these are machined off at the factory every 180 degrees to provide a precise reference point 90 degrees before top dead center (TDC) and bottom dead center (BDC). The TDC sensor detects TDC, BDC and engine speed. It is non-adjustable and secured by special shouldered bolts to the flywheel/drive housing.

Engine speed and crankshaft position are determined by the TDC sensor which sends a signal to the ignition control module (ICM). The ICM uses the information to set the ignition advance ratio, then opens and closes the primary circuit of the ignition coil. The collapsing magnetic field induces a high voltage in the coil secondary windings, which is transferred through the coil tower to

A-A Altitude advance
A-B Not used
A-C Ambient advance
A-D Battery voltage
A-E Ground
A-F Tachometer voltage
7. Ignition coil (+)
8. Ignition coil (−)
9. Coil (+) connector
10. Coil (−) connector

11. High voltage terminal
B-A Sensor
B-B Sensor
B-C Wire shield ground
M Distributor cap
N Ignition coil
C Vacuum capsule
E Ignition control module
P TDC sensor
V Flywheel

Components of Ducellier computer controlled ignition system

the distributor cap where it is distributed to the spark plugs by the rotor and secondary ignition wires. A vacuum sensor provides the computer with information on engine load conditions and a detonation sensor detects engine knock on turbo models. If equipped, the detonation sensor allows the computer to retard spark timing 6 degrees to control detonation.

SERVICE PRECAUTIONS

• Turn the ignition switch OFF when removing or installing any test leads or components.
• Do not attempt to remove the vacuum capsule from the ICM.
• Do not short circuit the high voltage current of the ICM body.
• Do not ground the ignition coil low or high voltage current.
• Do not ground high voltage secondary wires (coil or plug wires) to the ICM body during testing.

Performance Tests

Secondary Circuit Test

The ignition system can be checked for proper operation by removing the coil wire from the distributor cap and holding it 1/4 in. from a ground, using insulated pliers. Pick a ground point that is as far away from the coil and control module as possible. Cranking the engine should produce a spark. If no spark is produced during the secondary circuit test, it will be necessary to diagnose the primary ignition system malfunction.

If a spark is produced, reinstall the coil wire and remove a spark plug wire from a spark plug. Hold the plug wire 1/4 in. away from a ground and crank the engine. Use insulated pliers or heavy rubber glove to avoid the danger of shock from the high voltages produced during operation. If a spark is produced, check the spark plugs, engine fuel and mechanical systems. If no spark is produced, check the rotor, distributor cap, and the spark plug wire resistance.

Check all ignition system connections for loose or broken wires and corrosion on the terminals of the connectors.

---CAUTION---

DO NOT ground the coil or spark plug wires to the ICM body or serious damage will result.

Vacuum Sensor Test

Connect a suitable timing light and tachometer to the engine. Start the engine and allow it to reach normal operating temperature. Check the initial timing against the specifications listed on the underhood sticker and make sure it is correct. Disconnect the vacuum hose to the vacuum sensor on the computer and install a hand vacuum pump. Apply vacuum slowly and make sure the engine speed increases and the timing advances. Reconnect the vacuum hose and increase the engine speed to 3000 rpm. While holding the engine speed steady, pull off the vacuum hose to the sensor and make sure the engine speed drops. If the test results are as described, the vacuum sensor is operating properly. If no problem is found in the vacuum lines and the engine speed fails to drop or the timing fails to advance, replace the computer module and vacuum sensor as an assembly.

NOTE: Any attempt to remove the vacuum sensor will ruin it by breaking the thin connecting wire to the computer

Coil Voltage Test

Connect a voltmeter to the coil positive (+) terminal and ground with the coil connectors in place. Turn the ignition switch ON and make sure at least 9.5 volts are present. If less than 9.5 volts are noted, turn the ignition switch OFF and disconnect the 6 pin connector from the ICM. Connect a voltmeter to pin 1 (+) of the harness connector and ground and crank the engine while noting the reading. It should again show 9.5 volts. If not, check the battery voltage and the lead wires from the module to the ignition switch for loose or corroded connections and breaks or shorts to ground.

Diagnostic connector terminal identification and mounting location

NO IGNITION

Visually check:
- Spark plugs
- High voltage wires
- Distributor cap
- Ignition coil high voltage wire

Condition of connector contacts (A) and (B): Remove and insert them several times.

Clean the terminals if necessary. Do this before replacing any component.

PRELIMINARY TEST

Test to determine if the voltage is more than 9.5V between Terminal 7 (ignition coil +) and ground (ignition switch on).

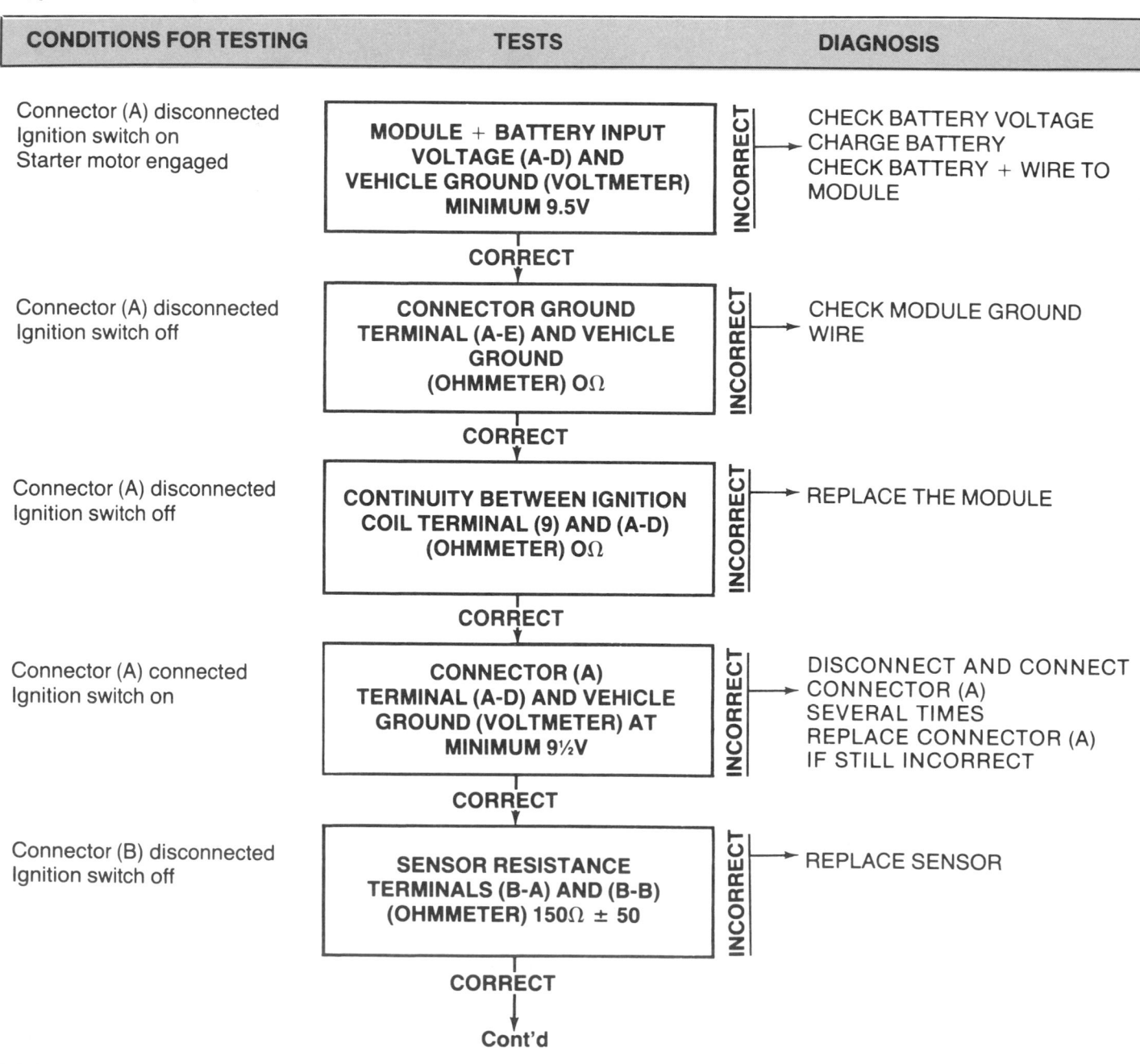

CONDITIONS FOR TESTING	TESTS		DIAGNOSIS
Connector (A) disconnected Ignition switch on Starter motor engaged	**MODULE + BATTERY INPUT VOLTAGE (A-D) AND VEHICLE GROUND (VOLTMETER) MINIMUM 9.5V**	INCORRECT	CHECK BATTERY VOLTAGE CHARGE BATTERY CHECK BATTERY + WIRE TO MODULE
	CORRECT		
Connector (A) disconnected Ignition switch off	**CONNECTOR GROUND TERMINAL (A-E) AND VEHICLE GROUND (OHMMETER) OΩ**	INCORRECT	CHECK MODULE GROUND WIRE
	CORRECT		
Connector (A) disconnected Ignition switch off	**CONTINUITY BETWEEN IGNITION COIL TERMINAL (9) AND (A-D) (OHMMETER) OΩ**	INCORRECT	REPLACE THE MODULE
	CORRECT		
Connector (A) connected Ignition switch on	**CONNECTOR (A) TERMINAL (A-D) AND VEHICLE GROUND (VOLTMETER) AT MINIMUM 9½V**	INCORRECT	DISCONNECT AND CONNECT CONNECTOR (A) SEVERAL TIMES REPLACE CONNECTOR (A) IF STILL INCORRECT
	CORRECT		
Connector (B) disconnected Ignition switch off	**SENSOR RESISTANCE TERMINALS (B-A) AND (B-B) (OHMMETER) 150Ω ± 50**	INCORRECT	REPLACE SENSOR
	CORRECT		
	Cont'd		

CONDITIONS FOR TESTING	TESTS	DIAGNOSIS

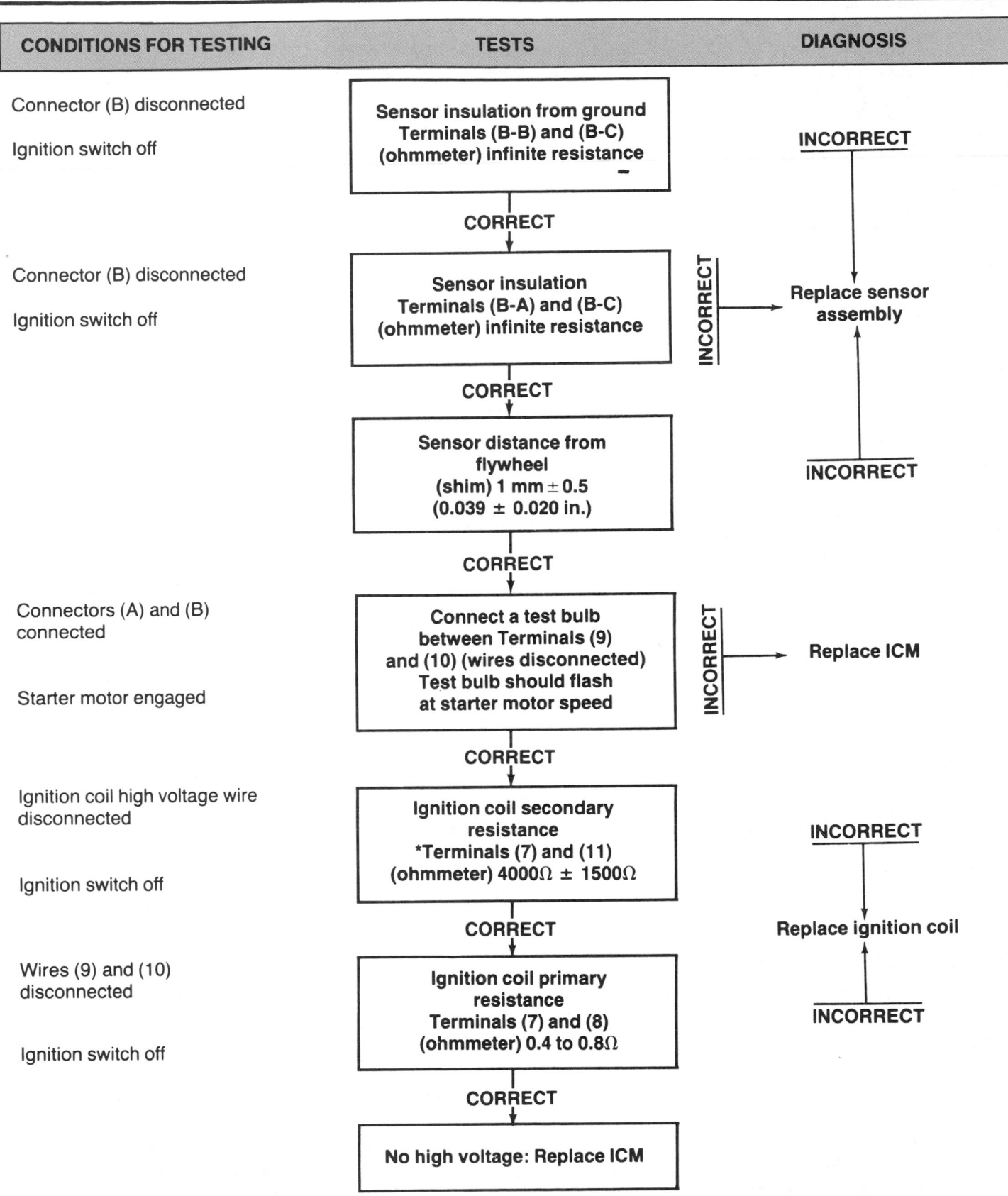

Connector (B) disconnected

Ignition switch off

→ **Sensor insulation from ground Terminals (B-B) and (B-C) (ohmmeter) infinite resistance** —

CORRECT ↓

Connector (B) disconnected

Ignition switch off

→ **Sensor insulation Terminals (B-A) and (B-C) (ohmmeter) infinite resistance** → INCORRECT → **Replace sensor assembly**

CORRECT ↓

→ **Sensor distance from flywheel (shim) 1 mm ± 0.5 (0.039 ± 0.020 in.)**

INCORRECT (up to Replace sensor assembly)

CORRECT ↓

Connectors (A) and (B) connected

Starter motor engaged

→ **Connect a test bulb between Terminals (9) and (10) (wires disconnected) Test bulb should flash at starter motor speed** → INCORRECT → **Replace ICM**

CORRECT ↓

Ignition coil high voltage wire disconnected

Ignition switch off

→ **Ignition coil secondary resistance *Terminals (7) and (11) (ohmmeter) 4000Ω ± 1500Ω** → INCORRECT → **Replace ignition coil**

CORRECT ↓

Wires (9) and (10) disconnected

Ignition switch off

→ **Ignition coil primary resistance Terminals (7) and (8) (ohmmeter) 0.4 to 0.8Ω** → INCORRECT (up to Replace ignition coil)

CORRECT ↓

No high voltage: Replace ICM

INCORRECT (top, Replace sensor assembly)

INCORRECT (Replace sensor assembly)

---

* High voltage wire disconnected from secondary terminal (11) on ignition coil.
If the resistance measured is infinite, ensure that the ohmmeter probe has good contact with the terminal.

CAUTION:
Do not switch wires (9) and (10) when connecting the ignition coil.

Red wire (9) connected to + (terminal 7)
Black wire (10) connected to - (terminal 8)

DIFFICULT STARTING BUT ENGINE OPERATES NORMAL AFTER ENGINE STARTS

Inspect visually or use tester:
- Spark plugs
- High voltage wires
- Distributor cap
- Ignition coil high voltage wire

Check high voltage with the starter motor engaged:
- Disconnect high voltage wire at distirbutor cap
- Hold the high voltage wire 2 cm (0.7 in.) from the cylinder block

CAUTION: DO NOT SHORT CIRCUIT THE HIGH VOLTAGE TO THE ICM BODY

Engage starter motor

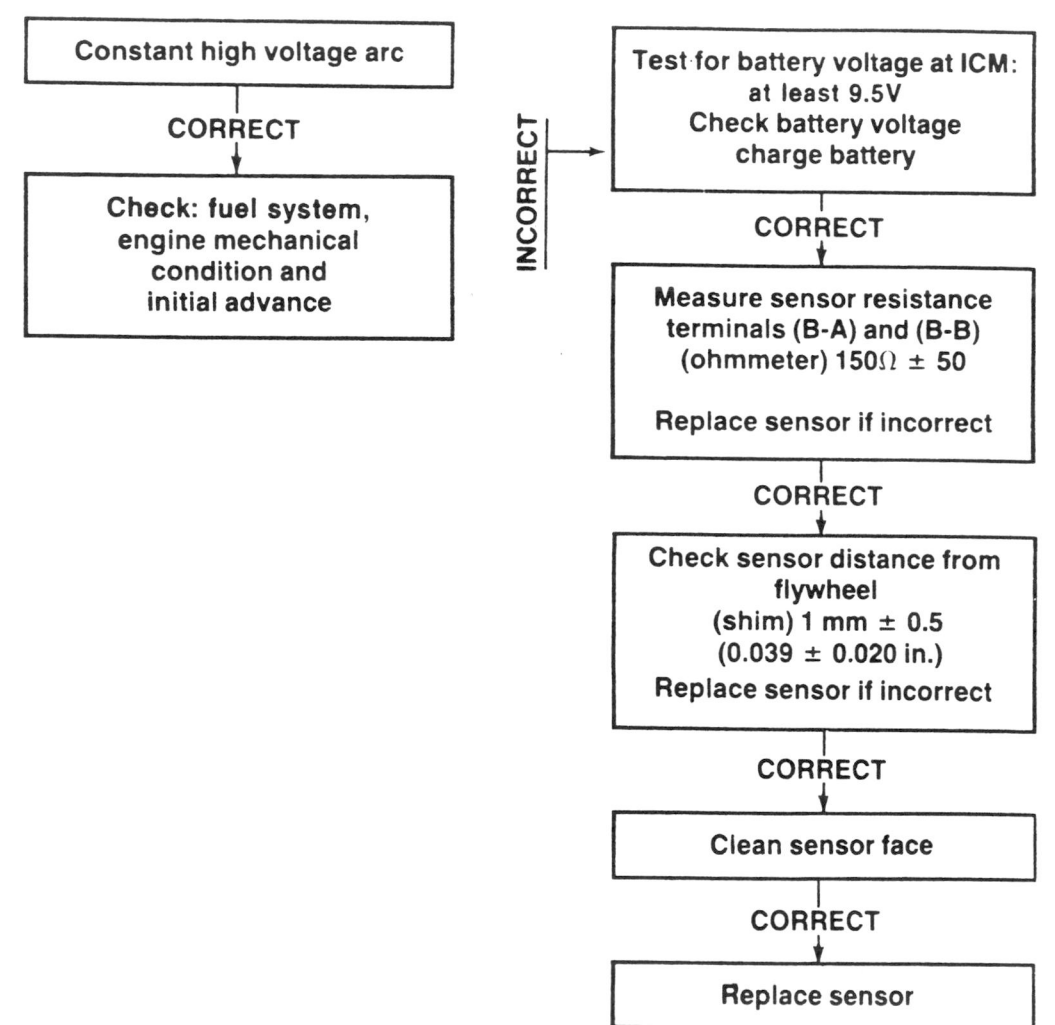

Constant high voltage arc
↓ CORRECT
Check: fuel system, engine mechanical condition and initial advance

← INCORRECT

Test for battery voltage at ICM: at least 9.5V
Check battery voltage charge battery
↓ CORRECT
Measure sensor resistance terminals (B-A) and (B-B) (ohmmeter) 150Ω ± 50

Replace sensor if incorrect
↓ CORRECT
Check sensor distance from flywheel
(shim) 1 mm ± 0.5
(0.039 ± 0.020 in.)
Replace sensor if incorrect
↓ CORRECT
Clean sensor face
↓ CORRECT
Replace sensor

CHECK MECHANICAL CONDITION OF VACUUM CAPSULE

Operate engine at a constant 3000 rpm
Disconnect vacuum hose from capsule.

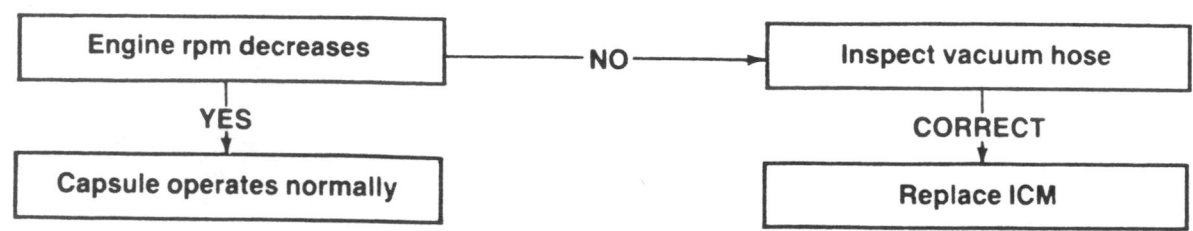

Engine rpm decreases — NO → Inspect vacuum hose
↓ YES   ↓ CORRECT
Capsule operates normally   Replace ICM

FORD SOLID STATE IGNITION SYSTEMS

General Information

Basically, four electronic ignition systems have been used in Ford Motor Company vehicles from 1977–84:

1. Dura Spark I
2. Dura Spark II
3. Dura Spark III
4. TFI (Thick Film Integrated)

In 1977, the Dura Spark systems, were introduced. Dura Spark I and Dura Spark II systems are nearly identical in operation, and virtually identical in appearance. The Dura Spark I uses a special control module which senses current flow through the ignition coil and adjust the dwell, or coil "on" time for maximum spark intensity. If the Dura Spark I module senses that the ignition is ON, but the distributor shaft is not turning, the current to the coil is turned OFF by the module. The Dura Spark II system does not have this feature—the coil is energized for the full amount of time that the ignition switch is ON. Keep this in mind when servicing the Dura Spark II system, as the ignition system could inadvertently "fire" while performing ignition system services (such as distributor cap removal) while the ignition is ON. All Dura Spark II systems (except the Escort, Lynx, EXP, and LN7) are easily identified by having a two-piece, flat topped distributor cap. Escort, Lynx, EXP, and LN7 models use a conventional, one-piece distributor cap.

In 1980, the new Dura Spark III system was introduced. This version is based on the previous sytems, but the input signal is controlled by the EEC system, rather than as a function of engine timing and distributor armature position. The distributor, rotor, cap, and control module are unique to this system: the spark plugs

Electronic module schematic-Dura Spark I system

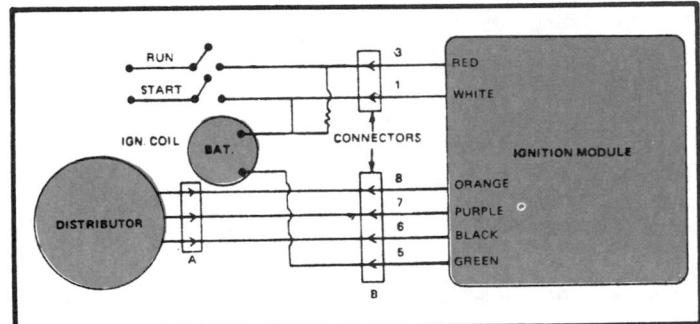

Electronic module schematic-Dura Spark II

Components of 1978-79 Dura Spark I system—V8 shown

Components of typical Dura Spark II ignition system—4 cylinder shown

1978 dual mode Dura Spark II system

Components of Dura Spark III ignition system

and plug wires are the same as those used with the Dura Spark II system. Although the Dura Spark II and III control modules are similar in appearance, they cannot be interchanged between systems.

The TFI (Thick Film Integrated) ignition system is used on 1982–84 Escort, Lynx, EXP, and LN7 models with automatic transaxles.

Previous models, and those with manual transaxles, use the Dura Spark II system. The main difference between Dura Spark II and TFI is not in operation, but in component usage. The TFI system uses a new distributor base-mounted, TFI ignition module, which is contained in a moulded thermo-plastic. Also, this system uses an E-Core ignition coil in lieu of the Dura Spark coil.

Components of Thick Film Integrated (TFI) ignition system

Typical Dura Spark ignition control modules

SPECIAL CONTROL MODULES

The 1978–79 Versailles with the modified Dura Spark II system, uses a special control module designed to function with the vehicles EEC system.

Some 1978 and later engines use a special Dura Spark Dual Mode ignition control module. The module is equipped with an altitude sensor, an economy modulator, or pressure switches (turbocharged engines only). This module, when combined with the additional switches and sensor, varies the base engine timing according to altitude and engine load conditions. Dura Spark Dual Mode ignition control modules have three wiring harness from the module.

1980–81 49-state and 1982 Canadian 2.3 liter engines with automatic transmissions have a Dual Mode Crank Retard ignition module, which has the same function as the Dura Spark II module plus an ignition timing retard function which is operational during engine cranking. The spark timing retard feature eases engine starting, but allows normal timing advance as soon as the engine is running. This module can be identified by the presence of a white connector shell on the four-pin connector at the module.

Some 1981 and later Dura Spark II systems used with some 255 and 302 cu. in. engines are equipped with a Universal Ignition Module (UIM) which includes a run-retard function. The operation of the module is basically the same as the Dura Spark Dual Mode module.

1980 and later cranking retard module, identified by white connector shell

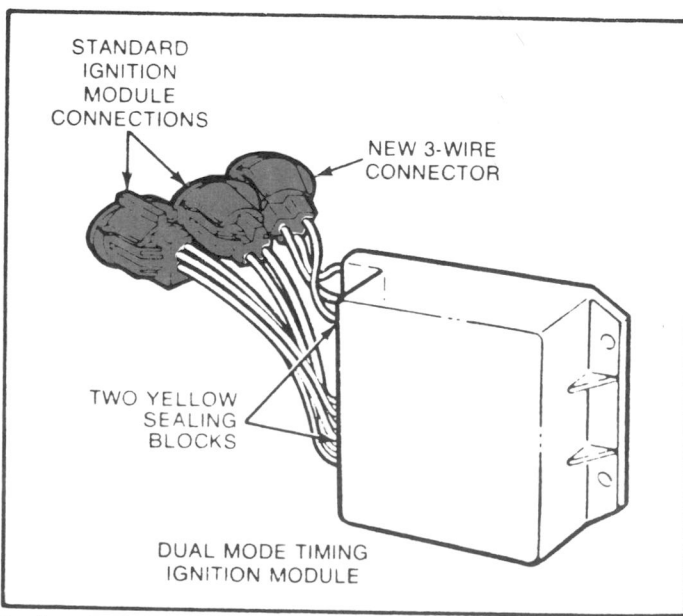

Dual mode electronic module

Refer to the accompanying chart for Ford Motor Company ignition system applications.

NOTE: When replacing the ignition control module, always use the old module as a reference to identify the wiring, connectors, and type of the new module.

FORD ELECTRONIC IGNITION APPLICATION CHART

Dura Spark I 1978–79	All California 302 cu. in. engines, except the Versailles
Dura Spark II 1978–79	All Versailles, and all engines except the California 302 cu. in. engine
1980–81	All models without EEC
1982–85	All models except: Lincoln and Mark VI and VII with the 302 cu. in engine Police models with the 351 cu. in. Escort, Lynx, EXP, and LN7 with automatic transaxles
Dura Spark III 1980–81 1982–85	All models with EEC Lincoln and Mark VI and VII with 302 cu. in. engine Police models with 351 cu. in. engine
TFI 1982–85	Escort, Lynx, EXP, and LN7 with automatic transaxles.

COMPONENTS

All solid state magnetic inductance ignition systems operate on the same basic principle. A magnetic field is provided by a permanent magnet which is part of the pick-up assembly. As an armature tooth approaches the pole piece, it reduces the reluctance of the magnetic circuit, thus increasing the field strength. The resultant alternating voltage is applied to the ignition module at a rate proportional to the engine speed. The signal-generating systems vary in detail but generally follow the pattern of a gear-shaped iron rotor or armature, driven by the distributor shaft, which rotates past the stationary pole piece.

Distributor Mounted Pick-Up

Spark advance is controlled by a centrifugal advance mechanism which varies armature position and by a vacuum advance diaphragm which varies the pick-up coil position exactly as in prior conventional distributors where the cam and breaker points were repositioned respectively.

Crankshaft Sensor

The sensor operates like the breakerless distributor pick-up coil and reluctor which make and break the ignition primary circuit. The tip contains a permanent magnet and wire coil. The current from the computer passes through the coil producing a magnetic field. The output wire carries voltage to the module. As the crankshaft rotates, the individual pulse ring lobes approach and finally align with the sensor tip. The metal lobe "cuts" the magnetic field. This interruption generates a voltage output signal of crankshaft position to the computer. This chapter describes the basic solid state ignition systems and the changes in the system.

Ignition Module

The ignition module is simply an electronic switching circuit which turns the primary circuit off and on in response to voltage pulses received from the magnetic pulse-signal generator. The ignition module shuts off the primary circuit each time it receives a pulse from the magnetic pick-up. Timing circuitry in the module leaves this circuit OFF just long enough for the coil to discharge into the secondary circuit, and then turns the primary ON again. (The time intervals for this switching are on the order of milliseconds.) Maximum time is allowed for the coil to charge. Internal resistance of coil windings prevents excessive current flow and overheating.

NOTE: Different ignition modules are used on different vehicle models. Many do not interchange.

CHANGES AND MODIFICATIONS

1978 Solid State Ignition System

For 1978, a number of innovations were introduced. Vehicles were built with the basic solid state ignition system which was essentially a (Duraspark II) system for cars and trucks (except super-duty engines). Dual-mode ignition modules and sensors were installed on some models. High-output (Duraspark I) systems were limited to 5.0L (302 CID) V-8 engines in cars built for California usage, except on Versailles. An electronic engine control system (EEC I) was incorporated on 5.0L (302 CID) V-8 engines installed in Versailles cars. This system controls a number of engine functions besides ignition.

1979 Solid State Ignition System

For 1979, EEC I is continued on the 5.0L (302 CID) V-8 engines in Versailles except in California. Also, an expanded version, EEC II, is installed on Fords with the 5.8L (351 W CID) V-8 engines built for use in California only and on Mercurys with the 5.8L (351 W CID) V-8 engines built for all 50 states. The high-output (Duraspark I) ignition system is used only on the 5.0L (302 CID) V-8 engines in cars built for California usage. Non-turbocharged 2.3L engines with automatic transmission have a "cranking retard" circuit built into the ignition module. The retard feature is actuated only during engine crank by the slow rpm signal of the distributor magnetic pick-up. This signal actuates a circuit in the ignition module to retard ignition timing up to 18 degrees.

The ignition control module with cranking retard can be identified by the white sealing block and white 4-pin connector. The module is not functionally interchangeable with other ignition control modules.

NOTE: Starting with some 1979 cars, emission control units are controlled by a computer. See "Engine Controls" for information on system testing

The Systems are called EEC I, EEC II and EEC III. All EEC units use an electrical control (advance) distributor. EEC I uses a crankshaft positioned (pick-up) attached to the rear of the crankshaft. On EEC II and III, the pick-up unit is mounted on the front of the engine.

NOTE: Refer to the "Engine Control" Section for service information on the EEC series.

1980 and Later Solid State Ignition System

1980–83 49 State 2.3 liter four cylinder engines with automatic transmission have a Dual Mode Crank Retard ignition module, which has the same function as a Dura Spark II module plus an ignition timing retard function which is operational during engine cranking: the spark timing retard enhances engine starting, but allows normal timing advance once the engine is running. The module can be identified by the presence of a white connector shell on the four pin connector at the module. Some 1981 and later models equipped with either the 255 or 302 cu in. engines are equipped with a Universal Ignition Module (UIM) which includes a run-retard function. This module basically performs the same functions as the Dual Mode Timing module. These include altitude and economy timing calibrations and engine knock control.

It is important to note that the amplifier module and coil on the Dura Spark II system are on when the ignition switch is on, and will generate a spark when the key is turned off. Certain service actions, such as removing the distributor cap with the ignition switch on, could cause the system to fire, inadvertently causing the engine to rotate. The Dura Spark I system automatically shuts down when it senses no distributor rotation.

OPERATION

NOTE: For a description of the EEC systems, refer to "Ford Electronic Engine Control systems" section.

With the ignition switch ON, the primary circuit is on and the ignition coil is energized. When the armature spokes approach the magnetic pickup coil assembly, they induce a voltage which tells the amplifier to turn the coil primary current off. A timing circuit in the amplifier module will turn the current on again after the coil field has collapsed. When the current is on, it flows from the battery through the ignition switch, the primary windings of the ignition coil, and through the amplifier module circuits to ground. When the current is off, the magnetic field built up in the ignition coil is allowed to collapse, inducing a high voltage into the second-

Special test jumper schematic

Removing primary wiring connector from coil

ary windings of the coil. High voltage is produced each time the field is thus built up and collapsed. When Dura Spark is used in conjunction with EEC, the EEC computer tells the Dura Spark module when to turn the coil primary current off or on. In this case, the armature position is only a reference signal of engine timing, used by the EEC computer in combination with other reference signals to determine optimum ignition spark timing.

The high voltage flows through the coil high tension lead to the distributor cap where the rotor distributes it to one of the spark plug terminals in the distributor cap. This process is repeated for every power stroke of the engine. Ignition system troubles are caused by a failure in the primary and/or the secondary circuit; incorrect ignition timing; or incorrect distributor advance. Circuit failures may be caused by shorts, corroded or dirty terminals, loose connections, defective wire insulation, cracked distributor cap or rotor, defective pick-up coil assembly or amplifier module, defective distributor points or fouled spark plugs. If an engine starting or operating trouble is attributed to the ignition system, start the engine and verify the complaint. On engines that will not start, be sure that there is gasoline in the fuel tank and that fuel is reaching the carburetor or fuel injectors. Then locate the ignition system problem using the following procedures.

Performance Tests

BASIC SYSTEM INSPECTION

Many times a quick check can locate the cause of a problem without going into full system checkout. Included are checks which may isolate the cause of the problem. Just as with a conventional breaker point ignition system, the first step is to verify that the problem exists and then to make some preliminary checks to find out whether the problem is in the ignition system or somewhere else. The following procedures are intended to provide quick checks to identify and locate some of the more frequently encountered problems.

There is also the possibility that there is an intermittent problem in the module or the magnetic pick-up. Some intermittent problem checks are included at the end of these quick checks.

1. Check battery for state of charge and for clean, tight battery terminal connections.

2. Inspect all wires and connectors for breaks, cuts, abrasions or burned spots. Repair or replace as necessary. Make sure all wires are connected correctly.

3. Unplug all connectors and inspect for corroded/burned contacts. Repair as necessary and plug connectors back together. Do not remove the lubricant compound in connectors.

4. Check for loose or damaged spark plug or coil wires. If boots or nipples are removed on 8 mm ignition wires, reline inside of each with new silicone di-electric compound.

5. Make a test jumper as shown in illustration. It is important to use only this test jumper when making these checks. Solid wire jumpers will not work for quick checks.

The following Dura Spark II troubleshooting procedures may be used on Dura Spark I systems with a few variations. The Dura Spark I module has internal connections which shut off the primary circuit in the run mode when the engine stalls. To perform the above troubleshooting procedures, it is necessary to by-pass these connections. However, with these connections by-passed, the current flow in the primary becomes so great that it will damage both the ignition coil and module unless a ballast resistor is installed in series with the primary circuit at the BAT terminal of the ignition coil. Such a resistor is available from Ford (Motorcraft part number DY-36). A 1.3 ohm, 100 watt wire-wound power resistor can also be used.

To install the resistor, proceed as follows:

NOTE: The resistor will become very hot during testing.

1. Release the BAT terminal lead from the coil by inserting a paper clip through the hole in the rear of the horseshoe coil connec-

Test connections for Dura Spark I system

tor and manipulating it against the locking tab in the connector until the lead comes free.

2. Insert a paper clip in the BAT terminal of the connector on the coil. Using jumper leads, connect the ballast resistor as shown.

3. Using a straight pin, pierce both the red and white leads of the module to short these two together. This will by-pass the internal connections of the module which turn off the ignition circuit when the engine is not running.

— CAUTION —

Pierce the wires only AFTER the ballast resistor is in place or you could damage the ignition coil and module.

4. With the ballast resistor and by-pass in place, proceed with the Dura Spark II troubleshooting procedures.

To perform the following tests, two special tools are needed; the ignition test jumper shown in the illustration and a modified spark plug. Use the illustration to assemble the ignition test jumper. The test jumper must be used when performing the following tests. The modified spark plug is basically a spark plug with the side electrode removed. Ford makes a special tool called a Spark Tester for this purpose, which besides not having a side electrode is equipped with a spring clip so that it can be grounded to engine metal. It is recommended that the Spark Tester be used as there is less chance of being shocked.

— CAUTION —

Dangerously high voltages are produced in ANY electronic ignition system. Always use insulated pliers and wear a heavy rubber glove when testing secondary system.

RUN MODE SPARK TEST

Step One

1. Remove distributor cap and rotor from distributor.

2. Crank engine to align one tooth of armature with magnet in pick-up coil (ignition OFF).

3. Remove coil wire from distributor cap, install a modified spark plug (side electrode removed) in the coil wire terminal and, using insulated pliers, hold the spark plug shell against the engine block.

4. Turn the ignition switch to RUN and tap the distributor body with a screwdriver handle. There should be a spark at the spark plug or coil wire terminal.

5. If there is a spark, the primary circuit is okay in the run mode. Check for a problem in the secondary circuit and/or perform the start mode spark test. If there is no spark, perform Step Two.

Step Two

1. Unplug the module connector(s) which contain(s) the green and black module leads.

2. To the harness side of the connector(s), connect the special test jumper between the leads which connects to the green and black leads of the module pigtails. Use paper clips in connector socket holes to make contact.

3. With the ignition switch turned to RUN, close the test jumper switch. Leave it closed for approximately one second, then open. Repeat this several times. There should be a spark each time this switch is opened. On Duraspark I systems, close the test switch for 10 seconds on the first cycle. After that, one second is adequate.

4. If there is no spark, the problem is most probably in the primary circuit through the ignition switch, coil, green lead, black lead or ground connection in the distributor. Perform Step Three.

5. If there is a spark, the primary circuit wiring and coil are probably okay. The problem is most probably in the distributor pick-up, the module bias power feed (red wire) or the module. Perform Step Six.

Step Three

1. Disconnect the test jumper lead from the black lead and con-

nect to a good ground on the engine. Turn the test jumper switch ON and OFF several times as in step 2.

2. If there is no spark, the problem is most probably in the green lead, the coil or the coil feed circuit, Perform Step Five.

3. If there is a spark, the problem is most probably in the black lead or the ground connection in the distributor. Perform Step Four.

Step Four

1. Connect an ohmmeter between the black lead and good ground on the engine. With the meter on its lowest scale, there should be no measurable resistance in the circuit.

2. If there is resistance, check the ground connection in the distributor and the black lead form the module. Repair or replace as necessary. Remove the meter, plug in all the connectors and repeat Step One.

3. If there is no resistance, the primary ground wiring is okay. Perform Step Six.

Step Five

1. Disconnect the test jumper from the green lead and the ground and connect it between the tach-test terminal of the coil and a good ground on the engine.

2. With the ignition switch turned to RUN, turn the jumper switch on. Hold it on for approximately one second and turn it off as in Step Two. Repeat this several times. There should be a spark each time the switch is turned off.

3. If there is no spark, the problem is most probably in the coil or in the primary circuit through the ignition switch to the coil battery terminal.

4. Check the coil for internal shorts or opens and for primary resistance (Duraspark I—.7 ohm, Duraspark II—1.17 ohm) and secondary resistance (Duraspark I—7.3–8.2 k ohms, Duraspark II—7.7–9.3 k ohms). Replace the coil if necessary.

5. Check the coil power circuit for opens, shorts or high resistance. Repair as necessary. Remove test jumper, plug in connectors and recheck Step One.

6. If there is a spark, the coil and its feed circuit are most probably okay. The problem may be in the green lead between the coil and the module. Check for open or short and repair as necessary. Remove the test jumper. Plug in all connectors and repeat Step One.

Step Six

1. Connect a voltmeter between the orange and purple leads on the harness side of the module connectors.

———————CAUTION———————

If the vehicle has a catalytic converter, disconnect the air supply line between the by-pass valve and the manifold before turning the engine with the ignition off. This will prevent damage to the catalytic converter. After testing, run the engine for at least 3 minutes before reconnecting the air supply line to clear excess fuel from the exhaust system.

NOTE: Do not use a voltmeter which is combined with a dwellmeter. Slight needle oscillations (1/2 volt) may not be detectable on this type of test unit.

2. Set the meter on its lowest scale and crank the engine. The meter needle should oscillate slightly (approximately 1/2 volt).

3. If the meter needle does not oscillate, check the circuit through magnetic pick-up (in the distributor) for open, shorts, shorts to ground and resistance. Resistance between the orange and purple leads should be 400—1,000 ohms and between each lead and the ground should be more than 70 k-ohms. Repair as necessary. Plug in all connectors and recheck Step One.

4. If the meter oscillates, the problem is most probably in the power feed to the module (red wire) or in the module itself. Perform Step Seven.

Step Seven

1. Remove all meters and jumpers. Plug in all connectors.

2. Turn the ignition switch to RUN and measure voltage to engine ground at the following:

a. Battery positive terminal, reading should be at least 12 volts.

b. The red lead of the module. Use a straight pin to pierce the insulation of the lead and connect the voltmeter to the pin.

3. These two readings should be within 1 volt of each other. If readings are not within one volt, check the circuit feeding power to the red lead for shorts, open, or high resistance. Repair as necessary and repeat Step One.

4. If readings are within one volt, the problem is probably in the module. Disconnect the module and connect a known-good module in its place. Repeat Step One. If this corrects the problem, reconnect the original module and recheck. If the problem returns, remove the old module and install the new one.

START MODE SPARK TEST

Step One

Remove the coil wire from the distributor cap, install the modified spark plug (side electrode removed) in the coil wire terminal. Using an insulated pliers, hold the spark plug shell against the engine block. Crank the engine (from the ignition switch). If there is a good spark, the problem is probably in the distributor cap, rotor, ignition cable(s) or spark plug(s). If there is no spark, proceed to Step Two.

Step Two

Measure battery voltage and voltage at the white wire of the module (use a straight pin to pierce the wire) while cranking the engine. These two readings should be within 1 volt of each other. If readings are not within one volt, check and repair the feed through the ignition switch to the white wire. Recheck for spark (Step One). If readings are within one volt, or if there is still no spark after the power feed to white wire is repaired, proceed to Step Three.

Step Three

Measure coil battery terminal voltage while cranking the engine (see catalytic converter caution). The reading should be within 1 volt of battery voltage. If the reading is not within one volt, check and repair the feed through the ignition switch to the coil. Recheck for spark (Step One). If the reading is within one volt, the problem is probably in the ignition module. Plug in a known-good module and recheck for spark (Step One).

NOTE: If all the above steps check out okay, checks should be made of the fuel system and of the engine itself.

TESTING FOR INTERMITTENT CONDITIONS

If the ignition system becomes operative in the course of performing these procedures and you have not made a repair, it is likely an intermittent connection or an intermittent ignition component has become functional. With the engine running, attempt to recreate the problem by wiggling the wires at the coil, module, distributor and other harness connectors. Start first with the connections you might have already disturbed. Also check the ground connection in the distributor. Disconnecting and reconnecting connectors may also be helpful.

———————CAUTION———————

Do not clean lubricant compound from connectors as it is required to prevent terminal corrosion.

Testing Pick-Up Coil

With the engine off, remove the distributor cap, rotor and adaptor if so equipped, and heat the stator pick-up coil by placing a 250-

watt heat lamp approximately 1 to 2 in. from it top surface. Apply heat for 5 to 10 minutes while monitoring pick-up coil continuity bctween the parallel blades of the disconnected distributor connector. The resistance should be 400—1,000 ohms. Tapping with a screwdriver handle may also be helpful. Reinstall the distributor cap. A reading less than 400 ohms would indicate a short, while an infinity reading would indicate an open.

Testing Ignition Module

With the engine running, heat module by placing a 250-watt heat lamp approximately 1 to 2 in. from the top surface of the module. Tapping may also be helpful.

———CAUTION———
The module temperature should not exceed 212°F (boiling). After the first 10 minutes of heating, check the temperature by applying a few drops of water to the module housing. Repeat this check every two minutes until the water droplets boil. Avoid tapping the module to the extent that the housing is distorted.

If this procedure results in ignition malfunction, substitute a known-good module. If the malfunction is corrected by the substitution validate that the original module is at fault by reconnecting it to the vehicle. A functional check of the original and known-good module can quickly be accomplished by using the run mode check.

QUICK CHECKS FOR DURASPARK I

The same quick checks that have been explained for basic solid state ignition can also be used for cars with Duraspark I with a few variations. The Duraspark I module has internal connections which shut off the primary circuit in the RUN mode when the engine stalls (no pulses coming from the pick-up coil). To perform the quick checks, it is necessary to by-pass these connections.

However, with these connections by-passed, the current flow in the primary circuit is so great that it will cause damage to both the ignition coil and the module unless it is controlled. To control primary current, install a ballast resistance in *series* with the primary circuit at the battery terminal of the ignition coil. (See Duraspark I Test Circuit.) Ford has such a resistor available as Motorcraft Part Number DY-36. A 1.3 ohm, 100 watt wire-wound power resistor can also be used.

———CAUTION———
This resistor will become very hot during testing.

1. Release the battery terminal lead from the coil.
2. Insert a paper clip in the battery terminal of the connector on the coil. Using alligator clips and jumper wires, install the ballast resistor.
3. Using a straight pin, pierce both the red and white leads of the module to short these two leads together. This will by-pass the internal connections of the module which turns off the ignition primary circuit when the engine is not running.

Ignition timing pick-up unit at the crankshaft pulley

Testing pick-up coil for intermittent operation

———CAUTION———
Never install this by-pass until after the ballast resistor is in place. The damage to the ignition coil and module may not show up immediately, but the damage will be there and will cause a later failure.

4. With the ballast resistor and by-pass in place, proceed with the quick checks described earlier for the basic solid state ignition system and Duraspark II.

NOTE: It may be necessary to leave the special jumper switch on for up to 10 seconds before turning it off to get a spark at the test spark plug.

Ignition Timing Adjustment

NOTE: The following points must be considered when checking timing on conventional type distributors. For vehicles equipped with the dual-mode ignition module using either the ignition barometric pressure switch assembly or the vacuum switch, disconnect the 3-pin switch assembly connector from the dual-mode timing ignition module. Failure to disconnect the switch will build in a 3–6° retard in the dual-mode ignition on V-8 engines and more on 6 cylinder engines.

1. Start the engine and allow the engine to warm up.
2. Set the timing idle speed to specification (per engine decal) to avoid centrifugal advance input.

3. Set initial timing to specifications using timing light. Use only the clamp-on type timing devices which have an inductive pick-up when checking the Duraspark I ignition system.

4. After adjusting the initial timing, check and if necessary, adjust curb idle and fast idle speeds.

CHECKING DUAL-MODE IGNITION SYSTEM (FUNCTIONAL TEST)

Perform the initial timing, then reconnect the 3-pin switch assembly connector to the module. Disconnect the vacuum line to the switch. Using an external vacuum source, apply vacuum to the switch and compare basic timing to the requirements.

VACUUM SWITCH APPLICATIONS

Applied Vacuum	Basic Timing
Greater than 10 in. Hg.	Per specifications
Between 6 and 10 in. Hg.	Per specifications or per specifications less 3–6°
Less than 6 in. Hg. or 0	Per specifications less 3–6°

BAROMETRIC PRESSURE SWITCH APPLICATIONS

Elevation	Basic Timing
Below 2400 ft.	Per specifications less 3–6°
2400 ft. to 4300 ft.	Per specifications or per specifications less 3–6°
Over 4300 ft.	Per specifications

NOTE: See the underhood Emission Control Sticker for base timing specifications on various models

3. If these requirements are not met, substitute a new vacuum switch or barometric pressure switch and recheck timing.

4. If the timing is okay after the switch substitution, reconnect the original switch to validate failure. If the timing is not correct with the original switch, replace the switch.

5. If the timing is outside specified limits after substituting the switch, reinstall the original switch and go on to the next step.

6. Substitute a new dual-mode ignition module and recheck the timing.

7. If the timing is okay after the module substitution, reconnect the original module to validate the failure.

8. If the timing is not okay with the original module, replace the module.

Engine Operates Well at Idle But Not at Increased RPM

1. Remove the distributor cap and inspect for the presence of the roll pin holding the armature on the distributor shaft. If the roll pin is missing, the armature may have rotated out of position relative to the distributor shaft, causing timing to be out of phase.

2. Check for the correct connection of the orange and purple wires between the distributor and the module. If the wires are reversed, the distributor timing is 22½ degrees out of phase.

3. If these checks are okay, perform further tests as described in the solid state ignition system.

Engine Starts and Runs, But Stalls as Normal Operating Temperature Is Reached

1. Run the engine until normal operating temperature is reached or until the engine quits, whichever occurs first.

2. While cranking the engine, check the voltage between the orange and purple wires at the ignition module. With the voltmeter at the lowest range, only a slight meter movement should be noted (approximately 1/2 volt).

3. With the ignition switch off, check the resistance between the purple and orange wires at the distributor. Resistance should be 400—1,000 ohms.

4. Again with the ignition switch off, check the resistance between the purple wire at the distributor and ground and between the orange wire and ground. In each case, the resistance should be over 70,000 ohms.

5. If any of these measurements are not within specification, replace the magnetic pick-up assembly.

Engine Quits Intermittently with Complete Loss of Ignition

Check the primary circuit ground resistance at the ignition module connector (black wire). The resistance should be 0 ohms. If the resistance is not 0 ohms, remove the distributor cap and inspect the attaching screw at the rubber plug where the wires enter the distributor housing. A loose or cross-threaded screw or a dirty/corroded connection at this screw can cause an intermittent high-resistance ground or a complete loss of ground.

THICK FILM INTEGRATED (TFI) SYSTEM TESTING

NOTE: After performing any test which requires piercing a wire with a straight pin, remove the straight pin and seal the holes in the wire with silicone sealer.

Ignition Coil Secondary Voltage Test

1. Disconnect the secondary (high voltage) coil wire from the distributor cap and install a spark tester (see Special Tools, located with the Dura Spark Troubleshooting) between the coil wire and ground.

2. Crank the engine—a good, strong spark should be noted at the spark tester. If spark is noted, but the engine will not start, check the spark plugs, spark plug wiring, and fuel system. If there is no spark at the tester check the ignition coil secondary wire resistance; it should be no more than 5000 ohms per inch.

3. Inspect the ignition coil for damage and/or carbon tracking.

4. With the distributor cap removed, verify that the distributor shaft turns with the engine; if it does not, repair the engine as required.

5. If the fault was not found in Step 2, 3, or 4, proceed to the next test.

Ignition Coil Primary Circuit Switching Test

1. Insert a small straight pin in the wire which runs from the coil negative (−) terminal to the TFI module, about one inch from the module.

—CAUTION—
The pin must not touch ground.

2. Connect a 12 volt test lamp between the straight pin and an engine ground.

3. Crank the engine, noting the operation of the test lamp. If the test lamp flashes, proceed to the next test. If the test lamp lights but does not flash, proceed to the Wiring Harness test. If the test lamp does not light at all, proceed to the Primary Circuit Continuity test.

Ignition Coil Resistance Test

Refer to the General Testing for an explanation of the resistance tests. Replace the ignition coil if the resistance is out of the specification range.

Wiring Harness Test

1. Disconnect the wiring harness connector from the TFI module; the connector tabs must be pushed to disengage the connector. Inspect the connector for damage, dirt, and corrosion.

2. Attach the negative lead of a voltmeter to the base of the distributor. Attach the other voltmeter lead to a small straight pin.

3. With the ignition switch in the RUN position, insert the straight pin into the No. 1 terminal of the TFI module connector. Note the voltage reading and proceed to b.

4. With the ignition switch in the RUN posiition, move the straight pin to the No. 2 connector terminal. Again, note the voltage reading, then proceed to c.

5. Move the straight pin to the No. 3 connector terminal, then turn the ignition switch to the START position. Note the voltage reading then turn the ignition OFF.

6. The voltage readings from Steps 3, 4 and 5 should all be at least 90% of the available battery voltage. If the readings are okay, proceed to the Stator Assembly and Module test. If any reading is less than 90% of the battery voltage, inspect the wiring, connector, and/or ignition switch for defects. If the voltage is low only at the No. 1 terminal, proceed to the ignition coil primary voltage test.

Stator Assembly and Module Test

1. Remove the distributor from the engine according to the procedure listed in the appropriate car section.

2. Remove the TFI module from the distributor as outlined under "Overhaul" in this section.

3. Inspect the distributor terminals, ground screw, and stator wiring for damage. Repair as necessary.

4. Measure the resistance of the stator assembly, using an ohmmeter. If the ohmmeter reading is 800—975 ohms; the stator is okay, but the TFI module must be replaced. If the ohmmeter reading is less than 800 ohms or more than 975 ohms; the TFI module is okay, but the stator assembly must be replaced.

5. Reinstall the TFI module and the distributor.

Primary Circuit Continuity Test

This test is performed in the same manner as the previous Wiring Harness test, but only the No. 1 terminal conductor is tested (ignition switch in RUN position). If the voltage is less than 90% of the available battery voltage, proceed to the next test.

Ignition Coil Primary Voltage Test

1. Attach the negative lead of a voltmeter to the distributor base.

2. Turn the ignition switch ON and connect the positive voltmeter lead to the negative (−) ignition coil terminal. Note the voltage reading and turn the ignition OFF. If the voltmeter reading is less than 90% of the available battery voltage, inspect the wiring between the ignition module and the negative (−) coil terminal, then proceed to the last test, which follows.

Ignition Coil Supply Voltage Test

1. Attach the negative lead of a voltmeter to the distributor base.

2. Turn the ignition switch ON and connect the positive voltmeter lead to the positive (+) ignition coil terminal. Note the voltage reading then turn the igntion OFF.

Ignition coil primary circuit switching test—TFI ignition system

Wiring harness test—TFI ignition system

Stator assembly and module test—TFI ignition system

3. If the voltage reading is at least 90% of the battery voltage, yet the engine will still not run: first, check the ignition coil connector and terminals for corrosion, dirt, and/or damage; second, replace the ignition switch if the connectors and terminals are okay. Connect any remaining wiring.

Coil primary voltage test—TFI ignition system

Coil supply voltage test—TFI ignition system

Overhaul

STATOR ASSEMBLY

Removal and Installation

EXCEPT ESCORT, LYNX, EXP, LN7

NOTE: If the engine is equipped with EEC, see the "Electronic Engine Controls" section for information on rotor alignment and identification.

1. Remove the distributor cap and rotor and disconnect the distributor harness plug. To remove the two-piece Dura Spark distributor cap, take off the top position, then the rotor, then the bottom adaptor.

2. Using a small gear puller or two awls, lift or pry the armature from the advance plate sleeve. Remove the roll pin.

3. Remove the large wire retaining clip from the base plate annular groove.

For 1977–81 models:

4. Remove the snap-ring which secures the vacuum advance link to the pick-up assembly.

5. Remove the magnetic pick-up assembly ground screw and lift the assembly from the distributor.

6. Lift the vacuum advance arm off the post on the pick-up assembly and move it out against the distributor housing.

For 1982 and later models:

7. Remove the ground screw which retains the ground strap.

8. Pull upward on the lead wires to remove the rubber grommet from the distributor base.

9. Remove the E-clip which retains the vacuum advance pull rod to the stator assembly.

10. Lift the pull rod off of the stator post and move the rod out against the distributor housing.

11. Remove the stator assembly.

Installation—all models:

12. Place the new pick-up assembly in position over the fixed base plate and slide the wiring in position through the slot in the side of the distributor housing.

13. Install the wire snap-ring securing the pick-up assembly to the fixed base plate.

14. Position the vacuum advance arm over the post on the pick-up assembly and install the snap-ring.

15. Install the grounding screw through the tab on the wiring harness and into the fixed base plate.

16. Install the armature on the advance plate sleeve making sure that the roll pin is engaged in the matching slots.

17. Install the distributor rotor cap.

18. Connect the distributor wiring plug to the vehicle harness.

ESCORT, LYNX, EXP, AND LN7

1. Remove the distributor cap from the distributor, and set it aside (spark plug wires intact).

2. Remove the distributor as outlined in the appropriate car section.

3. Remove the rotor from the distributor.

4. Carefully remove the drive coupling spring, using a small screwdriver.

5. Blow the dirt and oil from the drive end of the distributor with compressed air.

6. Paint matchmarks on the drive coupling and the shaft to indicate their relationship for reassembly. Align the drive pin with the slot in the base.

Exploded view of typical electronic distributor

Exploded view of 4 cylinder TFI distributor

7. Carefully support the distributor and drive out the roll pin using a 1/8 in. drift punch and hammer.

8. Remove the distributor drive coupling.

9. Check the end of the distributor shaft for burrs. If any are present, smooth them with emery paper and wipe the shaft clean. Withdraw the shaft assembly from the distributor.

10. Remove the two screws which retain the stator connector to the distributor bowl.

11. On TFI systems, remove the connector from the top of the TFI module.

12. Remove the three screws which retain the stator assembly to the distributor base. Carefully lift the stator assembly from the distributor base.

NOTE: While the distributor is disassembled, inspect all parts for damage, wear, and freedom of operation.

To install the stator assembly:

13. Assemble the stator retainer to the stator assembly by sliding the stator bumper into the groove in the bottom of the stator, with the horseshoe opening at the diaphragm rod pivot pin.

14. On TFI systems, place the connector on top of the module (with pins aligned). Press down on the connector to properly seat it.

15. Place the stator assembly over the distributor base bushing, with the diaphragm pivot pin positioned in front of the diaphragm mounting hole.

16. Align the holes in the stator retaining plate with the holes in the distributor base. Install the three stator retaining screws and torque the screws to 1.8—3.0 ft. lbs. Check the stator for free rotation.

17. Install the two screws which secure the connector to the base and torque the screws to 1.8—3.0 ft. lbs.

18. Place the two stator wires behind the wire guard of the connector. The wires must not be tangled or twisted.

19. Install the diaphragm assembly.

20. Apply a SMALL amount of Ford M2C162A (or its equivalent) lubricant to the distributor shaft below the armature.

21. Install the distributor shaft and the drive coupling, lining up the marks made during step 6.

22. Support the distributor securely and drive the roll pin into place. The end of the pin should be flush with the step in the drive coupling. Check for free movement of the drive coupling and the distributor shaft.

23. Install the drive coupling retaining spring.

24. Install the distributor assembly, following the procedure listed in the appropriate car section.

25. Install the distributor cap and the rotor.

TFI MODULE

Removal and Installation

1. Remove the distributor cap from the distributor, and set it aside (spark plug wires intact). Do not remove the wires from the cap.

2. Disconnect the TFI harness connector.

3. Remove the distributor after matchmarking it to the engine with chalk, etc.

4. Remove the two TFI module retaining screws.

5. To disengage the module terminals from the distributor base connector, pull the right side of the module down the distributor mounting flange and then back up. Carefully pull the module toward the flange and away from the distributor.

—CAUTION—

Step 5 must be followed EXACTLY; failure to do so will result in damage to the distributor/module connector pins.

To install the TFI module:

6. Coat the TFI module baseplate with a 1/32 in. layer of silicone grease (Ford No. D7AZ19A331-A or its equivalent).

7. Place the TFI module on the distributor base mounting flange. Position the module assembly toward the distributor bowl and carefully engage the distributor connector pins. Install and torque the two TFI module retaining screws to 9—16 inch lbs.

8. Install the distributor assembly.

9. Install the distributor cap and check the engine timing.

NOTE: It is recommended to use a new roll pin in the armature groove positioned 180° away from the original groove.

GM DELCO—REMY HIGH ENERGY IGNITION (HEI)

General Information

COMPONENTS AND OPERATION

The Delco-Remy High Energy Ignition (HEI) System is a breakerless, pulse triggered, transistor controlled, inductive discharge ignition system used on all GM passenger car engines as standard equipment. The ignition coil is located in the top of the distributor cap on all V6 and V8 engines and some 4 cylinder engines. Some inline 4 cylinder engines mount the coil externally on the engine block.

NOTE: Some distributors are equipped with a Hall effect switch, located inside the distributor cap.

The magnetic pick-up assembly located inside the distributor contains a permanent magnet, a pole piece with internal teeth, and a pick-up coil. When the teeth of the rotating timer core and pole piece align, an induced voltage in the pick-up coil signals the electronic module to open the coil primary circuit. As the primary current decreases, a high voltage is induced in the secondary windings of the ignition coil, directing a spark through the rotor and high voltage leads to fire the spark plugs. The dwell period is automatically controlled by the electronic module and is increased with increasing engine rpm. The HEI System features a longer spark duration which is instrumental in firing lean and EGR (Exhaust Gas Recirculation) diluted fuel/air mixtures. The condenser (capacitor) located within the HEI distributor is provided for noise (static) suppression purposes only and is not a regularly replaced ignition system component.

Beginning in 1980, three different modules are used. The original four terminal module is continued in use for most applications in 1980. Some 1980 models and most 1981 and later models are equipped with an Electronic spark timing (EST) distributor, which is part of the C-4 or CCC System (see the "Engine Controls" section). On these, the ignition timing is determined by the C-4 or CCC Electronic Control Module (ECM). The EST module has seven terminals. The EST distributor can be quickly identified: it has no vacuum advance diaphragm. The EST distributor can be equipped with an additional spark control, the Electronic Spark Control (ESC) system. This is a closed loop system that controls engine detonation by retarding the spark timing. The ESC is usually used on turbocharged engines. Some models are equipped with Electronic Module Retard (EMR). This system uses a five terminal module which retards ignition timing a calibrated number of crankshaft degrees. Distributors with this system are equipped with vacuum advance. When replacing modules on these three systems, be certain to obtain the correct part: the modules are not interchangeable.

The magnetic pick-up assembly located inside the distributor contains a permanent magnet, a pole piece with internal teeth, and

1. Cap cover attaching screw
2. Distributor cap cover
3. Coil attaching screw
4. Distributor coil
5. Coil to distributor cap seal
6. Distributor cap
7. Resistor brush
8. Module coil harness
9. Distributor rotor
10. Distributor ground lead

11. Rotor screw
12. Distributor mainshaft
13. Pole piece and plate retainer
14. Distributor pole piece and plate
15. Vacuum control attaching screw
16. Distributor vacuum control
17, 18. Capacitor and attaching screw
19. Vacuum control attaching screw
20. Felt washer
21. Distributor housing seal

22. Module
23. Distributor housing
24. Housing stem washer
25. Shaft spacer washer
26. Shaft thrust washer
27. Distributor drive gear
28. Module attaching screw
29. Washer
30. Gear attaching pin

Exploded view of HEI distributor with integrated coil

7/16" (11mm) FROM TIP OF SPARK PLUG

CONNECT TO GROUND

INSERT BOOT OVER PORCELAIN END OF ST-125

LEAVE HARNESS CONNECTED

To test for coil spark on integral coil models, cut a plug boot so that it fits as shown over the modified spark plug (ST-125). Fit the modified plug on the center terminal of the distributor cap and connect the plug to ground with a jumper wire

DISCONNECT PICK-UP COIL LEADS FROM MODULE TERMINAL

(TO BAT +)

TEST LIGHT

CONNECT VOLTMETER, "TACH" TERMINAL TO GROUND

Watch the voltmeter and momentarily connect a test light from the positive battery terminal to the appropriate module terminal

a pick-up coil. When the teeth of the rotating timer core and pole piece align, an induced voltage in the pick-up coil signals the electronic module to open the coil primary circuit. As the primary current decreases, a high voltage is induced in the secondary windings of the ignition coil, directing a spark through the rotor and high voltage leads to fire the spark plugs. The dwell period is automatically controlled by the electronic module and is increased with increasing engine rpm. The HEI System features a longer spark duration which is instrumental in firing lean and EGR diluted fuel/air mixtures. The condenser (capacitor) located within the HEI distributor is provided for noise (static) suppression purposes only and is not a regularly replaced ignition system component.

Performance Tests

NOTE: An accurate diagnosis is the first step to problem solution and repair. For several of the following steps, a modified spark plug (side electrode removed) is needed. GM makes a modified plug (tool ST 125) which also has a spring clip to attach it to ground. Use of this tool is recommended, as there is less chance of being shocked. If a tachometer is connected to the TACH terminal on the distributor, disconnect it before proceeding with this test.

Secondary Circuit Test

1. Check for spark at the spark plugs by attaching the modified spark plug to one of the plug wires, grounding the modified plug shell on the engine and cranking the starter. Wear heavy gloves, use insulated pliers and make sure the ground is good. If no spark on one wire, check a second. If spark is present, HEI system is good. Check fuel system, plug wires, and spark plugs. If no spark (except EST), proceed to next step. If no spark on EST distributor, disconnect the 4 terminal EST connector and recheck for spark. If spark is present, EST system service check, as outlined under "Engine Controls," should be performed. If no spark, proceed to Step 2.

NOTE: Before making any circuit checks with test meters, be sure that all primary circuit connectors are properly installed and that spark plug cables are secure at the distributor and at the plugs. Also check that the distributor through-bolts are tight; loose bolts can cause radio interference and poor performance.

2. Check voltage at the BAT terminal of the distributor while cranking the engine. If under 7V, repair the primary circuit to the ignition switch. If over 7V, proceed to Step 3.

3. With the ignition switch on, check voltage at the TACH terminal of the distributor or coil (external). If under 1V, coil connection or coil are faulty. If over 10V, proceed to Step 4. If 1 to 10V, replace module and check for spark from coil. See Step 4.

TESTING IGNITION COIL

IGNITION COIL

1 OHMMETER   2 OHMMETER   3 OHMMETER

To test the HEI ignition coil on external coil models, attach an ohmmeter as shown. Use the high scale for test No. 1; the reading should be very high or infinite. Use the low scale for test No. 2; the reading should be very low or zero. Use the high scale for test No. 3; the reading should not be infinite. If any test results are different, replace the coil.

4. On external coil models, disconnect coil wire from distributor and connect to grounded modified spark plug. On integral coils, remove distributor cap from distributor without removing its electrical connectors, remove the rotor, then modify a plug boot so that the modified plug can be connected directly to the center terminal of the distributor cap. Ground the shell of the modified plug to the engine block with a jumper wire. Make sure no wires, clothing, etc., are in the way of moving parts and crank the engine. On external coils, if no spark, check secondary coil wire continuity and repair. On both external and integral coils, if spark is present, inspect distributor cap for moisture, cracks, etc. If cap is OK, install new rotor. If no spark, proceed to Step 5.

5. Remove the pick-up coil leads from the module and check TACH terminal voltage with the ignition on. Watch the voltmeter and momentarily (not more than 5 seconds) connect a test light from the positive battery terminal to the appropriate module terminal: 4 terminal module, terminal "G" (small terminal); 5 terminal module (ESS or ESC), terminal "D"; 5 terminal module, (EMR) terminal "H"; 7 terminal module, terminal "P". If no drop in voltage, test the module, check module ground, and check for open in wires from cap to distributor. If OK, replace module. If voltage drops, proceed to next step.

NOTE: 4 terminal modules may be tested with simple tools, according to the Module Test procedure which follows. 5 and 7 terminal modules must be tested professionally.

6. Reconnect modified plug to ignition coil as instructed in step 4, and check for spark as the test light is removed from the appropriate module terminal (see step 5 for appropriate terminal). Do not connect test light for more than 5 seconds. If spark is present, problem is with pick-up coil or connections. Pick-up coil resistance should be 500—1500 ohms and not grounded. If no spark, proceed to next step.

7. On integral coil distributors, check the coil ground by attaching a test light from the BAT terminal of the cap to the coil ground wire. If the light lights when the ignition is on, replace the ignition coil and repeat Step 6. If the light does not light, repair the ground. On external coil models, replace the ignition coil and repeat Step 6. On both the integral and external coil distributors, if no spark is present, replace the module and reinstall the original coil. Repeat Step 6 again. If no spark is present, replace the original ignition coil with a good one.

MODULE TESTING

NOTE: This procedure applies only to 4 terminal HEI modules. 5 and 7 terminal modules must be tested with a suitable diagnostic tester.

1. Remove the module from the distributor as previously outlined. Connect a 12VDC test lamp between the B and C module terminals.

2. Connect a jumper wire from a 12VDC source to the B module terminal.

3. Connect the module ground terminal to a good ground. If the test lamp lights, the module is defective and must be replaced.

4. Connect a jumper wire between the B and G module terminals. The test lamp will light if the module is okay.

MODULE DRAW TEST

Test Condition	Current Draw
Key on, engine off	0.1 to 0.2 amp
Engine cranking	0.5 to 1.5 amps
Engine at idle	0.5 to 1.5 amps
Engine at 2,000 to 2,500 rpm	1.0 to 2.8 amps

NOTE: Exact values may vary.

To test the HEI ignition coil on integral models, connect the ohmmeter as shown in test No. 1. The reading should be zero or nearly zero. Connect the ohmmeter both ways as shown in test No. 2 with the meter on the high scale. Replace the coil if both readings are infinite.

HEI pick-up coil test. The ohmmeter in test No. 1 should read infinite at all times. The ohmmeter in test No. 2 should read 500-1500 ohms. On cavuum advance equipped models, attach an external vacuum source (hand pump) and run the vacuum advance unit through its range while making tests. The readings should not change. The ohmmeter unit may deflect if the vacuum unit causes the teeth to align.

Hall Effect Switch Test

The Hall Effect Switch, when used, is installed in the HEI distributor. The purpose of the switch is to measure engine speed and send the information to the Electronic control Module ECM. To remove the Hall Effect Switch, the distributor shaft must be removed from the distributor.

1. Remove the switch connectors from the switch.

2. Connect a 12 volt battery and voltmeter to the switch. Note and follow the polarity markings as indicated in the illustration.

3. Without the knife blade inserted, the voltmeter should read less than 0.5 volts. If not, the switch is defective.

4. With the knife blade inserted, the voltmeter should read within 0.5 volts of battery voltage. If not, the switch is defective.

Testing the four terminal HEI module. The numbers correspond to the steps in the testing procedure.

Testing the Hail Effect switch

* DIESEL CARS
  NO. 6 - SAME AS 5 ON GAS
  NO. 5 - FUEL SOLENOID
  NO. 4 - NOT USED

GROUND TERM

IGNITION SWITCH

HEADLAMP SWITCH

DASH CONNECTOR

DIAGNOSTIC CONNECTOR

G BLK
9 PPL DBL WHT
8 PPL
7 PPL
6 WHT
5 PNK DBL BLK
4 PINK
3 RED DBL BLK
2 RED DBL WHT
1 RED

RED
PINK
RED

7 OHMS

PINK

DIESEL FUEL SOL

DISTRIBUTOR

PINK
RED DBL WHT
RED

GENERATOR

SOLENOID

F.L

STARTER

PPL

POS   NEG

BATTERY

TROUBLESHOOTING
GM DELCO-REMY HIGH ENERGY IGNITION (H.E.I.)

ENGINE WILL NOT START

Use fiber or plastic spark plug wire removing tool to remove one spark plug lead. Hold the lead ¼" from dry area of engine block while cranking engine.

SPARK JUMPS

Problem is not ignition distributor. Check fuel system.

SPARK DOES NOT JUMP

Connect 12 volt test lamp to ground and to "BAT" terminal lead on distributor, ignition switch ON.

LAMP OFF

Repair open in pink wire from ignition switch to distributor.

LAMP ON

INSTRUCTIONS
1. Insure that ignition switch feed ("BAT") connector is properly attached.
2. Insure that all spark plug leads are properly connected.

INSURE THAT PROPER FUEL IS BEING DELIVERED TO ENGINE. CHECK ALL VACUUM HOSES FOR LEAKS

TEST A

TEST B

DETACH LEADS FROM MODULE ↓

ENGINE RUNS, BUT RUNS ROUGH

If an ignition oscilloscope is available go to next page.

ENGINE ROUGH AT IDLE ONLY

Problem is not ignition. Check:
1. vacuum hoses for leaks
2. carburetor mounting bolts (15 ft.-lb)
3. idle speed and timing

ENGINE ROUGH AT ALL SPEEDS

Remove cap and coil assembly by turning 4 latches. Inspect cap and rotor for arc-over.

ENGINE ROUGH AT PART THROTTLE AND HIGHER SPEEDS. OK AT IDLE AND OFF.

Replace module.

NO ARC-OVER

Connect ohmmeter, Step 1, Test A. Reading should be zero or nearly zero.

ARC-OVER

Replace cap or rotor as required.

READING NORMAL

Connect ohmmeter, Step 2, Test A. Use high scale. Reading should be high, but less than infinite.

READING HIGH

Replace coil

READING NORMAL

Remove coil and inspect for arc-over at spring and seal.

READING INFINITE

Replace coil

NO ARC-OVER

Connect test stand vacuum source to vacuum advance unit.

ARC-OVER

Replace cap, coil or seal as required.

VACUUM ADVANCE OPERATES

Connect ohmmeter Step 1, Test B. Operate vacuum advance through range. Ohmmeter should read infinite at all positions.

VACUUM ADVANCE INOPERATIVE

Replace vacuum advance.

READING NORMAL

Connect ohmmeter, Step 2, Test B. Should read 650 to 850 ohms in all vacuum advance positions.

READING NOT INFINITE

Replace pick-up coil

READING NORMAL

If no defects have been found at this time, replace module.

READING NOT NORMAL

Replace pick-up coil

Internal components of HEI distributor

Overhaul Procedure (Distributor in Engine)

IGNITION COIL

Removal and Installation

1. Disconnect the feed and module wire terminal connectors from the distributor cap.
2. Remove the ignition set retainer.
3. Remove the four coil cover-to-distributor cap screws and the coil cover.
4. Remove the four coil-to-distributor cap screws.
5. Using a blunt drift, press the coil wire spade terminals up out of distributor cap.
6. Lift the coil up out of the distributor cap.
7. Remove and clean the coil spring, rubber seal washer and coil cavity of the distributor cap.
8. Reverse the above procedures to install.

DISTRIBUTOR CAP

Removal and Installation

1. Remove the feed and module wire terminal connectors from the distributor cap.
2. Remove the retainer and spark plug wires from the cap.
3. Depress and release the four distributor cap-to-housing retainers and lift off the cap assembly.
4. Remove the four coil cover screws and cover.
5. Using a finger or a blunt drift, push the spade terminals up out of the distributor cap.
6. Remove all four coil screws and lift the coil, coil spring and rubber seal washer out of the cap coil cavity.
7. Using a new distributor cap, reverse the above procedures to assemble.

Pick-up coil and magnet removed from distributor

ROTOR

Removal and Installation

Disconnect the feed and module wire connectors from the distributor. Depress and release the four distributor cap to housing retainers and lift off the cap assembly. Remove the two rotor attaching screws and rotor. Reverse the procedure to install.

VACUUM ADVANCE UNIT

Removal and Installation

Remove the distributor cap and rotor as previously described. Disconnect the vacuum hose from the vacuum advance unit. Remove the two vacuum advance retaining screws, pull the advance unit outward, rotate and disengage the operating rod from its tang. Reverse the procedure to install.

CONTROL MODULE

Removal and Installation

Remove the distributor cap and rotor as previously described. Disconnect the harness connector and pick-up coil spade connectors from the module. Remove the two screws and module from the distributor housing. Coat the bottom of the new module with dielectric lubricant. Reverse the procedure to install.

DISTRIBUTOR

Removal and Installation

NOTE: The following is a general procedure for all distributor types. Refer to the underhood sticker for specific timing instructions on EST and other computer-controlled systems.

1. Disconnect the ground cable from the battery.
2. Disconnect the feed and module terminal connectors from the distributor cap. Tag all wires for reassembly.
3. Disconnect the hose at the vacuum advance, or EST connectors.
4. Depress and release the four distributor cap-to-housing retainers and lift off the cap assembly.
5. Using crayon or chalk, make locating marks on the rotor and module and on the distributor housing and engine for installation purposes.
6. Loosen and remove the distributor clamp bolt and clamp, and lift distributor out of the engine. Noting the relative position of the rotor and module alignment marks, make a second mark on the rotor to align it with the one mark on the module.
7. See the Overhaul Procedures for further distributor disassembly on the bench.
8. With a new O-ring on the distributor housing and the second mark on the rotor aligned with the mark on the module, install the distributor, taking care to align the mark on the housing with the one on the engine. It may be necessary to lift the distributor and turn the rotor slightly to align the gears and the oil pump driveshaft.
9. With the respective marks aligned, install the clamp and bolt finger-tight.
10. Install and secure the distributor cap.
11. Connect the feed and module connectors to the distributor cap.
12. Connect a timing light to the engine and plug the vacuum hose, or disconnect the EST connector, if equipped.
13. Connect the ground cable to the battery.
14. Start the engine and set the timing. Follow the underhood sticker instructions, if applicable.
15. Turn the engine OFF and tighten the distributor clamp bolt. Disconnect the timing light and unplug and connect the hose to the vacuum advance. Reconnect the EST connector, if equipped.

Pick-up coil removal

Module and harness removal

Module and harness installation

Overhaul Procedures (Distributor Removed)

DRIVEN GEAR REPLACEMENT

With the distributor removed, use a 1/8 in. pin punch and tap out the driven gear roll pin. Hold the rotor end of shaft and rotate the driven gear to shear any burrs in the roll pin hole. Remove the driven gear from the shaft. Reverse the procedure to install.

MAINSHAFT REPLACEMENT

With the driven gear and rotor removed, gently pull the mainshaft out of the housing. Remove the advance springs, weights and slide the weight base plate off the mainshaft. Reverse the procedure to install.

POLE PIECE, MAGNET OR PICK-UP COIL REPLACEMENT

With the mainshaft out of its housing, remove the three retaining screws, pole piece and magnet and/or pick-up coil. Reverse the removal procedure to install making sure that the pole piece teeth do not contact the timer core teeth by installing and rotating the mainshaft. Loosen the three screws and realign the pole piece as necessary.

ELECTRONIC TIMING CONTROLS

General Information

Before the development of computerized engine control systems, ignition timing advance has been regulated by mechanical weights which centrifugally varied the timing with engine speed (rpm), or vacuum advance devices which varied the timing according to throttle position (manifold vacuum). The electronic spark timing distributor replaces both the centrifugal and vacuum advance devices with an electronic control module which controls the ignition timing much more reliably and exactly. By monitoring engine operating conditions (such as rpm, load and temperature), the on-board computer is able to adjust the spark timing once each crankshaft revolution to the programmed setting for those instantaneous values and insure that the engine operates with peak efficiency at all times.

Under normal operating conditions, the on-board computer will control the spark advance. However, under certain operating conditions such as cranking or setting base timing, the distributor will operate in a bypass mode and timing will be maintained at a fixed, preset value programmed into the distributor module to aid engine starting. Some systems are programmed to advance or retard the spark timing according to engine temperature to meet different emission requirements for cold operation and some on-board computers incorporate a "limp home" mode that will allow the vehicle to be driven reasonably short distances should the timing control circuit fail.

Electronic spark timing has existed in different forms for a number of years, but all can be identified by their lack of vacuum connections and the absence of centrifugal flyweights. Since some early and late distributor control modules are similar in appearance, it is very important to carefully identify exactly which engine control system is being serviced in order to correctly diagnose problems and order replacement parts. The original General Motors HEI spark control module, for example, has a four terminal connector, while the later distributor modules have five or seven terminals. In addition to different calibrations, some spark control systems incorporate different functions and capabilities than earlier models, such as detonation sensors to retard the spark advance during periods of engine operation when detonation occurs. This is particularly critical for turbocharged engines where detonation under boost can cause serious engine damage.

GM Electronic Module Retard (EMR) System

This system is used on 1981 Chevrolet (engine code K) modules. EMR is a spark control system which uses an HEI module with five terminals. The ignition timing is electronically retarded when the HEI module is grounded through the EMR vacuum switch on all except California models. On California engines, the EMR module is controlled by the C4 system electronic control module (ECM). EMR retards the timing about 10 degrees during engine warm-up (coolant below 120 degrees F), but operates like a standard HEI module the rest of the time. On California models, the timing is retarded only when the coolant is between 66–130 degrees F, with the throttle open position below 45% and the engine speed above 400 rpm. When the retard circuit is open, there is no delay and the distributor fires the spark plugs as controlled by engine speed and vacuum. If the EMR-HEI module is removed and/or replaced for any reason, the ignition timing must be checked and set to specifications.

GM Electronic Spark Control (ESC) System

This modified spark control system is used on turbocharged engines to control engine detonation by automatically retarding ignition timing during periods of engine operation when detonation occurs. 1981 Chevrolet and Buick V6 and Pontiac V8 turbo engines use an HEI/EST/ESC system. Some 1981 Chevrolet and GMC C and K series light trucks with the 5.0L engine (code H) also use a modified HEI/ESC system.

The ESC system consists of a detonation sensor, controller and HEI distributor. The intake manifold transmits the vibrations caused by detonation to the sensor mounting location. The sensor detects the presence and intensity of detonation and feeds this information to the controller which evaluates the sensor signal and sends a command signal to the distributor to adjust timing. The HEI distributor has a modified electronic module which responds to signals from the controller and will retard timing up to 15 degrees to minimize detonation levels, if necessary.

Loss of the ESC knock sensor signal or loss of the ground at the ESC module terminal D would cause the ECM to control the EST as if no detonation were occurring; no timing retard would occur and spark knock would become severe under heavy engine load conditions. Loss of the ESC signal to the ECM would cause the ECM to constantly retard the spark timing, resulting in sluggish performance and causing a trouble code 43 to be set in the ECM memory. Code 43 indicates that the ECM terminal 4 (white connector) is receiving less than 6 volts for a 4 second period with the engine running. This is circuit 485, which normally provides a 6–16 volts signal from the ESC module to the ECM. When no code 43 is present, but the ESC is suspect as a cause of excessive spark knock, perform the ESC test procedures to check the system function.

NOTE: A slight amount of engine knock is normal on vehicles equipped with this system. Simulating an engine knock by tapping the engine block should normally cause an engine rpm drop due to retarded timing. If the rpm doesn't drop, either the timing is not retarding or is retarded all the time.

Testing pick-up coil in HEI system

GM Electronic Spark Timing (EST) System

Electronic spark timing is used on engines equipped with Computer Command Control (CCC) systems. The electronic control module (ECM) is used to advance or retard the ignition timing in place of the mechanical and vacuum advance units in the distributor. The system uses a seven pin HEI module which converts the pick-up coil signal into a crankshaft position signal that the ECM modifies to advance or retard the spark timing. Early Computer Control Command engines and 1982 CCC minimum function systems do not use EST. For more information, see the "Engine Controls" Section for a description of the GM Computer Command Control (C3) System.

EST DISTRIBUTOR DISASSEMBLY AND TESTING

Testing Coil in Cap

1. A 6-cyl. EST distributor with coil-in-cap is illustrated.
2. Detach the wiring connector from the cap, as shown.
3. Turn four latches and remove the cap and coil assembly from the lower housing.
4. Connect an ohmmeter as illustrated (1).
5. The reading should be zero or nearly zero. If not, replace the coil.
6. Connect the ohmmeter both ways as illustrated (2). Use the high scale. Replace the coil only if both readings are infinite.
7. If the coil is good, go to step 13.
8. If the coil fails the test, go to step 9.

Ignition Coil Removal and Inspection

9. Remove the ignition coil attaching screws and lift the coil with the leads from the cap.
10. Remove the ignition coil arc seal.
11. Clean with a soft cloth and inspect the cap for defects. Replace, if needed. Replace the cap if the electrodes are excessively burned or scored.
12. Assemble the new coil and cover to cap.

Testing Pickup Coil

13. On all distributors, remove the rotor and pickup coil leads from the module.
14. Connect the ohmmeter as illustrated (1) and (2).
15. If the vacuum unit is used, connect the vacuum source to the vacuum unit. Replace the unit if inoperative. Observe the ohmmeter throughout the vacuum range. Flex the leads by hand without vacuum to check for intermittent opens.
16. Test 1 should read infinite at all times. Test 2 should read steady at one value within 500—1,500 ohm range.

NOTE: The ohmmeter may deflect if the operating vacuum unit causes the teeth to align. This is not a defect.

17. If the pickup coil is defective, go to step 18. If okay, go to step 23.

Removing Shaft Assembly

18. Mark the distributor shaft and gear so they can be reassembled in the same position.
19. Drive out the roll pin, using a suitable punch.
20. Remove the gear and pull the shaft assembly from the distributor.

Electronic Module Retard (EMR) Diagnosis

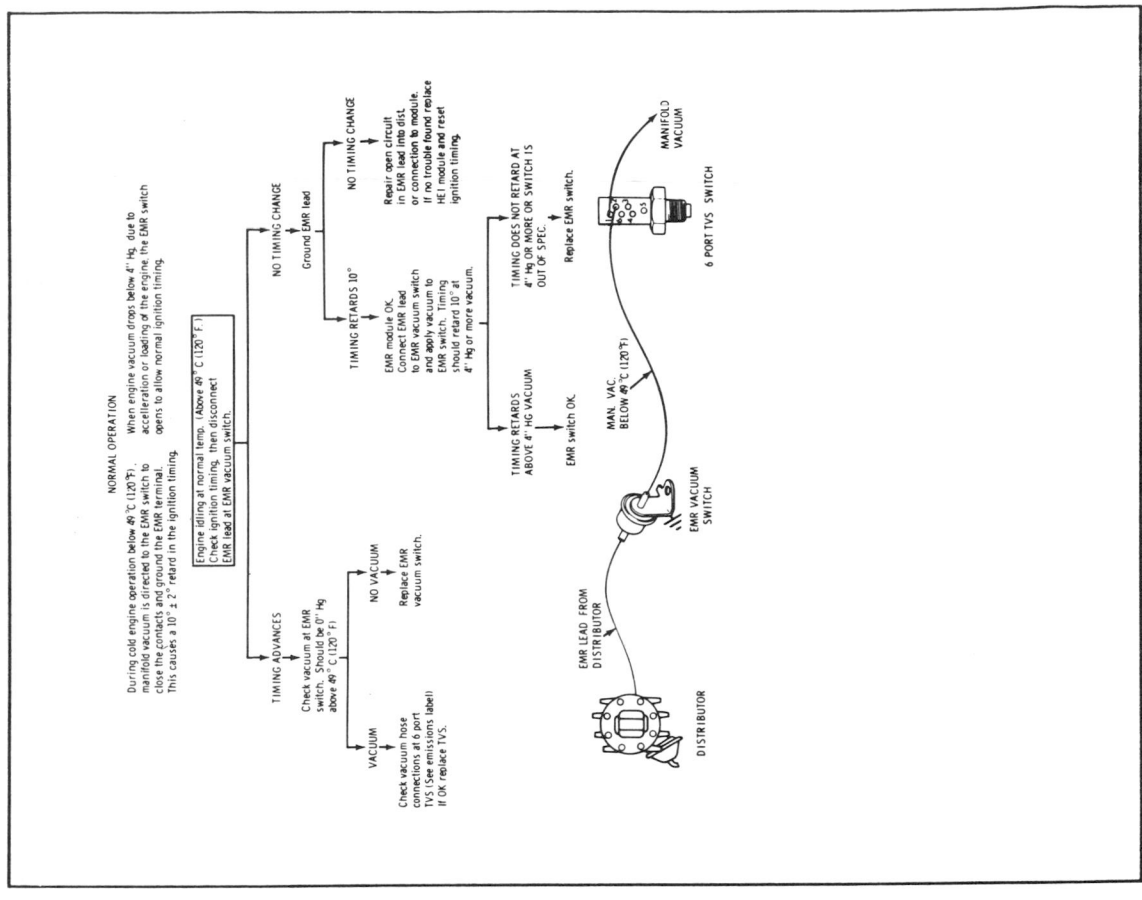

Electronic Module Retard (EMR) Diagnosis

- Engine idling at normal operating temperature
- Check ignition timing, then disconnect EMR lead at distributor

Timing Advances → Connect test light from bat + to EMR lead to ECM
- No light → Replace ECM
- Light → Disconnect connector from ECM
  - No light → Replace ECM
  - Light → Repair ground in EMR lead

No timing change → Ground distributor side of EMR lead
- Timing retards → No trouble found in EMR circuit
- No timing change → Check for open or grounded EMR lead to dist.
  - O.K. → Replace ignition module
  - Not O.K. → Repair lead

The system performance check should be performed after any repair to this system has been made.

EMR Module

C — To coil
B — Battery
R L H — Pick up coil
ECM

123

ESC Diagnostic Procedure—1978–79

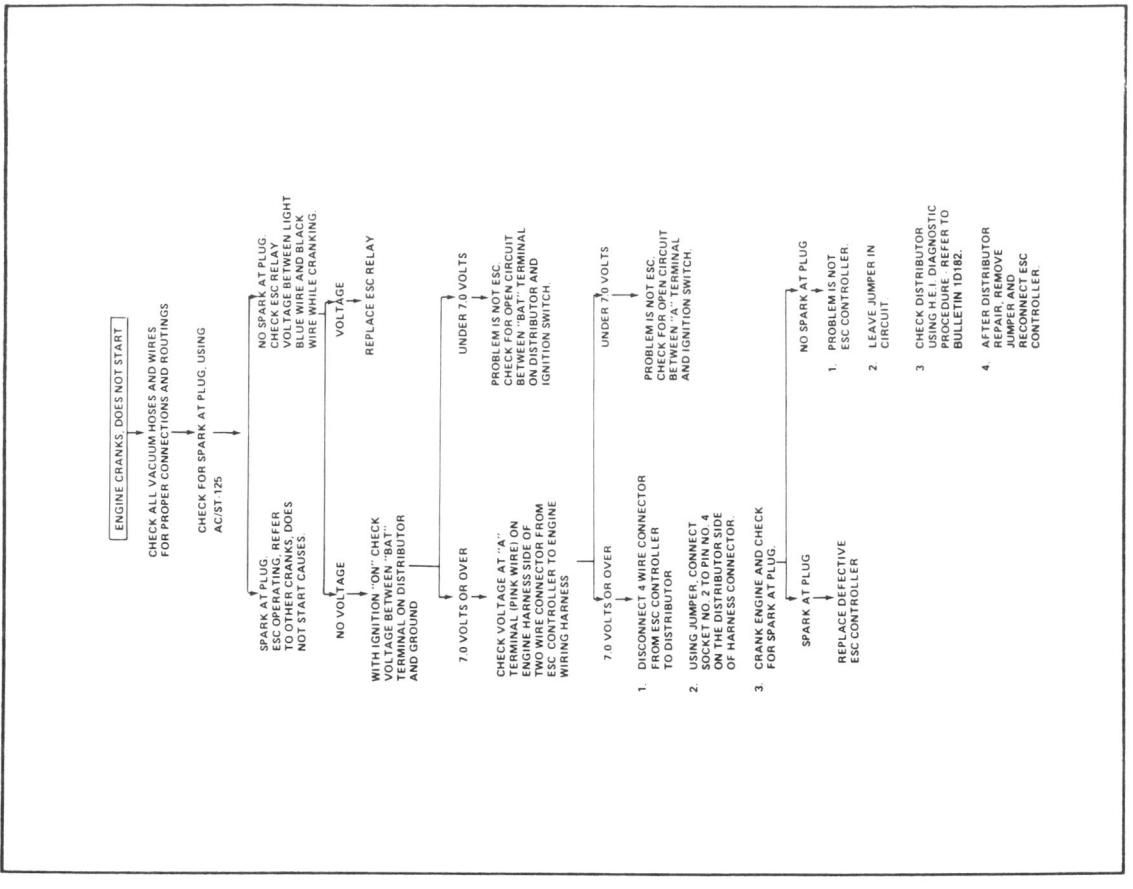

ENGINE CRANKS, DOES NOT START

CHECK ALL VACUUM HOSES AND WIRES FOR PROPER CONNECTIONS AND ROUTINGS

CHECK FOR SPARK AT PLUG, USING AC/ST 125

- SPARK AT PLUG — ESC OPERATING. REFER TO OTHER CAUSES, DOES NOT START CAUSES.
- NO SPARK AT PLUG — CHECK ESC RELAY VOLTAGE BETWEEN LIGHT BLUE WIRE AND BLACK WIRE WHILE CRANKING.
  - VOLTAGE
  - NO VOLTAGE — REPLACE ESC RELAY

WITH IGNITION "ON", CHECK VOLTAGE BETWEEN "BAT" TERMINAL ON DISTRIBUTOR AND GROUND

- 7.0 VOLTS OR OVER
- UNDER 7.0 VOLTS — PROBLEM IS NOT ESC. CHECK FOR OPEN CIRCUIT BETWEEN "BAT" TERMINAL ON DISTRIBUTOR AND IGNITION SWITCH.

CHECK VOLTAGE AT "A" TERMINAL (PINK WIRE) ON ENGINE HARNESS SIDE OF TWO WIRE CONNECTOR FROM ESC CONTROLLER TO ENGINE WIRING HARNESS

- 7.0 VOLTS OR OVER
- UNDER 7.0 VOLTS — PROBLEM IS NOT ESC. CHECK FOR OPEN CIRCUIT BETWEEN "A" TERMINAL AND IGNITION SWITCH.

1. DISCONNECT 4 WIRE CONNECTOR FROM ESC CONTROLLER TO DISTRIBUTOR
2. USING JUMPER, CONNECT SOCKET NO. 2 TO PIN NO. 4 ON THE DISTRIBUTOR SIDE OF HARNESS CONNECTOR.
3. CRANK ENGINE AND CHECK FOR SPARK AT PLUG.
   - SPARK AT PLUG — REPLACE DEFECTIVE ESC CONTROLLER
   - NO SPARK AT PLUG
     1. PROBLEM IS NOT ESC CONTROLLER
     2. LEAVE JUMPER IN CIRCUIT
     3. CHECK DISTRIBUTOR USING H.E.I. DIAGNOSTIC PROCEDURE. REFER TO BULLETIN 1D1B2.
     4. AFTER DISTRIBUTOR REPAIR, REMOVE JUMPER AND RECONNECT ESC CONTROLLER.

ESC Diagnostic Procedure—1978–79

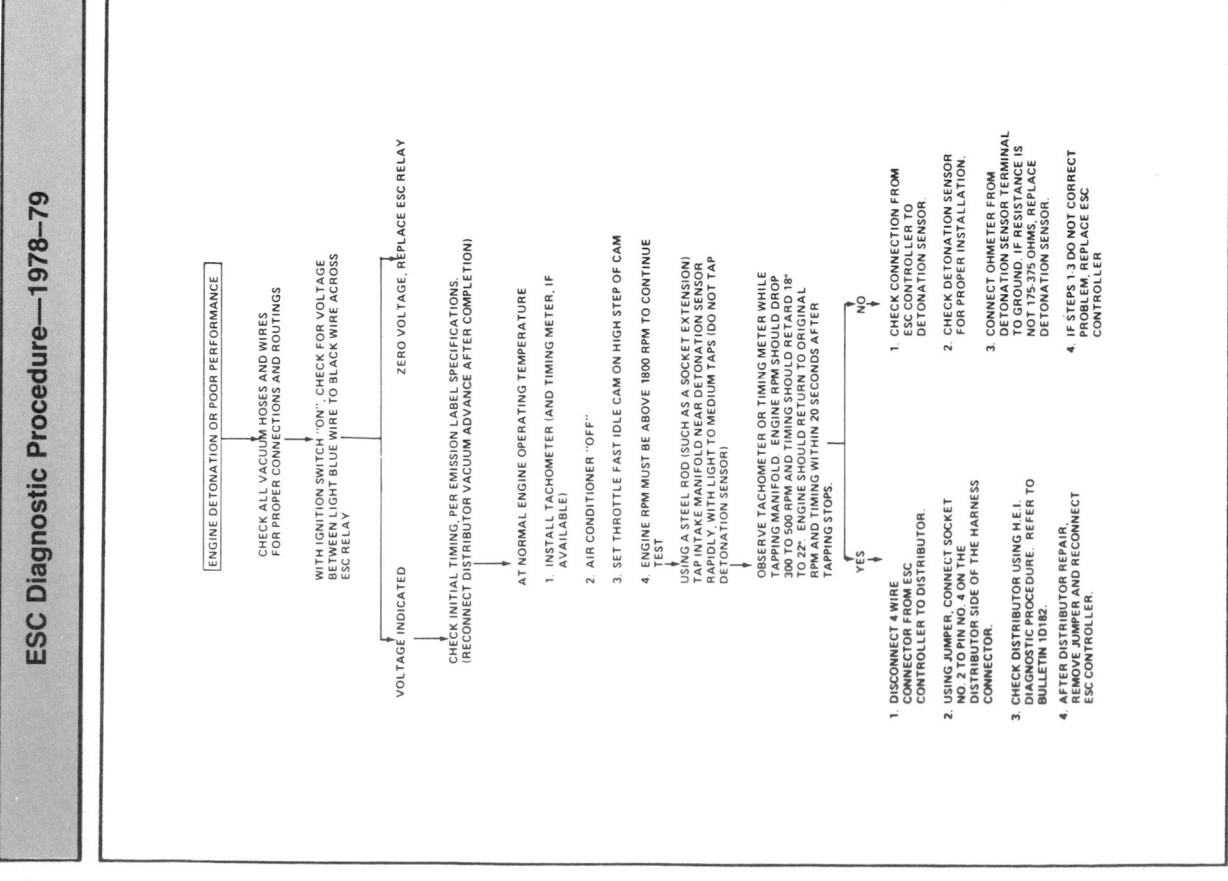

ENGINE DETONATION OR POOR PERFORMANCE

CHECK ALL VACUUM HOSES AND WIRES FOR PROPER CONNECTIONS AND ROUTINGS

WITH IGNITION SWITCH "ON", CHECK FOR VOLTAGE BETWEEN LIGHT BLUE WIRE TO BLACK WIRE ACROSS ESC RELAY

- VOLTAGE INDICATED
- ZERO VOLTAGE, REPLACE ESC RELAY

CHECK INITIAL TIMING, PER EMISSION LABEL SPECIFICATIONS. (RECONNECT DISTRIBUTOR VACUUM ADVANCE AFTER COMPLETION)

AT NORMAL ENGINE OPERATING TEMPERATURE

1. INSTALL TACHOMETER (AND TIMING METER, IF AVAILABLE)
2. AIR CONDITIONER "OFF"
3. SET THROTTLE FAST IDLE CAM ON HIGH STEP OF CAM
4. ENGINE RPM MUST BE ABOVE 1800 RPM TO CONTINUE TEST

USING A STEEL ROD (SUCH AS A SOCKET EXTENSION) TAP INTAKE MANIFOLD NEAR DETONATION SENSOR RAPIDLY, WITH LIGHT TO MEDIUM TAPS (DO NOT TAP DETONATION SENSOR)

OBSERVE TACHOMETER OR TIMING METER WHILE TAPPING MANIFOLD. ENGINE RPM SHOULD DROP 300 TO 500 RPM AND TIMING SHOULD RETARD 18° TO 22°. ENGINE SHOULD RETURN TO ORIGINAL RPM AND TIMING WITHIN 20 SECONDS AFTER TAPPING STOPS.

- YES
- NO
  1. CHECK CONNECTION FROM ESC CONTROLLER TO DETONATION SENSOR
  2. CHECK DETONATION SENSOR FOR PROPER INSTALLATION.
  3. CONNECT OHMMETER FROM DETONATION SENSOR TERMINAL TO GROUND. IF RESISTANCE IS NOT 175-375 OHMS, REPLACE DETONATION SENSOR.
  4. IF STEPS 1-3 DO NOT CORRECT PROBLEM, REPLACE ESC CONTROLLER

1. DISCONNECT 4 WIRE CONNECTOR FROM ESC CONTROLLER TO DISTRIBUTOR.
2. USING JUMPER, CONNECT SOCKET NO. 2 TO PIN NO. 4 ON THE DISTRIBUTOR SIDE OF THE HARNESS CONNECTOR.
3. CHECK DISTRIBUTOR USING H.E.I. DIAGNOSTIC PROCEDURE. REFER TO BULLETIN 1D1B2.
4. AFTER DISTRIBUTOR REPAIR, REMOVE JUMPER AND RECONNECT ESC CONTROLLER.

ESC Diagnostic Procedures—1980 Buick

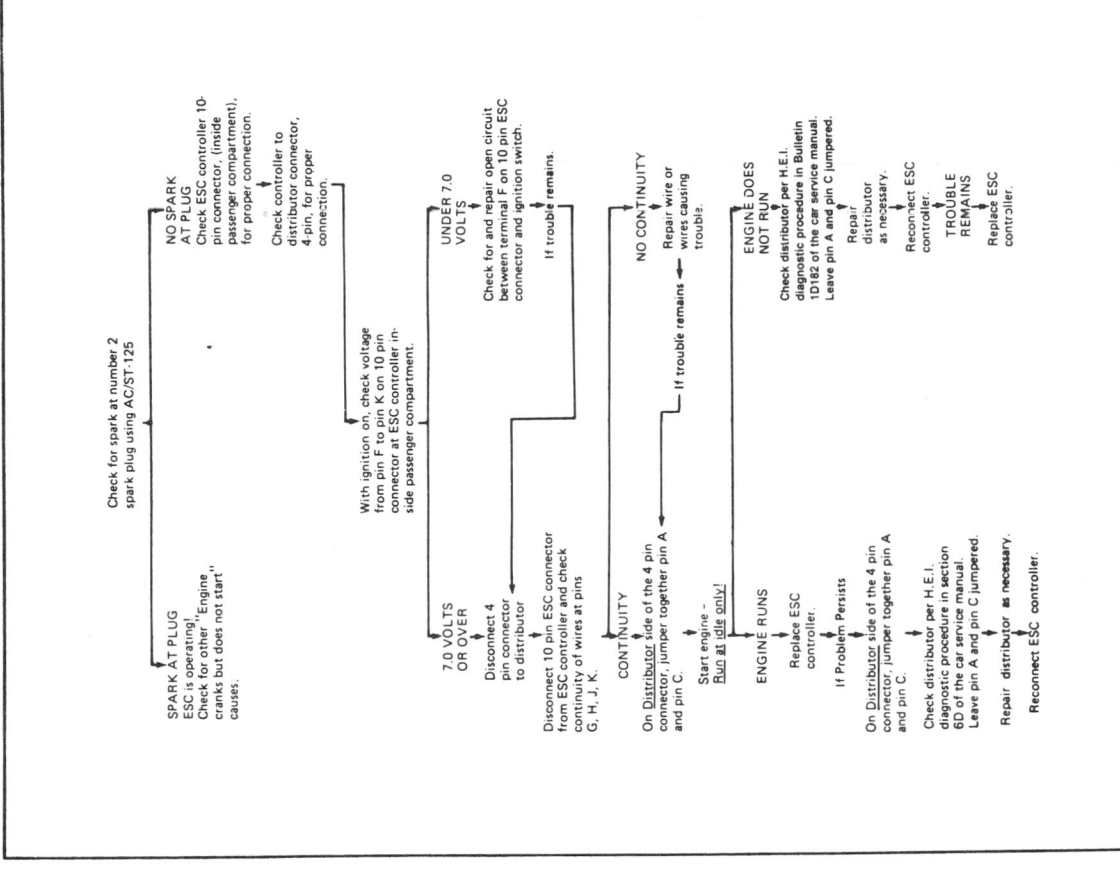

Check for spark at number 2 spark plug using AC/ST-125

SPARK AT PLUG
ESC is operating!
Check for other "Engine cranks but does not start" causes.

NO SPARK AT PLUG
Check ESC controller 10-pin connector, (inside passenger compartment), for proper connection.

Check controller to distributor connector, 4 pin, for proper connection.

With ignition on, check voltage from pin F to pin K on 10 pin connector at ESC controller inside passenger compartment.

7.0 VOLTS OR OVER
Disconnect 4 pin connector to distributor

UNDER 7.0 VOLTS
Check for and repair open circuit between terminal F on 10 pin ESC connector and ignition switch.

If trouble remains.

Disconnect 10 pin ESC connector from ESC controller and check continuity of wires at pins G, H, J, K.

CONTINUITY
On Distributor side of the 4 pin connector, jumper together pin A and pin C.

NO CONTINUITY
Repair wire or wires causing trouble.

If trouble remains

Start engine –
Run at idle only!

ENGINE RUNS
Replace ESC controller.

If Problem Persists

On Distributor side of the 4 pin connector, jumper together pin A and pin C.

Check distributor per H.E.I. diagnostic procedure in section 6D of the car service manual. Leave pin A and pin C jumpered.

Repair distributor as necessary.

Reconnect ESC controller.

ENGINE DOES NOT RUN
Check distributor per H.E.I. diagnostic procedure in Bulletin 1D182 of the car service manual. Leave pin A and pin C jumpered.

Repair distributor as necessary.

Reconnect ESC controller.

TROUBLE REMAINS
Replace ESC controller.

Engine Cranks, But Does Not Start—1980 Buick

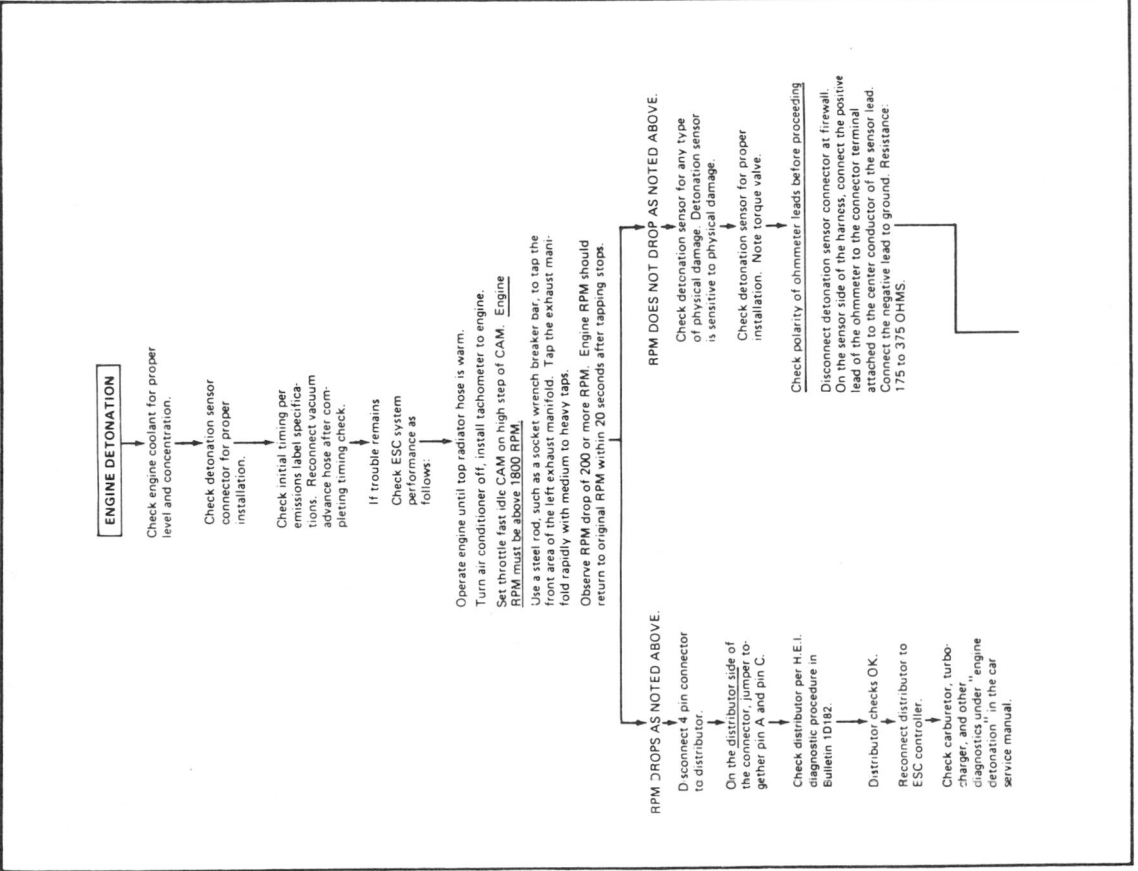

ENGINE DETONATION

Check engine coolant for proper level and concentration.

Check detonation sensor connector for proper installation.

Check initial timing per emissions label specifications. Reconnect vacuum advance hose after completing timing check.

If trouble remains

Check ESC system performance as follows:

Operate engine until top radiator hose is warm.

Turn air conditioner off, install tachometer to engine.

Set throttle fast idle CAM on high step of CAM. Engine RPM must be above 1800 RPM

Use a steel rod, such as a socket wrench breaker bar, to tap the front area of the left exhaust manifold. Tap the exhaust manifold rapidly with medium to heavy taps.

Observe RPM drop of 200 or more RPM. Engine RPM should return to original RPM within 20 seconds after tapping stops.

RPM DROPS AS NOTED ABOVE.

Disconnect 4 pin connector to distributor.

On the distributor side of the connector, jumper together pin A and pin C.

Check distributor per H.E.I. diagnostic procedure in Bulletin 1D182.

Distributor checks OK.

Reconnect distributor to ESC controller.

Check carburetor, turbocharger, and other diagnostics under "engine detonation" in the car service manual.

RPM DOES NOT DROP AS NOTED ABOVE.

Check detonation sensor for any type of physical damage. Detonation sensor is sensitive to physical damage.

Check detonation sensor for proper installation. Note torque valve.

Check polarity of ohmmeter leads before proceeding

Disconnect detonation sensor connector at firewall. On the sensor side of the harness, connect the positive lead of the ohmmeter to the connector terminal attached to the center conductor of the sensor lead. Connect the negative lead to ground. Resistance: 175 to 375 OHMS.

ESC Diagnosis (Cont'd.)—1980 Buick

ESC System—1980 Buick

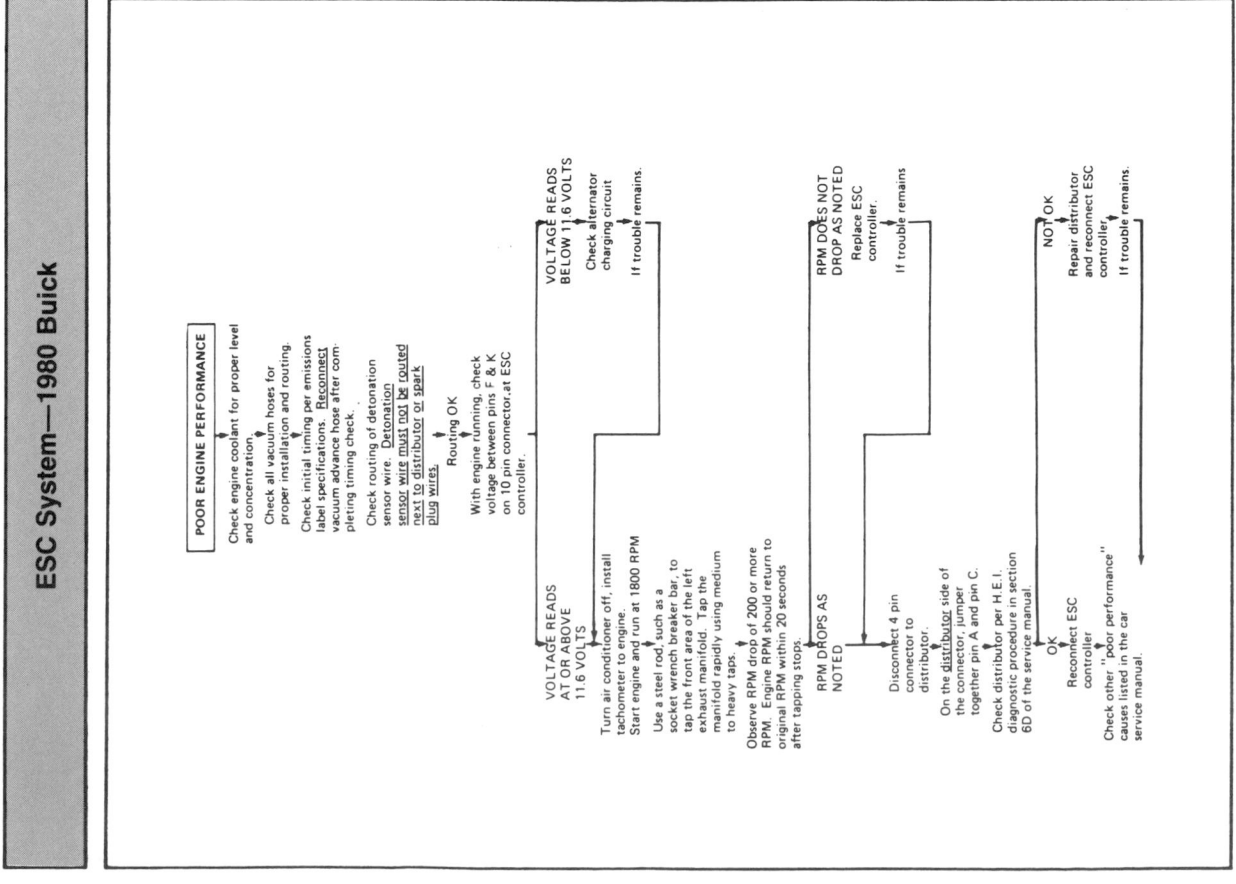

Engine Cranks, But Does Not Run

EST Diagnosis

ESC Check (EST Check Cont'd.)

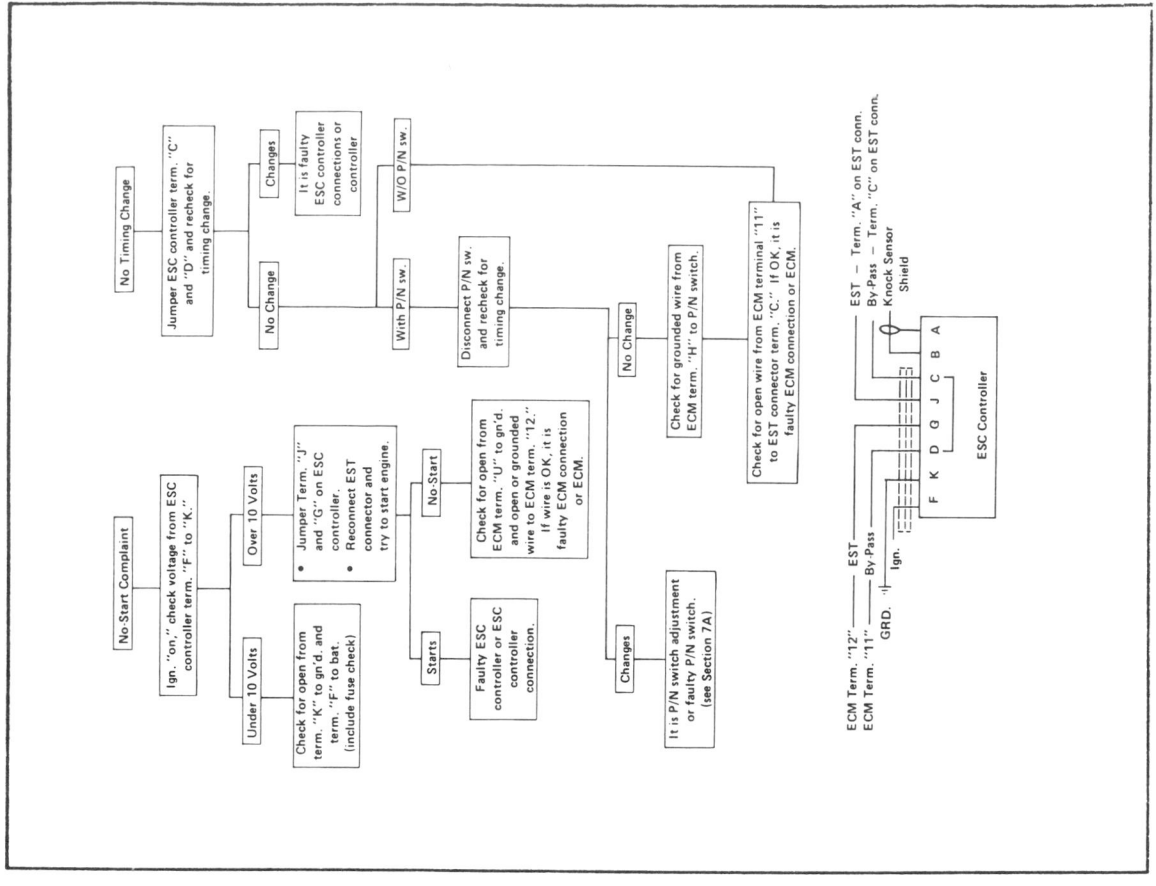

No Timing Change

Jumper ESC controller term. "C" and "D" and recheck for timing change.

Changes → It is faulty ESC controller connections or controller

No Change

W/O P/N sw.

With P/N sw. → Disconnect P/N sw. and recheck for timing change.

No Change → Check for grounded wire from ECM term. "H" to P/N switch.

Check for open wire from ECM terminal "11" to EST connector term. "C." If OK, it is faulty ECM connection or ECM.

Changes → It is P/N switch adjustment or faulty P/N switch. (see Section 7A)

No Start Complaint

Ign. "on," check voltage from ESC controller term. "F" to "K."

Over 10 Volts

Under 10 Volts → Check for open from term. "K" to gn'd. and term. "F" to bat. (include fuse check)

- Jumper Term. "J" and "G" on ESC controller.
- Reconnect EST connector and try to start engine.

No-Start → Check for open from ECM term. "U" to gn'd. and open or grounded wire to ECM term. "12." If wire is OK, it is faulty ECM connection or ECM.

Starts → Faulty ESC controller or ESC controller connection.

EST — Term. "A" on EST conn.
By-Pass — Term. "C" on EST conn.
Knock Sensor Shield

ECM Term. "12" ——— EST
ECM Term. "11" ——— By-Pass
GRD. —— Ign.

ESC Controller
F K D G J C B A

Engine Detonation

ESC PERFORMANCE DIAGNOSTIC

This chart should only be used after other causes of knock have been checked, i.e., timing, lack of EGR, engine temp., etc.

- Engine at fast idle, auto. trans in "park," manual trans. in "neutral."
- Note timing change as exhaust manifold is tapped with a hammer (nylon or similar mat'l.).

No retard → Disconnect knock sensor. Connect a jumper to knock sensor connector terminal and lay the jumper formed into a loop on top of the distributor, or hold it along a spark plug wire and note timing.

Retards → Measure resistance of sensor. Should be 175-375 ohms.

OK → Reconnect sensor. Disconnect ECS connector and check resistance from connector Term. "B" to "K." (175-375 ohms)

Not OK → Replace sensor

OK → Check for an open in wires to "B" and "K."

OK → Replace sensor

Not OK → Repair harness

OK → Repair sensor connection

Not OK → Repair harness

Retards

No trouble found

No retard → Reconnect sensor. Disconnect ESC connector and measure resistance from connector term. "B" to "K." Should be 175-375 ohms.

Not OK → Repair ESC harness

OK → Replace ESC controller

EST Diagnosis

Engine Cranks, But Does Not Run

Trouble Code 12
No Reference Pulses To The ECM (EST Distributor)

Check connections at four (4) terminal EST distributor connector.

- Not OK
  - Repair

- OK
  - With engine idling, connect digital voltmeter from ECM terminal "10" to ground. Check voltage at idle and at part throttle.
    - Increases at part throttle
      - Faulty ECM connections or ECM.
    - Doesn't increase at part throttle
      - Check for open or grounded reference lead from distributor module to ECM. If OK, replace HEI module.

9-26-80

TROUBLE CODE 42
EST BY PASS VOLTAGE LOW

- Disconnect four (4) terminal connector to distributor.
- Connect test light from Bat. + to by-pass terminal "C" in distributor side of connector.

- Light On
  - Check for grounded by-pass lead to distributor. If not grounded, replace HEI module.

- Light Off
  - Remove numbered terminal connector from ECM.
  - Connect test light from Bat. + to terminal "11" in connector removed from ECM.

  - Light On
    - Repair ground in by-pass lead from ECM to distributor.

  - Light Off
    - Check for a short between wires to ECM terminals 11 and 13. If shorted, replace ECM.

EST Diagnosis

ENGINE WON'T RUN COMPLAINT

Car will not run with distributor connected to ECM.

Leave EST Connector disconnected at distributor.

EST PERFORMANCE CHECK

Car will run with distributor connected to ECM.

- Trans. in park (A.T.) or Neutral (M.T.).
- Run engine at fast idle and note timing change as dist. EST connector is disconnected.

- Changes
  - Automatic Trans.
    - Engine idling in "Drive".
    - Note timing change as dist. EST Connector is disconnected, then reconnected.
    - Changes
    - No trouble found
  - Manual Trans.
    - With engine idling, check voltage output of map or vacuum sensor as vacuum hoses are disconnected and reconnected.
    - No Change—See Chart #34
    - Change

- No Change
  - With engine stopped, connect jumper from Term. "A" to "B" in dist. side of EST connector. Start engine ground "test" Term. and connect test light from Bat. + to term. "C" of EST connector.
    - Engine Stops
    - Engine Runs
      - Remove jumper between Term. "A" and "B".
        - Engine Runs
        - Engine Stops
          - Check for open or grounded distributor wire to term. "A" of EST connector. If wire OK, it is faulty HEI module connection or module.

          - Check distributor wires for:
            - Open to Mod. Term. "B."
            - Short between Mod. Term. "R" and "E." If wires OK, it is faulty HEI Mod conn. or Module.

Remove test light, reconnect four (4) Term. connector and — — —.

- No Start complaint
  - See following ESC check
    - With ESC
      - W/O P/N SW
        - No timing change
          - With P/N Sw
            - Disconnect P/N switch and recheck for timing change
              - No Change
                - Check for grounded wire from ECM Term. "H" to P/N sw.
              - Change
                - It is P/N sw adj. or faulty P/N switch. (See Section 7A.)
    - W/O ESC

- Check for open from ECM Term. "11" to EST Conn. Term. "C." If OK, it is faulty ECM Connector or ECM.

Check for open from ECM Term. "C" and open at ECM term. "12". If wire is OK, it is faulty ECM Term. "U" to gn'd and grounded wire to ECM term. "12". If wire is OK, it is faulty ECM connection or ECM.

PICK UP COIL

2.5L-L4

P N E R

+ C B

A B C D

10
11
12
13
U

Ignition coil separation from distributor cap—HEI system

HEI distributor with aluminum non-magnetic shield removed

21. Remove the three attaching screws and remove the magnetic shield.

22. Remove the retaining ring. Remove the pickup coil magnet and pole piece.

23. Remove the two module attaching screws and the capacitor attaching screw. Lift the module, capacitor and harness assembly from the base.

24. Disconnect the wiring harness from the module.

25. Check the module with an approved module tester.

26. Install the module, wiring harness and capacitor assembly. Use silicone lubricant on the housing under the module.

NOTE: The silicone helps cool the module in operation. Do not wipe the module clean.

Reassembly and Installation

27. Install the pickup coil assembly, shaft and gear, in the reverse of removal procedure.

28. Spin the shaft and, if used, operate the vacuum unit to insure that the teeth do not touch. To eliminate contact, loosen the three pickup screws. Then retighten and check for contact.

29. Assemble the rotor, cap assembly and attach wiring harness to cap.

Component Replacement

DISTRIBUTOR

Removal and Installation

1. Disconnect the ignition switch battery feed wire and the tachometer lead (if equipped) from the distributor cap. Also release the coil connectors from the cap. (Do not use a screwdriver or tool to release the locking tabs.)

2. Remove the distributor cap by turning the four latches counterclockwise. Move the cap out of the way. If necessary to remove the secondary wires from the cap, release the wire harness latches and remove the wiring harness retainer. The spark plug wire numbers are indicated on the retainer.

3. Remove the distributor clamp screw and hold-down clamp.

4. Note the position of the rotor. Then pull the distributor up until the rotor just stops turning counterclockwise. Again note the position of the rotor. To insure correct timing of the distributor, the distributor must be installed with the rotor correctly positioned.

CONTROL MODULE

Removal and Installation

1. Remove the distributor cap and rotor.

2. Disconnect the two pick-up leads from the module. (Observe the color code on the leads, as these cannot be interchanged.)

Exploded view of pick-up coil assembly

Module removal showing location of silicone lubricant

3. Remove the two module attaching screws.

4. Remove the module from the distributor base and remove the two wire connectors. Do not wipe grease from the module of distributor base if the same module is to be replaced. If a new module is to be installed, a package of silicone lubricant will be included with it. Spread the lubricant on the metal face of the module and on the distributor base where the module seats. This lubricant is important as it aids heat transfer for module cooling.

5. Installation is the reverse of removal.

PICK-UP COIL

Removal and Installation

1. Remove the distributor from the car.
2. Drive out the roll pin and remove the gear.
3. Remove the distributor shaft with rotor.
4. Remove the thin C-washer on top of the pickup coil assembly. Remove the pickup coil leads from the module and remove the pickup coil assembly. (Do not remove the three screws.)
5. Installation is the reverse of removal.

ELECTRONIC SPARK IGNITION SYSTEM DIAGNOSIS

Engine Cranks But Will Not Run

NOTE: IF A TACHOMETER IS CONNECTED TO THE TACHOMETER TERMINAL, DISCONNECT IT BEFORE PROCEEDING WITH THE TEST.

1. CHECK SPARK AT PLUG WITH ST-125 WHILE CRANKING (IF NO SPARK ON ONE WIRE, CHECK A SECOND WIRE).*

SPARK → CHECK FUEL, SPARK PLUGS, ETC.

NO SPARK (WITHOUT EST)

NO SPARK (WITH EST) → DISCONNECT 4 TERM. EST CONNECTOR AND RECHECK FOR SPARK.

NO SPARK

SPARK → SEE EST DIAGNOSIS

2. CHECK VOLTAGE AT DISTRIBUTOR "BAT" TERMINAL WHILE CRANKING

7 VOLTS OR MORE

UNDER 7 VOLTS → REPAIR PRIMARY CIRCUIT TO IGNITION SWITCH.

3. WITH IGNITION "ON" CHECK "TACH" TERMINAL VOLTAGE.

UNDER 1 VOLT → REPLACE IGNITION COIL

10 VOLTS OR MORE

1 TO 10 VOLTS → REPLACE MODULE AND CHECK FOR SPARK FROM COIL AS IN STEP 6.

4. CHECK FOR SPARK AT COIL OUTPUT TERMINAL WITH ST-125 WHILE CRANKING

SPARK → INSPECT CAP FOR WATER, CRACKS, ETC. IF OK, RE—PLACE ROTOR.

NO SPARK

SPARK → SYSTEM OK

NO SPARK → REPLACE IGN. COIL. IT TOO IS FAULTY.

5. REMOVE PICK-UP COIL LEADS FROM MODULE. CHECK TACH. TERM. VOLTAGE WITH "IGN" "ON". WATCH VOLTMETER AS TEST LIGHT IS MOMENTARILY CONNECTED FROM BAT. TO MODULE TERM:

4 TERM. MOD.	- TERM G
5 TERM. MOD. ESS OR ESC	- TERM. D
EMR	- TERM. H
7 TERM. MOD	- TERM. P

NOT MORE THAN 5 SECONDS.

NO DROP IN VOLTAGE → CHECK MODULE GRND. AND FOR OPEN IN WIRES FROM CAP TO DISTRIBUTOR. IF OK, REPLACE MOD.

VOLTAGE DROPS

6. CHECK FOR SPARK FROM COIL WITH ST-125 AS TEST LIGHT IS REMOVED FROM MODULE TERMINAL.

NO SPARK

SPARK → IT IS PICK-UP COIL OR CONNECTIONS. COIL RESISTANCE SHOULD BE 500-1500 OHMS AND NOT GROUNDED.

IF MODULE TESTER IS AVAILABLE, TEST MOD.

OK

BAD → REPLACE MOD.

CHECK IGN. COIL GROUND. IF OK, REPLACE IGN. COIL.

IF NO MODULE TESTER IS AVAILABLE

7. CHECK IGN. COIL GROUND CIRCUIT. IF OK, REPLACE IGN. COIL AND REPEAT STEP 6.

SPARK → SYSTEM OK

NO SPARK → COIL REMOVED IS OK, REINSTALL ORIGINAL COIL AND REPLACE MODULE.

*SOME EST PROBLEMS WILL RESULT IN ONE OR TWO SPARKS WHEN CRANKING IS STARTED, THEN SPARK WILL STOP. THIS IS CONSIDERED A "NO SPARK" CONDITION.

1978 TORONADO IGNITION SYSTEM

1978 Toronado ignition system wiring schematic

General Information

The Toronado EST ignition system does not use a standard HEI distributor. The distributor does not have a vacuum advance unit or mechanical advance weights. The rotor, ignition coil and pole piece are the same, but the pick-up coil and harness are different. There is a spark shield under the rotor to protect electronic circuits from false impulses. The system consists of the distributor, controller, temperature sensor and two separate harnesses. The engine coolant temperature sensor is different from the on-off switches used in other cars. It is part of the ignition system and resistance in the sensor changes with changes in coolant temperature. (Resistance lowers when temperature rises.)

The controller is an electronic unit that receives signals from the distributor pick-up coil, engine vacuum and atmospheric pressure. It then decides the most efficient advance based on the input signals and sends a signal to the distributor module to fire the spark plug. One of the electrical harnesses also contains the vacuum tube that connects the engine vacuum and to the controller in the car. The atmospheric pressure sensor in the controller is open to a port on top of the controller. There are two different controllers. The controllers used on California cars have different advance specifications. A "Check Ignition" light is located in the Instrument Panel Cluster and will come on under the following conditions:

- Ignition switch in the start position bulb check.
- If electrical system voltage is low and there is a heavy electrical load such as operation of power door lock, power windows, power seat, cigar lighter, rear window defogger, etc.

NOTE: The "Check Ignition" light will go off as soon as the electrical load is removed if the system voltage returns to normal.

- When checking the reference timing and the reference timing connector is grounded.
- If there should be a controller failure so the spark timing would not advance. Light will be on because of ground wire installed.
- If timing is incorrect, loosen distributor clamp bolt. Turn distributor clockwise to advance, counterclockwise to retard. Tighten clamp bolt.

Component Removal

CONTROLLER (UNDER GLOVE BOX)

Removal and Installation

1. Turn ignition off and disconnect connectors from controller.
2. Remove controller mounting bracket screws from lower edge of instrument panel.
3. Lower controller and disconnect vacuum connector and electrical connectors.
4. Remove controller to bracket screws and remove controller.
1. Position mounting bracket to controller so that electrical connectors will be down when bracket is installed in the car. Install bracket on controller, then install controller and bracket assembly.
2. Make sure ignition is off, then install connectors. Do not start engine until all mounting screws are tight.

Ajusting Ignition Timing (Magnetic Probe Timing Meter Preferred Method of Checking Timing.)

Connect a jumper wire to Reference Timing connector near controller assembly and ground other end of jumper. With transmission in "Park", drive wheels blocked, and parking brake applied, start engine and run at 1,100 RPM. Timing should be 20 degrees at 1,100 RPM (Exc. California 22 degrees at 1,100 RPM). "Check ignition" light should be on.

TEMPERATURE SENSOR (LEFT REAR OF INTAKE MANIFOLD)

Removal and Installation

1. Disconnect temperature sensor connector. (Press wide sides together to unlock tabs, then pull on harness and connector.)
2. Carefully turn radiator cap to release pressure on cooling system, then tighten cap.
3. Remove sensor.
4. Install new sensor, use thread sealer.
5. Install connector.

NOTE: If it is necessary to install a new vacuum tube, the tube must be placed inside the plastic conduit in the engine compartment. Connect the tube to the vacuum "T".

TO SET REFERENCE TIMING

1. CONNECT OPEN REFERENCE TIMING CONNECTOR (TAPED TO HARNESS) TO GROUND USING ABOUT A 2 FT. JUMPER WIRE.

2. CONNECT TIMING LIGHT OR METER AND TACHOMETER THEN START ENGINE. "CHECK IGNITION" LIGHT WILL BE ON IF GROUND WIRE WAS PROPERLY INSTALLED.

3. TIMING SHOULD BE 20 DEGREES AT 1100 RPM (CALIFORNIA 22 DEGREES AT 1100 RPM).

4. IF TIMING IS INCORRECT, LOOSEN DISTRIBUTOR CLAMP BOLT AND TURN DISTRIBUTOR TO ADJUST TIMING.

5. TIGHTEN DISTRIBUTOR CLAMP BOLT. REMOVE JUMPER WIRE. "CHECK IGNITION" LIGHT WILL GO OUT.

LOWER I.P. TIE-BAR

I.P. HARNESS EXTENSION

VACUUM TUBE AND CONNECTOR

IGNITION HARNESS ASM.

THE CONTROLLER ASSEMBLY IS LOCATED BELOW THE GLOVE BOX

REFERENCE TIMING CONNECTOR

CONTROLLER ASSEMBLY

Setting reference timing on Toronado

IGNITION SYSTEM DIAGNOSIS —TORONADO 1978

(MAKE SURE CONTROLLER CASE IS GROUNDED)

ENGINE DOES NOT START. CRANKS OK. BATTERY FULLY CHARGED.

Check for spark at plug with AC/ST-125 or J-26792

SPARK OK

Trouble is not ignition. Check spark plugs, cables and fuel system.

NO SPARK

Turn ignition key to "run" and check voltage at the following locations. (Look at circuit diagram for wire connections.)
1. Ignition wire to distributor. 12 volts or more is ok. Less than 12 volts, check ignition wire from distributor to ignition switch for loose or open connections. Also check ignition switch. (Should be 12 volts or more at ignition No. 1 terminal.)
2. Make sure controller case is grounded.
3. Check voltage at terminal J (PNK wire) in 4 wire connector at controller. 12 volts or more is ok. Less than 12 volts, check PNK wire from controller to ignition switch for loose or open connections.
4. Check voltage at terminal J (Brn wire) in 6 wire connector at controller. Should be .5 to 2 volts while cranking.

VOLTAGE OK

Check distributor cap, rotor ignition coil and module. (pickup coil is ok). Check wiring from controller to distributor for open circuit (see circuit diagram) Replace part that checks bad.

PICK-UP COIL
WHITE   DK. GRN.
MODULE – BROWN

VOLTAGE NOT OK

1. Turn ignition off and disconnect distributor harness connector from controller harness.
2. Connect ohmmeter to ground and touch probe to each of the three terminals in the distributor half of the connector. Each terminal should show 1000 ohms or more.

ONE OR MORE READINGS NOT OK

1. Check wires into distributor for short circuit.
2. If reading on module terminal was less than 1000 ohms and wire to module was not shorted, test module with tester J-24642.
3. If no trouble found, replace pickup coil and harness assembly.

ALL READINGS OK

Connect ohmmeter to the two pickup coil terminals in the connector shown in the drawing. Reading should be 500 to 1500 ohms.

READING NOT OK

Replace pickup coil and harness assembly

READING OK

1. Remove distributor cap, disconnect single wire terminal from module.
2. Connect ohmmeter to wire and to module terminal in the connector shown in the drawing. If wire is good, reading will be zero ohms resistance.

WIRE IS BAD (NO READING)

Replace pickup coil and harness assembly

WIRE IS GOOD (ZERO OHMS)

1. Connect jumper wire to ground and to wire removed from module.
2. Connect distributor harness connector.
3. Remove 6 wire connector from controller.
4. Connect ohmmeter to terminal E (Wht wire) and terminal C (DK grn) wire in harness connector. Resistance should be 500-1500 ohms.
5. Connect ohmmeter to ground and to terminal J (brn wire). Reading should be zero resistance.

ALL READINGS OK

Harness is ok, check to make sure controller is grounded. If ok, make sure ignition is turned off then replace controller. (Do not turn ignition key on until controller is grounded.)

ONE OR MORE READINGS NOT OK

Replace harness

IGNITION SYSTEM DIAGNOSIS
—TORONADO 1978

(MAKE SURE CONTROLLER CASE IS GROUNDED)

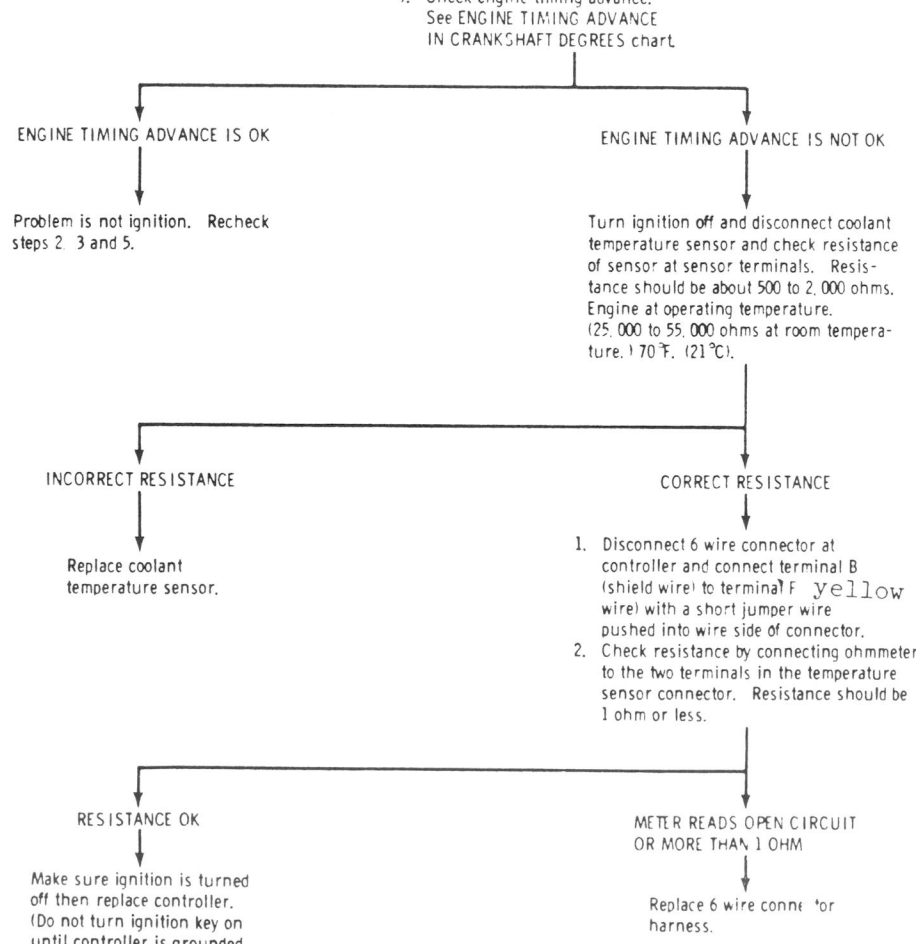

HARD STARTING, ROUGH ENGINE, POOR PERFORMANCE
(Battery fully charged - 12 Volts or more)

1. If CHECK IGNITION light is on (engine running), use diagnosis chart CHECK IGNITION LIGHT ON - ENGINE RUNNING.
2. If CHECK IGNITION light is off, check fuel system, choke, spark plugs and cables.
3. Check all vacuum hoses and white vacuum tube to controller for pinches or leaks.
4. Make sure harness connections to distributor, coolant sensor and controller are good and controller is grounded.

5. Connect voltmeter to ground and touch probe to ignition wire at distributor 12 volts or more is ok. If less, check ignition wire from distributor to ignition switch. Also check ignition switch. Refer to circuit diagram.
6. Connect voltmeter to ground and touch probe to terminal J (PNK wire) in 4 wire connector at controller. Should be 12 volts or more. If less, check PNK wire from controller to ignition switch for loose connections. Also check ignition switch.
7. Remove distributor cap, check rotor and cap for signs of arcing. Check module with J-24642.
8. Check reference timing.
9. Check engine timing advance. See ENGINE TIMING ADVANCE IN CRANKSHAFT DEGREES chart.

ENGINE TIMING ADVANCE IS OK

Problem is not ignition. Recheck steps 2, 3 and 5.

ENGINE TIMING ADVANCE IS NOT OK

Turn ignition off and disconnect coolant temperature sensor and check resistance of sensor at sensor terminals. Resistance should be about 500 to 2,000 ohms. Engine at operating temperature. (25,000 to 55,000 ohms at room temperature.) 70°F. (21°C).

INCORRECT RESISTANCE

Replace coolant temperature sensor.

CORRECT RESISTANCE

1. Disconnect 6 wire connector at controller and connect terminal B (shield wire) to terminal F yellow wire) with a short jumper wire pushed into wire side of connector.
2. Check resistance by connecting ohmmeter to the two terminals in the temperature sensor connector. Resistance should be 1 ohm or less.

RESISTANCE OK

Make sure ignition is turned off then replace controller. (Do not turn ignition key on until controller is grounded.

METER READS OPEN CIRCUIT OR MORE THAN 1 OHM

Replace 6 wire connector harness.

IGNITION SYSTEM DIAGNOSIS —TORONADO 1978

(MAKE SURE CONTROLLER CASE IS GROUNDED)

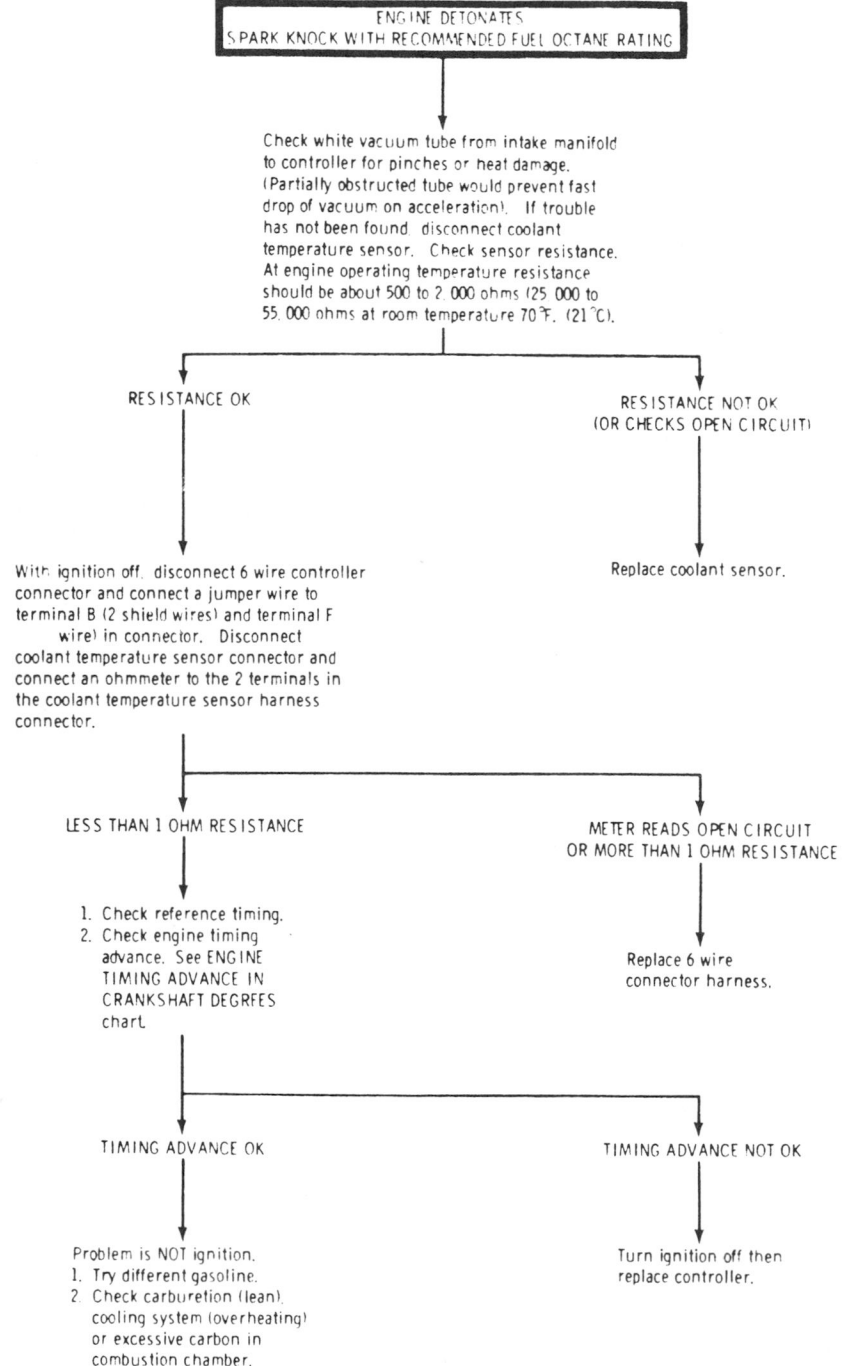

ENGINE DETONATES
SPARK KNOCK WITH RECOMMENDED FUEL OCTANE RATING

Check white vacuum tube from intake manifold to controller for pinches or heat damage. (Partially obstructed tube would prevent fast drop of vacuum on acceleration). If trouble has not been found, disconnect coolant temperature sensor. Check sensor resistance. At engine operating temperature resistance should be about 500 to 2,000 ohms (25,000 to 55,000 ohms at room temperature 70°F. (21°C).

RESISTANCE OK

RESISTANCE NOT OK
(OR CHECKS OPEN CIRCUIT)

With ignition off, disconnect 6 wire controller connector and connect a jumper wire to terminal B (2 shield wires) and terminal F wire) in connector. Disconnect coolant temperature sensor connector and connect an ohmmeter to the 2 terminals in the coolant temperature sensor harness connector.

Replace coolant sensor.

LESS THAN 1 OHM RESISTANCE

METER READS OPEN CIRCUIT
OR MORE THAN 1 OHM RESISTANCE

1. Check reference timing.
2. Check engine timing advance. See ENGINE TIMING ADVANCE IN CRANKSHAFT DEGREES chart.

Replace 6 wire connector harness.

TIMING ADVANCE OK

TIMING ADVANCE NOT OK

Problem is NOT ignition.
1. Try different gasoline.
2. Check carburetion (lean), cooling system (overheating) or excessive carbon in combustion chamber.

Turn ignition off then replace controller.

137

IGNITION SYSTEM DIAGNOSIS
—TORONADO 1978

(MAKE SURE CONTROLLER CASE IS GROUNDED)

HOT LIGHT ON (IGNITION KEY IN "RUN")

Check usual causes of hot light on - Low Coolant, Low Oil, etc. Correct if required.

If no trouble found, disconnect 2-wire connector at coolant temperature sensor, turn ignition switch to run position.

HOT LIGHT ON → Turn ignition switch off. Disconnect 3 wire connector. (See Fig. 1) Turn ignition switch to run position.

HOT LIGHT OFF → Replace coolant temperature sensor.

HOT LIGHT ON → Locate and repair short circuit in dk. green wire from 3 wire connector to instrument cluster and to ignition switch. (If car has multifunction tone generator refer to section 9 for diagnosis of HOT LIGHT.)

HOT LIGHT OFF →
1. Turn ignition off. Disconnect controller and temperature sensor 6 wire connector. Touch ohmmeter probes to the two terminals in the temperature sensor connector. Meter should show open circuit.
2. Connect ohmmeter to ground and to each terminal. Meter should show open circuit

ALL READINGS OK → Make sure ignition is turned off, then replace controller. Be sure controller case is grounded.

READINGS NOT OK → Wires are shorted. Replace harness.

"CHECK IGNITION" AND HOT LIGHT ON ENGINE RUNS ROUGH, NO POWER

Turn ignition off then replace controller.

"CHECK IGNITION" LIGHT ON (ENGINE RUNNING, BATTERY FULLY CHARGED)

Check reference timing wire (purple) at controller. The connector should be disconnected (not grounded)

Check voltage at controller 4 wire connector terminal J (pink wire) while engine is running, transmission in PARK, parking brakes applied.

VOLTAGE LESS THAN 11 VOLTS → Connect voltmeter to battery. Turn accessories off, run engine at fast idle.

LESS THAN 12 VOLTS → Check generator belt tension, if ok repair charging system.

12 VOLTS OR MORE → Check for loose connection from terminal J in controller 4 wire connector through instrument panel harness connectors to ignition switch. Repair as required.

VOLTAGE ABOVE 11 VOLTS → Turn ignition key to run position (engine off). Disconnect three wire connector. See Fig. 1

LIGHT OUT → Turn ignition key off then replace controller.

LIGHT ON → Circuit grounded between 3 wire connector and instrument cluster connector. Repair as required.

RADIO CONNECTOR

INSTRUMENT CLUSTER CONNECTORS

TO CONTROLLER
3 WIRE CONNECTOR

WIRING CLAMP

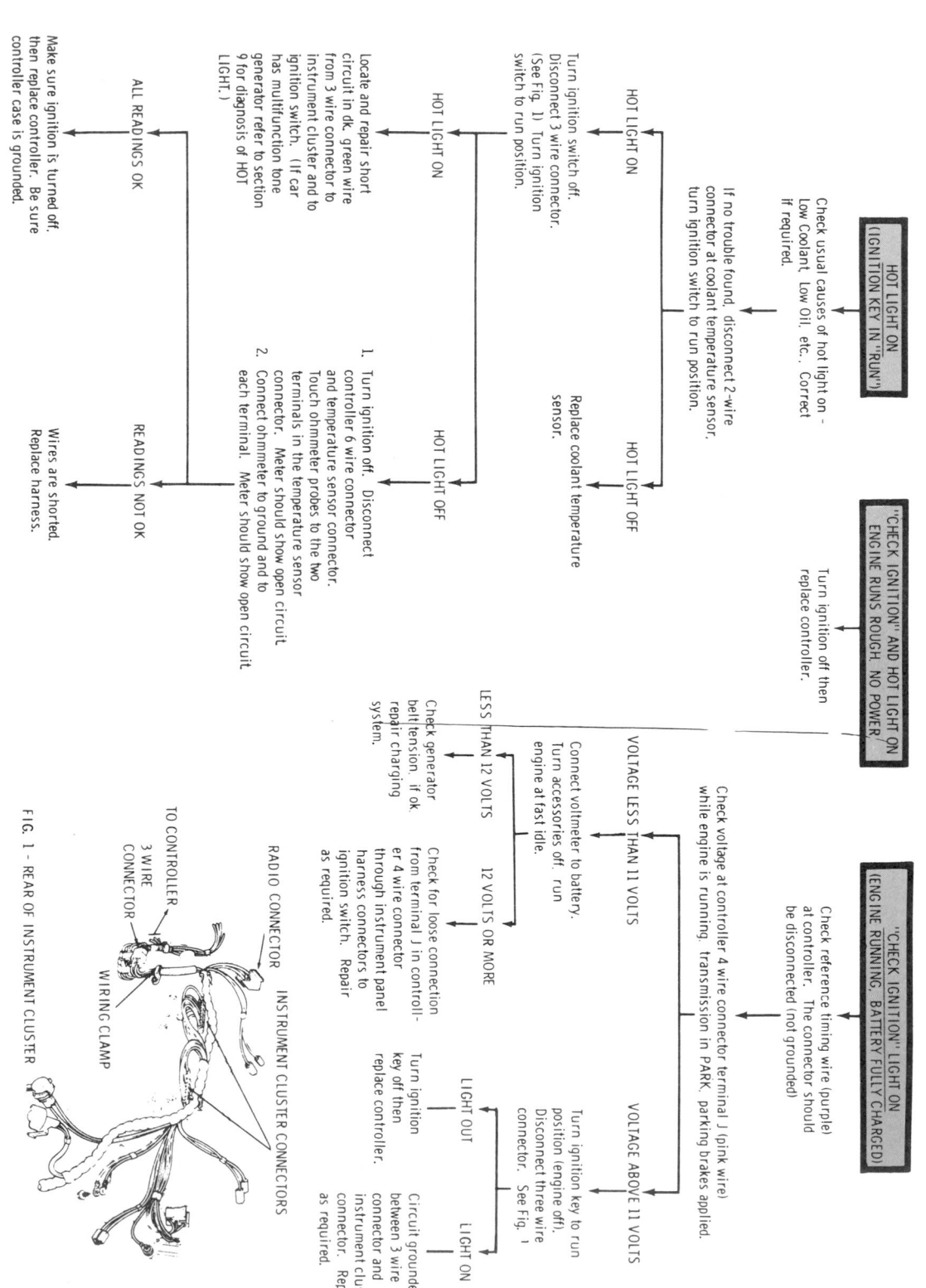

FIG. 1 - REAR OF INSTRUMENT CLUSTER

GM COMPUTER CONTROLLED COIL IGNITION (C3I) SYSTEM

General Information

COMPONENTS

The C3I system eliminates the need for a distributor to control the flow of current between the battery and spark plugs. In its place, an electromagnetic sensor consisting of a Hall effect switch, magnet and interruptor ring. The gear on the shaft of this sensor is connected directly to the camshaft gear. At the heart of this system is an electronic coil module that replaces the distributor and coil used on previous electronic ignition systems. A microprocessor within the module receives and processes signals from the crankshaft and camshaft and, by way of three interconnecting coils, distributes high voltage current to the spark plugs.

Electromagnetic sensors take position readings from the crankshaft and camshaft, then transmit these readings to the electronics package. Using the information relayed from the electronic control module, the microprocessor then selects and sequentially triggers each of the three interconnecting coils to fire the spark plugs at the proper crankshaft position. An electronic spark control (ESC) is incorporated into the system to adjust the spark timing according to engine load and operating conditions. This closed loop system includes a piezoelectric sensor which transforms engine detonation vibrations into an electrical signal which is then fed to the electronic control module. The ECM uses this and other information on engine speed (rpm), intake air mass, coolant temperature and converter clutch operation to adjust the spark advance for the most efficient performance with the lowest emissions. Because of this feature, there is no timing adjustment or regular maintenance required aside from periodic replacement of the spark plugs.

1	C³ IGNITION MODULE AND COIL ASSEMBLY
2	CAM SENSOR
3	CRANKSHAFT SENSOR

Computer Controlled Coil Ignition (C3I) components

Wiring schematic of C3I ignition system—V6 shown

1 CRANKSHAFT SENSOR
2 SENSOR RETAINING BOLT
3 CRANKSHAFT SENSOR HOUSING
4 CAMSHAFT POSITION SENSOR

C3I system crankshaft and camshaft position sensor locations

SYSTEM OPERATION

The C3I system uses a waste spark method of spark distribution. Companion cylinders are paired (1–4, 5–2, 3–6 on the 3.8L V6 engine) and the spark occurs simultaneously in both cylinders. The cylinder on the exhaust stroke requires very little of the available voltage to arc, so the remaining high voltage is used by the cylinder in the firing position (TDC/compression). This same process is repeated when the companion cylinders reverse roles. There are three separate coils combined in the sealed coil/module assembly on the V6 engine. Spark distribution is synchronized by a signal from the crankshaft sensor which the ignition module uses to trigger each coil at the proper time.

NOTE: The signal from the camshaft sensor is also used by the fuel injection electronic control module to trigger the fuel injectors, so a failed sensor can affect both the fuel and ignition system. A 7.5 amp ECM fuse is used to provide a low current source for the voltage to the sensors and internal circuitry; a 10 amp fuse provides voltage for the ignition coils.

This system also incorporates an electronic spark timing (EST) system similar to other Delco distributor ignition systems. All connectors are lettered to make circuit identification easier. Terminal C (Crankshaft sensor) provides the ECM with engine speed (rpm) and crankshaft position information by passing a signal to the ignition module and then to ECM terminal B5. A plate with three vanes is mounted to the harmonic balancer and the vanes pass through slots in the crankshaft sensor. As the vanes pass through the slots, the Hall effect switch triggers and sends a voltage signal to the ECM. The signal from the Hall effect switch is either high or low and is used to trigger the ignition module for proper engine timing. Both the camshaft and crankshaft signal must be received by the ignition module in order for the ECM to take over spark timing control from the ignition module. An open or grounded

Wiring schematic of C3I system used on the 3.8L turbocharged V6 engine circuit (terminal B) will set a trouble code 42 in the ECM memory and the engine will run in the bypass or "limp home" mode with the timing fixed at 10 degrees BTDC. The EST terminal A circuit triggers the HEI module by passing a reference signal which the ECM uses to advance or retard the timing according to the input from the crankshaft sensor. Cam terminal E is used by the ECM to determine when the No. 1 cylinder is on the compression stroke by a signal from the Hall effect camshaft position sensor. A loss of the cam signal will store a trouble code 41 if the engine is running and a loss of sensor signal during cranking will prevent the engine from starting.

The electronic control module uses information from the coolant sensor and mass air flow sensor in addition to engine speed to calculate the spark advance to allow more spark advance when the engine is cold or under minimum load. The ECM will retard the timing when the engine is hot or under a heavy load. When the system is running on the HEI module, it grounds the electronic spark timing signal. If the ECM detects voltage in the bypass circuit through a loss of ground for the EST signal, it sets a trouble code 42 and will not switch into the EST mode. When the engine reaches 400 rpm, the ECM applies 5 volts to the bypass circuit and the EST voltage will vary. If the bypass circuit is open, the ECM will store a trouble code 42.

Performance Tests
Overhaul Procedures

IGNITION COIL

Removal and Installation

1. Disconnect the negative battery cable.
2. Remove the spark plug wires.
3. Remove the Torx Screws holding the coil to the ignition module.
4. Tilt the coil assembly to the rear and remove the coil to module connectors.
5. Remove the coil assembly.
6. Installation is the reverse of removal.

IGNITION MODULE

Removal and Installation

1. Disconnect the negative battery cable.
2. Disconnect the 14-pin connector at the ignition module.
3. Remove the spark plug wires at the coil assembly.
4. Remove the nuts and washers securing the ignition module assembly to the mounting bracket.
5. Remove the Torx screws securing the ignition module to the coil.
6. Tilt the coil and disconnect the coil to module connectors.
7. Separate the coil and module.
8. Installation is the reverse of removal.

CRANKSHAFT SENSOR

Removal and Installation

NOTE: It is not necessary to remove the sensor bracket

1. Disconnect the negative battery cable.
2. Disconnect the sensor 3-way connector.
3. Raise the vehicle and support it safely.
4. Rotate the harmonic balancer so the slot in the disc is aligned with the sensor.
5. Loosen the sensor retaining bolt.
6. Slide the sensor outboard and remove through the notch in the sensor housing.
7. Install the new sensor in the housing and rotate the harmonic balancer so that the disc is positioned in the sensor.
8. Adjust the sensor so that there is an equal distance on each

Camshaft sensor adjustment

side of the disc. There should be approximately .030 in. (.76 mm) clearance between the disc and the sensor.

9. Tighten the retaining bolt and recheck the clearance.
10. Install remaining components in the reverse order of removal.

CAMSHAFT POSITION SENSOR

Removal and Installation

NOTE: If only the camshaft sensor is being replaced, it is not necessary to remove the entire assembly. The sensor is replaceable separately.

1. Disconnect the negative battery cable.
2. Disconnect the ignition module 14-pin connector.
3. Remove the spark plug wires at the coil assembly.
4. Remove the ignition module bracket assembly.
5. Disconnect the sensor 3-way connector.
6. Remove the sensor mounting screws, then remove the sensor.
7. Installation is the reverse of removal.

CAMSHAFT POSITION SENSOR DRIVE ASSEMBLY

Removal and Installation

1. Follow steps 1–6 of the cam sensor removal procedure. Note the position of the slot in the rotating vane.
2. Remove the bolt securing the drive assembly to the engine.
3. Remove the drive assembly.
4. Install the drive assembly with the slot in the vane. Install mounting bolt.
5. Install the camshaft sensor.
6. Rotate the engine to set the No. 1 cylinder at TDC/compression.
7. Mark the harmonic balancer and rotate the engine to 25 degrees after top dead center.
8. Remove the plug wires from the coil assembly.
9. Using weatherpack removal tool J-28742-A, or equivalent, remove terminal B of the sensor 3-way connector on the module side.
10. Probe terminal B by installing a jumper and reconnecting the wire removed to the jumper wire.
11. Connect a voltmeter between the jumper wire and ground.
12. With the key ON and the engine stopped, rotate the camshaft sensor counterclockwise until the sensor switch just closes. This is indicated by the voltage reading going from a high 5–12 volts to a low 0–2 volts. The low voltage indicates the switch is closed.
13. Tighten the retaining bolt and reinstall the wire into terminal B.
14. Install remaining components.

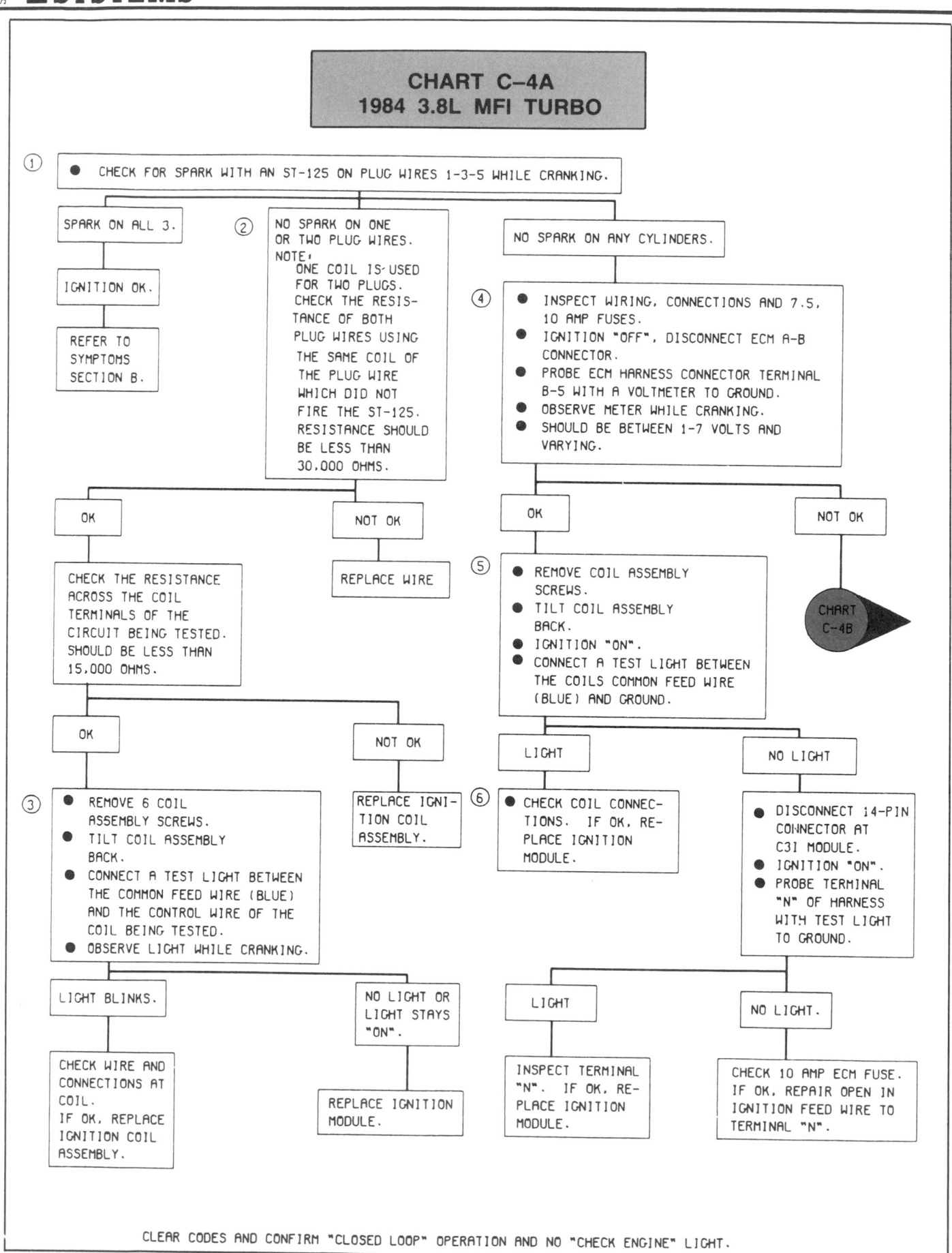

**CHART C-4A
1984 3.8L MFI TURBO**

① ● CHECK FOR SPARK WITH AN ST-125 ON PLUG WIRES 1-3-5 WHILE CRANKING.

SPARK ON ALL 3.

IGNITION OK.

REFER TO SYMPTOMS SECTION B.

② NO SPARK ON ONE OR TWO PLUG WIRES. NOTE: ONE COIL IS USED FOR TWO PLUGS. CHECK THE RESISTANCE OF BOTH PLUG WIRES USING THE SAME COIL OF THE PLUG WIRE WHICH DID NOT FIRE THE ST-125. RESISTANCE SHOULD BE LESS THAN 30,000 OHMS.

NO SPARK ON ANY CYLINDERS.

④ ● INSPECT WIRING, CONNECTIONS AND 7.5, 10 AMP FUSES.
● IGNITION "OFF", DISCONNECT ECM A-B CONNECTOR.
● PROBE ECM HARNESS CONNECTOR TERMINAL B-5 WITH A VOLTMETER TO GROUND.
● OBSERVE METER WHILE CRANKING.
● SHOULD BE BETWEEN 1-7 VOLTS AND VARYING.

OK

NOT OK

REPLACE WIRE

CHECK THE RESISTANCE ACROSS THE COIL TERMINALS OF THE CIRCUIT BEING TESTED. SHOULD BE LESS THAN 15,000 OHMS.

OK

⑤ ● REMOVE COIL ASSEMBLY SCREWS.
● TILT COIL ASSEMBLY BACK.
● IGNITION "ON".
● CONNECT A TEST LIGHT BETWEEN THE COILS COMMON FEED WIRE (BLUE) AND GROUND.

NOT OK

CHART C-4B

OK

NOT OK

REPLACE IGNITION COIL ASSEMBLY.

LIGHT

NO LIGHT

③ ● REMOVE 6 COIL ASSEMBLY SCREWS.
● TILT COIL ASSEMBLY BACK.
● CONNECT A TEST LIGHT BETWEEN THE COMMON FEED WIRE (BLUE) AND THE CONTROL WIRE OF THE COIL BEING TESTED.
● OBSERVE LIGHT WHILE CRANKING.

⑥ ● CHECK COIL CONNECTIONS. IF OK, REPLACE IGNITION MODULE.

● DISCONNECT 14-PIN CONNECTOR AT C3I MODULE.
● IGNITION "ON".
● PROBE TERMINAL "N" OF HARNESS WITH TEST LIGHT TO GROUND.

LIGHT BLINKS.

CHECK WIRE AND CONNECTIONS AT COIL. IF OK, REPLACE IGNITION COIL ASSEMBLY.

NO LIGHT OR LIGHT STAYS "ON".

REPLACE IGNITION MODULE.

LIGHT

INSPECT TERMINAL "N". IF OK, REPLACE IGNITION MODULE.

NO LIGHT.

CHECK 10 AMP ECM FUSE. IF OK, REPAIR OPEN IN IGNITION FEED WIRE TO TERMINAL "N".

CLEAR CODES AND CONFIRM "CLOSED LOOP" OPERATION AND NO "CHECK ENGINE" LIGHT.

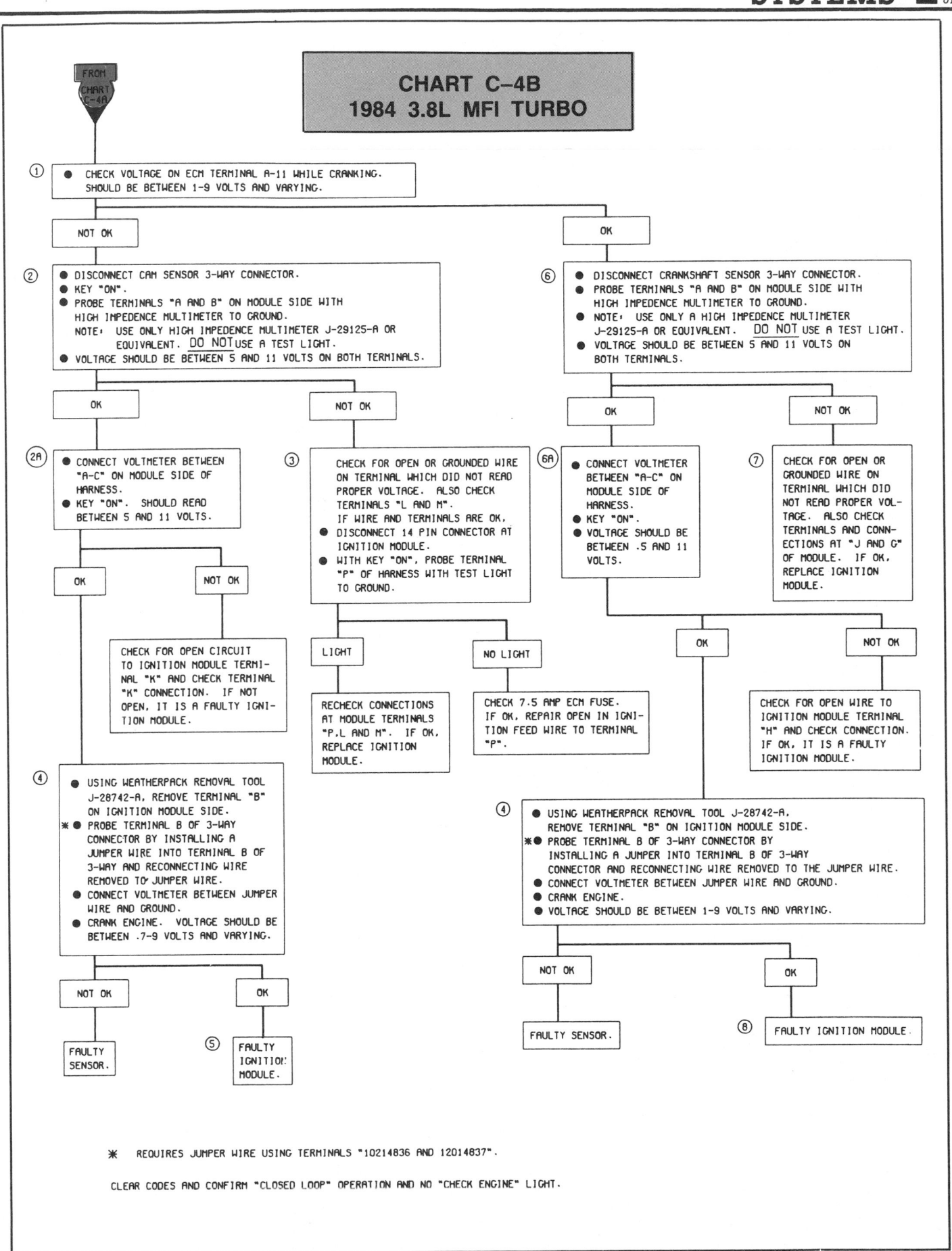

HITACHI ELECTRONIC IGNITION SYSTEM

General Information

COMPONENTS AND OPERATION

The Hitachi electronic ignition system uses a magnetic pulse/igniter distributor and a conventional ignition coil. The distributor cap, rotor, advance mechanism (vacuum and centrifugal) and secondary ignition wires are also of standard design. The system was first introduced on the 1979 Honda Accord and Prelude, and used an external module (igniter) mounted on the firewall. The distributor contains the stator, reluctor, and pulse generator (pick-up coil) which replaced the point assembly. Beginning with some 1980 models, the size of the igniter was reduced and located within the distributor and the shape of the stator was changed. The operation of the system still remains the same.

As the teeth of the reluctor align with the stator, a signal is generated by the pulse generator (pick-up coil) and sent to the igniter

Schematic of Hitachi ignition system used on 1979 Honda Accord models

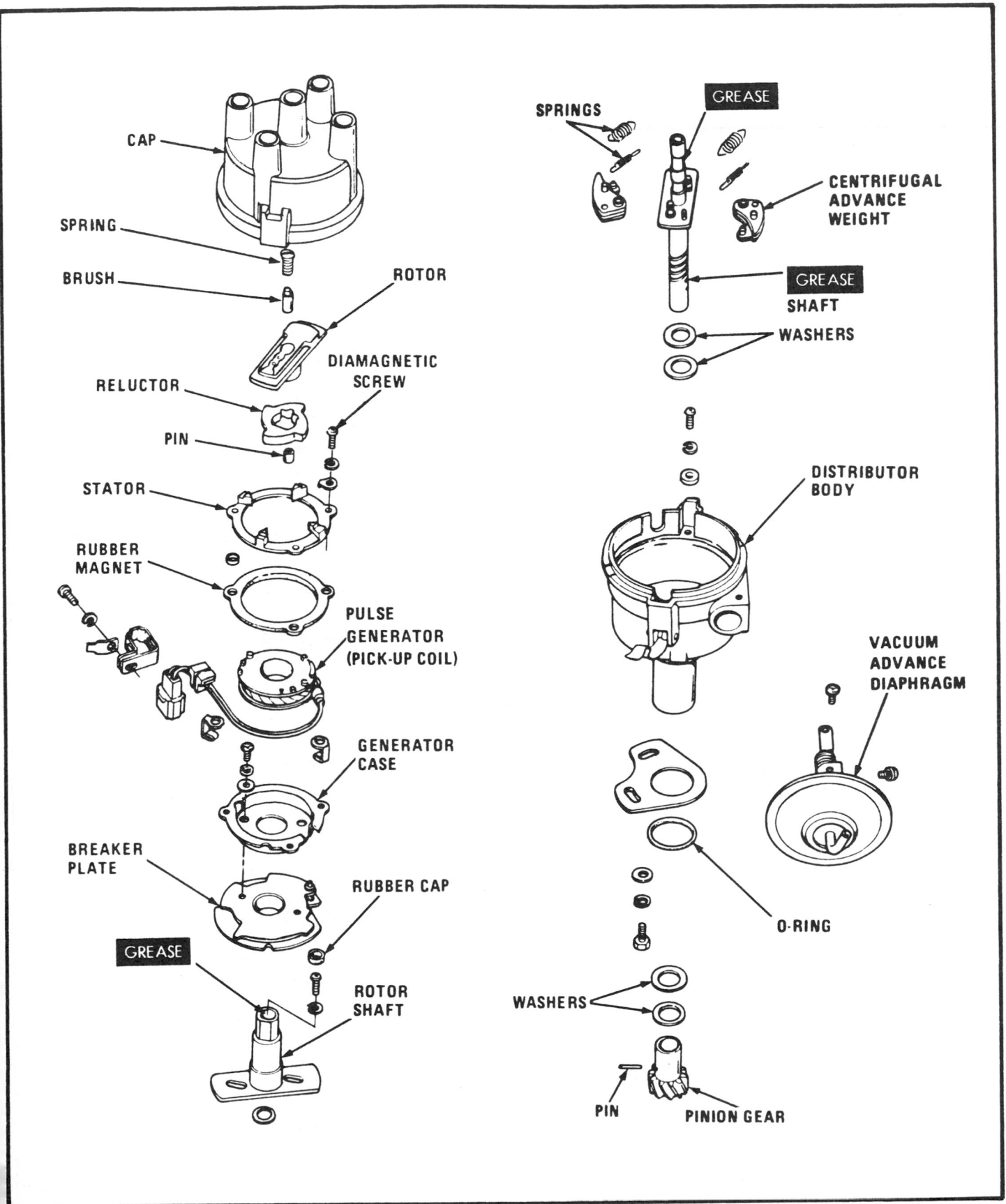

CAP

SPRING

BRUSH

ROTOR

RELUCTOR

DIAMAGNETIC SCREW

PIN

STATOR

RUBBER MAGNET

PULSE GENERATOR (PICK-UP COIL)

GENERATOR CASE

BREAKER PLATE

GREASE

RUBBER CAP

ROTOR SHAFT

SPRINGS

GREASE

CENTRIFUGAL ADVANCE WEIGHT

GREASE

SHAFT

WASHERS

DISTRIBUTOR BODY

VACUUM ADVANCE DIAPHRAGM

O-RING

WASHERS

PIN

PINION GEAR

Exploded view of 1979 Honda distributor

(module). The module, upon receiving the signal, opens the primary of the ignition coil. As the primary magnetic field collapses, a high voltage surge is developed in the secondary windings of the coil. This high voltage surge travels from the coil to the distributor cap and rotor through the secondary ignition wires to the spark plugs.

Performance Tests

When testing the Hitachi electronic ignition system, follow the following service precautions:

• Never reverse battery polarity.

• Do not let the pulse generator wires touch the secondary ignition wires with the engine running.

• Do not attempt any service procedures that will produce abnormal pulses in the system.

• Connect the pulse type tachometer to the negative terminal of the ignition coil.

• Make sure all wires and cables are connected properly.

Schematic of Hitachi ignition system used on 1980 and later Honda Accord models

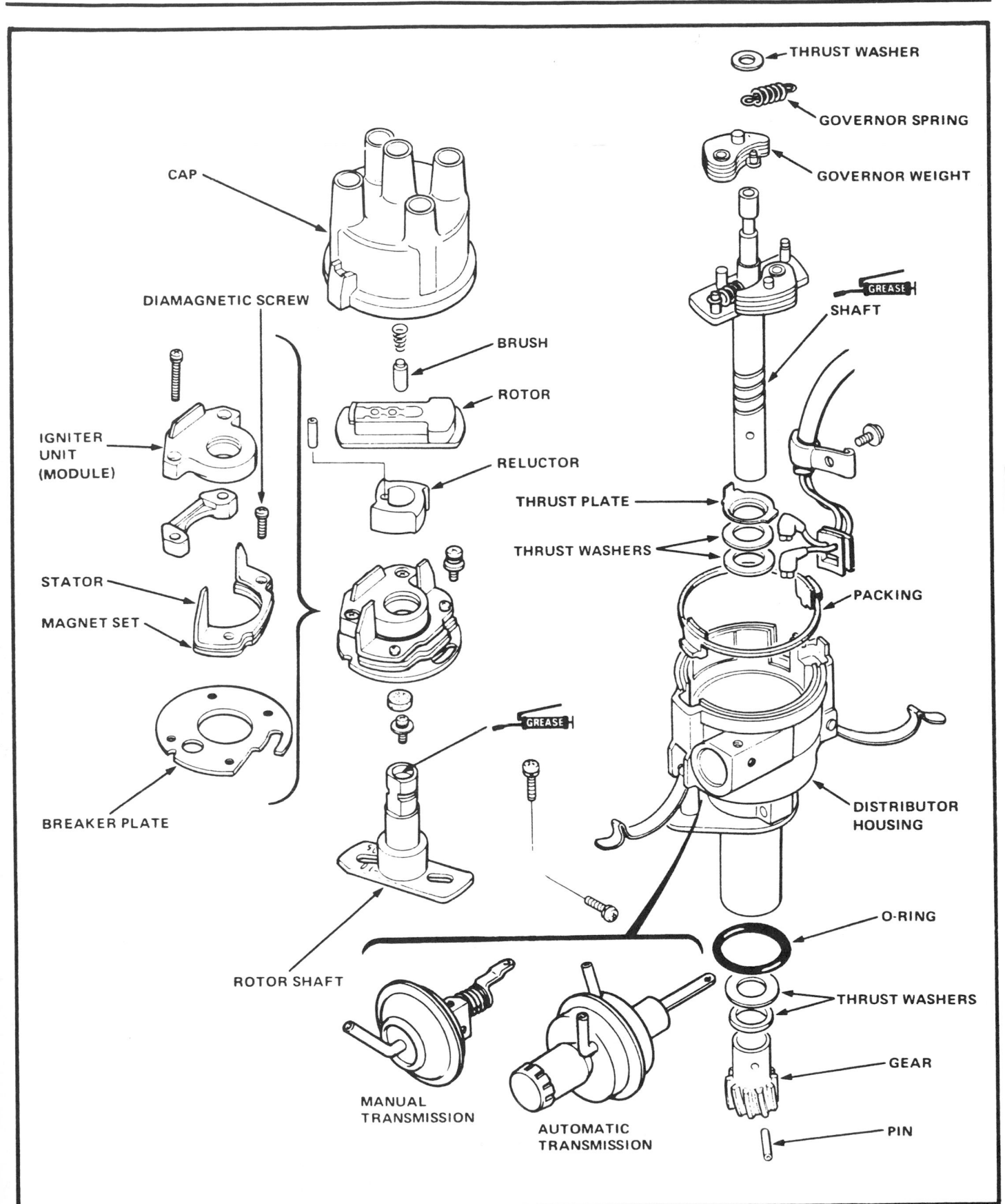

CAP

DIAMAGNETIC SCREW

BRUSH

ROTOR

RELUCTOR

IGNITER UNIT (MODULE)

STATOR

MAGNET SET

BREAKER PLATE

ROTOR SHAFT

GREASE

MANUAL TRANSMISSION

AUTOMATIC TRANSMISSION

THRUST WASHER

GOVERNOR SPRING

GOVERNOR WEIGHT

GREASE

SHAFT

THRUST PLATE

THRUST WASHERS

PACKING

DISTRIBUTOR HOUSING

O-RING

THRUST WASHERS

GEAR

PIN

Exploded view of 1981 Honda distributor

HITACHI PERFORMANCE TEST SPECIFICATIONS
(All measurements given in ohms)

| Manufac-turer | Year | Model | Coil Circuit | | Air Gap (in.) | Pick-Up Coil | Secondary Wires |
			Primary	Secondary			
Honda	1979	Accord, Prelude	1.78–2.08	8.8k–13.2k	.012 ①	⑤	25k
	1980–1984	All Models	1.0–1.3–	7.4k–11.0k–	.012 ①	—	25k
Mazda	1981–1984	GLC	1.03–1.27 ②	10.0k–30.0k	.012–.018	—	16k ③
Nissan (Datsun)	1978–1979	All Models	0.84–1.02	8.4k–12.7k	.008–.016 ④	720	30k
	1980	All Models	0.84–1.02	8.3k–12.3k	.012–.020 ①	400	30k
	1981–1984	210,310, 810,280ZX	0.84–1.02	8.3k–12.3k	.012–.020 ①	400	30k
	1981–1984	510,720, 200SX	1.04–1.27	8.3k–10.1k	.012–.020 ①	400	30k
	1982–1984	310	1.0–1.3	7.3k–11.0k	.012–.020	—	30k

NOTE: Exact resistance values may vary, but should fall within the range given

k = kilo-ohms
① Stator centered
② As measured at 68 degrees F (20 degrees C)
③ [+ −] 40% per meter (39.37 in.) of length
④ .012 in. preferred clearance
⑤ Trignition pulse generator resistance is 600–800 ohms
⑥ 1980 California   200SX, 510 models:
    Primary   1.04–1.27 ohms
    Secondary 8.3k–10.1k ohms

Air Gap Adjustment

Before performing any service or testing on the system, check the air gap between the stator and reluctor. The air gaps should be the same. If not, loosen the stator mounting screws and position the stator so that the air gaps are the same. When all adjustments are complete, tighten the mounting screws and recheck the air gaps.

Secondary Circuit Test

Check the ignition secondary circuit performance by removing the coil wire from the distributor cap and holding it ¼ in. away from ground, or use a suitable tester. Crank the engine while watching the end of the wire for spark. Hold the wire with insulated pliers and wear a heavy rubber glove during testing to avoid the chance of a dangerous shock from the high voltages produced by the system. If no spark is present, perform the primary circuit tests to isolate the problem in the ignition system.

If a spark is produced, reinstall the coil wire and remove a spark plug wire from the spark plug. Again, hold the wire ¼ in. from a ground or use a suitable tester and crank the engine. If a spark is produced, check the spark plugs, fuel delivery and mechanical systems. If no spark is produced, check the rotor, distributor cap, and spark plug wires.

Primary Circuit Test

1. Check the voltage between the positive (+) terminal of the coil and ground with the ignition ON. The voltage should be greater than 11 volts. If not, check the wiring between the ignition switch and the coil, then check the ignition switch for continuity.
2. Check the voltage between the negative (−) terminal of the coil and ground with the ignition ON. Again, the voltage should exceed 11 volts. If not, check the wiring between the coil and igniter, then follow the procedures under "Coil Resistance Test."
3. With the coil wire removed from the distributor cap and grounded, measure the voltage drop between the coil negative (−) and positive (+) terminals with the engine cranking. There should be 1–3 volts present. If not, check the coil resistance.
4. If the coil voltage drop is not correct, disconnect the igniter and check the voltage between the blue wire and ground with the

ignition ON. Check the voltage between the black/yellow wire and ground. If it is not above 11 volts, check the wiring from the ignition coil to the igniter.

5. On 1979 systems, check the continuity of both the red and blue wires between the igniter and pulse generator with an ohmmeter. If continuity exists, check the pulse generator resistance as described under "Pulse Generator Resistance Test." If the pulse generator resistance is not correct, replace the igniter and repeat the Secondary Circuit Test.

6. On 1980 and later systems, disconnect the wires from the igniter and check the continuity of the igniter as described under "Igniter Continuity Test." If the igniter fails the test, replace the igniter unit and repeat the Secondary Circuit Test.

7. If the system checks out but still fails to produce a spark at the coil wire, replace the igniter unit and repeat the test.

Testing voltage at igniter connector—1979 models

Pulse Generator Resistance Test

1979 MODELS

Connect an ohmmeter across the pulse generator terminals blue and red wires with the ignition OFF. The resistance should be 600–800 ohms. If not, replace the pulse generator assembly and retest.

Igniter Continuity Test

1980 AND LATER MODELS

Check the continuity of the igniter using an ohmmeter (R × 100 scale) with the wires disconnected from the igniter terminals. There should be continuity with the positive probe to the blue wire terminal and the negative probe to the black/yellow terminal. When the ohmmeter leads are reversed on the terminals, no continuity should be present. Replace the igniter if it fails the continuity test. If the igniter passes the continuity test, it does not necessarily mean the igniter is good, since the continuity test checks only a portion of the igniter. If spark is not present from the coil wire when the secondary circuit test is performed, replace the igniter and retest.

COIL RESISTANCE TEST

To measure the coil primary resistance, turn the ignition switch OFF and connect an ohmmeter (R × 1 scale) across the positive (+) and negative (−) terminals of the ignition coil. Record the resistance value as measured on the ohmmeter and compare the

1979 ACCORD & PRELUDE

1980-1982

Checking the air gap between the stator and reluctor

Testing voltage at igniter

Testing igniter continuity

Removing the reluctor

reading to the specifications chart. Replace the ignition coil if the resistance differs from the specified values.

To measure the coil secondary resistance, connect an ohmmeter (R × 1000 scale) to the coil tower and the positive (+) terminal on 1980 and later models. On 1979 models, connect the ohmmeter between the coil tower and the negative (−) terminal of the coil. Again, record and compare the resistance measurements with the specifications chart. If the secondary resistance differs from the values given in the specifications chart, replace the ignition coil.

RELUCTOR

Removal and Installation

Remove the distributor cap and rotor, then carefully pry the reluctor up using two screwdrivers or a suitable puller. Use rags to cushion the distributor housing and prevent possible damage. When installing the reluctor, be sure to drive in the pin with the gap away from the shaft.

HITACHI TRIGNITION SYSTEM

General Information

COMPONENTS AND OPERATION

The Hitachi electronic ignition system consists of an ignition coil, distributor cap rotor, transistor ignition unit (module) and breakerless distributor. The distributor has an iron (core reluctor on the distributor shaft and a pick-up coil, as well as conventional vacuum and centrifugal advance mechanisms. The ignition unit is mounted on a dash panel in the passengers compartment. In 1979, a hybrid Integrated Circuit (IC) ignition system was introduced and used up through 1981. The IC control unit is mounted to the exterior of the distributor housing. The distributor has a reluctor, pick-up coil and stator. A reduced IC unit was first used on 1980 California models. It was incorporated into the pick-up coil within the distributor and this system uses two sets of plugs with two ignition coil.

As the reluctor teeth align with the stator (pick-up coil), a signal is produced and transmitted to the control unit. The control unit interrupts the current flow in the coil primary circuit. As the magnetic field collapses in the primary windings of the coil, the high voltage is induced in the secondary coil windings. The high voltage in the secondary is transmitted through the coil wire to the distributor cap and rotor, then into a spark plug wire and from there to the plug.

Performance Tests

────CAUTION────

Always make sure the ignition switch is OFF before attempting any repairs or service to any electronic ignition system. Dangerous voltages are produced when the ignition is ON. Do not touch any secondary system components while the engine is running or being cranked and use insulated pliers to hold coil and ignition wires when testing for spark.

Secondary Circuit Test

Before testing the ignition system, make sure the battery has at least 9.5 volts when cranking the engine. If not, check the battery, charging and starting system first. Check the secondary circuit performance by removing the coil wire from the distributor cap and holding it ¼ in. away from a good ground with insulated pliers or a heavy rubber glove. Crank the engine while watching the coil wire for spark. If no spark is produced during the secondary test, inspect the ignition primary circuit wiring for loose or corroded connections. Check the air gap between the reluctor and pick-up coil and adjust if the measured gap does not agree with the specifications chart.

If there is spark at the coil wire during the secondary test, reinstall the coil wire into the distributor cap tower and remove a spark

Schematic of Hitachi integrated Circuit (IC) ignition system

Schematic of Hitachi Trignition system used on 1978 Datsun models

IGNITION SWITCH

FUSE

TO DISTRIBUTOR
(EX. SIDE)

FUSE

TO DISTRIBUTOR
(IN. SIDE)

BATTERY

$\oplus$ IGNITION COIL (A) $\ominus$

$\oplus$ IGNITION COIL (B) $\ominus$

I.C. IGNITION UNIT
& PICK-UP COIL

E B I

RELUCTOR

Schematic of Hitachi dual coil IC ignition system

plug wire. Again, using insulated pliers or heavy rubber glove, hold the plug wire ¼ in. away from a good ground, or use an ignition tester to check for spark while cranking the engine. If a spark is present, check the spark plugs, engine mechanical and fuel systems for a malfunction. If no spark is produced, check the rotor, distributor cap and spark plug wire resistance. Wire resistance should not exceed 30,000 ohms. If the measured resistance is greater than 30k ohms, replace the ignition wires and repeat the performance test.

NON-MAGNETIC
FEELER GAUGE

.008-.016"

Checking air gap—typical

Air Gap Adjustment

1978 MODELS

Using a non-magnetic (brass) feeler gauge, check the air gap between the reluctor and pick-up coil. The air gap should be between 0.008–0.016 in. (0.2–0.4mm) with a preferred setting of 0.012 in. (0.3mm). If the air gap is incorrect, loosen the pick-up coil mounting screw and adjust to specifications. Recheck the air gap after tightening the mounting screw.

1979 AND LATER MODELS

Inspect the reluctor air gap and make sure the stator is centered around the reluctor. If the stator is not centered, loosen the stator mounting screws and reposition until the stator is centered and the air gap is 0.012–0.020 in. (0.3–0.5mm). Tighten the stator screws and recheck adjustment.

Primary Circuit Test

1978 MODELS

NOTE: It is not necessary to disconnect the harness connectors when performing the tests. Probe all test connectors from the rear of the terminal cavity.

1. Check for voltage between terminal 4 and ground with the ignition ON. If the voltmeter reads 11 volts or less, check the wiring and connectors between the ignition unit and the ignition switch for loose connections or corrosion.

2. Turn the ignition switch to START and measure the voltage at terminal 4 with the engine cranking. Remove the coil wire from the distributor cap and ground it to prevent the engine from starting.

Testing 1978 Hitachi Trignition system

Make sure the coil wire is properly grounded. The voltmeter should read at least 9 volts. If not, check the wiring and connectors between the ignition switch and the ignition module, as well as the starting system.

3. Check the voltage drop between terminal 5 and the negative (−) battery post with the ignition switch turned to START and the coil wire grounded. If the voltage drop exceeds 1/2 volt, check the distributor ground, wiring from the chassis, ground and the battery terminal connections for looseness or corrosion.

4. Check the voltage between terminal 3 and ground with the ignition ON. The voltmeter should read more than 11 volts. If not, check the coil primary resistance and wiring, as well as the connectors between the ignition switch and ignition module, for looseness or corrosion.

1979-80 MODELS (EXCEPT CALIFORNIA)

1. Check the voltage between terminal 2 and ground with the ignition ON. The voltmeter should read more than 11 volts. If not, check the wiring and connectors between the IC ignition module and the ignition switch.

2. Turn the ignition switch to START and measure the voltage at terminal 2. Remove the coil wire from the distributor and ground it to prevent the engine from starting. Make sure the coil wire is grounded properly to prevent damage to the 10 module. The voltmeter should read more than 9 volts. If not, check the wiring and connectors between the ignition switch and the IC ignition module, as well as the starter.

3. Check the voltage drop between terminal 7 and the negative (−) battery post with the ignition switch turned to START. Ground the coil wire to prevent the engine from starting. If the voltage drop exceeds 1/2 volt, check the distributor ground, wiring from the battery terminals for looseness or corrosion.

4. Check the voltage between terminal 1 and ground with the ignition ON. The voltmeter should read more than 11 volts. If not, check the coil primary resistance, wiring and connectors between the ignition switch and the IC module for looseness or corrosion.

1980 CALIFORNIA AND 1981 AND LATER MODELS

1. Check the voltage between terminal B and ground. It should exceed 11 volts. If not, check the wiring and connectors between the ignition switch and the IC ignition module for looseness of corrosion.

2. With the voltmeter still connected, measure the voltage when the engine is cranked. Remove the coil wire from the distributor cap and ground it to prevent the engine from starting. Make sure the coil wire is grounded to prevent damage to the IC module. The voltmeter should read more than 9 volts. If not, check the wiring and connectors between the ignition switch and the IC ignition module for looseness or corrosion and check the starter.

3. Check the voltage drop between the distributor housing and ground while cranking the engine with the coil wire grounded. If the voltage drop exceeds 1/2 volt, check the distributor ground, wiring from the chassis ground to the battery and the battery terminals for looseness or corrosion.

4. Check the voltage between the E and I terminals of the IC ignition module and ground with the ignition switch ON. The voltage should exceed 11 volts. If not, check the coil primary resistance and the wiring and connectors between the ignition switch and the IC ignition module for looseness of corrosion.

Pick-Up Coil Tests
1978 MODELS

Check the resistance between terminals 1 and 2 with the ignition OFF. The ohmmeter should indicate 720 ohms. If not, check the wiring and connectors between the ignition module and pick-up coil in the distributor. To eliminate the wiring and connector, check the resistance of the pick-up coil at the distributor connector. If it is correct, it indicates the wiring and/or the connector is the problem. If incorrect, replace the pick-up. The output of the pick-up coil can be checked with a voltmeter connected to terminals 1 and 2. When the engine is cranked, the voltmeter should show a rythmic meter deflection. If not, check the reluctor, wiring, connectors and the pick-up coil.

Testing Hitachi Trignition system with IC ignition unit

Testing Hitachi dual coil ignition system

1979 AND LATER MODELS

Check the resistance between terminals 5 and 6 with an ohmmeter. The resistance should be 400 ohms. If not, replace the pick-up coil. To check the output of the pick-up coil, connect a voltmeter to the pick-up coil and set it on the lowest AC voltage scale. When the engine is cranked, the voltmeter should show a rythmic needle deflection. If not, check the reluctor, wiring, connectors and the pick-up coil.

Ignition Coil Test

ALL MODELS

Connect an ohmmeter (R × 1 scale) between the coil negative (−) and positive (+) terminals. The resistance should be 0.84–1.02 ohms. If not, replace the coil and retest.

NOTE: If the source of the problem cannot be located in any of the above tests, replace the ignition module and repeat the Performance Test.

LUCAS ELECTRONIC IGNITION SYSTEMS

Internal Amplifier Type

GENERAL INFORMATION

A distributor with a built-in electronic amplifier module has been used on 1978 and later 4- and 6-cylinder MG Midget and MGB, Triumph Spitfire and TR-7, and Jaguar XJ-6 models. The timing rotor (reluctor) is a molded plastic drum mounted on the distributor shaft beneath the rotor arm, into which a number of equally spaced ferrite rods are vertically embedded. The pick-up module (pick-up coil) is mounted on the base plate. The pick-up has an iron core wound with a primary and secondary winding connected to the amplifier module. The amplifer module has a multi-stage amplifier and power transistor connected to the ignition coil primary circuit. To prevent arcing and flashover from the high tension terminals of the distributor cap, a flashover shield is installed between the rotor and timing rotor. The amplifier module is contained in a metal housing attached to the distributor body. The distributor uses conventional centrifugal and vacuum advance mechanisms.

As the engine is cranked, the timing rotor (reluctor) passes the pick-up coil, producing a voltage which is applied to the amplifier (ignition module). The amplifier switches off the ignition coil primary, causing the rapid collapse of the coil's primary magnetic field across the secondary windings and producing the high secondary voltage. Some Lucas ignition systems use a non-ballasted coil, while other systems use a drive and ballast resistor in the primary circuit. The other primary systems use a ballast resistor unit, which consists of resistors and a printed board sealed and mounted in an aluminum heat sink.

Schematic of Lucas ignition system with 9BR ballast resistor. The unit consists of resistors and a printed circuit board sealed and mounted in an aluminum heat sink

Schematic of Lucas ignition system without ballast resistor

Exploded view of Lucas distributor with internal amplifier

Schematic of Lucas ignition system with ballast resistor

Voltage tests on Lucas ignition system without ballast resistor

Testing voltage at negative coil terminal and drive resistor

Testing output voltage at 9BR ballast resistor

Testing voltage at coil positive terminal

Testing voltage at 9BR ballast resistor output terminal

PERFORMANCE TESTS

Secondary Circuit Test

Remove the coil wire from the distributor cap. With the coil wire held 1/4 in. (6 mm) away from a ground (or using a suitable tester), crank the engine and check for a spark at the coil wire. If no spark is produced, it will be necessary to check the battery voltage and perform system diagnosis. If a good spark is produced, reinstall the coil wire and remove a spark plug wire. Hold the plug wire with insulated pliers or a heavy rubber glove 1/4 in. away from a ground and crank the engine. If a spark is produced, check the spark plugs, engine fuel and mechanical systems for a malfunction. If no spark is produced, check the rotor, distributor cap, and spark plug wires.

Primary Circuit Voltage Checks

1. Check the voltage at the amplifier input, drive resistor, and the ballast resistor with the ignition switch ON. On non-ballast resistor systems, check the voltage at the (+) terminal of the ignition coil. The voltage should exceed 11 volts. If not, check the ignition switch and wiring between the ignition switch and the check points for looseness or corrosion.

2. On systems that use a 9BR ballast resistor, check the voltage at the output center terminal of the resistor. It should exceed 9 volts. If not, replace the ballast resistor. On systems using ballast resistors, check the voltage at the positive (+) coil terminal and make sure it is about 4–8 volts. If the voltage is not within specifications, check the ballast resistor and wiring between the resistor and coil.

3. Check the voltage at the negative (−) coil terminal and make sure it is between 0.3–1.3 volts. If it is less than 0.3 volt, check the coil resistance. If it is above 1.3 volts, check the amplifier.

4. Check the voltage at the drive resistor or ballast resistor output. It should be 0.5–2.5 volts. If less than 0.5 volt, check the resistor. If above 2.5 volts, check the resistor, amplifier and wiring connecting the two together.

Air Gap Adjustment

The air gap should not normally require adjustment, but it should be checked when troubleshooting the ignition system. With the ferrite rods in the timing rotor equally spaced away from the pick-up, measure the clearance with a non-magnetic (brass) feeler gauge. Air gap should be 0.012-0.017 in. (0.3-0.4mm). If the air gap is incorrect, loosen the mounting screws on the pick-up and adjust as required to specifications.

Cranking Voltage Test

On systems with ballast resistors, check the voltage at the coil positive (+) terminal while cranking the engine. Use a jumper wire to ground the negative (−) coil terminal during test. The voltage should increase as the starter is engaged. If the voltage does not increase, check the voltage at the starter solenoid ignition terminal and the wiring between the solenoid and the coil positive (+) terminal. Check the ballast resistor also, if equipped with the 9BR system.

Amplifier Switching Test

Connect a voltmeter to the negative (−) coil terminal and crank the engine. The voltage should increase when the starter is engaged. If the voltage does not increase as described, replace the amplifier and retest the system.

External Amplifier Type Ignition System

GENERAL INFORMATION

This Lucas electronic ignition system consists of a pick-up assembly, reluctor, electronic module, coil and distributor. The amplifier is a solid state electronic module sealed in an aluminum case and

Schematic of Lucas electronic ignition system with external amplifier

Checking air gap on Lucas ignition system

Cranking voltage test at positive coil terminal

Amplifier switching test

connected to the coil primary by two leads. The distributor pick-up is connected to the amplifier (module) by two shielded wires and is grounded at the amplifier by the mounting bolts. No separate ballast resistor is used in the primary circuit and the current flow is controlled by the amplifier. The distributor consists of vacuum and centrifugal advance mechanisms, and anti-flash shield, rotor, reluctor and pick-up assembly. The pick-up is made up of a winding around a pole piece attached to a permanent magnet. The reluctor is mounted on the distributor shaft.

As the reluctor tooth passes by the pick-up, the magnetic field

Exploded view of Lucas external amplifier-type distributor

perform system diagnosis. If a good spark is produced, reinstall the coil wire and remove a spark plug wire. Hold the plug wire with insulated pliers or a heavy rubber glove ¼ in. away from a ground and crank the engine. If a spark is produced, check the spark plugs, engine fuel and mechanical system for a malfuction. If no spark is produced, check the rotor, distributor cap, and spark plug wires.

Primary Circuit Voltage Checks

1. Check the voltage at the amplifier input, drive resistor, and the ballast resistor with the ignition switch ON. On non-ballast resistor systems, check the voltage at the (+) terminal of the ignition coil. The voltage should exceed 11 volts. If not, check the ignition switch and wiring between the ignition switch and the check points for looseness or corrosion.

2. On systems that use a ballast resistor, check the voltage at the output center terminal of the resistor. It should exceed 9 volts. If not, replace the ballast resistor. On systems using ballast resistors,

Voltage test at coil positive terminal

Voltage test at coil negative terminal

strength around the pick-up winding increases, producing a voltage in the pick-up winding. This voltage signal is interpreted by the amplifier which switches the primary current flow off, inducing the high secondary voltage which travels through the coil wire, through the distributor cap and wires and finally to the spark plugs.

PERFORMANCE TESTS

Secondary Circuit Test

Remove the coil wire from the distributor cap. With the coil wire held ¼ in. 96 mm) away from a ground (or using a suitable tester), crank the engine and check for a spark at the coil wire. If no spark is produced, it will be necessary to check the battery voltage and

Adjusting air gap on Lucas distributor

Testing pick-up coil resistance

check the voltage at the positive (+) coil terminal and make sure it is about 4–8 volts. If the voltage is not within specifications, check the ballast resistor and wiring between the resistor and coil.

3. Check the voltage at the negative (−) coil terminal and make sure it is between 0.3–1.3 volts. If it is less than 0.3 volt, check the coil resistance. If it is above 1.3 volts, check the amplifier.

4. Check the voltage at the drive resistor or ballast resistor output. It should be 0.5–2.5 volts. If less than 0.5 volt, check the resistor. If above 2.5 volts, check the resistor, amplifier and wiring connecting the two together.

Coil Voltage Test

Connect a voltmeter to the positive (+) coil terminal and check the voltage with the ignition switch ON. It should read more than 11 volts. If not, check the wiring between the coil and the ignition switch for poor or corroded connections or broken, burned or shorted wires. Check the voltage at the negative (−) coil terminal with the ignition ON. Again, the voltage should exceed 11 volts. If not, disconnect the wire from the negative (−) coil terminal to the amplifier and check the voltage again. If the voltage is now correct, replace the amplifier. If the voltage is still low, replace the coil and repeat the test.

Pick-Up Coil Resistance Test

Turn the ignition switch OFF and disconnect the distributor pick-up coil from the amplifier. Measure the resistance of the pick-up

coil with an ohm-meter. It should be between 2200–4800 ohms. If the resistance is not within specifications, replace the pick-up coil. If the coil passes the resistance test, reconnect it to the amplifier and measure the voltage at the coil negative (−) terminal while cranking the engine. The voltage should drop. If not, replace the amplifier.

Air Gap Adjustment

The air gap between the reluctor and the pick-up coil should not normally need adjustment, but an air gap check should be part of any electrical trouble shooting procedure. Use a non-magnetic (brass) feeler gauge to check the air gap. It should be 0.008–0.014 in. (0.20–0.35mm). If the air gap requires adjustment, align a reluctor tooth with the pick-up and loosen both barrel nuts on the pick-up plate. Insert the feeler gauge between the tooth and the pick-up and adjust the plate until the correct gap is obtained. Once the adjustment is complete, tighten the barrel nuts and recheck the air gap.

MARELLI ELECTRONIC IGNITION SYSTEM

General Information

The Marelli electronic ignition system uses the same control module as the General Motors HEI system. The module and coil are mounted in a support which consists of a finned aluminum casting to provide cooling and the casting to provide cooling and the ground for the coil and the module. No ballast resistor is used with this system. The pick-up assembly consists of a pick-up coil, stator pole and permanent magnet. Primary voltage is supplied from the battery through the ignition switch. This voltage is regulated by the control module to supply a regulated current to the primary windings of the ignition coil. As the tooth of the reluctor passes through the magnetic field, an electrical impulse is induced in the pick-up and set to the control module where it interrupts the primary circuit, inducing a high voltage in the coil secondary windings which travels through the coil wire to the distributor cap and from there is distributed to the spark plugs. The distributor uses conventional vacuum and centrifugal advance mechanisms. The module controls the current flow in the coil by turning the coil primary on and off, providing for dwell change as engine speed (rmp) is increased or decreased.

Marelli coil and support assembly

Schematic of Marelli electronic ignition system

Exploded view of Marelli electronic distributor

Performance Tests

Secondary Circuit Test

Remove the coil wire from the distributor cap and hold it ¼ in. away from a good ground and crank the engine. Hold the coil wire with insulated pliers or wear a heavy rubber glove during testing to avoid the chance of a dangerous shock. A spark should be noted when the engine is cranked. If no spark is noted, check the coil voltage. If spark is present, install the coil wire in the distributor

Pick-up assembly used on Fiat models with Marelli distributor

tower and remove one spark plug wire. Hold the plug wire with insulated pliers or heavy rubber glove ¼ in away from a good ground and again crank the engine. If no spark is produced, check the rotor, distributor cap, spark plug wires, and spark plugs. If a good spark is present, check the engine mechanical and fuel systems to locate the source of the problem.

Coil Voltage Test

Connect a voltmeter to the B+ terminal of the coil and turn the ignition ON. The voltmeter should show more than 11 volts. If the voltage is lower than specified, check the ignition switch, wiring and connections between the coil and ignition switch for loose or corroded connections, broken wires, or a malfunction within the ignition switch itself.

Module Test

Remove the pick-up coil leads from the module. With the ignition ON, watch the voltmeter connected from the negative (−) coil terminal to ground as the test light is momentarily connected from the battery to the module terminal G. If the voltage does not drop, check the module ground and for an open circuit in the wires from the distributor to the coil. If no problem is found, replace the module and retest. If the voltage drops, check for spark from the coil with a tester or by holding the coil wire ¼ in. from a good ground as the test light is removed from the module terminal. If a spark is produced, it indicates a pick-up coil or connection problem. Check the pick-up coil resistance and make sure it's not grounded. If no spark is evident, check the ignition coil ground circuit and replace the ignition coil if no problem is found and retest the system. If a spark is still not produced, reinstall the original coil and replace the module.

Module Ground Test

Use an ohmmeter to test for continuity between the support assembly mounting stud and the battery negative (−) terminal with the ignition OFF. The resistance reading should be less than 0.2 ohm. If the resistance is greater than 0.2 ohm, check the support and mounting connections, then check the casing to make sure the hold down screws are clean and tight.

Testing coil voltage at positive terminal

Control module ground test

Control module testing

Pick-up coil resistance test

Coil Resistance Test

Disconnect the wires from the primary (B+ and −) coil terminals. Connect an ohmmeter across the primary terminals and check that the coil resistance measures 0.75–0.81 ohms. Check the secondary resistance by connecting the ohmmeter across the coil negative (−) terminal and the high voltage output (coil wire) tower. The resistance should measure 10,000–11,000 ohms. If either resistance value is not as specified, replace the coil.

Distributor Pick-Up Test

Disconnect the pick-up connector at the control module. Check the resistance of the pick-up coil with the ohmmeter. It should measure 700–800 ohms. Check the pick-up coil for a short to ground by connecting one of the ohmmeter leads to ground and the other to a pick-up coil lead. The resistance should be infinite. Using a non-magnetic (brass) feeler gauge, check the air gap between the stator pole and reluctor tooth. The air gap should be 0.020–0.024 in. (0.5–0.6mm). If the source of the problem still cannot be located, replace the control module and repeat the performance test.

Checking air gap

Pick-up coil ground test

MITSUBISHI ELECTRONIC IGNITION SYSTEM

Schematic of 1981 and later Mitsubishi electronic ignition system

General Information

The Mitsubishi electronic ignition system consists of an electronic ignition control module (igniter), ignition coil and distributor. Some models mount the control unit on the ignition coil, others mount it to the outside of the distributor housing. The control unit is made up of a power transistor chip, IC and thick film circuit. When the ignition is switched ON, the primary circuit of the ignition coil has current flowing and a magnetic field is built up around it. As the reluctor rotates inside the pick-up coil assembly, the teeth of the reluctor pass the stator and a signal is generated in the pick-up coil which is sent to the control unit. Upon receiving the signal, the control unit opens the primary circuit, the magnetic field collapses, and a high voltage is induced in the secondary windings of the coil. The high voltage travels through the coil wire to the distributor cap, then through the spark plug wires to the plugs.

Performance Tests

Secondary Circuit Test

Remove the coil wire from the center tower of the distributor cap and hold the end of the wire 1/4 in. away from a good ground with insulated pliers or a heavy rubber glove. Exercise caution as dangerous voltages are produced by any electronic ignition system.

Crank the engine and check for spark from the coil wire. If a spark is noted, the IC igniter and ignition coil can be considered good. Reinstall the coil wire and repeat the test using one spark plug wire held 1/4 in. away from a good ground with insulated pliers or by using a fabricated spark tester made from a spark plug and alligator clip soldered together. If no spark is produced in either test, check the distributor cap, rotor and spark plug wire resistance. If spark is present in both tests, check the engine mechanical and fuel systems for a malfunction.

NOTE: On 1980 Chrysler imports, insert a screwdriver tip between the reluctor and pick-up coil with the ignition ON to check for spark at the coil and plug wires. If no spark is produced when removing and inserting the screwdriver, check the control unit, pick-up coil, ignition coil and wires. Use a screwdriver with an insulated handle.

Primary Circuit Test

Check the coil voltage by connecting a voltmeter to the negative (−) terminal of the ignition coil with the ignition switch ON. It should read more than 11 volts. If the voltmeter reads 3 volts or less, the IC in the distributor is defective. If no voltage is present, check for an open circuit in the coil or connecting wiring. With the ignition ON, connect a jumper wire to the negative (−) coil terminal and momentarily touch it to ground while holding the coil wire 1/4 in. away from a good ground. There should be a spark at the

MITSUBISHI PERFORMANCE TEST SPECIFICATIONS
(All measurements given in ohms)

Manufacturer	Year	Model	Coil Circuit Primary	Coil Circuit Secondary	Air Gap (in.)	Pick-Up Coil	Secondary Wires
Chrysler Imports and 2.6L engine	1979–1984	All Models	0.7–0.85 ①	9k–11k	—	9k–11k ②	22k max
Ford Courier	1979–1984	2.3L Engine	0.81–0.99	8k–1.2k	.008–.024	760–840	570 per inch
	1980	2.0L ③	0.81–0.99	8k–1.2k	—	945–1155	570 per inch
	1981–1984	2.0L ④	1.15	9.8k	—	—	570 per inch
Mazda	1978–1980	GLC ⑤	1.28	13.5k	.010–.014	670–790	9.6k–22.4k
	1979	626, B2000	1.28	13.5k	.008	720–880	9.6k–22.4k
	1980–1984	626, B2000	0.81–0.99 ⑥	7k	—	945–1155	9.6k–22.4k
	1981–1984	RX-7	1.22–1.48 ⑦	16k	.020–.035	600–700	9.6k–22.4k

① Ballast resistor test should be 1.22–1.49 ohms
② 1981 and later should be 920–1120 ohms
③ Externally mounted igniter
④ Internally mounted igniter
⑤ Except 1979 GLC with 2.0L engine
⑥ 1982 626 should be 1.04–1.26 ohms
⑦ Leading and trailing coils

SECTION 4 ELECTRONIC IGNITION SYSTEMS

Schematic of 1980 Mitsubishi electronic ignition system

Control unit (model or igniter) mounted on the ignition coil

coil wire. If not, check the voltage at the positive (+) coil terminal with the ignition ON and make sure the reading exceeds 11 volts. If the voltage is OK, replace the coil and retest. If the voltmeter indicates 11 volts or less at the coil positive terminal, check the wiring and connectors for loose or corroded connections. Make sure the battery is fully charged and the battery terminals are clean and tight.

Ignition Coil Resistance Test
ALL MODELS
To check the coil primary resistance, use an ohmmeter (R × 1

Testing secondary ignition circuit

164

scale) to measure between the (+) and (−) terminals of the coil with the ignition (OFF). If the resistance is outside the specification, replace the coil. To check the coil secondary resistance, use an ohmmeter (R × 1000 scale) to measure the resistance between the coil secondary terminal (coil tower) and (−) terminal. The secondary resistance should be within the specification. If not, replace the coil.

Testing pick-up coil resistance on 1980 Chrysler models

Testing pick-up coil resistance on Mazda models

Pick-Up Coil Resistance Test

On systems with the control unit (module or igniter) mounted on the coil, turn the ignition OFF and disconnect the pick-up coil connector from the control unit. Using the ohmmeter (R × 10 scale), measure the resistance at the distributor connector between the terminals. If the pick-up coil resistance is not within the specification, replace the pick-up coil assembly. On all other systems, measure the resistance of the pick-up coil with an ohmmeter (R × 10 scale). If the resistance is not within the specification, replace the pick-up coil.

Control Unit Test

1980 CHRYSLER IMPORTS AND FORD COURIER WITH 2.0L ENGINE

Check for continuity between terminal (C) and reverse side (metallic surface) of the control unit. If control unit is installed in the distributor, check between the terminal (C) and distributor housing. Perform the continuity test in the same way as a diode test, reversing the ohmmeter leads to the continuity in the other direction. If there is continuity or an open circuit in both directions, replace the control unit. The continuity test checks only the switching section of the control unit. It is possible for the control unit to pass the test but still be defective. If the unit passes the test, but the system does not produce a spark from the coil wire, replace the control unit and retest.

FORD COURIER 1977–1982 2.3L ENGINE AND THE 1979 2.0L ENGINE

Connect a 3.4 watt test light between the ignition coil positive (+) and negative (−) terminals. Disconnect the connector between the module and distributor, then connect a jumper wire from the coil positive (+) terminal to the positive pin (red wire) on the module side of the disconnected electrical connector. With the ignition switch (ON), the test light should be on. When the jumper wire is disconnected, the test light should go out. If the ignition module does not test properly, replace the module.

1981–1982 CHRYSLER IMPORTS AND CHRYSLER DOMESTIC 2.6L ENGINE

Connect igniter unit and lamp. Apply signal voltage to the signal imput terminal of the igniter unit using an ohmmeter. The lamp should light when the signal is supplied from the ohmmeter and go

Testing pick-up coil resistance on 1981 and later Chrysler models

Testing control unit on Chrysler models

IGNITION MODULE

RED-WHITE WIRE

BLACK WIRE

YELLOW WIRE

RED WIRE

2-GREEN WIRE

1-RED WIRE

GREEN WIRE

2-WIRE CONNECTOR
(IGNITOR SIDE)

BLACK-RED WIRE

IGNITION SWITCH

BLACK WIRE

BATTERY

RED WIRE

YELLOW WIRE

GREEN WIRE

1   2

JUMPER WIRE

PICKUP COIL

DISTRIBUTOR

IGNITION COIL

TEST LIGHT
(3.4W)

Ignition module test connections for Ford Courier

LAMP
(12V. 3 TO 30W)

(+)

BATTERY

(−)

OHMMETER

Testing IC igniter on Chrysler models

out when the ohmmeter signal is removed. If the IC igniter fails to perform properly, replace it. This procedure is a simplified inspection check. Although the igniter may check good, it is possible that the igniter may not function properly. If, after completely checking out the ignition system, no malfunctions can be located and spark is still not present at the coil wire when the engine is cranked, replace the IC igniter and retest.

NOTE: When replacing the IC igniter do not wipe the grease of the back of the igniter. The grease helps dissipate heat from the igniter.

Igniter Module Test

MAZDA RX-7

With the igniter removed from the distributor, connect a test lamp as illustrated using a 12 volt battery and less than a 10 watt bulb. Quickly operate the switch and check to see if the light flashes off and on. If the light does not flash, replace the igniter.

Air Gap Adjustment

On the Mazda RX-7 and all models with the igniter mounted on the coil, align the reluctor with the pick-up coil and measure the air gap with a non-magnetic (brass) feeler gauge. If the air gap is not within 0.010–0.014 in. (0.25-0.35 mm), adjust by loosening the mounting screws and adjusting the pick-up coil base until the correct air gap is obtained. Tighten the mounting screws and recheck the air gap. On Ford Courier models with the 2.3L engine, the air gap should be 0.016 in. (0.4mm) and can be adjusted by bending the pick-up coil.

Testing IC igniter on Mazda models

NIPPONDENSO ELECTRONIC IGNITION SYSTEM

General Information

The Nippondenso Electronic Ignition System consists of an igniter (module) mounted on the ignition coil and a distributor. The distributor contains a signal generator (pick-up coil) and a signal rotor (reluctor). The distributor uses a vacuum and mechanical advance mechanism to advance the ignition timing. Some systems use a resistor mounted on the ignition timing. Some systems use a resistor mounted on the ignition coil or a resistor wire in the primary circuit. Other Nippondenso systems use no external resistors but rely on the igniter to limit the current flow in the ignition primary circuit. The coil and igniter assembly are mounted on the fender apron.

As the signal rotor (reluctor) rotates with the distributor shaft, the tooth of the signal rotor aligns with the signal generator (pick-up coil) and generates a voltage signal which is supplied to the igniter. This voltage signal causes the igniter (module) to open the primary circuit causing the magnetic field to collapse across the secondary windings inducing the high secondary voltage. The secondary voltage travels from the coil through the coil wire to the distributor cap and rotor and into the spark plug wire. The secondary voltage then jumps the gap of the spark plug, igniting the air-fuel mixture in the cylinder.

SERVICE PRECAUTIONS

• Do not disconnect the battery when the engine is running.
• The igniter must be properly grounded to prevent damaging it.
• Never allow the ignition coil terminals to touch ground since it could damage the igniter or ignition coil.
• Do not allow the ignition switch to remain (ON) for more than 10 minutes if the engine will not start.
• When using a tachometer on the system connect it to the (−) terminal of the coil and ground. Some tachometers are not compatible with this ignition system.
• Carefully remove the spark plug wires from the spark plugs by the rubber boots. Do not pull on or bend the wires.

Schematic of Nippondesno electronic ignition system used on California Toyota models

SIGNAL ROTOR (RELUCTOR)

WEIGHTS

THRUST WASHER

GOVERNOR SHAFT

O-RING

DISTRIBUTOR HOUSING

O-RING

WASHER

GEAR

DISTRIBUTOR CAP

ROTOR

DUST COVER

SIGNAL GENERATOR (PICK-UP COIL)

BREAKER PLATE

Gasket

VACUUM ADVANCE DIAPHRAGM

Exploded view of Nippondenso distributor used on Toyota models

For Federal

BATTERY

IGNITION SWITCH

IG

ST

RESISTOR

IGNITION COIL

SPARK PLUGS

DISTRIBUTOR

TO TACHOMETER

PICK-UP COIL

SIGNAL ROTOR

MAGNET

IGNITER

Schematic of Nippondenso electronic ignition system used on Federal Toyota models

168

NIPPONDENSO PERFORMANCE TEST SPECIFICATIONS
(All measurements given in ohms)

Manufac-turer	Year	Model	Coil Circuit		Air Gap (in.)	Signal Generator	Secondary Wires
			Primary	Secondary			
Toyota	1978	K and T Series Engines	1.3–1.7	12k–16k	.008–.016	130–190	25k max
	1979	A, 3T–C Series Engines	0.4–0.5	8.5k–11.5k	.008–.016	130–190	25k max
	1979	Celica	1.3–1.7	12k–16k	.008–.016	130–190	25k max
	1980	4M–E Engine	0.5–0.6	11.5k–15.5k	.008–.016	130–190	25k max
	1980	Celica ①	0.5–0.6	11.5k–15.5k	.008–.016	130–190	25k max
	1981–1982	Corolla	0.8–1.1	11.5k–15.5k	.008–.016	130–190	25k max
	1981	K Series Engines	1.3–1.7	10k–15k	.008–.016	130–190	25k max
	1982	Tercel, Celica	0.8–1.1	10.7k–14.5k	.008–.016	130–190	25k max
Chevrolet	1980–1981	LUV (Series 11)	.828–1.02	12.1k–14.8k	.008–.016	140–180	31.5k–73.5k

① Federal models only. California models are the same as the 1981 Corolla

Performance Tests

Secondary Circuit Test

Remove the coil wire from the distributor cap and use insulated pliers to hold the coil wire ¼ in. away from ground. Exercise caution as dangerous voltages are produced by any electronic ignition system. Crank the engine and watch for spark. If no spark is produced, go on to the ignition system performance diagnosis procedures. If a spark is produced, reconnect the coil wire into the distributor cap and remove a spark plug wire from a spark plug. Hold

Testing resistance wire

the spark plug wire with insulated pliers ¼ in. away from a good ground and again crank the engine and watch for spark. If no spark is produced, check the distributor cap, rotor and spark plug wire resistance. If a spark is produced, check the fuel and engine mechanical systems for malfunction.

Ballast Resistor Test

With the ignition OFF, check the resistance of the ballast resistor with an ohmmeter across the resistor terminals. If the resistance is not within specifications, replace the ballast resistor.

Testing ballast resistor wire resistance with an ohmmeter

Testing signal generator resistance

Checking air gap on Toyota models

Test connections for checking igniter operation on Toyota models

Resistor Wire Test

To measure the resistance of the resistor wire, disconnect the power supply connector at the igniter. With the ignition OFF, measure the resistance across the connector terminals with an ohmmeter. If the resistance is not within specifications, replace the wire harness.

Coil Tests

Check the coil for cracks or damage and for carbon tracking at the terminals. If any of these conditions are found, replace the ignition coil. Measure the primary coil resistance between the positive (+) and negative (−) terminals of the coil. Using an ohmmeter, measure the secondary coil resistance between the high tension center terminal and the (+) terminal of the coil. On the Chevrolet LUV, measure the resistance between the coil (−) terminal and the high tension center terminal. If either the primary or secondary resistance is not within specifications, replace the coil.

Testing coil voltage

Signal Generator (Pick-Up Coil) Resistance Test

Disconnect the signal generator connector at the distributor. Check the resistance of the signal generator with an ohmmeter across the signal generator terminals at the connector. The resistance of the signal generator should be 130–190 ohms. If it is not, replace the signal generator.

Air Gap Adjustment

Use a non-magnetic feeler gauge of the correct thickness to measure the air-gap between the signal rotor (reluctor) tooth and the signal generator (pick-up coil). The air-gap for all Nippondenso systems should be 0.2-0.4mm (0.008–0.016 in.) To adjust the air gap, loosen the two screws and move the signal generator until the air gap is correct. Tighten the screws and recheck the gap.

Igniter Tests

TOYOTA (K) AND (T) SERIES ENGINES 1978

Check the voltage between the coil (−) terminal and the resistor wire terminal with the ignition ON. The voltage present should be more than 11 volts. If the voltage is less than 11 volts, check the resistor wire and connector. Disconnect the distributor connector and connect an ohmmeter (1 or 10 ohms scale) to the disconnected distributor connector. Connect the (+) ohmmeter lead to the pink wire terminal of the connector and the (−) ohmmeter lead to the white wire terminal. When the ignition is turned ON, the voltage should be nearly zero and return to more than 11 volts when the ohmmeter leads are removed from the distributor connector. If the voltmeter readings are not correct, replace the igniter.

Coil voltage test—1979 models

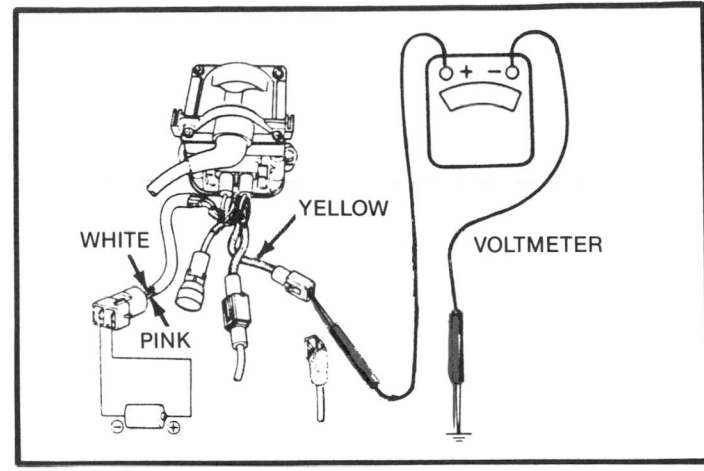

Testing igniter operation—1979 models

Voltage and Igniter Tests

TOYOTA (A) SERIES ENGINE 1979

Voltage Test

Disconnect the wiring connector (brown and yellow). Use a voltmeter to check the voltage between the brown wire and ground with the ignition ON. The voltage should be more than 11 volts. If the voltage is less than 11 volts, check the wiring and connector between the coil and the ignition switch.

Igniter Tests

With the brown connector reconnected, check the voltage between the tachometer wiring connector and ground with ignition (ON). The voltage should be more than 11 volts. Use a 1.5 volt dry cell battery to apply voltage to the distributor connector. Connect the positive (+) pole of the battery to the pink wire and the negative (−) pole of the battery to the white wire of the connector. The voltage at the tachometer terminal should drop to between 5 and 8 volts. In order to prevent damaging the power transistor of the igniter, DO NOT apply the voltage of the battery to the distributor connector for more than 5 seconds. If the voltage does not drop to within 5–8 volts, replace the igniter.

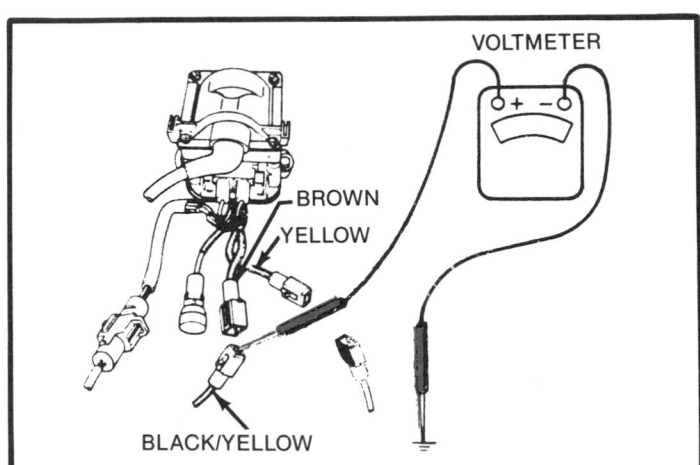

Testing coil input voltage on 1979 models

Voltage and Igniter Tests

TOYOTA CELICA 1979

Use a voltmeter to check the voltage between the positive (+) coil terminal and negative (−) coil terminal with the ignition ON. The voltage should be approximately 6 volts. Unplug the distributor connector and connect a 1.5 volt dry cell battery between the distributor connector terminals. Connect the battery (+) pole to the pink wire terminals. The voltage between the coil terminals should drop to zero with the battery connected and return to 6 volts when the battery is disconnected from the distributor connector.

Voltage and Igniter Tests

TOYOTA CELICA 1980 (FEDERAL)

Voltage Test

Connect a voltmeter between the resistor terminal and ground. With the ignition ON, the voltage should be above 11 volts. If the voltage is less than 11 volts, check the wiring and connector between the ballast resistor and the ignition switch.

Connect a 1.5 volt battery as shown for testing at the distributor connector

Igniter Tests

Connect the voltmeter to the coil negative (−) terminal and the other voltmeter lead to ground. Unplug the distributor connector and connect a 1.5 volt dry cell battery to the distributor connector. Connect the battery (+) pole to the white wire and the (−) pole of the battery to the pink wire terminal of the connector. The voltage at the coil should be more than 11 volts with the ignition ON. Reversing the battery terminals should result in the voltage dropping to between 1–2 volts. If the voltage does not drop when the battery is reversed, replace the igniter.

Voltage and Igniter Tests

CHEVROLET LUV SERIES 11 AND TOYOTA CELICA 1980 (CALIF.), 1981 AND 1982 COROLIA, 1980 4M-E ENGINE, 1981 (K) SERIES ENGINE, 1982 TERCEL AND CELICA

Check the voltage present between the coil positive (+) terminal

Toyota coil voltage check

LUV coil voltage check

and ground with the ignition ON. The voltage should be more than 11 volts. If it is not, check the wire and connector between the coil and the ignition switch. To check the igniter, connect the voltmeter to the negative (−) terminal of the coil and ground. The voltage should be more and 11 volts with the ignition switch ON. Using a 1.5 volt dry cell battery, apply voltage to the distributor connector. Connect the (+) pole of the battery to the pink wire terminal of the distributor connector and the (−) pole to the white wire terminal. In order to avoid damaging the power transistor of the igniter, DO NOT apply the voltage to the distributor connector for more than 5 seconds. The voltage at the coil negative (−) terminal should drop to between 5 and 8 volts when the voltage is applied to the distributor connector. If the voltage does not drop, replace the igniter.

Electronic Engine Controls 5 SECTION

INDEX

NOTE: Please refer to the Application Chart at the front of this Manual.

AMC COMPUTERIZED EMISSION CONTROL (CEC) SYSTEM

1980–81 Six Cylinder Engines
GENERAL INFORMATION

Three different feedback systems are used with AMC automobiles, two for four-cylinder engines and one for six-cylinder engines. Each system is designed to achieve the same objective: reduce undesirable exhaust emission in conjunction with either a three-way catalytic (TWC) converter or a duel bed (TWC and COC) converter, while maintaining fuel economy and good engine performance.

With all systems, the primary feedback data is provided by an oxygen sensor located in the exhaust system. This sensor provides a voltage that is proportional to the amount of oxygen present in the exhaust gas. This data is used by each system microprocessor to regulate and optimize the air/fuel mixture.

The C-4 system is used on four cylinder engines, 1981 and on selected four cylinder engines from 1982 and later. The Computerized Emission Control System (CEC) is used on all 1981 and later six cylinder engines and on selected four cylinder engines beginning with the 1982 and later models.

There are two primary modes of operation for the CEC feedback system, open loop and closed loop. The system will be in the open loop mode of operation (or a variation of it) whenever the engine operation conditions do not meet the programmed criteria for closed loop operation. During open loop operation, the air-fuel mixture is maintained at a programmed ratio that is dependent on the type of engine operation involved. The oxygen sensor data is

Computerized Emission Control (CEC) system wiring diagram—typical

Open and Closed Loop Modes of Operation

Metering pins in causes a rich mixture

not accepted by the system during this mode of operation. The following conditions involve open loop operation.
1. Engine start-up
2. Coolant temperature too low
3. Oxygen sensor temperature too low
4. Engine idling
5. Wide open throttle (WOT)
6. Battery voltage too low

When all input data meets the programmed criteria for closed loop operation, the oxygen content from the oxygen sensor is accepted by the computer. This results in an air-fuel mixture that will be optimum for the engine operating condition and also will correct any pre-existing mixture condition which is too lean or too rich.

NOTE: A high oxygen content in the exhaust gas indicates a lean air-fuel mixture. A low oxygen content indicates a rich air-fuel mixture. The optimum air-fuel mixture ratio is 14.7:1.

Micro Computer Unit (MCU)

The MCU monitors the oxygen sensor voltage and, based upon the mode of operation, generates an output control signal for the car-

buretor stepper motor. If the system is in the closed loop mode of operation, the air-fuel mixture will vary according to the oxygen content in the exhaust gas and engine operation. If the system is in the open loop mode of operation, the air-fuel mixture will be based on a predetermined ratio that is dependent on engine rpm.

Stepper Motor

The stepper motor controls the metering pins that vary the size of the air bleed orifices located in the carburetor body. The motor moves the pins in and out of the orifices in steps according to the control signal generated by the MCU. The motor has a range of 100 steps, but the normal operating area is mid-range. When the metering pins are stepped in the direction of the orifices, the air-fuel mixture becomes richer; when stepped away from the orifices, the mixture becomes leaner.

ENGINE SENSORS

Oxygen Sensor

This component of the system provides a variable voltage (millivolts) for the micro computer unit (MCU) that is proportional to the oxygen content in the exhaust gas. In addition to the oxygen sensor, the following data senders are used to supply the micro computer unit (MCU) with engine operation data.

Vacuum Switch

Two vacuum-operated electrical switches (ported and manifold) are used to detect and send throttle position data to the MCU.
1. Idle (closed)
2. Partial throttle
3. Wide open throttle (WOT)

Engine RPM Voltage

This voltage is supplied from a terminal on the distributor. Until a voltage equivalent to a predetermined rpm is received by the MCU, the system remains in the open loop mode of operation. The result is a fixed rich air-fuel mixture for starting purposes.

Coolant Temperature Switch

The temperature switch supplies engine coolant temperature data to the MCU. Until the engine is sufficiently warmed, the system remains in the open loop mode of operation (i.e., a fixed air-fuel mixture based upon engine rpm.)

CEC SYSTEM OPERATION

The open loop mode of operation occurs when starting the engine or the engine is cold, when the engine is idling, or when the engine is at wide open throttle (WOT). When any of these three conditions occur, the metering pins are driven to a predetermined programmed position for each condition. Because the positions are predetermined and no feedback relative to the results is accepted, this type of operation is referred to as open loop operation. The three open loop operations are characterized by the metering pins being driven to a position where they are stopped and remain stationary.

Open Loop Priorities

Each open loop operation has a specific metering pin position and, because more than one of the open loop triggering conditions can be present at one time, the MCU is programmed with a priority ranking for the operations. It complies with the input having the highest priority. The priorities are as follows:
1. Open loop 1, cold operation, starting engine
2. Open loop 2, wide open throttle (WOT)
3. Open loop 3, idle
4. Closed loop

Metering pins out causes a lean mixture

Open Loop Predetermined Position Variation

An additional function of the MCU is to correct for a change in ambient conditions (high altitude). During closed loop operation, the MCU stores the amount and direction that the metering pins are driven to correct the oxygen content. If the movements are consistently to the same position, the MCU will vary all three open loop predetermined positions a corresponding amount. This function allows the open loop air-fuel mixture ratios to be tailored to the existing ambient condition during each uninterrupted use of the system.

Closed Loop Operation

The CEC system controls the air-fuel ratio with movable air metering pins, visible from the top of the carburetor air horn, that are driven by a stepper motor. The stepper motor moves the metering pins in increments or small steps via electrical impulses generated by the MCU. The MCU causes the stepper motor to drive the metering pins to a richer or leaner position in reaction to the voltage input from the oxygen sensor.

The oxygen sensor voltage varies in reaction to changes in oxygen content present in the exhaust gas. Because the content of oxygen in the exhaust gas indicates the completeness of the combustion process, it is a reliable indicator of the air-fuel mixture that is entering the combustion chamber.

Because the oxygen sensor only senses oxygen, any air leak or malfunction between the carburetor and sensor may cause the sensor to provide an erroneous voltage output. This could be caused by a fouled spark plug, manifold air leak or malfunctioning secondary air check valve.

The engine operation characteristics never quite permit the MCU to compute a single metering pin position that constantly provides the optimum air-fuel mixture. Therefore, closed loop operation is characterized by constant movement of the metering pins because the MCU is forced constantly to make small corrections in the air-fuel mixture in an attempt to create a system null.

Engine Data Senders

The other components of the CEC system are not actually involved in the fuel metering. They provide input data to the MCU to trigger either the open loop or closed loop operation.

1. The open loop 1 vacuum switch is colored yellow. It is controlled by manifold vacuum through a CTO switch and has a normally open (NO) electrical contact that is closed by 3 ±.5 in. Hg vacuum.

2. The open loop 2 vacuum switch is colored blue. It is controlled by manifold vacuum and has a normally closed (NC) electrical switch that is opened by a 4 ± .5 in. Hg vacuum.

3. The open loop 3 vacuum switch is colored pink. It is controlled by carburetor ported vacuum and has a normally closed (NC) electrical switch that is opened by a 3 ± .5in. Hg vacuum.

4. The rpm voltage input is provided by a harness wire connected between the MCU and the negative terminal of the ignition coil.

NOTE: For the system to operate properly, all associated components and related systems must be intact and operational. This includes EGR valves, EGR related componentry, correct spark vacuum routing, etc.

Initialization (Start-up)

When the ignition system is turned off, the MCU is also turned off. It has no memory circuit for prior operation. As a result, it has an initialization function that is activated when the ignition is turned on.

The MC initialization function moves the metering pins to the predetermined starting position by first driving them all the way to the rich end stop and then driving them in the lean direction by a predetermined number of steps. No matter where they were before initialization, they will be at the predetermined position at the end of every initialization period.

Since open loop operation metering pin position is dependent on the initialization function, this function is the first operational check in the diagnostic procedure.

Diagnosis and Testing

The steps in each check and test systematically evaluate each component that could cause the operational problem experienced. The "okay" or "not okay" result of the steps determine additional steps or repairs which are necessary.

After completing a repair, repeat the operational check to insure the problem is solved.

Computerized Emission Control System Six Cylinder Engines 1982 and Later

SYSTEM OPERATION

The open loop mode of operation occurs when:
1. Starting engine, engine is cold or air cleaner air is cold.
2. Engine is at idle speed.
3. Carburetor is either at or near wide open throttle (WOT).

When any of these conditions occur, the metering pins are driven to a predetermined (programmed) position for each condition. Because the positions are predetermined and no feedback relative to the results is accepted, this type of operation is referred to as open loop operation. The five open loop operations are characterized by the metering pins being driven to a position where they are stopped and remain stationary.

Each operation (except closed loop) has a specific metering pin position and because more than one of the operation selection con-

ELECTRIC CHOKE (BLUE WIRE)
TACH (GREEN WIRE)

ELECTRIC CHOKE (BLUE WIRE)

TACH (GREEN WIRE)

1. 4 in. HG vacuum switch
2. Coolant temp. switch
3. 10 in. HG vacuum switch
4. WOT switch
5. Altitude jumper wire
6. Stepper motor A
7. Stepper motor B
8. Upstream solenoid
9. Divert solenoid
10. Vacuum switching solenoid
11. Idle speed relay
12. Thermal electric switch (TES)
13. Ground
14. B + (12v)
15. Sole-vac solenoid

Diagnostic connector found on 1982 and later six cylinder engines ditions can be present at one time, the MCU is programmed with a priority ranking for the operations. It complies with conditions that pertain to the operation having the highest priority. The priorities are as described below.

Cold Weather Engine Start-up and Operation

If the air cleaner air temperature is below the calibrated value of the thermal electric switch (TES), the stepper motor is positioned a predetermined number of steps rich of the initialization position and air injection is diverted upstream. Lean air/fuel mixtures are not permitted for a preset period following a cold weather start-up.

Open Loop 2, Wide Open Throttle (WOT)

Open Loop 2 is selected whenever the air cleaner air temperature is above the calibrated value of the thermal electric switch (TES) and the WOT switch has been engaged.

When the Open Loop 2 mode is selected, the stepper motor is driven to a calibrated number of steps rich of initialization and the air control valve switches air "downstream". However, if the "lean limit" circuit (with altitude jumper wire) is being used, the air is instead directed "upstream". The WOT timer is activated whenever OL2 is selected and remains active for a preset period of time. The WOT timer remains inoperative if the "lean limit" circuit is being used.

Open Loop 4

Open Loop 4 is selected whenever manifold vacuum falls below a predetermined level. During OL4 operation, the stepper motor is positioned at the initialization position. Air injection is switched "upstream" during OL4 operation. However, air is switched "downstream" if the extended OL4 timer is activated and if the "lean limit" circuit is not being used (without altitude jumper wire). Air is also switched "downstream" if the WOT timer is activated.

Open Loop 3

Open Loop 3 is selected when the ignition advance vacuum level falls below a predetermined level.

When the OL3 mode is selected, the engine rpm is also determined. If the rpm (tach) voltage is greater than the calibrated value, an engine deceleration condition is assumed to exist. If the rpm (tach) voltage is less than the calibrated value, an engine idle speed condition is assumed to exist.

Open Loop 1

Open Loop 1 will be selected if the air cleaner air temperature is above a calibrated value and open loop 2, 3 or 4 is not selected, and if the engine coolant temperature is below the calibrated value.

The OL1 mode operates in lieu of normal closed-loop operation during a cold engine operating condition. If OL1 operation is selected, one of two predetermined stepper motor positions are chosen, dependent if the altitude circuit (lean limit) jumper wire is installed.

With each engine start-up, a start-up timer is activated. During this interval, if the engine operating condition would otherwise trigger normal closed loop operation, OL1 operation is selected.

Closed Loop

Closed loop operation is selected after either OL1, OL2, OL3 or OL4 modes have been selected and the start-up timer has timed out. Air injection is routed "downstream" during closed loop operation. The predetermined "lean" air/fuel mixture ceiling is selected for a preset length of time at the onset of closed loop operation.

High Altitude Adjustment

An additional function of the MCU is to correct for a change in ambient conditions (e.g., high altitude). During closed loop operation the MCU stores the number of steps and direction that the metering pins are dirven to correct the oxygen content of the

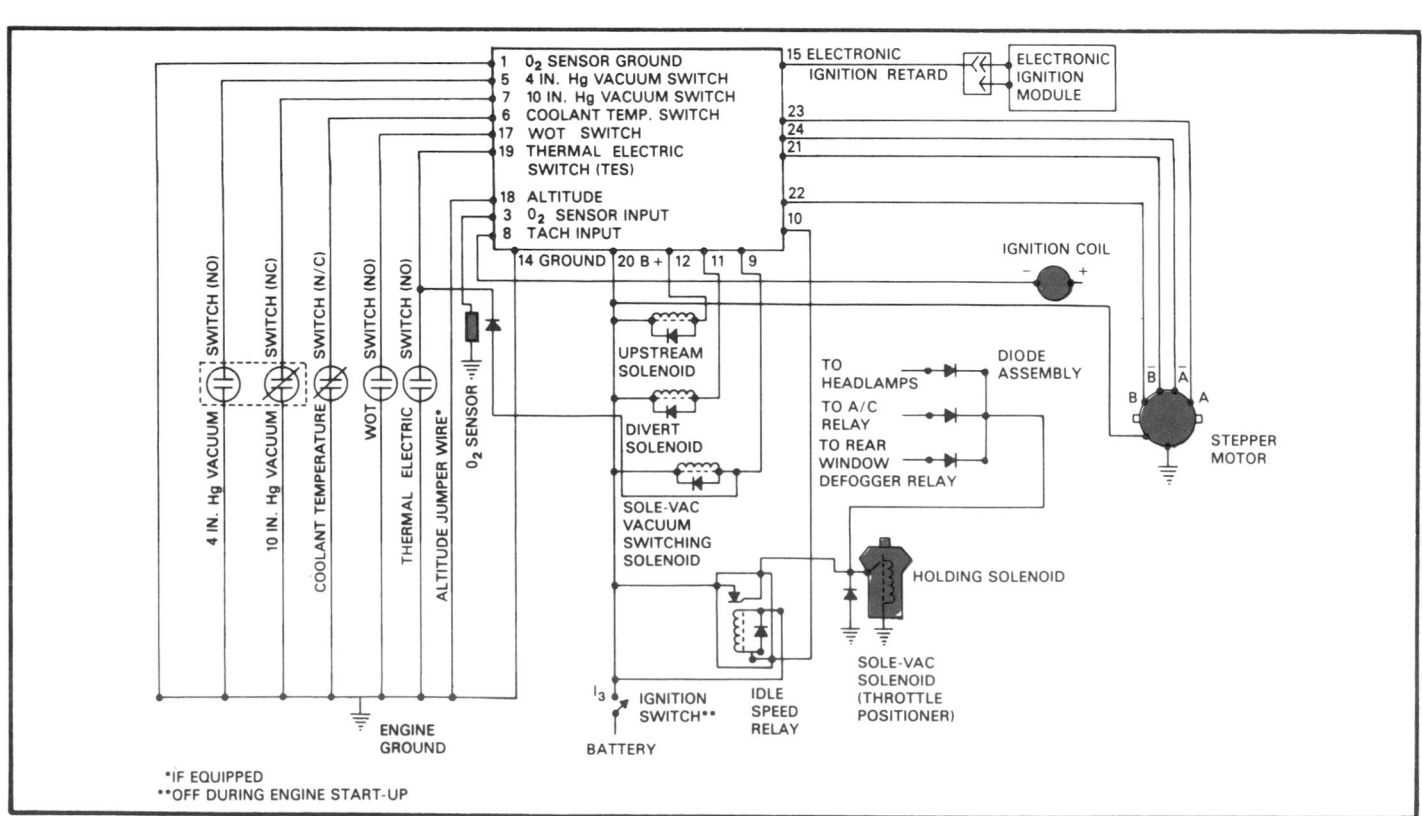

CEC wiring diagram for 1982 and later six cylinder engines

exhaust. If the movements are consistently to the same position, the MCU will vary all open loop operation predetermined metering pin positions a corresponding amount. This function allows the open loop air/fuel mixture ratios to be "tailored" to the existing ambient conditions during each uninterrupted use of the system. This optimizes emission control and engine performance.

Closed Loop Operation

The CEC system controls the air/fuel ratio with movable air metering pins, visible from the top of the carburetor air horn, that are driven by the stepper motor. The stepper motor moves the metering pins in increments or small steps via electrical impulses generated by the MCU. The MCU causes the stepper motor to drive the metering pins to a "richer" or "leaner" position in reaction to the voltage input from the oxygen content present in the exhaust gas. Because the content of oxygen in the exhaust gas indicates the completeness of the combustion process, it is a reliable indicator of the air/fuel mixture that is entering the combustion chamber.

Because the oxygen sensor only reacts to oxygen, any air leak or malfunction between the carburetor and sensor may cause the sensor to provide an erroneous voltage output. This could be caused by a manifold air leak or malfunctioning secondary air check value.

The engine operation characteristics never quite permit the MCU to compute a single metering pin position that constantly provides the optimum air/fuel mixture. Therefore, close loop operation is characterized by constant movement of the metering pins because the MCU is forced constantly to make small corrections in the air/fuel mixture in an attempt to create an optimum air/fuel mixture ratio.

Diagnosis and Testing

Idle Speed Control System

The idle speed control system is interrelated with the CEC system and must be diagnosed in conjunction with the CEC System. Refer to Diagnostic Tests 9, 10 and 11, if a malfunction occurs.

Electronic Ignition Retard

The electronic ignition retard function of the ignition control mod-

ule is interrelated with the CEC System and must be diagnosed in conjunction with the CEC System. Refer to Diagnostic Test 4 if a malfunction occurs.

Air Injection System

The air injection system is interrelated with the CEC System and must be diagnosed in conjunction with the CEC System. Refer to Diagnostic Tests 6, 7 and 8, if a malfunction occurs.

PRELIMINARY TESTS

Before performing the **Diagnostic Tests,** other engine associated systems that can affect air/fuel mixture, combustion efficiency or exhaust gas composition should be tested for faults. These systems include:
1. Basic carburetor adjustments
2. Mechanical engine operation (i.e., spark plugs, valves, rings)
3. Ignition system
4. Gaskets (intake manifold, carburetor or base plate); loose vacuum hoses or fittings

Initialization

When the ignition system is turned off, the MCU is also turned off. It has no long term memory circuit for prior operation. As a result, it has an initialization function that is activated when the ignition switch is turned On.

The MCU initialization function moves the metering pins to the predetermined starting position by first driving them all the way to the rich end stop and then driving them in the lean direction by a predetermined number of steps. No matter where they were before initialization, they will be at the correct position at the end of every initialization period.

Because each open loop operation metering pin position is dependent on the initialization function, this function is the first test in the diagnostic procedure.

NOTE: The CEC System should be considered as a possible source of trouble for engine performance, fuel economy and exhaust emission complaints only after normal tests that would apply to an automobile without the system have been performed.

DIAGNOSTIC TEST 1, CEC SYSTEM INITIALIZATION TEST

NOTE: WHEN APPLICABLE, DIAGNOSTIC CONNECTOR TERMINALS CAN BE USED AS TEST POINTS INSTEAD OF MCU HARNESS CONNECTOR TERMINALS.

REMOVE AIR CLEANER COVER.

WHILE OBSERVING METERING PINS, HAVE HELPER TURN IGNITION SWITCH TO ON POSITION WITHOUT STARTING ENGINE. METERING PINS SHOULD MOVE FULLY TOWARD THE FRONT OF ENGINE, REVERSE DIRECTION AND MOVE PARTIALLY BACK TOWARD REAR, STOP AND REMAIN STATIONARY.

NO   OK?   YES

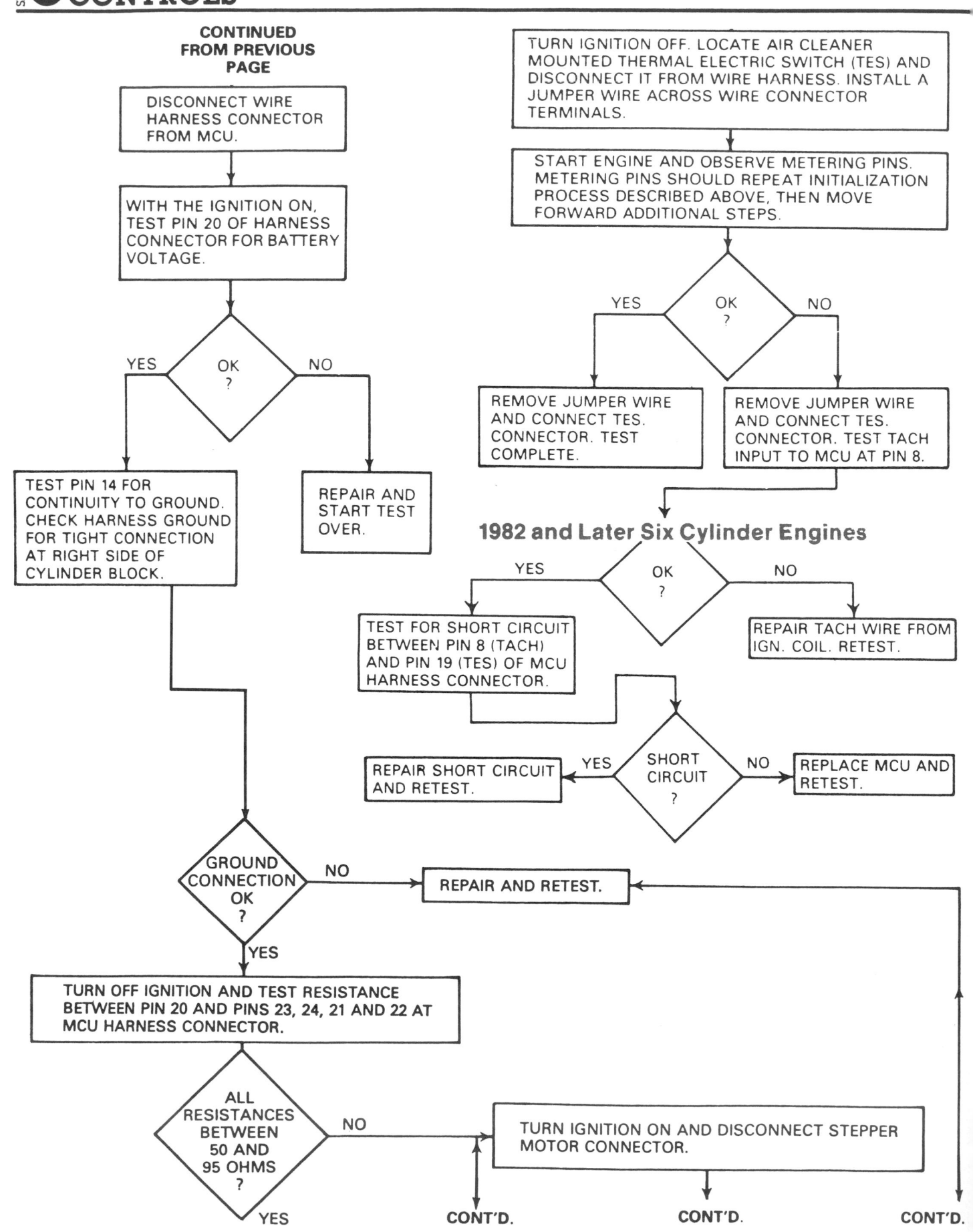

CONTINUED FROM PREVIOUS PAGE

DISCONNECT WIRE HARNESS CONNECTOR FROM MCU.

WITH THE IGNITION ON, TEST PIN 20 OF HARNESS CONNECTOR FOR BATTERY VOLTAGE.

OK ?

YES — TEST PIN 14 FOR CONTINUITY TO GROUND. CHECK HARNESS GROUND FOR TIGHT CONNECTION AT RIGHT SIDE OF CYLINDER BLOCK.

NO — REPAIR AND START TEST OVER.

GROUND CONNECTION OK ?

NO — REPAIR AND RETEST.

YES — TURN OFF IGNITION AND TEST RESISTANCE BETWEEN PIN 20 AND PINS 23, 24, 21 AND 22 AT MCU HARNESS CONNECTOR.

ALL RESISTANCES BETWEEN 50 AND 95 OHMS ?

NO — TURN IGNITION ON AND DISCONNECT STEPPER MOTOR CONNECTOR.

YES

TURN IGNITION OFF. LOCATE AIR CLEANER MOUNTED THERMAL ELECTRIC SWITCH (TES) AND DISCONNECT IT FROM WIRE HARNESS. INSTALL A JUMPER WIRE ACROSS WIRE CONNECTOR TERMINALS.

START ENGINE AND OBSERVE METERING PINS. METERING PINS SHOULD REPEAT INITIALIZATION PROCESS DESCRIBED ABOVE, THEN MOVE FORWARD ADDITIONAL STEPS.

OK ?

YES — REMOVE JUMPER WIRE AND CONNECT TES. CONNECTOR. TEST COMPLETE.

NO — REMOVE JUMPER WIRE AND CONNECT TES. CONNECTOR. TEST TACH INPUT TO MCU AT PIN 8.

1982 and Later Six Cylinder Engines

OK ?

YES — TEST FOR SHORT CIRCUIT BETWEEN PIN 8 (TACH) AND PIN 19 (TES) OF MCU HARNESS CONNECTOR.

NO — REPAIR TACH WIRE FROM IGN. COIL. RETEST.

SHORT CIRCUIT ?

YES — REPAIR SHORT CIRCUIT AND RETEST.

NO — REPLACE MCU AND RETEST.

CONT'D.   CONT'D.   CONT'D.

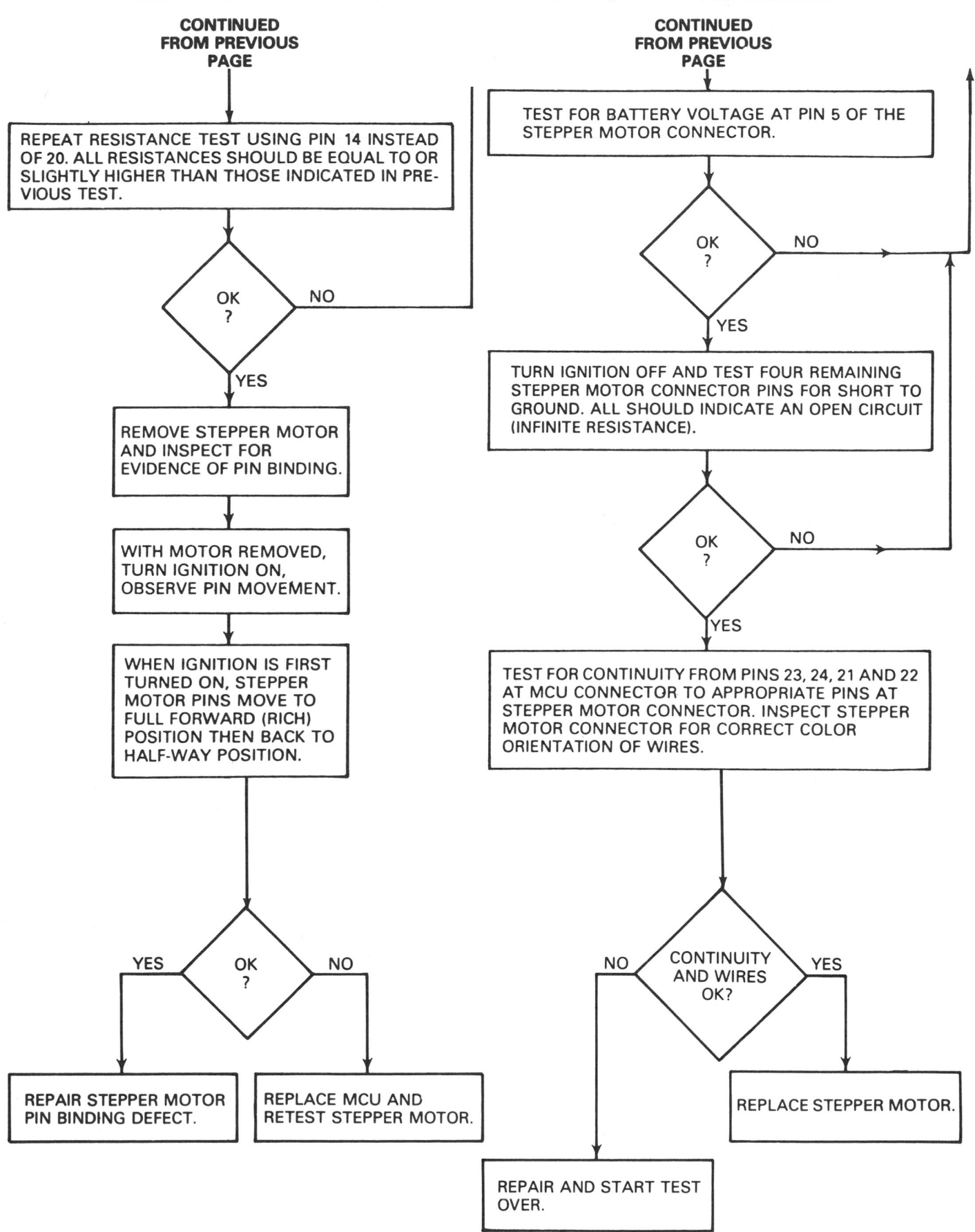

REPEAT RESISTANCE TEST USING PIN 14 INSTEAD OF 20. ALL RESISTANCES SHOULD BE EQUAL TO OR SLIGHTLY HIGHER THAN THOSE INDICATED IN PREVIOUS TEST.

OK ?

NO

YES

REMOVE STEPPER MOTOR AND INSPECT FOR EVIDENCE OF PIN BINDING.

WITH MOTOR REMOVED, TURN IGNITION ON, OBSERVE PIN MOVEMENT.

WHEN IGNITION IS FIRST TURNED ON, STEPPER MOTOR PINS MOVE TO FULL FORWARD (RICH) POSITION THEN BACK TO HALF-WAY POSITION.

YES

OK ?

NO

REPAIR STEPPER MOTOR PIN BINDING DEFECT.

REPLACE MCU AND RETEST STEPPER MOTOR.

TEST FOR BATTERY VOLTAGE AT PIN 5 OF THE STEPPER MOTOR CONNECTOR.

OK ?

NO

YES

TURN IGNITION OFF AND TEST FOUR REMAINING STEPPER MOTOR CONNECTOR PINS FOR SHORT TO GROUND. ALL SHOULD INDICATE AN OPEN CIRCUIT (INFINITE RESISTANCE).

OK ?

NO

YES

TEST FOR CONTINUITY FROM PINS 23, 24, 21 AND 22 AT MCU CONNECTOR TO APPROPRIATE PINS AT STEPPER MOTOR CONNECTOR. INSPECT STEPPER MOTOR CONNECTOR FOR CORRECT COLOR ORIENTATION OF WIRES.

NO

CONTINUITY AND WIRES OK?

YES

REPLACE STEPPER MOTOR.

REPAIR AND START TEST OVER.

DIAGNOSTIC TEST 2, CEC SYSTEM
OPEN LOOP SWITCH TEST
1982 and Later Six Cylinder Engines

NOTE: ENGINE SHOULD BE AT NORMAL OPERATING TEMPERATURE.

NOTE: CONTINUITY TESTING WITH MCU CONNECTED TO THE SYSTEM SHOULD INDICATE 2 OHMS. WHEN THE MCU IS DISCONNECTED FROM THE SYSTEM, ALL CONTINUITY SHOULD INDICATE LESS THAN 1 OHM. WHEN APPLICABLE, DIAGNOSTIC CONNECTOR TERMINALS CAN BE USED AS TEST POINTS INSTEAD OF MCU HARNESS CONNECTOR TERMINALS.

OPEN LOOP SWITCH TEST

USING A STANDARD VOLT-OHMMETER, TEST FOR CONTINUITY FROM THE DIAGNOSTIC CONNECTOR PIN 13 TO MCU CONNECTOR PIN 14.

OPEN CIRCUIT ?

NO → DISCONNECT VACUUM HOSE FROM SWITCH 2 OF VACUUM SWITCH ASSEMBLY.

YES → TEST FOR CONTINUITY BETWEEN PIN 2 AND MCU CONNECTOR PIN 14.

TRAPPED VACUUM ?

YES → REPAIR MALFUNCTION AND RETEST.

NO → DISCONNECT VACUUM SWITCH ASSEMBLY WIRE CONNECTOR AND RETEST CONTINUITY.

OPEN CIRCUIT ?

YES → REPLACE VACUUM SWITCH ASSEMBLY AND RETEST.

NO → DISCONNECT MCU HARNESS CONNECTOR AND RETEST.

OPEN CIRCUIT ?

YES → REPLACE MCU AND RETEST.

NO → REPAIR HARNESS SHORT CIRCUIT BETWEEN VACUUM SWITCH ASSEMBLY AND MCU. RETEST.

OPEN CIRCUIT ?

NO → ENGINE WARM ?

ENGINE WARM ?

YES → DISCONNECT COOLANT TEMPERATURE SWITCH CONNECTOR AND RETEST.

NO → DISCONNECT COOLANT TEMPERATURE SWITCH CONNECTOR AND RETEST.

YES → (from OPEN CIRCUIT ? after pin 2 test)

OPEN CIRCUIT ?

YES → REPLACE COOLANT TEMPERATURE SWITCH AND RETEST.

NO → DISCONNECT MCU CONNECTOR AND RETEST.

OPEN CIRCUIT ?

YES → REPLACE MCU AND RETEST.

NO → REPAIR HARNESS SHORT CIRCUIT BETWEEN COOLANT TEMPERATURE SWITCH AND MCU. RETEST.

CONT'D.

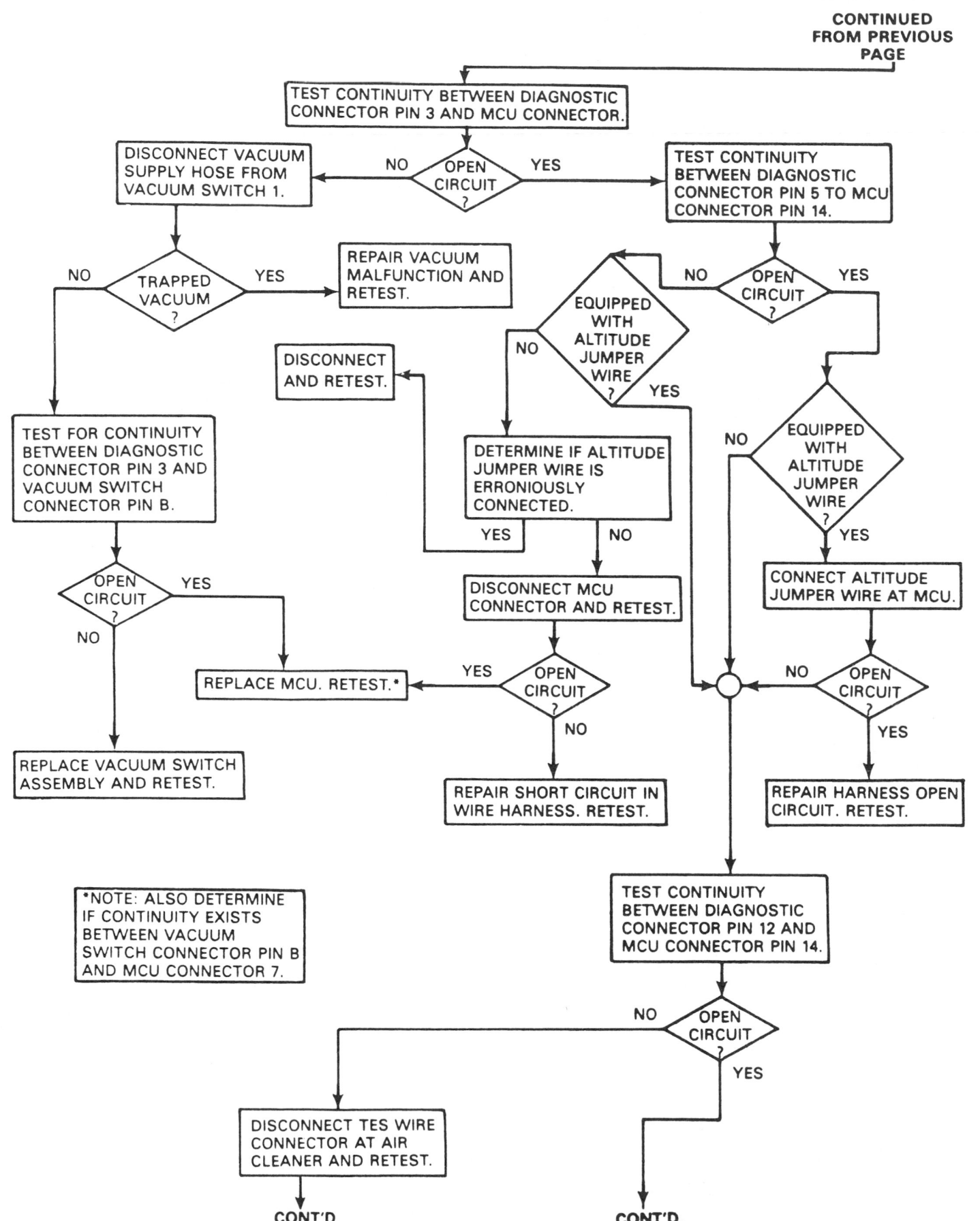

CONTINUED
FROM PREVIOUS
PAGE

TEST CONTINUITY BETWEEN DIAGNOSTIC
CONNECTOR PIN 3 AND MCU CONNECTOR.

DISCONNECT VACUUM
SUPPLY HOSE FROM
VACUUM SWITCH 1.

OPEN CIRCUIT? — NO / YES

TEST CONTINUITY
BETWEEN DIAGNOSTIC
CONNECTOR PIN 5 TO MCU
CONNECTOR PIN 14.

TRAPPED VACUUM? — NO / YES

REPAIR VACUUM
MALFUNCTION AND
RETEST.

OPEN CIRCUIT? — NO / YES

EQUIPPED WITH ALTITUDE JUMPER WIRE? — NO / YES

DISCONNECT
AND RETEST.

DETERMINE IF ALTITUDE
JUMPER WIRE IS
ERRONIOUSLY
CONNECTED.

EQUIPPED WITH ALTITUDE JUMPER WIRE? — NO / YES

TEST FOR CONTINUITY
BETWEEN DIAGNOSTIC
CONNECTOR PIN 3 AND
VACUUM SWITCH
CONNECTOR PIN B.

CONNECT ALTITUDE
JUMPER WIRE AT MCU.

OPEN CIRCUIT? — YES / NO

DISCONNECT MCU
CONNECTOR AND RETEST.

REPLACE MCU. RETEST.*

OPEN CIRCUIT? — YES / NO

OPEN CIRCUIT? — NO / YES

REPLACE VACUUM SWITCH
ASSEMBLY AND RETEST.

REPAIR SHORT CIRCUIT IN
WIRE HARNESS. RETEST.

REPAIR HARNESS OPEN
CIRCUIT. RETEST.

*NOTE: ALSO DETERMINE
IF CONTINUITY EXISTS
BETWEEN VACUUM
SWITCH CONNECTOR PIN B
AND MCU CONNECTOR 7.

TEST CONTINUITY
BETWEEN DIAGNOSTIC
CONNECTOR PIN 12 AND
MCU CONNECTOR PIN 14.

OPEN CIRCUIT? — NO / YES

DISCONNECT TES WIRE
CONNECTOR AT AIR
CLEANER AND RETEST.

CONT'D.

CONT'D.

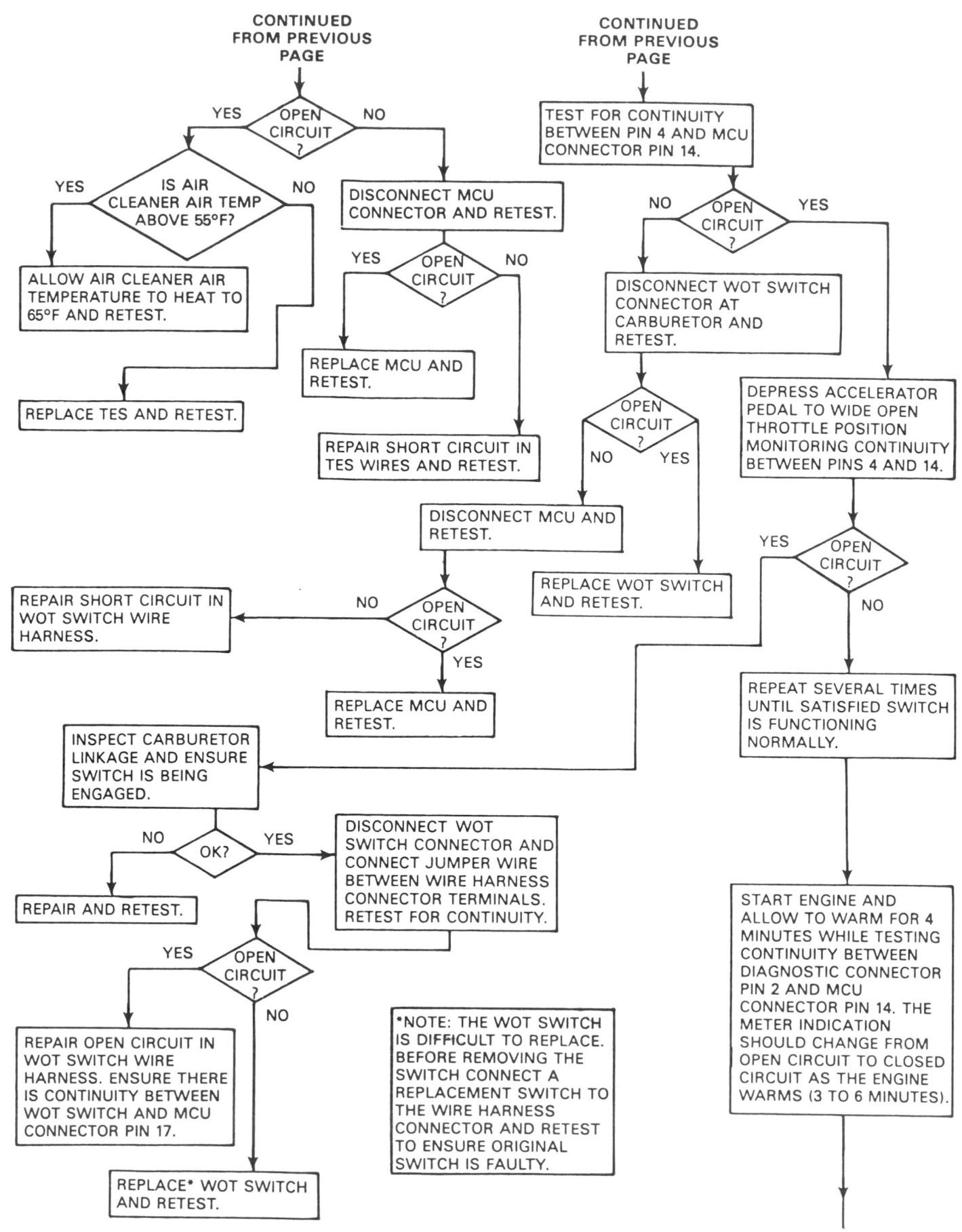

CONTINUED FROM PREVIOUS PAGE

CONTINUED FROM PREVIOUS PAGE

OPEN CIRCUIT ?

YES   NO

IS AIR CLEANER AIR TEMP ABOVE 55°F?

YES   NO

ALLOW AIR CLEANER AIR TEMPERATURE TO HEAT TO 65°F AND RETEST.

REPLACE TES AND RETEST.

DISCONNECT MCU CONNECTOR AND RETEST.

OPEN CIRCUIT ?

YES   NO

REPLACE MCU AND RETEST.

REPAIR SHORT CIRCUIT IN TES WIRES AND RETEST.

TEST FOR CONTINUITY BETWEEN PIN 4 AND MCU CONNECTOR PIN 14.

OPEN CIRCUIT ?

NO   YES

DISCONNECT WOT SWITCH CONNECTOR AT CARBURETOR AND RETEST.

OPEN CIRCUIT ?

NO   YES

DISCONNECT MCU AND RETEST.

REPLACE WOT SWITCH AND RETEST.

DEPRESS ACCELERATOR PEDAL TO WIDE OPEN THROTTLE POSITION MONITORING CONTINUITY BETWEEN PINS 4 AND 14.

OPEN CIRCUIT ?

YES   NO

REPAIR SHORT CIRCUIT IN WOT SWITCH WIRE HARNESS.

OPEN CIRCUIT ?

NO   YES

REPLACE MCU AND RETEST.

REPEAT SEVERAL TIMES UNTIL SATISFIED SWITCH IS FUNCTIONING NORMALLY.

INSPECT CARBURETOR LINKAGE AND ENSURE SWITCH IS BEING ENGAGED.

OK?

NO   YES

REPAIR AND RETEST.

DISCONNECT WOT SWITCH CONNECTOR AND CONNECT JUMPER WIRE BETWEEN WIRE HARNESS CONNECTOR TERMINALS. RETEST FOR CONTINUITY.

OPEN CIRCUIT ?

YES   NO

REPAIR OPEN CIRCUIT IN WOT SWITCH WIRE HARNESS. ENSURE THERE IS CONTINUITY BETWEEN WOT SWITCH AND MCU CONNECTOR PIN 17.

*NOTE: THE WOT SWITCH IS DIFFICULT TO REPLACE. BEFORE REMOVING THE SWITCH CONNECT A REPLACEMENT SWITCH TO THE WIRE HARNESS CONNECTOR AND RETEST TO ENSURE ORIGINAL SWITCH IS FAULTY.

START ENGINE AND ALLOW TO WARM FOR 4 MINUTES WHILE TESTING CONTINUITY BETWEEN DIAGNOSTIC CONNECTOR PIN 2 AND MCU CONNECTOR PIN 14. THE METER INDICATION SHOULD CHANGE FROM OPEN CIRCUIT TO CLOSED CIRCUIT AS THE ENGINE WARMS (3 TO 6 MINUTES).

REPLACE* WOT SWITCH AND RETEST.

CONTINUED FROM PREVIOUS PAGE

OK?
NO — YES

CONNECT JUMPER WIRE BETWEEN PINS A AND B OF COOLANT TEMPERATURE SWITCH CONNECTOR (HARNESS SIDE) AND RECHECK PINS 2 AND 14 ON DIAGNOSTIC CONNECTOR FOR CLOSED CIRCUIT.

REMOVE THROTTLE FROM FAST IDLE CAM POSITION AND ALLOW ENGINE TO RETURN TO NORMAL IDLE SPEED. ADJUST IDLE SPEED IF NECESSARY ACCORDING TO IDLE SPEED ADJUSTMENT PROCEDURE.

CLOSED?
NO — YES → REPLACE COOLANT SWITCH AND RETEST.

TEST CONTINUITY BETWEEN DIAGNOSTIC CONNECTOR PIN 1 AND MCU CONNECTOR PIN 14.

REPAIR CONTINUITY PROBLEM IN COOLANT SWITCH CIRCUIT. ENSURE THAT CONTINUITY ALSO EXISTS AT MCU PIN 6. RECHECK.

DETERMINE IF PORTED VACUUM IS AT VACUUM SWITCH 2. THERE SHOULD BE NO VACUUM AT IDLE SPEED. REPAIR AND RETEST.

OPEN?
NO — YES

INCREASE ENGINE SPEED TO 2000 RPM. TEST CONTINUITY BETWEEN PINS 1 AND 14. CONTINUITY SHOULD EXIST.

OK?
NO — YES

RETURN ENGINE TO IDLE SPEED. DISCONNECT VACUUM SWITCH ASSEMBLY AND PLACE JUMPER WIRE BETWEEN PINS A AND B OF VACUUM SWITCH CONNECTOR (HARNESS SIDE) AND RETEST CONTINUITY BETWEEN PINS 1 AND 14.

CONT'D.

CONT'D.

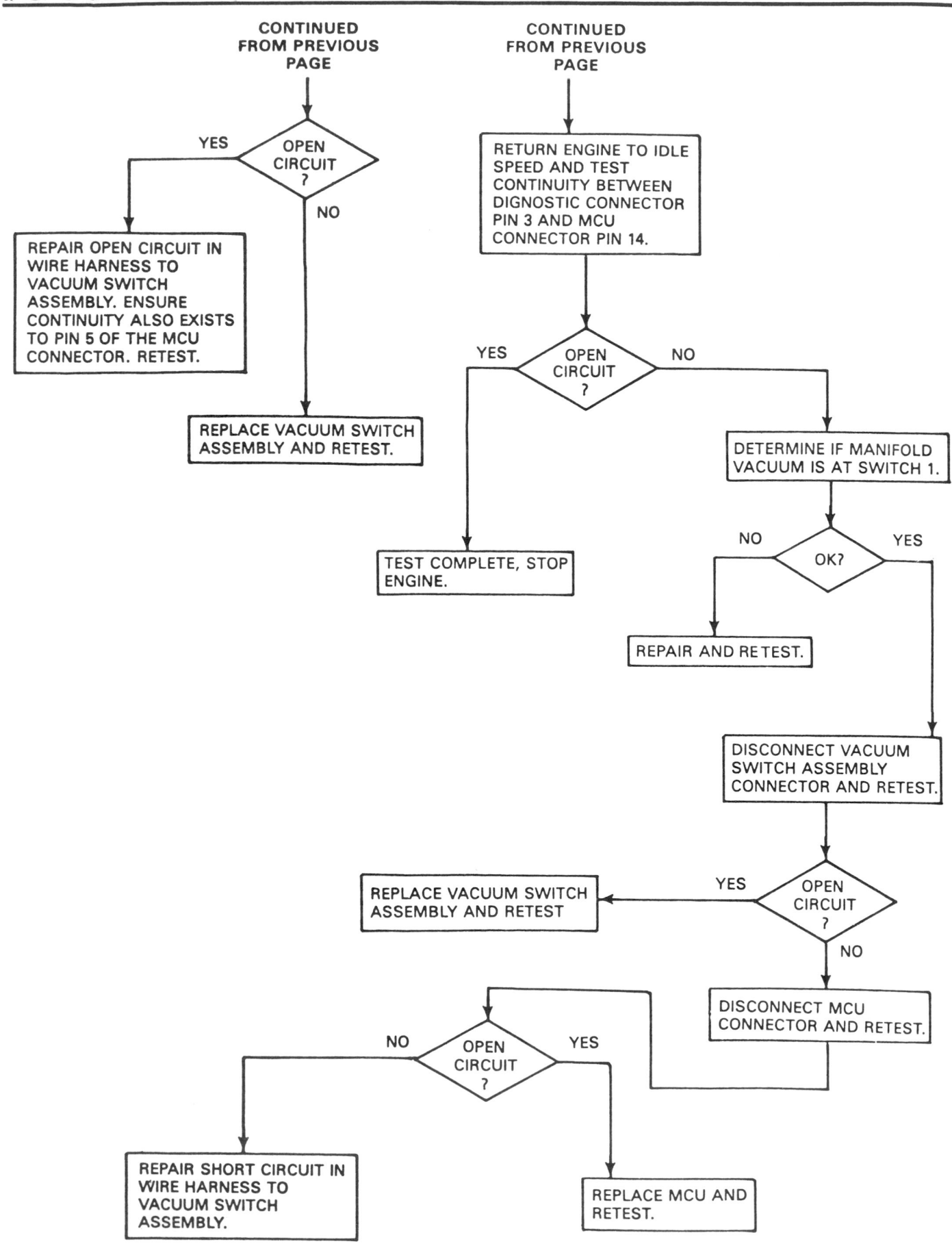

DIAGNOSTIC TEST 3, CEC SYSTEM
CLOSED LOOP OPERATIONAL TEST
1982 and Later Six Cylinder Engines

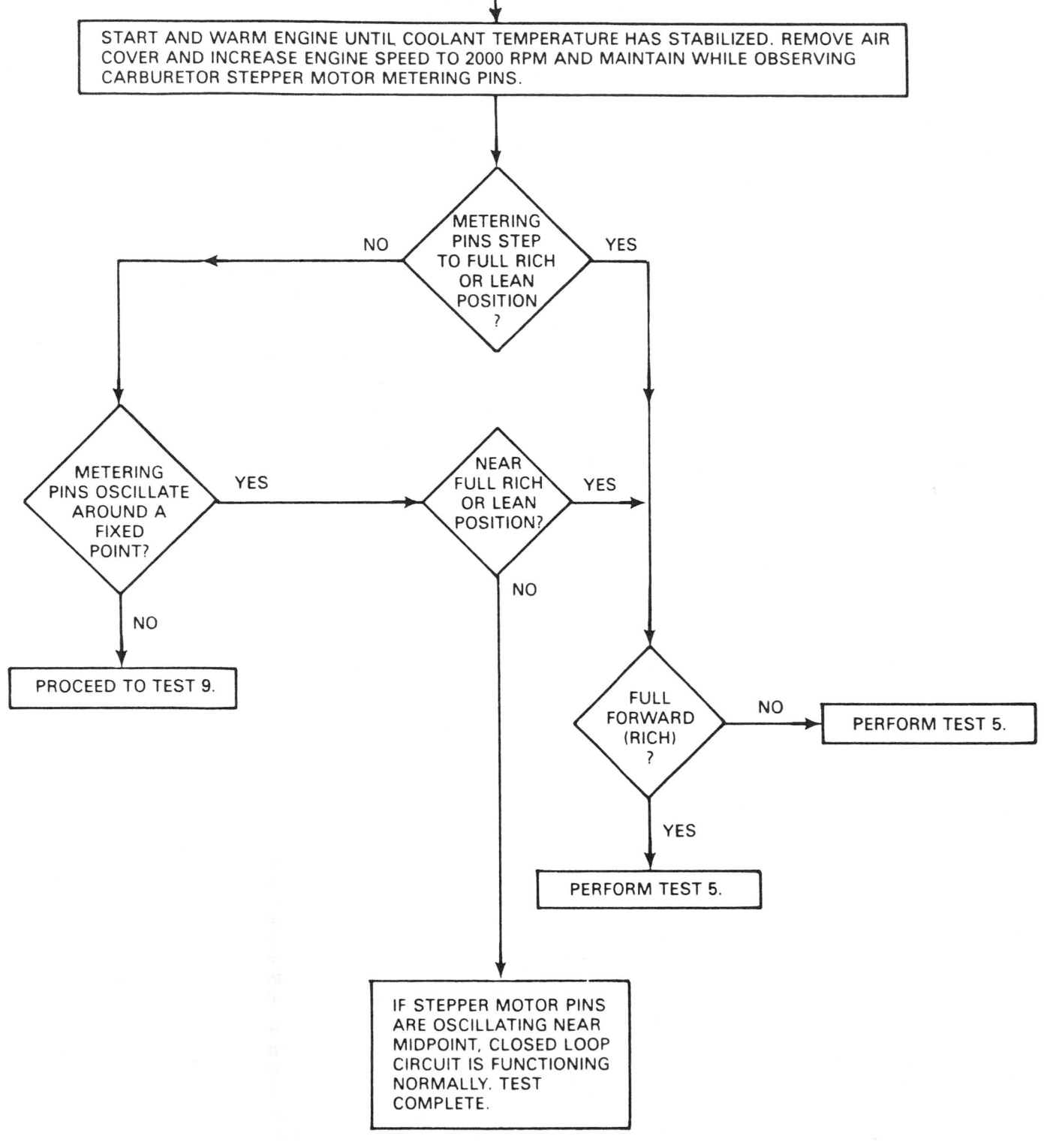

START AND WARM ENGINE UNTIL COOLANT TEMPERATURE HAS STABILIZED. REMOVE AIR COVER AND INCREASE ENGINE SPEED TO 2000 RPM AND MAINTAIN WHILE OBSERVING CARBURETOR STEPPER MOTOR METERING PINS.

METERING PINS STEP TO FULL RICH OR LEAN POSITION ?

NO

YES

METERING PINS OSCILLATE AROUND A FIXED POINT?

YES

NEAR FULL RICH OR LEAN POSITION?

YES

NO

NO

PROCEED TO TEST 9.

FULL FORWARD (RICH) ?

NO

PERFORM TEST 5.

YES

PERFORM TEST 5.

IF STEPPER MOTOR PINS ARE OSCILLATING NEAR MIDPOINT, CLOSED LOOP CIRCUIT IS FUNCTIONING NORMALLY. TEST COMPLETE.

DIAGNOSTIC TEST 4, CEC SYSTEM
ELECTRONIC IGNITION RETARD TEST
1982 and Later Six Cylinder Engines

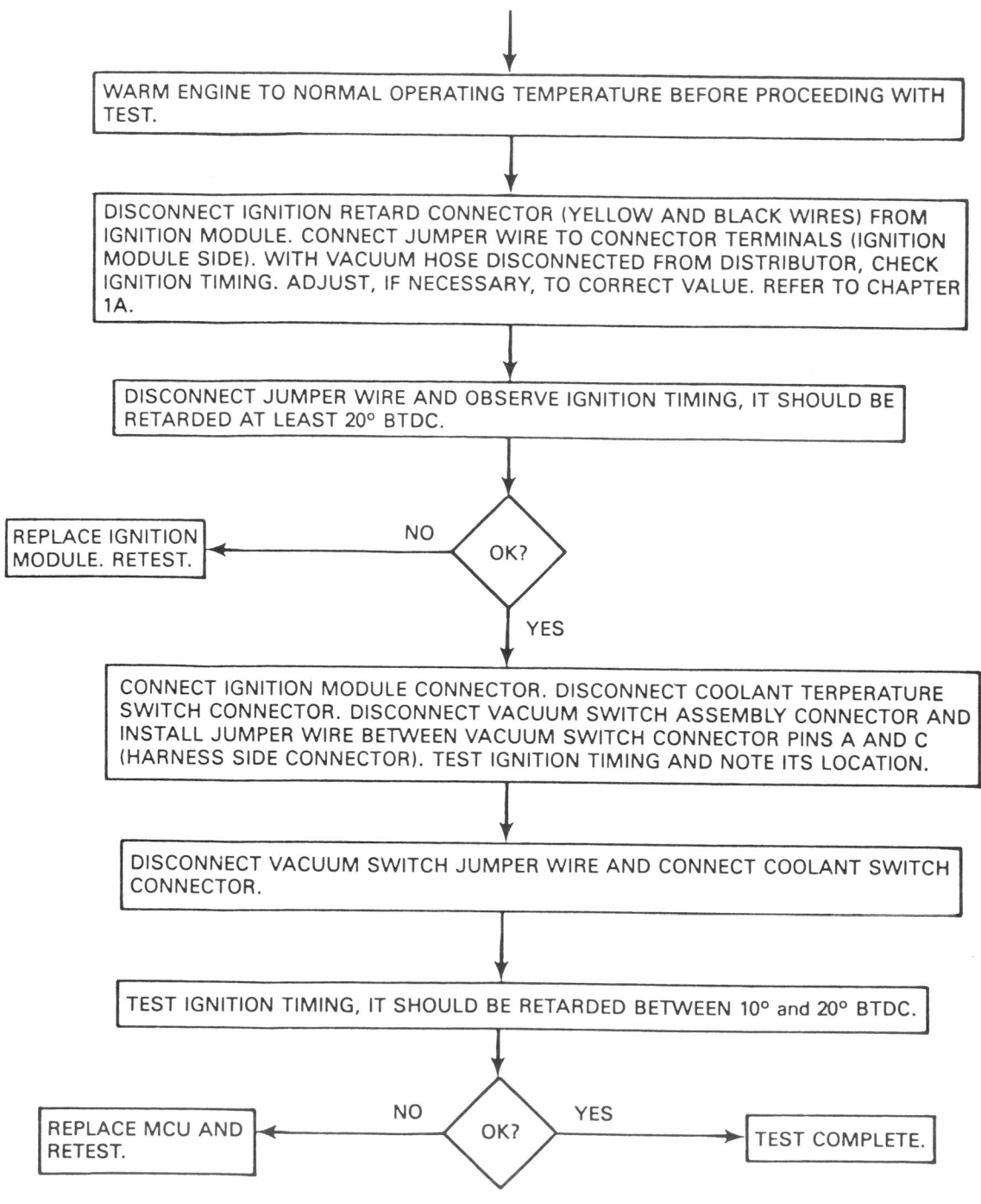

WARM ENGINE TO NORMAL OPERATING TEMPERATURE BEFORE PROCEEDING WITH TEST.

DISCONNECT IGNITION RETARD CONNECTOR (YELLOW AND BLACK WIRES) FROM IGNITION MODULE. CONNECT JUMPER WIRE TO CONNECTOR TERMINALS (IGNITION MODULE SIDE). WITH VACUUM HOSE DISCONNECTED FROM DISTRIBUTOR, CHECK IGNITION TIMING. ADJUST, IF NECESSARY, TO CORRECT VALUE. REFER TO CHAPTER 1A.

DISCONNECT JUMPER WIRE AND OBSERVE IGNITION TIMING, IT SHOULD BE RETARDED AT LEAST 20° BTDC.

REPLACE IGNITION MODULE. RETEST. ← NO — OK?

YES

CONNECT IGNITION MODULE CONNECTOR. DISCONNECT COOLANT TERPERATURE SWITCH CONNECTOR. DISCONNECT VACUUM SWITCH ASSEMBLY CONNECTOR AND INSTALL JUMPER WIRE BETWEEN VACUUM SWITCH CONNECTOR PINS A AND C (HARNESS SIDE CONNECTOR). TEST IGNITION TIMING AND NOTE ITS LOCATION.

DISCONNECT VACUUM SWITCH JUMPER WIRE AND CONNECT COOLANT SWITCH CONNECTOR.

TEST IGNITION TIMING, IT SHOULD BE RETARDED BETWEEN 10° and 20° BTDC.

REPLACE MCU AND RETEST. ← NO — OK? — YES → TEST COMPLETE.

DIAGNOSTIC TEST 5, CEC SYSTEM
OXYGEN SENSOR AND CLOSED LOOP TEST
1982 and Later Six Cylinder Engines

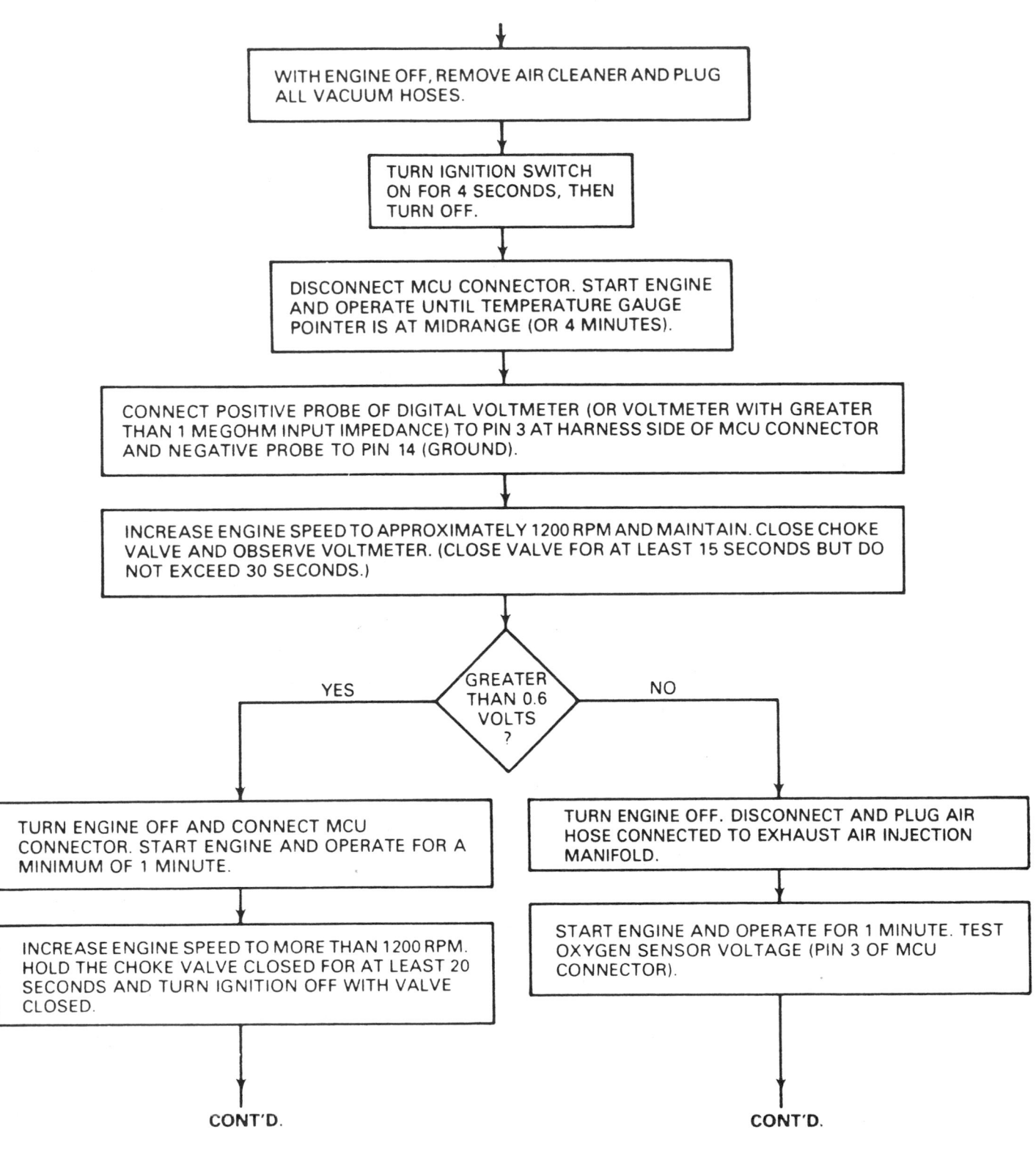

WITH ENGINE OFF, REMOVE AIR CLEANER AND PLUG ALL VACUUM HOSES.

TURN IGNITION SWITCH ON FOR 4 SECONDS, THEN TURN OFF.

DISCONNECT MCU CONNECTOR. START ENGINE AND OPERATE UNTIL TEMPERATURE GAUGE POINTER IS AT MIDRANGE (OR 4 MINUTES).

CONNECT POSITIVE PROBE OF DIGITAL VOLTMETER (OR VOLTMETER WITH GREATER THAN 1 MEGOHM INPUT IMPEDANCE) TO PIN 3 AT HARNESS SIDE OF MCU CONNECTOR AND NEGATIVE PROBE TO PIN 14 (GROUND).

INCREASE ENGINE SPEED TO APPROXIMATELY 1200 RPM AND MAINTAIN. CLOSE CHOKE VALVE AND OBSERVE VOLTMETER. (CLOSE VALVE FOR AT LEAST 15 SECONDS BUT DO NOT EXCEED 30 SECONDS.)

GREATER THAN 0.6 VOLTS ?

YES

NO

TURN ENGINE OFF AND CONNECT MCU CONNECTOR. START ENGINE AND OPERATE FOR A MINIMUM OF 1 MINUTE.

INCREASE ENGINE SPEED TO MORE THAN 1200 RPM. HOLD THE CHOKE VALVE CLOSED FOR AT LEAST 20 SECONDS AND TURN IGNITION OFF WITH VALVE CLOSED.

TURN ENGINE OFF. DISCONNECT AND PLUG AIR HOSE CONNECTED TO EXHAUST AIR INJECTION MANIFOLD.

START ENGINE AND OPERATE FOR 1 MINUTE. TEST OXYGEN SENSOR VOLTAGE (PIN 3 OF MCU CONNECTOR).

CONT'D.

CONT'D.

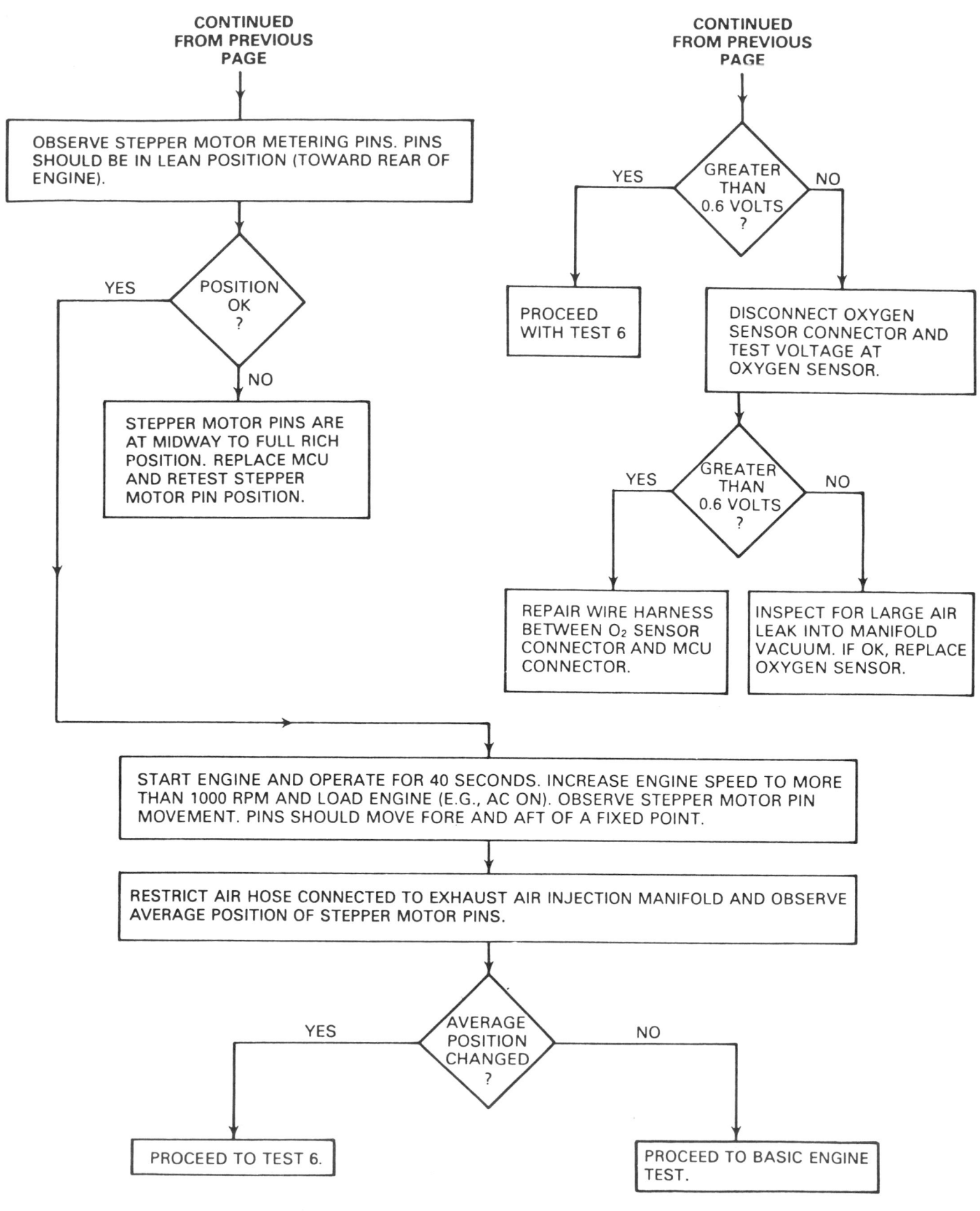

CONTINUED FROM PREVIOUS PAGE

OBSERVE STEPPER MOTOR METERING PINS. PINS SHOULD BE IN LEAN POSITION (TOWARD REAR OF ENGINE).

POSITION OK ?

YES

NO

STEPPER MOTOR PINS ARE AT MIDWAY TO FULL RICH POSITION. REPLACE MCU AND RETEST STEPPER MOTOR PIN POSITION.

CONTINUED FROM PREVIOUS PAGE

GREATER THAN 0.6 VOLTS ?

YES

NO

PROCEED WITH TEST 6

DISCONNECT OXYGEN SENSOR CONNECTOR AND TEST VOLTAGE AT OXYGEN SENSOR.

GREATER THAN 0.6 VOLTS ?

YES

NO

REPAIR WIRE HARNESS BETWEEN O$_2$ SENSOR CONNECTOR AND MCU CONNECTOR.

INSPECT FOR LARGE AIR LEAK INTO MANIFOLD VACUUM. IF OK, REPLACE OXYGEN SENSOR.

START ENGINE AND OPERATE FOR 40 SECONDS. INCREASE ENGINE SPEED TO MORE THAN 1000 RPM AND LOAD ENGINE (E.G., AC ON). OBSERVE STEPPER MOTOR PIN MOVEMENT. PINS SHOULD MOVE FORE AND AFT OF A FIXED POINT.

RESTRICT AIR HOSE CONNECTED TO EXHAUST AIR INJECTION MANIFOLD AND OBSERVE AVERAGE POSITION OF STEPPER MOTOR PINS.

AVERAGE POSITION CHANGED ?

YES

NO

PROCEED TO TEST 6.

PROCEED TO BASIC ENGINE TEST.

DIAGNOSTIC TEST 5A, CEC SYSTEM
BASIC ENGINE TEST
1982 and Later Six Cylinder Engines

IF THE RESULTS OF DIAGNOSTIC TESTS 1 THROUGH 5 INDICATE THAT THE CEC SYSTEM IS FUNCTIONING NORMALLY AND ENGINE PERFORMANCE REMAINS INADEQUATE, PERFORM THE FOLLOWING TEST.

DETERMINE WHICH DIRECTION, RICH OR LEAN, THAT STEPPER MOTOR METERING PINS CONSISTENTLY MOVE TOWARD.

NO — RICH ? — YES

- INSPECT FOR AIR LEAKS AT INTAKE MANIFOLD AND CARBURETOR GASKETS. INSPECT FOR FAULTY VACUUM HOSES OR FITTINGS. REPAIR SOURCE OF AIR LEAKS AND RETEST.
- CHECK FOR EXHAUST LEAKS AT OR NEAR O_2 SENSOR. REPAIR AND RETEST.

NO — LEAN ? — YES

IF METERING PINS VARY CONSISTENTLY WITHIN MIDRANGE, OPERATION IS NORMAL. TEST COMPLETE.

CHECK FOR FAULTY SPARK PLUG(S); MISADJUSTED IGNITION TIMING; AND MALFUNCTIONING IGNITION ADVANCE MECHANISMS.

YES — OK? — NO

ADJUST AND/OR REPLACE COMPONENTS AS NECESSARY. RETEST.

- CHECK CARBURETOR IDLE SPEED ADJUSTMENT AND CHOKE ADJUSTMENT. CHECK OPERATION OF CHOKE LINKAGE. ENSURE HOSES AND WIRES ARE NOT INTERFERRING WITH OR RESTRICTING CARBURETOR LINKAGE. REPAIR AS NECESSARY AND RETEST.
- INSPECT HEATED AIR TUBE FOR PROPER CONNECTION AT AIR CLEANER AND EXHAUST MANIFOLD HEAT STOVE. REPAIR AS NECESSARY AND RETEST.
- INSPECT EGR VALVE FOR CORRECT INSTALLATION AND PROPER OPERATION. REPAIR AS NECESSARY AND RETEST.
- INSPECT PCV VALVE FOR PROPER OPERATION. REPAIR AS NECESSARY AND RETEST.
- INSPECT VAPOR CANISTER FOR PROPER "PURGE" OPERATION AND CONDITION OF HOSES. REPAIR AS NECESSARY AND RETEST.

DIAGNOSTIC TEST 6, CEC SYSTEM
AIR INJECTION SYSTEM TEST
1982 and Later Six Cylinder Engines

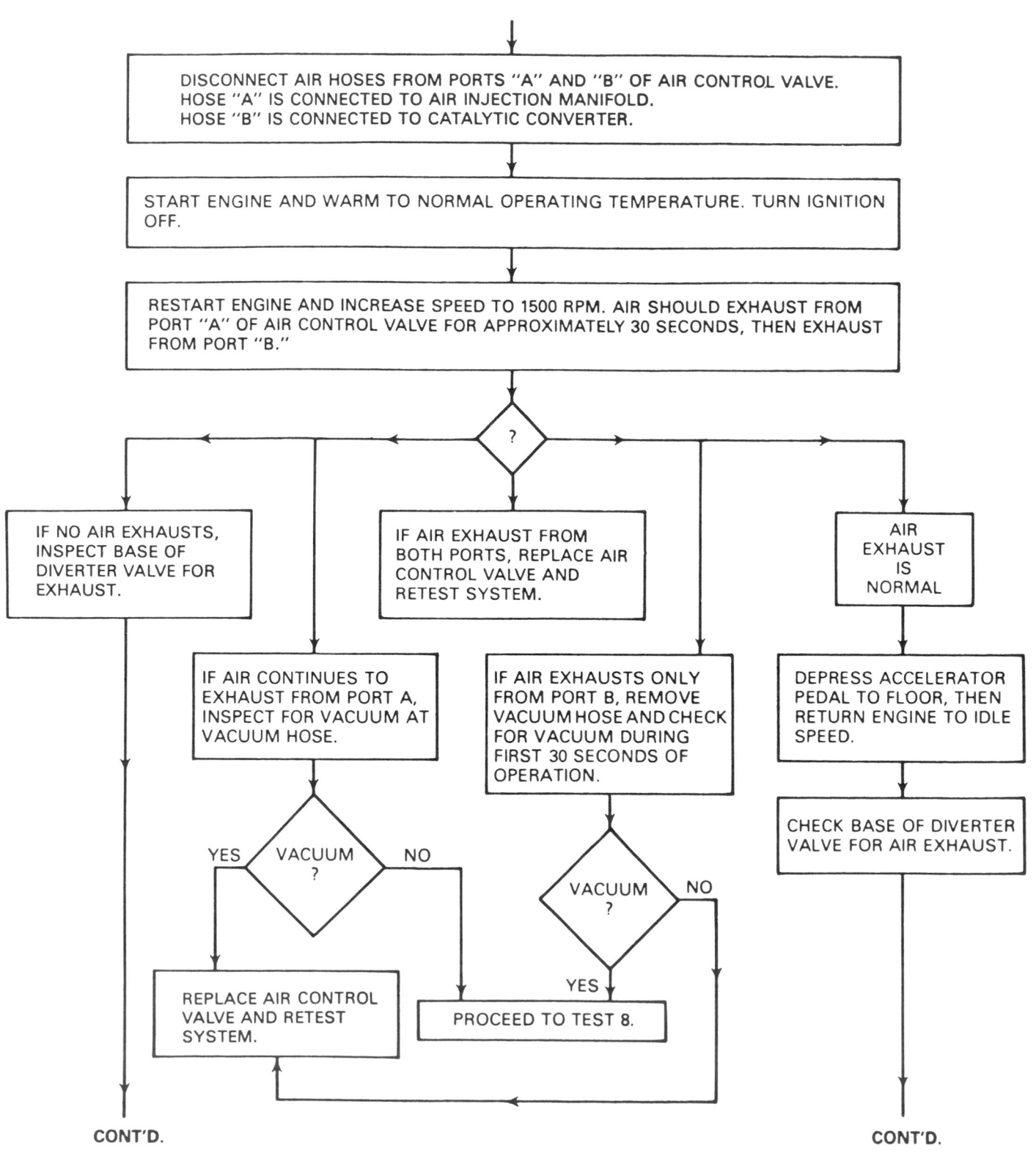

DISCONNECT AIR HOSES FROM PORTS "A" AND "B" OF AIR CONTROL VALVE.
HOSE "A" IS CONNECTED TO AIR INJECTION MANIFOLD.
HOSE "B" IS CONNECTED TO CATALYTIC CONVERTER.

START ENGINE AND WARM TO NORMAL OPERATING TEMPERATURE. TURN IGNITION OFF.

RESTART ENGINE AND INCREASE SPEED TO 1500 RPM. AIR SHOULD EXHAUST FROM PORT "A" OF AIR CONTROL VALVE FOR APPROXIMATELY 30 SECONDS, THEN EXHAUST FROM PORT "B."

?

IF NO AIR EXHAUSTS, INSPECT BASE OF DIVERTER VALVE FOR EXHAUST.

IF AIR EXHAUST FROM BOTH PORTS, REPLACE AIR CONTROL VALVE AND RETEST SYSTEM.

AIR EXHAUST IS NORMAL

IF AIR CONTINUES TO EXHAUST FROM PORT A, INSPECT FOR VACUUM AT VACUUM HOSE.

IF AIR EXHAUSTS ONLY FROM PORT B, REMOVE VACUUM HOSE AND CHECK FOR VACUUM DURING FIRST 30 SECONDS OF OPERATION.

DEPRESS ACCELERATOR PEDAL TO FLOOR, THEN RETURN ENGINE TO IDLE SPEED.

CHECK BASE OF DIVERTER VALVE FOR AIR EXHAUST.

VACUUM ?   YES   NO

VACUUM ?   NO

REPLACE AIR CONTROL VALVE AND RETEST SYSTEM.

PROCEED TO TEST 8.   YES

CONT'D.

CONT'D.

192

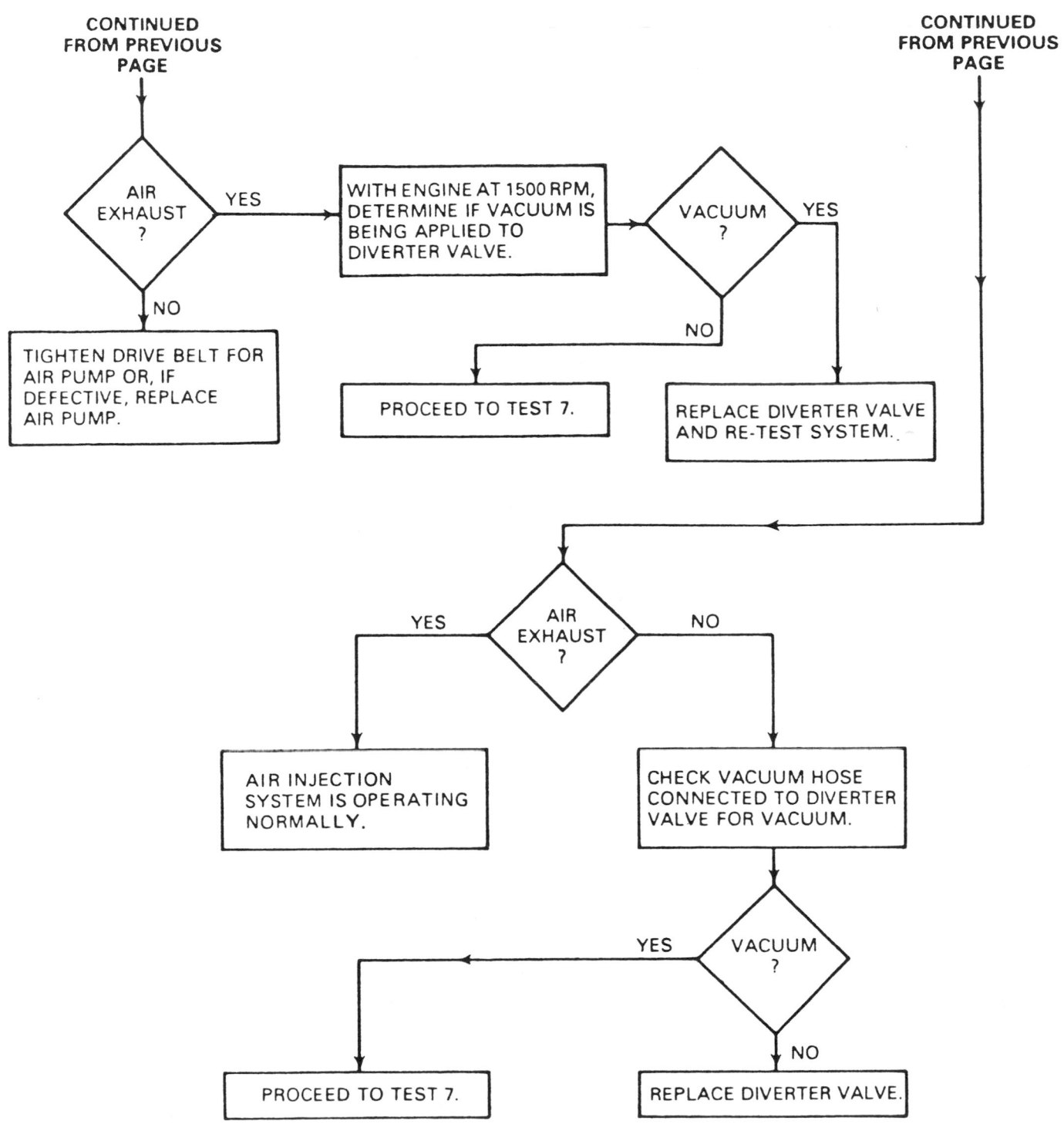

DIAGNOSTIC TEST 7, CEC SYSTEM
DIVERT SOLENOID TEST
1982 and Later Six Cylinder Engines

NOTE: WHEN APPLICABLE, DIAGNOSTIC CONNECTOR TERMINALS CAN BE USED AS TEST POINTS INSTEAD OF MCU CONNECTOR TERMINALS.

DETERMINE IF MANIFOLD VACUUM IS PRESENT AT PORT F OF DIVERT SOLENOID.

VACUUM OK ?

NO → SUPPLY MANIFOLD VACUUM AND PROCEED TO TEST 6.

YES

TURN IGNITION ON AND TEST FOR BATTERY VOLTAGE AT YELLOW WIRE TERMINAL OF SOLENOID CONNECTOR.

VOLTAGE OK ?

NO → REPAIR AND RETEST.

YES

TURN IGNITION OFF. DISCONNECT MCU CONNECTOR. WITH OHMMETER, MEASURE RESISTANCE BETWEEN PINS 20 AND 11 OF MCU WIRE HARNESS CONNECTOR.

RESISTANCE BETWEEN 50 AND 90 OHMS ?

NO →

YES

GREATER THAN 90 OHMS ?

YES →

NO

CONNECT MCU CONNECTOR. CONNECT JUMPER WIRE FROM PIN 19 TO CHASSIS GROUND.

IF RESISTANCE IS LESS THAN 50 OHMS, DISCONNECT DIVERT SOLENOID WIRE CONNECTOR AND TEST RESISTANCE BETWEEN PINS 20 AND 11.

DISCONNECT WIRE CONNECTOR FROM DIVERT SOLENOID. WITH APPROPRIATE LENGTH OF JUMPER WIRE, TEST CONTINUITY BETWEEN ORANGE WIRE TERMINAL AND MCU HARNESS CONNECTOR PIN 11.

CONT'D.

CONT'D.

CONT'D.

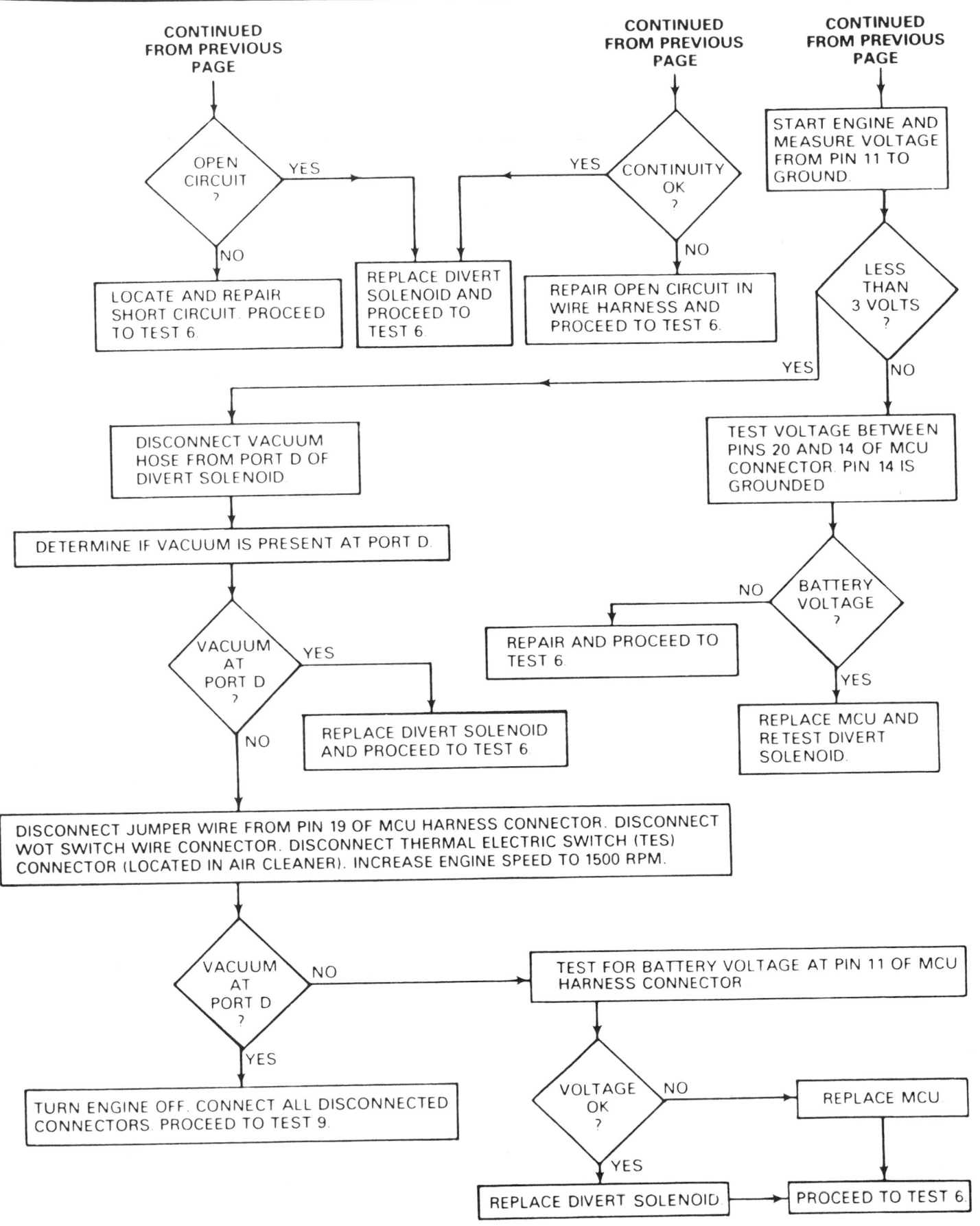

CONTINUED FROM PREVIOUS PAGE

CONTINUED FROM PREVIOUS PAGE

CONTINUED FROM PREVIOUS PAGE

START ENGINE AND MEASURE VOLTAGE FROM PIN 11 TO GROUND.

OPEN CIRCUIT ? — YES

NO

CONTINUITY OK ? — YES

NO

LOCATE AND REPAIR SHORT CIRCUIT. PROCEED TO TEST 6.

REPLACE DIVERT SOLENOID AND PROCEED TO TEST 6.

REPAIR OPEN CIRCUIT IN WIRE HARNESS AND PROCEED TO TEST 6.

LESS THAN 3 VOLTS ?

YES

NO

TEST VOLTAGE BETWEEN PINS 20 AND 14 OF MCU CONNECTOR. PIN 14 IS GROUNDED

DISCONNECT VACUUM HOSE FROM PORT D OF DIVERT SOLENOID.

DETERMINE IF VACUUM IS PRESENT AT PORT D.

BATTERY VOLTAGE ? — NO

YES

VACUUM AT PORT D ? — YES

NO

REPAIR AND PROCEED TO TEST 6.

REPLACE DIVERT SOLENOID AND PROCEED TO TEST 6

REPLACE MCU AND RETEST DIVERT SOLENOID.

DISCONNECT JUMPER WIRE FROM PIN 19 OF MCU HARNESS CONNECTOR. DISCONNECT WOT SWITCH WIRE CONNECTOR. DISCONNECT THERMAL ELECTRIC SWITCH (TES) CONNECTOR (LOCATED IN AIR CLEANER). INCREASE ENGINE SPEED TO 1500 RPM.

VACUUM AT PORT D ? — NO

YES

TEST FOR BATTERY VOLTAGE AT PIN 11 OF MCU HARNESS CONNECTOR

TURN ENGINE OFF. CONNECT ALL DISCONNECTED CONNECTORS. PROCEED TO TEST 9.

VOLTAGE OK ? — NO

YES

REPLACE MCU.

REPLACE DIVERT SOLENOID

PROCEED TO TEST 6.

195

DIAGNOSTIC TEST 8, CEC SYSTEM
UPSTREAM SOLENOID TEST
1982 and Later Six Cylinder Engines

NOTE: WHEN APPLICABLE, DIAGNOSTIC CONNECTOR TERMINALS CAN BE USED AS TEST POINTS INSTEAD OF MCU CONNECTOR TERMINALS.

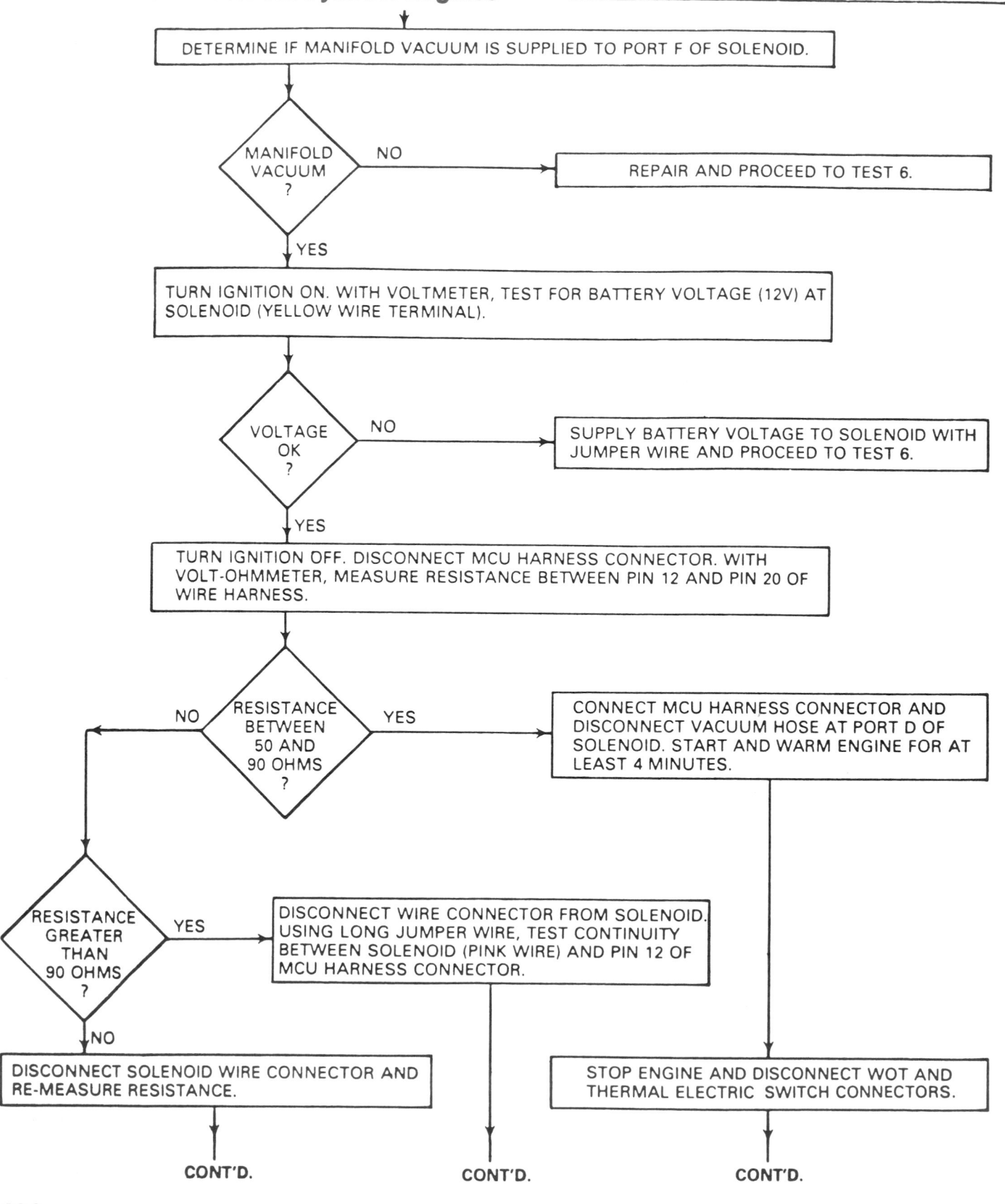

DETERMINE IF MANIFOLD VACUUM IS SUPPLIED TO PORT F OF SOLENOID.

MANIFOLD VACUUM ? — NO → REPAIR AND PROCEED TO TEST 6.

YES

TURN IGNITION ON. WITH VOLTMETER, TEST FOR BATTERY VOLTAGE (12V) AT SOLENOID (YELLOW WIRE TERMINAL).

VOLTAGE OK ? — NO → SUPPLY BATTERY VOLTAGE TO SOLENOID WITH JUMPER WIRE AND PROCEED TO TEST 6.

YES

TURN IGNITION OFF. DISCONNECT MCU HARNESS CONNECTOR. WITH VOLT-OHMMETER, MEASURE RESISTANCE BETWEEN PIN 12 AND PIN 20 OF WIRE HARNESS.

RESISTANCE BETWEEN 50 AND 90 OHMS ? — YES → CONNECT MCU HARNESS CONNECTOR AND DISCONNECT VACUUM HOSE AT PORT D OF SOLENOID. START AND WARM ENGINE FOR AT LEAST 4 MINUTES.

NO

RESISTANCE GREATER THAN 90 OHMS ? — YES → DISCONNECT WIRE CONNECTOR FROM SOLENOID. USING LONG JUMPER WIRE, TEST CONTINUITY BETWEEN SOLENOID (PINK WIRE) AND PIN 12 OF MCU HARNESS CONNECTOR.

NO

DISCONNECT SOLENOID WIRE CONNECTOR AND RE-MEASURE RESISTANCE.

STOP ENGINE AND DISCONNECT WOT AND THERMAL ELECTRIC SWITCH CONNECTORS.

CONT'D.   CONT'D.   CONT'D.

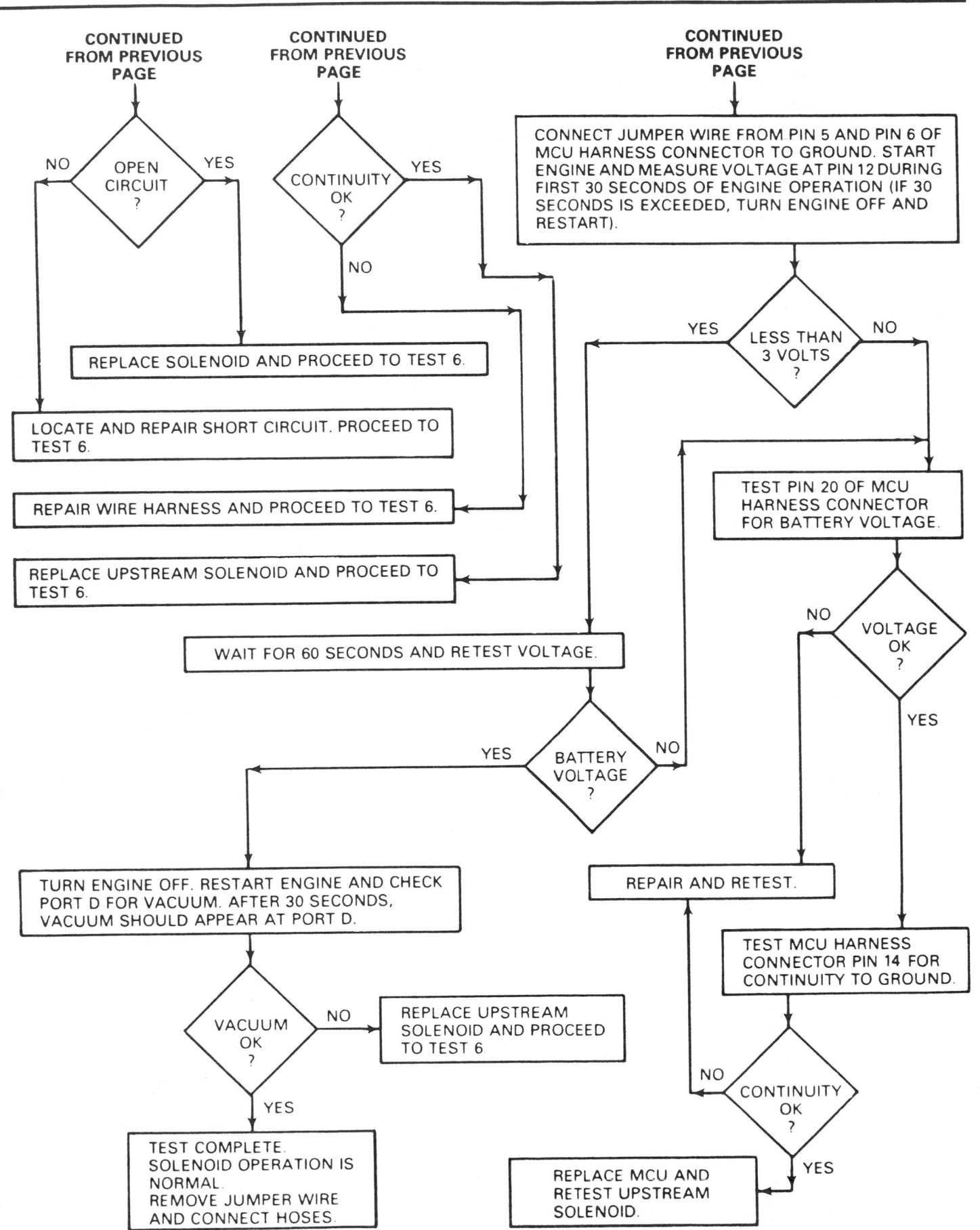

CONTINUED FROM PREVIOUS PAGE

CONTINUED FROM PREVIOUS PAGE

CONTINUED FROM PREVIOUS PAGE

OPEN CIRCUIT ?
NO
YES

CONTINUITY OK ?
YES
NO

CONNECT JUMPER WIRE FROM PIN 5 AND PIN 6 OF MCU HARNESS CONNECTOR TO GROUND. START ENGINE AND MEASURE VOLTAGE AT PIN 12 DURING FIRST 30 SECONDS OF ENGINE OPERATION (IF 30 SECONDS IS EXCEEDED, TURN ENGINE OFF AND RESTART).

REPLACE SOLENOID AND PROCEED TO TEST 6.

LESS THAN 3 VOLTS ?
YES
NO

LOCATE AND REPAIR SHORT CIRCUIT. PROCEED TO TEST 6.

REPAIR WIRE HARNESS AND PROCEED TO TEST 6.

TEST PIN 20 OF MCU HARNESS CONNECTOR FOR BATTERY VOLTAGE.

REPLACE UPSTREAM SOLENOID AND PROCEED TO TEST 6.

VOLTAGE OK ?
NO
YES

WAIT FOR 60 SECONDS AND RETEST VOLTAGE.

BATTERY VOLTAGE ?
YES
NO

TURN ENGINE OFF. RESTART ENGINE AND CHECK PORT D FOR VACUUM. AFTER 30 SECONDS, VACUUM SHOULD APPEAR AT PORT D.

REPAIR AND RETEST.

TEST MCU HARNESS CONNECTOR PIN 14 FOR CONTINUITY TO GROUND.

VACUUM OK ?
NO
YES

REPLACE UPSTREAM SOLENOID AND PROCEED TO TEST 6

CONTINUITY OK ?
NO
YES

TEST COMPLETE. SOLENOID OPERATION IS NORMAL. REMOVE JUMPER WIRE AND CONNECT HOSES.

REPLACE MCU AND RETEST UPSTREAM SOLENOID.

DIAGNOSTIC TEST 9, CEC SYSTEM IDLE SPEED CONTROL SYSTEM TEST
1982 and Later Six Cylinder Engines

NOTE: TEST MUST BE PERFORMED WITH ENGINE AT NORMAL OPERATING TEMPERATURE AND AFTER CEC SYSTEM DIAGNOSTIC TESTS ARE COMPLETED.

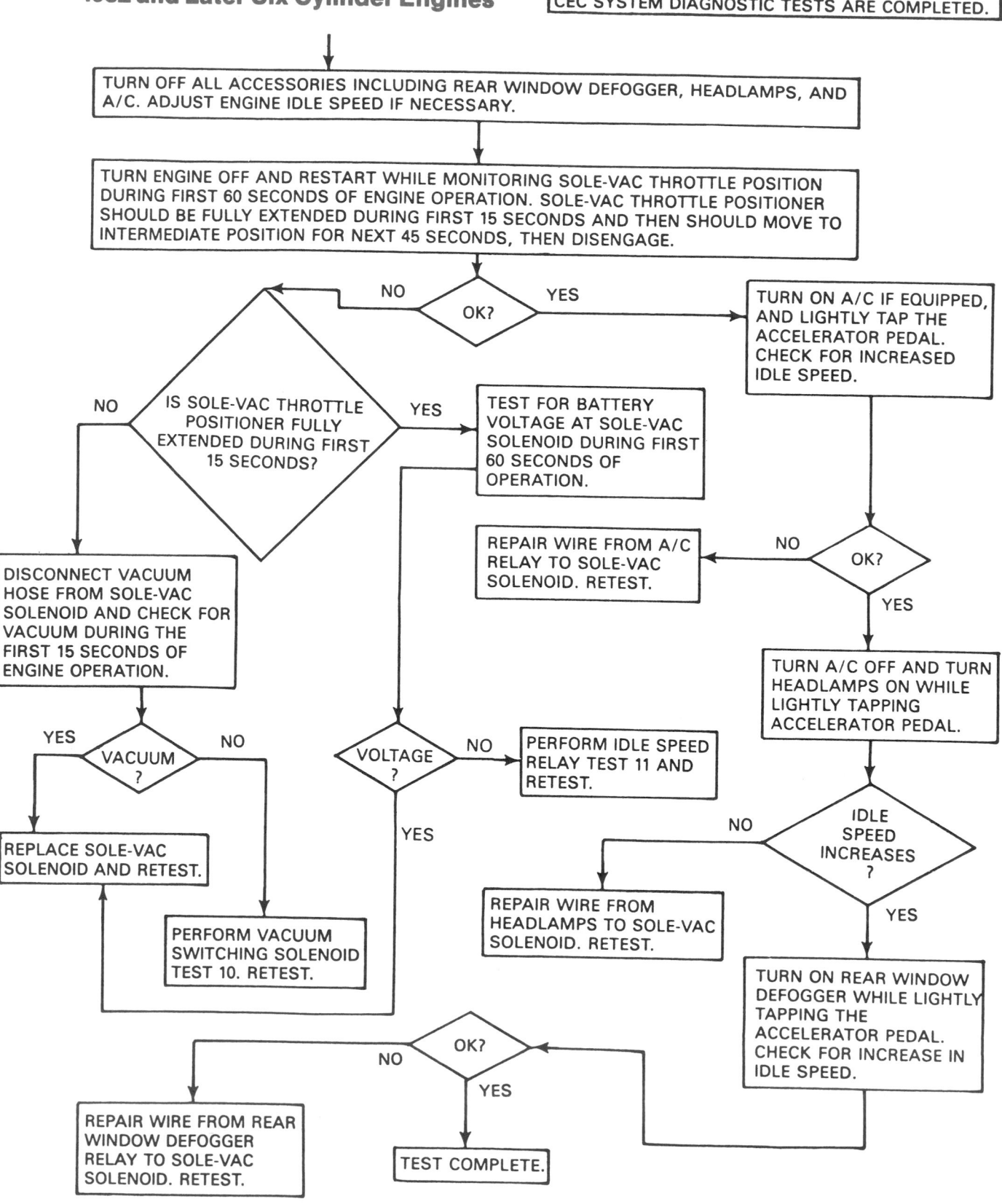

TURN OFF ALL ACCESSORIES INCLUDING REAR WINDOW DEFOGGER, HEADLAMPS, AND A/C. ADJUST ENGINE IDLE SPEED IF NECESSARY.

TURN ENGINE OFF AND RESTART WHILE MONITORING SOLE-VAC THROTTLE POSITION DURING FIRST 60 SECONDS OF ENGINE OPERATION. SOLE-VAC THROTTLE POSITIONER SHOULD BE FULLY EXTENDED DURING FIRST 15 SECONDS AND THEN SHOULD MOVE TO INTERMEDIATE POSITION FOR NEXT 45 SECONDS, THEN DISENGAGE.

OK?

IS SOLE-VAC THROTTLE POSITIONER FULLY EXTENDED DURING FIRST 15 SECONDS?

TURN ON A/C IF EQUIPPED, AND LIGHTLY TAP THE ACCELERATOR PEDAL. CHECK FOR INCREASED IDLE SPEED.

TEST FOR BATTERY VOLTAGE AT SOLE-VAC SOLENOID DURING FIRST 60 SECONDS OF OPERATION.

REPAIR WIRE FROM A/C RELAY TO SOLE-VAC SOLENOID. RETEST.

OK?

DISCONNECT VACUUM HOSE FROM SOLE-VAC SOLENOID AND CHECK FOR VACUUM DURING THE FIRST 15 SECONDS OF ENGINE OPERATION.

TURN A/C OFF AND TURN HEADLAMPS ON WHILE LIGHTLY TAPPING ACCELERATOR PEDAL.

VACUUM?

VOLTAGE?

PERFORM IDLE SPEED RELAY TEST 11 AND RETEST.

IDLE SPEED INCREASES?

REPLACE SOLE-VAC SOLENOID AND RETEST.

PERFORM VACUUM SWITCHING SOLENOID TEST 10. RETEST.

REPAIR WIRE FROM HEADLAMPS TO SOLE-VAC SOLENOID. RETEST.

TURN ON REAR WINDOW DEFOGGER WHILE LIGHTLY TAPPING THE ACCELERATOR PEDAL. CHECK FOR INCREASE IN IDLE SPEED.

OK?

REPAIR WIRE FROM REAR WINDOW DEFOGGER RELAY TO SOLE-VAC SOLENOID. RETEST.

TEST COMPLETE.

DIAGNOSTIC TEST 10, CEC SYSTEM
SOL-VAC VACUUM SWITCHING SOLENOID TEST
1982 and Later Six Cylinder Engines

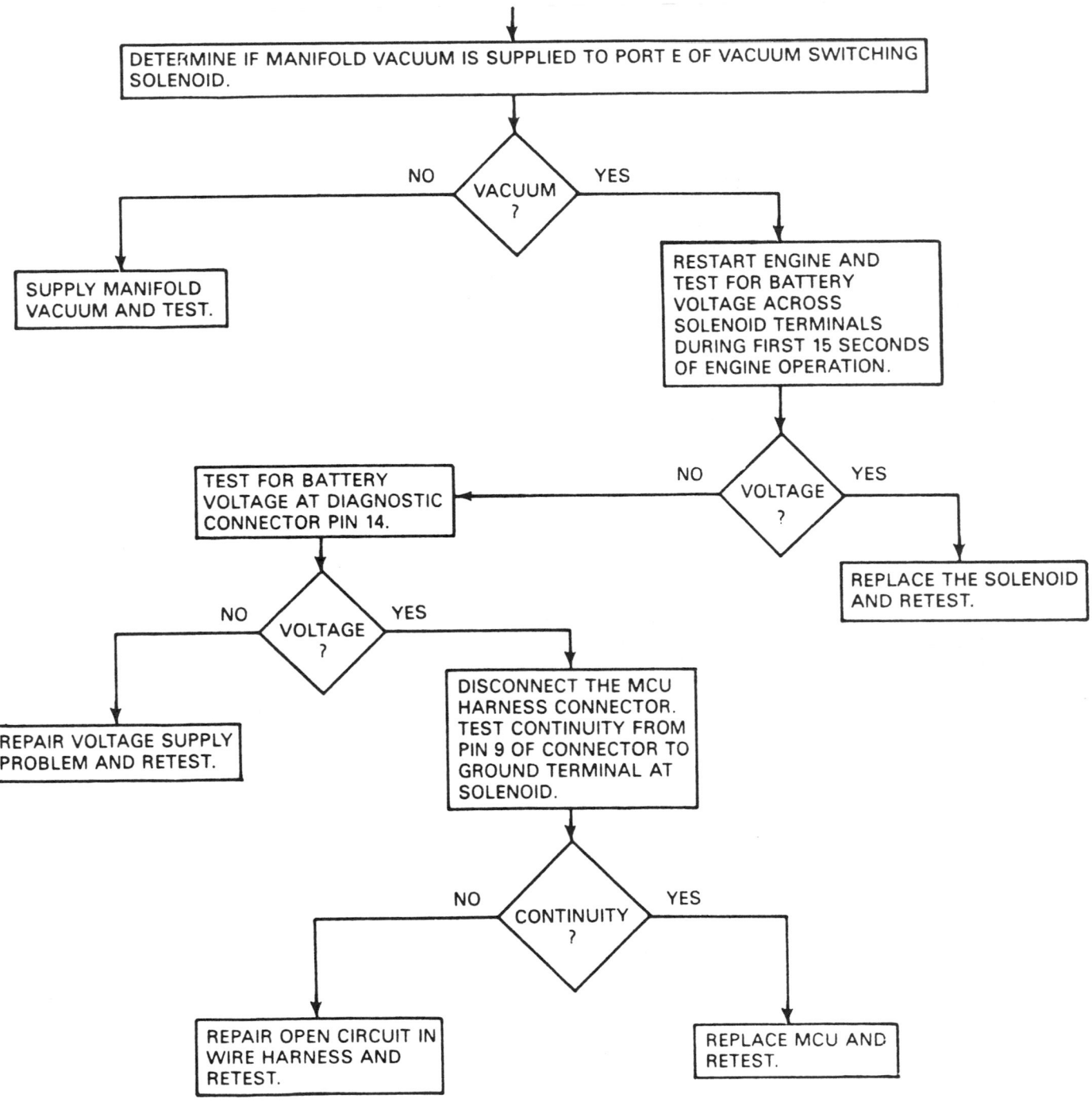

DETERMINE IF MANIFOLD VACUUM IS SUPPLIED TO PORT E OF VACUUM SWITCHING SOLENOID.

VACUUM ?

NO — SUPPLY MANIFOLD VACUUM AND TEST.

YES — RESTART ENGINE AND TEST FOR BATTERY VOLTAGE ACROSS SOLENOID TERMINALS DURING FIRST 15 SECONDS OF ENGINE OPERATION.

VOLTAGE ?

YES — REPLACE THE SOLENOID AND RETEST.

NO — TEST FOR BATTERY VOLTAGE AT DIAGNOSTIC CONNECTOR PIN 14.

VOLTAGE ?

NO — REPAIR VOLTAGE SUPPLY PROBLEM AND RETEST.

YES — DISCONNECT THE MCU HARNESS CONNECTOR. TEST CONTINUITY FROM PIN 9 OF CONNECTOR TO GROUND TERMINAL AT SOLENOID.

CONTINUITY ?

NO — REPAIR OPEN CIRCUIT IN WIRE HARNESS AND RETEST.

YES — REPLACE MCU AND RETEST.

DIAGNOSTIC TEST 11, CEC SYSTEM
SOL-VAC IDLE SPEED RELAY TEST
1982 and Later Six Cylinder Engines

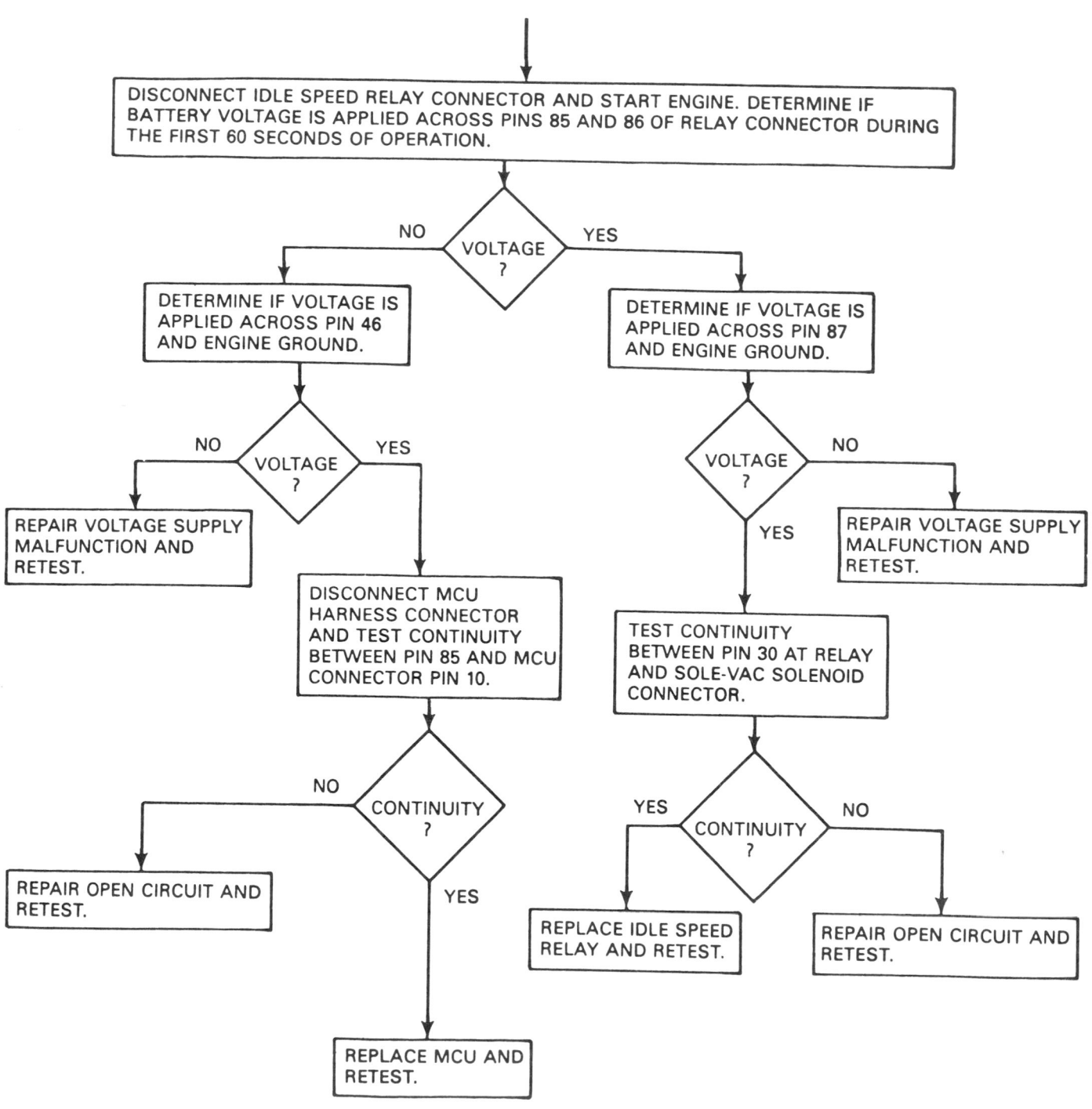

Computerized Emission Control System Four Cylinder Engines 1982 and Later

SYSTEM OPERATION

The open loop mode of operation occurs when:
1. Starting engine, engine is cold or air cleaner air is cold.
2. Engine is at idle speed, accelerating to partial throttle or decelerating from partial throttle to idle speed.
3. Carburetor is either at or near wide open throttle (WOT).

When any of these conditions occur, the MC solenoid provides a predetermined air/fuel mixture ratio for each condition. Because the air/fuel ratios are predetermined and no feedback relative to the results is accepted, this type of operation is referred to as open loop operation. All open loop operations are characterized by predetermined air/fuel mixture ratios.

Each operation (except closed loop) has a specific air/fuel ratio and because more than one of the engine operational selection conditions can be present at one time, the MCU is programmed with a priority ranking for the operations. It complies with the conditions that pertain to the operation having the highest priority. The priorities are as described below.

Cold Weather Engine Start-up and Operation

If the air cleaner air temperature is below the calibrated value (55°F or 13°C) of the thermal electric switch (TES), the air/fuel mixture is at a "rich" ratio. Lean air/fuel mixtures are not permitted for a preset period following a cold weather start-up.

ELECTRIC CHOKE (BLUE WIRE)
TACH (GREEN WIRE)

ELECTRIC CHOKE (BLUE WIRE)

TACH (GREEN WIRE)

1. Adaptive vacuum switch
2. WOT vacuum switch (cold)
3. Open loop coolant temperaure switch
4. WOT vacuum switch (warm) and enrichment coolant temperature switch
5. Open loop thermal electric switch (TES)
6. MC solenoid
13. Ground
14. B + (12v)
15.

Diagnostic connector found on 1982 and later four cylinder engines

CEC wiring diagram for 1982 and later four cylinder engines

201

At or Near Wide Open Throttle (WOT) Operation (Cold Engine)

This open loop operation occurs whenever the coolant temperature is below the calibrated switching value (95°F or 35°C) of the open loop coolant temperature switch and the WOT vacuum switch (cold) has been closed because of the decrease in manifold vacuum (i.e., less than 5 in. Hg or 17kPa).

When this open loop condition occurs the MC solenoid provides a rich air/fuel mixture for cold engine operation at wide open throttle.

NOTE: Temperature and switching vacuum levels are nominal values. The actual switching temperature or vacuum level will vary slightly from switch to switch.

At or Near Wide Open Throttle (WOT) Operation (Warm Engine)

This open loop operation occurs whenever the coolant temperature is above the calibrated switching temperature (135°F or 57°C) of the enrichment coolant temperature switch and the WOT vacuum switch (warm) has been opened because of the decrease in manifold vacuum (i.e., less than 3 in. Hg or 10kPa). When this open loop condition occurs the MC solenoid provides a rich air/fuel mixture for warm engine operation at wide open throttle.

Adaptive Mode of Operation

This open loop operation occurs when the engine is either at idle speed, accelerating from idle speed or decelerating to idle speed. If the engine rpm (tach) voltage is less than the calibrated value and manifold vacuum is above the calibrated switching level for the adaptive vacuum switch (i.e., switch closed), an engine idle condition is assumed to exist. If the engine rpm (tach) voltage is greater than the calibrated value and manifold vacuum is above the calibrated switching level of the adaptive vacuum switch (i.e., switch closed), an engine-deceleration-to-idle speed condition is assumed to exist. During the adaptive mode of operation the MC solenoid provides a predetermined air/fuel mixture.

Closed Loop

Closed loop operation occurs whenever none of the open loop engine operating conditions exist.

The MCU causes the MC solenoid to vary the air/fuel mixture in reaction to the voltage input from the oxygen sensor located in the exhaust manifold. The oxygen sensor voltage varies in reaction to changes in oxygen content present in the exhaust gas. Because the content of oxygen in the exhaust gas indicates the completeness of the combustion process, it is a reliable indicator of the air/fuel mixture that is entering the combustion chamber.

Because the oxygen sensor only reacts to oxygen, manifold air leak or malfunction between the carburetor and sensor may cause the sensor to provide an erroneous voltage output.

The engine operation characteristics never quite permit the MCU to compute a single air/fuel mixture ratio that constantly provides the optimum air/fuel mixture. Therefore, closed loop operation is characterized by constant variation of the air/fuel mixture because the MCU is forced constantly to make small corrections in an attempt to create an optimum air/fuel mixture ratio.

Diagnosis and Testing

The CEC System should be considered as a possible source of trouble for engine performance, fuel economy and exhaust emission complaints only after normal tests and inspections that would apply to an automobile without the system have been performed.

The steps in each test will provide a systematic evaluation of each component that could cause an operational malfunction. Refer to the Switch Calibrations chart during tests.

To determine if fault exists with the system, a system operational test is necessary. This test should be performed when the CEC System is suspected because no other reason can be determined for a specific complaint. A dwell meter, digital volt-ohmmeter, tachometer, vacuum gauge and jumper wires are required to diagnose system problems. Although most dwell meters should be acceptable, if one causes a change in engine operation when it is connected to the mixture control (MC) solenoid dwell pigtail wire test connector, it should not be used.

The dwell meter, set for the six-cylinder engine scale and connected to a pigtail wire test connector leading from the mixture control (MC) solenoid, is used to determine the air/fuel mixture dwell. When the dwell meter is connected, do not allow the connector terminal to contact any engine component that is connected to engine ground. This includes hoses because they may be electrically conductive. With a normally operating engine, the dwell at both idle speed and partial throttle will be between 10 degrees and 50 degrees and will be varying. Varying means the pointer continually moves back and forth across the scale. The amount it varies is not important, only the fact that is does vary. This indicates closed loop operation, indicating the mixture is being varied according to the input voltage to the MCU from the oxygen sensor. With wide open throttle (WOT) and/or cold engine operation, the air/fuel mixture ratio will be predetermined and the pointer will only vary slightly. This is open loop operation, indicating the oxygen sensor output has no effect on the air/fuel mixture. If there is a question whether or not the system is in closed loop operation, richening or leaning the air/fuel mixture will cause the dwell to vary more if the system is in closed loop operation.

TEST EQUIPMENT

The equipment required to perform the checks and tests includes a tachometer, a hand vacuum pump and a digital volt-ohmmeter (DVOM) with a minimum ohms per volt of 10 meg-ohms.

---CAUTION---

The use of a voltmeter with less than 10 meg-ohms per volt input impedance can destroy the oxygen sensor. Since it is necessary to look inside the carburetor with the engine running, observe the following precautions.

1. Shape a sheet of clear acrylic plastic at least .250 inches thick and 15 × 15 inches.

2. Secure the acrylic sheet with an air cleaner wing nut after the top of the air cleaner has been removed.

3. Wear eye protection whenever performing checks and tests.

4. When engine is operating, keep hands and arms clear of fan, drive pulleys and belts. Do not wear loose clothing. Do not stand in line with fan blades.

5. Do not stand in front of running car.

PRELIMINARY CHECKS 1981

Check A: Initialization (Start-up)

1. Remove air cleaner cover. Install plastic air cleaner cover in its place.

NOTE: Metering pins operate in tandem. Only the upper pin is visible.

2. While observing metering pins by looking down into carburetor, have a helper turn ignition switch to "ON" position without starting the engine.

3. Metering pins should move fully toward front of automobile, then reverse direction and move partially back toward rear. They will then stop and remain stationary for approximately 40 seconds, and then move in either direction.

4. If okay, continue with Step 7.

5. If not okay and pins do not move at all, perform Test 1.

6. If not okay and pins do not move at the end of 40 seconds, perform Test 2 starting with Step 3.

7. Turn ignition off.
8. Continue with Check B.

Check B: Open Loop 1 Cold Start Operation

This check should be performed with the coolant temperature below 100°F (38°C), to ensure the CTO diverts vacuum to the yellow vacuum switch. If the coolant temperature is above 100°F (38°C), cold operation may be simulated by removing the vacuum hose from the yellow vacuum switch and applying (and maintaining) a vacuum of 5 to 10 in. Hg to the switch.

1. Start engine and maintain engine rpm at 1,500.
2. At the end of initialization period (approximately 40 seconds if cold, but may vary if hot), metering pins should not move. Release vacuum applied to yellow vacuum switch (disconnect vacuum hose or vacuum pump, if used). The metering pins should move.
3. If okay, perform Check C.
4. If not okay, perform Test 2.

Check C: Open Loop 2 Wide Open Throttle (WOT)

1. While observing metering pins with engine at idle below 800 rpm and no vacuum applied to yellow vacuum switch, disconnect vacuum hose connected to blue vacuum switch.
2. Metering pins should move toward front of automobile, stop and remain stationary.
3. If okay, continue with Step 5.
4. If not okay, continue with Step 7.
5. Reconnect vacuum hose to blue vacuum switch.
6. Continue with Check D.
7. Reconnect vacuum hose to blue vacuum switch.
8. Continue with Test 3.

Check D: Open Loop 3 Idle

1. Turn engine off. Have a helper restart and idle engine below 800 rpm.
2. Observe metering pins during initialization function.
3. At the end of initialization period, metering pins should move forward, stop and remain stationary.
4. If okay, perform Check E.
5. If not okay, perform Test 4.

Check E: Closed Loop Warm Mid-Range

1. With no vacuum applied to yellow vacuum switch, increase engine speed slowly to 2,000 rpm while observing metering pins. Maintain 2,000 rpm and determine if metering pins start moving and continue in incremental steps.
2. If okay, CEC system is functioning normally. Continue with Step 5.
3. If not okay and metering pins do not move, perform Test 4.
4. If not okay and metering pins move fully to either stop and remain stationary, perform Test 5.
5. Turn engine off.
6. Install carpet pulled down during test procedures, if required.
7. Connect all vacuum hoses.
8. Install air cleaner cover.

OPERATION TESTS

Test 1: Failure to Initialize

1. Pull down forward edge of carpeting that extends up dash panel on passenger side to expose MCU and harness connectors.
2. Disconnect six-wire connector.
3. With voltmeter, check terminal 12 to determine if battery voltage is present at harness side of connector.
4. If okay, continue with Step 6.
5. If not okay, repair circuit and perform Check A.
6. Turn ignition off.

7. With ohmmeter, check terminal 10 for electrical continuity to ground.
8. If okay, continue with Step 10.
9. If not okay, repair ground circuit and perform Check A.
10. Disconnect four-wire connector.
11. Check electrical continuity between harness side connector terminal 12 of six-wire connector and each of four harness-side terminals of four-wire connector. All four indications should be nearly equal and between 50 and 95 ohms.
12. If okay, continue with Step 17.
13. If not okay, continue with Step 14.
14. Disconnect the five-wire connector on stepper motor and check electrical continuity between terminal 18 and motor housing and between other four terminals on stepper motor. Resistance to all four terminals should be nearly equal and between 53 and 85 ohms.
15. If okay, repair wiring defect in harness between stepper motor and MCU, then perform Check A.
16. If not okay, replace stepper motor and perform Check A.
17. Turn ignition on.
18. With voltmeter, check for presence of battery voltage on terminal 18, harness side of connector.
19. If okay, continue with Step 21.
20. If not okay, repair voltage supply circuit to stepper motor and perform Check A.
21. Turn ignition off.
22. Remove stepper motor, push metering pins further into motor. Install motor.
23. Connect the connector disconnected in Step 14.
24. While observing metering pins, have ignition turned on and check for metering rod movement. Pins should move.
25. If okay, replace stepper motor and perform Check A.
26. If not okay, replace MCU and perform Check A.

Test 2: Loop 1 Cold Start and Operation

NOTE: If an alternate vacuum source was used for Check B, start with step 4.

1. With the coolant temperature less than 100°F (38°C), check vacuum hose to yellow vacuum switch for vacuum. A vacuum of 5 in. Hg or more should be indicated.
2. If okay, continue with Step 4.
3. If not okay, repair vacuum leak or replace CTO valve and return to Check B.
4. Turn ignition off.
5. Pull down forward edge of carpeting extending up dash panel on passenger side to expose MCU and harness connectors.
6. Disconnect six-wire connector.
7. Check terminal 6 on harness connector for electrical continuity to ground. There should be no continuity (infinite resistance).
8. If okay, continue with Step 13.
9. If not okay, continue with Step 10.
10. Disconnect vacuum switch from harness and check feed wire (terminal 6) for electrical continuity to ground. There should be no continuity (infinite resistance).
11. If okay, repair short in harness and return to Check B.
12. If not okay, replace vacuum switch and return to Check B.
13. Apply and hold vacuum of 5-10 in. Hg to yellow vacuum switch.
14. Repeat check for electrical continuity to ground from terminal 6 of harness connector. There should be continuity.
15. If okay, replace MCU and return to Check B.
16. If not okay, continue with Step 17.
17. With vacuum still applied, check yellow wire at vacuum switch harness connector (switch side) for electrical continuity to ground. There should be continuity.
18. If okay, reconnect six-wire connector. Repair open circuity in harness and return to Check B.
19. If not okay, reconnect six-wire connector and replace vacuum switch. Return to Check B.

Test 3: Open Loop 2 Wide Open Throttle (WOT)

1. Pull down forward edge of carpeting extending up dash panel on passenger side to expose MCU and harness connector.
2. Disconnect six-wire connector.
3. Using ohmmeter with engine still at idle, test for electrical continuity to ground from terminal 7 on harness side of connector. There should be no continuity to ground (infinite resistance).
4. If okay, continue with Step 9.
5. If not okay, continue with Step 6.
6. Disconnect vacuum switches from engine compartment harness and test blue wire for electrical continuity to ground. There should be no continuity (infinite resistance).
7. If okay, repair short in harness and return to Check C.
8. If not okay, continue with Step 15.
9. Disconnect and plug vacuum hose to blue vacuum switch and retest terminal 7 for continuity to ground. There should be no continuity (infinite resistance).
10. If okay, replace MCU and return to Check C.
11. If not okay, continue with Step 12.
12. Disconnect blue vacuum switch from engine compartment harness and test blue wire for continuity to ground. There should be continuity.
13. If okay, repair open circuit in harness and return to Check C.
14. If not okay, replace switch and return to Check C.
15. Disconnect vacuum hose to blue vacuum switch and check for vacuum in hose. With engine still at idle, there should be a vacuum.
16. If okay, replace blue vacuum switch. Reconnect harness and vacuum hose and return to Check C.
17. If not okay, repair vacuum leak. Reconnect harness and vacuum hose and return to Check C.

Test 4: Open Loop 3 Idle and Closed Loop Switch-In

1. Pull down forward edge of carpeting extending up dash panel on passenger side to expose MCU and harness conductor.
2. Disconnect six-wire connector.
3. Check voltage at terminal 5 on harness side of connector. Voltage should be 7 volts ± 2 volts.
4. If okay, continue with Step 6.
5. If not okay, repair harness wiring to coil and return to Check D.
6. Check for electrical continuity to ground from terminal 9 on harness side of connector with engine at idle. There should be continuity.
7. If okay, continue with Step 15.
8. If not okay, continue with Step 9.
9. Check for vacuum at pink vacuum switch. There should be no vacuum at idle.
10. If okay, continue with Step 12.
11. If not okay, correct vacuum line routing or carburetor idle speed setting. Return to Check D.
12. Disconnect vacuum switch harness connector and check pink wire for electrical continuity to ground with no vacuum applied. There should be continuity.
13. If okay, repair open circuit in harness wiring and reconnect. Return to Check D.
14. If not okay, replace switch and reconnect harness. Return to Check D.
15. Increase engine speed to 1,500 rpm and recheck continuity. There should be no continuity.
16. If okay, return engine to idle. Replace MCU and return to Check D.
17. If not okay, continue with Step 18.
18. With engine still at 1,500 rpm, check vacuum hose at pink vacuum switch for vacuum. There should be more than 5 in. Hg.
19. If okay, continue with Step 21.
20. If not okay, return engine to idle. Repair vacuum hose routing and return to Check D.
21. Reconnect vacuum hose to pink switch.
22. Disconnect harness connection to vacuum switches.

23. With engine at 1,500 rpm, check pink wire for electrical continuity to ground at switch. There should be no continuity (infinite resistance).
24. If okay, repair short circuit in harness wiring and reconnect. Return to Check D.
25. If not okay, replace switch and reconnect harness. Return to Check D.

Test 5: Closed Loop Operation

---CAUTION---

The use of a voltmeter with less than 10 meg-ohms per volt input impedance in this test will destroy the oxygen sensor. A digital volt-ohm meter must be used.

1. Turn engine off.
2. Remove air cleaner assembly and plug vacuum hoses.
3. Turn ignition on for four seconds. Then turn off.
4. Disconnect stepper motor connector.
5. Disconnect oxygen sensor connector.
6. Using voltmeter with minimum of 10 meg-ohms per volt, connect positive (+) lead to pin 2 on oxygen sensor connector and negative (−) lead to pin 4. Set meter on 1-volt scale.
7. Start engine and warm up for four minutes.
8. Increase engine speed to 1,200 rpm and hold while closing choke butterfly valve. Keep valve closed for one minute, while observing voltmeter. Turn engine off.
9. While choke was closed, voltmeter should have indicated minimum of 0.6 volts. Turn ignition switch off.
10. If okay, replace MCU and continue with Step 19.
11. If not okay, continue with Step 12.
12. Disconnect and plug hose leading to exhaust manifold air distribution check valve at manifold.
13. Start engine and warm up for one minute.
14. Close choke valve with engine at 1,200 rpm and observe voltmeter. Turn ignition off.
15. While choke was closed, voltmeter should have indicated 0.6 volts or more.
16. If okay, replace air distribution check valve and continue with Step 18.
17. If not okay, replace oxygen sensor and continue with Step 18.
18. Unplug and reconnect hose to air distribution check valve.
19. Connect oxygen sensor to harness.
20. Connect stepper motor connector.
21. Install air cleaner (without cover) and vacuum hoses.
22. Start engine and return to Check E.

NOTE: If, after completing Test 5 and returning to Check E, the problem persists, it is not in the CEC system. Any other engine associated system that can affect mixture, combustion efficiency or exhaust gas composition can be at fault. These systems include the following.

1. Basic carburetor adjustments
2. Mechanical engine operation (plugs, valves and rings)
3. Ignition
4. Gaskets (intake manifold, carburetor or base plate)
5. Loose vacuum hoses or fittings

Component Replacement

Oxygen Sensor

1. Disconnect two-wire plug.
2. Remove sensor from exhaust pipe.
3. Clean threads in pipe.
4. Coat replacement sensor threads with antiseize compound.
5. Tighten sensor to 31 ft. lbs (42 Nm) torque.

---CAUTION---

Ensure that wire terminal ends are properly seated in plug prior to connecting plug.

NOTE: Do not push rubber boot down on sensor body beyond ½ inch above base. Oxygen sensor pigtail wires cannot be spliced or soldered. If broken, replace sensor.

Vacuum Switches

NOTE: The vacuum switches are not serviced individually. The complete assembly must be replaced as a unit.

1. Remove vacuum switch and bracket assembly from left inside fender panel.
2. Install replacement vacuum switch and bracket.
3. Connect electrical plug and vacuum hoses.

Computer

The computer unit is located in the passenger compartment beneath the dash panel on the right-hand side. Replace complete unit.

NOTE: The ECM bracket is insulated from automobile ground. Do not ground bracket.

-------- CAUTION --------

Ensure that the terminal ends are not forced out of position when connecting plug.

Stepper Motor (Carburetor)

-------- CAUTION --------

Avoid dropping metering pins and spring when removing motor.

1. Remove retaining screw and unit from carburetor.
2. Install replacement motor on carburetor with retaining screw. Tighten to 25 in.lbs. (2.8 Nm) torque.
3. Connect wire plug.
4. Install air cleaner.

Coolant Temperature Switch

1. Disconnect electrical connector.
2. Remove switch.
3. Install replacement switch. Tighten to 72 in. lbs. (7 Nm) torque.

DIAGNOSTIC TEST 1, CEC SYSTEM
SYSTEM OPERATIONAL TEST
1982 and Later Four Cylinder Engines

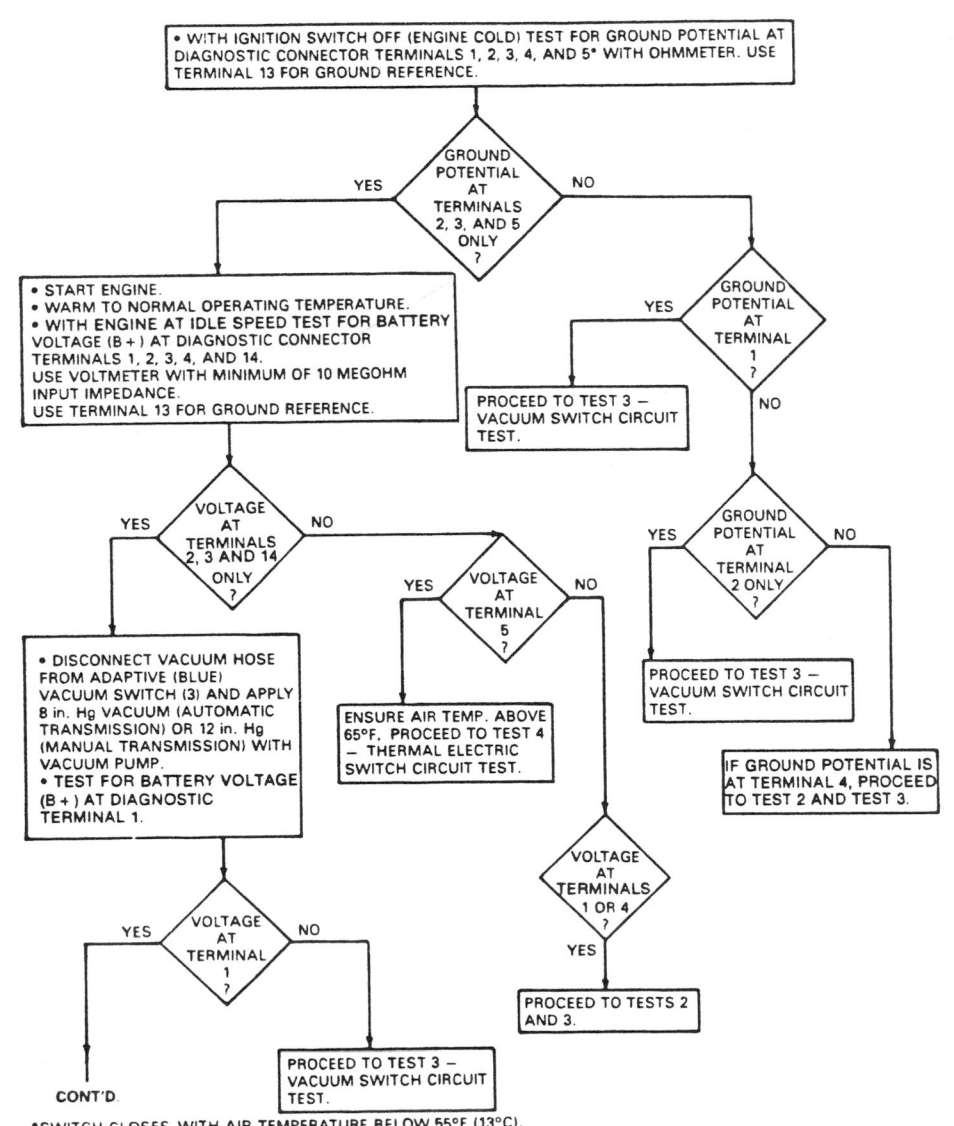

*SWITCH CLOSES WITH AIR TEMPERATURE BELOW 55°F (13°C).

CONTINUED
FROM PREVIOUS
PAGE

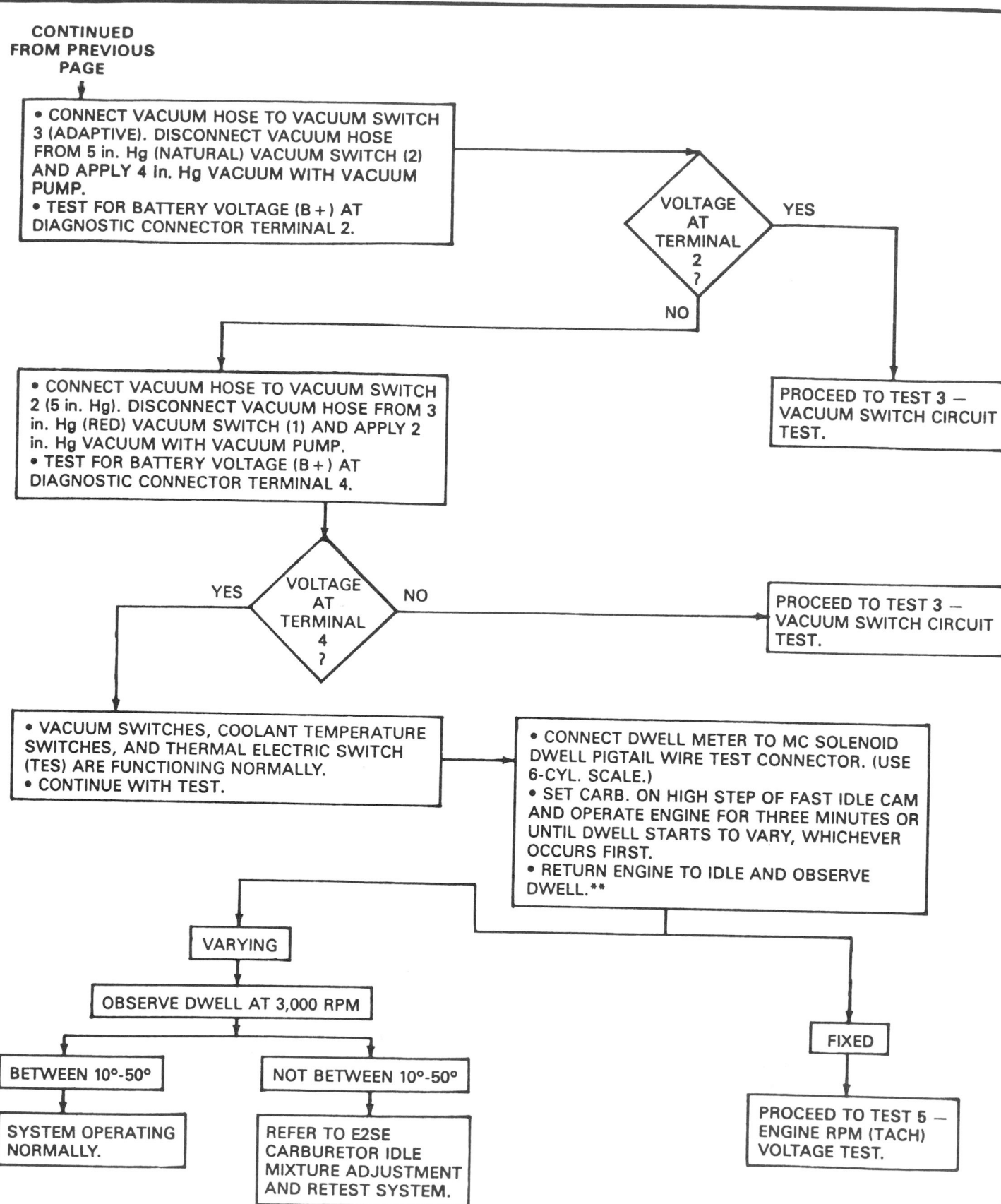

• CONNECT VACUUM HOSE TO VACUUM SWITCH 3 (ADAPTIVE). DISCONNECT VACUUM HOSE FROM 5 in. Hg (NATURAL) VACUUM SWITCH (2) AND APPLY 4 In. Hg VACUUM WITH VACUUM PUMP.
• TEST FOR BATTERY VOLTAGE (B+) AT DIAGNOSTIC CONNECTOR TERMINAL 2.

VOLTAGE AT TERMINAL 2?

YES

NO

PROCEED TO TEST 3 — VACUUM SWITCH CIRCUIT TEST.

• CONNECT VACUUM HOSE TO VACUUM SWITCH 2 (5 in. Hg). DISCONNECT VACUUM HOSE FROM 3 in. Hg (RED) VACUUM SWITCH (1) AND APPLY 2 in. Hg VACUUM WITH VACUUM PUMP.
• TEST FOR BATTERY VOLTAGE (B+) AT DIAGNOSTIC CONNECTOR TERMINAL 4.

VOLTAGE AT TERMINAL 4?

YES

NO

PROCEED TO TEST 3 — VACUUM SWITCH CIRCUIT TEST.

• VACUUM SWITCHES, COOLANT TEMPERATURE SWITCHES, AND THERMAL ELECTRIC SWITCH (TES) ARE FUNCTIONING NORMALLY.
• CONTINUE WITH TEST.

• CONNECT DWELL METER TO MC SOLENOID DWELL PIGTAIL WIRE TEST CONNECTOR. (USE 6-CYL. SCALE.)
• SET CARB. ON HIGH STEP OF FAST IDLE CAM AND OPERATE ENGINE FOR THREE MINUTES OR UNTIL DWELL STARTS TO VARY, WHICHEVER OCCURS FIRST.
• RETURN ENGINE TO IDLE AND OBSERVE DWELL.**

VARYING

OBSERVE DWELL AT 3,000 RPM

BETWEEN 10°-50°

NOT BETWEEN 10°-50°

FIXED

SYSTEM OPERATING NORMALLY.

REFER TO E2SE CARBURETOR IDLE MIXTURE ADJUSTMENT AND RETEST SYSTEM.

PROCEED TO TEST 5 — ENGINE RPM (TACH) VOLTAGE TEST.

**OXYGEN SENSOR TEMPERATURE MAY COOL AT IDLE CAUSING THE DWELL TO CHANGE FROM VARYING TO A FIXED INDICATION BETWEEN 10°-50°. IF THIS OCCURS, OPERATE THE ENGINE AT FAST IDLE TO HEAT THE SENSOR.

DIAGNOSTIC TEST 2, CEC SYSTEM
COOLANT TEMPERATURE SWITCH CIRCUIT TEST
1982 and Later Four Cylinder Engines

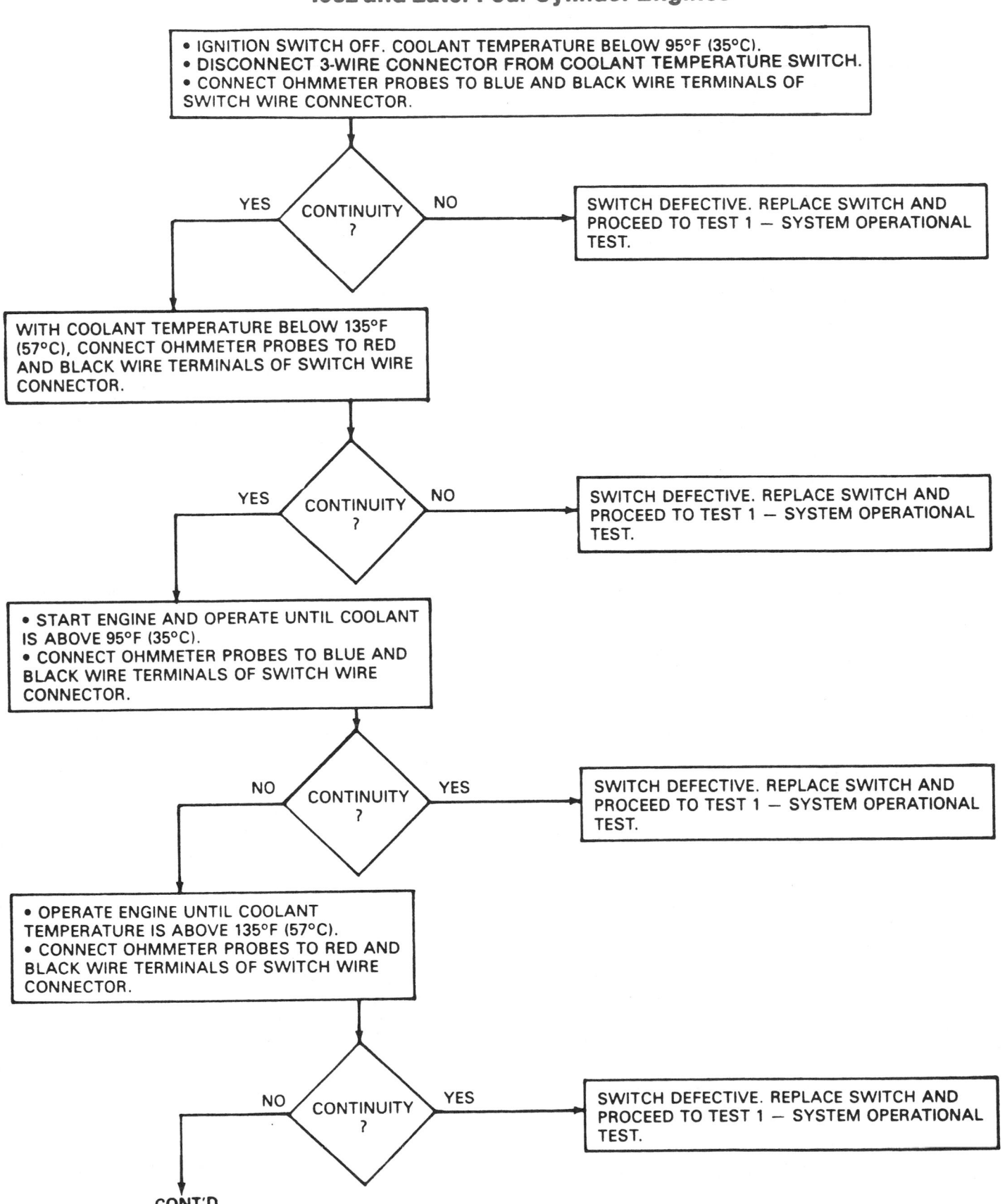

- IGNITION SWITCH OFF. COOLANT TEMPERATURE BELOW 95°F (35°C).
- DISCONNECT 3-WIRE CONNECTOR FROM COOLANT TEMPERATURE SWITCH.
- CONNECT OHMMETER PROBES TO BLUE AND BLACK WIRE TERMINALS OF SWITCH WIRE CONNECTOR.

CONTINUITY ?

YES

NO → SWITCH DEFECTIVE. REPLACE SWITCH AND PROCEED TO TEST 1 — SYSTEM OPERATIONAL TEST.

WITH COOLANT TEMPERATURE BELOW 135°F (57°C), CONNECT OHMMETER PROBES TO RED AND BLACK WIRE TERMINALS OF SWITCH WIRE CONNECTOR.

CONTINUITY ?

YES

NO → SWITCH DEFECTIVE. REPLACE SWITCH AND PROCEED TO TEST 1 — SYSTEM OPERATIONAL TEST.

- START ENGINE AND OPERATE UNTIL COOLANT IS ABOVE 95°F (35°C).
- CONNECT OHMMETER PROBES TO BLUE AND BLACK WIRE TERMINALS OF SWITCH WIRE CONNECTOR.

CONTINUITY ?

NO

YES → SWITCH DEFECTIVE. REPLACE SWITCH AND PROCEED TO TEST 1 — SYSTEM OPERATIONAL TEST.

- OPERATE ENGINE UNTIL COOLANT TEMPERATURE IS ABOVE 135°F (57°C).
- CONNECT OHMMETER PROBES TO RED AND BLACK WIRE TERMINALS OF SWITCH WIRE CONNECTOR.

CONTINUITY ?

NO

YES → SWITCH DEFECTIVE. REPLACE SWITCH AND PROCEED TO TEST 1 — SYSTEM OPERATIONAL TEST.

CONT'D.

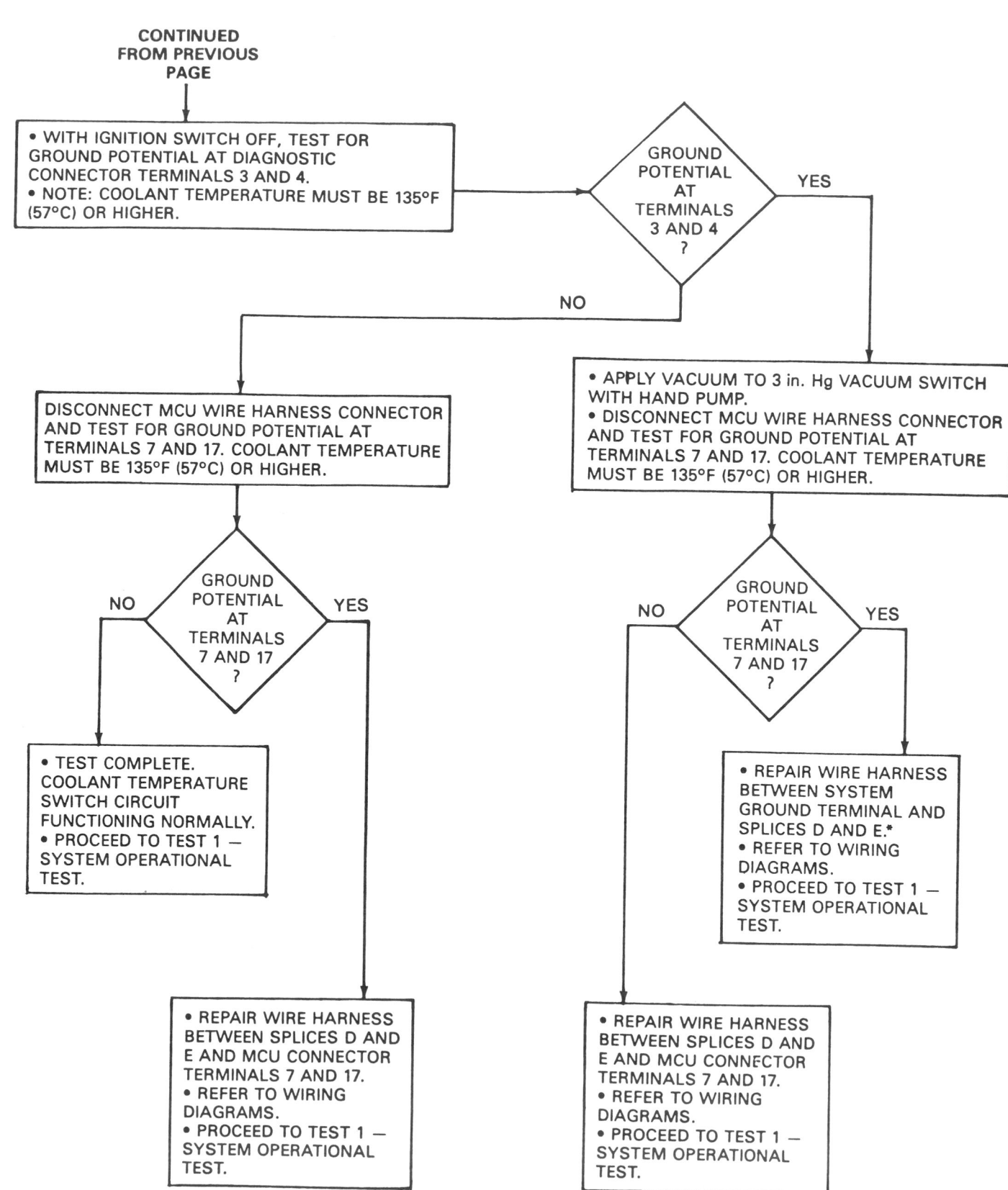

CONTINUED FROM PREVIOUS PAGE

- WITH IGNITION SWITCH OFF, TEST FOR GROUND POTENTIAL AT DIAGNOSTIC CONNECTOR TERMINALS 3 AND 4.
- NOTE: COOLANT TEMPERATURE MUST BE 135°F (57°C) OR HIGHER.

GROUND POTENTIAL AT TERMINALS 3 AND 4 ?

YES

NO

DISCONNECT MCU WIRE HARNESS CONNECTOR AND TEST FOR GROUND POTENTIAL AT TERMINALS 7 AND 17. COOLANT TEMPERATURE MUST BE 135°F (57°C) OR HIGHER.

- APPLY VACUUM TO 3 in. Hg VACUUM SWITCH WITH HAND PUMP.
- DISCONNECT MCU WIRE HARNESS CONNECTOR AND TEST FOR GROUND POTENTIAL AT TERMINALS 7 AND 17. COOLANT TEMPERATURE MUST BE 135°F (57°C) OR HIGHER.

GROUND POTENTIAL AT TERMINALS 7 AND 17 ?

NO   YES

GROUND POTENTIAL AT TERMINALS 7 AND 17 ?

NO   YES

- TEST COMPLETE. COOLANT TEMPERATURE SWITCH CIRCUIT FUNCTIONING NORMALLY.
- PROCEED TO TEST 1 — SYSTEM OPERATIONAL TEST.

- REPAIR WIRE HARNESS BETWEEN SYSTEM GROUND TERMINAL AND SPLICES D AND E.*
- REFER TO WIRING DIAGRAMS.
- PROCEED TO TEST 1 — SYSTEM OPERATIONAL TEST.

- REPAIR WIRE HARNESS BETWEEN SPLICES D AND E AND MCU CONNECTOR TERMINALS 7 AND 17.
- REFER TO WIRING DIAGRAMS.
- PROCEED TO TEST 1 — SYSTEM OPERATIONAL TEST.

- REPAIR WIRE HARNESS BETWEEN SPLICES D AND E AND MCU CONNECTOR TERMINALS 7 AND 17.
- REFER TO WIRING DIAGRAMS.
- PROCEED TO TEST 1 — SYSTEM OPERATIONAL TEST.

*INCLUDING 3 in. Hg WOT (RED) VACUUM SWITCH. REFER TO TEST 3.

DIAGNOSTIC TEST 3, CEC SYSTEM
VACUUM SWITCH CIRCUIT TEST
1982 and Later Four Cylinder Engines

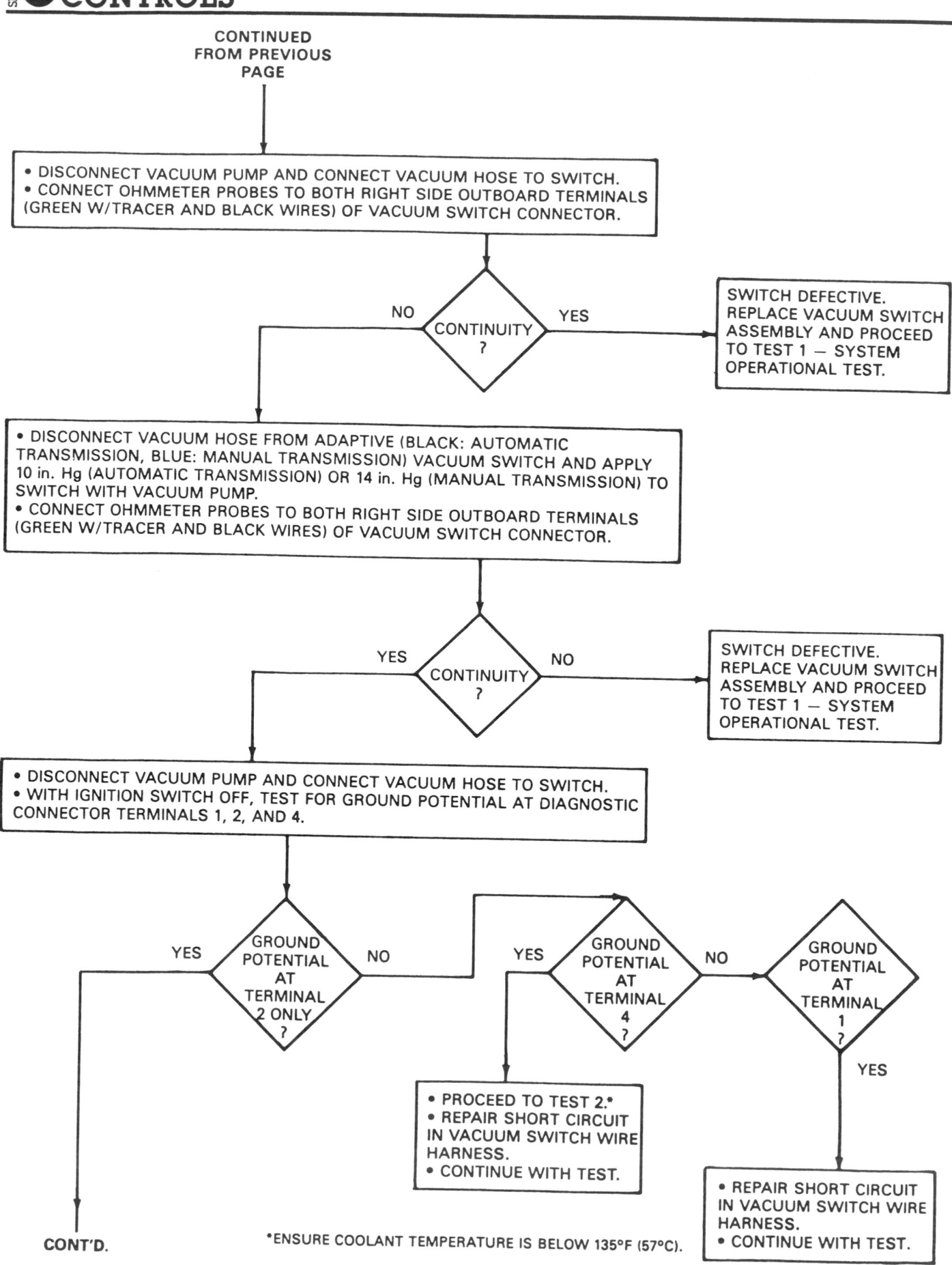

CONTINUED
FROM PREVIOUS
PAGE

• DISCONNECT VACUUM PUMP AND CONNECT VACUUM HOSE TO SWITCH.
• CONNECT OHMMETER PROBES TO BOTH RIGHT SIDE OUTBOARD TERMINALS (GREEN W/TRACER AND BLACK WIRES) OF VACUUM SWITCH CONNECTOR.

NO ← CONTINUITY ? → YES

SWITCH DEFECTIVE. REPLACE VACUUM SWITCH ASSEMBLY AND PROCEED TO TEST 1 — SYSTEM OPERATIONAL TEST.

• DISCONNECT VACUUM HOSE FROM ADAPTIVE (BLACK: AUTOMATIC TRANSMISSION, BLUE: MANUAL TRANSMISSION) VACUUM SWITCH AND APPLY 10 in. Hg (AUTOMATIC TRANSMISSION) OR 14 in. Hg (MANUAL TRANSMISSION) TO SWITCH WITH VACUUM PUMP.
• CONNECT OHMMETER PROBES TO BOTH RIGHT SIDE OUTBOARD TERMINALS (GREEN W/TRACER AND BLACK WIRES) OF VACUUM SWITCH CONNECTOR.

YES ← CONTINUITY ? → NO

SWITCH DEFECTIVE. REPLACE VACUUM SWITCH ASSEMBLY AND PROCEED TO TEST 1 — SYSTEM OPERATIONAL TEST.

• DISCONNECT VACUUM PUMP AND CONNECT VACUUM HOSE TO SWITCH.
• WITH IGNITION SWITCH OFF, TEST FOR GROUND POTENTIAL AT DIAGNOSTIC CONNECTOR TERMINALS 1, 2, AND 4.

YES ← GROUND POTENTIAL AT TERMINAL 2 ONLY ? → NO

YES ← GROUND POTENTIAL AT TERMINAL 4 ? → NO

GROUND POTENTIAL AT TERMINAL 1 ?
→ YES

• PROCEED TO TEST 2.*
• REPAIR SHORT CIRCUIT IN VACUUM SWITCH WIRE HARNESS.
• CONTINUE WITH TEST.

• REPAIR SHORT CIRCUIT IN VACUUM SWITCH WIRE HARNESS.
• CONTINUE WITH TEST.

CONT'D.

*ENSURE COOLANT TEMPERATURE IS BELOW 135°F (57°C).

CONTINUED
FROM PREVIOUS
PAGE

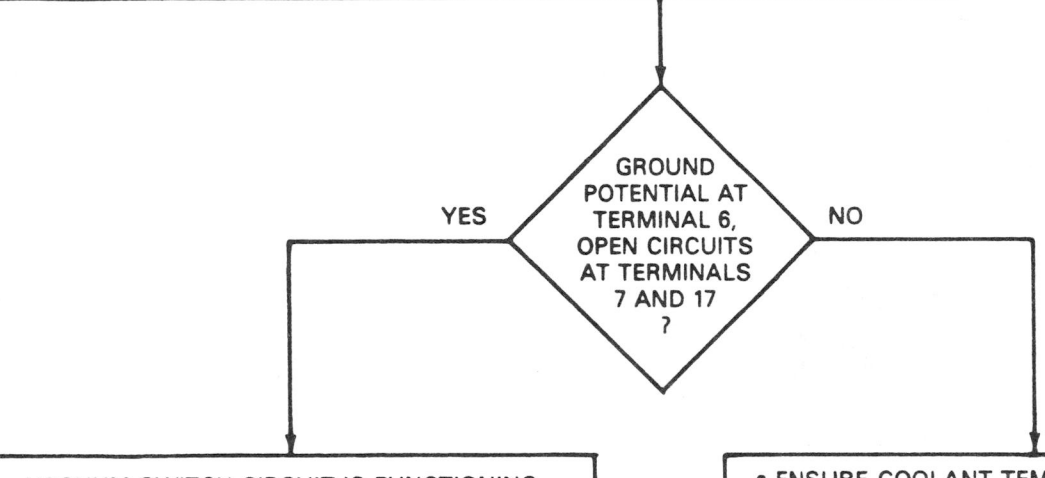

• START ENGINE AND OPERATE UNTIL COOLANT TEMPERATURE EXCEEDS 135°F (57°C).
• CONNECT VACUUM GAUGE TO MANIFOLD VACUUM SOURCE. DISCONNECT MCU WIRE HARNESS CONNECTOR.
• TEST FOR OPEN CIRCUIT AT MCU WIRE HARNESS CONNECTOR TERMINAL 5 WHILE ACCELERATING ENGINE AND DECREASING MANIFOLD VACUUM TO LESS THAN 9 in. Hg (AUTOMATIC TRANSMISSION) OR LESS THAN 13 in. Hg (MANUAL TRANSMISSION).
• TEST FOR GROUND POTENTIAL AT MCU WIRE HARNESS CONNECTOR TERMINAL 6 WHILE ACCELERATING ENGINE AND DECREASING MANIFOLD VACUUM TO LESS THAN 5 in. Hg.
• TEST FOR OPEN CIRCUIT AT MCU WIRE HARNESS CONNECTOR TERMINAL 17 WHILE ACCELERATING ENGINE AND DECREASING MANIFOLD VACUUM TO LESS THAN 3 in. Hg.

GROUND POTENTIAL AT TERMINAL 6, OPEN CIRCUITS AT TERMINALS 7 AND 17 ?

YES

NO

• VACUUM SWITCH CIRCUIT IS FUNCTIONING NORMALLY.
• CONNECT MCU CONNECTOR AND DISCONNECT VACUUM GAUGE.
• PROCEED TO TEST 1 — SYSTEM OPERATIONAL TEST.

• ENSURE COOLANT TEMPERATURE IS ABOVE 135°F (57°C).
• REFER TO TEST 2.
• INSPECT VACUUM HOSES AND FITTINGS. REPAIR AS NECESSARY.
• REPAIR WIRE HARNESS BETWEEN SPLICES B, C, AND E, AND MCU CONNECTOR. REFER TO WIRING DIAGRAMS.
• RETEST VACUUM SWITCH CIRCUIT.

DIAGNOSTIC TEST 4, CEC SYSTEM
THERMAL ELECTRIC SWITCH (TES) CIRCUIT TEST
1982 and Later Four Cylinder Engines

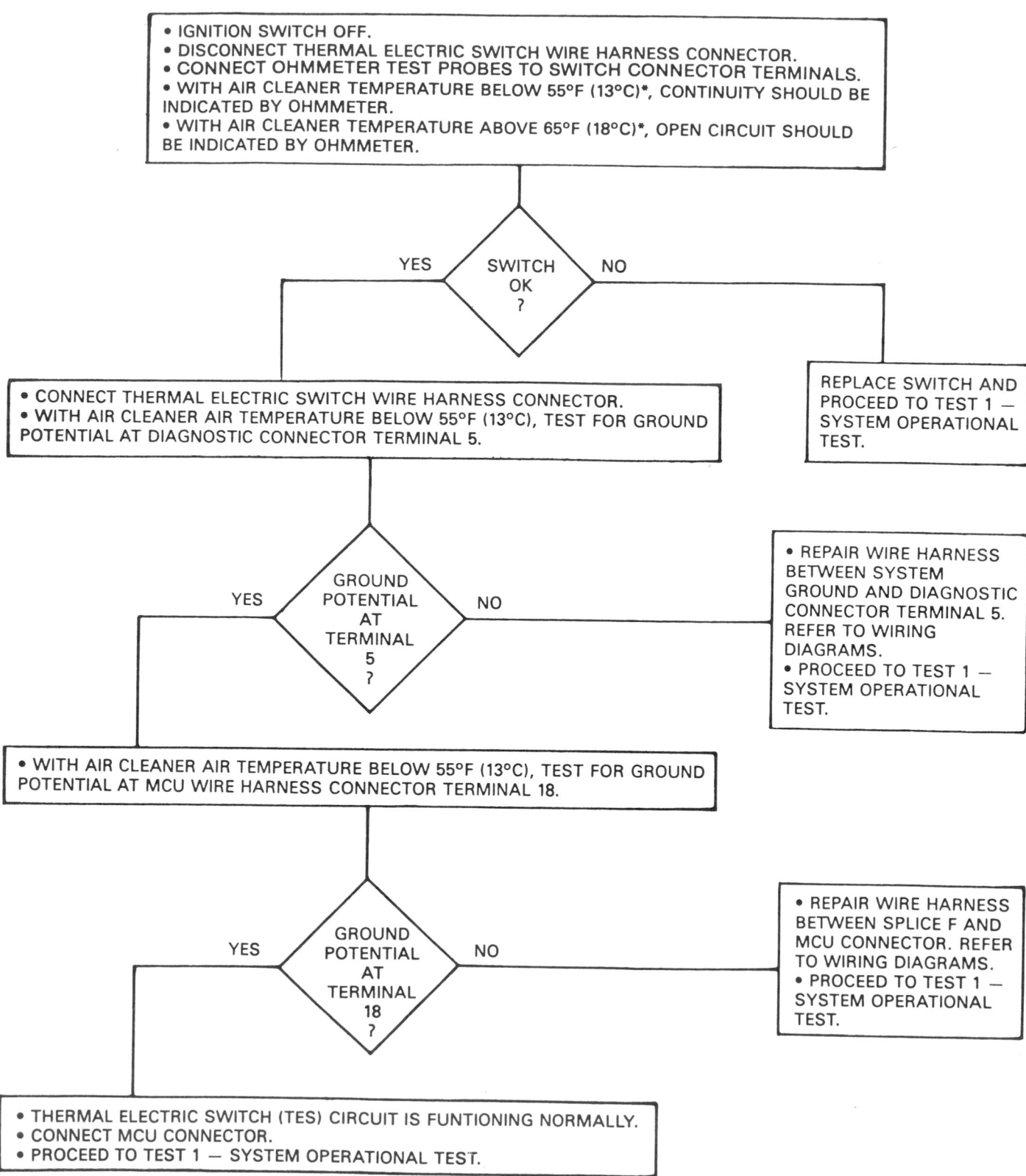

- IGNITION SWITCH OFF.
- DISCONNECT THERMAL ELECTRIC SWITCH WIRE HARNESS CONNECTOR.
- CONNECT OHMMETER TEST PROBES TO SWITCH CONNECTOR TERMINALS.
- WITH AIR CLEANER TEMPERATURE BELOW 55°F (13°C)*, CONTINUITY SHOULD BE INDICATED BY OHMMETER.
- WITH AIR CLEANER TEMPERATURE ABOVE 65°F (18°C)*, OPEN CIRCUIT SHOULD BE INDICATED BY OHMMETER.

SWITCH OK ?

YES / NO

NO → REPLACE SWITCH AND PROCEED TO TEST 1 — SYSTEM OPERATIONAL TEST.

YES →
- CONNECT THERMAL ELECTRIC SWITCH WIRE HARNESS CONNECTOR.
- WITH AIR CLEANER AIR TEMPERATURE BELOW 55°F (13°C), TEST FOR GROUND POTENTIAL AT DIAGNOSTIC CONNECTOR TERMINAL 5.

GROUND POTENTIAL AT TERMINAL 5 ?

YES / NO

NO →
- REPAIR WIRE HARNESS BETWEEN SYSTEM GROUND AND DIAGNOSTIC CONNECTOR TERMINAL 5. REFER TO WIRING DIAGRAMS.
- PROCEED TO TEST 1 — SYSTEM OPERATIONAL TEST.

YES →
- WITH AIR CLEANER AIR TEMPERATURE BELOW 55°F (13°C), TEST FOR GROUND POTENTIAL AT MCU WIRE HARNESS CONNECTOR TERMINAL 18.

GROUND POTENTIAL AT TERMINAL 18 ?

YES / NO

NO →
- REPAIR WIRE HARNESS BETWEEN SPLICE F AND MCU CONNECTOR. REFER TO WIRING DIAGRAMS.
- PROCEED TO TEST 1 — SYSTEM OPERATIONAL TEST.

YES →
- THERMAL ELECTRIC SWITCH (TES) CIRCUIT IS FUNTIONING NORMALLY.
- CONNECT MCU CONNECTOR.
- PROCEED TO TEST 1 — SYSTEM OPERATIONAL TEST.

*WITH DECREASING AIR TEMPERATURE, SWITCH CLOSES AT 55°F (13°C). WITH INCREASING AIR TEMPERATURE, SWITCH OPENS AT 65°F (18°C).

DIAGNOSTIC TEST 5, CEC SYSTEM
ENGINE RPM (TACH) VOLTAGE TEST
1982 and Later Four Cylinder Engines

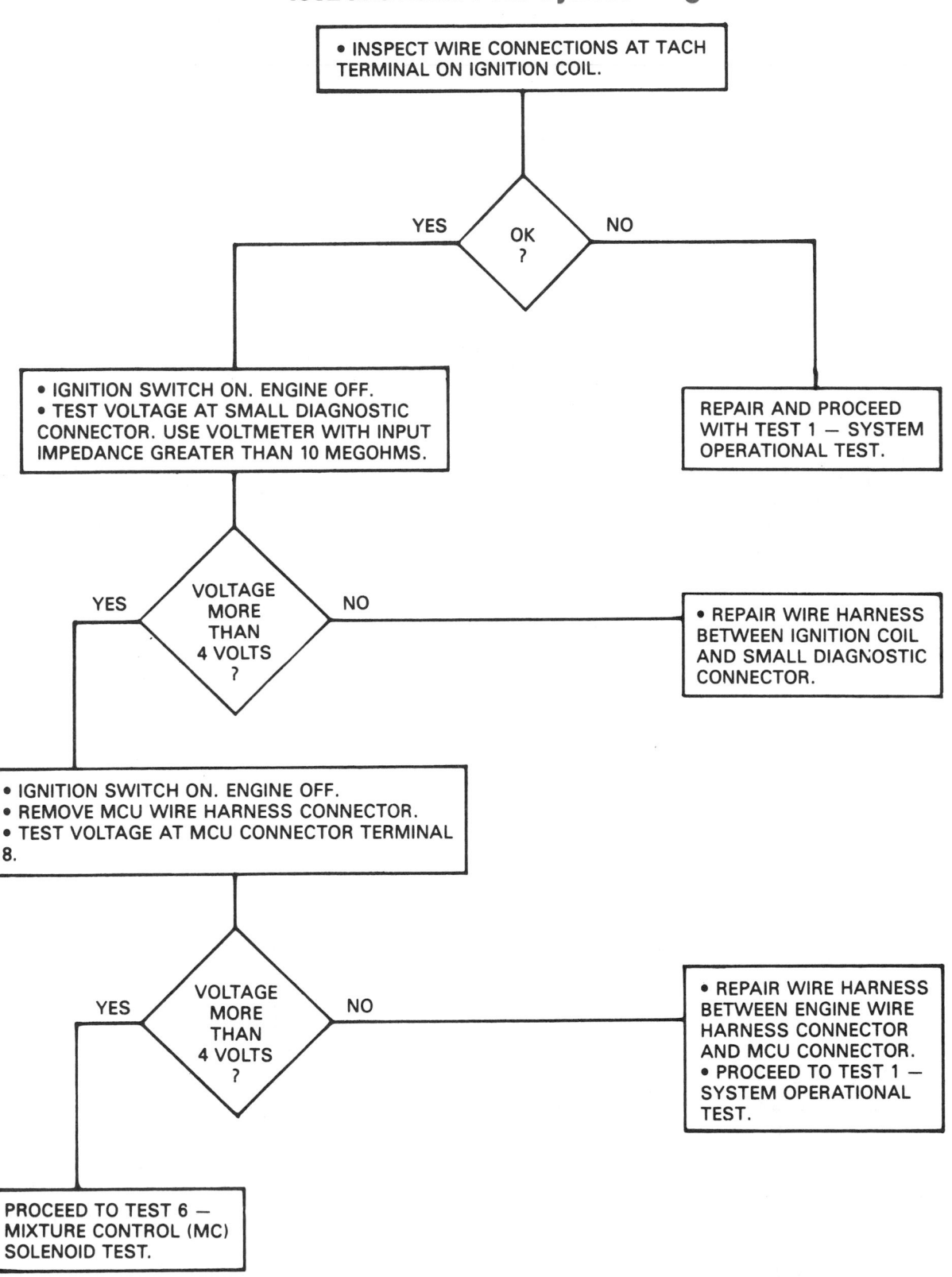

• INSPECT WIRE CONNECTIONS AT TACH TERMINAL ON IGNITION COIL.

OK ?

YES

NO

• IGNITION SWITCH ON. ENGINE OFF.
• TEST VOLTAGE AT SMALL DIAGNOSTIC CONNECTOR. USE VOLTMETER WITH INPUT IMPEDANCE GREATER THAN 10 MEGOHMS.

REPAIR AND PROCEED WITH TEST 1 — SYSTEM OPERATIONAL TEST.

VOLTAGE MORE THAN 4 VOLTS ?

YES

NO

• REPAIR WIRE HARNESS BETWEEN IGNITION COIL AND SMALL DIAGNOSTIC CONNECTOR.

• IGNITION SWITCH ON. ENGINE OFF.
• REMOVE MCU WIRE HARNESS CONNECTOR.
• TEST VOLTAGE AT MCU CONNECTOR TERMINAL 8.

VOLTAGE MORE THAN 4 VOLTS ?

YES

NO

• REPAIR WIRE HARNESS BETWEEN ENGINE WIRE HARNESS CONNECTOR AND MCU CONNECTOR.
• PROCEED TO TEST 1 — SYSTEM OPERATIONAL TEST.

PROCEED TO TEST 6 — MIXTURE CONTROL (MC) SOLENOID TEST.

DIAGNOSTIC TEST 6, CEC SYSTEM
MIXTURE CONTROL (MC) SOLENOID CIRCUIT TEST
1982 and Later Four Cylinder Engines

NOTE: USE VOLT METER WITH INPUT IMPEDANCE OF 10 MEGOHMS OR GREATER.

CONTINUED
FROM PREVIOUS
PAGE

CONTINUED
FROM PREVIOUS
PAGE

CONTINUED
FROM PREVIOUS
PAGE

• WHILE OBSERVING VOLTMETER, CREATE AIR LEAK BY DISCONNECTING VACUUM HOSE. THIS WILL CAUSE LEAN AIR/FUEL MIXTURE.
• CONNECT VACUUM HOSE. WHILE OBSERVING VOLTMETER, CLOSE CHOKE VALVE FOR 15 SECONDS. THIS WILL CAUSE RICH AIR/FUEL MIXTURE.

• IF VOLTAGE IS VARYING ABOVE 1 VOLT, RICH AIR/FUEL MIXTURE CONDITION EXISTS. REFER TO CARBURETOR MODELS E2SE/2SE SECTION AND REPAIR AS NECESSARY.
• RETEST SYSTEM.
• IF VOLTAGE IS VARYING BELOW 600 MV, LEAN AIR/FUEL MIXTURE CONDITION EXISTS. INSPECT FOR AIR LEAK INTO MANIFOLD VACUUM. REPAIR AS NECESSARY AND RETEST SYSTEM. IF NO AIR LEAK EXISTS, REPLACE OXYGEN SENSOR AND RETEST SYSTEM.
• IF VOLTAGE IS NOT VARYING, REPLACE OXYGEN SENSOR AND RETEST SYSTEM.

• REPAIR WIRE HARNESS BETWEEN IGNITION SWITCH AND SPLICE A. REFER TO WIRING DIAGRAMS.
• PROCEED WITH TEST 1 — SYSTEM OPERATIONAL TEST.

VARYING VOLTAGE DECREASES AND INCREASES WITH AIR/FUEL MIXTURE CHANGES ?

YES

NO

• OXYGEN SENSOR FUNCTIONING NORMALLY.
• REPLACE MCU AND REFER TO TEST 1 — SYSTEM OPERATIONAL TEST.

• REPLACE OXYGEN SENSOR.
• PROCEED WITH TEST 1 — SYSTEM OPERATIONAL TEST.

.250 INCH HOLE

5.5 INCHES

13 INCHES

Air cleaner cover dimensions

AMC COMPUTER CONTROLLED CATALYTIC CONVERTER (C-4) SYSTEM

General Information

The C-4 system incorporates a self-diagnostic feature that enables quicker determination of system malfunctions. This system is used with selected four cylinder engines, depending upon the emission requirements. The ECM (microprocessor) is the brains of the C4 System. It is programmed to determine the correct air/fuel mixture necessary for each engine operating mode. This is accomplished via the several data inputs and the standard data stored in the "read only memory" (ROM) circuit.

The ECM also contains a programmable read only memory (PROM) circuit (calibration unit) that has stored data unique to the automobile. The PROM contains the instructions the on-board computer needs to control engine operation under a variety of loads and conditions.

An oxygen sensor provides a variable voltage (100 to 900 mv) for the microprocessor (ECM) that is actually a voltage analog for the oxygen content in the exhaust gas. As the oxygen content increases (lean mixture), the voltage output from the sensor decreases proportionally and as the oxygen content decreases (rich mixture), the voltage output increases proportionally. The microprocessor uses the voltage data to control the mixture control (MC) solenoid in the model E2SE carburetor and maintain an optimum air/fuel mixture. In addition to the oxygen sensor, the following data sensors are used with the C4 System.

• Vacuum Switch Closed during engine idle and partial throttle (Adaptive Mode of Operation).

• Wide Open Throttle (WOT) Switch When a wide open throttle condition occurs, the decreased manifold vacuum (at 5 in. Hg) closes the WOT switch, which results in the mixture control solenoid being regulated to provide the rich air/fuel mixture necessary for the increased air flow (WOT Mode of Operation).

• Engine rpm Voltage from Distributor to The Mixture Control Solenoid is de-energized until the voltage is equivalent to 200 rpm. The result is a rich air/fuel mixture for engine starting (Inhibit or Starting Mode of Operation).

• Coolant Temperature Sensor During engine warmup, below 150°F (66°C), the electrical impedance of the Coolant Temperature Sensor is high. The result is the C4 Computer does not accept the Oxygen Sensor voltage output and a fixed air/fuel mixture is maintained (Open Loop Mode of Operation).

NOTE: In addition to the above data input to the C4 Computer, the computer also determines the temperature of the Oxygen Sensor by sensing its electrical impedance. Until the Oxygen Sensor is heated to a temperature of 600°F (320°C), a fixed air/fuel mixture is maintained (Open Loop Mode of Operation).

The Mixture Control (MC) Solenoid is an electro-mechanical device integral with the carburetor that regulates the air/fuel mixture according to "commands" from the ECM. One terminal of the MC Solenoid is connected to 12v (battery voltage) and the other is connected to the ECM. The ECM functions as a switch that provides either a ground for current flow to energize the MC Solenoid or an open circuit to de-energize the MC Solenoid. The ECM switches the MC Solenoid **ON** and **OFF** ten times a second. When the MC Solenoid is energized the needle is inserted into the jet and the result is a lean air/fuel mixture. When the solenoid is de-energized the needle is withdrawn from the jet and the result is a rich air/fuel mixture. The average or effective air/fuel mixture is determined by the length of time the solenoid is either energized or de-energized (period of dwell) during each **ON/OFF** cycle.

The C4 System utilizes an instrument panel mounted indicator lamp that will inform the driver of the need for service. If a malfunction occurs, the lamp will be illuminated and display **CHECK ENGINE**. The ECM also incorporates a diagnostic program that will flash a code identifying the malfunction when this function is activated.

Diagnosis and Testing

The C4 System should be considered as a possible source of trouble for engine performance, fuel economy and exhaust emission complaints only after normal tests and inspections that would apply to an automobile without the C4 System have been performed. An integral self-diagnostic system within the ECM detects the problems that are most likely to occur.

The diagnostic system will illuminate the CHECK ENGINE light if a fault exists. If the trouble code test pigtail wire (located under the dash) is manually connected to ground, the system will flash a trouble code if a fault has been detected.

As a routine system test, the test bulb will also be illuminated when the ignition switch is first turned **on** and the engine not started. If the test wire is grounded, the system will flash code 12, which indicates that the diagnostic system is functioning normal (i.e., no engine rpm voltage to the ECM). This consists of **one flash** followed by a pause and then **two flashes.** After a longer pause, the code will be repeated two more times. The cycle will repeat itself until the engine is either started or the ignition switch turned **off.** When the engine is started, the bulb will remian illuminated for a few seconds.

If the test wire is grounded with the engine operating and a fault has been detected by the system, the trouble code will be flashed three times. If more than one fault has been detected, the second trouble code will be flashed three times after the first code is flashed. The series of code flashes will then be repeated.

A trouble code indicates a problem within a specific circuit, for example, code 14 indicates a problem in the coolant temperature sensor circuit. This includes the coolant temperature sensor, wire harness, and Electronic Control Module (ECM). The procedure for determining which of the three is at fault is located in the Trouble Code 14 chart. For other trouble codes, refer to the applicable charts.

C4 electronic control module assembly

Because the self-diagnostic subsystem does not detect all possible faults, the absence of a flashed code does not always indicate that there is no problem with the system. To determine this, a system operational test is necessary. This test should be performed when the test bulb does not flash a trouble code but the C4 System is suspected because no other reason can be determined for a specific complaint. In addition to the test bulb, a dwell meter, test lamp, digital volt-ohmmeter, tachometer, vacuum gauge and jumper wires are required to diagnose system problems. A test lamp rather than a voltmeter should be used when so instructed.

NOTE: Although most dwell meters should be acceptable, if one causes a change in engine operation when it is connected to the mixture control (MC) solenoid dwell pigtail wire connector, it should not be used.

The dwell meter, set for the six-cylinder engine scale and connected to a pigtail wire connector leading from the mixture control (MC) solenoid at the carburetor, is used to determine the air/fuel mixture dwell. When the dwell meter is connected, do not allow the terminal to contact any engine component that is connected to engine ground. This includes hoses because they may be electrically conductive. With a normally operating engine, the dwell at both idle speed and partial throttle will be between 10 degrees and 50 degrees and will be varying. Varying means the pointer continually moves back and forth across the scale. The amount it varies is not important, only the fact that it does vary. This indicates closed loop operation, meaning the mixture is being varied according to the input voltage to the ECM from the oxygen sensor. With a wide open throttle (WOT) condition or cold engine operation, the air/fuel mixture ratio will be fixed and the pointer will not vary. This is open loop operation, richening or leaning the mixture will cause the dwell to vary if the system is in closed loop operation.

NOTE: Normally, system tests should be performed with the engine warm (upper radiator hose hot).

Trouble Code Memory

When a fault is detected in the system, the test bulb will be illuminated and a trouble code will be set in the memory of the ECM. However, if the fault is intermittent, the test bulb will be extinguished when the fault no longer exists, but the trouble code will remain in the ECM memory.

Long Term Memory

The ECM, with most C4 Systems, has a long term memory. With this provision, trouble codes are not lost when the ignition switch is turned off. Certain troubles may not appear until the engine has been operated 5 to 18 minutes at partial throttle. For this reason, and for intermittent troubles, a long term memory is desirable. To clear the long term memory, disconnect and connect the battery negative cable.

NOTE: Long term memory causes approximately a 13 ma battery drain with the ignition switch off.

Trouble Codes

The test bulb will only be illuminated under the conditions listed below when a malfunction exists. If the malfunction is eliminated, the bulb will be extinguished and the trouble code will be reset, except for one fault, trouble code 12. If the bulb is illuminated intermittently, but no trouble code is flashed, refer to this symptom within Driver Complaint.

1. Trouble Code 12 No rpm (tach) voltage to the ECM.
2. Trouble Code 13 Oxygen sensor circuit. The engine has to operate for approximately five minutes at partial throttle before this code will be flashed.
3. Trouble Code 14 Short circuit within coolant temperature sensor circuit. The engine has to operate two minutes before this code will be flashed.
4. Trouble Code 15 Open circuit within coolant temperature sensor circuit. The engine has to operate for approximately five minutes at partial throttle before this code will be flashed.
5. Trouble Codes 21 and 22 (at same time) WOT switch circuit has short circuit to ground.

6. Trouble Code 22 Adaptive vacuum or WOT switch circuit has short circuit to ground.
7. Trouble Code 23 Carburetor MC solenoid circuit has short circuit to ground or open circuit exists.
8. Trouble Code 44 Voltage input to ECM from oxygen sensor indicates continuous "lean" mixture. MC solenoid is regulated to produce continuous "rich" mixture. The engine has to operate approximately five minutes at partial throttle with a torque load and the C4 System in closed loop operation before this code will be flashed.
9. Trouble Codes 44 and 45 (at same time) Faulty Oxygen Sensor.
10. Trouble Code 45 Voltage input to ECM from oxygen sensor indicates continuous "rich" mixture. MC solenoid is regulated to produce continuous "lean" mixture. The engine has to operate approximately five minutes at partial throttle with a torque load and the C4 System in closed loop operation before this code will be flashed.
11. Trouble Code 51 Faulty calibration unit (PROM) or installation.
12. Trouble Codes 52 and 53 Test bulb off, intermittent ECM problem. Test bulb on, faulty ECM.
13. Trouble Code 54 Faulty MC Solenoid and/or ECM.
14. Trouble Code 55 Faulty oxygen sensor circuit or ECM.

When the test bulb is not illuminated with the engine operating, but a trouble code can be obtained, the situation must be evaluated to determine if the fault is intermittent or because of engine operating conditions.

For all malfunctions, except those represented by trouble codes 13, 44, and 45, the test bulb should be illuminated with the engine rpm below 800 after five minutes of operation.

If trouble codes other than 43, 44, and 45 can be obtained when the test bulb is not illuminated, the diagnostic charts cannot be used because the system is operating normally. All that can be performed is a physical inspection of the circuit indicated by the trouble code. The circuit should be inspected for faulty wire connections, frayed wires, etc., then the System Operational Test should be performed.

Trouble codes 13, 44, and 45 require engine operation at partial throttle with an engine torque load for an extended period of time before a code will be flashed. Trouble code 15 requires five minutes of engine operation before it will be flashed. The diagnostic chart should be used if these codes are flashed even though the test bulb is not illuminated with the engine at idle speed.

CALIBRATION UNIT (PROM)

The microprocessor (ECM) has a calibration unit called a PROM that is programmed with specific instructions for the engine. It is not a replaceable assembly.

Trouble code 51 indicates the PROM has been installed improperly or is defective. When codes 51 is flashed the ECM (microprocessor) should be replaced.

-----CAUTION-----
If trouble code 51 was caused by the PROM (calibration unit) being installed backwards, replace the ECM with another unit. Whenever the calibration unit is installed backwards and the ignition switch is turned on, the unit is destroyed.

C4 System Tests and Trouble Code Diagnosis
-----CAUTION-----
The self-diagnostic system does not detect all possible faults. The absence of a trouble code does not indicate there is not a malfunction with the system. To determine whether or not a system problem exists, an operational test is necessary.

NOTE: The System Operational Test should also be performed after all repairs on the C4 System have been completed.

C-4 Open And Closed Loop Modes

ECM Terminal Connections

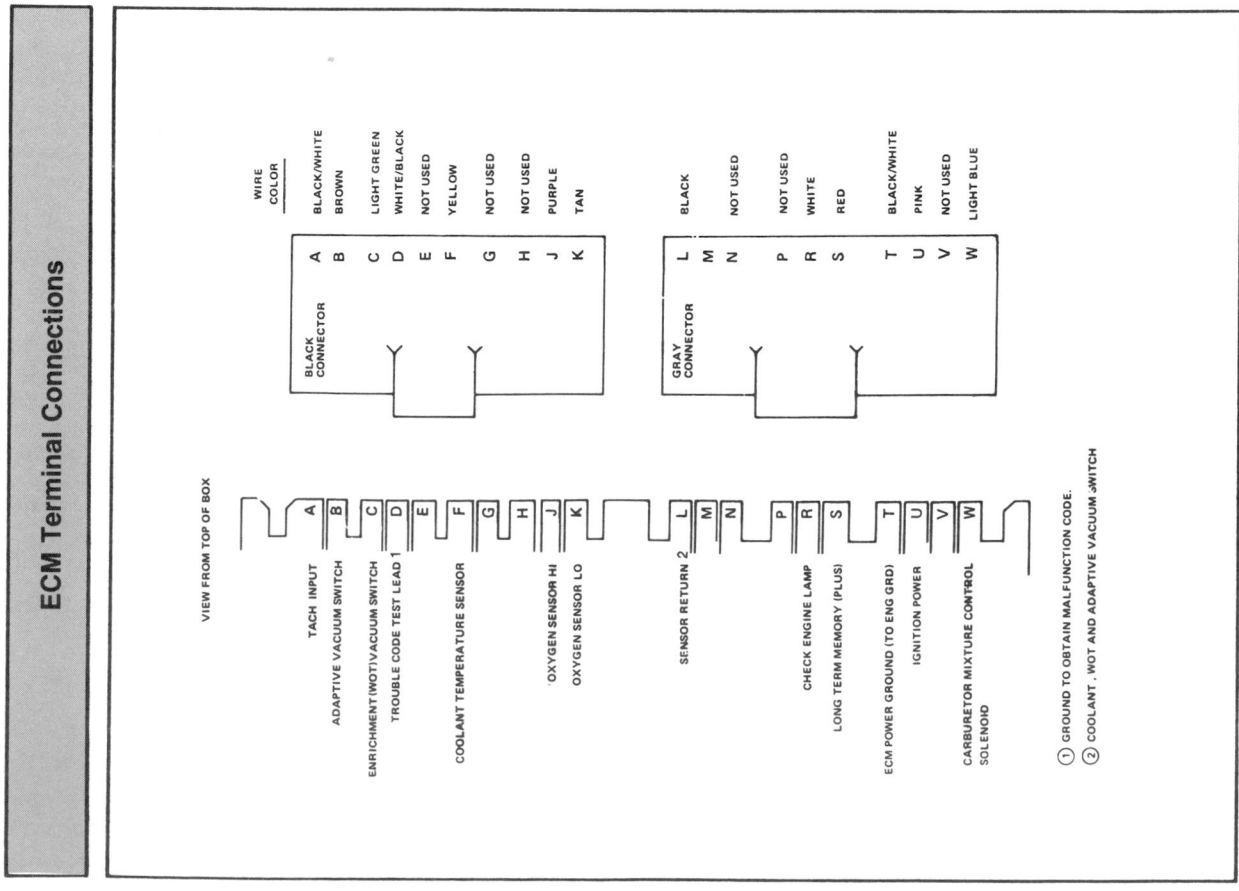

VIEW FROM TOP OF BOX

WIRE COLOR		
BLACK CONNECTOR	A	BLACK/WHITE
	B	BROWN
	C	LIGHT GREEN
	D	WHITE/BLACK
	E	NOT USED
	F	YELLOW
	G	NOT USED
	H	NOT USED
	J	PURPLE
	K	TAN
GRAY CONNECTOR	L	BLACK
	M	NOT USED
	N	NOT USED
	P	WHITE
	R	RED
	S	BLACK/WHITE
	T	BLACK/WHITE
	U	PINK
	V	NOT USED
	W	LIGHT BLUE

TACH INPUT
ADAPTIVE VACUUM SWITCH
ENRICHMENT (WOT)/VACUUM SWITCH
TROUBLE CODE TEST LEAD ①
COOLANT TEMPERATURE SENSOR
OXYGEN SENSOR HI
OXYGEN SENSOR LO
SENSOR RETURN ②
CHECK ENGINE LAMP
LONG TERM MEMORY (PLUS)
ECM POWER GROUND (TO ENG GRD)
IGNITION POWER
CARBURETOR MIXTURE CONTROL SOLENOID

① GROUND TO OBTAIN MALFUNCTION CODE.
② COOLANT, WOT AND ADAPTIVE VACUUM SWITCH

C-4 Trouble Diagnosis

C4 System Operational Test

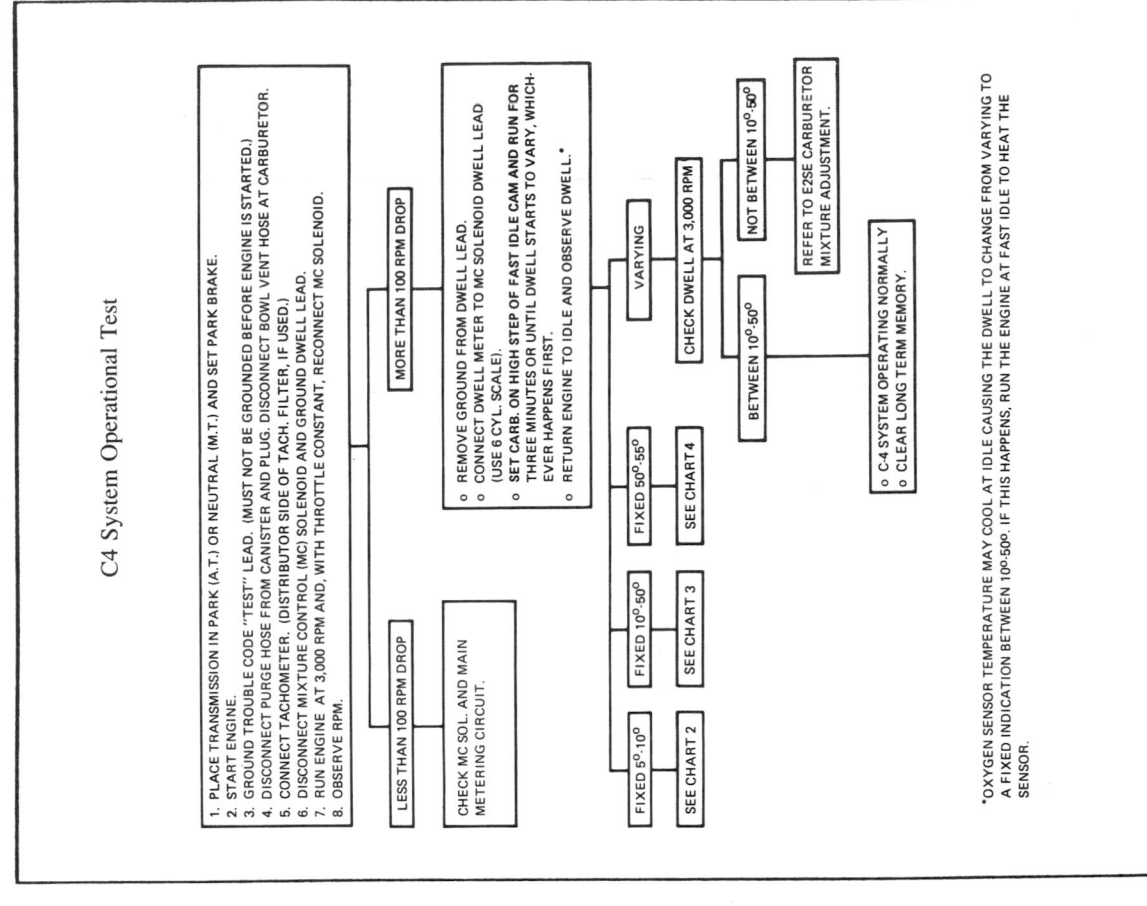

1. PLACE TRANSMISSION IN PARK (A.T.) OR NEUTRAL (M.T.) AND SET PARK BRAKE.
2. START ENGINE.
3. GROUND TROUBLE CODE "TEST" LEAD. (MUST NOT BE GROUNDED BEFORE ENGINE IS STARTED.)
4. DISCONNECT PURGE HOSE FROM CANISTER AND PLUG. DISCONNECT BOWL VENT HOSE AT CARBURETOR.
5. CONNECT TACHOMETER. (DISTRIBUTOR SIDE OF TACH. FILTER, IF USED.)
6. DISCONNECT MIXTURE CONTROL (MC) SOLENOID AND GROUND DWELL LEAD.
7. RUN ENGINE AT 3,000 RPM AND, WITH THROTTLE CONSTANT, RECONNECT MC SOLENOID.
8. OBSERVE RPM.

- REMOVE GROUND FROM DWELL LEAD.
- CONNECT DWELL METER TO MC SOLENOID DWELL LEAD (USE 6 CYL. SCALE).
- SET CARB. ON HIGH STEP OF FAST IDLE CAM AND RUN FOR THREE MINUTES OR UNTIL DWELL STARTS TO VARY, WHICH-EVER HAPPENS FIRST.
- RETURN ENGINE TO IDLE AND OBSERVE DWELL.*

- C-4 SYSTEM OPERATING NORMALLY
- CLEAR LONG TERM MEMORY.

*OXYGEN SENSOR TEMPERATURE MAY COOL AT IDLE CAUSING THE DWELL TO CHANGE FROM VARYING TO A FIXED INDICATION BETWEEN 10°-50°. IF THIS HAPPENS, RUN THE ENGINE AT FAST IDLE TO HEAT THE SENSOR.

C-4 Trouble Diagnosis

Dwell Fixed Between 5° And 10°

- GROUND TEST LEAD
- CONNECT DWELL METER TO MC SOLENOID (USE 6 CYL. SCALE)
- WITH ENGINE IDLING, CHOKE ENGINE

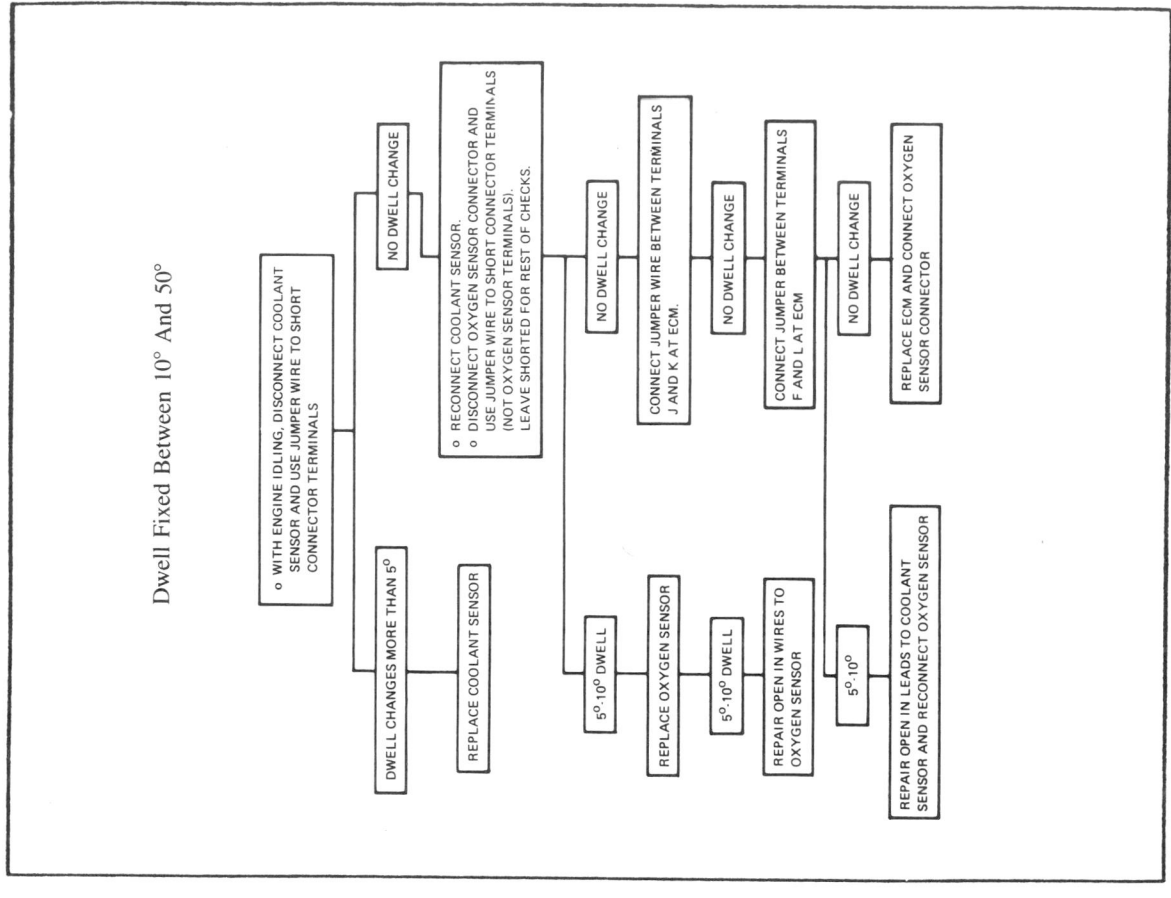

C-4 Trouble Diagnosis

Dwell Fixed Between 10° And 50°

C-4 Trouble Diagnosis

Dwell Fixed Between 50° And 55°

C-4 Trouble Diagnosis

Self-Diagnostic Circuit Test

KEY "ON," ENGINE "OFF," OBSERVE "CHECK ENGINE" LIGHT.

- LIGHT ON → GROUND "TEST" LEAD AND OBSERVE "CHECK ENGINE" LIGHT.
  - FLASHES CODE 12
    - REMOVE TEST LEAD GROUND.
    - ○ SET PARKING BRAKE WITH TRANS. IN PARK.
    - ○ RUN AND WARM ENGINE FOR 2 MINUTES (UNDER 800 RPM FOR AT LEAST 10 SEC.) AND OBSERVE "CHECK ENGINE" LIGHT AT IDLE.
      - LIGHT ON → GROUND TEST LEAD AND CHECK FOR TROUBLE CODE
      - LIGHT OFF → ○ RUN ENGINE ON HIGH STEP OF IDLE CAM AND REMOVE VACUUM HOSES FROM WOT AND CLOSED THROTTLE SWITCHES. ○ OBSERVE "CHECK ENGINE" LIGHT REPLACE HOSES BEFORE RETURNING ENGINE TO IDLE.
        - SEE APPLICABLE TROUBLE CODE DIAGNOSIS CHART. LEAVE TROUBLE CODE TEST LEAD GROUNDED WHILE USING DIAGNOSTIC CHARTS UNLESS OTHERWISE INSTRUCTED. IF MORE THAN ONE CODE IS FLASHED, START WITH THE LOWEST CODE. NOTE: ANYTIME AN ENGINE IS STARTED, EVEN A WARM ENGINE, IT MUST BE RUN AT PART THROTTLE FOR THREE MINUTES, OR UNTIL THE DWELL STARTS TO VARY BEFORE PROCEEDING WITH CHECKS.
          - LIGHT OFF → GROUND TEST LEAD AND CHECK FOR TROUBLE CODE
            - CODE → 13, 15, 44, 45
            - NO CODE → SEE CHART 22
          - LIGHT ON → ALL OTHER → TROUBLE IS INTERMITTENT. DIAGNOSTIC CODE CHARTS CAN NOT BE USED. MAKE PHYSICAL CHECK OF CIRCUIT INDICATED BY TROUBLE CODE. → REFER TO DRIVER COMPLAINTS
  - DOES NOT FLASH CODE 12 → GROUND TERMINAL "D" ON ECM CONNECTOR
    - FLASHES CODE 12 → REPAIR OPEN "TEST" LEAD
    - DOES NOT FLASH CODE 12 → REMOVE ECM CONNECTOR AND OBSERVE "CHECK ENGINE" LIGHT
      - LIGHT OFF → REPLACE ECM
      - LIGHT ON → REPAIR GROUNDED LEAD FROM BULB TO ECM TERM. "R" → REPEAT DIAGNOSTIC CIRCUIT CHECK
- LIGHT OFF → SEE TEST 6

NOTE: ALWAYS CHECK FOR CORRECT CONNECTIONS AT A UNIT BEFORE CONSIDERING IT DEFECTIVE.

C-4 Trouble Diagnosis

Test Bulb Circuit Inoperative

NOTE: LIGHT WILL NOT BE ILLUMINATED IF "TEST" LEAD IS GROUNDED BEFORE THE IGNITION IS TURNED ON. THE MC SOLENOID WILL ALSO CLICK.

CHECK FUSE AT FUSE BLOCK
- BLOWN FUSE → REPLACE FUSE - CHECK FOR CAUSE
- FUSE O.K. → INSPECT "CHECK ENGINE" LAMP CONNECTOR FOR PROPER CONNECTION. WITH IGNITION "ON" AND ENGINE "OFF," CHECK VOLTAGE BETWEEN LAMP CONNECTOR WHITE WIRE TERMINAL AND GROUND.
  - UNDER 10 VOLTS → CHECK VOLTAGE BETWEEN LAMP CONNECTOR PINK/BLACK WIRE TERMINAL AND GROUND.
    - OVER 10 VOLTS → CHECK BULB AND WIRE LEADS
    - UNDER 10 VOLTS → REPAIR OPEN WIRE LEAD BETWEEN FUSE AND LAMP CONNECTOR
  - OVER 10 VOLTS → CHECK VOLTAGE BETWEEN ECM TERMINAL "R" AND GROUND
    - OVER 10 VOLTS → CHECK VOLTAGE BETWEEN ECM TERMINAL "T" AND GROUND
      - UNDER 1 VOLT → CHECK VOLTAGE BETWEEN ECM TERMINAL "U" AND GROUND
        - OVER 10 VOLTS → TURN IGNITION OFF AND REPLACE ECM
        - UNDER 10 VOLTS → REPAIR OPEN IN WIRE LEAD BETWEEN TERMINAL "U" AND "CHECK ENGINE" LAMP CONNECTOR
      - OVER 1 VOLT → REPAIR ECM GROUND CONNECTION
    - UNDER 10 VOLTS → REPAIR OPEN IN WIRE LEAD BETWEEN ECM "R" TERMINAL AND "CHECK ENGINE" LAMP CONNECTOR.

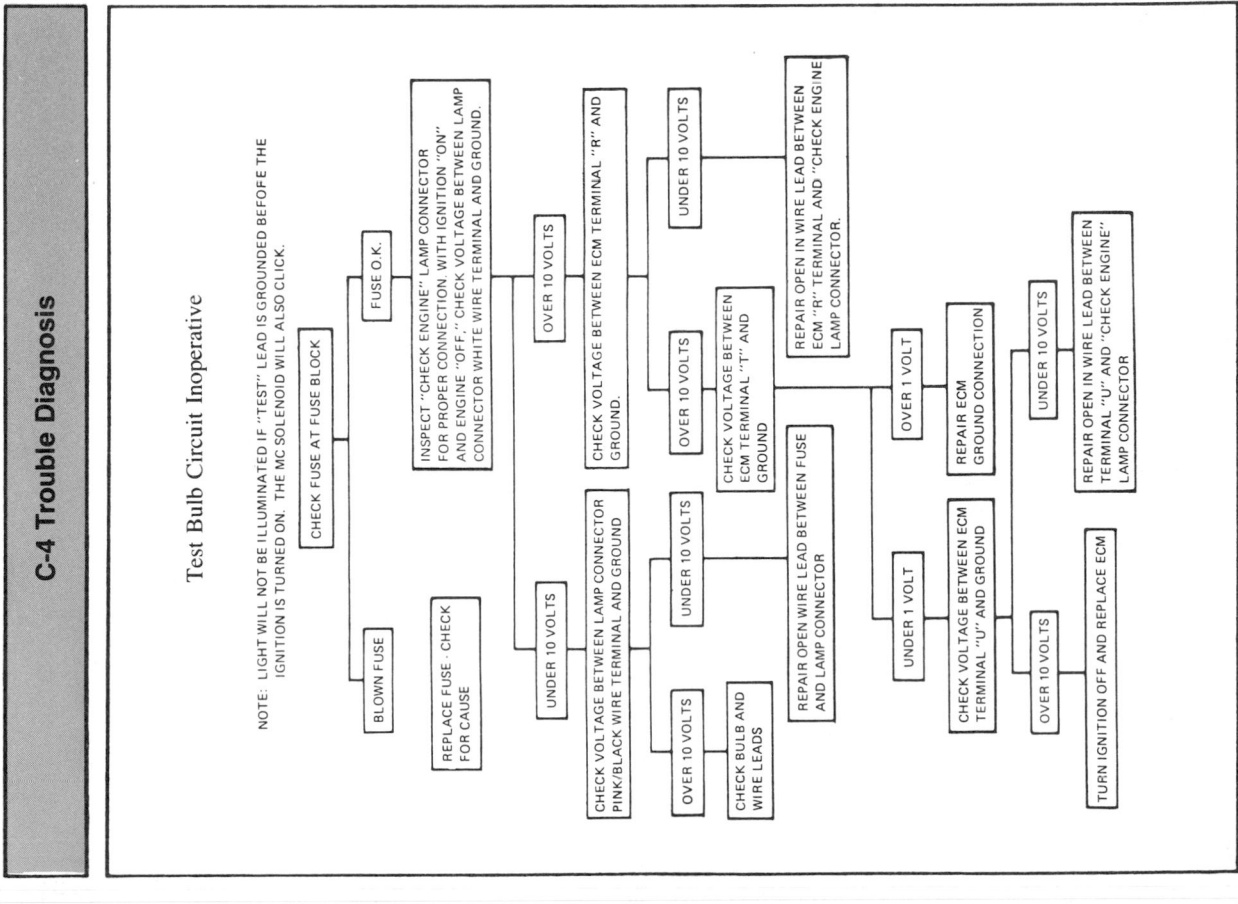

C-4 Trouble Diagnosis

Adaptive Vacuum Switch Circuit Test

Trouble Code 12

Trouble Code 13

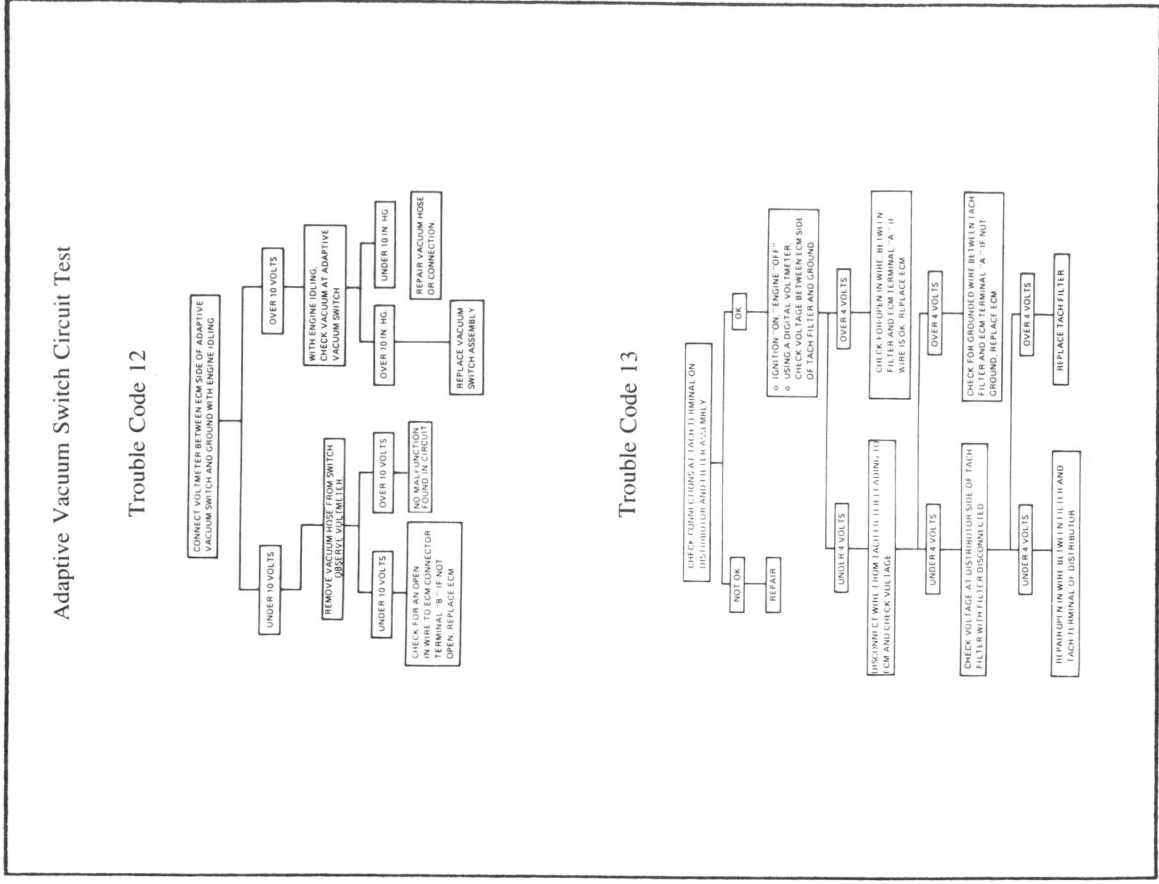

C-4 Trouble Diagnosis

Trouble Code 12

C-4 Trouble Diagnosis

Trouble Code 15

- GROUND "TEST" LEAD.
- CONNECT DWELL METER TO MC SOLENOID (USE 6 CYL. SCALE)
- STOP AND START ENGINE AND RUN AT PARTIAL THROTTLE FOR 3 MINUTES AND OBSERVE WELL.
- WITH ENGINE IDLING, REMOVE CONNECTOR FROM COOLANT SENSOR AND CONNECT WIRE BETWEEN CONNECTOR TERMINALS.

DWELL UNCHANGED
CHECK FOR AN OPEN IN WIRES BETWEEN COOLANT SENSOR AND ECM TERMINAL "F". IF WIRES ARE OK, REPLACE ECM.

DWELL CHANGED MORE THAN 5° FROM DWELL WITH SENSOR CONNECTED
CHECK COOLANT SENSOR CONNECTION. IF OK, REPLACE SENSOR.

C-4 Trouble Diagnosis

Trouble Code 14

NOTE: IF THE ENGINE COOLANT WARNING LIGHT IS "ON," CHECK FOR AN OVERHEATING CONDITION BEFORE PERFORMING THE FOLLOWING TEST.

- GROUND "TEST" LEAD.
- CONNECT DWELL METER TO MC SOLENOID.
- RUN ENGINE AT PARTIAL THROTTLE UNTIL DWELL STARTS TO VARY.
- WITH ENGINE IDLING, REMOVE CONNECTOR FROM COOLANT SENSOR.

DWELL FIXED → REPLACE COOLANT SENSOR

DWELL VARIES
REMOVE BLACK ECM CONNECTOR AND CONNECT TEST LIGHT BETWEEN TERMINAL "U" AND TERMINAL "F" OF CONNECTOR (NOT ECM).

LIGHT
CHECK FOR GROUNDED WIRE BETWEEN ECM TERMINAL AND COOLANT SENSOR. IF NOT GROUNDED REPLACE ECM.

NO LIGHT → REPLACE ECM

223

C-4 Trouble Diagnosis

Trouble Code 22

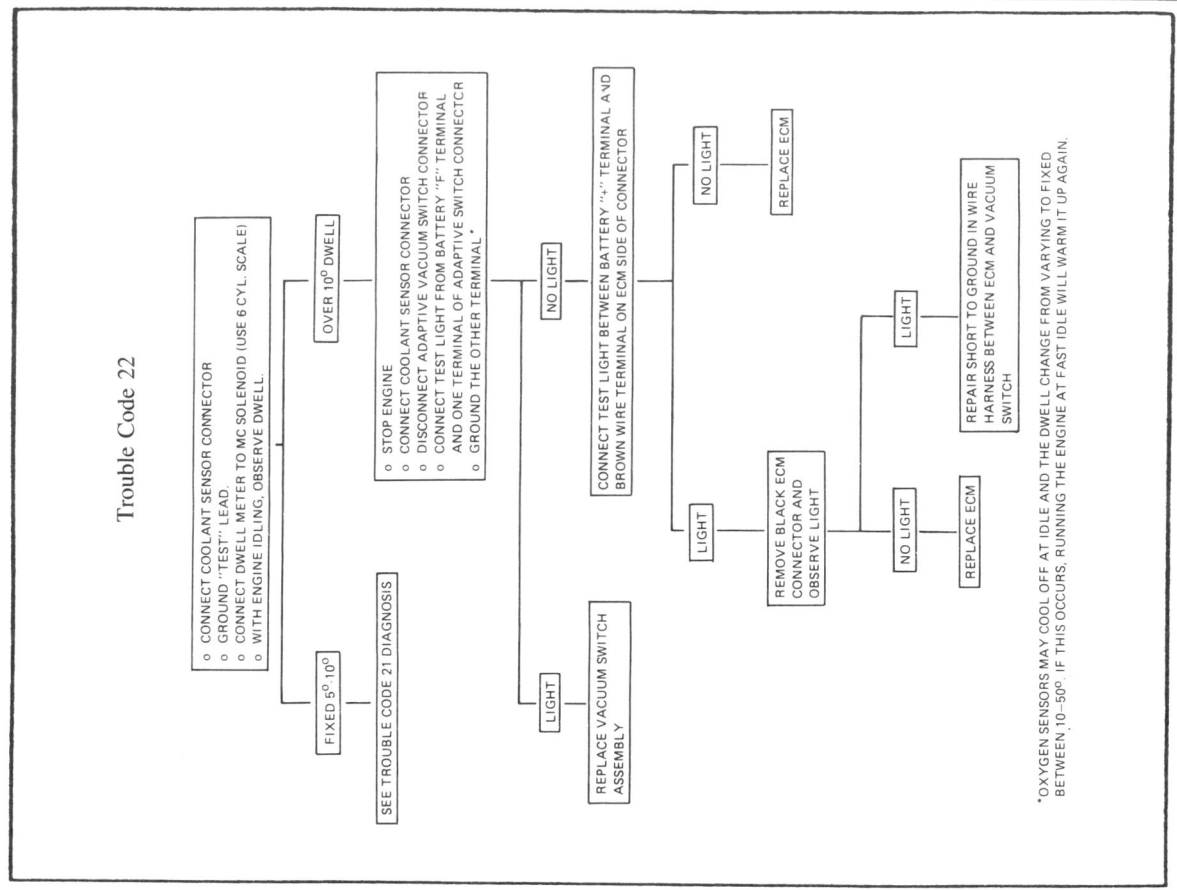

- CONNECT COOLANT SENSOR CONNECTOR
- GROUND "TEST" LEAD.
- CONNECT DWELL METER TO MC SOLENOID (USE 6 CYL. SCALE)
- WITH ENGINE IDLING, OBSERVE DWELL.

FIXED 5°-10° → SEE TROUBLE CODE 21 DIAGNOSIS

OVER 10° DWELL
- STOP ENGINE
- CONNECT COOLANT SENSOR CONNECTOR
- DISCONNECT ADAPTIVE VACUUM SWITCH CONNECTOR
- CONNECT TEST LIGHT FROM BATTERY "F" TERMINAL AND ONE TERMINAL OF ADAPTIVE SWITCH CONNECTOR
- GROUND THE OTHER TERMINAL.*

LIGHT → REPLACE VACUUM SWITCH ASSEMBLY

NO LIGHT → CONNECT TEST LIGHT BETWEEN BATTERY "+" TERMINAL AND BROWN WIRE TERMINAL ON ECM SIDE OF CONNECTOR

NO LIGHT → REPLACE ECM

LIGHT → REMOVE BLACK ECM CONNECTOR AND OBSERVE LIGHT

NO LIGHT → REPLACE ECM

LIGHT → REPAIR SHORT TO GROUND IN WIRE HARNESS BETWEEN ECM AND VACUUM SWITCH

*OXYGEN SENSORS MAY COOL OFF AT IDLE AND THE DWELL CHANGE FROM VARYING TO FIXED BETWEEN 10-50°. IF THIS OCCURS, RUNNING THE ENGINE AT FAST IDLE WILL WARM IT UP AGAIN.

C-4 Trouble Diagnosis

Trouble Code 21 And 22 Together

- GROUND "TEST" LEAD.
- CONNECT DWELL METER TO MC SOLENOID (USE 6 CYL. SCALE)
- WITH ENGINE IDLING, DISCONNECT WOT VACUUM SWITCH.

OVER 10° DWELL → CHECK VACUUM AT WOT SWITCH

OVER 10 IN. HG → REPAIR HOSE OR HOSE CONNECTIONS

UNDER 10 IN. HG → REPLACE VACUUM SWITCH ASSEMBLY

5°-10° DWELL → CONNECT A TEST LIGHT BETWEEN ECM TERMINALS "U" AND "C." NOTE: TERMINAL "U" IS VOLTAGE SOURCE.

NO LIGHT → REPLACE ECM

LIGHT → REMOVE BLACK ECM CONNECTOR AND OBSERVE TEST LIGHT

NO LIGHT → REPLACE ECM

LIGHT → REPAIR SHORT TO GROUND BETWEEN WOT SWITCH AND ECM

C-4 Trouble Diagnosis

Trouble Code 44

NOTE: IF CODE 44 AND 55 ARE BOTH FLASHED, REPLACE OXYGEN SENSOR AND PERFORM SYSTEM OPERATIONAL CHECK.

- GROUND ECM "TEST" LEAD
- CONNECT DWELL METER TO MC SOLENOID (USE 6 CYL. SCALE)
- RUN ENGINE ON HIGH STEP OF FAST IDLE CAM AND OBSERVE DWELL.

- BETWEEN 10°-50°
  - REPLACE OXYGEN SENSOR
- 5°-10°
  - WITH ENGINE IDLING, CHOKE ENGINE.
    - DWELL INCREASES
      - CHECK FOR AIR LEAK IN VACUUM LINES
        - NO LEAK
          - SEE E2SE CARBURETORS
        - LEAK
          - REPAIR AND RECHECK
    - NO DWELL CHANGE
      - DISCONNECT OXYGEN SENSOR AND CONNECT A TEST LIGHT BETWEEN BATTERY "+" AND TERMINAL AND WIRE TERMINAL IN CONNECTOR (NOT OXYGEN SENSOR TERMINAL)
        - DWELL INCREASES
          - CONNECT TEST LIGHT BETWEEN BATTERY "+" TERMINAL AND PURPLE LEAD TERMINAL IN CONNECTOR
            - LIGHT
              - CHECK FOR GROUNDED PURPLE WIRE TO ECM TERMINAL "J" IF NOT GROUNDED, REPLACE ECM.
            - NO LIGHT
              - REPLACE OXYGEN SENSOR
        - NO DWELL CHANGE
          - CHECK FOR A GROUND TAN WIRE TO ECM TERMINAL "K" IF NOT GROUNDED, REPLACE ECM

C-4 Trouble Diagnosis

Trouble Code 23

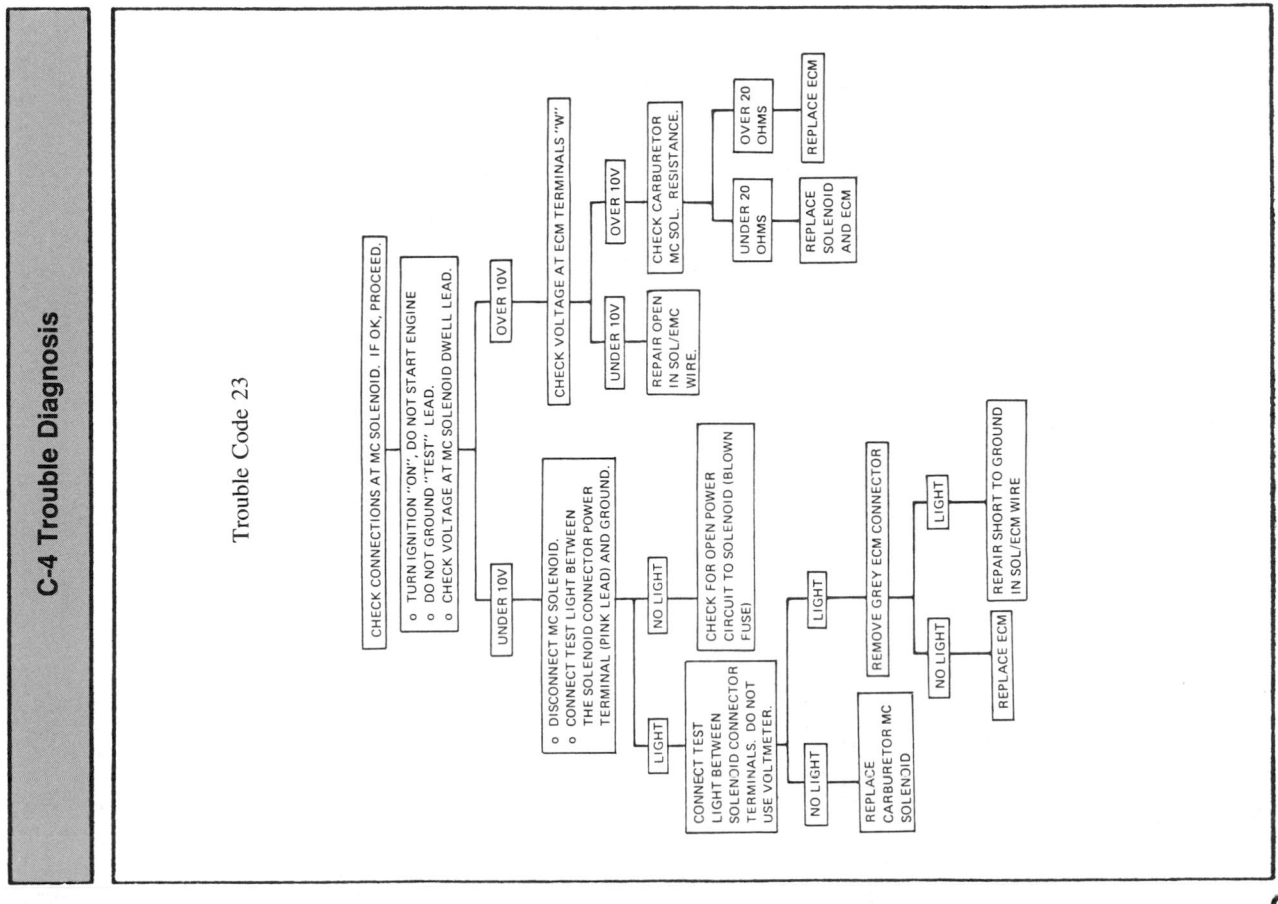

- CHECK CONNECTIONS AT MC SOLENOID. IF OK, PROCEED.
- TURN IGNITION "ON", DO NOT START ENGINE
  - DO NOT GROUND "TEST" LEAD.
  - CHECK VOLTAGE AT MC SOLENOID DWELL LEAD.
- OVER 10V
  - CHECK VOLTAGE AT ECM TERMINALS "W"
    - OVER 10V
      - CHECK CARBURETOR MC SOL. RESISTANCE.
        - UNDER 20 OHMS
          - REPLACE SOLENOID AND ECM
        - OVER 20 OHMS
          - REPLACE ECM
    - UNDER 10V
      - REPAIR OPEN IN SOL/EMC WIRE.
- UNDER 10V
  - DISCONNECT MC SOLENOID.
  - CONNECT TEST LIGHT BETWEEN THE SOLENOID CONNECTOR POWER TERMINAL (PINK LEAD) AND GROUND.
    - LIGHT
      - CONNECT TEST LIGHT BETWEEN SOLENOID CONNECTOR TERMINALS. DO NOT USE VOLTMETER.
        - NO LIGHT
          - REPLACE CARBURETOR MC SOLENOID
    - NO LIGHT
      - CHECK FOR OPEN POWER CIRCUIT TO SOLENOID (BLOWN FUSE)
        - LIGHT
          - REMOVE GREY ECM CONNECTOR
            - NO LIGHT
              - REPLACE ECM
            - LIGHT
              - REPAIR SHORT TO GROUND IN SOL/ECM WIRE

C-4 Trouble Diagnosis

Trouble Code 45

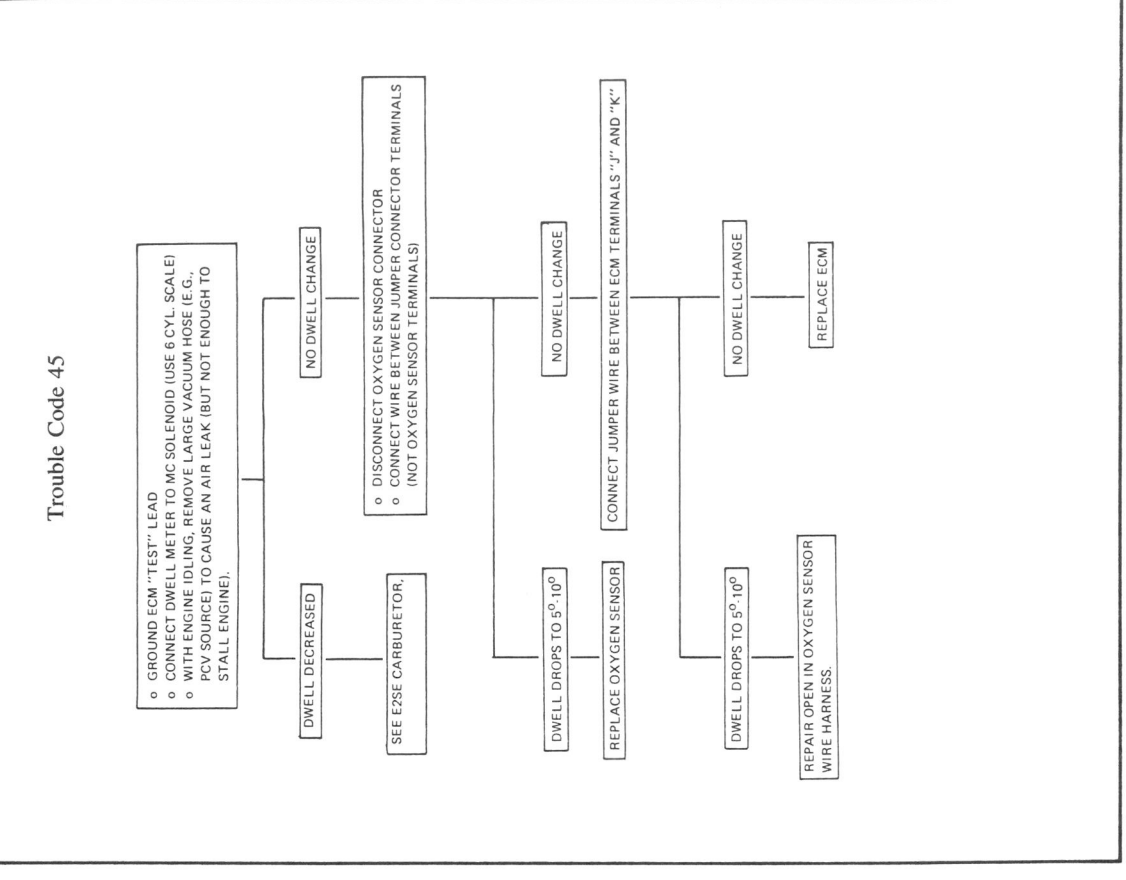

- GROUND ECM "TEST" LEAD
- CONNECT DWELL METER TO MC SOLENOID (USE 6 CYL. SCALE)
- WITH ENGINE IDLING, REMOVE LARGE VACUUM HOSE (E.G., PCV SOURCE) TO CAUSE AN AIR LEAK (BUT NOT ENOUGH TO STALL ENGINE).

DWELL DECREASED → SEE E2SE CARBURETOR,

NO DWELL CHANGE →
- DISCONNECT OXYGEN SENSOR CONNECTOR
- CONNECT WIRE BETWEEN JUMPER CONNECTOR TERMINALS (NOT OXYGEN SENSOR TERMINALS)

DWELL DROPS TO 5°-10° → REPLACE OXYGEN SENSOR

NO DWELL CHANGE → CONNECT JUMPER WIRE BETWEEN ECM TERMINALS "J" AND "K"

DWELL DROPS TO 5°-10° → REPAIR OPEN IN OXYGEN SENSOR WIRE HARNESS.

NO DWELL CHANGE → REPLACE ECM

C-4 Trouble Diagnosis

Trouble Code 51-55

TROUBLE CODE 51

IF SERVICE REPLACE-MENT CALIBRATION UNIT → CHECK TO ENSURE ALL PINS ARE FULLY INSERTED IN THE SOCKET AND ALIGNMENT IS CORRECT. IF OK, REPLACE CALIBRATION UNIT.

IF FACTORY INSTALLED CALIBRATION UNIT → REPLACE CALIBRATION UNIT

TROUBLE CODES 52-53

REPLACE ECM IF DISPLAY LIGHT ILLUMINATED. NO DISPLAY LIGHT, INTERMITTENT ECM MALFUNCTION.

TROUBLE CODE 54

CHECK MC SOLENOID RESISTANCE

LESS THAN 20 OHMS →
- REPLACE MC SOLENOID
- CLEAR MEMORY
- START ENGINE. CHECK ENGINE DISPLAY. OBSERVE

NO DISPLAY → PERFORM SYSTEM OPER-ATIONAL CHECK.

DISPLAY ILLUMINATED → GROUND TEST LEAD AND OBSERVE CODE. → SEE APPLICABLE CODE DIAGNOSIS

MORE THAN 20 OHMS →
- IGNITION "ON" ENGINE NOT STARTED
- DISCONNECT MC SOLENOID CONNECTOR
- CONNECT TEST LIGHT FROM GROUND TO DWELL LEAD ON MC SOLENOID
- DISCONNECT GRAY ECM CONNECTOR

NO LIGHT → REPLACE ECM

LIGHT → REPAIR SHORT TO POWER SOURCE IN BLUE WIRE LEADING TO ECM TERMINAL "W" CLEAR MEMORY AND CHECK FOR OTHER TROUBLE CODES.

TROUBLE CODE 55

CHECK FOR AN OPEN IN SENSOR RETURN WIRE TO ECM TERMINAL "L". IF OK, REPLACE ECM.

CADILLAC MODULATED DISPLACEMENT ENGINE (1981 MODELS)

General Information

Modulated displacement is an electromechanical system, controlled by a microprocessor, that calls up four, six or eight engine cylinders depending on driving requirements. The selective operation of four, six or eight cylinders is provided for by four engine valve selector units that are controlled through the use of a microprocessor (computer). In each case, as the number of cylinders in operation is reduced, the engine is effectively converted from 6.0 liter displacement with all eight cylinders in use, to 4.5 liters with six cylinders operating, to a 3.0 liter engine with four cylinders providing power. By varying the size of the engine in this manner, significant reductions are made in the amount of internal work the engine has to do.

NOTE: Idle speed is adjusted by turning adjusting screw, located at by-pass port of throttle housing.

The system automatically actuates only the number of cylinders needed to satisfy the demand. In doing so, the mechanical efficiency of the engine is improved. Four, six or eight cylinder selection is entirely automatic and operates according to driving demands. A digital instrument panel display of "active cylinders" is standard as part of a new MPG Sentinel system. This system also provides a display of average and instantaneous miles per gallon and expected fuel range.

Service is limited to replacement. An electrical check can be done without removing the valve cover. Connect a voltmeter and check voltage at the solenoid wire (engine running). Run the engine in all three modes, 8 cyl. - 6 cyl. - 4 cyl. If there is full voltage at the actuation solenoid, and the solenoid does not click, investigate the solenoid or the valve shifter.

---CAUTION---

If you choose to electrically test the valve shifter on the engine, it is important that both valves be in the closed position.

During active operation, the fulcrum point is near the center of the rocker arm. As the cam reaches its high point, the valve is brought to an open position, allowing a fuel charge to enter the cylinder. During the inactive stage, the valve will not open because the selector is commanded to release the rocker arm pivot, allowing it to move upward. This in effect shifts the fulcrum point to the tip of the stationary valve. With the valve being held closed by its spring, the cylinder is rendered inactive.

BLOCKING PLATE
BODY PROJECTIONS
BODY
FULCRUM
SELECTOR SPRING
VALVE SPRING

Modulated displacement engine valve assembly

ACTUATION SOLENOID

BLOCKING PLATE OPENING

Location of actuation solenoid on valve assembly

BOSCH DIGITAL IGNITION TIMING CONTROL (DITC) SYSTEM

General Information

The Bosch Digital Ignition Timing Control (DITC) is a computerized engine control system that provides exact ignition timing for maximum engine power with minimal emissions under all operating conditions. Components of the DITC system include:

- Computer control unit
- Ignition control unit
- Manifold pressure sensor
- Coolant temperature sensor
- Throttle switch
- Crankshaft sensor
- Oxygen sensor
- Distributor
- Ignition coil

As the crankshaft turns, a flywheel sensor counts the teeth on a flywheel ring gear. Each tooth on the flywheel ring causes two pulses to be sent to the control unit from the flywheel sensor, equivalent to 2 degrees of crankshaft rotation. A reference tooth with a soft iron insert causes two stronger pulses to tell the control unit when the engine is at TDC. In this manner, the DITC on-board computer can calculate both engine speed and the crankshaft angle of rotation continuously to make timing adjustments without the need for centrifugal or vacuum advance devices in the distributor itself. Since the computer control unit controls the timing, the only function of the distributor is to transfer the secondary voltage to the spark plugs.

The DITC computer also monitors various engine operating conditions through its engine sensors and uses this input data (voltage signals) to calculate timing advance and idle speed. On some models, an acceleration enrichment device replaces a speed relay. The device only allows air/fuel enrichment when the engine temperature is below 140 deg. F (60 deg. C) and the oxygen sensor is below operating temperature (about 480 deg. F). At normal operating temperature the enrichment device doesn't operate and the control unit handles fuel mixture control by sending a voltage signal to the oxygen sensor to increase the duty cycle to 75% for approximately 3 seconds.

NOTE: The oxygen sensor should be replaced every 30,000 miles. Reset the mileage counter, located in the left front wheel housing on Porsche models, by pressing the reset button with a small screwdriver.

Diagnosis and Testing

NOTE: At the time of publication, no test information for the DITC system was available from the manufacturer, but the following should be noted when troubleshooting ignition problems on vehicles equipped with the Bosch DITC system.

1. If a flywheel sensor fails the DITC system will not allow the engine to start.
2. If a temperature sensor fails the ignition timing will be retarded at all times.
3. If the throttle switch fails, the control unit will not retard the

timing during starting or deceleration and the idle speed will be too high.
4. If a pressure sensor fails (or the vacuum hose is disconnected or leaking) the ignition timing will be advanced.
5. If the wiring harness connector running to the left wheel housing is disconnected, the ignition timing will be retarded 7 degrees. This plug may be disconnected to eliminate detonation (engine ping) from low octane fuel.

IDLE SPEED ADJUSTMENT

The DITC system controls the engine idle speed by varying the ignition timing. All idle speed adjustments require the use of a timing light on a cold engine (temperature sensor below 120 deg. F (50 deg. C). Remove the temperature sensor from the intake manifold and install a plug in the sensor mounting hole. Leave the temperature sensor wire attached and lay the sensor aside. Attach a suitable timing light, then start the engine and allow it to reach normal operating temperature. Turn the air bypass screw (idle control screw) until the ignition timing mark is visible at the timing pointer edge, then make sure the idle speed is below 900 rpm. The timing mark may move due to the computer control signals. If necessary, adjust the CO level (using a suitable emission analyzer) at the same time the idle speed adjustment is made.

BOSCH DIGITAL MOTOR ELECTRONICS (DME) SYSTEM

General Information

The Bosch DME system uses various engine sensors that monitor intake air volume, engine rpm, crankshaft angle or rotation, coolant temperature, intake air temperature, throttle position and exhaust gas oxygen content. Signals from these sensors are sent to an electronic control unit (ECU), which is the brain of the DME system. The ECU is usually located under the instrument panel and controls the air/fuel ratio and ignition timing in one of two modes, called OPEN or CLOSED LOOP operation. The DME computer will switch from the open loop mode to the closed loop mode when the engine coolant temperature is above 113 deg. F and the oxygen sensor is above 480 deg. F. California models use a heated oxygen sensor to switch the DME system into closed loop operation sooner.

System Operation

The DME system consists of 4 sub-systems: Fuel Control, Data-Sensors, Electronic Control Unit (ECU), and Spark Timing. For fuel control, the DME system uses the Bosch Air Flow controlled (AFC) fuel injection system. The AFC system is electronically controlled by the ECU, which is programmed to regulate fuel injection based upon information received from various data sensors, along with the specific data for the engine stored in computer memory. The ECU generates control signals for the fuel pump relay, auxiliary air valve, cold start injector coil, and the cylinder port injector coils. These devices control cold idle, curb idle speed and mixture, air/fuel ratio and fuel supply.

Spark control allows the electronic control unit (ECU) to determine the exact instant that ignition is required, based upon information received from data sensors. At the optimum time, the ECU breaks the primary circuit of the ignition coil, producing a high voltage at coil center tower. This voltage surge fires the spark plug at the proper time for most efficient combustion, eliminating the need for vacuum and/or centrifugal advance. Each sensor furnishes electronic impulses to the ECU. Using this information, the

ECU computes spark timing, and correct amount of fuel necessary to maintain proper engine operation.

The function of each sensor is closely related in maintaining proper engine operation.

ENGINE SENSORS

Oxygen Sensor

This sensor is mounted in engine exhaust stream, in front of catalytic converter. It supplies a low voltage (under $1/2$ volt) when fuel mixture is lean (too much oxygen) and a higher voltage (up to 1 volt) when fuel mixture is rich (not enough oxygen). Oxygen sensor must be hot (over 480°F) to function properly and to allow ECU to accept its electrical signals. The oxygen sensor measures quantity of oxygen only. Some vehicles are equipped with an electrically heated oxygen sensor. This sensor reaches operating temperature sooner and begins to function earlier. The heated oxygen sensor has 3 wires, 2 for the heater element (power & ground), and a single wire for the oxygen sensor signal. The heating begins with ignition on (via fuel pump & DME relay terminal 87). The plugs from the sensor to the wiring harness are located near the flywheel sensor plugs (speed, reference mark).

---CAUTION---

No attempt should be made to measure oxygen sensor voltage output. Current drain of conventional voltmeter could permanently damage sensor, shift sensor calibration range and/or render sensor unusable. Do not connect jumper wire, test leads or other electrical connectors to sensor. Use these devices only on ECU side of harness after disconnecting sensor.

Reference Mark Sensor

The reference mark sensor is located on crankcase flange. This sensor detects crankshaft position in relation to top dead center, and sends this signal to the control unit. It is triggered by a bolt cemented into the flywheel.

Speed Sensor

The speed sensor is mounted on an adjustable bracket with the reference mark sensor. The speed sensor measures engine speed by counting the teeth on the starter ring gear. The speed sensor sends 2 voltage pulses to the control unit for each tooth that passes.

Coolant Temperature Sensor

This sensor is located in the coolant stream of the intake manifold, and supplies coolant temperature information to the ECU. This information affects the following engine systems: Air/fuel ratio (as engine coolant temperature varies with time during a cold start), spark timing, and engine temperature lamp operation.

Intake Air Temperature Sensor

This sensor is located in the air stream of the air flow meter, and supplies incoming air temperature information to the ECU. The ECU uses this along with other information in regulating the fuel injection rate.

Air Flow Sensor

This sensor is located in the air stream of the air flow meter, and supplies air volume information to the ECU. The ECU uses this and other information in regulating the fuel injection rate. The air flow meter incorporates a measuring flap, that opens against pressure of a spiral spring, and is connected to a potentiometer. The potentiometer transmits an elecrical signal determined by position of the measuring flap to form the ECU of engine load.

Throttle Switch

A contact-type throttle switch is located on the throttle body. It converts throttle position into electrical signals to inform ECU of throttle position. The potentiometer within the air flow meter prevents loss of engine power during sudden acceleration/deceleration by signaling the ECU of necessary fuel enrichment requirements.

High Altitude Switch

Switch is mounted under the dashboard, on driver's side of vehicle. In altitudes higher than 3300 ft. (1000 m) the high altitude switch closes, signaling the ECU to lean the fuel mixture.

Auxiliary Air Valve

Auxiliary air valve provides additional air during cold engine starts and warmup. It is located next to throttle body. The valve consists of an electrically heated bi-metal strip, movable disc and air by-pass channel. The heater coil on the bi-metal strip is energized by the fuel pump relay. Control of the valve is based upon engine temperature. The air by-pass channel is open when engine is cold and gradually closes as temperature rises. At predetermined temperatures, air by-pass channel is blocked and additional air flow stops.

Fuel Pressure Regulator

The pressure regulator is located at the end of the injection collection line. Pressure regulator maintains constant fuel pressure to the fuel injectors.

NOTE: For more information on DME fuel system components, see the Fuel Injection Section.

Electronic Control Unit (ECU)

The ECU monitors and controls all DME system functions. The ECU consists of input/output devices, Central Processing Unit (CPU), power supply and memories. The input/output devices of the ECU convert electrical signals received by data sensors and switches to digital signals for use by the CPU. Digital signals received by the CPU are used to perform all mathematical computations and logic functions necessary to deliver proper air/fuel mixture. The CPU also calculates spark timing information. The

Read Only Memory (ROM) of the ECU is programmed with specific information that is used by the ECU during open loop (spark timing and fuel injection rate). This information is also used when a sensor or other component fails in the system, allowing the vehicle to be driven in for repairs (limp-in mode).

Diagnosis & Testing

CAUTION

DME ignition system voltage is extremely high. Contact with current-carrying parts while engine is running could prove fatal. Always turn ignition switch OFF or remove battery ground cable when connecting testers or replacing system components. High voltage is particularly present at spark plug, distributor, and ignition coil connections and at terminal 1 of the control unit. Do not attempt to check ignition system by a sparking test of spark plugs. This may destroy ignition coil or control unit.

Complete testing of the DME system requires an oscilloscope, voltmeter, ohmmeter and special test leads to insert in multiple pin control unit connector. Therefore, system testing is limited. Check that all electrical connections are free of corrosion and securely attached. Check DME ground wire on engine flange and on clutch housing near speed and reference mark sensors. Be sure connections have good contact and are tight. Particularly check 9-pin connector above the brake booster, 4-pin connector on the air flow sensor, 3-pin connector on throttle switch, 35-pin connector on the control unit, 2-pin connector at temperature sensor, 1-pin (or 2-pin) connector for the oxygen sensor (on firewall above flywheel sensors), and two 3-pin connectors for flywheel sensors (attached to the intake manifold).

With ignition turned ON, but with engine not running, connect positive voltmeter lead to terminal 1 of control unit harness connector. Connect negative lead to ground. Voltmeter should register battery voltage. If not, check wiring back to battery.

Speed Sensor Test

NOTE: This is an alternate test when an oscilloscope is not available.

Using a Fresnel lens front LED from an electronics store, connect a 220-ohm-$\frac{1}{4}$ watt resistor in series with one of the LED terminals. Connect positive LED test lead to terminal 8 of control unit harness connector. Connect negative LED test lead to terminal 27 of same connector. Do not start the engine, but operate starter. LED will flicker dimly if speed sensor is sending a signal.

Reference Mark Sensor

Using same LED tester as used for speed sensor, connect positive lead to control unit harness connector terminal 25 and negative lead to terminal 26. Do not start engine, but operate starter. If sensor is sending a signal, LED should flicker dimly.

Primary Resistance Test

With ignition switch OFF, disconnect wires from primary terminals of ignition coil to isolate it from the system. Set ohmmeter for x1 scale. Connect ohmmeter leads to 2 primary terminals. Reading should be .4-.6. If not, replace ignition coil.

Secondary Resistance Test

With ignition switch still OFF, remove wire from coil tower. Set ohmmeter at x1000 scale. Connect ohmmeter leads to ignition coil positive terminal and coil tower. Reading should be 5,000-7,200 ohms. If not within specifications, replace ignition coil. Shielded resistance of spark plug connectors should be 3,000 ohms. Shielded resistance of distributor rotor, and of all distributor cap connections should be rotor.

Speed Sensor Adjustment

NOTE: Adjusting speed sensor automatically adjusts reference mark sensor. They cannot be adjusted separately.

The speed sensor bracket is mounted on the crankcase flange with 2 bolts. To adjust clearance, loosen bolts and turn sensor holder. Clearance should be .030-034 in. (.75-.85 mm). To adjust clearance with engine installed in vehicle, remove speed sensor. Using a depth gauge, measure distance from sensor holder's upper surface to tooth head on starter ring gear. Measure length of speed sensor. Subtract speed sensor length from holder-to-flywheel tooth distance. Difference should be .030-.034in. (.75-.85mm). If not to specifications, loosen screws and turn holder until holder-to-flywheel tooth distance is equal to the length of the sensor plus the specified clearance. Tighten screws, and install speed sensor in holder.

CHRYLSER ELECTRONIC FEEDBACK CARBURETOR (EFC) SYSTEM

General Information

The Chrysler Electronic Feedback Carburetor (EFC) system was introduced in mid-1979 on Volares and Aspens sold in California with the six cylinder engine. The system is a conventional one, incorporating an oxygen sensor, a three-way catalytic converter, an oxidizing catalytic converter, a feedback carburetor, a solenoid-operated vacuum regulator valve, and a Combustion Computer. Also incorporated into the system are Chrysler's Electronic Spark Control, and a mileage counter which illuminates a light on the instrument panel at 15,000 mile, (now 30,000 mile) intervals, signaling the need for oxygen sensor replacement.

Typical Chrysler combustion computer

Dual pick-up distributor

In Chrysler's system, "Combustion Computer" is a collective term for the Feedback Carburetor Controller and the Electronic Spark Control computer, which are housed together in a case located on the air cleaner. The feedback carburetor controller is the information processing component of the system, monitoring oxygen sensor voltage (low voltage/lean mixture, high voltage/rich mixture), engine coolant temperature, manifold vacuum, engine speed, and engine operating mode (starting or running). The controller examines the incoming information and then sends a signal to the solenoid-operated vacuum regulator valve (also located in the Combustion computer housing), which then sends the proper rich or lean signal to the carburetor.

The 1 bbl Holley R-8286A carburetor is equipped with two diaphragms, controlling the idle system and the main metering system. The diaphragms move tapered rods, which vary the size of the orifaces in the idle system air bleed and the main metering system fuel flow. A "lean" command from the controller to the vacuum regulator results in increased vacuum to both diaphragms, which simultaneously raise both the idle air bleed rod (increasing idle air bleed) and the main metering rod (reducing fuel flow). A "rich" command reduces vacuum level, causing the spring-loaded rods to move in the other direction, enrichening the mixture.

Both closed loop and open loop operation are possible in the EFC system. Open loop operation occurs under any one of the following conditions: coolant temperature under 150°F, oxygen sensor temperature under 660°F; low manifold vacuum (less than 4.5 in. Hg. engine cold, or less than 3.0 in. Hg. engine hot); oxygen sensor failure; or hot engine starting. Closed loop operation begins when engine temperature reaches 150°F.

Air injection is supplied by an air pump. At cool engine temperature, air is injected into the exhaust manifold upstream of both catalytic converters. At operating temperature, an air switching valve diverts air from the exhaust to an injection point downstream from the three-way catalyst, but upstream of the conventional oxidizing catalyst.

The 1980 and later system is used with Electronic Spark Advance (ESA). Differences lie in the deletion of some components within the combustion computer. The start timer, vacuum transducer count-up clock and memory throttle transducer, and ambient air temperature sensor are not used.

The feedback system for the six cylinder engines is essentially unchanged. The four and eight cylinder systems differ from the six mainly in the method used to control the carburetor mixture. Instead of having vacuum-controlled diaphragms to raise or lower the mixture rods, the carburetors are equipped with an electric solenoid valve, which is part of the carburetor.

Other differences between the systems are minor. On the four cylinder, the ignition sensor is the Hall Effect distributor, but it functions in the same manner as the six cylinder pick-up coil. eight cylinder uses two pick-up coils (a Start pick-up and a Run pick-up); troubleshooting is included in the "Lean Burn/Electronic Spark Control" section. The four and six cylinder engines use a 150°F switch with Combustion Computer 4145003, and a 98°F switch with Computer 4145088. The eight cylinder engine has a detonation sensor (see the "Lean Burn/Electronic Spark Control" section), and the six and eight cylinder engines have a charge temperature switch to monitor intake charge temperature. Below approximately 60°F, the switch prevents EGR timer function and EGR valve operation; additionally, on eight cylinder engines, air injection is routed upstream of the exhaust manifolds.

Finally, the replacement interval for the oxygen sensor has been doubled, from 15,000–30,000 miles. Replacement procedures and odometer resetting are the same as for the 1979 six cylinder system.

Diagnosis and Testing

The equipment necessary to test the EFC system includes:
1. Volt/ohm meter
2. Jumper wires
3. Auxiliary vacuum supply (hand held vaccum pump)
4. Fuel pressure gauge
5. Tachometer
6. Timing light
7. Oscilloscope
8. Vacuum gauge
9. Propane kit

PRELIMINARY CHECKS

1. Road test the vehicle and determine when the problem occurs. Narrow it down as far as possible to isolate the system, if possible.
2. Perform visual checks. Experience has shown that many problems are caused by loose connectors, frayed insulation, loose hose clamps, leaks in vacuum or fuel lines. A short visual check will help you spot these most common faults and save a lot of unnecessary test and diagnostic time. If there are no obvious faults that can be identified visually, proceed with the test sequence.
3. Perform test procedure. The procedure is broken down into four categories: Visual Inspection, No Start, Cold Driveability, and Warm Driveability. The customer complaint will tell you which one to use. Only use that procedure. There is no need to go through the No Start Test when the complaint is Warm Driveability.

Vacuum leaks will cause the system to operate richer than normal and the owner may complain about poor fuel economy. This may be indicated in the warm driveability procedure with a variable voltmeter reading of 4-14 volts. Because of a stock-up of tolerances, some engines may have good driveability but an O_2 solenoid voltage of 9-13 volts. Do not attempt to make any repairs. Fuel contamination of the crankcase will cause the oxygen feedback system to operate the engine leaner than normal. The owner complaint will be a surging condition. The warm driveability procedure should be followed after the visual inspection. If test 12 indicates a voltmeter reading between 0-5 volts, then fuel contamination of the crankcase can be suspected and/or extremely rich carburetion.

NOTE: High altitude areas may use lower closed loop voltage specifications.

Visual Inspection

In order for the ignition and fuel systems to function properly, all electrical, vacuum, or air hose connections must be complete and tight. Before proceeding with the test procedure, the following must be checked.

ELECTRICAL CONNECTIONS

Terminal in connectors must lock together. Look for connectors that are not fully plugged into each other or terminals that are not fully plugged into the insulator.

IGNITION SYSTEM COMPONENTS
1. Connectors at SCC.
2. Start and run pick-up coil connectors at distributor.
3. Spark plug wires.
4. Coil wire (cap and coil connections).
5. Connectors at coil.

Single pick-up distributor

6. Connectors at starter relay.
7. Connector at detonation sensor (5.2L-4bbl).

FUEL CONTROL SYSTEM

1. Connector at engine coolant sensor (3.7L-5.2L-4bbl) located in the front of the intake manifold.
2. Connect at charge temperature sensor (5.2L-2bbl) located in the rear of the intake manifold.
3. Connector at charge temperature switch (3.7L-5.2L-4bbl) located in the rear of the intake manifold.
4. Connector at oil pressure switch.
5. Connector and choke control.
6. Connectors at carburetor harness.
7. Carburetor ground switch.
8. Connectors at air switching and EGR solenoids.
9. Engine harness to main harness connector.
10. Oxygen sensor connectors.

NOTE: On 5.2L, there is a jumper harness used between oxygen sensor and computer harness.

11. Battery cables.
12. Battery ground on engine.
13. Engine to firewall ground strap.

Detonation sensor location—typical

DISTRIBUTOR
- Electronic Ignition
- Reduced Tolerances
- Permanently Lubricated

AIR INDUCTION

INCREASED CAM OVERLAP

CCEGR TEMPERATURE VALVE

CHARCOAL CANISTER

COOLANT CONTROL ENGINE VACUUM SWITCH

AIR PUMP AND COMBINATION DIVERTER/SWITCH VALVE

MODIFIED COMBUSTION CHAMBER AND REDUCED COMPRESSION RATIO

EXHAUST PORT AIR INJECTION

HEATED INTAKE AIR

MINI OXIDATION CATALYST

ELECTRONIC SPARK CONTROL COMPUTER

CLOSED CRANKCASE VENTILATION

OXIDATION CATALYTIC CONVERTER

ROLL-OVER VALVE

FUEL TANK

LEADED-FUEL RESTRICTOR

PRESSURE-VACUUM RELIEF FILLER CAP

EGR VACUUM AMPLIFIER

EGR DELAY SOLENOID

EGR DELAY TIMER

ORIFICE SPARK ADVANCE CONTROL VALVE (OSAC)

INTAKE MANIFOLD
- Improved Hot Spot

EXHAUST GAS RECIRCULATION
- EGR Control Valve
- EGR Vacuum Amplifier
- EGR Time Delay
- CTS (Charge Temperature Switch)

CARBURETOR
- Improved Distribution
- Faster Acting Choke, Electric Assist
- External Idle Mixture Limiter Caps
- Solenoid Idle Stop
- Control System
- Heat Shield

Chrysler combustion computer system

HOSE CONNECTIONS

All hoses must be fully and firmly fitted at their connections. Also, they cannot be pinched anywhere along their routing. Look for hoses that are not fully plugged on, or are pinched and cut.

PCV SYSTEM

1. Hose between carburetor and PCV valve.
2. PCV valve plugged into valve cover grommet.
3. Correct PCV valve. White in color.

Spark Control Computer (SCC)

1. Hose betwen vacuum transducer and carburetor.

NOTE: On 5.2L–2BBL this hose has a CVSCC (coolant vacuum switch cold closed) in it.

2. Air intake hose.

EGR System

1. Hose between carburetor and EGR amplifier.
2. Hose between intake manifold and EGR amplifier.
3. Hose between EGR amplifier and EGR solenoid.
4. Hose between EGR solenoid and EGR valve.

NOTE: Some 5.21-4BBL have a delay valve in this hose.

5. Hose between EGR amplifier and vacuum reservoir (3.7L only).

Air Switching System

1. Hose between intake manifold and air switching solenoid.
2. Hose between air switching solenoid and air switching/relief valve.
3. Hose between air switching/relief valve and plumbing to exhaust manifolds.
4. Hose between air switching/relief valve and plumbing to catalyst.

Evaporative Control System

1. Hose between carburetor bowl vent and canister.
2. Hose between canister and air cleaner.
3. Hoses between canister and air pump.
4. Hose between canister and fuel tank line.

NOTE: This hose has a shut off valve in it.

Choke System

Check the hose between carburetor and vacuum kick diaphragm.

Heated Air Door System

1. Hose between carburetor and air temperature sensor.
2. Hose between air temperature sensor and door diaphragm.
3. Hose between air cleaner and exhaust manifold heat stove.

Power Brake and/or Speed Control (Where Applicable)

1. Hose between carburetor and power brake booster.

NOTE: This hose has a charcoal canister in it.

2. Hose between power brake booster and speed control servo.

Heater/AC System

1. Vacuum hose at water valve.
2. Vacuum supply hose to instrument panel control.

OPERATION TESTS

NOTE: Three different troubleshooting procedures are included. Use the 1979 procedure only for the 1979 Aspens and Volares with six cylinder engines. Use the 1980–81 and 1982 and later procedures where applicable.

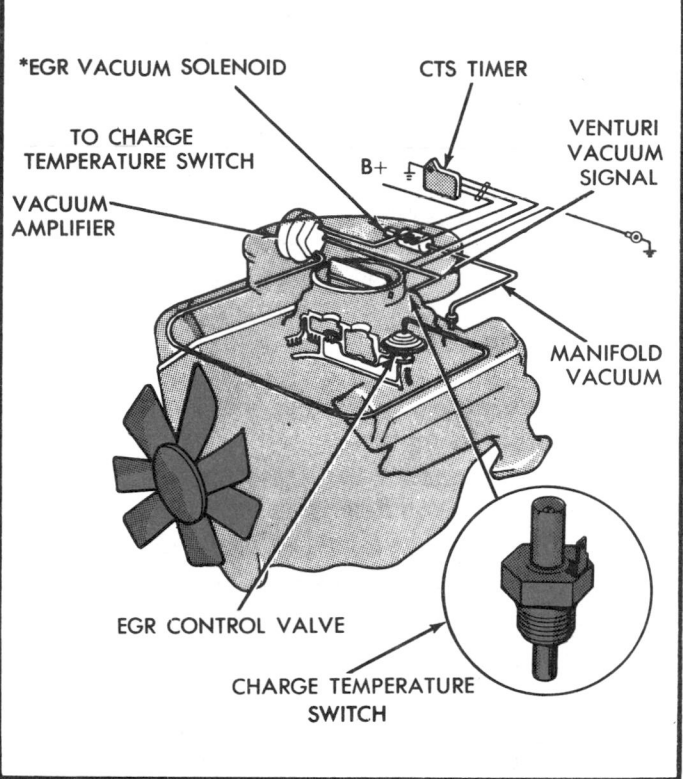

Charge temperature switch location

1979 MODELS

1. Warm the engine to normal operating temperature. Install a tee into the control vacuum hose which runs to the carburetor. Install the 0-5 in. vacuum gauge on the tee. Start the engine and allow it to idle. The vacuum gauge should read 2.5 in. for approximately 100 seconds, then fall to zero, then gradually rise to between 1.0 and 4.0 in. The reading may oscillate slightly.

2. If the vacuum reading is incorrect, increase the engine speed to 2,000 rpm. If vacuum reads between 1.0 and 4.0 in., return the engine to idle. If the reading is now correct, the system was not warmed up; originally, but is OK.

3. If the gauge is correct at 2,000 rpm but not at idle, the carburetor must be replaced.

Coolant switch—typical

Schematic of 1979 Chrysler electronic feedback carburetor system

4. If the vacuum is either above 4.0 in. or below 1.0 in., follow the correct troubleshooting procedure given next. Note that in most cases of system malfunction, control vacuum will be either 0 in. or 5.0 in.

Control Vacuum Above 4.0 In. Hg.

Start the engine, apply the parking brake, place the transmission in Neutral, and place the throttle on the next to lowest step of the fast idle cam.

1. Remove the PCV hose from the PCV valve. Cover the end of the hose with your thumb. Gradually uncover the end of the hose until the engine runs rough. If control vacuum gets lower as the hose is uncovered, the carburetor must be replaced; however, complete Step 2 before replacing it. If control vacuum remains high, continue with the tests.

2. Before replacing the carburetor, examine the heat shield. Interference may exist between the heat shield and the mechanical power enrichment valve lever. If so, the carburetor will be running rich. Correct the problem and repeat Step 1.

NOTE: A new heat shield is used starting in 1979 which has clearance for the enrichment lever. Earlier heat shields should not be used unless modified for clearance.

3. Disconnect the electrical connector at the solenoid regulator valve. Control vacuum should drop to zero. If not, replace the solenoid regulator valve.

4. Disconnect the oxygen sensor wire. Use the jumper wire to connect the *harness* lead to the negative battery terminal.

─────CAUTION─────
Do not connect the oxygen sensor wire to ground or the battery.

Control vacuum should drop to zero in approximately 15 seconds. If not, replace the Combustion Computer. If it does, replace the oxygen sensor. Before replacing either part, check the Computer to sensor wire for continuity.

Control Vacuum Below 1.0 In. Hg.

1. Start the engine and allow it to idle in Neutral. Disconnect the vacuum hose at the computer transducer and connect the hose to the 0-30 in. Hg. vacuum gauge. The gauge should show manifold vacuum (above 12 in.) If not, trace the hose to its source and then connect it properly to a source of manifold vacuum.

The following Steps should be made with the engine warm, parking brake applied, transmission in Neutral, and throttle placed on the next to lowest step of the fast idle cam.

2. Remove the air cleaner cover. Gradually close the choke plate until the engine begins to run roughly. If control vacuum increases to 5.0 in. as the choke is closed, go to Step 3. If control vacuum remains low, go to Step 4.

3. Disconnect the air injection hose from its connection to a metal tube at the rear of the cylinder head. Plug the tube. If control vacuum remains below 1.0 in. replace the carburetor. If control vacuum returns to the proper level, reconnect the air injection hose and disconnect the 3/16 in. vacuum hose from the air switching valve. If control vacuum remains below 1.0 in., replace the air switching valve. If control vacuum rises to the proper level, check all hoses for proper connections, then, if correct, replace the coolant vacuum switch.

4. Check that the bottom nipple of the solenoid regulator valve is connected to manifold vacuum. Disconnect the solenoid regulator electrical connector. Use the jumper wire to connect one terminal of the solenoid regulator lead to the positive battery terminal. Connect the other terminal of the solenoid regulator lead to ground. Control vacuum should rise above 5.0 in. If not, replace the solenoid regulator. If so, go to the next Step.

5. Disconnect the 5 terminal connector at the computer. The terminals are numbered 1 to 5, starting at the rounded end. Connect a jumper wire from terminal 2 in the harness to a ground. Control vacuum should rise to 5 in. If not, trace the voltage to the battery to discover where it is being lost. If so, go to the next Step.

NOTE: Wiring harness problems are usually in the connectors. Check them for looseness or corrosion.

6. Disconnect the oxygen sensor wire. Use a jumper wire to connect the *harness* lead to the positive battery terminal.

―――――――――CAUTION―――――――――

Do not connect the oxygen sensor wire to the battery or to a ground.

Control vacuum should rise to 5 in. in approximately 15 seconds. If not, replace the computer. If so, replace the oxygen sensor.

Ignition Timing

1. Ground the carburetor switch with a jumper wire.
2. Connect a timing light to the engine.
3. Start the engine. Wait one minute.
4. With the engine running at a speed not greater than the specified curb idle rpm (see the emission control sticker in the engine compartment), adjust the timing to specification.
5. Remove the ground wire after adjustment.

Curb Idle Adjustment

Adjust the curb idle only after ignition timing has been checked and set to specification.
1. Start the engine and run in Neutral on the second step of the fast idle cam until the engine is fully warmed up and the radiator becomes hot. This may take 5 to 10 minutes.
2. Disconnect and plug the EGR hose at the EGR valve.
3. Ground the carburetor switch with a jumper wire.
4. Adjust the idle rpm in Neutral to the curb idle rpm figure given on the emission control sticker in the engine compartment.
5. Reconnect the EGR hose and remove the jumper wire.

Oxygen Sensor Replacement

1. Disconnect the negative battery cable. Remove the air cleaner.
2. Disconnect the sensor electrical lead. Unscrew the sensor using Chrysler special tool C-4589.
3. Installation is the reverse. Before installation, coat the threads of the sensor with a nickel base anti-seize compound. Do not use other type compounds since they may electrically insulate the sensor. Torque the sensor to 35 ft. lbs.

Mileage Counter Reset

The mileage counter will illuminate every 15,000 miles, signaling the need for oxygen sensor replacement. After replacing the oxygen sensor, reset the counter as follows:
1. Locate the mileage counter. It is spliced into the speedometer cable, the boot.

Typical oxygen sensor

Resetting maintenance switch

2. Slide the rubber boot up the speedometer cable to expose the top of the mileage counter. Turn the reset screw on top of the counter to reset. Replace the boot.

1980–81 MODELS

ESA System Tests

1. Connect a timing light to the engine.
2. Disconnect and plug the vacuum hose at the vacuum transducer. Connect a vacuum pump to the transducer fitting and apply 14-16 in. Hg. of vacuum.
3. With the engine at normal operating temperature, raise the speed to 2,000 rpm. Wait one minute, then check the timing

5 ELECTRONIC ENGINE CONTROLS

advance. Specifications are as follows (timing in addition to basic advance):

1981 1.7A/T: 31″—39″
1981 1.7M/T Fed.: 34″—42″
                   39″—47″
1981 2.2M/T Fed.: 24″—32″
                   29″—37″
1981 2.2M/T Cal.: 19″—27″
1981 2.2A/T: 21″—29″
1981 6 cyl.: 16″—24″
1981 8 cyl.: 30″—38″

Air Switching System Tests

1. Remove the vacuum hose from the air switching valve, connect a vacuum gauge to the hose.

2. Start the engine. With the engine cold, engine vacuum should be present on the gauge until the engine coolant temperature is as follows:

1981 4 cylinder except 2.2L
49 States: 125°F
1981 4 cylinder 2.2L 49 states: 150°F
6 cylinder all: 150°F
8 cylinder with computer 4145003: 150°F
8 cylinder with computer 4145088: 98°F

On the 8 cylinder models, the charge temperature switch must be open and fuel mixture temperature above 60°F.

3. When the indicated temperatures are reached, vacuum should drop to zero. If no vacuum is present on the gauge before the temperature is reached:

On the four cylinder, check the vacuum supply and the Coolant Controlled Engine Vacuum Switch (CCEVS); on the six and eight cylinder, check the vacuum supply, air switching solenoid, coolant switch (and charge temperature switch on the eight), and the wiring and connections to the computer. If all these systems are OK, it is possible that the computer is faulty, preventing air switching.

4. With the engine warm on the four cylinder, no vacuum should be present; if there is vacuum, check the CCEVS.

5. With the engine warm on the six and eight: on the 1981 six, vacuum should be present for 65 seconds; on the 1981 Cal. eight for 20 seconds; on the 1981 Fed. 4bbl eight for 30 seconds; on the 1981 Fed. 2bbl eight for 90 seconds after the engine starts. After the period indicated, vacuum should drop to zero. If there is no vacuum, check as follows:

Connect a voltmeter to the light green wire on the air switching solenoid. On the eight cylinder, also disconnect the coolant switch and charge temperature switch. Start the engine; voltage should be

Carburetor switch

less than one volt. Allow the warm-up schedule to finish (time as specified at the beginning of this step). The solenoid should de-energize and the voltmeter should then read charging system voltage. If not, replace the solenoid and repeat the test. If the voltmeter indicates charging system voltage before the warm-up schedule finishes, replace the computer.

EFC Tests

Check all vacuum hose connections and the spark advance schedule before performing these tests. Check the resistance of all related wiring, and examine all electrical connections for soundness. On the four cylinder, connect a vacuum pump to the vacuum transducer and apply 10 (16-1981) in. Hg. of vacuum. On all engines, start the engine and allow it to reach normal operating temperature.

NOTE: After a hot restart, run the engine at 1,200-2,000 rpm for at least two minutes before continuing. DO NOT GROUND THE CARBURETOR SWITCH.

1. On the four and eight and 1981 six cylinder engines, disconnect the electrical connector from the regulator solenoid. Engine speed should increase at least 50 rpm. (If not, on the four cylinder only disconnect the four-way tee from the air cleaner temperature sensor and repeat the test. If no response, replace the computer.) Connect the regulator solenoid; engine speed should return to 1,200-2,000 rpm. Disconnect the six (twelve-1981 reardrive) pin connector from the computer, and connect a ground to the No.15 harness connector pin. Engine speed should drop 50 rpm. If not, check for carburetor air leaks, and service the carburetor as necessary.

2. With the engine cold, check the coolant switch. It should have continuity to ground on the four cylinder, or have a resistance of less than 10 ohms on the six and eight. With the engine warm (above 150°F) the switch should be open.

3. With the engine hot, disconnect the coolant temperature switch. *Do not ground the carburetor switch.* Maintain an engine speed of 1,200-2,000 rpm (use a tachometer). Disconnect the oxygen sensor electrical lead at the sensor and connect a jumper wire. The engine speed should increase (at least 50 rpm) for 15 seconds, then return to 1,200-2,000 rpm. (If not, on the four cylinder *only,* disconnect the four-way tee from the air cleaner temperature sensor, allowing the engine to draw in air. Repeat the test; if no response, replace the computer.) Next, connect the end of the jumper wire to the positive battery terminal; engine speed should drop. If the computer fails these tests, replace it. Reconnect the wires.

4. To test the oxygen sensor, run the engine at 1,200-2,000 rpm. Connect a voltmeter to the solenoid output wire which runs to the carburetor (18 DGN). Hold the choke plate closed. Over the next ten seconds, voltage should drop to 3 V. or less. If not, disconnect the air cleaner temperature sensor four-way tee and repeat the test. If no response, replace the computer.

Disconnect the PCV hose and/or the canister purge hose. Over the next ten seconds, voltage should be over 9 V. Voltage should then drop slightly, and remain there until the vacuum hoses are reconnected.

If the oxygen sensor fails these tests, replace it. Reconnect all wires.

1982 AND LATER SYSTEM TESTING

NOTE: The following tests can be made on the 1981 models with only slight modifications.

Prior to starting test sequence, check all vacuum hose connections. Refer to the vacuum hose routing diagram in the engine compartment for the correct hose routing. Check the resistance in all related wiring, giving specific attention to the connectors at the output devices and at the fuel control computer. Connect an auxiliary vacuum source to the vacuum transducer. Apply 16 inches of vacuum. Set the parking brake. Start the engine and let it warm up

Schematic of the Chrysler feedback carburetor system used on the 3.7L and 5.2L engines

until normal operating temperature is reached. After any hot start, maintain 1,500 RPM for at least two minutes before proceeding. Do not ground the carburetor switch.

Air Switching System Test

1. Remove vacuum hose for air switching/divertor valve and connect a vacuum gauge to hose.
2. Set the parking brake. Start engine and observe gauge reading.

ENGINE COLD

Engine vacuum should be present on gauge until engine coolant temperature and the charge temperature switch reach their normal operating conditions. When the temperature and time delay have been reached, vacuum should drop to zero. If no vacuum is present on gauge, check the vacuum supply, air switching solenoid, coolant switch, and charge temperature switch (CTS) and wiring and connections to computer. If they are okay, then it is possible that the computer is bad, preventing air switching to occur.

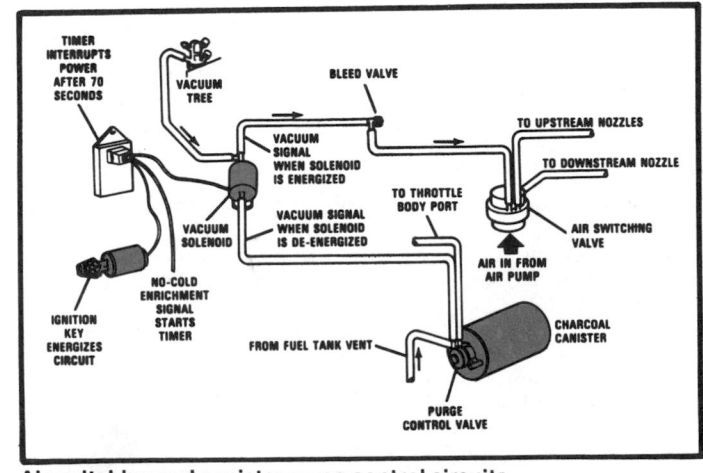

Air switching and canister purge control circuits

Typical vacuum solenoid/regulator

ENGINE WARM

Vacuum should be present for the specified period of time after the engine starts, and then should drop to zero. If there is no vacuum, check vacuum supply, air switching solenoid, engine temperature and charge temperature switch (CTS) and wiring and connections to computer. If they are okay, then it is possible that the computer is bad, preventing air switching to occur.

Connect a voltmeter to the light green wire on the air switching solenoid. With the engine at normal operating temperature and the engine off, start the engine. Voltage should be less than one volt. Allow the O_2 feedback air switching schedule to time out. This will permit the catalyst to reach normal operating temperature before the electronics begin fuel control operation. When the warmup schedule is completed, the solenoid will de-energize and the voltmeter will read charging system voltage. If not, replace the solenoid and repeat the procedure. If the voltmeter indicates charging system voltage before the warmup schedule is complete, replace the computer.

Air Switching Valve Test

1. Remove air supply hose from valve.
2. Remove vacuum hose from valve and install an auxiliary vacuum supply.
3. Start engine, air should be blowing out of side port. Apply vacuum to valve. Air should now be blowing out of bottom port.

Engine Temperature Sensor Tests

1. Turn ignition **Off** and disconnect wire from temperature switch.
2. Connect one lead of ohmmeter to a good ground on engine, or in the case of the charge temperature switch to its ground terminal.
3. Connect other lead of ohmmeter to center terminal of coolant switch.
4. Check for continuity using the following ohmmeter readings.
   a. **For Cold Engine:** Continuity should be present with a resistance less than 100 ohms. If not replace the switch. The charge temperature switch must be cooler than 60°F (15°C) in order to achieve this reading.

b. **For Hot Engine At Normal Operating Temperature:** Terminal reading should show no continuity, if it does, replace coolant switch.

Coolant Sensor Test

1. Connect the leads of ohmmeter to the terminals of the sensor.
2. With the engine cold and the ambient temperature less than 90°F (32°C) the resistance should be between 500 and 1,000 ohms.
3. With the engine hot (normal operating temperature) the resistance should be greater than 1,300 ohms.

Carburetor Regulator Test

Using a tachometer, maintain an engine speed of 1,500 rpm.
Disconnect the regulator solenoid connector from the solenoid. Average engine speed should increase a minimum of 50 rpm.
Reconnect the regulator solenoid connector. The engine speed should slowly return to 15,000 rpm. Disconnect the twelve pin connector at the fuel control computer. Connect a ground to harness connector pin 15. Engine speed should decrease a minimum of 50 rpm. If the engine speed does not change accordingly, service the carburetor (check for air leaks).

Electronic Fuel Control Computer Test

With the engine at normal operating temperature, make certain the carburetor switch is **not grounded.** Using a tachometer, maintain an engine speed of 1,500 rpm. Connect a voltmeter to the solenoid output wire going to the carburetor (green). Do not separate the connector from the wiring harness. Separate the connector at the oxygen sensor and connect a jumper wire to the harness end.

1. Connect the other end of the jumper wire to a good ground. An increase in engine speed should be observed (minimum of 50 rpm). Voltmeter should indicate more than 9 volts.
2. Hold the wire with one hand and with the other touch the battery positive terminal. Engine speed should decrease (minimum of 50 RPM). Voltmeter should now indicate less than 3 volts. If the computer fails both tests replace it. Reconnect the oxygen sensor wire.

Leave voltmeter connected to carburetor regulator solenoid.

Oxygen Sensor Test

The feedback electronics must be working properly for this test.
1. Set the parking brake. Run the engine at 1,500 RPM (carburetor switch **not** grounded).
2. Using the voltmeter connected to the solenoid output wire going to the carburetor (green).
3. **Full Rich Test:** Hold the choke blades(s) closed. During the next ten seconds the voltage should decrease to three volts or less and maintain that level. If engine does not respond, go to step 4.
4. **Full Lean Test:** Disconnect the PCV system. During the next ten seconds, the voltage should increase to nine volts and maintain that level. The voltage will remain at this level until vacuum hoses are reconnected.
5. If the sensor fails both tests 3 and 4, replace it. Reconnect all hoses and wires. Steps 2 and 3 should not be performed for longer than 90 seconds.

DIAGNOSIS PROCEDURES

Engine Cranks But Will Not Start

1. Choke not closing check binding or interferences hot and cold and with accessories on.
2. No ignition firing.

Engine Fires, Runs Up, Then Dies

1. Choke vacuum kick setting too wide.
2. EGR system on at start check CCEGR valve or CTS switch timer, and solenoid for proper operation also EGR valve.
3. Fast idle speed set too low or cam index incorrect.
4. Vacuum leak.

5. Inadequate fuel pump output.
6. Low fuel level in carb reset floats.

Engine Dies On Kickdown After Start

1. Check vacuum kick, cam index, hot fast idle speed mis-set.

Engine Fires, Runs Up, Then Idles Slowly With Black Smoke

1. Choke vacuum diaphragm leaks or is not receiving vacuum signal.
2. Choke vacuum kick setting too tight.
3. Cam index and/or hot fast idle mis-set too low.
4. EGR system on during warmup check CCEGR or CTS and timer.

Engine Fires, But Does Not Run Up And Dies When Key Is Released

1. Choke vacuum diaphragm leaks or is not receiving vacuum signal.
2. Choke linkage binding preventing proper closing or breathing of blade.
3. Timing mis-set.

Engine Stalls When Transmission Is Placed In Gear (Cold Engine)

1. Improper choke vacuum kick setting.
2. Fast idle speed or cam index mis-set.
3. Ignition timing vacuum advance OSAC.

Engine Stalls, Hesitates Or Sags During Acceleration Tip-Ins During First Mile

1. Choke vacuum kick setting.
2. Exhaust Manifold Heat Control Valve stuck open.
3. Choke control switch in high heat at low ambients.
4. Incorrect float heights low fuel level.
5. EGR on during warm-up defective CCEGR or CTS.
6. Weak or low output, carburetor accelerator pump.
7. Secondary lockout mis-set 4 bbl. carb.
8. Defective OSAC no vacuum advance.

Engine Hesitates Or Sags, Stalls After First Mile Of Warmup

1. Choke control switch in high heat at lower ambients.
2. Exhaust Manifold Heat Control Valve stuck open.
3. Weak or poor output accelerator pump.
4. Incorrect float heights low fuel level.
5. EGR on during warmup defective CCEGR or CTS (low ambients).
6. Ignition system PSAC, vacuum advance, etc.
7. Heated air inlet in cold position (Icing).

Hesitation Sag, Stumble With Slight Acceleration Pedal Movement (Engine Warm)

1. Vacuum leak hose off or misrouted or split.
2. Mis-set timing or defective distributor governor or vacuum advance.
3. Weak or defective accelerator pump in carburetor-output to only one bore results in backfire on 2- or 4-bbl. carburetor.
4. Incorrect float height in carb low fuel level.
5. Sticking or binding carburetor power valve (Holley) or metering rod carrier binding or sticking (Carter).
6. Heated inlet air stuck in either full hot or full cold position, due to binding door hinge or faulty sensor.
7. Carburetor transfer or idle system plugged or obstructed.
8. Plugged or restricted OSAC giving little or no vacuum advance.
9. Binding, bent or defective EGR valve or control system, resulting in excessive EGR rates.

Hesitation, Sag, Stumble With Heavy Accelerator Pedal Movement (Engine Warm)

1. Weak or defective accelerator pump.
2. Major vacuum leak.
3. Sticking or binding carburetor power valve or step-up rods.
4. Mis-set basic timing or distributor governor advance faulty.
5. Mis-set carburetor float levels low fuel.
6. Faulty fuel pump obstructed lines or filter.
7. Binding or bent carburetor float arms inadequate fuel.
8. Mis-set air valve spring tension on 4-bbl. carburetors causing premature opening.

Surge At Constant Speed
LOW SPEED

1. Vacuum leak hoses off.
2. Mis-set timing failed vacuum advance.
3. Defective ASAC plugged or restricted giving no vacuum advance.
4. Partially plugged idle or transfer system in carb including mis-set idle.
5. Incorrect float setting low fuel level.
6. Defective PCV stuck in high flow position.
7. Heated air system stuck in cold position at low ambient.

HIGH SPEED

1. Incorrect spark advance defective distributor or OSAC valve plugged.
2. Major vacuum leak.
3. Defective or sticking gradient power valve (Holley Carb).
4. Incorrect float setting low fuel level.
5. Restricted fuel supply.

GENERAL MOTORS COMPUTER CONTROLLED CATALYTIC CONVERTER (C-4) SYSTEM, AND COMPUTER COMMAND CONTROL (CCC) SYSTEM

General Information

The GM designed Computer Controlled Catalytic Converter System (C-4) System), is a revised version of the 1978-79 Electronic Fuel Control System (although parts are not interchangeable between the systems). The C-4 System primarily maintains the ideal air/fuel ratios at which the catalytic converter is most effective.

Some versions of the system also control ignition timing of the distributor.

The Computer Command Control System (CCC System), introduced on some 1980 California models and used on all 1981 and later carbureted car lines, is an expansion of the C-4 System. The CCC System monitors up to fifteen engine/vehicle operating conditions which it uses to control up to nine engine and emission

Air management system operation (cold engine mode)

Air management system operation (warm engine mode)

There are two operation modes for both the C-4 System and the CCC System: closed loop and open loop fuel control. Closed loop fuel control means the oxygen sensor is controlling the carburetor's air/fuel mixture ratio. Under open loop fuel control operating conditions (wide open throttle, engine and/or oxygen sensor cold), the oxygen sensor has no effect on the air/fuel mixture.

NOTE: On some engines, the oxygen sensor will cool off while the engine is idling, putting the system into open loop operation. To restore closed loop operation, run the engine at part throttle and accelerate from the idle to part throttle a few times.

Computer Controlled Catalytic Converter (C-4) System

COMPONENTS AND OPERATION

Major components of the system include an electronic Control Module (ECM), an oxygen sensor, an electronically controlled variable-mixture carburetor, and a three-way oxidation-reduction catalytic converter.

The oxygen sensor generates a voltage which varies with exhaust gas oxygen content. Lean mixtures (more oxygen) reduce voltage; rich mixtures (less oxygen) increase voltage. Voltage output is sent to the ECM.

An engine temperature sensor installed in the engine coolant outlet monitors coolant temperatures. Vacuum control switches and throttle position sensors also monitor engine conditions and supply signals to the ECM.

Typical electronic control module (on-board computer)

control systems. In addition to maintaining the ideal air/fuel ratio for the catalytic converter and adjusting ignition timing, the CCC System also controls the Air Management System so that the catalytic converter can operate at the highest efficiency possible. The system also controls the lockup on the transmission torque converter clutch (certain automatic transmission models only), adjusts idle speed over a wide range of conditions, purges the evaporative emissions charcoal canister, controls the EGR valve operation and operates the early fuel evaporative (EFE) system. Not all engines use all of the above sub-systems.

Basic cycle of closed loop operation

C4 system air/fuel metering control

The Electronic Control Module (ECM) monitors the voltage input of the oxygen sensor along with information from other input signals. It processes these signals and generates a control signal sent to the carburetor. The control signal cycles between ON (lean command) and OFF (rich command). The amount of ON and OFF time is a function of the input voltage sent to the ECM by the oxygen sensor. The ECM has a calibration unit called a PROM (Programable Read Only Memory) which contains the specific instructions for a given engine application. In other words, the PROM unit is specifically programed or "tailor made" for the system in which it is installed. The PROM assembly is a replacable component which plugs into a socket of the ECM and requires a special tool for removal and installation.

On some 231 cu. in. V6 engines, the ECM controls the Electronic Spark Timing System (EST), AIR control system, and on the Turbo-charged 231 cu.in. C-4 System it controls the early fuel evaporative system (EFE) and the EGR valve control (on some models). On some 350 cu. in. V8 engines, the ECM controls the electronic module retard (EMR) system, which retards the engine timing 10 degrees during certain engine operations to reduce the exhaust emissions.

NOTE: Electronic Spark Timing (EST) allows continuous spark timing adjustments to be made by the ECM. Engines with EST can easily be identified by the absence of vacuum and mechanical spark advance mechanisms on the distributor. Engines with EMR systems may be recognized by the presence of five connectors, instead of the HEI module's usual four.

To maintain good idle and driveability under all conditions, other input signals are used to modify the ECM output signal. Besides the sensors and switches already mentioned, these input signals include the manifold absolute pressure (MAP) or vacuum sensors and the barometric pressure (BARO) sensor. The MAP or vacuum sensors sense changes in manifold vacuum, while the BARO sensor senses changes in barometric pressure. One important function of the BARO sensor is the maintenance of good engine performance at various altitudes. These sensors act as throttle position sensors on some engines. See the following paragraph for description.

A Rochester Dualjet carburetor is used with the C-4 System. It may be an E2SE, E2ME, E4MC or E4ME model, depending on engine application. An electronically operated mixture control solenoid is installed in the carburetor float bowl. The solenoid controls the air/fuel mixture metered to the idle and main metering systems. Air metering to the idle system is controlled by an idle air bleed valve. It follows the movement of the mixture solenoid to control the amount of air bled into the idle system, enriching or leaning out the mixture as appropriate. Air/fuel mixture enrichment occurs when the fuel valve is open and the air bleed is closed. All cycling of this system which occurs ten times per second, is controlled by the ECM. A throttle position switch informs the ECM of open or closed throttle operation. A number of different switches are used, varying with application. The four cylinder engine (151 cu. in.) uses two vacuum switches to sense open throttle and closed throttle operation. The V6 engines (except the 231 cu. in. turbo V6) use two pressure sensors MAP (Manifold Absolute Pressure) and BARO (Barometric Pressure) as well as a throttle-actuated wide open throttle switch mounted in a bracket on the side of the float bowl. The 231 cu. in. turbo V6, and V8 engines, use a throttle position sensor mounted in the carburetor bowl cover under the accelerator pump arm. When the ECM receives a signal from the throttle switch, indicating a change of position, it immediately searches its memory for the last set of operating conditions that resulted in an ideal air/fuel ratio, and shifts to that set of conditions. The memory is continually updated during normal operation.

Some 173 cu. in. V6 engines are equipped with a Pulsair control solenoid which is operated by the ECM. Likewise, many C-4 equipped engines with AIR systems (Air Injection Reaction systems) have an AIR system diverter solenoid controlled by the

C4 system schematic

Air management control on 3.8L engines

ECM. These systems are similar in function to the AIR Management system used in the CCC System. See below for information. Most C-4 Systems include a maintenance reminder flag connected to the odometer which becomes visible in the instrument cluster at regular intervals, signaling the need for oxygen sensor replacement.

NOTE: The 1980 Cutlass with 260 cu in. V8 engine is equipped with a hybrid C-4 System which includes some functions of the CCC System (Air Management, EGR valve control, Idle speed control, canister purge control and transmission converter clutch).

C-4 Component Removal
ELECTRONIC CONTROL MODULE (ECM)

The electronic control module monitors the voltage output of oxygen sensor and input from the coolant temperature sensor, throttle position sensor and an engine speed sensor. The control module analyzes the reading in a microprocessor in comparison with programmed values and generates a control signal to the mixture control solenoid within the carburetor.

Typical C4 control unit location and mounting

Removal

NOTE: When reference is made to red or blue connectors it is not the color of the connector body, but the secondary lock color on the wire side or back side of the connector.

1. Remove the red and the blue connectors from the ECM.

C4 electronic control module assembly

2. Remove ECM mounting hardware. The brackets and locations will vary from one car model to another, but all are relatively simple assemblies.

3. Remove the ECM from the vehicle.

NOTE: A replacement ECM is supplied without a PROM unit. The old PROM should be reused in the new ECM. This will avoid mix ups in emission programming. If the old PROM is defective it can be replaced. A trouble code 51 indicates a defective PROM unit.

Diassembly

1. Remove the sheet metal screw holding the access cover closed and remove the access cover from the ECM.

C4 PROM removal using removal tool

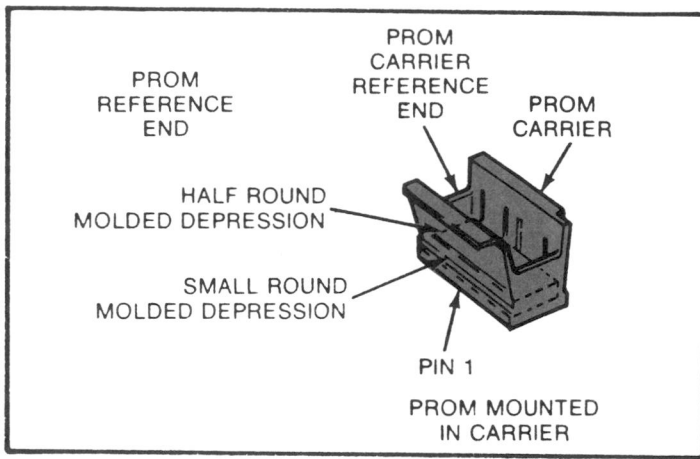

PROM reference markings used for proper installation

Installing the C4 PROM

242

C4 oxygen sensor

2. Pry the PROM unit from the ECM. A removal tool can be purchased from most electronics stores. Try to keep the PROM aligned during removal and installation to avoid bending the contact pins. Do not use excessive force to remove or install the PROM.

3. Match mark the reference end of the PROM or take notice of the ends of the PROM as it was installed. The reference end usually has a notch.

Assembly

1. Find the reference end of the PROM. If not marked look for the notch in the squared or symmetrical end of the carrier.

2. Align the PROM and carrier squarely over the socket and press firmly into the ECM socket. Using a piece of dowling or small blunt tool push down alternately on either end of the PROM to insure proper seating.

────────CAUTION────────

Do not install the PROM backwards and turn on the ignition, as this will destroy the PROM.

3. Replace the access cover on the ECM.

Installation

1. Install the ECM hardware and install the ECM unit in the passenger compartment.
2. Connect both connectors to the ECM following the red and blue color codes.
3. Start the engine and ground the diagnostic test lead.
4. Look for a trouble code 51. If code 51 occurs, the PROM is not fully seated, is installed backwards, the pins are bent or the unit is defective.

OXYGEN SENSOR

The C4 system uses a closed-end zirconia sensor placed in the engine exhaust stream. The sensor generates a weak voltage that varies with the oxygen content in the exhaust. As the oxygen increases indicating a lean fuel mixture, the voltage output falls. As the oxygen content decreases the sensor voltage rises, indicating a rich fuel mixture. When operating at 600°F or more the sensor generates from 200 millavolts (lean) to 800 millavolts (rich), at very low levels of current flow.

────────CAUTION────────

No attempt should be made to measure oxygen sensor voltage output. The current drain from any conventional voltmeter would be enough to permanently damage the sensor, shifting its calibration range, making it unusable. Also, connecting any jumper leads or test leads directly to the sensor can damage it. Make any test connections to the harness after disconnecting it from the sensor.

Removal and Installation

1. Disconnect the oxygen sensor electrical connector.

NOTE: The pigtail wire and connector are permanently attached to the oxygen sensor. Any attempt to remove them may damage the sensor. Care must be taken when handling the sensor. Keep the lower end of the sensor free of grease and dirt. Do not use solvents as they will damage the sensor. Do not roughly handle or drop the sensor as it may change the calibration.

2. Carefully back the sensor out of its threaded hole in the manifold.

NOTE: An anti-seize compound is used on all new sensors. If a sensor is to be reinstalled a special anti-seize compound must be applied to the threads.

────────CAUTION────────

If the silicone rubber boot is not positioned 5/16 in. away from the base of the sensor, the boot will melt during engine operation.

3. Before installation coat the threads of the sensor with GM part number 5613695 or equivalent anti-seize compound.
4. Install the sensor and torque it to 30 ft. lbs.
5. Install the electrical connector on the sensor pigtail.

Typical C4 oxygen sensor locations

COOLANT SENSOR

The coolant sensor supplies engine temperature information to the ECM. This allows for cold engine starting and good driveability during warm up. A cold engine signal causes the ECM signal to be modified. This keeps the system out of closed loop operation dur-

C4 engine temperature sensor

C4 vacuum control switches

C4 MAP and BARO locations—typical

Accelerator pump assembly—typical

ing engine warm up. These conditions must be met before the system will switch over to closed loop operation on hot restarts. First, an arbitrary 15 second waiting period is imposed by the ECM. Then a predetermined voltage reading, showing that the oxygen sensor is warmed up must be detected. Finally, the engine must heat up to normal operating temperature. When all three of these conditions are met, closed loop operation will occur.

Removal and Installation

The coolant sensor will be located on the intake manifold water jacket and may be near the thermostat housing. Removal should only be done on a cold engine to avoid a possible burn from the coolant when the sensor is loosened.

1. Disconnect the electrical connector from the terminals on the sensor.
2. Remove the threaded temperature sensor from the engine.
3. Check the sensor with coolant tip immersed in water at 59°F (15°C). The resistance across the terminals should check to 4114-4743 ohms. If not within specification, replace the sensor.
4. Install the threaded sensor and tighten it to 6 ft. lbs. (7 Nm).
5. Install the electrical connector on the sensor.

NOTE: Refer to the illustrations for removal information on the following engine sensors.

THROTTLE POSITION SENSOR

The throttle position sensor is mounted on the carburetor in such a way as to move when the throttle linkage is moved. The sensor provides a variable resistance, which indicates three different throttle positions to the ECM. The three positions are idle, part throttle and full throttle. The ECM uses this information to call up an "adaptive memory" of the most recent similar operating condition to avoid lost time in reaching stabilized closed loop operation.

BAROMETRIC PRESSURE SENSOR—BARO

The barometric pressure sensor provides an input signal to the ECM to allow for adjustments mixture and timing according to ambient barometric pressure. One important feature of this input is the maintenance of good engine performance at various altitudes, while reducing emissions.

MANIFOLD ABSOLUTE PRESSURE SENSOR—MAP

The manifold absolute sensor provides a signal to the ECM to allow adjustments of the engine operating conditions for changes in manifold vacuum, due to changing load conditions.

MIXTURE CONTROL M/C SOLENOID

The carburetors used with C4 systems are equipped with an electrically controlled solenoid. This mixture control solenoid monitors fuel flow and air bleed to control fuel mixtures to the rich or lean side, whichever is called for by the ECM. When the fuel valve is closed by the solenoid the air bleed is opened, resulting in leaner fuel mixtures. When the fuel valve is opened by the solenoid the air bleed is closed, resulting in richer fuel mixtures.

DISTRIBUTOR/ENGINE SPEED SENSOR

To assist in engine start up, the ECM reads engine speed through the tachometer connection on the HEI ignition distributor. The signal over rides other signals to maintain a rich command to the M/C solenoid at engine speeds below 200 rpm. When the engine starts and speed exceeds 200 rpm, the ECM begins cycling the M/C solenoid to control the fuel mixture.

VACUUM CONTROL SWITCHES

The vacuum control switches monitor the vacuum signal enabling the ECM to recognize closed throttle idle or open throttle operation. They are usually mounted on a bracket on or near the fender or firewall.

LEAN AUTHORITY LIMIT SWITCH

The lean authority limit switch monitors heated carburetor inlet air through an air cleaner thermal vacuum switch (TVS) and prevents the ECM from driving the carburetor too lean during cold operation.

Computer Command Control (CCC) System

COMPONENTS AND OPERATION

The CCC has many components in common with the C-4 system (although they should probably not be interchanged between systems). These include the Electronic Control Module (ECM, which is capable of monitoring and adjusting more sensors and components than the ECM used on the C-4 system, an oxygen sensor, an electronically controlled variable-mixture carburetor, a three way catalytic converter, throttle position and coolant sensors, a barometric pressure (BARO) sensor, a manifold absolute pressure (MAP) sensor, a "Check Engine" light on the instrument cluster, and an Electronic Spark Timing (EST) distributor, which on some engines (turbcharged) is equipped with an Electronic Spark Control (ESC) which retards ignition spark under some conditions (detonation, etc.).

Components used almost exclusively by the CCC System include the Air Injection Reaction (AIR) Management System, charcoal canister purge solenoid, EGR valve control, vehicle speed sensor (located in the instrument cluster), transmission torque converter clutch solenoid (automatic transmission models only), idle speed control, and early fuel evaporative (EFE) system.

NOTE: See the operation descriptions under C-4 System for those components (except the ECM) the CCC Systems shares with the C-4 System.

EST control circuit

The CCC System ECM, in addition to monitoring sensors and sending a control signal to the carburetor, also controls the following components or sub-systems: charcoal canister purge, AIR Management System, idle speed control, automatic transmission converter lockup, distributor ignition timing, EGR valve control, EFE control, and the air conditioner compressor clutch operation. the CCC ECM is equipped with a PROM assembly similar to the one used in the C-4 ECM. See above for description.

The AIR Management System is an emission control which provides additional oxygen either to the catalyst or the cylinder head ports (in some cases exhaust manifold). An AIR Management System, composed of an air switching valve and/or an air control valve, controls the air pump flow and is itself controlled by the ECM. A complete description of the AIR system is given elsewhere in this section. The major difference between the CCC AIR System

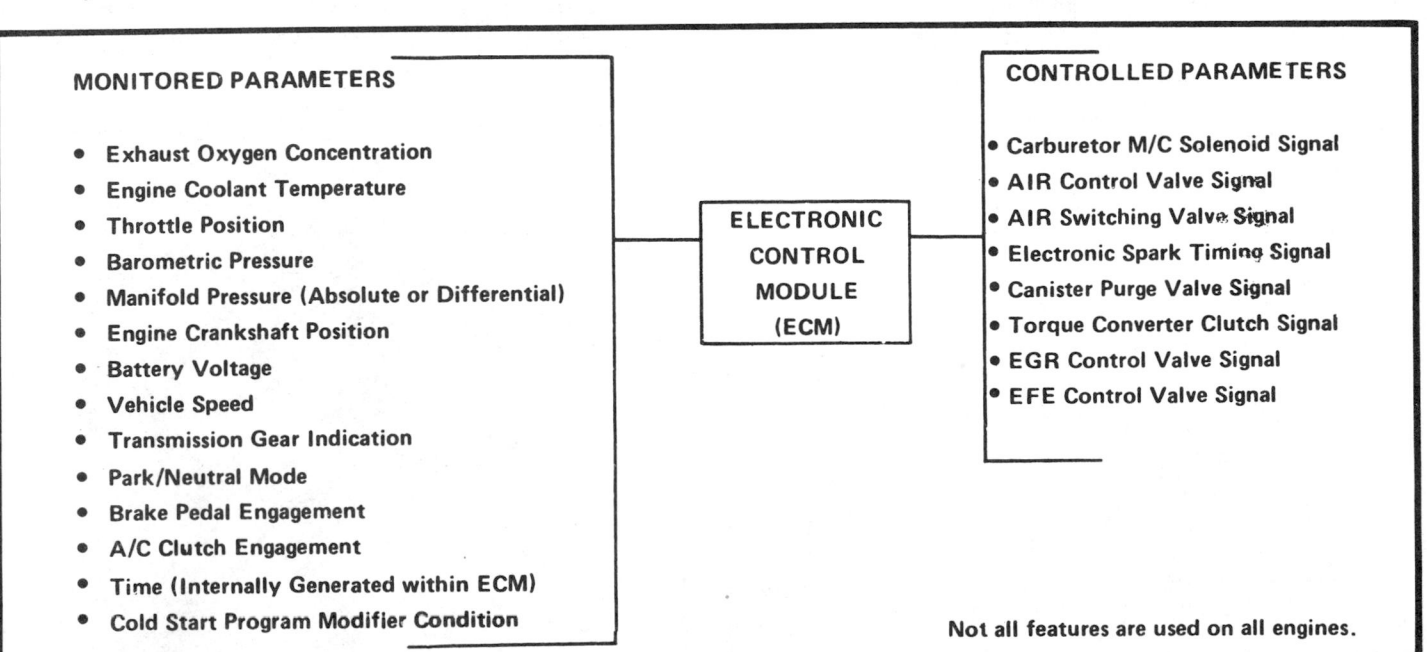

MONITORED PARAMETERS

- Exhaust Oxygen Concentration
- Engine Coolant Temperature
- Throttle Position
- Barometric Pressure
- Manifold Pressure (Absolute or Differential)
- Engine Crankshaft Position
- Battery Voltage
- Vehicle Speed
- Transmission Gear Indication
- Park/Neutral Mode
- Brake Pedal Engagement
- A/C Clutch Engagement
- Time (Internally Generated within ECM)
- Cold Start Program Modifier Condition

ELECTRONIC CONTROL MODULE (ECM)

CONTROLLED PARAMETERS

- Carburetor M/C Solenoid Signal
- AIR Control Valve Signal
- AIR Switching Valve Signal
- Electronic Spark Timing Signal
- Canister Purge Valve Signal
- Torque Converter Clutch Signal
- EGR Control Valve Signal
- EFE Control Valve Signal

Not all features are used on all engines.

General Motors CCC system schematic

Location of MAP and BARO sensors on C3 system—typical

ERG, EFE and Canister Purge solenoid valve

and the systems used on other cars is that the flow of air from the air pump is controlled electrically by the ECM, rather than by vacuum signal.

The charcoal canister purge control is an electrically operated solenoid valve controlled by the ECM. When energized, the purge control solenoid blocks vacuum from reaching the canister purge valve. When the ECM de-energizes the purge control solenoid, vacuum is allowed to reach the canister and operate the purge valve. This releases the fuel vapors collected in the canister into the induction system.

The EGR valve control solenoid is activated by the ECM in similar fashion to the canister purge solenoid. When the engine is cold, the ECM energizes the solenoid, which blocks the vacuum signal to the EGR valve. When the engine is warm, the ECM de-energizes the solenoid and the vacuum signal is allowed to reach and activate the EGR valve.

The Transmission Converter Clutch (TCC) lock is controlled by the ECM through an electrical solenoid in the automatic transmission. When the vehicle speed sensor in the instrument panel signals the ECM that the vehicle has reached the correct speed, the ECM energizes the solenoid which allows the torque converter to mechanically couple the engine to the transmission. When the brake pedal is pushed or during deceleration, passing, etc., the ECM returns the transmission to fluid drive.

The idle speed control adjusts the idle speed to load conditions, and will lower the idle speed under no-load or low-load conditions to conserve gasoline.

The Early Fuel Evaporative (EFE) system is used on some engines to provide rapid heat to the engine induction system to promote smooth start-up and operation. There are two types of systems: vacuum servo and electrically heated. They use different means to achieve the same end, which is to pre-heat the incoming air/fuel mixture. They are contolled by the ECM.

Typical pressure sensor construction

EGR and EGR bleed solenoids—3.8L engine

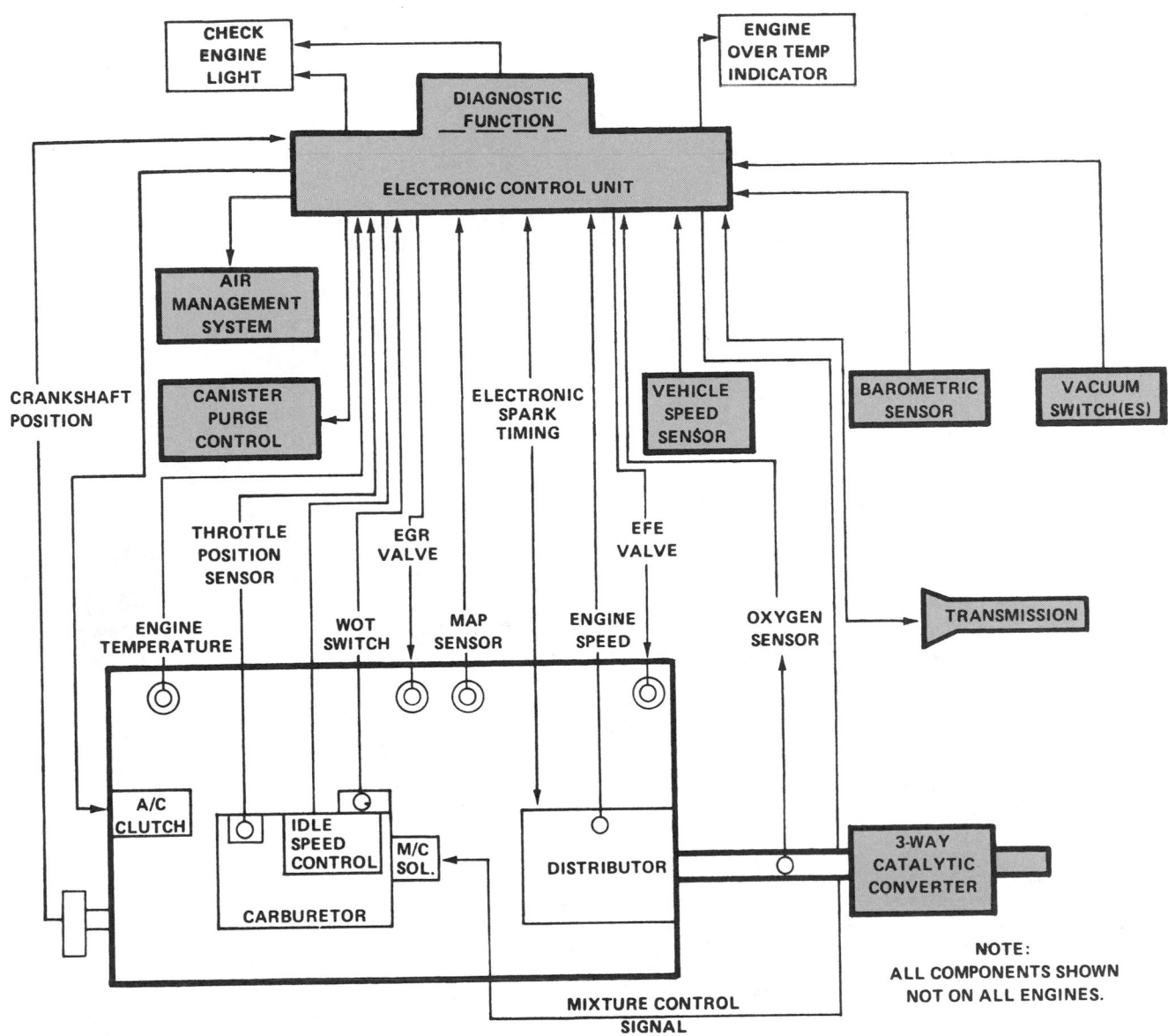

Computer Command Control (C3) system schematic

COMPUTER COMMAND CONTROL SYSTEM CARBURETORS

Three types of Rochester carburetors are used for system applications. The Varajet is a two barrel, staged opening carburetor. The Quadrajet is a four barrel staged opening carburetor. The Dualjet is a two barrel non-staged carburetor, essentially the primary side of a Quadrajet.

The metering rods and an idle bleed valve are connected to a 12 volt mixture control solenoid. The model E2SE carburetor, used with the computer command control system, is a controlled air-fuel ratio carburetor of a two barrel, two stage down-draft design with the primary bore smaller in size than the secondary bore. Air-fuel ratio control is accomplished with a solenoid controlled on/off fuel valve which supplements the preset flow of fuel which supplies the idle and main metering systems. The solenoid on/off cycle is controlled by a 12 volt signal from the computer. The solenoid also controls the amount of air bled into the idle system. The air bleed valve and fuel control valve work together so that the fuel valve is closed when the air bleed valve is open, resulting in a leaner air-fuel

mixture. Enrichment occurs when the fuel valve is open and air bleed valve closed.

The Quadrajet-Dualjet arrangement is such that the level of metering is dependent on the positioning of rods in the orifices. The Varajet system is different in that it features a non-moving-part main system for lean mixtures and a supplemental system to provide for rich mixture.

The mixture control solenoid actuates two spring-loaded rods, controlling fuel flow to the idle and main metering circuits of the carburetor. Energizing the solenoid lowers the metering rod into the main metering jet. This makes the air-fuel mixture in the Dualjet and Quadrajet carburetors leaner. The Varajet carburetor has a solenoid operated fuel control valve.

The mixture control solenoid changes the air-fuel ratio by allowing more or less fuel to flow through the carburetor. When no electrical signal is applied to the solenoid, maximum fuel flows to the idle and main metering circuits. When an electrical signal is applied to the solenoid, the mixture is leaned. (Leaning means reducing the amount of fuel mixed with the air.)

An Idle Speed Control—ISC is used on some engines to control idle speed while preventing stalls due to engine load changes. A

247

E2SE computer controlled carburetor mixture control solenoid—plunger pulses ten times per second

motor assembly mounted on the carburetor moves the throttle lever to open or close the throttle blades. The ECM monitors engine load to determine proper idle speed. To prevent stalling, the ECM monitors the air conditioning compressor switch, transmission, park/neutral switch and the ISC throttle switch. With this information the ECM will control the ISC motor and vary the engine idle as necessary.

Mixture control solenoid on E2ME and E4ME carburetors with C3 system

NOTE: For all information and service procedures, see the "Carburetors" Section.

Component Removal

ELECTRONIC CONTROL MODULE (ECM)

Removal

1. Remove the two connectors from the ECM. One is numbered and the other is lettered.
2. Remove ECM mounting hardware.

NOTE: The General Motors mounting hardware will vary with differing car divisions.

3. Remove ECM mounting hardware.

C3 electronic control module removal

C3 ECM service number location

248

NOTE: A replacement ECM is supplied without a PROM unit. The old PROM should be reused in the new ECM. This will avoid mix ups in emissions programming. If the old PROM is defective it can be replaced. A trouble code 51 indicates a defective PROM unit.

Disassembly

1. Remove the sheet metal screw holding the access cover closed and remove the access cover from the ECM.
2. Pry the PROM unit from the ECM. A removal tool can be purchased from most electronics stores. Try to keep the PROM aligned during removal and installation to avoid bending the contact pins.
3. Match mark the reference end of the PROM or take notice of the ends of the PROM as it was installed.

Assembly

1. Find the reference end of the PROM. If not marked look for the notch in the squared or symmetrical end of the carrier.
2. Align the PROM and carrier squarely over the socket and press firmly into the ECM socket. Using a piece of dowling or small blunt tool push down alternately on either end of the PROM to ensure proper seating.

──────────CAUTION──────────

Do not install the PROM backwards and turn on the ignition, as this will destroy the PROM.

──────────────────────────────

3. Replace the access cover on the ECM.

Installation

1. Install the ECM hardware and install the ECM unit in the passenger compartment.
2. Connect both connectors to the ECM following the number and letter codes.
3. Start the engine and ground the diagnostic test lead.
4. Look for a trouble code 51. If code 51 occurs, the PROM is not fully seated, is installed backwards, the pins are bent or the unit is defective.

OXYGEN SENSOR

The oxygen sensor located in the exhaust manifold compares the oxygen content in the exhaust stream to the oxygen content in the outside air. This shows that there is a passage from the top of the oxygen sensor to the inner chamber which permits outside air to enter. When servicing the sensor, do not plug or restrict the air passage.

C3 oxygen sensor locations

C3 PROM removal

C3 PROM installation

C3 PROM reference marks

A rich exhaust stream is low in oxygen content and will cause the oxygen sensor to send a rich signal, approximately one volt, to the computer. A lean exhaust stream will result in a lean signal, less than half a volt, from the oxygen sensor to the computer.

As the sensor temperature increases during engine warm-up, the sensor voltage also increases. Because the minimum voltage required to operate this circuit is half a volt, the computer will not use the oxygen sensor signal until the sensor has reached 600°F.

Removal and Installation

1. Disconnect the oxygen sensor electrical connector.

Exhaust Oxygen Sensor—typical

NOTE: The pigtail wire and connector are permanently attached to the oxygen sensor. Any attempt to remove them may damage the sensor. Care must be taken when handling the sensor. Keep the lower end of the sensor free of grease and dirt. Do not use solvents as they will damage the sensor. Do not roughly handle or drop the sensor as it may change the calibration.

2. Carefully back the sensor out of its threaded hole in the manifold. An anti-seize compound is used on all new sensors. If a sensor is to be reinstalled a special anti-seize compound must be applied to the threads. Do not allow the compound to contaminate the sensor probe.

—CAUTION—

If the silicone rubber boot is not positioned 5/16 in. away from the base of the sensor, the boot will melt during engine operation.

3. Before installation coat the threads of the sensor with GM part number 5613695 or equivalent anti-seize compound.
4. Install the sensor and torque it to 30.0 ft. lbs.
5. Install the electrical connector on the sensor pigtail.

Coolant temperature sensor found on all C3 systems

COOLANT TEMPERATURE SENSOR

The coolant temperature sensor in the engine block sends the EMC information on engine temperature which can be used to vary the air-fuel ratio as the engine coolant temperature varies with time during a cold start. It also accomplishes various switching functions at different temperatures (EGR, EFF, etc.) provides a switch point for hot temperature light indication and varies spark advance.

The coolant temperature sensor has a connector which lets the ground return lead surround the signal lead. This design provides an interference shield to prevent high voltage in the area (such as spark plug leads) from affecting the sensor signal to the computer.

NOTE: The ground return wire goes to the computer which internally grounds the wire.

Removal and Installation

The coolant sensor will be located on the intake manifold water jacket and may be near the thermostat housing.
1. Disconnect the electrical connector from the terminals of the sensor.
2. Remove the threaded temperature sensor from the engine.
3. Check the sensor with coolant tip immersed in water at 59°F (15°C). The resistance across the terminals should check to 4114-4743 ohms. If not within specifications, replace the sensor.
4. Install the threaded sensor and tighten it to 6 ft. lbs. (7 Nm.).
5. Install the electrical connector on the sensor.

IDLE SPEED CONTROL (ISC)

Removal and Installation

—CAUTION—

Do not connect or disconnect the ISC motor while the ignition is turned on, as it may damage the ECM.

1. With ignition off, disconnect the 4 terminal connector from the ISC motor assembly. Remove the throttle return spring and the two attaching screws from the ISC bracket. Remove the ISC motor and bracket assembly from the carburetor.
2. Install ISC assembly on the bracket and to the carburetor. Install the throttle return spring on the bracket.
3. Adjust the idle speed control to specification.

C3 idle speed control motor—typical

Adjustment

On L4 engines with air conditioning and 3.8L-V6 engines an idle speed control motor is used with the CCC system. The electronic control module, ECM, is used to control engine idle speed by controlling the ISC motor. The ISC motor in turn controls the ISC plunger to regulate idle speed. Additionally, the ISC acts as a dashpot on acceleration and throttle closing.

NOTE: Since curb idle is programmed into the ECM, no attempt should be made to use the ISC to set curb idle speed. The slow idle screw on the carburetor is used, only for setting base primary throttle valve position, for engine shutdown.

1. Rotate the ISC plunger clockwise to decrease rpm and counterclockwise to increase rpm. Adjust the plunger until specified maximum authority rpm is obtained.

2. Check the accuracy of the ISC adjustment (engine running) with the full 12 volts applied to the motor. The ISC motor will react with 12 volts applied. Do not test for an extended period of time, as this may damage the motor.

3. Remove the 12 volt power source, ground lead, tachometer and dwellmeter.

4. Turn off the ignition and install the 4 terminal harness connector to the ISC motor.

NOTE: Fully extending the ISC plunger by applying 12 volts direct to the motor will set an intermittant trouble code in the ECM. To clear the code disconnect the ECM pigtail lead from the positive battery terminal for a few seconds.

IDLE LOAD COMPENSATOR (ILC)

Adjustment

1. Prepare vehicle for adjustments—see emission label.
2. Connect tachometer (distributor side of TACH filter, if used).
3. Remove air cleaner and plug vacuum hose to Thermal Vacuum Valve (TVV).
4. Disconnect and plug vacuum hose to EGR.
5. Disconnect and plug vacuum hose to canister purge port.
6. Disconnect and plug vacuum hose to ILC.
7. Back out idle stop screw on carburetor 3 turns.
8. Turn A/C OFF.

---CAUTION---

Before, starting engine, place transmission in PARK, set parking brake, and block drive wheels.

---

9. With engine running (engine warm, choke off), transmission in drive, and ILC plunger fully extended (no vacuum applied), using Tool J-29607, BT-8022, or equivalent, adjust plunger to obtain 750 rpm E2MC models, 725 rpm E4MC models. Jam nut on plunger must be held with wrench to prevent damage to guide tabs.

10. Remove plug from vacuum hose, reconnect hose to ILC and observe idle speed. Idle speed should be 500 rpm in drive.

11. If rpm in step 10 is correct proceed to step 13, No further adjustment of the ILC is necessary.

12. If rpm in step 10 is not correct:
   a. Stop engine and remove the ILC. Plug vacuum hose to ILC.
   b. With the ILC removed, remove the rubber cap from the center outlet tube and then remove the metal plug (IF USED) from this same tube.
   c. Install ILC on carburetor and re-attach throttle return spring and any other related parts removed during disassembly. Remove plug from vacuum hose and reconnect hose to ILC.
   d. Using a spare rubber cap with hole punched to accept a .090″ (3/32″) hex key wrench, install cap on center outlet tube (to seal against vacuum loss) and insert wrench through cap to engage adjusting screw inside tube. Start engine and turn adjusting screw with wrench to obtain 550 rpm in drive. Turning the adjusting screw will change the idle speed.

Maximum adjustment of the ILC plunger

Typical idle load compensator

   e. Remove wrench and cap (with hole) from center outlet tube and install new rubber cap.
   f. Engine running, transmission in drive, observe idle speed. If a final adjustment is required, it will be necessary to repeat Steps 12a through 12e.

13. After adjustment of the ILC plunger, measure distance from the jam nut to tip of the plunger, dimension must not exceed 25 mm (1″).

14. Disconnect and plug vacuum hose to ILC. Apply vacuum source such as hand vacuum pump J-23768, BT-7517 or equivalent to ILC vacuum inlet tube to fully retract the plunger.

15. Adjust the idle stop on the carburetor float bowl to obtain 500 rpm in drive.

16. Place transmission in PARK and stop engine.

17. Remove plug from vacuum hose and install hose on ILC vacuum inlet tube.

18. Remove plugs and reconnect all vacuum hoses.

19. Install air cleaner and gasket.

20. Remove block from drive wheels.

---CAUTION---

If base throttle position is set at too high an rpm, the engine may diesel or run-on after ignition shutdown.

ISC rpm adjustment must be set for minimum authority first and maximum authority last. The minimum and maximum must be set whenever a new ISC assembly is installed.

MINIMUM AUTHORITY

1. Place the transmission in park or neutral, set parking brake and block drive wheels.

---CAUTION---

Do not disconnect or connect the ISC connector while the ignition is on, as it may damage the ECM.

2. Connect a tachometer to the distributor tach terminal and ground. Connect a dwellmeter to the mixture control solenoid dwell lead. Set the dwellmeter on the 6 cylinder scale, regardless of engine being tested.

3. Turn the air conditioning off.

4. Start the engine and run until it stabilizes in closed loop operation. The dwell meter needle will begin to vary.

5. Turn the ignition off and unplug the ISC connector at the ISC motor.

6. Fully retract the ISC plunger by applying 12 volts to the C terminal of the ISC motor and grounding the D terminal of the ISC motor.

NOTE: Do not apply 12 volts to the ISC motor for an extended period of time as it will damage the motor.

---CAUTION---

Do not connect a voltage source across terminal A and B of the ISC motor. Doing so will damage the internal throttle contact switch of the ISC assembly.

---

7. Start the engine and wait until dwellmeter needle starts to vary, indicating closed loop operation.

8. With ISC plunger fully retracted, adjust the carburetor idle stop rpm screw minimum authority specification.

9. Leave the tachometer and dwellmeter connected. Also, let the blocks remain at the drive wheels.

MAXIMUM AUTHORITY

1. Place the transmission in park or neutral, set the parking brake and block drive wheels if not already done.

2. Fully extend the ISC plunger by applying 12 volts to the D terminal of the motor connector and grounding the C terminal of the ISC motor connector.

---CAUTION---

Do not connect voltage across the A and B terminals of the ISC connector as it will damage the internal throttle contact switch.

Diagnosis and Testing

NOTE: The following explains how to activate the Trouble Code signal light in the instrument cluster and gives an explanation of what each code means. This is not a full C-4 or CCC System troubleshooting and isolation procedure.

Before suspecting the C-4 or CCC System or any of its components as faulty, check the ignition system including distributor, timing, spark plugs and wires. Check the engine compression, air cleaner, and emission control components not controlled by the ECM. Also check the intake manifold, vacuum hoses and hose connectors for leaks and the carburetor bolts for tightness.

The following symptoms could indicate a possible problem with the C-4 or CCC System:

• Detonation
• Stalls or rough idle (cold)
• Stalls or rough idle (hot)
• Missing
• Hesitation
• Surges
• Poor gasoline mileage
• Sluggish or spongy performance
• Hard starting—cold
• Hard starting—hot
• Objectionable exhaust odors
• Cuts out
• Improper idle speed (CCC System and C-4 equipped 1980 Cutlass with 260 cu. in. engine only)

A bulb and system check, the "Check Engine" light will come on when the ignition switch is turned to the ON position but the engine is not started.

The "Check Engine" light will also produce the trouble code or codes by a series of flashes which translate as follows. When the diagnostic test lead (C-4) or terminal (CCC) under the dash is grounded, with the ignition in the ON position and the engine not running, the "Check Engine" light will flash once, pause, then flash twice in rapid succession. This is a code 12, which indicates that the diagnostic system is working. After a longer pause, the code 12 will repeat itself two more times. The cycle will then repeat itself until the engine is started or the ignition is turned off.

NOTE: The C-4 equipped 1980 Cutlass with 260 cu. in. V8 engine has a test terminal similar to the kind used on the CCC System.

When the engine is started, the "Check Engine" light will remain on for a few seconds, then turn off. If the "Check Engine" light remains on, the self-diagnostic system has detected a problem. If the test lead (C-4) or test terminal (CCC) is then grounded, the trouble code will flash three times. If more than one problem is found, each trouble code will flash three times. Trouble codes will flash in numerical order (lowest code number to highest). The trouble codes series will repeat as long as the test lead or terminal is grounded.

A trouble code indicates a problem with a given circuit. For example, trouble code 14 indicates a problem in the cooling sensor circuit. This includes the coolant sensor, its electrical harness, and the Electronic Control Module (ECM).

Since the self-diagnostic system cannot diagnose every possible fault in the system, the absence of a trouble code does not mean the system is trouble-free. To determine problems within the system which do not activate a trouble code, a system performance check must be made.

In the case of an intermittant fault in the system, the "Check Engine" light will go out when the fault goes away, but the trouble code will remain in the memory of the ECM. Therefore, if a trouble code can be obtained even though the "Check Engine" light is not on, the trouble code must be evaluated. It must be determined if the fault is intermittant or if the engine must be at certain operating conditions (underload, etc.) before the "Check Engine" light will come on. Some trouble codes will not be recorded in the ECM until the engine has been operated at part throttle for about 5 to 18 minutes.

On the C-4 System, the ECM erases all trouble codes every time the ignition is turned off. In the case of intermittent faults, a long term memory is desirable. This can be produced by connecting the orange connector/lead from terminal "S" of the ECM directly to the battery (or to a "hot" fuse panel terminal). This terminal must be disconnected after diagnosis is complete or it will drain the battery.

On the CCC System, a trouble code will be stored until terminal "R" on the ECM has been disconnected from the battery for 10 seconds.

NOTE: On 1980 Cutlass with 260 cu. in. V8, the trouble code is stored in the same manner as on the CCC System. In addition, some 1980 Buicks have a long term constant memory similar to that used on the CCC System. In which case terminal S (terminal R on the 3.8 Liter V6) must be disconnected in the same manner as on the CCC System to erase the memory.

An easy way to erase the computer memory on the CCC System is to disconnect the battery terminals from the battery, If this method is used, don't forget to reset clocks and electronic preprogramable radios. Another method is to remove the fuse marked ECM in the fuse panel. Not all models have such a fuse.

Activating the Trouble Code

On the C-4 System activate the trouble code by grounding the trouble code test lead. Use the illustrations to locate the test lead under the instrument panel (usually a white and black wire or a wire with a green connector). Run a jumper wire form the lead to ground.

On the CCC System and the C-4 System used on the 1980 Cutlass with 260 cu. in. V8, locate the test terminal under the instrument

DWELL FIXED	STARTING/ WOT			WARM-UP			
DWELL VARYING		ACCELERATION		CRUISING IDLE	DECELERATION		
A/F MIXTURE	RICH	←————		VARYING	————→	LEAN	
DWELLMETER READING	0°	6°	15°	30°	45°	54°	60°
SOLENOID ON TIME	0%	10%	25%	50%	75%	90%	100%

ON
OFF
→| ONE |← CYCLE

Analyzing dwellmeter readings

DIAGNOSTIC GROUND (GREEN CONNECTOR)

ECM

R. H. KICK PAD

A AND B SERIES

CHECK ENGINE LIGHT

I P HARNESS CONNECTOR

VIN CODE A ONLY

DIAGNOSTIC GROUND (GREEN CONNECTOR)

F SERIES

CHECK ENGINE LIGHT

FUSE PNL.

ECM

DIAGNOSTIC GROUND (GREEN CONNECTOR)

DIAGNOSTIC BATTERY LEAD (FOR ECM MEMORY)

PLUG INTO CAVITY MARKED ING. NO. 1

H SERIES

C4 system diagnostic test leads

Trouble code activation terminals—locations vary

panel. Ground the test lead. On many systems, the test lead is situated side by side with a ground terminal. In addition, on some models, the partition between the test terminal and other ground terminal has a cut out section so that a spade terminal can be used to connect the two terminals.

NOTE: Ground the test lead or terminal according to the instructions given in "Basic Troubleshooting", above.

Code Clearing Procedure

DEFI AND DFI-EQUIPPED ENGINES

Use of an improper code clearing procedure following repairs may result in recurrence of the trouble code and illumination of the telltale indicator even though the problem has been corrected. To prevent misdiagnosis, the correct code clearing procedure must be followed exactly.

1. Enter the diagnostic mode by depressing the OFF and WARMER buttons on the ECC panel simultaneously until ".." appears.

2 Depress the OFF and HI buttons simultaneously. Hold until "0.0" or "00" appears.

3. When the ECC control panel displays "7.0" or "70", turn the ignition off for at least 10 seconds before re-entering the diagnostic mode.

NOTE: Unnecessary ECM replacement may result if the above procedure is not followed exactly.

Test Equipment

In order to perform the system checks a separate dwell meter and tachometer should be used. It will be necessary to read small changes in engine rpm while at the same time observing the dwell reading on the m/c solenoid. Other equipment needed includes a 12 volt test light, a vacuum pump/gauge and an assortment of jumper wires. When the dwell meter is used, it should be set on the 6 cylinder scale.

NOTE: Do not allow the dwell meter test leads to touch ground. This includes hoses, they are conductive enough to effect the dwell readings.

A 10 megohm digital type volt/ohmmeter will be required. Using this type of meter will prevent damage to the C4 system, when checking the more sensitive circuits. Most late model dwell meters will be compatible with the system. If no change in engine operation is caused by connecting a dwell meter, then the meter is acceptable for use in diagnosing the system. The duty cycle signal can vary from 10% (rich) to 90% (lean) and the m/c control chart gives information corresponding to several possible dwell readings.

On a normally operating engine, dwell readings, for idle and part throttle should be somewhere between 10° and 50° and will be varying. Varying means that the needle continually moves up and down the scale as slow as one time per second at idle and much faster at part throttle. The amount that the needle moves is not important, just the fact that it moves.

If a fixed dwell reading is observed, it may mean that the system is in open loop operation. In open loop operation the fixed dwell signals are programmed into the ECM. For example, on engine start up the engine and oxygen sensor must both be warmed up to the predetermined level before the system will go into closed operation (controlling the fuel mixture by reading oxygen content in the exhaust.) At the very least the engine would have to be in operation for three minutes before closed loop operation begins.

When diagnosing the C4 or CCC system, always start with the "Diagnostic Circuit Check Chart." The "Diagnostic Engine Performance Chart" covers some problems that may have to be checked before doing a complete systems performance check. The "Systems Performance Check" should always be the final check out for the system. Always run the "System Performance Check" after repairs have been made. All of the diagnostic charts will lead either to decision to replace a component of the system or to consult another diagnostic chart.

EXPLANATION OF TROUBLE CODES
GM C-4 AND CCC SYSTEMS
(Ground test lead or terminal AFTER engine is running.)

Trouble Code	Applicable System	Notes	Possible Problem Area
12	C-4, CCC		No tachometer or reference signal to computer (ECM). This code will only be present while a fault exists, and will not be stored if the problem is intermittent.
13	C-4, CCC		Oxygen sensor circuit. The engine must run for about five minutes (eighteen on C-4 equipped 231 cu in. V6) at part throttle (and under road load—CCC equipped cars) before this code will show.
13 & 14 (at same time)	C-4	Except Cadillac and 171 cu in. V6	See code 43.
13 & 43 (at same time)	C-4	Cadillac and 171 cu in. V6	See code 43.
14	C-4, CCC		Shorted coolant sensor circuit. The engine has to run 2 minutes before this code will show.
15	C-4, CCC		Open coolant sensor circuit. The engine has to operate for about five minutes (18 minutes for C-4 equipped 231 cu in. V6) at part throttle (some models) before this code will show.
21	C-4		Shorted wide open throttle switch and/or open closed-throttle switch circuit (when used).
	C-4, CCC		Throttle position sensor circuit. The engine must be run up to 10 seconds (25 seconds—CCC System) below 800 rpm before this code will show.
21 & 22 (at same time)	C-4		Grounded wide open throttle switch circuit (231 cu in. V6, 151 cu in. 4 cylinder).
22	C-4		Grounded closed throttle or wide open throttle switch circuit (231 cu in. V6, 151 cu in. 4 cylinder).
23	C-4, CCC		Open or grounded carburetor mixture control (M/C) solenoid circuit.
24	CCC		Vehicle speed sensor (VSS) circuit. The car must operate up to five minutes at road speed before this code will show.
32	C-4, CCC		Barometric pressure sensor (BARO) circuit output low.
32 & 55 (at same time)	C-4		Grounded +8V terminal or V(REF) terminal for barometric pressure sensor (BARO), or faulty ECM computer.
34	C-4	Except 1980 260 cu in. Cutlass	Manifold absolute pressure (MAP) sensor output high (after ten seconds and below 800 rpm).
34	CCC	Including 1980 260 cu in. Cutlass	Manifold absolute pressure (MAP) sensor circuit or vacuum sensor circuit. The engine must run up to five minutes below 800 RPM before this code will set.
35	CCC		Idle speed control (ISC) switch circuit shorted (over ½ throttle for over two seconds).
41	CCC		No distributor reference pulses to the ECM at specified engine vacuum. This code will store in memory.

EXPLANATION OF TROUBLE CODES
GM C-4 AND CCC SYSTEMS

(Ground test lead or terminal AFTER engine is running.)

Trouble Code	Applicable System	Notes	Possible Problem Area
42	CCC		Electronic spark timing (EST) bypass circuit grounded.
43	C-4		Throttle position sensor adjustment (on some models, engine must run at part throttle up to ten seconds before this code will set).
44	C-4, CCC		Lean oxygen sensor indication. The engine must run up to five minutes in closed loop (oxygen sensor adjusting carburetor mixture), at part throttle and under road load (drive car) before this code will set.
44 & 55 (at same time)	C-4, CCC		Faulty oxygen sensor circuit.
45	C-4, CCC	Restricted air cleaner can cause code 45	Rich oxygen sensor system indication. The engine must run up to five minutes in closed loop (oxygen sensor adjusting carburetor mixture), at part throttle under road load before this code will set.
51	C-4, CCC		Faulty calibration unit (PROM) or improper PROM installation in electronic control module (ECM). It takes up to thirty seconds for this code to set.
52 & 53	C-4		"Check Engine" light off: Intermittent ECM computer problem. "Check Engine" light on: Faulty ECM computer (replace).
52	C-4, CCC		Faulty ECM computer.
53	CCC	Including 1980 260 cu in. Cutlass	Faulty ECM computer.
54	C-4, CCC		Faulty mixture control solenoid circuit and/or faulty ECM computer.
55	C-4	Except 1980 260 cu. in. Cutlass	Faulty oxygen sensor, open manifold absolute pressure sensor or faulty ECM computer (231 cu in. V6). Faulty throttle position sensor or ECM computer (except 231 cu. in. V6). Faulty ECM computer (151 cu in. 4 cylinder)
55	CCC	Including 1980 260 cu in. Cutlass	Grounded + 8 volt supply (terminal 19 of ECM computer connector), grounded 5 volt reference (terminal 21 of ECM computer connector), faulty oxygen sensor circuit or faulty ECM computer.

Computer Controlled Catalytic Converter—C4

ECM TERMINAL CONNECTIONS

5.0 L—V8 AND 5.7 L—V8, VIN CODES H AND R

VIEW FROM TOP OF BOX

Terminal	Connection	Wire Color
A	TACHOMETER	BLACK
B		WHITE / NOT USED
C	LEAN LIMIT SWITCH	LT. GREEN
D	TROUBLE CODE TEST LEAD (Note 1)	WHITE/BLACK
E	THROTTLE POSITION SENSOR (TPS) REFERENCE	GREY
F	COOLANT TEMPERATURE SENSOR	YELLOW
G	THROTTLE POSITION SENSOR	DK. BLUE
H	OXYGEN SENSOR HI	NOT USED
J		PURPLE
K	OXYGEN SENSOR LO	TAN
L	SENSOR RETURNS (Note 2)	BLACK / GREY
M	ENGINE HOT LIGHT	DK. GREEN
N		NOT USED
P	PULSE AIR SOLENOID	BLACK/PINK
R	"CHECK ENGINE" LAMP	BROWN/WHITE
S	LONG TERM MEMORY (PLUS)	ORANGE
T	ECM POWER GROUND (TO ENG GRD)	BLACK/WHITE
U	IGNITION 1 POWER	PINK/BLACK
V		NOT USED
W	CARBURETOR MIXTURE CONTROL SOLENOID	LT. BLUE

NO. 12004832 NO. 12010123

Notes:
1. Ground to get malfunction code.
2. Connects to lo side of Throttle Position Sensor, Coolant Sensor, and Shield Connections.

Computer Controlled Catalytic Converter—C4

ECM TERMINAL CONNECTIONS

2.5L L-4 VIN CODE V

VIEW FROM TOP OF BOX

Terminal	Connection	Wire Color
A	TACHOMETER	BLACK/WHITE
B	CLOSED THROTTLE SWITCH	BROWN
C	ENRICHMENT (WOT) SWITCH	LIGHT GREEN
D	TROUBLE CODE TEST LEAD (Note 1)	WHITE/BLACK
E		NOT USED
F	COOLANT TEMPERATURE SENSOR	YELLOW
G		NOT USED
H	OXYGEN SENSOR HI	NOT USED
J		PURPLE
K	OXYGEN SENSOR LO	TAN
L	SENSOR RETURNS (Note 2)	BLACK / GREY
M		NOT USED
N		NOT USED
P		NOT USED
R	"CHECK ENGINE" LAMP	BROWN/WHITE
S	LONG TERM MEMORY (PLUS)	ORANGE
T	ECM POWER GROUND (TO ENG GRD)	BLACK/WHITE
U	IGNITION POWER	PINK/BLACK
V		NOT USED
W	CARBURETOR MIXTURE CONTROL SOLENOID	LIGHT BLUE

NO. 12004832 NO. 12010123

Notes:
1. Ground to get malfunction code.
2. Connects to lo side of Throttle Position Sensor, Coolant Sensor, and Shield Connections.

Computer Controlled Catalytic Converter—C4

DIAGNOSTIC ENGINE PERFORMANCE CHART

Preliminary Conditions: If the check engine light is not on, follow the procedures for checking a driveability complaint on any vehicle not equipped with a C4 system. When the generator or coolant light is on at the same time as the check engine light, check for a generator or coolant problem first. Inspect for poor connections at the coolant sensor, M/C solenoid and wiring. Check for loose vacuum hoses and connections and repair as needed.

Any time an engine is started, even a warm engine, it must be run at part throttle for 3 minutes or until the dwell starts to vary before proceeding with any checks.

Driver Complaint	Probable Cause	Correction or Additional Testing
Intermittent check engine light but no trouble code stored	1. Engine runs below 200 rpm	1. No correction—code not stored when caused by low rpm condition
	2. Poor electrical connection ☉ at the distributor tach to ECM "A" terminal	2. Repair or tighten connections
	3. Poor connection from the ☉ "T" ignition to the ECM "V" terminal	3. Repair or tighten connections
	4. Poor connection from the ☉ ECM "T" to terminal to ground	4. Repair or tighten connections
	5. Tach filter defective or faulty. The filter should have 14,000–18,000 ohms when checked with an end disconnected and an open circuit to ground	5. Replace tach filter
	6. Low battery voltage (less than 9 volts)	6. Recharge battery/repair charging system
Loss of long term memory	1. Defective 20 amp ECS fuse	1. Replace 20 amp ECS fuse
	2. Defective Electronic Control Module—ECM Momentarily ground the dwell lead with engine idling and test lead disconnected. This should produce a code 23, which should be retained after the engine is stopped and restarted. If voltage is present at the long term memory terminal "S" of the ECM, but the code is not stored, the ECM is defective	2. Replace the ECM
Backfire during warmup	1. A.I.R. pump diverter valve not shifting air to air cleaner for 5 seconds after engine start up or on quick deceleration	1. Replace the diverter valve
Poor gas mileage	1. Air management switch not shifting air pump output to the catalytic converter upon TVS signal after engine warmup	1. Replace air switch valve.
Full throttle performance complaint	1. Follow TPS chart number 4	1. Repair as check out indicates
All other complaints	1. Make systems perform-check on warm engine	1. Repair as check out indicates

NOTE: System performance checks should be performed after any repairs to the C4 system have been completed.
☉ On 3.8L V6 trace the circuit: Distributor module terminal "R" to terminal "C" and "R", and ECM terminal "10"; Bat. to ECM terminal "U" to ground.

Computer Controlled Catalytic Converter—C4

3.8L V6 **Connector**

View - Top of Box	View - Bottom of Box
Not used	Baro Sensor Output
5V Reference	TPS Sensor Output
MAP Sensor	Coolant temp. Sensor
8V Supply	Not Used
M/C Solenoid	Not Used
Not Used	Not Used
Not Used	Sensor Return
	Not Used
WOT sw.	Oxygen Sensor-Hi
Oxygen Sensor-Lo	Dist. Ref. Pulse-Hi
Dist. Ref. Pulse-Lo	Ign. Module By Pass
EST	Trouble Code Test Lead
Not Used	Not Used
"CHECK ENGINE" Lamp	Not Used
Not Used	Not Used
Not Used	Not Used
Ign. 1 Power	Long Term Memory (PLUS)
	Not Used
Air Select Sol.	EGR-EFE Solenoid-(Turbo Only)
Not Used	Ground (To Engine)

Connector: BLUE — 22 21 20 19 18 / 17 16 / 15 14 13 12 ; 1 2 3 4 5 / 6 7 / 8 9 10 11
RED — J H G / F E D C / B A ; K L M / N P R S / T U

258

Computer Controlled Catalytic Converter—C4

Computer Controlled Catalytic Converter—C4

Computer Controlled Catalytic Converter—C4

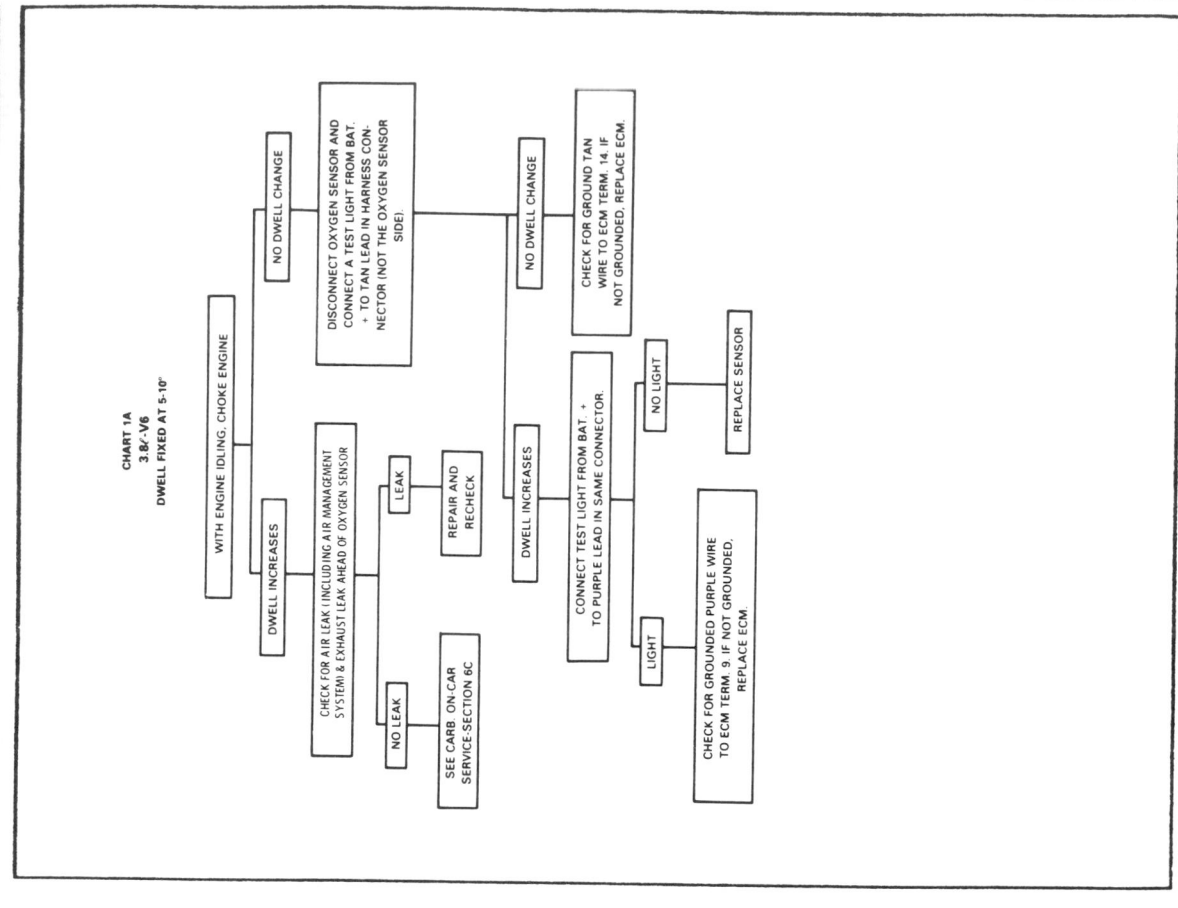

CHART 1A
3.8/·V6
DWELL FIXED AT 5-10°

Top chart (Chart 1A, 3.8/·V6):

WITH ENGINE IDLING, CHOKE ENGINE

- NO DWELL CHANGE
  - DISCONNECT OXYGEN SENSOR AND CONNECT A TEST LIGHT FROM BAT. + TO TAN LEAD IN HARNESS CONNECTOR (NOT THE OXYGEN SENSOR SIDE).
    - NO DWELL CHANGE
      - CHECK FOR GROUND TAN WIRE TO ECM TERM. 14. IF NOT GROUNDED, REPLACE ECM.
- DWELL INCREASES
  - CHECK FOR AIR LEAK (INCLUDING AIR MANAGEMENT SYSTEM) & EXHAUST LEAK AHEAD OF OXYGEN SENSOR
    - LEAK
      - REPAIR AND RECHECK
    - NO LEAK
      - SEE CARB. ON-CAR SERVICE-SECTION 6C
  - DWELL INCREASES
    - CONNECT TEST LIGHT FROM BAT. + TO PURPLE LEAD IN SAME CONNECTOR.
      - NO LIGHT
        - REPLACE SENSOR
      - LIGHT
        - CHECK FOR GROUNDED PURPLE WIRE TO ECM TERM. 9. IF NOT GROUNDED, REPLACE ECM.

Computer Controlled Catalytic Converter—C4

CHART NO..1 DWELL FIXED AT 5-10°

- Ground Test Lead
- Connect dwell meter to M/C Sol. - Use 6 cyl. scale
- With engine idling, choke engine.

- No dwell change
  - Disconnect oxygen sensor and connect a test light from Bat. + to purple lead from ECM.
    - No dwell change
      - No Light
        - Check for an open in oxygen sensor leads to ECM. If OK, replace ECM.
- Dwell increases
  - Check for air leak including "air-switch" valve stuck in exhaust port mode.
    - Air Leak
      - Repair & recheck
    - No Air Leak
      - See carb. on-car Service Section 6-C
  - Dwell reading increases
    - Replace oxygen sensor
  - Lamp Lights
    - Remove black ECM connector
      - Light off
        - Replace ECM
      - Light on
        - Repair ground in oxygen sensor harness.

Computer Controlled Catalytic Converter—C4

CHART NO. 3
DWELL FIXED AT 50-55°

- Ground "test" lead.
- Connect dwell meter to M/C Sol. - use 6 cyl. scale.
- With engine idling, remove large vacuum hose such as PCV source, to cause air leak to engine (but not enough to kill the engine).

→ **Dwell decreases** → See carb. on-car service - Section 6C.

→ **No dwell change**
- Disconnect oxygen sensor.
- Jumper connector terminals on leads to ECM (not oxyten sensor).

  → **Dwell drops to 5-10°** → Replace oxygen sensor

  → **No dwell change** → Connect jumper between ECM terminals J and K.

  → **Dwell drops to 5-10°** → Repair open in oxygen sensor leads.

  → **No dwell change** → Replace ECM

Computer Controlled Catalytic Converter—C4

CHART NO. 2   DWELL FIXED BETWEEN 10-50°

- With engine idling, disconnect coolant sensor and jumper harness connector term.

→ **Dwell varies over 5° from what it was with sensor connected.** → Replace Coolant Sensor

→ **No dwell change**
- Reconnect coolant sensor.
- Disconnect oxygen sensor and jumper connector terminals on leads to ECM (not oxygen sensor). Leave jumpered for rest of checks.

  → **5-10° dwell** → Replace oxygen sensor

  → **No dwell change** → Connect jumper between terminals J and K at ECM.

  → **5-10° dwell** → Repair open in leads to oxygen sensor.

  → **No dwell change** → Connect jumper between terminals F and L at ECM.

  → **5-10°** → Repair open in leads to coolant sensor and reconnect oxygen sensor.

  → **No dwell change** → Replace ECM and reconnect oxygen sensor.

Computer Controlled Catalytic Converter—C4

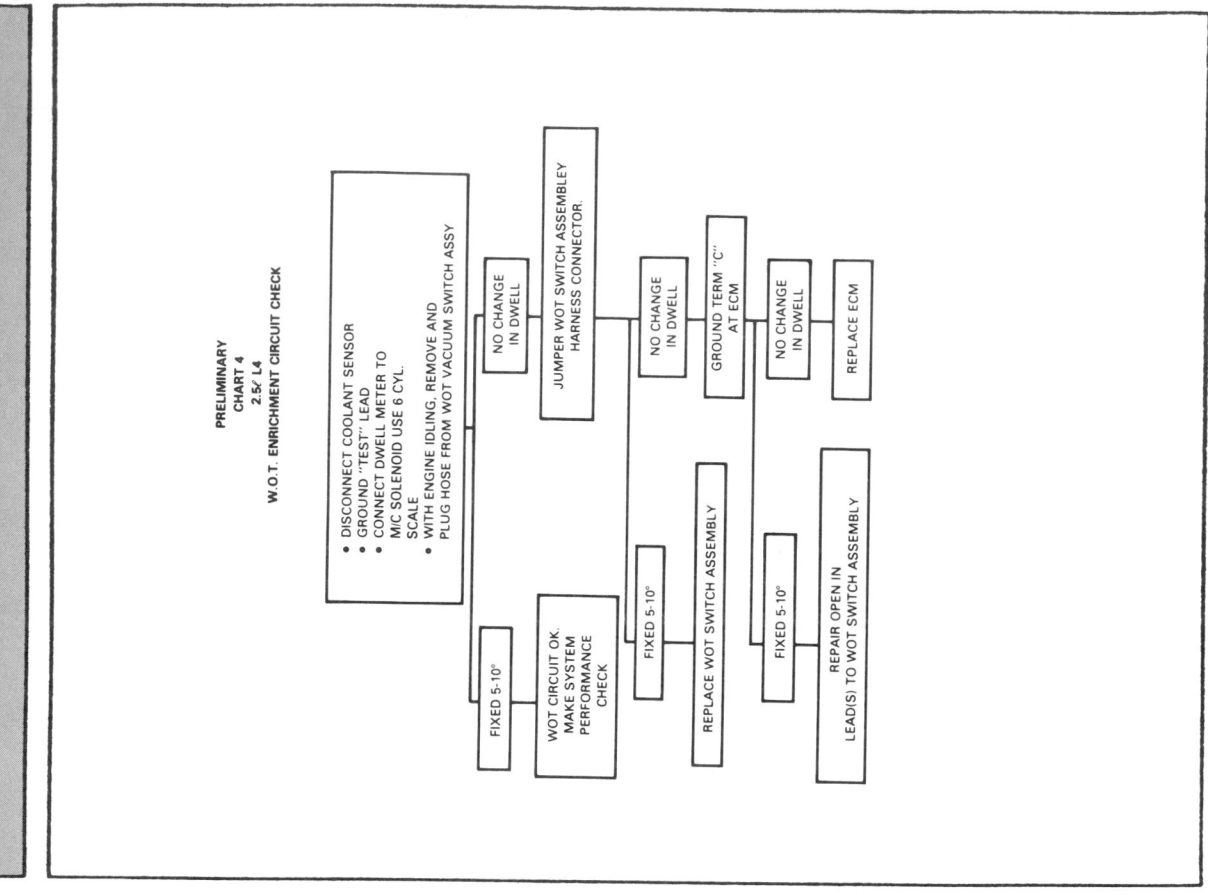

PRELIMINARY
CHART 4
2.5/ L4
W.O.T. ENRICHMENT CIRCUIT CHECK

- DISCONNECT COOLANT SENSOR
- GROUND "TEST" LEAD
- CONNECT DWELL METER TO M/C SOLENOID USE 6 CYL. SCALE
- WITH ENGINE IDLING, REMOVE AND PLUG HOSE FROM WOT VACUUM SWITCH ASSY

NO CHANGE IN DWELL
→ JUMPER WOT SWITCH ASSEMBLEY HARNESS CONNECTOR.
  → NO CHANGE IN DWELL → GROUND TERM "C" AT ECM → NO CHANGE IN DWELL → REPLACE ECM

FIXED 5-10"
WOT CIRCUIT OK. MAKE SYSTEM PERFORMANCE CHECK
→ FIXED 5-10" → REPLACE WOT SWITCH ASSEMBLY → FIXED 5-10" → REPAIR OPEN IN LEAD(S) TO WOT SWITCH ASSEMBLY

Computer Controlled Catalytic Converter—C4

CHART #4
3.8/-V6
WOT SWITCH CIRCUIT CHECK

- GROUND "TEST" LEAD.
- CONNECT DWELL METER TO M/C SOLENOID-USE 6 CYL. SCALE.
- WITH ENGINE IDLING, CLOSE WIDE OPEN THROTTLE (WOT) SWITCH BY PUSHING PLUNGER

NO CHANGE IN DWELL
→ JUMPER WOT SWITCH CONNECTOR TERMINALS.
  → NO CHANGE IN DWELL → GROUND TERMINAL "15" AT ECM → NO CHANGE IN DWELL → REPLACE ECM

FIXED 5-10
WOT SWITCH CIRCUIT OK MAKE SYSTEM PERFORMANCE CHECK
→ FIXED DWELL 5-10 → ADJUST OR REPLACE WOT SWITCH

FIXED 5-10 → REPAIR LEADS TO WOT SWITCH

Computer Controlled Catalytic Converter—C4

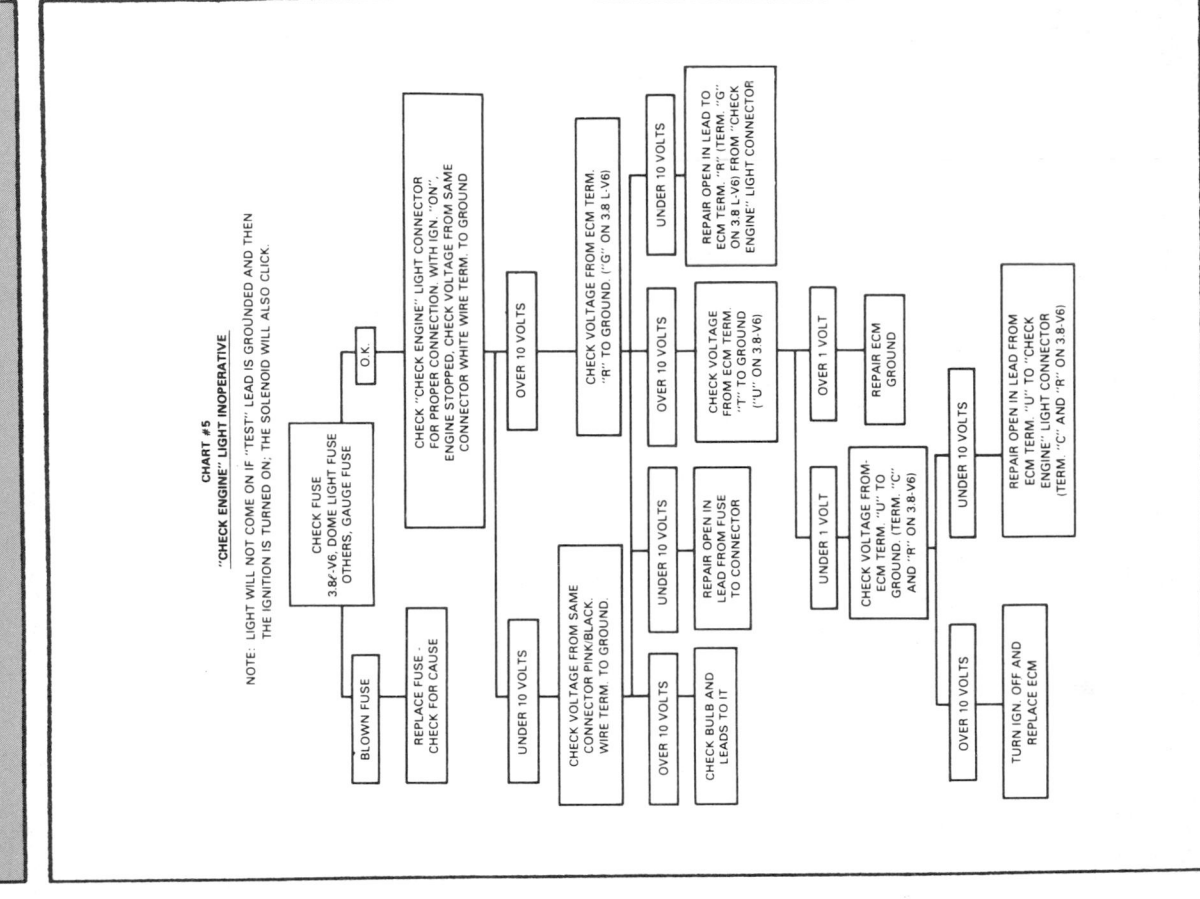

CHART #5

"CHECK ENGINE" LIGHT INOPERATIVE

NOTE: LIGHT WILL NOT COME ON IF "TEST" LEAD IS GROUNDED AND THEN THE IGNITION IS TURNED ON; THE SOLENOID WILL ALSO CLICK.

CHECK FUSE
3.8&-V6, DOME LIGHT FUSE
OTHERS, GAUGE FUSE

BLOWN FUSE

REPLACE FUSE -
CHECK FOR CAUSE

O.K.

CHECK "CHECK ENGINE" LIGHT CONNECTOR
FOR PROPER CONNECTION. WITH IGN. "ON",
ENGINE STOPPED, CHECK VOLTAGE FROM SAME
CONNECTOR WHITE WIRE TERM. TO GROUND

UNDER 10 VOLTS

CHECK VOLTAGE FROM SAME
CONNECTOR PINK/BLACK
WIRE TERM. TO GROUND

UNDER 10 VOLTS

CHECK BULB AND
LEADS TO IT

OVER 10 VOLTS

REPAIR OPEN IN
LEAD FROM FUSE
TO CONNECTOR

OVER 10 VOLTS

CHECK VOLTAGE FROM ECM TERM.
"R" TO GROUND. ("G" ON 3.8 L-V6)

UNDER 10 VOLTS

REPAIR OPEN IN LEAD TO
ECM TERM. "R" (TERM. "G"
ON 3.8 L-V6) FROM "CHECK
ENGINE" LIGHT CONNECTOR

OVER 10 VOLTS

CHECK VOLTAGE
FROM ECM TERM.
"T" TO GROUND
("U" ON 3.8-V6)

OVER 1 VOLT

REPAIR ECM
GROUND

UNDER 1 VOLT

CHECK VOLTAGE FROM
ECM TERM. "U" TO
GROUND. (TERM. "C"
AND "R" ON 3.8-V6)

OVER 10 VOLTS

TURN IGN. OFF AND
REPLACE ECM

UNDER 10 VOLTS

REPAIR OPEN IN LEAD FROM
ECM TERM. "U" TO "CHECK
ENGINE" LIGHT CONNECTOR
(TERM. "C" AND "R" ON 3.8-V6)

Computer Controlled Catalytic Converter—C4

CHART 4B

TPS WIDE OPEN THROTTLE CIRCUIT CHECK

ALL OTHERS

- GROUND "TEST" LEAD WITH IGNITION
  "ON" BUT ENGINE STOPPED
- CONNECT DWELL METER, SET ON
  6 CYL SCALE, SET ON M/C SOLENOID
- MOVE THROTTLE TO WIDE OPEN
  POSITION AND NOTE DWELL

3.8&-V6

- GROUND "TEST" LEAD WITH ENGINE
  RUNNING AT IDLE, TRANSMISSION
  IN NUETRAL, PARKING BRAKE
  SET AND DRIVE WHEELS BLOCKED.
- PUSH TPS PLUNGER DOWN AND
  NOTE DWELL

NO DWELL CHANGE

5-10°

ENRICHMENT CIRCUIT OK,
MAKE SYSTEM PERFORMANCE
CHECK

- DISCONNECT TPS HARNESS CONNECTOR FROM SENSOR
- CHECK VOLTAGE FROM HARNESS CONNECTOR TERMINAL
  "B" TO "C" WITH DIGITAL VOLTMETER.

OVER 2 VOLTS

ADJUST TPS

UNDER 2 VOLTS

CHECK FOR GROUND IN
WIRE TO ECM TERM. "G"
(TERM. "2", ON 3.8&-V6
IF NOT GROUNDED, REPLACE ECM

Computer Controlled Catalytic Converter—C4

CHART #7A
DIVERTER VALVE SYSTEMS CHECK
3.8ℓ-V6

AIR SHOULD BE DIVERTED TO AIR CLEANER FOR UP TO 5 SECONDS AFTER STARTING ENGINE THEN SWITCH TO EXHAUST PORTS UNTIL SYSTEM GOES CLOSED LOOP (APPROX. 10-60 SECONDS). IT THEN DIVERTS TO AIR CLEANER AGAIN. AIR WILL ALSO DIVERT TO AIR CLEANER DURING OPEN LOOP DECECERATIONS

NOT OK → • IGNITION "ON" ENGINE STOPPED.
• REMOVE CONNECTOR FROM DIVERT VALVE AND CONNECT A TEST LIGHT BETWEEN CONNECTOR TERMINALS.

NO LIGHT → GROUND "TEST" LEAD.
LIGHT → REPLACE DIVERT VALVE
NO LIGHT → CONNECT TEST LIGHT FROM CONNECTOR PINK WIRE TO GROUND
LIGHT → CHECK FOR AN OPEN IN WIRE FROM VALVE TO ECM. IF OK, CHECK RESISTANCE OF SOLENOID WINDING (SOLENOID IS POLARITY SENSITIVE). IF UNDER 40 OHMS IN BOTH DIRECTIONS, REPLACE SOLENOID AND ECM. IF OVER 40 OHMS IN BOTH WAYS REPLACE ECM ONLY
NO LIGHT → CHECK FOR BLOWN FUSE OR OPEN IN PINK WIRE

LIGHT → CHECK FOR GROUNDED WIRE FROM VALVE TO ECM. IF NOT GROUNDED, REPLACE ECM.

OK → NO TROUBLE FOUND

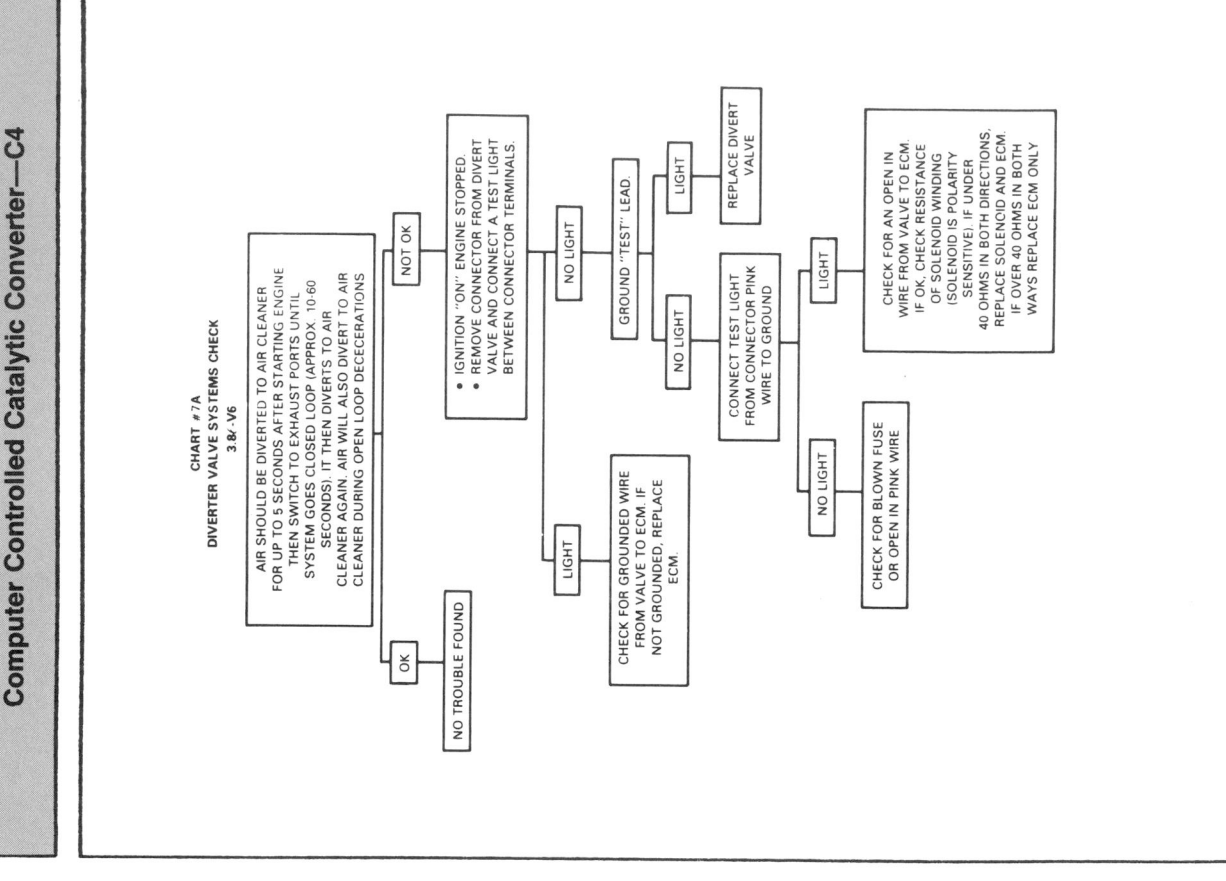

Computer Controlled Catalytic Converter—C4

CHART #7 5.0ℓ-V8 AND 5.7ℓ-V8
AIR MANAGEMENT SYSTEM CHECK

MAKE VISUAL INSPECTION OF HOSES AND CONNECTORS FOR LEAKS AND PROPER CONNECTIONS. REPAIR AS NECESSARY.

CHECK DIVERT VALVE OPERATION:
VALVE SHOULD NOT PUMP AIR TO AIR CLEANER HOSE AT PART THROTTLE, BUT SHOULD ON QUICK DECELERATION OR ANY TIME VACUUM SIGNAL DROPS BELOW 3" HG.

NOT OK → CHECK DIVERT VALVE SOLENOID CONTROL CIRCUIT. CHART 7 A

OK → CHECK SELECT VALVE OPERATION:
• START ENGINE AND RUN AT FAST IDLE.
• PULSATION SHOULD BE FELT IN HOSE TO EXHAUST PORTS UNTIL SYSTEM GOES TO CLOSED LOOP. THEN IT SHOULD SWITCH TO CATALYTIC CONVERTER HOSE.

NOT OK → CHECK SELECT VALVE SOLENOID CONTROL CIRCUIT

OK → NO TROUBLE FOUND

• IGNITION "ON", ENGINE STOPPED.
• REMOVE CONNECTOR FROM APPLICABLE VALVE AND CONNECT A TEST LIGHT BETWEEN CONNECTOR TERMINALS.

NO LIGHT → START ENGINE
LIGHT → REPLACE APPLICABLE VALVE
NO LIGHT → CONNECT TEST LIGHT FROM CONNECTOR PINK WIRE TO GROUND
LIGHT → CHECK FOR OPEN IN WIRE FROM VALVE TO ECM. IF OK, REPLACE ECM.
NO LIGHT → CHECK FOR BLOWN FUSE OR OPEN IN PINK WIRE

LIGHT → CHECK FOR GROUNDED WIRE FROM VALVE TO ECM IF NOT GROUNDED, REPLACE ECM

Computer Controlled Catalytic Converter—C4

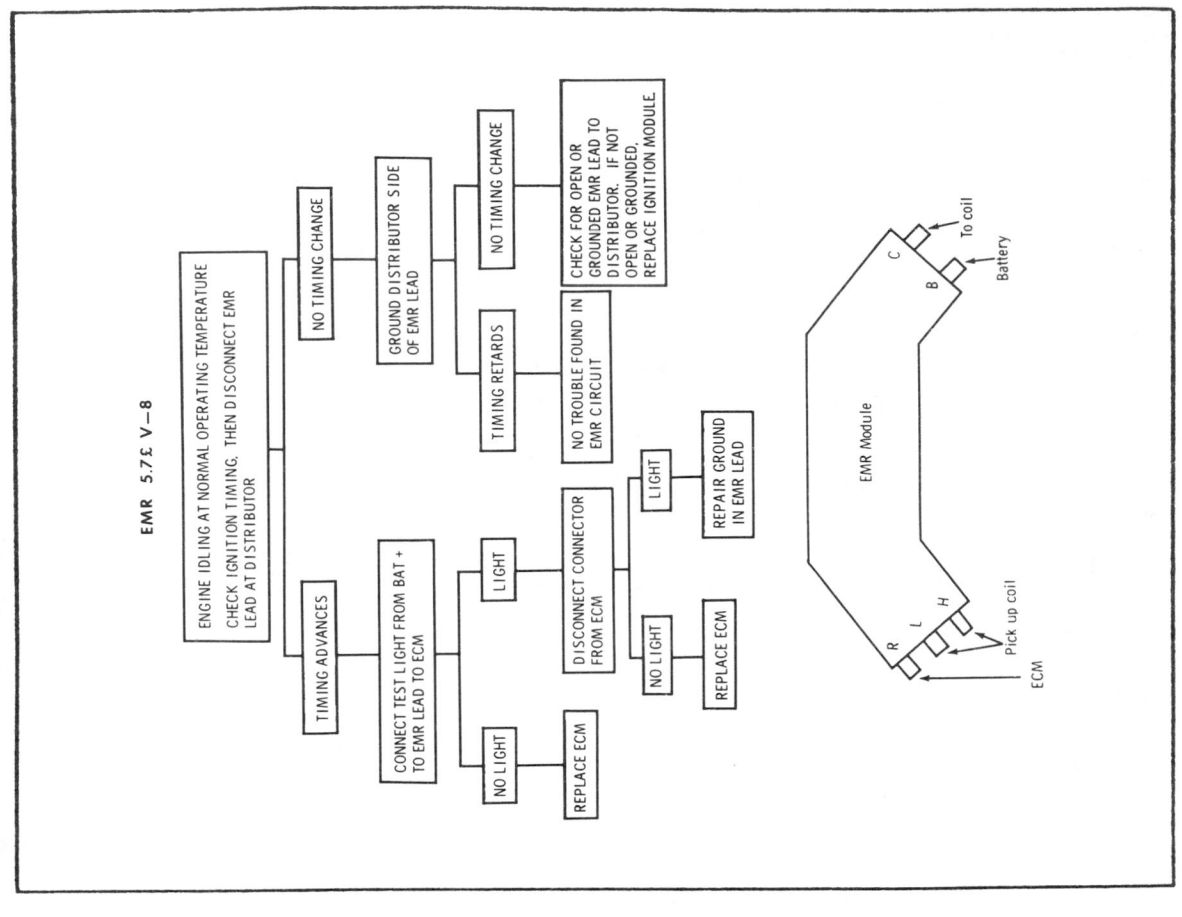

EMR 5.7£ V–8

ENGINE IDLING AT NORMAL OPERATING TEMPERATURE

CHECK IGNITION TIMING, THEN DISCONNECT EMR LEAD AT DISTRIBUTOR

- TIMING ADVANCES
  - CONNECT TEST LIGHT FROM BAT + TO EMR LEAD TO ECM
    - NO LIGHT
      - REPLACE ECM
    - LIGHT
      - DISCONNECT CONNECTOR FROM ECM
        - NO LIGHT
          - REPLACE ECM
        - LIGHT
          - REPAIR GROUND IN EMR LEAD

- NO TIMING CHANGE
  - GROUND DISTRIBUTOR SIDE OF EMR LEAD
    - NO TIMING CHANGE
      - CHECK FOR OPEN OR GROUNDED EMR LEAD TO DISTRIBUTOR. IF NOT OPEN OR GROUNDED, REPLACE IGNITION MODULE
    - TIMING RETARDS
      - NO TROUBLE FOUND IN EMR C CIRCUIT

EMR Module

To coil
Battery
C
B
R
L
H
Pick up coil
ECM

Computer Controlled Catalytic Converter—C4

**CHART #7B
DIVERTER VALVE CHECK
3.8£ V6**

- CHECK VACUUM AND AIR HOSES FOR CORRECT CONNECTIONS AND ROUTINE.
- CHECK DIVERTER VALVE MOUNTING AND CONDITION

  - NOT OK
    - REPAIR AND RETEST

  - OK
    - DISCONNECT VACUUM HOSE TO MAIN DIVERTER VALVE DIAPHRAGM NIPPLE
    - CHECK FOR DIVERTER FLOW FOR UP TO 5 SEC. WHEN HOSE IS RE-CONNECTED.

      - NO DIVERT FUNCTION
        - REPLACE DIVERTER VALVE

      - DIVERT FLOW OK
        - DIVERTER VALVE OK

      - DIVERT FLOW OVER 5 SEC.
        - BYPASS THE VACUUM DELAY VALVE.

          - DIVERTER FLOW UP TO 5 SEC.
            - REPLACE VACUUM DELAY VALVE

          - DIVERT FLOW OVER 5 SEC.
            - RE-INSTALL VACUUM DELAY VALVE
            - REPLACE DIVERTER VALVE

Computer Controlled Catalytic Converter—C4

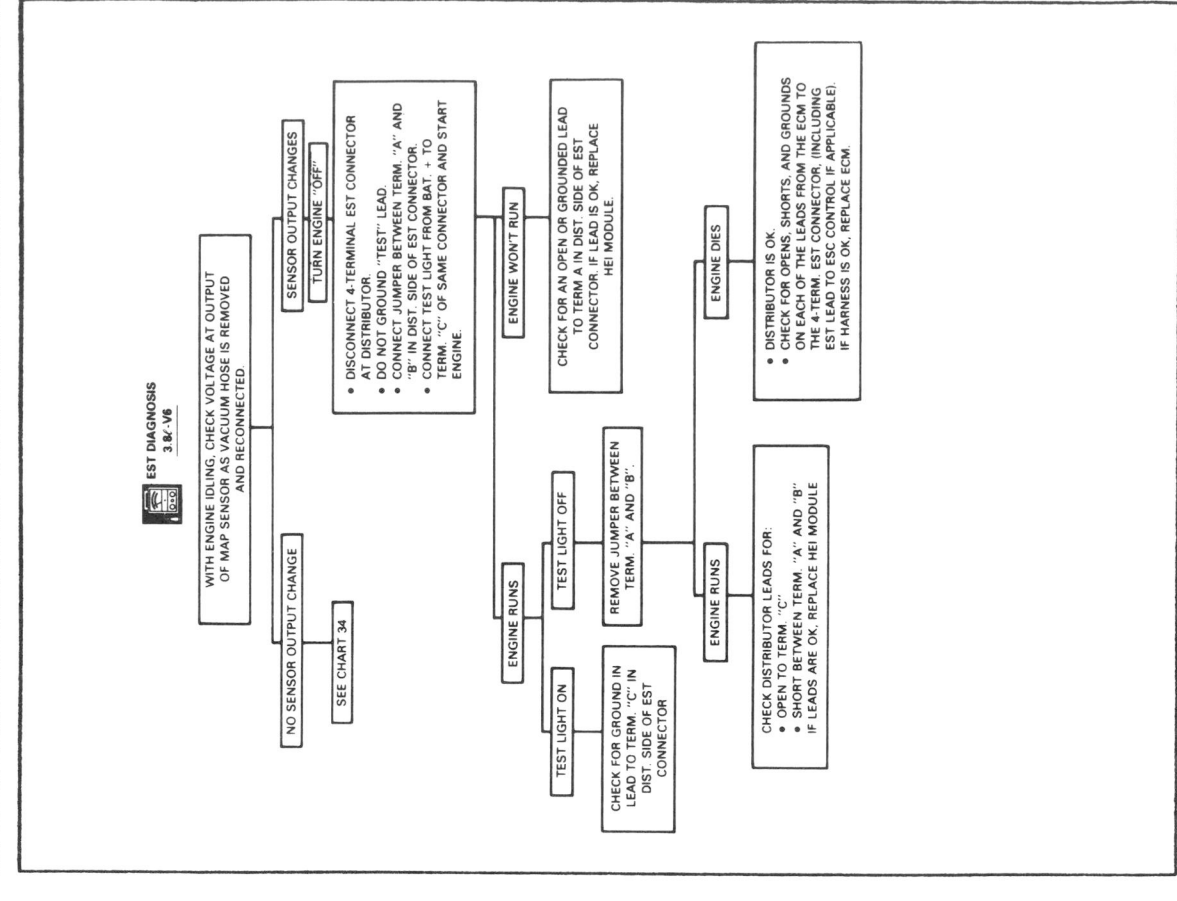

EST DIAGNOSIS
3.8ℓ-V6

WITH ENGINE IDLING, CHECK VOLTAGE AT OUTPUT OF MAP SENSOR AS VACUUM HOSE IS REMOVED AND RECONNECTED

SENSOR OUTPUT CHANGES

TURN ENGINE "OFF"

- DISCONNECT 4-TERMINAL EST CONNECTOR AT DISTRIBUTOR.
- DO NOT GROUND "TEST" LEAD.
- CONNECT JUMPER BETWEEN TERM. "A" AND "B" IN DIST. SIDE OF EST CONNECTOR.
- CONNECT TEST LIGHT FROM BAT. + TO TERM. "C" OF SAME CONNECTOR AND START ENGINE.

ENGINE WON'T RUN

CHECK FOR AN OPEN OR GROUNDED LEAD TO TERM. A IN DIST. SIDE OF EST CONNECTOR. IF LEAD IS OK, REPLACE HEI MODULE.

ENGINE DIES

- DISTRIBUTOR IS OK.
- CHECK FOR OPENS, SHORTS, AND GROUNDS ON EACH OF THE LEADS FROM THE ECM TO THE 4-TERM. EST CONNECTOR, (INCLUDING EST LEAD TO ESC CONTROL IF APPLICABLE) IF HARNESS IS OK, REPLACE ECM.

NO SENSOR OUTPUT CHANGE

SEE CHART 34

ENGINE RUNS

TEST LIGHT ON

CHECK FOR GROUND IN LEAD TO TERM. "C" IN DIST. SIDE OF EST CONNECTOR

TEST LIGHT OFF

REMOVE JUMPER BETWEEN TERM. "A" AND "B"

ENGINE RUNS

CHECK DISTRIBUTOR LEADS FOR:
- OPEN TO TERM. "C"
- SHORT BETWEEN TERM. "A" AND "B" IF LEADS ARE OK, REPLACE HEI MODULE

Computer Controlled Catalytic Converter—C4

TROUBLE CODE 12
2.5ℓ-L4, 5.0ℓ-V8, 5.7ℓ-V8

CHECK CONNECTIONS AT TACH. TERMINAL OF DIST. AND FILTER ASS'Y.

NOT OK

REPAIR

OK

- IGNITION "ON", ENGINE STOPPED.
- USING A DIGITAL VOLTMETER, CHECK VOLTAGE FROM ECM SIDE OF TACH FILTER TO GROUND.

OVER 4 VOLTS

CHECK FOR OPEN IN WIRE FROM FILTER TO ECM TERM. A. IF WIRE IS OK, REPLACE ECM.

OVER 4 VOLTS

CHECK FOR GROUNDED WIRE FROM TACH FILTER TO ECM TERM. A. IF NOT GROUNDED, REPLACE ECM.

OVER 4 VOLTS

REPLACE TACH. FILTER.

UNDER 4 VOLTS

DISCONNECT WIRE FROM TACH. FILTER TO ECM AND RECHECK VOLTAGE.

UNDER 4 VOLTS

CHECK VOLTAGE AT DIST. SIDE OF TACH. FILTER WITH FILTER DISCONNECTED.

UNDER 4 VOLTS

REPAIR OPEN IN WIRE FROM FILTER TO TACH. TERMINAL OF DISTRIBUTOR.

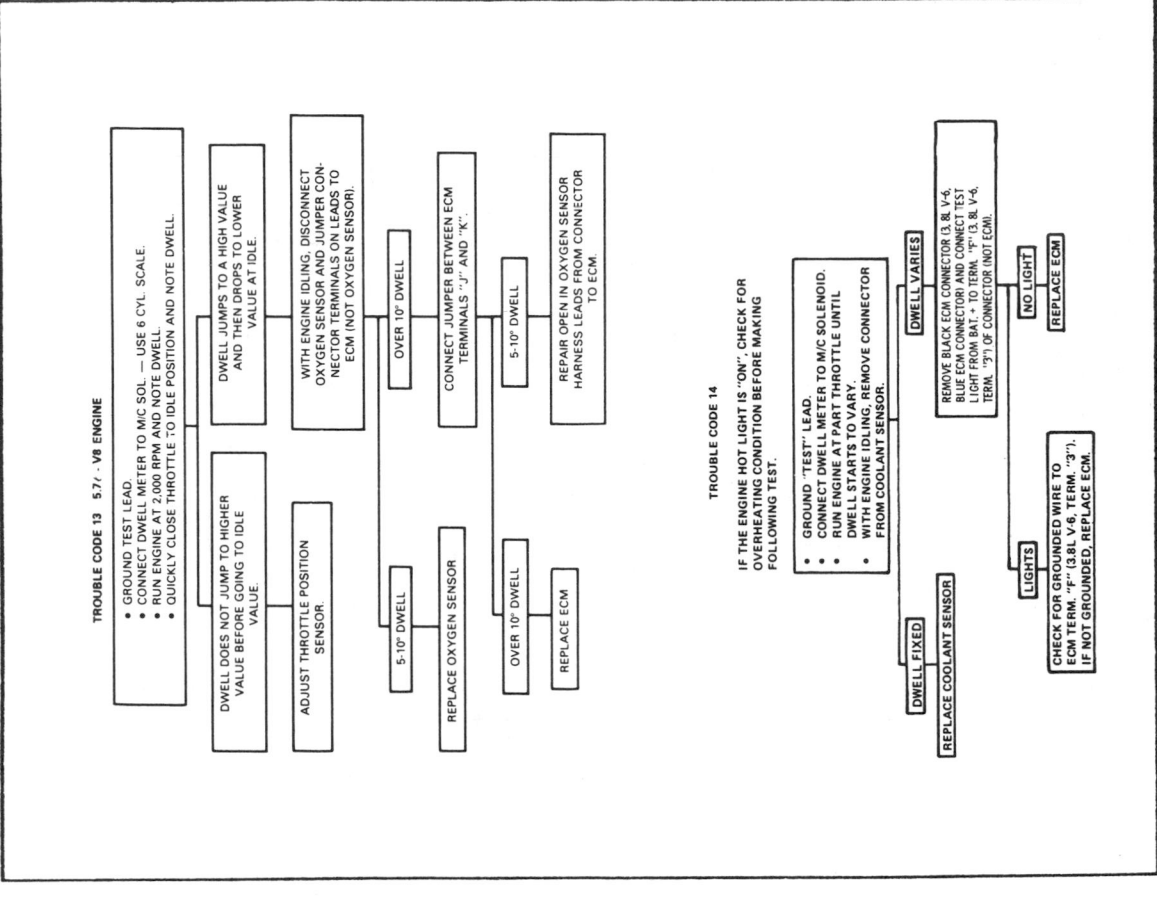

Computer Controlled Catalytic Converter—C4

TROUBLE CODE 13 5.7/- V8 ENGINE

- GROUND TEST LEAD.
- CONNECT DWELL METER TO M/C SOL. — USE 6 CYL. SCALE.
- RUN ENGINE AT 2,000 RPM AND NOTE DWELL.
- QUICKLY CLOSE THROTTLE TO IDLE POSITION AND NOTE DWELL.

DWELL DOES NOT JUMP TO HIGHER VALUE BEFORE GOING TO IDLE VALUE

ADJUST THROTTLE POSITION SENSOR.

DWELL JUMPS TO A HIGH VALUE AND THEN DROPS TO LOWER VALUE AT IDLE.

WITH ENGINE IDLING, DISCONNECT OXYGEN SENSOR AND JUMPER CONNECTOR TERMINALS ON LEADS TO ECM (NOT OXYGEN SENSOR).

5-10° DWELL

REPLACE OXYGEN SENSOR

OVER 10° DWELL

REPLACE ECM

OVER 10° DWELL

CONNECT JUMPER BETWEEN ECM TERMINALS "J" AND "K".

5-10° DWELL

REPAIR OPEN IN OXYGEN SENSOR HARNESS LEADS FROM CONNECTOR TO ECM.

TROUBLE CODE 14

IF THE ENGINE HOT LIGHT IS "ON", CHECK FOR OVERHEATING CONDITION BEFORE MAKING FOLLOWING TEST.

- GROUND "TEST" LEAD.
- CONNECT DWELL METER TO M/C SOLENOID.
- RUN ENGINE AT PART THROTTLE UNTIL DWELL STARTS TO VARY.
- WITH ENGINE IDLING, REMOVE CONNECTOR FROM COOLANT SENSOR.

DWELL FIXED

REPLACE COOLANT SENSOR

DWELL VARIES

REMOVE BLACK ECM CONNECTOR (3.8L V-6, BLUE ECM CONNECTOR) AND CONNECT TEST LIGHT FROM BAT. + TO TERM. "F" (3.8L V-6, TERM. "3") OF CONNECTOR (NOT ECM).

NO LIGHT

REPLACE ECM

LIGHTS

CHECK FOR GROUNDED WIRE TO ECM TERM. "F" (3.8L V-6, TERM. "3"). IF NOT GROUNDED, REPLACE ECM.

Computer Controlled Catalytic Converter—C4

TROUBLE CODE 12 3.8/- V6

CHECK CONNECTIONS AT 4-TERMINAL EST DISTRIBUTOR CONNECTOR.

OK

NOT OK

REPAIR

WITH ENGINE IDLING CONNECT DIGITAL VOLTMETER FROM ECM TERMINAL "0" TO GROUND. CHECK VOLTAGE AT IDLE AND PART THROTTLE.

INCREASE AT PART THROTTLE 0.5 VOLTS OR MORE

REPLACE ECM

INCREASE AT PART THROTTLE LESS THAN 0.5 VOLTS

CHECK FOR OPEN OR GROUNDED REFERENCE LEAD FROM DISTRIBUTOR TO ECM. CHECK CONNECTION AT HEI MODULE TERM. "R". IF LEAD(S) AND CONNECTION(S) ARE OK, REPLACE HEI MODULE.

TROUBLE CODE 13 EXCEPT 5.7/- V-8

- GROUND "TEST" LEAD.
- CONNECT DWELL METER TO M/C SOLENOID — USE 6 CYL. SCALE.
- WITH ENGINE IDLING, DISCONNECT OXYGEN SENSOR AND JUMPER CONNECTOR TERMINALS ON LEADS TO ECM (NOT OXYGEN SENSOR).

5-10° DWELL

REPLACE OXYGEN SENSOR

OVER 10° DWELL

REPLACE ECM

OVER 10° DWELL

CONNECT JUMPER BETWEEN ECM TERMINALS "J" AND "K", TERM. "9" 3.8L V6, AND "14"

5-10° DWELL

REPAIR OPEN IN OXYGEN SENSOR HARNESS LEADS FROM CONNECTOR TO ECM.

267

Computer Controlled Catalytic Converter—C4

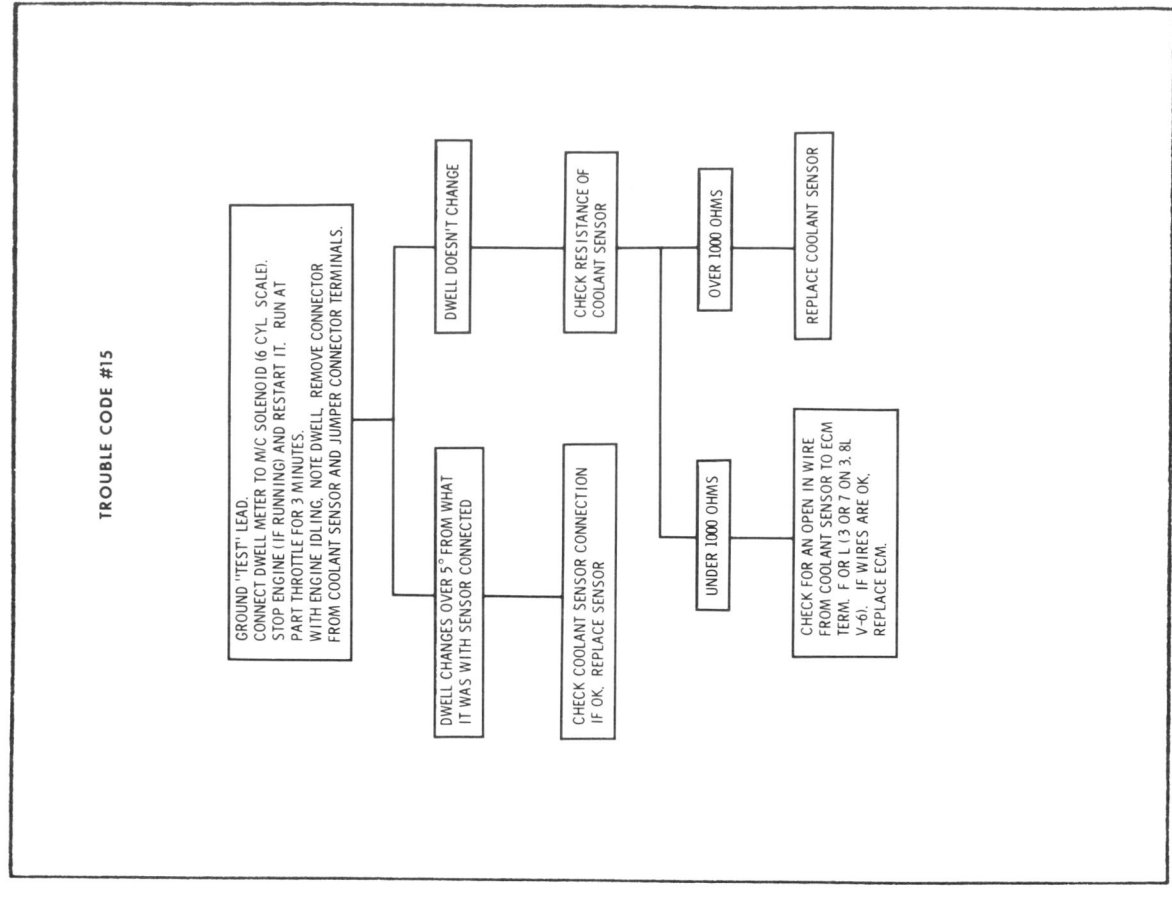

TROUBLE CODE #15

GROUND "TEST" LEAD.
CONNECT DWELL METER TO M/C SOLENOID (6 CYL. SCALE).
STOP ENGINE (IF RUNNING) AND RESTART IT. RUN AT
PART THROTTLE FOR 3 MINUTES.
WITH ENGINE IDLING, NOTE DWELL. REMOVE CONNECTOR
FROM COOLANT SENSOR AND JUMPER CONNECTOR TERMINALS.

- DWELL DOESN'T CHANGE
  - CHECK RESISTANCE OF COOLANT SENSOR
    - OVER 1000 OHMS
      - REPLACE COOLANT SENSOR
    - UNDER 1000 OHMS
      - CHECK FOR AN OPEN IN WIRE FROM COOLANT SENSOR TO ECM TERM. F OR L13 OR 7 ON 3.8L V-6). IF WIRES ARE OK, REPLACE ECM.
- DWELL CHANGES OVER 5° FROM WHAT IT WAS WITH SENSOR CONNECTED
  - CHECK COOLANT SENSOR CONNECTION. IF OK, REPLACE SENSOR

Computer Controlled Catalytic Converter—C4

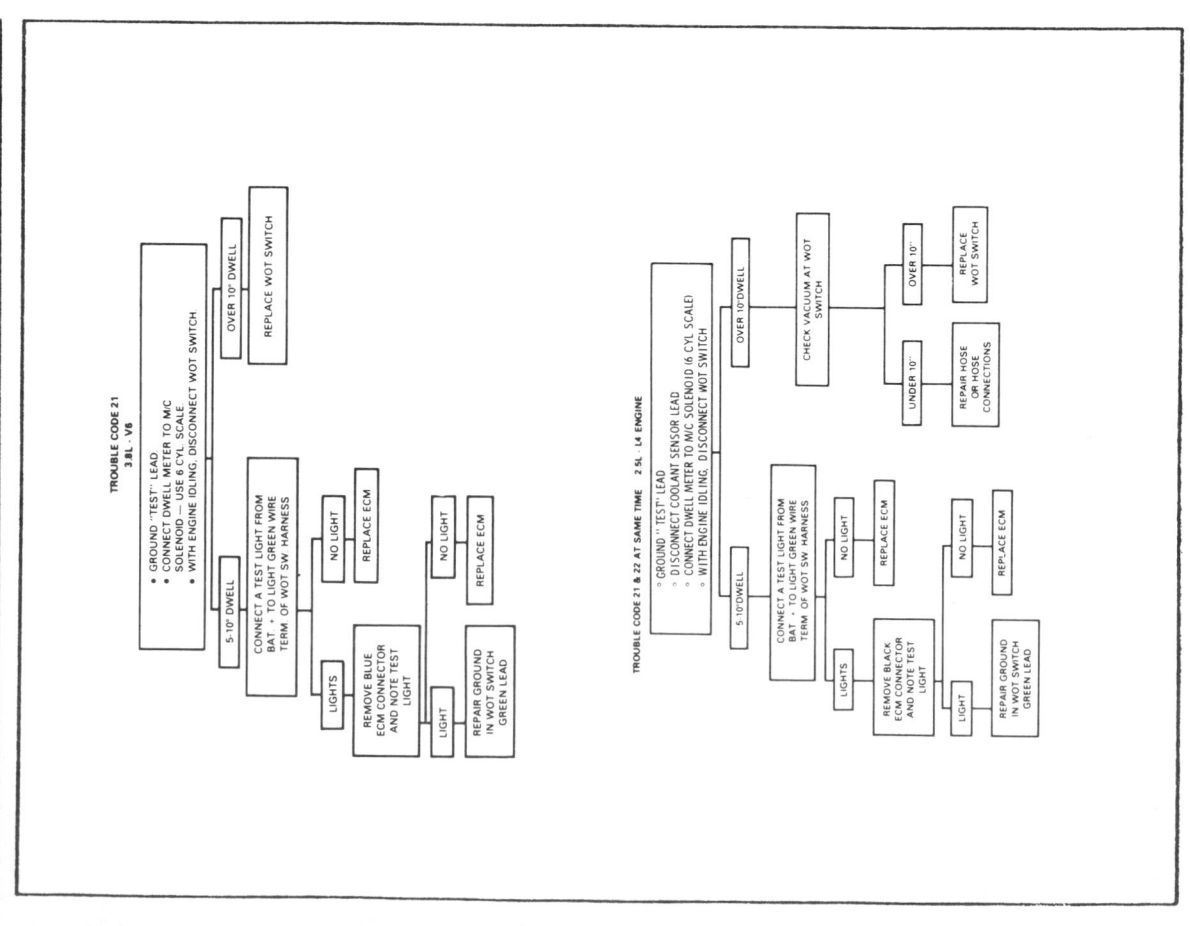

TROUBLE CODE 21
3.8L - V6

- GROUND "TEST" LEAD.
- CONNECT DWELL METER TO M/C SOLENOID—USE 6 CYL. SCALE.
- WITH ENGINE IDLING, DISCONNECT WOT SWITCH

- 5-10° DWELL
  - CONNECT A TEST LIGHT FROM BAT. + TO LIGHT GREEN WIRE TERM OF WOT SW HARNESS
    - LIGHTS
      - REMOVE BLUE ECM CONNECTOR AND NOTE TEST LIGHT
        - LIGHT
          - REPAIR GROUND IN WOT SWITCH GREEN LEAD
        - NO LIGHT
          - REPLACE ECM
    - NO LIGHT
      - REPLACE ECM
- OVER 10° DWELL
  - REPLACE WOT SWITCH

TROUBLE CODE 21 & 22 AT SAME TIME   2.5L - L4 ENGINE

- GROUND "TEST" LEAD
- DISCONNECT COOLANT SENSOR LEAD
- CONNECT DWELL METER TO M/C SOLENOID (6 CYL SCALE)
- WITH ENGINE IDLING, DISCONNECT WOT SWITCH

- 5-10° DWELL
  - CONNECT A TEST LIGHT FROM BAT. + TO LIGHT GREEN WIRE TERM OF WOT SW HARNESS
    - LIGHTS
      - REMOVE BLACK ECM CONNECTOR AND NOTE TEST LIGHT
        - LIGHT
          - REPAIR GROUND IN WOT SWITCH GREEN LEAD
        - NO LIGHT
          - REPLACE ECM
    - NO LIGHT
      - REPLACE ECM
- OVER 10° DWELL
  - CHECK VACUUM AT WOT SWITCH
    - UNDER 10°
      - REPAIR HOSE OR HOSE CONNECTIONS
    - OVER 10°
      - REPLACE WOT SWITCH

Computer Controlled Catalytic Converter—C4

TROUBLE CODE 21
THROTTLE POSITION SENSOR (TPS)
EQUIPPED ENGINES ONLY

CHECK FOR STUCK TPS PLUNGER; REPAIR AS
NECESSARY. IF OK, PROCEED BELOW:

- GROUND "TEST" LEAD.
- CONNECT DWELL METER TO M/C SOLENOID — USE 6-CYL. SCALE.
- DISCONNECT TPS HARNESS CONNECTOR FROM SENSOR.
- CHECK VOLTAGE FROM HARNESS CONNECTOR TERM. "A" TO "C"
  THEN "B–C" WITH A DIGITAL VOLTMETER AND IGN. "ON", ENGINE
  STOPPED.

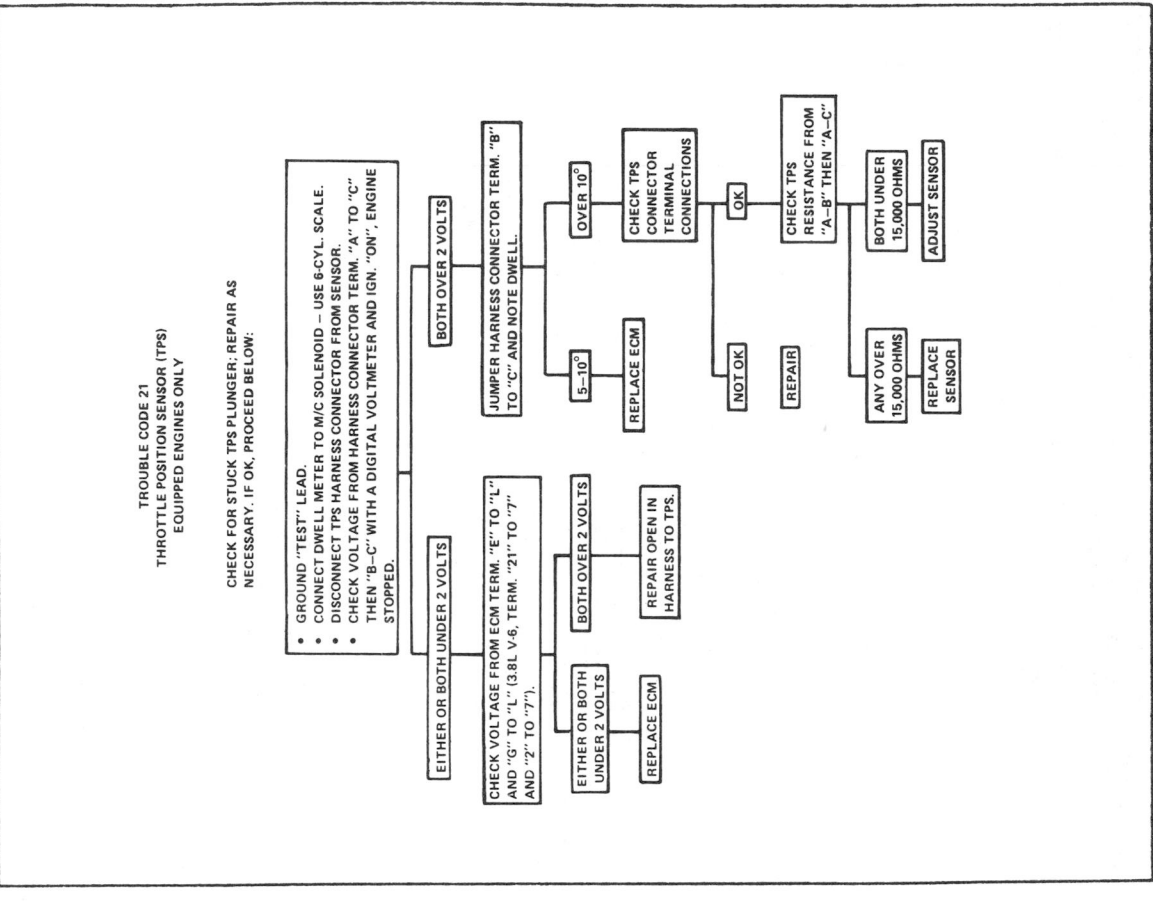

Computer Controlled Catalytic Converter—C4

TROUBLE CODE 22
2.5/-L4 ENGINE

- DISCONNECT COOLANT SENSOR
- GROUND "TEST" LEAD.
- CONNECT DWELL METER TO M/C
  SOLENOID — USE 6 CYL. SCALE.
- WITH ENGINE IDLING, NOTE DWELL.

OVER 10° DWELL

- STOP ENGINE
- RECONNECT COOLANT SENSOR
- DISCONNECT CLOSED THROTTLE
  VACUUM SWITCH.
- CONNECT TEST LIGHT FROM BAT. + TO ONE
  TERMINAL OF CLOSED THROTTLE SWITCH
  AND GROUND THE OTHER LEAD.

FIXED 5°-10°

SEE CHART 21
FOR 2.5/ L4

LIGHT

REPLACE IDLE
VACUUM SWITCH

NO LIGHT

CONNECT TEST LIGHT FROM BAT. + TO ECM
LEAD WITH WAS REMOVED FROM IDLE SWITCH

NO LIGHT

REPLACE ECM

LIGHT

REMOVE BLACK ECM
CONNECTOR AND
NOTE TEST LIGHT

NO LIGHT

REPLACE ECM

LIGHT

REPAIR GROUND IN
HARNESS

Computer Controlled Catalytic Converter—C4

TROUBLE CODE 23

CHECK CONNECTIONS AT M/C SOLENOID IF O.K.:

- TURN IGNITION "ON". ENGINE STOPPED.
- DO NOT GROUND "TEST" LEAD.
- CHECK VOLTAGE AT M/C SOLENOID DWELL LEAD.

UNDER 10V

- DISCONNECT M/C SOLENOID.
- CONNECT TEST LIGHT FROM THE SOL. CONNECTOR BATTERY TERMINAL PINK LEAD TO GROUND.

NO LIGHT → CHECK FOR OPEN B+ CIRCUIT TO SOLENOID (BLOWN FUSE)

LIGHTS → CONNECT TEST LIGHT BETWEEN SOL. CONNECTOR TERMINALS. DO NOT USE VOLTMETER.

LIGHTS → REMOVE GREY ECM CONNECTOR (3.8/-V6, BLUE CONNECTOR)

LIGHTS → REPAIR GROUND IN SOL/ECM LEAD

NO LIGHT → REPLACE ECM

NO LIGHT → REPLACE CARB M/C SOLENOID

OVER 10V

CHECK VOLTAGE AT ECM TERM. "W" (3.8/-V6, TERM. "18")

UNDER 10V → REPAIR OPEN IN SOL/ECM WIRE.

OVER 10V → CHECK CARBURETOR M/C SOL. RESISTANCE

UNDER 10 OHMS → REPLACE SOLENOID AND ECM

OVER 10 OHMS → REPLACE ECM

Computer Controlled Catalytic Converter—C4

CHART 32 3.8 £ V—6
TROUBLE CODE 32 (OR 32 AND 55)
4 TERM. BARO SENSOR

IGNITION "ON". ENGINE STOPPED. CHECK VOLTAGE FROM SENSOR TERM. "B" TO "C".

UNDER 2 VOLTS

DISCONNECT WIRE FROM TERM. "B". CHECK VOLTAGE FROM SENSOR TERM. "B" TO "C".

OVER 2 VOLTS → CHECK FOR GROUNDED WIRE TO ECM TERM. "1". IF NOT GROUNDED, REPLACE ECM.

UNDER 2 VOLTS → DISCONNECT SENSOR. CHECK VOLTAGE FROM HARNESS CONNECTOR TERM. "A" TO "C".

OVER 2 VOLTS → CHECK VOLTAGE FROM ECM TERM. "7".

OVER 2 VOLTS → REPAIR OPEN IN WIRES TO ECM TERMS. "19" OR "7".

UNDER 2 VOLTS → CHECK FOR GROUNDED WIRE TO ECM TERM. "19". IF NOT GROUNDED, IT IS FAULTY ECM CONNECTIONS OR ECM.

UNDER 2 VOLTS → CHECK VOLTAGE FROM HARNESS CONNECTOR TERM. "D" TO "C".

OVER 2 VOLTS → CHECK VOLTAGE FROM ECM TERM. "21" TO "7".

OVER 2 VOLTS → REPLACE SENSOR

UNDER 2 VOLTS → REPAIR OPEN IN WIRE TO ECM TERM. "21".

UNDER 2 VOLTS → CHECK FOR GROUNDED WIRE TO ECM TERM. "21". IF NOT GROUNDED, IT IS FAULTY ECM CONNECTIONS OR ECM.

OVER 2 VOLTS

CHECK VOLTAGE FROM ECM TERM. "1" TO "7".

UNDER 2 VOLTS → REPAIR OPEN IN WIRE TO ECM TERM. "1".

OVER 2 VOLTS → IT IS FAULTY ECM CONNECTIONS OR ECM.

```
19 ----- A 8volt
 1 ----- B output   (SENSOR)
(ECM) 7 or 22 ----- C low
21 ----- D Vref
```

Computer Controlled Catalytic Converter—C4

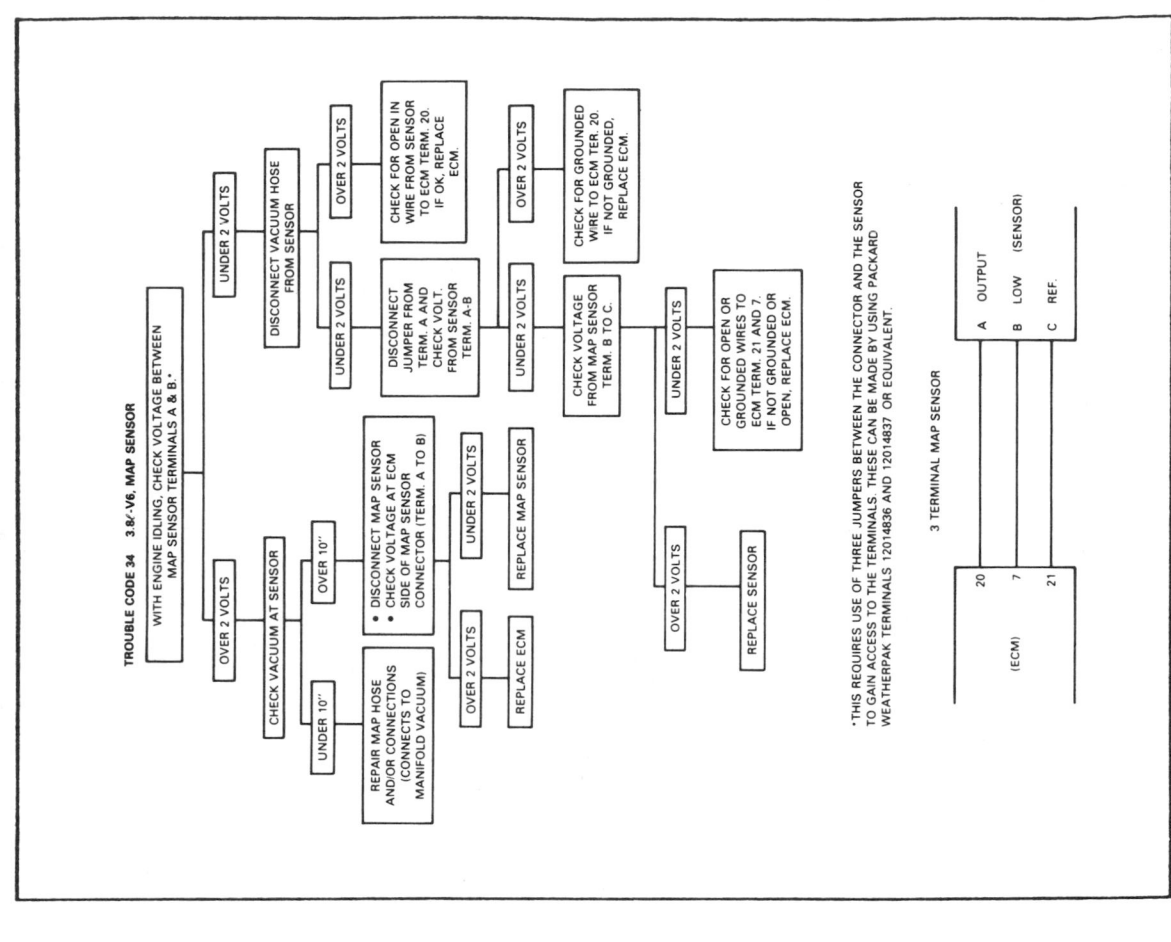

TROUBLE CODE 34   3.8/-V6, MAP SENSOR

WITH ENGINE IDLING, CHECK VOLTAGE BETWEEN MAP SENSOR TERMINALS A & B.*

- OVER 2 VOLTS
  - CHECK VACUUM AT SENSOR
    - UNDER 10"
      - REPAIR MAP HOSE AND/OR CONNECTIONS (CONNECTS TO MANIFOLD VACUUM)
    - OVER 10"
      - • DISCONNECT MAP SENSOR
      - • CHECK VOLTAGE AT ECM SIDE OF MAP SENSOR CONNECTOR (TERM. A TO B)
        - OVER 2 VOLTS
          - REPLACE ECM
        - UNDER 2 VOLTS
          - REPLACE MAP SENSOR

- UNDER 2 VOLTS
  - DISCONNECT VACUUM HOSE FROM SENSOR
    - UNDER 2 VOLTS
      - DISCONNECT JUMPER FROM TERM. A AND CHECK VOLT. FROM SENSOR TERM. A-B
        - UNDER 2 VOLTS
          - CHECK VOLTAGE FROM MAP SENSOR TERM. B TO C.
            - OVER 2 VOLTS
              - CHECK FOR OPEN OR GROUNDED WIRES TO ECM TERM. 21 AND 7. IF NOT GROUNDED OR OPEN, REPLACE ECM.
            - UNDER 2 VOLTS
              - REPLACE SENSOR
        - OVER 2 VOLTS
          - CHECK FOR GROUNDED WIRE TO ECM TER. 20. IF NOT GROUNDED, REPLACE ECM.
    - OVER 2 VOLTS
      - CHECK FOR OPEN IN WIRE FROM SENSOR TO ECM TERM. 20. IF OK, REPLACE ECM.

*THIS REQUIRES USE OF THREE JUMPERS BETWEEN THE CONNECTOR AND THE SENSOR TO GAIN ACCESS TO THE TERMINALS. THESE CAN BE MADE BY USING PACKARD WEATHERPAK TERMINALS 12014836 AND 12014837 OR EQUIVALENT.

3 TERMINAL MAP SENSOR

(ECM)		MAP SENSOR
20	A	OUTPUT
7	B	LOW (SENSOR)
21	C	REF.

Computer Controlled Catalytic Converter—C4

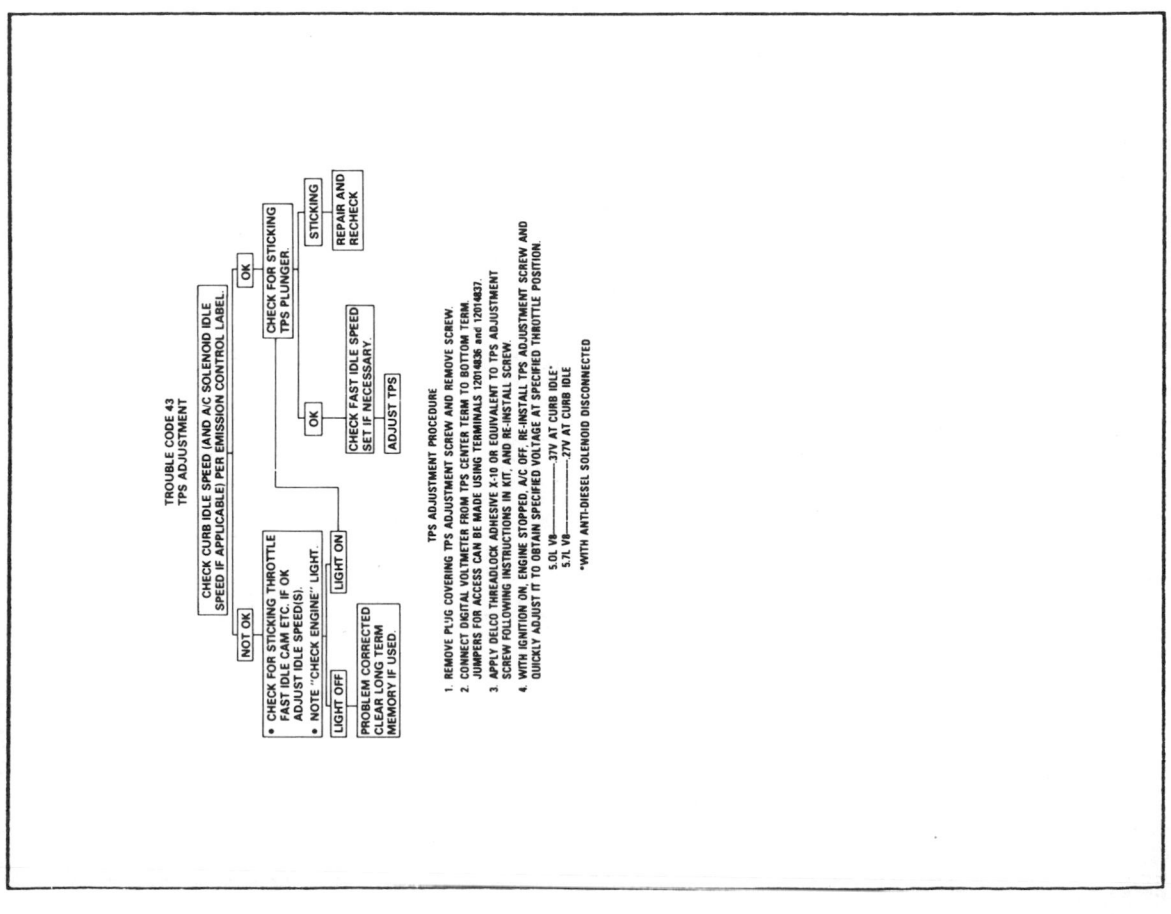

TROUBLE CODE 43
TPS ADJUSTMENT

CHECK CURB IDLE SPEED (AND A/C SOLENOID IDLE SPEED IF APPLICABLE) PER EMISSION CONTROL LABEL.

- NOT OK
  - • CHECK FOR STICKING THROTTLE FAST IDLE CAM ETC. IF OK ADJUST IDLE SPEED(S).
  - • NOTE "CHECK ENGINE" LIGHT.
    - LIGHT OFF
      - PROBLEM CORRECTED CLEAR LONG TERM MEMORY IF USED
    - LIGHT ON

- OK
  - CHECK FOR STICKING TPS PLUNGER.
    - OK
      - CHECK FAST IDLE SPEED SET IF NECESSARY.
        - ADJUST TPS
    - STICKING
      - REPAIR AND RECHECK

TPS ADJUSTMENT PROCEDURE

1. REMOVE PLUG COVERING TPS ADJUSTMENT SCREW AND REMOVE SCREW.
2. CONNECT DIGITAL VOLTMETER FROM TPS CENTER TERM TO BOTTOM TERM. JUMPERS FOR ACCESS CAN BE MADE USING TERMINALS 12014836 and 12014837.
3. APPLY DELCO THREADLOCK ADHESIVE X-10 OR EQUIVALENT TO TPS ADJUSTMENT SCREW FOLLOWING INSTRUCTIONS IN KIT, AND RE-INSTALL SCREW.
4. WITH IGNITION ON, ENGINE STOPPED, A/C OFF, RE-INSTALL TPS ADJUSTMENT SCREW AND QUICKLY ADJUST IT TO OBTAIN SPECIFIED VOLTAGE AT SPECIFIED THROTTLE POSITION.

5.0L V8 ————————— .37V AT CURB IDLE*
5.7L V8 ————————— .27V AT CURB IDLE
*WITH ANTI-DIESEL SOLENOID DISCONNECTED

Computer Controlled Catalytic Converter—C4

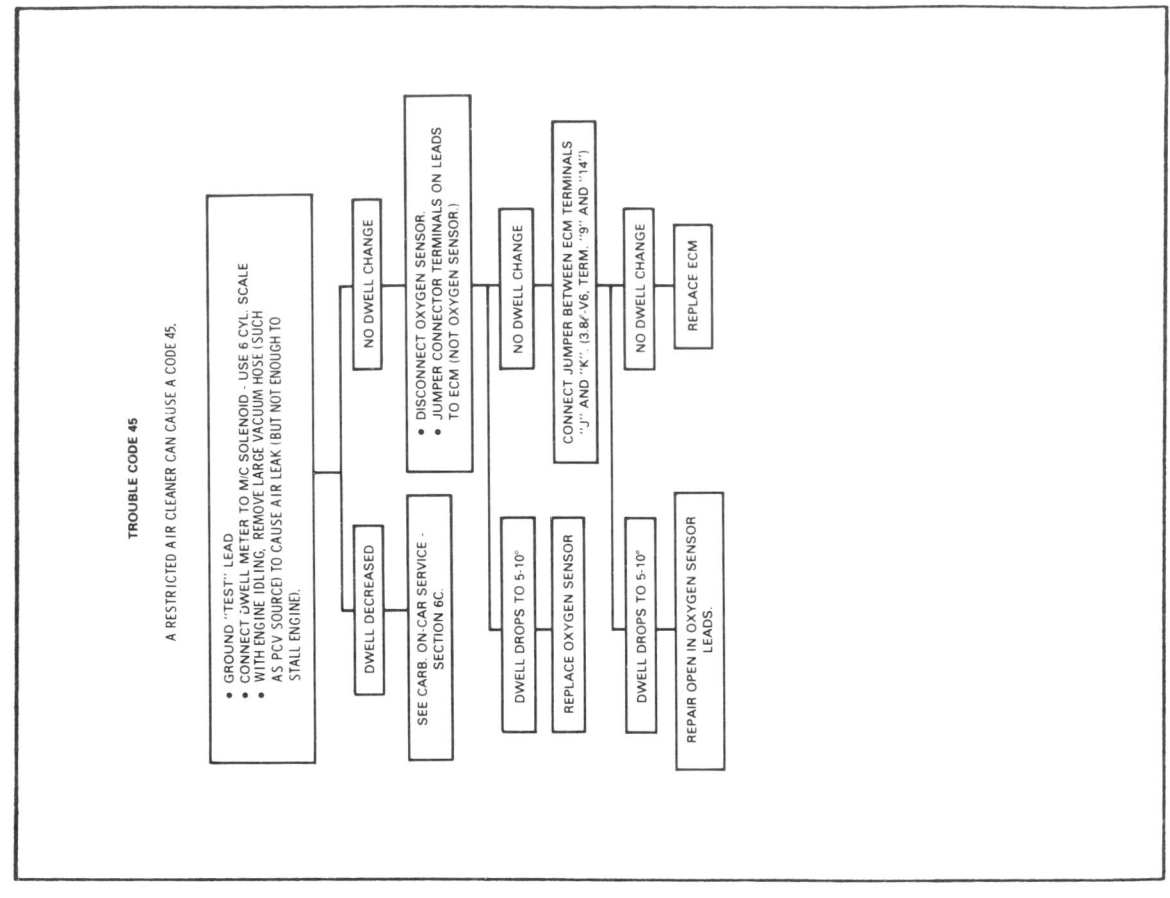

TROUBLE CODE 45

A RESTRICTED AIR CLEANER CAN CAUSE A CODE 45.

- GROUND "TEST" LEAD
- CONNECT DWELL METER TO M/C SOLENOID - USE 6 CYL. SCALE
- WITH ENGINE IDLING, REMOVE LARGE VACUUM HOSE (SUCH AS PCV SOURCE) TO CAUSE AIR LEAK (BUT NOT ENOUGH TO STALL ENGINE).

DWELL DECREASED → SEE CARB. ON-CAR SERVICE - SECTION 6C.

NO DWELL CHANGE →
- DISCONNECT OXYGEN SENSOR.
- JUMPER CONNECTOR TERMINALS ON LEADS TO ECM (NOT OXYGEN SENSOR)

DWELL DROPS TO 5-10° → REPLACE OXYGEN SENSOR

NO DWELL CHANGE → CONNECT JUMPER BETWEEN ECM TERMINALS "J" AND "K" (3.8/ V6, TERM. "9" AND "14")

DWELL DROPS TO 5-10° → REPAIR OPEN IN OXYGEN SENSOR LEADS.

NO DWELL CHANGE → REPLACE ECM

Computer Controlled Catalytic Converter—C4

TROUBLE CODE 44

CODE 44 AND 55 AT SAME TIME
CHECK FOR OPEN WIRE FROM OXYGEN SENSOR TO ECM. IF NOT OPEN. REPLACE OXYGEN SENSOR

- GROUND "TEST" LEAD
- CONNECT DWELL METER TO M/C SOLENOID-USE 6 CYL. SCALE
- RUN ENGINE ON HIGH STEP OF FAST IDLE CAM AND NOTE DWELL

BETWEEN 10-50° → REPLACE OXYGEN SENSOR

5-10° → WITH ENGINE IDLING, CHOKE ENGINE.

DWELL INCREASES → CHECK FOR AIR LEAK (INCLUDING AIR MANAGEMENT SYSTEM. - SEE SECTION 6E)

NO LEAK → SEE CARB. ON-CAR SERVICE-SECTION 6C

LEAK → REPAIR AND RECHECK

NO DWELL CHANGE → DISCONNECT OXYGEN SENSOR AND CONNECT A TEST LIGHT FROM BAT.+ TO TAN LEAD IN HARNESS CONNECTOR (NOT THE OXYGEN SENSOR SIDE.)

DWELL INCREASES → CONNECT TEST LIGHT FROM BAT.+ TO PURPLE LEAD IN SAME CONNECTOR

LIGHT → CHECK FOR GROUNDED PURPLE WIRE TO ECM TERM. J (3.8/ V6, TERM. "9") IF NOT GROUNDED. REPLACE ECM

NO LIGHT → REPLACE SENSOR

NO DWELL CHANGE → CHECK FOR OPEN TAN WIRE TO ECM TERM. K (3.8L V-6, TERM. "14"). IF NOT OPEN. REPLACE ECM

Computer Controlled Catalytic Converter—C4

TROUBLE CODE 55

2.5£ L-4

REPLACE ECM

ALL OTHERS EXCEPT 3.8£ V-6

GROUND "TEST" LEAD. DISCONNECT TPS CONNECTOR AND MEASURE VOLTAGE BETWEEN CONNECTOR TERMINALS "A" AND "C" WITH A DIGITAL VOLTMETER WITH IGN. "ON". ENGINE STOPPED.

- LESS THAN 2 VOLTS → DISCONNECT BLACK ECM CONNECTOR AND MEASURE VOLTAGE BETWEEN ECM TERMS. "E" AND "L" WITH A DIGITAL VOLTMETER.
  - UNDER 2 VOLTS → CHECK FOR OPEN IN SENSOR RETURN WIRE TO TERM. "L" ON ECM. IF NOT OPEN. REPLACE ECM
  - OVER 2 VOLTS → REPAIR GROUND IN WIRE TO TERM. "E"

- OVER 2 VOLTS → MEASURE RESISTANCE BETWEEN TERMINALS "A" AND "C" OF TPS WITH THROTTLE CLOSED.
  - UNDER 5,000 OHMS → REPLACE TPS
  - OVER 5,000 OHMS → CHECK FOR OPEN IN SENSOR RETURN WIRE TO TERM. "L" ON ECM. IF NOT OPEN, REPLACE ECM.

3.8£ V-6

DISCONNECT TEST LEAD DISCONNECT OXYGEN SENSOR AND NOTE "CHECK ENGINE LIGHT" WITH ENGINE IDLING

- OFF → CHECK FOR OPEN IN TAN WIRE TO ECM. IF NOT OPEN, REPLACE OXYGEN SENSOR.
- ON → CHECK VOLTAGE FROM ECM TERMS. "20" TO "7". AS VACUUM HOSE IS DISCONNECTED AND RECONNECTED WITH ENGINE IDLING.
  - NO CHANGE → SEE CHART 34
  - CHANGE → REPLACE ECM

Computer Controlled Catalytic Converter—C4

TROUBLE CODES 51 THRU 54

CODE 51

SERVICE REPLACEMENT UNIT

CHECK THAT ALL PINS ARE FULLY INSERTED IN THE SOCKET IF OK. REPLACE PROM

OEM UNIT

REPLACE PROM

CODES 52-53

REPLACE ECM IF LIGHT IS ON WITH CODE IF CODE BUT NO LIGHT, TROUBLE IS INTERMITTENT.

CODE 54

CHECK MC SOLENOID RESISTANCE

- OVER 10 OHMS
- UNDER 10 OHMS

- IGNITION "ON" ENGINE STOPPED CONNECT TEST LIGHT FROM GROUND TO DWELL LEAD AT MC SOLENOID WITH SOL. DISCONNECTED
- DISCONNECT BLACK CONNECTOR AT ECM (3.8 L-V6. BLUE CONNECTOR)
  - LIGHT → REPAIR SHORT TO BAT . IN BLUE WIRE TO ECM TERM "W" (3.8 L-V6. TERM. "18") CLEAR MEMORY AND CHECK FOR TROUBLE CODES
  - NO LIGHT → REPLACE ECM

- REPLACE SOLENOID
- CLEAR MEMORY
- START ENGINE AND CHECK FOR TROUBLE CODE
  - CODE → SEE APPLICABLE CODE CHART
  - NO CODE → MAKE SYSTEM PERFORM CHECK

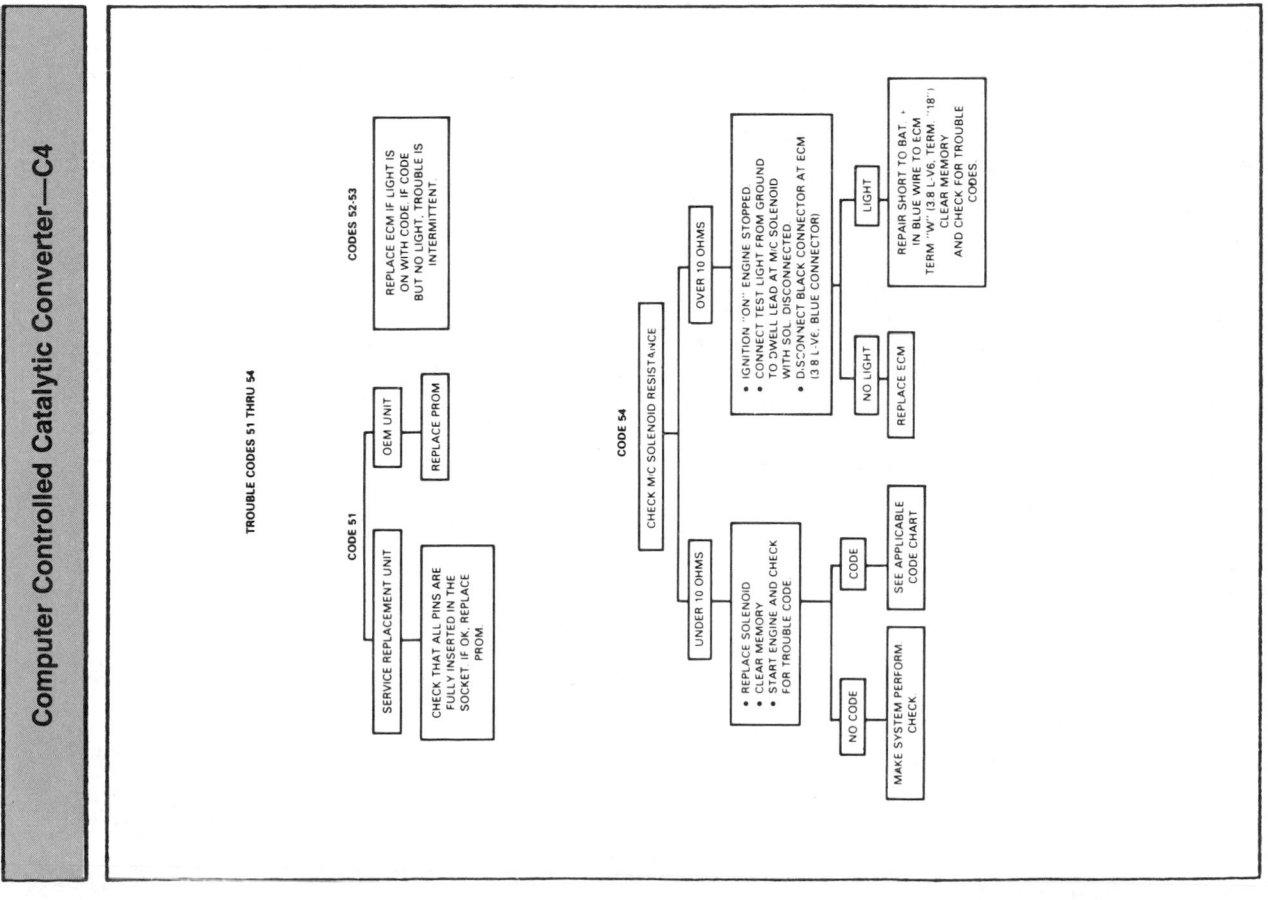

Computer Command Control (With EST)

ECM TERMINAL IDENTIFICATION

NOT ALL TERMINALS ARE USED ON ALL ENGINE APPLICATIONS

VIEW — TOP OF BOX   CONNECTOR   VIEW — BOTTOM OF BOX

Sensor Return — 22 | 1 — BARO Sensor Output

5V Reference — 21 | 2 — TPS Sensor Output (Jumpered to 20 on 3.8L V-6 VIN Code "K")

MAP or Vacuum Sensor Output (TPS on 3.8L VIN Code "K") — 20 | 3 — Coolant Temp. Sensor

8V Supply — 19 | 4 — Air Control Solenoid (1)

M/C Solenoid — 18 | 5 — Trouble Code Test Terminal

High Gear Switch or Cold — 17 | 6 — Not Used

Idle Lean Limit Switch — 16 | 7 — Sensor Return

Vehicle Speed Signal

Cold Start Program

Modifier ("E" Cell) — 15 | 8 — ISC Switch

Oxygen Sensor-Lo — 14 | 9 — Oxygen Sensor-Hi

Dist. Ref. Pulse-Lo — 13 | 10 — Dist. Ref. Pulse-Hi

EST — 12 | 11 — Ign. Module By-Pass

A/C On — J | K — Not Used

Park/Neutral Switch — H | L — Not Used

"Check Engine" Lamp — G | M — ISC Motor—Retract

ISC Motor-Extend — F | N — Not Used

Canister Purge Solenoid (2) — E | P — Transmission Converter Clutch

Not Used — D | R — Memory (Continuous Bat.) Long Term

Ign. 1 Power — C | S — Not Used

Air Switching Solenoid (1 + 3) — B | T — EGR Solenoid (EFE Heater Relay if used)

Ground (To Engine) — A | U — Ground (To Engine)

1. Air control and air switching terminals and their wire colors are reversed on 3.8L V-6 VIN Code K, 4.4L V-8 VIN Code J, 5.0L V-8 VIN Code H, and 5.7L V-8 VIN Code L & 6.

2. Also aux. EGR solenoid on 4.1L V-6 VIN Code 4 with aux. vac. pump, and EGR bleed solenoid on 3.8L V-6 VIN Code 3 Turbo in "E" car.

3. Divert valve on 3.8L V-6 VIN Code A that does not use a switching valve and pulse air valve on 1.6L L4 VIN Code 9.

Computer Command Control (With EST)

DIAGNOSTIC CIRCUIT CHECK

ALWAYS CHECK PROM FOR CORRECT APPLICATION AND INSTALLATION BEFORE REPLACING AN ECM. ALSO REMOVE TERMINAL(S) FROM ECM CONNECTOR FOR CIRCUIT INVOLVED. CLEAN TERMINAL CONTACT AND EXPAND IT SLIGHTLY TO INCREASE CONTACT PRESSURE AND RECHECK TO SEE IF PROBLEM IS CORRECTED.

Computer Command Control (With EST)

DRIVER COMPLAINT

ENGINE PERFORMANCE PROBLEM (ODOR, SURGE, FUEL ECONOMY . . .)
EMISSION PROBLEM

IF THE "CHECK ENGINE" LIGHT IS NOT ON, NORMAL CHECKS THAT WOULD BE PERFORMED ON CARS WITHOUT THE SYSTEM SHOULD BE DONE FIRST.

IF GENERATOR OR COOLANT LIGHT IS ON WITH THE CHECK ENGINE LIGHT, THEY SHOULD BE DIAGNOSED FIRST.

INSPECT FOR POOR CONNECTIONS AT COOLANT SENSOR, M/C SOLENOID, ETC., AND POOR OR LOOSE VACUUM HOSES AND CONNECTIONS. REPAIR AS NECESSARY.

- Intermittent Check Engine light but no trouble code stored.
  Check for intermittent connection in circuit from:
    - Ignition coil to ground and arcing at spark plug wires or plugs.
    - Bat. to ECM Terms. 'C' and 'R'.
    - ECM Terms. 'A' and 'U' to engine ground.
    - Loss of long-term memory.
  Grounding dwell lead for 10 seconds with "test" lead ungrounded should give Code 23 which should be retained after engine is stopped and ignition turned to "RUN" position. If it is not, ECM is defective.
  EST wires should be kept away from spark plug wires, distributor housing, coil and generator. Wires from ECM Term. 13 to dist. and the shield around EST wires should be a good ground.

- Open diode across A/C compressor clutch.

- Stalling, Rough Idle, or Improper Idle Speed. See idle speed control.

- Detonation (spark knock)
  Check:
    MAP or Vacuum Sensor output.
    EGR operation.
    TPS enrichment operation.
    HEI operation.

- Poor Performance and/or Fuel Economy. See EST diagnosis.

- Poor Full Throttle Performance See Chart 4 if equipped with TPS.

- ALL OTHER COMPLAINTS Make system performance check on warm engine (upper radiator hose hot).

The system performance check should be performed after any repairs to the system has been made.

Computer Command Control (With EST)

SYSTEM PERFORMANCE CHECK

1. Start engine.
2. Ground "test" term. (Must not be grounded before engine is started.)
3. Disconnect purge hose from canister and plug it. On E2SE carburetors, disconnect bowl vent at carburetor.
4. Connect tachometer.
5. Disconnect Mixture Control (M/C) Solenoid and ground M/C Solenoid dwell term.
6. Run engine at 3,000 RPM and, while keeping throttle constant, reconnect M/C Solenoid and note RPM. If car is equipped with an electric cooling fan, it may lower RPM when it engages.
7. Remove ground from M/C Solenoid dwell term. before returning to idle.

Less than 100 RPM drop
- Check that pink wire is attached to right-hand term. of M/C Solenoid Connector, as viewed from harness end.
- Check evaporator canister for being loaded with fuel and related valves, such as purge and bowl vents for leaks which would cause richness. Also check for fuel in crankcase. If OK, see Carb. On-Car Service, Section 6C.

Fixed under 10°	Fixed 10–50°	Fixed over 50°
See Chart #1	See Chart #2	See Chart #3

More than 100 RPM drop
- Connect dwell meter to M/C sol. dwell term. (6-cyl. scale).
- Set carb. on high step of fast idle cam. and run for one (1) minute or until dwell starts to vary, whichever happens first.
- Return engine to idle and note dwell.*

Varying
Check dwell at 3,000 RPM (on 2.8L V-6, Auto Trans. Only, disconnect and plug hose to vacuum sensor during check.)
- No trouble found in the "System."
- Clear long term memory.**

Between 10–50°
Check air management system.

Not between 10–50°
See Carb. Calibration Procedure including TPS adjust.

*Oxygen sensors may cool off at idle and the dwell change from varying to fixed. If this happens, running the engine at fast idle will warm it up again.

**See Code(s) Clearing Procedure.

Computer Command Control (With EST)

CHART NO. 1

DWELL FIXED UNDER 10°

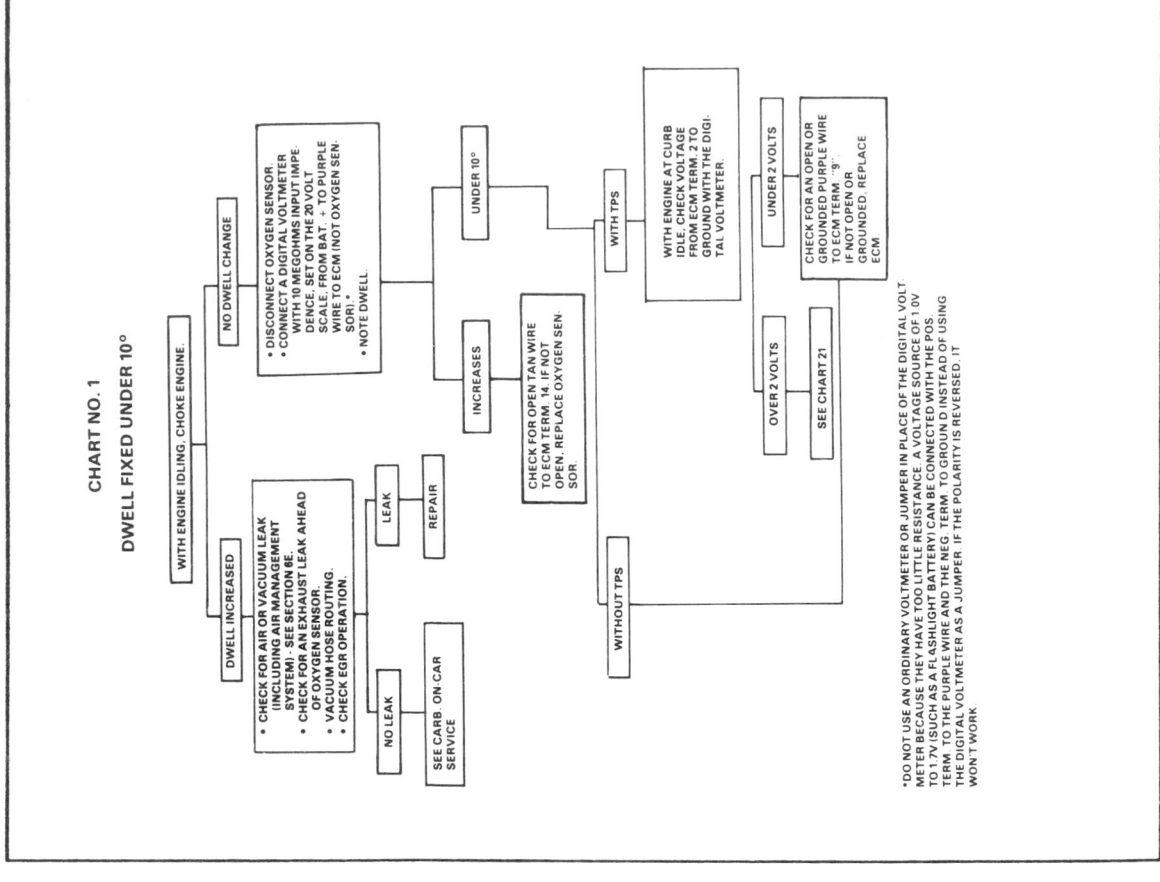

WITH ENGINE IDLING, CHOKE ENGINE.

NO DWELL CHANGE
- DISCONNECT OXYGEN SENSOR.
- CONNECT A DIGITAL VOLTMETER WITH 10 MEGOHMS INPUT IMPEDENCE. SET ON THE 20 VOLT SCALE. FROM BAT. + TO PURPLE WIRE TO ECM (NOT OXYGEN SENSOR).*
- NOTE DWELL.

UNDER 10°

WITH TPS

WITH ENGINE AT CURB IDLE, CHECK VOLTAGE FROM ECM TERM. 2 TO GROUND WITH THE DIGITAL VOLTMETER.

UNDER 2 VOLTS

CHECK FOR AN OPEN OR GROUNDED PURPLE WIRE TO ECM TERM. "9". IF NOT OPEN OR GROUNDED, REPLACE ECM

OVER 2 VOLTS

SEE CHART 21

INCREASES

CHECK FOR OPEN TAN WIRE TO ECM TERM. 14. IF NOT OPEN, REPLACE OXYGEN SENSOR

WITHOUT TPS

DWELL INCREASED
- CHECK FOR AIR OR VACUUM LEAK (INCLUDING AIR MANAGEMENT SYSTEM) - SEE SECTION 6E.
- CHECK FOR AN EXHAUST LEAK AHEAD OF OXYGEN SENSOR.
- VACUUM HOSE ROUTING.
- CHECK EGR OPERATION.

LEAK

REPAIR

NO LEAK

SEE CARB. ON CAR SERVICE

*DO NOT USE AN ORDINARY VOLTMETER OR JUMPER IN PLACE OF THE DIGITAL VOLT METER BECAUSE THEY HAVE TOO LITTLE RESISTANCE. A VOLTAGE SOURCE OF 1.0V TO 1.7V (SUCH AS A FLASHLIGHT BATTERY) CAN BE CONNECTED WITH THE POS. TERM. TO THE PURPLE WIRE AND THE NEG. TERM. TO GROUND IN D INSTEAD OF USING THE DIGITAL VOLTMETER AS A JUMPER. IF THE POLARITY IS REVERSED, IT WON'T WORK.

Computer Command Control (With EST)

CHART #2

DWELL FIXED BETWEEN 10° - 50°

(OPEN COOLANT OR OXYGEN SENSOR CIRCUIT)

CHECK FOR STICKING TPS PLUNGER AND ADJUSTMENT AND LOW COOLANT.

- RUN ENGINE AT PART THROTTLE FOR ONE MINUTE.
- WITH ENGINE IDLING, NOTE DWELL. REMOVE CONNECTOR FROM COOLANT SENSOR, AND JUMPER CONNECTOR TERMS.

NO DWELL CHANGE. RECONNECT COOLANT SENSOR.

- DISCONNECT OXYGEN SENSOR AND JUMPER CONNECTOR TERMS. ON LEADS TO ECM (NOT SENSOR). LEAVE JUMPERED FOR REST OF CHECKS.

NO DWELL CHANGE

CONNECT JUMPER BETWEEN TERMINALS 9 AND 14 AT ECM

NO DWELL CHANGE

JUMPER TERMINALS 3 AND 7 AT ECM

NO DWELL CHANGE

IT IS FAULTY CONNECTION TO ECM TERMS. 3, 7, 9, OR 14 OR FAULTY ECM. RE-CONNECT OXYGEN SENSOR

DWELL CHANGES OVER 5° FROM WHAT IT WAS WITH SENSOR CONNECTED

CHECK RESISTANCE OF COOLANT SENSOR.

OVER 1000 OHMS

REPLACE SENSOR

UNDER 1000 OHMS

RECONNECT COOLANT SENSOR AND NOTE DWELL

VARYING (CLOSED LOOP)

IT WAS BAD COOLANT SENSOR CONNECTION.

FIXED (OPEN LOOP)

UNDER 10°

IT IS FAULTY OXYGEN SENSOR CONNECTIONS OR SENSOR

UNDER 10°

REPAIR OPEN IN WIRES TO OXYGEN SENSOR

DWELL CHANGES OVER 5°

REPAIR OPEN IN WIRES TO COOLANT SENSOR. RECONNECT OXYGEN SENSOR

Computer Command Control (With EST)

(With Electronic Spark Timing)
(Rich Exhaust Indication)

CHART 3   DWELL FIXED OVER 50°

Run engine at fast idle, then with engine idling, remove large vacuum hose, such as PCV source to cause air leak to engine. (But not enough to stall the engine.)

Dwell Changes

- Check evap. canister for being loaded with fuel and related valves, such as purge and bowl vent, for leaks which would cause richness, also fuel in crankcase. If OK, see Carb. On-Car Service-Section 6C.

Dwell drops to under 10°

- Ign. "ON," engine stopped.
- Remove ground from O₂ harness connector and check voltage from that term. to ground with digital voltmeter.

Under 55V
It is faulty oxygen sensor.

Over 55V
Check wire from ECM term. "9" for short to Bat. +. If not shorted, it is faulty ECM.

No Dwell Change

- Disconnect oxygen sensor.
- Ground connector terminal on lead to ECM (not oxygen sensor.)

No Dwell Change
Replace ECM

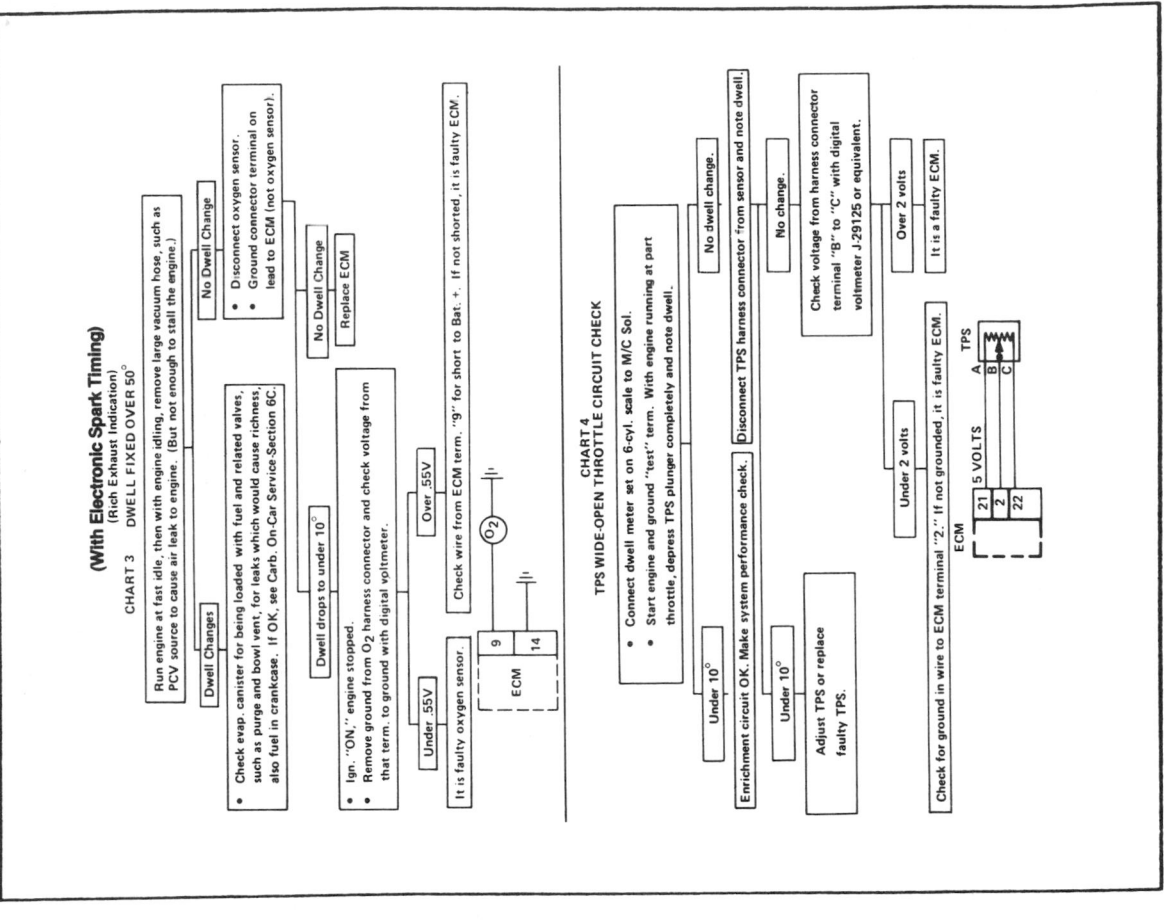

CHART 4
TPS WIDE-OPEN THROTTLE CIRCUIT CHECK

- Connect dwell meter set on 6-cyl. scale to M/C Sol.
- Start engine and ground "test" term. With engine running at part throttle, depress TPS plunger completely and note dwell.

No dwell change.
Enrichment circuit OK. Make system performance check.

No change.
Disconnect TPS harness connector from sensor and note dwell.

Under 10°

Under 10°
Adjust TPS or replace faulty TPS.

Check voltage from harness connector terminal "B" to "C" with digital voltmeter J-29125 or equivalent.

Under 2 volts

Over 2 volts
It is a faulty ECM.

Check for ground in wire to ECM terminal "2." If not grounded, it is faulty ECM.

Computer Command Control (With EST)

CHART #5   "CHECK ENGINE" LIGHT INOPERATIVE
(REMOTE LAMP DRIVER IN HARNESS)

- Ign. "on," engine stopped.
- Ground "Check Engine" lamp terminal in ALCL connector (Terminal "D") and note "Check Engine" light.

Light "On"
Check voltage from lamp driver terminal "C" to ground

Light "Off"
Check for a blown gage fuse and open in wire from ALCL to Instrument Panel (I.P.) "Check Engine" light terminal If not open it is faulty bulb or connection to it

Over 11 volts
Check for open from lamp driver terminal "D" to ground If not open, replace lamp driver.

6 to 11 volts
Ground lamp driver terminal "E" and note "Check Engine" light

Under 6 volts
Check voltage from driver terminal "B" to ground

Light "Off"
Repair open in wire to lamp driver terminal "E".

Light "On"
It is faulty lamp driver connection or driver.

Over 10 volts
- Remove wire from driver connector cavity "C"
- Reconnect lamp driver and note "Check Engine" light.

Under 10 volts
Repair open in circuit to gage fuse from terminal "B"

Light "Off"
It is faulty driver connections or driver.

Light "On"
Check for grounded wire from driver terminal "C" to ECM terminal "G." If not grounded, replace ECM

Computer Command Control (With EST)

Computer Command Control (With EST)

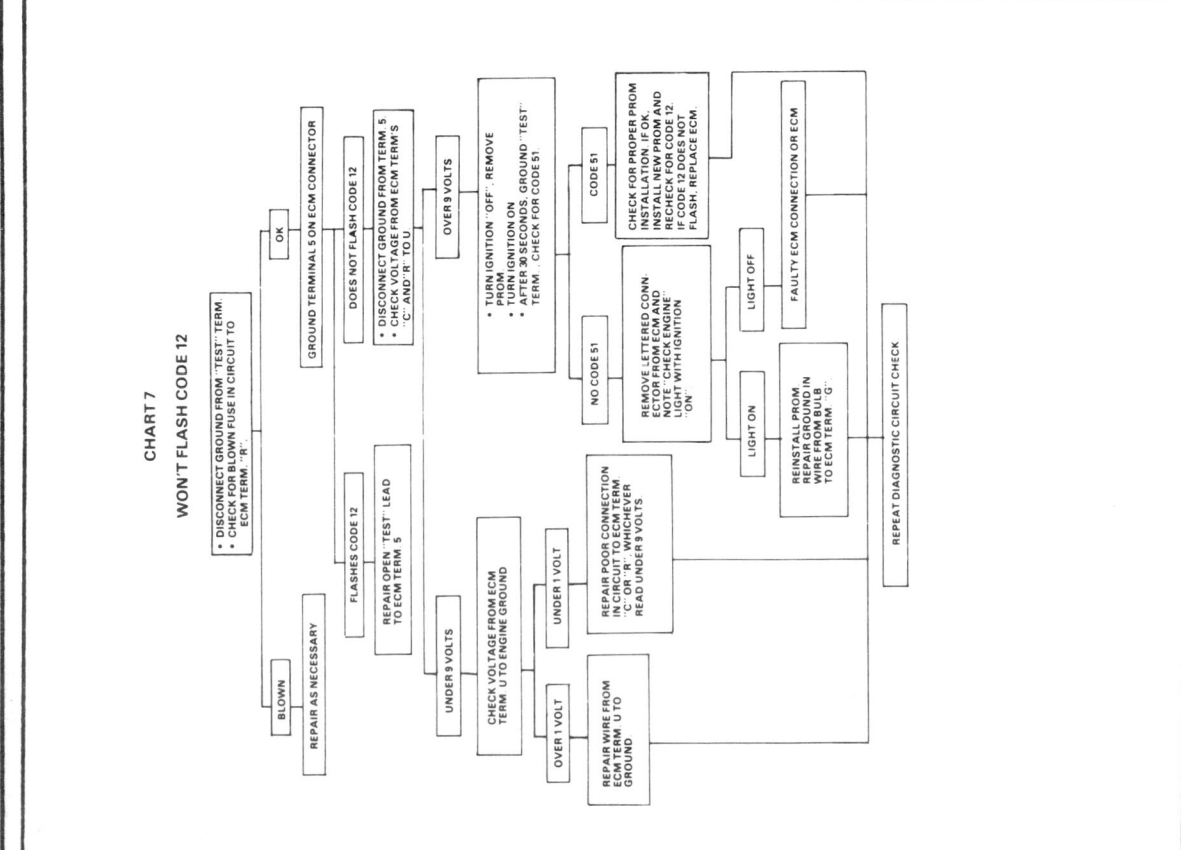

Computer Command Control (With EST)

CHART #13   TROUBLE CODE 13
OXYGEN SENSOR CIRCUIT

Check for sticking throttle position sensor.
If 13 and 21 are displayed, go to 21 first.
On 2.5L L4 if codes 13 and 34 are present, go to Chart #34 first.

- Ground "test" term.
- Connect dwell meter to M/C Solenoid — use 6-cyl. scale.
- With engine idling, disconnect oxygen sensor and jumper connector terminals on leads to ECM (not oxygen sensor).

Under 10° dwell → Faulty oxygen sensor connections or sensor.

Over 10° dwell → Connect jumper between ECM terminals "g" and "14."

- **Over 10° dwell** → Faulty ECM connections or ECM.
- **Under 10° dwell** → Repair open in oxygen sensor harness leads from connector to ECM.

TROUBLE CODE 14

IF 14 AND 21 ARE DISPLAYED, GO TO CHART 21 FIRST
ON 2.5 L4 AND 2.8 V 6 W. M.T. IF 14 AND 34 ARE DISPLAYED, GO TO CHART 34 FIRST.

IF THE ENGINE HOT LIGHT IS "ON", CHECK FOR OVERHEATING CONDITION BEFORE MAKING FOLLOWING TEST.

- GROUND "TEST" TERMINAL.
- CONNECT DWELL METER TO M/C SOLENOID (USE 6CYL. SCALE)
- RUN ENGINE A PART THROTTLE UNTIL DWELL STARTS TO VARY
- WITH ENGINE IDLING, REMOVE CONNECTOR FROM COOLANT SENSOR

DWELL FIXED → REPLACE COOLANT SENSOR

DWELL VARIES → REMOVE NUMBERED TERM. ECM CONNECTOR AND CONNECT TEST LIGHT FROM BAT + TO TERM. 3 OF CONNECTOR (NOT ECM).

- **LIGHTS** → REPAIR GROUNDED WIRE TO ECM TERM. "3"
- **NO LIGHT** → CHECK FOR SHORT BETWEEN ECM CONNECTOR & COOLANT SENSOR. IF NOT SHORTED, REPLACE ECM

Computer Command Control (With EST)

TROUBLE CODE 15   OPEN COOLANT SENSOR CIRCUIT

If codes "15" and "21" are displayed, go to trouble code "21" chart first

- Connect dwell meter to M/C sol. — use 6-cyl. scale.
- Start engine.
- Ground "test" term. and note dwell at part throttle.

Varying (closed loop). → Trouble is intermittent. Circuit not open at present. Make physical inspection of circuit for intermittent connection. Clear memory.

Fixed about 30°.
- Disconnect coolant sensor.
- Ignition "ON," engine stopped, check voltage between sensor connector terminals, should be over 4 volts.

OK → Check resistance of coolant sensor. Should be under 1000 ohms on warm engine.
- **OK** → It is poor sensor connection or low
- **Not OK** → Replace sensor.

Not OK → Check voltage from ECM term. "3" to "7" (sensor disconnected).
- **Under 4 volts** → It is faulty ECM connection or ECM.
- **Over 4 volts** → Check for open in ECM wires to ECM terms. "3" and "7."

SENSOR
UNDER 1000 OHMS HOT

5 VOLTS—ON OPEN CIRCUIT

3
7
ECM

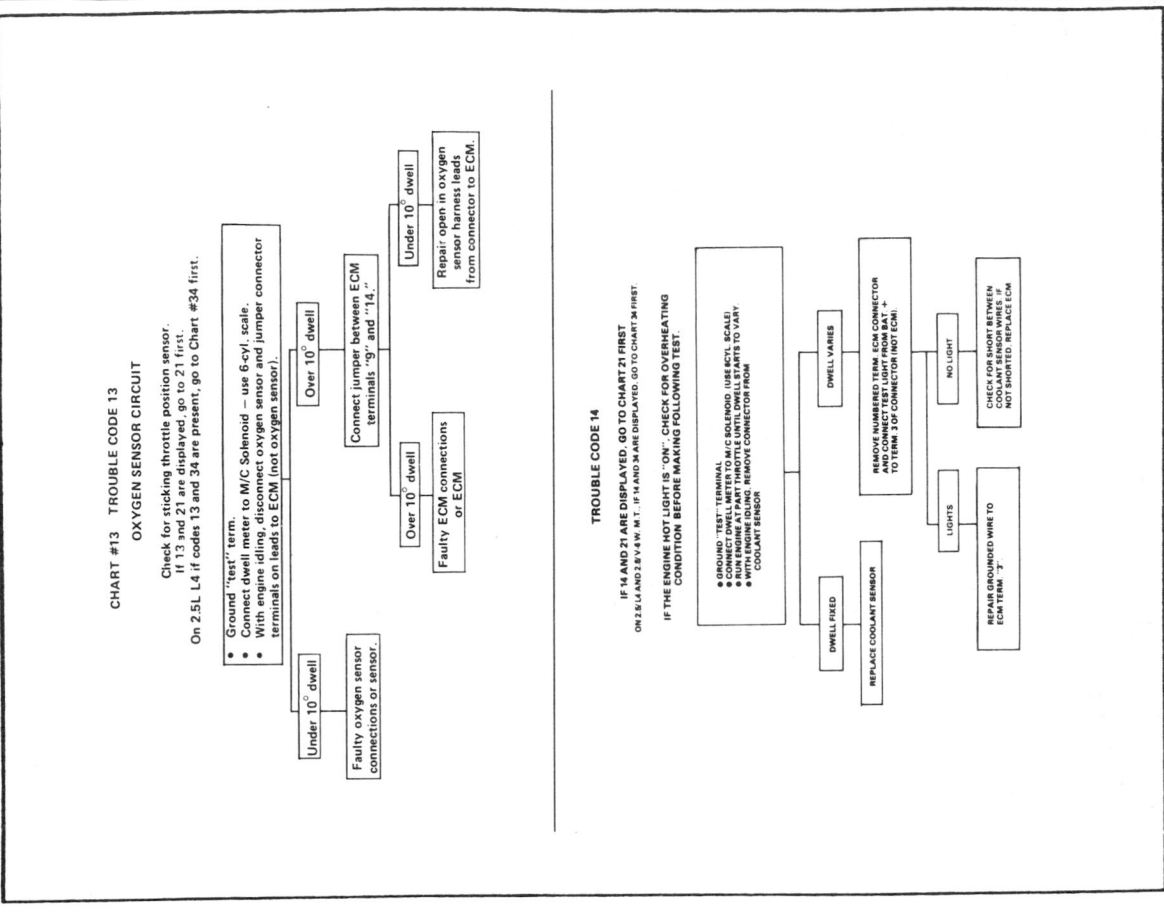

Computer Command Control (With EST)

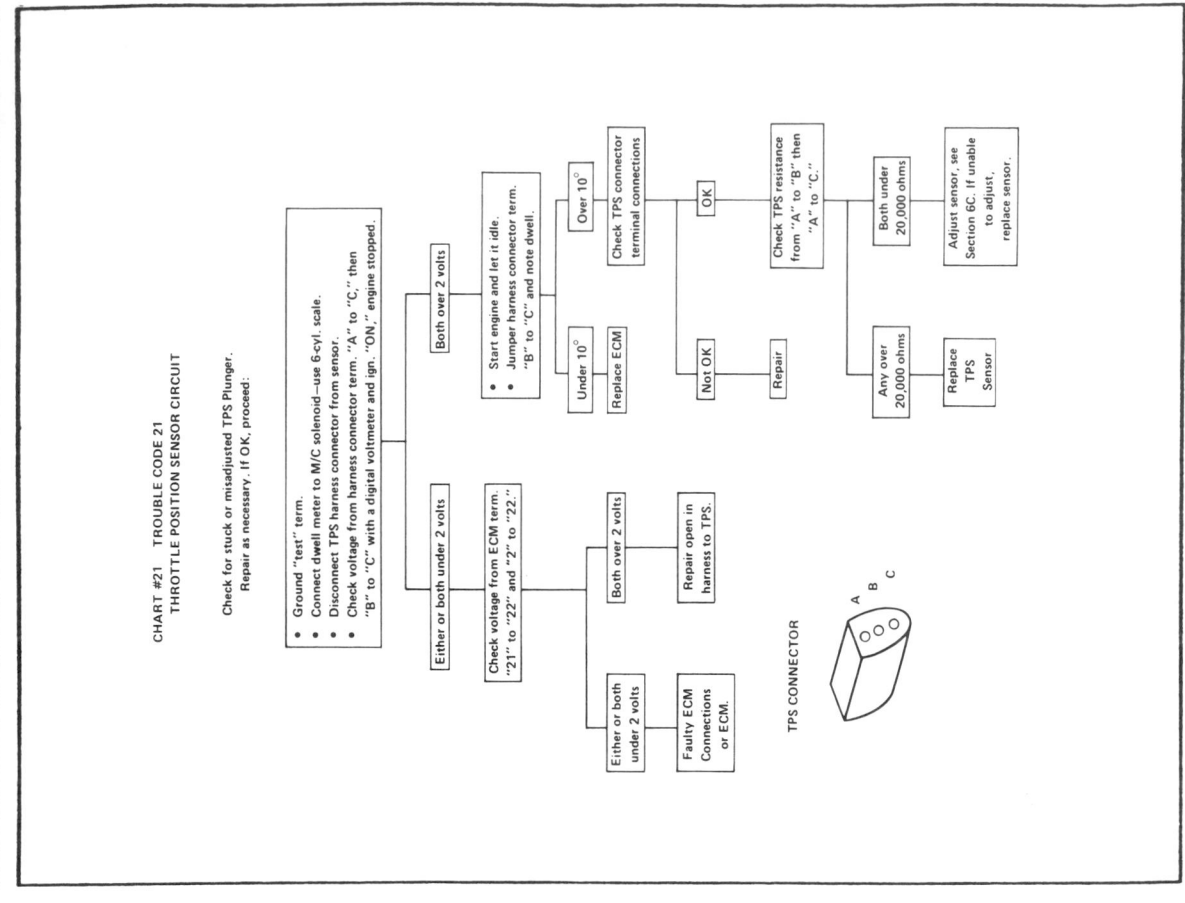

Computer Command Control (With EST)

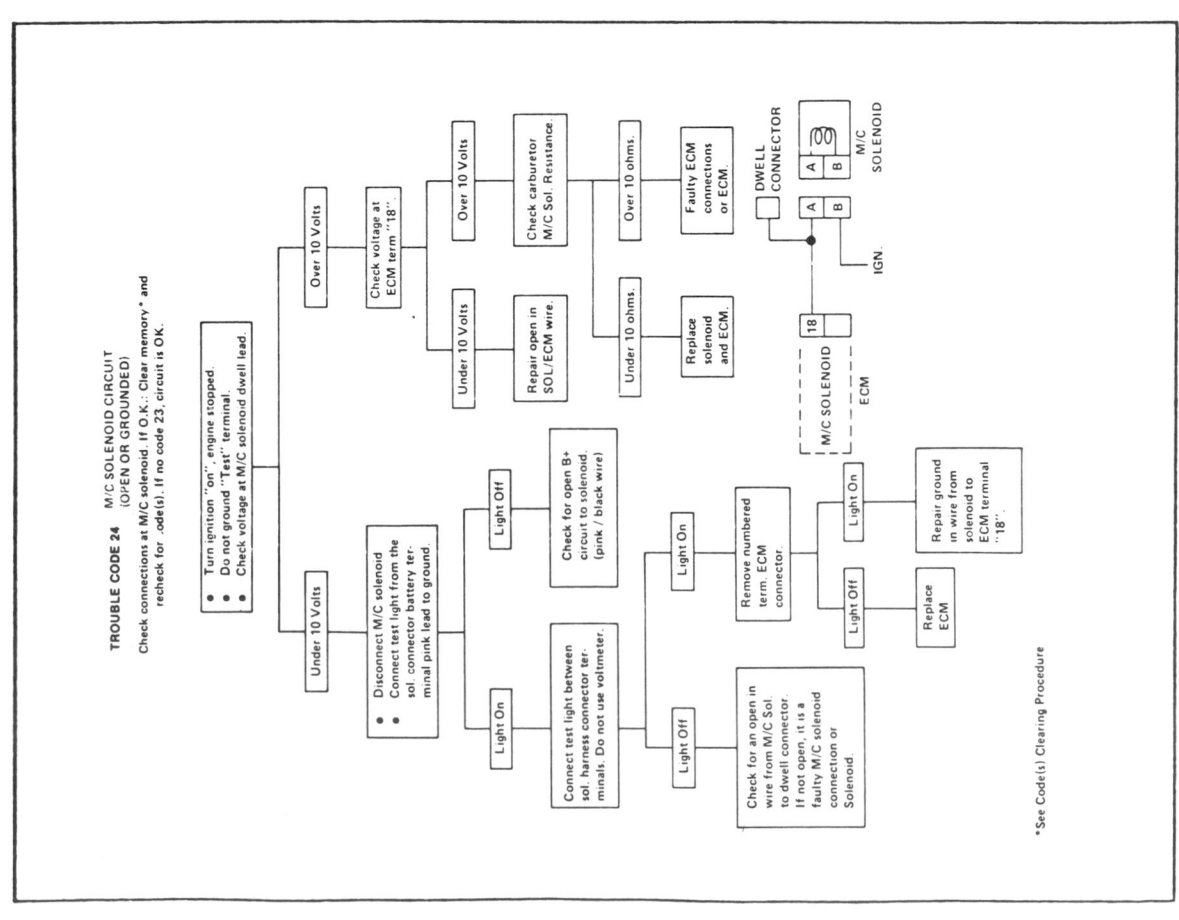

Computer Command Control (With EST)

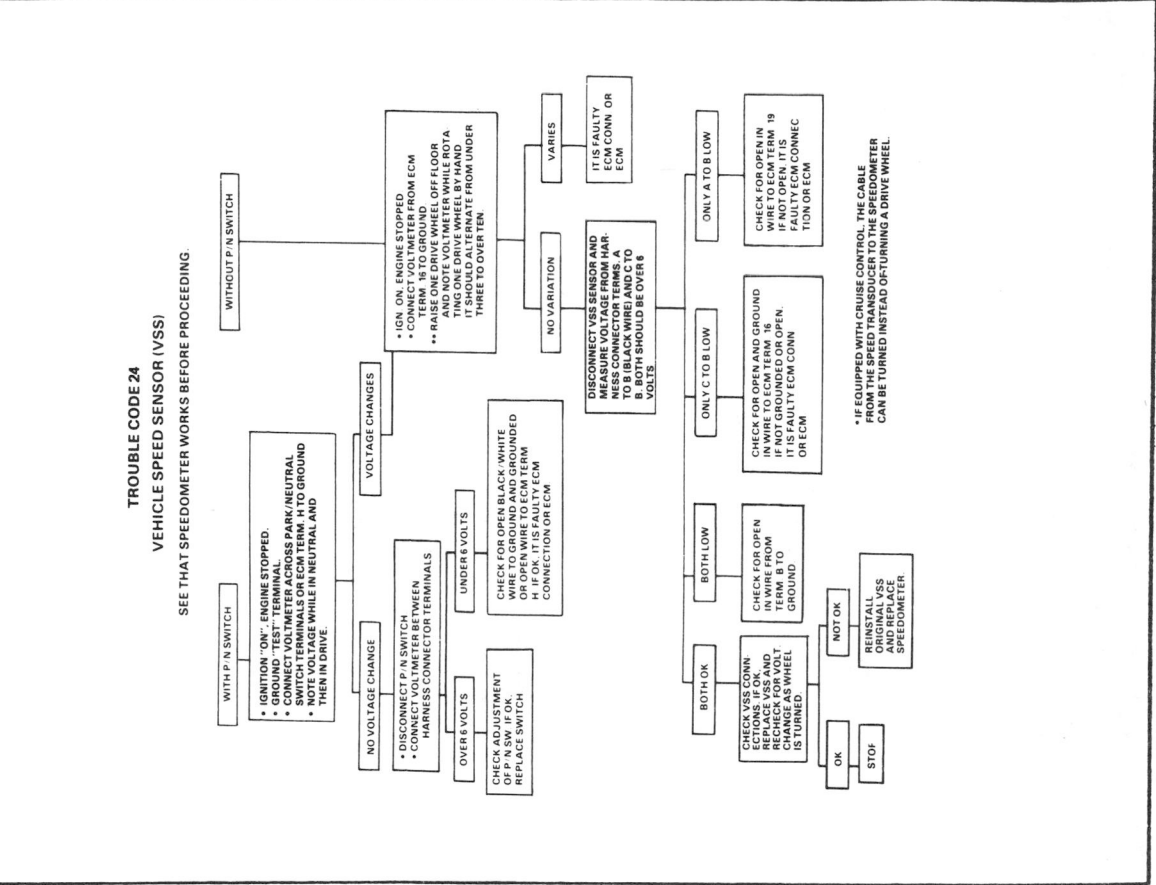

TROUBLE CODE 24

VEHICLE SPEED SENSOR (VSS)

SEE THAT SPEEDOMETER WORKS BEFORE PROCEEDING.

- IGNITION "ON," ENGINE STOPPED.
- GROUND "TEST" TERMINAL.
- CONNECT VOLTMETER ACROSS PARK/NEUTRAL SWITCH TERMINALS OR ECM TERM. H TO GROUND
- NOTE VOLTAGE WHILE IN NEUTRAL AND THEN IN DRIVE.

WITH P/N SWITCH

NO VOLTAGE CHANGE
- DISCONNECT P/N SWITCH
- CONNECT VOLTMETER BETWEEN HARNESS CONNECTOR TERMINALS

OVER 6 VOLTS — CHECK ADJUSTMENT OF P/N SW. IF OK, REPLACE SWITCH

UNDER 6 VOLTS — CHECK FOR OPEN BLACK/WHITE WIRE TO GROUND AND GROUNDED OR OPEN WIRE TO ECM TERM. H. IF OK, IT IS FAULTY ECM CONNECTION OR ECM

VOLTAGE CHANGES

WITHOUT P/N SWITCH

- IGN. ON, ENGINE STOPPED
- CONNECT VOLTMETER FROM ECM TERM. 16 TO GROUND
- RAISE ONE DRIVE WHEEL OFF FLOOR AND NOTE VOLTMETER WHILE ROTATING ONE DRIVE WHEEL BY HAND. IT SHOULD ALTERNATE FROM UNDER THREE TO OVER TEN

VARIES — IT IS FAULTY ECM CONN. OR ECM

NO VARIATION — DISCONNECT VSS SENSOR AND MEASURE VOLTAGE FROM HARNESS CONNECTOR TERMS. A TO B (BLACK WIRE) AND C TO B. BOTH SHOULD BE OVER 6 VOLTS

ONLY A TO B LOW — CHECK FOR OPEN IN WIRE TO ECM TERM 19. IF NOT OPEN IT IS FAULTY ECM CONNECTION OR ECM

ONLY C TO B LOW — CHECK FOR OPEN AND GROUND IN WIRE TO ECM TERM. 16. IF NOT GROUNDED OR OPEN, IT IS FAULTY ECM CONN OR ECM

BOTH LOW — CHECK FOR OPEN IN WIRE FROM TERM. B TO GROUND

BOTH OK — CHECK VSS CONNECTIONS. IF OK, REPLACE VSS AND RECHECK FOR VOLT CHANGE AS WHEEL IS TURNED

OK — STOP

NOT OK — REINSTALL ORIGINAL VSS AND REPLACE SPEEDOMETER

* IF EQUIPPED WITH CRUISE CONTROL, THE SPEEDOMETER CABLE FROM THE SPEED TRANSDUCER TO THE SPEEDOMETER CAN BE TURNED INSTEAD OF TURNING A DRIVE WHEEL.

Computer Command Control (With EST)

TROUBLE CODE 32

BARO SENSOR CIRCUIT LOW

- Ignition "on," engine stopped.
- Check voltage from sensor term. "B" to "A" and refer to chart value below.**

Above table Volts

Check for short between wires to Sensor terms. "B" and "C." If not shorted, replace Sensor.

Within table Volts

Apply 34 kPa (10 inches) of vacuum to sensor and note Voltage change

More than 2.3 Volt change — Replace Sensor

Less than 1.2 Volt change — Check for short between wires to Sensor term. "B" & "C." If not shorted replace Sensor.

1.2–2.3 Volt change — Remove Vacuum — Check Volts from ECM term. "1" to "22."

Over 2 Volts — It is faulty ECM Connection or ECM.

Under 2 Volts — Repair open in wire to ECM term. "22."

Below table Volts

Disconnect jumper from term. "B" and check Voltage from Sensor term. "B" to "A."

No change — Check Voltage Harness from sensor term. "C" to "A" with sensor disconnected

Increases — Check for grounded wire to ECM term. "1." If not grounded, replace ECM.

Under 4.5 Volts — Check Voltage from ECM term. "21" to "22."

Over 4.5 Volts — Replace Sensor

Under 4.5 Volts — Check for grounded wire to ECM term. "21." If not grounded, it is faulty ECM Conn. or ECM.

Over 4.5 Volts — Repair Open in wire to ECM term. "21" or "22."

sensor
- A low
- B output
- C volt. ref.

```
        sensor
   22   A low
ECM 1   B output
   21   C volt. ref.
```

High Pressure = High Voltage

**Altitude	Voltage Range
Below 1,000'	3.8 — 5.5V
1,000–2,000'	3.6 — 5.3V
2,000–3,000'	3.5 — 5.1V
3,000–4,000'	3.3 — 5.0V
4,000–5,000'	3.2 — 4.8V
5,000–6,000'	3.0 — 4.6V
6,000–7,000'	2.9 — 4.5V
7,000–8,000'	2.8 — 4.3V
8,000–9,000'	2.6 — 4.2V
9,000–10,000'	2.5 — 4.0V

Computer Command Control (With EST)

CHART #34

TROUBLE CODE 34
VACUUM SENSOR CIRCUIT

Check for over 34kPa (10 inches) of vacuum at sensor with engine idling. If not OK, repair.

Computer Command Control (With EST)

TROUBLE CODE 34 (NON TURBO)
MAP SENSOR CIRCUIT

Check for over 34 kPa (10 inches) vacuum at MAP sensor with engine idling. If not OK, repair hoses or connections.

Computer Command Control (With EST)

CHART #34A
TROUBLE CODE 34 (TURBO) MAP SENSOR CIRCUIT

Check for over 34 kPa (10 inches) vacuum at MAP sensor with engine idling. If not OK, repair hoses or connections.

- Ignition "on" engine stopped.
- Ground "test" term.
- Check voltage from sensor term. "B" to "A" and refer to chart value below. **

Above table volts
→ Check for short between wires to Sensor terms. "B" and "C." If not shorted, replace Sensor.

Within table volts
→ Apply 50 kPa (15 inches) of vacuum sensor and note Voltage change.
- More than 1.7 Volt change → Replace Sensor
- Less than 0.9 Volt change → Check for short between wires to Sensor term. "B" & "C." If not shorted, replace Sensor.
- 0.9-1.7 Volt change → Remove Vacuum. Check Volts from ECM term. "20" to "22."
  - Over 1 Volt → It is faulty ECM Connection or ECM.
  - Under 1 Volt → Repair open in wire to ECM term. "22."

Below table volts
→ Disconnect jumper from term. "B" and check Voltage from Sensor term. "B" to "A".
- Increases → Check for grounded wire to ECM term. "20." If not grounded, replace ECM
- No change → With sensor disconnected, check voltage from sensor harness term. "C" to "A".
  - Over 4.5 Volts → Replace Sensor
  - Under 4.5 Volts → Check Voltage from ECM term. "21" to "22."
    - Over 4.5 Volts → Repair Open in wire to ECM terms. "21." or "22."
    - Under 4.5 Volts → Check for grounded wire to ECM term. "21." If not grounded, it is faulty ECM Conn. or ECM.

sensor
A low
B output
C volt. ref.

	sensor
7 or 22	A low
ECM 20	B output
21	C volt. ref.

High Pressure = High Voltage

** Altitude	Voltage Range	
Below 1,000'	1.7 –	3.2V
1,000–2,000'	1.6 –	3.0V
2,000–3,000'	1.5 –	2.8V
3,000–4,000'	1.4 –	2.7V
4,000–5,000'	1.3 –	2.6V
5,000–6,000'	1.3 –	2.5V
6,000–7,000'	1.2 –	2.5V
7,000–8,000'	1.1 –	2.4V
8,000–9,000'	1.1 –	2.3V
9,000–10,000'	1.0 –	2.2V

Computer Command Control (With EST)

TROUBLE CODE 35
SHORTED IDLE SPEED CONTROL (ISC) CIRCUIT

Check for sticking TPS plunger — repair as necessary.

- Test terminal ungrounded.
- Run engine at 3000 RPM for 5 seconds and note "check engine" light.

Light "OFF"
→ Trouble is intermittent and system is OK at present. Make physical inspection of circuit. Clear memory.

Light "ON"
→
- Ignition "OFF."
- Disconnect ISC connector.
- Connect ohmmeter from Term. "A" to "B" on ISC motor assembly.
- Open throttle and note resistance.

- Under 10 ohms → Replace ISC motor
- Over 10 ohms →
  - Ign. "ON," engine stopped.
  - Check voltage from terminal "A" to "B" on harness connector.
    - Under 6 volts → Check for shorted or grounded wire from terminal "B" to ECM terminal "B". If not shorted or grounded, replace ECM.
    - Over 6 volts → Check adjustment of TPS (see Section 6C). If OK, replace ECM.

MOTOR
D C B A
ISC
ECM
B

Computer Command Control (With EST)

TROUBLE CODE 44 OR 44 AND 55 AT SAME TIME

CODE 44 AND 55 AT SAME TIME — CHECK FOR OPEN WIRE FROM ECM TERM. 14 TO GROUND. IF NOT OPEN REPLACE OXYGEN SENSOR.

- GROUND TEST TERMINAL
- CONNECT DWELL METER TO M/C SOLENOID - USE 6 CYLINDER SCALE
- RUN ENGINE AT 3000 RPM AND NOTE DWELL.

BETWEEN 15 - 50° (10-50° ON 3.8L V6 VIN CODE A OR 3)

UNDER 15° (UNDER 10 ON 3.8L V6 VIN CODE A OR 3)

REPLACE OXYGEN SENSOR

WITH ENGINE IDLING, CHOKE ENGINE

DWELL INCREASES

NO DWELL CHANGE

- CHECK FOR AIR LEAK (INCLUDING AIR MANAGEMENT SYSTEM)
- CHECK FOR EXHAUST LEAK AHEAD OF OXYGEN SENSOR

LEAK

REPAIR

NO LEAK

SEE CARB. ON CAR SERVICE SECTION

- DISCONNECT OXYGEN SENSOR.
- CONNECT A DIGITAL VOLTMETER WITH 10 MEGOHMS INPUT IMPEDENCE. SET ON THE 20 VOLT SCALE. FROM BAT. + TO PURPLE WIRE TO ECM (NOT OXYGEN SENSOR)*
- NOTE DWELL.*

INCREASES

REPLACE OXYGEN SENSOR

READS UNDER 10°

CHECK FOR GROUNDED PURPLE WIRE TO ECM TERM. 9 IF NOT GROUNDED. REPLACE ECM.

*DO NOT USE AN ORDINARY VOLTMETER OR JUMPER IN PLACE OF THE DIGITAL VOLTMETER BECAUSE THEY HAVE TOO LITTLE RESISTANCE. A VOLTAGE SOURCE OF 1.0 V TO 0.7 V SUCH AS A FLASHLIGHT BATTERY CAN BE CONNECTED WITH THE POS. TERM. TO THE PURPLE WIRE AND THE NEG. TERM. TO GROUND INSTEAD OF USING THE DIGITAL VOLTMETER AS A JUMPER. IF THE POLARITY IS REVERSED, IT WON'T WORK.

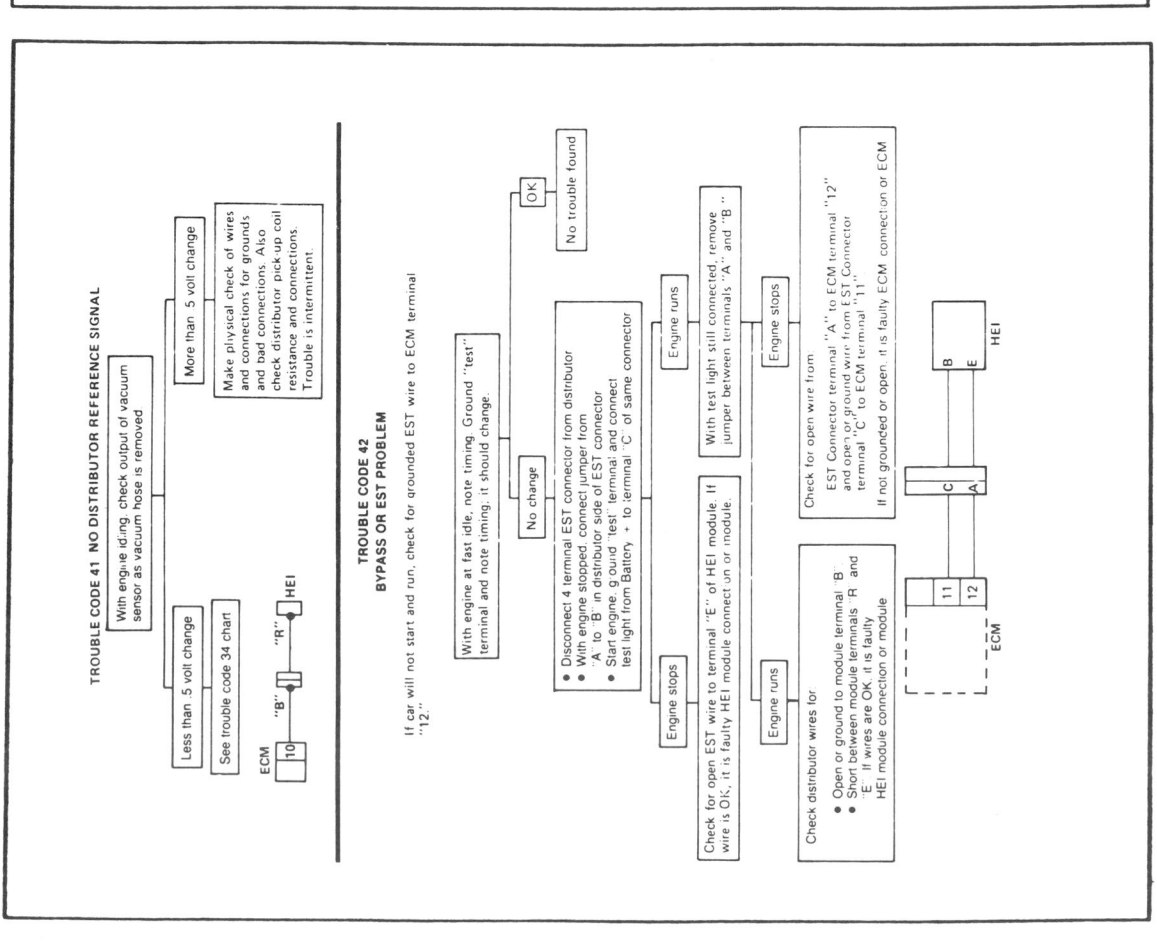

Computer Command Control (With EST)

TROUBLE CODE 41 NO DISTRIBUTOR REFERENCE SIGNAL

With engine idling check output of vacuum sensor as vacuum hose is removed

Less than 5 volt change

See trouble code 34 chart

More than 5 volt change

Make physical check of wires and connections for grounds and bad connections. Also check distributor pick-up coil resistance and connections. Trouble is intermittent.

ECM ["B" "R"] HEI
10

TROUBLE CODE 42 BYPASS OR EST PROBLEM

If car will not start and run, check for grounded EST wire to ECM terminal "12"

With engine at fast idle, note timing. Ground "test" terminal and note timing, it should change.

No change

Engine stops

- Disconnect 4 terminal EST connector from distributor
- With engine stopped, connect jumper from "A" to "B" in distributor side of EST connector
- Start engine g ound "test" terminal and connect test light from Battery + to terminal "C" of same connector

Engine runs

Engine runs

With test light still connected, remove jumper between terminals "A" and "B"

Engine stops

OK

No trouble found

Check for open wire from EST Connector terminal "A" to ECM terminal "12" and open wire from EST Connector terminal "C" to ECM terminal "11".

If not grounded or open, it is faulty ECM connection or ECM

Check for open EST wire to terminal "E" of HEI module. If wire is OK, it is faulty HEI module connect un or module.

Check distributor wires for
- Open or ground to module terminal "B"
- Short between module terminals "R" and "E". If wires are OK, it is faulty HEI module connection or module

ECM [11 12] C A | B E | HEI

Computer Command Control (With EST)

TROUBLE CODES 51 - 54

CODE 51

CHECK THAT ALL PINS ARE FULLY INSERTED IN THE SOCKET. IF OK, REPLACE PROM. CLEAR MEMORY, AND RECHECK. IF CODE 51 REAPPEARS, REPLACE ECM.

CODE 52 - 53
REPLACE ECM

CODE 54

CHECK M/C SOLENOID RESISTANCE

OVER 10 OHMS
- IGNITION "ON." ENGINE STOPPED.
- CONNECT TEST LIGHT FROM GROUND TO DWELL LEAD AT M/C SOLENOID WITH SOL. DISCONNECTED.
- DISCONNECT NUMBERED TERMINAL CONNECTOR AT ECM.

LIGHT

REPAIR SHORT TO BATT. + BLUE WIRE TO ECM TERM. 18. CLEAR MEMORY AND CHECK FOR TROUBLE CODES.

NO LIGHT

REPLACE ECM

UNDER 10 OHMS
- REPLACE SOLENOID
- CLEAR MEMORY
- START ENGINE AND CHECK FOR TROUBLE CODE

CODE

SEE APPLICABLE CODE CHART.

NO CODE

MAKE SYSTEM PERFORM. CHECK.

Computer Command Control (With EST)

CHART 45
TROUBLE CODE 45
(Rich Exhaust Indication)
- If M/C solenoid does not click with ign. "ON" and "TEST" term. grounded, and there is no Code 23 or 54, check for sticking M/C solenoid.
- If Code 54 is present, go to Chart 54 first.

- Connect dwell meter to M/C Sol. — use 6 cyl. scale. Run at 3000 RPM in Park or Neutral and note dwell.

Under 50°

Over 50°

Trouble is intermittent. System is OK at present. Clear memory.

With engine idling, note dwell. Remove large vacuum hose (such as PCV source) to cause an air leak (but not enough to stall engine).

Dwell Decreased

No Dwell Change

- Check that pink wire is attached to right-hand term. of M/C solenoid connector, as viewed from harness end.
- Check evaporator canister for being loaded with fuel and related valves, such as purge and bowl vent, for leaks which would cause richness, also fuel in crankcase.

- Disconnect oxygen sensor.
- Ground connector terminal on lead to ECM (not oxygen sensor).

No Dwell Change

Replace ECM

Dwell Drops to Under 10°

- Ignition "ON." engine stopped.
- Remove ground from O2 harness connector and check voltage from that term. to ground with digital voltmeter.

Over .55V

Check wire from ECM term. 9 for short to Bat. +. If not shorted, it is faulty ECM.

Under .55V

It is faulty oxygen sensor.

ECM 9 14

O2

Computer Command Control (With EST)

ENGINE CRANKS, BUT WILL NOT RUN (WITH INTEGRAL IGNITION COIL)

NOTE: Perform diagnostic circuit check before using this procedure. If a tachometer is connected to the tachometer terminal, disconnect it before proceeding with the test.

1. Check spark at plug with ST-125 while cranking (if no spark on one wire, check a second wire).
   - Spark → Check fuel, spark plugs, etc.
   - No Spark (Without EST)

2. Check voltage at distributor "bat" terminal while cranking.
   - 7 volts or more
   - Under 7 volts → Repair primary circuit to ignition switch

3. With ignition "on," check "tach" terminal voltage.
   - 7 volts or more
   - 1 to 10 Volts

4. Check for spark at coil output terminal with ST-125 while cranking.
   - 10 Volts or More
   - Spark → System OK
   - No Spark → Replace module and check for spark from coil as in Step 6

5. Remove pick up coil leads from module. Check "tach" term. voltage with "ign" "on." Watch voltmeter as test light is momentarily (not more than five (5) seconds) connected from bat. + to module term.
   - 4 Term Mod — Term "G"
   - 5 Term Mod — Term "D" or ESC — Term "D"
   - 7 Term Mod — Term "P"
   - Voltage Drops
   - No Drop in Voltage → Check module grnd and for open in wires from cap to distributor. If OK, replace mod.
   - Spark → It is pick up coil or connections. Coil resistance should be 500-1500 ohms and not grounded
   - No Spark → Replace ign. coil. If too, is faulty.

6. Check for spark from coil with ST-125 as test light is removed from module terminal
   - Spark
   - No Spark
     - If no module tester is available → Check ign coil ground circuit. If OK, replace ign coil and repeat Step 6
     - If module tester is available → test module
       - OK
       - Bad → Replace mod
       - Check ign coil ground. If OK, replace ign coil
   - Spark → System OK

7. Coil removed is OK, reinstall original coil and replace module

Under 1 Volt → It is faulty ign. coil connection or coil

Check color match of pick up coil connector and ign. coil lead. Inspect cap for water, cracks, etc. If OK, replace rotor.

IGN COIL / PICK-UP COIL
WHITE WIRE
RED WIRE
P/N 1876209

IGN COIL / PICK UP COIL
WHITE WIRE
GREEN WIRE
CLEAR, BLACK, BLUE CONNECTOR

IGN COIL / PICK-UP COIL
GREEN WIRE
RED WIRE
YELLOW WIRE
P/N 1875894
YELLOW CONNECTOR

Computer Command Control (With EST)

TROUBLE CODE 55 FAULTY OXYGEN SENSOR OR ECM

Check for corrosion at ECM edgeboard connectors and terms. If present, check for coolant sensor, windshield or heater core leaks. Repair leak, clean connector terms. and replace ECM. Also, check for 4 term. EST harness being too close to electrical signals, such as spark plug wires, distributor housing, generator, etc.

- Disconnect test terminal.
- Disconnect oxygen sensor and note "check engine" light with engine idling for less than one minute.
  - Light On
    - Ignition "ON," engine stopped. Check voltage from ECM Terminal "21" to "22."
      - Over 6 Volts
        - Turn ign. "OFF." Disconnect numbered connector from ECM. Ign. "ON," check voltage from connector Term. "21" to "22."
          - Voltage → Check for short in B+ wire to Term. "21."
          - 0 Volts → Replace ECM
      - Under 4 Volts
        - Check for ground in circuit to ECM Terminal "21" (includes shorted or grounded TPS Vacuum or Vehicle Speed Sensors). If not grounded or shorted, replace ECM.
  - Light Off
    - Disconnect O2 sensor. Ign. "ON," engine stopped. Check voltage from connector of purple wire disconnected from oxygen sensor.
      - 4 to 6 Volts
      - Over 1 Volt
        - Turn "OFF," ign. disconnect numbered ECM connector and then turn ign. "ON."
        - Check voltage from ECM harness connector Term. "9" to ground.
          - Over 1 Volt → Check for short from wire to ground. If not open, replace ECM.
          - Under 1 Volt → Check for open circuit from Term. "14" to ground. If not open, replace ECM.
      - Under 1 Volt
        - Check for intermittent ground in circuit to ECM Terminal "21" (includes TPS, MAP, BARO, and Vacuum Sensors). Clear codes and check for reoccurrence of Code 55. If it reappears, it could be faulty oxygen sensor (except on 4.3L VIN Code 'F' and 5.0 VIN Code 'Y').

O2 SENSOR 9
GROUND 14
5 VOLT REF 21
ECM

OXYGEN SENSOR

VACUUM SENSOR OR MAP
C
A — TPS

BARO SENSOR

Computer Command Control (With EST)

AIR MANAGEMENT SYSTEM CHECK

Engines which use dual bed converters and electric air control valves (EAC/ES).

On some applications, some air may divert to air cleaner, above 2000 RPM.

Make visual inspection of hoses and connectors for leaks and proper connections. Repair as necessary.

CHECK CONTROL VALVE OPERATION

- Start engine and do not ground "test" terminal.
- Quickly accelerate and decelerate engine. Valve should divert air to air cleaner outlet or atmosphere on deceleration only.

Check switching valve operation
- Run engine at part throttle (below 2000 rpm). Pulsations should be felt in outlet to exhaust ports until system goes closed loop, then switch to converter outlet.

OK → Ignition "ON," engine stopped check for a click at air control solenoid as "test" term. is grounded.
- Clicks
- No Click
- No trouble found

Not OK → Check switching valve sol. control circuit as follows:
- Ignition "ON," engine stopped. "TEST" term. ungrounded.
- Remove connector from applicable valve solenoid and connect a test light between harness connector terminals.
  - Light
  - No light

Check for grounded wire to ECM Term. "4" for control valve or Term. "B" for switching valve. If not grounded, replace ECM.
- No light → Check for open in pink wire circuit.
- Light on both term. → Repair short from bat. + to wire to ECM.
- Light on one term. → Connect test light from each term. of connector to ground.
  - Light on one term.
  - No light → Ground trouble code "test" term.
    - Light → It is faulty valve connections or valve.
    - No light → Check for open in wire to ECM Term. "4" for control valve or "B" for switching valve. If OK, check resistance of sol. If under 20 ohms, replace sol. and ECM. If not, it is faulty connection to ECM or ECM.

Check control valve solenoid control circuit as follows:
- Constant divert
- No divert → Check for at least 34 kPa (10") of vacuum at valve. If OK, replace valve.

ECM — 4 — B — AIR CONT. — AIR SWITCH — IGN.

Computer Command Control (With EST)

AIR MANAGEMENT CHECK WITH ELECTRIC DIVERT AND ELECTRIC SWITCHING VALVE. (ED/ES)

Check vacuum hoses condition and connection. Repair as necessary. On some applications, some air may divert to the air cleaner above 2000rpm.

- "Test" term. ungrounded.
- Start engine, running at part throttle, below 2000rpm, air should be felt at outlet to exhaust ports during Open Loop operation (from 6 seconds to 3 minutes on warm engine depending on application) and switch to converter when system goes Closed Loop.

Disconnect M/C sol. conn. at idle and air should divert to air cleaner after a few seconds.
- OK
- No divert → No trouble found. Clear memory.

Constant divert to air cleaner
- Ign. "ON," engine stopped. Disconnect Air Control solenoid electrical connector and connect test light between harness connector term. Note light.
  - Off → Replace air control valve.
  - On → Check for grounded wire from Air Control solenoid to ECM Term. "4." If wire is not grounded, replace ECM.

Constant converter air
- Check divert valve circuit as follows:
  - With remote sol.
    - With engine idling, check for at least 10" of vacuum at Air Control valve.
      - OK → It is faulty Air Control valve.
      - Not OK → It is faulty Air Control sol. conn. or sol.
  - With integral sol.
    - With engine idling, check for at least 10" of vacuum at valve. If OK, it is faulty valve conn. or valve.
- Check air switching valve cir. as follows:
  - Ign. "ON," engine stopped.
  - Ground "test" term.
  - Disconnect applicable sol. electrical connector and connect test light between harness conn. term. and note light.
    - Light On → Check for grounded wire from air switching valve to ECM Term. "B." If not grounded, replace ECM.
      - Light on both term. → Repair short from Bat. + to wire to ECM and replace ECM.
      - Light on one term. → Check for open in wire from applicable sol. to ECM Term. "4" for air control or Term. "B" for air switching. If not open, check resistance of applicable sol. If under 20 ohms, replace sol. and ECM. If not, it is faulty ECM connection or ECM.
    - Light Off → Connect test light from both wire term. to ground and note light.
      - Light On
      - No Light → Repair open in pink wire circuit to ign. switch.

Constant Port Air
- Ign. "ON," engine stopped. "Test" term. not grounded. Disconnect air switching valve sol. electrical conn. and connect test light between harness conn. term. and note light.
  - Light On → Check for grounded wire from air switching valve to ECM Term. "B." If not grounded, replace ECM.
  - Light Off → Replace air switching valve.

ECM — 4 — B — AIR CONT. — AIR SW. — IGN.

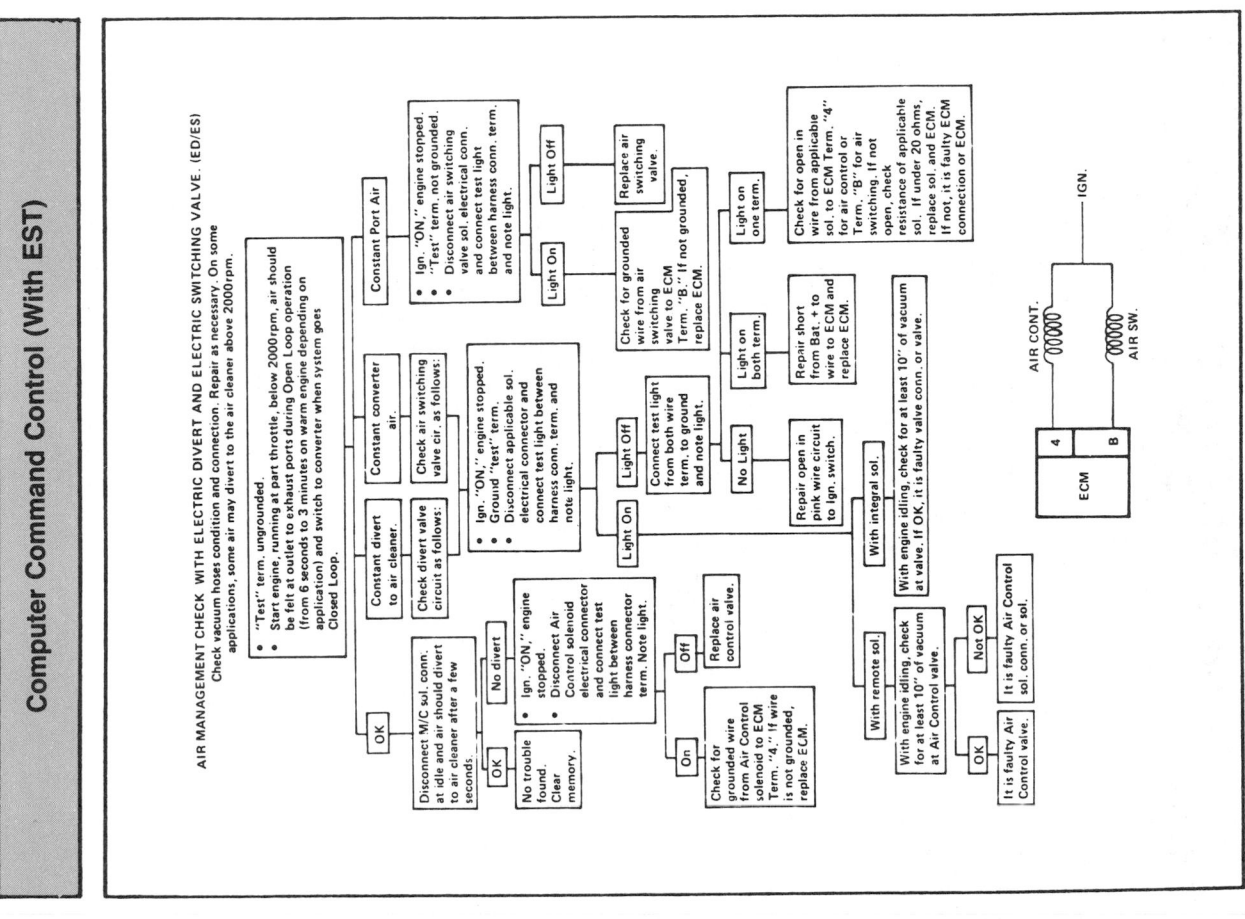

Computer Command Control (With EST)

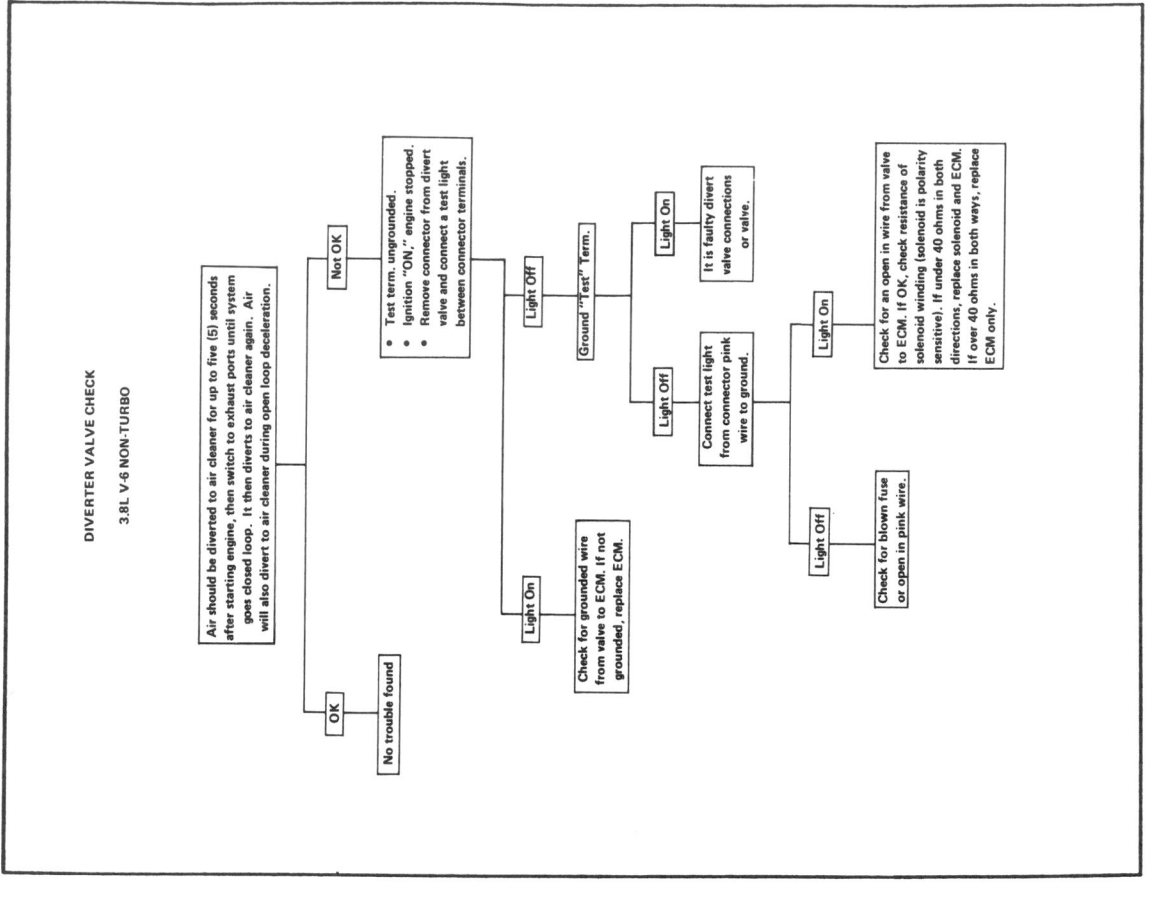

DIVERTER VALVE CHECK

3.8L V-6 NON-TURBO

Air should be diverted to air cleaner for up to five (5) seconds after starting engine, then switch to exhaust ports until system goes closed loop. It then diverts to air cleaner again. Air will also divert to air cleaner during open loop deceleration.

- OK → No trouble found

- Not OK →
  - Test term. ungrounded.
  - Ignition "ON," engine stopped.
  - Remove connector from divert valve and connect a test light between connector terminals.

  - Light On → Check for grounded wire from valve to ECM. If not grounded, replace ECM.

  - Light Off → Ground "Test" Term.
    - Light On → It is faulty divert valve connections or valve.
    - Light Off → Connect test light from connector pink wire to ground.
      - Light On → Check for an open in wire from valve to ECM. If OK, check resistance of solenoid winding (solenoid is polarity sensitive). If under 40 ohms in both directions, replace solenoid and ECM. If over 40 ohms in both ways, replace ECM only.
      - Light Off → Check for blown fuse or open in pink wire.

Computer Command Control (With EST)

PULSAIR SOLENOID CHECK

- With engine stopped, disconnect pulsair solenoid hose from air cleaner.
- Start car and feel for air pulsations at end of hose while engine is run until dwell starts to vary. Pulsations should be felt until dwell starts to vary and then should stop.

- OK → No trouble found in pulsair system.

- NOT OK →
  - Turn ignition "ON," engine stopped.
  - Ground "test" lead.
  - Push throttle to wide-open.

  - Pulsair Solenoid Clicks → Replace Pulsair Solenoid

  - No Click → Connect test light between Pulsair solenoid harness connector terminals with connector disconnected (throttle at idle position).

    - Light Off → Connect test light from Solenoid connector pink wire to ground and note light.
      - Light On → Check for open in wire from solenoid to ECM term. "B." If open, it is faulty ECM connector or ECM.
      - Light Off → Repair open in pink wire circuit.

    - Light On → Push throttle to wide-open position (ignition "ON," engine stopped)
      - Light On → Check for grounded wire from solenoid to ECM term. "B." If not grounded, replace ECM.
      - Light Off → It is faulty solenoid connector solenoid.

Computer Command Control (With EST)

Computer Command Control (With EST)

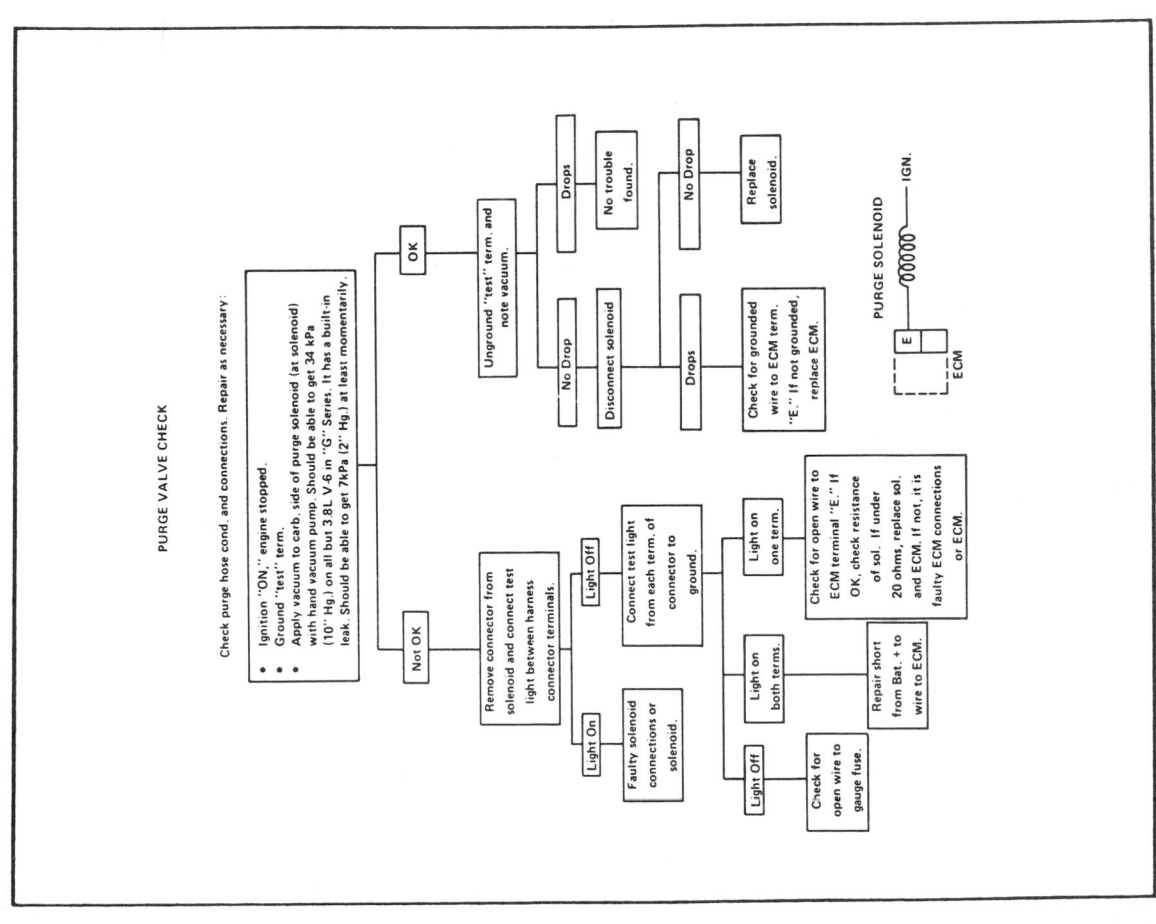

Computer Command Control (With EST)

ESC CHECK
(EST CHECK – CONTINUED)

No-Start Complaint

Ign. "on," check voltage from ESC controller term. "F" to "K."

- Under 10 Volts → Check for open from term. "K" to gn'd. and term. "F" to bat. (include fuse check).
- Over 10 Volts → Jumper Term. "J" and "G" on ESC controller. Reconnect EST connector and try to start engine.
  - Starts → Faulty ESC controller or ESC controller connection.
  - No-Start → Check for open from ECM term. "U" to gn'd. and open or grounded wire to ECM term. "12." If wire is OK, it is faulty ECM connection or ECM.

No Timing Change

Jumper ESC controller term. "C" and "D" and recheck for timing change.

- No Change → With P/N sw. → Disconnect P/N sw. and recheck for timing change.
  - Changes → It is P/N switch adjustment or faulty P/N switch. (see Section 7A)
  - No Change → Check for open wire from ECM terminal "11" to EST connector term. "C." If OK, it is faulty ECM connection or ECM.
- Changes → With P/N sw. / W/O P/N sw. → It is faulty ESC controller connections or controller.

Check for grounded wire fro.m ECM term. "H" to P/N switch.

ECM Term. "12" ——— EST
ECM Term. "11" ——— By-Pass
GRD. ——— Ign.

EST – Term. "A" on EST conn.
By-Pass – Term. "C" on EST conn.
Knock Sensor
Shield

F K D G J C B A
ESC Controller

Computer Command Control (With EST)

ESC PERFORMANCE DIAGNOSTIC

This chart should only be used after other causes of knock have been checked, i.e., timing, lack of EGR, engine temp., etc.

- Engine at fast idle, auto. trans. in "park," manual trans. in "neutral."
- Note timing change as exhaust manifold is tapped with a hammer (nylon or similar mat'l.).

- Retards → No trouble found
- No retard →
  - Disconnect knock sensor.
  - Connect a jumper to knock sensor connector terminal and lay the jumper formed into a loop on top of the distributor, or hold it along a spark plug wire and note timing.
    - Retards → Measure resistance of sensor. Should be 175-375 ohms.
      - OK →
        - Reconnect sensor.
        - Disconnect ECS connector and check resistance from connector Term. "B" to "K." (175-375 ohms)
        - Not OK → Check for an open in wires to "B" and "K."
          - OK → Replace sensor
          - Not OK → Repair harness
      - Not OK → Replace sensor → OK → Replace sensor → OK → Repair sensor connection
    - No retard →
      - Reconnect sensor.
      - Disconnect ESC connector and measure resistance from connector term. "B" to "K." Should be 175-375 ohms.
        - OK → Replace ESC controller
        - Not OK → Repair ESC harness

Computer Command Control (With EST)

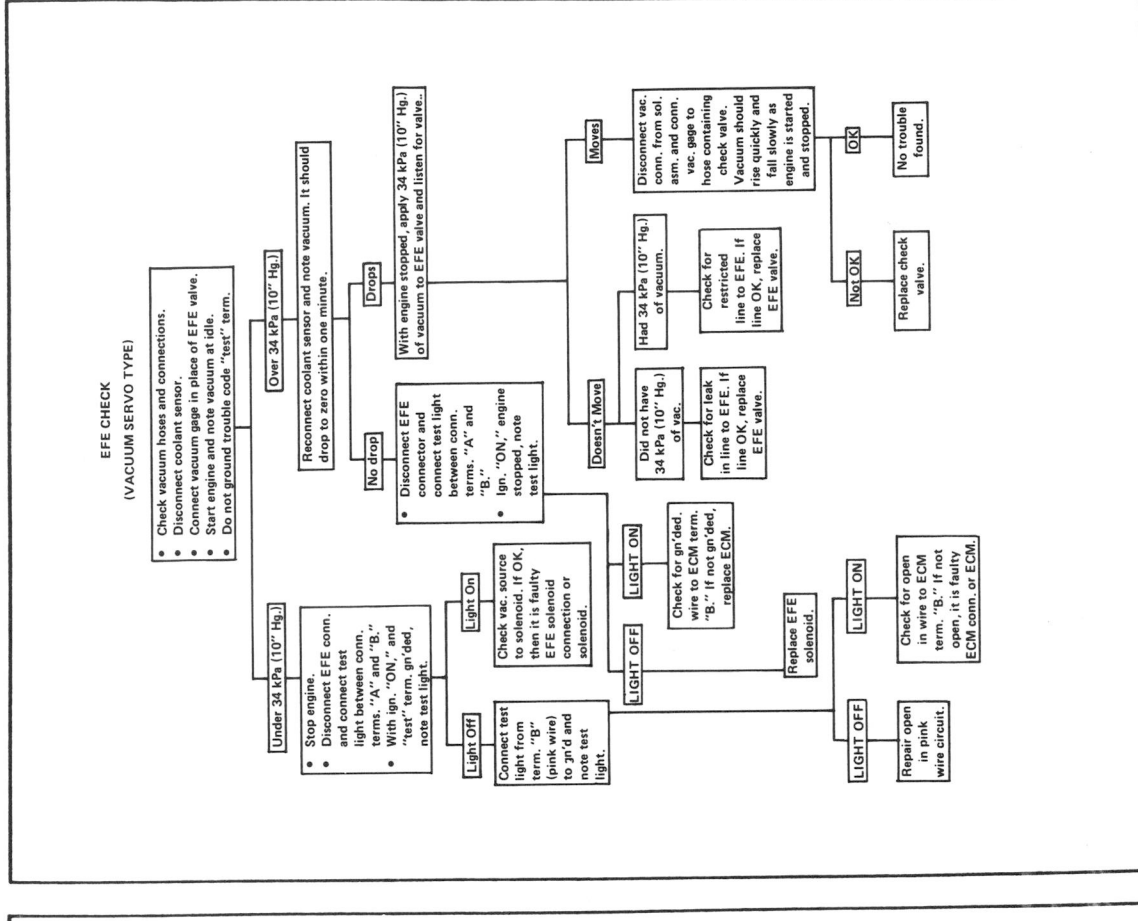

EFE CHECK
(VACUUM SERVO TYPE)

- Check vacuum hoses and connections.
- Disconnect coolant sensor.
- Connect vacuum gage in place of EFE valve.
- Start engine and note vacuum at idle.
- Do not ground trouble code "test" term.

Over 34 kPa (10" Hg.)

Reconnect coolant sensor and note vacuum. It should drop to zero within one minute.

No drop → Drops

Disconnect EFE connector and connect test light between conn. terms. "A" and "B." With ign. "ON," and "test" term. gn'ded, note test light.

With engine stopped, apply 34 kPa (10" Hg.) of vacuum to EFE valve and listen for valve.

Moves → Disconnect vac. conn. from sol. asm. and conn. vac. gage to hose containing check valve. Vacuum should rise quickly and fall slowly as engine is started and stopped.

OK → No trouble found.
Not OK → Replace check valve.

Doesn't Move → Had 34 kPa (10" Hg.) of vacuum.

Check for restricted line to EFE. If line OK, replace EFE valve.

Did not have 34 kPa (10" Hg.) of vac.

Check for leak in line to EFE. If line OK, replace EFE valve.

Under 34 kPa (10" Hg.)

- Stop engine.
- Disconnect EFE conn. and connect test light between conn. terms. "A" and "B." With ign. "ON," and "test" term. gn'ded, note test light.

Light On → Check vac. source to solenoid. If OK, then it is faulty EFE solenoid connection or solenoid.
Light Off → Connect test light from term. "B" (pink wire) to gn'd and note test light.

LIGHT ON → Check for gn'ded. wire to ECM term. "B." If not gn'ded, replace ECM.
LIGHT OFF → Replace EFE solenoid.

LIGHT ON → Check for open in wire to ECM term. "B." If not open, it is faulty ECM conn. or ECM.
LIGHT OFF → Repair open in pink wire circuit.

Computer Command Control (With EST)

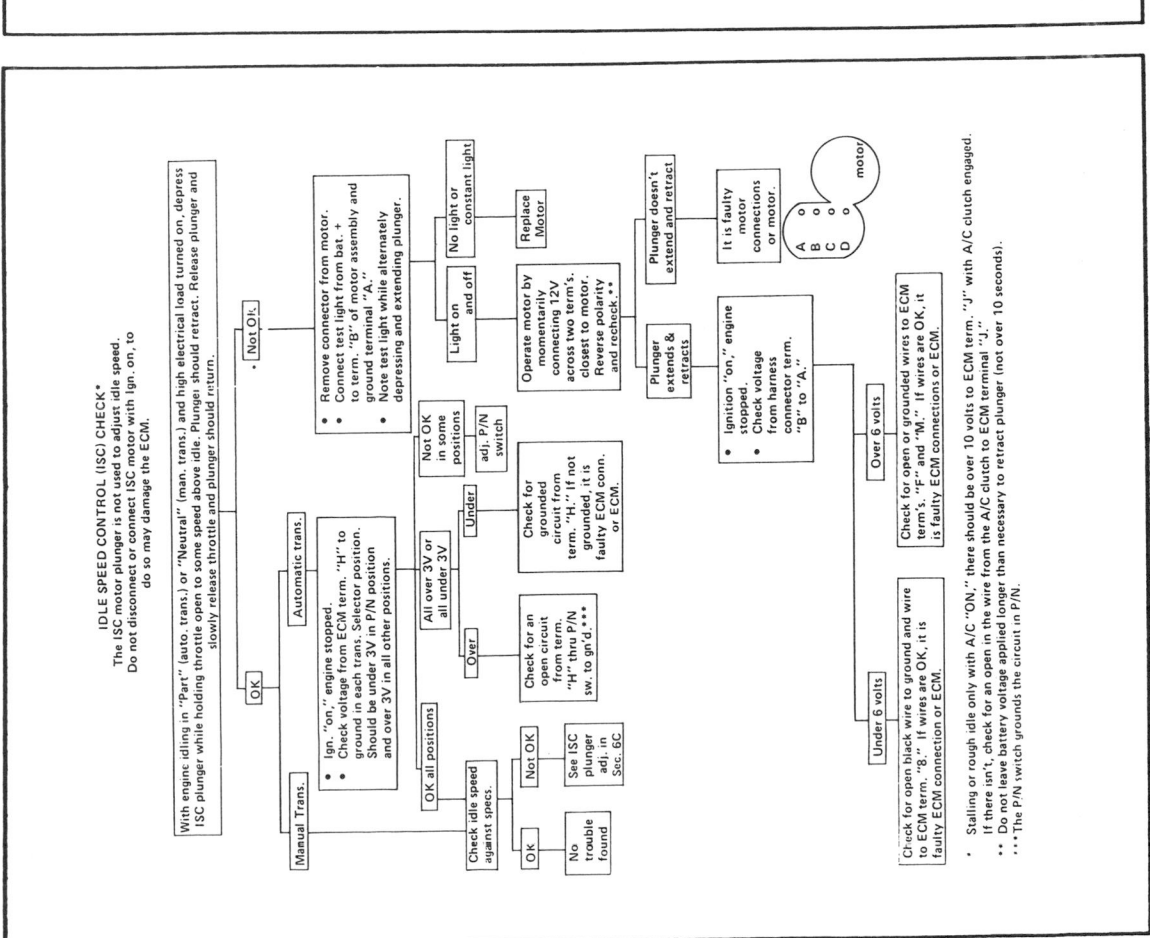

IDLE SPEED CONTROL (ISC) CHECK*
The ISC motor plunger is not used to adjust idle speed.
Do not disconnect or connect ISC motor with ign. on, to do so may damage the ECM.

With engine idling in "Park" (auto. trans.) or "Neutral" (man. trans.) and high electrical load turned on, depress ISC plunger while holding throttle open to some speed above idle. Plunger should retract. Release plunger and slowly release throttle and plunger should return.

OK → Manual Trans. / Automatic trans.
Not OK.

Manual Trans. → Check idle speed agianst specs.
OK → No trouble found.
Not OK → See ISC plunger adj. in Sec. 6C.

Automatic trans. → • Ign. "on," engine stopped.
• Check voltage from ECM term. "H" to ground in each trans. Selector position. Should be under 3V in P/N position and over 3V in all other positions.

OK all positions → All over 3V or all under 3V
Over → Check for an open circuit from term. "H" thru P/N sw. to gn'd.***
Under → Check for grounded circuit from term. "H." If not grounded, it is faulty ECM conn. or ECM.

Not OK in some positions → adj. P/N switch

• Remove connector from motor.
• Connect test light from bat. + to term. "B" of motor assembly and ground terminal "A."
• Note test light while alternately depressing and extending plunger.

Light on and off → Operate motor by momentarily connecting 12V across two term's. closest to motor. Reverse polarity and recheck.**

No light or constant light → Replace Motor

Plunger extends & retracts → • Ignition "on," engine stopped.
• Check voltage from harness connector term. "B" to "A."

Over 6 volts → Check for open or grounded wires to ECM term's. "F" and "M." If wires are OK, it is faulty ECM connections or ECM.
Under 6 volts → Check for open black wire to ground and wire to ECM term. "B." If wires are OK, it is faulty ECM connection or ECM.

Plunger doesn't extend and retract → It is faulty motor connections or motor.

motor
A B C D

* Stalling or rough idle only with A/C "ON," there should be over 10 volts to ECM term. "J" with A/C clutch engaged. If there isn't, check for an open in the wire from the A/C clutch to ECM terminal "J."
** Do not leave battery voltage applied longer than necessary to retract plunger (not over 10 seconds).
*** The P/N switch grounds the circuit in P/N.

Computer Command Control (With EST)

EGR VALVE CHECK
(EXCEPT 5.0L V-8)
- Start warm engine with coolant sensor disconnected.
- Ground test terminal.
- Push up on underside of EGR to open it and note RPM change as valve opens.

Computer Command Control (With EST)

HEATED EFE OPERATION CHECK
- Ignition "on," engine stopped.
- Disconnect coolant sensor.
- Disconnect connector at heater.
- Connect test light between harness connector terminals.

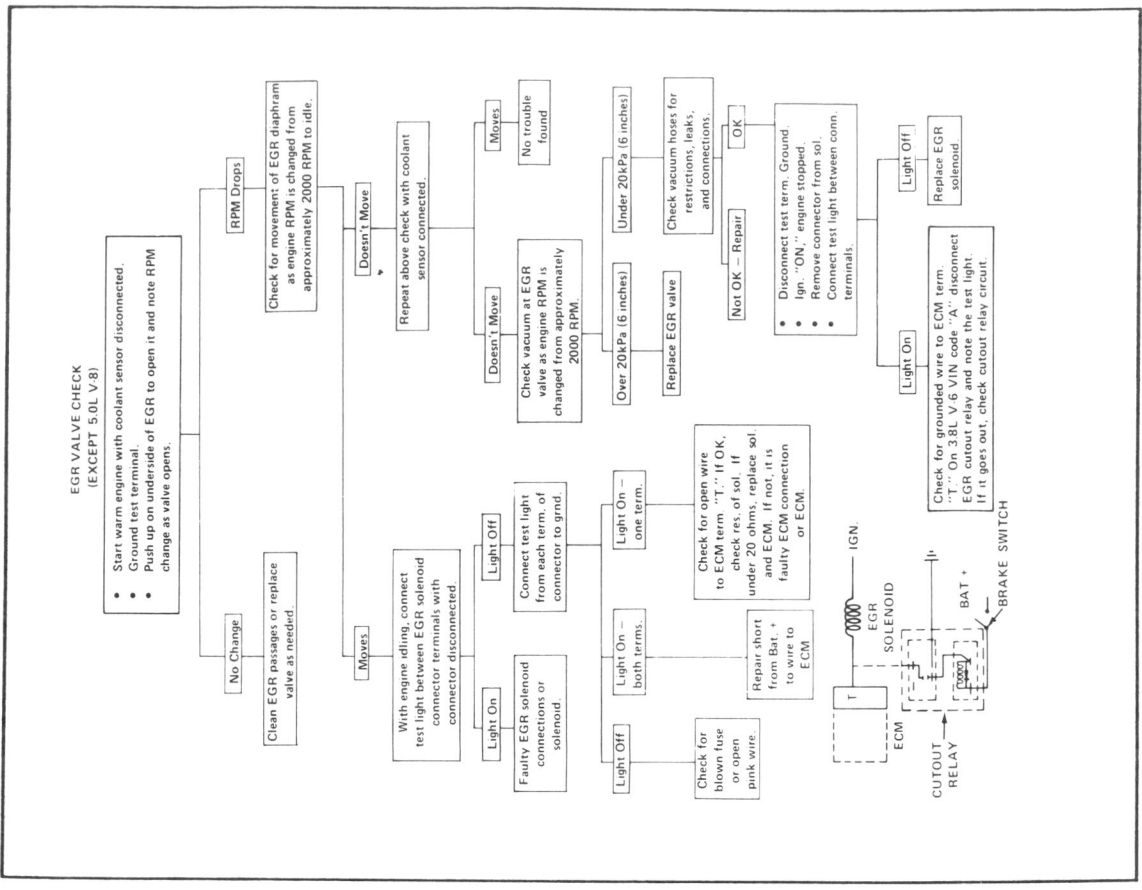

Computer Command Control (With EST)

TCC/EGR BLEED SOLENOID CHECK 5.0L V-8

- Ign. "ON," engine stopped.
- Remove hose from EGR valve and plug hose.
- Apply vacuum to carb. side of EGR bleed solenoid. Should be able to get at least 10".

Not OK. → Remove connector from sol. and connect test light between harness connector terminals and note light.
- **Off** → Replace EGR bleed solenoid.
- **On** → Check for grounded wire to ECM term. "T". If not grounded, replace ECM.

OK → Ground "test" term. and vacuum should drop.
- **OK** → No trouble found.
- **Not OK** → Remove connector from solenoid. Connect test light between harness connector terms. and note light.
  - **Off** → Connect test light from each term. of harness connector to ground and note light.
    - **No light** → Check for open in pink wire circuit.
    - **Light on both term.** → Repair short from bat. + to wire to ECM term. "T".
    - **Light on one terminal** → Check for open in wire to ECM term. "T". If wire is OK, check res. of sol. If under 20 ohms, replace sol. and ECM. If not, it is faulty ECM connection or ECM.
  - **On** → It is faulty sol. connector or solenoid.

IGN. — ECM — T

Transmission Converter Clutch (TCC)

ELECTRICAL DIAGNOSIS
(EXCEPT APPLICATIONS USING TCC/EGR BLEED SOLENOID)

Mechanical checks, such as linkage, oil level, etc., should be performed prior to using this chart. Also, check for a Code "24." If present, see Chart 24.

- Connect test light from T.C.C. test point in Term. "P" in ALCL connector to ground (in fuse block to grnd on "J" car).
- With drive wheels off floor, trans. in gear, increase speed to 35 MPH and note light.

Light on → It is faulty brake switch or adj.

Light off → Check for blown fuse. If OK, disconnect connector at trans. and connect test light from harness connector "A" to "B" term. on two term. connector ("A" to "D" on 4 term. connector) with ignition on, engine stopped, note test light.
- **Light off** → Connect test light from term. "A" to ground.
  - **Light off** → Connect test light from term. "A" to ground.
  - **Light on** → Check for ground in wire to ECM term. "P." If not grounded, replace ECM.

OK → Hold throttle position. Test light should go out as brake pedal is momentarily depressed.
- **Not OK** → Increase speed to 50-55 mph and note light.
  - **Light on** → Lightly depress parking brake and open throttle to maintain 50-55 mph for 5 sec. and note light.

Check volt. from ECM term. "2" to ground with digital V.M. with ign. on, eng. stopped, throttle wide open.
- **Under 1 volt** → Check for gnd'd in wire to ECM term. "2." If not grounded, replace ECM.
- **Over 1 volt** → Engine stopped. Ign. "ON," check volt from ECM term. "16" to gnd'd while turning one drive wheel by hand with the other on the floor. It should alternate from under 3 to over 10.

With 2 wires in trans. conn. → Check TPS adj. On 3.0L V-6 check TCC relay if OK, no trouble found.

With 3 wires in trans. conn. → Ign. "on," eng. stopped, check voltage from ECM term. "N" to ground.
- **Under 6 volts** → Check for open in wire from ECM term. "B." If not open, it is faulty conn. at trans. or open in trans. 4th gear sw.
- **Over 6 volts** → Check TPS adj. If OK, no elec. trouble found.

Connect test light between harness connecter term's. again. Ground trans. test point & note light.
- **Light off** → Repair open in wire from trans. to test point.
- **Light on** → It is faulty conn. at trans. or trans. sol. circuit.

Repair open in TCC brake switch circuit or adj. switch (3.0L V-6 check TCC cutout Relay).

Start engine and with trans. in "D," increase speed to 50-55 mph and note voltage reading.
- **Under 6 volts** → Ign. "ON," engine stopped. Disconnect trans. conn. and check volt from harness conn. term. "B" to ground.
  - **Over 6 volts** → Trans. 4th gear switch is grounded or not opening.
  - **Under 6 volts** → Check for grounded w're to ECM term. "17." If not grounded, it is faulty ECM conn. or ECM.
- **Not OK** → See Code chart 24.

OK → Check TPS adj. Check for low coolant level and higher than normal resistance in coolant sensor circuit. Check T.C.C. sol. resistance if under 20ohms, replace sol. and ECM. If OK, it is faulty ECM connection or ECM.

3RD GEAR SWITCH — BRAKE SWITCH — IGN — ECM

TRANSMISSION — TRANS. CONNECTOR

Computer Command Control—1982 Chevette W/O EST

DIAGNOSTIC CIRCUIT CHECK SYSTEM "A"

Trouble codes are lost when the ignition is turned off. Therefore, on "Check Engine" light complaints, codes should be checked before ignition is turned off, if possible. (See "trouble code memory")

Always check PROM for correct application and installation before replacing an ECM. Also, remove terminal(s) from ECM connector for circuit involved, clean terminal contact and expand it slightly to increase contact pressure and recheck to see f problem is corrected.

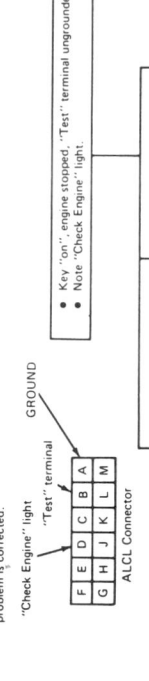

"Check Engine" light
"Test" terminal
GROUND
ALCL Connector

- Key "on", engine stopped. "Test" terminal ungrounded
- Note "Check Engine" light.

Light "Off"
See Chart No. 4

Light "On" steady.

Light flashes

Check for grounded wire to ECM terminal "16". If not grounded, it is faulty ECM.

Ground "test" terminal and note "Check Engine" light.

Does not flash code 12.
See Chart No. 6.

Flashes code 12

- Remove "test" terminal ground.
- Set parking brake with transmission in park (A.T.), neutral (M.T.) and block drive wheels.
- Run warm engine at specified curb idle for 1 minute and note "Check Engine" light.

Light "Off"
See driver complaints on following page.

Light "On"

- Ground "test" terminal and note "Check Engine" light.
- See Applicable trouble code chart.
- If more than one code is stored, start with lowest code unless one is 51, then start with it.

The system performance check should be performed after any repairs to the system have been made.

Computer Command Control—1982 Chevette W/O EST

DRIVER COMPLAINT SYSTEM "A"

ENGINE PERFORMANCE PROBLEM (ODOR, SURGE, FUEL ECONOMY . . .) EMISSION PROBLEM

IF THE "CHECK ENGINE" LIGHT IS NOT ON, NORMAL CHECKS THAT WOULD BE PERFORMED ON CARS WITHOUT THE SYSTEM SHOULD BE DONE FIRST.

IF GENERATOR OR COOLANT LIGHT IS ON WITH THE "CHECK ENGINE" LIGHT, THEY SHOULD BE DIAGNOSED FIRST.

INSPECT FOR POOR CONNECTIONS AT COOLANT SWITCH, M/C SOLENOID, ETC., AND POOR OR LOOSE VACUUM HOSES AND CONNECTIONS. REPAIR AS NECESSARY.

- Intermittent "Check Engine" light but no trouble code stored.

- Check for intermittent connection in circuit from:

  - Battery to ECM terminal "1".
  - ECM terminal "1" to engine ground.
  - ECM terminal "19" to distributor, including tach, filter.

- Open diode across A/C compressor clutch.

- Poor Full Throttle Performance.
  See chart No. 5 – TPS Enrichment Check.

- Cold Operation Problem
  See chart No. 3 – Grounded Coolant Switch Check.

- ALL OTHER COMPLAINTS
  Make system performance check on warm engine
  (Upper radiator hose hot).

Computer Command Control—1982 Chevette W/O EST

SYSTEM PERFORMANCE CHECK SYSTEM "A"

1. Start engine.
2. Do not ground trouble code "test" terminal.
3. Disconnect purge hose from cannister and plug it.
4. Connect tachometer to terminal "6" of engine electrical connector.
5. Disconnect mixture control (M/C) solenoid and ground M/C solenoid dwell lead.
6. Run engine at 3,000 RPM and while keeping throttle constant, reconnect M/C solenoid and note RPM.
7. Remove ground from dwell lead before returning to idle.

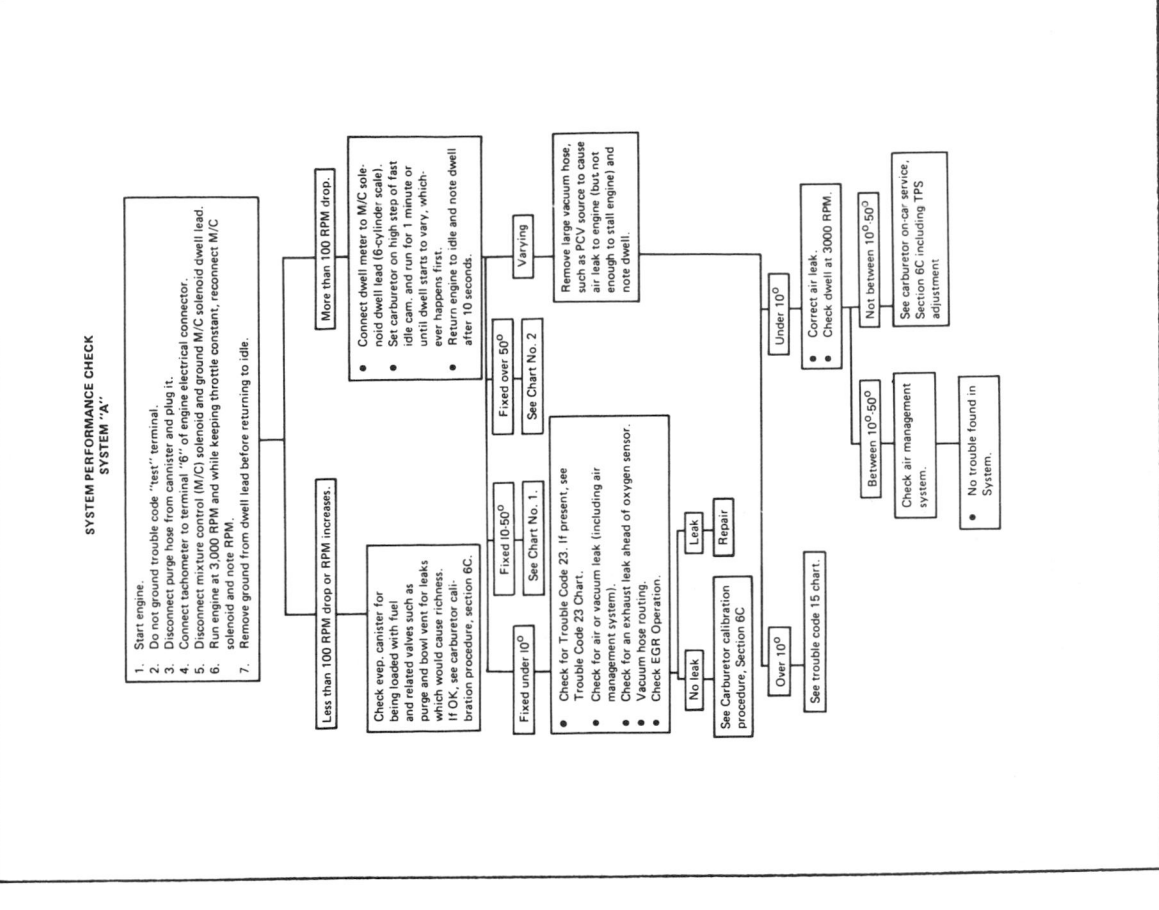

Less than 100 RPM drop or RPM increases.

Check evap. canister for being loaded with fuel and related valves such as purge and bowl vent for leaks which would cause richness. If OK, see carburetor calibration procedure, section 6C.

- Fixed under 10°
- Fixed 10-50° — See Chart No. 1.
- Fixed over 50° — See Chart No. 2.

Check for Trouble Code 23. If present, see Trouble Code 23 Chart.
- Check for air or vacuum leak (including air management system).
- Check for an exhaust leak ahead of oxygen sensor.
- Vacuum hose routing.
- Check EGR Operation.

- No leak → See Carburetor calibration procedure, Section 6C
- Leak → Repair

- Over 10°
- Under 10° → See trouble code 15 chart.

More than 100 RPM drop.

- Connect dwell meter to M/C solenoid dwell lead (6-cylinder scale).
- Set carburetor on high step of fast idle cam, and run for 1 minute or until dwell starts to vary, which-ever happens first.
- Return engine to idle and note dwell after 10 seconds.

Varying

Remove large vacuum hose, such as PCV source to cause air leak to engine (but, not enough to stall engine) and note dwell.

- Under 10°
  - Correct air leak.
  - Check dwell at 3000 RPM
    - Between 10°-50° → Check air management system.
    - Not between 10°-50° → See carburetor on-car service, Section 6C including TPS adjustment
  - No trouble found in System.

Computer Command Control—1982 Chevette W/O EST

CHART NO. 1 SYSTEM "A" DWELL FIXED 10°-50°

(Lean engine, open coolant switch, or open or grounded oxygen sensor circuit.)

Ground "test" terminal and note dwell.

Varying (Closed loop) — See Trouble Code 15 Chart

Fixed

With engine at part throttle, choke engine. (Disregard any dwell variation as throttle is being opened or closed.)

Dwell increased
- Check for Trouble Code 23. If present, see TC 23 Chart.
- Check for air or vacuum leak (including air management system)
- Check for an exhaust leak ahead of oxygen sensor.
- Vacuum hose routing.
- Check EGR Operation.

- Leak → Repair
- No leak → See carburetor on-car service-section 6C.

No dwell increase

- Disconnect oxygen sensor.
- Connect a digital voltmeter with 10 meg-ohms input impedence, set on the 20 volt scale, from battery + to purple wire to ECM (not oxygen sensor).*
- Note dwell.

Dwell increases

Check for open from ECM terminal "20" to ground (including ECM connections). If not open, it is faulty oxygen sensor connection or sensor.

No Dwell Change

Check for an open or grounded purple wire to ECM terminal "3". If not open or grounded, it is faulty ECM connection or ECM.

OXYGEN SENSOR

PURPLE — 3
TAN — 17 / 20
COOLANT SWITCH
ECM

*Do Not use an ordinary voltmeter or jumper in place of digital voltmeter, because they have too little resistance. A voltage source of 1.0V to 1.7V (such as a flashlight battery) can be connected with the positive terminal to the purple wire and the negative terminal to ground as a jumper. If the polarity is reversed, it won't work.

295

Computer Command Control—1982 Chevette W/O EST

CHART NO. 3
SYSTEM "A"
COOLANT SWITCH CIRCUIT CHECK

- Engine temperature must be below 80°F (27°C).
- Ignition "on", engine stopped.
- Disconnect coolant switch and check voltage from connector terminal to ground.

Under 10 volts
→ Check for open or grounded wire from coolant switch to ECM terminal "17": If not open or grounded, it is faulty ECM connection or ECM.

COOLANT SWITCH — 17 — ECM

Over 10 volts
→ Connect test light from Battery + to coolant switch terminal and note light.

Light ON → Replace Coolant Switch.

Light OFF → No trouble found.

Computer Command Control—1982 Chevette W/O EST

CHART NO. 2
SYSTEM "A"
DWELL FIXED OVER 50°
(RICH EXHAUST INDICATION)

Remove large vacuum hose such as PCV source to cause air leak to engine. (But not enough to stall engine.)

No dwell change.
→
- Disconnect oxygen sensor.
- Ground connector terminal on lead to ECM (not oxygen sensor.)

No dwell change. → Replace ECM.

Dwell decreases.
→ Check evap. canister for being loaded with fuel, and related valves such as purge and bowl vent for leaks which would cause richness, also fuel in crankcase. If OK, see carburetor calibration procedure, Section 6C.

Dwell decreases.
→ Check voltage on purple oxygen sensor wire from ECM with digital voltmeter, (sensor disconnected).

Over .5 volt → Repeat voltage check with ECM disconnected.

Under .5 volt → Replace oxygen sensor.

Over .5 volt → Check for short in harness to purple wire from oxygen sensor.

Under .5 volt → Replace ECM.

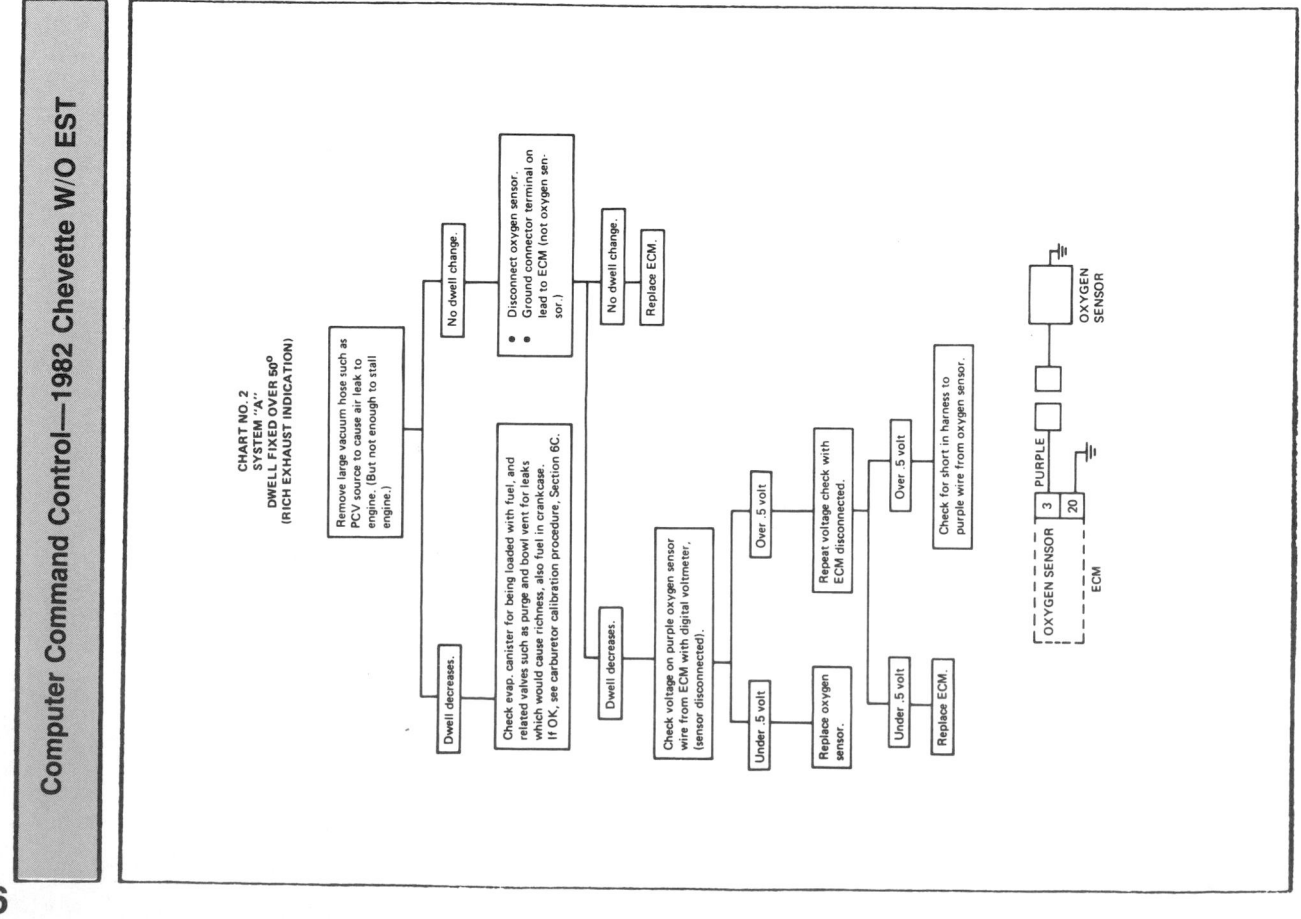

OXYGEN SENSOR — 3
ECM — 20
PURPLE
OXYGEN SENSOR

Computer Command Control—1982 Chevette W/O EST

CHART NO. 5
SYSTEM "A"
TPS ENRICHMENT CHECK

- Ground "test" terminal with ignition "on", engine running at part throttle.
- Connect dwell meter set on 6 cylinder scale to M/C solenoid.
- Depress TPS plunger completely and note dwell.

No dwell change

Under 10° *

Enrichment Circuit OK. Make System Performance Check.

*on high altitude vehicles enrichment circuit is approx 30° M/T or 40° A/T

Disconnect TPS Harness Connector from sensor and note dwell.

No change

Under 10° *

Adjust TPS or replace faulty TPS.

"Check voltage from harness connector terminal "B" to "C" with digital voltmeter J29125-A or equivalent.

Over 2 volts

It is faulty ECM.

Under 2 volts

Check for ground in wire to ECM terminal "5". If not grounded, it is faulty ECM.

WOT
IDLE
A
B
C
TPS

+5 VOLTS
15
5
8
ECM

Computer Command Control—1982 Chevette W/O EST

CHART NO. 4
SYSTEM "A"
"CHECK ENGINE" LIGHT INOPERATIVE

- Ignition "on", engine stopped.
- Ground "Check Engine" lamp terminal in ALCL connector (terminal "D") and note "Check Engine" light.

Light "OFF"

Check for blown gage fuse and open in wire from ALCL to Instrument Panel (I.P.) "Check Engine" light terminal. If not open, it is faulty bulb or connection to it.

Light "ON"

Check voltage from driver terminal "C" to ground.

Over 11 volts

Check for open from lamp driver terminal "D" to ground. If not open, replace lamp driver.

Light "OFF"

Repair open in driver wire to driver terminal "E".

6 to 11 volts

Ground driver terminal "E" and note "Check Engine" light.

Light "ON"

It is faulty driver connection or driver.

Under 6 volts

Check voltage from driver terminal "B" to ground.

Over 10 volts

- Remove wire from driver connector cavity "C".
- Reconnect driver and note "Check Engine" light.

Light "OFF"

It is faulty driver connections or driver.

Light "ON"

Check for grounded wire from driver terminal "C" to ECM terminal "2". If not grounded, replace ECM.

Under 10 volts

Repair open in circuit to gage fuse from terminal "B".

Tc Ignition in I.P.
C. E. Lamp
To ALCL—"D"

Lamp driver

F E D C B A
Driver Terminal

to gages

Ignition

4.7K
15K
12K

B
C
D
E

11
2
ECM

Computer Command Control—1982 Chevette W/O EST

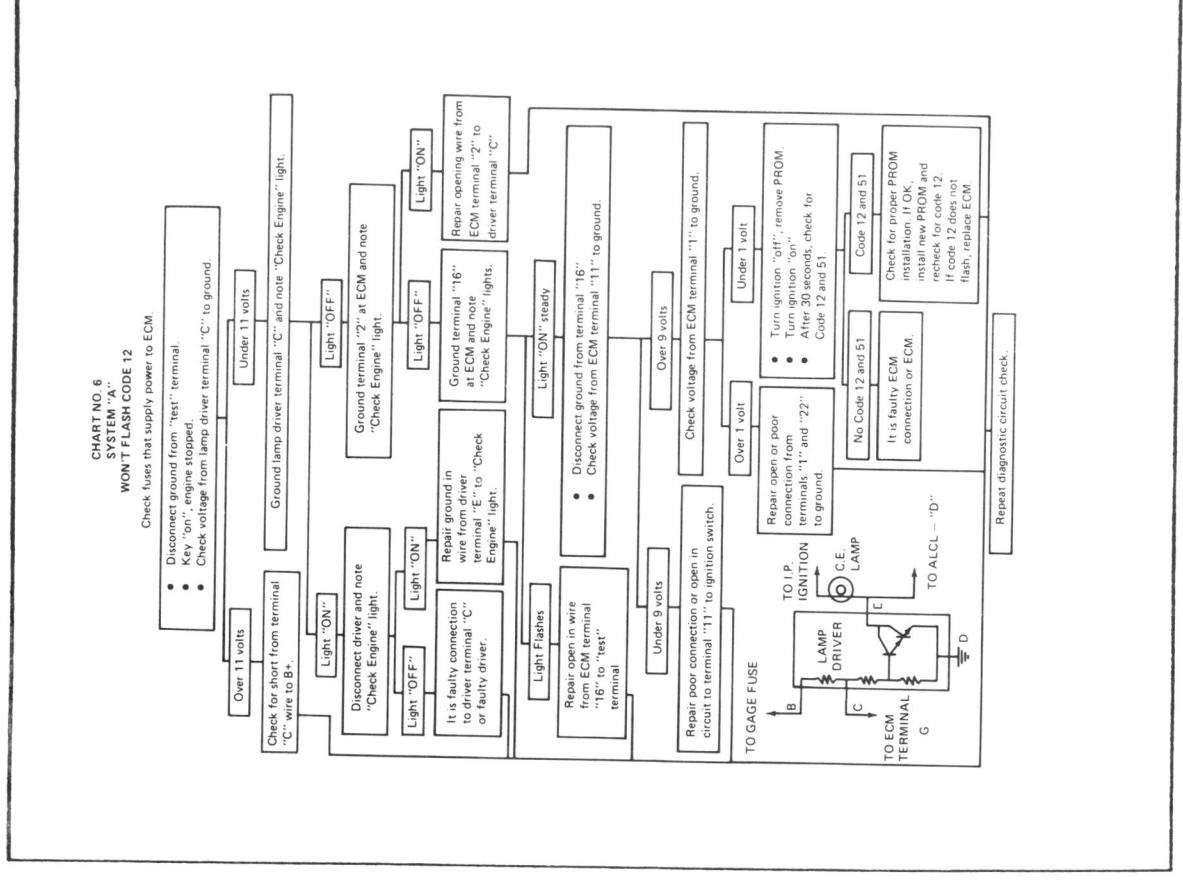

CHART NO. 6
SYSTEM "A"
WON'T FLASH CODE 12

Check fuses that supply power to ECM.

- Disconnect ground from "test" terminal.
- Key "on", engine stopped.
- Check voltage from lamp driver terminal "C" to ground.

Over 11 volts
Check for short from terminal "C" wire to B+.

Under 11 volts
Ground lamp driver terminal "C" and note "Check Engine" light.

Light "ON"
Disconnect driver and note "Check Engine" light.

Light "OFF"
It is faulty connection to driver terminal "C" or faulty driver.

Light "ON"
Repair ground in wire from driver terminal "E" to "Check Engine" light.

Light "OFF"
Ground terminal "2" at ECM and note "Check Engine" light.

Light "OFF"
Ground terminal "16" at ECM and note "Check Engine" lights.

Light "ON"
Repair opening wire from ECM terminal "2" to driver terminal "C".

Light Flashes
Repair open in wire from ECM terminal "16" to "test" terminal

Light "ON" steady
- Disconnect ground from terminal "16".
- Check voltage from ECM terminal "11" to ground.

Under 9 volts
Repair poor connection or open in circuit to terminal "11" to ignition switch.

Over 9 volts
Check voltage from ECM terminal "1" to ground.

Over 1 volt
Repair open or poor connection from terminals "1" and "22" to ground.

Under 1 volt
- Turn ignition "off", remove PROM
- Turn ignition "on"
  After 30 seconds, check for Code 12 and 51.

No Code 12 and 51
It is faulty ECM connection or ECM.

Code 12 and 51
Check for proper PROM installation. If OK, install new PROM and recheck for code 12. If code 12 does not flash, replace ECM

Repeat diagnostic circuit check.

TO I.P. IGNITION
C.E. LAMP
TO ALCL "D"
TO GAGE FUSE
LAMP DRIVER
TO ECM TERMINAL
G

Computer Command Control—1982 Chevette W/O EST

TROUBLE CODE IDENTIFICATION
SYSTEM "A"

The "CHECK ENGINE" light will only be "ON" if the malfunction exists under the conditions listed below. It takes up to five seconds minimum for the light to come on when a problem occurs. If the malfunction clears, the light will go out and a trouble code will be set in the ECM. Code 12 does not store in memory. If the light comes "on" intermittently, but no code is stored, go to the "Driver Complaint" section. Any codes stored will be erased when ignition is turned "OFF".

The trouble codes indicate problems as follows:

TROUBLE CODE 12 — No distributor reference pulses to the ECM. This code is not stored in memory and will only flash while the fault is present.

TROUBLE CODE 15 — Open coolant sensor circuit — The engine must run up to ten minutes before this code will set.

TROUBLE CODE 21 — Throttle position sensor circuit at WOT. The engine must run up to 10 seconds below 1000 RPM, before this code will set.

TROUBLE CODE 23 — M/C solenoid circuit. Must be in closed loop before this code will set.

TROUBLE CODE 44 — Lean exhaust indication — The engine must run up to one minute in closed loop and at part throttle above 2000 RPM before this code will set.

TROUBLE CODE 45 — Rich exhaust indication — The engine must run up to one minute, in closed loop and at part throttle above 2000 RPM before this code will set.

TROUBLE CODE 51 — Faulty calibration unit (PROM) or installation. Turns ECM off.

Computer Command Control—1982 Chevette W/O EST

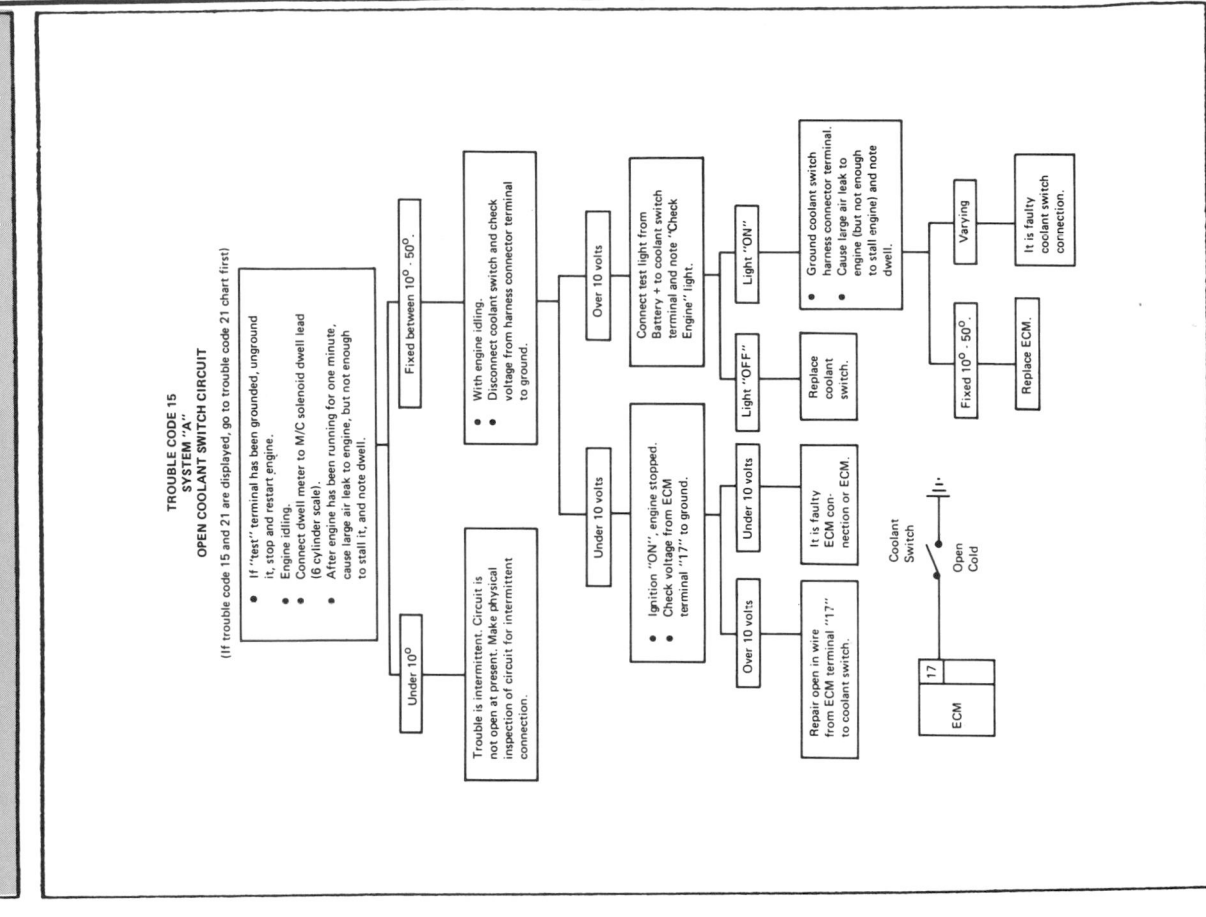

TROUBLE CODE 15
SYSTEM "A"
OPEN COOLANT SWITCH CIRCUIT
(If trouble code 15 and 21 are displayed, go to trouble code 21 chart first)

- If "test" terminal has been grounded, unground it, stop and restart engine. Engine idling.
- Connect dwell meter to M/C solenoid dwell lead (6 cylinder scale).
- After engine has been running for one minute, cause large air leak to engine, but not enough to stall it, and note dwell.

Fixed between 10° - 50°.

Under 10°

Trouble is intermittent. Circuit is not open at present. Make physical inspection of circuit for intermittent connection.

- With engine idling.
- Disconnect coolant switch and check voltage from harness connector terminal to ground.

Over 10 volts

Under 10 volts

- Ignition "ON", engine stopped. Check voltage from ECM terminal "17" to ground.

Over 10 volts

Under 10 volts

Repair open in wire from ECM terminal "17" to coolant switch.

It is faulty ECM connection or ECM.

Connect test light from Battery + to coolant switch terminal and note "Check Engine" light.

Light "ON"

Light "OFF"

Replace coolant switch.

- Ground coolant switch harness connector terminal.
- Cause large air leak to engine (but not enough to stall engine) and note dwell.

Varying

Fixed 10° - 50°

It is faulty coolant switch connection.

Replace ECM.

Coolant Switch

Open Cold

ECM 17

Computer Command Control—1982 Chevette W/O EST

TROUBLE CODE 12
SYSTEM "A"
NO DISTRIBUTOR REFERENCE PULSE TO THE ECM

Check connections at tach. filter assembly.

OK

Not OK

Repair

- Ignition "on", engine stopped.
- Using meter J29125-A, check voltage from ECM side of tach. filter to ground.

Over 4 volts

Under 4 volts

Check for open in wire from filter to ECM terminal "19". If wire is OK, it is faulty ECM connection or ECM.

Disconnect wire from tach. filter to ECM and recheck voltage at filter side of connector.

Over 4 volts

Under 4 volts

Check for grounded wire from tach. filter to ECM terminal "19". If not grounded, replace ECM.

Check voltage at tach. lead from distributor with it disconnected from tach. filter. (Use terminal "6" of engine electrical connector.)

Over 4 volts

Under 4 volts

Replace tach. filter.

Repair open in wire from filter to tach. terminal of distributor.

ECM 19

Tach. Filter

Dist.

Computer Command Control—1982 Chevette W/O EST

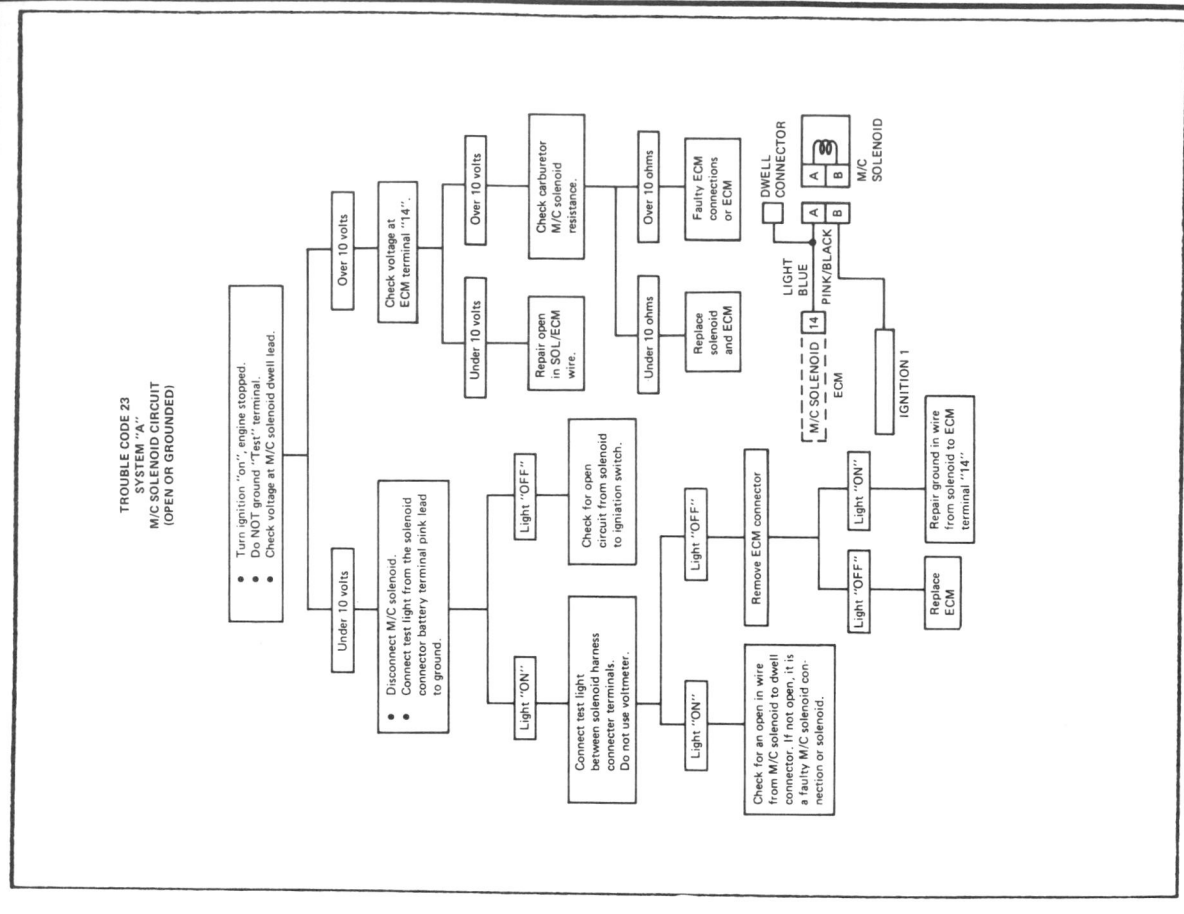

TROUBLE CODE 23
SYSTEM "A"
M/C SOLENOID CIRCUIT
(OPEN OR GROUNDED)

- Turn ignition "on", engine stopped.
- Do NOT ground "Test" terminal.
- Check voltage at M/C solenoid dwell lead.

Over 10 volts

Check voltage at ECM terminal "14".

- Over 10 volts → Check carburetor M/C solenoid resistance.
  - Over 10 ohms → Faulty ECM connections or ECM
  - Under 10 ohms → Replace solenoid and ECM
- Under 10 volts → Repair open in SOL/ECM wire.

Under 10 volts

- Disconnect M/C solenoid.
- Connect test light from the solenoid connector battery terminal pink lead to ground.

- Light "OFF" → Check for open circuit from solenoid to ignition switch.
  - Light "OFF" → Remove ECM connector
    - Light "ON" → Repair ground in wire from solenoid to ECM terminal "14".
    - Light "OFF" → Replace ECM
  - Light "ON" → Check for an open in wire from M/C solenoid to dwell connector. If not open, it is a faulty M/C solenoid connection or solenoid.
- Light "ON" → Connect test light between solenoid harness connecter terminals. Do not use voltmeter.

DWELL CONNECTOR   M/C SOLENOID

M/C SOLENOID 14   PINK/BLACK   B
ECM   LIGHT BLUE   A
IGNITION 1

Computer Command Control—1982 Chevette W/O EST

TROUBLE CODE 21
SYSTEM "A"
THROTTLE POSITION SENSOR CIRCUIT
(OPEN OR MISADJUSTED)

This may also set trouble code 44 if altitude compensation lead is grounded. Enrichment under this condition is about 30°.

Check for stuck or misadjusted TPS Plunger. Repair as necessary. If OK, proceed:

- Connect dwell meter to M/C solenoid — use 6 cylinder scale.
- Disconnect TPS harness connector from sensor.
- Check voltage from harness connector terminal "A" to "C", then "B" to "C" with a digital voltmeter J29125-A and ignition "ON", engine stopped.

Both over 2 volts.

- Start engine and let it idle.
- Jumper harness connector terminal "B" to "C" and note dwell.

- Over 10° → Check TPS connector terminal connections.
  - OK → Check TPS resistance from "A" to "B" then "A" to "C".
    - Both under 20,000 ohms. → Adjust TPS, see section 6C. If unable to adjust, replace TPS.
    - Any over 20,000 ohms. → Replace TPS Sensor
  - Not OK → Repair
- Under 10° → Replace ECM

Either or both under 2 volts.

Check voltage from ECM terminal "15" to "8" and "5" to "8".

- Both over 2 volts. → Repair open in harness to TPS.
- Either or both under 2 volts. → Faulty ECM Connections or ECM.

+5 VOLTS 15 GRAY 416 A W.O.T.
TPS 5 DK BLUE 417 B
GROUND 8 BLACK 452 C IDLE
ECM   TPS

Computer Command Control—1982 Chevette W/O EST

**TROUBLE CODE 45
SYSTEM "A"
RICH EXHAUST INDICATION**

If M/C solenoid does not click with ignition "ON" "TEST" terminal grounded and there is no trouble code 23, check for sticking solenoid.

- Over 50°.
- Under 50°.
- Trouble is intermittent. System is OK at present.

With engine idling, note dwell. Remove large vacuum hose (such as PCV source) to cause air leak (but not enough to stall engine).

- No dwell change.
- Dwell decreased.

Check that pink wire is attached to right-hand terminal of M/C solenoid connector, as viewed from harness end.
- Check evap. canister for being loaded with fuel and related valves such as purge and bowl vent for leaks which would cause richness, also fuel in crankcase. If OK, see carburetor calibration procedure, section 6C.

Disconnect oxygen sensor.
- Ground connector terminal on lead to ECM (not oxygen sensor).

- No dwell change.
- Dwell drops to under 10°.

Ground terminal "3" at ECM and note dwell.

- No dwell change.
- Dwell drops to under 10°.

Ignition "ON", engine stopped. Remove ground from O₂ harness connector and check voltage from that terminal to ground with digital voltmeter.

- It is faulty ECM.
- Repair open or short in wire from oxygen sensor to ECM terminal "3".

- Over .55 volts.
- Under .55 volts.
- It is faulty oxygen sensor.

Check wire from ECM terminal "9" for short to battery +. If not shorted, it is faulty ECM.

[ECM diagram: 3, 20, O₂]

**TROUBLE CODE 51
PROM PROBLEM**

Check that all PROM pins are fully seated in socket. If OK, replace PROM and recheck. If 51 reappears, replace ECM.

Computer Command Control—1982 Chevette W/O EST

**TROUBLE CODE 44
SYSTEM "A"
LEAN EXHAUST INDICATION**

If M/C solenoid does not click with ignition "ON" and "TEST" terminal grounded and there is no Code 23, check for sticking solenoid.

- Ground test terminal.
- Connect dwell meter to M/C solenoid — use 6-cylinder scale.
- Run engine at 3000 RPM and note dwell after one minute of running time.

- Under 10°.
- Between 10°-50°.
- Replace Oxygen Sensor

With engine at part throttle, choke engine.

- No dwell change.
- Dwell Increases

Check for air leak (including air management system).
- Check for exhaust leak ahead of oxygen sensor.

- Leak — Repair
- No leak
- See Carburetor Calibration Procedure Section 6C.

Disconnect oxygen sensor.
- Connect digital multimeter J29125-A or equivalent and set on the 20 volts scale, from battery + to purple wire to ECM (nct oxygen sensor).*
- Note dwell.*

- Dwell Increases
- Dwell Under 10°

Check for open circuit from ECM terminal "20" to ground. If not open, it is faulty oxygen sensor connector or oxygen sensor.

Check for grounded or open circuit to ECM terminal "3". If circuit is not open or grounded, it is faulty ECM connection or ECM.

[Diagram: OXYGEN SENSOR, PURPLE 3, TAN 20, ECM, OXYGEN SENSOR]

*Do not use an ordinary voltmeter or jumper in place of the digital voltmeter because they have too little resistance. A voltage source of 1.0V to 1.7V (such as a flashlight battery) can be connected with the positive terminal to the purple wire and the negative terminal to ground as a jumper. If the polarity is reversed, it won't work.

Computer Command Control—1982 Chevette W/O EST

ENGINE CRANKS BUT WILL NOT RUN SYSTEM "A"

IF A TACHOMETER IS CONNECTED TO THE TACHOMETER TERMINAL, DISCONNECT IT BEFORE PROCEEDING WITH THE TEST.

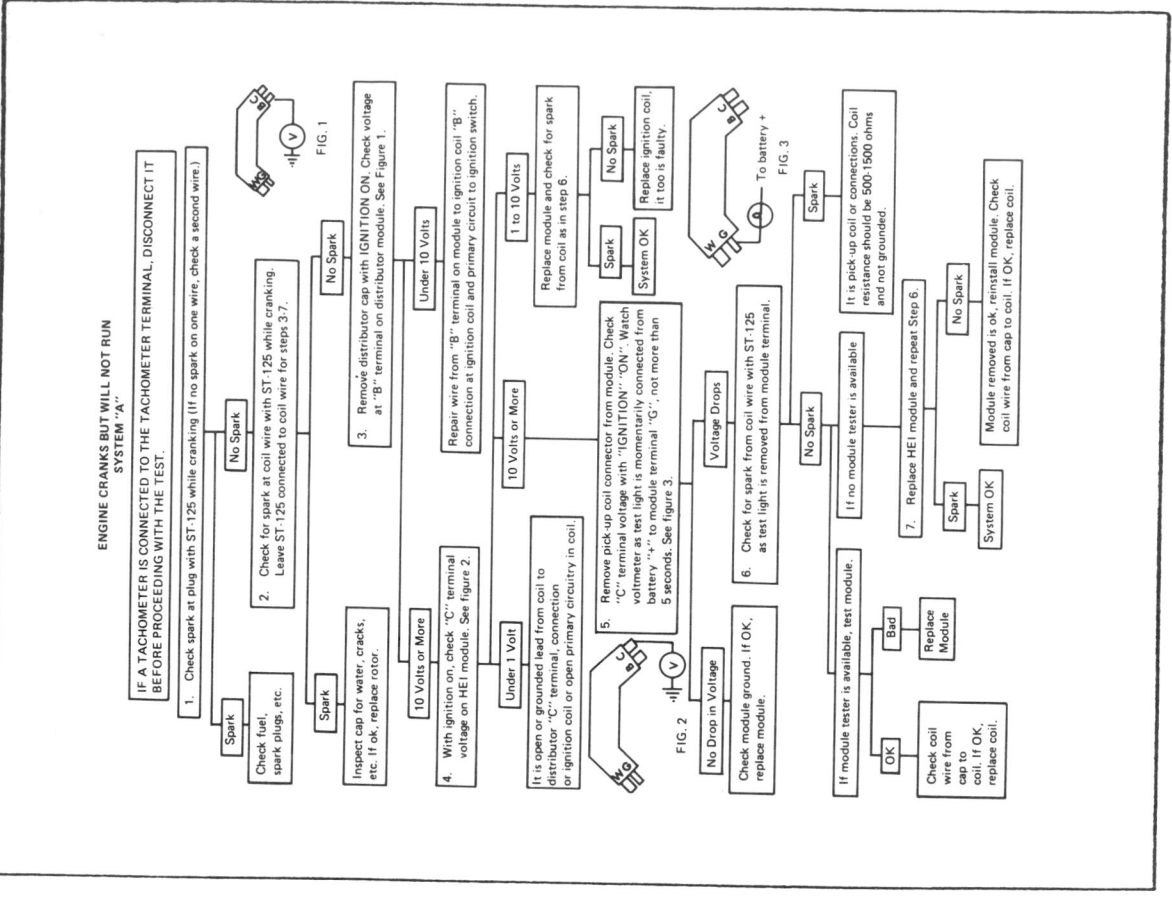

1. Check spark at plug with ST-125 while cranking (If no spark on one wire, check a second wire.)
   - Spark → Check fuel, spark plugs, etc.
   - No Spark

2. Check for spark at coil wire with ST-125 while cranking. Leave ST-125 connected to coil wire for steps 3-7.
   - Spark → Inspect cap for water, cracks, etc. If ok, replace rotor.
   - No Spark

3. Remove distributor cap with IGNITION ON. Check voltage at "B" terminal on distributor module. See Figure 1.
   - 10 Volts or More
   - Under 10 Volts → Repair wire from "B" terminal on module to ignition coil "B" connection at ignition coil and primary circuit to ignition switch.

4. With ignition on, check "C" terminal voltage on HEI module. See figure 2.
   - 10 Volts or More → It is open or grounded lead from coil to distributor "C" terminal, connection or ignition coil or open primary circuitry in coil.
   - Under 1 Volt

5. Remove pick-up coil connector from module. Check "C" terminal voltage with "IGNITION" "ON". Watch voltmeter as test light is momentarily connected from battery "+" to module terminal "G", not more than 5 seconds. See figure 3.
   - Voltage Drops → Check module ground. If OK, replace module.
   - No Drop in Voltage

6. Check for spark from coil wire with ST-125 as test light is removed from module terminal.
   - Spark → 1 to 10 Volts → Replace module and check for spark from coil as in step 6.
     - Spark → System OK
     - No Spark → Replace ignition coil, it too is faulty.
   - No Spark → If no module tester is available, test module.
     - If module tester is available, test module.
       - OK → Check coil wire from cap to coil. If OK, replace coil.
       - Bad → Replace Module

7. Replace HEI module and repeat Step 6.
   - Spark → System OK
   - No Spark → Module removed is ok, reinstall module. Check coil wire from cap to coil. If OK, replace coil.

It is pick-up coil or connections. Coil resistance should be 500-1500 ohms and not grounded.

FIG. 1

FIG. 2

FIG. 3

To battery +

Computer Command Control—1982 Chevette W/O EST

PULSAIR CONTROL VALVE CHECK SYSTEM "A"

Make physical check of pulsair hoses and connections.

- With engine stopped, disconnect pulsair valve hose from air cleaner. Disconnect the pulse air pipe from PCV air intake in rocker cover and plug that end of the pipe.
- Start car and feel for air pulsations at end of pipe while engine is idling. Pulsations should be felt within 15 seconds after starting and stop.
  - OK → No trouble found in pulse air system.
  - Not OK → Check for at least 10" of vacuum at valve with engine idling.
    - OK → Ground "test" terminal. Connect test light between Pulsair solenoid harness connector terminal with connector disconnected.
    - Not OK → Repair vacuum source.

Light "OFF":
- Connect test light from each solenoid harness connector terminal to ground and note light.
  - Light "ON" one terminal. → Check for open in wire from solenoid to ECM terminal "10". If not open, check resistance of pulsair valve solenoid. If under 30 ohms, replace solenoid and ECM; if not, it is faulty ECM connection or ECM.
  - Light "OFF". → Repair open in circuit from sol. to ignition switch.

Light "ON" both terminals. → Repair short to B+ and recheck. ECM may be damaged.

Light "ON":
- Unground "test" terminal and note light.
  - Light "OFF" → It is faulty solenoid connector or solenoid.
  - Light "ON" → Check for grounded wire from solenoid to ECM terminal 10. If not grounded, replace ECM.

ECM — 10

Control Valve

Ignition

Computer Command Control—1982 Chevette W/O EST

AIR MANAGEMENT CHECK SYSTEM "A"
WITH ELECTRIC DIVERT AND ELECTRIC SWITCHING VALVE

Check vacuum hoses condition and connection. Repair as necessary. On some applications, some air may divert to the air cleaner above 2000 RPM.

- "Test" term. ungrounded.
- Start engine, running at part throttle, below 2000 RPM, air should be felt at outlet to exhaust ports during Open Loop operation (approx. 15 sec.) on warm engine and switch to converter when system goes Closed Loop.

Constant Port Air.

- Ign. "on", engine stopped.
- "Test" term. not grounded.
- Disconnect air switching valve sol. electrical conn. and connect test light between harness conn. term. and note light.

Light "OFF" — Replace air switching valve.

Light "ON" — Check for grounded wire from air switching valve to ECM term. "10". If not grounded, replace ECM.

Light "ON" one terminal — Check for open in wire from applicable sol. to ECM term. "13" for air switch. or term. "10" for air switch. If not open, check resistance of applicable sol. If under 20 ohms, ECM. If not, it is faulty ECM connection or ECM.

Light "ON" both terminals — Repair short from Bat. + to wire to ECM and replace ECM.

Constant converter air.

Constant divert to air cleaner.

Check air switching valve cir. as follows:
- Ign. "on", engine stopped.
- Ground "test" term.
- Disconnect applicable sol. electrical connector and connect test light between harness conn. term. and note light.

Light "OFF" — Connect test light from both wire term. to ground and note light.

Light "ON"

Light "OFF" — Repair open in pink wire circuit to ignition switch.

With engine idling, check for at least 10" of vac. of valve. If OK, it is faulty valve conn. or valve.

OK

Check divert valve circuit as follows:

No divert

Disconnect M/C sol. conn. at idle and air should divert to air cleaner after a few seconds.

OK

No trouble found. Clear memory.

- Ign. "on", engine stopped.
- Disconnect Air control solenoid electrical connector and connect test light between harness connector terminal. Note light.

Light "OFF" — Replace air control valve.

Light "ON" — Check for grounded wire from Air divert solenoid to ECM term. "13". If wire is not grounded, replace ECM.

ECM — 13 Air Divert — 10 Air Switch — Ign.

ECM Connector Circuit Identification—Fuel Injection

FUEL INJECTION
ECM CONNECTOR CIRCUIT IDENTIFICATION

White Power Connector

Pin	Top	Pin	Bottom
24	Spare	1	Spare
23	E-Cell	2	Vehicle Speed Sensor
22	4th Gear Switch	3	Diagnostic Test ALCL
21	A/C Clutch	4	Electronic Spark Control
20	Check Engine Light	5	Park/Neutral Switch
19	Converter Clutch	6	Dual Injector Select
18	Fuel Pump Relay Drive	7	Serial Data
17	Fuel Pump Relay Signal	8	Injector #1
16	Switched Ignition	9	Injector #2
15	Battery	10	Battery
14	MAP Ground	11	5 Volt Reference
13	ECM Ground	12	ECM Ground

Black I/O Connector

Pin	Top	Pin	Bottom
22	EGR	1	Crank Signal
21	Spare	2	HEI Reference
20	Manifold Absolute Pressure Signal	3	HEI Dist Ground
19	EST Signal	4	Coolant Sensor Signal
18	I.A.C. Coil "A" Lo	5	T P S. Signal
17	I.A.C. Coil "A" Hi	6	3rd Gear Signal
16	Air Divert So.	7	A/C Realy or Hood Louvre Control
15	Oxygen Sensor Ground	8	Oxygen Sensor Signal
14	Air Switch Sol	9	Cooling Fan or Cannister Purge
13	I.A.C. Coil "B" Lo	10	EST Bypass
12	I.A.C. Coil "B" Hi	11	Coolant & TPS Ground

ALCL Connector: Diagnostic Terminal, Ground, T.C.C., A.I.R., Fuel Pump Test

CHART 1
Driver's Complaint

- Intermittent "check engine" light or stored codes.

NOTICE: Do not use diagnostic charts for intermittent problems. The fault must be present to locate the problem. If the fault is intermittent, use of the charts may result in the replacement of non-defective parts.

Most intermittent problems are caused by faulty electrical connectors or wiring. Diagnosis must include a careful visual and physical inspection of the indicated circuit wiring and connectors.

— Poor mating of the connector halves or terminals not fully seated in connector body (backed out "terminals").

— Improperly formed or damaged terminals. All connector terminals in problem circuit should be carefully reformed to increase contact tension.

— HEI distributor EST wires should be routed away from distributor, ignition coil, secondary wiring and generator.

— CKT 419 — "Check Engine Lamp" to ECM, short to ground.

— CKT 451 — Diagnostic connector to ECM, short to ground.

— Electrical system interference caused by a defective relay, ECM driven solenoid, or a switch causing a sharp electrical surge. Normally, the problem will occur when the defective component is operated.

— Open Air Conditioning clutch diode.

- Stalling, rough or improper idle speed — see Chart 11.

- Engine cranks but will not run — see Chart 4.

- Hard starting, poor performance, driveability or fuel economy—see Chart 7.

- Detonation (spark knock)
  — ESC Performance Chart 10, if applicable
  — EGR Chart 8.

Following any repairs or adjustments, always clear codes and confirm "Closed Loop" operation and no "Check Engine" light.

Diagnostic Circuit Check—Fuel Injection

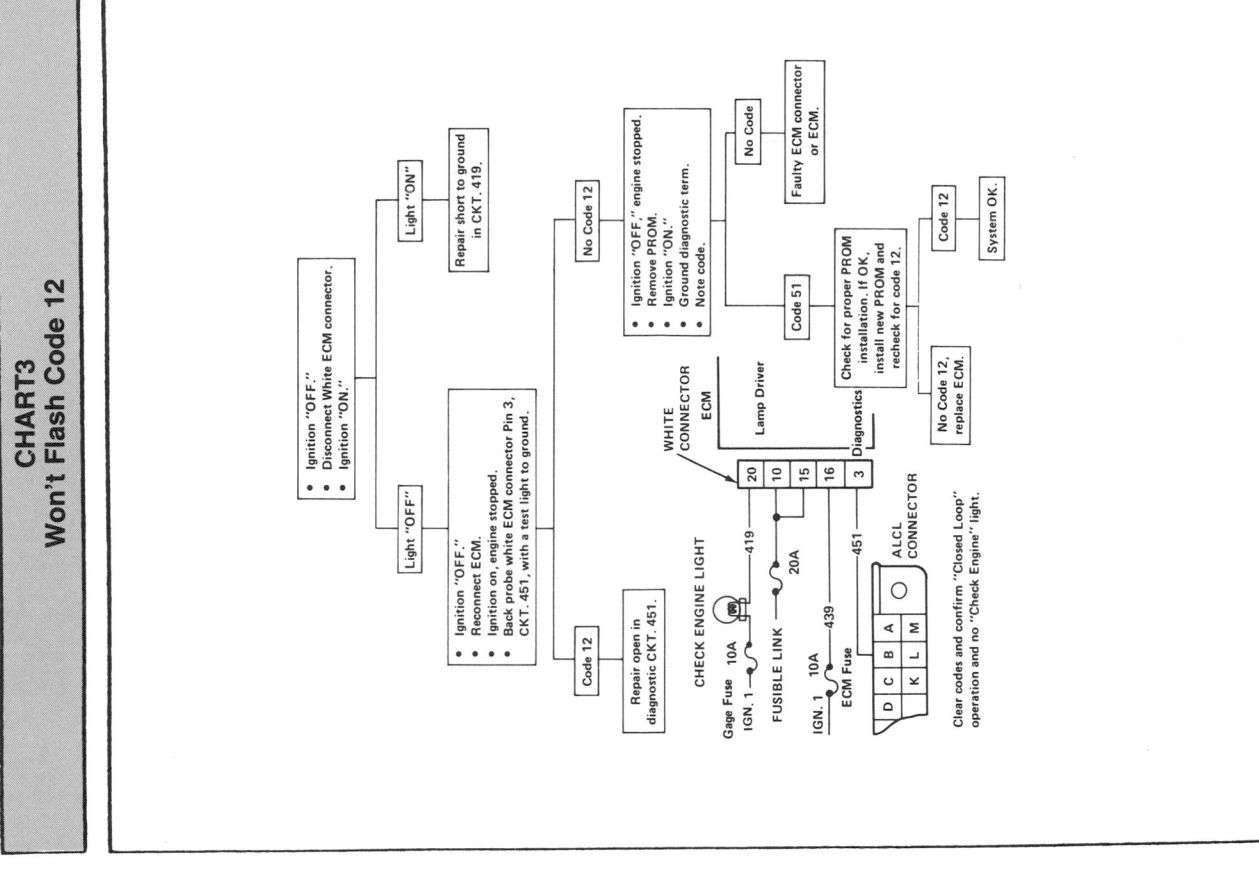

CHARTS 4 and 5
Fuel Injection Schematic—2.5L

CHART 4
2.5L Fuel Injection

CHART 5 — 2.5L Fuel System

*Notice: EFI system under pressure to avoid spillage. Refer to field service procedures for testing or making repairs requiring disassembly of fuel lines or fittings.

- Fuel quantity OK.
- Install fuel pressure gage.
- Note pressure while cranking.

Test Point One

- No pressure
  - Check fuel pump fuse. — OK
- Pressure but less than 10 psi. → See Chart 5A
- Above 12 psi.

- Disconnect oil pressure switch.
- Probe ALDL connector term. "G" with a test light to ground.
- Note light while cranking.

Light "ON" / Light "OFF"

- Apply battery voltage to ALDL term. "G."
- Listen for pump running at fuel tank.

Pump Runs → Check for restricted in-line fuel filter or pressure line. If OK, remove in tank pump assembly and check for restricted inlet filter or leaking pump rubber coupling. → Replace intank fuel pump.

Pump Not Running → Check for an open CKT 120 or open pump ground CKT 150. → CKT 120 and 150 OK.

- Remove pump relay.
- Ignition "ON," engine stopped.
- Probe harness connector terminal "E." bat. CKT 939 with a test light to ground.

Light "ON" / Light "OFF"

- Disconnect fuel pump at rear body connector.
- Ignition "OFF."
- Probe ALDL connector terminal "G," CKT 120, with a test light to 12 volts.

Light "ON" / Light "OFF" → Reconnect fuel pump. Ignition "ON." Recheck fuse.

Repair short to ground in CKT 120.

Fuel pump or pump harness shorted to ground.

Defective fuse or intermittent short to ground in CKT 120 OK fuel pump.

OK / Not OK

Above 12 psi.

RELAY HARNESS CONNECTOR — RELAY END VIEW
C B A / E D

- Connect test light between harness connector terminals "C" and "E." CKTS 450 and 940.
  - Light "ON" → Repair open CKT 940.
  - Light "OFF" → Repair open ground CKT 450.

- Connect test light between terminals "A" and "C." CKTS 465 and 450. Note light while cranking engine.
  - Light "OFF" → Check for open or short to CKT 465.
    - CKT 465 OK. / CKT 465 Not OK
  - Light "ON"

Repair CKT 465. If CKT was shorted to ground, recheck for "Light ON" between harness conn. Terms. "A" and "C" while cranking engine.

- Check resistance across pump relay Pins 1 and 3. Should measure 20 ohms or more.
  - OK → Replace ECM
  - Not OK → Replace pump relay and ECM, if

- Connect test light between harness connector terminals CKT 120 and CKT 940.
  - Light → Probe oil pressure switch harness connector terminal CKT 940 (pink wire) with test light to ground.
    - No Light → Repair open CKT 940, reconnect oil pressure switch and install new pump relay.
    - Light → Install new pump relay.
  - Repair open CKT 120 reconnect oil pressure switch and install new relay.

- No Light → Faulty ECM
- Light → Reconnect oil pressure switch.

CHART 5 (Page 2 of 2)

FUEL INJECTION
2.5L FUEL SYSTEM DIAGNOSIS

CAUTION: EFI fuel system under pressure. To avoid personal injury, use care when testing or making repairs requiring the disassembly of fuel line or fittings.

- Fuel tank quantity OK.
- Ignition "OFF" ten seconds.
- Note fuel pressure within two seconds after ignition "ON."

- No Pressure → See Page 1
- Has Pressure But Less Than 9 PSI
- Above 13 PSI

Check for restricted in-line filter.
- OK / Not OK → Replace filter and recheck.

- Ignition "OFF."
- Disconnect injector connector.
- Block fuel return line by pinching flexible hose.
- Check fuel pressure within two seconds after ignition "ON."

Above 13 PSI → Replace regulator and cover assembly.
Pressure But Less Than 9 PSI → Replace in-tank fuel pump.

- Disconnect injector connector.
- Disconnect fuel return line flexible hose.
- Attach 5/16 I.D. flex hose to throttle body side of return line. Insert the other end in an approved gasoline container.
- Note fuel pressure while cranking.

Above 13 PSI → Check for restricted fuel return line from throttle body. → Line OK → Replace regulator and cover assembly.
9-13 PSI → Locate and correct restricted fuel return line to fuel tank.

Diagram labels: RETURN LINE, PRESSURE LINE, IN-TANK PUMP, PUMP INLET FILTER, PRESSURE REGULATOR, FLEX HOSE, FILTER, INJECTOR, FUEL PRESSURE GAGE TEST POINT

CHART 7

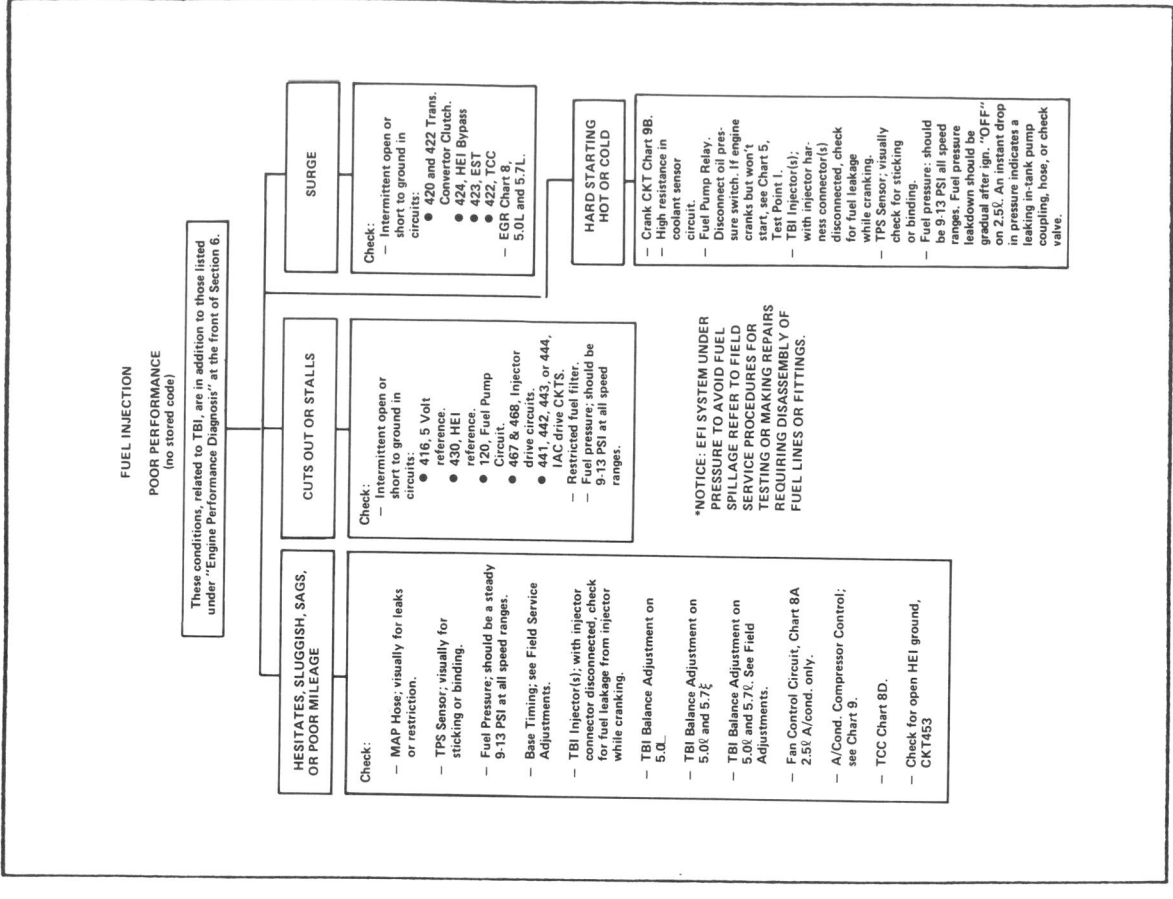

FUEL INJECTION

POOR PERFORMANCE
(no stored code)

These conditions, related to TBI, are in addition to those listed under "Engine Performance Diagnosis" at the front of Section 6.

HESITATES, SLUGGISH, SAGS, OR POOR MILEAGE

Check:

- MAP Hose; visually for leaks or restriction.
- TPS Sensor; visually for sticking or binding.
- Fuel Pressure; should be a steady 9-13 PSI at all speed ranges.
- Base Timing; see Field Service Adjustments.
- TBI Injector(s); with injector connector disconnected, check for fuel leakage from injector while cranking.
- TBI Balance Adjustment on 5.0ℓ.
- TBI Balance Adjustment on 5.0ℓ and 5.7ℓ.
- TBI Balance Adjustment on 5.0ℓ and 5.7ℓ. See Field Adjustments.
- Fan Control Circuit, Chart 8A 2.5ℓ A/cond. only.
- A/Cond. Compressor Control; see Chart 9.
- TCC Chart 8D.
- Check for open HEI ground, CKT453

CUTS OUT OR STALLS

Check:

- Intermittent open or short to ground in circuits:
  • 416, 5 Volt reference.
  • 430, HEI reference.
  • 120, Fuel Pump Circuit.
  • 467 & 468, Injector drive circuits.
  • 441, 442, 443, or 444, IAC drive CKTS.
- Restricted fuel filter.
- Fuel pressure; should be 9-13 PSI at all speed ranges.

*NOTICE: EFI SYSTEM UNDER PRESSURE TO AVOID FUEL SPILLAGE REFER TO FIELD SERVICE PROCEDURES FOR TESTING OR MAKING REPAIRS REQUIRING DISASSEMBLY OF FUEL LINES OR FITTINGS.

SURGE

Check:

- Intermittent open or short to ground in circuits:
  • 420 and 422 Trans. Convertor Clutch.
  • 423, HEI Bypass
  • 423, EST
  • 422, TCC
  EGR Chart 8, 5.0L and 5.7L.

HARD STARTING HOT OR COLD

- Crank CKT Chart 9B.
- High resistance in coolant sensor circuit.
- Fuel Pump Relay. Disconnect oil pressure switch. If engine cranks but won't start, see Chart 5, Test Point I.
- TBI Injector(s) with injector harness connector(s) disconnected, check for fuel leakage while cranking.
- TPS Sensor; visually check for sticking or binding.
- Fuel pressure: should be 9-13 PSI all speed ranges. Fuel pressure leakdown should be gradual after ign. "OFF" on 2.5ℓ. An instant drop in pressure indicates a leaking in-tank pump coupling, hose, or check valve.

Engine Cranks, But Will Not Run
Remote Coil

NOTE: Perform diagnostic circuit check before proceeding with this test.

NOTE: If a tachometer is connected to the tachometer terminal, disconnect it before proceeding with the test.

1. Check spark at plug with ST-125 while cranking (if no spark on one wire, check a second wire).

   Spark → Check fuel, spark plugs, etc.

   No Spark →

   2. Check for spark at coil wire with ST-125 while cranking. Leave ST-125 connected to coil wire for Steps 3–7.

   Spark →
   • Inspect cap for water, cracks, etc. If OK, replace rotor.

   No Spark →

   3. Remove dist. cap with ignition on. Check voltage at "+" term. on dist. module. See Figure 1.

   Under 10 volts → Repair wire from "+" term. on module to ign. coil "+" connection at ign. coil and primary circuit to ignition switch.

   10 volts or more →

   4. With ign. "ON" check "C" term. voltage on HEI module. See Figure 2.

   Under 1 volt → It is open or grounded lead from coil to dis. "C" term., connection or ign. coil or open primary circuit in coil.

   10 volts or more → Replace module and check for spark from coil as in Step 6.
   Spark → System OK
   No Spark → Replace ign. coil, it too is faulty.

   No Drop in Voltage → Check module ground. If OK, replace module.

   Voltage Drops →

   5. Remove pick-up coil connector from module. Check "C" connector voltage with "Ign. ON." Watch voltmeter as test light is momentarily connected from bat. + to module term. "P," not more than 5 sec. See Figure 3.

   Spark →
   6. Check for spark from coil wire with ST-125 as test light is removed from module term.
   Spark → System OK
   No Spark → It is pick-up coil or connections. Coil resistance should be 500-1500 ohms and not grounded.

   No Spark →
   If no module tester is available:
   7. Replace HEI module and repeat Step 6.

   If module tester is available, test mod.
   OK → Check coil wire from cap to coil. If OK, replace coil.
   Bad → Replace mod.

   Module removed is OK, reinstall module. Check coil wire from cap to coil. If OK, replace coil.

Figure 1

Figure 2

Figure 3
TO BAT. +

CHART 8C
Canister Purge Valve

- Ignition "ON," engine stopped.
- Ground diagnostic terminal.
- At the solenoid, apply 10" vacuum to throttle body side of purge solenoid.

Able to get and hold 10" vacuum.
- Remove ground from diagnostic terminal.
- Note vacuum.

→ Drops → No trouble found.

→ No Drop → Disconnect solenoid.

→ No Drop → Replace solenoid.

→ Drops → Repair short to ground in CKT 428.

→ CKT 428 OK. → Faulty ECM.

Unable to get or hold 10" vacuum.
- Disconnect purge solenoid. Connect test light between harness connector terminal.

→ No Light → Probe each harness connector terminal with a test light to ground.

→ Light → Faulty solenoid connection or solenoid.

Light On One Terminal → Check for open CKT 428.

Light Both Terminals → Repair short to voltage in CKT 428.

No Light → Check for open CKT 39.

CKT 428 OK. → Check resistance across solenoid. Should be 20 ohms or more.

→ OK → Faulty ECM connector or ECM.

→ Not OK → Replace both solenoid and ECM.

CANISTER PURGE SOLENOID
CANISTER PURGE
ECM
9
428
BLACK CONNECTOR
IGN. CKT 39

CHART 8A
Coolant Fan Control Circuit—2.5L With A/C

- Disconnect cooling fan temperature switch.
- Engine idling.
- Turn A/C "ON" and "OFF".
- Note cooling fan.

Turns "ON" and "OFF".
- Raise drive wheels.
- Idle engine with transmission in "DRIVE".
- A/C "ON."
- Probe temp. switch harness connector with a test light to 12 volts.
- Increase wheel speed to 35mph and note light.

→ Light Goes Out → CM fan control circuit OK, no trouble found.

→ Light Remains "ON"
- Ignition "ON," engine stopped.
- Back probe white ECM connector Terminal 2, CKT 437, with a voltmeter to ground.
- Manually rotate drive wheel and note voltage. Be sure opposite wheel does not turn.

→ Voltage Varies from Under 3 to Over 9 Volts → Faulty ECM.

→ Voltage Variation → See Code 24

Fan Does Not Turn "ON" and "OFF"
- Disconnect fan control relay.
- Engine idling.
- A/C "ON."
- Probe fan temp. switch harness connector with a test light to 12 volts.

→ Light "ON" → A/C "OFF."
- Reconnect fan relay.
- Probe fan temp. switch harness connector with a test light to ground.

→ Light "ON" → Check for short to ground in CKT 409 to fan relay.

→ Light "OFF" → ECM fan control CKT OK. No trouble found.

→ Light "OFF" → Check for faulty A/C mode switch or open CKT 409 to ECM.

→ A/C switch and CKT 409 OK. → Faulty ECM connector or ECM.

→ Light "OFF" → Check for open fan relay coil. See fan control relay diagnostics.

FAN CONTROL
ECM
9
BLACK CONNECTOR
409
A/C MODE SWITCH
FAN TEMP. SWITCH
IGN. 1
FAN CONTROL RELAY
A B C D
FAN MOTOR
M
BATTERY

CHART 9

FUEL INJECTION

CHART 8D
Transmission Converter Clutch (TCC)—Electrical Diagnosis

CHART 9B
Crank Signal

- Probe black ECM connector Pin 1 with test light to ground.
- Crank engine.
- Note test light.

Light During Crank

Crank Signal Circuit OK

No Light During Crank

Check Fuse

OK → Repair open in wire from ECM to ignition switch (Sol).

Not OK → Check wire from fuse to ECM for short to ground.

OK →
- Replace fuse.
- Crank engine.
- Recheck fuse.

OK → Defective fuse. Crank circuit OK.

Not OK → Replace ECM

ECM
CRANK
1
BLACK CONNECTOR
FUSE
10A
IGNITION SWITCH (SOL)

CHART 9A
Park/Neutral Switch—2.5L and 5.0L

- Ignition "ON" — Engine stopped.
- Transmission in "PARK."
- Connect voltmeter J-29125 to Circuit 434 (orn/blk wire) of P/N switch to ground. Do Not Use Test Light.

9-12 Volts

Check for open in ground CKT 450.

CKT 450 OK → Check switch adjustment. If OK, replace switch.

Less Than 1 Volt

- Move Transmission Selector into "Drive" and Note Voltage.

9-12 Volts → No Trouble Found

Less Than 1 Volt
- Disconnect P/N switch.
- Recheck voltage CKT 434 (orn/blk wire)

9-12 Volts → Check adjustment. If OK, replace switch.

Less than 1 volt. → Check for open CKT 434.

CKT 434 OK → Faulty ECM connector on ECM.

P/N
GROUND
ECM
WHITE CONNECTOR
5
12
434
450
PARK NEUTRAL SWITCH
I.P. CONNECTOR
B
A
I.P. CONNECTOR
CLOSED IN P/N POSITION

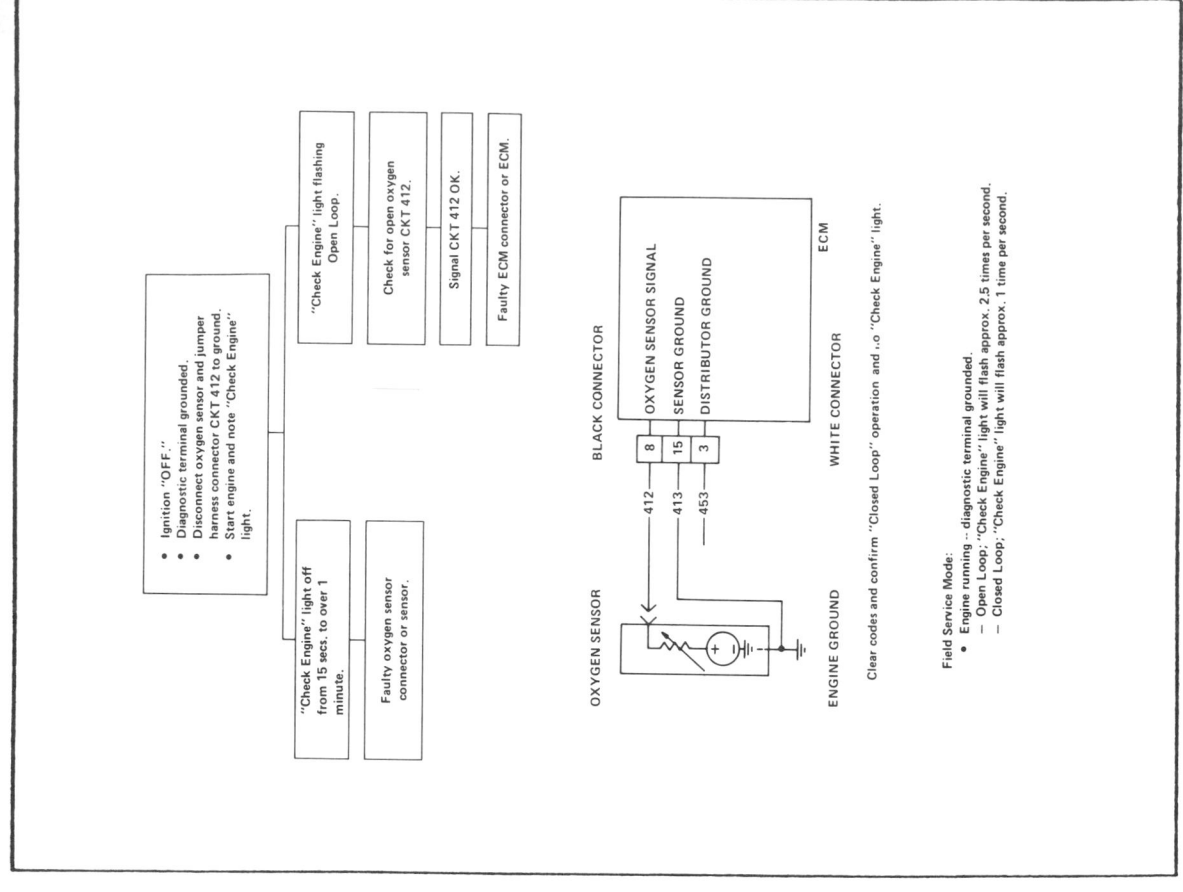

CODE 13
Oxygen Sensor Circuit

- Ignition "OFF".
- Diagnostic terminal grounded.
- Disconnect oxygen sensor and jumper harness connector CKT 412 to ground.
- Start engine and note "Check Engine" light.

| "Check Engine" light off from 15 secs. to over 1 minute. | "Check Engine" light flashing Open Loop. |

| Faulty oxygen sensor connector or sensor. | Check for open oxygen sensor CKT 412. |

Signal CKT 412 OK.

Faulty ECM connector or ECM.

OXYGEN SENSOR   BLACK CONNECTOR   ECM

412 — 8 — OXYGEN SENSOR SIGNAL
413 — 15 — SENSOR GROUND
453 — 3 — DISTRIBUTOR GROUND

ENGINE GROUND   WHITE CONNECTOR

Clear codes and confirm "Closed Loop" operation and no "Check Engine" light.

Field Service Mode:
- Engine running -- diagnostic terminal grounded.
  — Open Loop; "Check Engine" light will flash approx. 2.5 times per second.
  — Closed Loop; "Check Engine" light will flash approx. 1 time per second.

CHART 11
Idle Air Control

Connect tachometer. Idle engine at normal operating temperature and record RPM in Park or Neutral.

- Ignition "OFF".
- Disconnect IAC motor. Rear IAC motor on 5.0L.
- Start engine, note idle RPM in neutral.

| Idle RPM, No Increase | Idle RPM Increase |

- Ignition "OFF".
- Reconnect IAC.
- Start engine and note idle RPM in neutral.

Will not return to idle RPM recorded above.

Return to idle RPM recorded above.

- 5.0L and 5.7L reconnect rear IAC. Return to beginning of chart, and repeat test with front IAC motor.

Idle Air Control OK

Check:
- TBI air rate balance 5.0L and 5.7L.
- Vacuum leaks.
- Sticking or binding throttle shaft or accelerator linkage.
- Base idle air rate.
- Park/Neutral switch chart 9A.
- A/cond. clutch signal chart 9.
- EGR chart 8, 5.0L and 5.7L.
- Leaking injectors.

- Ignition "OFF".
- Jumper fuel pump test terminal to 12 volts.
- Ignition "ON" engine stopped.
- Ground diagnostic test terminal.
- Disconnect IAC, Disconnect both front and rear IAC motors on 5.0L and 5.7L.
- Connect a test light between each harness connector pin and ground.

| No light, one or more circuits. | Light flashes All circuits | Three circuits Dim/Bright, one circuit On/Off or Three circuits On/Off, one circuit Dim/Bright. |

| | Two circuits On/Off and Two circuits Dim/Bright | Faulty ECM. |

Repair open or short to ground in circuits with no light.

Replace IAC.

All circuits OK.

Check voltage at white ECM term 17. Should be above 8 volts.

| OK | Not OK |

Faulty ECM connectors or ECM.

Repair open circuit 120

FRONT IAC MOTOR 5.0L AND 5.7L

BLACK ECM CONNECTOR   ECM

441 — 17 — IAC COIL "A" HI
442 — 18 — IAC COIL "A" LO
443 — 12 — IAC COIL "B" HI
444 — 13 — IAC COIL "B" LO

IAC MOTOR

A B C D   IAC CONNECTOR

INTAKE MANIFOLD

Clear codes and confirm "Closed Loop" operation and no "Check Engine" light.

CODE 15
Coolant Sensor Circuit—Signal Voltage High

CODE 14
Coolant Sensor Circuit—Signal Voltage Low

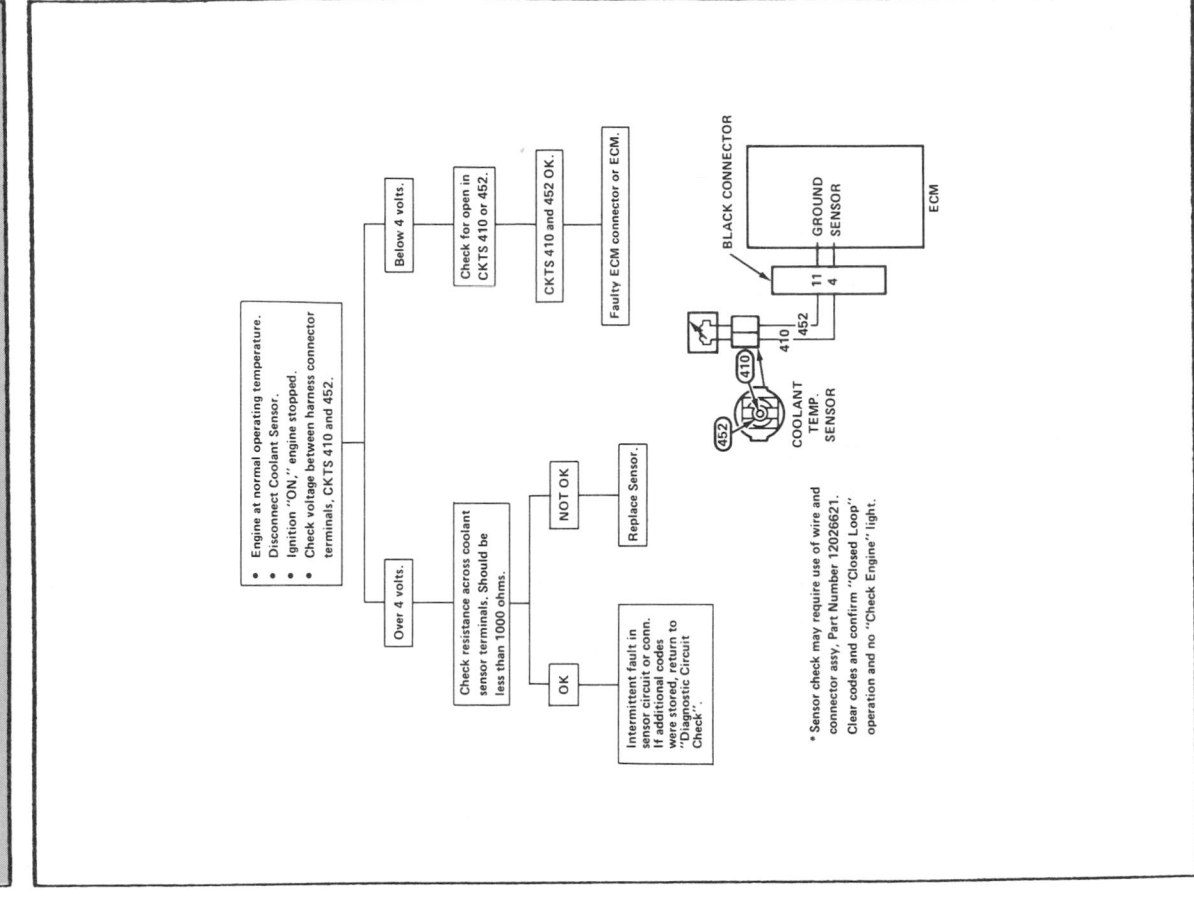

CODE 15 — Coolant Sensor Circuit—Signal Voltage High

- Engine at normal operating temperature.
- Disconnect Coolant Sensor.
- Ignition "ON," engine stopped.
- Check voltage between harness connector terminals, CKTS 410 and 452.

Over 4 volts.

Check resistance across coolant sensor terminals. Should be less than 1000 ohms.

OK → Intermittent fault in sensor circuit or conn. If additional codes were stored, return to "Diagnostic Circuit Check".

NOT OK → Replace Sensor.

Below 4 volts.

Check for open in CKTS 410 or 452.

CKTS 410 and 452 OK.

Faulty ECM connector or ECM.

BLACK CONNECTOR

11 452
4 410

GROUND
SENSOR

COOLANT TEMP. SENSOR

ECM

* Sensor check may require use of wire and connector assy, Part Number 12026621. Clear codes and confirm "Closed Loop" operation and no "Check Engine" light.

CODE 14 — Coolant Sensor Circuit—Signal Voltage Low

If the "Engine Hot" light is "ON," check for overheating condition before making following test.

- Engine stopped, Ignition "OFF".
- Diagnostic terminal ungrounded.
- Disconnect coolant sensor.
- Jumper harness connector signal CKT. 410 to ground, CKT. 452.
- Start engine and idle at normal operating temperature for 1 minute or until "Check Engine" light comes on.
- With engine idling, remove jumper from harness connector and run engine for 1 more minute.
- Stop engine, enter diagnostics and note code(s).

Code 14 only.

- Disconnect black ECM connector.
- Check signal CKT. 410 for short to CKT. 452 or chassis ground.

CKT. 410 OK

Replace ECM.

Both Code 14 and 15.

Replace coolant sensor.

BLACK CONNECTOR

11 452
4 410

GROUND
SENSOR

COOLANT TEMP. SENSOR

ECM

Clear codes and confirm "Closed Loop" operation and no "Check Engine" light.

CODE 22
Throttle Position Sensor—Signal Voltage Low

- Diagnostic terminal not grounded.
- Clear codes.
- Disconnect TPS and jumper CKTS 416 and 452.
- Start engine and idle for 1 minute or until "Check Engine" light comes on.
- Ignition "ON," engine stopped. Note code.

Code 22
- Remove jumper from CKTS 416 and 417.
- Check voltage between harness conn. Pins A and C using digital voltmeter. (J 29125)

Below 4 volts
Disconnect white ECM connector. Check for open or short to ground in CKT 416.

CKT 416 OK. Faulty ECM connector or ECM.

4-6 Volts
Check for open or short to ground in CKT 417.

CKT 417 OK. Faulty ECM connector or ECM.

Code 21
Check TPS Adjustment

Adjustment OK. Replace TPS.

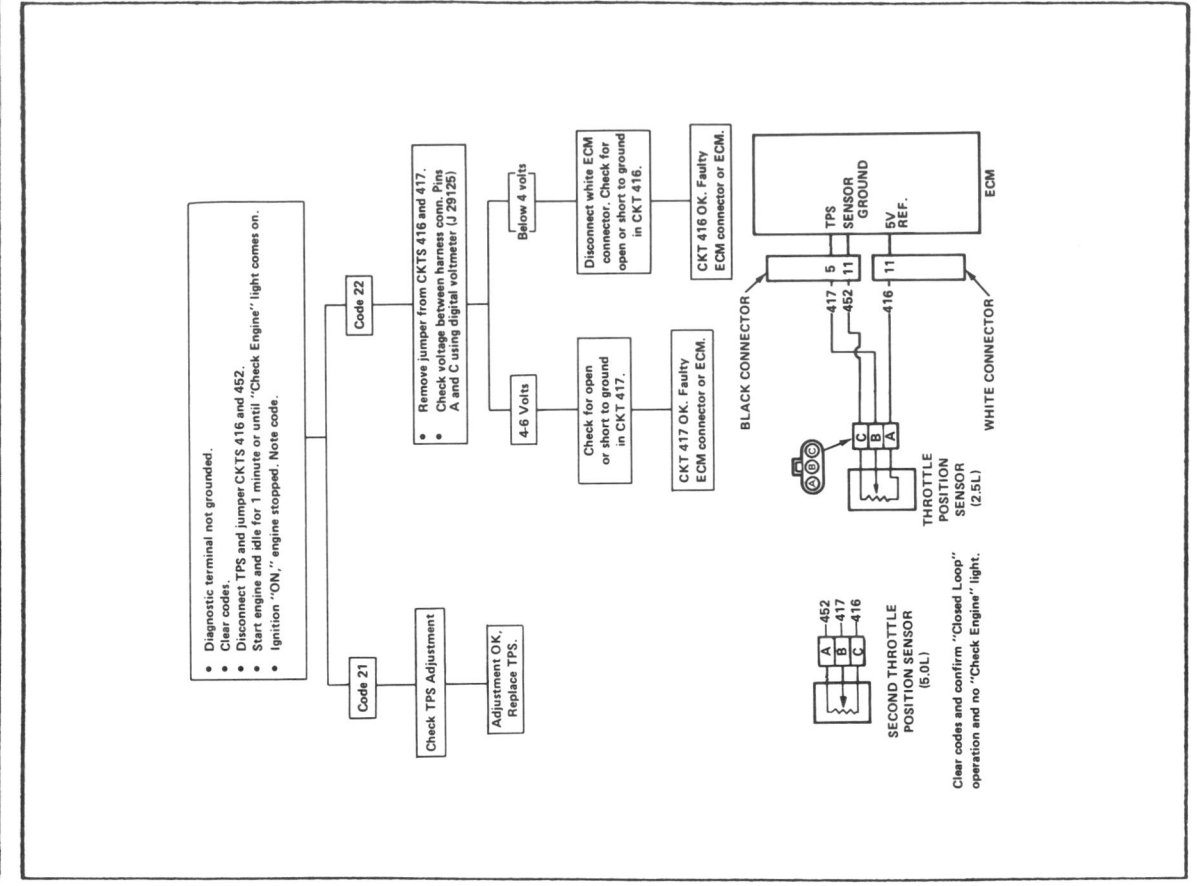

ECM
TPS
SENSOR GROUND
5V REF.

417 5
452 11
416 11

BLACK CONNECTOR
WHITE CONNECTOR

C B A
THROTTLE POSITION SENSOR (2.5L)

A — 452
B — 417
C — 416

SECOND THROTTLE POSITION SENSOR (5.0L)

Clear codes and confirm "Closed Loop" operation and no "Check Engine" light.

CODE 21
Throttle Position Sensor—Signal Voltage High

- Diagnostic terminal not grounded.
- Clear codes.
- Disconnect TPS sensor.
- Start engine and idle for 1 minute or until "Check Engine" light comes on.
- Ignition "ON," engine stopped.
- Ground Diagnostic Terminal and Note Code.

Code 21
Disconnect black ECM connector and probe harness connector Pin 5 with a test light to ground.

Light
Repair short to voltage CKT 417.

No light.
Replace ECM.

Code 22
Probe harness connector CKT 452 with test light to 12 volts.

No light.
Repair open CKT 452.

Light.
Replace TPS Sensor.

ECM
TPS
SENSOR GROUND
5V REF.

417 5
452 11
416 11

BLACK CONNECTOR
WHITE CONNECTOR

416 — C
417 — B
452 — A
THROTTLE POSITION SENSOR (2.5L)

A — 452
B — 417
C — 416

SECOND THROTTLE POSITION SENSOR (5.0L)

Clear codes and confirm "Closed Loop" operation and no "Check Engine" light.

CODE 33 — MAP Sensor

- Ignition "OFF," clear codes.
- Disconnect MAP sensor connector.
- Diagnostic terminal not grounded.
- Start engine and run for 1 minute or until "Check Engine" light comes on.
- Ignition "ON," engine stopped.
- Ground diagnostic terminal and note code.

CODE 34
- Check for plugged or leaking sensor vacuum line.
- Vacuum line OK.
- Replace Sensor.

CODE 33
- Check for open in ground CKT 469.
- CKT 469
- Check for short to voltage CKT 432.
- CKT 432 OK.
- Replace ECM.

MANIFOLD PRESSURE — MAP SENSOR

WHITE CONNECTOR
- 416 — 11 — 5 VOLTS
- 469 — 14 — GROUND
- 432 — 20 — SIGNAL
BLACK CONNECTOR — ECM

Clear codes and confirm "Closed Loop" operation and no "Check Engine" light.

CODE 24 — Vehicle Speed Sensor (VSS)—1982

NOTICE: A False Code 24 and "Check Engine" light may be set if engine is run above 1200 RPM in Neutral on vehicles equipped with manual transmission. To prevent misdiagnosis, disregard Code 24 if set under these circumstances.

- Speedometer working OK.
- Lift drive wheels.
- Back probe white ECM connector Pin 2, signal CKT 437 with a voltmeter to ground.
- Ignition "ON."
- Transmission in "NEUTRAL."
- Rotate drive wheel manually while observing voltage. Be sure opposite wheel does not turn.

Voltage varies from under 1.0 volt to over 10 volts.

Park/Neutral switch Chart 9A.

Park/Neutral switch OK.

- Clear codes.
- Diagnostic term. not grounded.
- Road test—At steady 40 MPH for one minute
- Note "Check Engine" light.

Light "ON"

No Light

VSS system OK. No trouble found.

- Stop engine.
- Ignition "ON."
- Ground diagnostic term.

Code 24

No Code 24

See chart for code indicated.

Faulty buffer connector or ECM.

No voltage variation

- Disconnect buffer amplifier.
- Ignition "ON."
- Probe harness connector Pin C with a voltmeter to ground. Should be 9-12 volts.

OK

Connect voltmeter between harness connector Pins B and C. Should be 9-12 volts.

OK

Connect voltmeter between harness connector Pins A & B. Should be 9-12 volts.

OK

Faulty connector or VSS.

Recheck voltage at white ECM connector Pin 2, CKT 437 as drive wheel is turned.

No voltage variation.

Reinstall original VSS and repair speedometer.

Not OK

Repair open CKT 39, Ignition 12 volts.

Not OK

Repair open ground CKT 450.

Not OK

Repair open or short to ground in signal CKT 437.

CKT 437 OK. Faulty ECM connector or ECM.

SPEED SENSOR — BUFFER AMP.

WHITE CONNECTOR
- 2 — VSS SIGNAL
- 12 — ENGINE GROUND
- 13 — 450 — ECM
437 — 450R — IGN

Clear codes and confirm "Closed Loop" operation and no "Check Engine" light.

CODE 42
Electronic Spark Timing (EST)

- Run engine at 1800 to 2200 RPM and note timing.
- Ground diagnostic terminal and note timing, it should change.

NO CHANGE

- Disconnect HEI distributor 4 way connector.
- Using two jumpers, reconnect HEI connector term. "B" to harness connector term. "B" and HEI connector term. "D" to harness connector term. "D".
- Start and idle engine.
- Probe chassis harness connector term. "A" CKT 423 with voltmeter J-29125. Voltage should vary 2.0 to 2.8

OK
- Ignition "OFF," engine stopped.
- Using third jumper, reconnect HEI connector term. "A" to harness connector term. "A".
- With engine idling, again probe CKT 423, with voltmeter to ground
- Voltage should be less than 1 volt.

NOT OK
Check for open or short to ground in EST CKT 423

CKT 423 OK
Faulty ECM connector or ECM.

NOT OK
Faulty wire or connector to HEI term. "E".
Wire and connector OK.
Replace HEI module

CHANGE
No trouble found. Infrequently a rare set of circumstances during engine crank could result in a "Check Engine" light after engine starts. The light will stay on until ignition "OFF" for 10 seconds and a normal restart. EST circuits 430 and 423 should be physically checked for proper harness routing, connectors and wiring for intermittent open or short to ground. If OK, no further repairs should be made.

Distributor 4-Way Connector
A B C D
E R B
HEI Module

Black Connector
423 19 EST
430 2 Reference
424 10 By Pass
453 3 Ground
ECM

OK
- Engine idling,
- Again probe term. "A" with a volt meter to gnd. Note voltage while probing HEI harness conn. term. "C." CKT 424, with a test light connected to 12V. Voltage should be 1.0 to 2.8 volts.

OK
- Stop engine, ignition off for 10 seconds.
- Using fourth jumper, reconnect HEI connector term. "C" to harness connector term. "C".
- Engine idling.
- Check voltage at term. "C," should be above 2 volts.

OK
EST OK No trouble found

NOT OK
Check for open or short to ground in CKT 424 to ECM

CKT 424 OK
Faulty ECM connector or ECM

NOT OK
Faulty HEI harness wire or connector to module term. "B." If OK, replace module

Clear codes and confirm "Open Loop" operation and no "Check Engine" light.

*This test requires the use of four jumpers using terminals 12014836 and 12014837.

CODE 34
MAP Sensor

- Ignition "OFF," clear codes.
- Disconnect MAP sensor and jumper harness connector pins "B" to "C."
- Diagnostic terminal not grounded.
- Start engine and run for 1 minute or until "Check Engine" light comes on.
- Ignition "ON," engine stopped.
- Ground diagnostic terminal and note code.

CODE 33
Replace sensor.

CODE 34

- Remove jumper from Pins "B" to "C."
- Check voltage between harness connector Pins "A" and "C" using voltmeter J-29125.

4 TO 6 VOLTS
Disconnect ECM black connector. Check for open or short to ground in CKT 432.

CKT 432 OK, faulty ECM connector or ECM.

BELOW 4 VOLTS
Check for open or short to ground in CKT 416.

CKT 416 OK, faulty ECM connector or ECM.

WHITE CONNECTOR
5 VOLTS
GROUND
SIGNAL
ECM
11
14
20
416
469
432
BLACK CONNECTOR

MANIFOLD PRESSURE
MAP SENSOR
A B C

Clear codes and confirm "Closed Loop" operation and no "Check Engine" light.

CODE 45 — Rich Exhaust Indication

- Ignition "OFF."
- Diagnostic terminal grounded.
- Disconnect oxygen sensor and jumper harness connector signal CKT 412 to ground.
- Start engine and note "Check Engine" light.

"Check Engine" Light from 15 secs. to over 1 minute.

System rich, check:
- Fuel pressure 9-13 PSI.
- Injector(s) for leakage or sticking.
- HEI shield CKT 453 for open circuit.
- Check for leakage or restriction in MAP hose.
- Check CCP, Chart 8C.

Steady Light.

Replace ECM.

Clear codes and confirm "Closed Loop" operation and no "Check Engine" light.
FIELD SERVICE MODE:
Open-Loop: "Check Engine" light flashes at a rate of 2 times per second.
Closed-Loop: "Check Engine" light flashes at a rate of 1 time per second.

BLACK CONNECTOR

OXYGEN SENSOR SIGNAL — 8 — 412
SENSOR GROUND — 15 — 413
DISTRIBUTOR GROUND — 3 — 453

ECM

OXYGEN SENSOR

ENGINE GROUND

CODE 44 — Lean Exhaust Indication

- Ignition "OFF."
- Diagnostic terminal grounded.
- Disconnect oxygen sensor.
- Start engine and note "Check Engine" light.

"Check Engine" light off from 15 secs. to over 1 minute.

- Measure voltage at oxygen sensor harness connector CKT 412 using J-29125 voltmeter or equivalent.
- Voltage should be .36 to .54 volts.

"Check Engine" light flashing Open Loop.

- Check for ground in wire from connector to sensor.
- Check for intake air leaks, including air management of TBI units on 5.0L and 5.7L.
- Check EGR, see Service Manual Section 6E or Chart 8 for 5.0L and 5.7L.
- Check fuel pressure. Should be 9-13 PSI.

All checks OK.

Faulty oxygen sensor.

OK.

Check for open oxygen sensor ground CKT 413.

CKT 413 OK.

Faulty ECM connector or ECM.

Not OK.

Check signal CKT 412 for open or short to ground.

CKT 412 OK.

Clear codes and confirm "Closed Loop" operation and no "Check Engine" light.
FIELD SERVICE MODE: Engine running, diagnostic terminal grounded.
Open-Loop: "Check Engine" light flashes at a rate of 2 times per second.
Closed-Loop: "Check Engine" light flashes at a rate of 1 time per second.

BLACK CONNECTOR

OXYGEN SENSOR SIGNAL — 8 — 412
SENSOR GROUND — 15 — 413
DISTRIBUTOR GROUND — 3 — 453

ECM

OXYGEN SENSOR

ENGINE GROUND

GENERAL MOTORS MAINTENANCE SCHEDULE—GASOLINE ENGINES — Typical

OWNER'S SERVICE LOG — MILES (km)

INSERT MONTH, DAY, AND MILEAGE (km) (i.e. MAY/5/76 12) IN COLUMN CLOSEST TO MILEAGE (km) WHEN SERVICE IS PERFORMED

ITEM NO.	SERVICES (FOR DETAILS, SEE NUMBERED PARAGRAPHS)	7,500 (12 000 km)	15,000 (24 000 km)	22,500 (36 000 km)	30,000 (48 000 km)	37,500 (60 000 km)	45,000 (72 000 km)
SECTION A — LUBRICATION AND GENERAL MAINTENANCE							
A-1	•CHASSIS LUBRICATION	X	X	X	X	X	X
A-2	•FLUID LEVELS CHECK	X	X	X	X	X	X
A-3	•ENGINE OIL CHANGE	X	X	X	X	X	X
A-4	•OIL FILTER CHANGE	X		X		X	
A-5	TIRE ROTATION	X	X	X			
A-6	REAR AXLE OR FINAL DRIVE LUBE CHECK	X		X	X	X	X
A-7	•COOLING SYSTEM CHECK — SEE EXPLANATION		X		X		X
A-8	WHEEL BEARING REPACK [1]				X		
A-9	FINAL DRIVE BOOTS AND SEALS CHECK				X		
A-10	AUTO. TRANS. FLUID & FILTER CHANGE				X		
SECTION B — SAFETY MAINTENANCE							
B-1	OWNER SAFETY CHECKS	X	X	X	X	X	X
B-2	TIRE, WHEEL AND DISC BRAKE CHECK	X	X	X	X	X	X
B-3	•EXHAUST SYSTEM CHECK	X	X	X	X	X	X
B-4	SUSPENSION AND STEERING CHECK	X	X	X	X	X	X
B-5	BRAKE AND POWER STEERING CHECK	X	X	X	X	X	X
B-6	•DRIVE BELT CHECK		X [2]	X	X	X	X [2]
B-7	DRUM BRAKE AND PARKING BRAKE CHECK		X	X	X	X	X
B-8	THROTTLE LINKAGE CHECK		X	X	X	X	X
B-9	BUMPER CHECK				X		
B-10	•FUEL CAP, TANK AND LINES CHECK	X		X		X	
SECTION C — EMISSION CONTROL MAINTENANCE † (SEE "SAMPLE LABEL" ON PAGE 1 FOR ENGINE FAMILY AND ENGINE SUFFIX EXPLANATION)							
C-1	CARBURETOR CHOKE & HOSES CHECK (EXCEPT FUEL INJECTION)	X			X [3]		X
C-2	ENGINE IDLE SPEED ADJUSTMENT (EXCEPT FUEL INJECTION)	X [4]			X		
C-3	EFE SYSTEM CHECK	X			X		
C-4	CARBURETOR (OR FUEL INJECTION THROTTLE BODY) MOUNTING TORQUE	X [4]			X		
C-5	THERMO CONTROLLED AIR CLEANER CHECK				X		
C-6	VACUUM ADVANCE SYSTEM & HOSES CHECK				X [4]		
C-7	SPARK PLUG WIRES CHECK				X		
C-8	IDLE STOP SOLENOID OR IDLE SPEED CONTROL (ISC) CHECK				X [4]		
C-9	SPARK PLUG REPLACEMENT				X		
C-10	ENGINE TIMING ADJUST. & DISTRIBUTOR CHECK				X [4]		
C-11	AIR CLEANER AND PCV FILTER ELEMENT REPLACEMENT				X		
C-12	PCV VALVE REPLACEMENT				X [4]		
C-13	OXYGEN SENSOR CHANGE				X [3][5]		
C-14	EGR VALVE REPLACEMENT				X [6]		
C-15	EGR SYSTEM CHECK (FUEL INJECTION ONLY)				X		

WHEN TO PERFORM SERVICES (MONTHS OR MILES WHICHEVER OCCURS FIRST)

Section A:
EVERY 12 MONTHS OR 7,500 MILES (12 000 km)
SEE EXPLANATION
EVERY 12 MONTHS OR 15,000 MILES (24 000 km)
EVERY 30,000 MILES (48 000 km)
SEE EXPLANATION

Section B:
EVERY 12 MONTHS OR 7,500 MILES (12 000 km)
EVERY 12 MONTHS OR 15,000 MILES (24 000 km)
EVERY 12 MONTHS OR 7,500 MILES (12 000 km)

Section C:
AT FIRST 6 MONTHS OR 7,500 MILES (12 000 km) — THEN AT 24-MONTH, 30,000-MILE (48 000 km) INTERVALS AS INDICATED IN LOG, EXCEPT C-1 WHICH REQUIRES SERVICE AT 45,000 MILES (72 000 km)
EVERY 30,000 MILES (48 000 km)

•ALSO A SAFETY SERVICE
•ALSO AN EMISSION CONTROL SERVICE

FOOTNOTES [1] NOT REQUIRED ON FRONT WHEEL DRIVE CARS [2] IN CALIFORNIA, A SEPARATELY DRIVEN AIR PUMP BELT CHECK IS RECOMMENDED BUT NOT REQUIRED AT 15,000 MILES (24 000 km) AND 45,000 MILES (72 000 km) [3] ONLY THESE EMISSION CONTROL MAINTENANCE ITEMS ARE CONSIDERED TO BE REQUIRED MAINTENANCE AS DEFINED BY THE CALIFORNIA AIR RESOURCES BOARD (ARB) REGULATION AND ARE, ACCORDING TO SUCH REGULATION, THE MINIMUM MAINTENANCE AN OWNER IN CALIFORNIA MUST PERFORM TO FULFILL THE MINIMUM REQUIREMENTS OF THE EMISSION WARRANTY. ALL OTHER EMISSION MAINTENANCE ITEMS ARE RECOMMENDED MAINTENANCE AS DEFINED BY SUCH REGULATION. GENERAL MOTORS URGES THAT ALL EMISSION CONTROL MAINTENANCE ITEMS BE PERFORMED [4] NOT APPLICABLE ON VEHICLES EQUIPPED WITH ELECTRONIC SPARK TIMING (EST) [5] REQUIRE THE OXYGEN SENSOR CHANGED AT THIS INTERVAL [6] ONLY ENGINE FAMILIES 14F4AE AND 14F4AEJ REQUIRE THIS CHANGE

**CODE 51
FUEL INJECTION**

> Check that all pins are fully inserted
> in the socket. If OK, replace PROM,
> clear memory, and recheck. If Code 51
> reappears, replace ECM.

**CODE 55
FUEL INJECTION**

> Replace Electronic
> Control Module (ECM)

Clear codes and confirm "Closed Loop" operation
and no "Check Engine" light.

GM ELECTRONIC FUEL CONTROL (EFC) SYSTEM

General Information

The EFC system is the forerunner of the C4 and CCC systems and was used on 1979 Vega, Monza, Astre and Sunbird models with 151 CID (2.5 L) engines, sold in California. EFC was not used on Canadian vehicles.

This system controls both the idle and main metering fuel mixture according to how much oxygen there is in the exhaust. Most tune-up men have used an infra-red exhaust gas analyzer to measure the carbon monoxide (CO) and hydrocarbon (HC) in the exhaust. The infra-red measures the actual pollutants, except nitrogen oxides (NOx). Since these pollutants are what we want to control, it would seem that the best way to control them would be to install an analyzer on every car. The electronic fuel control system does just that, but instead of using an infra-red analyzer, it uses an oxygen sensor.

The easiest thing to analyze in the exhaust is the amount of oxygen. Because repair shops are not used to analyzing oxygen with their exhaust gas analyzers, most emission control technicians do not realize that the exhaust contains any oxygen. But oxygen is always present in the exhaust to some degree. If the mixture is rich, the extra fuel will combine with the oxygen in the air and the exhaust will have very little oxygen. If the mixture is lean, there won't be enough fuel to use up all the oxygen and more of it will pass through the engine.

As the oxygen content of the exhaust goes up (lean mixture), the amount of CO goes down, because there is an excess of oxygen to combine with the CO and turn it into harmless CO_2 (carbon dioxide). However, if the mixture gets too lean there is a tendency to form more NOx. The electronic fuel control solves all these problems by controlling the mixture within very narrow limits.

The oxygen sensor has a zirconia element, and looks very much like a spark plug. It screws into the exhaust pipe close to the exhaust manifold. Zirconia, when combined with heat and oxygen, has the peculiar property of being able to generate current. The amount of current is very small, but it is enough that it will pass through a wire and can be amplified by electronics.

A small black box under the hood is the electronic control unit. It receives the electric signals from the oxygen sensor and amplifies them enough to operate a vacuum modulator. The vacuum modulator is a vibrating electrical device. Engine manifold vacuum connects to the modulator, and then goes to the carburetor. The amount of vacuum that the carburetor receives is controlled by the modulator.

Electronic fuel control on GM four cylinder engines

LEAN MIXTURE
O₂ IN EXHAUST
GAS

LOW SENSOR
VOLTAGE

CARBURETOR CONTROL
"LEANS" MIXTURE

VACUUM TO CARBURETOR
INCREASES

VACUUM TO CARBURETOR
DECREASES

HIGH SENSOR
VOLTAGE

CARBURETOR CONTROL
ENRICHENS MIXTURE

LESS O₂ IN
EXHAUST GAS

Closed loop cycle of EFC operation

The carburetor is specially constructed with an idle air bleed valve and a main metering fuel valve. Both of the valves are operated by vacuum diaphragms. The idle air bleed gives a richer mixture at low vacuum because a spring pushes the regulating needle into the bleed. At high vacuum, the diaphragm compresses the spring and pulls the needle out of the bleed, letting more air into the idle system, which leans the mixture.

The main metering fuel valve actually takes the place of the power valve. It is separate from the main metering jet. It works the same as a power valve, in that it can add fuel to the system or shut off, but it cannot change the amount of fuel going through the main metering jet.

The spring tension on both the diaphragms is adjustable with small screws. However, the main metering diaphragm is factory adjusted, and there are no specifications for adjusting it in the field. Both the idle diaphragm screw and the idle mixture screw on the carburetor are covered with press-in plugs. The idle mixture needle is covered by a cup plug that can be removed with a screw extractor. The screw extractor should fit the cup plug without drilling a hole. If a hole is drilled in the plug, the mixture needle will be damaged. The idle diaphragm plug is soft lead, and can be carefully pried out. Idle mixture settings are normally made only when the carburetor is overhauled. The necessary plugs are in the overhaul kit.

The Electronic Fuel Control is not a complicated system. Except for the vacuum checks, which need to be done only at time of carburetor overhaul, no maintenance is required.

EFC Component Removal

ELECTRONIC CONTROL UNIT (ECU)

The electronic control unit monitors the voltage output of the oxygen sensor and generates the control signal to the vacuum modulator. During cold engine operation an engine temperature switch signals the control unit limiting the extent of the carburetor lean out. A final control input is received from the vacuum input switch. Heavy engine load (low vacuum) causes the switch to signal the control unit, limiting the leanness of the fuel mixture. The electronic control unit is located in the engine compartment on the passenger side fender well.

Removal and Installation

1. Remove the vacuum canister (if equipped).
2. Disconnect ECU wire connector from the control unit.

3. Remove the four attaching screws and lift the control unit off the backing plate.
4. Install the control unit on the backing plate and tighten the attaching screws.
5. Connect the wiring harness to the control unit. Make sure a good connection is made.
6. Install the vacuum canister (if equipped).

OXYGEN SENSOR

The oxygen sensor is located in the exhaust crossover pipe and consists of a closed end zirconia sensor plus a wire connecting it to the electronic control unit. The wire can be removed from the sensor connector.

Removal and Installation

NOTE: The oxygen sensor may be difficult to remove when the engine temperature is below 120°F (48°C).

1. Disconnect the electrical connector clip at the oxygen sensor.
2. Spray penetrating oil on the sensor threads and allow to soak in.
3. Carefully back out the sensor and remove.
4. To install coat the sensor threads with anti-seize compound and carefully torque to 18 ft. lbs. (24 Nm).
5. Install the electrical connector clip to the oxygen sensor, using care not to bend the sensor terminal.

NOTE: If the oxygen sensor is being replaced per regular maintenance interval, the EFC "SENSOR" flag in the instrument panel must be reset—if equipped.

VACUUM MODULATOR

The vacuum modulator provides a modulated vacuum signal to the carburetor air bleed circuit. The vacuum modulator is located next to the control unit on the passenger fender well.

Removal and Installation

1. Unplug the electrical connector at the vacuum modulator.
2. Remove the three vacuum hoses, marking their position for correct reinstallation.
3. Remove the two attaching screws and remove the modulator and bracket.
4. Remove the two screw clips holding the bracket to the modulator and separate them.
5. Install the vacuum modulator to mounting bracket and tighten the two clips.
6. Install the mounting bracket to backing plate and tighten the two screws.
7. Connect the vacuum hoses to the correct fittings and connect the electrical connection.

FEEDBACK CARBURETOR

The carburetor is equipped with a feedback diaphragm and idle needle housing. This controls the idle air bleed into the carburetor according to signals received from the vacuum modulator. For all information and service procedures, see the "carburetor" section.

Trouble Diagnosis

NOTE: Do not disconnect the vacuum modulator electrical connector when testing. Probe into the connector touching the brown wire contact.

The operation of the Electronic Fuel Control system should be included when troubleshooting vehicles with the following symptoms.

• Detonation
• Stalls or rough idle cold

EFC electrical components

• Stalls or rough idle hot
• Missing
• Hesitation
• Surges
• Sluggish or spongy
• Poor gasoline mileage
• Hard starting cold
• Hard starting hot
• Excessive exhaust odor
• Cuts out

NOTE: When testing vacuum the readings will steadily decrease as the altitude above sea level increases. The vacuum readings may be as 1 in. Hg. to 1½ in. Hg. lower at 4,000 feet and higher.

─────────── CAUTION ───────────

When making tests by connecting a jumper wire to the positive battery terminal, use care to avoid ground shorts that could cause personal injury.

1. Before any tests are made, check the vacuum hoses for leaks, breaks, kinks, or improper connections. Inspect the wiring for breaks, shorts, or fraying. Be sure the electrical connector at the ECU is tight. Disconnect the wire from the vacuum switch (3B), and connect a test light between it and the positive battery terminal. Run the engine at 1500 rpm, with the transmission in Neutral. The test light should go on and off as the vacuum hose is removed and replaced at the switch. If not, replace the switch.

2. Turn the ignition switch ON (engine OFF).

3. The vacuum modulator should emit a steady clicking sound. If so, go to Step 4. If not, ground one end of a jumper wire to a ground, the other to the brown wire in the modulator connector (5B).

   a. If the modulator clicks once, check the ECU connector for tightness. If it's ok, remove the ECU connector and touch 5A with the jumper wire. If there's no click, there is an open in the brown wire. If it clicks once, replace the ECU.

   b. If the modulator does not click when the brown wire is grounded, connect a test light to a ground and the pink wire at the modulator (1D). If the test light goes on, replace the modulator. If not, there is an open in the pink wire.

4. If a clicking sound is heard, use a T-fitting to attach a vacuum gauge between the center port of the vacuum modulator and the carburetor. Start the engine, allow it to reach operating temperature, and let the engine idle. Automatic transmission should be in Drive (front wheels blocked, parking brake on), manual in Neutral.

   a. If the gauge reads above 7 in. Hg., replace the vacuum modulator.

   b. If the gauge reads 2–4 in. Hg., shift the transmission to Neutral or Park, with an automatic, and increase the engine speed to 3500 rpm. If the reading is still 2–4 in. Hg., the system is ok; either the ignition or fuel supply is faulty. If it reads below 2–4 in. Hg., the carburetor is faulty.

   c. If the gauge reads below 2–4 in. Hg., shift to Neutral or

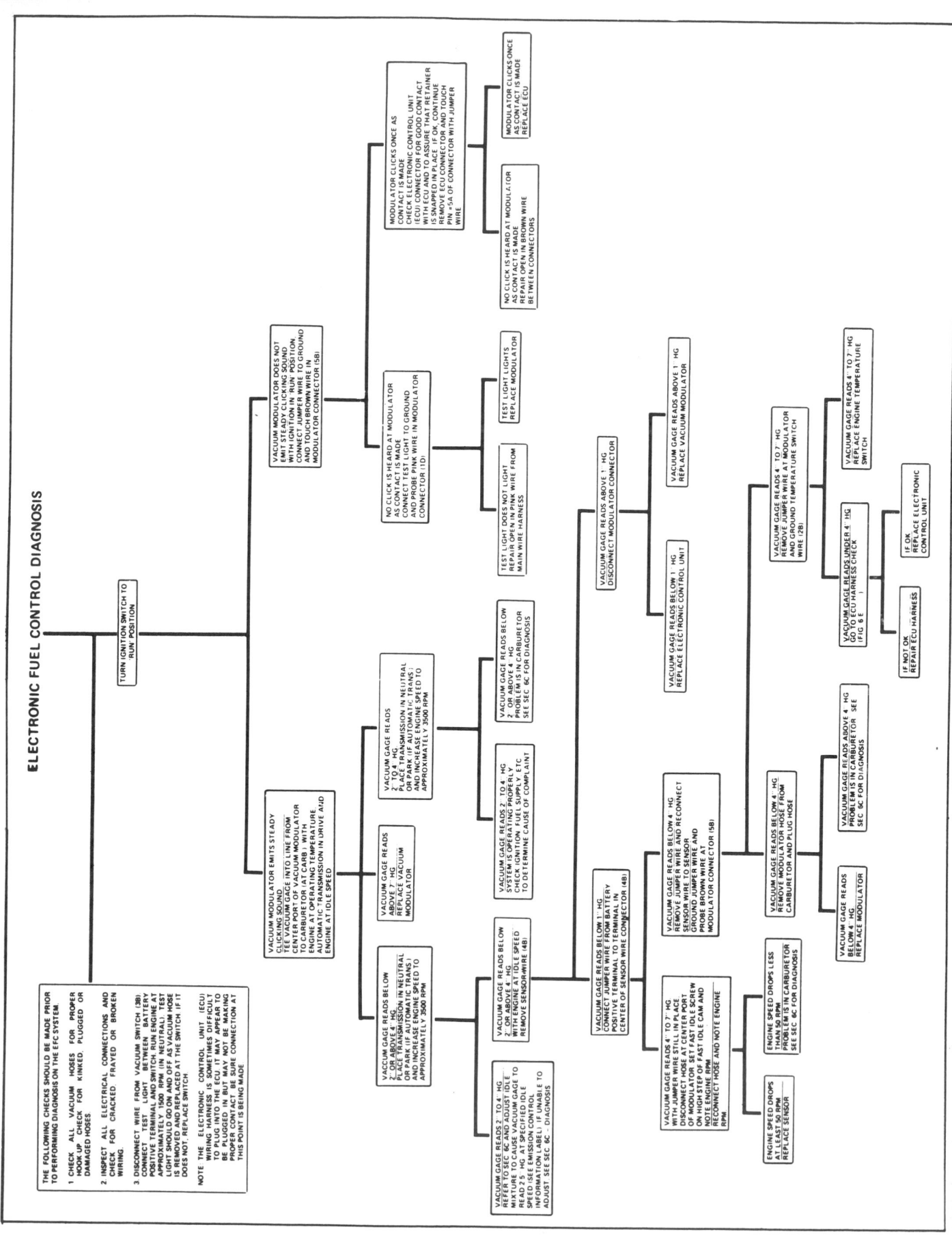

ELECTRONIC FUEL CONTROL DIAGNOSIS

THE FOLLOWING CHECKS SHOULD BE MADE PRIOR TO PERFORMING DIAGNOSIS ON THE EFC SYSTEM

1 CHECK ALL VACUUM HOSES FOR PROPER HOOK UP CHECK FOR KINKED PLUGGED OR DAMAGED HOSES

2 INSPECT ALL ELECTRICAL CONNECTIONS AND CHECK FOR CRACKED FRAYED OR BROKEN WIRING

3 DISCONNECT WIRE FROM VACUUM SWITCH (3B) CONNECT TEST LIGHT BETWEEN BATTERY POSITIVE TERMINAL AND SWITCH RUN ENGINE AT APPROXIMATELY 1500 RPM (IN NEUTRAL) TEST LIGHT SHOULD GO ON AND OFF AS VACUUM HOSE IS REMOVED AND REPLACED AT THE SWITCH IF IT DOES NOT, REPLACE SWITCH

NOTE THE ELECTRONIC CONTROL UNIT (ECU) WIRING HARNESS IS SOMETIMES DIFFICULT TO PLUG INTO THE ECU IT MAY APPEAR TO BE PLUGGED IN BUT MAY NOT BE MAKING PROPER CONTACT BE SURE CONNECTION AT THIS POINT IS BEING MADE

TURN IGNITION SWITCH TO RUN POSITION

VACUUM MODULATOR EMITS STEADY CLICKING SOUND TEE VACUUM GAGE INTO LINE FROM CENTER PORT OF VACUUM MODULATOR TO CARBURETOR (AT CARB) WITH ENGINE AT OPERATING TEMPERATURE AUTOMATIC TRANSMISSION IN DRIVE AND ENGINE AT IDLE SPEED

VACUUM MODULATOR DOES NOT EMIT STEADY CLICKING SOUND WITH IGNITION IN RUN POSITION CONNECT JUMPER WIRE TO GROUND AND TOUCH BROWN WIRE IN MODULATOR CONNECTOR (5B)

VACUUM GAGE READS BELOW 2˚ OR ABOVE 4˚ HG PLACE TRANSMISSION IN NEUTRAL OR PARK (IF AUTOMATIC TRANS) AND INCREASE ENGINE SPEED TO APPROXIMATELY 3500 RPM

VACUUM GAGE READS ABOVE 7˚ HG REPLACE VACUUM MODULATOR

VACUUM GAGE READS 2˚ TO 4˚ HG PLACE TRANSMISSION IN NEUTRAL OR PARK (IF AUTOMATIC TRANS) AND INCREASE ENGINE SPEED TO APPROXIMATELY 3500 RPM

NO CLICK IS HEARD AT MODULATOR AS CONTACT IS MADE CONNECT TEST LIGHT TO GROUND AND PROBE PINK WIRE IN MODULATOR CONNECTOR (1D)

MODULATOR CLICKS ONCE AS CONTACT IS MADE CHECK ELECTRONIC CONTROL UNIT (ECU) CONNECTOR FOR GOOD CONTACT WITH ECU AND TO ASSURE THAT RETAINER IS SNAPPED IN PLACE IF OK, CONTINUE REMOVE ECU CONNECTOR AND TOUCH PIN +5A OF CONNECTOR WITH JUMPER WIRE

NO CLICK IS HEARD AT MODULATOR AS CONTACT IS MADE REPAIR OPEN IN BROWN WIRE BETWEEN CONNECTORS

MODULATOR CLICKS ONCE AS CONTACT IS MADE REPLACE ECU

VACUUM GAGE READS BELOW 2˚ OR ABOVE 4˚ HG WITH ENGINE AT IDLE SPEED REMOVE SENSOR WIRE (4B)

VACUUM GAGE READS BELOW 2˚ OR ABOVE 4˚ HG PROBLEM IS IN CARBURETOR SEE SEC 6C FOR DIAGNOSIS

TEST LIGHT DOES NOT LIGHT REPAIR OPEN IN PINK WIRE FROM MAIN WIRE HARNESS

TEST LIGHT LIGHTS REPLACE MODULATOR

VACUUM GAGE READS 2˚ TO 4˚ HG SYSTEM IS OPERATING PROPERLY CHECK IGNITION FUEL SUPPLY ETC TO DETERMINE CAUSE OF COMPLAINT

VACUUM GAGE READS BELOW 1˚ HG DISCONNECT MODULATOR CONNECTOR

VACUUM GAGE READS ABOVE 1˚ HG REPLACE VACUUM MODULATOR

VACUUM GAGE READS 2˚ TO 4˚ HG MIXTURE IS LEAN ADJUST IDLE REFER TO SEC 6C AND ADJUST IDLE MIXTURE CO TO CENTER PORT READ 2˚5˚ HG AT SPECIFIED IDLE SPEED (SEE EMISSION CONTROL INFORMATION LABEL) IF UNABLE TO ADJUST SEE SEC 6C DIAGNOSIS

VACUUM GAGE READS BELOW 1˚ HG CONNECT JUMPER WIRE FROM BATTERY POSITIVE TERMINAL TO TERMINAL IN CENTER OF SENSOR WIRE CONNECTOR (4B)

VACUUM GAGE READS BELOW 1˚ HG REPLACE ELECTRONIC CONTROL UNIT

VACUUM GAGE READS 4˚ TO 7˚ HG WITH JUMPER WIRE STILL IN PLACE DISCONNECT HOSE AT CENTER PORT OF MODULATOR SET FAST IDLE SCREW ON HIGH STEP OF FAST IDLE CAM AND NOTE ENGINE RPM RECONNECT HOSE AND NOTE ENGINE RPM

VACUUM GAGE READS BELOW 4˚ HG REMOVE JUMPER WIRE AND RECONNECT SENSOR WIRE TO SENSOR GROUND JUMPER WIRE AND PROBE BROWN WIRE AT MODULATOR CONNECTOR (5B)

VACUUM GAGE READS ABOVE 4˚ HG SEE SEC 6C FOR DIAGNOSIS

VACUUM GAGE READS ABOVE 1˚ HG REMOVE JUMPER WIRE AT MODULATOR AND GROUND TEMPERATURE SWITCH (2B)

VACUUM GAGE READS 4˚ TO 7˚ HG REPLACE ENGINE TEMPERATURE SWITCH

ENGINE SPEED DROPS LESS THAN 50 RPM PROBLEM IS IN CARBURETOR SEE SEC 6C FOR DIAGNOSIS

VACUUM GAGE READS BELOW 4˚ HG REMOVE MODULATOR HOSE FROM CARBURETOR AND PLUG HOSE

VACUUM GAGE READS UNDER 4˚ HG GO TO ECU HARNESS CHECK (FIG 6 E)

ENGINE SPEED DROPS AT LEAST 50 RPM REPLACE SENSOR

VACUUM GAGE READS BELOW 4˚ HG REPLACE MODULATOR

VACUUM GAGE READS ABOVE 4˚ HG SEE SEC 6C FOR DIAGNOSIS

IF OK REPLACE ELECTRONIC CONTROL UNIT

IF NOT OK REPAIR ECU HARNESS

ECU WIRE HARNESS CONTINUITY CHECK

1. ENGINE AT NORMAL OPERATING TEMPERATURE.
2. KEY IN "ON" POSITION.
3. ENGINE NOT RUNNING.
4. REMOVE MAIN WIRE HARNESS AT ECU AND TEST AS FOLLOWS.

TEST LIGHT		RESULT	ACTION
CLIP LEAD	PROBE		
GROUND	1A	LIGHTS	OK
		NO LIGHT	CHECK WIRING, CONNECTIONS FUSIBLE LINK, ETC. REPAIR
POSITIVE BATTERY TERMINAL	2A	LIGHTS	OK
		NO LIGHT	UNPLUG CONNECTOR WIRE AT COLD OVERRIDE SWITCH AND GROUND CONNECTOR WIRE. LIGHTS—WIRE OK, REPLACE SWITCH. NO LIGHT—WIRING PROBLEM, REPAIR.
POSITIVE BATTERY TERMINAL	3A	LIGHTS	OK
		NO LIGHT	UNPLUG WIRE CONNECTOR AT VACUUM SWITCH AND GROUND CONNECTOR WIRE. LIGHT—WIRE OK, REPLACE SWITCH. NO LIGHT—WIRING PROBLEM, REPAIR.

CAUTION: BEFORE CHECKING TEST POINT 4A, REMOVE WIRE CONNECTOR AT 02 SENSOR AND GROUND THE WIRE CONNECTOR. APPLYING 12 VOLTS TO THE SENSOR MAY DAMAGE THE SENSOR.

TEST LIGHT		RESULT	ACTION
POSITIVE BATTERY TERMINAL	4A	LIGHTS	OK
		NO LIGHT	CHECK WIRING, REPAIR.
GROUND	5A	LIGHTS	OK
		NO LIGHT	1. IF 1A WAS OK, WIRING PROBLEM OR DEFECTIVE VACUUM MODULATOR. 2. IF 1A WAS NOT OK, CORRECT 1A PROBLEM AND THEN RECHECK 5A.
POSITIVE BATTERY TERMINAL	6A	LIGHTS	OK
		NO LIGHT	CHECK WIRING, GROUND EYELET AT ENGINE BLOCK, REPAIR.

Electronic fuel control continuity check

Park, with automatic transmission, and increase the engine speed to 3500 rpm. If it now reads 2–4 in. Hg., adjust the idle speed to read 2–4 in. at normal idle, according to the emission sticker in the engine compartment. If the reading is still below that figure, go to the next Step.

5. Remove the oxygen sensor wire (4B).

a. If the vacuum gauge reads above 1 in. Hg., disconnect the modulator connector. If the vacuum falls below 1 in. Hg., replace the ECU. If it stays above 1 in. Hg., replace the vacuum modulator.

b. If it reads below 1 in. Hg., connect a jumper wire from the positive battery terminal to the oxygen sensor terminal (4B). Go to the next Step.

6. If the gauge reads below 4 in. Hg., go to Step 7. If it reads 4–7 in. Hg., leave the jumper connected, and disconnect the vacuum hose at the center port of the modulator. Set the fast idle screw on the high step of the cam and note the engine rpm. Reconnect the hose and note the rpm.

a. If the engine speed drops 50 rpm or more when the hose is reconnected, replace the oxygen sensor.

b. If it drops less than 50 rpm, the problem is in the carburetor.

7. If after Step 5b the gauge still reads below 4 in. Hg., remove the jumper wire and reconnect the oxygen sensor wire. Ground the jumper wire and connect the other end to the brown wire at the modulator connector (5B).

a. If the gauge reads 4–7 in. Hg., go to the next Step.

b. If the gauge reads below 4 in. Hg., remove and plug the modulator vacuum hose from the carburetor. If the reading is still below 4 in. Hg., replace the modulator. If it is above 4 in. Hg., the problem is in the carburetor.

8. If the gauge reads 4–7 in. Hg., in Step 7a, remove the jumper wire at the modulator, and ground the engine temperature switch wire (2B).

a. If the vacuum gauge reads 4–7 in. Hg., replace the temperature switch.

b. If it reads under 4 in. Hg., go to the ECU Wiring Harness Continuity Check (diagram). If after the check the reading is still below 4 in. Hg., repair the ECU harness. If not, replace the ECU.

Electronic Wastegate Controls

1984 AND LATER MODELS

The wastegate is used on turbocharged engines and is normally closed, but opens to bleed off exhaust gases to prevent an over-boost condition. The wastegate will open when pressure is applied to the actuator and is controlled by a wastegate control solenoid valve that is pulsed on and off by the ECM. Under normal driving conditions, the control solenoid is energized all of the time and closes off the manifold to the wastegate actuator. This allows for rapid increase in boost pressure. As boost increases, the increase in pressure is detected by the MAP sensor and the ECM will read the signal and pulse the wastegate control valve, causing the wastegate to open and bleed off the excess boost pressure to prevent possible engine damage. As the boost pressure decreases, the ECM closes the control valve and the wastegate actuator pressure bleeds off through the vent in the control valve.

NOTE: If the MAP sensor detects an overboost condition, the ECM will reduce fuel delivery to prevent engine damage.

A code 31 will be set when the manifold pressure exceeds about 15 psi of boost as determined by the MAP sensor for two seconds and a code 33 has not previously been set. A trouble code 31 will illuminate the SERVICE ENGINE SOON light for as long as the overboost condition exists and for ten seconds after the condition disappears. The trouble code will be stored in the memory if the condition exists long enought to illuminate the SERVICE ENGINE SOON light.

Testing

An overboost condition could be caused by the actuator circuit shorted to ground, a sticking wastegate actuator or wastegate, control valve stuck in the closed position, cut or pinched hose or a defective ECM. An underboost condition can be caused by the wastegate actuator sticking open, wastegate sticking open, control valve sticking open, no ignition signal to the control valve or an open circuit to the ECM, or a defective ECM.

1. With the key OFF, the control valve solenoids is open and should allow pressure to be applied to the wastegate actuator.

2. When 15 psi is applied to the valve and then removed, the actuator should slowly move back and close the wastegate. If the pressure does not bleed off, the vent in the control valve solenoid could be plugged.

3. With the ignition ON and the diagnostic terminal grounded, the control valve solenoid should be energized, closing off the manifold to the wastegate actuator.

4. Check the electrical control portion of the system with the ignition ON and the engine off. The solenoid should not be energized. With the key ON and the diagnostic terminal grounded, the solenoid should be energized.

FORD MICROPROCESSOR CONTROL UNIT (MCU) SYSTEM

General Information

The system is equipped to supply input signals to the microprocessor control unit module (MCU). These inputs originate from the exhaust gas oxygen sensor, cold temperature vacuum switch, idle tracking switch and the rpm tach input from the coil.

The MCU module continuously monitors the input signals and computes the correct operating mode for a given condition. Output signals from the MCU module are applied to control the vacuum solenoid regulator, thermactor bypass control solenoid and the thermactor diverter control solenoid (manual transmission only).

The primary function of the 2.3L MCU module is to control the vacuum regulator solenoid. The MCU module sends ten signals per second to the vacuum regulator solenoid in a timed duty cycle. By varying the "ON" time to the "OFF" time of the cycle, the MCU module is able to maintain or change the air-fuel mixture.

The MCU module does not control ignition timing. The system uses a conventional distributor and coil. The MCU system has three operating modes. These modes are system initialization (start-up), open loop and closed loop.

System Initialization (Start-Up)

The MCU module will initialize when battery power is applied to the computer prior to engine cranking and again immediately with engine starting. During initialization, the duty cycle to the vacuum regulator solenoid is maintained at 50%. After starting, initialization lasts for only a fraction of second. Then, the MCU system goes into the open or closed loop.

Open Loop

The system is in the open loop mode when either the cold termperature vacuum switch or idle tracking switch is activated. In the open loop mode, the MCU module will control the duty cycle with "ON" time signals to the vacuum regulator solenoid. These will provide a calibrated air-fuel mixture.

Closed Loop

With the proper signals from the idle tracking switch and the cold temperature switch, the MCU module changes to the closed loop mode for close range monitoring and control of the air-fuel ratio. The exhaust gas oxygen sensor monitors the exhaust gas to determine if the engine is running rich or lean. This information is used by the MCU module to adjust the carburetor to the air-fuel ratio desired for the operating condition.

Signals from the MCU module, which produce carburetor adjustments, are calibrated. This provides a damping effect to minimize over-correction and abrupt changes.

SYSTEM COMPONENTS

MCU Module

The MCU is the brain of the system. It is a solid-state, programmed micro-computer. It takes the information inputs and uses its program to provide output control signals to the control solenoids. The MCU module receives its power from the battery through the ignition switch.

The module is located either in the engine compartment or under the instrument panel to the left of the steering column. It appears similar to an ignition switch module, but differences in the wiring connectors prevent interchangeability.

Typical oxygen sensor construction

With the eingine cold or at idle, the air-fuel ratio is at a preset level. When the engine is warm and off idle, the air-fuel mixture is adjusted by a signal from the exhaust gas oxygen sensor. These adjustments are made by an "ON-OFF" control signal from the module. For example, when the sensor signals a rich mixture, control "ON" time is increased, while "ON" time is decreased for a lean mixture.

System components used on four cylinder engine

Electric fuel pump wiring diagram—turbocharged models only

Cold Temperature Vacuum Switch

The cold temperature switch is a normally closed switch, with vacuum controlled through a ported vacuum switch (PVS). The MCU system will enter a closed loop mode when the cold temperature switch is activated, provided the vehicle is operating at part throttle.

When the engine is cold, the PVS valve blocks vacuum from the cold temperature vacuum switch. The switch position provides a

Typical electric fuel pump

ground path as a signal to the control unit. When the engine is above 95°F, the PVS valve opens to allow ported vacuum to activate the normally closed switch. With the contacts opened, the ground path signal to the control unit is interrupted.

Idle Tracking Switch

The idle tracking switch is a limit switch used to detect the throttle in the idle position. It is normally closed but opens at closed throttle, sending the MCU system into an open loop mode. The idle tracking switch is mounted on the rear of the carburetor.

Exhaust Gas Oxygen Sensor

The exhaust gas oxygen sensor is threaded into the exhaust manifold, directly in the path of the exhaust gas stream. The sensor provides information to the computer about the air-fuel ratio, indicated by the oxygen concentration in the exhaust gases.

When it senses a rich mixture, the sensor generates a high voltage signal to the computer. A low voltage is generated when a lean mixture (high oxygen level in the exhaust) is sensed. The voltage signal is used by the MCU module for adjustment of the duty cycle during the closed loop mode of operation.

Vacuum Solenoid Regulator

The vacuum solenoid regulator controls manifold vacuum which has been regulated to 5 in Hg. This solenoid receives ten signals per second from the MCU module. The vacuum applied to the metering rod of the carburetor is controlled by varying the duty cycle ("ON-OFF" ratio of the MCU signal).

At 100% duty cycle, 5 in. Hg. vacuum is applied to the metering rod, producing a full lean condition. At 0% duty cycle, the metering rod diaphragm is vented to the atmosphere, producing a full rich condition.

Tachometer Input

The rpm signal to the computer is taken from the "tach" terminal of the ignition coil. This circuit is identified by the dark green-yellow dot wire. This negative signal is used by the computer to determine the amount of damping to use changing the duty signals to the carburetor. These signals are used only in the closed loop mode of operation.

THERMACTOR AIR SYSTEM

The thermactor air system is used to operate the three-way catalytic converter system. The thermactor air system consists of the air pump, bypass and diverter valves and the air control solenoids.

Thermactor air control solenoids

The 2.3l MCU-equipped engine with manual transmission (non-turbo) has a managed thermactor system. When the thermactor air is not bypassed to the atmosphere, it is directed upstream or downstream by the diverter valve. In this application, the diverter valve is controlled by a MCU-controlled solenoid.

The automatic transmission and turbocharged 2.3l engine do not have an air diverter solenoid or a managed thermactor air system. Routing for the thermactor air is determined by engine performance, mode and operating temperature. The valves are pre-calibrated. During normal engine operation, thermactor air is directed downstream. This provides fresh air to the catalyst for the oxidation of HC and CO gases in the exhaust.

Thermactor air venting to the atmosphere is controlled by the idle tracking switch to protect the vehicle from overtemperature during extended idling. Venting begins after 2–2½ minutes of uninterrupted idle. To reduce the excessive amounts of HC and CO during warm-up, thermactor air is directed upstream during this period. The termactor air valves are located at the right front of the engine.

Thermactor Air Pump

The air pump is an impeller-type centrifugal air filter fan. Heavier than air contaminants are thrown from the air intake by centrifugal force. This type of air pump does not have a pressure relief valve because this function is controlled by the thermactor bypass valve.

Thermactor Bypass Solenoid and Diverter Solenoid

The bypass valve operation and diverter valve operation for non-turbocharged engines with manual transmissions are controlled by the termactor air control solenoids. The solenoids route vacuum in three possible directions: bypass, upstream or downstream.

In the bypass mode, air is vented to the atmosphere. In the upstream mode, air is injected into the exhaust manifold. In the downstream mode, air is directed into the three-way catalyst between the two catalyst stages.

IGNITION SYSTEM

A conventional ignition system is used with the MCU-equipped 2.3l engine. The ignition system includes the Duraspark® II coil and ignition module, and a conventional distributor. The MCU system does not control ignition timing. The primary function of the MCU system is the monitoring and adjustment of the air-fuel ratio. The two separate systems complement each other to produce performance in a wide range of operating conditions.

FUEL SYSTEM

Carburetor Control

Controlled vacuum from the vacuum regulator solenoid is channeled to the cavity above the metering rod diaphragm. With no vacuum present, the valve spring causes the valve to move to its lowest (richest) position, where maximum fuel can pass through the orifice. As vacuum is applied to the diaphragm, spring pressure is overcome and the metering rod rises, making the mixture leaner.

Vacuum Solenoid/Regulator

The component that supplies the vacuum signal to the carburetor feedback valve is the vacuum solenoid/regulator. When current from the control module is applied to the solenoid coil, the armature moves upward until it rests on its upper seat. This blocks the atmospheric pressure passage and opens the vacuum passage to the output port. The output vacuum will now reach a constant 5 in. Hg. When current is removed from the coil, the armature moves downward until it rests against its lower seat. This opens the atmospheric passage and closes the vacuum passage, causing the output vacuum to drop to zero.

In operation, the armature actually cycles up and down ten times per second, according to the signal received from the module. The output vacuum is an average value, related to the length of time the armature spends in each position. For example, if the solenoid is

Fuel metering system

energized half the time, the reading would be ½ of 5 in. Hg. of 2½ in. Hg.

The metering valve is calibrated so that the maximum vacuum signal supplied to the diaphragm by the regulator/solenoid (5 in. Hg.) raises the rod to its highest (leanest) position.

Feedback Fuel Valve Piston and Diaphragm Assembly

If the feedback fuel valve piston and diaphragm assembly is removed for any reason during servicing of the Holley Model 6500 carburetor, it is essential that this procedure is followed during reassembly to insure proper operation.

1. Apply one drop of Loctite® or equivalent to the threads in each of the three tapped reatining screw holes.
2. Position the feedback fuel diaphragm and piston assembly over the spring so that the attaching screw holes align with the tapped holes in the upper body (air horn). Make sure the diaphragm is properly installed. One end of the spring should be over the end of the adjustment screw, the other end centered within the cupped washer of the diaphragm and piston assembly.
3. Install and tighten the three retaining screws.

Solenoid Test with Engine Running

1. Connect a voltmeter to the vacuum solenoid at the regulator input lead.
2. Start the engine and observe the voltmeter reading. Increase engine rpm until the reading jumps to approximately 12 volts. Hold it at that rpm.
3. Slowly reduce engine rpm and check to see if the voltmeter pulsates. This proves that the solenoid is getting signals from the module.

MICROPROCESSOR SYSTEM DIAGNOSTIC TESTS

DIAGNOSING NO START CONDITION

Procedure	Result	Action
Battery Voltage Check Ignition key off.	a. 10-16 volts b. Less than 10, more than 16 volts	a. Battery good, go to the next step. b. Service the charging system.
Harness Check Disconnect ignition coil connector and ignition module. Check circuit 11 (dark green with yellow dot) tach terminal for short to ground.	a. No short b. Short to ground	a. Reconnect ignition coil connector and ignition modules. Check for fuel to carburetor and spark to spark plugs. b. Go to next step.
MCU Module Check Disconnect the MCU module and check circuit 11 for short to ground.	a. No short b. Short to ground	a. Replace module and retest. b. Repair harness.

DIAGNOSING COLD ENGINE CONDITION
If condition occurs only when engine is cold, perform this test first

Procedure	Result	Action
Ported Vacuum Switch (PVS) (PVS) Check This test must be performed without starting the engine and with the PVS temperature below 80°F. Disconnect the hose from the cold temperature switch and leave disconnected. Remove the vacuum hose from the carburetor port. Apply vacuum to the hose.	a. Vacuum is held b. Vacuum is not held	a. PVS is good. b. Check for leaks. If there are no leaks, replace PVS and repeat vacuum test.

MCU SELF-TEST PROGRAM
Preliminary Testing

1. A routine pre-test can produce immediate results and help identify a service condition needing correction.
2. With the engine off, place transmission in Park or Neutral. Set the parking brake and block the wheels.
3. Turn off all accessories.
4. Check the vacuum hoses for tight connections.
5. Check the wiring harness, tach lead to coil and MCU components for bad connections and physical damage.
6. Start the engine and warm to operating temperature.
7. While engine is warming, check for vacuum leaks and for exhaust leaks around the exhaust manifold and the exhaust gas oxygen sensor.

MICROPROCESSOR SYSTEM DIAGNOSTIC TESTS
MCU SELF-TEST PROGRAM
Test Preparations

1. Perform the PVS check and the preliminary checks first.
2. With the engine off, ground the brown single-pin connector. On Fairmont, Zephyr, Mustang, and Capri, this connector is located along the right side dash panel, engine side. On Pinto and Bobcat, it is located along the left side dash panel, engine side.
3. Connect voltmeter across the thermactor air bypass solenoid. Use the 0–15 volt scale.
4. Connect a tachometer to the engine.
5. System is now ready to test.

MCU self-test connectors

MICROPROCESSOR SYSTEM DIAGNOSTIC TEST

MCU SELF-TEST PROGRAM
Test Preparations

Procedure	Result	Action
Cold Temperature Vacuum Switch Check With the engine off, turn the ignition key to "RUN". Observe the voltmeter for a pulse code signal. Allow 5 seconds for signal to start after first pulse.	a. Pulses steadily b. One pulse c. Steady high or low reading	a. Switch is good. Go to next step. b. Check switch for continuity. c. Recheck jumper wire at brown test connector and ground. Check voltmeter connections. If same results, substitute a good switch.
Cold Temperature Vacuum Switch Check Disconnect vacuum hose from switch and apply 10" Hg. vacuum to the switch. (If vacuum will not hold, check for leaks and replace switch if necessary.) Turn the ignition key to "RUN" and observe the voltmeter for pulse code signal.	a. One pulse b. Pulses steadily	a. Switch is good. Go to next step. b. Check switch for continuity.
Spark Port Vacuum Check Start the engine and run at 2500 to 2800 rpm. Check for vacuum at cold temperature vacuum switch. There should be greater than 5" vacuum at the switch.	a. Vacuum at hose b. No vacuum at hose	a. Go to the next step. b. Check hoses, PVS and carburetor port for restriction, contamination, damage or vacuum leaks. Repair as needed and go to next step.

MICROPROCESSOR SYSTEM DIAGNOSTIC TESTS

MCU SELF-TEST PROGRAM

Procedure	Result	Action
Idle Tracking Switch Check Turn the ignition key off and reconnect the hose to the cold temperature vacuum switch. Start the engine and observe the voltmeter. Increase engine speed (2800 rpm max.) until voltmeter reading jumps to about 12 volts. Immediately release the throttle. Observe the voltmeter, which will drop to 0 after about 20 seconds. Observe the pulse code signal.	a. One pulse b. Pulses more than once or pulses steadily c. Reading does not jump to 12 volts	a. Switch is good. On non-turbo-charged engines with manual transmissions, go to the next step. On all others, skip the next step and go to the following step. b. Check the idle tracking switch. c. Check the tachometer lead.
Managed Thermactor Air Test With the engine off, remove the self-test ground wire and connect the voltmeter across the air diverter solenoid. Start the engine and immediately observe the voltmeter. Then increase engine speed to 2200 rpm and observe the voltmeter.	a. 11.5 volts at idle and less than 2.5 volts at 2200 rpm b. All other readings	a. Diverter solenoid is good. Connect the self-test jumper and the voltmeter to bypass the solenoid. Go to the next step. b. Check the air diverter.
MCU System Running Test Turn the engine off and restart the engine. Observe the voltmeter. Increase engine speed until the meter jumps to about 12 volts and hold that engine speed. Observe the voltmeter and return the engine to idle when the reading drops to 0. Observe the pulse code signal.	a. Pulses steadily b. One pulse c. Two or three pulses	a. MCU sub-system is good. The test is completed, remove test equipment. b. Go to the idle tracking switch check. c. Go to the fuel control check.

FUEL CONTROL CHECK
Test Preparation and Preliminary Testing

1. Remove the grounding jumper wire from the brown self-test connector.
2. Inspect the choke plate for freedom of movement.
3. Recheck for vacuum leaks and burned or damaged wiring.
CHILTON CAUTION: Do not hold the throttle open with any device since this will activate the idle tracking switch.
4. Turn the ignition key to "RUN" with the engine off.
5. Listen or feel for clicking at the vacuum solenoid regulator.
6. If there is steady clicking, skip the first four steps of the fuel control test procedure.
7. If there is irregular clicking or no clicking at all, begin with the first step of the test procedure.

MCU harness connectors

MICROPROCESSOR SYSTEM DIAGNOSTIC TESTS

FUEL CONTROL CHECK

Procedure	Result	Action
Exhaust Gas Oxygen Sensor Test Check continuity from pin 77 to pin VSR.	a. Continuity b. No continuity	a. Check the harness. b. Repair open in circuit 77 (dark blue with yellow hash).
Check continuity from pin 77 to ground.	a. Continuity b. No continuity	a. Repair short in circuit 77. b. Go to the next step.
Check continuity from pin 687 to pin BATT.	a. Continuity b. No continuity	a. Go to the next step. b. Repair open in circuit 687 (gray with yellow stripe).
Measure vacuum solenoid regulator resistance. It should be 30 ohms.	a. 30 to 75 ohms b. Less than 30 or more than 75 ohms	a. Replace the MCU module. b. Replace the vacuum solenoid regulator.
Leave voltmeter on pin 77 and ground. Disconnect the thermactor air supply hose to the diverter valve and plug the opening at the diverter valve. Run the engine at 2500 to 2800 rpm, while holding the choke about ¾ closed for 10 to 20 seconds. Do not hold the choke closed for more than 20 seconds.	a. 2.5 volts or more b. Less than 2.5 volts	a. Go to the next step. b. Check thermactor catalytic converter emission system.
Tee vacuum gauge into hose to feedback port of carburetor. Run engine at 2500 to 2800 rpm.	a. Less than 2.5" vacuum b. More than 2.5" vacuum	a. Skip the next two steps. b. Go to the next step.
Connect voltmeter from pin 77 to ground. Run the engine at 2500 to 2800 rpm.	a. 2.5 volts or more b. Less than 2.5 volts	a. Replace the vacuum solenoid regulator. b. Go to the next step.
Leave voltmeter between pin 77 and ground, and reconnect the vacuum hose. Unplug the exhaust gas oxygen sensor from the harness. Run the engine at 2500 to 2800 rpm.	a. 10 or more volts b. Less than 10 volts	a. Check stepper motor needle travel. b. Replace MCU module.
Connect voltmeter to pin 77 and ground. Run the engine at 2500 to 2800 rpm.	a. 10 or more volts b. Less than 10 volts	a. Skip the next step. b. Go to the next step.
Remove tee and attach the vacuum gauge directly to the hose from the center port of the vacuum solenoid regulator. Run the engine at idle speed.	a. 4" vacuum b. Less than 4" vacuum	a. Check the carburetor feedback system. b. Check the hose between the vacuum solenoid regulator and carburetor. Check the vacuum source to VSR and if less than 10", repair. If 10" or more, replace the vacuum solenoid regulator.

Oxygen sensor circuit

MICROPROCESSOR SYSTEM DIAGNOSTIC TESTS

FUEL CONTROL CHECK

Procedure	Result	Action
Disconnect the exhaust gas oxygen sensor from the harness. Check continuity from pin 74 to pin EGO.	a. Continuity b. No continuity	a. Go to the next step. b. Repair open in circuit 94 (dark green with purple hash).
Check continuity from pin 74 to ground.	a. Continuity b. No continuity	a. Repair short in circuit 94. b. Go to the next step.
Check continuity from pin EGO to ground.	a. Continuity b. No continuity	a. Go to the next step. b. Repair open circuit.
Connect MCU to harness. Leave the voltmeter connected from pin 77 to ground and run the engine at idle. Carefully run a jumper from pin EGO to the positive terminal of the battery. Increase the engine speed to 2500 to 2800 rpm.	a. Less than 2.5 volts b. 2.5 volts or more	a. Replace the exhaust gas oxygen sensor. b. Replace the MCU module.

COLD TEMPERATURE VACUUM SWITCH CIRCUIT TESTS

Procedure	Result	Action
With the key off, check for continuity from pin 73 to ground.	a. Continuity b. No continuity	a. Replace the MCU module. b. Unplug the switch and ground wire 73 (orange with light blue hash) at the switch connector. If there is continuity, go to the next step. If there is no continuity, repair open in circuit 73.
With the key off, check for continuity from ground to pin B.	a. Continuity b. No continuity	a. Repair open in circuit 57 (black base). b. Replace cold temperature vacuum switch.
With the key off, apply 10" vacuum to the cold temperature vacuum switch. Check for continuity from pin 73 to ground.	a. No continuity b. Continuity	a. Replace the MCU module. b. Unplug the switch. If there is still continuity, repair short in circuit 73. If there is no continuity, replace the switch.

Cold temperature vacuum switch circuit

MICROPROCESSOR SYSTEM DIAGNOSTIC TESTS

IDLE TRACKING SWITCH CIRCUIT TESTS

Procedure	Result	Action
CHILTON CAUTION: Before performing the following tests, be sure the idle tracking switch is in proper position for throttle at idle. The throttle arm should fully depress the switch.		
With the key off and the throttle closed, check for continuity from pin 189 to ground.	a. No continuity b. Continuity	a. Replace the MCU module. b. Unplug the idle tracking switch. If there is still continuity, repair short in wire 189 (light blue with pink dots). If there is no continuity, replace the switch.
With the key off and the throttle open, check for continuity from pin 189 to ground.	a. Continuity b. No continuity	a. Go to the last step. b. Unplug the switch and ground wire 189 at the connector. If there is continuity, go to the next step. If there is no continuity, repair open in wire 189.
With the key off, check for continuity from ground to pin A.	a. No continuity b. Continuity	a. Repair open in circuit 57 (black base). b. Replace the idle tracking switch.
With the key off, measure the resistance from pin 189 to pin 687. (Should be 120 ohms.)	a. 90 to 150 ohms b. Less than 90 or more than 150 ohms	a. Replace MCU module. b. Repair or replace harness resistor.

Idle tracking switch circuit

MICROPROCESSOR SYSTEM DIAGNOSTIC TESTS

THERMACTOR AIR DIVERTER SOLENOID CIRCUIT TESTS

Procedure	Result	Action
With the key off, check for continuity from pin 200 to pin H.	a. Continuity b. No continuity	a. Go to the next step. b. Repair open in circuit 200 (white with black hash).
With the key off, check for continuity from pin 200 to ground.	a. No continuity b. Continuity	a. Go to the next step. b. Repair short in circuit 200.
With the key off, check for continuity from pin 687 to pin J.	a. Continuity b. No continuity	a. Go to the next step. b. Repair open in circuit 687 (gray with yellow stripe).
With the key off, measure the resistance of the air diverter solenoid. It should be 30 to 75 ohms.	a. 30 to 75 ohms. b. 0 to 30 or more than 75 ohms.	a. Solenoid is good, go to the next step. b. Replace the solenoid.
With the key off, check for continuity from pin 201 to ground.	a. No continuity b. Continuity	a. Go to the next step. b. Repair short in circuit 201.
CHILTON CAUTION: Before continuing with the following tests, be sure the idle tracking switch is in the proper position for throttle at idle. The throttle arm should fully depress the idle tracking switch. If not in the correct position, the idle tracking switch can cause air diverter solenoid circuit problems.		
With the key off and the throttle open, check for continuity from pin 189 to ground.	a. Continuity b. No continuity	a. Skip the next step and go to the following step. b. Unplug the idle tracking switch and ground wire 189 at the connector. If there is continuity, go back to the third step of this procedure. If there is no continuity, repair open in wire 189.
With the key off, check for continuity from ground to pin A.	a. No continuity b. Continuity	a. Repair open in circuit 57 (black). b. Replace idle tracking switch.
With the key off, measure the resistance from pin 189 to pin 687. It should be 120 ohms.	a. 90 to 150 ohms. b. Less than 90 or more than 150 ohms	a. Replace the MCU module. b. Repair or replace the harness resistor.

Air diverter solenoid circuit

MICROPROCESSOR SYSTEM DIAGNOSTIC TESTS

THERMACTOR AIR BY-PASS RESISTANCE TESTS

Procedure	Result	Action
With the key off, check for continuity from pin 201 to pin D.	a. Continuity b. No continuity	a. Go to the next step. b. Repair open in circuit 201 (brown connector, self-test trigger).
With the key off, check for continuity from pin 687 to the positive battery terminal.	a. Continuity b. No continuity	a. Go to the next step. b. Repair open in circuit 687 (gray with yellow stripe).
With the key off, check for continuity from pin 687 to pin E.	a. Continuity b. No continuity	a. Go to the next step. b. Repair open in circuit 687.
With the key off, check for continuity from pin 57 to ground.	a. Continuity b. No continuity	a. Go to the next step. b. Repair open in circuit 57 (black base).
With the key off, check for continuity from pin 190 to pin F.	a. Continuity b. No continuity	a. Go to the next step. b. Repair open in circuit 190 (white with red dot).
With the key off, check for continuity from pin 190 to ground.	a. No continuity b. Continuity	a. Go to the next step. b. Repair open in circuit 190.
With the key off, measure the resistance of the air by-pass solenoid.	a. 30 to 75 ohms b. 0 to 30 or more than 75 ohms	a. The solenoid is good, replace the MCU module. b. Replace the solenoid.

TACHOMETER LEAD TEST

Procedure	Result	Action
With the key off, check for continuity from pin 11 to the tach terminal.	a. Continuity b. No continuity	a. Wiring is good, replace the MCU module. b. Repair open in circuit 11 (dark green with yellow dot).

Non-turbo automatic transmission

Turbocharged models

Feedback carburetor electrical circuits

MCU/EGO CONNECTOR

74
57

MCU MODULE

74 (DARK GREEN/YELLOW HASH)

EXHAUST GAS OXYGEN SENSOR (EGO)

EGO SELECT LINE (57)

11 (DARK GREEN/YELLOW DOT)

TO IGNITION COIL
(TACH TERMINAL)

73 (ORANGE/LT. BLUE HASH)

201

120 R 189

189 (LT. BL./PINK DOT)

57 (BLACK BASE)

ENGINE GROUND

COLD TEMPERATURE VACUUM SWITCH

N C

57
73

189
57

IDLE TRACKING SWITCH
(OPEN AT IDLE)

N C

687 (GRAY/YELLOW STRIPE)

TO IGNITION SWITCH (RUN ONLY)

73 11

201   189

687   57

MCU CONNECTOR

HARNESS CONNECTOR
LOCATED UNDER DASH

190 (WHITE/RED)

SERVICE CODE
CONNECTOR (GRAY)

190
687

THERMACTOR AIR BYPASS SOLENOID

190
200   77

CONNECTOR

200 (WHITE/BLACK)

THERMACTOR AIR DIVERTER SOLENOID
(2.3L NON-TURBO MANUAL TRANS. ONLY)

201   57

190

687

77 (DARK BLUE/YELLOW HASH)

SELF TEST TRIGGER
CONNECTOR (BROWN)

687
77

VACUUM SOLENOID REGULATOR

NOTE BLACK PINS ARE NOT USED

Non-turbo manual transmission models

FORD ELECTRONIC ENGINE CONTROLS (EEC) I

General Information

The system is called the electronic engine control (EEC I) system, and consists of an electronic control assembly (ECA) and seven sensors, a DuraSpark II ignition module and coil, a unique distributor assembly and an air pressure operated EGR system.

To monitor ambient conditions and the function of the vehicle and engine, two pressure sensors, two temperature sensors and three position sensors are required. The sensors monitor the following.

- Manifold absolute pressure
- Barometric pressure
- Engine coolant temperature
- Inlet air temperature
- Crankshaft position
- Throttle position
- EGR valve position

The sensors monitor these various engine and ambient conditions and send electrical signals to the ECA for processing. The computer computes the correct ignition timing, EGR flow rate and digital volt-ohmmeter is accurate and has a high input impedance unit for gathering EEC I system data. Digital readout minimizes errors, giving technicians necessary accuracy for EEC diagnosis.

An advance timing light compatible with the Dura Spark II ignition system, a pressure/vacuum gauge and a tachometer are also required for diagnosis of the EEC I system.

Fail-Safe Mode

If for some reason the ECA should not function properly, it goes into what is called the limited operation strategy (LOD) mode. In the LOS mode, spark advance is held constant at 10 degrees BTDC. EGR and thermactor systems are deactivated. This allows operation of the vehicle, although with reduced performance, until repairs can be made.

EEC I SYSTEM COMPONENTS

Electronic Control Assembly (ECA)

The electronic control assembly (ECA) is the brain of the EEC system, and is a solid-state, micro-computer consisting of a processor assembly and a calibration assembly. This assembly is located in the passenger compartment under the instrument panel, just to the left of the steering column.

Power Relay

A power relay attached to the lower right hand side of the ECA mounting bracket supplies battery voltage to the EEC I system. It also protects the ECA from possible damage due to reversed voltage polarity.

Calibration Assembly

The calibration assembly is attached to the top of the processor assembly with two screws, and contains the memory and programming for processing assembly. It is capable of providing calibration information for that particular vehicle, for use by the processor assembly, storing calculations for the processor assembly and recalling information from its memory when asked.

Unique calibration assemblies are required for differences in engine calibrations (i.e. 49 state, California etc.).

Processor Assembly

The processor assembly is housed in an aluminim case. It contains circuits designed to continuously sample the seven sensor input signals, to convert the sampled signal to a form usable by the computer section in calculations, to perform ignition timing, thermactor and EGR flow calculations and to send electrical output control

Power relay and ECA attachment

signals to the ignition module and control solenoids to adjust timing, EGR flow rate and the thermactor air flow. The processor assembly also provides a continuous reference voltage (about 9 volts) to the sensors.

Crankshaft Pulse Ring

In operation, the crankshaft position sensor works somewhat like the breakerless distributor pickup coil. The pulse ring passes through the magnetic field at the tip of the sensor. When a lobe of the pulse ring passes the tip of the sensor, an output signal is generated and sent to the electronic control assembly (ECA). As the crankshaft turns, the computer interprets the electrical impulses to determine the exact position of the crankshaft at any given time.

Electronic control assembly

INLET AIR
TEMP SENSOR

ELECTRONIC
CONTROL
ASSEMBLY
(ECA)

CALIBRATION
ASSEMBLY
PROCESSOR
ASSEMBLY

MODEL 2700 VV
CARBURETOR

LOCATED IN
PASSENGER
COMPARTMENT

POWER RELAY

THROTTLE
POSITION
SENSOR

BAROMETRIC
PRESSURE SENSOR

ENGINE COOLANT
TEMP SENSOR

MANIFOLD ABSOLUTE
PRESSURE SENSOR

EGR VENT SOLENOID
VALVE

EGR PRESSURE
SOLENOID VALVE

EGR VALVE ACTUATOR
AND POSITION SENSOR

THERMACTOR AIR BY-PASS
SOLENOID

DURA-SPARK II
IGNITION MODULE

CRANKSHAFT
POSITION SENSOR

Typical EEC I system

From the frequency of the pulses, the ECA can determine the engine rpm. By knowing these two factors, the computer will determine the appropriate ignition timing advance required for best engine operation.

The crankshaft position sensor is held in place by a retaining clip and screw. An O-ring near the tip of the sensor seals the lower opening in the rear of the engine block. Once the sensor is locked in place, no field adjustment is necessary.

A broken sensor, open wiring or a sensor not completely seated in the engine will prevent the ECA from receiving a position signal. The ECA will not send a firing signal to the ignition module, thus disabling the ignition system and preventing the engine from starting.

Throttle Position Sensor (TP)

The throttle positioner (TP) sensor is a potentionmeter, mounted on the carburetor and actuated by the throttle linkage to provide an output signal proportional to throttle angle.

Throttle position sensor (TP)

With a reference voltage applied, the TP sensor output is interpreted as one of the following modes, closed throttle (idle or deceleration), part throttle (cruise) or wide open throttle (maximum acceleration).

ADJUSTMENT

Set the throttle to the idle position (against the idle set screw). Connect a 0–10 digital voltmeter between the connector terminal with the green wire (positive) and the terminal with the black wire. Rotate the sensor counter-clockwise to obtain a reading on the voltmeter of 1.89 ± .180 volts. (An alternate method of setting the throttle potentiometer is to rotate it counter-clockwise until a ratiometric reading of 0.21 ± is obtained). Tighten the mounting screws. Rotate the throttle to wide open position and release. Recheck the sensor output at idle. Adjust as required.

As a final check, rotate the throttle to a wide open condition and release. The throttle must return to an idle condition unassisted. Reconnect to wire harness.

EGR SYSTEM COMPONENTS

The amount of EGR gas flow is controlled by the computer which utilizes air pressure from the thermactor system bypass valve to

Crankshaft position sensor (CP)

operate the EGR valve. When the EGR valve is open, exhaust gas from the exhaust manifold is allowed to flow into the intake manifold, becoming part of the combustion cycle and reducing NOx emissions.

EGR Valve and Sensor Assembly

The EGR valve used with the EEC I system resembles the valve used with non-EEC I system applications, but is air pressure operated rather than vacuum operated. The EGR valve attaches to a spacer that mounts under the carburetor on the intake manifold. The valve controls the flow of gases through a tapered pintle valve and seat. A position sensor built into the valve provides an electrical signal to the ECA that indicates EGR valve position.

EGR valve and spacer

EGR gas cooler

Unlike conventional system EGR valves, the EEC I system EGR valve is completely sealed, and no pintle valve movement can be seen when the valve is installed on the spacer. The valve and position sensor are serviced as a unit.

EGR Cooler Assembly

In order to provide improved flow characteristics, better engine operation and EGR valve durability, an external EGR gas cooler is used to reduce EGR gas temperature. The cooler assembly is

Air operated EGR valve

mounted over the right valve cover and uses engine coolant to reduce the temperature of exhaust gases routed from the exhaust manifold to the EGR valve.

Dual EGR Control Solenoids

EGR valve movement is controlled by two solenoid valves mounted on a bracket above the left hand valve cover. To properly control the air pressure used to operate the EGR valve and to allow for application, hold and release of the air pressure requires two types of solenoid valve. The first is a vent valve which is normally open; that is, the outlet port is normally connected to the inlet port when the solenoid is not operated. The other is a pressure valve which is normally closed; that is, the outlet port is normally blocked when the solenoid is not operated.

OPERATION

The EGR valve is operated by air pressure supplied from the thermactor by pass valve. The pressure and vent solenoid valves work together under the direction of the computer to increase EGR flow by applying air pressure to the EGR valve, maintain EGR flow by trapping air pressure in the system and decrease EGR flow by venting system pressure to the atmosphere.

With data received from the various sensors, the computer determines the correct amount of EGR flow required, checks the position of the EGR valve pintle and decides if a change in position is required. In response to these calculations, the ECA puts the EGR system into one of the modes. The ECA samples and calculates these changes about 10 times each second for improved economy and driveability under all conditions.

Manifold Absolute Pressure Sensor (MAP)

The manifold absolute pressure (MAP) sensor is mounted on the left rocker arm cover and minitors the changes in intake manifold pressure which result from changes in engine load, speed and atmospheric pressure. (Manifold absolute pressure is defined as barometric pressure minus manifold vacuum). The MAP sensor contains a pressure sensing element and electronic circuits that convert pressure sensed by the unit into an electric signal for the ECA. This signal is used by the ECA to determine part throttle spark advance and EGR flow rate.

Barometric Pressure Sensor (BP)

The BP sensor is mounted on the engine compartment side of the dash panel and senses barometric pressure. The pressure is then converted into an electrical signal and fed to the ECA for computations. From this input, the ECA is able to determine EGR flow requirements, depending on the altitude at which the vehicle is being driven.

Manifold absolute pressure (MAP) sensor

Barometric pressure sensor (BP)

Coolant temperature sensor (ECT)

Coolant Temperature Sensor (ECT)

The engine coolant temperature sensor is installed in the rear of the intake manifold and converts engine coolant temperature into an electrical signal for the ECA to process. The sensor consists of a brass housing which contains a thermistor (variable resistor which decreases its resistance as the temperature rises) that measures engine temperature.

The coolant temperature sensor takes the place of the cooling PVS and EGR PVS used in the conventional system. When the engine coolant temperature reaches a predetermined value stored in the system's memory, the ECA will cut off all EGR flow. In addition, if the engine coolant overheats from prolonged idle, the ECA will advance the engine initial ignition timing for increased engine idle speed and improved cooling system efficiency.

Thermactor Air Bypass Solenoid

The thermactor control solenoid is a normally closed valve that functions the same as the EGR pressure solenoid valve. The upper port is connected to the thermactor bypass valve top (actuator) port and the lower port is connected to manifold vacuum. When the ECA energizes the thermactor air bypass solenoid, manifold vacuum is applied to the bypass valve and thermactor air is injected into the cylinder head exhaust ports. When the ECA de-energizes the thermactor air bypass solenoid, the valve closes and the bypass valve dumps thermactor air into the atmosphere. The ECA uses information from the inlet air temperature sensor and the throttle position sensor to determine when to inject air and when to dump air into the atmosphere.

Inlet Air Temperature Sensor (IAT)

The inlet air temperature sensor is similar in construction and function to the coolant temperature sensor, except for the design of the sensor tip which monitors air temperature. The sensor is mounted in the air cleaner body near the duct and valve assembly and is sensitive to changes in inlet air temperature. As inlet air temperature rises, the resistance of the sensing thermistor decreases, allowing the ECA to keep constant check on the temperature. With this information, the ECA can determine the proper spark advance and

EEC I distributor cap and rotor

Inlet air temperature sensor (IAT)

thermactor system air flow. At high inlet air temperatures the ECA will modify ignition timing advance as necessary to prevent spark knock.

IGNITION SYSTEM

The ignition system used with the EEC I system uses a DuraSpark II ignition module and ignition coil to generate the required high voltage spark. Routing the secondary voltage to the appropriate spark plugs is accomplished with a distributor designed for the EEC I system.

Distributor

The EEC I distributor does not have conventional mechanical or vacuum advance mechanisms as do other Ford distributors. Instead, all ignition timing is controlled by the electronic control assembly (ECA), which is capable of firing the spark plug at any point from top dead center (TDC) to 60 degrees before top dead center (BTDC). This increased spark advance capability requires greater separation of adjacent distributor cap electrods to prevent cross fire.

Bi-Level Rotor and Distributor Cap

The distributor rotor and cap electrodes have been designed to handle the additional advance capability, by using a two-level design. Both the rotor and cap have upper and lower electrode levels. As the rotor turns, one of the high-voltage electrode pick-up arms aligns with one spoke of the distributor cap center electrode plate. This allows high voltage to pass from the plate, through the rotor to a terminal on the distributor cap and out to the spark plug.

The numbers molded into the top of the cap are spark plug wire identification numbers. However, due to the unique construction of the distributor cap and rotor, the wires are not arranged in the cap in firing order.

NOTE: Do not attempt to remove any silicone coating from the rotor lower electrode blades or from the distributor cap electrodes.

Component Removal

ELECTRONIC CONTROL ASSEMBLY (ECA)

The Electronic Control Assembly (ECA) is mounted behind the instrument panel on the driver's side to the left of the steering column near the brake pedal support. The ECA is attached to its mounting bracket with three screws. If the ECA requires replacement, loosen only the two left hand screws and remove the one right hand screw. There are slots which allow the unit to slide out and away from the left hand mounting screws. The bottom side of the ECA has 3 wiring harness connectors which are easily removed for diagnostic work and test equipment connection. The harness connector bodies are polarized (keyed) to prevent improper connection. Each connector body is color coded (Black 7-pin, Blue 10-pin, Red 9-pin) and each has pin identification letters on the side of the connector. Also, corresponding colored dots are located on the bottom side of the ECA to aid in reconnection of the three wiring harness connectors.

DISTRIBUTOR ROTOR

In order to obtain maximum timing advance without crossfire to adjacent distributor cap electrodes, it is important that proper distributor rotor alignment be established, using the special rotor alignment tool designed for this purpose. Since there is no mechanical advance mechanism or adjustments under the rotor, there is no need to remove the rotor except to replace it.

Removal

1. Remove the distributor cap by loosening the two spring clips holding the cap to the distributor adaptor.

2. Rotate the crankshaft sufficiently to align the distributor rotor upper blade (with slot) with the locating slot in the distributor adaptor, so the distributor rotor alignment Tool T78P-12200-A, or equivalent will drop into place. If the rotor or adapter is damaged and alignment is not possible, position the crankshaft with number 1 piston at compression TDC by aligning the zero mark on the damper with the timing pointer on the front cover.

3. Remove the rotor alignment tool and remove the two screws attaching the rotor to the distributor shaft. Remove the rotor.

—————————————CAUTION—————————————

Do not rotate the crankshaft after the rotor has been removed.

Installation

NOTE: When replacing the rotor, coat the lower electrode blades approximately $1/32$ in. thick on all sides (outboard of the plastic) with D7AZ-19A331-AA silicon grease or equivalent.

1. Place the new rotor on the distributor shaft with the slot in the upper blade pointing to the locating notch in the distributor adapter. Install, but do not tighten both rotor attaching screws.

2. Position the rotor alignment Tool T78P-12200-A, or equivalent, in the distributor adapter so that the tang on the underside of the tool engages the locating notch in the distributor adapter and the slot in the rotor at the same time.

3. Tighten both rotor attaching screws to 15–20 in. lb.

4. Remove the rotor alignment tool and reinstall the distributor cap. Seat both cap-to-adapter spring clips.

DISTRIBUTOR

The EECI distributor is locked in place during engine assembly and no rotational adjustment is possible. A slot in the distributor base mounting flange fits around the distributor clamp hold-down bolt, preventing movement. Adjustment is not required, since all timing is controlled by the ECA.

Removal

1. Remove the distributor cap and insert the rotor alignment Tool T78P-12200-A, or equivalent, by following Steps 1 and 2 under Rotor Removal.

2. With the rotor alignment tool inserted, loosen the distributor hold-down bolt and clamp. Remove alignment tool.

3. Slowly remove the distributor assembly from the engine block, noting the position of the rotor blade with respect to the distributor base when the cam and distributor drive gear are felt to disengage.

—————————————CAUTION—————————————

Do not rotate the crankshaft after the distributor has been removed from the engine.

Installation

1. Position the distributor in the block so that when fully seated the following conditions are met:

   a. The slot on the distributor base hold-down flange is aligned with the clamp bolt hole in the block, and

   b. the slot in the upper blade of the rotor is approximately aligned with the slot in the adapter.

If alignment is not possible when the distributor is fully seated, raise the distributor out of the block enough to disengage the cam gear and rotate the distributor shaft slightly to allow the next tooth on the distributor drive gear to engage the cam gear. Repeat this procedure until conditions outlined in (a) and (b) are satisfied.

2. Install the distributor-to-block clamp and bolt and tighten to 15–18 ft. lbs. (20–24 Nm) torque.

3. Align the rotor and install the distributor cap following procedures outlined under Rotor Installation Steps 1–4.

NOTE: When installing a new distributor cap, coat the brass center electrode plate tip surfaces with D7AZ-19A331-AA silicon grease or equivalent (Dow 111 or G.E. G-627 compound).

PROCESSOR ASSEMBLY

Removal and Installation

1. Disconnect the battery negative cable.
2. Disconnect the three processor/wiring harness connectors.
3. Remove the assembly (loosen and remove the screws which mount the processor to its bracket).
4. Separate the calibration assembly from the processor.
5. Install the calibration assembly on the new processor (tighten mounting screws).
6. Install the assembly and connect the wiring harness connectors making certain that the connectors latch in place.
7. Connect the battery negative cable.
8. Verify EECI Subsystem Operates properly by performing Subsystem checkout.

CALIBRATION ASSEMBLY

Removal and Installation

1. Disconnect the battery negative cable.
2. Disconnect the three processor/wiring harness connectors.
3. Remove the assembly (loosen and remove screws which mount the processor to its bracket).
4. Separate the calibration assembly from the processor.
5. Install the new calibration assembly on the processor (tighten (2) mounting screws).
6. Install the assembly and connect the wiring harness connectors making certain that the connectors latch in place.
7. Connect the battery negative cable.
8. Verify EECI Subsystem operates properly by performing Subsystem checkout.

MANIFOLD ABSOLUTE SENSOR PRESSURE (MAP)

Removal and Installation

1. Disconnect the vacuum hose and electrical connector from the MAP sensor.
2. Remove the sensor from the mounting bracket by removing the two bracket stud nuts.
3. Install the new sensor on the bracket studs and install the nuts.
4. Connect the vacuum hose and electrical connector.
5. Verify that the EECI Subsystem operates properly by performing Subsystem checkout.

BAROMETRIC PRESSURE (BP) SENSOR

Removal and Installation

1. Disconnect the electrical connector.
2. Remove the sensor by loosening and removing the two retaining screws.
3. Install the new sensor using two retaining screws.
4. Connect the electrical connector.
5. Verify that the EECI Subsystem operates properly by performing subsystem checkout.

CRANKSHAFT POSITION SENSOR

Removal

1. Disconnect the Sensor (blue) connector from the wiring harness.
2. After the engine and exhaust system have cooled sufficiently, raise the vehicle.

3. Remove the transmission filler tube by removing the attaching bolt. Use drain pan to catch any fluid that leaks out.
4. Remove the engine ground strap bolt from engine block.
5. Lower the vehicle.
6. Loosen the Phillips head (Allen head on later models) screw, part of the sensor retainer clamp assembly. Using an offset screwdriver or other similar hooked tool to pull the sensor from its seated position.
7. When screw is thoroughly disengaged, remove the sensor and retainer clamp from the engine block.

Installation

1. Snap the retainer clamp assembly onto the sensor.
2. Lubricate O-ring with engine oil. Carefully start sensor with the retainer clamp assembly into block so as not to damage the O-ring. The sensor must be fully seated by alternately pushing on the sensor hat section, but not the wires, with finger pressure and tightening retainer assembly screw. Do not rely on retainer clamp assembly pressure alone to seat sensor, as clamp will be damaged.

NOTE: Failure to fully seat and retain the sensor will cause malfunction of sensor operation, and a possible no start condition.

3. Tighten the retainer clamp screw to 60 to 108 in. lbs. (7-1 Nm).
4. Connect the sensor plug to the wiring harness.
5. Raise the vehicle.
6. Install the engine ground strap.
7. Install the transmission filler tube.
8. Lower the vehicle.
9. Refill the transmission and check the filler tube for leaks.
10. Verify that the EECI Subsystem is operating properly by performing Subsystem checkout.

INLET AIR TEMPERATURE (IAT) SENSOR

Removal and Installation

1. Remove the air cleaner cover.
2. Disconnect the electrical connector.
3. Remove the retainer clip and remove the sensor.
4. Place the new sensor in the mounting hold and secure using the retainer clip.
5. Connect the electrical connector.
6. Install the air cleaner cover.
7. Verify that the EECI Sub-system operates properly by performing subsystem checkout.

ENGINE COOLANT TEMPERATURE (ECT) SENSOR

Removal and Installation

1. Disconnect the transmission kickdown rod from the carburetor linkage and position out of the way.
2. Disconnect the electrical connector.
3. Remove the sensor using $13/16$ inch crow foot wrench.
4. If the sensor is new, check the sensor threads for the presence of Teflon tape. Wrap with $1\,1/4$ turns of Teflon tape if missing. If the sensor is being re-installed, clean threads and wrap with $1\,1/4$ turns of Teflon tape.
5. Install the sensor using a $13/16$ inch crow foot wrench. Tighten to 8-18 ft. lbs. (10-14 Nm) torque.
6. Connect the electrical connector.
7. Install the transmission kickdown rod to the carburetor linkage.
8. Verify that the EECI subsystem operates properly by performing subsystem checkout.

EGR VALVE POSITION (EVP) SENSOR

Removal and Installation

1. Remove the air cleaner.

2. Disconnect the choke tube and fresh air, return tube from the carburetor.

3. Disconnect the sensor electrical connector.

4. Disconnect the EGR pressure line.

5. Cut the EGR cooler tube clamp.

6. Remove the EGR valve assembly.

7. Clean the gasket surface.

8. Install a new gasket.

9. Install the EGR cooler tube gasket and clamp.

10. Install the new EGR valve assembly.

11. Crimp the cooler tube clamp.

12. Install the EGR pressure line.

13. Connect the EVP sensor electrical connector.

14. Connect the choke tube and fresh air return to the carburetor.

15. Install the air cleaner.

16. Verify that the EECI subsystem operates properly by performing subsystem checkout.

THROTTLE POSITION SENSOR

Removal and Installation

1. Loosen the two screws holding throttle sensor to the carburetor sensor bracket.

2. Disengage the connector from wiring harness and remove the potentiometer assembly.

3. Attach the actuator (DE4E-9B991-AA or equivalent) to the throttle lever, using one hex head, 3 x 48 UNC screw. Tighten to 5 in. lbs. (.5 Nm).

4. Mount the position sensor bracket to the throttle body using two 1/4 x 20 hex head screws. Tighten to 70-105 in. lbs. (7-11 Nm).

5. Insert the throttle position sensor through the pilot hole in the bracket and insure that the sensor shaft coupling engages the actuator correctly. Attach the sensor to the bracket using two 6 x 32 Phillips/washer head screws. Finger tighten to facilitate rotation of the sensor within the adjustment slots.

6. Set the throttle to the idle position (against the idle set screw). Apply 9.0 VDC ± 10 percent between the connector terminal with the orange wire (positive) and the terminal with the black wire (negative). Connect a 0-10 VDC voltmeter between the connector terminal with the green wire (positive) and the terminal with the black wire. Rotate the sensor counterclockwise to obtain a reading on the voltmeter of 1.89 VDC ± 8.10 BDC. (An alternate method of setting the throttle potentiometer is to rotate it until a reading of 0.21 ± .02 is obtained). Tighten the mounting screws to 8-1°0 in. lbs. (.9-1 Nm). Rotate the throttle to wide open position and release. Recheck the sensor output at idle. Adjust as required.

7. As a final check, rotate the throttle to a wide open condition and release. The throttle must return to an idle condition unassisted.

8. Reconnect sensor to wire harness.

Diagnosis and Testing

NOTE: This procedure is intended for the Electronic Engine Control sub-system installed on the 1979 5.0L engine.

TEST EQUIPMENT

Several special service tools are necessary to test the EECI system, including:

• Digital volt/ohm meter (DVOM) Rotunda Model #T78L-50-DVOM or T79L-50-DVOM (or equivalent)

• Rotunda Model #T78L-50-EEC-1 or equivalent tester including test fixtures.

• Tachometer: with a 0 to 3000 RPM range.

• Vacuum/Pressure Gauge with a range of 0-25 + 5, − 0 in. Hg, 0-15 ± psi

• Timing light Rotunda #27-0002 (or equivalent) or magnetic pick up timing and advance meter.

• Speed control tool, Snap-On, #GA-437 (or equivalent).

Visual Inspection

1. Remove air cleaner assembly and inspect all vacuum and pressure hoses for proper connection to fittings, or broken, cracked or pinched hoses.

2. Inspect the EEC Sub-System harness and electrical connections for loose or detached connectors, broken or detached wires, terminals not completely seated in the connector, partially broken or frayed wires at connectors, shorting between wires, corrosion.

3. Inspect the sensors for evidence of physical damage.

Test Equipment Hookup

1. Turn ignition KEY OFF.

2. Disconnect the harness from the Electronic Control Assembly (ECA).

3. Connect the test equipment to vehicle per the manufacturer's instructions.

4. Check the battery voltage level and verify the reading is greater than the value stated on face plate.

5. If the voltage is low consult the tester manual. Set the DVOM switch to "TESTER" position.

CAUTION

When using DVOM with selector switch in "TESTER" position, test leads MUST BE removed from DVOM "TEST LEADS" jacks.

---

6. Air cleaner cover or assembly may be removed as required for testing or check-out.

Engine Will Not Start

1. Set the TESTER TEST SELECTOR SWITCH (TSS) to position 9 and ignition key to RUN position. (Verify engine is not running).

2. If the reading 10.5 (volts) or more, proceed to Step 4.

3. If the reading is less than 10.5 (volts), check for a discharged battery, an open wire from the battery to the ECA power relay (Circuit 175), open wire from the ignition switch to the ECA power relay coil (Circuit 20), an open wire from the ECA to the ECA power relay (Circuit 361), a shorted or inoperative ECA power relay or the ECA or power relay not securely fastened to its mounting bracket (Provides return path for ECA power relay); or an open EEC ground wire (Circuit 57).

4. Disconnect harness wire from the "S" terminal on the Starter Relay and set TSS switch on TESTER to position 22.

5. Hold Ignition Key in START position and observe DVOM reading (volts). If reading is 9.0 or greater, reconnect EEC harness wire to "S" terminal on Starter relay and proceed to Step 6. If reading is less than 9.0, check for an open or short in harness Circuits 32 and 57. Repair or replace as required and retest.

6. Depress and hold the NO START switch on TESTER. Set ignition key to "start" position while attempting to start engine.

7. If vehicle starts, release the NO START button and turn key OFF.

8. Turn IGNITION KEY OFF. To check for positive CP lead shorted to engine, set the TSS switch to position 10 and observe DVOM reading. If reading is less than 100 (ohms) replace the CP sensor and retest. If reading is 100 (ohms) or greater, proceed to next step.

CAUTION

Be sure new CP sensor is fully inserted into engine mounting hole.

---

9. Temporarily install known, good ECA Processor Assembly with original Calibration Assembly. Turn key to START. If engine starts normally, turn key OFF. Install new ECA Processor Assembly and original Calibration assembly. Test for proper EEC operation by performing tests as outlined under "Engine Runs."

10. If engine still does not start, temporarily install known, good Calibration Assembly on original ECA Processor Assembly. If engine starts, install new Calibration Assembly on original Processor Assembly. Test for proper EEC operation. If engine still does

not start, install new Processory and Calibration assembly and retest.

11. If vehicle fails to start, release the NO START button and proceed to the next step.

12. Turn the ignition key OFF. Set the TSS switch to position 10 to check out the Crankshaft Position sensor and its harness wires.

13. Disconnect Crankshaft Position (CP) connector and install the blue continuity test fixture to the wiring harness. Measure the resistance. If the reading is between 170 and 230 ohms proceed to Step 14. If the reading is less than 170 or Greater than 230 (ohms) check circuits 349 and 350 for an open or short. Repair the harness as required and retest.

14. Remove the test fixture and reconnect the CP connector. If the reading is less the 100 or greater than 550 ohms, replace the CP sensor and retest.

—CAUTION—
Be sure new CO sensor is fully inserted into engine mounting hole.

15. Set the TSS switch to position 11 and connect the black, four pin continuity test fixture to the four-blade wiring harness connector at the ignition module. If reading is between 7-13 (ohms), disconnect test fixture and reconnect harness. If the reading is less than 7 ohms, check for short in circuits 57 and 144. If reading is greater than 13 ohms, check for open in circuits 57 and 155. Repair harness as required and retest.

Engine Runs

NOTE: This procedure assumes that the other diagnostic procedures have been run in accordance with the appropriate routines.

1. Block both front wheels.
2. Put the parking brake ON and set transmission selector to PARK.
3. Turn off all vehicle electrical loads (i.e. radio, air conditioner, heater and lights).
4. Disconnect the harness wire from terminal "S" of the Starter Relay. Set the tester test selector switch (TSS) to position 22. Verify reading is greater than 9 (volts) with ignition key to START position. If not proceed to Step 1 of "V Ref. Not Within Limits". If 9 (volts) or greater, reconnect wire to terminal "S" of Starter Relay and proceed to the next step.
5. Start the engine. Let engine run until the thermostat is open and the upper radiator hose is hot and pressurized. Check that throttle is off fast idle and in normal idle, in neutral.
6. Turn the engine OFF. Then turn the ignition key to the RUN position, engine OFF.
7. Set the tester test selector switch (TSS) to position T and the DVOM Selector Switch to TESTER. Turn ingnition key to RUN position (engine OFF).
8. Using the TSS switch on the special tester, gather the data for test sequence I and record it on the Diagnostic Data Chart. Be sure the throttle is completely off fast idle. If the reference voltage is out of limits, proceed immediately to subroutines. If Vref is within limits, complete gathering and recording data. Then proceed to the following steps for TEST SEQUENCE II.

NOTE: Complete all data gathering per TEST SEQUENCES I and II prior to performing any diagnostic subroutine, except as noted on the Data Chart.

9. Prior to starting TEST SEQUENCE II, turn ignition key OFF. Disconnect Manifold Absolute Pressure (MAP) and Inlet Air Temperature (IAT) Sensors from wiring harness.
10. Install CONTINUITY TEST FIXTURES as follows:
MAP Sensor: Install YELLOW fixture to the harness MAP Sensor connector.
IAT Sensor: Install BROWN fixture to the harness IAT Sensor connector.

—CAUTION—
Check for correct pin orientation prior to mating.

11. Operate engine at idle in PARK until the thermostat is open and the upper radiator hose is hot and pressurized. Gather data for TEST SEQUENCE II per the following steps and record it on the Diagnostic Data Chart.

12. With engine at idle, in NEUTRAL obtain data for TSS switch positions 2 and 6 in TEST SEQUENCE II. If either reading is out of limits, perform appropriate diagnostics steps listed in Data Chart before continuing.

13. Set TSS switch to position 7 and be prepared to make the indicated timed measurement. Raise engine speed briefly to 1600-1800 rpm. Begin timing, per TEST SEQUENCE II of Data Chart, when throttle is released for return to idle.

14. Install a suitable speed control tool (available from after-market sources). Using tool, set engine speed to 1600 ± 50 rpm. Obtain EVP and Spark Advance data per Diagnostics Data Chart.

15. Remove speed control tool and turn ignition KEY to OFF.

16. Remove MAP and IAT continuity test fixtures (brown and yellow) and reconnect MAP and IAT sensors to harness.

17. Review the test data. If all data is within limits the system is operating properly, or the problem is no longer present.

18. If one or more of the test points are out of limits, perform the subroutine indicated at the bottom of the appropriate column. The subroutines should be used in sequence from left to right.

NOTE: If the initial system check or a subroutine is completed and the problem is not found and corrected, proceed as follows. Turn engine off, remove all test equipment and reconnect all vacuum, air, and electrical connections. Verify that the initial problem still exists. If it does, repeat the initial system check and/or the appropriate subroutine of this procedure.

COMPONENT TROUBLESHOOTING (SUB-ROUTINES)

Reference Voltage (Vref) Not Within Limits

1. Turn the TSS switch to position 9, ignition key in RUN position and DVOM switch to TESTER. If the battery voltage is less than 10.5 (volts) check for:

- A discharged battery
- Open wire from the battery to the ECA power relay (circuit 175).
- Open wire from ignition switch to the ECA power relay coil (circuit 20).
- Open wire from the ECA to the power relay (circuit 361).
- Inoperative ECA power relay
- Repair or replace the defective item as required and retest.
- If the battery voltage is greater than 10.5 (volts) proceed to the next step.

2. Disconnect the Engine Coolant Temperature (ECT) sensor at its connector and set the TSS switch to position 1. If the reference voltage is between 8.5 and 9.5 volts, replace ECT sensor and retest. If the reference voltage does not come within limits, proceed to the next step.

3. Disonnect the Inlet Air Temperature Sensor (IAT) at its connector. If the reference voltage is between 8.5 and 9.5 volts, replace IAT Sensor and retest. If the reference voltage does not come within limits, proceed to the next step.

4. Disconnect the EGR Valve Position (EVP) Sensor at its connector. If the reference voltage is between 8.5 and 9.5 volts, replace the EGR Valve assembly and retest. If the reference voltage does not come within limits, proceed to the next step.

5. Disconnect the Throttle Position (TP) Sensor at its connector. If the reference voltage is between 8.5 and 9.5 volts, replace TP Sensor and retest. If the reference voltage does not come within limits, proceed to the next step.

6. Disconnect the Manifold Absolute Pressure (MAP) Sensor at its connector. If the reference voltage is between 8.5 and 9.5 volts, replace MAP Sensor·and retest. If the reference voltage does not come within limits, proceed to the next step.

7. Disconnect the Barometric Pressure (BP) Sensor at its connector. If the reference voltage is beween 8.5 and 9.5 volts, replace BP Sensor and retest. If the reference voltage does not come within limits, proceed to the next step.

8. Disconnect the blue (10 pin) harness connector from the TESTER. If the reference voltage is within 8.5-9.5 volts check circuits 351 (A, B, C and D), 354 or 357 for a short or check circuits 359 (A thru F) for an open. Repair the circuit and retest.

9. If reference voltage now within limits, install new ECA Calibration Assembly and retest.

10. If reference voltage does not come within limits, install new ECA Processor assembly (Reinstall original Calibration Assembly). Retest.

11. Reconnect all sensors to the harness and the harness to the TESTER. Complete gathering and recording data per TEST SEQUENCES I and II of Diagnostics Data Chart.

Manifold Absolute Pressure (MAP) Sensor—Not Within Limit

1. On the DIAGNOSTIC DATA CHART, compare the MAP and BP sensor reading of TEST SEQUENCE I. If the MAP reading is within 0.75 volts of the BP reading, both sensors are ok. **DO NOT CHANGE THEM** — the out of tolerance condition is the result of variations in local air pressure. If the MAP reading differs form the BP reading by 0.75 volts or more, proceed to step VI-D2b.

2. Verify that the Ignition switch is OFF and disconnect MPA sensor. Connect the yellow continuity test fixture to the wiring harness. Set the TSS switch to position 13, and DVOM switch to TESTER. If the reading is between 170 and 230 ohms, proceed to the next step. If the reading is less than 170 ohms or more than 230 ohms, repair short or open in circuit 358 and/or 359 of wiring harness and retest.

3. Set the TSS switch to position 12. If the reading is less than 170 ohms or more than 230 ohms, repair short or open in circuit 351 and/or 359 of wiring harness and retest. If the reading is between 170 and 230 ohms, inspect the sensor connector. If bad, repair. If good, replace MAP sensor and retest. If the voltage is still out of limits, replace ECA Processor Assembly (Reinstall the original Calibration Assembly). Retest.

4. Turn tester function switch to OFF and disconnect the test equipment.

———CAUTION———
Remove continuity test fixture.

5. If MAP reading is not within limits during TEST SEQUENCE II, turn Ignition key OFF. Remove YELLOW continuity test fixture from MAP connector of harness. Using DVOM on 200 ohm range, check resistance between adjacent pins of YELLOW test fixture.
• If resistance is less than 170 ohms or greater than 230 ohms, repair or replace test fixture (refer to tester instruction manual) and repeat TEST SEQUENCE II.
• If resistance is within 170 to 230 ohms, carefully align pins of YELLOW test fixture with MAP connector of harness and reconnect. Repeat TEST SEQUENCE II.

Throttle Position Sensor (TP)—Not Within Limits

1. Verify that the ignition switch is OFF. Set the TSS switch to position 12, and the DVOM switch to TESTER. Disconnect the TP connector and connect yellow continuity test fixture to the TP sensor harness connector. If the reading is between 170 and 230 ohms, proceed to the next step. If the reading is less than 170 ohms or more than 230 ohms, repair the short or open in circuit 351 and/or 359 and retest.

2. Set the TSS switch to position 14. If the reading is between 170 and 230 ohms proceed to the next step. If the reading is less than 170 ohms or more than 230 ohms, repair the short or open in circuit 355 and/or 359 and retest.

3. Connect DVOM between circuit 351 and circuit 359 for the TP Sensor connector. Set DVOM switch to 200 x 1000 ohms range. If the reading is less than 3 (x 1000 ohms or more than 5 (x 1000) ohms), replace the sensor and retest. If the reading is between 3 and 5 (x 1000 ohms), proceed to the next step.

4. Connect DVOM between circuit 355 and circuit 359 of the connector. Set DVOM switch to 2000 (ohms) range and verify the throttle is in the closed position (i.e., off high cam). If the reading is less than 580 ohms, or greater than 1100 ohms, readjust by loosening the bolt and turning the TP sensor until the reading is within limits. If not able to set to this range replace the TP senosr and retest.

NOTE: Torque mounting screws to 8-10 in. lbs. (.904-1.13 Nm).

If the reading is between 580 and 1100 ohms reconnect the sensor to the harness. Set the TSS switch to position 3, key to RUN position and DVOM to TESTER. Adjust the sensor by loosening the bolt and turning the TP sensor until the VOLTMETER reads 1.82 ± 0.11 volts. Retest. If the sensor cannot be adjusted to obtain the proper voltage, replace the ECA Processor Assembly (Reinstall the original Calibration Assembly). Retest.

5. Turn DVOM switch to OFF and disconnect the test equipment.

———CAUTION———
Remove continuity test fixture.

Barometric Pressure (BP) Sensor—Not Within Limits

1. On the BP and Diagnostic Data Chart review the MAP reading of Test Sequence 1. If the BP reading is within 0.75 volts of the MAP reading both sensors are OK. **DO NOT CHANGE THEM** — the out of tolerance condition is the result of variations in local air pressure. If the BP reading differs from the MAP reading by 0.75 volts or more, proceed to step VI-D4b.

2. Verify that the ignition switch is "OFF" and disconnect BP sensor. Connect the yellow continuity test fixture to wiring harness. Set the TSS switch to position 12 and DVOM to TESTER. If the reading is less than 170 ohms or more than 230 ohms repair short or open in circuit 351 and/or 359 of wiring harness and retest. If the reading is between 170 and 230 ohms proceed to next step.

———CAUTION———
Remove continuity test fixture. Connect sensor to harness.

3. Set the TSS switch to position 15. If reading is less than 170 ohms or more than 230 ohms, repair short or open in circuit 356 and/or 359 of wiring harness and retest. If the reading is between 170 and 230 ohms, inspect the sensor leads and connector. If bad, repair. If good, replace BP sensor and retest. If the voltage is still out of limits, replace the ECA Processory Assembly (Reinstall the original Calibration Assembly). Retest.

4. Turn DVOM switch to OFF and disconnect test equipment.

———CAUTION———
Remove continuity test fixture.

Engine Coolant Temperature (ECT) Sensor—Not Within Limits

1. Verify the ignition switch is OFF. Set the TSS switch to position 16, DVOM to TESTER. Disconnect the ECT connector and connect the blue continuity test fixture to the wiring harness ECT connector. If the reading is between 170 and 230 ohms, proceed to the next step. If the reading is less than 170 ohms or more than 230 ohms, repair the short or open in circuit 354 or 359 and retest.

2. Connect the DVOM between the two pins of the ECT sensor connector. Set DVOM switch to 200 x 1000 ohms scale. If reading is greater than 6 x 1000 ohms, verify engine coolant temperature. If coolant temperature is below 160°F (71°C) follow diagnostic routine and retest. If coolant temperature is above 160°F (71°C) replace the sensor and retest.

If reading is less than 1.5 (x 1000 ohms) verify engine coolant temperature. If coolant temperature is above 220°F (104°C) follow diagnostic routine and retest. If coolant temperature is below 220°F (104°C), replace the sensor and retest. If reading is between 1.5 and 6.0 (x 1000 ohms), replace ECA Processor Assembly (Reinstall original Calibration Assembly). Retest.

3. Turn TESTER FUNCTION switch to OFF and disconnect test equipment.

Inlet Air Temperature (IAT)—Not Within Limits

1. Verify the Ignition switch is OFF. Set the TSS switch to position 17. Disconnect the IAT connector and connect the blue continuity test fixture to the wiring harness. If the reading is between 170 and 250 ohms, proceed to the next step. If the reading is less than 170 ohms, or more than 230 ohms, repair the short or open in circuit 357 and/or 359 and retest.

2. Connect the DVOM between circuit 357 and circuit 359 of the IAT sensor connector. Set DVOM switch to 200 x 1000 ohms scale. If the reading is less than 6.5 (x 1000 ohms) or greater than 45 (x 1000 ohms), check air cleaner temperature control per SSD-9, if the temperature control is ok replace the IAT sensor and retest.

If the reading is between 6.5 and 45 (x 1000 ohms), replace the ECA Processor Assembly (Reinstall original Calibration Assembly). Retest.

———————CAUTION———————
Remove continuity test fixture. Connect sensor to harness.

3. Turn tester function switch to OFF and disconnect test equipment.

4. If IAT reading is **not** within limits during TEST SEQUENCE II, turn ignition key OFF. Remove BROWN continuity test fixture from IAT connector of harness. Using DVOM an 200 x 1000 ohms range, check resistance between pins of BROWN TEST FIXTURE. If resistance is less than 23.3 (x 1000 ohms) or greater than 25.3 (x 1000 ohms), repair or replace test fixture (refer to tester instruction manual) and repeat TEST SEQUENCE II. If resistance is within 23.3–25.3 (x 1000 ohms), carefully align pins of brown test fixture with IAT connector of harness and reconnect. Repeat TEST SEQUENCE II.

Thermactor Air-Bypass Solenoid Actuator—Not Within Limits

1. To verify Throttle Position sensor detects changes in throttle position, set TSS switch to position 3, DVOM to Tester position and the ignition key to the RUN position.

2. Set throttle to the Wide Open Throttle position and observe DVOM reading. If reading is 5.0 (volts) or greater, TP sensor is OK. If reading is less than 5.0 (volts). Remove and replace TP sensor and retest.

3. Turn Ignition Key OFF. Set DVOM switch to the 200 ohm position and install external test leads in DVOM test jacks.

4. Disconnect harness connector from TAB solenoid. Measure resistance of solenoid coil by inserting DVOM probes into solenoid electrical contacts and observing DVOM reading. If reading is between 50 and 90 ohms, solenoid coil is OK. Remove DVOM leads from both coil and DVOM and re-install harness connector on solenoid. If reading is less than 50 ohms or more than 90 ohms, install new TAB solenoid, reconnect the harness and retest.

5. Set the TSS switch to position 7, DVOM to the TESTER position and the ignition key in the RUN position. If reading is greater than 10.5 volts proceed to the next step.

If reading is less than 10.5 volts check circuit 361. With a DVOM measure the voltage between circuit 361 and the engine block. If reading is less than 10.5 volts repair open or short in circuit 361 and retest. If circuit 361 reading is greater than 10.5 (volts), repair open or short in circuit 100 and retest.

6. Temporarily install known, good ECA Processor Assembly (Reinstall original Calibration Assembly) and retest. If system tests OK, instal! new ECA Processor (Reinstall original Calibration

Assembly) and retest. If problem still exists, temporarily install known good ECA Calibration Assembly on to original Processor Assembly and retest. If system tests OK, install new Calibration Assembly and retest. If problem still exists, install new ECA Processor and new ECA Calibration Assembly and retest.

NOTE: Whenever a component has been repaired or replaced a retest is required.

EGR Valve Position (EVP) Sensor—Not Within Limits

1. Turn "off" engine and disconnect the EVP sensor. Connect the yellow continuity test fixture to the wiring harness. Set the TSS switch to position 12, DVOM switch to TESTER. If the reading is less than 170 ohms or more than 230 ohms, repair the short or open in circuit 351 and/or 359 of the harness and retest. If the reading is between 170 and 230 ohms proceed to the next step.

2. Set the TSS switch to position 18. If the reading is less than 170 ohms or more than 230 ohms, repair the short or open in circuit 352 and/or 359 of the harness and retest. If the reading is between 170 and 230 (ohms), proceed to the next step.

———————CAUTION———————
Remove continuity test fixture before proceeding.

3. Disconnect the EGR air hose from the AIR BYPASS VALVE (small hose on side of valve) and connect the PRESSURE GAUGE to the fitting. Leave EGR hose disconnected during this step. Run the engine at about 1600 rpm in PARK.

If the pressure is greater than 1.5 psi proceed to the next step. If the pressure is less than 1.5 psi, check the AIR BYPASS VALVE and THERMACTOR AIR PUMP. Repair or replace as required and retest.

4. Connect a known good test hose between the small port at the side of AIR BYPASS VALVE and the EGR valve assembly. Run the engine at about 1600 RPM in PARK with the TSS switch in position 8. If the reading is 6.4 volts or less, replace the EGR valve and sensor assembly and retest. If the voltage is greater than 6.4 volts, reinstall the original hoses and proceed to the next procedure. Reconnect all pressure and vacuum hoses to their proper connection.

EGR Solenoid Valve Check

1. Turn the key to RUN (engine OFF). Set the TSS to position 19. Depress and hold the EGR PRESSURE test button on TESTER while reading DVOM.

   a. If the reading is less than 1.0 volt, check for open in harness circuits 361 or 362 or short in harness circuit 362 to ground. Repair or replace as required and retest. If harness circuits 361 and 362 are OK, install new solenoid valve assembly and retest.

   b. If the reading is greater than 5.0 volts, check for short between harness circuits 362 and 361. Repair or replace as required and retest. If harness is OK, replace the solenoid valve assembly and retest.

   c. If the reading is between 1 and 5 volts, proceed to the next step.

2. Set the TSS to position 20 and depress and hold the EGR VENT button on TESTER. If the reading is less than 1.0 volt, check for open in harness circuits 360 or 361 or short in harness circuit 360 to ground. Repair or replace as required and retest. If harness circuits 360 and 361 are OK, install new solenoid valve assembly and retest. If reading is greater than 5.0 volts, check for short between harness circuits 360 and 361. Repair or replace as required and retest. If harness is OK, replace the solenoid valve assembly and retest. If the reading is between 1.0 and 5.0 (volts), proceed to the next step.

3. Disconnect the pressure hose from the input side of the EGR pressure solenoid and insert pressure gauge into hose. Operate engine, in NEUTRAL, at 1100 ± 100 rpm and observe pressure gauge. If pressure is less than 0.5 psi, check Thermactor system per

SSD-5. Repair or replace Thermactor system parts as required and retest. If pressure is greater than 0.5 psi, proceed to next step.

4. Disconnect the pressure hose from the output side of the EGR pressure solenoid (lower fitting) and connect a pressure gauge to the solenoid. Leave pressure hose disconnected. Run the engine at 1100 ± 100 rpm with the transmission selector in NEUTRAL or PARK.

If the pressure is greater than 0.5 psi after 5 seconds, replace the solenoid valve assembly and retest. If the pressure is less than 0.5 psi, proceed to the next step.

5. Reconnect the pressure hose to the output side of EGR pressure solenoid. Disconnect the EGR valve pressure hose at the hose tee and connect the pressure gauge to the tee. Leave EGR valve hose disconnected. Run the engine at about 1100 ± 100 rpm with the transmission selector in NEUTRAL or PARK. Depress and hold the EGR PRESSURE and EGR VENT test buttons, on the TESTER, until the pressure stabilizes. Then release the EGR PRESSURE button. If the maximum pressure is less than 0.5 psi or decreases more than 0.5 psi in 5 seconds, replace the EGR solenoid assembly or hoses and fittings and retest.

If the maximum pressure is greater than 0.5 psi and decreases less than 0.5 psi in 5 seconds, proceed to the next step. With the engine at 1100 ± 100 rpm and EGR valve hose still disconnected, press and hold the EGR PRESSURE and VENT buttons until the pressure stabilizes. Release EGR PRESSURE button, then release the EGR VENT button. The pressure should drop **IMMEDIATELY**. If the pressure remains within 0.5 psi of the maximum reading for 5 seconds, replace the EGR solenoid assembly and retest. If the pressure drops immediately to less than half of the maximum reading, replace the EGR valve assembly and retest. If after retest, the EVP data is still out of limits, proceed to the next step.

6. Temporarily install known good ECA Calibration Assembly on to original ECA Processor Assembly and retest. If system now operates properly, install new Calibration Assembly onto original Processor Assembly and retest. If the problem still exists, temporarily install known good ECA Processor (Reinstall original Calibration Assembly). Retest. If system now operates properly, install new ECA Processor Assembly (reinstall original Calibration Assembly) and retest. If problem still exists, install new ECA Processor Assembly and new ECA Calibration Assembly. Retest.*

Spark Advance (in degrees) Not Within Limits

NOTE: If vehicle is equipped with Dual Mode Ignition System, verify correct dual mode operation before performing the following procedures. If repair or replacement of any Ignition system component(s) was necessary, retest EEC sub-system to verify original problem has been corrected.

1. Run engine at idle, in PARK, to check base engine timing per the following steps.
2. Depress and hold NO START button on TESTER while reading spark advance using Timing Light.
   a. If spark advance is less than 8 degrees BTDC or more than 12 degrees BTDC, check alignment of Timing Pointer and position of Crankshaft Position Pulse Ring (see Engine Shop Manual).
   b. If spark advance is within 8 degrees to 12 degrees BTDC, temporarily install known good ECA Calibration Assembly on original ECA Processor and Retest. If SPARK ADVANCE is now **in limits** in Test Sequence III, install **new** Calibration Assembly on to original Processor Assembly and retest. If SPARK ADVANCE is still **not within limits** of Test Sequence III, temporarily install a known good ECA Processor assembly (reinstall original Calibration Assembly) and retest.

If SPARK ADVANCE is now **in** limits in Test Sequence III, install **new** ECA Processor Assembly (reinstall original Calibration Assembly) and retest. If SPARK ADVANCE is still **not** within limits of Test Sequence III, install **new** ECA Processor and **new** ECA Calibration Assembly and retest.

Crank Signal—Not Within Limits

1. Verify correct vehicle battery voltage.
2. Disconnect harness wire from the "S" terminal on the Starter Relay and set TESTER TSS to position 22.
3. With Ignition Key in START position, verify reading is 9.0 volts or greater.
4. If reading is less than 9.0 volts, check for an open or short in harness circuits 32 and 57. Repair as required and retest.

—CAUTION—
Reconnect harness wire to "S" terminal on Starter Relay.

FORD ELECTRONIC ENGINE CONTROLS (EEC) II

General Information

The system is composed of seven sensors, an electronic control assembly, several control solenoids, a vacuum-operated thermactor air system and an exhaust gas recirculation system (EGR). In addition, the system features a carburetor equipped with a controllable air-fuel mixture and an exhaust gas oxygen sensor that provides a rich/lean signal to the electronic control assembly.

The EEC II system features a four lobe pulse ring, integral with the crankshaft damper, and a crankshaft position sensor attached to the timing pointer bracket. The distributor has no advance or retard mechanism, since spark timing is controlled by the electronic control assembly according to engine operating conditions and individual vehicle calibration. Calibration is controlled by the calibration assembly, which is attached to the electronic control assembly.

Power for the EEC II system is provided by the power relay, which is mounted on the same bracket as the electronic control assembly.

SYSTEM OPERATION

The EEC II has a total of the following seven sensors.
- Barometric pressure (BP) sensor
- Engine coolant temperature (ECT) sensor
- Crankshaft position (CP) sensor
- Throttle position (TP) sensor
- EGR valve position (EVP) sensor
- Exhaust gas oxygen (EGO) sensor
- Manifold absolute pressure (MAP) sensor

NOTE: MAP sensor and the BP sensor are contained in a single unit.

During engine starting and operation, the electronic control assembly (ECA) constantly monitors these sensors to determine the required timing advance, EGR flow rate, thermactor air mode and air-fuel ratio for any given instant of vehicle operation.

The ECA then sends output commands for the following:
- Ignition module, for spark timing

EEC II system components

- Throttle kicker solenoid
- EGR control solenoids
- Canister purge solenoids
- Feedback carburetor actuator (FBCA), to adjust air-fuel mixture
- Thermactor solenoids, to direct thermactor air flow

The continuous adjustment of ignition timing, EGR flow rate, and air-fuel ratio results in optimum engine performance under all vehicle operating conditions.

Fail-Safe

If for some reason there is a failure in the ECA, the system goes into the limited operational strategy (LOS) mode. In this mode, the ECA commands are cut off and the engine operates with initial spark advance only, regardless of sensor input signals. The engine can be operated until repairs are made, but poor performance may be experienced as long as the system is in the LOS mode.

SYSTEM COMPONENTS

Electronic Control Assembly (ECA)

The ECA consists of two parts, the processor assembly and the

calibration assembly. The calibration assembly is a memory storage device and is attached to the top of the processor assembly by two screws. It performs three functions.

1. Provides calibration information unique to the vehicle for use by the processor assembly.
2. Stores data calculated by the processor assembly.
3. Recalls appropriate data from the memory bank when required.

The processor assembly performs four important functions within a fraction of one second.

1. Chooses one of seven sensor input signals for analysis.
2. Converts signals to permit computer use of information in calculation.
3. Performs spark, thermactor, EGR and air-fuel mixture calculations, and adjusts canister purge and throttle kicker.
4. Sends electrical output control signals to the ignition module and control solenoids to adjust calibration timing, EGR flow rate, thermactor air mode, carburetor mixture, throttle kicker mode and canister purge mode.

The processor assembly compensates for such variables as altitude, engine rpm, ambient temperature, etc. It also contains a separate power supply which provides a continuous 8–10 volts to the sensors.

CRANKSHAFT POSITION (CP) SENSOR

BAROMETRIC AND MANIFOLD ABSOLUTE PRESSURE (B/MAP) SENSOR

ENGINE COOLANT TEMPERATURE (ECT) SENSOR

THROTTLE POSITION (TP) SENSOR

EGR VALVE POSITION (EVP) SENSOR

EXHAUST GAS OXYGEN (EGO) SENSOR

EGR SYSTEM VENT (EGRV) AND CONTROL (EGRC) SOLENOID/VALVES

FEEDBACK CARBURETOR ACTUATOR (FBCA)

IGNITION MODULE SIGNAL (IMS)

THROTTLE KICKER SOLENOID (TKS)

THERMACTOR AIR DIVERTOR (TAD) AND THERMACTOR AIR BYPASS (TAB) SOLENOID/VALVES

EEC II system schematic

ECA MOUNTING BRACKET

POWER RELAY

PROCESSOR ASSEMBLY

CALIBRATION ASSEMBLY

EEC II electronic control assembly

Crankshaft position sensor (CP)

Canister purge solenoid (CANP)

aneroid capsule into a voltage signal proportional to intake manifold pressure.

Crankshaft Position Sensor

The crankshaft position sensor is mounted on the front of the engine block and is held in place by a retaining clip and screw. The tip of the sensor contains an electromagnet, whose magnetic field is cut by the rotating lobes on the pulse ring. This action generates an output voltage to the ECA.

Positioning of the pulse ring is critical, since this determines basic engine timing. The pulse ring is a press fit on the crankshaft damper, and cannot be removed or adjusted. It is set for a basic timing of 10 ° BTDC

Exhaust Gas Oxygen Sensor

1. The sensor shield covers the sensor body and protrudes into the stream of exhaust gases in the manifold.

2. Exhaust gases flow into the shield and contact the sensor body through slits in the shield.

3. Atmospheric pressure is admitted through a vent to the end of the sensor body opposite the exhaust gases.

4. The sensor body generates a voltage, due to pressure difference between vent air and oxygen in the exhaust gases.

   a. In a rich mixture, low oxygen pressure generates higher output voltage (0.6 volt or greater).

   b. In a lean mixture, high oxygen pressure generates a lower output voltage (0.2 volt or less).

Canister Purge (CANP) Solenoid

The canister purge solenoid is a combination valve/solenoid, located in the canister vent line. Operated by a signal from the ECA, it controls the flow of vapors during engine operating modes. Operation depends on calibration, but is also influenced by engine coolant temperature, engine rpm, the time since engine start-up throttle position.

Throttle Kicker Solenoid (TKS) and Actuator (TKA)

The vacuum-operated actuator which increases idle rpm, is energized when the solenoid receives a signal from the computer. Idle speed is increased during air conditioning system operation or when engine temperature is too high or too low.

Feedback Carburetor Actuator (FBCA)

The FBCA is a stepper motor mounted in the model 7200 VV carburetor. It has 120 steps, with a total range of .400 in. in and out. Setting of the air-fuel mixture is dependent on calibration of the computer, so the air-fuel ratio changes constantly due to sensor signals to the ECA.

EGR System
GENERAL INFORMATION

The EGR system is similar to those found on vehicles not equipped with EEC II. Opening and closing of the valve, which can not be seen when the EGR assembly is mounted on the engine, is controlled by the ECA signal to the EGR valve position sensor. When

Exhaust gas oxygen sensor—typical

ECA Replacement

The complete assembly, including the processor and calibration devices, is mounted under the dashboard, behind the instrument panel near the brake pedal support.

1. Loosen the two left hand mounting screws and remove the right hand screw.
2. Slide the unit out away from the left hand mounting screws.
3. Disconnect the wiring harness connector, which can be tested from the engine compartment.

Throttle Position Sensor

The throttle position sensor is a variable resistor control coupled to the carburetor throttle shaft, mounted on a special carburetor bracket. When reference voltage is applied, the developed signal is proportional to the throttle plate angle. This information is supplied to the ECA, indicating closed, part, or wide open throttle.

Throttle position (TP) sensor

Adjustment

---CAUTION---

Use only a digital-type voltmeter, as conventional meters are not sensitive enough to gather EEC II system data. Also, use of a standard 9-volt ohmmeter may damage the computer calibration unit or the EGR position sensor.

Engine coolant temperature (ECT) sensor

EGR valve position sensor

1. If sensor needs replacement, correct positioning is essential false throttle angle information will be fed to the ECA.
2. Turn ignition to the run position with the engine off.
3. Adjust the sensor by loosening the mounting screws and turning the sensor until voltage is between 1.85 and 2.35. Tighten the screws to 8–10 lbs.

Coolant Temperature Sensor

The coolant temperature sensor consists of a thermistor in a brass housing with the integral harness connector extending from the body. It is mounted in the heater outlet fitting, in front of the intake manifold, near the left rocker arm cover. As the temperature rises in the cooling system, the resistance of the sensor decreases, sending a stronger signal to the ECA. This sensor replaces the coolant temperature switch and the EGR proted vacuum switch in vehicles not equipped with EEC II.

EGR Valve Position Sensor

The EGR valve position sensor is mounted on the EGR valve and measures the linear position the metering rod in the fixed orifice. The developed signal to the ECA varies with the amount of EGR valve opening.

NOTE: At higher altitudes, the EGR signal may be eliminated to maintain proper engine performance.

Barometric Pressure Sensor

The barometric pressure sensor is mounted on the right fender apron. It monitors engine compartment barometric pressure, which varies with changing climate or altitude. This information is then fed to the ECA.

Barometric manifold absolute pressure sensor (B/MAP)

Manifold Pressure Sensor

The manifold pressure sensor monitors changes in intake manifold pressure by means of an aneroid capsule. As manifold pressure changes due to changes in engine load and speed, and barometric pressure, electronic units in the sensor convert the position of the

Feedback carburetor actuator

Throttle kicker solenoid and actuator

the EGR valve is open, it allows exhaust gases to be reburned in the engine, reducing the formation of nitrous oxides (NO_x).

COMPONENTS AND OPERATION

EGR Valve and Sensor Assembly

The EGR valve and sensor assembly is made up of the pintle valve and seat assembly, the actuator diaphragm and housing assembly, and the EGR valve position sensor (EVP).

The EGR valve is operated by vacuum from the EGR control (EGRC) and EGR vacuum (EGRV) solenoid/valves. These solenoid/valves work together to apply vacuum to the EGR valve and increase EGR, to maintain vacuum and EGR, or to vent vacuum to the atmosphere and shut off EGR.

Increase EGR flow system diagram

The vacuum from the control solenoid/valves pulls on the actuator diaphragm which is attached to the pintle valve. The pintle valve is tapered so that EGR flow is determined by its position.

The EGR valve position sensor monitors the position of the pintle valve and feeds this information to the ECA. The ECA then determines whether to increase, maintain or shut off EGR flow.

EGR Cooler Assembly

The EGR cooler assembly is a heat exchanger used with the electronic control assembly to provide improved flow characteristics and better engine operation. It uses engine coolant to cool exhaust gases passing from the exhaust manifold through the EGR valve to the intake manifold.

EGR Control Solenoids

The EGR control solenoids, mounted in a bracket above the left rocker arm cover, control actual vacuum to the EGR valve. Closest to the rear of the engine is the normally open EGR vacuum (EGRV) solenoid. Next to it is the normally closed EGR control (EGRC) solenoid.

Since the vacuum valve is normally open, its output port is open to the atmosphere in the de-energized mode, closed in the energized

EGR system used with the EEC II system

"NORMALLY OPEN" E.G.R. SOLENOID 'VACUUM CONTROL' OPERATION

NO POWER

SYSTEM VACUUM VENTED TO ATMOSPHERE

SOLENOID DE-ENERGIZED

POWER APPLIED

ENERGIZES SOLENOID

PULLS PLUNGER DOWN

AND CLOSES OFF VENT PORT

SOLENOID ENERGIZED

"NORMALLY CLOSED" E.G.R. SOLENOID 'VACUUM CONTROL' OPERATION

SUPPLY VACUUM IS BLOCKED

SOLENOID DE-ENERGIZED

ENERGIZES SOLENOID

AND ALLOWS VACUUM TO FLOW TO OUTLET

PULLS PLUNGER UP

SOLENOID ENERGIZED

EGR solenoid valve operation

COMPUTER RECOGNIZES THE NEED FOR DECREASED E.G.R. FLOW

POWER REMOVED FROM BOTH SOLENOIDS

DE-ENERGIZES SOLENOID

DE-ENERGIZES SOLENOID

TO PREVENT ADDITIONAL VACUUM FROM ENTERING

CONSTANT VACUUM SOURCE FROM INTAKE MANIFOLD

NORMALLY OPEN 'VENT VALVE'

NORMALLY CLOSED VACUUM CONTROL

AND PLUNGER LIFTS TO OPEN VENT PORT

E.G.R. VALVE & SENSOR ASSEMBLY

Decrease EGR flow system operation

mode. The control valve is normally closed, so its output port is closed in the de-energized mode and open to system vacuum in the energized mode.

Thermactor Air System

COMPONENTS AND OPERATION

Thermactor Air Pump

The thermactor air pump is engine-driven and supplies air to the bypass/diverter valve. It is located on a bracket on the lower right front of the engine.

Air Bypass/Diverter Valve

The bypass/diverter valve is used to route air in three directions. It routes air downstream to the catalytic converter mid-bed, upstream to the exhaust manifold and bypass to the atmosphere. Air routing is controlled by the ECA, depending on engine temperature, sensor input, calibration and the ECA program.

Normal operation of the system is as follows.
1. Upstream during engine start-up.
2. Downstream during engine operation.

PINTLE POSITION SENSOR

DIAPHRAGM RETURN SPRING

VACUUM HOSE FITTING

DIAPHRAGM

PINTLE VALVE SEAT

PINTLE

Cross section of typical EGR valve

COMPUTER RECOGNIZES THE NEED FOR INCREASED E.G.R. FLOW

POWER APPLIED TO BOTH SOLENOIDS

ENERGIZES SOLENOID

ENERGIZES SOLENOID

CONSTANT VACUUM SOURCE FROM INTAKE MANIFOLD

AND PLUNGER LIFTS TO ALLOW VACUUM FLOW TO E.G.R. VALVE

NORMALLY OPEN 'VENT VALVE'

AND CLOSES VENT PORT

NORMALLY CLOSED 'VACUUM CONTROL'

Maintain EGR flow system diagram

COLD ENGINE
BYPASS DIVERTER VALVE

CHECK VALVE

COC

CHECK VALVE

EXHAUST MANIFOLD

CATALYTIC CONVERTER

HOT ENGINE
BYPASS DIVERTER VALVE

CHECK VALVE

CHECK VALVE

EXHAUST MANIFOLD

CATALYTIC CONVERTER

Air diverter system

BYPASS

THERMACTOR

CHECK VALVE

EXHAUST MANIFOLD

DIVERTER

TO EGR SOLENOIDS (VACUUM SUPPLY)

TO INTAKE MANIFOLD (VACUUM SUPPLY)

THERMACTOR SOLENOID VALVES

VACUUM RESERVOIR

CHECK VALVE

TO CATALYTIC CONVERTER

(TAD) (TAB)

Thermactor control diagram

EGR CONTROL SOLENOIDS

COOLER OUTLET FITTING

EGR VALVE

EGR COOLER

WATER PUMP HOUSING

COOLER INLET FITTING

EGR cooler assembly

THERMACTOR AIR BYPASS SOLENOID

THERMACTOR AIR DIVERTER SOLENOID

TO BYPASS DIAPHRAGM

TO DIVERTER DIAPHRAGM

TO VACUUM SUPPLY

Thermactor solenoid valve

Air bypass/diverter valve

Dual bed catalytic converter

3. Bypass after a certain time at closed-throttle operation, or if the EGO sensor inputs exceed a certain time period (for catalyst protection).

4. Bypass at wide open throttle.

Ignition System

Ignition systems for the EEC II equipped vehicles use a Duraspark® III ignition module and a Duraspark® II coil to generate a high voltage spark. Since the computer controls all ignition timing, there are no vacuum or centrifugal advance mechanisms in the ignition module. The only function of the distributor is to transmit high voltage from the coil to the correct spark plug.

NOTE: For all ignition system testing on Duraspark® III components, see the "Electronic Ignition" section.

BI-LEVEL ROTOR AND DISTRIBUTOR CAP

Since the EEC II system allows up to 36° distributor advance, the new design rotor and cap allow additional advance capability without crossfire. The bi-level rotor and cap have two levels of secondary voltage distribution. As the rotor turns, one of the high voltage electrode pick-up arms aligns with one spoke of the distributor cap center electrode plate, allowing high voltage to be transmitted from the plate through the rotor, cap and plug wire. The correct firing order is 1-3-7-2-6-5-4-8.

NOTE: Engine firing order can not be read off the distributor cap.

---CAUTION---

Proper rotor alignment must be established to obtain maximum allowable spark advance without crossfiring to adjacent distributor cap electrodes.

Component Removal

ELECTRONIC CONTROL ASSEMBLY (ECA)

The Electronic Control Assembly (ECA) is mounted behind the instrument panel on the driver's side to the left of the steering column near the brake pedal support. The ECA is attached to its mounting bracket with three screws. If the ECA requires replacement, loosen only the two left hand screws and remove the one right hand screw. There are slots which allow the unit to slide out and away from the left hand mounting screws. The bottom side of the ECA has a 32-pin wiring harness connector which is easily removed for diagnostic work and test equipment connection. The harness connector is keyed to prevent improper connection.

DISTRIBUTOR ROTOR

In order to obtain maximum timing advance without crossfire to adjacent distributor cap electrodes, it is important that proper distributor rotor alignment be established, using the special rotor alignment tool designed for this purpose. Since there is no mechanical advance or adjustments under the rotor, there is no need to remove the rotor except to replace it.

Electronic control assembly (ECA) 32 pin harness connector

Removal

1. Remove the distributor cap by loosening the two spring clips holding the cap to the distributor adaptor.

2. Rotate the crankshaft sufficiently to align the distributor rotor upper blade (with slot) with the locating slot in the distributor adaptor, so the distributor rotor alignment Tool T78P-12200-A, or equivalent will drop into place. If the rotor or adapter is damaged and alignment is not possible position the crankshaft with number 1 piston at compression TDC by aligning the zero mark on the damper with the timing pointer on the front cover.

3. Remove the rotor alignment tool and remove the two screws attaching the rotor to the distributor shaft. Remove the rotor.

—CAUTION—

Do not rotate the crankshaft after the rotor has been removed.

Installation

NOTE: When replacing the rotor, coat the lower electrode blades approximately $1/32$ in. thick on all sides (outboard of the plastic) with D7AZ-19A331-AA silicon grease or equivalent.

1. Place the new rotor on the distributor shaft with the slot in the upper blade pointing to the locating notch in the distributor adapter. Install, but do not tighten both rotor attaching screws.

2. Position the rotor alignment Tool T78P-12200-A or equivalent in the distributor adapter so that the tang on the underside of the tool engages the locating notch in the distributor adapter and the slot in the rotor at the same time.

3. Tighten both rotor attaching screws to 15-20 in lb.

4. Remove the rotor alignment tool and reinstall the distributor cap. Seat both cap-to-adapter spring clips.

DISTRIBUTOR

The EEC II distributor is locked in place during engine assembly and no rotational adjustment is possible. A slot in the distributor base mounting flange fits around the distributor base mounting flange fits around the distributor clamp hold-down bolt, preventing movement. Adjustment is not required, since all timing is controlled by the ECA.

Removal

1. Remove the distributor cap and insert the rotor alignment Tool T78P-12200-A or equivalent, by following Steps 1 and 2 under Rotor Removal.

2. With the rotor alignment tool inserted, loosen the distributor hold-down bolt and clamp. Remove alignment tool.

3. Slowly remove the distributor assembly from the engine block, noting the position of the rotor blade with respect to the distributor base when the cam and distributor drive gear are felt to disengage.

—CAUTION—

Do not rotate the crankshaft after the distributor has been removed from the engine.

Installation

1. Position the distributor in the block so that when fully seated the following conditions are met:

   a. The slot on the distributor base hold-down flange is aligned with the clamp bolt hole in the block, and

   b. the slot in the upper blade of the rotor is approximately aligned with the slot in the adapter.

   If alignment is not possible when the distributor is fully seated, raise the distributor out of the block enough to disengage the cam gear and rotate the distributor shaft slightly to allow the next tooth on the distributor drive gear to engage the cam gear. Repeat this procedure until conditions outlined in (a) and (b) are satisfied.

2. Install the distributor-to-block clamp and bolt and tighten to 15–18 ft. lbs. (20–24 Nm) torque.

3. Align the rotor and install the distributor cap following procedures outlined under Rotor Installation Steps 1–4).

NOTE: When installing a new distributor cap, coat the brass center electrode plate tip surfaces with D7AZ-19A331-AA silicon grease or equivalent (Dow 111 or G.E. G-627 compound).

PROCESSOR ASSEMBLY

Removal and Installation

1. Disconnect the battery negative cable.

2. Disconnect the three processor/wiring harness connectors.

3. Remove the assembly (loosen and remove the screws which mount the processor to its bracket.

4. Separate the calibration assembly from the processor.

5. Install the calibration assembly on the new processor (tighten the mounting screws).

6. Install the assembly and connect the wiring harness connectors making certain that the connectors latch in place.

7. Connect the battery negative cable.

8. Verify EECI Subsystem Operates properly by performing Subsystem checkout.

CALIBRATION ASSEMBLY

Removal and Installation

1. Disconnect the battery negative cable.

2. Disconnect the three processor/wiring harness connectors.

3. Remove the assembly (loosen and remove the screws which mount the processor to its bracket).

4. Separate the calibration assembly from the processor.

5. Install the new calibration assembly on the processor (tighten (2) mounting screws).

6. Install the assembly and connect the wiring harness connectors making certain that the connectors latch in place.

7. Connect the battery negative cable.

8. Verify EECI Subsystem operates properly by performing Subsystem checkout.

MANIFOLD ABSOLUTE PRESSURE (MPA) SENSOR

Removal and Installation

1. Disconnect the vacuum hose and electrical connector from the MAP sensor.

2. Remove the sensor from the mounting bracket by removing the two bracket stud nuts.

3. Install the new sensor on the bracket studs and install the nuts.

4. Connect the vacuum hose and electrical connector.

5. Verify that the EECI Subsystem operates properly by performing Subsystem checkout.

BAROMETRIC PRESSURE (BP) SENSOR

Removal and Installation

1. Disconnect the electrical connector.

2. Remove the sensor by loosening and removing the two retaining screws.

3. Install the new sensor using two retaining screws.

4. Connect the electrical connector.

5. Verify that the EECI Subsystem operates properly by performing subsystem checkout.

CRANKSHAFT POSITION SENSOR

Removal and Installation

1. Disconnect the sensor connector from the wiring harness.
2. Loosen the Phillips head (Allen head on later models) screw, part of the sensor retainer clamp assembly. Using an offset screwdriver or other similar hooked tool to pull the sensor from its seated position.
3. When screw is thoroughly disengaged, remove the sensor and retainer clamp from the engine block.
4. To install the assembly, snap the retainer clamp assembly onto the sensor.
5. Lubricate O-ring with engine oil. Carefully start sensor with the retainer clamp assembly into block so as not to damage the O-ring. The sensor must be fully seated by alternately pushing on the sensor hat section, but not the wires, with finger pressure and tightening retainer assembly screw. Do not rely on retainer clamp assembly pressure alone to seat sensor, as clamp will be damaged.

NOTE: Failure to fully seat and retain the sensor will cause malfunction of sensor operation, and a possible no start condition.

6. Tighten the retainer clamp screw to 60–108 in lbs. (7–12 Nm).
7. Connect the sensor plug to the wiring harness.
8. Verify that the EECI Subsystem is operating properly by performing Subsystem checkout.

INLET AIR TEMPERATURE (IAT) SENSOR

Removal and Installation

1. Remove the air cleaner cover.
2. Disconnect the electrical connector.
3. Remove the retainer clip and remove the sensor.
4. Place the new sensor in the mounting hold and secure using the retainer clip.
5. Connect the electrical connector.
6. Install the air cleaner cover.
7. Verify that the EECI Sub-system operates properly by performing subsystem checkout.

ENGINE COOLANT TEMPERATURE (ECT) SENSOR

Removal and Installation

1. Disconnect the transmission kickdown rod from the carburetor linkage and position out of the way.
2. Disconnect the electrical connector.
3. Remove the sensor using $^{13}/_{16}$ inch crow foot wrench.
4. If the sensor is new, check the sensor threads for the presence of Teflon tape. Wrap with $1^1/_4$ turns of Teflon tape if missing. If the sensor if being re-installed, clean threads and wrap with $1^1/_4$ turns of Teflon tape.
5. Install the sensor using a $^{13}/_{16}$ inch crow foot wrench. Tighten to 8–18 ft. lbs. (10–14 Nm) torque.
6. Connect the electrical connector.
7. Install the transmission kickdown rod to the carburetor linkage.
8. Verify that the EECI subsystem operates properly by performing subsystem checkout.

EGR VALVE POSITION (EVP) SENSOR

Removal and Installation

1. Remove the air cleaner.
2. Disconnect the choke tube and fresh air, return tube from the carburetor.
3. Disconnect the sensor electrical connector.
4. Disconnect the EGR pressure line.
5. Cut the EGR cooler tube clamp.
6. Remove the EGR valve assembly.

7. Clean the gasket surface.
8. Install a new gasket.
9. Install the EGR cooler tube gasket and clamp.
10. Install the new EGR valve assembly.
11. Crimp the cooler tube clamp.
12. Install the EGR pressure line.
13. Connect the EVP sensor electrical connector.
14. Connect the choke tube and fresh air return to the carburetor.
15. Install the air cleaner.
16. Verify that the EECI subsystem operates properly by performing subsystem checkout.

THROTTLE POSITION SENSOR

Removal and Installation

1. Loosen the two screws holding throttle sensor to the carburetor sensor bracket.
2. Disengage the connector from wiring harness and remove the potentiometer assembly.
3. Attach the actuator (D84E-9B991-AA or equivalent) to the throttle lever, using one hex head, 3 x 48 UNC screw. Tighten to 5 in. lbs. (.5 Nm).
4. Mount the position sensor bracket to the throttle body using two $^1/_4$ x 20 hex head screws. Tighten to 70–105 in. lbs. (7–11 Nm).
5. Insert the throttle position sensor through the pilot hole in the bracket and insure that the sensor shaft coupling engages the actuator correctly. Attach the sensor to the bracket using two 6 x 32 Phillips/washer head screws. Finger tighten to facilitate rotation of the sensor within the adjustment slots.
6. Set the throttle to the idle position (against the idle set screw). Apply 9.0 VDC ± 10 percent between the connector terminal with the orange wire (positive) and the terminal with the black wire (negative). Connect a 0–10 VDC voltmeter between the connector terminal with the green wire (positive) and the terminal with the black wire. Rotate the sensor counterclockwise to obtain a reading on the voltmeter of 1.89 VDC ± .180 BDC. (An alternate method of setting the throttle potentionmeter is to rotate is until a reading of 0.21 ± .02 is obtained). Tighten the mounting screws to 8–10 in. lbs. (.9–1 Nm). Rotate the throttle to wide open position and release. Recheck the sensor output at idle. Adjust as required.
7. As a final check, rotate the throttle to a wide open condition and release. The throttle must return to an idle condition unassisted.
8. Reconnect sensor to wire harness.

Diagnosis and Testing

NOTE: Performance testing of the EECII system requires the use of a special tester, although some simple continuity checks with an ohmmeter are possible.

Continuity Check with an Ohmmeter

Vehicle Power must be OFF. No Power on connections being measured for continuity. A continuity check with an ohms measurement checks circuits that should be almost 0.0 ohms for current flow and/or high resistance. Harness wires, ground connections, and connector pins and sockets are checked for Continuity from end to end.

CAUTION

An ohmmeter can damage a circuit if its voltage or current exceed the capability of the circuit being tested. It is **not** recommended that any ohmmeter with an ohms circuit voltage greater than 0.2 be used on any EEC system component. It is **not** recommended that **any** ohmmeter of any kind be used to test the Exhaust Gas Oxygen (EGO) Sensor.

SENSORS | IGNITION MODULE | ACTUATORS

EXHAUST GAS OXYGEN (EGO)

(SHELL GROUNDED)

BLACK
ORANGE
GREEN

(TKS) THROTTLE KICKER SOLENOID

TO IGNITION COIL "TACH" TERMAINAL

THROTTLE POSITION (TP)

(CANP) CANISTER PURGE SOLENOID

BATTERY

ENGINE COOLANT TEMPERATURE (ECT)

(TAD) THERMACTOR AIR DIVERTER SOLENOID

POWER RELAY

EGR VALVE POSITION (EVP)

(TAB) THERMACTOR AIR BYPASS SOLENOID

(EGRC) EGR CONTROL SOLENOID

BAROMETRIC AND MANIFOLD ABSOLUTE PRESSURE (B/MAP)

(EGRV) EGR VENT SOLENOID

(FBCA) FEEDBACK CARBURETOR ACTUATOR

CP SHIELD

CRANKSHAFT POSITION (CP)

FBC-2 FBC-1 FBC-3 FBC-4

SOCKET NUMBER

TO STARTER SOLENOID

TO A/C CLUTCH (MERCURY 49 STATES)

1. RED/LIGHT BLUE
2. GRAY
3. ORANGE/WHITE
4. BROWN/LIGHT GREEN
5. DARK GREEN/LIGHT GREEN
6. VACANT
7. BLACK
8. BLACK (SYSTEM GROUND)
9. LIGHT GREEN/BLACK DOT
10. GRAY/YELLOW HASH
11. TAN/LIGHT GREEN DOT

12. TAN/RED DOT
13. DARK GREEN
14. VACANT
15. VACANT
16. VACANT
17. ORANGE/YELLOW HASH
18. DARK BLUE
19. BLACK/WHITE
20. LIGHT GREEN/BLACK
21. LIGHT GREEN/YELLOW
22. DARK BLUE/LIGHT GREEN

23. DARK GREEN/PURPLE HASH
24. RED (SYSTEM POWER)
25. RED/LIGHT GREEN
26. WHITE/RED DOT
27. TAN/LIGHT BLUE DOT
28. TAN/ORANGE DOT
29. YELLOW
30. VACANT
31. BLACK/YELLOW HASH
32. VACANT

TOP

VACANT
VACANT
VACANT
VACANT
VACANT
VACANT

EEC II wiring diagram

Continuity Checks With the EECII Tester and Digital Volt-Ohmmeter (DVOM)

The EECII tester with DVOM attached and in TESTER position can be used to check harness continuity. Refer to the tester switch chart contained in the EECII tester operator's manual. To check the continuity of a particular harness wire, first determine which pin on the 32 pin connector is connected to that wire. Find the pin number of the Tester Switch Chart, and set the tester switches to the position that has that wire at a Test Point.

NOTE: Use only switch positions that have numbered (pin number) connections to Both Test Point A and Test Point B. Lettered connections are internal to tester and cannot be used for continuity checks.

Locate the opposite end of the vehicle harness wire connected to the Test Point A pin (at Sensor, Solenoid, Etc.). Connect a jumper from it to a convenient connection of the harness wire connected to Test Point B. Push the tester Ohms button. If the reading is 2.0 Ohms or less, continuity is OK. This checks continuity of both wires. If the reading is over 2.0 Ohms, there is a break in one of the wires. Select another switch position that is convenient and with one of the same pin connections. Leave the jumper on the common wire, and connect it to the new wire at the end furthest from the ECA. Push the tester ohms button. **If this continuity check reading is 2.0 Ohms or less, then the wire common to** both checks is OK. The wire or it's connecting pins not common to both checks is defective. If the reading is greater than 2.0 Ohms, the wire common to both checks is probably defective.

Continuity Check With DVOM as Ohmmeter Alone

NOTE: Do not use any ohmmeter with an ohms circuit voltage greater than the Rotunda DVOM ohms circuit voltage (0.2 Volts) on any EEC component. Do not use any ohmmeter of any kind to test the Exhaust Gas Oxygen (EGO) sensor.

Obtain a '0' reading for the ohmmeter by shorting the ohmmeter leads together, using 200 ohm scale. Subtract this reading from other continuity readings obtained to get true low ohms continuity reading. Use the 200 Ohms scale of the DVOM.

THREE METHODS OF CONNECTION

1. Connect one test lead of the DVOM to one end of the harness wire to be tested or a direct connection to it. Connect the other test lead of the DVOM to the other end of the harness wire or a direct connection to it.

2. Jumper one end of the harness wire to be tested or it's direct connection to a known good wire (either in the harness or another wire supplied externally). Connect one test lead to the other end of the harness wire or it's direct connection. Connect the other test lead to the opposite end of the known good wire from the jumper.

3. Connect a jumper to one end of the harness wire to be tested or it's direct connection. Connect the other end of the jumper to Vehicle ground. Connect one test lead of the DVOM to the other end of the harness wire of it's direct connection. Connect the other test lead to the Vehicle ground.

A reading of 001.0 Ohms or less indicates good continuity. A reading of more than 001.0 Ohms indicates a defective harness wire, pin, or connection. When checking continuity of injector wires, be sure to subtract the '0' reading, and use 00.3 ohms as specification for good continuity.

1. EEC-II (ECA)
   A. PROCESSOR ASSEMBLY
   B. CALIBRATION ASSEMBLY
2. BMAP SENSOR
3. EGR VALVE POS. SENSOR
4. EGR VALVE
5. EGR VALVE SOLENOID ACTUATORS
6. THERMACTOR SOLENOID VALVES
7. THROTTLE KICKER SOLENOID
8. IGNITION MODULE
9. TP SENSOR
10. THROTTLE KICKER ACTUATOR
11. FBC ACTUATOR
12. CANP SOLENOID VALVE
13. ECT SENSOR
14. CP SENSOR
15. EGO SENSOR
16. EEC POWER RELAY
17. STARTER SOLENOID

(a) AIR CONDITIONER CLUTCH
(b) "S" TERMINAL

EEC II test connections and component locations

Short Circuit Check With an Ohmmeter

Vehicle power must be OFF. No power on connections being measured for a short circuit. A short circuit check, with an ohms measurement, is a check for false circuit paths of current flow that can cause false voltage and/or current readings, overloads and, in many cases, defective components. The most common short on a vehicle is short-to-ground. Since ground is any conductive material with a direct conductive material connection to the vehicle frame and body, it is always present and therefore the most likely to make contact with a separate electrical connection.

Short Circuit Check With EEC-II Tester

To check for a short circuit with the EECII tester and DVOM connected to ECA and vehicle, refer to the Tester Switch Chart contained within the manufacturer's operator's manual. To check for a short circuit in a particular Gas harness wire, first determine which pin on the 32 pin connector is connected to that wire. Find the pin number of the Tester Switch Chart, and set the tester switches to the position that has that wire at Test Point A.

NOTE: Use only switch positions that have numbered (pin number) connections to Both Test Point A and Test Point B. Lettered connections are internal to tester and cannot be used for short circuit checks.

Two of the 32 pin connector wires are directly attached to Vehicle ground: No. 7 (ERTN) on the Engine Block and No. 8 (Power Ground) on the body. Two other wires of the connector are connected to No. 8 within the ECA unit only: No. 2 (CP–) and No. 19 (SRTN). A short circuit of either of these wires to ground could produce intermittent noise-type faults that will be difficult to diagnose. A short circuit check is the only practical way to determine if this particular problem exists. With the ECA, Tester, and Vehicle all connected and power off, push the ohms button. An ohms reading below specification indicates a short circuit or partial short circuit between the two wires. If within specification, its OK. If above specification, there is an open or high resistance connection.

If below specification, it is necessary to segregate components. Disconnect the component connected to the wire under test (SENSOR, Solenoid, etc.). Push the ohms button again, for most connections the reading should be overrange if there is no short circuit. If the wire being tested is not connected to any vehicle component other than the one disconnected, the reading should be overrange (greater than 200 ohms). If the reading is overrange, then the short is in the disconnected component. If it is not overrange, then disconnect the ECA unit and push the ohms button again. If the reading is now overrange the short is in the ECA. If the reading is still not overrange, then the short is in the harness wire. Harness wires with multiple connections (Vref. No. 3 and Batt. Power No. 24) require multiple disconnection or special procedures to detect short circuits. A short-to-ground, as mentioned previously, in wires No. 19 and No. 2 can be detected by unplugging the ECA and using positions B-7 or B-9. The reading should be overrange with the ECA disconnected and less than 2.0 Ohms with the ECA connected.

Short Circuit Check With DVOM as Ohmmeter Alone

NOTE: Do not use any ohmmeter with an ohms circuit voltage greater than the Rotunda DVOM ohms circuit voltage (0.2 volts) on any EEC system component. Do not use any ohmmeter of any kind to test the Exhaust Gas Oxygen (EGO) Sensor.

Use The DVOM 2000 Ohms range. Connect a test lead to each of the two circuits that are to be checked for a short. If the vehicle component connected to one of the circuits is disconnected, there should be an overrange (greater than 2000) Ohms reading for most circuits. If the reading is less than 2000 Ohms, there is a "short-circuit". Unplug the ECA. If the reading is still less than "over-range" the short is in the harness wire. Harness wires with multiple connections (Vref No. 3 and Batt. Power No. 24) require multiple disconnection or special procedures to detect short circuits. A

short-to-ground, as mentioned previously, in wires No. 19 and No. 2 can be detected by unplugging the ECA and checking then for a short-to-ground. The reading should be overrange with the ECA disconnected and less than 2.0 Ohms with the ECA connected.

ECA Relay and Solenoid Operation

Each of the relays and solenoids that are energized by the processor assembly of the ECA have two wire connections. One wire supplies battery power to the Solenoid (or relay) from the Battery through the ECA Power Relay. When the ignition key is tuned to RUN or START, battery voltage (within 0.4 volts) is at each of the Solenoids or Relays. The Second wire at each Solenoid or relay is the ECA control line. Each Solenoid or Relay control line has an individual pin in the ECA 32 pin connector and connects through its darlington configuration circuit to ground in the ECA unit. The Fuel Pump relay and the two fuel injector solenoids have separate darlington circuits. Each of the other solenoids connect to its darlington circuit in one of two quad darlington output chips.

All relays and solenoids are ON with the Darlington circuits energized and 1.5 volts or less from the Control line to ground. All Relays and Solenoids are OFF with the Darlington circuits de-energized and battery voltage (within 0.4 volts) from the control line to ground.

Multiple Sensor Failures

NOTE: If more than one (BP and MAP are counted as one— BMAP) Sensor has failed with readings above 9.0 or below 0.5 and Vref. Is within specification, it is probable that one of the common lines supplying all the sensors is open.

If all passive sensors, BMAP, EVP, TP, ECT, or ACT have readings above 9.0, it is probable that either the SRTN circuit No. 359 (pin No. 19) is open in the harness, before connection to the sensor nearest the ECA or the Sensor Return Line (SRTN) Connection in the processor to PWR GND. Circuit No. 57 (Pin No. 8) is open. Use TSS position B-9, to check SRTN continuity to PWR.GND. (Refer to Section 21—continuity check). If open, replace processor assembly using original calibration assembly, and retest. **Whenever a component has been serviced or replaced. Reconnect and retest to verify condition has been corrected.** If not open, check continuity from pin 19 to nearest sensor SRTN pin. If open, service, and retest. If not open, proceed with individual sensor checks per the sections specified in RH Column of Data Sheet.

If more than one but not all of the passive sensors BMAP, EVAP, TP, ACT, and ECT have readings above 9.0, it is probable that SRTN circuit No. 359 (pin No. 19) is open in the harness between a sensor within specification and one with a reading above 9.0. Check continuity of STRN and, if open, and retest. If no SRTN open is found, proceed with individual Sensor Checks per the sections specified in the RH column of the data sheet for the out-of-specification sensor. **If all or more than one** of the three and four wire passive sensors, BMAP, TP, and EVP have readings below 0.5, it is probable that Vref. circuit No. 351 (Pin No. 3) is open. Check Vref. continuity between pin No. 3 and nearest sensor (if all are below 0.5) or between a sensor with a in-specification reading and a sensor with less than 0.5 readings (if more than one but not all are below 0.5). If open is found, service, and retest. If there is no open, proceed with individual sensor checks per the sections specified in the RH column of the data sheet for the out-of-specification sensors.

Multiple Failures—Solenoids and Fuel Pump Relay

If more than one solenoid or fuel pump relay fails, it is probable that either the common power line supplying the solenoids and the FP relay is open, or has high resistance, or one or more of the common output driver circuits in the processor has failed. If more than one solenoid or FP relay does not work, but their ON voltage is below 1.5 volts (OK), and/or if the OFF voltage of more than one solenoid is below 8.0 volts and their 'on' voltage is below 1.5 volts (OK), it is probable that the power line circuit No. 361 is open to these solenoids or FP relay. Solenoids EGRC, EGRV, TAB, TAD, CANP, FP relay, and INJ. No. 1 and INJ. No. 2 can fail in this pattern. Check circuit No. 361 for continuity from ECA power relay to the low voltage or non-working solenoid or FP relay and continuity to pin No. 24. If open or high resistance, service, and retest.

NOTE: Whenever a component has been serviced or replaced. Reconnect and retest to verify condition has been corrected.

If no open or high resistance is found, proceed with individual defective solenoid or FP relay circuit checks per the sections specified in RH column of the data sheet.

If the ON voltage of more than one non-injector solenoid and EGRC, EGRV, TAB, TAD, CANP is above 1.5 volts, it is probable that the common processor output control circuit of the failed solenoid or FP relay is defective. The TAB, TAD, CANP, and TKS solenoids are controlled by one common quad output processor circuits. The EGRC and EGRV are controlled by another. A common high ON voltage (above 1.5) on TAB, TAD, CANP, and TK (if equipped) or on EGRC and EGRV indicates a failed processor driver circuit.

---CAUTION---

A short circuit in a solenoid or its harness wiring can result in the ECA unit solenoid driver being burned out. Therefore, any test result indicating a faulty Solenoid Driver circuit in the ECA unit can also indicate faults in the Solenoid or its harness wiring. An intermittent solenoid fault can burn-out its ECA driver and test OK later. Every precaution should be taken to check out the Solenoid and its associated harness before installing a new ECA, when the ECA failure is in a solenoid driver circuit.

If the Solenoid Failure pattern indicates a common output driver failure, after checking each of the defective solenoids circuits for shorts per the warning note, and using the techniques described in Section 22—short circuit check, replace processor assembly, using the original calibration assembly and retest. If the Solenoid failure pattern does not indicate a common output driver failure, or if after processor replacement, the failures are still present, reinstall the original processor (if replaced), and proceed with individual defective solenoid or FP relay circuit checks per the sections specified in the RH Column of the data sheet. FP Relay and injectors INJ. No. 1 and ING. No. 2 have individual output circuits, therefore, they are not part of the pattern of common output driver circuit failures.

FORD ELECTRONIC ENGINE CONTROLS (EEC) III

General Information

The Ford EEC III system is found on 1980–82 models. The system is designed to regulate specific emission control functions, based on sensor voltage inputs. The computer calculates appropriate voltages to energize control solenoids or trigger the Dura Spark III ignition module. The solenoids cause desired vacuum or air flow to operate the EGR valve or divert pumped air to the catalytic con-

CARBON
CANISTER

EFI
BALLAST
RELAY

FUEL
CHARGING
ASSEMBLY

EEC-III
ELECTRONIC
CONTROL ASSEMBLY

POWER
RELAY

ELECTRIC IN-TANK
FUEL PUMP

FUEL
SUPPLY
LINE

SECONDARY
FILTER

FUEL
RETURN
LINE

EFI VACUUM
BALLAST
SWITCH

PRIMARY
FILTER

INERTIA
SWITCH

Electronic fuel injection (EFI) system

vertcr, for example, and the module controls the spark advance timing curve. As engine operating conditions vary, sensor voltages change and the computer recalculates input data into output voltages. In this manner, the computer directs the engine emission control system components to continuously control exhaust emission performance.

The EEC III system uses two basic types of fuel delivery systems; either a feedback carburetor or electronic throttle body fuel injection. Basically, the two systems differ in the method of controlling the air-fuel ratio, but the computer and most components are the same. The feedback carburetor contains an electronically controlled actuator which varies fuel mixture and uses a conventional fuel pump. The electronic fuel injection system uses an electric fuel pump which supplies high pressure fuel to a fuel charging assembly consisting of a throttle body and two electronically controlled fuel injectors.

Both systems include several engine sensors, an electronic control assembly, several control solenoids and a vacuum operated thermactor air pumping system and exhaust gas recirculation (EGR). A four-lobe crankshaft pulse ring and crankshaft position sensor provide engine speed an crankshaft angle of rotation data to the on-board computer. The distributor has no advance or retard mechanism; the computer determines timing depending on the engine operation conditions and individual, preprogrammed system calibration. A calibration assembly, attached to the electronic control unit, contains specific instructions for "tailored" engine performance. Since the information stored in the calibration assembly is specific to each type of engine, they are not interchangeable.

NOTE: All system electrical power feeds through a power relay that is usually mounted on the control assembly mounting bracket, or as close to the control unit as possible.

SYSTEM OPERATION

The EEC III system uses the following engine sensors:
• Throttle position sensor (TPS)
• Barometric pressure and manifold absolute pressure (B/MAP) sensors (contained in a single housing)
• Engine coolant temperature (ECT) sensor
• Crankshaft position (CP) sensor
• EGR valve position (EVP) sensor
• Exhaust gas oxygen (EGO) sensor
• Manifold charging temperature sensor (electronic fuel injection only)

During engine starting and operation, the electronic control assembly constantly monitors these sensors to determine required timing advance, EGR flow rate, thermactor air mode and air-fuel ratio for any given instant of vehicle operation. The EEC III system makes adjustments constantly. The electronic control assembly sends output commands to the:
• Ignition module, for spark timing advance
• Throttle kicker solenoid, if equipped, for idle speed control
• EGR control solenoids, to control EGR flow rate
• Canister purge solenoid, to stop or allow fuel vapors into the intake manifold
• Feedback carburetor actuator or fuel injectors, to adjust air-fuel mixture
• Thermactor solenoids, to direct thermactor air flow to the catalytic converter.

The continuous control and adjustment of ignition timing, EGR flow rate and air-fuel ratio results in optimum engine performance with minimum emissions under all vehicle operating loads, temperatures and conditions.

LOS Mode (Fail Safe)

If for some reason there is a failure in the electronic control assembly, the system goes into what's called the Limited Operational Strategy (LOS) mode. In this mode, the electronic control assembly output commands are cut off, and the engine operates with a fixed 10° BTDC spark advance only, regardless of sensor input signals. The engine can be operated until repairs are made, but poor performance may be experienced as long as the system is in the LOS mode. This back-up system is sometimes referred to as the "limp home" mode, and is intended for emergency use, not prolonged operation.

SYSTEM COMPONENTS

Sensor and Solenoid Connectors

All other sensor and solenoid connectors on the EEC III system are the "pull apart" type that feature a release tab attached to the male side of the connector. This assures that proper contact between the sockets and pins in the connector will be maintained.

Electronic control assembly

Electronic control assembly power relay

To disconnect these connectors, lift the tab on the side of the connector slightly to decrease its holding pressure and separate the two connector halves. To reconnect the connectors, simply align the two connector halves and press them together. The holding tab on the side of the connector is designed to provide pressure to hold the two halves together.

NOTE: The ignition switch should be OFF when disconnecting any electrical connectors on computer-controlled systems.

Electronic Control Assembly

The electronic control assembly controls the various functions of the entire engine control system. A separate relay powers the assembly. The control unit delivers 8.1–9.9 reference volts (Vref) to the sensors. It then collects the voltage data from the sensors, calculates output voltages and sends voltage signals to the various emission control solenoids.

The electronic control assembly performs all of its functions continuously throughout all phases of engine operation. This precision adjustment enables engine operation with extremely good control of undesirable exhaust emission gases, while maintaining a good driveability and fuel economy.

PROCESSOR ASSEMBLY

The processor assembly contains several groups of extremely small electronic devices that each perform specific functions. The processor performs five functions:
  1. Analyzes sensor input voltages
  2. Converts voltages to digital input for computer calculations
  3. Selects operating strategy or mode
  4. Calculates ignition timing, EGR flow, air-fuel mixture ratio, charcoal canister purge, throttle kicker and other output voltage values
  5. Sends voltage signals to the various emission control solenoids and ignition module to cause emissions control functions.

CALIBRATION ASSEMBLY

The calibration assembly is a memory storage device (ROM) and is attached to the top side of processor assembly. It performs two functions:
  1. Provides calibration information unique to the vehicle for use by the processor assembly. This includes such variables as weight, transmission and axle ratio.
  2. Recalls appropriate data from memory bank, when required, to allow the processor to compensate for various conditions.

Power Relay

A separate electrical relay provides the source of EEC III current. From a common battery positive terminal, a fusible link carries voltage to one relay terminal. The relay is normally open. With the ignition switch in the RUN position, current travels through a single relay diode to the pull-in coil and grounds through the relay case attached to the steering column. The relay connects battery or system voltage to the computer. In the event of reversed polarity, which would damage electronic components in the control assembly, the relay diode prevents reversed flow and immediately opens the relay.

MONITORING SYSTEM

The monitoring system measures key engine operating conditions by gathering information from:
• Barometric and manifold absolute pressure sensor (B/MAP)
• Engine coolant temperature sensor (ECT)
• Throttle position sensor (TPS)
• Crankshaft position sensor (CP)
• EGR valve pintle position sensor (EVP)
• Exhaust gas oxygen sensor (EGO)
• Manifold charging temperature sensor (electronic fuel injection only).

Each of these sensors measures a mechanical condition. It then converts the information to an electrical voltage signal. The sen-

CRANKSHAFT POSITION (CP) SENSOR

ENGINE COOLANT TEMPERATURE (ECT) SENSOR

BAROMETRIC AND MANIFOLD ABSOLUTE PRESSURE (B/MAP) SENSOR

THROTTLE POSITION (TP) SENSOR

EGR VALVE POSITION (EVP) SENSOR

EXHAUST GAS OXYGEN (EGO) SENSOR

THERMACTOR AIR CONTROL SOLENOIDS

THERMACTOR BYPASS/DIVERTER VALVE

THERMACTOR AIR PUMP

IGNITION COIL

CANISTER PURGE SOLENOID

EGR VALVE

DUAL EGR CONTROL SOLENOIDS

EEC III CONTROL ASSEMBLY

DISTRIBUTOR

EGR SYSTEM VENT (EGRV) AND CONTROL (EGRC) SOLENOID/VALVES

THROTTLE KICKER SOLENOID (TKS)

DURA SPARK IGNITION MODULE

FEEDBACK CARBURETOR ACTUATOR (FBCA)

IGNITION MODULE SIGNAL (IMS)

THERMACTOR AIR DIVERTER (TAD) AND THERMACTOR AIR BYPASS (TAB) SOLENOID/VALVES

EEC III system schematic

sors provide the monitoring necessary to control the engine combustion process, reacting mechanically to pressure, temperature and position variations. They constantly adjust voltage signals to the electronic control assembly, allowing continual evaluation of operating conditions.

Barometric and Manifold Absolute Pressure Sensor

The barometric pressure and manifold absolute pressure sensor assembly contains two sensors. Each sensor converts a pressure

measurement into an electrical voltage signal. The assembly is mounted on the fender apron or firewall.

The barometric pressure sensor reacts to normal atmospheric pressure. The computer uses this voltage signal to determine EGR flow requirements depending on the altitude at which the vehicle operates. The manifold absolute pressure sensor converts the intake manifold vacuum signal to an electrical voltage. The computer reads the voltages which indicate changes in engine load and atmospheric pressure, then reacts to control distributor spark advance at part throttle. It also controls EGR valve flow and air-fuel mixture ratio.

Exhaust Gas Oxygen Sensor

The exhaust gas oxygen sensor monitors the overall effectiveness of the engine exhaust emission control system. It does this by measuring the presence of oxygen in the exhaust gas. Unlike the other sensors in the monitoring system which provide computer input about operating conditions, the exhaust gas oxygen sensor provides voltage data about engine operation output. The oxygen sensor must be warmed up to operate properly.

---CAUTION---

Attempting to measure the oxygen sensor voltage output with an analog voltmeter can destroy the sensor.

Barometric and manifold absolute pressure sensor

VENT   MANIFOLD

Exhaust gas oxygen (EGO) sensor

FRONT OF VEHICLE

HEX

TEFLON TAPE WRAPPED

Engine coolant temperature sensor

Engine Coolant Temperature Sensor

The engine coolant temperature sensor measures coolant temperature for the computer. The sensor threads into the heater water outlet at the front of the intake manifold.

Crankshaft Pulse Ring

The pulse ring position establishes reference timing for the engine. The lobes positioned on the crankshaft align with the sensors at 10° in advance of TDC. This sets timing at 10° BTDC.

The crankshaft pulse ring is located on the crankshaft vibration damper inside hub. It is installed during manufacturing and cannot be removed or adjusted. The ring contains four lobes equally spaced at 90°. Since the crankshaft rotates twice for each distributor revolution, four lobes suffice for 8 cylinder operation.

Crankshaft Sensor

The crankshaft sensor mounts immediately in front of the cylinder block aligned with the crankshaft pulse ring. The sensor identifies the actual position (angle of rotation) of the crankshaft, then produces a corresponding electrical voltage signal to the computer. The sensor operates like the breakerless distributor pick-up coil and reluctor which make and break the ignition primary circuit. The tip contains a permanent magnet and wire coil. The current from the computer passes through the coil, producing a magnetic field. The output wire carries voltage to the ECA. As the crankshaft rotates, the individual pulse ring lobes approach and finally align with the sensor tip. The metal lobe "cuts" the magnetic field. This interruption generates a voltage output signal of crankshaft position to the computer. As the crankshaft rotates and a pulse ring lobe approaches the sensor, sensor voltage increases then sharply decreases and returns to base level. This occurs once each time a lobe cuts the sensor magnetic field. Crankshaft position sensor identifies the correct ignition firing.

NOTE: An inoperative sensor, connector or wiring harness will prevent engine starting.

EGR Valve Pintle Position Sensor

The EGR valve pintle position sensor monitors the amount of EGR valve pintle movement. It converts this mechanical movement into an electrical voltage input to the computer. The computer reads the voltage which is proportional to the amount of exhaust gas flowing into the intake manifold. The computer measures EGR flow through the sensor signals.

The valve contains a completely enclosed diaphragm and spring.

Exhaust gas oxygen sensor installation

It reveals no pintle movement during operation. As the diaphragm and pintle move, a plunger operates within the sensor. The computer sends a reference voltage to the EGR valve position sensor. The pintle movement causes the sensor to move, which changes the sensor output voltage. The signal returns to the computer where EGR flow is calculated. Depending on the voltage input from the EGR valve and other sensors, the computer can change the amount of EGR flow by controlling electrical voltage signals to the EGR valve vacuum solenoids, which in turn control EGR vacuum.

NOTE: The EGR valve position sensor does not move or control the EGR valve. The valve pintle, as always, operates by vacuum applied to the diaphragm. The sensor produces an electrical signal that describes the position of the EGR valve to the computer. The computer controls the solenoids which actually control EGR flow. The sensor only monitors valve position.

Throttle Position Sensor

The throttle position sensor indicates driver demand through use of a potentiometer. A potentiometer is a variable resistor control. As the driver operates the accelerator and throttle shaft, the sensor delivers voltage signals depending on electrical resistance; more throttle—more voltage.

Three operating modes are sensed. They are closed throttle (idle or deceleration), part throttle (normal operation) and wide open throttle (maximum acceleration). The computer applies a set voltage to the sensor as a reference. It then classifies the output which depends on the resistance caused by one of the three modes. The ECA identifies driver demand and reacts to control spark advance, EGR flow, air-fuel ratio and thermactor air flow.

Throttle position sensor

Throttle position sensor adjustment

The throttle position sensor is mounted on a slotted bracket that provides proper adjustment. If replaced, the sensor must be correctly positioned or the ECA will read the wrong signal for the mode.

Crankshaft position sensor showing mounting assembly

EGR valve and position sensor

Dual bed catalytic converter—typical

Feedback carburetor actuator

Feedback carburetor

THROTTLE SENSOR ADJUSTMENT

1. Key ON, engine OFF.
2. Verify throttle is off fast idle cam. Loosen sensor screws.
3. Remove vacuum hose from throttle kicker actuator.
4. Attach a suitable voltmeter to the sensor connector terminals.
5. Adjust sensor until voltmeter reads between 1.8 and 2.4 volts.

Catalytic Converter

The EEC III system contains a three-way catalytic converter for final processing of undesirable exhaust emission gases. The on-board computer's precise control enables use of the three-way catalyst. Without it, the lean mixtures required would not be possible and converter efficiency would drop.

The EEC III converter contains two different catalysts. Each is a porous honeycomb construction coated with a catalytic material. The honeycomb shape maximizes available surface area to improve converter efficiency. The forward element is coated with a rhodium/platinum catalyst designed to reduce oxides of nitrogen (NOx), unburned hydrocarbons (HC), and carbon monoxide (CO). The front element is called a three-way catalyst. The rear converter is coated with a platinum/paladium catalyst and is called a conventional oxidation catalyst.

A catalyst is a substance that initiates a chemical reaction that would otherwise not occur. It also enables the reaction to proceed under milder conditions than otherwise possible. In the case of engine exhaust gases, the engine emission control systems minimize the output of undesirable pollutants. The "engine-out" emissions would be too high to comply with current emission standards. Once in the exhaust system, both temperature and additional air for oxidation are too low to complete the processing of pollutants into less harmful gases. The catalysts, rhodium/platinum and platinum/paladium, enable the gases to continue oxidizing with available air. The result is a conversion of NOx into nitrogen dioxide and HC and CO into carbon dioxide and water. Some other gases also result in small concentrations, but the bottom line is lower harmful emissions.

OPERATION

Exhaust gases enter the converter and flow first through the three-way catalyst. They pass through a "midbed" of air injected from the thermactor air pump and into the oxidizing catalyst. The combined effect of the chemical reactions and mixing with air results in a heat-generating reaction, providing an acceptable reduction of pollutants and exhaust air quality which complies with emission regulations.

Under some conditions when rich mixtures (such as cold enrichment and wide open throttle) could enter the converter, the thermactor air might result in overreaction and converter overheating. In these cases, thermactor air is redirected to treat exhaust gases at the manifold ports or bypassed to the atmosphere.

The exhaust gas oxygen sensor plays a key role in monitoring exhaust air quality. Combined with the computer control voltages, the complete system effectively controls undesirable pollutants under all engine operating conditions.

NOTE: The three-way catalyst depends on precise control of the exhaust gas oxygen content to achieve the best efficiency.

FEEDBACK CARBURETOR

Feedback Carburetor Actuator

The feedback carburetor actuator consists of a solenoid stepper motor which controls a metering rod position. The metering rod varies the vacuum level applied to the carburetor fuel reservoir. The degree of vacuum acting on the fuel affects how easily it leaves the main discharge tube. Control of this function controls the carburetor air-fuel mixture ratio.

The computer sends a voltage signal that actuates the feedback stepper motor. Based on voltage inputs from the exhaust gas oxygen sensor, barometric pressure and manifold absolute pressure sensors, etc., the electronic control assembly computes an output timed voltage to the feedback actuator. This achieves the desired air-fuel ratio, as the length of the signal determines movement.

The actuator stepper motor is mounted on the carburetor's right side. It contains 120 steps in a total linear travel range of 0.400 in. The computer sequentially energizes four separate armature windings to obtain the necessary vacuum metering rod position. The motor varies the position of this metering valve to achieve the desired effect on the air-fuel ratio. The extended position provides a rich air-fuel mixture. Admitting vacuum to the fuel chamber lowers the pressure above the fuel and results in a leaner air-fuel mixture.

NOTE: During cranking and immediately after starting, the computer sets the feedback actuator to initial position, depending on calibration. As engine operation continues, the computer modulates the actuator, based on sensor voltage inputs.

Throttle Kicker

A throttle kicker is used to control engine idle speed for different engine operations. The assembly includes a solenoid valve which controls the vacuum signal to a vacuum actuator. The computer provides the output voltage signal to operate the throttle kicker solenoid. When energized, the actuator diaphragm extends a carburetor throttle stop to increase engine idle speed.

The computer operates the solenoid for the following conditions:

1. Below a specified temperature to improve warm-up idle performance;

2. Above a specified temperature to increase engine cooling as needed;

3. With the air conditioning unit on to improve idle quality while under additional compressor load;

4. Above a specified altitude to improve idle quality.

The thermactor bypass-diverter valve contains three outlet passages: downstream to the catalytic converter, upstream to the exhaust manifold and bypass to the atmosphere. During normal engine temperature, thermactor air is directed downstream to the catalyst. The computer controls the desired routing based on coolant temperature for a calibrated time and other sensor inputs. The ECA energizes the bypass solenoid when time at closed throttle exceeds a calibrated time value. If time between the EGO lean/rich sensor exceeds a set time value, it also bypasses. These two calibrated functions are intended to protect the catalytic converter from damage and/or for vehicle safety. The computer also energizes the bypass solenoid during wide open throttle (WOT).

3. Examine each portion of the EEC III wiring harness. Check for the following at each location:

• Proper connection to sensors and solenoids (locked)
• Loose or disconnected connectors
• Broken or disconnected wires
• Partially seated connectors
• Broken or frayed wires
• Shorting between wires
• Corrosion

4. Inspect sensors for obvious physical damage.

5. Operate engine and inspect exhaust manifold and exhaust gas oxygen sensor for leaks.

6. Repair faults as necessary. Reinstall air cleaner. If the problem has not been corrected, proceed to self-test.

ON-BOARD DIAGNOSIS SYSTEM

The EEC III system is equipped with a self-test feature to aid in diagnosing possible problems. The self-test is a set of instructions programmed in the computer memory of the calibration assembly. When the program is activated, the computer performs a system test. This verifies the proper connection and operation of the various sensors and actuators. The self-test program controls vehicle operation during the test sequence.

Basically, the self-test program does the following:

1. Sends commands to the solenoids and checks for proper response.

2. Checks for reasonable readings from the sensors.

Vacuum throttle kicker

Thermactor air bypass and diverter solenoids

Fuel vapor canister purge occurs above a calibrated cold temperature and below a set overheat temperature, with engine rpm above a calibrated speed and after a set delay period following engine starting. The canister does not purge with the engine at closed throttle. Also, once the canister purge solenoid activates or deactivates, a slight delay may occur in the change of purge operation.

Diagnosis and Testing

Before attempting any repairs or extensive diagnosis, visually examine the vehicle for obvious faults.

1. Remove air cleaner assembly. Check for dirt, foreign matter or other contamination in and around filter element. Replace if necessary.

2. Examine vacuum hoses for proper routing and connection. Also check for broken, cracked or pinched hoses or fittings.

Triggering self-test mode

CARBON CANISTER

DIVERTER VALVE

MANIFOLD ABSOLUTE PRESSURE SENSOR

THERMACTOR AIR DIVERTER SOLENOID (TAD)

THERMACTOR AIR BYPASS SOLENOID (TAB)

FRONT OF ENGINE

FUEL TANK VENT LINE

THERMO VENT VALVE

AIR CLEANER COLD WEATHER MODULATOR

SOLENOID VALVE CARBURETOR BOWL VENT

MANIFOLD VACUUM

CANISTER PURGE SOLENOID

EGR VALVE

CARBURETOR

VACUUM CHECK VALVE

PCV VALVE

THROTTLE KICKER ACTUATOR

AIR CLEANER BI-METAL

AIR CLEANER DUCT VALVE

EGR VENT SOLENOID

VACUUM RESERVOIR

EGR CONTROL SOLENOID

THROTTLE KICKER SOLENOID

THERMO VENT VALVE
SOLENOID VALVE CARB BOWL VENT
(TVV)

EEC III vacuum schematic

371

5 ELECTRONIC ENGINE CONTROLS

3. Produces numbered codes that either outline a possible trouble area or of "all okay" operation.

Unfortunately, reading the EEC III trouble codes requires the use of a special tester with a variety of adapters. The EEC III diagnostic tester is also required for all pinpoint test procedures.

Self-Test Operation

The EEC diagnostic tester includes provisions for the self-test feature. In this case, monitor the test panel for flashes of the thermactor solenoids operation. The series of light flashes represent a service code. The test can also be accomplished using a vacuum pump and gauges. In this case, on must actually monitor the solenoids for pulses or observe corresponding vacuum signals caused by the pulses. In all cases, the starting method for the self-test is the same.

Activate the self-test only after proper engine preparation. The engine should be run until the radiator hose is hot and pressurized. With the engine running at idle, connect a vacuum pump to the barometric sensor vent outlet. Pump down the sensor vacuum to 20 in. Hg and hold for 5 seconds. This low reading is below any possible normal barometric pressure and it triggers the self-test to start. The self-test is not conclusive by itself, but is used in conjunction with the Quick Test procedures to diagnose EEC III system operation.

At first, the program pulses the throttle kicker solenoid and then holds it on during the entire test. The test lasts about one minute. After completion of the test, the program deactivates the throttle kicker solenoid. Any malfunctions recorded are indicated by thermactor solenoid pulses. Following the completion of all the service codes, the canister purge solenoid is energized for about fifteen seconds.

Service Codes

The service codes are a series of pulses on both thermactor solenoids at the same time. Each pulse is on for one-half second and off for a one-half second. This sequence represents the number one (1). The solenoids are off for a full second before starting the second digit of the code. In the case of the multiple service codes, the

solenoids are off for five full seconds between two-digit codes. An example follows.

Service code 23 throttle position sensor, would follow this pattern:

1. One-half second on; one-half second off
2. One-half second on; one full second off (2)
3. One-half second on; one-half second off
4. One-half second on; one-half second off
5. One-half second on; five full seconds off (3)

NOTE: The vehicle remains in self-test for 15 seconds after completing the last code. It then returns to normal operation.

When beginning diagnosis, consider the final code first. In the above case of 23 then 41, begin with diagnosis of code 41-fuel control lean, and then continue with code 23-throttle position sensor.

EXPLANATION OF CODE

Service codes are a series of pulses on both the thermactor air lights (TAB and TAD). The pulses form two-digit numbers. Each pulse is on for 1/2 second then off for 1/2 second for each count. A full second pause separates the digits, a 5-second pause separates service code numbers.

Code Number	Malfunction
11	EEC system okay
12	Engine rpm is out of specifications
21	Engine coolant temperature sensor (ECT) fault
22	Manifold absolute pressure sensor (MAP) fault
23	Throttle position sensor (TP) fault
31	EGR position sensor (EVP) fails to open
32	EGR position sensor (EVP) fails to close
41	Fuel control lean
42	Fuel control rich
43	Engine temperature reading below 120 deg. F
44	Thermactor air system (TAB and TAD) fault

372

Quick Test

1

PRE-CHECK PROCEDURES AND VEHICLE PRE-START PREPARATION

Before hooking up the equipment to diagnose the EEC system, make the following pre-checks:

1. Remove the air cleaner assembly, and reinstall it after visual inspection is complete.

2. Check* all engine vacuum hoses for:
   - Proper routing per vacuum schematic,
   - Proper connections to fittings,
   - Broken, cracked, pinched hoses or fittings.

3. Check* the EEC system wiring harness electrical connections for:
   - Proper connections,
   - Loose or detached connectors,
   - Corrosion,
   - Partially broken or frayed wires at connectors,
   - Shorting between wires,
   - Broken or detached wires,
   - Terminals not completely seated in connectors,
   - And proper routing and lay of harness.

4. Check ECA, sensors, actuators, and pulse ring lobes for physical damage and the CP sensor for proper seating.

5. Perform all safety steps required to start and run an unattended vehicle.

6. Turn OFF all vehicle electrical loads, such as the radio, lights, air conditioner, etc.

7. Be sure vehicle doors are shut whenever readings are made.

8. Start engine and idle until the upper radiator hose is hot and pressurized and the throttle is off fast idle.

*See wiring and vacuum diagrams and location diagram.

Quick Test

NOTE: SET ADAPTER SWITCH TO NORMAL.

FBC

EFI

EEC III TESTER CONNECTED TO ECA THROUGH EFI ADAPTER HARNESS

EEC III TESTER CONNECTED TO ECA

d. If tester lights are lit with the ignition OFF, check for a short between the vehicle battery and ECA power (circuit 361) or an open in the EEC ground (circuit 57 and 60). Refer to Pinpoint Test B8 .

e. Turn the ignition key to RUN, and press and hold the "Test Light" button. All the lights on the control panel should light up.

NOTE: Do not remove the air cleaner unless required for access.

Quick Test

4. Connect DVOM to Tester.

a. Place DVOM inside Tester case.

b. Plug DVOM into Tester jack. Tighten ring finger tight.

c. Pull UP On-Off switch.

d. Set DVOM to "Battery Test."
   — If reading is less than 6.2, replace battery (heavy duty 9V alkaline or mercury).

e. Set DVOM to TESTER position. Both SS and LOS buttons OFF (black flag) on Tester.

IMPORTANT: DVOM external test leads are bypassed when DVOM switch is in TESTER position.

5. Connect Tester to vehicle.

a. Make sure ignition key is OFF.

b. Turn EEC connector retaining bolt counterclockwise with 10MM socket with universal and nutdriver handle. Disconnect EEC-III harness from Electronic Control Assembly.

c. Connect Tester (EFI Adapter) as shown. Do not overtighten, 4.5 N•m (40 lb-in) maximum.

Quick Test

NOTE: If engine does not start or stalls after start, refer to No Start Pinpoint Test A1 that pertains to either EFI or FBC, depending on which type of vehicle you are working on.

9. While the engine is operating, check for leaks around the exhaust manifold, EGO sensor, and vacuum hose connections.

10. Turn ignition key OFF.

11. Service items as required, reinstall air cleaner, and proceed to equipment hookup.

Quick Test

☐2

TEST EQUIPMENT HOOK-UP AND CHECK-OUT

1. Key to OFF position.

2. Connect timing light.

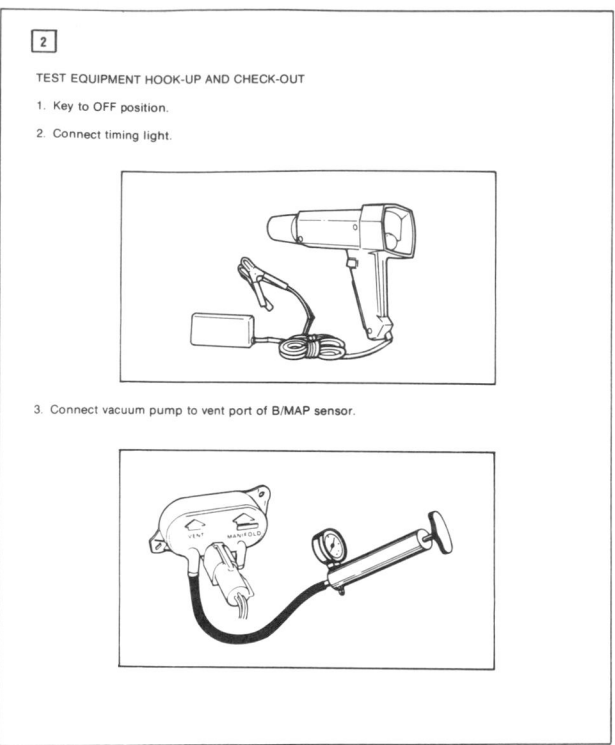

3. Connect vacuum pump to vent port of B/MAP sensor.

Quick Test

	TEST STEP	RESULT ▶	ACTION TO TAKE
8	ENGINE COOLANT TEMPERATURE SENSOR (ECT) — ENGINE AT NORMAL OPERATING TEMPERATURE	DVOM Reading:	
	• Tester to A-5	Between 0.75-2.60V ▶	GO to ☐9
		Under 0.75V or more than 2.60V ▶	GO to ☐E1
9	AIR CHARGE TEMPERATURE SENSOR (ACT), EFI ONLY	DVOM Reading:	
	SKIP THIS TEST FOR FBC • Tester to A-6	Between 1.0-5.6V ▶	GO to ☐10
		Under 1.0 or more than 5.6V ▶	GO to ☐S1
10	MANIFOLD ABSOLUTE PRESSURE SENSOR (MAP) • Tester to A-7 ——— Fill in appropriate limits for your local elevation. (For future reference.)	ELEVATION (FT.) LIMITS DVOM Reading: 0-1500 7.6-8.4 1501-2500 7.2-8.1 2501-3500 6.9-7.8 3501-4500 6.7-7.3 4501-5500 6.6-7.2 5501-6500 6.3-7.0 6501-7500 6.1-6.7 7501-8500 5.8-6.5 8501-9500 5.6-6.3 9501-10500 5.4-6.0 DVOM Reading Does not correspond to your local elevation ▶	GO to ☐11 GO to ☐F1

Quick Test

	TEST STEP	RESULT ▶	ACTION TO TAKE
3	BATTERY VOLTAGE (VPWR)	DVOM Reading:	
	• Tester to A-1	10.5 V or more ▶	GO to ☐4
	• DVOM switch to Tester	Under 10.5V ▶	GO to ☐B1
	• Turn key to RUN, engine OFF		
4	CRANKING SIGNAL VOLTAGE, EFI ONLY	DVOM Reading:	
	SKIP THIS TEST FOR FBC • Tester to A-2	1.0V or less ▶	GO to ☐5
		Over 1.0V ▶	GO to ☐R1
5	SENSOR REFERENCE VOLTAGE (VREF)	DVOM Reading:	
	• Tester to A-3	Between 8.0-10.0V ▶	GO to ☐6
		Under 8.0 or more than 10.0V ▶	GO to ☐C1
6	THROTTLE POSITION SENSOR (TP)	DVOM Reading:	
	• Tester to A-4	Between 1.8-2.8V ▶	GO to ☐7
		Under 1.8 or more than 2.8V ▶	GO to ☐D1
7	THROTTLE POSITION SENSOR MOVEMENT CHECK	DVOM Reading:	
	• Tester to A-4 • Depress accelerator pedal, and check TP value. Release pedal	6V or more then returns to 1.8-2.8 ▶	GO to ☐8
		Under 6V while depressed or does not return to 1.8 to 2.8 ▶	GO to ☐D2

Quick Test

	TEST STEP	RESULT ▶	ACTION TO TAKE
11	BAROMETRIC PRESSURE SENSOR (BP) • Tester to A-8 ——— Fill in appropriate limits for your local elevation. (For future reference.)	0-1500 7.6-8.4 1501-2500 7.2-8.1 2501-3500 6.9-7.8 3501-4500 6.7-7.3 4501-5500 6.6-7.2 5501-6500 6.3-7.0 6501-7500 6.1-6.7 7501-8500 5.8-6.5 8501-9500 5.6-6.3 9501-10500 5.4-6.0 DVOM Reading does not correspond to your local elevation ▶	GO to ☐12 GO to ☐F1
12	EGR VALVE POSITION SENSOR (EVP)	DVOM Reading:	
	• Tester to A-9	Between 1.40-2.45V ▶	WITH factory air, GO to ☐13 WITHOUT factory air, GO to ☐15
		Under 1.40 or more than 2.45V ▶	GO to ☐G1
13	FACTORY AIR CONDITIONING, A/C OFF • Tester to B-10	DVOM Reading: A/C OFF	
		1V or less ▶	GO to ☐14
		More than 1V ▶	GO to ☐J17
14	FACTORY AIR CONDITIONING, A/C ON • Tester to B-10	DVOM Reading: A/C ON	
		9V or more ▶	TURN A/C OFF, GO to ☐15
		Under 9V ▶	GO to ☐J18

Quick Test

TEST STEP	RESULT ▶	ACTION TO TAKE
15 SOLENOID VALVE ACTUATOR CHECK		
• Turn key to RUN — engine OFF	Light pattern is correct ▶	GO to 16
Light pattern should be:	If light pattern is not correct and wrong pattern was	
TAB NO / YES	TAB ▶	GO to K1
TAD UP / DOWN	TAD ▶	GO to K1
CANP ON / OFF	CANP ▶	GO to L1
EFI TKS ON / OFF FBC TKS ON / OFF	TKS ▶	GO to J1
EGRV ON / OFF	EGRV ▶	GO to G6
EGRC ON / OFF	EGRC ▶	GO to G6

Quick Test

TEST STEP	RESULT ▶	ACTION TO TAKE
18 START SELF-TEST	TESTER LIGHT:	
• Release vacuum on vent port of the B/MAP Sensor	TKS light goes from ON to OFF for 2 seconds and then back ON indicating Self-Test start ▶	GO to 19
• Observe TKS lights		
• Observe throttle kicker activation (throttle kicker movement may be as small as 1/16"). If no movement observed, GO to J11	1st ON TKS OFF 2nd ON TKS OFF 3rd ON TKS OFF FOR 2 SECS.	
NOTE: If engine stalls during Self-Test, GO to P1	TKS light not as above ▶	GO to J8
19 CHECK TIMING WITH TIMING LIGHT	Timing:	
• Make certain throttle kicker actuator is extended when checking timing	27°-33° BTDC ▶	GO to 20
	Under 27° or more than 33° BTDC ▶	GO to M1
20 CHECK CP LIGHT	TESTER LIGHT:	
• Engine at idle	CP ▶	GO to 21
• Observe CP light on Tester	CP ▶	GO to A20 (EFI) A17 (FBC)
NOTE: CP light should be on when engine is running.		

Quick Test

TEST STEP	RESULT ▶	ACTION TO TAKE
16 BP AND MAP SHORT CHECK	ELEVATION (FT.) LIMITS DVOM Reading:	
• Start engine. Bring to normal operating temperature and idle.	0-1500 7.6-8.4 1501-2500 7.2-8.1 2501-3500 6.9-7.8 3501-4500 6.6-7.2 4501-5500 6.3-7.0 5501-6500 6.3-7.0 6501-7500 6.1-6.7 7501-8500 5.8-6.5 8501-9500 5.6-6.3 9501-10500 5.4-6.0 ▶	GO to 16a
• Tester to A-8	—	
• Fill in appropriate limits for your local elevation. (For future reference.)	A-8 DVOM Reading: does not correspond to your local elevation ▶	GO to F6
16a • Tester to A-7	A-7 within 2.0-6.4 ▶	GO to 17
	A-7 not within 2.0-6.4 ▶	GO to F8
17 TRIGGER SELF-TEST	DVOM Reading:	
• Tester to A-8	2.85V or less ▶	GO to 18
• Apply vacuum to vent port of B/MAP Sensor until DVOM reading is under 2.85V.	More than 2.85V ▶	CHECK pump; if OK, replace B/MAP Sensor.
• Hold vacuum for 8 seconds		
NOTE: If engine stalls, go to P1		

Quick Test

TEST STEP	RESULT ▶	ACTION TO TAKE
21 CHECK IMS LIGHT	TESTER LIGHT:	
• Engine at idle	IMS ▶	GO to 22
• Observe IMS light on Tester	IMS ▶	TURN engine OFF, GO to A17 (EFI) A14 (FBC)
NOTE: IMS light should be on anytime engine is running.		
22 WARM-UP EGO SENSOR, RUN SELF-TEST	TESTER LIGHT:	
• Turn key to OFF	TKS light goes from ON to OFF	
• Start engine and run above 1800 rpm for about 2 minutes	FROM ON TKS OFF	
• Return to idle	TO ON TKS OFF ▶	GO to 23
• Trigger Self-Test (see Steps 17 and 18)		
• Wait for Self-Test to complete by watching TKS light switch from ON to OFF after 30 seconds to 3 minutes	TKS light stays on or intermittently goes OFF and ON during Self-Test ▶	GO to J16

Quick Test

	TEST STEP	RESULT	▶	ACTION TO TAKE
23	RECORD SERVICE CODES	Service Code(s) Displayed ON:		
	• Read and record all Service Code(s) displayed on TAB and TAD Lights	Both TAB and TAD Lights and CANP Light went ON	▶	GO to 24
	• Service Code(s) are complete when CANP light goes from OFF to ON	Either TAB or TAD Lights	▶	GO to K8
	NOTE: Refer to Fig. 1 for instructions on how to read Service Code(s).	No Service Code(s) Displayed	▶	GO to K7
		CANP Light did not go ON	▶	GO to L7
24	CHECK SERVICE CODE(S), AND GO TO APPROPRIATE DIAGNOSTIC PROCEDURE			
	• Using the lowest numbered Service Code from Step 23, find the number in the RESULTS column, and proceed to the appropriate diagnostic procedure indicated in the ACTION TO TAKE column	**CODE** **TEST**		
		11 —	▶	GO IMMEDIATELY to 25
		12 RPM	▶	GO to N1
		21 ECT	▶	GO to E7
		22 MAP	▶	GO to F7
		23 TP	▶	GO to D11
		24 ACT	▶	GO to S7
		31 EGR	▶	GO to G12
		32 EGR CLOSED	▶	GO to G12
		41 FUEL LEAN	▶	GO to H1
		42 FUEL RICH	▶	GO to H1
		43 ENGINE COLD	▶	GO to E7
		44 THERMAC-TOR	▶	GO to K10

No Start Problem — Pinpoint Test — A (EFI)

	TEST STEP	RESULT	▶	ACTION TO TAKE
A1	CHECK FOR FUEL LEAKS			
	NO LIGHTED TOBACCO NEARBY	Fuel not leaking	▶	GO to A2
	• Remove air cleaner			
	• Inspect and service any: — Loose connections — Corrosion — Water or other foreign matter in fuel — Fuel Leaks	Fuel being injected	▶	CHECK for short to ground in circuits 95 and 96* in harness or processor. If none found, replace injectors.
	• Watch for leaks* as you pressurize fuel system (Turn key ON and OFF five times with one second periods ON before switching OFF)	Fuel is leaking elsewhere than from injectors	▶	REPLACE leaking component*
	• Key OFF			*If no short or leaking found, GO to A34
	*WARNING: If fuel starts leaking or injectors discharge, IMMEDIATELY turn key OFF. No Smoking. NOTE: This step requires two technicians			
A2	TRY TO START ENGINE			
		Engine cranks, but does not start or stalls out	▶	GO to A3
		Engine does not crank	▶	REFER to Group 28 of the Shop Manual.
				If battery were discharged and you suspect the EEC-III system, charge the battery, and perform the QUICK TEST

Quick Test

	TEST STEP	RESULT	▶	ACTION TO TAKE
25	"GOOSE" ENGINE — EFI ONLY			
	SKIP THIS TEST FOR FBC			
	• Quickly accelerate while canister purge Light is ON	TAB pulsed	▶	GO to 26
	• Observe TAB and TAD Lights after canister purge Light goes OFF	TAD pulsed	▶	GO to H15 (EFI)
	• CANP Light will stay on for only 15 seconds; this step must be performed during this time, or test is invalid			
26	EEC-III SELF-TEST, OK			
	• The EEC-III system has passed its operational check. If a problem still exists, refer to Problem/Symptom List.			
	• Disconnect Tester			
	• Reconnect any disconnected hoses and wiring harness connectors			

No Start Problem — Pinpoint Test — A (EFI)

	TEST STEP	RESULT	▶	ACTION TO TAKE
A3	CHECK EEC-III SYSTEM	DVOM Reading:		
	• Turn key to OFF	10.50V or more	▶	GO to A4
	• Connect Tester	Less than 10.50V	▶	GO to B1
	• Tester to A1			
	• Disconnect injectors electrically			
	• DVOM switch to Tester			
	• Turn key to RUN — engine OFF			
A4	SENSOR REFERENCE VOLTAGE (VREF)	DVOM Reading:		
	• Tester to A-3	Between 8-10V	▶	GO to A5
		Under 8V or more than 10V	▶	GO to C1
A5	THROTTLE POSITION SENSOR (TP)	DVOM Reading:		
	• Tester to A-4	Between 1.8-2.8V	▶	GO to A6
		Under 1.8 or more than 2.8V	▶	GO to D1
A6	THROTTLE POSITION SENSOR MOVEMENT CHECK	DVOM Reading:		
	• Tester to A-4	6V or more	▶	GO to A7
	• Depress accelerator pedal	Under 6V	▶	GO to D2

No Start Problem		Pinpoint Test	A (EFI)

TEST STEP	RESULT ▶	ACTION TO TAKE
A7 ENGINE COOLANT TEMPERATURE SENSOR (ECT) — ENGINE AT NORMAL OPERATING TEMPERATURE • Tester to A-5	DVOM Reading: Between 0.83V-7.4V ▶ Under 0.83V ▶ More than 7.4V ▶	GO to A8 GO to E3 GO to E5
A8 AIR CHARGE TEMPERATURE SENSOR (ACT) • Tester to A-6	DVOM Reading: Between 0.83V-6.9V ▶ Under 0.83 or more than 6.9V ▶	GO to A9 GO to S1
A9 MANIFOLD ABSOLUTE PRESSURE SENSOR (MAP) • Tester to A-7 _____ • Fill in appropriate limits for your local elevation. (For future reference.)	ELEVATION (FT.) LIMITS DVOM Reading: 0-1500 7.6-8.4 1501-2500 7.2-8.1 2501-3500 6.9-7.8 3501-4500 6.7-7.3 4501-5500 6.6-7.2 5501-6500 6.3-7.0 6501-7500 6.1-6.7 7501-8500 5.8-6.5 8501-9500 5.6-6.3 9501-10500 5.4-6.0 DVOM Reading does not correspond to your local elevation. ▶	GO to A10 GO to F1

No Start Problem		Pinpoint Test	A (EFI)

TEST STEP	RESULT ▶	ACTION TO TAKE
A12a CHECK FOR FULL EGR • Disconnect EGR valve vacuum hose at EGR solenoid assembly DISCONNECT VACUUM LINE • Attempt to start engine	Engine does not start or stalls when starting ▶ Engine starts ▶	GO to A13 GO to G12
A13 CRANKING SIGNAL VOLTAGE • Tester to A-2	DVOM Reading: 1V or less ▶ Over 1V ▶	GO to A14 GO to R1
A14 CHECK CP AND IMS SIGNALS AND POWER TO STARTER VOLTAGE • Tester connected • Tester to A-2 • Observe DVOM reading and Tester CP and IMS lights while cranking engine for 5 seconds	WHILE CRANKING DVOM Reading: Under 6.5V on A-2 ▶ 6.5V or more on A-2 AND TESTER LIGHTS IMS ☼ CP ☼ ▶ IMS ● CP ☼ ▶ IMS ☼ CP ● ▶ IMS ● CP ● ▶	GO to R1 GO to A15 GO to A17 GO to A20 GO to A20

No Start Problem		Pinpoint Test	A (EFI)

TEST STEP	RESULT ▶	ACTION TO TAKE
A10 CHECK MANIFOLD VACUUM ON ENGINE CRANK • Tester to A-7 • Key to RUN, and observe initial DVOM reading • Crank engine, and note reading **NOTE:** Do not depress gas pedal during test.	DIFFERENCE IN READINGS: 0.4V or more ▶ Under 0.4V ▶	GO to A11 GO to F1
A11 CHECK BMAP SENSOR • Tester to A-8 • Compare reading with MAP reading A19	DIFFERENCE BETWEEN THE TWO READINGS: 0.75V or less ▶ More than 0.75V ▶	GO to A12 GO to F1
A12 CHECK EGR VALVE POSITION SENSOR AND EGR LIGHTS • Tester to A-9 ● EGRV ☼ ON OFF ● EGRC ☼ ON OFF	DVOM Reading: 1.4 to 2.45 ▶ Under 1.4 or over 2.45 ▶ If lights are not as shown ▶	GO to A12a GO to G1 GO to G6

No Start Problem		Pinpoint Test	A (EFI)

TEST STEP	RESULT ▶	ACTION TO TAKE
A15 CHECK FOR SPARK • Reconnect coil harness clip • Disconnect the Spark Plug wire to cylinder No. 2 or No. 4 • Connect spark tester between spark plug wire and engine ground • Crank engine • Reconnect the spark plug wire to the spark plug	Spark ▶ No spark ▶	CHECK rotor, CP ring, and damper for proper alignment. If OK, go to A29 GO to A16
A16 CHECK IGNITION MODULE • Disconnect Ignition Module harness. Install Rotunda Test Adapter T79P-12-127A. • Turn key to RUN • Connect the spark tester between the cap end of the ignition coil wire and engine ground • Repeatedly touch battery terminal with the orange diagnosis test lead, and check for ignition sparks (at coil) when the lead is touched to battery positive • Turn key to OFF • Remove test adapter, and reconnect the ignition module • Reconnect the coil wire to the distributor cap	No Spark ▶ Spark at coil ▶	REFER to Ignition System in Part 29-02 CHECK for open in Circuit 144 from EEC harness to Ignition Module. If OK, replace processor

No Start Problem	Pinpoint Test	A (EFI)

TEST STEP	RESULT ▶	ACTION TO TAKE
A17 CHECK IGNITION MODULE • Disconnect Ignition Module • Crank engine for 5 seconds, and observe CP and IMS light after 3 seconds of cranking	TESTER LIGHTS: [IMS ●] [CP ░] ▶ [IMS ░] [CP ●] ▶	GO to A18 RECONNECT Ignition Module REFER to Ignition System in Part 29-02
A18 CHECK WIRING HARNESS TO IGNITION MODULE • Disconnect processor assembly from vehicle harness • Tester to B-11 • Turn key to RUN — engine OFF • Turn key to OFF	DVOM Reading: 0.5V or less ▶ More than 0.5V ▶	GO to A19 SERVICE short to voltage source in wire 144 (orange/yellow hash) RECONNECT Ignition Module
A19 CHECK HARNESS • Turn key to OFF • Tester to 3-11 • Depress and hold Ohms button • Reconnect Ignition Module	DVOM Reading: 1000 ohms or more ▶ Under 1000 ohms ▶	REPLACE Processor Assembly SERVICE short-to-ground in wire 144 (orange/yellow hash)
A20 CHECK CP SENSOR • Turn key to OFF • Tester to A-10 • Depress and hold Ohms button	DVOM Reading: Between 100 and 640 ohms ▶ Under 100 or more than 640 ohms ▶	GO to A21 GO to A24

No Start Problem	Pinpoint Test	A (EFI)

TEST STEP	RESULT ▶	ACTION TO TAKE
A24 CHECK CP SENSOR RESISTANCE • Disconnect CP sensor from vehicle harness	DVOM Reading: Between 100-640 ohms ▶ Under 100 or more than 640 ohms ▶	GO to A25 REPLACE CP Sensor
A25 CHECK CP+ TO GROUND SHEATH RESISTANCE • Measure resistance from CP+ in sensor to both CP shield connectors (sensor and harness) for shorts	No short ▶ Short ▶	GO to A26 REPLACE CP Sensor
A26 CHECK CP SENSOR HARNESS FOR SHORT • Turn key to OFF • Tester to A-10 • Disconnect Processor Assembly from Tester • DVOM switch to Tester • Depress and hold Ohms button	DVOM Reading: +1 (overrange, no shorts) ▶ Under 1999 ohms (Short) ▶	GO to A27 SERVICE short in harness between circuits 350 and 349

No Start Problem	Pinpoint Test	A (EFI)

TEST STEP	RESULT ▶	ACTION TO TAKE
A21 CHECK FOR PHYSICAL DAMAGE • Check CP Sensor and pulse ring for damage, such as missing lobes, sensor cracks, damaged wiring, etc. • Check for proper CP Sensor seating	No damage and seating is proper ▶ Damage or improper seating ▶	GO to A22 SERVICE as required
A22 CHECK PROCESSOR ASSEMBLY • Disconnect processor assembly from vehicle harness • Crank engine for 5 seconds, and observe CP light after 3 seconds of cranking	TESTER LIGHT: [CP ●] ▶ [CP ░] ▶	GO to A23 REPLACE Processor Assembly
A23 CHECK CP HARNESS FOR CONTINUITY • Turn key to OFF • Tester to A-10 • Disconnect CP Sensor from vehicle harness • Jumper a wire between CP+ (349) and CP- (350) in CP harness • Depress and hold Ohms button	DVOM Reading: 5 ohms or more ▶ Under 5 ohms ▶	SERVICE wire 350 (gray) or wire 349 (dark blue) for open circuit or high resistance REPLACE CP Sensor

No Start Problem	Pinpoint Test	A (EFI)

TEST STEP	RESULT ▶	ACTION TO TAKE
A27 CHECK CP HARNESS FOR CONTINUITY • Turn key to OFF • Tester to A-10 • Disconnect CP Sensor from vehicle harness • Jumper a wire between CP+ and CP- in harness • Depress and hold Ohms button	DVOM Reading: 5 ohms or less ▶ More than 5 ohms ▶	GO to A28 SERVICE circuits 350 (gray) or 349 (dark blue) for open circuit or high resistance
A28 CHECK CP SENSOR HARNESS FOR SHORTS FROM CP+ TO GROUND (CIRCUIT 60)	DVOM Reading: 5 ohms or more ▶ Under 5 ohms ▶	REPLACE Processor Assembly SERVICE short in Harness

No Start Problem	Pinpoint Test	A (EFI)

TEST STEP	RESULT ▶	ACTION TO TAKE
A29 FUEL PUMP CHECK NO SMOKING NEARBY • Disconnect ignition coil connector • Disconnect both fuel injector electrical connections at the injectors • Connect pressure gauge to Schraeder valve on Throttle Body injector bar • Note initial pressure reading • Observe pressure gauge as you pressurize fuel system (turn key to RUN for 1 second, then turn key to OFF. Repeat 5 times) • Turn key to OFF WARNING: If fuel starts leaking or injectors discharging, turn key OFF immediately. No smoking. Reconnect ignition coil connector. GO to [A1]	PRESSURE GAUGE READING: Increase ▶ Did not increase ▶	GO to [A31] TURN key OFF, reconnect ignition coil connector, and go to [A30]

No Start Problem	Pinpoint Test	A (EFI)

TEST STEP	RESULT ▶	ACTION TO TAKE
A33 CHECK FOR FUEL DISCHARGE WITH INJECTORS DISCONNECTED • Crank engine for 3 seconds • Watch pressure gauge and injectors	Pressure does not drop, AND Injectors do not discharge ▶ Pressure drops, AND Injectors discharge ▶	GO to [A34] TURN key OFF immediately CHECK for hydraulic lockup or fuel fouled spark plugs RECONNECT ignition coil REPLACE leaking injector(s) with the same color code
A34 CHECK SIGNAL AT DRIVER SIDE INJECTOR • Reconnect injectors • Connect a 12 V Test Light across 2 pins on the driver side of Throttle Body connector • Turn key to RUN	TEST LIGHT: Off ▶ On ▶	GO to [A35] REMOVE Test Light GO to [A41]

No Start Problem	Pinpoint Test	A (EFI)

TEST STEP	RESULT ▶	ACTION TO TAKE
A30 CHECK INERTIA SWITCH • Locate inertia switch (in trunk) • Push the button of Inertia switch to turn it on • Watch pressure gauge as you attempt to pressurize fuel system NOTE: If switch will not turn "ON", replace it.	PRESSURE GAUGE READING: Increases ▶ Did not increase ▶	GO to QUICK TEST GO to [Q2]
A31 CHECK FUEL DELIVERY • Pressurize fuel system • Turn key to OFF • Wait for pressure to become steady • Read pressure gauge	PRESSURE GAUGE READING: Between 35 and 45 psi ▶ Over 45 psi or under 35 psi ▶	GO to [A32] RECONNECT ignition coil. REFER to Part 24-29 of the Shop Manual
A32 CHECK FOR LEAK DOWN • Wait 2 minutes after pressure gauge reading of test Step [A31] then note drop in gauge reading	PRESSURE DROP: 4 psi drop or less in 2 min. ▶ More than 4 psi drop in 2 min. ▶	GO to [A33] RECONNECT ignition coil. REFER to Part 24-29 of the Shop Manual

No Start Problem	Pinpoint Test	A (EFI)

TEST STEP	RESULT ▶	ACTION TO TAKE
A35 CHECK PROCESSOR OUTPUT TO DRIVER SIDE INJECTOR • Crank engine • Leave test light connected as in [A34]	TEST LIGHT: Flickers ▶ Does not flicker ▶	GO to [A36] DISCONNECT Test Light GO to [A41]
A36 CHECK SIGNAL AT PASSENGER SIDE INJECTOR • Connect the 12V Test Light across 2 pins on the passenger side of Throttle Body right connector • Turn key to RUN	TEST LIGHT: Off ▶ On ▶	GO to [A37] DISCONNECT Test Light GO to [A41]
A37 CHECK PROCESSOR OUTPUT TO PASSENGER SIDE INJECTOR • Crank engine • Leave test light connected as in [A36]	TEST LIGHT: Flickers ▶ Does not flicker ▶	GO to [A38] DISCONNECT Test Light GO to [A41]

379

No Start Problem	Pinpoint Test	A (EFI)

TEST STEP	RESULT ▶	ACTION TO TAKE
A38 CHECK ONE INJECTOR'S PRESSURE	**PRESSURE DROP:**	
• Disconnect one injector electrically (leave other one connected) • Pressurize fuel system • Disable fuel pump by disconnecting Inertia Switch or disconnecting Fuel Pump Relay • Observe pressure gauge reading • Crank engine for 2 seconds • Turn key to OFF • Wait 5 seconds then observe pressure gauge reading drop	Between 2 and 16 psi drop (1 to 8 psi drop per second of cranking) ▶	GO to A39
	Less than 2 or more than 16 psi drop (less than 1 or more than 8 psi drop per second of cranking) ▶	GO to A40
A39 CHECK OTHER INJECTOR'S PRESSURE	**PRESSURE DROP:**	
• Reactive fuel pump • Reconnect injector, and disconnect the other one • Repeat A38 for this injector	Between 2 and 16 psi drop (1 to 8 psi drop per second of cranking) ▶	RECONNECT ignition coil Spark plug and fuel is present. Check to make sure plugs are not fouled and all plugs are firing and the rotor is turning. Be sure there is no mechanical problem like distributor cross-fire, flooding, or improper fuel.
	Less than 2 or more than 16 psi drop (less than 1 or more than 8 psi drop per second of cranking) ▶	GO to A40

No Start Problem	Pinpoint Test	A (EFI)

TEST STEP	RESULT ▶	ACTION TO TAKE
A41 CHECK FOR INJECTOR SHORT-TO-GROUND		
• Turn key to OFF • Reconnect ignition coil connector • Reconnect injectors properly • Check each pin on Throttle Body connector for short-to-ground	No short at any pin ▶	GO to A45
	Short at one or more pins ▶	GO to A42
A42 CHECK FOR PROCESSOR SHORT-TO-GROUND		
• Turn key to OFF • Disconnect harness from Processor Assembly • Check each pin of Throttle Body for short-to-ground (See A41)	No short any pin ▶	REPLACE Processor Assembly
	Short at one or more pins ▶	GO to A43
A43 CHECK FOR SHORT-TO-GROUND IN DRIVER SIDE INJECTOR		
(Processor disconnected) • Disconnect driver side injector • Check each pin of Throttle Body connector for short-to-ground (See A41)	No short at any pin ▶	REPLACE driver side injector
	Short at one or more pins ▶	GO to A44

No Start Problem	Pinpoint Test	A (EFI)

TEST STEP	RESULT ▶	ACTION TO TAKE
A40 ISOLATE IMPROPER FUEL DELIVERY	**PRESSURE DROP:**	
• Remove the connected electrical connector from the injector, and connect it to the other injector	Between 2 and 16 psi (1 to 8 psi per second of cranking) ▶	REPLACE the Disconnected injector with same color code RECONNECT both injectors correctly RETEST.
	Less than 2 or more than 16 psi (less than 1 or more than 8 psi per second of cranking) ▶	GO to A41
• Reactivate fuel pump • Pressurize fuel system • Disable fuel pump by turning off Inertia Switch or disconnecting Fuel Pump Relay • Observe pressure gauge reading • Crank engine for 2 seconds • Turn key to OFF • Wait 5 seconds then observe pressure gauge reading drop		

No Start Problem	Pinpoint Test	A (EFI)

TEST STEP	RESULT ▶	ACTION TO TAKE
A44 CHECK FOR SHORT-TO-GROUND IN PASSENGER SIDE INJECTOR		
(Left injector disconnected) • Disconnect passenger side injector • Check each pin on Throttle Body connector again for short-to-ground	No short at any pin ▶	REPLACE passenger side injector
	Short at one or more pins	SERVICE short circuit
A45 CHECK INJECTOR CIRCUITS TO BATTERY VOLTAGE	**DVOM Reading:**	
• Using DVOM Test Leads, measure voltage between battery negative and each injector signal line	1V or less for both lines ▶	GO to A46
	Over 1V for either line ▶	SERVICE short in circuit 95 or 96 between battery positive and circuit(s) out of limits
A46 CHECK RESISTANCE OF INJECTORS HARNESS AND PROCESSOR CONNECTION	**DVOM Reading:**	
• Using DVOM Test Leads, measure resistance from 361 to 95 and from 361 to 96	Under 2 ohms ▶	GO to A47
	2 or more ohms ▶	GO to A49

No Start Problem	Pinpoint Test	A (EFI)

TEST STEP	RESULT ▶	ACTION TO TAKE
A47 CHECK FOR SHORT BETWEEN INJECTOR LINES • Disconnect harness from Processor Assembly • Using DVOM Test Leads, measure resistance between pins — 12 and 28 — 24 and 28 (left injector) — 24 and 12 (right injector) on Harness connector	DVOM Reading: 2 or more ohms for each pair of pins Under 2 ohms for one or more pair of pins	GO to A49 NOTE which lines. GO to A48
A48 ISOLATE OBSERVED SHORT TO INJECTORS OR HARNESS • Disconnect both injectors electrically • Using DVOM Test Leads, measure resistance (200 x 1000 scale) between pins: — 12 and 28 — 24 and 28 (left injector) — 24 and 12 (right injector) on Harness connector	DVOM Reading: 10,000 ohms or more for each pair of pins Under 10,000 ohms for one or more pair of pins	REPLACE injector(s) connected to the pin(s) that were shorted in A47 (replace with the same color code) SERVICE short in harness

No Start Problem	Pinpoint Test	A (EFI)

TEST STEP	RESULT ▶	ACTION TO TAKE
A57 CHECK FOR OPEN IN PASSENGER SIDE INJECTOR HARNESS • Disconnect passenger side injector electrically • Connect jumper wire across injector harness pins • Using DVOM Test Leads measure resistance between pins 24 and 12 of Harness connector	DVOM Reading: 5 or less ohms Over 5 ohms	REPLACE passenger side injector SERVICE open in circuit 95 or 361 to injector

No Start Problem	Pinpoint Test	A (EFI)

TEST STEP	RESULT ▶	ACTION TO TAKE
A49 CHECK FOR OPENS IN LINES TO INJECTORS • Using DVOM Test Leads, measure resistance (200 Ohms Scale) between pins: — 24 and 28 (driver side injector) — 24 and 12 (passenger side injector) on Harness connector	DVOM Reading: 4 or less ohms for each line Over 4 ohms between 24 and 28 Over 4 ohms between 24 and 12 Over 4 ohms on both	REPLACE Processor Assembly GO to A50 GO to A51 SERVICE open in Circuit 361
A50 CHECK FOR OPEN IN DRIVER SIDE INJECTOR HARNESS • Disconnect driver side injector electrically • Connect jumper wire across injector harness pins • Using DVOM Test Leads measure resistance between pins 24 and 28 on Harness connector	DVOM Reading: 5 or less ohms Over 5 ohms	REPLACE driver side injector SERVICE open in circuit 96 or 361 to injector

No Start Problem	Pinpoint Test	A (FBC)

TEST STEP	RESULT ▶	ACTION TO TAKE
A1 TRY TO START ENGINE	Engine cranks but does not start Engine does not crank	GO to A2 REFER to Group 28 of the Shop Manual If battery were discharged, and you suspect the EEC-III system, charge the battery and perform the QUICK TEST.
A2 CHECK FOR HOT SPARK AT A SPARK PLUG • Disconnect the Spark Plug wire to cylinder No. 2 or No. 4 • Connect the spark plug tester between the spark plug wire and engine ground • Crank engine • Reconnect the spark plug wire to the spark plug	Spark No spark	GO to A3 GO to A10

Panel 1 (Top Left)

No Start Problem	Pinpoint Test	A (FBC)

TEST STEP	RESULT ▶	ACTION TO TAKE
A3 CHECK FOR EGR	Engine does not start or starts and stalls ▶	GO to A7
• Disconnect vacuum hose to EGR valve at EGR solenoid assembly	Engine starts ▶	GO to A4
• Attempt to start engine		
DISCONNECT VACUUM LINE 361 360 362 361		
• Reconnect EGR vacuum hose		
A4 DETERMINE IF EGR FAULT IS ELECTRICAL OR MECHANICAL		
• Disconnect EGRC and EGRV solenoids electrically	Engine does not start or starts and stalls ▶	REPLACE EGR Solenoid Assembly
• Attempt to start engine	Engine starts ▶	GO to A5
A5 ISOLATE ELECTRICAL PROBLEM WITH EGR CIRCUIT	DVOM Reading:	
• Reconnect EGRC and EGRV solenoids electrically	Under 5 ohms ▶	GO to A6
• Disconnect Processor Assembly from vehicle harness	More than 5 ohms ▶	REPLACE Processor Assembly
• Turn key to OFF		
• Using DVOM, measure ohms (x200 scale) between circuits 360 and chassis ground, also 362 and chassis ground		

Panel 2 (Top Right)

No Start Problem	Pinpoint Test	A (FBC)

TEST STEP	RESULT ▶	ACTION TO TAKE
A9 CHECK COMPUTED TIMING	DVOM Reading:	
• Connect tester	Between +3 and −3 ▶	CHECK rotor and damper alignment, correct alignment problem, then retest
• Tester at D-9		
• DVOM switch to Tester	Greater than +3 or less than −3 ▶	REPLACE Calibration Assembly. Run QUICK TEST. If still OK, replace Processor Assembly using original Calibration Assembly, and repeat QUICK TEST
• Crank engine		
A10 CHECK IGNITION MODULE		
• Disconnect Ignition Module harness. Install Rotunda Test Adapter T79P-12-127A.	Spark at coil ▶	GO to A13
• Turn key to RUN — Engine OFF		
• Connect the spark tester between the cap end of the ignition coil wire and engine ground		
• Repeatedly touch battery terminal with the orange diagnostic test lead, and check for ignition sparks (at coil) when the lead is touched to battery positive	No spark ▶	REFER to Ignition Systems Diagnostics in Group 29
• Turn the key to OFF		
• Remove the test adapter, and connect the ignition module		
• Reconnect the coil wire to the distributor cap		
A11 CHECK EEC-III SYSTEM	DVOM Reading:	
• Turn key to OFF	10.50 V or more ▶	GO to A14
• Connect Tester	Less than 10.50 V ▶	GO to B1
• Tester at A1		
• DVOM switch to Tester		
• Turn key to RUN — engine OFF		

Panel 3 (Bottom Left)

No Start Problem	Pinpoint Test	A (FBC)

TEST STEP	RESULT ▶	ACTION TO TAKE
A6 DETERMINE IF SHORT OBSERVED IS IN HARNESS OR EGR SOLENOID	DVOM Reading:	
• Disconnect EGRC and EGRV electrically	Less than 5 ohms ▶	REPLACE EGR Solenoid Assembly
• Using DVOM, measure ohms (X200 scale) between both pins of EGRC and EGRV and ground	More than 5 ohms ▶	SERVICE short-to-ground in circuits 362 and/or 360 in vehicle harness
A7 CHECK FOR EGR	DVOM Reading:	
• Connect EEC Tester	Less than 2.45 ▶	GO to A8
• Turn key ON	More than 2.45 ▶	REFER to Part 29-15
• Tester to A9		
A8 CHECK VEHICLE TIMING		
• Reconnect EVP Sensor	Between 7° BTDC and 13° BTDC ▶	CHECK Fuel Delivery System for problem EEC is OK
• Crank engine		
• While cranking engine, measure engine timing using timing light	Greater than 13° BTDC or less than 7° BTDC ▶	GO to A9
NOTE: If vehicle starts with EEC Tester connected, replace EEC Processor		

Panel 4 (Bottom Right)

No Start Problem	Pinpoint Test	A (FBC)

TEST STEP	RESULT ▶	ACTION TO TAKE
A12 CHECK FOR CP AND IGNITION MODULE SIGNALS (IMS)	IMS CP ▶	GO to A13
• Crank engine for 5 seconds while observing CP and IMS lights	IMS CP ▶	GO to A14
	IMS CP ▶	GO to A17
	IMS CP ▶	GO to A17
A13 CHECK IMS WIRE FOR CONTINUITY	TESTER LIGHTS:	
• Disconnect Ignition Module three-pin connector	IMS CP ▶	SERVICE harness wire 144 (orange/yellow hash) for open circuit
• Jumper IMS Wire 144 (orange) from Ignition Module connector to ground	IMS CP ▶	REPLACE Processor Assembly
• Crank engine for 5 seconds, and observe CP and IMS lights after 3 seconds of cranking		
• Reconnect ignition module		
A14 CHECK IGNITION MODULE	TESTER LIGHTS:	
• Disconnect Ignition Module	IMS CP ▶	GO to A15
• Crank engine for 5 seconds and observe CP and IMS light after 3 seconds of cranking	IMS CP ▶	RECONNECT ignition module REFER to Ignition Systems in Part 29-02
A15 CHECK WIRING HARNESS TO IGNITION MODULE	DVOM Reading:	
• Disconnect Processor Assembly from vehicle harness	1V or less ▶	GO to A16
• Tester to B-11	More than 1V ▶	SERVICE short to voltage source in wire 144 (orange/yellow hash) RECONNECT ignition module
• Turn key to RUN — engine OFF		
• Turn key to OFF		

| No Start Problem | | | Pinpoint Test | A (FBC) |

TEST STEP	RESULT	►	ACTION TO TAKE
A16 CHECK HARNESS	DVOM Reading:		
• Turn key to OFF	5 ohms or more	►	REPLACE Processor Assembly
• Tester to B-11			
• Depress and hold Ohms button	Under 5 ohms	►	SERVICE short-to ground in wire 144 (orange/yellow hash)
• Reconnect ignition module			
A17 CHECK CP SENSOR	DVOM Reading:		
• Turn key to OFF	Between 100 and 640 ohms	►	GO to A18
• Tester to A-10	Under 100 or more than 640 ohms	►	GO to A21
• Depress and hold Ohms button			
A18 CHECK FOR PHYSICAL DAMAGE			
• Check CP Sensor and pulse ring for damage, such as missing lobes, sensor cracks, damaged wiring, etc.	No damage or improper seating	►	GO to A19
• Check for proper CP Sensor seating	Damage or improper seating	►	SERVICE as required
A19 CHECK PROCESSOR ASSEMBLY	TESTER LIGHT:		
• Disconnect Processor Assembly from vehicle to harness	[• CP]	►	GO to A20
• Crank engine for 5 seconds, and observe CP light after 3 seconds of cranking	[CP]	►	REPLACE Processor Assembly

| No Start Problem | | | Pinpoint Test | A (FBC) |

TEST STEP	RESULT	►	ACTION TO TAKE
A23 CHECK CP SENSOR HARNESS FOR SHORT	DVOM Reading:		
• Turn key to OFF	5 ohms or less	►	GO to A24
• Tester to A-10	More than 5 ohms	►	SERVICE short in Harness between circuits 350 and 349
• Disconnect Processor Assembly from Tester			
• DVOM switch to Tester			
• Depress and hold Ohms button			
A24 CHECK CP HARNESS FOR CONTINUITY	DVOM Reading:		
• Turn key to OFF	5 ohms or more	►	GO to A25
• Tester to A-10	Under 5 ohms	►	SERVICE circuits 350 (grey) or 349 (dark blue) for open circuit or high resistance
• Disconnect CP Sensor from vehicle harness			
• Jumper a wire between CP+ and CP– in harness			
• Depress and hold Ohms button			
A25 CHECK CP SENSOR HARNESS FOR SHORTS FROM CP+ TO GROUND (Circuit 60)	DVOM Reading:		
	5 ohms or more	►	REPLACE Processor Assembly
	Under 5 ohms	►	SERVICE short in Harness

(A24 diagram labels: CP+ (349), CP– (350), CP SENSOR HARNESS CONNECTOR)

(A25 diagram labels: CP HARNESS CONNECTOR, CP–, CIRCUIT 60 HARNESS CONNECTOR, 200 OHMS)

| No Start Problem | | | Pinpoint Test | A (FBC) |

TEST STEP	RESULT	►	ACTION TO TAKE
A20 CHECK CP HARNESS FOR CONTINUITY	DVOM Reading:		
• Turn key to OFF	5 ohms or more	►	SERVICE wire 350 (grey) or wire 349 (dark blue) for open circuit or high resistance
• Tester to A-10			
• Disconnect CP Sensor from vehicle harness			
• Jumper CP+ to CP– in vehicle harness connection			
• Depress and hold Ohms button	Under 5 ohms	►	REPLACE CP Sensor
A21 CHECK CP SENSOR RESISTANCE	DVOM Reading:		
	Between 100-640 ohms	►	GO to A22
	Under 100 or more than 640 ohms	►	REPLACE CP Sensor
A22 CHECK CP+ TO GROUND SHEATH RESISTANCE			
• Measure resistance from CP+ at Sensor to both CP shield connectors (sensor and harness) for shorts	No short	►	GO to A23
	Short	►	REPLACE CP Sensor

(A20 diagram labels: CP– (349), CP (350), CP SENSOR HARNESS CONNECTOR)

(A21 diagram label: 2000 OHMS)

(A22 diagram labels: CP+, CP SENSOR CONNECTOR, CP SENSOR GROUND SHEATH CONNECTOR, HARNESS CIRCUIT 60, 200 OHMS)

| Vehicle Battery | | | Pinpoint Test | B |

This Test Checks:
• Vehicle Battery Voltage
• Circuits 16, 57, 60, 38 and 361
• Power Relay
• Processor Assembly

(Diagram labels: 38 B-O, 361 R, 16 R-LG, TO IGNITION SWITCH "RUN", 361 R, POWER RELAY, 38 B-O, 8, 24, 57 BK, GROUND, 60 B-LGD, 57 BK, BATTERY)

TEST STEP	RESULT	►	ACTION TO TAKE
B1 BATTERY VOLTAGE CHECK	DVOM Reading:		
• Turn key to RUN — engine OFF	12V or more	►	GO to B2
	Under 12V	►	SERVICE discharged Battery
B2 CHECK POWER GROUND (60) WIRE	DVOM Reading:		
• Disconnect CP sensor from vehicle harness	0.7V or more	►	GO to B3
	Under 0.7V	►	GO to B4

(B1 diagram label: 20 VOLTS D.C.)

(B2 diagram labels: CP HARNESS, CP (GRAY WIRE), BATTERY, 20 VOLTS D.C.)

Vehicle Battery — Pinpoint Test B

TEST STEP	RESULT	▶	ACTION TO TAKE
B3 CHECK ECA, CP−, AND POWER GROUND CONTINUITY • Turn key to OFF • Tester to B-7 • DVOM switch to tester • Depress and hold Ohms button	DVOM Reading: 2 ohms or more Under 2 ohms	▶ ▶	REPLACE Processor Assembly CHECK circuits 57 and 60 for open circuit or bad connection SERVICE as required
B4 CHECK POWER RELAY OUTPUT VOLTAGE (CIRCUIT 361) • Leave Power Relay connected	DVOM Reading: 10.5V or less More than 10.5V	▶ ▶	GO to B5 CHECK Circuit 361 for open circuit or bad connection

Vehicle Battery — Pinpoint Test B

TEST STEP	RESULT	▶	ACTION TO TAKE
B8 KEY OFF, POWER RELAY CHECK NOTE: This check is made if any tester lights are lit when the tester is connected to the vehicle and the key is OFF during equipment hook-up prior to the QUICK TEST. NOTE: Do not disconnect power relay • Connect probe to Circuit 16 at Power Relay	DVOM Reading: 9V or less More than 9V	▶ ▶	GO to B9 SERVICE problem in Circuit 16 from Ignition Switch to Power Relay
B9 POWER RELAY CHECK • Disconnect Power Relay from harness	Tester lights OFF Tester lights ON	▶ ▶	REPLACE Power Relay CHECK for short in circuit 361 to battery voltage

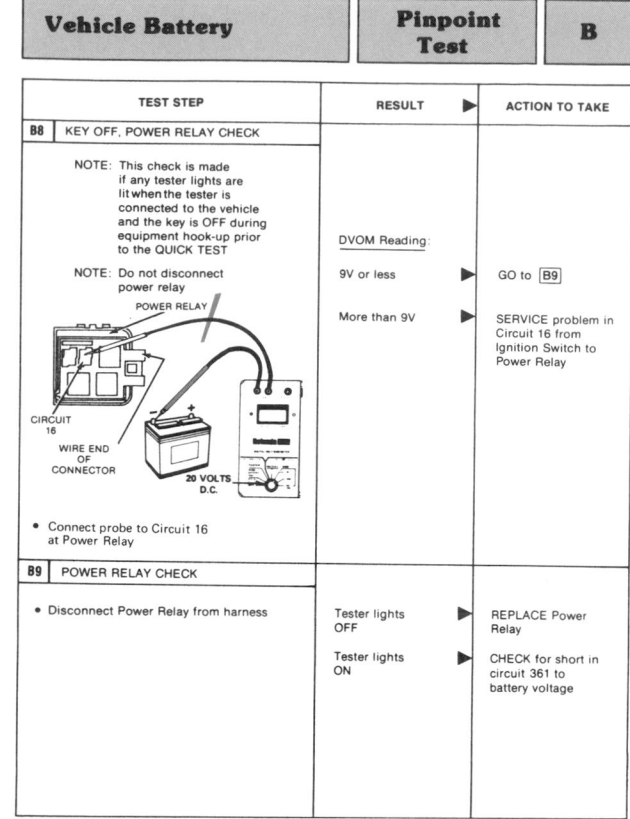

Vehicle Battery — Pinpoint Test B

TEST STEP	RESULT	▶	ACTION TO TAKE
B5 CHECK FOR POWER (CIRCUIT 38) AT POWER RELAY	DVOM Reading: 10.5V or more Under 10.5V	▶ ▶	GO to B6 CHECK circuit 38 for open circuit or bad connection If open, check for short-to-ground in Circuit 38 before replacing fuse link
B6 CHECK IGNITION SWITCH (CIRCUIT 16) POWER	DVOM Reading: 9V or more Under 9V	▶ ▶	GO to B7 SERVICE problem in Circuit 16 from Ignition Switch to Power Relay
B7 CHECK POWER RELAY GROUND	DVOM READING: More than 1 Volt Under 1 Volt	▶ ▶	SERVICE ground wire (circuit 60) in harness REPLACE power relay

Reference Voltage — Pinpoint Test C

This Test Checks
- Circuits 38, 351, 356, 358, 359, and 361
- Processor Assembly
- B/MAP, TP, and EVP Sensors

TEST STEP	RESULT	▶	ACTION TO TAKE
C1 VREF VOLTAGE CHECK • Turn key to RUN — engine OFF • Tester to A-3 • DVOM to Tester	DVOM Reading: 10V or more 8V or less	▶ ▶	GO to C2 GO to C4
C2 CHECK FOR SHORT TO BATTERY VOLTAGE • Turn key to OFF • Tester to A-3	DVOM Reading: 0.5V or less More than 0.5V	▶ ▶	GO to C3 SERVICE short between VREF (351) and Battery power circuits (361/38)

Reference Voltage	Pinpoint Test	C

TEST STEP	RESULT ▶	ACTION TO TAKE
C3 CHECK FOR SHORT TO PROCESSOR POWER (VPWR) • Disconnect Processor Assembly from Tester • Turn key to RUN — engine OFF • Tester to A-3	DVOM Reading: 0.5V or less ▶ More than 0.5V ▶	REPLACE Processor Assembly SERVICE short between VREF (351) and battery power (pin 24) in EEC-III harness
C4 CHECK FOR SHORTED B/MAP SENSOR • Disconnect B/MAP Sensor • Turn key to RUN — engine OFF • Tester to A-3	DVOM Reading: 8V or less ▶ More than 8V ▶	GO to C5 REPLACE B/MAP Sensor
C5 CHECK FOR SHORTED THROTTLE POSITION SENSOR • Disconnect Throttle Position Sensor from vehicle harness • Turn key to RUN — engine OFF • Tester to A-3	DVOM Reading: 8V or less ▶ More than 8V ▶	GO to C6 REPLACE TP Sensor RECONNECT B/MAP Sensor

Throttle Position Sensor	Pinpoint Test	D

This Test Checks
• TP Sensor
• Sensor Harness

TEST STEP	RESULT ▶	ACTION TO TAKE
D1 ADJUST TP SENSOR NOTE: This step is performed when TP Sensor voltage is out of specification. • Key to RUN — engine OFF • Tester to A-4 • DVOM switch to Tester position • Verify throttle is off fast idle cam • Remove vacuum hose from throttle kicker actuator • Adjust Sensor until DVOM reads between 1.8 and 2.40 volts. Reading is 2.40 with vacuum removed from TK	DVOM Reading: Between 1.80-2.40V ▶ Under 1.80 or more than 2.40V ▶	RECONNECT vacuum hose to TK Actuator REPEAT QUICK TEST ADJUST to lowest possible value RECONNECT vacuum hose to Throttle Kicker Actuator GO to D3

LOOSEN MOUNTING SCREWS — TURN SENSOR UNTIL READING IS BETWEEN 1.8 AND 2.4 — TIGHTEN MOUNTING SCREWS

Reference Voltage	Pinpoint Test	C

TEST STEP	RESULT ▶	ACTION TO TAKE
C6 CHECK FOR SHORTED EVP SENSOR • Disconnect EVP Sensor from vehicle harness • Key ON • Tester to A-3	DVOM Reading: 8V or less ▶ More than 8V ▶	GO to C6a REPLACE EVP Sensor RECONNECT TP and B/MAP Sensors
C6a CHECK VPWR AND GROUND HARNESS CONTINUITY • Turn key OFF • Disconnect EEC connector from tester • DVOM to 200 ohm scale • Check continuity from: Pin 8 to battery "−" terminal; Pin 24 to circuit 361 at power relay	DVOM Reading: Less than 1 ohm ▶ More than 1 ohm ▶	GO to C7 SERVICE open circuit or bad connection in harness
C7 CHECK FOR EEC HARNESS SHORTS • Disconnect Harness connector from Tester, and check for short circuits between VREF (pin 3) on connector and remaining 31 pins	DVOM Reading: 10,000 ohms or more ▶ Under 10,000 ohms ▶	REPLACE Processor Assembly SERVICE short RECONNECT all Sensors

Throttle Position Sensor	Pinpoint Test	D

TEST STEP	RESULT ▶	ACTION TO TAKE
D2 CHECK TP SENSOR LINKAGE NOTE: This step is performed when TP Sensor value does not increase above 6 volts during QUICK TEST. • Check TP Sensor Linkage connection to the throttle actuator Linkage for physical movement when throttle is depressed.	TP Sensor Linkage movement observed ▶ NO TP Sensor Linkage movement observed ▶	Replace TP Sensor and retest CORRECT mechanical faults
D3 CHECK FOR VREF AND SRTN AT TP HARNESS CONNECTOR • Disconnect TP Sensor • Measure VREF to SRTN in harness connector	DVOM Reading: 8.00 to 10.00 volts ▶ Under 8.00 or over 10.00 volts ▶	GO to D4 SERVICE open or short or bad connection in VREF or SRTN in harness

VREF (CIRCUIT 351)
SRTN (CIRCUIT 359)
20 VOLTS

385

Throttle Position Sensor	Pinpoint Test	D

TEST STEP	RESULT ▶	ACTION TO TAKE
D4 CHECK TP SENSOR HARNESS CONTINUITY • Turn key to OFF • Disconnect EEC harness from tester	DVOM Reading: 5 ohms or less ▶ More than 5 ohms ▶	GO to D5 SERVICE open circuit or bad connection in Harness

CHECK CONTINUITY OF THESE WIRES
VREF (351) — PIN 3
TP (355) — PIN 5
SRTN (359) — PIN 19

Throttle Position Sensor	Pinpoint Test	D

TEST STEP	RESULT ▶	ACTION TO TAKE
D7 CHECK RESISTANCE BETWEEN TP SENSOR SIGNAL AND SRTN	DVOM Reading: Between 550 and 1100 ohms ▶ Under 550 or more than 1100 ohms ▶	GO to D8 ADJUST TP Sensor Resistance. If Resistance cannot be adjusted, REPLACE TP Sensor
D8 CHECK RESISTANCE OF TP SENSOR AS ACCELERATOR PEDAL IS FULLY DEPRESSED • DVOM to 200 x 1000 • Test leads as shown in D7 • Depress Accelerator Pedal	DVOM Reading: 2100 ohms or more ▶ Under 2100 ohms ▶	GO to D9 REPLACE TP Sensor

Throttle Position Sensor	Pinpoint Test	D

TEST STEP	RESULT ▶	ACTION TO TAKE
D5 CHECK FOR SHORT BETWEEN TP SIGNAL LINE AND CHASSIS GROUND AT SENSOR • Turn key to OFF • Disconnect TP Sensor	DVOM Reading: 1900 ohms or more ▶ Under 1900 ohms ▶	GO to D6 SERVICE or replace TP Sensor

| **D6** CHECK FOR FULL SENSOR RESISTANCE | DVOM Reading:

Between 3000 and 5000 ohms ▶

Under 3000 or more than 5000 ohms ▶ | GO to D7

REPLACE TP Sensor |

Throttle Position Sensor	Pinpoint Test	D

TEST STEP	RESULT ▶	ACTION TO TAKE
D9 CHECK FOR SHORT TO VEHICLE POWER IN HARNESS • Disconnect EEC harness from tester • Turn key to ON • Check for shorts to power on all pins of TP Harness connector	DVOM Reading: 1V or less ▶ More than 1V ▶	GO to D10 SERVICE short circuit to Power in Harness

| **D10** CHECK TP HARNESS FOR SHORTS

• Check for Short circuits between pin 5 (TP) and the other 31 pins in the ECA connector | DVOM Reading:

10.000 ohms or more ▶

Less than 10.000 ohms ▶ | REPLACE Processor Assembly

SERVICE short(s) in EEC Harness |

Throttle Position Sensor	Pinpoint Test	D

TEST STEP	RESULT ▶	ACTION TO TAKE
D11 SERVICE CODE 23 RECEIVED DURING QUICK TEST • Set engine at idle (OFF fast idle cam) • Tester to A-4 • DVOM switch to Tester • Inspect TP sensor and harness for bad connections. Wiggle sensor harness while observing DVOM	DVOM Reading: Between 1.8 and 2.8V ▶ DVOM jumps to: 1.8V or less, 2.8V or more ▶ DVOM remains at: 1.8 or less or to 2.8V or more ▶	REPLACE Processor Assembly SERVICE bad or intermittent connection GO to D1

Engine Coolant Temperature Sensor	Pinpoint Test	E

TEST STEP	RESULT ▶	ACTION TO TAKE
E2 START ENGINE TO BRING ECT WITHIN LIMITS • Tester to A-5 • DVOM switch to Tester • Start Engine • Check that upper radiator hose is hot and pressured • Increase rpm to attempt bringing ECT Sensor reading between 0.75 and 2.60 volts (5-10 minutes)	DVOM Reading: Between 0.75 and 2.60V ▶ Under 0.75 or more than 2.60V ▶ More than 2.60V ▶	REPEAT QUICK TEST GO to E3 GO to E5
E3 CHECK ECT SENSOR RESISTANCE • Turn key to ON • Switch tester to A-5 • Disconnect harness from ECT Sensor • Read DVOM (A-5) • Measure Sensor Resistence	DVOM Reading: More than 8.00 ▶ Less than 8.00 ▶	CHECK the engine for overheating, and let cool down. If this fails to correct the problem, replace the sensor and retest GO to E4

Engine Coolant Temperature Sensor	Pinpoint Test	E

This Test Checks

• ECT Sensor   • Processor Assembly

• ECT Sensor Wiring Harness   • Calibration Assembly

ENGINE COOLANT TEMP. SENSOR

359 B-W   354 LG-Y

ENGINE COOLANT TEMPERATURE SENSOR

19   359 B-W

21   354 LG-Y

TEST STEP	RESULT ▶	ACTION TO TAKE
E1 CHECK ENGINE OPERATING TEMPERATURE NOTE: This step is performed when the ECT sensor and circuit indicate that the engine coolant temperature is not within the normal operating range of a hot engine. • What does the operating temperature of the engine appear to be?	Appears to be at normal operating temperature ▶ Overheated ▶ Less than normal operating temperature ▶	GO to E2 GO to Routine No. 217 GO to Routine No. 216

Engine Coolant Temperature Sensor	Pinpoint Test	E

TEST STEP	RESULT ▶	ACTION TO TAKE
E4 CHECK ECT SENSOR HARNESS FOR SHORTS • Turn key to OFF • Check for Shorts between pin 21 (ECT) and remaining pins in EEC Harness connector	DVOM Reading: 10,000 ohms or more ▶ Under 10,000 ohms ▶	REPLACE Processor Assembly SERVICE short in EEC Harness

200 X 1000 OHMS   EEC HARNESS CONNECTOR   PIN 21

TEST STEP	RESULT ▶	ACTION TO TAKE
E5 CHECK FOR SHORT CIRCUIT TO POWER • Turn key to RUN — engine OFF • Disconnect EEC harness from Tester • Turn key to RUN, engine OFF • Using DVOM (20 volt scale), measure voltage between circuit 354 and ground, also circuit 359 and ground	DVOM Reading: 0.20V or less ▶ More than 0.20V ▶	GO to E6 SERVICE Short Circuit to Power

354 (LG/Y)   359 (BK/W)   20 VOLTS D.C.

Engine Coolant Temperature Sensor		Pinpoint Test	E

TEST STEP	RESULT	▶	ACTION TO TAKE
E6 CHECK ECT SENSOR HARNESS CONTINUITY	DVOM Reading:		
• Turn key to OFF	5 ohms or less	▶	GO to E6a
	More than 5 ohms	▶	SERVICE open circuit or bad connection in ECT Sensor Harness
• Check Continuity of Both Wires: ECT (354) — PIN 21 SRTN (359) — PIN 19			

ECT SENSOR HARNESS CONNECTOR

ECT 354 (LG/Y)

PIN 19 (359 BK/W)

SRTN 359 (BK/W)

PIN 21 354 (LG/Y)

EEC HARNESS CONNECTOR

200 OHMS

Engine Coolant Temperature Sensor		Pinpoint Test	E

TEST STEP	RESULT	▶	ACTION TO TAKE
E7 SERVICE CODE 21 AND/OR 43 RECEIVED DURING QUICK TEST			
• Tester to A-5 • Start engine • Engine at idle, off high cam • DVOM switch to Tester • Service Code 21 indicates temperature not between 50°F-250°F • Service Code 43 indicates temperature below 120°F • Inspect ECT Sensor and harness for bad connections. Wiggle Sensor harness at both ends while observing DVOM	DVOM remains between: 0.7-4V	▶	REPLACE Processor Assembly. Run QUICK TEST. If Service Code 21 and/or 43 are still displayed in QUICK TEST, replace Calibration Assembly using original Processor Assembly.
	DVOM jumps to: 0.7 or less or 4V or more	▶	SERVICE bad or intermittent connection
	DVOM remains at: 0.7 or less or 4V or more	▶	GO to E1

Engine Coolant Temperature Sensor		Pinpoint Test	E

TEST STEP	RESULT	▶	ACTION TO TAKE
E6a CHECK ECT SENSOR RESISTANCE	DVOM Reading:		
• Measure sensor resistance	Between 1100 ohms and 8000	▶	REPLACE Processor
	8000 ohms or more or less than 1100 ohms	▶	REPLACE ECT Sensor

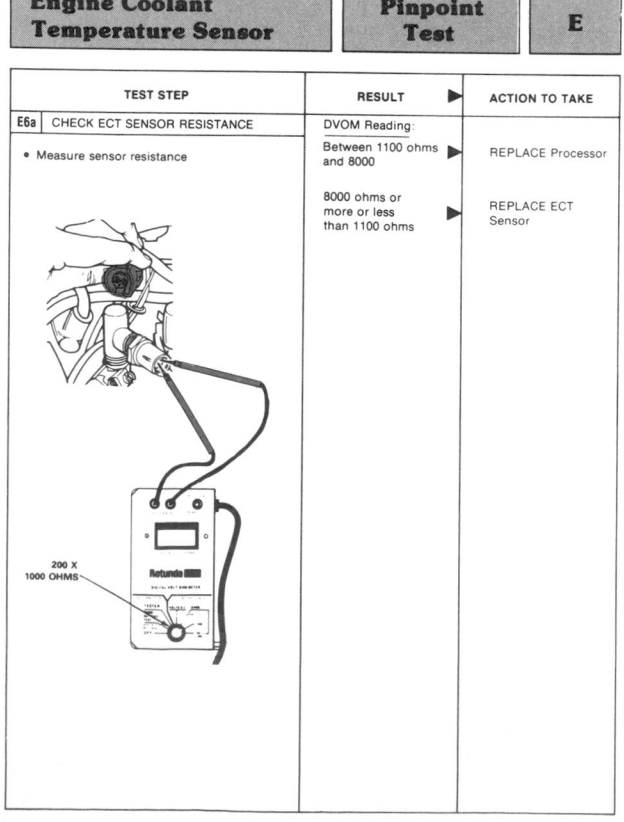

200 X 1000 OHMS

B/Map Sensor		Pinpoint Test	F

This Test Checks:
• B/MAP Sensor
• Processor Assembly
• Calibration Assembly
• Circuits 351, 356, 358, and 359

BAROMETRIC/ MANIFOLD ABSOLUTE PRESSURE SENSOR

NOTE: Check to be sure the vacuum hose from the manifold port of the B/MAP sensor goes directly to manifold vacuum, and also make sure that no hoses are connected to the vent port. Refer to Wiring and Vacuum Diagrams.

TEST STEP	RESULT	▶	ACTION TO TAKE
F1 CHECK PROCESSOR ASSEMBLY	DVOM Reading:		
NOTE: This step is performed when the B/MAP Sensor test fails during QUICK TEST. • Turn key to RUN — engine OFF • Depress Tester SS button (green flag) • DVOM switch to Tester • Tester to A-7 (MAP check) • Tester to A-8 (BP check)	A-7 MAP between 6.4-6.9V and A-8 BP between 8.0-8.5V	▶	GO to F2
	Reading(s) out of above specification	▶	REPLACE Processor Assembly

B/Map Sensor		Pinpoint Test	F

TEST STEP	RESULT ▶	ACTION TO TAKE
F2 CHECK SENSOR CONNECTIONS • Turn key to OFF • Check Sensor and harness for corrosion or bad connections	Good Connections ▶ Corroded or bad Connections ▶	GO to F3 SERVICE as required
F3 CHECK B/MAP SENSOR HARNESS CONTINUITY AND SWITCHED WIRES • Disconnect B/MAP Sensor. • Disconnect Processor. CHECK CONTINUITY OF THESE WIRES: VREF (351) — PIN 3 MAP (358) — PIN 20 SRTN (359) — PIN 19 BP (356) — PIN 22	DVOM Reading: 5 ohms or less ▶ More than 5 ohms ▶	GO to F4 SERVICE open circuit or bad connections in Harness

B/Map Sensor		Pinpoint Test	F

TEST STEP	RESULT ▶	ACTION TO TAKE
F6 CHECK FOR BP SIGNAL SHORTED TO MAP SIGNAL IN HARNESS NOTE: This test is performed when a shorted BP or MAP signal is indicated during the QUICK TEST • Disconnect B/MAP Sensor • Turn key to RUN — engine OFF • SS button ON (green flag) 	DVOM Reading: Less than 2000 ohms ▶ More than 2000 ohms (overrange) ▶	SERVICE short in EEC Harness between BP (356) and MAP (358) circuits CHECK to make sure that no hoses are connected to the vent port of the B/MAP Sensor; if none, replace B/MAP Sensor
F7 SERVICE CODE 22 RECEIVED DURING SELF-TEST • DVOM switch to Tester • Tester to A-7 • Start engine and bring to normal idle	DVOM Reading: 6.4V or less ▶ More than 6.4V ▶	REPLACE Processor Assembly RUN QUICK TEST If still not correct, replace Calibration Assembly using original Processor Assembly GO to F8

B/Map Sensor		Pinpoint Test	F

TEST STEP	RESULT ▶	ACTION TO TAKE
F4 CHECK BP CIRCUIT 356 FOR SHORTS • Check for short circuits between pin 22 and other 31 pins of EEC harness connector	DVOM Reading: 10,000 ohms or more ▶ Under 10,000 ohms ▶	GO to F5 SERVICE as required
F5 CHECK BP CIRCUIT 356 FOR SHORTS • Check for shorts between pin 22 and the 31 other pins of the EEC harness connector	DVOM Reading: 10,000 ohms or more ▶ Under 10,000 ohms ▶	REPLACE B/MAP Sensor SERVICE harness short as required

B/Map Sensor		Pinpoint Test	F

TEST STEP	RESULT ▶	ACTION TO TAKE
F8 CHECK B/MAP SENSOR FOR VACUUM LEAKS • Tester to A-7 • Apply 24 kPa (7 in. Hg.) to Sensor • DVOM switch to Tester	DVOM Reading: 6.4V or less ▶ More than 6.4V ▶	SERVICE low vacuum condition in vacuum hoses or engine REPLACE B/MAP Sensor

EGR Valve Position Sensor		Pinpoint Test	G

This Test Checks

- EVP Sensor
- EGR Valve Assembly
- EVP Sensor Harness
- Processor Assembly
- Calibration Assembly

TEST STEP	RESULT ▶	ACTION TO TAKE
G1 CHECK EVP SENSOR HARNESS CONTINUITY	DVOM Reading:	
• Turn key OFF, and disconnect EVP harness from sensor	8-10 volts ▶	GO to G2
• Turn key to RUN with engine OFF, and, using DVOM as shown, measure VREF to SRTN at harness connector	Less than 8 or more than 10 Volts ▶	SERVICE open wire or bad connection in harness (SRTN 359 or VREF 351)

EGR Valve Position Sensor		Pinpoint Test	G

TEST STEP	RESULT ▶	ACTION TO TAKE
G4 CHECK EGR VALVE ASSEMBLY	DVOM Reading:	
• Substitute known good sensor and EGR valve assembly	Less than 1.40V OR More than 2.45V ▶	REPLACE Processor Assembly
• Turn key to RUN, engine OFF		
• Connect sensor	Between 1.40V and 2.45V ▶	GO to G5
• Tester to A-9		
NOTE: Sensor and valve assembly does not have to be installed on engine to perform test.		
G5 CHECK ORIGINAL EGR VALVE ASSEMBLY AND SENSOR	DVOM Reading:	
• Install original EGR valve assembly and EVP sensor	1.40V or less ▶	REPLACE EVP sensor
• Reconnect sensor	More than 2.45V ▶	REPLACE EGR valve assembly. If EGR valve and sensor still not within the ignition key ON specification in QUICK TEST, Step 12, replace EVP sensor
• Tester to A-9		

EGR Valve Position Sensor		Pinpoint Test	G

TEST STEP	RESULT ▶	ACTION TO TAKE
G2 CHECK EVP SENSOR HARNESS CONTINUITY	DVOM Reading:	
• Turn key OFF	5 ohms or less ▶	GO to G3
• Disconnect EEC harness connector at tester	More than 5 ohms ▶	SERVICE open wire or bad connection in harness

CHECK CONTINUITY FROM EVP HARNESS CONNECTOR TO EEC HARNESS CONNECTOR:

EVP (352 BR-LB) — PIN 4

TEST STEP	RESULT ▶	ACTION TO TAKE
G3 CHECK EVP HARNESS EVP CIRCUIT 352 FOR SHORTS	DVOM Reading:	
	10,000 ohms or more ▶	GO to G4
	Less than 10,000 ohms ▶	SERVICE short in Harness
• Check between pin 4 of harness connector and remaining 31 pins		

EGR Valve Position Sensor		Pinpoint Test	G

TEST STEP	RESULT	ACTION TO TAKE
G6 KEY ON LIGHT TEST FAILURE DURING QUICK TEST	TESTER LIGHTS:	
NOTE: This step is performed when light test fails during QUICK TEST preliminary steps	EGRV ON / OFF and/or EGRC ON / OFF ▶	GO to G7
• Observe EGRV and EGRC lights	EGRV ON / OFF • and/or EGRC ON / OFF • ▶	GO to G9
G7 CHECK EGRC/EGRV HARNESS FOR OPEN	DVOM Reading:	
• Check 362 (EGRC Problem) or 360 (EGRV Problem)	10V or less ▶	GO to G8
	More than 10V ▶	SERVICE open circuit in 360 or 362 from processor to solenoid connector
• Keep Harness connected		
• DVOM 20 volt scale		
• Key ON		
G8 CHECK FOR SOLENOID OPEN	DVOM Reading:	
• Check circuit 361 at both harness connects	10V or more on both ▶	REPLACE Solenoid Assembly
	Under 10V on either ▶	SERVICE open circuit in VPWR circuit 361
• Keep Harness connected		
• DVOM 20 volt scale		

EGR Valve Position Sensor — Pinpoint Test — G

TEST STEP	RESULT ▶	ACTION TO TAKE
G9	DVOM Reading:	
• DVOM switch to Tester	0.1 or less ▶	GO to G10
• Tester to C-6 if during QUICK TEST	More than 0.1 ▶	REPLACE Processor Assembly. RUN QUICK TEST
EGRC ● / ON — OFF		If still not OK, replace Calibration Assembly using original Processor Assembly
• Tester to C-7 if during QUICK TEST		
EGRV ● / ON — OFF		
• Turn key to run, engine off		
G10 CHECK SOLENOID SHORT TO GROUND	TESTER LIGHTS:	
• Disconnect the Solenoid showing incorrect light indications during QUICK TEST	EGRC ● / ON — OFF and/or EGRV ● / ON — OFF ▶	GO to G11
	EGRC / ON — OFF and/or EGRV / ON — OFF ▶	REPLACE Solenoid Assembly
G11 CHECK FOR HARNESS SHORTS	DVOM Reading:	
• Turn key to OFF	10.000 ohms or more ▶	REPEAT QUICK TEST
	Under 10.000 ohms ▶	SERVICE short circuit as required

• Check for short circuits between pin 13 (EGRV) or pin 29 (EGRC) and remaining 31 pins as applicable

EGR Valve Position Sensor — Pinpoint Test — G

TEST STEP	RESULT ▶	ACTION TO TAKE
G14 CHECK EGR VALVE FOR MOVEMENT	DVOM Reading:	
• Turn key to RUN	Steadily increasing* to 8V or more ▶	GO to G16
• Tester to A-9	Under 8V ▶	GO to G15
• DVOM switch to Tester		
• Disconnect vacuum hose to the EGR valve at the EGR solenoids	*NOTE: Look for jumps in DVOM reading that may be caused by a sensor that's worn in one area. If so, replace sensor. (e.g., Reading increases to 3.04, then jumps to 0.00, then up 3.22)	
• Connect a vacuum pump to the hose going to EGR valve		
• Slowly apply vacuum while observing DVOM reading		
G15 CHECK EVP SENSOR	DVOM Reading:	
• Disconnect EVP Sensor from EGR valve	8V or more ▶	REPLACE EGR valve
• Slowly depress shaft on EVP Sensor	Under 8V ▶	REPLACE EVP Sensor

EGR Valve Position Sensor — Pinpoint Test — G

TEST STEP	RESULT ▶	ACTION TO TAKE
G12 CHECK FOR SHORTS	DVOM Reading:	
NOTE: This step is performed when Service Code 31 or 32 is obtained during Self-Test or vehicle stalls during Self-Test.	30 ohms or more ▶	GO to G14
	Under 30 ohms ▶	GO to G13
• Turn key to OFF		
• Check both solenoids		
• Do not disconnect harness connectors		
G13 CHECK FOR SOLENOID SHORTS	DVOM Reading:	
• Check both Solenoids	30 ohms or more ▶	SERVICE short circuit to power in Harness
• Disconnect harness connectors	Under 30 ohms ▶	REPLACE Solenoid

EGR Valve Position Sensor — Pinpoint Test — G

TEST STEP	RESULT ▶	ACTION TO TAKE
G16 CHECK EGR VALVE FOR LEAKING	DVOM Reading:	
• Apply 20 kPa (6 In. Hg.) to EGR valve	Reading changes 1V or less in 5 seconds; ▶	GO to G17
• Observe DVOM reading for 5 seconds	Changes more than 1V in 5 seconds ▶	SERVICE Leaks or replace EGR Valve
G17 CHECK EGR CLOSING RESPONSE	DVOM Reading:	
• Quickly release vacuum while observing DVOM	2.45V or less ▶	GO to G18
	More than 2.45V ▶	GO to Part 29-15
• Repeat G16 and G17 a few times, looking for a repeatable closed reading that might be caused by a sticky valve or sensor		

EGR Valve Position Sensor	Pinpoint Test	G

TEST STEP	RESULT ▶	ACTION TO TAKE
G18 CHECK EGR CONTROL SOLENOID FOR LEAKS • Connect vacuum gauge to solenoid assembly where hose to EGR valve went • Start engine. • Depress and hold EGRV button for 5 seconds while observing vacuum gauge	Vacuum Gauge Reading: 3.4 kPa (1 in. Hg.) or less More than 3.4 kPa (1 in. Hg.) ▶	GO to G19 REPLACE EGR Solenoid assembly
G19 CHECK EGR CONTROL SOLENOID • Simultaneously depress and hold Tester EGRV and EGRC buttons while observing vacuum gauge	Vacuum Gauge Reading: 34 kPa (10 in. Hg.) or less ▶ More than 34 kPa (10 in. Hg.) ▶	RELEASE buttons, and GO to G20 Continue to hold buttons, and GO to G21

EGR Valve Position Sensor	Pinpoint Test	G

TEST STEP	RESULT ▶	ACTION TO TAKE
G22 TEST PROCESSOR ASSEMBLY • Release EGRV button on Tester • Observe vacuum gauge	Vacuum Gauge Reading: 1.7 kPa (1.5 in. Hg.) or less ▶ More than 1.7 kPa (1.5 in. Hg.) ▶	REPLACE Processor Assembly Run QUICK TEST If still not OK, replace Calibration Assembly using original Processor Assembly CHECK vacuum hoses as shown on vacuum schematic If OK, replace Solenoid assembly

EGR Valve Position Sensor	Pinpoint Test	G

TEST STEP	RESULT ▶	ACTION TO TAKE
G20 CHECK VACUUM SOURCE • Connect vacuum gauge to vacuum source	Vacuum Gauge Reading: 34 kPa (10 in. Hg.) or more ▶ Under 34 kPa (10 in. Hg.) ▶	CHECK hoses at EGR Solenoids for leaks or obstructions. If no leaks found, REPLACE Solenoid Assembly SERVICE vacuum leak or problem in vacuum system
G21 CHECK EGR VENT SOLENOID FOR LEAKS • Release EGRC button on tester • Continue Holding EGRV Solenoid button on Tester for 5 seconds while observing vacuum gauge	Vacuum Gauge Reading: Reading changes 5 kPa (1.5 in. Hg.) or less in 5 seconds; ▶ Reading changes more than 5 kPa (1.5 in. Hg.) in 5 seconds ▶	GO to G22 CHECK for hose leaks. If no leaks found, replace Solenoid.

Fuel Control	Pinpoint Test	H (EFI)

This Test Checks
• EGO Sensor Connections
• Vacuum Systems
• EGO Sensor
• Fuel Injectors
• EGO Sensor Harness
• Processor Assembly
• Calibration Assembly

TEST STEP	RESULT ▶	ACTION TO TAKE
H1 CHECK FOR SERVICE CODE(S) 41, 42, OR 43 • Was Service Code 43 displayed? • Turn key to OFF	ALONG WITH 41 OR 42 SERVICE CODE 43: Also displayed ▶ Not displayed ▶	 GO to E7 GO to H2
H2 CHECK FOR SERVICE CODE(S) 44 • Was Service Code 44 displayed?	ALONG WITH 41 or 42, SERVICE CODE 44: Not displayed ▶ Also displayed ▶	 GO to H4 GO to H3

Fuel Control		Pinpoint Test	H (EFI)

TEST STEP	RESULT	▶	ACTION TO TAKE
H3 CHECK THERMACTOR SYSTEM	SERVICE CODE(S) 41 AND 42.		
• Disconnect hose from Thermactor Pump to Thermactor Valve at pump	Neither displayed	▶	RECONNECT hose to Thermactor Pump GO to K10
• Repeat Self-Test (QUICK TEST 22 , 23 , 24)	Either code displayed	▶	GO to H4
H4 FUEL PUMP PRESSURE CHECK	PRESSURE GAUGE READING:		
NO SMOKING NEARBY			
• Disconnect coil by removing the ignition coil connector from coil	Between 35 to 45 psi	▶	GO to H5
• Disconnect both fuel injectors electrical connectors at the injectors	Under 35 or over 45 psi	▶	GO to Part 24-29 of the Shop Manual
• Pressurize fuel system* (turn key to RUN wait 1 second, then turn key to OFF) Repeat 5 times			
• Turn key to OFF			
• Watch pressure reading drop off several psi then hold steady			
*WARNING: If fuel starts leaking or injectors discharge, turn key OFF immediately. No smoking			

Fuel Control		Pinpoint Test	H (EFI)

TEST STEP	RESULT	▶	ACTION TO TAKE
H8 CHECK FUEL PRESSURE REGULATOR	PRESSURE GAUGE READING:		
• Reconnect ignition coil connector	35 to 45 psi	▶	GO to H9
• Reconnect inertia switch or fuel pump relay	less than 35 or more than 45	▶	CHECK to make sure the fuel lines, the supply and return, are free from kinks. Especially, check the rubber hose on the return line into the fuel tank. If OK, go to Part 24-29 of the Shop Manual, and check the pressure regulator and throttle body for proper operation.
• Reconnect injectors			
• Start engine, let idle			
• Observe pressure gauge			
H9 CHECK FOR MARGINAL INJECTOR(S)	RPM Difference:		
• Disconnect and plug vacuum hose to EGR valve			
• Engine to 1,800 RPM and hold that Throttle position	100 RPM or less	▶	GO to H10
• Disconnect left injector electrically	More than 100 RPM	▶	REPLACE both injectors
• Note RPM when it stabilizes (at about 1,200)			
• Reconnect left injector			
• Stabilize RPM at 1,800			
• Disconnect right injector, note RPM when it stabilizes			
• Reconnect right injector			
• Engine to idle			
• Note the difference between the two RPM readings			

Fuel Control		Pinpoint Test	H (EFI)

TEST STEP	RESULT	▶	ACTION TO TAKE
H5 CHECK FOR LEAK DOWN	PRESSURE GAUGE READING:		
• Observe pressure drop 2 minutes after performing Step H4 pressure	4 psi drop or less	▶	GO to H6
	More than 4 psi	▶	GO to Part 24-29 of the Shop Manual
H6 CHECK ONE INJECTOR'S PRESSURE	PRESSURE GAUGE READING:		
• Reconnect one injector electrically; leave other one connected	Between 2 and 16 psi drop (1 to 8 psi per second of cranking)	▶	GO to H7
• Pressurized fuel system			
• Disable fuel pump by disconnecting Inertia Switch or disconnecting Fuel Pump Relay	Under 2 or more than 16 psi drop (Under 1 or more than 8 psi per second of cranking)	▶	GO to A40
• Observe pressure gauge reading			
• Crank engine for 2 seconds			
• Turn key to OFF			
• Wait 5 seconds then observe pressure drop			
H7 CHECK OTHER INJECTOR'S PRESSURE	PRESSURE GAUGE READING:		
• Reactivate fuel pump	Between 2 and 16 psi drop (1 to 8 psi per second of cranking)	▶	GO to H8
• Disconnect injector, and connect the other one			
• Repeat H6 for this injector	Under 2 or more than 16 psi drop (Under 1 or more than 8 psi per second of cranking)	▶	GO to A40

Fuel Control		Pinpoint Test	H (EFI)

TEST STEP	RESULT	▶	ACTION TO TAKE
H10 CHECK EGO SENSOR GROUND	DVOM Reading:		
• Turn key to OFF	5 ohms or less	▶	GO to H11
• Tester to B-8	More than 5 ohms	▶	CHECK and service EGO Sensor Ground wire or open circuit bad connection
• Depress and hold Ohms button			
H11 ECA LEAN EGO TEST CHECK			
• Reconnect coil			
• Reconnect vacuum hose to EGR valve	Code 41 displayed and DVOM reading increased slightly during test	▶	GO to H12
• Reconnect injector(s)			
• Turn EFI cable adapter EGO simulation switch to lean			
• Repeat Self-Test Quick Test 22 , 23 , 24	Code 42 displayed or DVOM reading not increased during test	▶	REPLACE Processor Assembly RUN QUICK TEST If still not OK, replace Calibration Assembly using original Processor Assembly
• Tester to C-2			
• Observe DVOM reading and Service Code(s) on TAB/TAD tester lights			

393

Fuel Control — Pinpoint Test — H (EFI)

TEST STEP	RESULT	▶	ACTION TO TAKE
H12 ECA RICH EGO TEST • Turn EGO simulation switch to rich • Tester to C-3 • Repeat Self-Test • Observe DVOM reading and Service Code(s) on TAB TAD	Code 42 displayed and DVOM reading decreased slightly	▶	GO to H13
	Code 41 displayed or DVOM reading not decreased	▶	REPLACE Processor Assembly RUN QUICK TEST If still OK, replace Calibration Assembly using original Processor Assembly
H13 CHECK EGO HARNESS FOR CONTINUITY • Turn key to OFF • Disconnect the processor and the EGO sensor from the harness • Measure harness continuity	DVOM Reading		
	5 ohms or less	▶	GO to H14
	More than 5 ohms	▶	SERVICE open circuit RECONNECT all disconnected hoses and electrical connectors

Fuel Control — Pinpoint Test — H (FBC)

This Test Checks:

EGO Sensor Connections	EGO Sensor Harness
Vacuum Systems	Processor Assembly
EGO Sensor	Calibration Assembly
Choke Relay	Stepper Motor

TEST STEP	RESULT	▶	ACTION TO TAKE
H1 SERVICE CODE 41 (FUEL SYSTEM LEAN) OR 42 (FUEL SYSTEM RICH) RECEIVED DURING SELF-TEST • Turn key to OFF • Visually inspect EGO Sensor for poor or corroded connections	Connections good	▶	GO to H2
	Connections poor or corroded		Service as required
H2 FUEL ROUTING		▶	If lowest Service Code were 41 — EGO always Lean. Make sure EGO was properly warmed up prior to entering Self-Test A. A cold EGO will look lean. GO to H3 If Service Code were 42 — EGO always rich, GO to H9

Fuel Control — Pinpoint Test — H (EFI)

TEST STEP	RESULT	▶	ACTION TO TAKE
H14 CHECK FOR SHORT • Check for short circuit between pin 23 and all the other 31 pins	DVOM Reading:		
	∞	▶	REPLACE EGO Sensor RUN QUICK TEST If still fails, REPLACE Processor Assembly
	Under 200,000 ohms	▶	SERVICE short circuit(s) in harness
H15 RECHECK RESPONSE TO "GOOSE" DURING QUICK TEST • Repeat Self-Test • When CANP light comes on, "Goose" engine • When CANP light goes OFF, watch TAB/TAD lights	TAB pulsed* [NO / YES]	▶	EEC System, OK
	TAD pulsed* [UP / DOWN] *Blinked ON and OFF, once	▶	REPLACE Processor Assembly RUN QUICK TEST If still not OK, replace Calibration Assembly using original Processor Assembly

Fuel Control — Pinpoint Test — H (FBC)

TEST STEP	RESULT	▶	ACTION TO TAKE
H3 FORCE CARBURETOR RICH	[EGO RICH LEAN] With CVR Rod Depressed	▶	GO to H4
	[EGO RICH LEAN] With CVR Rod Depressed	▶	CHECK carburetor for vacuum leaks If no leaks, GO to H6

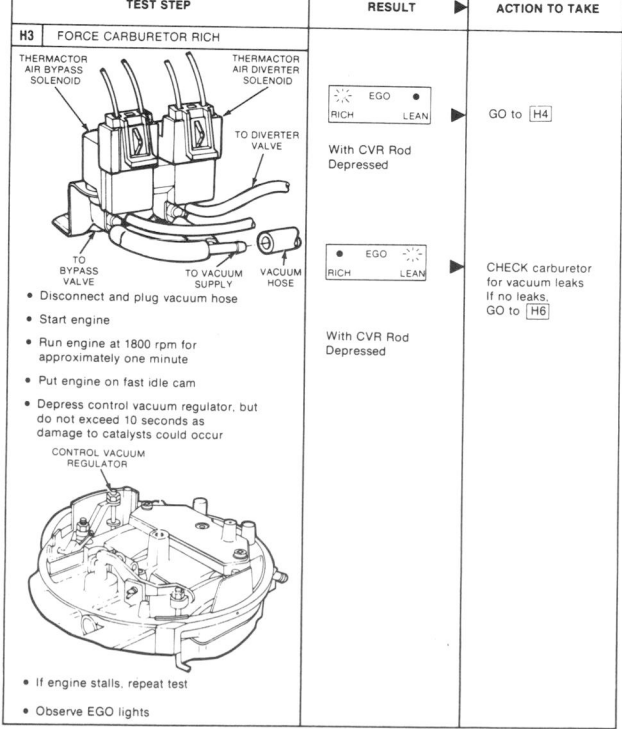

- Disconnect and plug vacuum hose
- Start engine
- Run engine at 1800 rpm for approximately one minute
- Put engine on fast idle cam
- Depress control vacuum regulator, but do not exceed 10 seconds as damage to catalysts could occur
- If engine stalls, repeat test
- Observe EGO lights

Fuel Control		Pinpoint Test	H (FBC)

TEST STEP	RESULT ▶	ACTION TO TAKE
H4 CHECK FBCA MOTOR MOVEMENT		
• Turn the ignition key to OFF	Extended 0.5 in. ▶ or more	REINSTALL FBCA motor, and GO to [H5]
• Carefully remove FBCA motor from carburetor		
• Connect the electrical harness to the FBCA motor	Under 0.5 in. ▶ extension	GO to [H14]
• Turn key to RUN with the engine off		
• Observe the FBCA motor shaft		

FBCA MOTOR

Fuel Control		Pinpoint Test	H (FBC)

TEST STEP	RESULT ▶	ACTION TO TAKE
H6 CHECK EGO SENSOR GROUND	DVOM Reading:	
• Turn key to OFF	5 ohms or less ▶	GO to [H6a]
• Tester to B-8	More than ▶ 5 ohms	CHECK and service EGO sensor ground wire or open circuit or bad connection
• Depress and hold ohms button		

Fuel Control		Pinpoint Test	H (FBC)

TEST STEP	RESULT ▶	ACTION TO TAKE
H5 CHECK THERMACTOR AND CARBURETOR	Tester Lights:	
• Turn key to OFF		
• Keeping the engine off, turn the key to RUN to initialize the FBCA motor full rich	● EGO ⚬ RICH LEAN ▶	CHECK carburetor for proper operation, and verify that the FBCA motor extended during initialization. If not, check for proper pintle movement.
• Turn key to OFF		
• Disconnect harness from FBCA motor		
• Start engine, and bring it to normal operating temperature	⚬ EGO ● RICH LEAN	
• Put engine on fast idle cam for one minute	— OR —	RECONNECT thermactor hose, and check for proper vacuum connections at thermactor solenoid. Refer to Pinpoint Test J or to Part 29-35. The thermactor could cause a lean (41) condition when connected. If still not OK, replace the Processor Assembly, and retest. If still not OK, replace the calibration assembly using the original Processor, and retest.
• Observe EGO lights	● EGO ⚬ RICH LEAN	

Fuel Control		Pinpoint Test	H (FBC)

TEST STEP	RESULT ▶	ACTION TO TAKE
H6a CHECK EGO SENSOR	DVOM Reading:	
• Turn key to OFF		
• Disconnect EGO sensor	0.5V or more with ▶ CVR depressed	GO to [H7]
• Start engine		
• Run engine on high cam, fast idle, for one minute, then depress the control vacuum regulator, but do not exceed 10 seconds	Under 0.5V with ▶ CVR depressed	REPLACE EGO sensor
• Switch DVOM to 20 volt scale		
NOTE: If engine stalls, repeat this test.		

CONTROL VACUUM REGULATOR

USE CUP LEADS TO CONNECT

20 VOLTS D.C.

Fuel Control		Pinpoint Test	H (FBC)

TEST STEP	RESULT ▶	ACTION TO TAKE
H7 CHECK EGO HARNESS FOR CONTINUITY • Disconnect EEC harness from tester • Measure from EGO harness connector to Pin 23 • DVOM to 200 ohms	DVOM Reading: 5 ohms or less ▶ More than 5 ohms ▶	GO to H8 SERVICE open circuit. Reconnect all disconnected hoses and electrical connections
H8 CHECK FOR SHORT Check for short circuit between pin 23 and the other 31 pins	DVOM Reading: 10,000 ohms or more ▶ Under 10,000 ohms ▶	REPLACE processor and RETEST SERVICE short circuit(s) in harness

Fuel Control		Pinpoint Test	H (FBC)

TEST STEP	RESULT ▶	ACTION TO TAKE
H11 FORCE CARBURETOR LEAN • Run engine on fast idle cam for one minute • Remove vacuum hose from PCV valve • Disconnect and plug vacuum hose at canister purge valve • Observe EGO lights	Tester Lights: ● EGO RICH/LEAN ▶ — OR — EGO RICH/LEAN ▶	GO to H11a GO to H12
H11a CHECK FBCA MOTOR MOVEMENT • Turn key to OFF • Reconnect thermactor vacuum hose • Carefully remove the FBCA motor from the carburetor • Connect the electrical harness to the FBCA motor • Turn the key to RUN, but keep engine off • Observe the FBCA motor's shaft	Under 0.5 inch extension ▶ Extended 0.5 inch or more ▶	GO to H14 RECONNECT the FBCA motor, vacuum hoses and PCV valve. Check the canister purge per 29-20. Check the bowl vent per Group 24. If all OK, replace processor and retest

FBCA MOTOR

Fuel Control		Pinpoint Test	H (FBC)

TEST STEP	RESULT ▶	ACTION TO TAKE
H9 CHECK ELECTRICAL CHOKE • Start engine, bring it to normal operating temperature and idle	DVOM Reading: 10V or more ▶ Under 10V ▶	CHECK to be sure the choke enrichment rod is seated, indicating choke off. If OK, GO to H10 SERVICE harness and/or choke relay. Run QUICK TEST. If still not OK, refer to Choke Adjustment Procedure in Part 29-02
H10 CHECK EGO SENSOR GROUND • Turn key to OFF • Tester to B-8 • DVOM switch to tester • Depress and hold ohms button	DVOM Reading: 5 ohms or less ▶ More than 5 ohms ▶	GO to H11 CHECK and service EGO Sensor Ground wire for open circuit or bad connection

GROUND · 20 VOLTS D.C.

Fuel Control		Pinpoint Test	H (FBC)

TEST STEP	RESULT ▶	ACTION TO TAKE
H12 CHECK EGO SENSOR • Turn engine off • Disconnect EGO sensor • Start engine • Run engine at fast idle for one minute with the PCV still disconnected • Measure the EGO voltage	DVOM Reading: 0.5V or less ▶ More than 0.5V ▶	GO to H13 REPLACE EGO sensor

20 VOLTS D.C.

Fuel Control		Pinpoint Test	H (FBC)

TEST STEP	RESULT ▶	ACTION TO TAKE
H13 CHECK FOR SHORT • Disconnect the EEC harness from tester • Check for short circuit between Pin 23 and the other 31 remaining pins to possibly find the short to the voltage source	DVOM Reading: 10,000 ohms or more ▶ Under 10,000 ohms	REPLACE processor, and retest. EGO always reads rich SERVICE short circuit(s) in harness
H14 CHECK FBCA MOTOR VOLTAGE • Disconnect the processor assembly from tester • Turn the key to RUN, keep the engine off • DVOM switch to tester • Tester to: 1st — C-2 2nd — C-3 3rd — C-4 4th — C-5	DVOM Reading: 10V or more on any position ▶ 10V or more on any position ▶	GO to H15 GO to H16

Fuel Control		Pinpoint Test	H (FBC)

TEST STEP	RESULT ▶	ACTION TO TAKE
H17 CHECK FBCA MOTOR HARNESS FOR SHORT CIRCUITS • Disconnect EGRC, EGRV, TAB, TAD, TKS, and CANP harnesses from their solenoids • Check for short circuits between the five pins shown and each of the other 31 remaining pins on the EEC connector	DVOM Reading: 10,000 ohms or more ▶ Less than 10,000 ohms ▶	GO to H18 SERVICE short circuit(s)
H18 CHECK FBCA MOTOR RESISTANCE • Check between 361 (V BATT) and each of the other four pins on the FBCA motor	DVOM Reading: Between 32-150 ohms for each measurement ▶ Less than 32 ohms or more than 150 ohms for any measurement ▶	RECONNECT FBCA motor, and replace Processor Assembly RUN QUICK TEST If still not OK, replace Calibration Assembly using original Processor Assembly REPLACE FBCA motor

Fuel Control		Pinpoint Test	H (FBC)

TEST STEP	RESULT ▶	ACTION TO TAKE
H15 CHECK FBCA MOTOR POWER CIRCUIT 361 • Disconnect FBCA motor	DVOM Reading: 10V or more ▶ Under 10V ▶	GO to H16 SERVICE open circuit
H16 CHECK FBCA MOTOR HARNESS CONTINUITY • Turn key to OFF • Disconnect FBCA motor from vehicle harness • Check continuity of the five stepper motor harness circuits	DVOM Reading: 5 ohms or less ▶ More than 5 ohms ▶	GO to H17 SERVICE open circuit in harness

Throttle Kicker		Pinpoint Test	J

This Test Checks
• TK Solenoid Valve
• TK Actuator
• Circuits 69, 361, and 347

TEST STEP	RESULT ▶	ACTION TO TAKE
J1 TKS LIGHTS INCORRECT DURING QUICK TEST • Turn key to RUN, but keep engine off • Observe TKS lights	TESTER LIGHTS: TKS ON/OFF OR EFI TKS ON/OFF TKS ON/OFF OR FBC TKS ON/OFF	GO to J2 GO to J4 GO to J6

SECTION 5 ELECTRONIC ENGINE CONTROLS

Throttle Kicker	Pinpoint Test	J

TEST STEP	RESULT ▶	ACTION TO TAKE
J2 CHECK FOR OPEN IN HARNESS • Turn key to RUN, but keep engine off 	DVOM Reading: 10V or less ▶ More than 10V ▶	GO to J3 SERVICE Open Harness in circuit 69
J3 CHECK FOR OPEN TK SOLENOID • Disconnect TKS solenoid from harness • Measure voltage at TK harness connector	DVOM Reading: 10V or less ▶ More than 10V ▶	SERVICE Open in circuit 361 REPLACE TK Solenoid

Throttle Kicker	Pinpoint Test	J

TEST STEP	RESULT ▶	ACTION TO TAKE
J6 CHECK FOR SHORT BETWEEN TKS CIRCUIT 69 AND VPWR 361 • Turn key to OFF 	DVOM Reading: 45 ohms or less ▶ More than 45 ohms ▶	GO to J7 REPLACE processor assembly. Run QUICK TEST. If still not OK, replace calibration assembly using original processor assembly

Throttle Kicker	Pinpoint Test	J

TEST STEP	RESULT ▶	ACTION TO TAKE
J4 CHECK TKS SOLENOID FOR SHORT-TO-GROUND • Disconnect harness connectors from Throttle Kicker Solenoid Assembly • Observe Tester TKS lights	TKS LIGHTS: ON ☀ TKS OFF ▶ ON · TKS OFF ▶	GO to J5 REPLACE TKS Solenoid Assembly
J5 CHECK FOR EEC HARNESS SHORT-TO-GROUND • Turn key off • Check between pin 25 and the remaining 31 pins for a short	DVOM Reading: 10,000 ohms or more ▶ Under 10,000 ohms ▶	REPLACE Processor Assembly RUN QUICK TEST If still not OK, replace Calibration Assembly using original Processor Assembly SERVICE Harness short

Throttle Kicker	Pinpoint Test	J

TEST STEP	RESULT ▶	ACTION TO TAKE
J7 CHECK FOR SHORTED SOLENOID OR CIRCUIT 69 SHORTED TO POWER • Disconnect harness connectors to TKS solenoid • Measure ohms 	DVOM Reading 45 ohms or less ▶ More than 45 ohms ▶	REPLACE the TK solenoid valve assembly and processor assembly SERVICE short circuit in TK harness from Circuit 69 to power, and replace processor assembly
J8 CHECK THE PROCESSOR AND CALIBRATION ASSEMBLY • Turn key to OFF • Disconnect the processor from the tester • Turn the key to ON, but keep the engine off • Observe the TKS lights	ON · TKS OFF ▶ ON ● TKS OFF ▶ ON · TKS OFF ▶	GO to J2 CHECK to make sure the self-test was triggered. Replace processor, and retest If not OK, replace the calibration assembly using the original processor, and retest GO to J9

398

Throttle Kicker		**Pinpoint Test**	**J**

TEST STEP		RESULT	▶	ACTION TO TAKE
J9 CHECK FOR TK SOLENOID SHORT CIRCUIT TO GROUND				
• Turn key to OFF		No short	▶	GO to J10
	69 (R/LG)	Short	▶	REPLACE the TK solenoid valve assembly
	200 OHMS CHASSIS GROUND			
J10 CHECK FOR EEC HARNESS SHORT-TO-GROUND		DVOM Reading:		
• Check between pin 25 and the remaining 31 pins		10,000 ohms or more	▶	RECONNECT and retest
		Less than 10,000 ohms	▶	SERVICE short circuit in harness
	25 200 X 1000 OHMS EEC HARNESS CONNECTOR			

Throttle Kicker		**Pinpoint Test**	**J**

TEST STEP	RESULT	▶	ACTION TO TAKE
J14 CHECK TK SOLENOID VALVE VACUUM SUPPLY			
• Start engine, bring to normal operating temperature and idle	More than 34 kPa (10 in. Hg.)	▶	GO to J15
CHECK FOR VACUUM HERE MANIFOLD VACUUM HOSE TKS	Less than 34 kPa (10 in. Hg.)	▶	SERVICE source of vacuum
J15 CHECK TK HARNESS WIRE CONTINUITY	DVOM Reading:		
• Check between TKS (69) and pin 25	5 ohms or less	▶	REPLACE TK solenoid valve assembly
• Also check VPWR (361) to pin 24			
VPWR 361 (R) TKS 69 (R/LG) PIN 24 PIN 25 200 OHMS EEC HARNESS CONNECTOR	More than 5 ohms	▶	SERVICE harness open circuit or bad connection
J16 CHECK FOR LOOSE CONNECTIONS			
NOTE: This step is performed if TKS light stays on or intermittently turns OFF and ON during QUICK TEST	TKS wiring or connector faulty	▶	SERVICE connections or mechanical problem as required.
• Start engine, bring to normal operating temperature and idle	TKS wiring good	▶	INSPECT TK actuator for mechanical binding. If OK, replace calibration assembly
• Trigger Self-Test. Refer to QUICK TEST			
• Wiggle harness wires and connectors			

Throttle Kicker		**Pinpoint Test**	**J**

TEST STEP		RESULT	▶	ACTION TO TAKE
J11 CHECK THROTTLE KICKER ACTUATOR (TKA)				
• Disconnect TKA vacuum hose at TKS. Apply 34 kPa (10-inches of vacuum) with pump or engine vacuum		TKA extends fully and quickly	▶	GO to J12
	TKA	TKA does not extend fully and quickly	▶	CHECK hose, mechanical connections SERVICE or replace TK Actuator as required
J12 CHECK TO BE SURE THE TK ACTUATOR RETRACTS				
• Remove vacuum from TK Actuator Assembly		Actuator remains extended	▶	CHECK TK Actuator for mechanical binding. Service or replace as required
• Observe Actuator		Actuator retracts immediately	▶	RECONNECT vacuum hoses to TKS and TKS solenoid, and GO to J13
J13 CHECK THROTTLE KICKER VACUUM		Vacuum Gauge Showing:		
• Tee vacuum gauge into vacuum line to TK actuator				
• Start engine. Bring to normal operating temperature and idle		More than 34 kPa (10 in. Hg.)	▶	KICKER should operate. Retest
• Trigger Self-Test (see QUICK TEST)		Less than 34 kPa (10 in. Hg.)	▶	GO to J14
• Observe vacuum gauge				

Throttle Kicker		**Pinpoint Test**	**J**

TEST STEP	RESULT	▶	ACTION TO TAKE
J17 CHECK AIR CONDITIONING CLUTCH SWITCH INPUT FOR SHORT TO POWER	DVOM Reading:		
NOTE: This step is performed when factory A/C clutch input is more than 1V with A/C OFF during QUICK TEST.	1V or less	▶	REPLACE processor assembly
• Disconnect Processor Assembly			
• Turn key to RUN — engine OFF	More than 1V	▶	Either service circuit 347 for short to power or A/C system as outlined in Group 36 of Shop Manual
• Tester to B-10			
• DVOM to Tester			
V BATT 347 BK/YH A/C CLUTCH (ACCS) SWITCH PIN 31 A/C CLUTCH 347 EEC HARNESS CONNECTOR			
J18 CHECK AIR CONDITIONING CLUTCH SWITCH INPUT			
NOTE: This step is performed when factory A/C clutch input is less than 9V with A/C ON during QUICK TEST	A/C clutch engages	▶	SERVICE open circuit in harness (circuit 347) from EEC harness connector Pin 31 to A/C switch
• Does A/C clutch engage?	A/C does not engage	▶	SERVICE A/C system. Refer to Group 36 of Shop Manual

Thermactor Air — Pinpoint Test — K

This Test Checks:

- TAB and TAD Solenoid Valve Assemblies
- Circuits 99, 100, and 361
- Vacuum Supply
- Processor Assembly
- Calibration Assembly

TEST STEP	RESULT ▶	ACTION TO TAKE
K1 TAB/TAD LIGHTS INCORRECT DURING QUICK TEST • Turn key to RUN – Engine OFF • Observe Tester TAB and TAD lights	TESTER LIGHTS: Either [TAB NO • YES] or (but not both) [TAD UP • DOWN] ▶	GO TO K4
	Either [TAB NO • YES] or [TAD UP • DOWN] ▶	GO to K2
K2 CHECK FOR OPEN IN HARNESS • Check circuit 99 (TAD problem) or 100 (TAB problem) for power	DVOM Reading: 10V or less ▶	GO to K3
	More than 10V ▶	SERVICE open in circuit 99 or 100 in harness from Thermactor solenoids to EEC connectors

Thermactor Air — Pinpoint Test — K

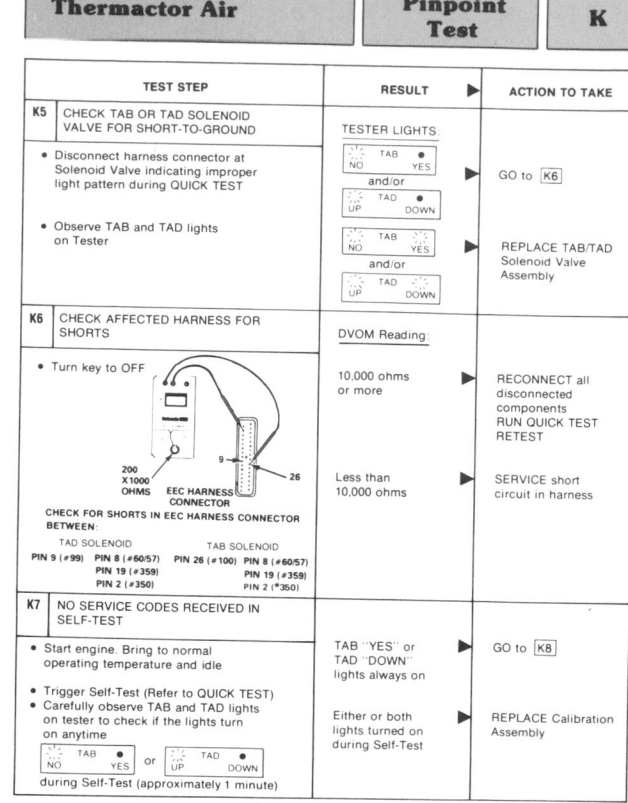

TEST STEP	RESULT ▶	ACTION TO TAKE
K5 CHECK TAB OR TAD SOLENOID VALVE FOR SHORT-TO-GROUND • Disconnect harness connector at Solenoid Valve indicating improper light pattern during QUICK TEST • Observe TAB and TAD lights on Tester	TESTER LIGHTS: [TAB NO • YES] and/or [TAD UP • DOWN] ▶	GO to K6
	[TAB NO • YES] and/or [TAD UP • DOWN] ▶	REPLACE TAB/TAD Solenoid Valve Assembly
K6 CHECK AFFECTED HARNESS FOR SHORTS • Turn key to OFF	DVOM Reading: 10,000 ohms or more ▶	RECONNECT all disconnected components RUN QUICK TEST RETEST
	Less than 10,000 ohms ▶	SERVICE short circuit in harness
CHECK FOR SHORTS IN EEC HARNESS CONNECTOR BETWEEN: TAD SOLENOID: PIN 9 (#99), PIN 8 (#60/57), PIN 19 (#359), PIN 2 (#350) TAB SOLENOID: PIN 26 (#100), PIN 8 (#60/57), PIN 19 (#359), PIN 2 (#350)		
K7 NO SERVICE CODES RECEIVED IN SELF-TEST • Start engine. Bring to normal operating temperature and idle • Trigger Self-Test (Refer to QUICK TEST) • Carefully observe TAB and TAD lights on tester to check if the lights turn on anytime	TAB "YES" or TAD "DOWN" lights always on ▶	GO to K8
	Either or both lights turned on [TAB NO • YES] or [TAD UP • DOWN] during Self-Test (approximately 1 minute) ▶	REPLACE Calibration Assembly

Thermactor Air — Pinpoint Test — K

TEST STEP	RESULT ▶	ACTION TO TAKE
K3 CHECK FOR OPEN SOLENOID • Check circuit 361 for power at both Solenoids	DVOM Reading: 10V or less on either ▶	SERVICE harness open in circuit 361
	More than 10V on both ▶	REPLACE TAB/TAD Solenoid valve assembly
K4 CHECK PROCESSOR AND CALIBRATION ASSEMBLY • DVOM switch to Tester • Tester switch to C-8 if TAB "NO" light were lit • Tester switch to C-9 if TAD "UP" light were lit • If both TAB "NO" and TAD "UP" lights are lit, position Tester to C-8 and then to C-9, and observe DVOM for each position	DVOM Reading: 0.1 or less ▶	GO to K5
	More than 0.1 ▶	REPLACE Processor Assembly RUN QUICK TEST If still not OK, replace Calibration Assembly using original Processor Assembly

Thermactor Air — Pinpoint Test — K

TEST STEP	RESULT ▶	ACTION TO TAKE
K8 CHECK SOLENOID RESISTANCE • Turn key to OFF NOTE: Do **not** disconnect harness from solenoid. • Check resistance across terminals of solenoid(s) that did **not** flash.	DVOM Reading: 45-90 ohms ▶	REPLACE Processor Assembly
	Less than 45 or more than 90 ohms ▶	GO to K9
K9 CHECK SOLENOID FOR SHORT • Disconnect harness on Solenoid that did **not** flash in Step K7 Check resistance of Solenoid	DVOM Reading: 45-90 ohms ▶	SERVICE short in harness
	Less than 45 ohms or more than 90 ohms ▶	REPLACE TAB/TAD solenoid valve assembly
K10 SERVICE CODE 44 RECEIVED DURING SELF-TEST • Start engine; run at idle • Also check for obstructions or leaks in vacuum hose or tee to solenoid	More than 34 kPa (10 in. Hg.) present ▶	GO to K11
	Less than 34 kPa (10 in. Hg.) vacuum present ▶	SERVICE vacuum problem

Thermactor Air	Pinpoint Test	K

	TEST STEP	RESULT ▶	ACTION TO TAKE
K11	CHECK FOR SWITCHING OF TAB/TAD SOLENOID VALVE		
	• Reconnect vacuum hose • Make sure the engine is at normal operating temperature and idle • Trigger Self-Test • Check for manifold vacuum pulsing CHECK FOR MANIFOLD VACUUM PULSING ON AND OFF	Vacuum pulsing from more than 34 kPa (10 in. Hg.) to less than 3.4 kPa (1 in. Hg.) on TAB and TAD	GO to K12
		No vacuum at TAB or TAD	GO to K13
		Steady manifold vacuum at TAB or TAD, or vacuum never goes less than 3.4 kPa (1 in. Hg.) on TAB or TAD	REPLACE TAB/TAD solenoid valve assembly
K12	HOSE CHECK		
	• Inspect hoses from TAB/TAD solenoid for leaks, cracks, pinches, etc.	Hoses good	REFER to Part 29-15
		Hoses faulty	SERVICE or replace hoses as required

Thermactor Air	Pinpoint Test	K

	TEST STEP	RESULT ▶	ACTION TO TAKE
K14	CHECK FOR BAD CONNECTIONS OR HARNESS	DVOM Reading:	
	• Turn key to OFF • Check resistance between solenoid harness and EEC connector pins	5 ohms or less at each position	REPLACE Processor Assembly
		More than 5 ohms at any position	INSPECT circuits indicating more than 5 ohms resistance for corrosion, bad connections, etc. SERVICE or replace as required
	• Check resistance between:		

	SOLENOID HARNESS	EEC HARNESS CONNECTOR
(TAB)	361	24
	100	26
(TAD)	361	24
	99	9

Thermactor Air	Pinpoint Test	K

	TEST STEP	RESULT ▶	ACTION TO TAKE
K13	CHECK FOR RELAY ENERGIZED	DVOM Reading:	
	• Start engine, bring to normal operating temperature and idle • Trigger Self-Test, wait 40 seconds • Observe DVOM when solenoid (TAB or TAD) is turned on for 4-6 seconds CONNECT ACROSS TERMINALS THAT DID NOT PULSE VACUUM. 20 VOLTS D.C. NOTE: Do not disconnect harness from solenoid	8V or less	GO to K14
		More than 8V	REPLACE TAB/TAD solenoid valve assembly

Canister Purge	Pinpoint Test	L

This Test Checks

- CANP Solenoid Valve Assembly
- Circuits 101 and 361
- Processor Assembly
- Calibration Assembly

	TEST STEP	RESULT ▶	ACTION TO TAKE
L1	CANP LIGHT INCORRECT AT KEY ON IN QUICK TEST	TESTER LIGHTS:	
	• Turn key to RUN, but keep engine OFF • Observe CANP light on Tester	CANP ON / OFF	GO to L2
		CANP ON / OFF	GO to L4
L2	CHECK HARNESS FOR OPEN CIRCUIT	DVOM Reading:	
	361 / 101 / CANP HARNESS CONNECTOR • DVOM 20 volt scale • Red probe to 101 and other to ground	10V or less	GO to L3
		More than 10V	SERVICE open circuit in harness circuit 101
L3	CHECK CANP SOLENOID FOR OPEN CIRCUIT	DVOM Reading:	
	361 / 101 • DVOM 20 volt scale • Red probe to 361 and other to ground	10V or less	SERVICE harness open circuit in power circuit 361
		More than 10V	REPLACE CANP solenoid valve assembly

Canister Purge	Pinpoint Test	L

TEST STEP	RESULT ▶	ACTION TO TAKE
L4 CHECK FOR MALFUNCTION IN PROCESSOR ASSEMBLY OR IN CALIBRATION ASSEMBLY • Tester to C-10 • DVOM switch to tester	DVOM Reading: 0.1V or less ▶ More than 0.1V ▶	GO to L5 REPLACE Processor Assembly RUN QUICK TEST If still not OK, replace Calibration Assembly using original Processor Assembly
L5 CHECK CANP SOLENOID FOR SHORT-TO-GROUND • Disconnect harness connector from CANP solenoid • Observe CANP light on tester	CANP ● ON OFF ▶ CANP ON OFF ▶	GO to L6 SERVICE connector leads, or replace CANP solenoid valve assembly as required
L6 CHECK CANP HARNESS FOR SHORT • Turn key to OFF EEC HARNESS CONNECTOR 200X 1000 OHMS CHECK FOR SHORTS BETWEEN: PIN 10 (101) — 2 (350) 8 (50) 19 (359)	DVOM Reading: 10,000 ohms or more ▶ Under 10,000 ohms ▶	RECONNECT all circuits RETEST SERVICE short as required

Spark Advance Out-of-Limits	Pinpoint Test	M

This Test Checks

• Processor Assembly
• Calibration Assembly
• CP Sensor Wiring

TEST STEP	RESULT ▶	ACTION TO TAKE
M1 CHECK COMPUTER TIMING • Tester to D-9 to read computer Timing • DVOM switch to Tester • Start engine, bring to normal operating temperature and idle • Trigger Self-Test (See QUICK TEST)	DVOM Reading: Between 17-23 ▶ Less than 17 or more than 23 ▶	GO to M2 REPLACE Processor Assembly. Run QUICK TEST If still not OK, replace Calibration Assembly
M2 CHECK THAT LOBE ON PULSE RING IS CENTERED ON CP SENSOR • Turn key to OFF • Align 10° BTDC mark on vibration damper with timing pointer by cranking engine CP-SENSOR PULSE RING	Lobe centered on CP Sensor ▶ Lobe not centered on CP Sensor ▶	GO to M3 Mechanical engine problem. Check timing pointer, vibration damper, pulse ring, etc. SERVICE or replace as required

Canister Purge	Pinpoint Test	L

TEST STEP	RESULT ▶	ACTION TO TAKE
L7 CANP LIGHT FAILED TO TURN-ON DURING SELF-TEST • Turn key to OFF CANP SOLENOID VALVE • Do not disconnect from harness	DVOM Reading: 45-90 ohms ▶ Under 45 ohms or over 90 ohms ▶	REPLACE processor assembly GO to L8
L8 CHECK SOLENOID FOR SHORT TO POWER • Turn key to OFF CANP SOLENOID VALVE • Disconnect CANP Solenoid from harness • Measure resistance of CANP Solenoid	DVOM Reading: 45-90 ohms ▶ Under 45 ohms or over 90 ohms ▶	SERVICE harness short to power REPLACE CANP solenoid valve assembly

Spark Advance Out-of-Limits	Pinpoint Test	M

TEST STEP	RESULT ▶	ACTION TO TAKE
M3 CHECK CP SENSOR FOR SWITCHED WIRE CONNECTIONS • Remove leads from CP Sensor connector and reverse REVERSE • Start engine, bring to normal operating temperature and idle • Trigger Self-Test (See QUICK TEST) • Recheck timing with timing light during Self-Test	Timing: Between 27°-33° BTDC ▶ Less than 27° or more than 33° BTDC ▶	CHECK circuit schematic to see if harness is correct. If not OK, reverse CP leads, and correct harness. If OK, RUN QUICK TEST Disconnect CP Sensor and reconnect leads to original positions GO TO M4
M4 CHECK COMPUTER TIMING • Tester to D-9, to read Computer Timing • DVOM switch to Tester • Trigger Self-Test (See QUICK TEST)	DVOM Reads: Computer Timing not between 17 and 23 ▶ Computer Timing between 17 and 23 ▶	REPLACE Calibration Assembly RUN QUICK TEST If still not OK, replace Processor Assembly using original Calibration Assembly Mechanical problem CHECK crankshaft pointer, pulse ring, CP sensor retainer, vibration dampener, etc.

RPM Failed Self-Test	Pinpoint Test	N

This Test Checks		
Engine RPM's		

TEST STEP	RESULT ▶	ACTION TO TAKE
N1 SERVICE CODE 12 RECEIVED DURING SELF-TEST	DVOM Reading:	
NOTE: This Service Code occurs because the processor interprets the rpm as too high or too low for Self-Test. If rpm is out of limits, other tests within Self-Test may fail. Therefore, this problem must be corrected first.	2.4V or less ▶ More than 2.4V ▶	GO to N2 RUN QUICK TEST
• Tester to A-9 (EVP) • DVOM switch to Tester • Start engine, bring to normal operating temperature and idle • All accessories OFF		
N2 CHECK CURB IDLE ADJUSTMENT		
• Check "A/C ON" and "A/C OFF" idle specifications per emission decal on engine	Idle within specification ▶	GO to N3
NOTE: If difficult to adjust idle, check for vacuum leaks	Idle not within specification ▶	CORRECT Curb Idle Adjustment per decal
N3 CHECK RPM WITH TACHOMETER		
• Connect Tachometer	No Service Codes ▶	RUN QUICK TEST
• Trigger Self-Test	Service Code 12 and rpm NOT between 700-1200 ▶	RESET Throttle Kicker "ON" RPM REFER to Idle Speed Setting Procedure in Part 29-02
• Observe rpm on Tachometer when throttle kicker is ON		
• Note Service Codes	Service Code 12 and rpm between 700-1200 ▶	GO to N4

Stall During Self-Test	Pinpoint Test	P

This Test Checks		
• EGR Valve	• Vacuum System	

TEST STEP	RESULT ▶	ACTION TO TAKE
P1 CHECK EGR VALVE		
• Disconnect vacuum hose at EGR Valve	(EFI) ▶	CHECK rotor registry, then GO to A29
• Start engine, bring to normal operating temperature and idle	Vehicle stalls (FBC) ▶	GO to P2
• Trigger Self-Test	Vehicle does not stall ▶	EGR problem; Refer to PINPOINT TEST G12 RECONNECT vacuum hose
P2 CHECK FOR VACUUM LEAKS FOR EFI — SKIP THIS TEST		
• Reconnect Vacuum hose at EGR valve	Vehicle stalls ▶	GO to P3
• Turn ignition key to OFF, to RUN and then to OFF again to initialize the FBCA Motor	Vehicle does not stall ▶	IF Service Code 41 is output, check for vacuum leaks that would cause lean carburetor condition. Otherwise, check the carburetor per Group 24 of the Shop Manual
• Remove harness connector from FBCA Motor		
• Start engine		
• Run engine at 1800-2000 rpm for approximately 60 seconds to heat EGO Sensor		
• Trigger Self-Test		

FBCA MOTOR

RPM Failed Self-Test	Pinpoint Test	N

TEST STEP	RESULT ▶	ACTION TO TAKE
N4 CHECK OTHER SERVICE CODES		
• Check other Service Codes noted in Step N3	Only Service Code 12 ▶	REPLACE processor using original calibration assembly, and retest. If not OK, replace the calibration assembly using original processor, and retest
	Codes higher than 12 ▶	Refer to QUICK TEST the next higher Service Code number direction

Stall During Self-Test	Pinpoint Test	P

TEST STEP	RESULT ▶	ACTION TO TAKE
P3 CHECK BOWL VENT SOLENOID		
IF EFI, SKIP THIS TEST	Vehicle stalls ▶	CHECK rotor registry per Ignition Systems in Part 29-02
DISCONNECT & PLUG	Vehicle does not stall ▶	CHECK bowl vent per Group 24 in the Shop Manual
TO CARBURETOR		
• Disconnect and plug hose from carburetor to Bowl Vent Solenoid		
• Start engine		
• Trigger Self-Test		

| Fuel Pump Relays | Pinpoint Test | Q (EFI) |

This Test Checks
Cause of Low/No Fuel Pressure

TEST STEP	RESULT ▶	ACTION TO TAKE
Q1 INERTIA SWITCH CHECK		
• Locate Inertia Switch	PRESSURE INCREASES TO:	
• Check connections on switch	More than 35 psi ▶	RUN QUICK TEST (page 5)
• Push top button to turn on Inertia Switch	35 psi or less ▶	GO to Q2
• Pressurize fuel system (turn key to RUN for 1 second, then turn OFF) repeat 5 times		
• Observe fuel pressure gauge		

| Fuel Pump Relays | Pinpoint Test | Q (EFI) |

TEST STEP	RESULT ▶	ACTION TO TAKE
Q5 CHECK FOR POWER TO FUEL PUMP	DVOM Reading:	
• Use DVOM Test Leads to measure voltage on circuit 787 at the Inertia Switch to fuel pump	Under 6V ▶	GO to Q6
• LOS button ON	6V or more ▶	GO to Q17
Q6 CHECK FOR POWER TO INERTIA SWITCH	DVOM Reading:	
• Use DVOM to measure voltage on circuit 787 at Inertia Switch to fuel pump relay	6V or more ▶	REPLACE Inertia Switch
• LOS button ON	Under 6V ▶	GO to Q7

| Fuel Pump Relays | Pinpoint Test | Q (EFI) |

TEST STEP	RESULT ▶	ACTION TO TAKE
Q2 CHECK IF FUEL PUMP RUNS		
• Turn key to RUN, but keep engine OFF	Pump runs briefly ▶	GO to Q11
• Listen* for fuel pump to run briefly when key is first turned on	Pump does not run ▶	GO to Q3
*You may want to open gas filler cap to hear the pump. No smoking		
Q3 RECHECK IF FUEL PUMP RUNS		
• Tester hooked up	Pump runs ▶	REPLACE Calibration Assembly. Retest. If not OK, replace Processor
• Press tester LOS button to "ON" (green flag), and leave LOS button "ON" during entire PINPOINT TEST	Pump does not run ▶	GO to Q4
• Turn key to RUN, but keep engine OFF		
• Listen closely for fuel pump; it should run constantly		
Q4 CHECK VOLTAGE ON WIRE TO PROCESSOR	DVOM Reading:	
• Tester to C-4 (the processor grounds this lead to turn on the fuel pump)	Under 2.0V ▶	GO to Q5
• LOS button ON	2.0V or more ▶	GO to Q14

| Fuel Pump Relays | Pinpoint Test | Q (EFI) |

TEST STEP	RESULT ▶	ACTION TO TAKE
Q7 CHECK FOR VOLTAGE OUT OF FUEL PUMP RELAY	DVOM Reading:	
• Use DVOM Test Leads to measure voltage on circuit 787 at Fuel Pump Relay	Under 6V ▶	GO to Q8
• LOS button ON	6V or more ▶	SERVICE open in circuit 787 from fuel pump relay to inertia switch
Q8 CHECK FOR VOLTAGE INTO FUEL PUMP RELAY	DVOM Reading:	
• Use DVOM Test Leads to measure voltage on circuit 787A at the Ballast Bypass Relay	Under 6V ▶	GO to Q9
	6V or more ▶	GO to Q19

Fuel Pump Relays		Pinpoint Test		Q (EFI)

TEST STEP	RESULT ▶	ACTION TO TAKE
Q9 CHECK FOR VOLTAGE INTO BALLAST BYPASS RELAY • Use DVOM Test Leads to measure voltage on circuit 37B at the Ballast Bypass Relay	DVOM Reading: More than 10V ▶ Less than 10V ▶	GO to Q10 SERVICE open or bad connection in circuit 37B to power. If fuse link is blown, service short to ground in 787, 787A, 787B, 37, or the fuel pump itself; this must be serviced prior to fixing the fuse link

BALLAST BYPASS RELAY
20 VOLTS D.C.
CIRCUIT 37

Fuel Pump Relays		Pinpoint Test		Q (EFI)

TEST STEP	RESULT ▶	ACTION TO TAKE
Q11 CHECK FOR VOLTAGE DROP ACROSS FUEL PUMP BALLAST BYPASS RELAY • Use DVOM Test Leads to measure voltage from circuit 37 to circuit 787A at Ballast Bypass Relay	DVOM Reading: More than 1V ▶ 1V or less ▶	GO to Q12 GO to Part 24-29 in the Shop Manual, and check for clogged fuel line, filter, or defective Throttle Body
Q12 CHECK FOR RELAY ENERGIZED • Use DVOM Test Leads to measure voltage on circuit 57A at Ballast Bypass Relay	DVOM Reading: Under 10V ▶ 10V or more ▶	GO to Q13 REPLACE Ballast Bypass Relay

BALLAST BYPASS RELAY
CIRCUIT 37
CIRCUIT 787A
20 VOLTS D.C.

BALLAST BYPASS RELAY
CIRCUIT 57A
20 VOLTS D.C.

Fuel Pump Relays		Pinpoint Test		Q (EFI)

TEST STEP	RESULT ▶	ACTION TO TAKE
Q10 CHECK OUTPUT OF BALLAST BYPASS RELAY • Use DVOM Test Leads to measure voltage on circuit 787A at the Ballast Bypass Relay	DVOM Reading: 6V or more ▶ Under 6V ▶	SERVICE open in circuit 787A between bypass relay and fuel pump relay, circuit 787A. If reading were between 6V and 10V, GO to Q11. Relay is open or energized or contacts opened SERVICE open in circuit 37A ballast resistor. Also, ballast bypass relay is energized or contacts open, GO to Q11

BALLAST BYPASS RELAY
20 VOLTS D.C.
CIRCUIT 787A

Fuel Pump Relays		Pinpoint Test		Q (EFI)

TEST STEP	RESULT ▶	ACTION TO TAKE
Q13 CHECK VACUUM SWITCH • Disconnect Vacuum Swich from vehicle harness • Use DVOM Test Leads to check for short-to-ground in circuit 57A	DVOM Reading: More than 10V ▶ 10V or less ▶	REPLACE Vacuum Switch SERVICE short in circuit 57A
Q14 ISOLATE REASON FOR HIGH VOLTAGE (AT TESTER C-4) • Turn key to off • Disconnect fuel pump relay • Disconnect Adapter Harness from processor assembly • Turn key to RUN, but keep engine off • Tester to C-4	DVOM Reading: Under 1V ▶ 1V or more ▶	GO to Q15 SERVICE short to power in circuit 97 or fuel pump relay

200 OHMS

Fuel Pump Relays		Pinpoint Test	Q (EFI)

TEST STEP	RESULT	▶	ACTION TO TAKE
Q15 CHECK FOR SHORTED FUEL PUMP RELAY COIL			
• Measure resistance of fuel pump relay coil	More than 40 ohms	▶	GO to Q15
	Less than 40 ohms	▶	REPLACE Relay
Q16 CHECK FOR SHORT TO 787A IN RELAY COIL			
	No short	▶	REPLACE Processor Assembly, and RUN QUICK TEST. If still not OK, replace Calibration Assembly using original Processor Assembly
	Short	▶	REPLACE fuel pump relay
Q17 CHECK WIRES TO FUEL PUMP			
• Visually check wires to fuel Pump for bad connections or opens	Problem identified as bad wiring	▶	SERVICE as needed
	Problem not seen in wiring	▶	GO to Q18

Fuel Pump Relays		Pinpoint Test	Q (EFI)

TEST STEP	RESULT	▶	ACTION TO TAKE
Q19 CHECK FOR VOLTAGE TO RELAY COIL	DVOM Reading:		
• Use DVOM Test Leads to measure voltage on circuit 361 at the Fuel Pump Relay	More than 10V	▶	GO to Q20
	10V or less	▶	SERVICE open in circuit 361 between Power Relay and Fuel Pump Relay
Q20 CHECK PROCESSOR SIDE OF RELAY COIL			
• Use DVOM test leads to measure voltage on circuit 97 at the fuel pump relay	More than 2V	▶	SERVICE open in circuit 97
	2V or less	▶	REPLACE Fuel Pump Relay

Fuel Pump Relays		Pinpoint Test	Q (EFI)

TEST STEP	RESULT	▶	ACTION TO TAKE
Q18 CHECK WIRES TO FUEL PUMP	DVOM Reading:		
• Use DVOM to measure voltage on each of the two pins of the fuel pump. Measure voltage between one of the pins and ground, then between the other pin and ground	Under 6V on both pins	▶	SERVICE open in circuit 787 between Inertia Switch and Fuel Tank
• Do not disconnect connector from fuel tank	6V or more for both	▶	SERVICE open in circuit 57 ground wire
	One reads more than 7V and other reads under 7V	▶	REPLACE Fuel Pump Assembly

CAUTION: Fuel supply lines will remain pressurized for long periods of time after key is turned OFF. This pressure must be relieved before servicing of the fuel system has begun. A valve is provided on the throttle body for this purpose. Remove air cleaner, and relieve system pressure by depressing pin in relief valve CAUTIOUSLY; fuel will be expelled into throttle body

Fuel Pump Relays		Pinpoint Test	Q (EFI)

TEST STEP	RESULT	▶	ACTION TO TAKE
Q21 CHECK FUEL PUMP RELAY			
NOTE: This check is made if Fuel Pump is always ON	Fuel Pump OFF	▶	GO to Q22
• Turn key to OFF	Fuel Pump RUNS	▶	SERVICE short to power in circuit 787 between Fuel Pump Relay and Fuel Pump
• Disconnect Fuel Pump Relay			
• Listen for Fuel Pump			
Q22 CHECK CIRCUIT 97 FOR SHORT-TO-GROUND IN HARNESS	DVOM Reading:		
• Using DVOM, check for a short between circuit 97 and ground at fuel pump relay harness connector	Short	▶	GO to Q23
• Check at the relay connector with relay disconnected	No short	▶	REPLACE Fuel Pump Relay
Q23 CHECK CIRCUIT 97 FOR SHORT-TO-GROUND WITH ECA DISCONNECTED	DVOM Reading:		
• Disconnect harness from Processor Assembly	150 ohms or less	▶	SERVICE short-to-ground in wire 97
• Tester to C-4			
• Press Ohms button DVOM	More than 150 ohms	▶	REPLACE Processor Assembly. If still not OK, replace calibration assembly using original processor

Fuel Pump Relays	Pinpoint Test	Q (EFI)

TEST STEP	RESULT ▶	ACTION TO TAKE
Q24 CHECK FUEL PUMP VOLTAGE	DVOM Reading:	
NOTE: This check is made if Fuel Pump is always noisy • Engine at idle • Measure Fuel Pump voltage at Inertia Switch	Under 10V ▶	CHECK Fuel Pump mechanically if noise is excessive
	10V or more ▶	GO to Q25
Q25 CHECK VOLTAGE ON CIRCUIT 361 AT THE BALLAST BYPASS RELAY	DVOM Reading:	
• Use DVOM Test Leads to measure voltage on circuit 361 at the ballast bypass relay	10V or more ▶	GO to Q26
	Under 10V ▶	SERVICE open circuit in 361

Fuel Pump Relay	Pinpoint Test	Q (EFI)

TEST STEP	RESULT ▶	ACTION TO TAKE
Q29 CHECK "FUEL PUMP BALLAST BYPASS" RELAY	DVOM Reading:	
• Disconnect ballast bypass relay from the harness • Use DVOM Test Lead to measure voltage on circuit 787A at relay connector	10V or more ▶	SERVICE short to power in circuit 787 between Ballast Bypass Relay and Fuel Pump Relay
	Under 10V ▶	REPLACE the Ballast Bypass Relay
Q30 FUEL PUMP BALLAST WIRE CHECK	DVOM Reading:	
NOTE: This check is made if vehicle starts but quickly stalls • Turn key to OFF • Disconnect Ballast Bypass Relay from harness • Use DVOM Test Leads to measure resistance of Ballast wire	3 ohms or less ▶	GO to A1
	Over 3 ohms ▶	SERVICE open circuit or bad connection in Ballast wire circuit 37A

Fuel Pump Relays	Pinpoint Test	Q (EFI)

TEST STEP	RESULT ▶	ACTION TO TAKE
Q26 CHECK IF BALLAST BYPASS RELAY IS ENERGIZED	DVOM Reading:	
• Measure voltage on Circuit 57A at the relay	10V or more ▶	GO to Q27
	Under 10V ▶	GO to Q29
Q27 CHECK HOSE TO VACUUM SWITCH		
• Check hose from manifold to Vacuum Switch for good connections, leaks, cracks, blockage, etc.	Hose good ▶	GO to Q28
	Hose faulty ▶	SERVICE hose
Q28 CHECK VACUUM SWITCH VOLTAGE	DVOM Reading:	
• Use DVOM Test Leads to measure voltage from each Vacuum Switch connector pin to ground (leave switch connected) with vehicle at idle	Both readings 10V or more ▶	SERVICE open in ground wire 57B
	Both readings under 10V ▶	SERVICE open or bad connection in circuit 57A between Ballast Bypass Relay and vacuum switch (57A)
	One reading 10V or more and other reading under 10V ▶	REPLACE vacuum switch

Cranking Signal	Pinpoint Test	R (EFI)

This Test Checks

Crank Signal Circuit

TEST STEP	RESULT ▶	ACTION TO TAKE
R1 CHECK CRANKING SIGNAL WITH KEY ON		
• Turn key to RUN, but keep engine OFF • Tester to A-2 (Cranking Signal)	DVOM Reads: Under 1V ▶	GO to R3
	1V or more ▶	GO to R2
R2 CHECK FOR SHORT TO POWER		
• Turn key to OFF • Disconnect harness from Tester • Using DVOM Test Leads measure resistance (200 x 1000 ohms range) between: — Pins 1 and 24 (circuit 361) — Pins 1 and 3 (circuit 351)	No short ▶	CHECK for proper chassis ground to engine and engine ground to battery If OK, RUN QUICK TEST
	Shorted ▶	SERVICE short

Cranking Signal	Pinpoint Test	R (EFI)

TEST STEP	RESULT ▶	ACTION TO TAKE
R3 CHECK FOR OPENS		
• Disconnect wire from Starter Relay "S" terminal • Tester at A-2 • Turn key to START	DVOM Reading: More than 6.5V ▶ 6.5V or less ▶	RUN QUICK TEST GO to R4
R4 CONTINUE CHECK FOR OPENS		
• Key OFF • Disconnect Tester from EEC harness • Using DVOM Test Leads, measure resistance (200 ohm range) between: — Pin 1 to Starter Relay "S" wire (circuit 32); — Pin 8 to Battery Negative (circuit 57)	DVOM Reading: Under 5 ohms ▶ 5 or more ohms ▶	GO to R5 SERVICE open circuit RECONNECT "S" terminal RUN QUICK TEST
R5 CHECK FOR CRANK SHORT-TO-GROUND		
• Using DVOM Test Leads, measure resistance between: — Pin 1 to Battery Negative	DVOM Reading: More than 10,000 ohms ▶ Under 10,000 ohms ▶	RECONNECT Tester RECONNECT Starter "S" terminal RUN QUICK TEST SERVICE short-to-ground in circuit 32 RECONNECT Tester RECONNECT Starter "S" terminal RUN QUICK TEST

PIN 1

200X1000 OHMS

Air Charge Temperature	Pinpoint Test	S (EFI)

TEST STEP	RESULT ▶	ACTION TO TAKE
S3 CHECK ACT SENSOR RESISTANCE		
• Disconnect harness from ACT sensor • Switch tester to A-6 • Read DVOM	DVOM Reading: Less than 8.00 ▶ More than 8.00 ▶	GO to S4 CHECK engine for overtemperate, and let cool down. If this fails to correct problem, replace ACT sensor, and retest
S4 CHECK ACT SENSOR HARNESS FOR SHORTS		
• Turn key to OFF • Use DVOM Test Leads to check for short from pin 6 (ACT) to all remaining 31 connector pins	DVOM Reading: More than 10,000 ohms ▶ 10,000 or less ohms ▶	REPLACE ACT SENSOR, and run QUICK TEST. If problem still exists, REPLACE Processor Assembly SERVICE short(s) in EEC harness
S5 CHECK FOR ACT SHORT TO POWER		
• Disconnect EEC Harness from Tester • Turn key to RUN, but keep engine OFF • Use DVOM Test Leads to measure voltage from each Sensor harness pin to chassis ground	DVOM Reading: Under 0.2V on both pins ▶ 0.2V or more on either pin ▶	GO to S6 SERVICE harness short to power

359 B-W

357 LG-P

200 x 1000 OHMS

Air Charge Temperature	Pinpoint Test	S (EFI)

This Test Checks

• Air Charge Temperature (ACT)
• Sensor and Harness

359 B-W

357 LG-P

AIR CHARGE TEMPERATURE SENSOR

359 B-W

6

19

357 LG-P

TEST STEP	RESULT ▶	ACTION TO TAKE
S1 CHECK ENGINE TEMPERATURE		
• What does the operating temperature of the engine appear to be by observation (ignoring tester readings)	ENGINE TEMPERATURE: Overheated ▶ Below normal ▶ At normal operating ▶	GO to Part 29 Routine 217 GO to Part 29 Routine 216 GO to S2
S2 ATTEMPT TO BRING AIR CHARGE TEMPERATURE WITHIN LIMITS		
• Tester to A-6 (ACT) • Start engine, increase RPM and hold for 5 to 10 minutes • Observe DVOM	DVOM Reading: Between 1.0V and 5.6V ▶ Under 1.0V ▶ More than 5.6V ▶	RUN QUICK TEST GO to S3 GO to S5

Air Charge Temperature	Pinpoint Test	S (EFI)

TEST STEP	RESULT ▶	ACTION TO TAKE
S6 CHECK ACT SENSOR HARNESS CONTINUITY		
• Turn key to OFF • Use DVOM Test Leads to check continuity from Sensor connector to the ECA harness connector pins 19 and 6	DVOM Reading: Under 5.0 ohms ▶ 5.0 or more ohms ▶	GO to S6a SERVICE open or bad harness connection
S6a CHECK ACT SENSOR RESISTANCE		
• Turn key to OFF • Disconnect harness from ACT Sensor • Use DVOM Test Leads to measure resistance across sensor pins	DVOM Reading: 1,700-60,000 ohms ▶ Under 1,700 or over 60,000 ohms ▶	REPLACE processor REPLACE ACT sensor
S7 LOCATE CAUSE OF CODE 24		
(EGA has interpreted air temperature to be outside the 40-240°F range) • Engine at idle • Tester to A-6 (ACT) • While observing DVOM, wiggle ACT Sensor and harness, checking for bad connections	DVOM Reading: Remains Under 1.0V or more than 5.6V ▶ Jumps to under 1.0V or more than 5.6V ▶ Remains between 1.0-5.6V ▶	GO to S1 SERVICE connection REPLACE Processor Assembly

357   359

6   19

200x 1000 OHMS

FORD EEC IV ENGINE CONTROL SYSTEM

General Information

The EEC IV system is similar to other Ford engine control systems in that the center of the system is a microprocessor called an Electronic Control Assembly (ECA). The ECA receives data from sensors, switches, relays and other electronic components and issues commands (output signals) to control engine functions. The ECA is calibrated to optimize emissions, fuel economy and driveability.

The ECA in the EEC IV system is a microprocessor like other EEC systems, but the calibration modules are located within the ECA assembly instead of being attached to the outside, as in previous models. The harness connectors are edge-card type connectors, providing a more positive connection and allowing probing from the rear while connected. The ECA is usually mounted in the passenger compartment under the front section of the center console.

NOTE: The EEC IV system does not control the pulse air injection (Thermactor air pump) or the upshift lamp.

The EEC IV system electronically controls the fuel injectors for air/fuel ratio control, spark timing, deceleration fuel cut-off, EGR function (on or off), curb and fast idle speed, evaporative emissions purge, A/C cut-off during wide open throttle, cold engine start and enrichment, electric fuel pump and self-test engine diagnostics.

FUEL DELIVERY SYSTEM

The fuel sub-system consists of a high-pressure electric fuel pump to deliver fuel from the tank, a fuel filter to remove contaminants from the fuel, a Fuel Charging Manifold Assembly, a fuel pressure regulator, and solid and flexible fuel supply and return lines. The Fuel Charging Manifold Assembly incorporates four electronically controlled fuel injectors. One injector is mounted directly above each intake port in the lower intake manifold. All injectors are energized simultaneously and fire once every crankshaft revolution. The injectors spray a predetermined quantity of fuel into the intake airstream. A constant pressure drop is maintained across the injector nozzles through a pressure regulator which is referenced to intake manifold pressure (vacuum). The regulator is connected parallel to the fuel injectors and positioned on the far end of the fuel rail. Fuel supplied by the pump, but not required by the engine, passes through the regulator and returns to the fuel tank through a fuel return line.

NOTE: The pressure regulator reduces fuel pressure to 39–40 psi under normal operating conditions. At idle or high manifold vacuum condition, fuel pressure is reduced to about 30 psi.

The fuel pressure regulator is a diaphragm operated relief valve in which one side of the diaphragm senses fuel pressure and the other side senses manifold vacuum. Normal fuel pressure is established by a spring preload applied to the diaphragm. Control of the fuel system is maintained through the EEC power relay and the EEC IV control unit, although electrical power is routed through the fuel pump relay and an inertia switch. The fuel pump relay is normally located on a bracket somewhere above the Electronic Control Assembly (ECA) and the Inertial Switch is located in the left rear kick panel. The fuel pump is usually mounted on a bracket at the fuel tank.

The inertia switch opens the power circuit to the fuel pump in the event of a collision. Once tripped, the switch must be reset manu-

1.6L EFI-EEC IV engine—front view

Fuel charging manifold assembly

1.61 EFI-EEC IV engine—rear view

Cross section of fuel injector

ally by pushing the reset button on the assembly. Check that the inertia switch is reset before diagnosing power supply problems.

Fuel Injectors

The fuel injectors used with the EFI-EEC IV system are electro-mechanical (solenoid) type, designed to meter and atomize fuel delivered to the intake ports of the engine. The injectors are mounted in the lower intake manifold and positioned so that their spray nozzles direct the fuel charge in front of the intake valves. The injector body consists of a solenoid actuated pintle and needle valve assembly. The control unit sends an electrical impulse that activates the solenoid, causing the pintle to move inward off the seat and allow the fuel to flow. The amount of fuel delivered is controlled by the length of time the injector is energized since the fuel flow orifice is fixed and the fuel pressure drop across the injector tip is constant. Correct atomization is achieved by controlling the pintle at the point where the fuel enters the pintle chamber. All injectors are energized simultaneously and spray once every crankshaft revolution, delivering a predetermined quantity of fuel into the intake airstream.

NOTE: Exercise care when handling fuel injectors during service. Be careful not to lose the pintle cap and replace damaged O-rings to assure a tight seal. Never apply direct battery voltage to test an EFI fuel injector.

The injectors receive high pressure fuel from the fuel manifold (fuel rail) assembly. The complete assembly includes a single, pre-

formed tube with four injector connectors, mounting flange for the pressure regulator, mounting attachments to locate the manifold and provide the fuel injector retainers and Schrader® quick disconnect fitting used to perform fuel pressure tests.

AIR INDUCTION SYSTEM

The EFI-EEC IV air subsystem components include the air cleaner assembly, air flow (vane) meter, throttle air bypass valve and air ducts that connect the air system to the throttle body assembly. The throttle body regulates the air flow to the engine through a single butterfly-type throttle plate controlled by conventional accelerator linkage. The throttle body has an idle adjustment screw (throttle air bypass valve) to set the throttle plate position, a PCV fresh air source upstream of the throttle plate, individual vacuum taps for PCV and control signals and a throttle position sensor that provides a voltage signal for the EEC IV control unit.

The hot air intake system uses a thermostatic flap valve assembly whose components and operation are similar to previous hot air intake systems. Intake air volume and temperature are measured by the vane meter assembly which is mounted between the air cleaner and throttle body. The vane meter consists of two separate devices; the vane airflow sensor (VAF) uses a counterbalanced L-shaped flap valve mounted on a pivot pin and connected to a variable resistor (potentiometer). The control unit measures the amount of deflection of the flap vane by measuring the voltage signal from the potentiometer mounted on top of the meter body; larger air volume moves the vane further and produces a higher voltage signal. The vane air temperature (VAT) sensor is mounted in the middle of the air stream just before the flap valve. Since the mass (weight) of a specific volume of air varies with pressure and temperature, the control unit uses the voltage signal from the air temperature sensor to compensate for these variables and provide a more exact measurement of actual air mass that is necessary to calculate the fuel required to obtain the optimum air/fuel ratio under a wide range of operating conditions. On the EEC IV system, the VAT sensor affects spark timing as a function of air temperature.

NOTE: Make sure all air intake connections are tight before testing. Air leaking into the engine through a loose bellows connection can result in abnormal engine operation and affect the air/fuel mixture ratio.

Throttle Air Bypass Valve
FUEL INJECTION ONLY

The throttle air bypass valve is an electro-mechanical (solenoid) device whose operation is controlled by the EEC IV control unit. A variable air metering valve controls both cold and warm idle airflow in response to commands from the control unit. The valve operates by bypassing a regulated amount of air around the throttle plate; the higher the voltage signal from the control unit, the more air is bypassed through the valve. In this manner, additional air can be added to the fuel mixture without moving the throttle plate. At curb idle, the valve provides smooth idle for various engine coolant temperatures, compensates for A/C load and compensates for transaxle load and no-load conditions. The valve also provides fast idle for start-up, replacing the fast idle cam, throttle kicker and anti-dieseling solenoid common to carbureted models.

NOTE: Curb and fast idle speeds are proportional to engine coolant temperature and controlled through the EEC IV control unit. Fast idle kick-down will occur when the throttle is depressed, or after approximately 15–20 seconds after coolant temperature reaches 160°F.

ELECTRONIC ENGINE CONTROL SYSTEM

The electronic engine control sub-system consists of the ECA and various sensors and actuators. The ECA reads inputs from engine sensors, then outputs a voltage signal to various components (actuators) to control engine functions.

Components of EFI-EEC IV air intake system

The period of time that the injectors are energized (on-time or "pulse width") determines the amount of fuel delivered to each cylinder. The longer the pulse width, the richer the fuel mixture.

NOTE: **The operating reference voltage (Vref) between the ECA and its sensors and actuators is five volts. This allows these components to work during the crank operation even though the battery voltage drops.**

The components which make up the EEC-IV electronic control system include:
• Electronic control assembly (ECA)—the on-board computer for the EEC IV

• Systems input (sensors)—devices that are designed to measure engine operating conditions
• System outputs (actuators)—control devices that the ECA uses to adjust various engine parameters

In order for the ECA to properly control engine operation, it must first receive current status reports on various operating conditions. The control unit constantly monitors crankshaft position, throttle plate position, engine coolant temperature, exhaust gas oxygen level, air intake volume and temperature, A/C (On/Off), ATX or MTX status-load or no-load (1.6L only), Spark knock (detonation) (2.3L only) and Barometric pressure (2.3L only).

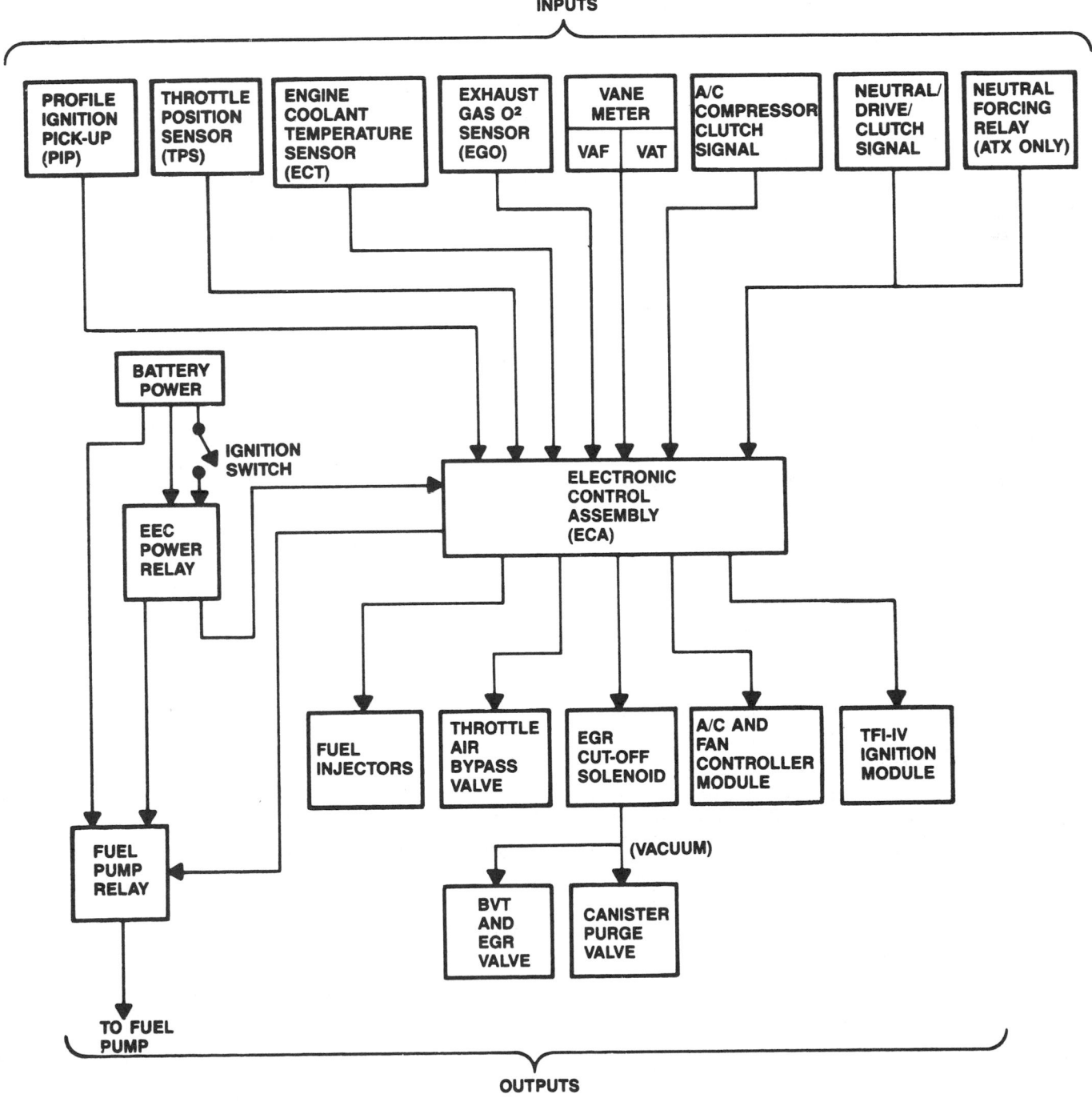

EFI-EEC IV system inputs and outputs

Universal Distributor

The primary function of the EEC-IV system universal distributor is to direct the high secondary voltage to the spark plugs. In addition, the universal distributor supplies crankshaft position and frequency information to the ECA using a profile ignition pick-up (PIP) sensor in place of the magnetic pickup or the crankshaft position sensor used on other models. This distributor does not have any mechanical or vacuum advance. The universal distributor assembly is adjustable for resetting base timing, if required.

NOTE: The PIP replaces the crankshaft position sensor found on other EEC IV models.

The PIP sensor has an armature with four windows and four metal tabs that rotates past the stator assembly (Hall effect switch). When a metal tab enters the stator assembly, a positive signal (approximately 10 volts) is sent to the ECA, indicating the 10° BTDC crankshaft position. The ECA calculates the precise time to energize the spark output signal to the TFI module. When the TFI module receives the spark output signal, it shuts off the coil primary current and the collapsing field energizes the secondary output.

NOTE: Misadjustment of the base timing affects the spark advance in the same manner as a conventional solid-state ignition system.

Throttle Position Sensor (TPS)

The TPS is mounted on the throttle body. This sensor provides the ECA with a signal that indicates the opening angle of the throttle plate. The sensor output signal uses the 5-volt reference voltage (Vref) previously described. From this input, the ECA controls:
1. Operating mode
   —Wide-open throttle (WOT)
   —Part throttle (PT)
   —Closed throttle (CT)
2. Fuel enrichment at WOT
3. Additional spark advance at WOT
4. EGR and Canister Purge cut off (1.6L only) during WOT, deceleration and idle
5. A/C cut off during WOT (30 seconds maximum) (1.6L only)
6. Cold start kickdown
7. Fuel cut off during deceleration
8. WOT dechoke during crank mode (starting)

On the EEC-IV system, the TPS signal to the ECA only changes the spark timing during the WOT mode. As the throttle plate rotates, the TPS varies its voltage output. As the throttle plate moves from a closed throttle position to a WOT position, the voltage output of the TPS will change from a low voltage (approximately 1.0 volt) to a high voltage (approximately 4.75 volts). The TPS used is not adjustable and must be replaced if it is out of specification. The EEC-IV programming compensates for differences between sensors.

Engine Coolant Temperature (ECT) Sensor

The ECT sensor is located in the heater supply tube at the rear of the engine on 1.6L engines. On 2.3L engines the ECT is located in the lower intake manifold. The ECT is a thermistor (changes resistance as temperature changes). The sensor detects the temperature of engine coolant and provides a corresponding signal to the ECA. From this signal, the ECA will modify the air/fuel ratio (mixture), idle speed, spark advance, EGR and Canister purge control. When the engine coolant is cold, the ECT signal causes the ECA to provide enrichment to the air/fuel ratio for good cold driveaway as engine coolant warms-up, the voltage will drop.

NOTE: On 2.3L HSC engines, the EEC IV system also controls the upshift light and thermactor air system.

Exhaust Gas Oxygen (EGO) Sensor

The EGO sensor on the EEC IV system is a little different from others used and is mounted in its own mounting boss, located between the two downstream tubes in the header near the exhaust system on the 1.6L engine. On the 2.3L engine the EGO sensor is mounted in the turbocharger exhaust elbow. The EGO sensor works between zero and one volt output, depending on the presence (lean) or absence (rich) of oxygen in the exhaust gas. A voltage reading greater than 0.6 volts indicates a rich air/fuel ratio, while a reading of less than 0.4 volt indicates a lean ratio.

CAUTION

Never apply voltage to the EGO sensor because it could destroy the sensor's calibration. This includes the use of an ohmmeter. Before connecting and using a voltmeter, make sure it has a high-input impedance (at least 10 megohms) and is set on the proper resistance range. Any attempt to use a powered voltmeter to measure the EGO voltage output directly will damage or destroy the sensor.

Operation of the sensor is the same as that for the sensor used on other models. One difference that should be noted is that the rubber protective cap used on top of the sensor on the other models has been replaced with a metal cap.

Vane Meter

FUEL INJECTION ONLY

The vane meter is actually two sensors in one assembly—a vane airflow (VAF) sensor and a vane air temperature (VAT) sensor. This meter measures airflow to the engine and the temperature of the air stream. The vane meter is located behind the air cleaner on the 1.6L engine. On the 2.3L engine it is located under the air cleaner.

Airflow through the body moves a vane mounted on a pivot pin. The more air flowing through the meter, the further the vane rotates about the pivot pin. The air vane pivot pin is connected to a variable resistor (potentiometer) on top of the assembly. The vane meter uses the 5-volt reference voltage. The output of the potentiometer to the ECA varies between zero and Vref (5 volts), depending on the volume of air flowing through the sensor. A higher volume of air will produce a higher voltage output. The volume of air measured through the meter has to be converted into an air mass value. The mass (weight) of a specific volume of air varies with pressure and temperature. To compensate for these variables, a temperature sensor in front of the vane measures incoming air temperature. The ECA uses the air temperature and a programmed pressure value to convert the VAF signal into a mass airflow value. This value is used to calculate the fuel flow necessary for the optimum air/fuel ratio. The VAT also affects spark timing as a function of air temperature.

A/C Clutch Compressor (ACC) Signal

Anytime battery voltage is applied to the A/C clutch, the same signal is also applied to the ECA. The ECA then maintains the engine idle speed with the throttle air bypass valve control solenoid (fuel injection), or throttle kicker (carburetor), to compensate for the added load created by the A/C clutch operation. Shutting down the A/C clutch will have a reverse effect. The ECA will maintain the engine idle speed at 850 rpm (ATX) or 950 rpm (MTX) on 1.6L engines, and 900 rpm for 2.3L engines.

Clutch Engaged Switch and Transaxle Neutral Switch (Manual Transaxle) or Neutral Start Switch (Automatic Transaxle)

1.6L ENGINE ONLY

On models equipped with a manual transaxle, two switches wired in parallel are used to indicate the load or no-load condition of the transaxle to the ECA. These are the clutch engaged switch and the transaxle neutral switch. The clutch engaged switch is a two position switch that is closed when the clutch is depressed. It is mounted on the clutch pedal lever. The other switch used on manual transaxle models is mounted on the clutch shift linkage. The transaxle neutral switch is a microswitch that is closed only when the transaxle is in the neutral position. On automatic transaxle models, the neutral start switch provides the ECA with an indication of whether or not the transaxle is in gear.

A Vref voltage on the line between the switch and the ECA is an indication that the switch is open and the transaxle is in Drive or Reverse. No voltage (one volt or less) on the line (switch closed) is an indication that the transaxle is in Park or Neutral.

The ECA adjusts the air bypass, as required to maintain the engine idle speed at 850 rpm for the load or no-load conditions. A neutral forcing relay is energized in the start mode to provide the no-voltage signal on the Vref line.

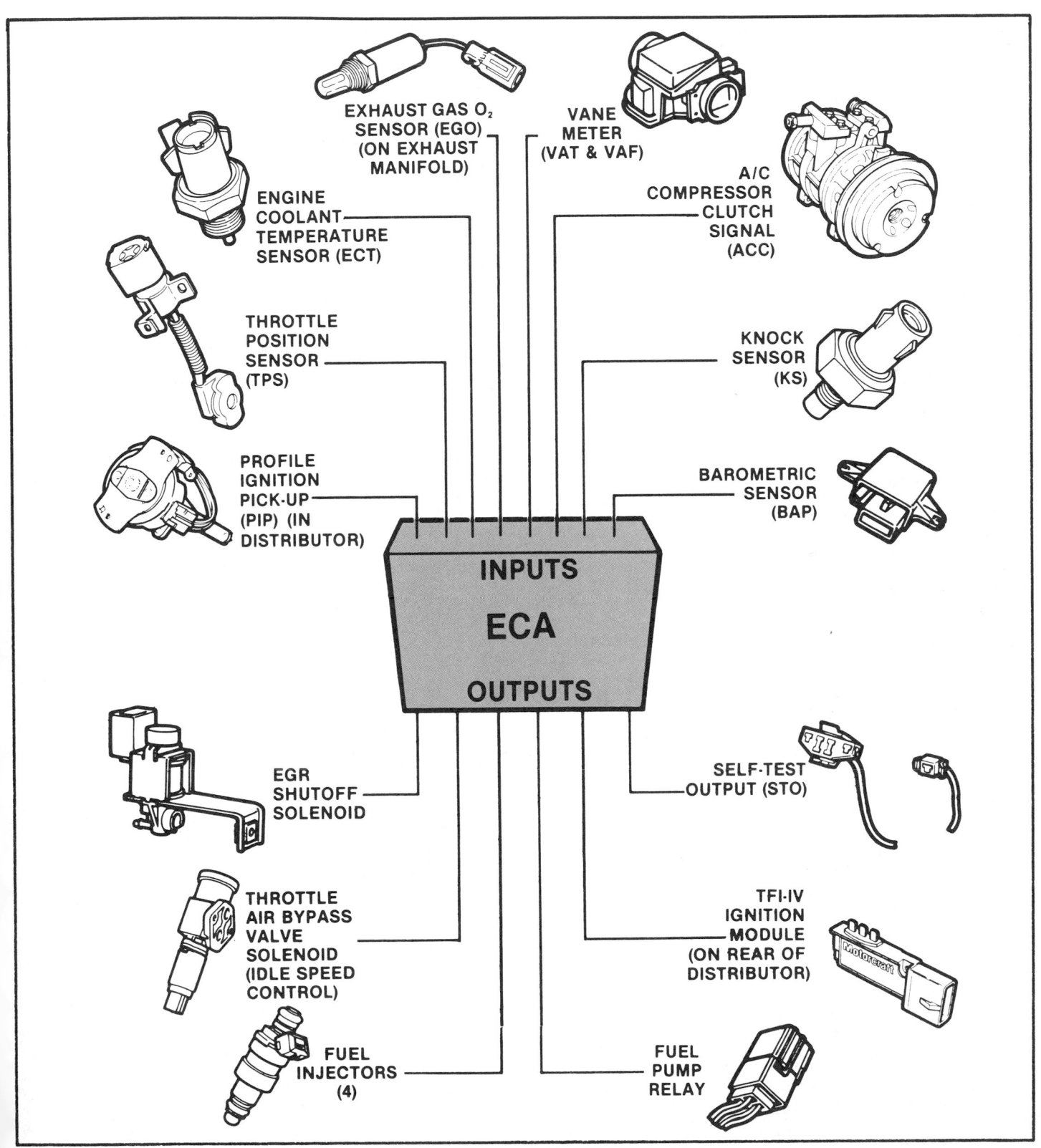

2.3L engine inputs and outputs—fuel injection shown

Neutral Forcing Relay

1.6L ENGINE WITH AUTOMATIC TRANSMISSION

In the START mode, the neutral forcing relay is energized and pulls the neutral/drive input signal down to less than one volt. The ECA reads this as a no-load condition on the engine and maintains idle speed accordingly. This improves cold start characteristics of the engine. Without the relay, the neutral/drive input to the ECA in the Start mode, would remain high (approximately five volts) due to the battery voltage through the ignition switch. This would be improperly interpreted as being a load condition (transaxle in Drive or Reverse) by the ECA and the engine idle speed would be improperly adjusted for the starting mode.

Knock Sensor (KS)

2.3L ENGINE ONLY

The knock sensor is used to detect detonation. In situations of excessive knock the ECA receives a signal from this sensor and retards the spark accordingly. The operation of the knock sensor during boost on turbocharged models improves the engine's durability. It is mounted in the lower intake manifold at the rear of the engine.

Barometric (BAP) Sensor

2.3L ENGINE ONLY

The barometric sensor is used to compensate for altitude variations. From this signal, the ECA modifies the air/fuel ratio, spark timing, idle speed, and EGR flow. The barometric sensor is a design that produces a frequency based on atmospheric pressure (altitude). The barometric sensor is mounted on the right-hand fender apron.

EGR Shut-Off Solenoid

The electrical signal to the EGR shut-off solenoid is controlled by the ECA. The signal is either ON or OFF. It is Off during cold start, closed throttle or WOT. It is On at all other times.

The solenoid is the same as the EGR control solenoid used on previous EEC systems. It is mounted on the LH side of the dash panel in the engine compartment on 1.6L engines and on the RH shock tower in the engine compartment on 2.3L engines. The solenoid is normally closed, and the control vacuum from the solenoid is applied to the EGR valve on the 2.3L engine. On the 1.6L engine the vacuum is applied to a tee which goes to both the EGR valve and a backpressure variable transducer (BVT). Vacuum from this line is also applied to the canister purge valve.

NOTE: The canister purge valve is controlled by vacuum from the EGR solenoid. The purge valve is a standard-type valve and operates the same as in previous systems.

Thick Film Ignition (TFI-IV) Module

The TFI-IV ignition module has six connector pins at the engine wiring harness that supply the following signals:
- Ignition switch in RUN position
- Engine cranking
- Tachometer
- PIP (crankshaft position to ECA)
- Spark advance (from ECA)
- Internal ground from the ECA to the distributor

The TFI-IV module supplies the spark to the distributor through the ignition coil and calculates the duration. It receives its control signal from the ECA (spark output).

Throttle Air Bypass Valve Solenoid

FUEL INJECTION ONLY

The throttle air bypass valve solenoid, is an electro-mechanical device controlled by the ECA. It incorporates a solenoid which positions a variable area metering valve. In response to commands from the ECA, the valve controls both cold and warm idle airflow. The position of the solenoid, and therefore, also the bypass valve and the amount of bypassed air, is determined by the On/Off time of current applied to the solenoid by the ECA.

The valve operates by passing a variable amount of air around the throttle plate. The air inlet of the valve is in front of the throttle plate and the air outlet is behind the plate. In this manner, additional air can be added to the mixture without moving the throttle plate. At curb idle, the valve provides smooth idle for various engine coolant temperatures, compensates for A/C load, and on the 1.6L engine it compensates for transaxle load and no-load conditions. The valve also provides fast idle for start-up. In operation, the throttle air bypass valve replaces the fast idle cam, the throttle kicker, the anti-dieseling solenoid, and other throttle-position modulators. Therefore, there are no curb idle or fast idle adjustments. As in curb idle operation, the fast idle speed is proportional to engine coolant temperature. Fast idle kick-down will occur when the throttle is kicked. A time-out feature in the ECA will also automatically kick-down fast idle to curb idle after a time period of approximately 15–25 seconds; after coolant has reached approximately 71°C (160°F). The signal duty cycle from the ECA to the valve will be at 100% (maximum current) during the crank to provide maximum air flow to allow no touch starting at any time (engine cold or hot).

A/C and Cooling Fan Controller Module

1.6L ENGINE ONLY

An A/C and cooling fan controller module, is provided on EEC models to control operation of the A/C compressor and the engine cooling fan. This module is unique to this application, and is mounted under the instrument panel on the RH side. The A/C and cooling fan controller module receives inputs form the ECA, the coolant temperature switch and the stop-lamp switch. The module provides output signals to control operation of the A/C compressor and the engine cooling fan. It acts similar to a WOT switch in controlling these components.

The signal for turning On the A/C compressor comes through the clutch cycling pressure switch to the controller module. The module then applies the operating voltage to the compressor. During periods of WOT operation, the ECA applies an input to the controller module that disables the signal the the A/C compressor. This WOT signal from the ECA also de-energizes the cooling fan motor if the engine coolant temperature is below 105°C (221°F).

NOTE: The engine coolant temperature switch applies a ground signal to the controller module if the coolant temperature exceeds 105°C (221°F). This ground overrides the ECA WOT signal, and prevents the engine cooling fan from shutting off.

The ECA also contains a time-out feature for the WOT signal. After approximately 30 seconds, the WOT signal is stopped whether or not the WOT condition has ended. However, re-cycling from WOT to part throttle and back to WOT will again shut off the A/C for 30 seconds. Stepping on the brake (on models with power brakes) also provides a cut-off signal to the A/C compressor and to the engine cooling fan for approximately 3–5 seconds. Battery voltage applied through the stoplamp switch is applied to the controller module.

EEC IV SYSTEM OPERATION

CRANK MODE

The crank mode is entered after initial engine starting, or after engine stall when key is in START. A special operation program is used in the crank mode to aid engine starting. After engine start, one of the run modes is entered and normal engine operation is performed. If the engine stumbles during a run mode, the underspeed mode is entered to help it recover from the stumble and prevent stalling. When cranking the engine, the fuel control is in the open loop mode (no feedback to the ECA) of operation and the ECA sets engine timing at 10–15° BTDC (for the correct timing specification, refer to the Engine Emissions Decal under the hood.

On fuel injected (EFI) models, the injectors fire in a simultaneous, double-fire manner (fires twice every crankshaft revolution) to provide the base crank air-fuel control. The throttle air bypass fast idle solenoid is set to open the bypass valve to provide the fast idle/no-touch start. On models with a feedback carburetor, the air/fuel ratio is controlled through the feedback solenoid. On the 2.3L engine, the EGR cut-off solenoid is not energized, so EGR valve is Off. On the 1.6L engine the EGR cut-of solenoid is not energized, so both the EGR valve and the canister purge valve are off.

NOTE: On 2.3L HSC engines, the vapor canister purge solenoid is teed with the Thermactor Air Divert (TAD) solenoid, so when thermactor air is upstream, the canister purge is off.

On 1.6L ATX models in the crank mode, the neutral forcing relay provides a signal to the ECA Vref line to hold this line at one volt or less and to indicate that the transaxle is in Park or Neutral. If the engine coolant is cold, the ECT sensor signal to the ECA causes the ECA to richen the fuel mixture. In this operation, the ECT sensor is performing as a choke system to improve the cold start reaction and to provide good cold driveaway characteristics.

At start-up, the throttle position sensor (TPS) keeps the ECA informed on the position of the throttle plate. When the throttle is kicked after start-up, the ECA will bring the engine down from fast idle by changing the signal to the throttle air bypass valve.

UNDERSPEED MODE

Operation in the underspeed mode (under 600 rpm on 1.6L, and under 500 rpm on 2.3L) is similar to that previously described for the crank mode. The system switches from the underspeed mode to the normal run mode when the required rpm is reached. The underspeed mode is used to provide a good pulse width to the injectors and ignores any signal from the vane meter. During this mode, the vane meter used on fuel injection models flutters and the signal generated would vary with the flutter. Therefore, the vane meter signal is ignored by the ECA in the underspeed mode.

CLOSED THROTTLE MODE (IDLE OR DECELERATION)

In the closed throttle mode, the air/fuel ratio is trimmed by either varying the pulse width of the output from the ECA to the injectors, or by varying the duty cycle of the feedback solenoid on carbureted models, to obtain the desired mixture. To calculate what this output signal should be, the ECA evaluates inputs from the ECT sensor, the vane meter, the TPS, the EGO sensor, the PIP sensor and the A/C clutch. These sensors inform the ECA of the various conditions that must be evaluated in order for the ECA to determine the correct air/fuel ratio for the closed-throttle condition present. Therefore, with the input from the EGO sensor, the system is maintained in closed-loop operation at idle. If the EGO sensor fails to switch rich/lean, the ECA programming assumes the EGO sensor has cooled off, and the system goes to open-loop fuel control. Under a deceleration condition, the TPS signal indicates closed throttle and the ECA shut-off fuel for improved fuel economy and emissions. The injectors are turned back on, as required, to prevent engine stalling.

NOTE: The point at which the injectors are turned back On will occur at different rpm's, depending on calibration factors and engine temperature, although the injectors are turned back On if the throttle is opened.

Ignition timing is also determined by ECA using these same inputs. The ECA has a series of tables programmed into the assembly at the factory. These tables provide the ECA with a reference of desired ignition timing for the various operating conditions reflected by the sensor inputs. The throttle air bypass valve position is determined by the ECA as a function of RPM, ECT, A/C On or Off, neutral/drive (1.6L only), throttle mode and time since start-up inputs. On the 1.6L both the EGR valve and the canister purge valve are Off during a closed-throttle condition. On the 2.3L

engine the EGR valve is Off. The signal from the TPS to the ECA indicates that the throttle plate is closed, and the ECA de-energizes the EGR shut-off solenoid to close the EGR valve and on the 1.6L the canister purge valve.

PART THROTTLE MODE (CRUISE)

The air/fuel mixture ratio and ignition timing are calculated in the same manner as previously described for the closed throttle mode. The fuel control system remains in closed-loop during part throttle operation, as long as the EGO sensor is operational. In part throttle operation, the throttle air bypass valve is positioned to provide an electronic dashpot function in the event the throttle is closed. Again, as in the closed throttle mode, the ECA makes this determination based on the inputs from the applicable sensors. The TPS provides the throttle plate position signal to the ECA. With the throttle plate being in a partial open position, the ECA energizes the EGR shut-off solenoid to open the EGR valve, and on the 1.6L to allow purge vapors to flow into the intake manifold.

WIDE-OPEN THROTTLE MODE (WOT)

Control of the air/fuel ratio in WOT mode is the same as in part, or closed throttle situations, except that fuel control switches to open-loop, and the fuel injector pulse width is increased to provide additional fuel enrichment. This pulse width increase is applied as a result of the WOT signal from the TPS to the ECA. This signal from the TPS also causes the ECA to remove the energizing signal from the EGR shut-off solenoid (if present). More spark advance is added in WOT for improved performance. In addition, on the 1.6L engine, the A/C clutch and cooling fan are turned Off to aid performance.

COLD OR HOT ENGINE OPERATION

This modified operation changes the normal engine operation output signals, as required, to adjust for uncommon engine operating conditions. These include cold or excessively hot engine.

LIMITED OPERATION STRATEGY (LOS)

In this operation, the ECA provides the necessary output signals to allow the vehicle to "limp home" when an electronic malfunction occurs. The EGR valve and on the 1.6L, the canister purge valve are shut-Off, the air bypass valve goes to a fixed voltage, timing is locked at the fixed timing (depends on calibration, refer to Engine Emissions Decal on the vehicle), and the injector pulse width is constant.

Diagnosis and Testing

Like all earlier EEC systems, the EFI-EEC IV system has a self-test capability. The primary tools needed for the self-test are an analog voltmeter or Ford Self-Test Automatic Readout (STAR) tester, a timing light, vacuum gauge, spark tester, tachometer, jumper wire, fuel pressure gauge and hand vacuum pump. There are two testing procedures, the Quick Test and the Pinpoint Test. The Quick Test is a functional check of EEC IV system operation. The Pinpoint Test is an individual component check. Perform the Quick Test first to isolate the problem; then perform the Pinpoint Test to verify any component failure before replacing any part. After all tests and services are completed, repeat the entire Quick Test to make sure the system is working properly.

NOTE: The 2.3L system is similar to the 1.6L, with the addition of a "keep alive" memory in the ECA that retains any intermittent trouble codes stored within the last 20 engine starts. With this system, the memory is not erased when the ignition is switched OFF. In addition, the 2.3L EEC IV system incorporates a knock sensor to detect engine detonation (mounted in the lower intake manifold at the rear of the engine), and a barometric pressure sensor to compensate for altitude variations. The barometric pressure sensor is mounted on the right fender apron.

EEC IV SYSTEM QUICK TEST

The ECA stores the self-test program in its permanent memory. When activated, it checks the EEC IV system by testing its memory integrity and processing capability, and it verifies that various sensors and actuators are connected and operating properly. The self-test is divided into three categories: Key ON/Engine OFF, Engine Running, and Continuous Testing.

NOTE: The Key ON/Engine OFF and Engine Running tests are intended to detect hard failures only. Intermittent faults are detected by Continuous Testing.

Before connecting any equipment to diagnose the EEC system, make the following checks:
1. Check the air cleaner and ducting.
2. Check all vacuum hoses for proper routing, tight connections and breaks or damage.
3. Check the EEC system wiring harness connections for looseness, corrosion, broken or frayed wires, shorted connections, proper routing and tight connections. Shake or wiggle wires to check connections while performing continuity tests.
4. Check control module, sensors and actuators for physical damage.
5. Turn OFF all electrical accessories and make sure all doors are closed when taking readings.
6. Start and warm up the engine before testing any further.

Analog Voltmeter Hookup

1. Turn ignition key OFF.
2. Connect a jumper wire from pin 5 self-test input to pin 2 signal return on self-test connector.
3. Set analog voltmeter on a DC voltage range to read from 0–15 volts DC. Connect voltmeter from battery (+) to pin 4 self-test output in the self-test connector.

4. Connect a timing light according to manufacturer's instructions.

NOTE: If a STAR tester is available, follow the manufacturer's instructions to connect it to the system. The STAR tester will give a digital trouble code readout.

Service Codes

The EEC IV system relays service information to the technician via the self-test service codes. These codes are two digit numbers representing the results of the self-test. The code impulses can be read as sweeps or pulses of the needle on an analog voltmeter, or as an actual digital number readout on the STAR test equipment. The pulse format is usually 1/2 second ON time for each digit of a trouble code, 2 seconds OFF time between digits, 4 seconds OFF time between codes and 6 seconds OFF time before and after the 1/2 second separator pulse. All testing is complete when the codes have been repeated once.

NOTE: Engine ID and Fast Codes are issued at the beginning of the engine running and self-test modes. Some meters in service may detect these codes as a short burst (meter deflection) but they serve no purpose in the field.

With the Key ON/Engine OFF and Engine Running tests, the EEC IV system components are checked by applying voltage with the engine at rest and running. A fault must be present in the system at the time of testing to be detected and registered as a trouble code. The Continuous Self-Test has the ability to store a service code indicating a suspected problem. The information from this test must be retrieved prior to turning the key off as the codes are erased each time the ignition switch is turned off. In the continuous test mode, the technician is able to monitor the self-test output while operating the engine. With the self-test NOT triggered and an analog voltmeter attached to the Self-Test Output, observe the meter while wiggling, moving or tapping the system harness, connectors or sensors. If an intermittent problem is present, the meter will deflect each time a failure or short occurs and a service code will be stored. These codes can then be retrieved by performing a normal self-test.

Quick Test

1.0 VISUAL CHECK AND VEHICLE PREPARATION

Correct test results for the Quick Test are dependent on the proper operation of related non-EEC components/systems. It may be necessary to correct any defects in these areas before EEC will pass Quick Test. Refer to Diagnostic Routines, Section 2 for service.

Before hooking up any equipment to diagnose the EEC system, make the following checks:

- Verify the condition of air cleaner and ducting.
- Check all engine vacuum hoses for leaks or pinched lines.
- Check the EEC system wiring harness electrical connections for loose or detached connectors, wires and terminals.
- Check EEC-IV module, sensors and actuators for physical damage.
- Perform all safety steps required to start and run operational vehicle tests.
- Apply the emergency brake, place shift lever in Park, Neutral for manual transmission. (Do not move these during testing.)
- Turn Off all vehicle electrical loads, such as the radio, lights, air conditioner, etc. Be sure vehicle doors are shut whenever readings are made.
- Verify engine coolant is at the specified level.
- Start engine and idle until the upper radiator hose is hot and pressurized.

  NOTE: If the engine will not start or starts and stalls, continue with this Step (1.0), and on through Steps 2.0, 3.0, and 4.0 of Quick Test.
- Turn ignition key Off.
- In the case of intermittent problems, complete Quick Test (Steps 2.0, 3.0, 4.0, 5.0 and 6.0) on through Continuous Testing.

2.0 EQUIPMENT HOOK-UP

- Turn ignition key to Off.
- Connect timing light.
- Connect STAR cable to vehicle Self-Test connector.
- STAR power switch On, release STAR pushbutton (no colon).

STAR HOOKUP
(WITH ADAPTER CABLE ASSEMBLY)

LED LIGHT

VEHICLE SELF-TEST CONNECTORS

STAR SERVICE CONNECTORS

Quick Test

TEST STEP	RESULT ▶	ACTION TO TAKE
4.0 CHECK TIMING		
• Release STAR pushbutton (no colon).	Timing is 27-33 degrees BTDC ▶	GO to 5.0 .
• Restart engine.	Timing is not 27-33 degrees BTDC ▶	GO to Q1 .
• STAR pushbutton depressed (colon showing).		
• Check timing while in Self-Test.		

NOTE: If engine stalls while testing, GO to Pinpoint Test T, Diagnostics by Symptom.

16° BTDC 8° 0°

0°

PULLEY

33° 27°

Quick Test

TEST STEP	RESULT ▶	ACTION TO TAKE
3.0 KEY ON, ENGINE OFF SELF TEST		
• Place transmission in Neutral or Park, set parking brake, A/C control off, turn key to run. Depress STAR pushbutton (colon showing). Observe and record the service codes as outputed on the STAR. This step applies to service codes received before code 10 is displayed.	Code 11 ▶	CONTINUE to Quick Test Step 4.0 . For no starts GO to Pinpoint Step A1 .
When more than one service code is received, always start with the 1st code received.	No Codes ▶	GO to Pinpoint Test Step P1 , No Codes.
NOTE: Do not move shift lever or clutch during test.	Service Code 15 ▶	REPLACE processor and RETEST.
• If an intermittent vehicle condition is present, continue with this step (3.0) and on through step 6.0 of quick test.	Service Code 21 ▶	GO to Pinpoint Test F .
	Service Code 23 ▶	GO to Pinpoint Test E .
	Service Code 24 ▶	GO to Pinpoint Test Step D10 .
	Service Code 26 ▶	GO to Pinpoint Test D .
	Service Code 67 ▶	GO to Pinpoint Test V .
	Any codes other than those listed above. ▶	GO to Pinpoint Test P .

NOTE: Before proceeding to a specific Pinpoint Test, read the instructions at the start of the Pinpoint Tests.

Quick Test

TEST STEP	RESULT ▶	ACTION TO TAKE
5.0 ENGINE RUNNING TEST		
• Release STAR pushbutton (no colon). Run engine at 2000 rpm for 2 minutes (EGO warm up)	No code SERVICE CODES ▶	GO to Pinpoint Test P .
• Restart engine and idle.	11 System OK ▶	If the drive symptom is still present, GO to Pinpoint Test T , Diagnostics by Symptom.
• Depress STAR pushbutton (colon displayed).		If the concern was of an intermittent nature, GO to Step 6.0 , Continuous Testing; otherwise, testing is complete.
• Code #20 will be displayed followed within 60 seconds by the service codes. Observe and record these service codes. This step applies to service codes received before code 10 is displayed.		EEC-IV System OK.
• If the engine stalls while testing, go to Pinpoint Test T, Diagnostics by Symptom.	12 ▶	GO to Pinpoint Test K .
• When more than one service code is received, always start with the first code received.	13 ▶	GO to Pinpoint Test K .
	21 ▶	GO to Pinpoint Test F .
	23 ▶	GO to Pinpoint Test E .
	24 ▶	GO to Pinpoint Test Step D10 .
	26 ▶	GO to Pinpoint Test D .
	41 ▶	GO to Pinpoint Test Step H8 .
	42 ▶	GO to Pinpoint Test Step H5 .

EEC IV-1.6L Engine Diagnosis

Quick Test

6.0	CONTINUOUS TESTING

NOTE: Service codes are lost when ignition key is turned off.

IMPLEMENTING CONTINUOUS TEST

- Key Off.
- Connect STAR cable to vehicle Self-Test connector. STAR power switch On and pushbutton switch out (no colon).
- Key On, Engine Off or Engine Running. Take safety precautions for working on a running engine. If engine stalls, do not turn the key Off or restart engine or else service codes would be lost.
- Wiggle, move, twist, the vehicle harness, tap shake or otherwise exercise sensor, (i.e., start from cold, monitor through warm up, etc.). Monitor STAR indicator light while doing the above. If at any time the indicator light goes Off or blinks, this indicates an intermittent short or open has occurred in a sensor circuit.

  (NOTE: Sensor circuit could be the harness, sensor, or processor.)
- Once the intermittent has been induced, the indicator light goes Off and the appropriate service code has also been stored. Do not turn the key Off, or codes will be lost. Depress STAR pushbutton (colon showing) (Engine Running or Key On), and observe the service code(s).

  NOTE: Self-Test can only be run once without turning the ignition key Off, so do not miss reading any service codes.
- Vehicle may be operated with STAR connected to verify if STAR indicator light goes Off when symptom occurs. If light does go Off, do not turn ignition key Off or codes will be lost. Depress STAR pushbutton (colon showing) to read out service codes.

These codes indicate a short or open circuit has been detected in the following monitored circuits:

```
21 — ECT, CKT 354, LG/Y (J1 pin 7)
     Sig Rtn, CKT 359, BK/W (J1 pin 12)
23 — TPS, CKT 355, DG/LG (J1 pin 9)
     Sig Rtn, CKT 359, BK/W (J1 pin 12)
     Vref, CKT 351, O/W (J1 pin 11)
24 — VAT, CKT 357, LG/P (J1 pin 10)
     Sig Rtn, CKT 359, BK/W (J1 pin 12)
26 — VAF, CKT 200, W/BK (J1 pin 10)
     Sig Rtn, CKT 359, BK/W (J1 pin 12)
     Vref, CKT 351, O/W (J1 pin 11)
```

In the event one of these service codes are received from the Continuous Test, disassemble the associated harness connectors (circuits indicated above) and inspect for improper crimps, over-insulation, etc. If OK, repeat the Continuous Test. This time, move, wiggle and tap the harness while observing the Continuous Test monitor. If the fault cannot be isolated, substitute the affected sensor. If the fault is still present, substitute the processor using the original sensor.

A fuel control service code will be stored whenever the fuel system is forced from closed loop* into open loop* fuel control due to lack of EGO sensor activity. This lack of activity could be rich or lean for more than 15 seconds while in closed loop fuel control.

Pinpoint Tests

INSTRUCTIONS FOR USING THE PINPOINT TESTS

- Do not run any of the following Pinpoint Tests unless you are so instructed by the Quick Test. Each Pinpoint Test assumes that a fault has been detected in the system with direction to enter a specific repair routine. Doing any Pinpoint Test without direction from Quick Test may produce incorrect results and replacement of Non-Defective components.
- Correct test results for Quick Test are dependent on the proper operation of related non-EEC components/systems. It may be necessary to correct any defects in these areas before EEC will pass the Quick Test. Refer to the Diagnostic Routines, Section 2 for service.
- Do not replace any parts unless the test result indicates they should be replaced.
- When more than one service code is received, always start service with the first code received.
- Do not measure voltage or resistance at the control module or connect any test lights to it, unless otherwise specified.
- Isolate both ends of a circuit, and turn key Off whenever checking for shorts or continuity, unless specified.
- Disconnect solenoids and switches from the harness before measuring for continuity, resistance, or energizing by way of 12v source.
- In using the Pinpoint Tests follow each step in order, starting from the first Step in the appropriate test. Follow each Step until the fault is found.
- After completing any repairs to the EEC system, verify all components are properly reconnected and repeat the functional test (Retest).
- An open is defined as any resistance reading greater than 5 ohms unless otherwise specified.
- A short is defined as any resistance reading less than 10,000 ohms to ground unless otherwise specified.

The standard Ford color abbreviations are:

BK	Black	O	Orange
BR	Brown	PK	Pink
DB	Dark Blue	P	Purple
DG	Dark Green	R	Red
GY	Gray	T	Tan
LB	Light Blue	W	White
LG	Light Green	Y	Yellow
N	Natural		

Where two colors are shown for a wire, the first color is the basic color of the wire. The second color is the dot, hash, or stripe marking. If **D** or **H** is given, the second color is dots or hash marks. If there is no letter after the second color, the wire has a stripe.

For example:

BR/O is a brown wire with an orange stripe.

R/Y D is a red wire with yellow dots.

BK/W H is a black wire with white hash marks.

Quick Test

6.0	CONTINUOUS TESTING — Continued

41 — EGO indicated the fuel system was lean for more than 15 seconds when the system should have been in closed loop fuel control.

42 — EGO indicated the fuel system was rich for more than 15 seconds when the system should have been in closed loop fuel control.

*CLOSED LOOP — Fuel control under the influence of the EGO sensor.

*OPEN LOOP — Fuel control NOT under the influence of the EGO sensor.

Before attempting to correct a fuel control code, 41/42, diagnose all other drive complaints first, eg., rough idle, misses, etc.

NOTE: The fuel control code may help in this diagnosis.

Using the fuel control service code, isolate the cause of the fuel control problem.

Some areas to check are:

- **Unmetered Air:** Vacuum leaks/intake air leaks.
  - — Canister Purge System
  - — PCV System
  - — Engine sealing
  - — Air leaks between VAF meter and throttle body.
- **EGO Fuel Fouled:** Whenever an over-rich fuel condition has been experienced (fuel fouled spark plugs), make a thorough check of the ignition system. In the event the EGO sensor is suspected of being fuel fouled (low output, slow response), run the vehicle at sustained high speeds (within legal limits) followed by a few hard accells. This will burn off EGO contamination and restore proper EGO operation.
- **Fuel Pressure:** Perform Pinpoint Test Steps A-11 and A-12 only.
- **Ignition System:** Always in default spark (10 degrees). Refer to Quick Test Step 4.0.
- **Improper Fueling:** Lead fouled EGO sensor.
- **TP Sensor:** Not moving (mechanical damage). Connect DVOM to J1 pin 9 CKT 355 DG/LG and to J1 pin 12, CKT 359 BK/W. Key to Run observe DVOM while moving the throttle. Reading must increase with increase in throttle opening. If not correct, REPLACE as necessary.

No Start Problem	Pinpoint Test	A

A

STOP-WARNING

You may have reached this point because of a fault in a non-EEC System and/or component. To prevent the replacement of good components, be aware that the following non-EEC areas may be at fault:

- Fuel, quantity and quality.
- Ignition, general condition, moisture, cracks, damage, etc.
- Engine, internal, valves, timing belt, camshaft.
- Starter and battery circuit.

This Pinpoint Test is intended to diagnose only the following:

- Spark (as related to EEC-IV).
- Fuel delivery (as related to EEC-IV).

EEC IV-1.6L Engine Diagnosis

No Start Problem	Pinpoint Test	A

TEST STEP	RESULT	▶	ACTION TO TAKE
FUEL PRESSURE CHECK			
WARNING: Stop this test at the first sign of a fuel leak. **CAUTION: No open flame — No smoking during fuel delivery checks.**			
A1 INSTALL FUEL PRESSURE GAUGE			
● Refer to illustration A.	Fuel Leaks	▶	CORRECT as necessary before proceeding.
● Cycle the ignition switch from Off to Run several times, attempting to pressurize the fuel system. **(Check for fuel leaks.)**	No Fuel Leaks	▶	GO to A2.
A2 TRY TO START THE ENGINE			
● Key to Start position (attempt to start the engine).	Engine cranks but does not start or cranks and attempts to start but will not continue to run, runs rough or misses	▶	GO to A3*.
	Engine does not crank	▶	Check for hydraulic lock, then starting/charging system. Refer to Shop Manual Groups 28 & 31.
*NOTE: Clearing a flooded engine is accomplished by holding the throttle wide open.			

No Start Problem	Pinpoint Test	A

TEST STEP	RESULT	▶	ACTION TO TAKE
A5 IGNITION MODULE SIGNAL (IMS) CHECK			
● DVOM on 20v range. Connect DVOM to J2 pin 14 to chassis ground.	Yes	▶	EEC OK service, no spark condition per TFI routines.
● Crank engine, record reading.	No	▶	CONTINUE to A6.
● Reading is 3.0v-6.0v.			

CKT. 60, BK/LG IGN. GND. — PIN 6
CKT. 324 Y/LG D. IMS* — PIN 2
CKT. 349 DB. D.O.S.* — PIN 1
CONNECTOR VIEWED FROM REAR (WIRE SIDE)
AT TFI
*IMS — IGNITION MODULE SIGNAL
*DOS — DISTRIBUTOR OUTPUT SIGNAL

A6 HARNESS CHECK (IMS CKT)			
● Refer to illustration, Step A5.			
● Key Off, J2 disconnected.	Greater than 2000 ohms	▶	CONTINUE to A7.
● Check circuit 324, J2 pin 14, for shorts to ground.	Less than 2000 ohms	▶	Isolate short if in vehicle harness. SERVICE as required if in TFI module per Section 15.
A7 DISTRIBUTOR OUTPUT SIGNAL CHECK (DSO)			
● Refer to illustration, Step A5.			
● DVOM to 20v range. Disconnect J1 and J2.	Yes	▶	INSPECT processor connectors for bent, damaged, or corroded terminals. SERVICE as required. If OK, REPLACE processor.
● Connect DVOM to J1 pin 14, and J2 pin 5.			
● Crank engine, record reading.	No	▶	CONTINUE to A8A.
● Reading is 3.0v-6.0v.			

No Start Problem	Pinpoint Test	A

TEST STEP	RESULT	▶	ACTION TO TAKE
A3 SPARK CHECK (AT SPARK PLUG)			
● Using a modified spark plug*,check for spark at a plug wire while cranking.	Yes	▶	GO to A9.
● Good hot spark.	No	▶	GO to A4.
*Spark plug with side electrode removed.			
A4 SPARK CHECK (AT IGNITION COIL)			
● Refer to illustration, Step A3.			
● Remove high tension coil wire from the **distributor** and install the modified spark plug*. Check for spark while cranking.	Yes	▶	GO to TFI diagnosis for cap, rotor, wires.
● Good hot spark.	No	▶	GO to A5.
*Spark plug with side electrode removed.			

No Start Problem	Pinpoint Test	A

TEST STEP	RESULT	▶	ACTION TO TAKE
A8A HARNESS CHECK, DISTRIBUTOR SIGNAL CIRCUIT 349			
● Refer to illustration Step A5.			
● Disconnect vehicle harness from TFI at the distributor and J1 from the processor.	No shorts or opens	▶	CONTINUE to A8B.
● Check distributor signal J1 pin 14, circuit 349, dark blue for opens or shorts to grounds or other circuits.	Shorts or opens	▶	SERVICE harness as required.
A8B HARNESS CHECK, IGNITION GROUND CIRCUIT 60			
● Check ignition ground J2 pin 5, circuit 60, black-lt.green dot, to TFI connector pin 6 for opens.	No opens	▶	GO to TFI routines, Section 15.
	Opens	▶	SERVICE harness as necessary.
A9 FUEL PUMP CHECK			
NO SMOKING NEARBY	PRESSURE GAUGE READING:		
● Disconnect all four injector electrical connections at the injectors.	Increased	▶	GO to A11.
	Did not increase	▶	TURN key Off, and CONTINUE to A10.
● Connect pressure gauge to Schraeder valve on injector bar. (Refer to illustration A.)			
● Note initial pressure reading.			
● Observe pressure gauge as you pressurize fuel system (turn key to Run for 1 second, then turn key to Off. Repeat 5 times).			
● Turn key to Off.			
● Reconnect all injectors.			
WARNING: If fuel starts leaking, turn key Off immediately. No smoking.			

EEC IV-1.6L Engine Diagnosis

No Start Problem		Pinpoint Test	A

TEST STEP	RESULT	▶	ACTION TO TAKE
A10 CHECK INERTIA SWITCH	PRESSURE GAUGE READING:		
• Locate fuel pump inertia switch. Refer to owner's manual for location.	Increases	▶	REPEAT Quick Test.
• Push the button of inertia switch to reset it.	Did not increase	▶	GO to **S1**.
• Watch pressure gauge as you attempt to pressurize fuel system. Refer to illustration A.			
NOTE: If switch will not reset to On, replace it.			
A11 CHECK FUEL DELIVERY			
• Pressurize fuel system, Step A9.	Between 35 and 45 psi	▶	GO to **A12**.
• Turn key to Off.			
• Wait for pressure to become steady.	Over 45 psi or under 35 psi	▶	VERIFY ignition coil is connected. REFER to Shop Manual Group 24, for leaking injectors or fuel regulator.
• Read pressure gauge.			
A12 CHECK FOR LEAK DOWN			
• With key off verify all injectors are connected.	4 psi drop or less in 2 minutes	▶	GO to **A13**.
• Wait 2 minutes after pressure gauge reading of Step A11, then note drop in gauge reading.	More than 4 psi drop in 2 minutes	▶	TURN key Off immediately. CHECK for hydraulic lockup or fuel fouled spark plugs. REFER to Shop Manual Group 24 for leaking injector and/or fuel regulator.

No Start Problem		Pinpoint Test	A

TEST STEP	RESULT	▶	ACTION TO TAKE
A15 SERVICING THE SUSPECT INJECTOR/ CIRCUIT			
Refer to illustration, Step A14.			
• Remove the fuel pump relay.	More than 1.0 volt difference	▶	DISCONNECT J1 and J2, INSPECT for corrosion, damaged pins, etc. RECONNECT and RETEST. If problem is still present, REPLACE processor.
• Using the DVOM, measure the average voltage at circuit 95 J2 pin 3 to circuit 361 J2 pin 11 during crank (record reading).	Less than 1.0 volt difference	▶	GO to **A16**.
• Also measure the average voltage at circuit 96 J2 pin 4 to circuit 361 J2 pin 11 during crank (record reading).			
• Reconnect fuel pump relay.			
A16 RESISTANCE CHECK OF THE INJECTOR HARNESS			
Refer to illustration, Step A14.			
• Key Off, DVOM 20 ohms range. Disconnect injectors 2, 3, and 4 electrically.	Yes	▶	CONTINUE to **A17**.
• Through the vehicle harness, measure the resistance of injector #1 cyl. 1 at J2 pin 3 to J2 pin 11 and record reading.	No	▶	CHECK the harness on the suspect injector. If OK, REPLACE the suspect injector. Verify all the injectors are connected at the END of testing.
• Disconnect injector #1 cyl. 1. Reconnect injector #2 cyl. 2. Read resistance at J2 pin 3 to J2 pin 11, record reading.			
• Disconnect injector #2 cyl. 2. Reconnect injector #3 cyl. 3. Read resistance at J2 pin 4 to J2 pin 11, record reading.			
• Disconnect injector #3 cyl. 3. Reconnect injector #4 cyl. 4. Read resistance at J2 pin 4 to J2 pin 11 and record reading.			
• All four readings are 2.0 ohms to 3.5 ohms.			

No Start Problem		Pinpoint Test	A

TEST STEP	RESULT	▶	ACTION TO TAKE
A13 FUEL DELIVERY TEST	PRESSURE GAUGE READING:		
• Pressurize the fuel system as in Step A9. Note: Verify fuel quality, air and/or water will also pressurize and look like acceptable fuel delivery.	Pressure is approximately 10-20 psi at the end of 5 second crank cycle. Refer to note below	▶	The EEC system is not the fault of the No Start. Fuel and spark are present. REFER to the Shop Manual for other No Start Routines. If complaint was runs rough or misses, CONTINUE to **A14**.
• Disable the electric fuel pump (disconnect fuel pump relay).			
• Crank engine for 5 seconds.			
• Take pressure reading at end of 5 second crank.			
• Reconnect fuel pump relay after testing.	Pressure is more or less than specified	▶	GO to **A14**.
NOTE: The colder the engine, the greater the pressure drop. (i.e., an engine coolant temperature of 200°F equals approximately a 10 psi drop in 5 seconds. 60°F equals approximately a 20 psi drop in 5 seconds.			
A14 INJECTOR DRIVER SIGNAL CHECK			
• Requires standard non-powered 12v test lamp.			

CKT. 95 T P D (INJ. A)
CKT. 96 T O D (INJ. B) → TO INJECTORS
CKT. 361 R (V. BATT.) → VEHICLE BATTERY
CONNECTOR AS VIEWED FROM THE REAR (WIRE SIDE)

• Connect test lamp from J2 pin 11 to J2 pin 3.	Dim glow at light on both tests	▶	Normal GO to **A15**.
• Crank engine, observe test lamp results.	No light on one or both tests	▶	VERIFY 12v battery power at J2 pin 11. SERVICE ckt 361 as required. If OK, REPLACE processor.
• Repeat above test from J2 pin 11 to J2 pin 4.	Bright light on one or both tests	▶	CHECK circuits 95 and 96 for shorts to ground. SERVICE as required. If OK, REPLACE processor.

No Start Problem		Pinpoint Test	A

TEST STEP	RESULT	▶	ACTION TO TAKE
A17 ISOLATING A FAULTY INJECTOR	All readings not within 4 psi of each other	▶	REPLACE injector that is not within 4 psi of the others.
• Electrically disconnect all injectors at the intake manifold.			
• Pressurize the fuel system as in Step A9.	All four readings are within 4 psi of each other	▶	VERIFY all the non-EEC Diagnostic Routines that apply to your drive complaint have been properly performed then: DISCONNECT J1 and J2. INSPECT for corrosion, damaged pins, etc., and RETEST. If fault is still present, REPLACE the processor.
• Connect the injector for cylinder #1 only.			
• Crank the engine for 5 seconds.			
• Observe the pressure gauge and record reading immediately at the end of the 5 second crank cycle.			
• Disconnect injector for cylinder #1.			
• Repeat above procedure for injectors 2, 3, or 4 (be sure to connect only one injector at a time).			

EEC IV-1.6L Engine Diagnosis

Vehicle Battery	Pinpoint Test	B

STOP-WARNING

You may have reached this point because of a fault in a non-EEC System and/or component. To prevent the replacement of good components, be aware that the following non-EEC areas may be at fault.

- Ignition Switch
- Voltage Regulator
- Battery Cables
- Ground Straps
- Alternator

This Pinpoint Test is intended to diagnose only the following:

- Vehicle Battery Voltage
- Circuits 37, 57, 60, 359, 361, and 640
- Power Relay
- Processor Assembly

Vehicle Battery	Pinpoint Test	B

TEST STEP	RESULT ▶	ACTION TO TAKE
B4 GROUND FAULT ISOLATION		
Refer to illustration B.		
• DVOM 20v range. Processor connected. Key to Run.	Both readings less than 0.5v ▶	CONTINUE to B5 .
• Take a voltage reading from battery negative (−) post to J2 pin 1.	One or both readings greater than 0.5v ▶	Circuit with greater than 0.5v has high resistance or open. CORRECT faulty ground circuit, circuit 57.
• Repeat above check from battery negative (−) post to J2 pin 2.		
B5 PROCESSOR GROUND FAULT ISOLATION		
Refer to illustration B.		
• Key Off. Processor connected. DVOM on 200 ohm range.	Both reading less than 1 ohm ▶	CONTINUE to B6 .
• Make a resistance measurement from J1 pin 12 to J2 pin 1.	One or both readings greater than 1 ohm ▶	DISCONNECT J1 and J2. INSPECT for corrosion damaged pins etc., and RETEST. If fault is still present, REPLACE processor.
• Repeat above test from J1 pin 12 to J2 pin 2.		
B6 HARNESS CHECK (SIGNAL RETURN)		
Refer to illustration B		
• Key Off. Processor connected. DVOM 200 ohm range.	Reading is less than 5 ohms ▶	System OK, RETEST.
• Make a resistance measurement from J1 pin 12 to circuit 359 blk/wh signal return in the Self-Test connector.	Reading is 5 ohms or greater ▶	CORRECT cause of resistance in the harness circuit 359.

Vehicle Battery	Pinpoint Test	B

TEST STEP	RESULT ▶	ACTION TO TAKE
B1 BATTERY VOLTAGE CHECK		
• Key to Run, engine Off.	Greater than 10.5v ▶	GO to B2 .
• Measure voltage across battery terminals.	10.5v or less ▶	SERVICE discharged battery. REFER to Group 31, Shop Manual.
B2 BATTERY POWER GROUND CHECK		
• Refer to illustration B.		
• Key to Run, engine Off, DVOM on 20v range. Processor connected.	Less than 0.50v ▶	CONTINUE to B3 .
• Take a voltage reading from battery negative (−) post to signal return circuit 359 Blk/Wh in the Self-Test connector.	Greater than 0.50v ▶	CONTINUE to B4 .
• Voltage reading is less than 0.5v.		
B3 12V BATTERY POWER CHECK AT PROCESSOR		
• Refer to illustration B.		
• Key to Run, engine Off.		
• DVOM 20v range. Processor connected. Key to Run.	Both readings less than 0.5v ▶	GO to C1 .
• Take a voltage reading from battery positive (+) post to J2 pin 11.	One or both readings greater than 0.5v ▶	CONTINUE to B7 .
• Repeat above check from battery positive (+) post to J2 pin 12.		

Vehicle Battery	Pinpoint Test	B

TEST STEP	RESULT ▶	ACTION TO TAKE
B7 12V BATTERY POWER FAULT ISOLATION		
• Refer to illustration B.		
• DVOM 20v range. Processor connected. Key to Run, engine Off.		
• DVOM negative (−) lead to battery negative (−) post. Make the following voltage checks:		
• In the event an open fusible link is found, check for shorts to ground before replacing the fusible link.		
NOTE: Key must remain in Run position for all remaining checks.		
a. Check circuit 37, yellow at EEC power relay.	Greater than 10.5v ▶	CONTINUE to b .
	10.5v or less ▶	CHECK circuit 37. Power relay to battery positive (+) for opens. Before servicing CHECK CKT 37 and 361 for shorts to ground.
b. Check circuit 640, Red/Yel H. at the power relay.	Greater than 10.5v ▶	CONTINUE to c .
	10.5v or less ▶	CHECK 10 amp fuse location 18, then for open in ignition switch start/run circuits 640, 16, ignition switch and circuit 37.
c. Check circuit 57, Blk at the power relay.	0.5v or less ▶	CONTINUE to d .
	Greater than 0.5v ▶	CORRECT open ground in circuit 57.
d. Check circuit 361, Red at the EEC power relay.	10.5v or more ▶	CORRECT open in circuit 361 from EEC power relay to J2 pin 11 and/or 12.
	Less than 10.5v ▶	REPLACE power relay.

EEC IV-1.6L Engine Diagnosis

Reference Voltage (Vref)	Pinpoint Test	C

C

STOP-WARNING

This Pinpoint Test is intended to diagnose only the following:

- Circuits 37, 57, 351, 359, 361 and 640
- Processor Assembly
- VAF, and TP Sensor

Reference Voltage	Pinpoint Test	C

TEST STEP	RESULT ▶	ACTION TO TAKE
C5 CHECK FOR SHORTED THROTTLE POSITION SENSOR		
• Do not disconnect processor.	DVOM READING	
• Disconnect Throttle Position (TP) sensor from vehicle harness.	4.0v or less ▶	GO TO C6 .
• Turn key to Run, engine Off.	More than 4.0v ▶	REPLACE TP sensor.
• With DVOM, measure between connector terminals J1-11 and J1-12.		
C6 CHECK FOR SHORTED VANE AIR METER		
• Do not disconnect processor.	DVOM READING	
• Disconnect VAF sensor from vehicle harness.	4.0v or less ▶	GO TO C7 .
• Key On.	More than 4.0v ▶	REPLACE VAF Meter.
• With DVOM, measure between connector terminals J1-11 and J1-12.		RECONNECT TP sensor.
C7 CHECK VPWR AND GROUND HARNESS CONTINUITY		
• Refer to illustration C.		
• Turn key Off.	DVOM READING	
	All circuits less than 1 ohm ▶	GO to C8 .
• Disconnect EEC processor from vehicle harness.	Any circuit more than 1 ohm ▶	SERVICE open circuit or bad connection in harness.
• DVOM to 200 ohm scale.		
• Check continuity from J2-1 and J2-2 to battery negative (−) post, J2-11 and J2-12 to circuit 361 (red) terminal on power relay.		
C8 CHECK FOR EEC HARNESS SHORTS		
	DVOM READING	
• Disconnect harness connector from module and check for short circuits between VREF (J1-11) on connector and remaining pins on connectors J1 and J2. Verify TP and VAF/VAT sensors are still disconnected.	10,000 ohms or more ▶	REPLACE processor assembly.
	Under 10,000 ohms ▶	SERVICE short. RECONNECT all sensors.

Reference Voltage	Pinpoint Test	C

TEST STEP	RESULT ▶	ACTION TO TAKE
C1 VEHICLE BATTERY POWER CIRCUIT CHECK		
• Refer to illustration C.		
• DVOM 20v range, J1 and J2 connected to processor.	Greater than 10.5v ▶	CONTINUE to C2 .
• Probe from J2 pin 11 to circuit 359, signal return Blk/Wh, in the Self-Test connector.	10.5v or less ▶	GO to Pinpoint Test B1 .
• Key in Run, reading must be greater than 10.5v.		
C2 VREF VOLTAGE CHECK		
• Refer to illustration C.	DVOM READING	
• Turn key to Run, engine Off.	More than 6.0v ▶	GO to C3 .
• With DVOM, measure between J1-11 and J1-12 at the back of the module connector (leave connected).	Less than 4.0v ▶	GO to C5 .
	4.0 to 6.0v ▶	RETEST system.
C3 CHECK FOR SHORT TO BATTERY VOLTAGE		
• Refer to illustration C.	DVOM READING	
• Turn key to Off.	0.5v or less ▶	GO to C4 .
• Leave DVOM connected as in Step C2.	More than 0.5v ▶	SERVICE short between VREF and battery power circuits.
C4 CHECK FOR SHORT TO PROCESSOR POWER (VPWR)		
• Refer to illustration C.	DVOM READING	
• Disconnect processor assembly from harness.	0.5v or less ▶	REPLACE processor assembly.
• Turn key to Run, engine Off.	More than 0.5v ▶	SERVICE short between VREF and battery power in EEC-IV harness.
• With DVOM, measure between connector terminals J1-11 and J1-12.		

Vane Air Flow/Temp	Pinpoint Test	D

STOP-WARNING

You may have reached this point because of a fault in a non-EEC System and/or component. To prevent the replacement of good components, be aware that the following non-EEC areas may be at fault:

- Check for unmetered air (air leaks) between VAF meter and throttle body.
- Vacuum leaks (PCV system, CANP system engine sealing).

This Pinpoint Test is intended to diagnose only the following:

- VAF meter
- Processor
- Harness circuits 190, 280, 351, 359.

VAF Sensor Total Resistance (Vref. to Sig R + M is 560 ohms)	VAT Typical Resistance and Voltages for a given temperature
	40°F = 5000 ohms = 3.6v
	100°F = 1200 ohms = 2.3v
	200°F = 240 ohms = 0.7v
	240°F = 150 ohms = 0.42v

EEC IV-1.6L Engine Diagnosis

Vane Air Flow Meter	Pinpoint Test	D

TEST STEP	RESULT ▶	ACTION TO TAKE
D1 VANE AIR FLOW (VAF) METER CODE 26		
• Refer to illustration D. • Connect DVOM to J1 pin 10 and J1 pin 12. • Rerun appropriate (*) Self-Test while monitoring DVOM.	Yes ▶	DISCONNECT J1 and J2, INSPECT for corrosion, damaged pins, etc. RECONNECT and RETEST. If problem is still present, REPLACE the processor.
• DVOM reads key On engine Off .20v to .50v. Key On engine Running 1.35v to 2.70v.	No ▶	CONTINUE to D2 .
D2 VAF METER CIRCUIT CHECK		
• Refer to illustration D.	No opens or shorts to ground. ▶	REPLACE Vane Air Flow meter **(NOTE: also contains VAT sensor as one unit).**
• Check circuits 200, 351 and 359 for opens and shorts to ground. Sensor and processor must be disconnected.	Open or short to ground ▶	REPAIR harness.
• It is necessary to disconnect the TP sensor when performing this Step. Reconnect all sensors after testing.		
(*) Appropriate Self-Test refers to key On, engine Off, or Engine Running, whichever led to this Pinpoint Test.		

Throttle Position	Pinpoint Test	E

E

J-2 / J-1 CONNECTORS AS VIEWED FROM THE REAR (WIRE SIDE)

PIN 9 / PIN 11 / PIN 12

CKT. 355 DG/LG (TP)
CKT. 351 O/W (V REF.)
CKT. 359 BK/W (SIG RTN)

TP SENSOR

STOP-WARNING

You may have reached this point because of a fault in a non-EEC System and/or component. To prevent the replacement of good components, be aware that the following non-EEC areas may be at fault:

• Idle Speeds/Throttle Stop Adustment
• Binding Throttle Shaft/Linkage or Cruise Control Linkage

This Pinpoint Test is intended to diagnose only the following:

• TP Sensor
• Sensor Harness Circuits 351, 355, and 359
• Processor Assembly
• TP Sensor total resistance (Vref. to Signal Return) is 3800 ohms

Vane Air Flow Meter	Pinpoint Test	D

TEST STEP	RESULT ▶	ACTION TO TAKE
D10 VANE AIR TEMP SENSOR: CODE 24		
CAUTION: Code 24 could result from problems with the heated inlet air system. Check for proper operation.		
• Refer to illustration D. • Disconnect J1 from the processor.	DVOM reading is between 100 ohms (270 F) and 4000 ohms (40 F) ▶	CONTINUE to D11 .
• Make a resistance measurement at disconnected J-1 from J-1 pin 8 to J1 pin 12.	DVOM reading is under 100 ohms (270 F) or over 4000 (40 F) ▶	CHECK circuits 357 and 359 for opens, SERVICE as required if no opens in CKT 357 & 359 CKT OK. REPLACE the VAF/VAT meter.
NOTE: Ambient temperature must be greater than 40°F for this test.		
D11 VANE AIR TEMP SENSOR CHECK		
• Refer to illustration D. • DVOM 200,000 ohms scale.	Greater than 10K (no shorts) ▶	DISCONNECT J1 and J2. INSPECT for corrosion damaged pins, etc. RECONNECT and RETEST, Code 24 still present. REPLACE processor.
• With VAT/VAF meter and processor disconnected from the harness, check circuit 357 for short to ground.	10K or less (short to ground) ▶	CORRECT short to ground in CKT 357.

Throttle Position Sensor	Pinpoint Test	E

TEST STEP	RESULT ▶	ACTION TO TAKE
E1 TP SENSOR CODE 23		
• Refer to illustration E. • Disconnect ISC solenoid and verify curb idle per emission decal. Adjust as necessary. Disregard this step for No Starts. • Connect DVOM to J1 pin 9 and J1 pin 12. • Rerun and appropriate (*) Self-Test while monitoring DVOM.	Yes ▶	DISCONNECT J1 and J2. INSPECT for corrosion, damaged pins, etc. RECONNECT and RETEST. If problem is still present, REPLACE processor.
• DVOM reads .50v to 1.30v during test.	No ▶	CONTINUE to E2 .
E2 VREF VOLTAGE CHECK		
• Refer to illustration E. • Key On, engine Off. DVOM to 20v range. Processor connected.	Yes ▶	CONTINUE to E3 .
• Make a voltage measurement at J1 pin 11, (Vref) to J1 pin 12, (signal return).	4.0v or less ▶	GO to Pinpoint Test C5 .
• DVOM reads 4.0v to 6.0v.	6.0v or more ▶	GO to Pinpoint Test C3 .
E3 TP CIRCUIT CHECK		
• Refer to illustration E. • Key Off sensor disconnected, check harness circuits 351, 355 and 359 for opens and shorts to ground.	No shorts to ground or opens ▶	REPLACE TP sensor. **NOTE: TP sensor is not adjustable.**
• It is necessary to disconnect the VAF/VAT sensor when performing this Step. Reconnect all sensors after testing.	Shorts to ground or opens ▶	REPAIR harness.
(*) Appropriate Self-Test refers to key On, engine Off, or Engine Running, whichever led to this Pinpoint Test.		

EEC IV-1.6L Engine Diagnosis

Engine Coolant		Pinpoint Test	F

STOP-WARNING

You may have reached this point because of a fault in a non-EEC System and/or component. To prevent the replacement of good components, be aware that the following non-EEC areas may be at fault:

- Coolant Level
- Oil Level
- Block or Obstructed Air Flow
- Engine Not at Normal Operating Temperature
- Electro-Drive Cooling Fan

This Pinpoint Test is intended to diagnose only the following:

- ECT Sensor
- Harness Circuits 354 and 359
- Processor Assembly

ECT SENSOR typical resistance and voltage for given temperature:

40°F	=	155,000 ohms	=	3.7v
60°F	=	95,000 ohms	=	3.3v
200°F	=	2,350 ohms	=	.55v
240°F	=	1,300 ohms	=	.30v

Fuel Control		Pinpoint Test	H

TEST STEP	RESULT ▶	ACTION TO TAKE

H

STOP-WARNING

You may have reached this point because of a fault in a non-EEC System and/or component. To prevent the replacement of good components, be aware that the following non-EEC areas may be at fault:

- Ignition Coil
- Distributor Cap
- Distributor Rotor
- Fouled Spark Plugs
- Spark Plug Wires
- CANP Problems
- PCV Valves (see note below).

- EGR Valve and Gasket
- Air Filter
- Fuel Contamination, Engine Oil
- Poor Power Ground
- Fuel Pressure
- Manifold Leaks, Intake/Exhaust
- Engine Not at Normal Operating Temperatures

This Pinpoint Test is intended to diagnose only the following:

- EGO Sensor
- Harness Circuits 89, 94, 95, 96, 361
- EGO Sensor Connection

- Vacuum Systems
- Fuel Injectors
- Processor Assembly

— CODE 42 start at H-5.
— CODE 41 start at H-8.

NOTE: Fuel contaminated engine oil may affect 4-1, 4-2 Service Codes, so if it is suspected, remove the PCV from the valve cover, and rerun the Quick Test. If the problem is corrected, then change the engine oil and filter.

Engine Coolant Temperature Sensor (ECT)		Pinpoint Test	F

TEST STEP	RESULT ▶	ACTION TO TAKE
F1 VERIFY REFERENCE VOLTAGE		
• Refer to illustration F. • DVOM 20v range. Processor connected. Key On, engine Off. • Take voltage measurement at J1 pin 11 to J1 pin 12.	4.0v to 6.0v ▶	CONTINUE to **F2**.
	Not 4.0v to 6.0v ▶	GO to Pinpoint Test **C1**.
F2 ENGINE COOLANT TEMP SENSOR CHECK		
To pass the key On, engine Off test, the engine coolant **must** be 50-240°F. To pass the key On, engine Running test, the engine coolant **must** be 165-240°F.		
• Refer to illustration F. • Disconnect J1 from the processor. • DVOM on 200,000 ohms range. • Make a resistance measurement at disconnected J1 pin 7 to J1 pin 12. • Is the reading from **For No Starts:** 1300 ohms (240°F) to 58,000 ohms (50°F). **For Engine Runs:** (at normal operating temperature) 1300 ohms (240°F) to 4450 ohms (165°F).	Yes ▶	CONTINUE to **F3**.
	No ▶	CHECK circuits 354 and 359 for opens. SERVICE as required. If OK, REPLACE the ECT sensor.
F3 ECT HARNESS CHECK		
• Refer to illustration F. • DVOM 200,000 ohms range. • With J1 disconnected, check circuit 354, J1-7 for shorts to ground.	Greater than 10K ohms (no shorts) ▶	DISCONNECT J1 and J2. INSPECT for corrosion, damaged pins, etc. and RECONNECT and RETEST. If code 21 is still present, REPLACE processor.
	10K ohms or less (short to ground present) ▶	ISOLATE and CORRECT short to ground in harness circuit 354 or sensor and RETEST.

Fuel Control		Pinpoint Test	H

TEST STEP	RESULT ▶	ACTION TO TAKE
H1 FUEL PRESSURE CHECK		
• Refer to illustration H. • Install fuel pressure gauge. • Start and Run engine fuel pressure must be 25-45 psi **For No Starts:** • If engine will not run, cycle the key from Off to On several times. • Fuel pressure must remain at 40 psi ± 5 psi for 60 seconds after final key Off.	Fuel pressure is within specifications ▶	GO to **H2**.
	Fuel pressure is not as specified ▶	REFER to the Shop Manual for electric fuel pump and fuel regulator check.

EEC IV-1.6L Engine Diagnosis

Fuel Control	Pinpoint Test	H

TEST STEP	RESULT ▶	ACTION TO TAKE
H2 HARNESS/INJECTOR RESISTANCE CHECK		

TEST STEP	RESULT ▶	ACTION TO TAKE
• Refer to illustration H2. • Key Off, DVOM 200 ohms range. Disconnect injectors for cylinders 2, 3, and 4 electrically.	Yes ▶	OK. Continue to **H3**.
• Through the vehicle harness, measure the resistance of injector #1 cyl. 1 at J2 pin 3 to J2 pin 11 record reading.	No ▶	SERVICE the harness/connectors on the suspect injector for opens or shorts. If OK, REPLACE injector.
• Disconnect injector #1 cyl. 1. Reconnect injector #2 cyl. 2. Read resistance at J2 pin 3 to J2 pin 11 record reading. • Disconnect injector #2 cyl. 2. Reconnect injector #3 cyl. 3. Read resistance at J2 pin 4 to J2 pin 11 record reading. • Disconnect injector #3 cyl. 3. Reconnect injector #4 cyl. 4. Read resistance at J2 pin 4 to J2 pin 11 record reading. • All four (4) readings are 2.0 ohms to 3.5 ohms. • Verify all injectors are connected at end of testing.		

Fuel Control	Pinpoint Test	H

TEST STEP	RESULT ▶	ACTION TO TAKE
H4 INJECTOR BALANCE TEST		

TEST STEP	RESULT ▶	ACTION TO TAKE
• Connect tachometer to engine. Run engine at 2000 rpm. May be necessary to disconnect ISC and use throttle body stop screw to set engine speed.	Yes ▶	Fuel delivery OK. Problem is with area common to all cylinders, i.e.: Air/vac leak, fuel contamination, EGR.
• Disconnect and reconnect the injectors one at a time; note rpm drop for each injector. • Does each injector produce at least a 150 rpm drop? • Reset curb idle and verify ISC connection at end of testing.	No ▶	REPLACE suspect injector.
H5 FUEL CONTROL — ALWAYS RICH, CODE 42		
• Refer to illustration Step H2.		
• Disconnect vehicle harness at the EGO sensor. Using a jumper wire, ground circuit 94. EGO Sensor input to the engine block.	Yes ▶	GO to **H7**.
• Rerun the engine running test.	No ▶	GO to **H6**.
• Service Code 41 results.		

Fuel Control	Pinpoint Test	H

TEST STEP	RESULT ▶	ACTION TO TAKE
H3 INJECTOR DRIVE SIGNAL CHECK		
Requires standard non-powered 12v test lamp. • Refer to illustration H2. • Connect test lamp from J-2 pin 11 to J2 pin 3.	Dim glow at light on both tests ▶	Normal GO to **H4**.
• Crank or start engine.	No light on one or both tests ▶	VERIFY 12v battery power at J2 pin 11. If OK, REPLACE processor.
• Repeat above test from J2 pin 11 to J2 pin 4.	Bright light on one or both tests ▶	CHECK circuits 95 and 96 for shorts to ground. If OK, REPLACE processor.

Fuel Control	Pinpoint Test	H

TEST STEP	RESULT ▶	ACTION TO TAKE
H6 HARNESS CHECK		
• Refer to illustration Step H2. • Verify continuity of circuit 89 org, J1 pin 5 to EGO ground.	Yes ▶	DISCONNECT J1 and J2. INSPECT for damage or corrosion. If OK, REPLACE processor.
• Verify continuity of circuit 94, J1 pin 6 to EGO connector. • Both circuits less than 5 ohms.	No ▶	CORRECT harness.
H7 EGO CHECK		
• Refer to illustration Step H2. • DVOM on 20v range.	Yes ▶	EGO sensor OK. GO to **H1**.
• With EGO sensor disconnected from the harness, connect a DVOM from EGO sensor to engine ground.	No ▶	REPLACE EGO sensor and RETEST.
• Run the engine at 2000 rpm for 2 minutes while observing DVOM. Disconnect the manifold vacuum hose indicated. Refer to illustration, Step H7. • Meter indicates less than 0.4 volts.		

EEC IV-1.6L Engine Diagnosis

Fuel Control		Pinpoint Test	H

TEST STEP	RESULT ▶	ACTION TO TAKE
H8 FUEL CONTROL — ALWAYS LEAN, CODE 41		
• Refer to illustration H2.		
• Key Off. DVOM to 20v range. Disconnect EGO sensor from vehicle harness. Connect DVOM to EGO sensor and engine ground. Remove air cleaner to gain access to air meter inlet. Using a standard wood lead pencil, prop the air meter door part-way open.	Yes ▶ No ▶	GO to **H9**. REPLACE EGO sensor.
• Start the engine and run at approximately 2000 rpm for 2 minutes.		
• Does the DVOM read greater than 0.5v at the end of 2 minutes?		
H9 HARNESS CHECK EGO CIRCUIT		
• Verify EGO circuits 89 and 94 for continuity.	OK ▶ Not OK ▶	DISCONNECT J1 & J2. INSPECT for corrosion, dent/ damaged pins, etc. SERVICE as required. If OK, REPLACE processor & RETEST. REPAIR/CORRECT and RETEST.

Idle Speed Control (ISC)		Pinpoint Test	K

TEST STEP	RESULT ▶	ACTION TO TAKE
K IDLE SPEED CONTROL		

Code 12 Failed elevated rpm check.
Code 13 Failed at idle rpm check.
 	
CAUTION: If the engine exhibits rough running and/or idle, correct these conditions before diagnosing Idle Speed Control (ISC).
Rough running/misses may be caused by:
  • Ignition System
    Refer to Section 15.
  • Fuel System
    Refer to Pinpoint Test Steps H1 through H4 of EEC diagnostics
  • EGR System, Section 6.		

K1 CODE 13; FOR CODE 12 GO TO K2		
• Refer to illustration K. • Verify curb idle per emission decal.	Curb idle OK ▶ Curb idle not OK ▶	CONTINUE to **K2**. CORRECT and RETEST.

Idle Speed Control		Pinpoint Test	K

K

IDLE SPEED CONTROL SOLENOID (ISC)

STOP-WARNING

You may have reached this point because of a fault in a non-EEC System and/or component. To prevent the replacement of good components, be aware that the following non-EEC areas may be at fault:

- Engine Not at Operating Temperature
- Engine Over Operating Temperature
- Improper Idle Speeds/Throttle Stop Adj.
- A/C Input (Electrical Problems)
- Throttle Linkage
- Inlet Air Problems (heat stove)
- Cruise Control Linkage

This Pinpoint Test is intended to diagnose only the following:

- RPM in Self-Test only
- ISC Actuator
- Harness Circuits 57, 67, 68, 36
- Processor Assembly

Idle Speed Control (ISC)		Pinpoint Test	K

TEST STEP	RESULT ▶	ACTION TO TAKE
K2 ISC CIRCUIT RESISTANCE CHECK		
• Refer to illustration K2.		
• Disconnect processor from vehicle harness.		
• Key Off, DVOM 200 ohms range, ISC solenoid connected.	6-14 ohms ▶	CONTINUE to **K4**.
• Measure ISC actuator resistance at J2-9 to J2-10.	Less than 6 ohms or greater than 14 ohms ▶	CONTINUE to **K3**.
K3 ISC SOLENOID RESISTANCE CHECK		
• Refer to illustration K2.		
• Key Off, DVOM 200 ohms range. ISC harness disconnected at actuator.	Less than 6 ohms or greater than 14 ohms ▶	REPLACE ISC.
• Measure ISC solenoid resistance at the actuator.	6-14 ohms ▶	ISOLATE and CORRECT short to V battery, CKT 361 and CKT 267 and/or 68.

EEC IV-1.6L Engine Diagnosis

Idle Speed Control (ISC)	Pinpoint Test	K

TEST STEP	RESULT ▶	ACTION TO TAKE
K4 VBATT TO ISC		
• Refer to illustration K2.		
• ISC solenoid connected, Key On, Engine Off, DVOM 20V range.	10.5v or less ▶	CORRECT open in harness CKT 361.
• Measure CKT 361 (Red) at ISC to engine ground.	Greater than 10.5v ▶	CONTINUE to K5 .
K5 CHECK FOR CKTS 67 & 68		
• Refer to illustration K2.		
• Key On, Engine Off. DVOM 20v range.	10.5v or greater ▶	CONTINUE to K6 .
• Take a voltage measurement from CKT 67 GY/WH at ISC actuator to engine ground.	Less than 10.5v ▶	ISOLATE and CORRECT short in harness CKT 67 or 68.
K6 CHECK FOR ISC SIGNAL AT ACTUATOR		
• Refer to illustration K2.		
• Vehicle prepared for Quick Test.	Meter reading varies during Quick Test ▶	REPLACE ISC actuator.
• DVOM on 20v range and connected to rear of ISC harness connector (leave harness connected).	Meter reading does not vary during Quick Test ▶	CONTINUE to K7 .
• Start engine and observe during Quick Test.		
K7 CHECK FOR ISC SIGNAL AT THE PROCESSOR		
• Refer to illustration K2.		
• Vehicle prepared for Quick Test.	Meter reading varies during Quick Test ▶	ISOLATE and CORRECT opens in harness CKTS 67 or 68.
• DVOM 20v range.	Meter reading does not vary during Quick Test ▶	DISCONNECT J1 & J2. INSPECT for bent, damaged, corrosion etc. CORRECT as necessary. If OK, REPLACE processor.
• Connect DVOM to J2 pin 11 and J2 pin 9.		
• Start engine and observe the DVOM during Self-Test.		

Vehicle Stalls In Self-Test	Pinpoint Test	P

TEST STEP	RESULT ▶	ACTION TO TAKE
P1 NO CODES, METER ALWAYS HIGH OR ALWAYS LOW, OR INCOMPLETE/ INCORRECT CODES		
• Refer to illustration P.		
• Key to Run, engine Off. Processor connected.	6.0v or more ▶	GO to Pinpoint Test Step C2 .
• DVOM on 20v range. Take a voltage reading from J1 pin 11, to J1 pin 12.	4.0v or less ▶	GO to Pinpoint Test Step C1 .
	4.0v to 6.0v ▶	CONTINUE to Pinpoint Test Step P2 .
P2 BATTERY POWER GROUND CHECK (NEGATIVE SUPPLY)		
• Refer to illustration P.		
• Key to Run, engine Off.	Less than 0.5v ▶	CONTINUE to P3 .
• DVOM on 20v range. Take a voltage reading from battery negative (−) post to signal return circuit 359, blk/wh in the Self-Test connector.	Greater than 0.5v ▶	GO to Pinpoint Test Step B4 .

No Codes/ Improper Codes	Pinpoint Test	P

STOP-WARNING

This Pinpoint Test is intended to diagnose only the following:

• Processor
• Harness circuits 57, 89, 100, 201, 361, 359

Vehicle Stalls In Self-Test	Pinpoint Test	P

TEST STEP	RESULT ▶	ACTION TO TAKE
P3 BATTERY POWER CHECK (POSITIVE SUPPLY)		
• Refer to illustration P.		
• Key to Run, engine Off. Processor connected. DVOM on 20v range.	Both readings less than 0.50v ▶	CONTINUE to P4 .
• Take a voltage reading from the battery positive (+) post to J2 pin 11, record reading.	One or both readings greater than .50v ▶	GO to Pinpoint Test Step B7 .
• Repeat above from battery positive (+) post to J2 pin 12.		
P4 SELF-TEST INPUT CHECK		
• Refer to illustration P.		
• Disconnect J-1 from processor.	Less than 5 ohms ▶	GO to P5 .
• With DVOM, check Self-Test input circuit 100 w/ red dot from Self-Test pigtail connector to J1-13.	5 ohms or more ▶	CORRECT open in circuit 100.
P5 SELF-TEST OUTPUT CIRCUIT CHECK		
• Refer to illustration P.		
• Disconnect J-2 from the processor.	5 ohms or more ▶	CORRECT open in circuit 201.
• With DVOM, check Self-Test output circuit 201 tan-red at Self-Test connector to J2-18.	Less than 5 ohms ▶	CONTINUE to P6 .
P6 CHECK EGO SENSOR GROUND		DVOM READING
• Refer to illustration P.		
• Turn key Off.	5 ohms or less ▶	DISCONNECT J1 and J2, INSPECT for corrosion, damaged pins, etc. RECONNECT and RETEST. If problem is still present, REPLACE processor.
• Disconnect EEC processor.		
• Connect DVOM between EGO ground point on the engine and J1-5.	More than 5 ohms ▶	CHECK and SERVICE EGO sensor ground wire or open circuit bad connection.

EEC IV-1.6L Engine Diagnosis

Spark Advance Out of Limits	**Pinpoint Test**	**Q**

STOP-WARNING

You may have reached this point because of a fault in a non-EEC System and/or component. To prevent the replacement of good components, be aware that the following non-EEC areas may be at fault:

- Base engine timing
- Base engine problems, cam timing, distributor index
- TFI Module

This Pinpoint Test is intended to diagnose only the following:

- Processor
- Harness circuit 324

Fuel Pump Circuit	**Pinpoint Test**	**S**

STOP-WARNING

You may have reached this point because of a fault in a non-EEC System and/or component. To prevent the replacement of good components, be aware that the following non-EEC areas may be at fault:

- Fuel Lines
- Fuel Filters
- Throttle Body
- Contaminated Fuel
- Fuel Pump

This Pinpoint Test is intended to diagnose only the following:

- Fuel Pump Relay
- Harness Circuits 37, 57, 97, 361, and 787
- Inertia Switch
- Processor Assembly

Spark Advance Out of Limits	**Pinpoint Test**	**Q**

TEST STEP	RESULT	▶	ACTION TO TAKE
Q1 SPARK ADVANCE NOT 30 ± 3 IN SELF-TEST			
• Refer to illustration Q. NOTE: Verify the system is in Self-Test. The Self-Test program lasts about 40 seconds. Once the Self-Test is completed the system returns to normal engine strategy and spark timing will no longer be locked at 30.			
• With the engine at idle, use a jumper wire to ground J2 pin 14 to chassis.	Yes	▶	Ignition module signal circuit OK. CONTINUE to **Q2**.
• Does the engine stall?	No	▶	CHECK for open in harness circuit 324. If OK, GO to TFI diagnostics, Section 15.
Q2 VERIFY BASE TIMING			
• Refer to illustration Q.			
• With the engine Off, disconnect the ignition module signal at inline connector.	Yes	▶	DISCONNECT J1 and J2 and INSPECT for corrosion, bent pins, etc. RECONNECT and RETEST. If the problem is still present, REPLACE the processor.
• Start engine and check timing.			
• Is timing to 10°BTDC ± 3°?	No	▶	ADJUST timing, refer to Shop Manual Group 23.

Fuel Pump Circuit	**Pinpoint Test**	**S**

TEST STEP	RESULT	▶	ACTION TO TAKE
S1 NO FUEL PUMP PRESSURE			
• Check if fuel pump runs.			
• Cycle key from Off to Run, repeat several times. (Do not enter start mode). Fuel pump should run briefly each time the key enters Run.	Pump runs	▶	GO to Shop Manual, Section 24-35.
	Pump does not run	▶	GO to **S2**.
S2 VERIFY EEC SYSTEM BATTERY POWER			
• Refer to illustration S.			
• Key in run, engine off.	10.5v or more	▶	GO to **S3**.
• Use DVOM to measure battery voltage at J2 pin 11 and pin 12. Negative meter lead to a good chassis ground.	Less than 10.5v	▶	GO to **B1**, vehicle battery check.
S3 VERIFY EEC SYSTEM GROUND			
• Refer to illustration Step S.			
• Key in Run position, engine off.	Less than 1.0v on both circuits	▶	Ground OK. GO to **S4**.
• One lead of meter (neg.) to neg. battery post. With other meter lead, probe J2 pin 1 and then pin 2.	1.0v or more on either or both circuits	▶	CORRECT faulty ground circuit 57 (high resistance indicated by voltage reading).
NOTE: J2, Pin 1 and pin 2 both go to vehicle battery negative post. We are looking for a voltage drop in the ground circuit.			

EEC IV-1.6L Engine Diagnosis

Fuel Pump Circuit	Pinpoint Test	S

TEST STEP	RESULT	ACTION TO TAKE
S4 RESISTANCE CHECK OF FUEL PUMP RELAY		
• Locate and disconnect the fuel pump relay. • With DVOM on 200 ohms range, measure the resistance of the fuel pump relay coil (across the two small pins).	Reading is 50-100 ohms ►	CONTINUE to Pinpoint S5.
	Reading is lower than 50 ohms or above 100 ohms ►	REPLACE fuel pump relay.

Fuel Pump Circuit	Pinpoint Test	S

TEST STEP	RESULT	ACTION TO TAKE
S5 FUEL PUMP CIRCUIT CHECK (Continued)		
f. Locate inertia switch. Take voltage reading at both terminals (circuit 787, pk-bk hash) during crank mode.	Greater than 10.5v at both terminals during crank ►	CONTINUE to g.
	10.5v or less at one terminal during crank ►	REPLACE inertia switch.
	10.5v or less at both terminals during crank ►	LOCATE open in circuit 787 between inertia switch and fuel pump relay.
g. Circuit 787, pk-bk, H at the fuel pump.	Greater than 10.5v during crank ►	CONTINUE to h.
	10.5v or less during crank ►	CORRECT open in 787 circuit between inertia switch and fuel pump.
h. Circuit 57, blk at the fuel pump. During crank mode (negative meter lead to a good chassis ground).	Greater than 1.0v ►	CORRECT faulty ground circuit from fuel pump to chassis ground.
	1.0v or less ►	REFER to Shop Manual, Group 24, fuel pump, service.

Fuel Pump Circuit	Pinpoint Test	S

TEST STEP	RESULT	ACTION TO TAKE
S5 FUEL PUMP CIRCUIT CHECK		
• Refer to illustration S. • Locate fuel pump relay. • Key to Run, engine off. • Using the DVOM negative lead to chassis ground, make the following voltage checks at the points indicated. • In the event an open fusible link is found, check for cause (short to ground) before replacing fuse link. Refer to illustration S.		
a. Circuit 361, red at fuel pump relay.	Greater than 10.5v ►	CONTINUE.
	10.5v or less ►	CHECK circuit 361 back to the EEC power relay for open. If OK, GO to B1.
b. Circuit 37, yellow at fuel pump relay.	Greater than 10.5v ►	CONTINUE.
	10.5v or less ►	LOCATE open in circuit 37 between fuel pump relay and vehicle battery positive post.
c. Circuit 97, tan, light green dot, at fuel pump relay.	Greater than 10.5v during crank ►	CONTINUE.
	10.5v or less ►	REPLACE pump relay.
d. Circuit 97, tan-light green dot, at the fuel pump relay during crank mode.	1.0v or less during crank ►	CONTINUE.
	Greater than 1.0v during crank ►	CHECK circuit 97 to processor for opens. If OK, REPLACE processor.
e. Circuit 787, pink/blk, hash, at fuel pump relay during crank mode.	Greater than 10.5v during crank ►	CONTINUE.
	10.5v or less during crank ►	REPLACE fuel pump relay.

Diagnostics By Symptom	Pinpoint Test	T

TEST STEP	RESULT	ACTION TO TAKE
T DIAGNOSTICS BY SYMPTOM		
• Engine stalls or stalls in Self-Test, runs rough, misses.	►	• Poor power/ground circuit connections. • Ignition system, dist. cap, rotor, wires, coil and plugs. • EGR valve (stuck open), Pinpoint Test Step T4. Then A1.
• High idle speeds on every restart.	►	Pinpoint Test T2.
• Incorrect/incomplete service codes.	►	Pinpoint Test P1.
• Stalls on decel, stalls at idle.	►	Pinpoint Test T1.
• Intermittent drive complaints.	►	REFER to Quick Test Step 7.0, Continuous Testing.
T1 EGR VALVE CHECK		
• Disconnect and plug the vacuum hose from the EGR valve.	Vehicle does not stall ►	REFER to Section 6 for EGR Service.
• Start the engine and bring to normal operation temperature.	Vehicle stalls ►	GO to Pinpoint Test K1.
• Perform Quick Test.		

EEC IV-1.6L Engine Diagnosis

Diagnostics By Symptom	Pinpoint Test	T

TEST STEP	RESULT ▶	ACTION TO TAKE
T2 HIGH IDLE SPEEDS ON EVERY RESTART		
• Verify system is not in Self-Test all the time.		
• Key Off, connect analog voltmeter to Self-Test connector. **Do not** insert jumper for Self-Test.	Any pulsing codes ▶	CONTINUE to T3.
• Key to On; observe voltmeter.	No pulsing codes ▶	VERIFY ISC per Pinpoint Test K1.
T3 CHECK SELF-TEST INPUT FOR SHORT TO GROUND		
• Refer to illustration T2.		
• DVOM to 200,000 ohm range. Disconnect J1 from the processor.	Reading is 10,000 ohms to infinity (+1) ▶	DISCONNECT J1 and J2. CHECK for corrosion and damaged pins. If fault is still present, REPLACE processor.
• Take a resistance reading from J1 pin 13 to chassis ground.		
• Reconnect J1 at end of testing.	Reading is less than 10,000 ohms ▶	SERVICE harness short to ground in circuit 100.

Diagnostics By Symptom	Pinpoint Test	T

TEST STEP	RESULT ▶	ACTION TO TAKE
T6 RESISTANCE CHECK OF EGR SOLENOID		
• Key off, disconnect EGR solenoid harness connector.	45-90 ohms ▶	CONTINUE to T7.
• With DVOM on 200 ohms scale, measure EGR solenoid resistance.	Not 45-90 ohms ▶	REPLACE EGR solenoid.
T7 CHECK CKT 361 AT EGR SOLENOID		
• Key on, EGR solenoid and processor connected, DVOM on 20 volt range.	Reading is lower than 10.5v ▶	CHECK harness terminals for poor connection/crimps. If OK, CORRECT open in CKT 361 (red).
• Measure the voltage at the yellow wire at the EGR solenoid connector.	DVOM reading more than 10.5v ▶	CHECK CKT 362 (yellow) for opens. If OK, DISCONNECT J1 & J2. INSPECT for corrosion, damaged pins, etc. RECONNECT and RETEST. If problem is still present, REPLACE the processor.

Diagnostics By Symptom	Pinpoint Test	T

TEST STEP	RESULT ▶	ACTION TO TAKE
T4 EGR ON-OFF FUNCTION CONTROL		
• Locate EGR On-Off solenoid and remove and plug the vacuum lines connected to it.	Will not hold a vacuum ▶	CONTINUE to T5.
• Connect a hand vacuum pump to the lower port.	Will not release the vacuum ▶	CONTINUE to T6.
• Start the engine and bring to normal operating temperature, then idle an additional 3 minutes, at idle apply a minimum of 10 inches hg. to the valve with hand vacuum pump.	Traps vacuum at idle and bleeds off on accel. ▶	EEC Control system OK. CHECK Non-EEC Components BVT, EGR Valve.
• At this point system should trap the vacuum.		
• While observing the vacuum gauge rapidly accelerate the engine, the vacuum should bleed off during the accel.		
T5 EGR SOLENOID WILL NOT HOLD A VACUUM		
• Disconnect harness from EGR solenoid.	Does not hold vacuum ▶	REPLACE EGR solenoid.
• Reapply minimum 10 inches vacuum to EGR solenoids.	Holds vacuum ▶	CHECK CKT 362 (yellow) J2 pin 17, for shorts to ground. If OK, disconnect J1 & J2. Inspect for corrosion, damaged pins, etc. RECONNECT and RETEST. If problem is still present, REPLACE the processor.

Neutral Drive Switch A/C Input	Pinpoint Test	V

STOP-WARNING

You may have reached this point because of a fault in a non-EEC System and/or component. To prevent the replacement of good components, be aware that the following non-EEC areas may be at fault:

• Neutral Drive SW
• Gear/Clutch Linkage

This Pinpoint Test is intended to diagnose only the following:

• Processor
• Harness Circuits 150, 347, 359 and 69
• Gear/Clutch SW
• Neutral Forcing Relay

EEC IV-1.6L Engine Diagnosis

Neutral Drive Switch A/C Input		Pinpoint Test	V

	TEST STEP	RESULT ▶	ACTION TO TAKE
V	NEUTRAL DRIVE — A/C INPUT CHECK CODE 67		
	MTX Application start at Step V1. ATX Application start at Step V3.		
V1	NEUTRAL DRIVE INPUT CHECK (MTX)		
	• Refer to illustration V.		
	• Verify A/C is Off, if so equipped.	Yes ▶	CONTINUE to V5.
	• Verify transaxle is in Neutral, clutch released.	No ▶	CONTINUE to V2.
	• With ignition Off, disconnect J1 and make a resistance measurement from J1 pin 1 to J1 pin 12.		
	• Is the DVOM reading less than 5 ohms?		
V2	GEAR/CLUTCH SWITCH CHECK		
	• Refer to illustration V.		
	• Locate the gear switch (on transaxle) and the clutch switch (under dash).	Yes ▶	CORRECT open in vehicle harness circuits (150 Dg/w or 359 Bk/w).
	• Disconnect the vehicle harness and take a resistance reading across each switch.	No ▶	REPLACE defective switch. RECONNECT and RETEST.
	• Reading is 5 ohms or less at each switch?		

Neutral Drive Switch A/C Input		Pinpoint Test	V

	TEST STEP	RESULT ▶	ACTION TO TAKE
V3	NEUTRAL DRIVE INPUT CHECK (ATX)		
	• Refer to illustration V.		
	• Verify heater control is in Off position, if so equipped.	Yes ▶	CONTINUE to V5.
	• Verify transaxle is in Neutral or Park.	No ▶	CONTINUE to V4.
	• Key On, engine Off.		
	• With DVOM set on 20v range, make a voltage measurement from the rear of the still connected J1 pin 1 circuit 150 Dg/w to chassis ground.		
	• Reading is less than .50v.		
V4	N/DR SWITCH CHECK		
	• Refer to illustration V.		
	• Locate the N/DR switch on the transaxle.	Yes ▶	CORRECT open in vehicle harness circuit 150 Dg/w.
	• Disconnect the vehicle harness from the N/DR switch and take a resistance reading across the contacts.	No ▶	REPLACE defective N/DR switch.
	• Reading is less than 5 ohms across the switch.		
V5	A/C INPUT CHECK		
	• Refer to illustration V.		
	• Key On, A/C control in the Off position. Make a voltage measurement at the rear of J1 pin 2 circuit 347 Bk/y has to chassis ground.	Greater than 1.0v ▶	CORRECT short to power in circuit 347, J1 pin 2.
	• Reading must be less than 1.0v.	1.0v or less ▶	REPLACE processor.

Appendix A

This appendix describes the use of an analog VOM to read Self-Test Service Codes. It is to be used when the Diagnostic Routines, in Section 2, instruct you to perform EEC-IV diagnostics and a STAR readout device is not available.

EQUIPMENT HOOK-UP

CAUTION: Do not turn ignition key off if the vehicle is towed in or is suspected of having an intermittent failure. Fault codes could be stored in the Continuous Memory.

• Turn ignition key to Off.
• Connect a jumper wire from Self-Test Input (STI) to Signal Return on the Self-Test Connector (see diagram below).

NOTE: The jumper wire is connected any time the Quick-Test procedure instructs the user to depress the pushbutton on the front of the STAR unit.

• Connect an analog VOM from battery positive (+) to Self-Test Output (STO) in the Self-Test Connector (see diagram). Set the VOM on DC voltage range that will read at least 15 volts.

Self-Test harness connector (colored RED) — located on passenger side under the hood.

NOTE: Connector viewed looking at its mating surface (not harness side).

Appendix A

SERVICE CODE DESCRIPTION

The EEC-IV system communicates service information by generating Self-Test Service Codes. These service codes are two-digit numbers representing the results of the Self-Test.

The service codes are transmitted on the Self-Test Output wire (STO) and can easily be observed on an Analog Voltmeter in the form of needle pulses (sweeps).

When a Service Code is observed on the Analog Voltmeter, it will appear as a pulsing or sweeping movement of the voltmeter's needle across the dial face of the voltmeter. The meter needle will start from a low or "zero" (0) position. Each time the needle goes high and then returns a single pulse (sweep) has been displayed. Example: Self-Test's Service Code 3-2 will appear on the voltmeter as three needle pulses (sweeps), then after a two-second pause, the needle will pulse (sweep) twice more.

EEC IV-1.6L Engine Diagnosis

Electrical — Schematic

EEC-IV Module Connector PIN Usage

CONNECTOR	CIRCUIT	WIRE COLOR	APPLICATION
J1 — 1	614	GY/O	N/D Switch
J1 — 2	347	BK/YH	A/C Clutch
J1 — 3			N/C
J1 — 4			N/C
J1 — 5	89	O	EGO Ground
J1 — 6	94	DG/PH	EGO
J1 — 7	354	LG/Y	ECT
J1 — 8	357	LG/P	VAT
J1 — 9	355	DG/LG	TAP
J1 — 10	200	W/BK	VAF
J1 — 11	351	O/W	V. REF
J1 — 12	359	BK/W	Sig. Rtn.
J1 — 13	100	W/RD	STI
J1 — 14	349	DB	PIP
J1 — 15			N/C
J1 — 16			N/C
J1 — 17			N/C
J1 — 18			N/C
J1 — 19	97	T/LGD	Fuel Pump
J1 — 20	57	BK	Case Ground
J2 — 1	57	BK	Pwr. Grd.
J2 — 2	57	BK	Pwr. Grd.
J2 — 3	95	T/RD	Inj. A
J2 — 4	96	T/OD	Inj. B
J2 — 5	60	BK/LGD	Ign. Grd.
J2 — 6			N/C
J2 — 7			N/C
J2 — 8			N/C
J2 — 9	68	O/BK	ISC
J2 — 10	67	GY/WH	LOS, ISC
J2 — 11	361	R	V-Pwr.
J2 — 12	361	R	V-Pwr.
J2 — 13			N/C
J2 — 14	324	Y/LGD	SPOUT
J2 — 15	69	R/LG	A/C WOT Cut-off
J2 — 16			N/C
J2 — 17	362	Y	EGR On/Off
J2 — 18	201	T/R	STO
J2 — 19			N/C
J2 — 20			N/C

Electrical — Schematic

Vacuum — Schematic

MTX TYPICAL

EEC IV-1.6L Engine Diagnosis

Vacuum — Schematic

ATX TYPICAL

EEC IV-1.6L Engine Diagnosis

Quick Test

2.0	EQUIPMENT HOOK-UP

Using STAR Tester, Rotunda 07-0004, or equivalent*

- Turn ignition key to Off.
- Connect timing light.
- Connect the color coded adapter cable leads to the STAR Tester.
- Connect the adapter cable's service connectors to the vehicle's appropriate Self-Test connectors.
- Turn power switch On, release STAR push button (no colon showing).

NOTE: STAR must be used with adapter cable 07-0010 or permanent system damage may result.

- Self-Test is activated by depressing STAR push button (colon showing).

Using Analog Voltmeter Rotunda 59-0010 or equivalent

- Turn ignition key to Off.
- Connect a jumper wire from Self-Test Input (STI) to Pin 2 Signal Return on Self-Test Connector.
- Set analog VOM on a DC voltage range to read from 0 to 15 volts DC. Connect VOM from battery (positive) to Pin 4 Self-Test Output (STO) in the Self-Test Connector.
- Self-Test is activated by installing a jumper from STI to Signal Return (pin 2) at the Self-Test connector.

*Must be used with adapter harness Rotunda 07-0010 only.

NOTE: For additional Quick Test information, refer to the Appendix in this Section.

EEC IV-2.3L EFI Turbocharged Engine Diagnosis

Quick Test

1.0	VISUAL CHECK AND VEHICLE PREPARATION

Correct test results for the Quick Test are dependent on the proper operation of related non-EEC components and systems. It may be necessary to correct faults in these areas before EEC will pass Quick Test. Refer to Diagnostic Routines, Section 2 for service.

Before hooking up any equipment to diagnose the EEC system, make the following checks:

1. Verify the condition of air cleaner and ducting. These components may be removed and reinstalled as necessary for service and/or inspection.

2. Check all engine vacuum hoses for:
   - Leaks or pinched hoses.
   - Proper emission routing per VECI decal.

3. Check the EEC system wiring harness electrical connections for:
   - Proper connections.
   - Loose or detached connectors, wires and terminals.
   - Corrosion.
   - Proper routing and lay of harness.

It may be necessary to disconnect or disassemble the connector assembly to perform some of the inspections. (Note the location of each pin before disassembly.)

4. Check control module, sensors and actuators for physical damage.

5. Perform all safety steps required to start and run operational vehicle tests.

6. Apply the emergency brake. Place shift lever in Park; Neutral for manual transmission.

7. Turn Off all electrical loads, such as the radio, lamps, air conditioner, etc. Be sure doors are closed whenever readings are made.

8. Verify engine coolant is at the specified level.

9. Start engine and idle until the upper radiator hose is hot and pressurized and the throttle is off fast idle. While the engine is operating, check for leaks around the exhaust manifold, EGO sensor, and vacuum hose connections.

   NOTE: If the engine will not start or starts and stalls, continue with this Step (1.0), and on through Steps 2.0, 3.0, and 4.0 of the Quick Test. If the engine idles rough and/or runs rough, go to Pinpoint Test X.

10. Turn ignition key Off.

11. Service items as required, and proceed to equipment hook-up.

12. If the problem is intermittent, occurs only at road load, or under some particular vehicle conditions, proceed through to Continuous Testing.

Quick Test

TEST STEP	RESULT	▶	ACTION TO TAKE
3.0 KEY ON — ENGINE OFF SELF-TEST			

Correct test results for Quick Test are dependent on the proper operation of related non-EEC-IV components/systems. It may be necessary to correct any faults in these areas before EEC-IV will pass Quick Test. Refer to Diagnostic Routines in Section 2 of this manual for proper servicing.

Code Format

O N D E M A N D	S ② E P A R A T O R	C O N T I N U O U S

- Verify the vehicle has been properly prepared per Quick Test Steps 1.0 and 2.0.
- Place transmission in Neutral or Park Set parking brake. Place A/C or heater control to Off. All electrical loads off.
- Activate Self-Test.
- Place key in Run to start Self-Test.
- Observe and record all Service Codes. The output format will be:
  — Fast codes①
  — On demand codes
  — Separator code②
  — Continuous codes
- Continuous Service Codes recorded in this step will be referenced later in Quick Test Step 6.0.

① Fast Codes serve no purpose in the field, therefore this will be the only place they are referenced. STAR has been designed to ignore these codes, and the analog meter may display them as a slight meter deflection.

② STAR displays a 10 in place of a 1 for the single digit separator code, therefore the separator code is expressed in the results column as 1(0).

RESULT	ACTION TO TAKE
11 —1(0)— 11 ▶	GO to Quick Test Step **4.0**.
Any Code —1(0)— 11 ▶	GO to Quick Test Step **3.1**.
Any Code —1(0)— Any Code ▶	RECORD On Demand continuous codes. GO to Quick Test Step **3.1**.
11 —1(0)— Any Code ▶	RECORD continuous codes. GO to Quick Test Step **4.0**.
No codes or invalid display of codes ▶	GO to Pinpoint Test Step **P1**.

EEC IV-2.3L EFI Turbocharged Engine Diagnosis

Quick Test

TEST STEP	RESULT	▶	ACTION TO TAKE
3.1 KEY ON — ENGINE OFF SELF-TEST	On Demand Service Codes		
• Using the On Demand Service Codes from Key On — Engine Off Quick Test Step 3.0, follow the instructions in the Action To Take column in this Step.	15	▶	REPLACE Processor. REPEAT Quick Test.
	21	▶	GO to Pinpoint Test Step **F1**.
• When more than one service code is received, always start service with the first code received.	22	▶	GO to Pinpoint Test Step **R1**.
• Whenever a repair is made, REPEAT Quick Test.	23	▶	GO to Pinpoint Test Step **E1**.
	24	▶	GO to Pinpoint Test Step **D1**.
	26	▶	GO to Pinpoint Test Step **G1**.
	51	▶	GO to Pinpoint Test Step **F6**.
	53	▶	GO to Pinpoint Test Step **E3**.
	54	▶	GO to Pinpoint Test Step **D5**.
	56	▶	GO to Pinpoint Test Step **G3**.
	61	▶	GO to Pinpoint Test Step **F8**.
	63	▶	GO to Pinpoint Test Step **E8**.
	64	▶	GO to Pinpoint Test Step **D7**.
	66	▶	GO to Pinpoint Test Step **G8**.
	67	▶	GO to Pinpoint Test Step **W1**.
	Any code not listed above	▶	RERUN Self-Test and VERIFY codes. GO to Pinpoint Test Step **P1**.

Quick Test

TEST STEP	RESULT	▶	ACTION TO TAKE
5.0 ENGINE RUNNING SELF-TEST	DYNAMIC RESPONSE ② ENGINE ID ENGINE RESPONSE ON DEMAND		
NOTE: If vehicle is a No Start, GO directly to Pinpoint Test A1.			
• Deactivate Self-Test.			
• Start and Run engine at greater than 2000 RPM for 2 minutes. This warms up EGO sensor. Ignore any code output at this time.			
• Turn Engine Off.			
• Verify Self-Test is activated.			
• Start the engine. The Engine Running Test will progress as follows:			
— Engine ID code. ①			
— Run Test.			
— Dynamic Response Ready Code 1(0) or 1 pulse occurs at this time, perform a brief W.O.T. ②	2(0) — 1(0) — 11	▶	If the drive symptom is still present, GO to Pinpoint Test **X**. Diagnostics by Symptom. If the symptom was of an intermittent nature, GO to Quick Test Step **6.0**. (Continuous Codes) otherwise testing is complete, EEC IV system is OK.
— Engine Running Service Codes.			
— End of Test.			
• If engine stalls in Self-Test, GO to Pinpoint Test Step **X1**.	2(0) — 1(0) — Any Code	▶	GO to Quick Test Step **5.1**.
① Engine ID code is equal to half of the number of cylinders (a code of 2 equals a 4 cylinder engine) except for STAR tester which adds a zero to all single digit readings (20 equals a 4 cylinder engine).	No Codes or Invalid Codes	▶	REPEAT Self-Test and verify SERVICE codes. Then GO to Pinpoint Test **P1**.
② STAR displays a 10 in place of a 1 for the single digit separator code; therefore the Dynamic Response Ready code is expressed in the results column as 1(0).			

Quick Test

TEST STEP	RESULT	▶	ACTION TO TAKE
4.0 CHECK TIMING			
• If vehicle is a no start, go directly to Pinpoint Test A NO STARTS.			
• Key Off.			
• Verify Self-Test trigger has been activated.			
• Restart engine and check timing while in Self-Test.	Timing is not 27-33 degrees BTDC	▶	GO to **Q1**.
NOTE: If engine stalls while testing, go to Pinpoint Test X, Diagnostics by Symptom.	Timing is 27-33 degrees BTDC	▶	GO to Quick Test Step **4.1**.

Quick Test

TEST STEP	RESULT	▶	ACTION TO TAKE
5.1 ENGINE RUNNING SELF-TEST	Engine Running Service Codes		
• Using the Service Codes from Engine Running Self-Test Step 5.0, follow the instructions in the Action To Take column in this Step.	12	▶	GO to Pinpoint Test Step **N1**.
	13	▶	GO to Pinpoint Test Step **N7**.
• When more than one service code is received, always start service with the first code received.	21	▶	GO to Pinpoint Test Step **F1**.
• Whenever a repair is made, REPEAT Quick Test.	22	▶	GO to Pinpoint Test Step **R1**.
	23	▶	GO to Pinpoint Test Step **E1**.
	24	▶	GO to Pinpoint Test Step **D1**.
	26	▶	GO to Pinpoint Test Step **G1**.
	31	▶	GO to Pinpoint Test Step **H1**.
	34	▶	GO to Pinpoint Test Step **V1**.
	41	▶	GO to Pinpoint Test Step **H8**.
	42	▶	GO to Pinpoint Test Step **H5**.
	73	▶	GO to Pinpoint Test Step **E13**.
	76	▶	GO to Pinpoint Test Step **G13**.
	77	▶	GO to Pinpoint Test Step **T1**.
	Any code not listed above	▶	GO to Pinpoint Test Step **P1**.

EEC IV-2.3L EFI Turbocharged Engine Diagnosis

Quick Test

6.0 CONTINUOUS TESTING

1. **Unless instructed otherwise, do not disconnect any sensor with the key On or a Service Code may be stored.**
2. Should Keep Alive power, Pin 1 (circuit 37), to the processor, be interrupted momentarily, all stored Continuous Codes may be erased (e.g., disconnecting the processor to connect the Breakout Box).
3. Should Keep Alive power, Pin 1 (circuit 37), fail (and remain an open circuit), invalid codes may be received during Continuous Test.
4. The correct method for clearing the processor's memory of stored Continuous Codes, is to exit Key On — Engine Off Quick Test during the code output sequence Perform Key On — Engine Off Self-Test at the point where the service codes begin. Exit Self-Test by unlatching STAR push button or removing the Self-Test Jumper.
5. Before utilizing stored continuous information, first, verify that the On Demand Key On — Engine Off and Engine Running Quick Tests indicate a pass (Service Code 11). If during testing or retesting, an On Demand code is detected, this must be repaired first, since some hard failures also request a code in the continuous memory. Once On Demand testing is completed, clear the memory of Continuous Codes and operate the vehicle to verify the previous repair. If a drive complaint still exists. REPEAT Quick Test and follow the directions of Continuous Testing, beginning with Quick Test Step 6.1.

TEST STEP	RESULT	▶	ACTION TO TAKE
6.1 CONTINUOUS TEST			
● Does the results of both On Demand Tests (Key On — Engine Off and Engine Running) result in a pass code 11.	Yes	▶	GO to 6.2 .
	No	▶	RETURN to Step 1.0 of Quick Test and make necessary repairs, indicated in Test Steps 3.0 and 5.0 before continuing.
6.2 KEY ON-ENGINE OFF CONTINUOUS TESTING			
● Prepare the vehicle for Key On — Engine Off Quick Test per Steps 1.0, 2.0, and 3.0.			
● Perform Key On — Engine Off Quick Test. When the service codes begin, exit the Self-Test program (via unlatching STAR or removing the jumper from STI to Signal Return). Exiting Quick Test during code output will erase codes stored in the continuous memory.			
● Do not activate Self-Test.	Continuous Monitor Test indicates a failure	▶	GO to 6.4 .
● Place key in Run, Engine Off. You are now in Engine Off Continuous Monitor Mode, the STO will be activated (indicated by STAR LED going out or Analog Meter Movement) whenever a monitored sensor is interrupted. Perform Continuous Monitor Test. (Refer to Continuous Monitor Test in Appendix.)	Continuous Monitor Test does not indicate a failure	▶	GO to 6.3 .

Quick Test

TEST STEP	RESULT	▶	ACTION TO TAKE
6.3 KEY ON — ENGINE RUNNING CONTINUOUS TESTING			
● Activate Self-Test and perform Engine Running Quick Test Step 5.0. After the service code output has been completed, do not turn the engine Off or deactivate Self-Test. At this time the system will enter and remain in the Continuous Monitor Mode until Self-Test is deactivated or engine is turned Off. Perform Continuous Monitor Test. Refer to Continuous Monitor Test in Appendix.	Continuous Monitor Test indicates a failure	▶	GO to 6.4 .
	Continuous Monitor Test does not indicate a failure	▶	Fault is not in a monitored EEC sensor circuit. EEC functional testing is complete. Refer to Pinpoint Test X , diagnostics by symptom, for additional service information.

Quick Test

TEST STEP	RESULT	▶	ACTION TO TAKE
6.4 CONTINUOUS TEST SERVICE CODES			
● Using the Service Codes from Continuous Testing Step 6.4 or 6.5, make necessary repair as indicated by the service code in the results column.	14	▶	GO to Pinpoint Test Step Y1 .
NOTE: For additional help in locating intermittent faults, refer to the "Additional Service Aids" Section following the Quick Test routine.	21	▶	GO to Pinpoint Test Step F1 .
	22	▶	GO to Pinpoint Test Step R1 .
	41	▶	GO to Pinpoint Test Step H11 .
	42	▶	GO to Pinpoint Test Step H11 .
	51	▶	GO to Pinpoint Test Step F10 .
	53	▶	GO to Pinpoint Test Step E3 .
	54	▶	GO to Pinpoint Test Step D5 .
	56,	▶	GO to Pinpoint Test Step G3 .
	61	▶	GO to Pinpoint Test Step F6 .
	63	▶	GO to Pinpoint Test Step E8 .
	64	▶	GO to Pinpoint Test Step D7 .
	66	▶	GO to Pinpoint Test Step G8 .

Pinpoint Tests

INSTRUCTIONS FOR USING THE PINPOINT TESTS

● Do not run any of the following Pinpoint Tests unless you are so instructed by the Quick Test. Each Pinpoint Test assumes that a fault has been detected in the system with direction to enter a specific repair routine. Doing any Pinpoint Test without direction from Quick Test may produce incorrect results and replacement of Non-Defective components.

● Correct test results for Quick Test are dependent on the proper operation of related non-EEC components/systems. It may be necessary to correct any defects in these areas before EEC will pass the Quick Test. Refer to the Diagnostic Routines, Section 2 for service.

● Do not replace any parts unless the test result indicates they should be replaced.

● When more than one service code is received, always start service with the first code received.

● Do not measure voltage or resistance at the control module or connect any test lights to it, unless otherwise specified.

● Isolate both ends of a circuit, and turn key Off whenever checking for shorts or continuity, unless specified.

● Disconnect solenoids and switches from the harness before measuring for continuity, resistance, or energizing by way of 12-volt source.

● In using the Pinpoint Tests, follow each Step in order, starting from the first Step in the appropriate test. Follow each Step until the fault is found.

● After completing any repairs to the EEC system, verify all components are properly reconnected and repeat the functional test (Retest).

● An open is defined as any resistance reading greater than 5 ohms unless otherwise specified.

● A short is defined as any resistance reading less than 10,000 ohms to ground, unless otherwise specified.

The standard Ford wire color abbreviations are:

BK	Black	O	Orange
BR	Brown	PK	Pink
DB	Dark Blue	P	Purple
DG	Dark Green	R	Red
GY	Gray	T	Tan
LB	Light Blue	W	White
LG	Light Green	Y	Yellow
N	Natural		

Where two colors are shown for a wire, the first color is the basic color of the wire. The second color is the dot, hash, or stripe marking. If D or H is given, the second color is dots or hash marks. If there is no letter after the second color, the wire has a stripe.

For example:

BR/O is a brown wire with an orange stripe.

R/Y D is a red wire with yellow dots.

BK/W H is a black wire with white hash marks.

EEC IV-2.3L EFI Turbocharged Engine Diagnosis

No Start Problem	Pinpoint Test	A

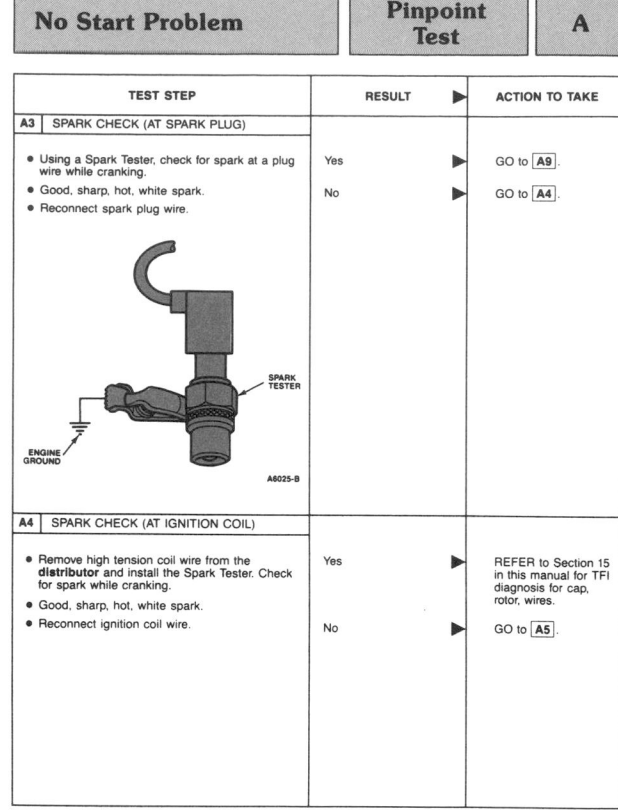

STOP-WARNING

You may have reached this point because of a fault in a non-EEC System and/or component. To prevent the replacement of good components, be aware that the following non-EEC areas may be at fault:

- Fuel, quantity and quality.
- Ignition, general condition, moisture, cracks, damage, etc.
- Engine, internal, valves, timing belt, camshaft.
- Starter and battery circuit.

This Pinpoint Test is intended to diagnose only the following:

- Spark (as related to EEC-IV).
- Fuel delivery (as related to EEC-IV).

No Start Problem	Pinpoint Test	A

TEST STEP	RESULT	▶	ACTION TO TAKE
A3 SPARK CHECK (AT SPARK PLUG)			
• Using a Spark Tester, check for spark at a plug wire while cranking. • Good, sharp, hot, white spark. • Reconnect spark plug wire.	Yes	▶	GO to **A9**.
	No	▶	GO to **A4**.
A4 SPARK CHECK (AT IGNITION COIL)			
• Remove high tension coil wire from the **distributor** and install the Spark Tester. Check for spark while cranking. • Good, sharp, hot, white spark. • Reconnect ignition coil wire.	Yes	▶	REFER to Section 15 in this manual for TFI diagnosis for cap, rotor, wires.
	No	▶	GO to **A5**.

No Start Problem	Pinpoint Test	A

TEST STEP	RESULT	▶	ACTION TO TAKE
FUEL PRESSURE CHECK			
WARNING: Stop this test at the first sign of a fuel leak. **CAUTION: No open flame — No smoking during fuel delivery checks.**			
A1 CHECK FOR FUEL LEAKS			
• Check fuel system for leaks.	Fuel Leaks	▶	CORRECT as necessary before proceeding.
	No Fuel Leaks	▶	GO to **A2**.
A2 TRY TO START THE ENGINE			
• Key to Start position (attempt to start the engine).	Engine cranks but does not start or cranks and attempts to start but will not continue to run, runs rough or misses	▶	GO to **A3***.
	Engine does not crank	▶	REFER to Section 28-02 in the Powertrain Shop Manual, Volume D for Engine Does Not Crank diagnosis.

*NOTE: Clearing a flooded engine is accomplished by holding the throttle wide open.

No Start Problem	Pinpoint Test	A

TEST STEP	RESULT	▶	ACTION TO TAKE
A5 IGNITION MODULE SIGNAL (IMS) CHECK			
• Key Off. Install Breakout Box. • Leave processor disconnected. • DVOM on 20 volt range. Connect DVOM between Breakout Box pins 56 and 16. • Crank engine, record reading. • Reading is 3.0 volts-6.0 volts.	Yes	▶	GO to **A6**.
	No	▶	GO to **A7**.
A6 CONTINUITY CHECK OF CIRCUITS 6 AND 349			
• Key OFF, Breakout Box connected, processor disconnected. • DVOM on 2,000 ohm scale. • Disconnect TFI module connector at distributor. • Check continuity between Breakout Box pin 16 and TFI connector terminal 6. • Check continuity between Breakout Box pin 56 and TFI connector terminal 1.	Both circuits less than 5 ohms	▶	REFER to Section 15, in this manual for TFI diagnosis.
	One or both circuits 5 ohms or greater	▶	REPAIR circuit(s) as necessary. REPEAT Quick Test.
A7 DISTRIBUTOR OUTPUT SIGNAL CHECK (DSO)			
• Refer to illustration, Step A5. • DVOM to 20 volt range. Disconnect Breakout Box connector from processor. • Connect DVOM to pin 36 and pin 16. • Crank engine, record reading. • Reading is 3.0 volts-6.0 volts.	Yes	▶	REFER to Section 15 in this manual for TFI diagnosis.
	No	▶	GO to **A8**.

EEC IV-2.3L EFI Turbocharged Engine Diagnosis

No Start Problem	Pinpoint Test	A

TEST STEP	RESULT ▶	ACTION TO TAKE
A8 CHECK FOR SHORT IN CIRCUIT 324		
• Key OFF, Breakout Box installed, processor disconnected. • DVOM on 2,000 ohm scale. • Connect TFI module connector to distributor. • Connect DVOM between Breakout Box pins 36 and 16. • DVOM reads greater than 2,000 ohms.	Yes ▶ No ▶	REFER to Section 15 in this manual for TFI diagnosis. DISCONNECT TFI module connector at distributor. If short is still present, REPAIR harness. If short is not present, refer to Section 15 in this manual for TFI diagnosis.
A9 FUEL PUMP CHECK		
NO SMOKING NEARBY • Disconnect all four injector electrical connections at the injectors. • Connect pressure gauge to Schrader valve on injector bar. Refer to Fig. A for valve location. • Note initial pressure reading. • Observe pressure gauge as you pressurize fuel system (turn key to Run for 1 second, then turn key to Off, repeat 5 times). • Turn key to Off. • Reconnect all injectors. **WARNING: If fuel starts leaking, turn key Off immediately. No smoking.**	PRESSURE GAUGE READING: Increased ▶ Did not increase ▶	GO to **A11**. GO to **A10**.
A10 CHECK INERTIA SWITCH		
• Locate fuel pump inertia switch. Refer to owner's manual for location. • Push the button of inertia switch to reset it. • Watch pressure gauge as you again attempt to pressurize fuel system. **NOTE: If switch will not reset to On, replace it.**	PRESSURE GAUGE READING: Increases ▶ Did not increase ▶	REPEAT Quick Test. GO to **S1**.

No Start Problem	Pinpoint Test	A

TEST STEP	RESULT ▶	ACTION TO TAKE
A14 INJECTOR DRIVER SIGNAL CHECK		
• Requires standard non-powered 12 volt test lamp. • Connect Breakout Box. • Connect test lamp from pin 37 to pin 58. • Crank engine, observe test lamp results. • Repeat above test from pin 37 to pin 59.	Dim glow at light on both tests ▶ No light on one or both tests ▶ Bright light on one or both tests ▶	Normal. GO to **A15**. VERIFY 12 volt battery power at pin 37 SERVICE circuit 361 as required. If OK, REPLACE processor. REPEAT Quick Test. CHECK circuits 95 and 96 for shorts to ground. SERVICE as required. If OK, REPLACE processor. REPEAT Quick Test.
BREAKOUT BOX PIN NO. PIN 58 ◯——— CKT. 95 T/PD (1" IA) ——— PIN 59 ◯——— CKT. 96 T/OD (1" IB) ——— PIN 37 ◯——— C361 R (BOTT.) ———		
A15 SERVICING THE SUSPECT INJECTOR/CIRCUIT		
• Refer to illustration, Step A14. • Remove the fuel pump relay. • Using the DVOM, measure the average voltage between pin 58 and pin 37, during crank (record reading). • Also, measure the average voltage between pin 59 and pin 37 during crank (record reading). • Reconnect fuel pump relay.	More than 1.0 volt difference between circuits 95 and 96 ▶ Less than 1.0 volt difference between circuits 95 and 96 ▶	DISCONNECT processor. INSPECT for corrosion, damaged pins, etc. RECONNECT and REPEAT Quick Test. If problem is still present, REPLACE processor. GO to **A16**.

No Start Problem	Pinpoint Test	A

TEST STEP	RESULT ▶	ACTION TO TAKE
A11 CHECK FUEL DELIVERY		
• Pressurize fuel system as in Step A9. • Turn key to Off. • Wait for pressure to become steady. • Read pressure gauge.	Between 35 and 45 psi ▶ Over 45 psi or under 35 psi ▶	GO to **A12**. VERIFY ignition coil is connected. REFER to Section 24-29, Power-train Shop Manual for leaking injectors or fuel regulator.
A12 CHECK FOR LEAK DOWN		
• Wait 2 minutes after pressure gauge reading of Step A11, then note drop in gauge reading.	4 psi drop or less in 2 minutes ▶ More than 4 psi drop in 2 minutes ▶	GO to **A13**. TURN key Off immediately. CHECK for hydraulic lockup or fuel fouled spark plugs. REFER to Section 24-29, Power-train Shop Manual, for leaking injectors and/or fuel regulator.
A13 FUEL DELIVERY TEST		
• Pressurize the fuel system as in Step A9. **NOTE: Verify fuel quality, air and/or water will also pressurize and look like acceptable fuel delivery.** • Disable the electric fuel pump (disconnect fuel pump relay). • Crank engine for 5 seconds. • Take pressure reading at end of 5 second crank. • Reconnect fuel pump relay after testing. **NOTE: The colder the engine, the greater the pressure drop (i.e., an engine coolant temperature of 200°F equals approximately a 10 psi drop in 5 seconds; 60°F equals approximately a 20 psi drop in 5 seconds).**	PRESSURE GAUGE READING: Pressure is approximately 10-20 psi at the end of 5 second crank cycle. Refer to note below ▶ Pressure is more or less than specified ▶	The EEC system is not the fault of the No Start. Fuel and spark are present. REFER to Section 2, in this manual for No Start diagnosis. If complaint was runs rough or misses, GO to **A14**. GO to **A14**.

No Start Problem	Pinpoint Test	A

TEST STEP	RESULT ▶	ACTION TO TAKE
A17 ISOLATING A FAULTY INJECTOR		
• Electrically disconnect all injectors at the intake manifold. • Pressurize the fuel system as in Step A9. • Connect the injector for cylinder No. 1 only. • Crank the engine for 5 seconds. • Observe the pressure gauge and record reading immediately at the end of the 5 second crank cycle. • Disconnect injector for cylinder No. 1. • Repeat above procedure for injectors Nos. 2, 3 and 4 (be sure to connect only one injector at a time).	All readings not within 4 psi of each other ▶ All four readings are within 4 psi of each other ▶	REPLACE injector(s) not within 4 psi of the others. REPEAT Quick Test. VERIFY all the non-EEC Diagnostic Routines that apply to your drive complaint have been properly performed, then DISCONNECT processor. INSPECT for corrosion, damaged pins, etc., and REPEAT Quick Test. If fault is still present, REPLACE the processor. REPEAT Quick Test.

EEC IV-2.3L EFI Turbocharged Engine Diagnosis

| Vehicle Battery | | Pinpoint Test | B |

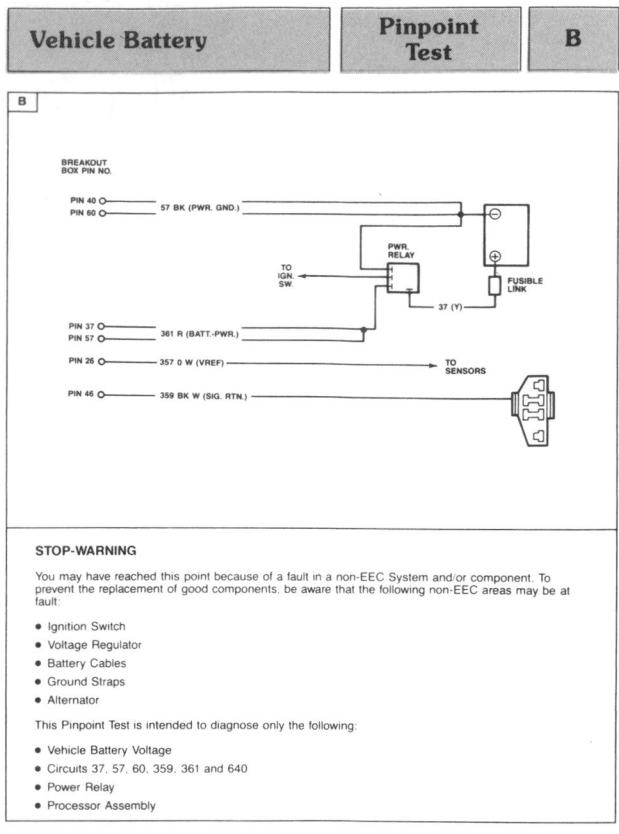

B

BREAKOUT
BOX PIN NO.

PIN 40 ○—
PIN 60 ○— 57 BK (PWR. GND.)

PWR. RELAY

TO IGN. SW.

FUSIBLE LINK

37 (Y)

PIN 37 ○—
PIN 57 ○— 361 R (BATT.-PWR.)

PIN 26 ○— 357 O W (VREF) TO SENSORS

PIN 46 ○— 359 BK W (SIG. RTN.)

STOP-WARNING

You may have reached this point because of a fault in a non-EEC System and/or component. To prevent the replacement of good components, be aware that the following non-EEC areas may be at fault:

- Ignition Switch
- Voltage Regulator
- Battery Cables
- Ground Straps
- Alternator

This Pinpoint Test is intended to diagnose only the following:

- Vehicle Battery Voltage
- Circuits 37, 57, 60, 359, 361 and 640
- Power Relay
- Processor Assembly

| Vehicle Battery | | Pinpoint Test | B |

TEST STEP	RESULT	▶	ACTION TO TAKE
B5 PROCESSOR GROUND FAULT ISOLATION			
• Refer to illustration B. • Connect breakout box. • Key Off. Processor connected. DVOM on 200 ohm range. • Make a resistance measurement between pin 46 and pin 40. • Repeat above test between pin 46 and pin 60.	Both readings less than 1 ohm	▶	GO to B6 .
	One or both readings greater than 1 ohm	▶	DISCONNECT processor. INSPECT for corrosion, damaged pins, and REPEAT Quick Test. If fault is still present, REPLACE processor. REPEAT Quick Test.
B6 HARNESS CHECK (SIGNAL RETURN)			
• Refer to illustration B. • Key Off. Processor connected. DVOM 200 ohm range. • Make a resistance measurement between pin 37 and circuit 359 Sig. Ret. in the Self-Test connector.	Reading is less than 5 ohms	▶	System OK, REPEAT Quick Test.
	Reading is 5 ohms or greater	▶	CORRECT cause of resistance in the harness circuit 359. REPEAT Quick Test.

| Vehicle Battery | | Pinpoint Test | B |

TEST STEP	RESULT	▶	ACTION TO TAKE
B1 BATTERY VOLTAGE CHECK			
• Key to Run, engine Off. • Measure voltage across battery terminals.	Greater than 10.5 volts	▶	GO to B2 .
	10.5 volts or less	▶	SERVICE discharged battery. REFER to Section 31-02, Shop Manual, Volume B.
B2 BATTERY POWER GROUND CHECK			
• Refer to illustration B. • Key to Run, engine Off, DVOM on 20 volt range. Processor connected. • Take a voltage reading from battery negative post to signal return circuit 359 in the Self-Test connector. • Voltage reading is less than 0.5 volts.	Less than 0.5 volts	▶	GO to B3 .
	Greater than 0.5 volts	▶	GO to B4 .
B3 12V BATTERY POWER CHECK AT PROCESSOR			
• Refer to illustration B. • Key to Run, engine Off. • DVOM 20 volt range. Processor connected. Key to Run. • Take a voltage reading from battery positive post to pin 37. • Repeat above check from battery positive post to pin 57.	Both readings less than 0.5 volts	▶	GO to C1 .
	One or both readings greater than 0.5 volts	▶	GO to B7 .
B4 GROUND FAULT ISOLATION			
• Refer to illustration B. • Connect breakout box. • DVOM 20 volt range. Processor connected. Key to Run. • Take a voltage reading from battery negative post to pin 40. • Repeat above check from battery negative post to pin 60.	Both readings less than 0.5 volts	▶	GO to B5 .
	One or both readings greater than 0.5 volts	▶	Circuit with greater than 0.5 volts has high resistance or open. CORRECT faulty ground circuit 57. REPEAT Quick Test.

| Vehicle Battery | | Pinpoint Test | B |

TEST STEP	RESULT	▶	ACTION TO TAKE
B7 12V BATTERY POWER FAULT ISOLATION			
• Refer to illustration B. • In the event an open fusible link is found, check for shorts to ground before replacing the fusible link. • DVOM 20 volt range. Processor connected. Key to Run, engine Off. • DVOM negative lead to battery negative post. Make the following voltage checks: **NOTE: Key must remain in Run position for all remaining checks.**			
a. Check circuit 37, yellow at EEC power relay.	Greater than 10.5 volts	▶	GO to b .
	10.5 volts or less	▶	CHECK circuit 37. Power relay to battery positive for opens. Before servicing, CHECK circuit 37 and 361 for shorts to ground.
b. Check circuit* at the power relay.	Greater than 10.5 volts	▶	GO to c .
	10.5 volts or less	▶	CHECK 10 amp fuse location 18, then for open in ignition switch start/run circuits,* ignition switch and circuit 37.
c. Check circuit** at the power relay.	0.5 volts or less	▶	GO to d .
	Greater than 0.5 volts	▶	CORRECT open ground in circuit **
d. Check circuit 361, Red at the EEC power relay.	10.5 volts or more	▶	CORRECT open in circuit 361 from EEC power relay to pins 37 and 57. If circuit 361 is OK, REPLACE processor.
* Circuit 175 BK/Y D — Mustang/Capri Circuit 20 W/LB A — Thunderbird/Cougar ** Circuit 57 BK — Mustang/Capri Circuit 60 BK/LG D — Thunderbird/Cougar	Less than 10.5 volts	▶	REPLACE power relay.

EEC IV-2.3L EFI Turbocharged Engine Diagnosis

Reference Voltage (Vref) | Pinpoint Test | C

C

BREAKOUT
BOX PIN NO.

PIN 40 O ——— 57 BK (PWR GRD)
PIN 60 O

PWR.
RELAY

TO
IGN.
SW.

FUSIBLE
LINK

37 (Y)

PIN 37 O ——— 361 R (BATT. PWR.)
PIN 57 O

PIN 26 O ——— 357 O/W (VREF) ———► TO SENSORS

PIN 46 O ——— 359 BK/W (SIG. RTN.)

STOP-WARNING

This Pinpoint Test is intended to diagnose only the following:

- Circuits 37, 57, 351, 359, 361 and 640
- Processor Assembly
- VAF, and TP Sensor

Reference Voltage | Pinpoint Test | C

	TEST STEP	RESULT ▶	ACTION TO TAKE
C5	CHECK FOR SHORTED THROTTLE POSITION SENSOR		
	• Do not disconnect processor. • Disconnect Throttle Position (TP) sensor from vehicle harness. • Turn key to Run, engine Off. • With DVOM, measure between Breakout Box pin 26 and pin 46.	DVOM READING 4.0 volts or less ▶ More than 4.0 volts ▶	GO to C6. REPLACE TP sensor. REPEAT Quick Test.
C6	CHECK FOR SHORTED VANE AIR METER		
	• Do not disconnect processor. • Disconnect VAF sensor from vehicle harness. • Key On. • With DVOM, measure between Breakout Box pin 26 and pin 46.	DVOM READING 4.0 volts or less ▶ More than 4.0 volts ▶	GO to C7. REPLACE VAF Meter. RECONNECT TP sensor. REPEAT Quick Test.
C7	CHECK VPWR AND GROUND HARNESS CONTINUITY		
	• Refer to illustration C. • Turn key Off. • Disconnect EEC processor from Breakout Box. Leave Breakout Box connected to harness. • DVOM to 200 ohm scale. • Check continuity from pin 40 and pin 60 to battery negative post, pin 37 and pin 57 to circuit 361 terminal on power relay.	DVOM READING All circuits less than 1 ohm ▶ Any circuit more than 1 ohm ▶	GO to C8. SERVICE open circuit or bad connection in harness. RE-CONNECT all sensors. REPEAT Quick Test.
C8	CHECK FOR EEC HARNESS SHORTS		
	• With Breakout Box connected to vehicle harness, disconnect harness connector from module and check for short circuits between VREF pin 26 and remaining pins on Breakout Box. Verify TP and VAF/VAT sensors are still disconnected.	DVOM READING 10,000 ohms or more ▶ Under 10,000 ohms ▶	REPLACE processor assembly. REPEAT Quick Test. SERVICE short. RECONNECT all sensors. REPEAT Quick Test.

Reference Voltage | Pinpoint Test | C

	TEST STEP	RESULT ▶	ACTION TO TAKE
C1	VEHICLE BATTERY POWER CIRCUIT CHECK		
	• Refer to illustration C. • DVOM 20 volt range, Breakout Box connected to processor and vehicle harness. • Measure voltage between pin 37 and pin 40. • Key in Run, reading must be greater than 10.5 volts.	Greater than 10.5 volts ▶ 10.5 volts less ▶	GO to C2. GO to Pinpoint Test B1.
C2	VREF VOLTAGE CHECK		
	• Refer to illustration C. • Connect Breakout Box. • Turn key to Run, engine Off. • With DVOM, measure between pin 26 and pin 46 with processor connected.	DVOM READING More than 6.0 volts ▶ Less than 4.0 volts ▶ 4.0 to 6.0 volts ▶	GO to C3. GO to C5. REPEAT Quick Test.
C3	CHECK FOR SHORT TO BATTERY VOLTAGE		
	• Refer to illustration C. • Turn key to Off. • Leave DVOM connected as in Step C2.	DVOM READING 0.5 volts or less ▶ More than 0.5 volts ▶	GO to C4. SERVICE short between VREF and battery power circuits. REPEAT Quick Test.
C4	CHECK FOR SHORT TO PROCESSOR POWER (VPWR)		
	• Refer to illustration C. • Disconnect processor assembly from Breakout Box harness. • Turn key to Run, engine Off. • With DVOM, measure between Breakout Box pin 26 and pin 46.	DVOM READING 0.5 volts or less ▶ More than 0.5 volts ▶	REPLACE processor assembly. REPEAT Quick Test. SERVICE short between VREF and battery power in EEC-IV harness. REPEAT Quick Test.

Vane Air Temp. (V.A.T.) | Pinpoint Test | D

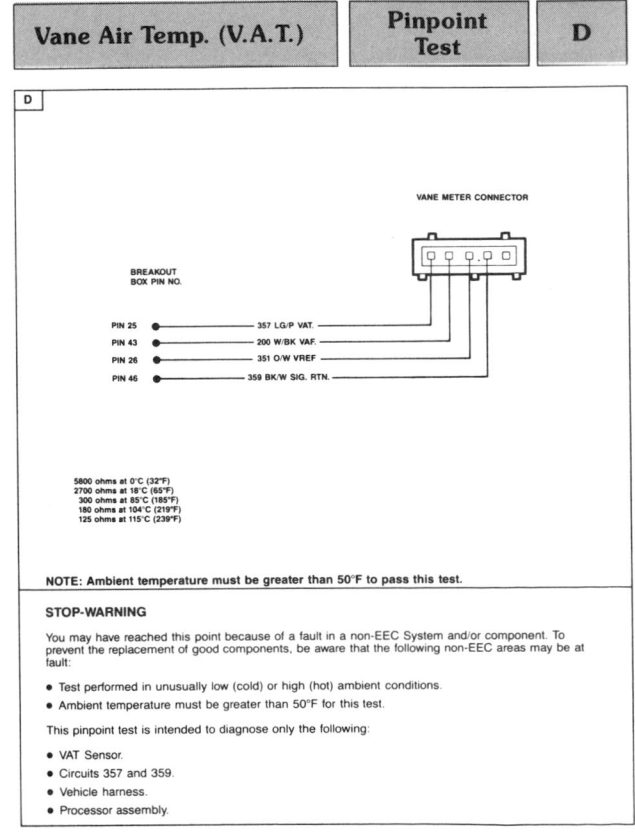

D

VANE METER CONNECTOR

BREAKOUT
BOX PIN NO.

PIN 25 ● ——— 357 LG/P VAT.
PIN 43 ● ——— 200 W/BK VAF.
PIN 26 ● ——— 351 O/W VREF
PIN 46 ● ——— 359 BK/W SIG. RTN.

5800 ohms at 0°C (32°F)
2700 ohms at 18°C (65°F)
300 ohms at 85°C (185°F)
180 ohms at 104°C (219°F)
125 ohms at 115°C (239°F)

NOTE: Ambient temperature must be greater than 50°F to pass this test.

STOP-WARNING

You may have reached this point because of a fault in a non-EEC System and/or component. To prevent the replacement of good components, be aware that the following non-EEC areas may be at fault:

- Test performed in unusually low (cold) or high (hot) ambient conditions.
- Ambient temperature must be greater than 50°F for this test.

This pinpoint test is intended to diagnose only the following:

- VAT Sensor.
- Circuits 357 and 359.
- Vehicle harness.
- Processor assembly.

EEC IV-2.3L EFI Turbocharged Engine Diagnosis

439

SECTION 5 ELECTRONIC ENGINE CONTROLS

Vane Air Temp (V.A.T.)	Pinpoint Test	D

TEST STEP	RESULT ▶	ACTION TO TAKE
D1 CHECK VAT TO SIG. RET. VOLTAGE		
• Disconnect VAT/VAF connector. • DVOM to 20 volt range. • Key On — Engine Off. • Make a voltage measurement at the VAT harness connector from VAT signal circuit 357 to Sig. Ret. circuit 359.	Between 4.0-6.0 volts ▶	GO to D2 .
	Less than 4.0 volts ▶	GO to D3 .
	More than 6.0 volts ▶	GO to Pinpoint Test Step C1 .
D2 VAT SENSOR CHECK		
NOTE: Ambient temperature must be greater than 28°C (50°F) to pass this test. • Key Off, DVOM 200,000 ohms range. • Make a resistance measurement at the VAT sensor (refer to Fig. D). **SPECIFICATION** • Key On — Engine Off Test. 10°C (50°F) = 3700 ohms. 115°C (239°F) = 125 ohms. • Key On — Engine Running Test. 28°C (50°F) = 3700 ohms. 115°C (239°F) = 125 ohms. • Is the resistance reading within specification?	No ▶ Yes ▶	REPLACE VAT/VAF meter assembly. REPEAT Quick Test. REPLACE processor. REPEAT Quick Test.
D3 CONTINUITY CHECK OF CIRCUITS 357 AND 359		
• Key Off. • Connect Breakout Box to Harness, leave processor disconnected. • DVOM to 200 ohm range. • Check continuity of VAT circuit 357 from harness connector to pin 25 of Breakout Box, also Sig. Ret. circuit 359 harness connector to pin 46 of the Breakout Box.	Both less than 5 ohms ▶ Either or both circuits more than 5 ohms ▶	GO to D4 . REPAIR circuit(s) with a reading of more than 5 ohms and retest. REPEAT Quick Test.
D4 CHECK VAT CIRCUITS FOR SHORTS		
• Key Off. • DVOM on 200,000 ohms range. • Breakout Box connected to vehicle harness, processor not connected. • Measure the resistance of Breakout Box pin 25 to Breakout Box pins 40, 46 and 60.	One or more reading less than 10,000 ohms ▶ All three reading greater than 10,000 ohms ▶	REPAIR circuits, with a reading of less than 10,000 ohms. REPEAT Quick Test. GO to D2 .

Throttle Position Sensor (TPS)	Pinpoint Test	E

E
BREAKOUT BOX PIN NO.

PIN 26 —— 351 O/W VREF
PIN 47 —— 355 RG/LG TP
PIN 46 —— 359 BK/W SIG. RTN.

TP SENSOR
VREF
SIG. RTN.
END VIEW OF HARNESS CONNECTOR

• Key On — Engine Off; closed throttle reading, 0.25-1.40 volts.
• Total Sensor Resistance 3800 ohms.

STOP-WARNING

You may have reached this point because of a fault in a non-EEC System and/or component. To prevent the replacement of good components, be aware that the following non-EEC areas may be at fault:

• Throttle or Speed Control Linkage Binding.
• Idle Speed/Throttle Stop Adjustment.

This Pinpoint is intended to diagnose only the following:

• TP Sensor.
• Sensor harness circuits 351, 355 and 359.

Vane Air Temp (V.A.T.)	Pinpoint Test	D

TEST STEP	RESULT ▶	ACTION TO TAKE
D5 VAT INPUT ALWAYS HIGH **Code 54**		
• Refer to Fig. D. • Key Off. • Generate opposite code by inserting a jumper between harness connector VAT circuit 357 and Sig. Rtn. 359. • Perform Key On — Engine Off Quick Test Step 3.0. • Is Code 64 present?	Yes ▶ No ▶	REPLACE VAT sensor. REPEAT Quick Test. REMOVE jumper wire. GO to D6 .
D6 CHECK CONTINUITY OF CIRCUITS 357 AND 359		
• Key Off. • Connect Breakout Box to harness, leave processor disconnected. • DVOM to 200 ohms range (verify jumper from Step D10 has been removed). • Check continuity of VAT circuit 357 from harness connector to pin 25 of the Breakout Box, also Sig. Return circuit 359 harness connector to pin 46 of the Breakout Box.	Both circuits less than 5 ohms ▶ Either or both circuits greater than 5 ohms ▶	REPLACE the processor. REPEAT Quick Test. REPAIR circuits with a reading of greater than 5 ohms. REPEAT Quick Test.
D7 VAT INPUT ALWAYS LOW **Code 64**		
• Key Off. • Generate opposite code by disconnecting vehicle harness connector from VAT/VAF and perform Key On — Engine Off Quick Test. • Is Code 54 present?	Yes ▶ No ▶	REPLACE VAT/VAF sensor. REPEAT Quick Test. GO to D8 .
D8 VAT CIRCUIT SHORT CHECK		
• Key Off. • Disconnect processor from vehicle harness. • Install Breakout Box. Leave processor and VAT/VAF Sensors disconnected. • DVOM 200,000 ohms range. • Measure the resistance between Breakout Box pin 25 and pins 40, 46, and 60.	One or more readings less than 10,000 ohms ▶ All three readings greater than 10,000 ohms ▶	REPAIR circuits with a reading of less than 10,000 ohms. REPEAT Quick Test. REPLACE processor. REPEAT Quick Test.

Throttle Position Sensor (TPS)	Pinpoint Test	E

TEST STEP	RESULT ▶	ACTION TO TAKE
E1 TP SENSOR SIGNAL OUT OF LIMITS **CODE 23**		
NOTE: Code 23 indicates the TP sensor input to the processor is out of the closed throttle limits (0.25-1.40 volts). There are no opens or shorts in the TP circuit or a code 53 (Sig. always high) or 63 (Sig. always low) would have been generated. • Verify the throttle linkage is at mechanical/ closed throttle. Check for: binding throttle linkage, speed control linkage, vacuum line/ electrical harness interference, etc.	The throttle plate is mechanically closed ▶ The throttle plate is not mechanically closed ▶	GO to E2 . REPAIR as necessary. REPEAT Quick Test.
E2 THROTTLE PLATE OPENING CHECK		
• Verify the Throttle Plate opening RPM Set Point. Refer to the VECI decal.	No adjustment needed ▶ RPM adjustment needed ▶	REPLACE TP Sensor. **NOTE: TP Sensor is non-adjustable. When out of specification, it must be replaced.** ADJUST as necessary. REPEAT Quick Test.
E3 TP SIGNAL INPUT ALWAYS HIGH **CODE 53**		
• Refer to Fig. E. • Key Off. • Disconnect TP Sensor. Inspect for damaged pins, corrosion, loose wires, etc. Repair as necessary. • With DVOM on 20 volt scale, make a voltage measurement from TP Sensor connector (harness side) circuit 359 BK/W, to battery positive. • Reading is 10 volts or more.	Yes ▶ No ▶	GO to E4 . GO to E6 .
E4 TP SENSOR SIGNAL CHECK		
• Refer to Fig. E. • TP Sensor disconnected. • Key On — Engine Off. • Make a voltage measurement between TP Sensor harness connector circuit 355 DG/LG, and circuit 359 BK/W.	Less than 4.0 volts ▶ 4.0 volts or more ▶	GO to E5 . GO to E7 .

EEC IV-2.3L EFI Turbocharged Engine Diagnosis

Throttle Position Sensor (TPS) — Pinpoint Test E

TEST STEP	RESULT ▶	ACTION TO TAKE
E5 GENERATE OPPOSITE FAULT		
• With TP Sensor disconnected, perform Key On — Engine Off Quick Test (Step 3.0). • Is code 63 present?	Yes ▶	REPLACE TP Sensor. REPEAT Quick Test.
	No ▶	REPLACE processor. REPEAT Quick Test.
E6 ISOLATE SIGNAL RETURN CIRCUIT FAULT		
• Refer to Fig. E. • Key Off. • Connect Breakout Box to vehicle harness. Do not connect the TP Sensor Processor. • DVOM to 200 ohms range. • Check continuity between circuit 359 BK/W from TP Sensor harness connector and Breakout Box pin 46.	5 ohms or less ▶	REPLACE processor. REPEAT Quick Test.
	Greater than 5 ohms ▶	REPAIR open in circuit 359. REPEAT Quick Test.
E7 TP SENSOR SHORTED TO POWER		
• Refer to Fig. E. • Disconnect processor from vehicle harness, leave TP Sensor disconnected. • DVOM to 20 volt scale. • Key On — Engine Off. • Make a voltage measurement between TP Sensor harness connector circuit 355 DG/LG and circuit 359 BK/W.	4.0 volts or more ▶	Correct short in harness circuit 355 to 359 or 361. REPEAT Quick Test.
	Less than 4.0 volts ▶	REPLACE processor. REPEAT Quick Test.
E8 VREF CHECK: **CODE 63** ALWAYS LOW		
• Refer to Fig. E. • Key On. • Disconnect TP Sensor. • DVOM to 20 volt range. • Take a voltage reading between TP harness connector circuit 351 O/W and circuit 359 BK/W.	4.0-6.0 volts ▶	GO to E9 .
	Less than 4.0 volts ▶	GO to E12 .
	More than 6.0 volts ▶	RECONNECT TP sensor. GO to Pinpoint Test Step C1 .

Throttle Position Sensor (TPS) — Pinpoint Test E

TEST STEP	RESULT ▶	ACTION TO TAKE
E13 TP SENSOR MOVEMENT IN ENGINE RESPONSE TEST: **CODE 73**		
NOTE: Code 73 indicates the TP Sensor did not exceed 25% of its rotation in the Engine Response Check. • Key Off. • Install Breakout Box. • DVOM to 20 volt range. • Connect DVOM to Breakout Box pin 47 and pin 46. • Perform Engine Running Quick Test (Step 5.0). • Verify DVOM reading exceeds 3.5 volts during brief WOT at Engine Response Check.	DVOM exceeds 3.5 volts during Engine Response Check ▶	REPLACE processor. REPEAT Quick Test.
	DVOM does not exceed 3.5 volts during Engine Response Check ▶	VERIFY TP Sensor is properly attached to throttle body. If OK, REPLACE TP Sensor. REPEAT Quick Test.

Throttle Position Sensor (TPS) — Pinpoint Test E

TEST STEP	RESULT ▶	ACTION TO TAKE
E9 GENERATE OPPOSITE CODE		
• Refer to Fig. E. • Key Off. • With TP Sensor disconnected, jumper TP Sensor circuit 355 DG/LG to circuit 351 O/W at the harness connector. • Perform Key On — Engine Off Quick Test (Step 3.0). • Is code 53 present?	Yes ▶	REPLACE TP Sensor. REPEAT Quick Test.
	No code 53 or no codes ▶	REMOVE jumper. GO to E10 .
E10 CHECK CIRCUIT 355 FOR SHORT TO GROUND		
• Refer to Fig. E. • Key Off. • DVOM to 200,000 ohms range. • Take a resistance reading between the harness connector TP Sensor circuit 355 DG/LG and circuit 359 BK/W.	10,000 ohms or more ▶	GO to E11 .
	Less than 10,000 ohms ▶	REPAIR short in circuit 355. REPEAT Quick Test.
E11 CONTINUITY CHECK OF CIRCUIT 355		
• Refer to Fig. E. • Key Off. • Install Breakout Box (processor may be left disconnected). • DVOM 200 ohm range. • Take a resistance measurement between TP harness connector circuit 355 DG/LG and Breakout Box pin 47.	Less than 5 ohms ▶	REPLACE processor. REPEAT Quick Test.
	5 ohms or more ▶	REPAIR open in circuit 355. REPEAT Quick Test.
E12 CONTINUITY CHECK OF CIRCUIT 351		
• Refer to Fig. E. • Key Off. • Install Breakout Box (processor may be left disconnected). • DVOM to 200 ohm range. • Take a resistance reading between TP harness connector circuit 351 O/W and Breakout Box pin 26.	Less than 5 ohms ▶	REPLACE processor. REPEAT Quick Test.
	5 ohms or more ▶	REPAIR open in circuit 351. REPEAT Quick Test.

Engine Coolant Temperature Sensor (ECT) — Pinpoint Test F

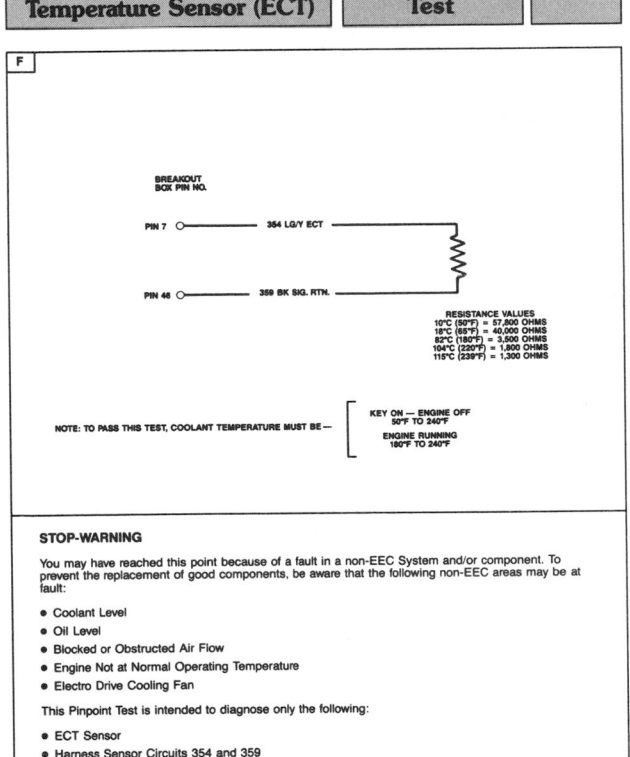

BREAKOUT BOX PIN NO.

PIN 7 — 354 LG/Y ECT

PIN 46 — 359 BK SIG. RTN.

RESISTANCE VALUES
 10°C (50°F) = 57,800 OHMS
 18°C (65°F) = 40,000 OHMS
 82°C (180°F) = 3,500 OHMS
 104°C (220°F) = 1,800 OHMS
 115°C (239°F) = 1,300 OHMS

NOTE: TO PASS THIS TEST, COOLANT TEMPERATURE MUST BE —
 KEY ON — ENGINE OFF 50°F TO 240°F
 ENGINE RUNNING 180°F TO 240°F

STOP-WARNING

You may have reached this point because of a fault in a non-EEC System and/or component. To prevent the replacement of good components, be aware that the following non-EEC areas may be at fault:

• Coolant Level
• Oil Level
• Blocked or Obstructed Air Flow
• Engine Not at Normal Operating Temperature
• Electro Drive Cooling Fan

This Pinpoint Test is intended to diagnose only the following:

• ECT Sensor
• Harness Sensor Circuits 354 and 359
• Processor Assembly

EEC IV-2.3L EFI Turbocharged Engine Diagnosis

Engine Coolant Temperature Sensor (ECT)	Pinpoint Test	F

TEST STEP	RESULT ▶	ACTION TO TAKE
F1 START ENGINE TO BRING ECT WITHIN LIMITS: **SERVICE CODE 21** • Start engine and operate. • Check that upper radiator hose is hot and pressurized. Verify engine is at normal operating temperature. • Perform Quick Test before continuing.	Code 21 still present ▶ No code 21 ▶ Vehicle stalls ▶	GO to F2. SERVICE any other codes as necessary. Do not service code 21 at this time. REFER to Section 2, in this manual for diagnostics by symptom.
F2 CHECK ECT TO SIG. RTN. VOLTAGE • Refer to Fig. E. • Disconnect ECT and inspect both connectors. • DVOM on 20 volt scale. • Key On — Engine Off • Measure voltage between harness connector circuits 354 LG/Y and 359 BK/W.	DVOM reading between 4.0 volts and 6.0 volts Less than 4.0 volts ▶ More than 6.0 volts ▶	GO to F3. GO to F4. GO to Pinpoint Test Step C1.
F3 ECT SENSOR CHECK **NOTE: Vehicle may have cooled down. Always warm vehicle up before taking ECT resistance measurements.** • Key Off. • DVOM on 200,000 ohm scale. • Take a resistance measurement of the ECT sensor. • Is the resistance reading from: — 1,300 ohms to 58,000 ohms for Engine Off test. — 1,300 ohms to 3,500 ohms for Engine Running.	Yes ▶ No ▶	REPLACE processor. REPEAT Quick Test. REPLACE the sensor. REPEAT Quick Test.

Engine Coolant Temperature Sensor (ECT)	Pinpoint Test	F

TEST STEP	RESULT ▶	ACTION TO TAKE
F7 CHECK CONTINUITY OF CIRCUITS 354 AND 359 • Refer to Fig. F. • Key Off. • Remove jumper wire. • Install Breakout Box to harness. Leave processor disconnected. • DVOM on 200 ohm scale. • Measure continuity of ECT sensor circuit 354 LG/Y to Breakout Box pin 7, and circuit 359 BK/W to pin 46.	Either circuit with resistance more than 5 ohms ▶ Both resistances 5 ohms or less ▶	REPAIR open in harness. REPEAT Quick Test. REPLACE processor. REPEAT Quick Test.
F8 ECT INPUT LOW • Disconnect ECT connector. • Induce opposite failure (open). • Run Key On — Engine Off Quick Test (Step 3.0). • Is code 51 present? **NOTE: Any time shorts or opens are present during testing a code will be generated in continuous test.**	Code 51 present ▶ No code 51 present ▶	REPLACE ECT. REPEAT Quick Test. GO to F9.
F9 CHECK ECT CIRCUIT FOR SHORTS TO GROUND • Key Off and wait 10 seconds. • Install Breakout Box to harness, leave processor disconnected. • DVOM on 200,000 ohm scale. • ECT disconnected. • Measure resistance of Breakout Box pin 7 to pins 40 and 60.	Any resistance less than 10,000 ohms ▶ Both resistances 10,000 ohms or more ▶	REPAIR harness short. REPEAT Quick Test. REPLACE processor. REPEAT Quick Test.

Engine Coolant Temperature Sensor (ECT)	Pinpoint Test	F

TEST STEP	RESULT ▶	ACTION TO TAKE
F4 CHECK CONTINUITY OF CIRCUITS 354 AND 359 • Refer to Fig. F. • Key Off. • Disconnect processor 60 pin connector and inspect both connectors. • Connect Breakout Box to harness. Leave processor disconnected. • DVOM on 200 ohm scale. • Measure continuity of ECT circuit 354 LG/Y to pin 7, and circuit 359 BK/W to pin 46.	Both circuits less than 5 ohms ▶ One or both circuits greater than 5 ohms ▶	GO to F5. REPAIR harness. REPEAT Quick Test.
F5 CHECK ECT CIRCUIT FOR SHORTS TO GROUND • Refer to Fig. F. • Key Off. • DVOM on 200,000 ohm scale. • Measure resistance of pin 7 to pins 40 and 60.	More than 10,000 ohms ▶ Any reading 10,000 ohms or less ▶	GO to F3. REPAIR short to ground. REPEAT Quick Test.
F6 ECT INPUT HIGH: **SERVICE CODE 51** • Refer to Fig. F. • Key Off. • Disconnect ECT connector. Inspect ECT sensor and connector. • Generate opposite code by inserting a jumper wire across vehicle harness ECT terminals 354 LG/Y and 359 BK/W. • Run Key On — Engine Off Quick Test (Step 3.0). • Is code 61 present? **NOTE: Any time shorts or opens are present during testing, a code will be generated in continuous test.**	Code 61 present ▶ No code 61 ▶	REPLACE ECT. REPEAT Quick Test. GO to F7.

Vane Air Flow (VAF)	Pinpoint Test	G

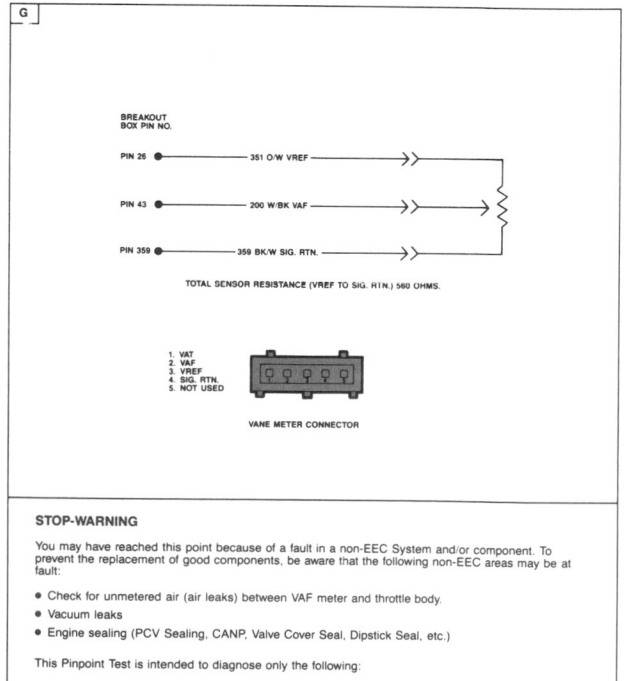

STOP-WARNING

You may have reached this point because of a fault in a non-EEC System and/or component. To prevent the replacement of good components, be aware that the following non-EEC areas may be at fault:

• Check for unmetered air (air leaks) between VAF meter and throttle body.
• Vacuum leaks
• Engine sealing (PCV Sealing, CANP, Valve Cover Seal, Dipstick Seal, etc.)

This Pinpoint Test is intended to diagnose only the following:

• VAF Meter
• Processor
• Harness Circuits 351, 359 and 200.

EEC IV-2.3L EFI Turbocharged Engine Diagnosis

Vane Air Flow (VAF) — Pinpoint Test G

TEST STEP	RESULT ►	ACTION TO TAKE
G1 VAF OUT OF LIMITS: CODE 26		
NOTE: Code 26 (Key On — Engine Off, or Engine Running) indicates the Vane Air Flow Input to the processor is out of closed (Engine Not Running) or at idle limits (Engine Off 0.15-0.50 volts; Engine at idle 1.50-2.70 volts). There have been no opens or shorts in the VAF circuit or a code 56 (signal always high) or 66 (signal always low) would have been generated. • Check for unmetered air leaks. (Vacuum leaks after the vane meter.) • Remove air cleaner element. Check for contamination that may impede vane meter movement. • Is service code 26 received during Key On — Engine Off Quick Test?	Yes ► No ►	REPLACE VAF meter. REPEAT Quick Test. GO to G2.
G2 VAF METER CHECK		
• Key Off. • Install Breakout Box. Reconnect processor and VAF meter. • DVOM 20 volt scale. • Connect DVOM leads between Breakout Box pin 43 and pin 46. • Key On. • Place an unsharpened (new) standard wood lead pencil in vane meter as shown. • Pencil must pass completely through vane meter. • DVOM will read 2.8 volts to 3.7 volts.	Yes ► No ►	Vane meter is capable of outputting an acceptable signal. The VAF code 26 has been caused by incorrect engine speed or on unmetered air leak (vacuum leak). REPAIR as necessary. REPEAT Quick Test. REPLACE VAF meter. REPEAT Quick Test.

PENCIL

VANE METER

Vane Air Flow (VAF) — Pinpoint Test G

TEST STEP	RESULT ►	ACTION TO TAKE
G7 VAF SIGNAL SHORTED TO POWER		
• Refer to Fig. G. • Key Off, connect Breakout Box. • Leave processor and VAF disconnected from vehicle harness. • DVOM to 200,000 ohm scale. • Make a resistance measurement between pin 43 and pin 26, 35 and 57.	Any readings greater than 10,000 ohms ► All readings greater than 10,000 ohms ►	REPAIR short in harness circuit 200 to 359 or 361. REPEAT Quick Test. REPLACE processor. REPEAT Quick Test.
G8 VAF SIGNAL ALWAYS LOW: CODE 66		
• Refer to Fig. G. • Key to Off. • Disconnect VAF harness from VAF meter. • DVOM to 20 volt scale. • Measure voltage between VAF meter harness connector circuit 351 D/W and circuit 359 BK/W.	4.0 volts-6.0 volts ► Less than 4.0 volts ► More than 6.0 volts ►	GO to G9. GO to G12. GO to Pinpoint Test Step C1.
G9 FORCE OPPOSITE CODE		
• Refer to Fig. G. • Key Off. • With VAF meter disconnected, jumper VAF signal circuit 200 W/BK to circuit 351 D/W at the harness connector. • Perform Key On — Engine Off Quick Test. • Is code 56 present? NOTE: Disregard all other codes at this time.	Code 56 present ► No code 56 or no codes ►	REPLACE VAF meter. REPEAT Quick Test. GO to G10.
G10 CHECK VAF CIRCUIT 200 FOR SHORT TO GROUND		
• Refer to Fig. G. • Key Off. VAF still disconnected. • DVOM 200,000 ohms scale. • Take a resistance reading between VAF harness connector circuit 200 W/BK and circuit 359 BK/W.	10,000 ohms or more ► Less than 10,000 ohms ►	GO to G11. REPAIR short in circuit 200. REPEAT Quick Test.

Vane Air Flow (VAF) — Pinpoint Test G

TEST STEP	RESULT ►	ACTION TO TAKE
G3 VAF METER SIGNAL ALWAYS HIGH: CODE 56		
• Refer to Fig. G. • Key Off. • Disconnect VAF sensor. • DVOM on 20 volt scale. • Make a voltage measurement between VAF sensor connector (harness side) circuit 359 BK/W and battery positive post. • Reading is 10 volts or more.	Yes ► No ►	GO to G4. GO to G6.
G4 VAF SENSOR INPUT CHECK		
• Refer to Fig. G. • VAF Sensor disconnected. • Key On — Engine Off. • DVOM 20 volt scale. • Make a voltage measurement between the VAF harness connector VAF circuit 200 W/BK and circuit 359 BK/W.	Less than 4.0 volts ► 4.0 volts or more ►	GO to G5. GO to G7.
G5 FORCE OPPOSITE FAULT		
• With VAF meter disconnected, perform Key On — Engine Off Quick Test (Step 3.0). • Is code 66 present? NOTE: Disregard all other codes at this time.	Yes ► No ►	REPLACE VAF/VAT meter. REPEAT Quick Test. REPLACE processor. REPEAT Quick Test.
G6 ISOLATE SIGNAL RETURN CIRCUIT FAULT		
• Refer to Fig. G. • Key Off. • Connect Breakout Box to vehicle harness. Do not connect the VAF meter or processor. • DVOM to 200 ohm scale. • Check continuity between circuit 359 from VAF harness connector and Breakout Box pin 46.	5 ohms or less ► More than 5 ohms ►	REPLACE processor. REPEAT Quick Test. REPAIR open in circuit 359. REPEAT Quick Test.

Vane Air Flow (VAF) — Pinpoint Test G

TEST STEP	RESULT ►	ACTION TO TAKE
G11 CONTINUITY CHECK OF CIRCUIT 200		
• Key Off. • Connect Breakout Box. • Processor may be left disconnected. • DVOM 200 ohm scale. • Measure the resistance between VAF harness connector circuit 200 W/BK and Breakout Box pin 43.	Less than 5 ohms ► 5 ohms or more ►	REPLACE processor. REPEAT Quick Test. REPAIR open in circuit 200. REPEAT Quick Test.
G12 CONTINUITY CHECK OF CIRCUIT 351		
• Refer to Fig. G. • Key Off. • Connect Breakout Box. • Processor may be left disconnected. • DVOM to 200 ohm scale. • Measure the resistance between VAF harness connector 351 and Breakout Box pin 26.	Less than 5 ohms ► 5 ohms or more ►	REPLACE processor. REPEAT Quick Test. REPAIR open in circuit 351. REPEAT Quick Test.
G13 VAF READING DOES NOT INCREASE IN DYNAMIC RESPONSE TEST: CODE 76		
NOTE: A punch or snap of the throttle may not be sufficient to pass this test. Be sure to move to WOT and return. • Connect Breakout Box. • DVOM on 20 volt scale connected to Breakout Box pins 43 and 46. • Perform Engine Running Quick Test Step 4.0. while monitoring DVOM. • After Dynamic Response code 1(0) operator does brief WOT. DVOM reading should increase more than 2.0 volts at this time. • Observe service code at end of Engine Running Quick Test.	DVOM did increase more than 2.0 volts at Dynamic Response Test, but code 76 still present ► DVOM did not increase 2.0 volts at WOT ►	REPLACE processor. REPEAT Quick Test. CHECK air cleaner and ducting for obstructions. If OK, REPLACE vane air flow meter. REPEAT Quick Test.

EEC IV-2.3L EFI Turbocharged Engine Diagnosis

443

Fuel Control — Pinpoint Test — H

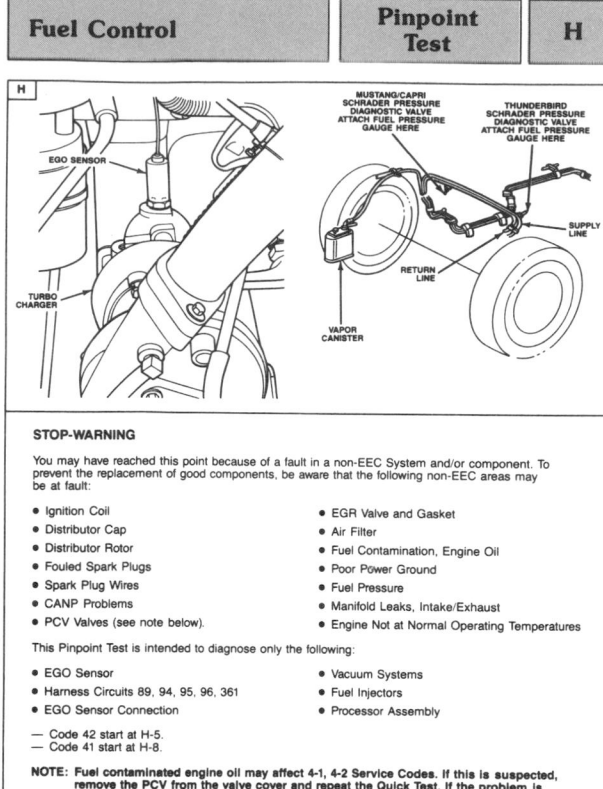

STOP-WARNING

You may have reached this point because of a fault in a non-EEC System and/or component. To prevent the replacement of good components, be aware that the following non-EEC areas may be at fault:

- Ignition Coil
- Distributor Cap
- Distributor Rotor
- Fouled Spark Plugs
- Spark Plug Wires
- CANP Problems
- PCV Valves (see note below).

- EGR Valve and Gasket
- Air Filter
- Fuel Contamination, Engine Oil
- Poor Power Ground
- Fuel Pressure
- Manifold Leaks, Intake/Exhaust
- Engine Not at Normal Operating Temperatures

This Pinpoint Test is intended to diagnose only the following:

- EGO Sensor
- Harness Circuits 89, 94, 95, 96, 361
- EGO Sensor Connection

- Vacuum Systems
- Fuel Injectors
- Processor Assembly

— Code 42 start at H-5.
— Code 41 start at H-8.

NOTE: Fuel contaminated engine oil may affect 4-1, 4-2 Service Codes. If this is suspected, remove the PCV from the valve cover and repeat the Quick Test. If the problem is corrected, then change the engine oil and filter.

Fuel Control — Pinpoint Test — H

	TEST STEP	RESULT	▶	ACTION TO TAKE
H5	FUEL CONTROL — ALWAYS RICH: CODE 42			
	NOTE: Non-EEC areas could cause a code 42. Check for: — Fuel contaminated engine oil — Ignition caused misfire — CANP problems • Refer to Fig. H. • Disconnect vehicle harness at the EGO sensor. Using a jumper wire, ground vehicle harness circuit 94, EGO Sensor input to the engine block. • Repeat the Engine Running Self-Test. • Service code 41 results.	Yes No	▶ ▶	GO to [H7] Go to [H6]
H6	HARNESS CHECK			
	• Refer to Fig. H. • Check continuity of EGO ground circuit 890 between Breakout Box pin 49 and EGO ground at engine block. • Check continuity of EGO circuit 94 DGIP H, between Breakout Box pin 29 and EGO harness connector. • Both circuits less than 5 ohms.	Yes No	▶ ▶	DISCONNECT processor connector. INSPECT for damage or corrosion . If OK, REPLACE processor. REPEAT Quick Test. CORRECT harness circuit with resistance greater than 5 ohms.
H7	EGO CHECK			
	• Refer to Fig. H. • DVOM on 20 volt range. • With EGO sensor disconnected from the harness, connect a DVOM from EGO sensor to engine ground. • Run the engine at 2000 rpm for 2 minutes. While observing DVOM, disconnect the manifold vacuum hose indicated below. • Meter indicates less than 0.4 volts.	Yes No	▶ ▶	EGO sensor OK. GO to [H1] REPLACE EGO sensor. REPEAT Quick Test.

REMOVE THIS HOSE FOR STEP H7

FRONT OF ENGINE

Fuel Control — Pinpoint Test — H

	TEST STEP	RESULT	▶	ACTION TO TAKE
H1	FUEL PRESSURE CHECK			
	• Install fuel pressure gauge. • Start and run engine. Fuel pressure must be 172-310 kPa (25-45 psi). **For No Starts:** • If engine will not run, cycle the key from Off to On several times. • Fuel pressure must remain at 276 ± 34 kPa (40 ± 5 psi) for 60 seconds after final key Off.	Fuel pressure is within specifications Fuel pressure is not as specified	▶ ▶	GO to [H2]. REFER to the Shop Manual for electric fuel pump and fuel pressure regulator check.
H2	HARNESS/INJECTOR RESISTANCE CHECK			

BREAKOUT BOX PIN NO.

PIN 49 — 89 O (EGO GND.)
PIN 29 — 94 DG/P H (EGO)

PIN 58 — 95 T/PK D (INJ. A)
PIN 59 — 96 T/O D (INJ. D)
PIN 37 — 361A R (PWR)
PIN 57 — 361B R (PWR)

EGO GROUND
EGO
INJ. B   INJ. A
TO IGN. SWITCH 37
EEC POWER RELAY   BATTERY

- Connect Breakout Box to harness.
- Key Off, DVOM 200 ohms range. Disconnect injectors for cylinders 2, 3, and 4 electrically.
- Through the vehicle harness, measure the resistance of injector No. 1, between pin 37 and pin 58, record reading.
- Disconnect injector No. 1. Reconnect injector No. 2. Read resistance between pin 37 and pin 58, record reading.
- Disconnect injector No. 2. Reconnect injector No. 3. Read resistance between pin 37 and pin 59, record reading.
- Disconnect injector No. 3. Reconnect injector No. 4. Read resistance between pin 37 and pin 59, record reading.
- All four (4) readings are 2.0 ohms to 3.5 ohms.
- Verify all injectors are connected at end of testing.

RESULT	▶	ACTION TO TAKE
Yes	▶	GO to [H3]
No	▶	SERVICE the harness/connectors on the suspect injector for opens or shorts. If OK, REPLACE injector. REPEAT Quick Test.

Fuel Control — Pinpoint Test — H

	TEST STEP	RESULT	▶	ACTION TO TAKE
H8	FUEL CONTROL — ALWAYS LEAN: CODE 41			
	NOTE: Vacuum/air leaks in non-EEC areas could cause a code 41. Check for: — Leaking vacuum actuator (eg: A/C control motor) — Engine sealing — EGR system — PCV system — Unmetered air leak between air meter and throttle body — Lead contaminated EGO sensor • Refer to Fig. H. • Key Off. DVOM to 20 volt range. Disconnect EGO sensor from vehicle harness. Connect DVOM to EGO sensor and engine ground. Remove air cleaner to gain access to air meter inlet. Using a standard wood lead pencil, prop the air meter door part-way open. • Start the engine and run at approximately 2000 rpm for 2 minutes. • Does the DVOM read greater than 0.5 volts at the end of 2 minutes?	Yes No	▶ ▶	Go to [H9] REPLACE EGO sensor. REPEAT Quick Test.
H9	HARNESS CHECK EGO CIRCUITS			
	• Check continuity of EGO circuit 89, Breakout Box pin 49 to engine block ground. Also circuit 94, pin 29 to harness connector DG/PH at EGO sensor. • Both circuits less than 5 ohms.	(OK) ▶ (⊘) ▶		GO to [H10]. REPAIR/CORRECT as necessary. REPEAT Quick Test.
H10	CHECK EGO CIRCUIT FOR SHORT TO GROUND			
	• Key Off. • DVOM to 200,000 ohms range. • Disconnect EGO sensor at harness. • Measure the resistance between Breakout Box pin 29 and pin 40.	Reading is 150,000 ohms or more Reading is less than 150,000 ohms	▶ ▶	EGO input circuit OK. DISCONNECT processor connector. INSPECT for corrosion or damaged pins. If OK, REPLACE processor. REPEAT Quick Test. CORRECT cause of resistance to ground. REPEAT Quick Test.

EEC IV-2.3L EFI Turbocharged Engine Diagnosis

Fuel Control	Pinpoint Test	H

H11 CONTINUOUS TESTING: CODE 41/42

41 — EGO indicated the fuel system was lean for more than 15 seconds when the system should have been in closed loop fuel control.

42 — EGO indicated the fuel system was rich for more than 15 seconds when the system should have been in closed loop fuel control.

*CLOSED LOOP — Fuel control under the influence of the EGO sensor.

*OPEN LOOP — Fuel control NOT under the influence of the EGO sensor.

Before attempting to correct a fuel control code, 41/42, diagnose all other drive complaints first, eg., rough idle, misses, etc.

NOTE: The fuel control code may help in this diagnosis.

Using the fuel control service code, isolate the cause of the fuel control problem.

Some areas to check are:

- Unmetered Air: Vacuum leaks/intake air leaks.
  — Canister Purge System
  — PCV System
  — Engine sealing
  — Air leaks between VAF meter and throttle body

- EGO Fuel Fouled: Whenever an over-rich fuel condition has been experienced (fuel fouled spark plugs), make a thorough check of the ignition system. In the event the EGO sensor is suspected of being fuel fouled (low output, slow response), run the vehicle at sustained high speeds (within legal limits) followed by a few hard accelerations. This will burn off EGO contamination and restore proper EGO operation.

- Fuel Pressure: Perform Pinpoint Test Step **H1**.

- Ignition System: Always in default spark (10 degrees). Refer to Quick Test Step 4.0.

- Improper Fueling: Lead fouled EGO sensor.

- TP Sensor: Not moving (mechanical damage). Connect DVOM to pin 47 circuit 355 DG/LG and to pin 46 circuit 359 BK/W. Key to Run. Observe DVOM while moving the throttle. Reading must increase with increase in throttle opening. If not correct, REPLACE as necessary.

- If at this point, the drive concern is still present, perform Pinpoint Test Steps H-2 through H-4 only.

Detonation/Spark Knock	Pinpoint Test	K

TEST STEP	RESULT	▶	ACTION TO TAKE
K1 DETONATION/SPARK KNOCK	Knock level remains the same with sensor disconnected	▶	GO to **K2**.
NOTE: The 2.3 EFI Turbo with EEC-IV is capable of retarding spark advance based on information from an engine mounted knock sensor. • Drive the vehicle and verify the detonation complaint. • Disconnect the vehicle harness from the knock sensor at the engine. • Drive the vehicle again. If the knock level has increased, the knock sensor circuit is working.	Knock level increases with sensor disconnected	▶	CHECK base timing, fuel octane, EGR operation, engine/coolant temperature, boost pressure, Self-Test timing.
K2 VERIFY KNOCK SENSOR INPUT, CIRCUITS 310 AND 359			
• Key Off. Disconnect knock sensor. • Connect Breakout Box. • DVOM to 200 ohm scale. • Make a resistance measurement between knock sensor harness-connector circuit 310 Y/RD and Breakout Box pin 23. • Also make a measurement from knock sensor harness connector circuit 359 BK/W and Breakout Box pin 46.	Both readings less than 5 ohms	▶	REPLACE knock sensor. REPEAT Step **K1**. If the knock level remains the same, REPLACE the processor.
	One or both readings greater than 5 ohms	▶	REPAIR circuit(s) with greater than 5 ohms and REPEAT Step **K1**.

Detonation/Spark Knock	Pinpoint Test	K

STOP-WARNING

You may have reached this point because of a fault in a non-EEC System and/or component. To prevent the replacement of good components, be aware that the following non-EEC areas may be at fault:

- Low Grade (Octane) Fuel
- Base Timing (Ignition/Engine)
- Over Temperature

This Pinpoint Test is intended to diagnose only the following:

- Knock Sensor
- Harness Circuit 310 and 351
- Processor Assembly

Idle Speed Control (ISC)	Pinpoint Test	N

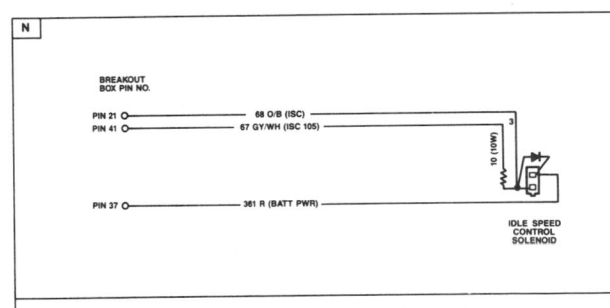

CAUTION: If the engine exhibits rough running and/or idle, correct these conditions before diagnosing Idle Speed Control (ISC). Rough running/misses may be caused by:

- **Ignition System** Refer to Section 15, in this manual.
- **Fuel System** Refer to Pinpoint Test Steps H1 through H4 in this Section.
- **EGR System, Section 6, in this manual.**

STOP-WARNING

You may have reached this point because of a fault in a non-EEC System and/or component. To prevent the replacement of good components, be aware that the following non-EEC areas may be at fault:

- Engine not up to operating temperature
- Engine over operating temperature
- Improper Idle Speed/Throttle Stop Adjustment
- A/C input (electrical problem)
- Throttle/Speed Control Linkage

This Pinpoint Test is intended to diagnose only the following:

- RPM in Self-Test only
- ISC actuator
- Harness Circuits 57, 67, 68, 36
- Processor Assembly

EEC IV-2.3L EFI Turbocharged Engine Diagnosis

Idle Speed Control (ISC) — Pinpoint Test — N

TEST STEP	RESULT ▶	ACTION TO TAKE
N1 DETERMINE CAUSE OF CODE 12		
• Does engine exhibit other symptoms besides ISC problem (miss, rough idle, surge).	Yes ▶	GO to Pinpoint Test Step X1.
	No ▶	GO to N2.
N2 IDLE SPEED CONTROL (ISC) SOLENOID RESISTANCE CHECK		
• Key Off. • Disconnect ISC harness. • DVOM 200 ohm scale. • Measure ISC solenoid resistance.	7-13 ohms ▶	GO to N3.
	Not 7-13 ohms ▶	REPLACE ISC solenoid. REPEAT Quick Test.
N3 ISC SHORT TO CASE (GROUND) CHECK		
• Key Off. • ISC harness disconnected. • DVOM 200,000 ohm scale. • Check for short from either ISC pin to ISC housing.	Greater than 10,000 ohms ▶	GO to N4.
	10,000 ohms or less ▶	REPLACE ISC solenoid. REPEAT Quick Test.
N4 ISC POWER CHECK		
• ISC harness connected. • Key On — Engine Off. • DVOM 20 volt scale. • Measure vehicle power at ISC connector, circuit 361.	Greater than 10.5 volts ▶	GO to N5.
	10.5 volts or less ▶	REPAIR open in circuit 361 from ISC to EEC power relay. REPEAT Quick Test.
N5 ISC CONTROL CIRCUIT CHECK		
• Key Off. • Harness disconnected at ISC. • Connect Breakout Box. • DVOM 200 ohm range. • Check continuity from circuit 68 to Breakout Box pin 21.	Less than 5 ohms ▶	GO to N6.
	5 ohms or greater ▶	REPAIR open/high resistance in circuit 68. REPEAT Quick Test.

Idle Speed Control (ISC) — Pinpoint Test — N

TEST STEP	RESULT ▶	ACTION TO TAKE
N9 CHECK FOR CODE 13		
• Was code 13 present in Step N10 above? (Disregard any other codes.)	Yes ▶	REPLACE processor. REPEAT Quick Test.
	No ▶	GO to N10.
N10 CHECK CIRCUITS 67 AND 68 FOR SHORTS		
• Key Off. • Disconnect processor 60 pin connector and ISC harness connector. • DVOM 2000 ohm scale. • Check for short from ISC harness circuits 67 and 68.	Greater than 1000 ohms ▶	REPLACE processor. REPEAT Quick Test.
	1000 ohms or less ▶	REPAIR short in circuit(s) 67 and/or 68. REPEAT Quick Test.

PIN 41 GY/W — 57 — RESISTANCE WIRE
PIN 21 O/BL — 68
TO POWER RELAY

Idle Speed Control (ISC) — Pinpoint Test — N

TEST STEP	RESULT ▶	ACTION TO TAKE
N6 CHECK FOR ISC SIGNAL AT ACTUATOR		
• Refer to Fig. N. • Vehicle prepared for Quick Test. • DVOM on 20 volt scale and connected to rear of ISC harness connector (leave harness connected); red probe to Red wire, black probe to GY/WH wire. • Start engine and observe DVOM during Quick Test.	Meter reading varies during Quick Test. ▶	REPLACE ISC actuator. REPEAT Quick Test.
	Meter reading does not vary during Quick Test. ▶	GO to N7.
N7 CHECK FOR ISC SIGNAL AT THE PROCESSOR		
• Refer to Fig. N. • Vehicle prepared for Quick Test. • DVOM 20 volt scale. • Connect DVOM to Breakout Box pin 21 and to pin 40. • Start engine and observe the DVOM during Self-Test.	Meter reading varies during Quick Test. ▶	REPAIR opens in harness circuits 67 or 68. REPEAT Quick Test.
	Meter reading does not vary during Quick Test. ▶	DISCONNECT processor and INSPECT for bent, damaged, corroded pins, etc. CORRECT as necessary. If OK, REPLACE processor. REPEAT Quick Test.
N8 RPM DOES NOT DROP TO LESS THAN 1500 AT END OF TEST: CODE 13		
• Disconnect ISC harness connector. • Connect engine tachometer. • Repeat Engine Running Quick Test. • At end of test, record service codes for future use. • Does RPM remain below 1500 RPM during test?	Yes ▶	GO to N9.
	No ▶	CHECK engine vacuum hoses. REFER to VECI decal. CHECK that throttle plates are fully closed, CHECK throttle linkage and/or speed control linkage for binding. If OK, REPLACE ISC. REPEAT Quick Test.

No Codes/ Improper Codes — Pinpoint Test — P

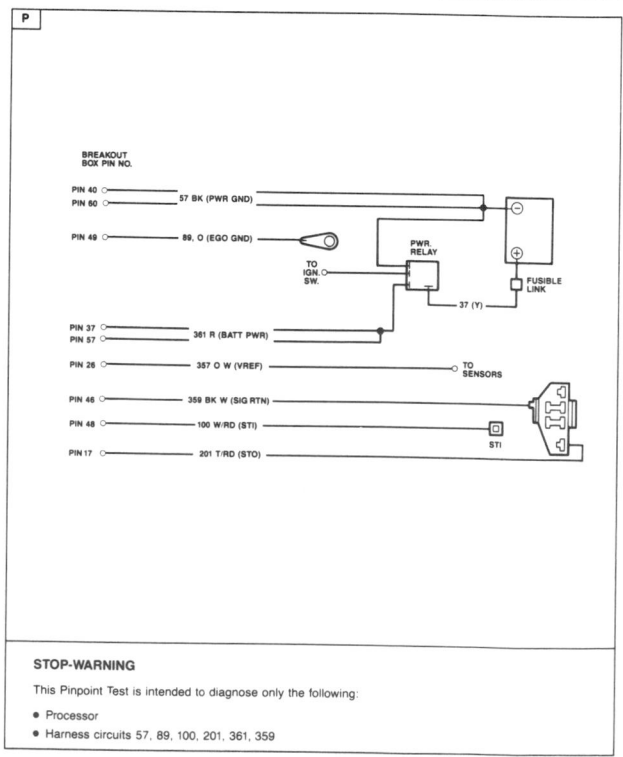

P

BREAKOUT BOX PIN NO.

PIN 40, PIN 60 — 57 BK (PWR GND)
PIN 49 — 89, O (EGO GND)
TO IGN. SW. — PWR. RELAY — FUSIBLE LINK
PIN 37, PIN 57 — 361 R (BATT PWR) — 37 (Y)
PIN 26 — 357 O W (VREF) — TO SENSORS
PIN 46 — 359 BK W (SIG RTN)
PIN 48 — 100 W/RD (STI) — STI
PIN 17 — 201 T/RD (STO)

STOP-WARNING

This Pinpoint Test is intended to diagnose only the following:

• Processor
• Harness circuits 57, 89, 100, 201, 361, 359

EEC IV-2.3L EFI Turbocharged Engine Diagnosis

No Codes/ Improper Codes		Pinpoint Test	P

TEST STEP	RESULT ▶	ACTION TO TAKE
P1 NO CODES, METER ALWAYS HIGH OR ALWAYS LOW, OR INCOMPLETE/ INCORRECT CODES		
• Refer to Fig. P. • Key On — Engine Off. Processor connected. • DVOM on 20 volt range. • Disconnect TP sensor and make voltage measurement between harness connector circuits 351 O/W and 359 BK/W.	6.0 volts or more ▶	GO to Pinpoint Test Step C2 .
	4.0 volts or less ▶	GO to Pinpoint Test Step C1 .
	4.0 to 6.0 volts ▶	RECONNECT TP sensor. GO to P2 .
P2 BATTERY POWER GROUND CHECK (NEGATIVE SUPPLY)		
• Refer to Fig. P. • Key On — Engine Off. • DVOM on 20 volt range. Take a voltage reading from battery negative post to circuit 359 BK/W in the Self-Test connector.	Less than 0.5 volts ▶	GO to P4 .
	Greater than 0.5 volts ▶	GO to Pinpoint Test Step B4 .
P3 SELF-TEST INPUT CHECK		
• Refer to Fig. P. • Connect Breakout Box. • With DVOM 200 ohm range, check Self-Test input circuit 100 W/R D from Self-Test pigtail connector to Breakout Box pin 48.	Less than 5 ohms ▶	GO to P4 .
	5 ohms or more ▶	REPAIR open in circuit 100. REPEAT Quick Test.
P4 SELF-TEST OUTPUT CIRCUIT CHECK		
• Breakout Box connected. • Using DVOM, check Self-Test output circuit 201 T/R at Self-Test connector to Breakout Box pin 17.	5 ohms or more ▶	REPAIR open in circuit 201. REPEAT Quick Test.
	Less than 5 ohms ▶	GO to P5 .

Spark Advance Out of Limits		Pinpoint Test	Q

STOP-WARNING

You may have reached this point because of a fault in a non-EEC System and/or component. To prevent the replacement of good components, be aware that the following non-EEC areas may be at fault:

• Base engine timing
• Base engine problems, cam timing, distributor index
• TFI Module

This Pinpoint Test is intended to diagnose only the following:

• Processor
• Harness circuit 324

No Codes/ Improper Codes		Pinpoint Test	P

TEST STEP	RESULT ▶	ACTION TO TAKE
P5 CHECK EGO SENSOR GROUND		
• Turn key Off. • Breakout Box connected. • Connect DVOM between EGO ground point on the engine and Breakout Box pin 49.	DVOM READING 5 ohms or less ▶	DISCONNECT processor connector. INSPECT for corrosion, damaged pins, etc. RECONNECT and REPEAT Quick Test. If problem is still present, REPLACE processor. REPEAT Quick Test.
	More than 5 ohms ▶	REPAIR EGO sensor ground wire or open circuit bad connection. REPEAT Quick Test.

Spark Advance Out of Limits		Pinpoint Test	Q

TEST STEP	RESULT ▶	ACTION TO TAKE
Q1 SPARK ADVANCE NOT 30° ± 3° IN SELF-TEST		
NOTE: Verify the system is in Self-Test. The Self-Test program lasts about 40 seconds. Once the Self-Test is completed, the system returns to normal engine strategy and spark timing will no longer be locked at 30. • Connect Breakout Box. • With the engine at idle, use a jumper wire to ground Breakout Box pin 36 to chassis. • Does the engine stall?	Yes ▶	Ignition module signal circuit OK, GO to Q2 .
	No ▶	CHECK for open in harness circuit 324. If OK, GO to TFI diagnostics, Section 15, in this manual.
Q2 VERIFY BASE TIMING		
• With the engine Off, disconnect the ignition module signal at inline connector. • Start engine and check timing. • Is timing to 10°BTDC ± 3°? **NOTE:** In the event base calibrated timing has been changed, there will be an emission modification decal on the vehicle. In this case, Self-Test timing will be the new base timing plus 20° ± 3° BTDC. Example: Self Timing = (Base + 20°) ± 3° BTDC.	Yes ▶	DISCONNECT processor connector and INSPECT for corrosion, bent pins, etc. RECONNECT and REPEAT Quick Test. If the problem is still present, REPLACE the processor. REPEAT Quick Test.
	No ▶	ADJUST timing, refer to Section 15, in this manual.

EEC IV-2.3L EFI Turbocharged Engine Diagnosis

Barometric Pressure Sensor	Pinpoint Test	R

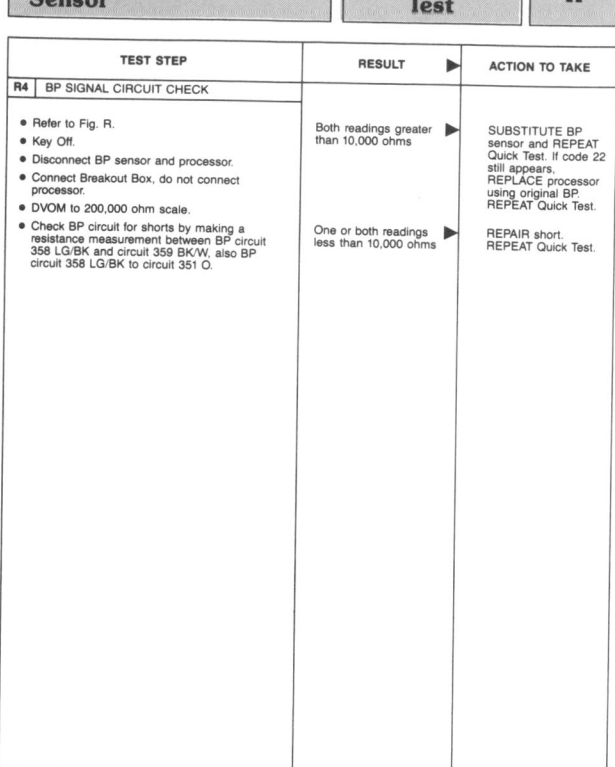

STOP-WARNING

You may have reached this point because of a fault in a non-EEC System and/or component. To prevent the replacement of good components, be aware that the following non-EEC areas may be at fault:

This Pinpoint Test is intended to diagnose only the following:

- An active BP Sensor (will not detect an out of range sensor)
- Harness circuits 100, 357 and 359.
- Processor Assembly

Barometric Pressure Sensor	Pinpoint Test	R

TEST STEP	RESULT ▶	ACTION TO TAKE
R4 BP SIGNAL CIRCUIT CHECK		
• Refer to Fig. R. • Key Off. • Disconnect BP sensor and processor. • Connect Breakout Box, do not connect processor. • DVOM to 200,000 ohm scale. • Check BP circuit for shorts by making a resistance measurement between BP circuit 358 LG/BK and circuit 359 BK/W, also BP circuit 358 LG/BK to circuit 351 O.	Both readings greater than 10,000 ohms ▶	SUBSTITUTE BP sensor and REPEAT Quick Test. If code 22 still appears, REPLACE processor using original BP. REPEAT Quick Test.
	One or both readings less than 10,000 ohms ▶	REPAIR short. REPEAT Quick Test.

Barometric Pressure Sensor	Pinpoint Test	R

TEST STEP	RESULT ▶	ACTION TO TAKE
R1 BP SENSOR: **CODE 22**		
• Refer to Fig. R. **NOTE:** The output signal of the Barometric Pressure Sensor is digital in nature and cannot be monitored without special equipment. Therefore, perform a harness check prior to substituting the BP Sensor. • Disconnect BP sensor. • Key On. • DVOM 20 volt scale. • Measure the voltage between BP Sensor harness connector circuit 351 O and battery negative post.	4.0 to 6.0 volts ▶	GO to R2 .
	Less than 4.0 volts or greater than 6.0 volts ▶	GO to Pinpoint Test Step C1 .
R2 SIGNAL RETURN CHECK		
• Refer to Fig. R. • BP sensor disconnected. • Key On. • DVOM to 20 volt scale. • Measure the voltage between BP harness connector circuit 359 BK/W and battery positive post.	10.0 volts or more ▶	GO to R3 .
	Less than 10.0 volts ▶	REPAIR open in circuit 359. REPEAT Quick Test.
R3 CHECK BP SIGNAL CIRCUIT FOR OPENS		
• Refer to Fig. R. • Key Off. • Disconnect BP sensor. • DVOM to 200,000 ohm scale. • Make a resistance measurement between BP circuit 358 LG/BK and circuit 359 BK/W, also BP circuit 358 LG/BK to circuit 351 O.	Both readings greater than 10,000 ohms ▶	Substitute BP sensor and REPEAT Quick Test. If code 22 still appears, REPLACE processor using original BP Sensor. REPEAT Quick Test.
	One or both readings less than 10,000 ohms ▶	GO to R4 .

Fuel Pump Circuit	Pinpoint Test	S

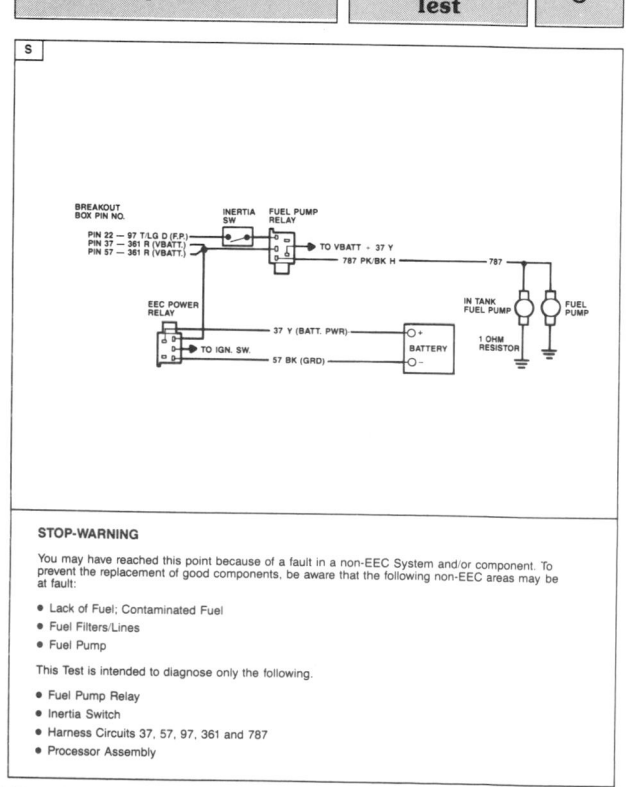

STOP-WARNING

You may have reached this point because of a fault in a non-EEC System and/or component. To prevent the replacement of good components, be aware that the following non-EEC areas may be at fault:

- Lack of Fuel; Contaminated Fuel
- Fuel Filters/Lines
- Fuel Pump

This Test is intended to diagnose only the following.

- Fuel Pump Relay
- Inertia Switch
- Harness Circuits 37, 57, 97, 361 and 787
- Processor Assembly

EEC IV-2.3L EFI Turbocharged Engine Diagnosis

Fuel Pump Circuit	Pinpoint Test	S

TEST STEP	RESULT ▶	ACTION TO TAKE
S1 NO FUEL PUMP PRESSURE		
• Check if fuel pump runs. • Cycle key from Off to Run, repeat several times. (Do not enter start mode). Fuel pump should run briefly each time the key enters Run.	Pump runs ▶	GO to Shop Manual Section 24-35.
	Pump does not run ▶	GO to **S2**.
S2 VERIFY EEC SYSTEM BATTERY POWER		
• Refer to Fig. S. • Connect Breakout Box. • Key On — Engine Off. • Use DVOM to measure battery voltage at pin 37 and pin 57. Negative meter lead to a good chassis ground.	10.5 volts or more ▶	GO to **S3**.
	Less than 10.5 volts ▶	GO to Pinpoint Test Step **B1**.
S3 VERIFY EEC SYSTEM GROUND		
• Refer to Fig. S. • Key On — Engine Off. • Negative lead of meter to battery negative post. With positive meter lead, probe Breakout Box pin 40 and then pin 60. NOTE: Pin 40 and pin 60 both go to vehicle battery negative post. We are looking for a voltage drop in the ground circuit.	Less than 1.0 volts on both circuits ▶	Ground OK. GO to **S4**.
	1.0 volts or more on either or both circuits ▶	REPAIR faulty ground circuit 57 (high resistance indicated by voltage reading).

Fuel Pump Circuit	Pinpoint Test	S

TEST STEP	RESULT ▶	ACTION TO TAKE
S5 FUEL PUMP CIRCUIT CHECK		
• Refer to Fig. S. • Locate fuel pump relay. • Key On — Engine Off. • Using the DVOM negative lead to chassis ground, make the following voltage checks at the points indicated. • In the event an open fusible link is found, check for cause (short to ground) before replacing fuse link.		
a. Circuit 361 R, at fuel pump relay.	Greater than 10.5 volts ▶	GO to b.
	10.5 volts or less ▶	CHECK circuit 361 back to the EEC power relay for open. If OK, GO to **B1**.
b. Circuit 37 Y, at fuel pump relay.	Greater than 10.5 volts ▶	GO to c.
	10.5 volts or less ▶	REPAIR open in circuit 37 between fuel pump relay and vehicle battery positive post.
c. Circuit 97 T/LG D, at fuel pump relay.	Greater than 10.5 volts ▶	GO to d.
	10.5 volts or less ▶	REPLACE pump relay.
d. Circuit 97 T/LG D, at the fuel pump relay during crank.	1.0 volt or less during crank ▶	GO to e.
	Greater than 1.0 volt during crank ▶	REPAIR circuit 97 open. If OK, REPLACE processor.
e. Circuit 787 P/BH, at fuel pump relay during crank mode.	Greater than 10.5 volts during crank ▶	GO to f.
	10.5 volts or less during crank ▶	REPLACE fuel pump relay.

Fuel Pump Circuit	Pinpoint Test	S

TEST STEP	RESULT ▶	ACTION TO TAKE
S4 RESISTANCE CHECK OF FUEL PUMP RELAY		
• Locate and disconnect the fuel pump relay. • DVOM on 200 ohm scale. • Measure the resistance of the fuel pump relay coil (across the two small pins).	Reading is 50-100 ohms ▶	GO to **S5**.
	Reading is lower than 50 ohms or above 100 ohms ▶	REPLACE fuel pump relay.

Fuel Pump Circuit	Pinpoint Test	S

TEST STEP	RESULT ▶	ACTION TO TAKE
S5 FUEL PUMP CIRCUIT CHECK (Continued)		
f. Locate inertia switch. Take voltage reading at both terminals (circuit 787 P/BH) during crank mode.	Greater than 10.5 volts at both terminals during crank ▶	GO to g.
	10.5 volts or less at one terminal during crank ▶	REPLACE inertia switch.
	10.5 volts or less at both terminals during crank ▶	REPAIR open in circuit 787 between inertia switch and fuel pump relay.
g. Circuit 787 P/BK H, at both fuel pumps.	Greater than 10.5 volts during crank at both fuel pumps ▶	GO to h.
	10.5 volts or less during crank at either fuel pump ▶	REPAIR open in 787 circuit between inertia switch and fuel pump.
h. Circuit 57, blk at both fuel pumps, during crank mode (negative meter lead to a good chassis ground).	Greater than 1.0 volt at either fuel pump ▶	CORRECT faulty (greater than 1 volt) ground circuit from fuel pump to chassis ground.
	1.0 volt or less at both fuel pumps ▶	REFER to Section 24-35, in Turbo Shop Manual supplement for fuel pump service.

EEC IV-2.3L EFI Turbocharged Engine Diagnosis

Dynamic Response Test	Pinpoint Test	T

OPERATOR PERFORMS BRIEF WOT

RPM INCREASE
GREATER THAN 3000 RPM

STOP-WARNING

You may have reached this point because of a fault in a non-EEC System and/or component. To prevent the replacement of good components, be aware that the following non-EEC areas may be at fault:

- Operator did not perform Brief Wot at dynamic response code
- Mechanical engine problems; engine will not accelerate

This Pinpoint Test is intended to diagnose only the following:

- Throttle movement (greater than 3/4 throttle)
- Vane Air Flow (greater than 50% open)
- RPM increase (greater than 2000 RPM increase)

EGR On-Off Control	Pinpoint Test	V

EGR SHUTOFF SOLENOID LOCATED UNDER SHIELD - RH FENDER APRON

EGR VALVE

BREAK OUT BOX PIN NO.

PIN 35 — 362 Y

PIN 37 — 361 R

EGR ON/OFF SOLENOID RESISTANCE 65-110 OHMS

STOP-WARNING

You may have reached this point because of a fault in a non-EEC System and/or component. To prevent the replacement of good components, be aware that the following non-EEC areas may be at fault:

- Air or Vacuum Leaks
- EGR Flow restrictions
- EGR Valve

This Pinpoint Test is intended to diagnose only the following:

- Circuits 361 and 362
- EGR Solenoid
- Presence of Manifold Vacuum
- Processor Assembly

Dynamic Response Test	Pinpoint Test	T

TEST STEP	RESULT ▶	ACTION TO TAKE
T1 SYSTEM FAILED TO RECOGNIZE BRIEF W.O.T.: **CODE 77**		
NOTE: A brief snap of the throttle may not be sufficient to pass this test. Be sure to go to W.O.T. and return.		
• Repeat Engine Running Test of Quick Test. Be sure operator is familiar with the engine running format which proceeds as follows: — With Self-Test activated restart the engine. — ID code 2 (0) start of test. — Dynamic response Code 1 (0) perform brief W.O.T. — Testing over. — Service code output begins.	Code 77 still present ▶ No Code 77 ▶	REPLACE processor. REPEAT Quick Test. Dynamic Response Test passed. REPAIR service code(s) received as necessary.

EGR On-Off Control	Pinpoint Test	V

TEST STEP	RESULT ▶	ACTION TO TAKE
V1 EGR FLOW CHECK: **CODE 34**		
NOTE: Code 34 may be the result of a high volume monoxi-vent system (reduces backpressure). If this is suspected perform the test in a well ventilated area, without monoxi-vent connected.		
Vacuum Check • Install vacuum gauge at EGR valve. • Start and idle engine. • Is the vacuum gauge reading less than 3.4 kPh (1 in. Hg)?	Yes ▶ No ▶	GO to **V3**. GO to **V2**.
V2 SOLENOID CHECK		
• Electrically disconnect the EGR solenoid. • Restart and idle the engine. • Is the vacuum gauge reading less than 3.4 kPh (1 in. Hg)?	Yes ▶ No ▶	REPAIR short in circuit 362. If OK replace processor. REPEAT Quick Test. REPLACE EGR solenoid. REPEAT Quick Test.
V3 CHECK VALVE MOVEMENT AND VACUUM		
• Check electrical connection to EGR solenoid. • With vacuum gauge at the EGR valve, perform Engine Running Quick Test and observe: 1. Vacuum changes in test. 2. Valve stem movement in Quick Test.	Valve moves and vacuum increases to greater than 27 kPa (8 in. Hg) ▶ Vacuum greater than 27 kPa (8 in. Hg) but No valve movement ▶ Vacuum less than 27 kPa (8 in. Hg) ▶	EEC system OK. REFER to Diagnostic Routines, Sec. 2 to service EGR system. EEC system OK. REFER to Diagnostic Routines, Sec. 2 to service EGR system. GO to **V4**.
V4 CORRECTING LACK OF ENGINE VACUUM		
• With engine at idle check for manifold vacuum at the lower port of the EGR solenoid.	Vacuum present ▶ Vacuum present ▶	RECONNECT line. GO to **V5**. REPAIR cause of low manifold vacuum at EGR solenoid.

EEC IV-2.3L EFI Turbocharged Engine Diagnosis

EGR On-Off Control		Pinpoint Test	V

TEST STEP	RESULT ▶	ACTION TO TAKE
V5 EGR SOLENOID CHECK		
• Key Off. • Disconnect vehicle harness from EGR solenoid. • With DVOM on 200 ohm scale measure the resistance of the EGR solenoid.	65-110 ohms ▶	GO to V6.
	Not 65-110 ohms ▶	REPLACE EGR solenoid. REPEAT Quick Test.
V6 CHECK CIRCUIT 361		
• Refer to Fig. V. • Key On — Engine Off. • With DVOM on 20 volt range check the voltage at the EGR harness connector circuit 361.	10.5 volts or greater ▶	GO to V7.
	Less than 10.5 volts ▶	REPAIR cause of low battery voltage at circuit 361.
V7 CONTINUITY CHECK OF CIRCUIT 361		
• Key Off. • Connect Breakout Box. • With DVOM on 200 ohm scale, check continuity of circuit 362 Y between Breakout Box pin 35 and harness connector at EGR solenoid. • Less than 5 ohms.	Yes ▶	GO to V8.
	No ▶	REPAIR cause of resistance in circuit 362. REPEAT Quick Test.
V8 EGR CYCLE CHECK		
• Refer to Fig. V. • DVOM to 20 volt scale, connect to back of EGR on-off solenoid connector (leave harness connected to EGR solenoid). • Enter output cycle test (refer to Appendix). • DVOM should indicate greater than 10.5 volts when Self-Test output is activated (STAR LED "off" — Analog meter 12 volts) and less than 1.0 volt when Self-Test output is deactivated, (STAR LED on analog meter 0 volt). • Are these conditions correct?	Yes ▶	REPLACE solenoid. REPEAT Quick Test.
	No ▶	REPLACE processor. REPEAT Quick Test.

A/C Input		Pinpoint Test	W

TEST STEP	RESULT ▶	ACTION TO TAKE
W1 A/C ON: **CODE 67**		
NOTE: Code 67 indicates the processor is receiving a signal (12 volts), that the A/C clutch is energized during Key On — Engine Off Quick Test. Verify the Heater-A/C control is Off. If Code 67 is received with Heater A/C control in the Off position, continue with this Pinpoint Test.		
• Refer to Fig. W. • Key Off. • Connect Breakout Box. • Key On. • DVOM 20 volt scale. • Measure the voltage between Breakout Box pins 10 and 40.	2.0 volts or less with A/C Off ▶	REPLACE processor. REPEAT Quick Test.
	Greater than 2.0 volts with A/C Off ▶	REPAIR short to power in A/C clutch circuit. REPEAT Quick Test.
W2 LACK OF FAST IDLE ASSIST WITH A/C ON		
NOTE: The A/C clutch input to the EEC provides the EEC processor information indicating whether the A/C clutch is energized or not. This information provides an increase in idle speed, to accommodate the additional load of the A/C system. A code 67 with A/C off, indicates a failure in this circuit. We can also force a 67 code to validate the integrity of the circuit.		
• Prepare vehicle Key On — Engine Off Quick Test. • Perform Key On — Engine Off Quick Test with A/C system On. • A good A/C clutch input circuit will produce a code 67.	Code 67 received ▶	System OK.
	No Code 67 ▶	GO to W3.
W3 A/C CLUTCH INPUT FAULT		
• Key Off. • Connect Breakout Box. • Key On — A/C system On. • DVOM 20 volt scale. • Measure the voltage between Breakout Box pins 10 and 40.	2.0 volts or less with A/C On ▶	REPAIR open in vehicle harness A/C circuit.
	Greater than 2.0 volts with A/C On ▶	REPLACE processor. REPEAT Quick Test.

A/C Input		Pinpoint Test	W

W

BREAK OUT BOX PIN NO.

PIN 40 ⊙———— 347 BK/Y H ————⊙ TO A/C CLUTCH

STOP-WARNING

You may have reached this point because of a fault in a non-EEC System and/or component. To prevent the replacement of good components, be aware that the following non-EEC areas may be at fault:

• Heater/A/C Controller

• A/C Compressor Circuits

This Pinpoint Test is intended to diagnose only the following:

• A/C Clutch (ACC) circuit 347

• Processor Assembly

Diagnostics By Symptom		Pinpoint Test	X

TEST STEP	RESULT ▶	ACTION TO TAKE
X1 DIAGNOSTICS BY SYMPTOM		
• Engine stalls. • Stalls in Self-Test. • Runs rough. • Misses.	▶	• Poor power/ground connections. • Ignition system distributor cap, rotor, wires, coil, plugs. • Base Engine — Valves, cam timing, compression etc. • Fuel delivery — Pinpoint steps H1-H4.
• Detonation/spark knock.	▶	GO to Pinpoint Test step K1.
• High idle speeds on each restart may be accompanied by detonation for up to 3-5 minutes after a restart.	▶	GO to Pinpoint Test step X2.
• Lack of fast idle assist with A/C On.	▶	GO to Pinpoint Test step W2.

EEC IV-2.3L EFI Turbocharged Engine Diagnosis

Diagnostics By Symptom	Pinpoint Test	X

TEST STEP	RESULT ▶	ACTION TO TAKE
X2 HIGH IDLE SPEEDS ON EVERY RESTART		
• Verify system is not in Self-Test all the time.		
• Key Off, connect analog voltmeter to Self-Test connector. **Do not** insert jumper for Self-Test.	Any pulsing codes ▶	GO to X3.
• Key to On; observe voltmeter.	No pulsing codes ▶	GO to Pinpoint Test Step N1.
X3 CHECK SELF-TEST INPUT FOR SHORT TO GROUND		
• Connect Breakout Box, leave processor disconnected. • DVOM to 200,000 ohm range. • Take a resistance reading from Breakout Box pin 17 to chassis ground. • Reconnect system at end of testing.	Reading is 10,000 ohms or greater	DISCONNECT, CHECK for corrosion and damaged pins. If fault is still present, REPLACE processor. REPEAT Quick Test
	Reading is less than 10,000 ohms	REPAIR harness short to ground in circuit 100. REPEAT Quick Test.

Erratic Ignition	Pinpoint Test	Y

TEST STEP	RESULT ▶	ACTION TO TAKE
Y1 ERRATIC IGNITION: CODE 14		
NOTE: Code 14 indicates two successive mistimed distributor output pulses were inputed to the processor, resulting in a possible engine miss or stall. • Check vehicle for: — loose wires/connectors — Arcing secondary ignition components, (coil, cap, rotor, wires, plugs, etc.) — On-board transmitter (2-way radio).* • Are any of the above present? *Verify all 2-way radio installations carefully follow manufacturer's installation procedures regarding the routing of antenna and power leads.	Yes ▶	REPAIR as necessary. REPEAT Quick Test.
	No ▶	Code 14 may have been caused by external electro-magnetic interference. REPEAT Quick Test.

EEC IV-2.3L EFI Turbocharged Engine Diagnosis

Quick Test

1.0	VISUAL CHECK AND VEHICLE PREPARATION

Correct test results for the Quick Test are dependent on the proper operation of related non-EEC-IV components systems. It may be necessary to correct any faults in these areas before EEC-IV will pass the Quick Test. Refer to Diagnostic Routines, Section 2 in this manual for service.

Before hooking up any equipment to diagnose the EEC-IV system, make the following checks:

1. Verify the condition of air cleaner and ducting. These components may be removed as necessary for service and/or inspection.

2. Check all engine vacuum hoses for:
   • Proper routing as shown on the VECI decal.

3. Check the EEC system wiring harness electrical connections for:
   • Proper connections.
   • Loose or detached connectors, wires and terminals.
   • Corrosion.
   • Proper routing and position of harness.

   NOTE: It may be necessary to disconnect or disassemble the connector assemblies to perform some of the inspections. (Note the location of each pin before disassembly.)

4. Check control module, sensors and actuators for physical damage.

5. Perform all safety steps required to Start and Run operational vehicle tests.

6. Apply the emergency brake. Place shift lever in Park for automatic transmission; Neutral for manual transmission.

7. Turn off all electrical loads such as: radio, lamps, air conditioner, etc. Be sure doors are closed whenever readings are made.

8. Verify engine coolant is at the specified level.

9. Start engine and idle until the upper radiator hose is hot and pressurized and the throttle is off fast idle. While the engine is operating, check for leaks around the exhaust manifold, EGO sensor, and vacuum hose connections.

   NOTE: If the engine will not start, or starts and stalls, continue with Steps 1.0 through 4.0 of the Quick Test.

10. Turn key Off.

11. Service items as required, and proceed to equipment hook-up.

12. If the problem is intermittent, occurs only at road load, or under some particular vehicle conditions, proceed through to Continuous Testing.

Quick Test

2.0	EQUIPMENT HOOK-UP

Using STAR Tester, Rotunda 07-0004, or equivalent*

• Turn ignition key to Off.

• Connect the color coded adapter cable leads to the STAR Tester.

• Connect the adapter cable's service connectors to the vehicle's appropriate Self-Test connectors.

• Turn power switch On, release STAR push button (no colon showing).

• Self-Test is activated by depressing STAR push button (colon showing).

Using Analog Voltmeter Rotunda 59-0010 or equivalent

• Turn ignition key to Off.

• Connect a jumper wire from Self-Test Input (STI) to Pin 2 Sig. Ret. on Self-Test Connector.

• Set analog VOM on a DC voltage range to read from 0 to 15 volts DC. Connect VOM from battery (+) to Pin 4 Self-Test Output (STO) in the Self-Test Connector.

• Self-Test is activated by installing a jumper from STI to Sig. Ret. pin 2 at the Self-Test connector.

***Must be used with adapter harness Rotunda 07-0010 only.**

NOTE: For additional Quick Test information, refer to the Appendix in this Section.

EEC IV-2.3L HSC Engine Diagnosis

Quick Test

	TEST STEP	RESULT	▶	ACTION TO TAKE
3.0	KEY ON — ENGINE OFF SELF-TEST			

Correct test results for Quick Test are dependent on the proper operation of related non-EEC-IV components/systems. It may be necessary to correct any faults in these areas before EEC-IV will pass Quick Test. Refer to Diagnostic Routines in Section 2 of this manual for proper servicing.

Code Format

ON DEMAND — SEPARATOR — CONTINUOUS

- Verify the vehicle has been properly prepared per Quick Test Steps 1.0 and 2.0.
- Place transmission in Neutral or Park. Set parking brake. Place A/C or heater control to Off.
- Activate Self-Test.
- Place key in Run to start Self-Test.

NOTE: Do not depress throttle during Self-Test.

- Observe and record all Service Codes. The output format will be:
  — Fast codes①
  — On demand codes
  — Separator code②
  — Continuous codes
- Continuous Service Codes recorded in this step will be referenced later in Quick Test Step 6.0.

① Fast Codes serve no purpose in the field, therefore this will be the only place they are referenced. STAR has been designed to ignore these codes, and the analog meter may display them as a slight meter deflection.

② STAR displays a 10 in place of a 1 for the single digit separator code, therefore the separator code is expressed in the results column as 10.

NOTE: If vehicle is being serviced because Shift Indicator Lamp is always On or always Off, Go to Pinpoint Test Step Z1.

TEST STEP	ON DEMAND	SEPARATOR	CONTINUOUS	▶	ACTION TO TAKE
(Fast codes)	11	-1(0)	-11	▶	GO to Quick Test Step 4.0 .
	Any Code	-1(0)	-11	▶	GO to Quick Test Step 3.1 .
	Any Code	-1(0)	Any Code	▶	RECORD continuous codes. GO to Quick Test Step 3.1 .
	11	-1(0)	Any Code	▶	RECORD continuous codes. GO to Quick Test Step 4.0 .
	No codes or invalid display of codes			▶	GO to Pinpoint Test Step P1 .

Quick Test

	TEST STEP	RESULT	▶	ACTION TO TAKE
4.0	CHECK TIMING			

- Engine Running Self-Test must be activated while checking or adjusting spark timing.
- Connect timing light.
- Start engine and check timing for no longer than 25 seconds.

NOTE: If timing is OK, you do not have to recheck timing during remaining tests.

- Refer to VECI decal for base engine timing.
- To calculate timing:
  (Base timing + 20°) ± 3° = Initial Timing

Example

Base timing is 10°.

(10° + 20°) ± 3° = 30° ± 3°

RESULT	▶	ACTION TO TAKE
Timing is: (Base + 20°) ± 3° BTDC	▶	GO to Quick Test Step 5.0 .
Timing is not: (Base + 20°) ± 3° BTDC	▶	GO to Pinpoint Test Step Q2 .
Vehicle does not start	▶	GO to Pinpoint Test Step A1 .
Vehicle stalls while checking timing, during the first 25 seconds	▶	GO to Pinpoint Test Step P16 .

Quick Test

	TEST STEP	RESULT	▶	ACTION TO TAKE
3.1	KEY ON — ENGINE OFF SELF-TEST			

- Using the On Demand Service Codes from Key On — Engine Off Quick Test Step 3.0, follow the instructions in the Action To Take column in this Step.
- When more than one service code is received, always start service with the first code received.
- Whenever a repair is made, REPEAT Quick Test.

NOTE: Before proceeding to the specified Pinpoint Test, read the instructions on how to use them at the beginning of the Pinpoint Tests in this section.

RESULT (On Demand Service Codes)	▶	ACTION TO TAKE
15 Memory	▶	REPLACE Processor and RETEST.
21 ECT	▶	GO to Pinpoint Test Step F1 .
22 MAP	▶	GO to Pinpoint Test Step G3 .
23 TP	▶	GO to Pinpoint Test Step E1 .
51 ECT Open	▶	GO to Pinpoint Test Step F7 .
53 TP Open	▶	GO to Pinpoint Test Step E4 .
61 ECT Low (Closed)	▶	GO to Pinpoint Test Step F9 .
63 TP Low (Closed)	▶	GO to Pinpoint Test Step E10 .
No Codes or Invalid Codes	▶	GO to Pinpoint Test Step P1 .

Quick Test

	TEST STEP	RESULT	▶	ACTION TO TAKE
5.0	ENGINE RUNNING SELF-TEST			

NOTE: On calibrations with a vacuum delay valve, there is a tee and restrictor in the Thermactor Vacuum Control line. The restrictor must be uncapped during Engine Running Self-Test.

- Start and Run engine at greater than 2000 RPM for 2 minutes. This warms up EGO sensor. Ignore any code output at this time.
- Turn Engine Off and wait 10 seconds.
- Verify Self-Test is activated.
- Start the engine. The Engine Running Self-Test will progress as follows:
  — Engine ID code.①
  — Run Test.
  — If a Dynamic Response Ready Code 10 or 1 pulse occurs at this time, perform a brief W.O.T.
  — Engine Running Service Codes.
  — End of Test.

① Engine ID code is equal to half of the number of cylinders (a code of 2 equals a 4 cylinder engine) except for STAR tester which adds a zero to all single digit readings (20 equals a 4 cylinder engine).

② STAR displays a 10 in place of a 1 for the single digit code, therefore the Dynamic Response Ready code is expressed in the results column as 10.

TEST STEP RESULT	ENGINE ID	DYNAMIC RESPONSE READY	ON DEMAND	▶	ACTION TO TAKE
	Engine ID	-1(0)	-11	▶	If there is a drive complaint of low vehicle RPM or occasional stalling during light loads. (Example: When A/C is on). GO to Pinpoint Test Step R1 . If CONTINUOUS codes have been received, GO to Quick Test Step 6.0 .
	Engine ID	-1(0)	Any Code	▶	GO to Quick Test Step 5.1 .
	No Codes or Invalid Codes			▶	REPEAT Self-Test and verify Dynamic Response Test was performed. If no codes after second Self-Test, GO to Pinpoint Test P1 .
	Vehicle stalls during Self-Test			▶	GO to Pinpoint Test Step P16 .

EEC IV-2.3L HSC Engine Diagnosis

Quick Test

TEST STEP	RESULT	▶	ACTION TO TAKE
5.1 ENGINE RUNNING SELF-TEST	Engine Running Service Codes		
NOTE: If vehicle continues to have a drive symptom, even after receiving the pass service code (11) during the Key On — Engine Off and Engine Running Self-Tests, refer to Section 2, in this manual, for further vehicle diagnosis.	12 RPM	▶	GO to Pinpoint Test Step R1.
• Using the Service Codes from Engine Running Self-Test Step 5.0, follow the instructions in the Action To Take column in this Step.	21 ECT	▶	GO to Pinpoint Test Step F1.
• When more than one service code is received, always start service with the first code received.	22 MAP	▶	GO to Pinpoint Test Step G1.
• Whenever a repair is made, REPEAT Quick Test.	23 TP	▶	GO to Pinpoint Test Step E1.
	31 EGR	▶	GO to Pinpoint Test Step H1.
	32 EGR	▶	GO to Pinpoint Test Step H9.
	33 EGR	▶	GO to Pinpoint Test Step H9.
	34 EGR	▶	GO to Pinpoint Test Step H9.
	35 EGR	▶	GO to Pinpoint Test Step R1.
	41 Fuel Lean	▶	GO to Pinpoint Test Step J1.
	42 Fuel Rich	▶	GO to Pinpoint Test Step J15.
	43 Cold EGO	▶	GO to Pinpoint Test Step J27.
	44 Thermactor Inoperative	▶	GO to Pinpoint Test Step L1.
	45 TAD	▶	GO to Pinpoint Test Step L1.

Quick Test

TEST STEP	RESULT	▶	ACTION TO TAKE
5.1 ENGINE RUNNING SELF-TEST (Cont'd.)	Engine Running Service Codes		
	46 TAB	▶	GO to Pinpoint Test Step L1.
	47 EGO Rich, Fuel Lean	▶	GO to Pinpoint Test Step J15.
	72 No MAP Change	▶	GO to Pinpoint Test Step M1.
	73 No PIP Change	▶	GO to Pinpoint Test Step M4.
	77 W.O.T. Not Performed	▶	GO to Pinpoint Test Step M1.
	No Codes or Invalid Codes	▶	GO to Pinpoint Test Step P1.

Quick Test

6.0 | CONTINUOUS TESTING

1. Unless instructed otherwise, do not disconnect any sensor with the key On or a Service Code will be stored in the Continuous Test.

2. Should Keep Alive power, Pin 1 (circuit 37), to the processor, be interrupted momentarily, all stored Continuous Codes will be erased (e.g., disconnecting the processor to connect the Breakout Box).

3. Should Keep Alive power, Pin 1 (circuit 37), fail (and remain an open circuit), invalid codes may be received during Continuous Test.

4. The correct method for clearing the processor's memory of stored Continuous Codes, is to exit Key On — Engine Off Quick Test during the code output sequence (perform Key On — Engine Off Self-Test at the point where the service codes begin). Exit Self-Test by unlatching STAR pushbutton or removing the Self-Test Jumper.

5. Before utilizing stored continuous information, first, verify that the On Demand Key On — Engine Off and Engine Running Quick Tests indicate Service Code 11. If during testing or retesting, an On Demand code is detected, this must be repaired first, since some hard failures also request a code in the continuous memory. Once On Demand testing is completed, clear the memory of Continuous Codes and operate the vehicle to verify the previous repair. If a drive complaint still exists, continue to Step 6.

6. Before repairing any Continuous Test Service Codes, verify a pass (Service Code 11) was received from both On Demand Tests (Key On — Engine Off and Engine Running).

7. Repair only those Continuous Service Codes not repeated from both On Demand Tests (Key On — Engine Off or Engine Running).

Example

	On Demand Key On — Engine Off	Separator	Continuous
First Test Result (Key On — Engine Off)	51	1(0)	41, 51, 64

	Engine I.D.	Dynamic Response	On Demand Engine Running
First Test Result (Engine Running)	3(0)	1(0) (W.O.T.)	41

• Repair the On Demand Key On — Engine Off Service Code 51 first. Next, repair the On Demand Engine Running Service Code 41.

• Note that Service Codes 41 and 51 have been repaired in the On Demand tests. The identical 41 and 51 codes in Continuous Test can now be deleted because of the repairs made in the On Demand Test.

• Repair only Continuous Service Code 64, utilizing Continuous Test procedures.

8. Determine codes to be serviced in Continuous Test procedures.

9. Continue to Quick Test Step 6.1.

Quick Test

6.1 | CLEAR CONTINUOUS CODES

1. Prepare the vehicle for Key On — Engine Off Quick Test as described in Steps 1.0, 2.0, and 3.0.

2. Record all Continuous Test Service Codes.

3. Perform Key On — Engine Off Self-Test. When the first Service Code begins to be outputted, exit the Self-Test program by immediately de-activating Self-Test. (Unlatch STAR pushbutton or remove the jumper from STI to Sig. Ret.) This action will erase any Continuous Codes. Then GO to Quick Test Step 6.2.

EEC IV-2.3L HSC Engine Diagnosis

Quick Test

TEST STEP	RESULT ▶	ACTION TO TAKE
6.2 CONTINUOUS TEST SERVICE CODES	Continuous Service Codes	
• Verify proper test equipment hook-up per Quick Test Step 2.0. • Self-Test de-activated. Do not activate Self-Test unless instructed. • Key On — Engine Off: — You are now in the continuous monitor mode (Wiggle Test mode). STO will be activated whenever a fault is detected. A fault is indicated when the STAR L.E.D. turns off. (Or meter deflection of 10.5 volts or more.) • Remain in Continuous Monitor Mode and service Continuous Code per appropriate Pinpoint Test. NOTE: An additional diagnostic aid is available in Engine Running Self-Test. After completion of Engine Running Self-Test, leave STI grounded. You are now in Continuous Monitor Mode during Engine Running. Fault indication is the same as Key On — Engine Off. NOTE: Record all Continuous Test service codes before removing or replacing the processor. The Continuous Test service codes will be erased from memory whenever the processor is disconnected.	11 ▶ 21 ▶ 22 ▶ 31 ▶ 51 ▶ 53 ▶ 61 ▶ 63 ▶ No Code ▶ Invalid Codes ▶	If problem is still intermittent, GO to Pinpoint Test Step X3, otherwise Testing complete. GO to Pinpoint Test Step U1. GO to Pinpoint Test Step U2. GO to Pinpoint Test Step U3. GO to Pinpoint Test Step U4. GO to Pinpoint Test Step U7. GO to Pinpoint Test Step U5. GO to Pinpoint Test Step U6. GO to Pinpoint Test Step P1. GO to Pinpoint Test Step X1.

Pinpoint Tests

INSTRUCTIONS FOR USING THE PINPOINT TESTS

- Do not run any of the following Pinpoint Tests unless you are so instructed by the Quick Test. Each Pinpoint Test assumes that a fault has been detected in the system with direction to enter a specific repair routine. Doing any Pinpoint Test without direction from Quick Test may produce incorrect results and replacement of Non-Faulty components.
- Correct test results for Quick Test are dependent on the proper operation of related non-EEC components/systems. It may be necessary to correct any faults in these areas before EEC will pass the Quick Test. Refer to the Diagnostic Routines, Section 2 in this manual for service.
- The Output State Test is used to aid the technician in diagnosing each output actuator. Connect the VOM to the desired actuator per Pinpoint Test instruction. The VOM will read battery voltage indicating actuator On and by depressing the throttle, the VOM will read 0 volts. (High reading = greater than 10.5 volts - low reading = less than 2.0 volts). Refer to Appendix A in this Section.
- Do not replace any parts unless the test result indicates they should be replaced.
- When more than one service code is received, always start service with the first code received.
- Do not measure voltage or resistance at the control module or connect any test lamps to it, unless otherwise specified.
- Connectors shown in schematics are shown as viewed from the front of the connector. Take all measurements by probing from the rear of the connector (harness side).
- Isolate both ends of a circuit, and turn key Off whenever checking for shorts or continuity, unless specified.
- Disconnect solenoids and switches from the harness before measuring for continuity, resistance, or energizing by way of 12-volt source.
- In using the Pinpoint Tests, follow each Step in order, starting from the first Step in the appropriate test. Follow each Step until the fault is found.
- After completing any repairs to the EEC system, verify all components are properly reconnected and repeat the Quick Test.
- An open is defined as any resistance reading greater than 5 ohms, unless otherwise specified.
- A short is defined as any resistance reading less than 10,000 ohms to ground, unless otherwise specified.

CAUTION: Never probe the processor connector.

The standard Ford color abbreviations are:

BK	Black	O	Orange
BR	Brown	PK	Pink
DB	Dark Blue	P	Purple
DG	Dark Green	R	Red
GY	Gray	T	Tan
LB	Light Blue	W	White
LG	Light Green	Y	Yellow
N	Natural		

Where two colors are shown for a wire, the first color is the basic color of the wire. The second color is the dot, hash, or stripe marking. If D or H is given, the second color is dots or hash marks. If there is no letter after the second color, the wire has a stripe.

For example:

BR/O is a brown wire with an orange stripe.

R/Y D is a red wire with yellow dots.

BK/W H is a black wire with white hash marks.

No Start Problem — Pinpoint Test — A

STOP-WARNING

You may have reached this point because of a fault in a non-EEC System and/or component. To prevent the replacement of good components, be aware that the following non-EEC areas may be at fault:

- Fuel, quantity and quality
- Ignition, general condition, moisture, cracks, damage, etc.
- Engine, internal, valves, timing belt, camshaft
- Starter and battery circuit

This Pinpoint Test is intended to diagnose only the following:

- Spark (as related to EEC-IV)

No Start Problem — Pinpoint Test — A

TEST STEP	RESULT ▶	ACTION TO TAKE
A1 ATTEMPT TO START ENGINE		
• Attempt to start engine.	Engine cranks, but does not start or stalls out ▶	GO to A2.
	Engine does not crank ▶	REFER to Section 31 of the Tempo/Topaz Shop Manual, Volume G.
A2 CHECK FOR SPARK AT PLUGS		
• Disconnect coil harness clip. • Disconnect the spark plug wire to any accessible cylinder. • Connect spark tester, D81P-6666-A or equivalent, between spark plug wire and engine ground. • Crank engine. • Reconnect the spark plug wire to the spark plug.	Spark ▶ No spark ▶	REFER to Section 2 in this manual, for further diagnostics. GO to A3.
A3 CHECK FOR SPARK AT COIL		
• Remove high tension coil wire from distributor and install sparktester. Check for spark while cranking.	Spark ▶ No spark ▶	REFER to Section 15 in this manual for further diagnostics. RECONNECT coil harness clip. GO to A4.
A4 CHECK FOR POWER TO PROCESSOR		
• Key Off. • Disconnect processor connector. Inspect for damaged pins, corrosion, pins pushed out, frayed wires, etc. Repair if necessary. • Connect Breakout Box and reconnect processor. • DVOM on 20 volt scale. • Key On — Engine Off. • Measure voltage from Breakout Box pin 37 to pin 40 and from Breakout Box pin 57 to pin 60.	Either voltage reading less than 10.5 volts ▶ Both voltage readings 10.5 volts or more ▶	GO to Pinpoint Test Step B1. GO to A5.

EEC IV-2.3L HSC Engine Diagnosis

No Start Problem	Pinpoint Test	A

TEST STEP	RESULT ▶	ACTION TO TAKE
A5 CHECK CONTINUITY OF IGNITION GROUND CIRCUIT		
• DVOM on 2,000 ohm scale. • Measure resistance from pin 16 to pin 40 and from pin 16 to pin 60.	Less than 5 ohms ▶	GO to **A6**.
	5 ohms or more ▶	REPAIR open circuit. REPEAT Quick Test.
A6 CHECK OUTPUT FROM DISTRIBUTOR		
• DVOM on 20 volt scale. • Connect one lead of DVOM to pin 56 and the other to pin 16. • Key On. • Observe voltage while cranking.	Between 3.0-6.0 volts ▶	GO to **A9**.
	Under 3.0 volts or more than 6.0 volts ▶	GO to **A7**.
A7 CONTINUITY CHECK OF CIRCUIT 349		
• Key Off. • DVOM on 2,000 ohm scale. • Disconnect processor. • Connect DVOM from pin 56 of Breakout Box to circuit 349 on the TFI connector. • Measure resistance.	5 ohms or less ▶	GO to **A8**.
	More than 5 ohms ▶	REPAIR open circuit 349. REPEAT Quick Test.
A8 CHECK CIRCUIT 349 FOR SHORTS		
• Key Off. • Disconnect TFI connector. • DVOM on 200,000 ohm scale. • Measure resistance from Breakout Box pin 56 to Breakout Box pins 26, 40, 46 and 57.	Any resistance 10,000 ohms or less ▶	REPAIR circuit 349. REPEAT Quick Test.
	All resistance more than 10,000 ohms ▶	GO to **A9**.

Vehicle Battery	Pinpoint Test	B

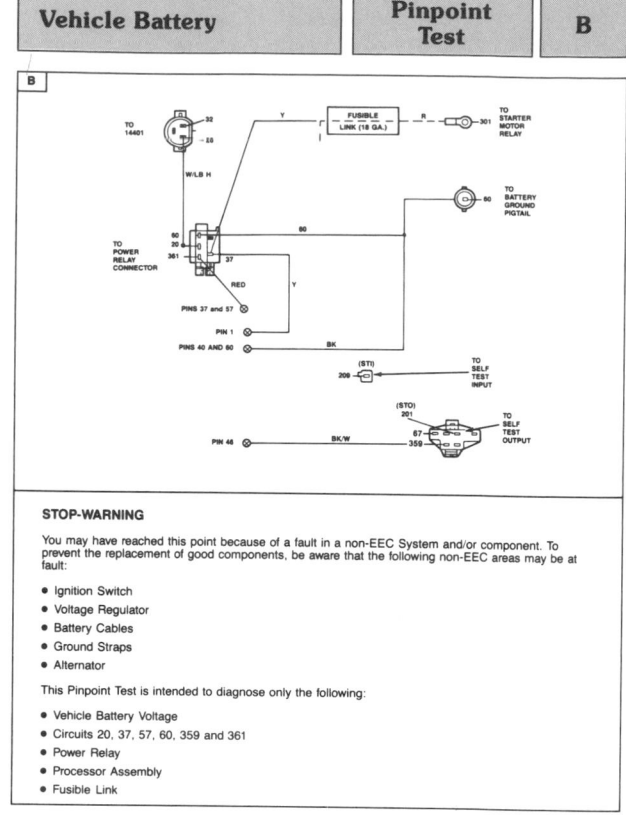

STOP-WARNING

You may have reached this point because of a fault in a non-EEC System and/or component. To prevent the replacement of good components, be aware that the following non-EEC areas may be at fault:

- Ignition Switch
- Voltage Regulator
- Battery Cables
- Ground Straps
- Alternator

This Pinpoint Test is intended to diagnose only the following:

- Vehicle Battery Voltage
- Circuits 20, 37, 57, 60, 359 and 361
- Power Relay
- Processor Assembly
- Fusible Link

No Start Problem	Pinpoint Test	A

TEST STEP	RESULT ▶	ACTION TO TAKE
A9 CHECK FOR SHORT ON CIRCUIT 324		
• Key Off. • Disconnect TFI. • Disconnect processor. • DVOM on 200,000 ohm scale. • Measure resistance of Breakout Box pin 36 to pins 26, 40, 46 and 57.	Any resistance less than 10,000 ohms ▶	REPAIR circuit 324. REPEAT Quick Test.
	All resistances 10,000 ohms or more ▶	GO to **A10**.
A10 ATTEMPT TO START ENGINE		
• TFI connected. • Disconnect processor from harness. • Turn key to start.	Starts ▶	REPLACE processor. REPEAT Quick Test.
	No start ▶	REFER to Section.

Vehicle Battery	Pinpoint Test	B

TEST STEP	RESULT ▶	ACTION TO TAKE
B1 BATTERY VOLTAGE CHECK		
• Key On — Engine Off. • DVOM on 20 volt scale. • Measure voltage across battery terminals.	Greater than 10.5 volts ▶	GO to **B2**.
	10.5 volts or less ▶	SERVICE discharged battery. REFER to Section 31-02, Tempo/Topaz Shop Manual, Volume G.
B2 BATTERY POWER GROUND CHECK		
• Key On — Engine Off. • DVOM on 20 volt scale. • Processor connected. • Measure voltage from battery negative post to Sig. Ret. circuit 359 in the Self-Test connector. • Is voltage reading less than 0.5 volt?	Less than 0.5 volt ▶	GO to **B3**.
	0.5 volt or more ▶	GO to **B4**.
B3 12 VOLT BATTERY POWER CHECK AT PROCESSOR — CHECK FOR VOLTAGE DROP		
• DVOM 20 volt range. • Disconnect processor. • Install Breakout Box. • Connect processor. • Key On — Engine Off. • Measure voltage from battery positive post to pin 37. • Repeat above check from battery to pin 57. • Both readings indicate a voltage reading (drop) of less than 0.5 volts.	Both readings less than 0.5 volt ▶	GO to Pinpoint Test Step **C1**.
	One or both readings 0.5 volt or more ▶	Go to **B7**.
B4 GROUND FAULT ISOLATION		
• DVOM 20 volt range. Processor connected. • Key On — Engine Off. • Measure voltage from battery negative post to pin 40. • Repeat above check from battery negative post to pin 60.	Both readings less than 0.5 volt ▶	GO to **B5**.
	One or both readings 0.5 volt or more ▶	Circuit with greater than 0.5 volt has high resistance or open. CORRECT faulty ground circuit. REPEAT Quick Test.

EEC IV-2.3L HSC Engine Diagnosis

Vehicle Battery	Pinpoint Test	B

TEST STEP	RESULT ▶	ACTION TO TAKE
B5 PROCESSOR GROUND FAULT ISOLATION • Key Off, processor connected, DVOM on 200 ohm range. • Make a resistance measurement from Breakout Box pin 46 to pin 40. • Repeat above test from pin 46 to pin 60.	Both readings less than 5 ohms ▶ One or both readings greater than 5 ohms ▶	GO to B6 . DISCONNECT processor connector from module and inspect for corrosion, damaged pins, etc. REPAIR as necessary and REPEAT Quick Test. If fault is still present, REPLACE processor.
B6 HARNESS CHECK (SIGNAL RETURN) • Key Off, processor connected. • DVOM on 200 ohm range. • Measure resistance from Breakout Box pin 46 to harness circuit 359 (Sig. Ret.) in the Self-Test connector.	Reading is less than 5 ohms ▶ Reading is 5 ohms or greater ▶	System OK. REPEAT Quick Test. CORRECT cause of resistance in harness circuit 359.
B7A 12 VOLT BATTERY POWER FAULT ISOLATION • DVOM on 20 volt range. • Processor connected. • Key On — Engine Off. • Connect DVOM negative lead to battery negative post. Connect positive lead to circuit 37 at EEC power relay. • Measure voltage. NOTE: In the event an open fusible link is found, check for shorts to ground before replacing the fusible link.	Greater than 10.5 volts ▶ 10.5 volts or less ▶	GO to B7B . CHECK circuit 37 power relay to battery , positive post for opens. Before servicing, CHECK circuits 37 and 361 for shorts to ground. REPAIR as necessary. REPEAT Quick Test.

Reference Voltage	Pinpoint Test	C

STOP-WARNING

This Pinpoint Test is intended to diagnose only the following:

• Circuits 37, 60, 351, 359, 361
• Processor Assembly
• TP, MAP and EVP Sensors

Vehicle Battery	Pinpoint Test	B

TEST STEP	RESULT ▶	ACTION TO TAKE
B7B 12 VOLT BATTERY POWER FAULT ISOLATION • DVOM on 20 volt range. • Processor connected. • Key On — Engine Off. • DVOM negative lead to negative post. Connect positive lead to circuit 20 at EEC power relay.	Greater than 10.5 volts ▶ 10.5 volts or less ▶	Leave key in On position. GO to B7C . CHECK for open in ignition switch circuits 16, 37 and 20. REPAIR as necessary. REPEAT Quick Test.
B7C 12 VOLT BATTERY POWER FAULT ISOLATION • DVOM on 20 volt range. • Processor connected. • Key On — Engine Off. • DVOM negative lead to negative post. Connect positive lead to circuit 60 at EEC power relay.	0.5 volt or less ▶ Greater than 0.5 volt ▶	Leave key in On position. GO to B7D . REPAIR open or ground in circuit 60. REPEAT Quick Test.
B7D 12 VOLT BATTERY POWER FAULT ISOLATION • DVOM on 20 volt range. • Processor connected. • Key On — Engine Off. • DVOM negative lead to negative post. Connect positive lead to circuit 361 at EEC power relay.	10.5 volts or more ▶ Less than 10.5 volts ▶	REPAIR open in circuit 361 from EEC power relay to processor connector pins 37 and 57. REPEAT Quick Test. REPLACE power relay. REPEAT Quick Test.

Reference Voltage	Pinpoint Test	C

TEST STEP	RESULT ▶	ACTION TO TAKE
C1 VEHICLE BATTERY POWER CIRCUIT CHECK • Key Off. • Disconnect processor. Connect Breakout Box. Reconnect processor. • Measure voltage from Breakout Box pin 37 between circuit 359 (Sig. Ret.) in the Self-Test connector. • Key On — Engine Off. Reading must be greater than 10.5 volts.	More than 10.5 volts ▶ 10.5 volts or less ▶	GO to C2 . GO to Pinpoint Test Step B1 .
C2 VREF VOLTAGE CHECK • DVOM on 20 volt scale. • Disconnect processor from Breakout Box. • Key On — Engine Off. • With DVOM, measure from pin 26 to pin 46 at Breakout Box.	6.0 volts or more ▶ 4.0 volts or less ▶	GO to C3 . GO to C5 .
C3 CHECK FOR SHORT TO BATTERY VOLTAGE • Turn key to Off. • Leave DVOM connected as in Step C2.	DVOM Reading: 0.5 volt or less ▶ More than 0.5 volt ▶	GO to C4 . SERVICE short between VREF and battery power circuits. REPEAT Quick Tests.
C4 CHECK FOR SHORT TO PROCESSOR POWER (VPWR) • Disconnect processor assembly from harness. • Key On — Engine Off. • DVOM on 20 volt scale. • With DVOM, measure between connector terminals pin 26 and pin 46.	DVOM Reading: 0.5 volt or less ▶ More than 0.5 volt ▶	REPLACE processor assembly. REPEAT Quick Test. SERVICE short between VREF and battery power in EEC-IV harness. REPEAT Quick Test.

EEC IV-2.3L HSC Engine Diagnosis

Reference Voltage	Pinpoint Test	C

TEST STEP	RESULT ▶	ACTION TO TAKE
C5 CHECK FOR SHORTED THROTTLE POSITION SENSOR	DVOM Reading:	
• Disconnect Throttle Position sensor from vehicle harness. • Key On — Engine Off. • With DVOM, measure voltage between Breakout Box pin 26 to pin 46.	4.0 volts or less ▶ More than 4.0 volts ▶	GO to **C6**. REPLACE TP sensor. REPEAT Quick Test.
C6 CHECK FOR SHORTED MAP SENSOR	4.0 volts or less ▶	GO to **C7**.
• Disconnect MAP sensor from vehicle harness. • Key On — Engine Off. • DVOM on 20 volt scale. • With DVOM, measure voltage between Breakout Box pin 26 to pin 46.	More than 4.0 volts ▶	REPLACE MAP sensor. RECONNECT TP sensor. REPEAT Quick Test.
C7 CHECK FOR SHORTED EGR VALVE POSITION SENSOR (EVP)	4.0 volts or less ▶	GO to **C8**.
• Disconnect EVP sensor from vehicle harness. • Key On — Engine Off. • DVOM on 20 volt scale. • Measure voltage between Breakout Box pin 26 and pin 46.	Greater than 4.0 volts ▶	REPLACE EVP sensor. CONNECT TP and MAP sensors. REPEAT Quick Test.
C8 CHECK VPWR AND GROUND HARNESS CONTINUITY	DVOM Reading:	
• Turn key Off. • Disconnect EEC connector from module. • DVOM to 200 ohm scale. • Check continuity from pins 40 and 60 to battery negative terminal and pins 37 and 57 to circuit 361 terminal on power relay.	All circuits less than 5 ohms ▶ Any circuit more than 5 ohms ▶	GO to **C9**. SERVICE open circuit or faulty connection in harness. REPEAT Quick Test.

Throttle Position Sensor	Pinpoint Test	E

STOP-WARNING

You may have reached this point because of a fault in a non-EEC System and/or component. To prevent the replacement of good components, be aware that the following non-EEC areas may be at fault:

• Idle Speeds/Throttle Stop Adjustment
• Binding Throttle Shaft/Linkage or Speed Control Linkage
• Choke/High Cam System

This Pinpoint Test is intended to diagnose only the following:

• TP Sensor
• Sensor Harness Circuits 351, 355, and 359
• Processor Assembly

Reference Voltage	Pinpoint Test	C

TEST STEP	RESULT ▶	ACTION TO TAKE
C9 CHECK FOR EEC HARNESS SHORTS	DVOM Reading:	
• Key Off. • DVOM on 200,000 ohm scale. • Disconnect harness connector from module and check for short circuits between VREF pin 26 on connector to pins 20, 40 and 60. • Reconnect all sensors.	10,000 ohms or more ▶ Under 10,000 ohms ▶	REPLACE processor assembly. REPEAT Quick Test. SERVICE short. REPEAT Quick Test.

Throttle Position Sensor	Pinpoint Test	E

TEST STEP	RESULT ▶	ACTION TO TAKE
E1 CHECK TP SENSOR: **SERVICE CODE 23**		
• Key Off. • Is TP sensor connector properly seated?	Yes ▶ No ▶	GO to **E2**. INSTALL TP sensor connector correctly. REPEAT Quick Test.
E2 CHECK SIGNAL RETURN FOR OPEN		
• Disconnect TP sensor. • Connect the DVOM positive test lead to TP harness circuit 351 and negative test lead to harness circuit 359. • Key On — Engine Off. • Measure voltage.	Between 4.0-6.0 volts ▶ Greater than 6.0 volts ▶ Less than 4.0 volts ▶	GO to **E3**. GO to Pinpoint Test Step **C1**. GO to **E14**.
E3 GENERATE CODE 63		
• Repeat Key On — Engine Off Self-Test with sensor disconnected.	Service code 63 ▶ Service 23 code ▶	REPLACE TP sensor. REFER to Section 4 in this Manual. REPEAT Quick Test. GO to **E4**.
E4 VOLTAGE CHECK		
• DVOM on 20 volt scale. • Key On — Engine Off. • Connect positive test lead to TP harness input circuit 355 and negative test lead to ground. • Observe voltage reading.	More than 2.0 volts ▶ 2.0 volts or less ▶	REPAIR harness short. REPEAT Quick Test. REPLACE processor. REPEAT Quick Test.

EEC IV-2.3L HSC Engine Diagnosis

Throttle Position Sensor	Pinpoint Test	E

TEST STEP	RESULT ▶	ACTION TO TAKE
E5 CHECK SIGNAL RETURN LINE FOR OPEN: **SERVICE CODE 53** • Key Off and wait 10 seconds. • Disconnect TP sensor connector. Inspect for damaged pins, corrosion, loose wires. Repair as necessary. • DVOM on 20 volt scale. • Connect DVOM positive test lead to battery positive terminal and negative test lead to harness circuit 359. • Observe voltage reading.	10 volts or more ▶ Less than 10 volts ▶	GO to E6. GO to E8.
E6 CHECK TP SIGNAL LINE FOR VOLTAGE • Leave TP sensor disconnected. • DVOM on 20 volt scale. • Connect DVOM positive test lead to circuit 355 and negative lead to circuit 359 in the harness. • Key On — Engine Off. • Measure voltage on circuit 355.	Less than 4.0 volts ▶ 4.0 volts or more ▶	GO to E7. GO to E9.
E7 GENERATE CODE 63 • With TP sensor disconnected, perform Key On — Engine Off Self-Test. • Check for code 63.	Code 63 present ▶ No code 63 present ▶	REPLACE TP sensor. REFER to Section 4 in this Manual. REPEAT Quick Test. REPLACE processor. REPEAT Quick Test.
E8 CHECK SIGNAL RETURN CIRCUIT FOR OPEN • Key Off and wait 10 seconds. • DVOM on 2,000 ohm scale. • Correct Breakout Box, leave processor disconnected. • Measure continuity of circuit 359 to Breakout Box pin 46.	Less than 5 ohms ▶ 5 ohms or more ▶	REPLACE processor. REPEAT Quick Test. REPAIR open circuit. REPEAT Quick Test.

Throttle Position Sensor	Pinpoint Test	E

TEST STEP	RESULT ▶	ACTION TO TAKE
E13 CHECK CONTINUITY OF CIRCUITS 355 AND 351 • Key Off — and wait 10 seconds. • Connect Breakout Box; leave processor disconnected. • DVOM on 2,000 ohm scale. • Check continuity of circuit 355 to Breakout Box pin 47. Check continuity of circuit 351 to Breakout Box pin 26.	Either reading more than 5 ohms ▶ Both readings 5 ohms or less ▶	REPAIR faulty circuit. REPEAT Quick Test. REPLACE processor. REPEAT Quick Test.
E14 CHECK CONNECTORS • Disconnect TP sensor from harness. • Carefully inspect both connectors for corrosion to terminals. • Disconnect processor from harness. • Carefully inspect both connectors for corrosion to terminals.	(OK) ▶ (OK̸) ▶	GO to E15. CLEAN and REPAIR connectors as necessary. GO to E16.
E15 • Reconnect processor. • DVOM on 20 volt scale. • Key On — Engine Off. • Measure voltage across circuit 351 and circuit 359 at sensor harness connector.	Less than 4.0 volts ▶ 4.0 volts or more ▶	GO to E16. VREF OK. Testing complete.
E16 CHECK RESISTANCE • Disconnect processor. • Connect Breakout Box and leave processor disconnected. • Measure resistance from TP sensor harness connector circuit 359 to pin 46 of Breakout Box. • Measure resistance from TP sensor harness connector circuit 351 to pin 26 of Breakout Box.	Either reading less than 5 ohms ▶ Either reading 5 ohms or more ▶	REPLACE processor. REPEAT Quick Test. REPAIR harness for possible opens, faulty connections, poor terminal to wire crimps, etc. REPEAT Quick Test.

Throttle Position Sensor	Pinpoint Test	E

TEST STEP	RESULT ▶	ACTION TO TAKE
E9 CHECK TP SIGNAL FOR SHORT TO POWER • Key Off. • DVOM on 200,000 ohm scale. • Connect Breakout Box, leave processor disconnected. • Measure resistance of Breakout Box pin 47 to Breakout Box pins 26 and 57.	Either resistance 10,000 ohms or less ▶ Both resistances more than 10,000 ohms ▶	REPAIR harness short. REPEAT Quick Test. REPLACE processor. REPEAT Quick Test.
E10 CHECK FOR VREF TO TP SIGNAL INPUT: **SERVICE CODE 63** • Key Off. • Disconnect TP sensor. Inspect for damaged pins, corrosion and pins pushed out. Repair as necessary. • DVOM on 20 volt scale. • Connect positive test lead to circuit 351 and negative test lead to circuit 359. • Key On — Engine Off.	Reading between 4.0 volts and 6.0 volts ▶ Reading less than 4.0 volts ▶ Reading 6.0 volts or more ▶	GO to E11. GO to E13. GO to Pinpoint Test Step C1.
E11 GENERATE CODE 53 • Key Off. • Jumper circuit 351 to circuit 355. • Perform Key On — Engine Off Self-Test. • Check for code 53.	Code 63 present ▶ No code 53 or no codes present ▶	REPLACE TP sensor. REFER to Section 4 in this Manual. REPEAT Quick Test. TURN Key Off. GO to E12.
E12 CHECK RESISTANCE OF CIRCUIT 355 TO GROUND • Key Off. • Disconnect processor 60 pin connector and inspect for damaged pins, corrosion, loose wires. Repair as necessary. • DVOM on 200,000 ohm scale. • Connect one test lead to circuit 355 at the TP sensor connector and the other test lead to ground.	Less than 10,000 ohms ▶ 10,000 ohms or more ▶	REPAIR circuit short. REPEAT Quick Test. GO to E13.

Engine Coolant Temperature Sensor	Pinpoint Test	F

STOP-WARNING

You may have reached this point because of a fault in a non-EEC System and/or component. To prevent the replacement of good components, be aware that the following non-EEC areas may be at fault:

• Coolant Level
• Oil Level
• Blocked or Obstructed Air Flow
• Engine Not at Normal Operating Temperature
• Electro-Drive Cooling Fan

This Pinpoint Test is intended to diagnose only the following:

• ECT Sensor
• Harness Circuits 354 and 359
• Processor Assembly

EEC IV-2.3L HSC Engine Diagnosis

Engine Coolant Temperature Sensor	Pinpoint Test	F

TEST STEP	RESULT ▶	ACTION TO TAKE
F1 START ENGINE TO BRING ECT WITHIN LIMITS: **SERVICE CODE 21** • Start engine and operate at 2000 RPM for 5 minutes. • Check that upper radiator hose is hot and pressurized. • REPEAT Engine Running Self-Test.	Code 21 present ▶ No code 21 present ▶	GO to **F2**. CONTINUE pinpoint tests as necessary.
F2 CHECK VREF TO SIG. RET. • Key On — Engine Off. • DVOM on 20 volt scale. • Disconnect ECT connector and connect DVOM to circuit 359 and circuit 354 at harness connector. • Observe voltage.	DVOM reading between 4.0 volts and 6.0 volts ▶ Less than 4.0 volts ▶ More than 6.0 volts ▶	GO to **F3**. GO to **F4**. GO to Pinpoint Test Step **C1**.
F3 ECT SENSOR CHECK NOTE: Vehicle may have cooled down. Always warm vehicle up before taking ECT resistance measurement. • DVOM on 200,000 ohm scale. • Make a resistance measurement of the ECT sensor. • Is the resistance reading from: — 1300 ohms (240 F) to 7450 ohms (140 F) for Key On — Engine Off Self-Test. — 1550 ohms (230 F) to 4250 ohms (170 F) for Engine Running Self-Test.	Yes ▶ No ▶	REPLACE processor. REPEAT Quick Test. REPLACE ECT sensor. REPEAT Quick Test.
F4 CHECK CONTINUITY OF HARNESS CIRCUITS 354 AND 359 • Key Off. • Disconnect processor 60 pin connector and inspect for corrosion, damaged pins, bent pins, etc. • Install Breakout Box, leave processor disconnected. • DVOM 2,000 ohm scale. • Measure continuity of harness circuit 354 to pin 7, and harness circuit 359 to pin 46.	Both resistances less than 5 ohms ▶ Either resistance more than 5 ohms ▶	GO to **F5**. REPAIR harness. REPEAT Quick Test.

Manifold Absolute Pressure Sensor	Pinpoint Test	G

STOP-WARNING

You may have reached this point because of a fault in a non-EEC System and/or component. To prevent the replacement of good components, be aware that the following non-EEC areas may be at fault:

• Usually High/Low Atmospheric Barometer Reading
• Kinked or Obstructed Vacuum Lines
• Basic Engine (Valves, Vacuum Leaks, Timing, Carburetor, etc.)

This Pinpoint Test is intended to diagnose only the following:

• MAP Sensor
• Harness Circuits 351, 356 and 359
• Processor Assembly

Engine Coolant Temperature Sensor (ECT)	Pinpoint Test	F

TEST STEP	RESULT ▶	ACTION TO TAKE
F5 CHECK ECT SIGNAL HARNESS FOR SHORTS TO GROUND • Key Off. • DVOM on 200,000 ohm scale. • Measure resistance of pin 7 to pins 40 and 60.	More than 10,000 ohms ▶ 10,000 ohms or less ▶	GO to **F3**. REPAIR short to ground. REPEAT Quick Test.
F6 ECT INPUT HIGH: **SERVICE CODE 51** • Key Off. • Disconnect ECT connector. Inspect connectors for corrosion, damaged, bent pins, etc. • Create opposite failure by inserting a jumper wire across ECT harness connector. • Perform Key On — Engine Off Self-Test.	Code 61 present ▶ No code 61 present ▶	REPLACE ECT sensor. REPEAT Quick Test. GO to **F7**.
F7 CHECK CONTINUITY OF HARNESS CIRCUIT 354 AND 359 • Remove jumper wire. • Connect Breakout Box, leave processor disconnected. • DVOM on 2,000 ohm scale. • Measure continuity of harness circuit 354 to Breakout Box pin 7, and harness circuit 359 to Breakout Box pin 46.	Either resistance more than 5 ohms ▶ Both resistances 5 ohms or less ▶	REPAIR open in harness. REPEAT Quick Test. REPLACE processor. REPEAT Quick Test.
F8 ECT INPUT LOW: **SERVICE CODE 61** • Disconnect ECT connector. • Perform Key On — Engine Off Self-Test. • Check for code 51.	Code 51 present ▶ No code 51 present ▶	REPLACE ECT sensor. REPEAT Quick Test. GO to **F9**.
F9 CHECK ECT FOR SHORT TO GROUND • Connect Breakout Box. Leave processor disconnected. • DVOM on 200,000 ohm scale. • Disconnect ECT. • Measure resistance of Breakout Box pin 7 to Breakout Box pins 40 and 60. NOTE: Any time shorts or opens are present during testing, a code will be generated in the Continuous Test.	Either resistance less than 10,000 ohms ▶ Both resistances 10,000 ohms or more ▶	REPAIR short to ground. REPEAT Quick Test. REPLACE processor. REPEAT Quick Test.

Manifold Pressure Sensor	Pinpoint Test	G

TEST STEP	RESULT ▶	ACTION TO TAKE
G1 MAP SENSOR OUT OF LIMITS: **SERVICE CODE 22** • Verify all accessories are off. • Check vacuum line to MAP sensor for opens, kinks or restriction. • Check for vacuum leaks in engine system. Refer to VECI decal.	Faults or leaks ▶ No faults or leaks ▶	REPAIR as necessary. REPEAT Quick Test. RETEST. GO to **G2**.
G2 CHECK FOR ENGINE RUNNING CODES • Check for Engine Running codes 31 or 41.	Code 31 present ▶ Code 41 present ▶ No code 31 or 41 present ▶	GO to Pinpoint Test Step **H1**. GO to Pinpoint Test Step **J1**. GO to **G3**.
G3 APPLY VACUUM TO MAP SENSOR • Disconnect vacuum line and attach vacuum pump to MAP sensor nipple. • Apply 70 kPa (20 in. Hg.) of vacuum to MAP sensor.	Holds vacuum ▶ Does not hold vacuum ▶	GO to **G4**. REPLACE sensor. CONNECT vacuum line. REPEAT Quick Test.
G4 CHECK VREF TO SIG. RET. VOLTAGE • Key On — Engine Off. • MAP connector disconnected. • DVOM on 20 volt scale. • Connect positive test lead to harness circuit 351 and negative test lead to harness circuit 359.	Between 4.0-6.0 volts ▶ Less than 4.0 volts ▶ More than 6.0 volts ▶	GO to **G5**. GO to **G10**. GO to Pinpoint Test Step **C1**.

EEC IV-2.3L HSC Engine Diagnosis

Manifold Pressure Sensor		Pinpoint Test	G

	TEST STEP	RESULT ▶	ACTION TO TAKE
G5	CHECK SIG. RET. TO MAP SIGNAL VOLTAGE		
	• Key On — Engine Off. • MAP connector disconnected. • Connect DVOM positive test lead to harness circuit 358 and negative test lead to harness circuit 359.	Less than 4.0 volts ▶ 4.0 volts or more ▶	GO to G6. GO to G8.
G6	CHECK CONTINUITY OF HARNESS CIRCUITS 359, 358 AND 351		
	• Key Off. • Disconnect processor 60 pin connector and inspect for corrosion, damaged pins, bent pins, etc. • DVOM on 2,000 ohm scale. • Measure continuity from MAP circuit 359 to Breakout Box pin 46, circuit 351 to pin 26 and circuit 358 to pin 45.	All resistances 5 ohms ▶ or less Any resistance more ▶ than 5 ohms	GO to G7. REPAIR open circuit in harness. REPEAT Quick Test.
G7	CHECK CIRCUITS 351 AND 358 FOR SHORTS TO GROUND		
	• Key Off. • DVOM on 200,000 ohm scale. • Processor disconnected. • Measure resistance of harness circuit 351 to pins 40 and 60, and harness circuit 358 to pins 40 and 60.	All resistances 10,000 ▶ ohms or more Any resistance less ▶ than 10,000 ohms	GO to G8. REPAIR circuit short to ground. REPEAT Quick Test.
G8	CHECK MAP SIGNAL AND VREF FOR SHORTS TO OTHER CIRCUITS		
	• Key Off and wait 10 seconds. • Connect Breakout Box to harness, leave processor disconnected. • MAP sensor disconnected. • DVOM on 200,000 ohm scale. • Measure resistance of Breakout Box pin 45 to pins 2 through 60.	Resistance more than ▶ 10,000 ohms to all pins Resistance 10,000 ▶ ohms or less on any pin	GO to G9. REPAIR harness short and RETEST.

EGR Valve Position		Pinpoint Test	H

STOP-WARNING

You may have reached this point because of a fault in a non-EEC System and/or component. To prevent the replacement of good components, be aware that the following non-EEC area may be at fault:

• Damaged EGR Valve

This Pinpoint Test is intended to diagnose only the following:

• EVP Sensor
• Harness Circuits 351, 352, 359, 360, 361, 362
• EGR Solenoids
• EGR Valve Assembly
• Processor Assembly

Manifold Pressure Sensor		Pinpoint Test	G

	TEST STEP	RESULT ▶	ACTION TO TAKE
G9	TEST PROCESSOR WITH A SUBSTITUTE MAP SENSOR		
	• Plug in substitute MAP sensor and hook-up vacuum line. Run Self-Test in test mode where sensor failed.	No code 22 ▶ Code 22 present ▶	INSTALL substitute sensor. REPEAT Quick Test. REPLACE processor. REMOVE substitute sensor. REPEAT Quick Test with original sensor.
G10	CHECK CONNECTORS		
	• Disconnect MAP sensor from harness. • Carefully inspect both connectors for corrosion to terminals. • Disconnect processor from harness. • Carefully inspect both connectors for corrosion to terminals.	⃝K ▶ ⃝K̸ ▶	GO to G11. CLEAN and REPAIR connectors as necessary. GO to G11.
G11	CHECK MAP SENSOR		
	• Reconnect processor. • DVOM on 20 volt scale. • Key On — Engine Off. • Measure voltage across harness circuit 351 and circuit 359.	Less than 4.0 volts ▶ 4.0 volts or more ▶	GO to G12. VREF OK. Testing complete.
G12	CHECK HARNESS RESISTANCE		
	• Disconnect processor. • Connect Breakout Box, leave processor disconnected. • DVOM on 200 ohm scale. • Measure resistance from sensor harness connector circuit 359 to pin 46. • Measure resistance from sensor harness connector circuit 351 to pin 26.	Either reading less ▶ than 5 ohns Either reading 5 ohms ▶ or more	REPLACE processor. REPEAT Quick Test. REPAIR harness for possible open, misconnections, poor terminal to wire crimps, etc. REPEAT Quick Test.

EGR Valve Position		Pinpoint Test	H

	TEST STEP	RESULT ▶	ACTION TO TAKE
H1	PERFORM ENGINE RUNNING TEST WITH EGR VACUUM LINE DISCONNECTED AT EGR VALVE, AND PLUG EGR VACUUM LINE: **SERVICE CODE 31**		
	• Perform Engine Running Self-Test. • Check for code 31.	Code 31 present ▶ No code 31 present ▶	GO to H2. GO to H10.
H2	CHECK SENSOR RESISTANCE		
	• Key Off • DVOM on 200,000 ohm scale. • Measure resistance from circuit 351 (pin 1) to circuit 352 (pin 3) on the sensor and from circuit 359 (pin 2) to circuit 352 (pin 3) on the sensor.	Both resistance ▶ readings between 100 ohms and 5,500 ohms Either resistance ▶ reading less than 100 ohms or more than 5,500 ohms	GO to H3. REPLACE EVP sensor. RECONNECT EGR vacuum line. REPEAT Quick Test.
H3	APPLY VACUUM TO EGR VALVE. CHECK FOR EVP MOVEMENT		
	• Key Off. • DVOM on 200,000 ohm scale. • Disconnect vacuum line from EGR valve. • Connect vacuum pump to EGR valve. • Measure resistance of EVP sensor circuits 351 (pin 1) to sensor circuit 352 (pin 3) while gradually increasing vacuum to 33 kPa (10 in. Hg.). • Observe resistance as vacuum increases.	EVP sensor reading ▶ gradually decreases from no more than 5,500 ohms to no less than 100 ohms EVP sensor readings ▶ of less than 100 ohms or more than 5,500 ohms EVP sensor readings ▶ do not decrease or unable to hold vacuum	GO to H4. REPLACE EVP sensor. REPEAT Quick Test. REPLACE EGR valve. REPEAT Quick Test.

EEC IV-2.3L HSC Engine Diagnosis

EGR Valve Position — Pinpoint Test — H

TEST STEP	RESULT ▶	ACTION TO TAKE
H4 MEASURE VREF TO SIG. RET. VOLTAGE • DVOM on 20 volt scale. • Key On — Engine Off. • Connect DVOM positive test lead to harness circuit 351 and negative test lead to harness circuit 359.	Voltage reading between 4.0-6.0 volts ▶ Voltage reading less than 4.0 volts ▶ Voltage reading more than 6.0 volts ▶	GO to H5. GO to H9. Go to Pinpoint Test Step C1.
H5 MEASURE VREF TO SIGNAL INPUT VOLTAGE • DVOM on 20 volt scale. • Key On — Engine Off. • Connect DVOM positive test lead to harness circuit 351 and negative test lead to harness circuit 352.	Voltage reading between 4.0-6.0 volts ▶ Voltage reading less than 4.0 volts ▶	GO to H10. GO to H6.
H6 CHECK HARNESS CIRCUIT 352 FOR SHORTS • Key Off. • Disconnect 60 pin processor connector and inspect both connectors. • DVOM on 200,000 ohm scale. • Measure resistance of harness circuit 352 to harness circuit 359, and harness circuit 352 to ground.	Either resistance reading less than 10,000 ohms ▶ Both resistance readings 10,000 ohms or more ▶	REPAIR circuit short. REPEAT Quick Test. GO to H7.

EGR Valve Position — Pinpoint Test — H

TEST STEP	RESULT ▶	ACTION TO TAKE
H11 OUTPUT STATE CHECK • Depress and release throttle several times (cycle) while observing voltmeter installed on the solenoid being tested. • Connect negative test lead to output circuit 360 and positive test lead to EGRV solenoid circuit 361. Record voltage while depressing and releasing throttle. • Install negative test lead to output circuit 362 and positive test lead to EGRC solenoid circuit 361. Record voltage while depressing and releasing throttle.	Both outputs cycle On and Off ▶ Either output does not cycle On or Off ▶	REMAIN in output state check. GO to H12. GO to H16.
H12 CHECK SOLENOIDS FOR VACUUM CYCLING • Install vacuum pump to the EGRC solenoid bottom port and install a vacuum gauge to the output port. Disconnect vent vacuum line. • While cycling outputs On and Off (by depressing and releasing throttle) observe the vacuum gauge at the output. **NOTE: Maintain vacuum at source.**	Vacuum cycles On and Off ▶ Vacuum does not cycle On or Off ▶	CONTINUE to H13. REPLACE solenoid assembly. REPEAT Quick Test.

Diagram labels:
TO EGR CONTROL VACUUM PORT (BOTTOM PORT) — VACUUM PUMP — DISCONNECT AND CAP MANIFOLD VACUUM LINE — VACUUM GAUGE — TO EGR VALVE — EGR CONTROL — EGR VENT — DISCONNECT VENT VACUUM LINE

EGR Valve Position — Pinpoint Test — H

TEST STEP	RESULT ▶	ACTION TO TAKE
H7 MEASURE CONTINUITY OF CIRCUITS 351, 352 AND 359 • Key Off. • Connect Breakout Box to harness, leave processor disconnected. • DVOM on 2,000 ohm scale. • Measure continuity of Breakout Box pin 46 to harness circuit 359, pin 26 to harness circuit 351 and pin 27 to harness circuit 352.	Any resistance readings of 5 ohms or more ▶ All resistance readings less than 5 ohms ▶	REPAIR faulty circuits. REPEAT Quick Test. GO to H8.
H8 MEASURE CIRCUIT 352 FOR SHORTS TO OTHER CIRCUITS • Key Off. • EVP sensor disconnected. • Measure resistance of Breakout Box pin 27 to pin 26 and pin 37.	Either reading 10,000 ohms or less ▶ Both readings more than 10,000 ohms ▶	REPAIR circuit short. REPEAT Quick Test. REPLACE processor. REPEAT Quick Test.
H9 SOLENOID RESISTANCE • Key Off. • Disconnect solenoid. • Connect DVOM across the terminals on both the EGRV and EGRC solenoids. • Measure resistance.	Resistance between 30 and 70 ohms ▶ Less than 30 or more than 70 ohms ▶	RECONNECT the solenoids. GO to H10. REPLACE the solenoid assembly. REPEAT Quick Test.
H10 OUTPUT STATE CHECK • Key Off. • DVOM on 20 volt scale. • Connect negative test lead to STO and positive lead to battery positive post. • Perform Key On — Engine Off Self-Test until the completion of Continuous Test. • DVOM will indicate 0 volts. • Depress and release accelerator. • DVOM will change to a high reading. (High voltage reading = greater than 10.5 – low voltage reading = less than 2.0 volts.)	Reading changed to high ▶ Reading did not change to high ▶	GO to H11. GO to Pinpoint Test Step P19.

EGR Valve Position — Pinpoint Test — H

TEST STEP	RESULT ▶	ACTION TO TAKE
H13 VACUUM LINE INSPECTION • Key Off. • Refer to VECI decal. • Check EGR vacuum supply line, check EGR vent vacuum line, and check EGR control vacuum line. • Check the above vacuum lines for kinks, cracks, blockage, restrictions, etc.	(OK) ▶ (not OK) ▶	GO to H14. REPAIR as necessary. REPEAT Quick Test.
H14 EVP RESISTANCE CHECK • Disconnect EVP sensor connector and inspect both connectors for corrosion, bent pins, pins not properly seated. • DVOM on 200,000 ohm scale. • Connect a vacuum pump to EGR valve. • Connect DVOM to EVP sensor, one lead to circuit 351 (pin 1) and the other lead to circuit 352 (pin 3). • Observe resistance, while gradually increasing the vacuum pump to 33 kPa (10 in. Hg.).	Reading decreases between 5,500 ohms and 100 ohms ▶ Reading does not decrease or resistance is greater than 5,500 ohms or less than 100 ohms ▶	REPLACE processor. REPEAT Quick Test. GO to H15.
H15 EGR SENSOR MOVEMENT • Remove EVP sensor from EGR valve. • DVOM on 200,000 ohm scale. • Measure resistance from pin 1 to pin 3. Use your finger to gradually move the EVP sensor shaft. • Look for sudden jumps in resistance reading.	Reading decreases ▶ Reading does not decrease or jumps suddenly ▶	REPLACE EGR valve assembly. REPEAT Quick Test. REPLACE EVP sensor. REPEAT Quick Test.
H16 CHECK FOR VOLTAGE ON CIRCUIT 361 • Key On — Engine Off. • DVOM on 20 volt scale. • Measure voltage across both EGR solenoids, (circuit 361 to battery ground).	Both voltage readings more than 10.5 volts ▶ Either voltage reading less than 10.5 volts ▶	GO to H17. REPAIR harness circuit open. REPEAT Quick Test.

EEC IV-2.3L HSC Engine Diagnosis

EGR Valve Position	**Pinpoint Test**	**H**

TEST STEP	RESULT ▶	ACTION TO TAKE
H17 CHECK CONTINUITY • Key Off. • Disconnect processor 60 pin connector and inspect both connectors. • Connect Breakout Box to harness, leave processor disconnected. • DVOM on 2,000 ohm scale. • Measure continuity of Breakout Box pin 33 to harness circuit 361 (EGR Vacuum solenoid). • Measure continuity of Breakout Box pin 52 to harness circuit 362 (EGR solenoid).	Both resistance readings less than 5 ohms ▶ Either resistance reading 5 ohms or more ▶	GO to H18. REPAIR open circuit. REPEAT Quick Test.
H18 CHECK FOR SHORT • Key Off. • Disconnect EGR soleniod connectors. • Measure resistance from Breakout Box pin 33 to pins 40, 46 and 57. • Measure resistance from Breakout Box pin 52 to pins 40, 46 and 57.	All resistance readings more than 10,000 ohms ▶ Any resistance reading of 10,000 ohms or less ▶	GO to H19. REPAIR circuit short. REPEAT Quick Test.
H19 CHECK RESISTANCE OF SOLENOIDS • DVOM on 2,000 ohm scale. • Measure resistance of both EGR solenoids.	Both resistance readings between 30 ohms and 70 ohms ▶ Either resistance readings more than 70 ohms or less than 30 ohms ▶	REPLACE processor. REPEAT Quick Test. REPLACE EGR solenoid assembly. REPEAT Quick Test.

Fuel Control	**Pinpoint Test**	**J**

TEST STEP	RESULT ▶	ACTION TO TAKE
J1 VERIFY VEHICLE WAS PREPARED AS DESCRIBED IN QUICK TEST: SERVICE CODE 41 • Was vehicle run more than 2 minutes immediately before testing?	No ▶ Yes ▶	PREPARE vehicle. REPEAT Quick Test. GO to J2.
J2 CHECK SYSTEM FOR OBVIOUS FAULTS • Is EGO sensor connector hooked-up? • Is EGO ground disconnected or corroded? • Are there intake manifold leaks or exhaust manifold leaks?	⊗ ▶ OK ▶	REPAIR fault. REPEAT Quick Test. GO to J3.
J3 CHECK EGO SENSOR HARNESS • Disconnect EGO sensor and processor. • DVOM on 200,000 ohm scale. • Connect DVOM positive test lead to sensor connector circuit 94 and negative test lead to ground. • Measure resistance.	Resistance less than 1,000 ohms ▶ Resistance 1,000 ohms or more ▶	REPAIR short. REPEAT Quick Test. CONNECT EGO sensor. GO to J4.
J4 ATTEMPT TO REMOVE SERVICE CODE 41 TO ISOLATE CAUSE • Connect EGO sensor. • Disconnect thermactor air supply hose at the air pump and cap the hose. • Perform Engine Running Self-Test. • Check for code 41.	No code 41 present ▶ Code 41 present ▶	REPAIR any other service codes first per appropriate Pinpoint Test. Leave thermactor disconnected. GO to J5.

Fuel Control	**Pinpoint Test**	**J**

| PIN 37 ○——— R ———361— TO FEEDBACK CARBURETOR |
| PIN 58 ○——— T/LG D ———97— |
| PIN 49 ○——— O ———89— TO GROUND |
| PIN 29 ○——— DG/P H ———94— TO EGO SENSOR |

VACUUM REGULATOR SOLENOID

EXHAUST GAS OXYGEN SENSOR

STOP-WARNING

You may have reached this point because of a fault in a non-EEC System and/or component. To prevent the replacement of good components, be aware that the following non-EEC areas may be at fault:

- Fouled Spark Plugs
- Distributor Cap and Rotor
- Ignition Coil
- Spark Plug Wires
- CANP Problems
- PCV Valve
- Oil Contamination
- EGR Valve and Gasket
- Air Filter
- Fuel Filter
- Fuel Pump and Pressure
- Manifold Leak, Intake/Exhaust
- Engine Not at Normal Operating Temperature
- Carburetor
- Choke, Sticking/Electrical

This Pinpoint Test is intended to diagnose only the following:

- EGO Sensor Connection
- EGO Sensor
- Harness Circuits 89, 94, 97, and 361
- Impact of Thermactor Air
- FBC/Solenoid
- Vacuum System (EEC Only)
- Choke Circuit
- Processor Assembly
- Distributor Modulator Valve (Vacuum Switch Assembly)

Fuel Control	**Pinpoint Test**	**J**

TEST STEP	RESULT ▶	ACTION TO TAKE
J5 CHECK FEED BACK CARBURETOR (FBC) SOLENOID FOR PROPER OPERATION • Disconnect FCS solenoid connector. • Perform Engine Running Self-Test. NOTE: Ignore all other codes at this time.	No code 41 present ▶ Code 41 present ▶	GO to J7. Leave FCS solenoid disconnected. GO to J6.
J6 FORCE SYSTEM RICH • Run vehicle for 2 minutes at part throttle. • Perform Engine Running Self-Test with choke plate 3/4 closed. (Do not stall engine).	No code 41 present ▶ Code 41 present ▶	EEC system OK. HOOK-UP all disconnected parts. REFER to Section 4 in this manual for Carburetor Diagnostics. GO to J11.
J7 CHECK PROCESSOR OUTPUT • Connect FCS. • Key Off. • Connect Breakout Box. • Disconnect processor. • DVOM on 200,000 ohm scale. • Measure resistance from pin 58 to pins 20, 40 and 46.	10,000 ohms or more ▶ Less than 10,000 ohms ▶	GO to J8. REPAIR harness short on circuit 97. REPEAT Quick Test.
J8 CHECK VACUUM • Check all FCS vacuum hoses to carburetor for leaks, blockages, and proper connection. REFER to VECI decal.	⊗ ▶ OK ▶	REPAIR or REPLACE hoses as necessary. REPEAT Quick Test. GO to J9.
J9 FORCE SYSTEM RICH • Run vehicle for 2 minutes at part throttle. • Hold the choke plate 3/4 closed while running Self-Test. Do not stall engine. • Check for code 41.	Code 41 present ▶ No code 41 present ▶	REPLACE FCS. REPEAT Quick Test. GO to J10.

EEC IV-2.3L HSC Engine Diagnosis

Fuel Control — Pinpoint Test J

TEST STEP	RESULT ▶	ACTION TO TAKE
J10 CHECK FCS SOLENOID • DVOM on 2,000 ohm scale. • Disconnect FCS. • Connect DVOM between circuit 97 in the FBC harness and engine ground. • Connect DVOM between circuit 360 in the FCS harness and engine ground.	Either reading less than 1,000 ohms ▶ Either reading 1,000 ohms or more ▶	REPLACE FCS solenoid. REPEAT Quick Test. REPLACE processor. REPEAT Quick Test.
J11 CHECK FOR EGO SENSOR SHORT TO GROUND • Key Off. • Processor connected. • Disconnect EGO sensor. • DVOM on 200,000 ohm scale. • Measure resistance of harness circuit 94 to battery ground.	More than 10,000 ohms ▶ 10,000 ohms or less ▶	GO to J12. REPLACE processor. REPEAT Quick Test.
J12 FORCE EGO RICH • Start vehicle and run for 2 minutes. • DVOM on 20 volt scale. • Disconnect EGO sensor. • With engine running, hold choke plate 3/4 closed and measure voltage between EGO sensor and ground.	Voltage 0.45 volt or more ▶ Voltage less than 0.45 volt ▶	GO to J13. REPLACE EGO sensor. REPEAT Quick Test.
J13 CHECK FOR EGO SENSOR SHORT TO VREF • Key On — Engine Off. • DVOM on 20 volt scale. • Connect DVOM positive test lead to circuit 94 and negative lead to battery ground. • Measure voltage.	Voltage reading less than 2 volts ▶ Voltage reading 2 volts or more ▶	GO to J14. REPAIR harness short to VREF. REPEAT Quick Test.
J14 CHECK CONTINUITY • Key Off. • Connect Breakout Box. • DVOM on 1,000 ohm scale. • Measure resistance from pin 29 to circuit 94, and resistance from pin 49 to pin 40 or 60.	Both resistances less than 5 ohms ▶ Either resistance 5 ohms or more ▶	REPLACE processor. REPEAT Quick Test. REPAIR faulty circuit. REPEAT Quick Test.

Fuel Control — Pinpoint Test J

TEST STEP	RESULT ▶	ACTION TO TAKE
J19 ENTER OUTPUT STATE CHECK. REFER TO APPENDIX A. • Key Off. • DVOM on 20 volt scale. • Connect DVOM negative test lead to STO and positive test lead to battery positive. • Jumper STI. • Perform Key On — Engine Off until the completion of the continuous test codes. DVOM will indicate 0 volts. • Depress and release the throttle. • Did DVOM reading change to a high voltage reading? **NOTE: Any reference to state change will be indicated by cycling from Off (less than 2 volts) to On (more than 10 volts).**	Yes ▶ No ▶	REMAIN in Output State Check. GO to J20. DEPRESS throttle to WOT and release. If STO voltage does not go high, GO to Pinpoint Test Step P19.
J20 CHECK FCS SOLENOID ELECTRICAL OPERATION • DVOM on 20 volt scale. • Connect positive test lead to circuit 361 on FCS solenoid and negative test lead to FCS circuit 97. • While observing VOM, depress and release the throttle several times to cycle output On and Off.	FCS output cycles On and Off ▶ FCS output does not cycle On and Off ▶	GO to J23. GO to J21.
J21 CHECK FOR POWER TO FCS SOLENOID • Connect one lead of the DVOM to circuit 361 of the FCS and the other to battery ground. • DVOM on 20 volt scale. • Key On — Engine Off. • Measure voltage.	10 volts or more ▶ Less than 10 volts ▶	GO to J22. REPAIR open in circuit. REPEAT Quick Test.
J22 CHECK CONTINUITY OF CIRCUIT 97 • Disconnect 60 pin connector. Inspect connectors for damaged pins, corrosion, frayed wires and pins pushed out. Repair as necessary. • Connect Breakout Box, leave processor disconnected. • DVOM on 200,000 ohm scale. • Measure continuity from circuit 97 to Breakout Box pin 58.	More than 5 ohms ▶ 5 ohms or less ▶	REPAIR open in circuit 97. REPEAT Quick Test. REPLACE processor. REPEAT Quick Test.

Fuel Control — Pinpoint Test J

TEST STEP	RESULT ▶	ACTION TO TAKE
J15 CHECK FOR PROPER CHOKE OPERATION: **SERVICE CODE 42/47** • Check for choke plate sticking or binding.	(OK) ▶ (⊘) ▶	GO to J16. SERVICE choke as required. REFER to Section 4 in this manual. REPEAT Quick Test.
J16 GENERATE KNOWN FAULT CONDITION • Disconnect EGO sensor connector. • Repeat Engine Running Self-Test. • Check for code 41. Ignore all other codes at this time.	Code 41 present ▶ No code 41 present ▶	GO to J17. GO to J26.
J17 ISOLATE PCV • Connect EGO sensor. • Repeat Engine Running Self-Test. • Remove vacuum hose from PCV. Leave PCV in rocker arm cover. • Check for code 42/47.	Code 42/47 present ▶ No code 42/47 present ▶	REPLACE EGO sensor. REPEAT Quick Test. GO to J18.
J18 CHECK SOLENOID RESISTANCE • Key Off. • DVOM on 2,000 ohm scale. • Disconnect FCS solenoid. • Connect DVOM across the terminals on the solenoid. • Measure resistance.	Resistance between 30 and 60 ohms ▶ Less than 30 or more than 60 ohms ▶	RECONNECT FCS solenoid. GO to J19. REPLACE FCS solenoid. REPEAT Quick Test.

Fuel Control — Pinpoint Test J

TEST STEP	RESULT ▶	ACTION TO TAKE
J23 CHECK RESISTANCE OF FEEDBACK CARBURETOR SOLENOID • Verify FCS is properly connected. • DVOM on 200 ohm scale. • Disconnect FCS connector and inspect for corrosion. Clean if necessary. • Measure resistance of solenoid.	DVOM reading between 30 and 65 ohms ▶ DVOM reading less than 30 or more than 65 ohms ▶	GO to J24. REPLACE FCS solenoid. REPEAT Quick Test.
J24 CHECK VACUUM HOSES • Check all vacuum hoses from the FCS solenoid to the carburetor for leaks, blockages, and proper connections. Refer to VECI decal.	(⊘) ▶ (OK) ▶	REPAIR hoses as required. REPEAT Quick Test. RECONNECT all vacuum hoses to carburetor. GO to J25.
J25 FORCE A LEAN CONDITION • Connect EGO sensor. • Connect FCS solenoid. • Run engine for 2 minutes. • Perform Engine Running Self-Test. • With engine running, disconnect vacuum hose from PCV. Leave PCV in rocker arm cover. • Check for code 42/47.	No code 42/47 present ▶ Code 42/47 present ▶	REFER to Section 4. in this manual for Carburetor Diagnostics. REPLACE FCS solenoid. REPEAT Quick Test.
J26 CHECK FOR CIRCUIT 97 SHORT TO GROUND • Connect EGO sensor. • Disconnect 60 pin connector. Inspect for damaged pins, corrosion and frayed wires. Repair as necessary. • DVOM on 20 volt scale. • Connect Breakout Box to harness, leave processor disconnected. • Key On — Engine Off. • Connect DVOM between pin 29 and battery ground.	More than 0.4 volt ▶ 0.4 volt or less ▶	REPAIR short in circuit 94. REPEAT Quick Test. REPLACE processor. REPEAT Quick Test.

EEC IV-2.3L HSC Engine Diagnosis

Fuel Control		Pinpoint Test	J

TEST STEP	RESULT ▶	ACTION TO TAKE
J27 EGO COOL DOWN HAS OCCURRED: **SERVICE CODE 43**		
• Run vehicle at 2000 RPM for 2 minutes. • Perform Engine Running Self-Test. • Check for code 43.	No code 43 present ▶	SERVICE other codes as necessary.
	Code 43 present ▶	GO to J28 .
J28 CHECK SYSTEM FOR EXHAUST LEAKS		
• Any exhaust leaks present?	(OK) ▶	REPAIR as necessary. REPEAT Quick Test.
	(OK) ▶	GO to J29 .
J29 CHECK SYSTEM FOR IDLE QUALITY		
• Start vehicle, let engine idle. • Does the idle quality deteriorate and remain constantly poor, during the test and after the test?	Idle quality remains poor ▶	REFER to Section 4, in this manual.
	Idle quality OK ▶	REPLACE EGO sensor. REPEAT Quick Test.

Air Management System		Pinpoint Test	L

TEST STEP	RESULT ▶	ACTION TO TAKE
L1 CHECK THERMACTOR: **SERVICE CODE 44**		
• Visually verify that restrictor teed into the TAD vacuum line is uncapped and restrictor is free from contamination.	(OK) ▶	Leave restrictor uncapped. GO to L2 .
	(⊗) ▶	SERVICE as required. REPEAT Quick Test.
L2 WARM UP ENGINE		
• Start engine and bring to operating temperature. • Verify upper radiator hose is hot and pressurized. • Key Off. • Ground STI. • Perform Engine Running Self-Test and record all service codes.	Service code 11 present ▶	REPEAT Quick Test.
	Service code 44 or 46 present ▶	GO to L3 .
	Any other service codes present ▶	REPAIR codes as necessary. REPEAT Quick Test.
L3 MEASURE TAB/TAD SOLENOID RESISTANCE		
• Key Off and wait 10 seconds. • DVOM on 2,000 ohm scale. • Disconnect TAB/TAD solenoid. • Connect DVOM across the terminals on the solenoid. • Measure resistance.	Resistance between 50 and 110 ohms ▶	RECONNECT TAB/TAD solenoid. GO to L4 .
	Less than 50 or more than 110 ohms ▶	REPLACE TAB/TAD solenoid assembly. REPEAT Quick Test.

Air Management System		Pinpoint Test	L

STOP-WARNING

You may have reached this point because of a fault in a non-EEC System and/or component. To prevent the replacement of good components, be aware that the following non-EEC areas may be at fault:

• Thermactor System
  — Belt
  — Pump
  — Valve

This Pinpoint Test is intended to diagnose only the following:

• TAB and TAD Solenoid Valve Assemblies
• Harness Circuits 99, 100 and 361
• Vacuum Supply
• Processor Assembly

Air Management System		Pinpoint Test	L

TEST STEP	RESULT ▶	ACTION TO TAKE
L4		
• Key Off and wait 10 seconds. • DVOM on 20 volt scale. • Connect DVOM negative test lead to STO and positive test lead to battery positive. • Jumper STI. • Perform Key On — Engine Off Self-Test until the completion of the continuous test codes. • DVOM will indicate 0 volts. • Depress and release the throttle. • Did DVOM reading change to a high voltage reading? **NOTE: Any reference to state change will be indicated by cycling from Off (less than 2.0 volts) to On (10.5 volts or more).**	Yes ▶	GO to L5 .
	No ▶	DEPRESS throttle to wide open and RELEASE. If STO voltage does not go high, GO to Pinpoint Test Step P19 .
L5 CHECK TAB/TAD SOLENOID ELECTRICAL OPERATION		
• Depress and release throttle several times (cycle) while observing voltmeter installed on the solenoid being tested. • Install negative test lead to output circuit 100 and positive test lead to TAB solenoid circuit 361. Record voltage while cycling outputs On and Off. • Install negative test lead to output circuit 99 and positive test lead to TAD solenoid circuit 361. Record voltage while cycling outputs On and Off.	Both outputs cycle On and Off ▶	GO to L6 .
	Either output does not cycle On and Off ▶	GO to L7 .
L6 CHECK TAB/TAD SOLENOIDS FOR VACUUM CYCLING		
• Apply 67 kPa (20 in. Hg.) to the TAB solenoid bottom port and install a vacuum gauge to the output (upper) port. • While cycling outputs On and Off (by depressing and releasing throttle) observe the vacuum gauge at the output. **(NOTE: Maintain vacuum at source.)** • Perform the same test with the TAD solenoid.	Vacuum cycles On and Off ▶	EEC system OK. REFER to Section 2 in this manual for further diagnostics.
	Vacuum does not cycle On and Off ▶	REPLACE TAB/TAD solenoid assembly. REPEAT Quick Test.

EEC IV-2.3L HSC Engine Diagnosis

Air Management System	Pinpoint Test	L

TEST STEP	RESULT ▶	ACTION TO TAKE
L7 CHECK FOR VOLTAGE ON CIRCUIT 361		
• Key On — Engine Off. • DVOM on 20 volt scale. • Measure voltage on both thermactor solenoids, circuit 361. Positive test lead to circuit 361 and negative test lead to ground.	Both voltage readings ▶ more than 10.5 volts	GO to L8 .
	Either voltage reading ▶ less than 10.5 volts	REPAIR harness circuit open. REPEAT Quick Test.
L8 CHECK CONTINUITY		
• Key Off. • Disconnect processor 60 pin connector and inspect both connectors. • Connect Breakout Box to harness, leave processor disconnected. • DVOM on 2,000 ohm scale. • Measure continuity of circuit 100 TAB solenoid, from Breakout Box pin 51 to solenoid. • Measure continuity of circuit 99 TAD solenoid, from Breakout Box pin 11 to solenoid.	Both resistance ▶ readings less than 5 ohms	GO to L9 .
	Either resistance ▶ reading 5 ohms or more	REPAIR open circuit. REPEAT Quick Test.
L9 CHECK FOR SHORT		
• Key Off. • Disconnect both thermactor solenoid connectors. • Measure resistance from Breakout Box pin 51 to pins 40, 46 and 57. • Measure resistance from Breakout Box pin 11 to pins 40, 46 and 57.	All resistance readings ▶ more than 10,000 ohms	GO to L10 .
	Any resistance ▶ readings of 10,000 ohms or less	REPAIR circuit short. REPEAT Quick Test.
L10 CHECK RESISTANCE OF SOLENOIDS		
• Key Off. • DVOM on 2,000 ohm scale. • Measure resistance across both thermactor solenoids.	Both resistance ▶ readings between 50 and 110 ohms	REPLACE processor. REPEAT Quick Test.
	Either resistance ▶ readings more than 50 ohms or less than 110 ohms	REPLACE solenoid assembly. REPEAT Quick Test.

No Codes/Invalid Codes	Pinpoint Test	P

TEST STEP	RESULT ▶	ACTION TO TAKE
P1 NO CODES/INVALID CODES		
NOTE: Verify automatic transmission is fully seated in park. • Disconnect processor. • Disconnect MAP sensor. • Connect Breakout Box. • Reconnect processor. • DVOM on 20 volt range. • Key On — Engine Off. • Measure voltage between MAP circuit 351 and battery ground.	6.0 volts or more ▶	GO to Pinpoint Test Step C1 .
	4.0 volts or less ▶	GO to P6 .
	4.0 volts to 6.0 volts ▶	GO to P2 .
P2 ENGINE RUNNING SELF-TEST WITH MAP SENSOR DISCONNECTED		
• Disconnect MAP. • Repeat Engine Running Self-Test. • Check for codes.	No codes ▶	GO to P3 .
	Codes ▶	REPLACE MAP sensor. REPEAT Quick Test.
P3 CHECK CIRCUIT 89 FOR SHORT TO GROUND		
• Key Off. • DVOM on 2,000 ohm scale. • Connect Breakout Box. Reconnect processor. • Connect one lead of the DVOM to Breakout Box pin 49 and the other to engine ground.	Less than 5 ohms ▶	GO to P4 .
	5 ohms and greater ▶	REPAIR open in circuit 89 to engine block. REPEAT Quick Test.
P4 CHECK SELF-TEST CONNECTOR		
• Disconnect processor and inspect both connectors, repair and retest if necessary. • Measure continuity from pin 46 of Breakout Box to circuit 359 of the Self-Test connector, also from pin 48 to circuit 209 (STI) and from pin 17 to circuit 201 (STO).	Both resistances ▶ 5 ohms or less	GO to P5 .
	Either resistance more ▶ than 5 ohms	REPAIR circuit open. REPEAT Quick Test.

RPM Failed Self-Test	Pinpoint Test	M

TEST STEP	RESULT ▶	ACTION TO TAKE
M1 CHECK CONNECTORS: **SERVICE CODE 72**		
• Check that MAP sensors are properly connected and completely seated.	⊘OK ▶	GO to M2 .
	⊗ ▶	REPAIR as necessary. REPEAT Quick Test.
M2 MAP SENSOR DYNAMIC RESPONSE DID NOT CHANGE ENOUGH DURING DYNAMIC RESPONSE TEST		
• Tee a vacuum gauge in the vacuum line to the MAP sensor. • Repeat Engine Running Self-Test. • Record all codes while observing vacuum gauge.	Vacuum decreased ▶ more than 24 kPa (7 in. Hg.) and code 72 is present	REPLACE MAP sensor. REPEAT Quick Test.
	Vacuum decreased ▶ more than 24 kPa (7 in. Hg.) and code 72 is not present	DISCONNECT vacuum equipment. REPEAT Engine Running Self-Test. VERIFY WOT test was performed.
	Vacuum decreased 24 ▶ kPa (7 in. Hg.) or less	CHECK vacuum line for proper routing per VECI decal. CHECK for blockage, kink, etc. Make necessary repairs. REPEAT Quick Test.
M3 CHECK CONNECTORS: **SERVICE CODE 73**		
• Check that TP sensor is properly connected and completely seated.	⊘OK ▶	GO to M4 .
	⊗ ▶	REPAIR as necessary. REPEAT Quick Test.
M4		
• Disconnect TP sensor. • DVOM on 200,000 ohm scale. • Connect DVOM leads across sensor connector between circuit 355 and circuit 359. • Observe resistance measurement while moving throttle to WOT position.	DVOM increases to ▶ 1,000 ohms or more	REPEAT Engine Running Self-Test and verify that a WOT test was performed
	DVOM increases less ▶ than 1,000 ohms	REPLACE TP sensor. REPEAT Quick Test.

No Codes/Invalid Codes	Pinpoint Test	P

TEST STEP	RESULT ▶	ACTION TO TAKE
P5 CHECK FOR SHORT TO GROUND		
• Key Off. • Disconnect processor. • Measure resistance from Breakout Box pin 17 to pin 40.	10,000 ohms or less ▶	REPAIR circuit 201 short. REPEAT Quick Test.
	More than 10,000 ▶ ohms	GO to P9 .
P6 KEY ON — ENGINE OFF SELF-TEST WITH MAP SENSOR DISCONNECTED		
• Disconnect MAP. • Perform Key On — Engine Off Self-Test. • Check for codes.	Codes ▶	GO to P7 .
	No codes ▶	GO to P8 .
P7 CHECK CONTINUITY		
• Disconnect processor and inspect both connectors, repair and retest if necessary. • Connect Breakout Box, leave processor disconnected. • Measure continuity from pin 26 to MAP sensor harness circuit 351.	More than 5 ohms ▶	REPAIR circuit open. REPEAT Quick Test.
	5 ohms or less ▶	REPLACE processor. REPEAT Quick Test.
P8 CHECK POWER CIRCUIT FOR SHORT TO GROUND		
• Disconnect processor. • Connect Breakout Box, leave processor disconnected. • Key On — Engine Off. • Connect positive DVOM test lead to pin 37 and negative lead to pin 40.	10.5 volts and less ▶	GO to Pinpoint Test Step B1 .
	More than 10.5 volts ▶	GO to Pinpoint Test Step C1 .
P9 CHECK CONTINUITY		
• Key Off. • DVOM on 20 volt scale. • Connect DVOM negative lead to battery negative post and the positive lead to circuit 37 at EEC power relay.	Greater than 10.5 volts ▶	GO to P10 .
	10.5 volts or less ▶	REPAIR circuit 37 open. REPEAT Quick Test.

EEC IV-2.3L HSC Engine Diagnosis

Vehicle Stalls in Self-Test		Pinpoint Test	P

TEST STEP	RESULT	▶	ACTION TO TAKE
P10 CHECK EEC POWER RELAY			
• Key Off. • DVOM on 20 volt scale. • Check circuit 20 at the power relay. • DVOM neg. (−) lead to engine ground.	Greater than 10.5 volts	▶	REPLACE power relay. REPEAT Quick Test.
	10.5 volts or less	▶	GO to P11 .
P11 CHECK CIRCUIT 20			
• DVOM on 20 volt scale. • Check circuit 20 at the power relay. • Key On — Engine Off. • DVOM negative lead to engine ground.	Greater than 10.5 volts	▶	GO to P13 .
	10.5 volts or less	▶	CHECK for open in ignition switch start run circuits 20, 16 and 37.
P12 CHECK CIRCUIT 60			
• DVOM on 20 volt range. • Key On — Engine Off. • Check circuit 60 at power relay. • DVOM neg. (−) lead to engine ground.	0.50 volt or less	▶	GO to P14 .
	Greater than 0.50 volt	▶	REPAIR open to circuit 60.
P13 CHECK CIRCUIT 361			
• DVOM 20 volt range. • Key Off. • Disconnect power relay. • Connect DVOM positive lead to harness connector circuit 361 and negative lead to ground.	10.5 volts or more	▶	REPAIR short between circuit 361 and circuit 37.
	Less than 10.5 volts	▶	EEC System OK. REFER to Section 2, in this manual.

Vehicle Stalls in Self-Test		Pinpoint Test	P

TEST STEP	RESULT	▶	ACTION TO TAKE
P18 FORCE FUEL RICH			
• Key Off. • Disconnect FCS solenoid connector. • Deactivate Self-Test. • Start engine and maintain at 2,000 RPM for 2 minutes. • Perform Engine Running Self-Test. • Check for code 41.	Code 41 present	▶	CHECK for vacuum leaks. REFER to Section 2, in this manual for diagnostics by symptom.
	No code 41 present	▶	GO to Pinpoint Test Step J1 .
P19 CHECK FOR CODES 23, 53 OR 63			
• Key Off. • Perform Key On — Engine Off Self-Test. • Leave key On to enter Output State Check. Refer to Appendix A. • Are codes 23, 53 or 63 present?	Yes	▶	GO to Quick Test Step 3.1 , and service appropriate code as instructed.
	No	▶	LEAVE key On. GO to P20 .
P20 ATTEMPT TO ENTER OUTPUT STATE CHECK			
• Depress throttle wide open and release several times. • Observe STO. Should cycle On and Off (VOM reading should cycle high and low).	Cycles On and Off	▶	CHECK throttle and throttle linkage for sticking and binding. REPAIR as necessary. REPEAT Quick Test.
	Does not cycle On and Off	▶	REPLACE TP sensor. REPEAT Quick Test.

Vehicle Stalls in Self-Test		Pinpoint Test	P

TEST STEP	RESULT	▶	ACTION TO TAKE
P14			
• Activate Key On — Engine Off Self-Test. • When the first service code is outputted, immediately de-activate Self-Test. This action, if performed as specified, will erase the continuous codes. • Perform Key On — Engine Off Self-Test and record all codes from continuous. Valid codes are: 11, 22, 31, 51, 53, 61, 63.	Valid codes listed	▶	GO to Quick Test Step 3.1 , for appropriate Pinpoint Test Step. REPAIR service code.
	Invalid codes listed	▶	GO to P15 .
P15			
• Disconnect processor harness connector, and inspect both connectors for damaged pins, corrosion, frayed wires, etc. Repair as necessary. • Connect Breakout Box, leave processor disconnected. • DVOM 20 volt scale. • Key On — Engine Off. • Measure voltage from pin 1 to pin 40 and pin 60.	10 volts or more	▶	REPLACE processor. REPEAT Quick Test.
	Less than 10 volts	▶	REPAIR open to circuit 37. REPEAT Quick Test.
P16 TRY TO MAINTAIN ENGINE OPERATION DURING ENGINE RUNNING SELF-TEST			
• Key Off and wait 10 seconds. • Connect tachometer. • Perform Engine Running Self-Test and try to maintain engine RPM at 2,000 RPM. • Does the engine stall?	Engine stalls	▶	REFER to Section 2, in this manual.
	Engine does not stall	▶	RECORD Engine Running service codes. GO to Step P17 .
P17 CHECK FOR VACUUM LEAKS			
• Check for vacuum leaks. • Refer to VECI decal. • Check for codes: 31, 33, 41. NOTE: Ignore all codes other than the above.	No codes present	▶	GO to P1 .
	Code 31 present	▶	GO to Pinpoint Test Step H1 .
	Code 33 present	▶	GO to Pinpoint Test Step H9 .
	Code 41 present	▶	GO to P19 .

Spark Timing Check		Pinpoint Test	Q

Q

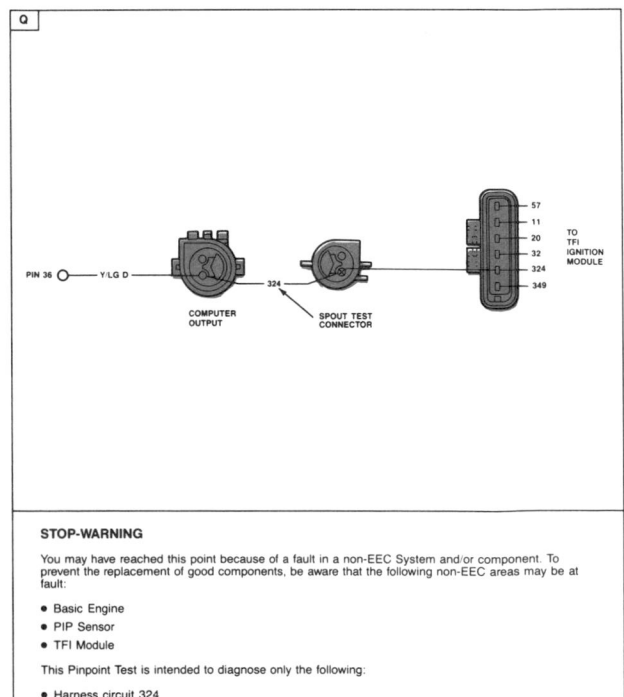

STOP-WARNING

You may have reached this point because of a fault in a non-EEC System and/or component. To prevent the replacement of good components, be aware that the following non-EEC areas may be at fault:

• Basic Engine
• PIP Sensor
• TFI Module

This Pinpoint Test is intended to diagnose only the following:

• Harness circuit 324
• Base Timing
• Processor Assembly

EEC IV-2.3L HSC Engine Diagnosis

Spark Timing Check	Pinpoint Test	Q

TEST STEP	RESULT ▶	ACTION TO TAKE
Q1 CHECK SPARK TIMING		
• Engine Running Self-Test must be activated while checking or adjusting timing Running Test. **NOTE:** Self-Test allows 25 seconds to check engine timing after engine starts. • Check if timing is base + 20° (±3°) BTDC.	(OK) ▶	GO to Quick Test Step 5.0 .
	(OK̸) ▶	GO to Q2 .
Q2 CHECK SPARK OUTPUT (SPOUT) CIRCUIT TO THE TFI MODULE		
• Locate and disconnect spout test connector at distributor. • Connect jumper wire to ground for circuit 324 which goes to distributor. • Start engine. • Install jumper wire from distributor test connector to ground.	Vehicle stalls ▶	GO to Q3 .
	Vehicle does not stall	CHECK for 324 circuit open to TFI module. REPAIR as necessary. If circuit OK, fault is not in the EEC-IV TFI system. Refer to TFI Diagnosis in Section 15, in this manual.
Q3 CHECK BASE TIMING		
• Disconnect jumper wire. • Leave spout connector disconnected. • Start engine. • Check base timing.	Timing is ±3° from base ▶	GO to Q4 .
	Timing is off by more than ±3° from base ▶	REFER to Section 15 in this manual for engine timing instructions.

Throttle Kicker	Pinpoint Test	R

TEST STEP	RESULT ▶	ACTION TO TAKE
R1 CHECK ACCESSORIES OFF		
• Are all accessories off?	(OK) ▶	GO to R2 .
	(OK̸) ▶	TURN all accessories Off. REPEAT Quick Test.
R2 CHECK VACUUM		
• Apply 70 kPa (20 in. Hg.) of vacuum to throttle kicker. • Verify vacuum holds.	(OK) ▶	GO to R3 .
	(OK̸) ▶	REPLACE TK. REPEAT Quick Test.
R3 RUN ENGINE RUNNING SELF-TEST		
• While vacuum is applied to throttle kicker, perform Engine Running Self-Test.	Service code 35 present ▶	EEC system OK. REFER to Section 4 in this manual for idle adjustment.
	All other service codes ▶	GO to R4 .
R4 TK SOLENOID RESISTANCE		
• Key Off. • Disconnect solenoid. • DVOM on 2,000 ohm scale. • Connect DVOM across the terminals on the solenoid. • Measure resistance.	Resistance between 50 and 110 ohms ▶	RECONNECT TK solenoid. GO to R5 .
	Less than 50 or more than 110 ohms ▶	REPLACE TK solenoid. REPEAT Quick Test.

Spark Timing Check	Pinpoint Test	Q

TEST STEP	RESULT ▶	ACTION TO TAKE
Q4 CHECK HARNESS FOR CONTINUITY		
• Key Off and wait 10 seconds. • Connect Breakout Box to harness. Leave processor disconnected. • DVOM on 2,000 ohm scale. • Measure continuity from Breakout Box pin 36 to circuit 324 at distributor test connector.	DVOM reading 5 ohms or less ▶	REPLACE processor. CONNECT spout circuit. CHECK timing per Q1 .
	DVOM reading more than 5 ohms ▶	REPAIR open circuit. CONNECT spout test connector. CHECK timing per Q1 . If problem still present, REFER to Section 15, in this manual for diagnosis.

Throttle Kicker	Pinpoint Test	R

TEST STEP	RESULT ▶	ACTION TO TAKE
R5		
• Key Off. • DVOM on 20 volt scale. • Connect VOM negative test lead to STO and positive test lead to battery positive. • Jumper STI. • Perform Key On — Engine Off Self-Test until the completion of the continuous test codes. • VOM will indicate "0" volts. • Depress and release the throttle. • Did VOM reading change to a high voltage reading? **NOTE:** Any reference to state change will be indicated by cycling from Off (2.0 volts or less) to On (10.5 volts or greater).	Yes ▶	GO to R6 .
	No ▶	DEPRESS throttle to WOT and RELEASE. If STO voltage does not go high, GO to Pinpoint Test Step P19 .
R6		
• Connect VOM across the TK solenoid. • Depress and release accelerator. • VOM reading will change high to low.	Yes ▶	GO to R7 .
	No ▶	REPAIR circuit open. REPEAT Quick Test.
R7		
• Depress and release accelerator. • DVOM should change low to high.	Yes ▶	EEC electrical circuit to TK solenoid OK. GO to R8 .
	No ▶	REPAIR circuit 361 for short. REPEAT Quick Test.
R8 CHECK VACUUM HOSES		
• Check vacuum hoses from throttle kicker solenoid to vacuum source and to the throttle kicker.	Leaks, blockages found ▶	REPAIR hoses as required. REPEAT Quick Test.
	No leaks or blockage found ▶	GO to R9 .

EEC IV-2.3L HSC Engine Diagnosis

Throttle Kicker		Pinpoint Test	R

TEST STEP	RESULT ▶	ACTION TO TAKE
R9 CHECK FOR VACUUM • Engine Running. • Check TK solenoid output, vacuum is present when the solenoid is energized by 12 volts.	Vacuum present ▶ Vacuum not present ▶	GO to R10. REPLACE TK solenoid. REPEAT Quick Test.
R10 CHECK CONTINUITY • Key Off. • Disconnect TK solenoid connector. • Disconnect processor. Connect Breakout Box to harness, leave processor disconnected. • DVOM on 200 ohm scale. • Measure continuity between Breakout Box pin 53 and circuit 69 at the TK solenoid connector. • Measure continuity between Breakout Box pin 37 and circuit 361 at the TK solenoid connector.	Both resistances are less than 5 ohms ▶ Either resistance is 5 ohms or greater ▶	REPLACE processor. REPEAT Quick Test. REPAIR circuit. REPEAT Quick Test.

Wiggle Test		Pinpoint Test	U

TEST STEP	RESULT ▶	ACTION TO TAKE
U4 CHECK ECT SENSOR: **SERVICE CODE 51** • Observe VOM for indication of a service code (high meter deflection). • Lightly tap on ECT sensor (simulate road shock). • Wiggle ECT connector. • Is a service code indicated?	Yes ▶ No ▶	DISCONNECT and INSPECT connectors. If connector and terminals are good, REPLACE ECT sensor. REPEAT Quick Test. GO to U8. REFER to Figure U4.
U5 CHECK ECT SENSOR: **SERVICE CODE 61** • Observe VOM for indication of a service code (high meter deflection). • Lightly tap on ECT sensor (simulate road shock). • Wiggle ECT connector. • Is a service code indicated?	Yes ▶ No ▶	DISCONNECT and INSPECT connectors. If connector and terminals are good, REPLACE ECT sensor. REPEAT Quick Test. GO to U8. REFER to Figure U5.
U6 EXERCISE TP SENSOR: **SERVICE CODE 63** • Observe VOM for indication of a service code (high meter deflection). • Move throttle slowly to WOT position. • Release throttle slowly to closed condition. • Lightly tap on TP sensor (simulate road shock.) • Wiggle TP sensor connectors. • Is a service code indicated?	Yes ▶ No ▶	DISCONNECT and INSPECT connectors. If connector and terminals are good, REPLACE TP sensor. REPEAT Quick Test. GO to U8. REFER to Figure U6.

Wiggle Test		Pinpoint Test	U

TEST STEP	RESULT ▶	ACTION TO TAKE
U1 TEST DRIVE VEHICLE: **SERVICE CODE 21** • Key Off and wait 10 seconds. • Disconnect all Self-Test equipment and prepare vehicle for test drive. • Drive vehicle. Try to simulate different drive modes or mode in which drive complaint is noticed. Attempt to maintain drive complaint mode for one minute or more, if possible. • Upon completion of drive evaluation, repeat Key On — Engine Off Self-Test. • Is code 21 present in the continuous test results?	Yes ▶ No ▶	VERIFY thermostat operating properly. If OK, REPLACE the ECT sensor. REPEAT Quick Test. Unable to duplicate fault. Code 21 testing complete.
U2 EXERCISE MAP SENSOR: **SERVICE CODE 22** • Observe VOM for indication of a service code (high meter deflection). • Connect a vacuum pump to the MAP sensor. • Slowly apply 84 kPa (25 in. Hg.) vacuum to the MAP sensor. • Slowly bleed vacuum off the MAP sensor. • Lightly tap on MAP sensor (simulate road shock). • Wiggle MAP connector. • Is a service code indicated?	Yes ▶ No ▶	DISCONNECT and INSPECT connectors. If connector and terminals are good, REPLACE MAP sensor. REPEAT Quick Test. GO to U8. REFER to Figure U2.
U3 EXERCISE EVP SENSOR: **SERVICE CODE 31** • Observe VOM for indication of a service code (high meter deflection). • Connect a vacuum pump to the EGR valve. • Slowly apply 33 kPa (10 in. Hg.) vacuum to the EGR valve. • Slowly bleed vacuum off the EGR valve. • Lightly tap on EVP sensor (simulate road shock). • Wiggle EVP sensor connector. • Is a service code indicated?	Yes ▶ No ▶	DISCONNECT and INSPECT connector. If connector and terminals are good, REPLACE EVP sensor. REPEAT Quick Test. GO to U8. REFER to Figure U3.

Wiggle Test		Pinpoint Test	U

TEST STEP	RESULT ▶	ACTION TO TAKE
U7 EXERCISE TP SENSOR: **SERVICE CODE 53** • Observe VOM for indication of a service code (high meter deflection). • Move throttle slowly to WOT position. • Release throttle slowly to closed position. • Lightly tap on TP sensor (simulate road shock). • Wiggle TP connector. • Is a service code indicated?	Yes ▶ No ▶	DISCONNECT and INSPECT connectors. If connector and terminals are good, REPLACE ACT sensor. REPEAT Quick Test. GO to U8. REFER to Figure U7.
U8 CHECK EEC-IV HARNESS • Observe voltmeter. • Utilizing referenced figure from the step that directed you here, grasp the harness as close to the sensor connector as possible. Wiggle, shake or bend a small section of the EEC-IV system harness while working your way to the bulkhead. Also wiggle, shake or bend the EEC-IV harness from the bulkhead to the processor. • Is a service code indicated?	Yes ▶ No ▶	ISOLATE fault and make necessary repairs. REFER to appropriate figure. REPEAT Quick Test. GO to U9.
U9 CHECK PROCESSOR AND HARNESS CONNECTORS • Key Off and wait 10 seconds. • Disconnect processor 60 pin connector. • Inspect both connectors and connector terminals for obvious damage or faults.	⊗ ▶ OK ▶	REPAIR as necessary. REPEAT Quick Test. Unable to duplicate fault at this time. If intermittent problem still exists, DRIVE, EVALUATE and CHECK for continuous codes. REPAIR as necessary. REPEAT Quick Test.

EEC IV-2.3L HSC Engine Diagnosis

Wiggle Test	Pinpoint Test	U

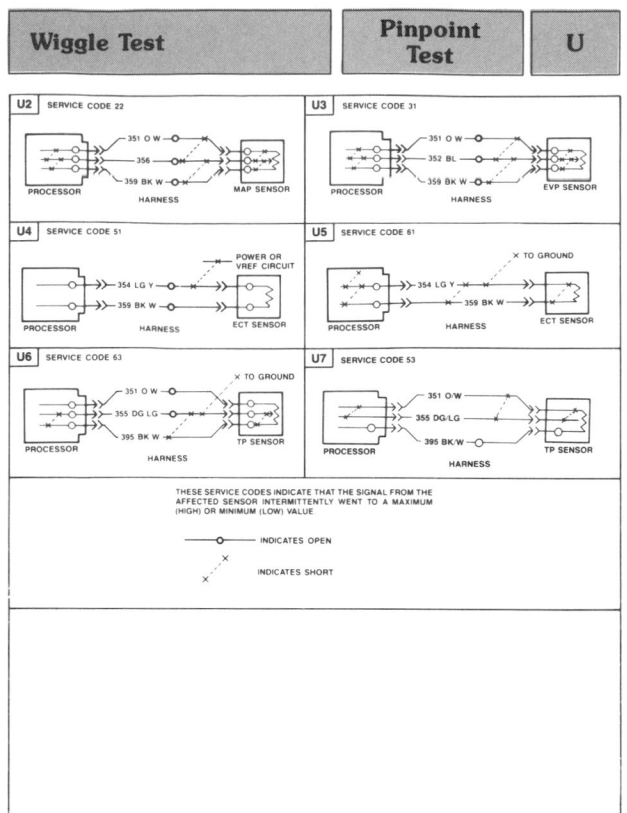

U2 SERVICE CODE 22	U3 SERVICE CODE 31
U4 SERVICE CODE 51	U5 SERVICE CODE 61
U6 SERVICE CODE 63	U7 SERVICE CODE 53

THESE SERVICE CODES INDICATE THAT THE SIGNAL FROM THE AFFECTED SENSOR INTERMITTENTLY WENT TO A MAXIMUM (HIGH) OR MINIMUM (LOW) VALUE.

—o— INDICATES OPEN

—x— INDICATES SHORT

Invalid Codes — Continuous Test	Pinpoint Test	X

TEST STEP	RESULT ▶	ACTION TO TAKE
X4		
• Check power circuit to Keep Alive Memory for voltage. • Key to Off. • Disconnect processor and inspect both 60 pin connectors. • Connect Breakout Box to harness, leave processor disconnected. • DVOM on 20 volt scale. • Connect positive test lead to Breakout Box pin 1 and negative test lead to Breakout Box pin 60. • Key On. • Observe voltage reading.	DVOM reading less than 10 volts ▶ DVOM reading 10 volts or more ▶	REPAIR open to power. REPEAT Quick Test. REPLACE processor. REPEAT Quick Test.

FUSIBLE LINK

PIN 1 — STARTER RELAY POSITIVE POST

Invalid Codes — Continuous Test	Pinpoint Test	X

TEST STEP	RESULT ▶	ACTION TO TAKE
X1 INSPECT ENGINE COMPARTMENT WIRING FOR PROPER ROUTING		
• Are any EEC components or EEC wiring close to ignition components or wires (High Electrical Energy Sources)?	Yes ▶ No ▶	REROUTE wires. GO to X2 GO to X2.
X2 ERASE CONTINUOUS CODES		
• Key On — Engine Off. • Activate Self-Test until the first code is outputted, then immediately deactivate Self-Test. This action, if performed as specified, will erase the continuous codes. • Turn key Off. • Perform Key On — Engine Off Self-Test and record codes from continuous test. • Valid codes are: 11, 22, 31, 51, 53, 61 and 63. • Any invalid codes?	Invalid codes ▶ All codes valid ▶	GO to X3 GO to Quick Test Step 6.0.
X3 GENERATE FAULT IN KEEP ALIVE MEMORY		
• Key Off. • Deactivate Self-Test. • Disconnect ECT sensor. • Key On and wait 15 seconds. • Key Off. • Connect ECT sensor. • Activate Self-Test. • Key On and record codes. • Is code 51 present in continuous test codes?	Yes ▶ No ▶	Keep Alive Memory is functioning properly. REPEAT Quick Test. GO to X4.

Shift Indicator Light (SIL)	Pinpoint Test	Z

TEST STEP	RESULT ▶	ACTION TO TAKE
Z1 DETERMINE SIL FAULT		
NOTE: Before proceeding with this Pinpoint Test, service code 11 (pass) must be present for both Key On — Engine Off and engine running quick test. • Check SIL operation by driving vehicle.	SIL is always Off ▶ SIL is on intermittently or always On ▶	GO to Z2 GO to Z4
Z2 CHECK CONTINUITY OF CIRCUIT 201 TO TOP GEAR SWITCH		
• Key Off and wait 10 seconds. • Disconnect harness from top gear switch. • DVOM on 200 ohms scale. • Measure continuity of top gear harness connector circuit 201 to Self-Test connector circuit connector.	Reading is less than 5 ohms ▶ Reading is 5 ohms or greater ▶	GO to Z3 REPAIR open in circuit 201 to top gear switch. RECONNECT harness and RETEST SIL function.
Z3 CHECK TOP GEAR SWITCH FOR OPEN		
• Key Off and harness disconnected from top gear switch. • Transmission in 1st gear. • DVOM on 200 ohm scale. • Measure continuity of top gear switch.	Reading is less than 5 ohms ▶ Reading is 5 ohms or more ▶	CHECK fuse and bulb. If OK REPAIR open in circuit 46 or 640. RECONNECT harness to top gear switch and RETEST SIL operation. REPLACE top gear switch. RECONNECT harness and RETEST SIL operation.

EEC IV-2.3L HSC Engine Diagnosis

Shift Indicator Light (SIL)	Pinpoint Test	Z

TEST STEP	RESULT ▶	ACTION TO TAKE
Z4 CHECK TOP GEAR SWITCH FOR CONTINUITY		
• Key Off and wait 10 seconds. • Disconnect harness from top gear switch. • DVOM on 200 ohm scale. • Transmission in top gear. • Measure continuity of top gear switch.	Reading is less than 5 ohms ▶	REPLACE top gear switch. RECONNECT harness and RETEST SIL operation.
	Reading is 5 ohms or greater ▶	REPAIR short to ground in circuit 46. RECONNECT harness and RETEST SIL operation.

Additional Diagnostic Aids (Cont'd.)

Continuous Monitor Test

This test is intended as an aid in diagnosing intermittent failures in the sensor input circuits. The Self-Test output is energized whenever the continuous test mode senses a fault and de-energized when the system is OK.

• Key On — Engine Off Continuous Monitor Mode:

To enter this mode, "verify" Self-Test is not activated and then turn the key to run. Self-Test output will be activated whenever a continuous fault is detected and if the duration is long enough, a fault code will be stored.

• Engine Running Continuous Monitor Mode

This mode of testing is entered immediately after the service codes from the Engine Running position of Quick Test (Step 4.0) because the engine running test can be entered only once per ignition cycle. An alternate quick method (eliminates waiting for Self-Test to complete its cycle) is to enter the running test, exit, and re-enter (do not shut the engine off). This will put you in the Engine Running Continuous Monitor Mode.

The Continuous Monitor Mode will allow the technician to activate these test modes and then attempt to re-create the intermittent failure (Tap, move, wiggle the harness and/or top, temperature cycle [start the engine cold and allow to warm up]), the suspected sensor.

If the Self-Test Monitor indicates a fault (short or open) the corresponding service code will be stored. Now with the knowledge of the affected circuits, a close check of the harness and associated connectors can be made.

Exercise Sensors While Observing Continuous Test Monitor

• Move TP through its range.
• Apply Vac to MAP/BP.
• Apply Vac to EGR Valve (moves EVP).
• Fuel.

Observe Continuous Test Monitor for an indication that the fault was simulated.

Additional Diagnostic Aids

Output State Check:

This test is performed in the Key On — Engine Off test after the continuous codes have been sent. Do not disable Self-Test but momentarily depress the throttle to the floor and release.

All aux. EEC outputs including Self-Test will be activated at this time. Another throttle depression will turn them off. This cycle may be repeated as many times as necessary, but if left activated for more than ten (10) minutes, will return to the de-energized condition.

This feature allows the technician to force the processor to activate these outputs for additional diagnostics.

How to Perform Output State Check

• Connect VOM to Self-Test Output (STO).
• Initialize Key On — Engine Off On-Demand Self-Test.

When the continuous service codes are completed, the VOM will read 0 volts.

• Depress accelerator to turn On or Off all actuators.

    On = High Meter Reading
    Off = 0 volts Low Meter Reading

• Disconnect VOM from the Self-Test Output (STO).
• Reconnect VOM to the appropriate actuator.
• Measure proper actuator output state voltage.

Example Test	Results	Action to Take
		Only perform "Action to Take" with specific instructions to do so.
A. When STO is ≥ 10 volts. Is actuator reading ≥ 10 volts?	Yes No	
B. Depress accelerator to change STO to < 10 volts. Is actuator reading < 10 volts?	Yes No	
C. Measure resistance of solenoid (50-110 ohms).	No Yes	

NOTE: Remember — you can cycle actuators On or Off as often as necessary.

However, actuators are On only for 10 minutes and will automatically turn off. If this should happen, you will need to re-initialize the Key On — Engine Off Self-Test to re-energize actuator.

How To Use Continuous Tests

• Remember: The intermittent service codes are unique service codes in the "Continuous Test" and were not displayed (repeated) from the Key On — Engine Off Self-Test.
• Initiate Key On — Engine Off Self-Test.
• Repair all Key On — Engine Off service codes.
• The service codes that are displayed (repeated) in both the Continuous Test and Key On — Engine Off test are also considered repaired. Only the **unique** service code(s) displayed in the "Continuous Test" are considered the intermittent service codes.

How to interpret the intermittent service codes in the Continuous Test. **See Figure 14.**

• Connect a VOM to the Self-Test output.
• After the last repeated code from the continuous test — remove the Self-Test input jumper.

NOTE: Remember to keep your eyes on the VOM for any movement which will indicate where the intermittent is located.

EXAMPLE: How to Use the Continuous Test (Systematically)

If a service code "21" was displayed — "Engine Coolant Temperature Sensor"

• Visually inspect the sensor **very closely.**
• Lightly TAP on the sensor.
• Push/Pull on the sensor harness connector (do not disconnect — yet).
• Test and Wiggle (shake) harness vigorously.
• If VOM has not given a positive indication of an intermittent, disconnect the sensor from the harness as **slowly as possible.** Remove terminals from the connector. Visually inspect terminals at both ends for corrosion, bad crimps, properly seated terminals, etc.
• Reconnect after inspection.
• Disconnect processor from harness as slowly as possible.
• Inspect terminals.
• Only remove terminals associated with the sensor being inspected.
• If the VOM does not give a positive intermittent indication — reconnect the connector and erase the Continuous Test service codes.
• To erase the continuous service codes:
   — Initiate Key On — Engine Off Self-Test.
   — Remove jumper from the Self-Test input terminal as soon as the **first** service code is received (even if an "11" is the first code).
   — Rerun Self-Test with jumper to verify services have been erased.

EEC IV-2.3L HSC Engine Diagnosis

Vacuum — Schematic

Electrical — Schematic

EEC IV-2.3L HSC Engine Diagnosis

Feedback Carburetors 6 SECTION

INDEX

NOTE: Please refer to the Application Chart at the front of this Manual.

FEEDBACK CARBURETORS

General Information

The need for better fuel economy combined with increasingly strict emission control regulations dictate a more exact control of the engine air/fuel mixture. A number of computer controlled carburetor systems have been developed in response to these needs. They are described in the following sections.

Essentially, all of these systems operate on the same principle. By controlling the air/fuel mixture exactly, more complete combustion can occur in the engine, and more thorough oxidation and reduction of the exhaust gases can be achieved in the catalytic converter.

The systems under discussion use variations of the same basic components: an oxygen sensor, to monitor exhaust gas oxygen content; a variable-mixture carburetor; a three-way catalytic converter capable of oxidizing HC and CO and reducing NOx; an air injection system to supply the converter with additional oxygen for the oxidation reaction; and a computer to monitor the process and adjust it according to continually changing engine and environmental conditions.

These systems operate in the following manner: The oxygen sensor, installed in the exhaust manifold upstream of the catalytic converter, reads the oxygen content of the exhaust gases. It generates an electrical signal and sends it to the computer. The computer then decides how to adjust the mixture to keep it at the correct air/fuel ratio. For example, if the mixture is too lean, the computer signals the carburetor that more fuel is needed. The computer signal activates a mixture control device on the carburetor, which enrichens the mixture accordingly. The monitoring process is a continual one, so that fine mixture adjustments are going on at all times.

The object of all of the systems is to maintain the optimum air/fuel mixture, which is chemically correct for theoretically complete combustion. The stoichiometric ratio is 14.7:1 (air to fuel). At that point, the catalytic converter's efficiency is greatest in oxidizing and reducing HC, CO, and NOx into carbon dioxide (CO_2), water (H_2O), and free oxygen and nitrogen (O_2 and N_2 respectively).

Most of the systems have two modes of operation: closed loop and loop. Closed loop operation occurs when the converter and oxygen sensor have warmed to efficient levels. All sensors become interdependent in this mode: the oxygen sensor sends signals to the computer, which signals the carburetor, which adjusts the mixture, which changes the oxygen sensor's readings, which go back to the computer, and so on. A continual and ongoing feedback of information and adjustment is achieved. Open loop operation generally takes place when the engine is still cold. In this mode, the computer simply provides a predetermined and invariable signal; the signal may affect only the carburetor air/fuel ratio, although in most installations it also provides a fixed spark advance signal to the electronic ignition module as well. In open loop operation, no signals are accepted by the computer.

Specific components used in these systems vary a great deal. The air injection system may be either an air pump or a pulse air design. Air injection may be into the exhaust manifold or directly into the catalytic converter. Mixture control on the carburetor can be a direct linkage to the metering valve or rods, or may be a vacuum control.

The Chrysler and Ford designs, and most 1980 and later G.M. C-4 and CCC systems, include electronic ignition as part of the system. Spark advance is controlled by the computer; the distributor pick-up and electronic ignition module are incorporated as signal devices for the computer, which decides when to order ignition firing as a function of interpretation of all sensor inputs.

One thing all of the systems have in common is a certain amount of nonadjustability. Mixture is always nonadjustable in these installations. If a mixture screw is provided on the carburetor, it is concealed under a staked-in plug, or locked in place. In many cases, ignition timing is also non-adjustable; idle speed, choke setting and fast idle rpm may also be either fixed during manufacture or under the control of the computer, and therefore not adjustable.

Unfortunately, most of the systems are so sophisticated and complicated that they do not respond favorably to conventional troubleshooting techniques. Problems with these devices almost invariably require the use of special test equipment and careful diagnosis procedures.

CAUTION

The use of improper test equipment can damage some computerized systems. See the "Tools" section for details.

AMERICAN MOTORS FEEDBACK SYSTEMS

General Information

American Motors introduced feedback systems on all cars (except Eagle) in 1980. Two different, but similar, systems are used. The four cylinder engine uses the G.M. C-4 feedback system, which is covered earlier in this section. Component usage is identical to that of the G.M. 151 cu. in four cylinder engine, including an oxygen sensor, a vacuum switch (which is closed at idle and partial throttle positions), a wide open throttle switch, a coolant temperature sensor (set to open at 150°F), an Electronic Control Module (ECM) equipped with modular Programmable Read Only Memory (PROM), and a mixture control solenoid installed in the air horn on the E2SE carburetor. A "Check Engine" light is included on the instrument panel as a service and diagnostic indicator.

The six cylinder engine is equipped with a Computerized Emission Control (CEC) System. 1980 CEC components include an oxygen sensor; two vacuum switches (one ported and one manifold) to detect three operating conditions: idle, partial throttle, and wide open throttle; a coolant temperature switch: a Micro Computer Unit (MCU), the control unit for the system which monitors all data and sends an output signal to the carburetor; and a stepper motor installed in the main body of the BBD carburetor, which varies the position of the two metering pins controlling the size of the air bleed orifices in the carburetor. The MCU also interprets signals from the distributor (rpm voltage) to monitor engine rpm.

On 1981 and later models with CEC, the number of sensors has been increased. Three vacuum operated electric switches, two mechanically operated electric switches, one engine coolant switch and an air temperature operated switch are used to detect and send engine opeating data to the MCU concerning the following engine operating conditions; cold engine start-up and operation; wide open throttle; idle (closed throttle); and partial and deep throttle.

Both AMC systems are conventional in operation. As in other feedback systems, two modes of operation are possible: open loop and closed loop. Open loop operation occurs during engine starting, cold engine operation, cold oxygen sensor operation, engine idling, wide open throttle operation, and low battery voltage operation. In open loop, a fixed air/fuel mixture signal is provided by the ECM or MCU to the carburetor, and oxygen sensor data is ignored. Closed loop operation occurs at all other times, and in this mode all signals are used by the control unit to determine the optimum air/fuel mixture.

Carter BBD feedback carburetor assembly—typical

Labels in image:
- BOWL VENT TO CANISTER
- BOWL VENT TO CANISTER
- TO EGR VACUUM AMPLIFIER
- DUTY CYCLE SOLENOID
- SOLENOID IDLE STOP
- TO CCEV VALVE
- TO CRANKCASE PCV VALVE
- TO CHOKE DIAPHRAGM
- TO POWER BRAKE
- TO AIR CLEANER HEATED INLET AIR CLEANER
- BOWL VENT SOLENOID

CARTER BBD FEEDBACK CARBURETOR

General Information

The Carter model BBD dual venturi carburetor utilizes three basic fuel metering systems. The idle System provides a mixture for idle and low speed performance; the Accelerator Pump System provides additional fuel during acceleration; the Main Metering System, provides an economical mixture for normal cruising conditions. In addition to these three basic systems, there is a fuel inlet system that constantly supplies the fuel to the basic metering systems, and a choke system (with electric assist) which temporarily enriches the mixture to aid in starting and running a cold engine.

The function of the O^2 Feedback Solenoid is to provide limited regulation of the fuel-air ratio of a feedback carburetor in response to electrical signals from the on-board computer. It performs this task by metering air-flow and operates in parallel with a conventional fixed main metering jet. The O^2 feedback solenoid includes, in addition to a protective case, such attaching surfaces and passageways as are required for the directing and containing of airflow when the solenoid assembly is correctly installed in a feedback carburetor designed for its use. If problems are experienced with the electronic feedback carburetor system, the system and its related components must be checked before carburetor work is begun. Close attention should be given to vacuum hose condition, hose connections, and any area where leaks could develop. In addition, the related wiring and its connectors must be checked for excessive resistance. In normal service, the mixture should not require adjustment. The idle set rpm can be checked without removal of the tamper resistant plug.

NOTE: Tampering with the carburetor is a violation of Federal Law. Adjustment of the carburetor idle air-fuel mixture can only be done under certain circumstances.

Adjustment should only be considered if an idle defect exists after normal diagnosis has revealed no other faulty condition, such as, incorrect idle speed, faulty hose or wire connection, etc. Also, it is important to make sure the on-board computer systems are operating properly. Adjustment of the carburetor idle air-fuel mixture should also be performed after a major carburetor overhaul. Upon completion of the carburetor adjustment, it is important to reinstall the plug.

Fuel Inlet System

All fuel enters the fuel bowl through the fuel inlet fitting in the bowl. The fuel inlet needle seats directly in the fuel inlet seat. The fuel inlet needle is controlled by dual floats and are hinged by a float fulcrum pin. The fuel inlet system must constantly maintain the specified level of fuel as the basic fuel metering systems are calibrated to deliver the proper mixture only when the fuel is at this level. When the fuel level in the bowl drops, the float also drops permitting additional fuel to flow past the fuel inlet needle into the bowl. The float chamber is vented to the vapor canister.

Idle System

Fuel used during curb idle and low speed operation flows through the main metering jet into the main well. Fuel continues into an idle fuel pick up tube where the fuel is mixed with air which enters

Low speed fuel control circuit on Carter BBD feedback carburetor

through idle by pass air bleeds located in the venturi cluster screws. At curb idle the fuel and air mixture flows down the idle channel and is further mixed or broken up by air entering the idle channel through the transfer slot which is above the throttle valve at curb idle. The idle system is equipped with a restrictor in the idle channel, located between the transfer slot and the idle port, which limits the maximum attainable idle mixture.

High speed fuel control circuit on Carter BBD feedback carburetor

During low speed operation the throttle valve moves exposing the transfer slot and fuel begins to flow through the transfer slot as well as the idle port. As the throttle valves are opened further and engine speed increases the air flow through the carburetor also increases. This increased air flow creates a low pressure area in the venturi and the main metering system begins to discharge fuel.

Accelerator Pump System

When the throttle valves are opened suddenly the air flow through the carburetor responds almost immmediately. However, there is a brief time interval or lag before the fuel can overcome its inertia and maintain the desired fuel-air ratio. The piston type accelerating pump system mechanically supplies the fuel necessary to overcome this deficiency for a short period of time. Fuel enters the pump cylinder from the fuel bowl through a port in the bottom of the pump well below the normal position of the pump piston. When the engine is turned off, fuel vapors in the pump cylinder are vented through the area between the pump piston and pump cup.

As the throttle lever is moved, the pump link is operated through a system of levers. A pump drive spring pushes the pump piston down. Fuel is forced through a passage around the pump discharge check ball and out the pump discharge jets which are located in the venturi cluster.

Main Metering System

As the engine approaches cruising speed the increased air flow through the venturi creates low pressure area in the venturi of the carburetor. Near atmospheric pressure present in the fuel bowl causes the fuel to flow to the lower pressure area created by the venturi and magnified by the booster venturi. Fuel flows through the main jet into the main well. The air enters through the main well air bleeds. The mixture of fuel and air being lighter than raw fuel, responds faster to changes in venturi vacuum and is also more readily vaporized when discharged into the venturi.

Exhaust Gas Recirculation System (EGR)

All BBD carburetors have an additional vacuum port for the exhaust gas recirculation system. The EGR system is controlled by the venturi vacuum control system. This system utilizes a venturi port in the side of the carburetor above the throttle valve.

SERVICE PROCEDURES

Oxygen Sensor Replacement

1. Disconnect the two wire plug.
2. Remove the sensor from the exhaust manifold on the four cylinder, or the exhaust pipe on the six.
3. Clean the threads in the manifold or pipe.
4. Coat the threads of the replacement sensor with an electrically-conductive antiseize compound. Do not use a conventional antiseize compound, which may electrically insulate the sensor.
5. Install the sensor. Installation torque is 25 ft. lbs. for the four cylinder, 31 ft. lbs. for the six cylinder.
6. Connect the sensor lead. Do not push the rubber boot into the sensor body more than 1/2 inch above the base.
7. If the sensor's pigtail is broken, replace the sensor. The wires cannot be spliced or soldered.

Vacuum Switch Replacement

The vacuum switches are mounted in a bracket bolted to the left inner fender panel in the engine compartment. They are not replaceable individually; the complete unit must be replaced.

1. Tag all the vacuum hoses, then disconnect them from the switches. Disconnect the electrical plugs. The four cylinder has two plugs and the six has one.
2. Remove the switch and bracket assembly from the fender panel.
3. Installation is the reverse.

Stepper Motor Replacement

The BBD stepper motor is installed in the side of the main body of the carburetor.

1. Remove the air cleaner case.
2. Disconnect the electrical plug.
3. Remove the retaining screw and remove the motor from the side of the carburetor. Be careful not to drop the metering pins or the spring when removing the motor.
4. Installation is the reverse.

CARBURETOR

Removal and Installation

1. Remove the air cleaner.
2. Disconnect the fuel and vacuum lines. It might be a good idea to tag them to avoid confusion when the time comes to put them back.
3. Disconnect the choke rod.
4. Disconnect the accelerator linkage.
5. Disconnect the automatic transmission linkage.
6. Unbolt and remove the carburetor.
7. Remove the base gasket.
8. Before installation, make sure that the carburetor and manifold sealing surfaces are clean.
9. Install a new carburetor base gasket.
10. Install the carburetor and start the fuel and vacuum lines.
11. Bolt down the carburetor evenly.
12. Tighten the fuel and vacuum lines.
13. Connect the accelerator and automatic transmission linkage. If the transmission linkage was disturbed, it will have to be adjusted.
14. Connect the choke rod.
15. Install the air cleaner. Adjust the idle speed and mixture. Depending on the vintage, it may not be necessary (or possible) to adjust the idle mixture.

Disassembly

1. Place carburetor on repair stand to protect throttle valves from damage and to provide a stable base for working.
2. Remove retaining clip from accelerator pump arm link and remove link.

3. Remove step-up piston cover plate and gasket from top of air horn.
4. Remove the screws and locks from the accelerator pump arm and the vacuum piston rod lifter. Then slide the pump lever out of the air horn. The vacuum piston and step-up rods can now be lifted straight up and out of the air horn as an assembly.
5. Remove vacuum hose from between carburetor main body and choke vacuum diaphragm at main body tap.
6. Remove choke diaphragm, linkage and bracket assembly and place to one side to be cleaned as a separate item.
7. Remove retaining clip from fast idle cam link and remove link from choke shaft lever.
8. Remove fast idle cam retaining screw and remove fast idle cam and linkage.

Step-up piston and metering rods showing location of assembly in the float bowl

Step-up piston assembly and related components

Exploded view of accelerator pump lever

477

Exploded view of Carter BBD float assembly

Remove and install main metering jets carefully from the float bowl

9. Remove air horn retaining screws and lift air horn straight up and away from main body. Discard gasket.

10. Invert the air horn and compress accelerator pump drive spring and remove "S" link from pump shaft. Pump assembly can now be removed.

11. Remove fuel inlet needle valve, seat, and gasket from main body.

12. Lift out float fulcrum pin retainer and baffle. Then lift out floats and fulcrum pin.

13. Remove main metering jets.

14. Remove venturi cluster screws, then lift venturi cluster and gaskets up and away from main body. Discard gaskets. Do not remove the idle orifice tubes or main vent tubes from the cluster. They can be cleaned in a solvent and dried with compressed air.

15. Invert carburetor and drop out accelerator pump discharge and intake check balls.

16. Using procedure outlined in "Propane Assisted Idle Set Procedure" in the adjustment area at the end of this section. Remove idle mixture screws from throttle body.

17. Remove screws that attach throttle body to main body. Separate bodies.

18. Test freeness of choke mechanism in air horn. The choke shaft must float free to operate correctly. If choke shaft sticks, or appears to be gummed from deposits in air horn, a thorough cleaning will be required.

19. The carburetor now has been disassembled into three main units: the air horn, main body, and throttle body. Components are disassembled as far as necessary for cleaning and inspection.

Cleaning Carburetor Parts

Efficient carburetion depends greatly on careful cleaning and inspection during overhaul, since dirt, gum, water, or varnish in or on the carburetor parts are often responsible for poor performance.

Overhaul the carburetor in a clean, dustfree area. Carefully disassemble the carburetor, referring often to the exploded views. Keep all similar and lookalike parts segregated during disassembly and cleaning to avoid accidental interchange during assembly. Make a note of all jet sizes.

When the carburetor is disassembled, wash all parts (except diaphragms, electric choke units, pump plunger, and any other plastic, leather, fiber, or rubber parts) in clean carburetor solvent. Do not leave parts in the solvent any longer than is necessary to sufficiently loosen the deposits. Excessive cleaning may remove the special finish from the float bowl and choke valve bodies, leaving these parts unfit for service. Rinse all parts in clean solvent and blow them dry with compressed air or allow them to air dry. Wipe clean all cork, plastic, leather, and fiber parts with a clean, lint-free cloth.

Blow out all passages and jets with compressed air and be sure that there are no restrictions or blockages. Never use wire or similar tools to clean jets, fuel passages, or air bleeds. Clean all jets and valves separately to avoid accidental interchange.

Inspection and Reassembly

THROTTLE BODY

Check throttle shaft for excessive wear in throttle body. If wear is extreme, it is recommended that throttle body assembly be replaced

Air horn and throttle body components

478

rather than installing a new shaft in old body. Install idle mixture screws in body. The tapered portion must be straight and smooth. If tapered portion is grooved or ridged, a new idle mixture screw should be installed to insure having correct idle mixture control.

MAIN BODY

1. Invert main body and place insulator in position, then place throttle body on main body and align. Install screws and tighten securely.

2. Install accelerator pump discharge check ball (5/32 inch diameter) in discharge passage. Drop accelerator pump intake check ball (3/16 inch diameter) into bottom of the pump cylinder.

3. To check the accelerator pump system; fuel inlet and discharge check balls, proceed as follows:

4. Pour clean gasoline into carburetor bowl, approximately 1/2 inch deep. Remove pump plunger from container of mineral spirits and slide down into pump cylinder. Raise plunger and press lightly on plunger shaft to expel air from pump passage.

5. Using a small clean brass rod, hold discharge check ball down firmly on its seat. Again raise plunger and press downward. No fuel should be emitted from either intake or discharge passage. If any fuel does emit from either passage, it indicates the presence of dirt or a damaged check ball or seat. Clean passage again and repeat test. If leakage is still evident, stake check ball seats (place a piece of drill rod on top of check ball and lightly tap drill rod with a hammer to form a new seat), remove and discard old balls, and install new check balls. The fuel inlet check ball is located at bottom of the plunger well. Remove fuel from bowl.

6. Install discharge check ball. Install new gaskets on venturi cluster, then install in position in main body. Install cluster screws and tighten securely.

7. Install main metering jets.

FLOAT

The carburetors are equipped with a synthetic rubber tipped fuel inlet needle. The needle tip is viton, which is not affected by gasoline and is stable over a wide range of temperatures. The tip is flexible enough to make a good seal on the needle seat, and to give increased resistance to flooding.

NOTE: The use of the synthetic rubber tipped inlet needle requires that care be used in adjusting the float setting. Care should be taken to perform this accurately in order to secure the best performance and fuel economy.

Location of accelerator pump intake and discharge check balls

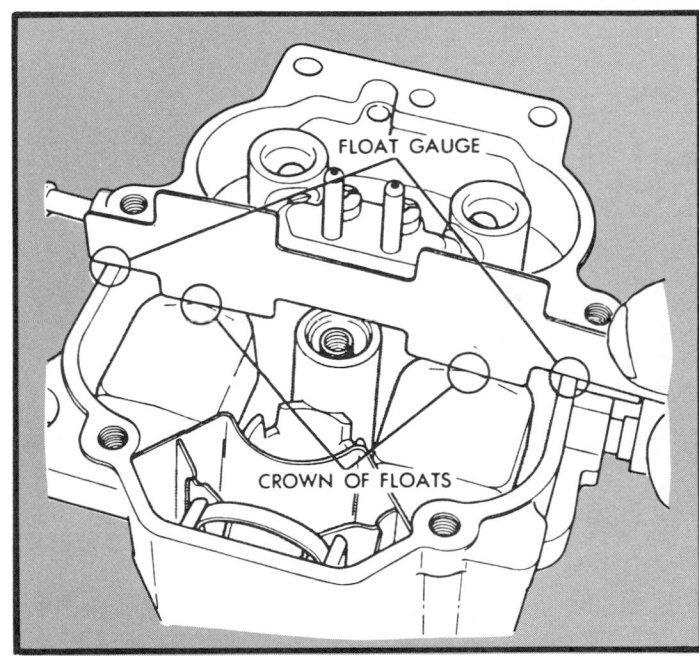

Checking float setting on Carter BBD models

When replacing the needle and seat assembly (inlet fitting), the float level must also be checked, as dimensional difference between the old and new assemblies may change the float level. Refer to carburetor adjustments for adjusting procedure.

1. Install floats and fulcrum pin.

2. Install fulcrum pin retainer and baffle.

3. Install fuel inlet needle valve, seat and gasket in main body.

AIR HORN

1. Place the accelerator pump drive spring on pump plunger shaft then insert shaft into air horn. Compress spring far enough to insert "S" link.

2. Install the pump lever, vacuum piston rod lifter and accelerator pump arm in the air horn.

3. Drop intake check ball into pump bore. Install baffle into main body. Place step-up piston spring in piston vacuum bore.

Hold down the check ball with a small brass rod when testing accelerator pump intake and discharge

Adjusting or qualifying the step-up piston—see the text for details

Position a new gasket on the main body and install air horn.

4. Install air horn retaining screws and tighten alternately, a little at a time, to compress the gasket securely.

5. To qualify the step-up piston, adjust gap by turning the allen head calibration screw on top of the piston. See the adjustment section for proper measurement. Record number of turns and direction to obtain this dimension for this must be reset to its original position after the vacuum step-up piston adjustment has been made.

6. Carefully position vacuum piston metering rod assembly into bore in air horn making sure metering rods are in main metering jets. Then place the two lifting tangs of the plastic rod lifter under piston yoke. Slide shaft of the accelerator pump lever through rod lifter and pump arm. Install two locks and adjusting screws, but do not tighten until after adjustment is made.

Adjusting the step-up piston assembly on Carter BBD models

7. Install fast idle cam and linkage. Tighten retaining screw securely.

8. Connect accelerator pump linkage to pump lever and throttle lever. Install retaining clip.

CHOKE VACUUM DIAPHRAGM

Inspect the diaphragm vacuum fitting to insure that the passage is not plugged with foreign material. Leak check the diaphragm to determine if it has internal leaks. To do this, first depress the diaphragm stem, then place a finger over the vacuum fitting to seal the opening. Release the diaphragm stem. If the stem moves more than 1/16 inch in 10 seconds, the leakage is excessive and the assembly must be replaced.

Install the diaphragm assembly on the air horn as follows:
1. Engage choke link in slot in choke lever.
2. Install diaphragm assembly, secure with attaching screws.
3. Inspect rubber hose for cracks before placing it on correct carburetor fitting. Do not connect vacuum hose to diaphragm fitting until after vacuum kick adjustment has been made.
4. Loosen choke valve attaching screws slightly. Hold valve closed, with fingers pressing on high side of valve. Tap valve lightly with a screw driver to seat in air horn. Tighten attaching screws securely and stake by squeezing with pliers.

CHOKE VACUUM KICK

The choke diaphragm adjustment controls the fuel delivery while the engine is running. It positions the choke valve within the air horn by action of the linkage between the choke shaft and the diaphragm. The diaphragm must be energized to measure the vacuum kick adjustment. Vacuum can be supplied by an auxiliary vacuum source.

CHOKE UNLOADER

The choke unloader is a mechanical device to partially open the choke valve at wide open throttle. It is used to eliminate choke enrichment during cranking of an engine. Engines which have been flooded or stalled by excessive choke enrichment can be cleared by use of the unloader. Refer to carburetor adjustments for adjusting procedure.

FAST IDLE SPEED

Fast idle engine speed is used to overcome cold engine friction, stalls after cold starts and stalls due to mixture icing. Make adjustment to the specifications. Refer to carburetor adjustment section for procedure.

SOLENOID IDLE STOP

Solenoid idle stops are used on vehicles equipped with either air conditioning or a heated backlite. The SIS is energized when either of those two accessories are turned on. The SIS will not change the throttle position, however, when rough engine idle occurs and the throttle is opened by the driver, the SIS will maintain a position that increases the idle speed.

BBD CARBURETOR ADJUSTMENTS

Float Setting Adjustment

1. Install floats with fulcrum pin and pin retainer in main body.
2. Install needle, seat and gasket in body and tighten securely.
3. Invert main body (catch pump intake check ball) so that weight of floats only, is forcing needle against seat. Hold finger against retainer to fully seat fulcrum pin.
4. Using a straight-edge scale, check float setting. The measurement from the surface of the fuel bowl to the crown of each float at center should be as indicated in specifications.
5. If an adjustment is necessary, hold the floats on the bottom of the bowl and bend the float lip toward or away from the needle. Recheck the setting again then repeat the lip bending operation as required. When bending the float lip, do not allow the lip to push against the needle as the synthetic rubber tip can be compressed sufficiently to cause a false setting which will affect correct level of fuel in the bowl.

Bend the float lever as indicated to adjust the fuel level

Qualifying Step-Up Piston Adjustment

If the step-up piston assembly is removed or the mechanical rod lifter adjustment is disturbed, the step-up piston must be readjusted or "Qualified". Qualifying places the step-up piston in a "mean" or central position.

1. Remove step-up piston cover plate and gasket.
2. Remove rod lifter lock screw and remove step-up piston assembly.
3. Adjust gap in the step-up piston by turning the allen head calibration screw on top of the piston. See specifications for proper measurement. Record number of turns and direction to obtain this dimension, for this must be reset to its original position after the vacuum step-up piston adjustment has been made.
4. Install step-up piston assembly and rod lifter lock screw.
5. Proceed to Vacuum Step-Up Piston Adjustment.

Vacuum Step-Up Piston Adjustment

1. Back off idle speed screw until throttle valves are completely closed. Count number of turns so that screw can be returned to its original position.
2. Fully depress step-up piston while holding moderate pressure on the rod lifter tab. While in this position, tighten rod lifter lock screw.
3. Release piston and rod lifter, then return idle speed screw to its original position.
4. Reset the allen head calibration screw on top of the step-up piston to its original position as recorded under Qualifying Step-Up Piston Adjustment.

NOTE: If this adjustment is changed the Step-Up Piston must be Re-Qualified.

Measuring the accelerator pump stroke on Carter BBD models

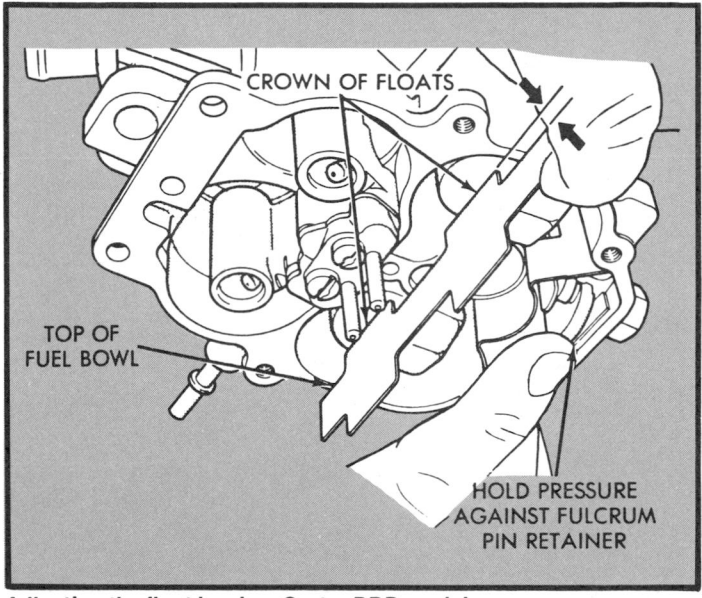

Adjusting the float level on Carter BBD models

Insert the gauge between the top of the bowl vent and seat when making bowl vent valve adjustment

Accelerator Pump Stroke Measurement (at Idle)

To establish an approximate curb idle on newly assembled carburetors, back off idle speed screw to completely close the throttle valve (fast idle cam must be in open choke position). Then turn the idle speed screw clockwise until it just contacts stop. Then continue to turn two complete turns.

1. Be sure accelerator pump "S" link is in the outer hole of the pump arm if arm has two holes.
2. Measure the distance between surface of air horn and top of accelerator pump shaft this measurement must be as shown in specifications.
3. To adjust pump travel, loosen pump arm adjusting lock screw and rotate sleeve until proper measurement is obtained, then tighten lock screw.

Choke unloader adjustment—Carter BBD models

Choke vacuum kick adjustment on Carter BBD models

Bowl Vent Valve Adjustment (On Vehicle at Curb Idle)

NOTE: The accelerator pump stroke adjustment and the idle speed must be properly set before making this adjustment.

1. Remove the step-up piston cover plate and gasket.
2. Measure by inserting specified gauge between the top of the bowl vent and the seat.
3. Adjust by bending the bowl vent lever tab. Support the bowl vent lever assembly before bending the bowl vent tab.
4. Install the step-up piston cover plate and gasket.

Choke Vacuum Kick Adjustment

1. Open throttle, close choke then close throttle to trap fast idle cam at closed choke position.
2. Disconnect vacuum hose from carburetor and connect to hose

from auxiliary vacuum source with small length of tube. Apply a vacuum of 15 or more inches of mercury.

3. Apply sufficient closing force on choke lever to completely compress spring in diaphragm stem without distorting linkage. Note: solid rod stem of diaphragm extends to an internal stop as spring compresses.

4. Measure by inserting specified gauge between top of choke valve and air horn wall at throttle lever side.

5. Adjust by changing diaphragm link length (open or close U-bend).

6. Check for free movement between open and adjusted positions. Correct any misalignment or interference by rebending link and readjust.

7. Reinstall vacuum hose on correct carburetor fitting.

Fast Idle Cam Position Adjustment

1. With fast idle speed adjusting screw contacting second highest speed step on fast idle cam, move choke valve towards closed position with light pressure on choke shaft lever.

2. Measure by inserting specified gauge between top of choke valve and air horn wall at throttle lever side.

3. Adjust by bending fast idle connector rod at angle until correct valve opening has been obtained.

Choke Unloader Adjustment

1. Hold throttle valves in wide open position.
2. Lightly press finger against control lever to move choke valve toward closed position.
3. Measure by inserting specified gauge between top of choke valve and air horn wall at throttle lever side.
4. Adjust by bending tang on throttle lever.

Solenoid Idle Stop Adjustment

Before checking or adjusting any idle speed, check ignition timing and adjust if necessary. Disconnect and plug the vacuum hose at the EGR valve. On vehicles equipped with a carburetor ground switch, connect a jumper wire between the switch and a good ground. On models not equipped with a Spark Control Computer (SCC), disconnect and plug the vacuum hoses from the carburetor at the heated air temperature sensor and at the OSAC valve and

Fast idle cam position adjustment—insert gauge as shown

remove the air cleaner. The air cleaner may be propped up on SCC equipped vehicles but not removed. Disconnect and plug the 3/16 inch diameter control hose at the canister. Remove the PCV valve from the cylinder head cover and allow the valve to draw underhood air. Connect a tachometer to the engine.

1. On Canadian vehicles equipped with a 318, 5.2L engine, proceed to Idle Set RPM Adjustment.

2. Turn on air conditioning and set blower on low. Disconnect the air conditioning compressor clutch wire.

3. On non-air conditioned vehicles, connect a jumper wire between the battery positive post and the solenoid idle stop lead wire.

---CAUTION---

Use care in jumping to the proper wire on the solenoid. Applying battery voltage to other than the correct wire will damage the wiring harness.

---

4. Open the throttle slightly and allow the solenoid plunger to extend.

5. Adjust engine rpm to the correct specification by turning the screw on the throttle lever.

6. Turn off air conditioning and reconnect clutch wire or disconnect solenoid jumper wire. Do not remove carburetor ground switch wire.

7. Proceed to Idle Set RPM Adjustment.

Idle Set RPM Adjustment

NOTE: This adjustment is to be performed only after the Solenoid Idle Stop Adjustment Procedure.

1. Disconnect the engine harness lead from the O² sensor and ground the engine harness lead.

---CAUTION---

Care should be exercised so that no pulling force is put on the wire attached to the O² sensor. Use care in working around the sensor as the exhaust manifold is extremely hot.

---

2. Remove and plug the vacuum hose at the vacuum transducer on the SCC. Connect an auxiliary vacuum supply to the vacuum transducer and set at 16 inches of vacuum.

3. Allow the engine to run for two minutes to allow the effect of disconnecting the O² sensor to take place.

4. If the idle set rpm is not correct, turn the screw on the solenoid to obtain the correct rpm.

5. Proceed to Fast Idle Speed Adjustment Procedure.

Fast Idle Speed Adjustment

NOTE: This adjustment is to be performed only after the Solenoid Idle Stop and Idle Set RPM Adjustments have been completed.

1. Open the throttle slightly and place the fast idle adjusting screw on the second highest step of the fast idle cam.

2. With the choke fully open, adjust the fast idle speed screw to obtain the correct fast idle rpm.

3. Return to idle then reposition the adjusting screw on the second highest step of the fast idle cam to verify speed. Readjust if necessary.

4. Return to idle and turn off engine. Unplug and reconnect vacuum hoses at the EGR valve and canister. Remove the tachometer. Remove all ground and jumper wires. Reinstall the air cleaner and, if disconnected, unplug and reconnect vacuum hoses from the carburetor to the heated air temperature sensor, and OSAC valve on the air cleaner. If disconnected, reconnect vacuum line on SCC. Reconnect O² sensor wire if disconnected.

NOTE: Idle speed with engine in normal operating condition (everything connected) may vary from set speeds. Do not readjust.

Fast idle speed adjustment—Carter BBD models

Concealment Plug Removal

1. Remove carburetor from engine.

2. Remove throttle body from carburetor.

3. Place the throttle body in a vise with the concealment plugs facing up and the gasket surfaces protected from the vise jaws.

4. Drill a 5/64 inch pilot hole at a 45° angle towards concealment plugs as shown in illustration.

5. Redrill hole to 1/8 inch.

6. Install a blunt punch into the hole and drive out the plug. Repeat procedure on the opposite side.

7. Reinstall the carburetor on the engine. The carburetor does not have to be removed to install new concealment plugs.

8. Proceed to propane assisted idle set procedure.

Propane Assisted Idle Set Procedure

NOTE: Tampering with the carburetor is a violation of Federal law. Adjustment of the carburetor idle air fuel mixture can only be done under certain circumstances, as explained below. Upon completion of the carburetor adjustment, the concealment plug must be replaced.

This procedure should only be used if an idle defect still exists after normal diagnosis has revealed no other faulty conditions such

Removing plugs to adjust idle mixture—see text for details

as incorrect basic timing, incorrect idle speed, faulty hose or wire connections, etc. Also, it is important to make sure the on-board computer systems are operating properly. Adjustment of the carburetor air fuel mixture should be performed after a major carburetor overhaul.

1. Remove the concealment plug. Set the parking brake and place the transmission in neutral. Turn all lights and accessories off. Connect a tachometer to the engine. Start the engine and allow it to warm up on the second highest step of the fast idle cam until normal operating is reached. Return engine to idle.

2. Disconnect and plug the vacuum hose at the EGR valve. On vehicles equipped with a carburetor ground switch, connect a jumper wire between the switch and a good ground. On vehicles not equipped with a Spark Control Computer (SCC), disconnect and plug the vacuum hoses at the heated air temperature sensor and at the OSAC valve. Remove the air cleaner except on vehicles equipped with SCC where the air cleaner cannot be removed but may be propped up.

3. Disconnect the hose from the heated air door sensor at the carburetor and install the propane supply hose in its place.

4. With the propane bottle upright and in a safe location, remove the PCV valve from the cylinder head cover and allow the valve to draw underhood air. Disconnect and plug the 3/16 inch diameter control hose from the canister.

5. Disconnect engine harness lead from the O^2 sensor and ground the engine harness lead.

---CAUTION---

Care should be exercised so that no pulling force is put on the wire attached to the O^2 sensor. Use care in working around the sensor as the exhaust manifold is extremely hot.

6. Remove and plug the vacuum line at the vacuum transducer at the SCC. Connect an auxiliary vacuum supply to the vacuum transducer and apply 16 inches of vacuum.

7. Allow the engine to run for two minutes to allow the effect of disconnecting the O^2 sensor to take place.

8. Open the propane main valve. Slowly open the propane metering valve until the maximum engine rpm is reached. When too much propane is added, engine rpm will decrease. "Fine tune" the metering valve to obtain the highest engine rpm.

9. With the propane still flowing, adjust the idle speed screw on the solenoid to obtain the correct propane rpm. Again, "fine tune" the metering valve to obtain the highest engine rpm. If there has been a change in the maximum rpm, readjust the idle speed screw to the specified propane rpm.

10. Turn off the propane main valve and allow the engine speed to stabilize. Slowly adjust the mixture screws by equal amounts, pausing between adjustments to allow engine speed to stabilize, to obtain the smoothest idle at the correct idle set rpm.

11. Turn on the propane main valve and "Fine tune" the metering valve to obtain the highest engine rpm. If the maximum engine speed is more than 25 rpm different than the specified propane rpm, repeat Steps 8–12.

12. Turn off propane main and metering valves. Remove the propane supply hose and reinstall the heated air sensor hose. Reinstall new concealment plug. If installed, remove O^2 sensor ground wire and reconnect O^2 sensor. If disconnected, reconnect vacuum line on SCC. Perform the Solenoid Idle Stop, Idle Set RPM, and Fast Idle Speed Adjustment Procedures.

Float Adjustment - On Vehicle

1. Remove air cleaner assembly and air cleaner gasket.
2. Remove air cleaner mounting bolt assembly.
3. Remove choke assembly.
4. Disconnect vacuum kick diaphragm hose.
5. Remove retaining clip from accelerator pump arm link and remove link.
6. Remove fast idle cam retaining clip and remove link.
7. Remove step-up piston cover plate and gasket from top of air horn.
8. Remove metering rod lifter lock screw.
9. Lift step-up piston and metering rod assembly straight up and out of the air horn.
10. Remove air horn retaining screws.
11. Lift air horn straight up and away from main body.
12. Remove float baffle.
13. Overfill the float bowl by depressing the float manually or from an external supply to within 1/4 to 3/8 inch from the top of the fuel bowl. This will provide adequate inlet needle seating force.
14. Using two wrenches, back off flare nut and tighten inlet fitting to 200 inch pounds (23 N m).
15. Firmly seat the float pin retainer by hand while measuring height. The measurement from the surface of the fuel bowl to the crown of each float at center should be as indicated in specifications. If adjustment is necessary, hold the floats on the bottom of the bowl and bend the float lip toward or away from the needle.

NOTE: When bending the float lip, do not allow the lip to push against the needle as the synthetic rubber tip can be compressed sufficiently to cause a false setting which will affect correct level of fuel in the bowl.

16. Install float baffle.
17. Install air horn on main body. Be sure the leading edge of the accelerator pump cup is not damaged as it enters the pump bore. Alternately tighten attaching screws to compress gasket evenly.
18. Alternately tighten attaching screws to compress gasket evenly.
19. Install step-up piston and metering rod assembly in air horn.
20. Install metering rod lifter lock screw.
21. Back off idle speed screw until throttle valves are completely closed. Count the number of turns so that screw can be returned to its original position.
22. Fully depress step-up piston while holding light pressure on metering rod lifter tab and tighten lock screw.
23. Install step-up piston cover plate and gasket.
24. Return idle speed screw to its original position.
25. Install fast idle cam link and retaining clip.
26. Install accelerator pump arm link and retaining clip.
27. Connect vacuum kick hose.
28. Install choke assembly.
29. Install air cleaner mounting bolt assembly.
30. Install air cleaner gasket and air cleaner.
31. Check idle speed with tachometer. If adjustment is necessary, refer to Emission Control Information Label in engine compartment for proper specifications.

CARTER BBD SPECIFICATIONS
Chrysler Products

Year	Model ②	Float Level (in.)	Accelerator Pump Travel (in.)	Bowl Vent (in.)	Choke Unloader (in.)	Choke Vacuum Kick	Fast Idle Cam Position	Fast Idle Speed (rpm)	Automatic Choke Adjustment
'78	8136S	¼	0.500①	0.080	0.280	0.110	0.070	1500	Fixed
	8137S	¼	0.500①	0.080	0.280	0.100	0.070	1600	Fixed

CARTER BBD SPECIFICATIONS
Chrysler Products

Year	Model ②	Float Level (in.)	Accelerator Pump Travel (in.)	Bowl Vent (in.)	Choke Unloader (in.)	Choke Vacuum Kick	Fast Idle Cam Position	Fast Idle Speed (rpm)	Automatic Choke Adjustment
'78	8177S	¼	0.500①	0.080	0.280	0.100	0.070	1600	Fixed
	8175S	¼	0.500①	0.080	0.280	0.160	0.070	1400	Fixed
	8143S	¼	0.500①	0.080	0.280	0.150	0.070	1500	Fixed
'79	8198S	¼	0.500①	0.080	0.280	0.100	0.070	1600	Fixed
	8199S	¼	0.500①	0.080	0.280	0.100	0.070	1600	Fixed
'80	8233S	¼	0.500①	0.080	0.280	0.130	0.070	1500	Fixed
	8235S	¼	0.500①	0.080	0.280	0.130	0.070	1700	Fixed
	8237S	¼	0.500①	0.080	0.280	0.110	0.070	1500	Fixed
	8239S	¼	0.500①	0.080	0.280	0.110	0.070	1500	Fixed
	8286S	¼	0.500①	0.080	0.280	0.100	0.070	1400	Fixed
'81-'82	8290S	¼	0.500①	0.080	0.280	0.100	0.070	1600	Fixed
	8291S	¼	0.500①	0.080	0.280	0.130	0.070	1400	Fixed
	8292S	¼	0.500①	0.080	0.280	0.130	0.070	1600③	Fixed
'83	8290S	¼	0.470①	0.080	0.280	0.100	0.070	1600	Fixed
	8291S	¼	0.470①	0.080	0.280	0.130	0.070	1400	Fixed
	8369S	¼	0.500①	0.080	0.280	0.130	0.070	1500	Fixed
'84	8385S	¼	0.470①	0.080	0.280	0.130	0.070	1400	Fixed
	8369S	¼	0.500	0.080	0.280	0.130	0.070	1500	Fixed

CARTER BBD SPECIFICATIONS
American Motors

Year	Model ①	Float Level (in.)	Accelerator Pump Travel (in.)	Choke Unloader (in.)	Choke Vacuum Kick	Fast Idle Cam Position	Fast Idle Speed (rpm)	Automatic Choke Adjustment
'78	8128	¼	0.496	0.280	0.150	0.110	1600	Index
	8129	¼	0.520	0.280	0.128	0.095	1500	1 Rich
'79	8185	¼	0.470	0.280	0.140	0.110	1600	1 Rich
	8186	¼	0.520	0.280	0.150	0.110	1500	1 Rich
	8187	¼	0.470	0.280	0.140	0.110	1600	1 Rich
	8221	¼	0.530	0.280	0.150	0.110	1600	1 Rich
'80	8216	¼	0.520	0.280	0.140	0.090	1850	2 Rich
	8246	¼	0.520	0.280	0.140	0.095	1850	2 Rich
	8247	¼	0.520	0.280	0.150	0.095	1700	1 Rich
	8248	¼	0.520	0.280	0.150	0.095	1700	1 Rich
	8253	¼	0.470	0.280	0.128	0.095	1850	2 Rich
	8256	¼	0.470	0.280	0.128	0.093	1850	2 Rich
	8278	¼	0.542	0.280	0.140	0.093	1850	Index

CARTER BBD SPECIFICATIONS
American Motors

Year	Model ①	Float Level (in.)	Accelerator Pump Travel (in.)	Choke Unloader (in.)	Choke Vacuum Kick	Fast Idle Cam Position	Fast Idle Speed (rpm)	Automatic Choke Adjustment
'81	8310	¼	0.525	0.280	0.140	0.095	1850	Index
	8302	¼	0.500	0.280	0.128	0.095	1850	1 Rich
	8303	¼	0.500	0.280	0.128	0.090	1700	1 Rich
	8306	¼	0.500	0.280	0.128	0.090	1700	1 Rich
	8307	¼	0.500	0.280	0.128	0.095	1850	1 Rich
	8308	¼	0.500	0.280	0.128	0.095	1850	2 Rich
	8309	¼	0.520	0.280	0.128	0.093	1700	2 Rich
'82	8338	¼	0.520	0.280	0.140	0.095	1850	1 Rich
	8339	¼	0.520	0.280	0.140	0.095	1850	1 Rich
'83	8360	¼	0.520	0.280	0.140	0.095	1850	Fixed
	8364	¼	0.520	0.280	0.140	0.095	1700	Fixed
	8367	¼	0.520	0.280	0.140	0.095	1700	Fixed
	8362	¼	0.520	0.280	0.140	0.095	1850	Fixed
'84	8383	¼	0.520	0.280	0.140	0.095	1850	½–1½ Rich
	8384	¼	0.520	0.280	0.140	0.095	1700	½–1½ Rich

① Model numbers located on the tag or casting

CHRYSLER ELECTRONIC FEEDBACK CARBURETOR

The Chrysler Electronic Feedback Carburetor (EFC) system was introduced in mid 1979 on Volarés and Aspens sold in California with the six cylinder engine. The system is a conventional one, incorporating an oxygen sensor, a three-way catalytic converter, an oxidizing catalytic converter, a feedback carburetor, a solenoid-operated vacuum regulator valve, and a Combustion Computer. Also incorporated into the system are Chrysler's Electronic Spark Control, and a mileage counter which illuminates a light on the instrument panel at 15,000 mile intervals, signaling the need for oxygen sensor replacement.

In Chrysler's system, "Combustion Computer" is a collective term for the Feedback Carburetor Controller and the Electronic Spark Control computer, which are housed together in a case located on the air cleaner. The feedback carburetor controller is the information processing component of the system, monitoring oxygen sensor voltage (low voltage/lean mixture, high voltage/rich mixture), engine coolant temperature, manifold vacuum, engine speed, and engine operating mode (starting or running). The controller examines the incoming information and then sends a signal to the solenoid-operated vacuum regulator valve (also located in the Combustion Computer housing), which then sends the proper rich or lean signal to the carburetor.

The 1 bbl Holley R-8286A carburetor (and 1 bbl Holley 6145 on later models) is equipped with two diaphragms, controlling the idle system and the main metering system. The diaphragms move tapered rods, which vary the size of the orifices in the idle system air bleed and the main metering system fuel flow. A "lean" command from the controller to the vacuum regulator results in increased vacuum to both diaphragms, which simultaneously raise both the idle air bleed rod (increasing idle air bleed) and the main

metering rod (reducing fuel flow). A "rich" command reduces vacuum level, causing the spring-loaded rods to move in the other direction, enrichening the mixture.

Both closed loop and open loop operation are possible in the EFC system. Open loop operation occurs under any one of the following conditions: coolant temperature under 150°F; oxygen sensor temperature under 660°F; low manifold vacuum (less than 4.5 in. Hg. engine cold, or less than 3.0 in Hg. engine hot): oxygen sensor failure; or hot engine starting. Closed loop operation begins when engine temperature reaches 150°F.

Air injection is supplied by an air pump. At cold engine temperature, air is injected into the exhaust manifold upstream of both catalytic converters. At operating temperature, an air switching valve diverts air from the exhaust to an injection point downstream from the three-way catalyst, but upstream of the conventional oxidizing catalyst.

In 1980, the system was modified slightly and used on all California models, and on all 318 4-bbl. V8's nationwide. The 1980 and later system is used with Electronic Spark Advance (ESA), not Electronic Spark Control (ESC)—see the previous description in this section and the Electronic Ignition Systems section in this book for details. Differences lie in the deletion of some components within the combustion computer. The start timer, vacuum transducer count-up clock and memory throttle transducer, and ambient air temperature sensor are not used.

The feedback system for the six cylinder engines is essentially unchanged. The four and eight cylinder systems differ from the six mainly in the method used to control the carburetor mixture. Instead of having vacuum-controlled diaphragms to raise or lower the mixture rods, the carburetors are equipped with an electric solenoid valve, which is part of the carburetor. These later carburetors include the Carter BBD and Carter Thermo-Quad.

Other differences between the systems are minor. On the four cylinder, the ignition sensor is the Hall Effect distributor, but it functions in the same manner as the six cylinder pick-up coil. The eight cylinder uses two pick-up coils (a Start pick-up and a Run pick-up); troubleshooting is included in the "Lean Burn/Electronic Spark Control" section. The four and six cylinder engines use a 150°F coolant switch; the eight cylinder uses a 150°F switch with Combustion Computer 4145003, and a 98°F switch with Computer 4145088. The eight cylinder uses a 150°F switch with Combustion Computer 4145003, and a 98°F switch with Computer 4145088. The eight cylinder engine has a detonation sensor (see the "Lean Burn/Electronic Spark Control" section), and the six and eight cylinder engines have a charge temperature switch to monitor intake charge temperature. Below approximately 60°F, the switch prevents EGR timer function and EGR valve operation; additionally, on eight cylinder engines, air injection is routed upstream of the exhaust manifolds.

Finally, the replacement interval for the oxygen sensor has been doubled, from 15,000 to 30,000 miles. Replacement procedures and odometer resetting are the same as for the 1979 six cylinder system.

Note that two completely different troubleshooting procedures have been included here. Use the "1979" procedure only for 1979 Aspens and Volarés with the six cylinder engine. Use the "1980 and Later" procedure as applicable.

Troubleshooting

1979 MODELS

Troubleshooting requires the use of a few special tools. A 0–5 in. Hg. vacuum gauge accurate within ½ in. Hg.; a 0–30 in. Hg. vacuum gauge; a hand vacuum pump with vacuum gauge; two short lengths of 3/16 in. I.D. vacuum hose; two 3/16 in. vacuum tees; and a jumper wire approximately five feet long.

Before performing any tests, check all vacuum hoses for leaks, breaks, kinks, or improper connections, all electrical connections for soundness, and all wires for fraying or breaks. Check for leakage at both the intake and exhaust manifolds.

1. Warm the engine to normal operating temperature. Install a tee into the control vacuum hose which runs to the carburetor. Install the 0–5 in. vacuum gauge on the tee. Start the engine and allow it to idle. The vacuum gauge should read 2.5 in. for approximately 100 seconds, then fall to zero, then gradually rise to between 1.0 and 4.0 in. The reading may oscillate slightly.

2. If the vacuum reading is incorrect, increase the engine speed to 2000 rpm. If vacuum reads between 1.0 and 4.0 in., return the engine to idle. If the reading is now correct, the system was not warmed up, originally, but is OK.

3. If the gauge is correct at 2000 rpm but not at idle, the carburetor must be replaced.

4. If the vacuum is either above 4.0 in. or below 1.0 in., follow the correct troubleshooting procedure given next. Note that in most cases of system malfunction, control vacuum will be either 0 in. or 5.0 in.

Control Vacuum Above 4.0 In. Hg.

Start the engine, apply the parking brake, place the transmission in Neutral, and place the throttle on the next to lowest step of the fast idle cam.

1. Remove the PCV hose from the PCV valve. Cover the end of the hose with your thumb. Gradually uncover the end of the hose until the engine runs rough. If control vacuum gets lower as the hose is uncovered, the carburetor must be replaced; however, complete Step 2 before replacing it. If control vacuum remains high, continue with the tests.

2. Before replacing the carburetor, examine the heat shield. Interference may exist between the heat shield and the mechanical power enrichment valve lever. If so, the carburetor will be running rich. Correct the problem and repeat Step 1.

NOTE: A new heat shield is used starting in 1979 which has clearance for the enrichment lever. Earlier heat shields should not be used unless modified for clearance.

3. Disconnect the electrical connector at the solenoid regulator valve. Control vacuum should drop to zero. If not, replace the solenoid regulator valve.

4. Disconnect the oxygen sensor wire. Use the jumper wire to connect the *harness* lead to the negative battery terminal.

——————————CAUTION——————————
Do not connect the oxygen sensor wire to ground or to the battery.

Control vacuum should drop to zero in approximately 15 seconds. If not, replace the Combustion Computer. If it does, replace the oxygen sensor. Before replacing either part, check the Computer to sensor wire for continuity.

Control Vacuum Below 1.0 In. Hg.

1. Start the engine and allow it to idle in Neutral. Disconnect the vacuum hose at the computer transducer and connect the hose to the 0–30 in. Hg. vacuum gauge. The gauge should show manifold vacuum (above 12 in.). If not, trace the hose to its source and then connect it properly to a source of manifold vacuum.

NOTE: The following Steps should be made with the engine warm, parking brake applied, transmission in Neutral, and throttle placed on the next to lowest step of the fast idle cam.

2. Remove the air cleaner cover. Gradually close the choke plate until the engine begins to run roughly. If control vacuum increases to 5.0 in. as the choke is closed, go to Step 3. If control vacuum remains low, go to Step 4.

3. Disconnect the air injection hose from its connection to a metal tube at the rear of the cylinder head. Plug the tube. If control vacuum remains below 1.0 in., replace the carburetor. If control vacuum returns to the proper level, reconnect the air injection hose and disconnect the 3/16 in. vacuum hose from the air switching valve. If control vacuum remains below 1.0 in., replace the air switching valve. If control vacuum rises to the proper level, check all hoses for proper connections, then, if correct, replace the coolant vacuum switch.

4. Check that the bottom nipple of the solenoid regulator valve is connected to manifold vacuum. Disconnect the solenoid regulator electrical connector. Use the jumper wire to connect one terminal of the solenoid regulator lead to the positive battery terminal. Connect the other terminal of the solenoid regulator lead to ground. Control vacuum should rise above 5.0 in. If not, replace the solenoid regulator. If so, go to the next step.

5. Disconnect the 5 terminal connector at the computer. The terminals are numbered 1 to 5, starting at the rounded end. Connect a jumper wire from terminal 2 in the harness to a ground. Control vacuum should rise to 5 in. If not, trace the voltage to the battery to discover where it is being lost. If so, go to the next step.

NOTE: Wiring harness problems are usually in the connectors. Check them for looseness or corrosion.

6. Disconnect the oxygen sensor wire. Use a jumper wire to connect the *harness* lead to the positive battery terminal.

——————————CAUTION——————————
Do not connect the oxygen sensor wire to the battery or to a ground.

Control vacuum should rise to 5 in. in approximately 15 seconds. If not, replace the computer. If so, replace the oxygen sensor.

Ignition Timing

1. Ground the carburetor switch with a jumper wire.
2. Connect a timing light to the engine.

3. Start the engine. Wait one minute.

4. With the engine running at a speed not greater than the specified curb idle rpm (see the emission control sticker in the engine compartment), adjust the timing to specification.

5. Remove the ground wire after adjustment.

Curb Idle Adjustment

Adjust the curb idle only after ignition timing has been checked and set to specification.

1. Start the engine and run in Neutral on the second step of the fast idle cam until the engine is fully warmed up and the radiator becomes hot. This may take 5 to 10 minutes.

2. Disconnect and plug the EGR hose at the EGR valve.

3. Ground the carburetor switch with a jumper wire.

4. Adjust the idle rpm in Neutral to the curb idle rpm figure given on the emission control sticker in the engine compartment.

5. Reconnect the EGR hose and remove the jumper wire.

Oxygen Sensor Replacement

1. Disconnect the negative battery cable. Remove the air cleaner.

2. Disconnect the sensor electrical lead. Unscrew the sensor using Chrysler special tool C-4589.

3. Installation is the reverse. Before installation, coat the threads of the sensor with a nickel base anti-seize compound. Do not use other type compounds since they may electrically insulate the sensor. Torque sensor to 35 ft. lbs.

Mileage Counter Reset

The mileage counter will illuminate every 15,000 miles, signaling the need for oxygen sensor replacement. After replacing the oxygen sensor, reset the counter as follows:

1. Locate the mileage counter. It is spliced into the speedometer cable, covered by a rubber boot.

2. Slide the rubber boot up the speedometer cable to expose the top of the mileage counter. Turn the reset screw on top of the counter to reset. Replace the boot.

1980 AND LATER MODELS

ESA System Tests

1. Connect a timing light to the engine.

2. Disconnect and plug the vacuum hose at the vacuum transducer. Connect a vacuum pump to the transducer fitting and apply 14–16 in. Hg. of vacuum.

3. With the engine at normal operating temperature, raise the speed to 2000 rpm. Wait one minute, then check the timing advance. Specifications are as follows (timing in addition to basic advance):

1980 4 cyl. M/T: 20°–28°	1982 8 cyl.: 30°–38°
1980 4 cyl. A/T: 31°–39°	1983 1.7 M/T: 26°–34°
1981 1.7 A/T: 31°–39°	1983 2.2 Can.: 20°–28°
1981 1.7 M/T Fed.: 34°–42°	1983 2.2 Fed.: 24°–32°
39°–47°	1983 2.2 Hi. Alt.: 30°–38°
1981 2.2 M/T Fed.: 24°–32°	1983 2.2 Cal. M/T: 30°–38°
29°–37°	1983 2.2 Cal. A/T: 27°–35°
1981 2.2 M/T Cal.: 19°–27°	1983 225 Fed.: 10°–18°
1981 2.2 A/T: 21°–29°	1983 225 Calif.: 4°–12°
1980 6 cyl.: 10°–18°	1983 318-2 USA: 26°–34°
1980 8 cyl.: 15°–23°	1983 318-2 Can.: 21°–29°
1981 6 cyl.: 16°–24°	1983 318-4 Can.: 21°–29°
1981 8 cyl.: 30°–38°	1983 318-4 Fed.: 16°–22°
1982 1.7 A/T Fed.: 51°–59°	1983 318 EFI: 16°–24°
1982 1.7 M/T: 46°–54°	
1982 2.2 A/T: 41°–49°	
1982 2.2 M/T: 43°–51°	
1982 6 cyl.: 16°–24°	
1982 8 cyl.: EFI 19°–27°	

Air Switching System Tests

1. Remove the vacuum hose from the air switching valve; connect a vacuum gauge to the hose.

2. Start the engine. With the engine cold, engine vacuum should be present on the gauge until the engine coolant temperature is as follows:
1980 four cylinder M/T: 98°F
1980 four cylinder A/T: 135°F
1981–83 four cylinder 2.2L
California: 125°F
1981–83 four cylinder 2.2L 49 states:
150°F
6 cylinder all: 150°F
8 cylinder with computer 4145003: 150°F
8 cylinder with computer 4145088: 98°F
On the 8 cylinder models, the charge temperature switch must be open and fuel mixture temperature above 60°F.

3. When the indicated temperatures are reached, vacuum should drop to zero. If no vacuum is present on the gauge before the temperature is reached:
On the four cylinder, check the vacuum supply and the Coolant Controlled Engine Vacuum Switch (CCEVS); on the six and eight cylinder, check the vacuum supply, air switching solenoid, coolant switch (and charge temperature switch on the eight), and the wiring and connections to the computer. If all these systems are OK, it is possible that the computer is faulty, preventing air switching.

4. With the engine warm on the four cylinder, no vacuum should be present; if there is vacuum, check the CCEVS.

5. With the engine warm on the six and eight: on the 1980 six, vacuum should be present for 100 seconds; on the 1981 six for 65 seconds; on the 1980 eight with 4145003 for 25 seconds; on the 1980 eight with 4145088 for 90 seconds; on the 1981 Cal. eight for 20 seconds; on the 1981 Fed. 4 bbl. eight for 30 seconds; on the 1981 Fed. 2 bbl. eight for 90 seconds after the engine starts. After the period indicated, vacuum should drop to zero. If there is no vacuum, check as follows:
Connect a voltmeter to the light green wire on the air switching solenoid. On the eight cylinder, also disconnect the coolant switch and charge temperature switch. Start the engine; voltage should be less than one volt. Allow the warm-up schedule to finish (time as specified at the beginning of this step). The solenoid should de-energize and the voltmeter should then read charging system voltage. If not, replace the solenoid and repeat the test. If the voltmeter indicates charging system voltage before the warm-up schedule finishes, replace the computer.

6. Test the air switching valve: remove the air supply hose from the valve. Remove the vacuum hose from the valve and connect a vacuum pump to the fitting. Start the engine; air should be discharged from the side port. When vacuum is applied, discharge from the side port should cease, and air should then be discharged from the bottom port.

EFC Tests

Check all vacuum hose connections and the spark advance schedule before performing these tests. Check the resistance of all related wiring, and examine all electrical connections for soundness. On the four cylinder, connect a vacuum pump to the vacuum transducer and apply 10 (16–1981) in. Hg. of vacuum. On all engines, start the engine and allow it to reach normal operating temperature.

NOTE: After a hot restart, run the engine at 1200–2000 rpm for at least two minutes before continuing. DO NOT GROUND THE CARBURETOR SWITCH.

1. On the four and eight and 1981 six cylinder engines, disconnect the electrical connector from the regulator solenoid. Engine speed should increase at least 50 rpm. (If not, on the four cylinder only disconnect the four-way tee from the air cleaner temperature sensor and repeat the test. If no response, replace the computer.) Connect the regulator solenoid; engine speed should return to 1200–

2000 rpm. Disconnect the six (twelve-1981 reardrive) pin connector from the computer, and connect a ground to the #15 harness connector pin. Engine speed should drop 50 rpm. If not, check for carburetor air leaks, and service the carburetor as necessary.

On 1980 six cylinders, tee a 0–5 in. Hg. vacuum gauge into the vacuum regulator supply line to the carburetor. Disconnect the regulator wiring. With the engine idling and no voltage to the regulator, vacuum should be zero, and engine speed should increase by at least 50 rpm. Using a jumper wire, apply battery voltage to one terminal of the regulator, and ground the other terminal, vacuum should rise to 5 in. Hg., and engine speed should drop at least 50 rpm. If not, replace the regulator and repeat the test; if still faulty, replace the computer.

2. With the engine cold, check the coolant switch. It should have continuity to ground on the four cylinder, or have a resistance of less than 10 ohms on the six and eight. With the engine warm (above 150°F) the switch should be open.

3. With the engine hot, disconnect the coolant temperature switch. *Do not ground the carburetor switch.* Maintain an engine speed of 1200–2000 rpm (use a tachometer). Disconnect the oxygen sensor electrical lead at the sensor and connect a jumper wire to the harness end of the connector. Ground the other end of the jumper wire. The engine speed should increase (at least 50 rpm) for 15 seconds, then return to 1200–2000 rpm. (If not, on the four cylinder *only*, disconnect the four-way tee from the air cleaner temperature sensor, allowing the engine to draw in air. Repeat the test; if no response, replace the computer.) Next, connect the end of the jumper wire to the positive battery terminal; engine speed should drop. If the computer fails these tests, replace it. Reconnect the wires.

4. To test the oxygen sensor, run the engine at 1200–2000 rpm. Connect a voltmeter to the solenoid output wire which runs to the carburetor (18 DGN). Hold the choke plate closed. Over the next ten seconds, voltage should drop to 3 V. or less. If not, disconnect the air cleaner temperature sensor four-way tee and repeat the test. If no response, replace the computer.

Disconnect the PCV hose and/or the canister purge hose. Over the next ten seconds, voltage should be over 9 V. Voltage should then drop slightly, and remain there until the vacuum hoses are reconnected.

If the oxygen sensor fails these tests, replace it. Reconnect all wires.

Holley 6145 Feedback Carburetor

GENERAL INFORMATION

The Holley Model 6145 carburetor is a single venturi concentric downdraft electronic feedback carburetor designed for use on 225/3.7 engines. The fuel bowl completely surrounds the venturi. Dual nitrophyl floats control a fuel level which permits high angularity operation to meet the most severe driving conditions. The closed-cell nitrophyl material also eliminates the possibility of malfunction due to a punctured metal float.

Principal sub-assemblies include a bowl cover, carburetor body and throttle body. A thick gasket between the throttle body and main body retards heat transfer to the fuel to resist fuel percolation in warm weather. To correctly identify the carburetor model, always check the part number stamped on the main body or attached tag. The carburetor includes four basic fuel metering systems. The idle system provides a mixture for smooth idle and a transfer system for low speed operation. The main metering system provides an economical mixture for normal cruising conditions. A fuel regulator solenoid responsive to the oxygen sensor. The accelerator system provides additional fuel during acceleration. The power enrichment system provides a richer mixture when high power output is desired.

Holley 6145 feedback carburetor

In addition to these four basic systems, there is a fuel inlet system that constantly supplies the fuel to the basic metering systems. A choke system temporarily enriches the mixture to aid in starting and running a cold engine. If problems are experienced with the Electronic Feedback Carburetor System, the system and its related components must be checked before carburetor work is begun. Close attention should be given to vacuum hose condition, hose connections, and any area where leaks could develop. In addition, the related wiring and its connectors must be checked for excessive resistance. Refer to group 25 Emission Control Systems for system operation and service diagnosis. In normal service, the mixture should not require adjustment. The idle set rpm can be checked without removal of the tamper resistant plug.

NOTE: Tampering with the carburetor is a violation of Federal Law. Adjustment of the carburetor idle air-fuel mixture can only be done under certain circumstances.

Adjustment should only be considered if an idle defect still exists after normal diagnosis has revealed no other faulty condition, such as, incorrect idle speed, faulty hose or wire connection, etc. Also, it is important to make sure the Combustion Computer systems are operating properly. Adjustment of the carburetor idle air-fuel mixture should also be performed after a major carburetor overhaul. Upon completion of the carburetor adjustment, it is important to reinstall the plug. The proper procedure is outlined later in this group.

Fuel Inlet System

All fuel enters the fuel bowl through the fuel inlet fitting in the carburetor body. The "Viton" tipped fuel inlet needle seats directly in the fuel inlet fitting. The needle is retained by a cap that permits the fuel to flow out holes in the side of the cap. The design of the fuel bowl eliminates the necessity of a fuel baffle. The fuel inlet needle is controlled by a dual lung nitrophyl float (a closed cellular buoyant material which cannot collapse or leak) and a stainless steel float lever which is hinged by a stainless steel float shaft.

The fuel inlet system must constantly maintain the specified level of fuel as the basic fuel metering systems are calibrated to deliver the proper mixture only when the fuel is at this level. When the fuel level in the bowl drops the float also drops permitting additional fuel to flow past the fuel inlet needle into the bowl. All carburetors with external bowl vents are vented to the vapor canister.

O² FEEDBACK SOLENOID

The function of the O² Feedback Solenoid is to provide limited regulation of the fuel-air ratio of a feedback carburetor in response to electrical signals from the Spark Control Computer. It performs this task by metering main system fuel, and operates in parallel with a conventional fixed main metering jet. In the power-off mode the solenoid valve spring pushes upward through the main system fuel valve. At this point, the solenoid controlled main metering orifice is fully uncovered, so the richest condition exists within the carburetor for any given airflow. In the power-on mode the field windings are energized and a magnetic flux path is established from the armature, through the armature bushing, the solenoid case and the pole piece, returning once again to the armature. This attraction between the pole piece and the armature assembly moves the valve operating push rod and main system valve downward against the valve spring. This movement continues until the main system valve bottoms on the main system valve seat and stops before the armature contacts the pole piece. In this position, the solenoid controlled main metering orifice is fully sealed. These conditions remain unchanged until the electrical signal from the Spark Control Computer to the solenoid is switched off. This solenoid position offers the leanest condition within the carburetor for any given airflow.

Main system fuel may be regulated between the richest and leanest limits by controlling the amount of time that the solenoid is in the power-on position. Under normal operating conditions a voltage signal (12 volts nominally) is applied to the field windings at a frequency of 10 Hz. By controlling the duration of this voltage signal the ratio of power-on time to total time, referred to as duty cycle is established. The O² feedback solenoid includes, in addition to a protective case, such attaching surfaces and passageways as are required for the directing and containing of main system fuel when the solenoid assembly is correctly installed in a feedback carburetor designed for its use.

Idle System

Fuel used during curb idle and low speed operation flows through the main metering jet into the main well. An angular connecting idle well intersects the main well. An idle tube is installed in the idle well. Fuel travels up the idle well and mixes with air which enters through the idle air bleed located in the bowl cover. At curb idle the fuel and air mixture flows down the idle channel and is further mixed or broken up by air entering the idle channel through the transfer slot which is above the throttle plate at curb idle. The idle system is equipped with a restrictor in the idle channel, located between the transfer slot and the idle port, which limits the maximum attainable idle mixture. During low speed operation the throttle plate moves exposing the transfer slot and fuel begins to flow through the transfer slot as well as the idle port. As the throttle plates are opened further and engine speed increases, the air flow through the carburetor also increases. This increased air flow creates a vacuum or depression in the venturi and the main metering system begins to discharge fuel.

Idle fuel control circuit on Holley 6145 feedback carburetor

Main Metering System

As the engine approaches cruising speed, the increased air flow through the venturi creates a low pressure area in the venturi of the carburetor. Near-atmospheric pressure present in the fuel bowl causes the fuel to flow to the lower pressure area created by the venturi and magnified by the dual booster venturi. Fuel flows through the main jet into the main well. Then, air enters through high speed air bleed and mixes in the main well through holes in the main well tube. The mixture of fuel and air being lighter than raw fuel responds faster to changes in venturi vacuum and is also more readily vaporized when discharged into the venturi.

The main discharge nozzle passage is a part of the dual booster venturi which is an integral part of the main body casting. The main metering system is calibrated to deliver a lean mixture for best overall economy. When additional power is required a vacuum operated power system enriches the fuel-air mixture.

Power Enrichment System (Modulated Power Valve)

During high speed (or low manifold vacuum) the carburetor must provide a mixture richer than is needed when the engine is running at cruising speed under no great power requirements. Added fuel for power operation is supplied by a vacuum modulated power enrichment system. A vacuum passage in the throttle body transmits manifold vacuum to the vacuum piston chamber in the bowl cover. Under light throttle and light load conditions, there is sufficient vacuum acting on the vacuum piston to overcome the piston spring tension. When the throttle valves are opened to a 55° angle, vacuum that is acting on the piston is bled to atmosphere and manifold vacuum is closed off, which in turn insures proper mixture for this throttle opening. The vent port is right in line with the throttle shaft. The throttle shaft has a small hole drilled through it. When the throttle valve is opened to 55° the hole in the throttle shaft will line up with the port in the base of the carburetor and vent the piston vacuum chamber to atmosphere allowing the spring loaded piston to open the power valve. As engine power demands are reduced, and the throttle valve begins to close, manifold vacuum increases. The increased vacuum acts on the vacuum piston, overcoming the tension of the piston spring. This closes the power valve and shuts off the added supply of fuel which is no longer required.

Accelerating Pump System

When the throttle plates are opened suddenly, the air flow through the carburetor responds almost immediately. However, there is a brief time interval or lag before the fuel can overcome its inertia and maintain the desired fuel-air ratio. The piston type accelerating pump system mechanically supplies the fuel necessary to overcome this deficiency for a short period of time. Fuel enters the pump cylinder from the fuel bowl through the pump cup with the fuel level well above the normal position of the pump piston.

Main metering system on Holley 6145 models

Accelerator pump system on Holley 6145 models

As the throttle lever is moved, the pump link operating through a system of levers pushing the pump piston down seating the pump cup against the face of the stem. Fuel is forced through a passage around the pump discharge needle valve and out the pump discharge jet which is drilled in the main body. When the pump is not in operation, vapors or bubbles forming in the pump cylinder can escape around the pump stem through the inlet of the floating piston cup.

Power enrichment system with modulated power valve

Automatic choke system showing vacuum connection

Automatic Choke System

The automatic choke provides richer fuel-air mixture required for starting and operating a cold engine. A bi-metal spring inside the choke housing, which is installed in a well in the intake manifold, pushes the choke valve toward the closed position. When the engine starts, manifold vacuum is applied to the choke diaphragm through a rubber hose from the throttle body. The adjustment of the choke valve opening when the engine starts by the choke diaphragm, is called vacuum kick. Manifold vacuum alone is not strong enough to provide the proper degree of choke opening during the entire choking period. The impact of in rushing air past the offset choke valve provides the additional opening force. As the engine warms up, manifold heat transmitted to the choke housing relaxes the bi-metal spring until it eventually permits the choke to open fully. An electric heater assists engine heat to open the choke rapidly in summer temperatures.

Exhaust Gas Recirculation (EGR System)

The venturi vacuum control system utilizes a vacuum tap at the throat of the carburetor venturi to provide a control signal for the Exhaust Gas Recirculation (EGR) system.

Carburetor Service Procedures

A thorough road test and check of minor carburetor adjustments should precede major carburetor service. Specifications for some adjustments are listed on the Vehicle Emission Control Information label found in each engine compartment.

Many performance complaints are directed at the carburetor. Some of these are a result of loose, misadjusted or malfunctioning engine or electrical components. Others develop when vacuum hoses become disconnected or are improperly routed. The proper approach to analyzing carburetor complaints should include a routine check of such areas.

1. Inspect all vacuum hoses and actuators for leaks. Refer to the vacuum hose routing diagram label located under the hood in the engine compartment for proper hose routing.
2. Tighten intake manifold bolts and carburetor mounting bolts to specifications.
3. Perform cylinder compression test.
4. Clean or replace spark plugs as necessary.

5. Test resistance of spark plug cables. Refer to "Ignition System Secondary Circuit Inspection," Engine Electrical Section.
6. Inspect ignition primary wire and vacuum advance operation. Test coil output voltage, primary and secondary resistance. Replace parts as necessary. Refer to "Ignition System" and make necessary adjustment.
7. Reset ignition timing.
8. Check carburetor idle mixture and speed adjustment. Adjust throttle stop screw to specifications.
9. Test fuel pump for pressure and vacuum.
10. Inspect manifold heat control valve in exhaust manifold for proper operation.
11. Remove carburetor air filter element and blow out dirt gently with an air hose. Install a new recommended filter element if necessary.
12. Inspect crankcase ventilation system.
13. Road test vehicle as a final test.

Cleaning Carburetor Parts

There are many commercial carburetor cleaning solvents available which can be used with good results. The choke diaphragm, choke heater and some plastic parts of the carburetor can be damaged by solvents. Avoid placing these parts in any liquid. Clean the external surfaces of these parts with a clean cloth or a soft brush. Shake dirt or other foreign material from the stem (plunger) side of the diaphragm. Compressed air can be used to remove loose dirt but should not be connected to the vacuum diaphragm fitting.

NOTE: If the commercial solvent or cleaner recommends the use of water as a rinse, HOT water will produce better results. After rinsing, all trace of water must be blown from the passages with air pressure. Never clean jets with a wire, drill, or other mechanical means, because the orifices may become damaged, causing improper performance. When checking parts removed from the carburetor, it is recommended that new parts be installed whenever the old parts are questionable.

Carburetor Removal

———————CAUTION———————

Do not attempt to remove the carburetor from the engine of a vehicle that has just been road tested. Allow the engine to cool sufficiently to prevent accidental fuel ignition or personal injury.

1. Disconnect battery ground cable.
2. Remove air cleaner.
3. Remove fuel tank pressure vacuum filler cap. The fuel tank should be under a small pressure.
4. Place a container under fuel inlet fitting to catch any fuel that may be trapped in fuel line.
5. Disconnect fuel inlet line using two wrenches to avoid twisting the line.
6. Disconnect throttle linkage, choke linkage and all vacuum hoses.
7. Remove carburetor mounting bolts or nuts and carefully remove carburetor from engine compartment. Hold carburetor level to avoid spilling fuel from fuel bowl.

Carburetor Installation

1. Inspect the mating surfaces of carburetor and intake manifold. Be sure both surfaces are clean and free of nicks, burrs or other damage. Place a new flange gasket on manifold surface.

NOTE: Some flange gaskets can be installed up-side down or backwards. To prevent this, match holes in the flange gasket to holes on bottom of carburetor, then place gasket properly on intake manifold surface.

2. Carefully place carburetor on manifold without trapping choke rod under carburetor linkage.
3. Install carburetor mounting bolts or nuts and tighten alternately, a little at a time, to compress flange gasket evenly. The nuts

or bolts must be drawn down tightly to prevent vacuum leakage between carburetor and intake manifold.

4. Connect throttle and choke linkage and fuel inlet line.

5. Check carefully for worn or loose vacuum hose connections. Refer to the vacuum hose routing diagram label located under the hood in the engine compartment.

6. Check to be sure the choke plate opens and closes fully when operated.

7. Check to see that full throttle travel is obtained.

8. Install air cleaner. The air cleaner should be cleaned or replaced at this time to insure proper carburetor performance.

9. Connect battery cable.

10. Check carburetor idle mixture adjustment. Refer to Emission Control Label in engine compartment.

---CAUTION---

The practice of priming an engine by pouring gasoline into the carburetor air horn for starting after servicing the fuel system, should be strictly avoided. Cranking the engine, and then priming by depressing the accelerator pedal several times should be adequate.

Diagnosing carburetor complaints may require that the engine be started and run with the air cleaner removed. While running the engine in this mode it is possible that the engine could backfire. A backfiring situation is likely to occur if the carburetor is malfunctioning, but removal of the air cleaner alone can lean the air fuel ratio in the carburetor to the point of producing an engine backfire. The battery cable should be removed from the negative terminal of the battery before any fuel system component is removed. This precaution will prevent the possibility of ignition of fuel during servicing.

Disassembly

1. Place carburetor assembly on repair stand to prevent damage to throttle valves and to provide a suitable base for working.

2. Remove wire retainer and bowl vent assembly.

3. Remove Solenoid Idle Stop (SIS).

4. Remove the fast idle cam retaining clip, fast idle cam and link. Disconnect link.

5. Remove choke vacuum diaphragm, link and bracket assembly. Disengage link from slot in choke lever. Place the diaphragm to one side and clean as special items.

6. Remove nut and washer from throttle shaft. Remove throttle lever and link. Note the hole position of lever.

7. Remove screws and duty cycle solenoid.

8. Remove the bowl cover screws. Separate the bowl cover from the carburetor body by tapping with a plastic hammer or handle of a screwdriver. Do not pry cover off with screwdriver blade. Lift bowl cover straight up until vacuum piston stem, accelerator pump, and main well tube are clear of the main body.

9. Remove the bowl cover gasket. If any gasket material is remaining on either surface, remove with a suitable cleaner. Do not use a metal scraper such as a carbon scraper or screwdriver on either the bowl cover surface or carburetor body surface. A nylon or hard plastic material such as a delrin body moulding remover, may be used as a suitable scraper.

10. Remove the accelerating pump operating rod retainer screw and retainer.

11. Remove accelerator pump assembly retaining screw and pump assembly.

12. Rotate the pump operating rod and remove from bowl cover.

13. Remove the pump operating rod grommet.

14. The power piston assembly retaining ring is staked in position and care must be taken at removal. Remove staking with a suitable sharp tool then remove the vacuum piston from the bowl cover by depressing the piston and allowing it to snap up against the retaining ring.

SOLENOID IDLE STOP (SIS)

Remove the solenoid idle stop with its bracket

Exploded view of bowl vent solenoid assembly

FAST IDLE LINK

FAST IDLE CAM

RETAINING CLIP

Removing fast idle cam and link—typical

Note accelerator pump linkage position before disassembly

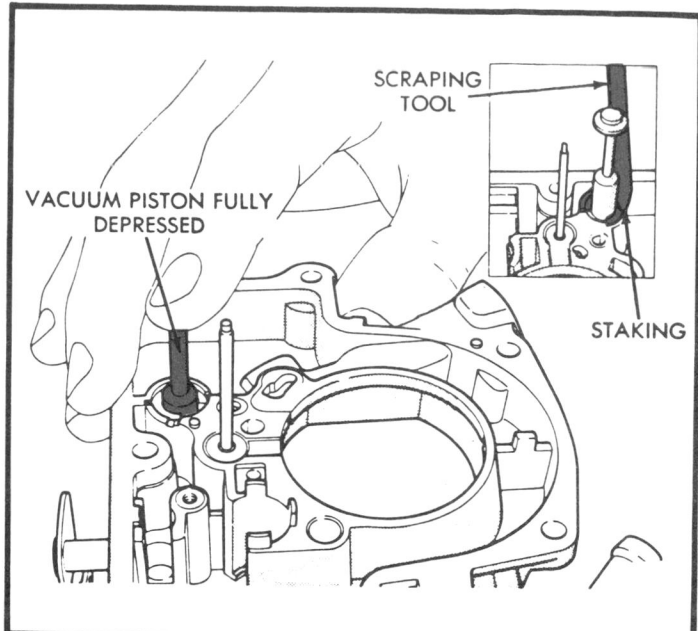

Exercise caution when removing vacuum piston—see text for details

15. This completes disassembly of the bowl cover. The main well tube cannot be removed and must be blown out carefully from both inside and outside of the cover. Remove the fuel inlet fitting valve assembly from the main body. Separate the gaskets from the parts.

16. Remove the spring float shaft retainer, float shaft and float assembly.

17. Turn the main body upside down and remove the pump discharge check ball and weight.

18. Remove the main jet with Special Tool Number C-3748. A 3/8 inch or wider screwdriver can also be used, but be sure it has a good square blade.

19. Carefully depress the power valve needle with a 3/8 inch wide screwdriver until screwdriver blade is squarely seated in slot on top of the valve. Remove valve. The power valve assembly consists of seat needle and spring. All of these components of the service power valve should be used if replacement is required.

20. This completes disassembly of the main body. Remove the three main body-to-throttle body screws. Separate the throttle body from the main body and remove the gasket.

Inspection and Reassembly

THROTTLE BODY

1. Check throttle shaft for excessive wear in body. If wear is

Exploded view of accelerator pump assembly

extreme, it is recommended that carburetor assembly be replaced rather than installing a new shaft in old body.

2. Install idle mixture screw and spring in body. (The tapered portion of the screw must be straight and smooth. If tapered portion is grooved or ridged, a new idle mixture screw should be installed to insure having correct idle mixture control).

3. Using a new gasket, install throttle body to main body, torque screws to 30 inch pounds (3 Nm).

BOWL COVER

1. Before installing the vacuum piston assembly in bowl cover, be sure and remove all staking from the retainer cavity. Install the spring and piston in the vacuum cylinder, seat the retainer and stake lightly with a suitable tool.

2. Test the accelerator pump discharge check ball and seat prior to assembly by coating the pump piston with oil, or filling the fuel bowl with clean fuel. Install accelerating pump discharge check ball and weight. Hold the discharge check ball and weight down with a small brass rod and operate the pump plunger by hand. If the check ball and seat are leaking, no resistance will be experienced when operating the plunger. If the valve is leaking, remove weight and stake the ball using a suitable drift punch. Exercise care when staking the ball to avoid damaging the bore containing the pump weight. After staking the old ball, remove and replace with new ball from tune-up kit. Install weight and re-check for leaks. If no leaks, remove check ball and weight from main body and install accelerator pump, pump operating rod, and rod retainer in bowl cover.

Accelerator pump discharge check ball and weight installation

MAIN BODY

1. Install power valve assembly in bottom of fuel bowl and tighten securely. Be sure needle valve operates freely.

2. Install main metering jet with special tool, C-3748, or equivalent.

3. Install float shaft and position the assembly in the float shaft cradle. Insert retaining spring. Check float alignment to prevent binding against bowl casting.

NOTE: A nitrophyl float can be checked for fuel absorption by lightly squeezing between fingers. If wetness appears on surface or float feels heavy (check with known good float), replace the float assembly.

Location of main jet and power valve in float bowl

4. Place a new gasket on fuel inlet fitting and install assembly into main body, tighten securely. When replacing the needle and seat assembly (inlet fitting), the float level must also be checked, as dimensional difference between the old and new assemblies may change the float level. If necessary, adjust as follows:

5. Place bowl cover gasket on top of the fuel bowl. Hold gasket in place and invert the bowl (refer to carburetor adjustments). Place a straight edge across the gasket surface. The portion of the float lungs farthest from the fuel inlet should just touch the

Correct method of staking the vacuum piston retaining washer

straight edge. If adjustment is necessary, bend the float tang to obtain this adjustment.

6. Insert check ball and weight into accelerator pump discharge well.

7. Install bowl cover gasket on air horn.

8. Carefully position bowl cover on the fuel bowl. Be sure the leading edges of the accelerator pump cup are not damaged as it enters the pump bore. Be careful not to damage the main well tube.

9. Install seven bowl cover screws and tighten alternately, a little at a time, to compress the gasket evenly (30 in lb).

10. Position a new O² feedback solenoid gasket on the air horn. Install new "O" Ring seal on duty cycle solenoid. Lubricate lightly with petroleum jelly and carefully install solenoid into carburetor. Install and tighten mounting screws securely. Route wire and tighten screw.

11. Install fast idle cam and link.

12. Install choke vacuum diaphragm.

13. Install Solenoid Idle Stop (SIS).

14. Install bowl vent assembly.

CHOKE UNLOADER

The choke unloader is a mechanical device designed to partially open the choke valve at wide open throttle. It is used to eliminate choke enrichment during cranking of an engine. Engines which have flooded or stalled by excessive choke enrichment can be cleared by use of the unloader. Refer to carburetor adjustments for adjusting procedure.

CHOKE VACUUM DIAPHRAGM

Inspect the diaphragm vacuum fitting to insure that the passage is not plugged with foreign material. Leak check the diaphragm to determine if it has internal leaks. To do this, first depress the diaphragm stem, then place a finger over the vacuum, fitting to seal the opening. Release the diaphragm stem. If the stem moves more than 1/16 inch in 10 seconds, the leakage is excessive and the assembly must be replaced.

CHOKE VACUUM KICK

The choke diaphragm adjustment controls the fuel delivery while the engine is running. It positions the choke valve within the air horn by action of the linkage between the choke shaft and the diaphragm. The diaphragm must be energized to measure the vacuum kick adjustment. Vacuum can be supplied by an auxiliary vacuum source.

FAST IDLE SPEED

Fast idle engine speed is used to overcome cold engine friction, stalls after cold starts and stalls due to carburetor icing. Adjustment must be made to specifications. If adjustment is necessary with less than 300 miles/500 km on the odometer, the specifications must be reduced 75 RPM. Refer to carburetor adjustments for procedure.

Float Setting Adjustment

1. Install float shaft and position the assembly in the float shaft cradle.

2. Install retaining spring and place bowl cover gasket on top of the fuel bowl.

3. Hold gasket in place and invert the bowl.

4. Place a straight edge across the gasket surface. The portion of the float lungs, farthest from the fuel inlet, should just touch the straight edge. If adjustment is necessary, bend the float tang.

Adjusting float level on Holley 6145 feedback carburetor

MODEL 6145
Chrysler Corporation

Year	Carb. Part No. ①	Float Level (in.)	Accelerator Pump Adjustment (in.)	Bowl Vent Clearance (in.)	Fast Idle (rpm)	Choke Unloader Clearance (in.)	Vacuum Kick (in.)	Fast Idle Cam Position (in.)	Choke
'81	R-9129A	②	1.615③	④	2000	.250	.150	.090	Fixed
'82	R-9936A	②	1.616③	④	1950	.250	.150	.090	Fixed
	R-9695A	②	1.615③	④	1950⑤	.250	.150	.090	Fixed
'83	R-40042A	②	1.615③	④	2000	.250	.150	.090	Fixed

① Located on a tag attached to the carburetor
② Flush with the top of the main body casting to .050" above
③ Position #2
④ Not Adjustable
⑤ Cordoba and Mirada—2000 rpm

Choke Vacuum Kick Adjustment

1. Open throttle, close choke then close throttle to trap fast idle cam at closed choke position.

2. Disconnect vacuum hose from carburetor and connect to hose of auxiliary vacuum source with small length of tube. Apply a vacuum of 15 or more inches of mercury.

3. Apply sufficient closing force on choke lever to completely compress spring in diaphragm stem without distorting linkage. Cylindrical stem of diaphragm extends to a stop as spring compresses.

4. Measure by inserting specified gauge between top of choke valve and air horn wall at throttle lever side.

5. Insert a 5/64 inch allen wrench into the choke diaphragm and turn to adjust the choke vacuum kick.

INSERT A 5/64 INCH ALLEN WRENCH INTO VACUUM DIAPHRAGM TO ADJUST VACUUM KICK

LIGHT CLOSING PRESSURE ON CHOKE LEVER

GAUGE

Choke vacuum kick adjustment—Holley 6145

FAST IDLE SPEED SCREW ON SECOND HIGHEST STEP OF CAM

BEND LINK HERE TO ADJUST

LIGHT CLOSING PRESSURE ON CHOKE LEVER

GAUGE

Fast idle cam position adjustment—Holley 6145

6. Check for free movement between open and adjusted positions. Correct any misalignment or interference by rebending link and readjust.

7. Replace vacuum hose on correct carburetor fitting.

LIGHT CLOSING PRESSURE ON CHOKE LEVER

GAUGE

BEND UNLOADER TANG HERE FOR ADJUSTMENT

THROTTLE LEVER IN WIDE OPEN POSITION

Choke unloader adjustment—Holley 6145

Fast Idle Cam Position Adjustment

1. With fast idle speed adjusting screw contacting second highest speed step on fast idle cam, move choke valve towards closed position with light pressure on choke shaft lever.

2. Measure by inserting specified gauge between top of choke valve and air horn wall at throttle lever side.

3. Adjust by bending fast idle connector rod at angle until correct valve opening has been obtained.

Choke Unloader Adjustment

1. Hold throttle valves in wide open position.

2. Lightly press finger against control lever to move choke valve toward closed position.

3. Measure by inserting specified gauge between top of choke valve and air horn wall at throttle lever side.

4. Adjust by bending tang on throttle lever.

MEASUREMENT POINTS CENTER TO CENTER

BEND LINK TO ADJUST

Accelerator pump stroke adjustment—Holley 6145

Solenoid idle stop adjustment—Holley 6145

Accelerator Pump Piston Stroke Adjustment

Position the throttle in the curb idle position with the accelerator pump operating link in the proper slot in the throttle lever. Measure the pump operating link as shown in above illustration. This measurement must be to specifications.

Solenoid Idle Stop Adjustment

Before checking or adjusting any idle speed, check ignition timing and adjust if necessary. Disconnect and plug the vacuum hose at the EGR valve. Also, connect a jumper wire between the carburetor switch and a good ground. Disconnect and plug the 3/16 inch diameter control hose at the canister. The air cleaner cannot be removed but may be propped up to provide access to the carburetor. Remove the PCV valve from the cylinder head cover and allow the valve to draw underhood air. Connect a tachometer to the engine.

1. Turn on air conditioning and set the blower on low.
2. Disconnect the air conditioning clutch wire.
3. On non-airconditioned models, connect a jumper wire between the battery positive post and the SIS lead wire.

─────────CAUTION─────────

Use care in jumping to the proper wire on the solenoid. Applying battery voltage to other than the correct wire will damage the wiring harness.

Fast idle speed adjustment—Holley 6145

4. Open throttle slightly to allow the solenoid plunger to extend.
5. Remove the adjusting screw and spring from the solenoid.
6. Insert a 1/8 inch allen wrench into the solenoid and adjust to the correct engine speed.
7. Turn off air conditioning and replace clutch wire or remove jumper wire.
8. Replace solenoid screw and spring.
9. Proceed to Idle Set RPM Adjustment.

Idle Set RPM Adjustment

NOTE: This adjustment is to be performed only after the Solenoid Idle Stop Adjustment Procedure.

1. Remove the exhaust manifold heat shield for access to the O^2 sensor.
2. Disconnect the engine harness lead from the O^2 sensor and ground the engine harness lead.

─────────CAUTION─────────

Care should be exercised so that no pulling force is put on the wire attached to the O^2 sensor. Use care in working around the sensor as the exhaust manifold is extremely hot.

Remove and plug the vacuum line at the vacuum transducer on the Spark Control Computer (SCC). Connect an auxiliary vacuum supply to the vacuum transducer and set at 16 inches of vacuum.

3. Allow the engine to run for two minutes to allow the effect of disconnecting the O^2 sensor to take place.
4. Adjust the idle set screw on the solenoid to obtain the correct idle set rpm.
5. Proceed to the Fast Idle Speed Adjustment.

Fast Idle Speed Adjustment

NOTE: This adjustment is to be performed only after the Solenoid Idle Stop and Idle Set RPM Adjustment Procedures.

1. Open throttle slightly and place the fast idle speed screw on the second highest step of the fast idle cam.
2. With the choke fully open, adjust the fast idle speed screw to obtain the correct fast idle rpm.
3. Return to idle then reposition the adjusting screw on the second highest step of the fast idle cam to verify fast idle speed. Readjust if necessary.
4. Return to idle and turn off the engine. Unplug and reconnect the vacuum hoses at the EGR valve and canister. Reconnect the vacuum line at the SCC. Install exhaust manifold heat shield. Remove the tachometer, reinstall the PCV valve, reconnect the O^2 sensor, and remove the ground wire.

NOTE: The idle speed with the engine in normal operating condition (everything connected) may vary from set speeds. DO NOT READJUST.

Concealment Plug Removal

1. Remove carburetor from engine.
2. Remove throttle body from the carburetor.
3. Clamp the throttle body in a vise with the gasket surfaces protected from the vise jaws.
4. Drill a 5/64 inch hole in the casting surrounding the idle mixture screw, then redrill the hole to 1/8 inch.
5. Insert a blunt punch into the hole and drive out the plug.
6. Reassemble the carburetor and reinstall it on the engine.
7. Proceed to Propane Assisted Idle Set Procedure.

NOTE: Tampering with the carburetor is a violation of Federal law. Adjustment of the carburetor idle air fuel mixture can only be done under certain circumstances, as explained below. Upon completion of the carburetor adjustment, it is important to restore the plug.

This procedure should only be used if an idle defect still exists after normal diagnosis has revealed no other faulty condition such as incorrect basic timing, incorrect idle speed, faulty wire or hose connections, etc. Also, it is important to make sure that the combustion computer systems are operating properly. Adjustment of the carburetor idle air fuel mixture should be performed after a major carburetor overhaul.

1. Remove concealment plug. Set the parking brake and place transmission in neutral. Turn all lights and accessories off. Connect a tachometer to the engine. Remove exhaust manifold heat shield for access to the O² sensor. Start engine and allow it to warm up on the second highest step of the fast idle cam until normal operating temperature is reached. Return engine to idle.

2. Disconnect and plug the vacuum hose at the EGR valve. Connect a jumper wire between the carburetor switch and a good ground. Do not remove the air cleaner. The air cleaner may be propped up to provide access to the carburetor.

3. Disconnect vacuum supply hose from the choke diaphragm at the tee and install propane supply hose in its place. Other connections at the tee must remain in place.

4. With the propane bottle upright and in a safe location, remove the PCV valve from the valve cover and allow the valve to draw underhood air. Disconnect and plug the 3/16 inch diameter control hose from the canister.

5. Disconnect the engine harness lead from the O² sensor and ground the engine harness lead.

---CAUTION---

Care should be exercised so no pulling force is put on the wire attached to the O² sensor. Use care in working around the sensor as the exhaust manifold is extremely hot.

6. Remove and plug the vacuum line at the vacuum transducer on SCC. Connect an auxiliary vacuum supply to vacuum transducer and set at 16 inches of vacuum. Allow engine to run for two minutes to allow the effect of disconnecting the O² sensor to take place.

7. Open propane main valve. Slowly open propane metering valve until maximum engine rpm is reached. When too much propane is added, engine rpm will decrease. "Fine tune" the metering valve to obtain the highest engine rpm.

8. With the propane still flowing, adjust the idle speed screw on solenoid to obtain the specified propane rpm. Again, "fine tune" the metering valve to obtain the highest engine rpm. If there has been a change in the maximum rpm, readjust the idle speed screw to the specified propane rpm.

9. Turn off propane main valve and allow engine to run for one minute to stabilize. Slowly adjust the mixture screw, pausing between adjustments to allow the engine to stabilize, to achieve the smoothest idle at the specified idle set rpm.

10. Turn on propane main valve. "Fine tune" metering valve to obtain the highest engine rpm. If the maximum engine speed is more than 25 rpm different than the specified propane rpm, repeat Steps 7-9.

11. Turn off propane main valve and metering valve.

12. Remove the propane supply hose and reinstall the vacuum supply hose from the choke. Remove O² sensor ground wire and reconnect O² sensor. Reconnect vacuum line on SCC.

13. Install concealment plug and perform Solenoid Idle Stop, Idle Set RPM, and Fast Idle Speed Adjustments.

Float Setting (On Vehicle)

1. Remove air cleaner assembly and air cleaner gasket.
2. Remove bowl vent hose.
3. Disconnect choke assembly.
4. Remove fast idle cam retaining clip, cam and link.
5. Remove vacuum choke diaphragm (vacuum kick), link, and hose.
6. Remove nut and washer from throttle shaft. Remove throttle lever and link. Note the hole position of lever.
7. Remove seven bowl cover screws and lift bowl cover straight up until vacuum piston stem, accelerator pump, and main well tube are clear of the main body.
8. Depress float manually to allow residual line pressure to over-

Removing idle mixture plugs from Holley 6145

fill the bowl to within 1/8-1/4 inch below the top of the fuel bowl. If line pressure is not enough to fill the bowl, use an external supply.

9. Using two wrenches, back off flare nut and tighten inlet fitting to recommended torque (170 inch-pounds) (19 N m).

10. Place bowl cover gasket on top of fuel bowl.

11. Firmly seat the float pin retainer by hand while measuring float height with a straight edge across the gasket surface. The portion of the float lungs farthest from the fuel inlet should just touch the straight edge. If adjustment is necessary, bend the float tang.

12. Remove bowl cover gasket. Drain fuel from accelerator

Adjusting float level on the car. Make sure the float pin retainer is properly seated

pump well with syringe type tool. This is done to prevent the discharge check ball and weight from leaving its position during assembly of the bowl cover.

13. Position bowl cover gasket on bowl cover. Carefully install bowl cover on main body. Be sure the leading edge of the accelerator pump cup is not damaged as it enters the pump bore and that the weight and discharge check ball remains in place. Be careful not to damage the main well tube.

14. Install seven bowl cover screws and tighten alternately to compress the gasket evenly.

15. Install pump rocker arm and linkage assembly.
16. Install vacuum kick diaphragm, link and hose.
17. Install fast idle cam retaining clip, cam and link.
18. Install bowl vent hose.
19. Connect choke assembly.
20. Install air cleaner and gasket.
21. Check idle speed with tachometer. If adjustment is necessary, use the "Propane Procedure."

Holley 6520 Carburetor

GENERAL INFORMATION

Holley model 6520 is a staged dual venturi carburetors. The primary bore or venturi is smaller than the secondary bore. The secondary stage is operated by a vacuum controlled diaphragm. The primary stage includes a curb idle and transfer system, diaphragm type accelerator pump system, main metering system, and power enrichment system. On model 6520 carburetors there is also an O_2 Feedback Solenoid that is responsive to the oxygen sensor. The secondary stage includes a main metering system and power system. Both the primary and secondary venturi draw fuel from a common fuel bowl. The electric automatic choke has a bimetal two stage heating element. In normal service the mixture should not require adjustment. The idle RPM can be checked without removing the tamper resistant plug.

Fuel Inlet System

Fuel under pressure from the fuel pump enters the fuel bowl through the fuel inlet line. The fuel inlet needle is controlled by a dual lung monocellular nitrophyl float (a closed cell buoyant material which cannot collapse or leak). A fuel inlet needle clip hooks over the front lever to insure the needle is pulled off the seat when the float drops. When the fuel level in the bowl drops the float drops permitting additional fuel to flow past the fuel inlet needle into the bowl. These carburetors are vented to the vapor canister.

Idle System

Fuel used during curb idle and low speed operation flows from the fuel through the primary main jet into the main well. From the main well it flows into the idle well and through the idle tube. Air enters through the primary idle air bleed. This air-fuel mixture

Holley 6520 feedback carburetor assembly

moves down the idle passages and past the idle transfer slot. This slot serves as an additional air bleed during curb idle operation. The air-fuel mixture then moves past the idle mixture adjusting screw tip which controls the amount of the mixture at curb idle. At speeds above idle the throttle valve exposes the transfer slot to vacuum and the air-fuel mixture is drawn out of the transfer slot as well as the idle passage.

Main Metering System 6520 Models

As the throttle valves continue opening, the airflow through the carburetor increases and creates a low pressure area in the venturi. This low pressure causes fuel to flow from the fuel bowl through the main jets and into the main wells. In addition to the main jet, fuel also enters the main well through another parallel circuit. Fuel flow in this circuit is regulated by the O_2 feedback solenoid. Air fom the main air bleed mixes with the fuel through holes in the sides of the main well tube. The mixture is then drawn from the main well tube and discharged through the venturi nozzle. By controlling the amount of fuel released, the solenoid regulates the total air-fuel mixture. The solenoid acts in direct response to the engine demand. As airflow through the carburetor increases, the amount of air-fuel mixture discharged also increases and the idle system tapers off.

ACCELERATOR PUMP SYSTEM

A diaphragm type accelerator pump system is located in the side of the carburetor body. When the throttle valves are opened quickly, air flow through the carburetor responds rapidly. Since fuel is heavier than air, there is a very brief time lag before fuel flow can sustain the proper air-fuel ratio. During this lag the accelerating pump system mechanically supplies the required additional fuel, until the proper air-fuel ratio can be maintained by the other metering systems.

When the throttle valves are closed, the diaphragm returns against its cover. Fuel is drawn through the inlet, past the inlet ball check valve and into the pump chamber. A discharge check ball prevents air from being drawn into the pump chamber. The moment the throttle valves are opened, the diaphragm rod is pushed inward, the diaphragm forces fuel from the pump chamber into the discharge passage. The intake check ball prevents fuel from returning to the fuel bowl. Fuel under pressure unseats the discharge check ball and is forced through the pump discharge valve where it sprays into the primary venturi through the pump discharge nozzle. Excess fuel and pump chamber vapors are discharged back into the fuel bowl through a restriction.

Manifold vacuum is applied to the power valve diaphragm from a passage in the base of the carburetor body. The passage connects to the air horn and the top of the power valve diaphragm. During idle and normal driving conditions, manifold vacuum is high enough to overcome the power valve spring tension, and the valve remains closed. When manifold vacuum drops below a predetermined level the diaphragm spring overcomes the vacuum and the diaphragm stem depresses the power valve stem. Fuel then flows through the power valve, power valve restriction, and into the main well. As engine load requirements decrease, manifold vacuum increases and overcomes the diaphragm spring. The spring in the power valve assembly then closes the valve.

SECONDARY PROGRESSION SYSTEM

Secondary metering circuit becomes operational when primary throttle opening exceeds 45°

SECONDARY POWER ENRICHMENT SYSTEM

The secondary system is also provided with an air velocity operated power system for full power operation. As the secondary throttle valve approaches wide open position, air velocity through the secondary venturi creates a low pressure at the discharge port. Fuel flows from the bowl through a restricted vertical channel. As this occurs, air enters through a calibrated air bleed and mixes with the fuel. This mixture is discharged through the discharge passage.

Main metering system on Holley 6520 feedback carburetor

Altitude Compensation System

Some models are equipped with an altitude compensation system. Less dense air at higher altitudes is compensated for by the use of variable air bleeds which act in parallel with the normal fixed air bleeds in the carburetor idle, primary, and secondary circuits. These air bleeds consist of tapered needles which are moved in orifices by an aneroid bellows. The bellows is contained in an altitude compensation module which is mounted in the engine compartment. Outside air passes through an air filter, through the compensation module, and into the carburetor. The system is calibrated so that there is no air flow until atmospheric pressure is below a preset level. Air flow gradually increases as atmospheric pressure decreases.

Solenoid Kicker System

The solenoid kicker is the combination of a position-holding solenoid, and a vacuum diaphragm assembly. When the engine is running, the solenoid is extended to hold the throttle at curb idle.

Typical altitude compensation system

Solenoid kicker system showing vacuum and electrical connections

When the engine is off, the solenoid retracts, allowing the throttle to close to prevent after-running (dieseling). Curb idle is adjusted with a screw on top of the solenoid. The diaphragm assembly extends when manifold vacuum is applied to open the throttle a fixed amount above the idle position. For any assembly, the stroke is fixed, but different calibrations may have different strokes. Manifold vacuum is supplied to the kicker by a three-port solenoid valve which receives its control signal from the ESA/EFC module. Control inputs which may trigger the kicker include: air conditioning "ON", electrically heated rear window defroster (EBL) "ON", and high engine coolant temperature at start up, which actuation ceases after a specified time period.

Electronic Feedback Control (EFC) System

The EFC system is essentially an emissions control system which utilizes an electronic signal, generated by an exhaust gas oxygen sensor to precisely control the air-fuel mixture ratio in the carburetor. This in turn allows the engine to produce exhaust gases of the proper composition to permit the use of a three-way catalyst. The three-way catalyst is designed to convert the three pollutants (1) hydrocarbons (HC), (2) carbon monoxide (CO), and (3) oxides of Nitrogen (NOx) into harmless substances.

There are two operating modes in the EFC system:

Open Loop—air fuel ratio is controlled by information programmed into the computer at manufacture.

Closed Loop—air fuel ratio is varied by the computer based on information supplied by the oxygen sensor.

When the engine is cold, the system will be operating in the open loop mode. During that time, the air fuel ratio will be fixed at a richer level. This will allow proper engine warm up. Also, during this period, air injection (from the air injection pump) will be injected upstream in the exhaust manifold.

OXYGEN (O₂) SOLENOID

The function of the O₂ Feedback Solenoid is to provide limited regulation of the fuel-air ratio of a feedback carburetor in response to electrical signals from the Spark Control Computer. It performs this task by metering main system fuel, and operates in parallel with a conventional fixed main metering jet. In the power-off mode the solenoid valve spring pushes upward through the main system fuel valve. At this point, the solenoid controlled main metering orifice is fully uncovered, so the richest condition exists within the carburetor for any given airflow. In the power-on mode the field windings are energized and a magnetic flux path is established from the armature, through the armature bushing, the solenoid case and the pole piece, returning once again to the armature.

This attraction between the pole piece and the armature assembly moves the valve operating push rod and main system valve downward against the valve spring. This movement continues until the main system valve bottoms on the main system valve seat and stops before the armature contacts the pole piece. In this position, the solenoid controlled main metering orifice is fully sealed. These conditions remain unchanged until the electrical signal from the Spark Control Computer to the solenoid is switched off. This solenoid position offers the leanest condition within the carburetor for any given airflow.

Main system fuel may be regulated between the richest and leanest limits by controlling the amount of time that the solenoid is in the power-on position. Under normal operating conditions a voltage signal (12 volts nominally) is applied to the field windings at a frequency of 10Hz. By controlling the duration of this voltage signal to the ratio of power-on time to total time, referred to as duty cycle is established.

The O₂ feedback solenoid includes attaching surfaces and passageways as are required for the directing and containing of main system fuel when the solenoid assembly is correctly installed in a feedback carburetor designed for its use.

OXYGEN SENSOR

The oxygen sensor is a device which produces electrical voltage. The sensor is mounted in the exhaust manifold and must be heated by the exhaust gas before producing a voltage. When there is a large amount of oxygen present (lean mixture) the sensor produces a low voltage. When there is a lesser amount present, it produces a higher voltage. By monitering the oxygen content and converting it to electrical voltage, the sensor acts as a rich-lean switch. The voltage is transmitted to the Spark Control Computer. The computer sends a signal to the Oxygen Feedback Solenoid mounted on the carburetor to change the air-fuel ratio back to stoichiometric.

Vacuum Operated Secondary System

The VOS system uses a vacuum diaphragm to operate the secondary throttle blade. At lower speeds and engine loads the throttle blade remains closed. When engine speed increases to a point where more breathing capacity is needed, the vacuum controlled secondary throttle blade begins to open. Venturi vacuum from the primary and secondary venturi act on the vacuum diaphragm. At high engine speeds when engine requirements approach the capacity of the primary bore, the increased primary venturi moves the diaphragm which compresses the diaphragm spring. This action moves the diaphragm link and lever which causes the secondary throttle blade to open. The position of the secondary throttle blade depends on the strength of the vacuum signal. This is determined by the air flow through the primary and secondary bores. As the air flow increases, a greater secondary throttle blade opening will result and the secondary bore will supply a greater portion of the engine's requirements. As higher speeds are reached, the secondary throttle blade will be wide open. The restriction in the vacuum passage to the secondary diaphragm limits the rate at which the secondary blade will open. This allows the vacuum to build up slowly at the diaphragm, resulting in an controlled secondary throttle blade opening rate. The secondary throttle blade begins to open where vacuum is created at the primary and secondary vacuum pick up holes. This vacuum assists in the operation of the secondary diaphragm.

When engine speed is reduced, venturi vacuum in the throttle bores becomes weaker, reducing the vacuum level in the secondary diaphragm chamber. As vacuum drops, the load from the diaphragm spring will start closing the secondary blade. The diaphragm spring is assisted by the design of the secondary blade. The blade is slightly offset. When the blades are closing, the combined force of manifold vacuum and the air stream has greater effect on the larger, upstream areas of the blade, forcing the blades to a closed position. The vacuum control solenoid bleeds off vacuum from the diaphragm during warm up and low air flow conditions. Secondary throttle blade operation can only occur if certain conditions occur simultaneously. Coolant temperature must be above 140°F, 30 seconds must have elapsed since start up, engine speed must be above 1800 rpm and manifold vacuum must be below 8 inches Hg.

Electric Choke Assembly

An electric heater and switch assembly is sealed within the choke housing. Electrical current is supplied through the oil pressure switch. A minimum of 2.7 kPa (4PSI) oil pressure is necessary to close the contacts in the oil pressure switch and feed current to the automatic choke system. Electrically must be present when the engine is running to open the choke and keep it open.

Typical electric choke system

NOTE: Use care when removing the choke thermostat not to lose the plastic bushing located between the thermostat loop and pin. The loop and bushing must be placed over the pin during assembly. Choke assembly removal is not necessary during normal service. The choke assembly must never be immersed in fluid as damage to the internal switch and heater assembly will result.

Vacuum secondary system on Holley 6520 feedback carburetor

The heater can be tested with a direct B+ connection. The choke valve should reach the open position within five minutes.

─────CAUTION─────

Operation of any type, including idling should be avoided if there is any loss of choke power. Under this condition, any loss of power to the choke will cause the choke to remain fully on during the operation of the vehicle. This will cause a very rich mixture to burn and result in abnormally high exhaust system temperatures, which may cause damage to the catalyst or other underbody parts of the car. It is advised that the electric choke power not be disconnected to trouble shoot cold start problems.

CARBURETOR OVERHAUL

Disassembly

1. Disconnect and remove the choke operating rod and choke rod seal.

Removing feedback solenoid from the air horn

Mark the location of the mounting screws before removing the WOT cut-out switch

Location of primary and secondary main metering jets—note sizes before removal

2. Remove the two solenoid retaining screws and remove the solenoid from the carburetor.

3. Remove the vacuum control valve and filter assembly.

4. Remove the wiring clip from the top of the carburetor.

5. Remove the two 02 feedback solenoid retaining screws and gently lift the solenoid from the air horn.

6. Remove the clip securing the vacuum control rod to the link and remove the vacuum control mounting screws. Remove the vacuum control diaphragm.

7. Remove the wide open throttle (WOT) cutout switch mounting screws after marking the location for proper reassembly. Remove the harness mounting screws and open the retaining clip.

8. Remove the air horn mounting screws and separate the air horn assembly from the carburetor body.

9. Remove the float level pin, float and float inlet needle.

10. Remove the fuel inlet seal and gasket.

11. Remove the main secondary metering jet after noting its size to make sure it is installed in its proper position on reassembly.

Location of primary and secondary high speed bleed—note sizes before removal

12. Remove the primary metering jet, again after noting its size to insure proper reassembly.

13. Remove the secondary high speed bleed and secondary main well tube after noting sizes for reassembly.

14. Remove the primary high speed bleed and primary main well tube after noting sizes for reassembly.

15. Remove the discharge nozzle screw, discharge nozzle and gasket.

16. Invert the carburetor body and drop out accelerator pump discharge weight ball and check ball.

NOTE: Both balls are the same size.

17. Remove the accelerator pump cover screws. Remove the cover, accelerator pump diaphragm and spring.

18. Remove the choke diaphragm cover screws and remove the cover and spring.

19. Rotate the choke shaft and lever assembly counterclockwise.

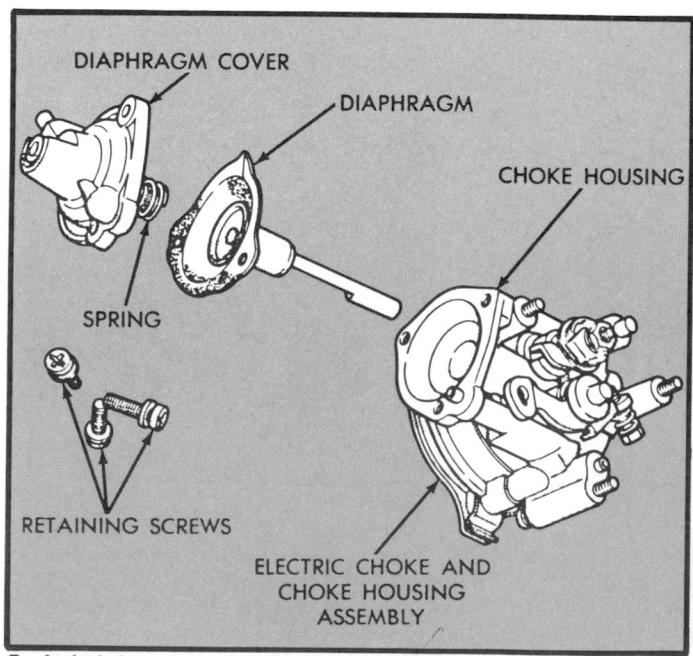

Exploded view of choke diaphragm assembly on Holley 6520 models

Rotate the choke diaphragm assembly clockwise and remove it from the housing. Remove the end of the lower screw from the housing.

NOTE: If the choke assembly is to be replaced, the diaphragm cover must also be replaced.

20. See the concealment plug removal procedure for removal of the idle mixture screw from the carburetor body.

Assembly

1. If the entire choke assembly was removed, position it on the carburetor and install the three retaining screws. If the choke diaphragm was serviced rotate the choke shaft counter-clockwise. Insert the diaphragm with a clockwise motion. Position spring and cover over diaphragm and install the retaining screws. **Make certain the fast idle link has been installed properly.**

2. Install accelerator pump spring, diaphragm cover and screws.

3. Install accelerator pump discharge check ball in discharge passage. Check accelerator and seat prior to assembly by filling the fuel bowl with clean fuel. Hold discharge check ball down with a small brass rod and operate pump plunger by hand. If the check ball and seat are leaking, no resistance will be experienced when operating plunger. If valve is leaking, stake ball using a suitable drift punch.

—CAUTION—

Exercise care when staking ball to avoid damaging bore containing the pump weight. After staking old ball, remove and replace with new ball from tune-up kit. Install weight ball and recheck for leaks.

4. Install new gaskets, discharge nozzle and screw.

5. Install primary main well tube and high speed bleed (primary).

6. Install secondary main well tube and secondary high speed bleed.

7. Install primary main metering jet (on this carburetor the primary main metering jet will have a smaller number stamped on it than the secondary main metering jet).

8. Install secondary main metering jet (on this carburetor the secondary main metering jet will have a larger number stamped on it than the primary main metering jet).

9. Install needle and set assembly.

10. Invert air horn and insert gauge or drill .480 in. (12.2 mm) between air horn and float.

11. Using a small screwdriver bend tang to adjust dry float level.

12. Position depth gauge and check float drop.

13. Using a small screwdriver bend tang to adjust float drop to 1 7/8 in. (48 mm).

14. Position new gasket on air horn; install choke rod seal and choke operating rod.

15. Carefully locate air horn to carburetor. Install new choke operating rod retainers on choke shaft lever and fast idle cam pickup lever and connect choke operating rod.

16. Install and tighten the 5 airhorn to carburetor body screws evenly in stages to 30 inch lbs. (3 N m).

17. Install and tighten idle stop solenoid screws. Reinstall anti-rattle spring.

18. Install wide open throttle cut-out switch, move switch so that air conditioning clutch circuit is open in throttle position 10° before to wide open.

19. Position a new O₂ feedback solenoid gasket on the air horn. Install new "O" ring seal on O₂ feedback solenoid. Lubricate lightly with petroleum jelly and carefully install solenoid into carburetor. Install and tighten mounting screws securely. Route wiring through clamp.

20. Install vacuum solenoid.

21. Install vacuum control valve.

22. Install and tighten harness mounting screw.

Typical oxgen feedback solenoid

MODEL 6520
Chrysler Corporation

Year	Carb. Part No. ①	Accelerator Pump	Dry Float Level (in.)	Float Drop (in.)	Vacuum Kick (in.)	Fast Idle RPM
'81	R-9052A	#2 hole	.480	1.875	.070	1400②
	R-9053A	#2 hole	.480	1.875	.070	1400②
	R-9054A	#2 hole	.480	1.875	.040	1400②
	R-9055A	#2 hole	.480	1.875	.040	1400②
	R-9060A	#2 hole	.480	1.875	.030	1100②
	R-9061A	#2 hole	.480	1.875	.030	1100②
	R-9602A	#2 hole	.480	1.875	.035	1500②
	R-9603A	#2 hole	.480	1.875	.035	1500②
	R-9125A	#2 hole	.480	1.875	.030	1200②
	R-9126A	#2 hole	.480	1.875	.030	1200②

FEEDBACK CARBURETORS
SECTION 6

MODEL 6520
Chrysler Corporation

Year	Carb. Part No. ①	Accelerator Pump	Dry Float Level (in.)	Float Drop (in.)	Vacuum Kick (In.)	Fast Idle RPM
'81	R-9604A	#2 hole	.480	1.875	.035	1600②
	R-9605A	#2 hole	.480	1.875	.035	1600②
'82	R-9822A	#2 hole	.480	1.875	.080	1400
	R-9823A	#2 hole	.480	1.875	.080	1400
	R-9824A	#2 hole	.480	1.875	.065	1400
	R-9503A	#3 hole	.480	1.875	.085	1300
	R-9504A	#3 hole	.480	1.875	.085	1300
	R-9505A	#3 hole	.480	1.875	.100	1600
	R-9506A	#3 hole	.480	1.875	.100	1600
	R-9750A	#3 hole	.480	1.875	.085	1300
	R-9751A	#3 hole	.480	1.875	.085	1300
	R-9509A	#3 hole	.480	1.875	.085	1600
	R-9510A	#3 hole	.480	1.875	.085	1600
	R-9752A	#3 hole	.480	1.875	.100	1600
	R-9753A	#3 hole	.480	1.875	.100	1600
	R-9507A	#3 hole	.480	1.875	.085	1300
	R-9508A	#3 hole	.480	1.875	.085	1300
'83	R-40003A	#3 hole	.480	1.875	.070	1400
	R-40004A	#3 hole	.480	1.875	.080	1500
	R-40005A	#3 hole	.480	1.875	.080	1350
	R-40006A	#3 hole	.480	1.875	.080	1275
	R-40007A	#3 hole	.480	1.875	.070	1400
	R-40008A	#3 hole	.480	1.875	.070	1600
	R-40010A	#3 hole	.480	1.875	.080	1500
	R-40012A	#3 hole	.480	1.875	.070	1600
	R-40014A	#3 hole	.480	1.875	.080	1275
	R-40080A	#2 hole	.480	1.875	.045	1400
	R-40081A	#3 hole	.480	1.875	.045	1400
'84	R-400641A	#3 hole	.480	1.875	.080	1500
	R-400651A	#3 hole	.480	1.875	.080	1600
	R-400811A	#2 hole	.480	1.875	.080	1500
	R-400821A	#2 hole	.480	1.875	.080	1600
	R-40071A	#3 hole	.480	1.875	.080	1500
	R-40122A	#2 hole	.480	1.875	.080	1500

① Located on tag attached to the carburetor
② With radiator fan running

506

CARBURETOR ADJUSTMENTS

Float Setting Adjustment

Invert the air horn and, with the gasket removed, insert a .480 inch (12.2mm) gauge between the air horn and the float. Bend the tang with a small screwdriver to obtain the proper level.

Float Drop Adjustment

Position the depth gauge and check the float drop. Bend the tang with a small screwdriver to adjust the float drop to the correct level.

Dry float level adjustment—Holley 6520 feedback carburetor

Bend the tang to adjust the float level

Fast Idle Adjustment

1. Unplug the connector at the radiator fan and install a jumper wire so that the fan will run continuously.
2. Remove the PCV valve from the moulded rubber connector, allow the PCV valve to draw underhood air.
3. Disconnect and plug the vacuum connector at the CVSCC.
4. Install a tachometer.
5. Ground the carburetor switch with a jumper wire.
6. Disconnect O₂ system test connector located on left fender shield by shock tower.
7. Start the engine and run until normal operating temperature is obtained.

Measuring float drop on Holley 6520 models

Adjusting float drop on Holley 6520 models

8. Open throttle slightly and place adjustment screw on slowest speed step of fast idle cam.
9. With the choke valve fully open, adjust the fast idle speed to the above specifications. Return to idle then replace adjusting screw on the slowest speed step of fast idle speed cam to verify fast idle speed, readjust if necessary.
10. Turn off engine, remove jumper wire and reconnect the radiator fan. Unplug and reconnect the vacuum connector. Reinstall the PCV valve and remove tachometer. Reconnect O₂ system test connector.

Choke Vacuum Kick Adjustment

1. Open throttle, close choke, then close throttle to trap fast idle system at closed choke condition.
2. Disconnect vacuum hose from carburetor and replace with hose from auxiliary vacuum source. Apply a vacuum of 15 in. Hg.
3. Apply sufficient closing force to position choke valve at smallest opening possible without distorting linkage system. An internal spring will compress to a stop inside choke system.
4. Measure by inserting drill or gauge in center of area between

SLOWEST
SPEED STEP

Fast idle speed adjustment—Holley 6520

top of choke valve and air horn wall at primary throttle end of carburetor. See Specifications above for drill or gauge size to be used.

5. Adjust by rotating allen head screw in center of diaphragm housing.

6. Replace vacuum hose on carburetor fitting.

Concealment Plug Removal

1. Remove air cleaner cross over assembly.
2. Remove canister purge and diverter valve vacuum hoses.
3. Center punch at a point ¼ inch from end of mixture screw housing.

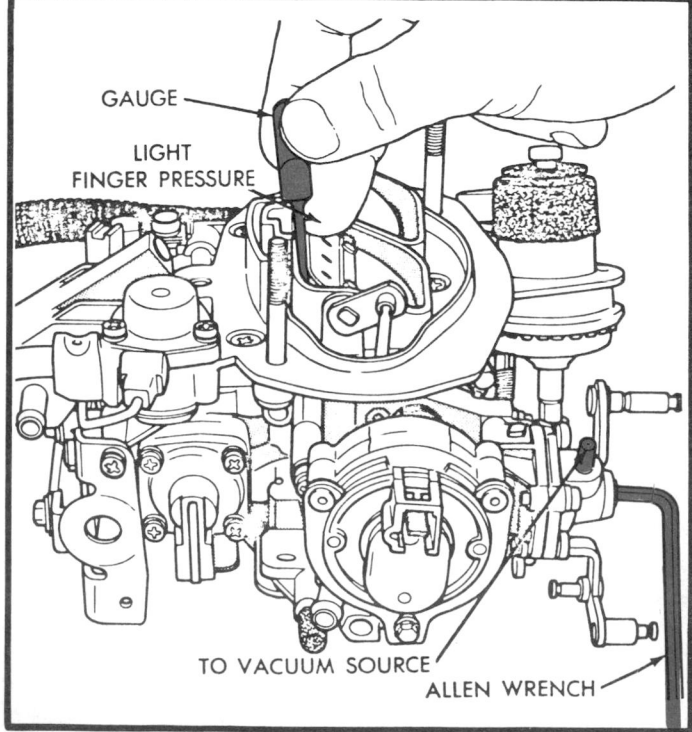

GAUGE

LIGHT
FINGER PRESSURE

TO VACUUM SOURCE   ALLEN WRENCH

Choke vacuum kick adjustment

HOLE
LOCATION

CONCEALMENT PLUG

Drill a hole as indicated to remove the idle mixture plug

4. Drill through outer housing with ³/₁₆ inch drill bit.
5. Pry out concealment plug and save for reinstallation.

Propane Idle Set Procedure

1. Remove concealment plug. Set the parking brake and place transaxle in neutral. Turn off all lights and accessories. Connect a tachometer to the engine. Start the engine and allow it to warm up on the second highest step on the fast idle cam until normal operating temperature is reached. Return engine to idle.

2. Disconnect and plug the vacuum connector at CVSCC. Disconnect the vacuum hose to the heated air door sensor at the three way connector, and in its place, install the supply hose from the propane bottle. Make sure that both valves are fully closed and that the bottle is upright and in a safe location.

3. Unplug the connector at the radiator fan and install a jumper wire so that the fan will run continuously. Remove the PCV valve from the molded rubber connector and allow the valve to draw underhood air. Connect a jumper wire between the carburetor switch and ground. On 6520 equipped vehicles disconnect the O₂ test connector located on the left fender shield.

4. Open the propane main valve. With the air cleaner in place, slowly open the propane metering valve until maximum engine

CONCEALED SCREW   ALLEN WRENCH

Adjusting idle mixture—Holley 6520

RPM is reached. When too much propane is added, engine speed will decrease. "Fine Tune" the metering valve for the highest engine RPM.

5. With the propane still flowing, adjust the idle speed screw on top of the solenoid to get the specified RPM. "Fine Tune" the propane metering valve to get the highest engine RPM. If there has been a change in the maximum RPM, readjust the idle speed to the specified propane RPM.

6. Turn off the propane main valve and allow engine speed to stabilize. With air cleaner in place, slowly adjust the mixture screw to achieve the specified idle set RPM. Pause between adjustments to allow engine speed to stabilize.

7. Turn on the main propane valve. "Fine Tune" the metering valve to get the highest engine RPM. If the maximum engine speed is more than 25 RPM different than the specified propane RPM repeat Steps 4–7.

8. Turn off both valves on propane bottle. Remove propane supply hose and reinstall the vacuum hose.

9. Reinstall the concealment plug. The plug can be installed with the carburetor on the engine.

10. Perform the fast idle speed adjustment procedure starting at Step 7.

Anti-dieseling adjustment—Holley 6520

FORD FEEDBACK CARBURETOR ELECTRONIC ENGINE CONTROL

General Information

This system, first used on 1978 Pinto and Bobcat models sold in California with the 2.3 liter four cylinder engine, actually consists of three subsystems: a two part catalytic converter, a Thermactor (air pump) system, and an electronically controlled feedback carburetor.

The converter consists of two catalytic converters in one shell. The front section is designed to control all three engine emissions (NOx, HC, and CO). The rear section acts only on HC and CO. There is a space between the two sections which serves as a mixing chamber. Air is pumped into this area by the Thermactor system to assist in the oxidation of HC and CO.

The Thermactor system is the same as that found on conventional Ford models, with the addition of a second air control valve and a second exhaust check valve.

An electronically controlled feedback carburetor is used to precisely calibrate fuel metering. The air/fuel ratio is externally controlled and variable. It is adjusted according to conditions by the Electronic Control Unit ECU), 1978–79, or the Microprocessor Control Unit (MCU), 1980 and later. There are two modes of operation: closed loop control and open loop control. Under closed loop operation, each component in the chain is sensitive to the signals sent by the other components. This means that the carburetor mixture is being controlled by the vacuum regulator/solenoid, which is adjusted by the control unit, which is receiving signals from the oxygen sensor in the exhaust manifold, which is measuring a mixture determined by the carburetor, and so on. In this case, the feedback loop is complete. Under open loop operation, the carburetor air/fuel mixture is controlled directly by the control unit according to a predetermined setting. Open loop operation takes place when the coolant temperature is below 125°F, or when the throttle is closed, during idle or deceleration.

The control unit receives signals from the exhaust gas oxygen sensor, the throttle angle vacuum switch, and the cold temperature vacuum switch, analyzes them, and sends out commands to the vacuum solenoid/regulator, which in turn adjusts, by means of vacuum, the height of the carburetor fuel metering rod. In this way, the fuel mixture is adjusted according to conditions. The control unit also varies the transition time from rich to lean (and vice

Typical feedback solenoid location

versa) according to engine rpm. The rpm signal is taken from the coil connector TACH terminal.

There are two differences between the ECU, used in 1978 and 1979, and the MCU, used in 1980 and later models. The MCU is programmable, enabling it to be used with many different engine calibrations. Additionally, the MCU controls the Thermactor solenoid values, thus directing the air flow to the exhaust manifold, the catalytic converter mixing chamber, or the atmosphere when air flow is not needed or wanted.

Because of the complicated nature of the Ford sytem, special diagnostic tools are necessary for troubleshooting and repair. No attempt at testing or repair should be made unless both the Feedback Control Tester (Ford part No. T78L-50-FBC-1) and a digital volt/ohmmeter (Ford part No. T78L-50-DVOM) are available. A tachometer, vacuum gauge, hand vacuum pump and gauge, and a special throttle rpm tool are also required for diagnosis. No trouble-shooting procedures will be given here, since they are supplied with the testing equipment.

Carter Model YFA Feedback Carburetor

ADJUSTMENTS

Float Adjustment

1. Invert the air horn assembly and check the clearance from the top of the float to the surface of the air horn with a T-scale. The air horn should be held at eye level when gauging and the float arm should be resting on the needle pin.

2. Do not exert pressure on the needle valve when measuring or adjusting the float. Bend the float arm as necessary to adjust the float level.

CAUTION

Do not bend the tab at the end of the float arm as it prevents the float from striking the bottom of the fuel bowl when empty and keeps the needle in place.

Metering Rod Adjustment

1. Remove the air horn. Back out the idle speed adjusting screw until the throttle plate is seated fully in its bore.

2. Press down on the upper end of the diaphragm shaft until the diaphragm bottoms in the vacuum chamber.

3. The metering rod should contact the bottom of the metering rod well. The lifter link at the outer end nearest the springs and at the supporting link should be bottomed.

4. On models not equipped with an adjusting screw, adjust by bending the lip of the metering rod is attached.

5. On models with an adjusting screw, turn the screw until the metering rod just bottoms in the body casting. For final adjustment, turn the screw one additional turn clockwise.

Fast Idle Cam Adjustment

1. Put the fast idle screw on the second highest step of the fast idle cam against the shoulder of the high step.

2. Adjust by bending the choke plate connecting rod to obtain the specified clearance between the lower edge of the choke plate and the air horn wall.

Choke Unloader Adjustment

1. With the throttle valve held wide open and the choke valve held in the closed position, bend the unloader tang on the throttle lever to obtain the specified clearance between the lower edge of the choke valve and their air horn wall.

Automatic Choke Adjustment

1. Loosen the choke cover retaining screws.

TOP VIEW

LEFT SIDE VIEW

CENTER VIEW

BOTTOM VIEW

RIGHT SIDE VIEW

Carter YFA feedback carburetor assembly—1 bbl shown

Component locations on Carter YFA feedback carburetor

2. Turn the choke cover so that the index mark on the cover lines up with the specified mark on the choke housing.

Choke Plate Pulldown Adjustment—1983–84

PISTON TYPE CHOKE

NOTE: This adjustment requires that the thermostatic spring housing and gasket (choke cap) are removed. Refer to the "Choke Cap" removal procedure below.

1. Remove the air cleaner assembly, then the choke cap.
2. Bend a 0.026 in. diameter wire gauge at a 90 degree angle approximately 1/8 in. from one end. Insert the bent end of the gauge between the choke piston slot and the right hand slot in the choke housing. Rotate the choke piston lever counterclockwise until the gauge is shut in the piston slot.
3. Apply light pressure on the choke piston lever to hold the gauge in place. Then measure the clearance between the lower edge of the choke plate and the carburetor bore using a drill with the diameter equal to the specified pulldown clearance.

Metering rod adjustment—typical

Float level adjustment—typical

Choke unloader adjustment—Carter YFA feedback carburetor

Piston type choke plate pulldown adjustment

Diaphragm type choke plate pulldown adjustment

4. Bend the choke piston lever to obtain the proper clearance.
5. Install the choke cap.

DIAPHRAGM TYPE CHOKE

1. Activate the pulldown motor by applying an external vacuum source.
2. Close the choke plate as far as possible without forcing it.
3. Using a drill of the specified size, measure the clearance between the lower edge of the choke plate and the air horn wall.
4. If adjustment is necessary, bend the choke diaphragm link as required.

Choke Cap Removal

1983–84

NOTE: The automatic choke has two rivets and a screw, retaining the choke cap in place. There is a locking and indexing plate to prevent misadjustment.

1. Remove the air cleaner assembly from the carburetor
2. Check choke cap retaining ring rivets to determine if mandrel is well below the rivet head. If mandrel appears to be at or within the rivet head thickness, drive it down or out with a 1/16 inch diameter punch.
3. Use a 1/8 inch diameter of No. 32 drill (.128 inch diameter) for drilling the rivet heads. Drill into the rivet head until the rivet head comes loose from the rivet body.
4. After the rivet head is removed, drive the remaining portion of the rivet out of the hole with a 1/8 inch diameter punch.

NOTE: This procedure must be followed to retain the hole size.

5. Repeat Steps 1–4 for the remaining rivet.
6. Remove the screw in the conventional manner.

Choke Cap Installation

1. Install choke cap gasket.
2. Install the locking and indexing plate.
3. Install the notched gasket.
4. Install choke cap, making certain that bimetal loop is positioned around choke lever tang.

CARTER YF, YFA SPECIFICATIONS
American Motors

Year	Model ①	Float Level (in.)	Fast Idle Cam (in.)	Unloader (in.)	Choke
'78–'79	7201	0.476	0.195	0.275	Index
	7228	0.476	0.195	0.275	1 Rich
	7229	0.476	0.195	0.275	1 Rich
	7235	0.476	0.195	0.275	Index
	7267	0.476	0.195	0.275	1 Rich
	7232	0.476	0.201	0.275	2 Rich
	7233	0.476	0.201	0.275	1 Rich
'83–'84	7700	0.600	0.175	0.370	Fixed
	7701	0.600	0.175	0.370	Fixed
	7702	0.600	0.175	0.370	Fixed
	7703	0.600	0.175	0.370	Fixed

① Model numbers located on the tag or casting

CARTER YF, YFA, YFA-FB SPECIFICATIONS
Ford Motor Co.

Year	Model ①	Float Level (in.)	Fast Idle Cam (in.)	Choke Plate Pulldown (in.)	Unloader (in.)	Dechoke (in.)	Choke
'78	D7BE-AA,AB,BA	25/32	0.140	—	0.250	—	Index
	D7BE-FA,HB, GB,GC	25/32	0.140	—	0.250	—	2 Rich
	D7BE-NA,DA	25/32	0.140	—	0.250	—	1 Rich
'79	D9BE-RA D9DE-CB,DB, AA,BA,CA,EA	25/32	0.140	—	0.250	—	1 Rich
'80	DEDE-GA,HA EODE-JA,NA, LA,MA	25/32	0.140	—	0.250	—	2 Rich
'83	E3ZE-LA	0.650	0.140	0.260	—	0.220	—
	E3ZE-MA	0.650	0.140	0.260	—	0.220	—
	E3ZE-TB	0.650	0.140	0.240	—	0.220	—
	E3ZE-UA	0.650	0.140	0.240	—	0.220	—
	E3ZE-VA	0.650	0.140	0.260	—	0.220	—
	E3ZE-YA	0.650	0.140	0.260	—	0.220	—
	E3ZE-NB	0.650	0.160	0.260	—	0.220	—
	E3ZE-PB	0.650	0.160	0.260	—	0.220	—
	E3ZE-ASA	0.650	0.160	0.260	—	0.220	—
	E3ZE-APA	0.650	0.140	0.240	—	0.220	—
	E3ZE-ARA	0.650	0.140	0.240	—	0.220	—
	E3ZE-ADA	0.650	0.140	0.260	—	0.220	—
	E3ZE-AEA	0.650	0.140	0.260	—	0.220	—
	E3ZE-ACA	0.650	0.140	0.260	—	0.220	—
	E3ZE-ATA	0.650	0.160	0.260	—	0.220	—
	E3ZE-ABA	0.650	0.140	0.260	—	0.220	—
	E3ZE-UB	0.650	0.140	0.240	—	0.220	—
	E3ZE-TC	0.650	0.140	0.240	—	0.220	—
'84	E4ZE-HC,DB	0.650	0.140	0.260	—	0.270	—
	E4ZE-MA,NA	0.650	0.140	0.240	—	0.270	—
	E4ZE-PA,RA	0.650	0.140	0.260	—	0.270	—

① Model number located on the tag or casting

5. While holding cap in place, actuate choke plate to make certain bimetal loop is properly engaged with lever tang. Set retaining clamp over choke cap and orient clamp to match holes in casting (holes are not equally spaced). Make sure retaining clamp is not upside down.

6. Place rivet in rivet gun and trigger lightly to retain rivet (1/8 inch diameter 1/2 inch long 1/4 inch diameter head).

7. Press rivet fully into casting after passing through retaining clamp and pop rivet (mandrel breaks off).

8. Repeat this step for the remaining rivet.

9. Install screw in conventional manner. Tighten to (17–20 lb-in.)

Choke Plate Clearance (Dechoke) Adjustment

1. Remove the air cleaner assembly.

2. Hold the throttle plate fully open and close the choke plate as far as possible without forcing it. Use a drill of the proper diameter to check the clearance between the choke plate and air horn.

3. If the clearance is not within specification, adjust by bending the arm on the choke lever of the throttle lever. Bending the arm downward will decrease the clearance, and bending it upward will increase the clearance. **Always recheck the clearance after making any adjustment.**

Dechoke adjustment—Carter YFA

Mechanical fuel bowl vent adjustment

Mechanical Fuel Bowl Vent Adjustment

1. Start the engine and wait until it has reached normal operating temperature before proceeding.

2. Check engine idle rpm and set to specificatons.

3. Check DC motor operation by opening throttle off idle. The DC motor should extend. Release the throttle, and the DC motor should retract when in contact with the throttle lever.

4. Disconnect the idle speed motor in the idle position.

5. Turn engine Off.

6. Open the throttle lever so that the throttle lever actuating lever does not touch the fuel bowl vent rod.

7. Close the throttle lever to the idle set position and measure the travel of the fuel bowl vent rod at point A. The distance measured represents the travel of the vent rod from where there is no contact with the actuating lever to where the actuating lever moves the vent rod to the idle set position. The travel of the vent rod at point A should be 0.100–0.150 in. (2.54–3.81 mm).

8. If adjustment is required, bend the throttle actuating lever at notch shown.

9. Reconnect the idle speed control motor.

Motorcraft 2700 VV Carburetor

GENERAL INFORMATION

In exterior appearance, the variable venturi carburetor is similar to conventional carburetors and, like a conventional carburetor, it uses a normal float and fuel bowl system. However, the similarity ends there. In place of a normal choke plate and fixed area venturis, the 2700 VV carburetor has a pair of small oblong castings in the top of the upper carburetor body where you would normally expect to see the choke plate. These castings slide back and forth across the top of the carburetor in response to fuel-air demands. Their movement is controlled by a spring-loaded diaphragm valve regulated by a vacuum signal taken below the venturis in the throttle bores. As the throttle is opened, the strength of the vacuum signal increases, opening the venturis and allowing more air to enter the carburetor.

Fuel is admitted into the venturi area by means of tapered metering rods that fit into the main jets. These rods are attached to the venturis, and, as the venturis open or close in response to air demand, the fuel needed to maintain the proper mixture increases

MOTORCRAFT MODEL 2700 VV SPECIFICATIONS
Ford Products

Year	Model	Float Level (in.)	Float Drop (in.)	Fast Idle Cam Setting (notches)	Cold Enrichment Metering Rod (in.)	Control Vacuum (in. H2O)	Venturi Valve Limiter (in.)	Choke Cap Setting (notches)	Control Vacuum Regulator Setting (in.)
'78	Pinto, Bobcat	1³⁄₆₄	1¹⁵⁄₃₂	4 Rich/2nd step	.125	5.0	¹³⁄₃₂	Index	—
	All other	1³⁄₆₄	1¹⁵⁄₃₂	1 Rich/3rd step	.125	5.0	⁶¹⁄₆₄	Index	—
'79	D9ZE-LB	1³⁄₆₄	1¹⁵⁄₃₂	1 Rich/2nd step	.125	①	②	Index	.230
	D84E-KA	1³⁄₆₄	1¹⁵⁄₃₂	1 Rich/3rd step	.125	5.5	⁶¹⁄₆₄	Index	—
'80	All	1³⁄₆₄	1¹⁵⁄₃₂	1 Rich/4th step	.125	③	④	⑤	.075
'81	EIAE-AAA	1.010-1.070	1.430-1.490	1 Rich/4th step	⑥	③	④	Index	—
	D9AE-AZA	1.015-1.065	1.435-1.485	1 Rich/4th step	.125	③	④	Index	—

① Venturi Air Bypass 6.8-7.3
　Venturi Valve Diaphragm 4.6-5.1
② Limiter Setting .38-.42
　Limiter Stop Setting .73-.77
③ See text
④ Opening gap: 0.99-1.01
　Closing gap: 0.94-0.98
⑤ See underhood decal
⑥ 0°F—0.490 @ starting position
　75°F—0.475 @ starting position

or decreases as the metering rods slide in the jets. In comparison to a conventional carburetor with fixed venturis and a variable air supply, this system provides much more precise control of the fuel-air supply during all modes of operation. Because of the variable venturi principle, there are fewer fuel metering systems and fuel passages. The only auxiliary fuel metering systems required are an idle trim, accelerator pump (similar to a conventional carburetor), starting enrichment, and cold running enrichment.

ADJUSTMENTS

NOTE: Adjustment, assembly and disassembly of this carburetor require special tools for some of the operations. Some 1978–81 models equipped with the 2700 VV carburetor experienced engine stalling, stumbling and poor performance. According to a Ford Motor Company service bulletin No. 81–9–10 issued in May of 1981, this condition may be caused by fluids trapped in the venturi valve diaphragm cavity which eventually deteriorate the diaphragm, resulting in a leak.

A quick check to verify if the above condition exists is to visually observe the venturi valve action while running the engine. Throttle movement from idle to just above idle should show a corresponding movement of the venturi valves. If no venturi valve action is observed and the valves are not sticking, there may be a leak in the diaphragm (stalls may be encountered while performing this check).

Float Level Adjustment

1. Remove and invert the upper part of the carburetor, with the gasket in place.
2. Measure the vertical distance between the carburetor body, outside the gasket, and the bottom of the float.
3. To adjust, bend the float operating lever that contacts the needle valve. Make sure that the float remains parallel to the gasket surface.

Float Drop Adjustment

1. Remove and hold upright the upper part of the carburetor.
2. Measure the vertical distance between the carburetor body, outside the gasket, and the bottom of the float.
3. Adjust by bending the stop tab on the float lever that contacts the hinge pin.

Float drop adjustment—2700 VV

Fast Idle Speed Adjustment

1. With the engine warmed up and idling, place the fast idle lever on the step of the fast idle cam specified on the engine compartment sticker or in the specifications chart. Disconnect and plug the EGR vacuum line.
2. Make sure the high speed cam positioner lever is disengaged.
3. Turn the fast idle speed screw to adjust to the specified speed.

Fast Idle Cam Adjustment

You will need a special tool for this job: Ford calls it a stator cap (#T77L-9848-A). It fits over the choke thermostatic lever when the choke cap is removed.

1. Remove the choke coil cap. On 1980 California model and all 1981 and later models, the choke cap is riveted in place. The top

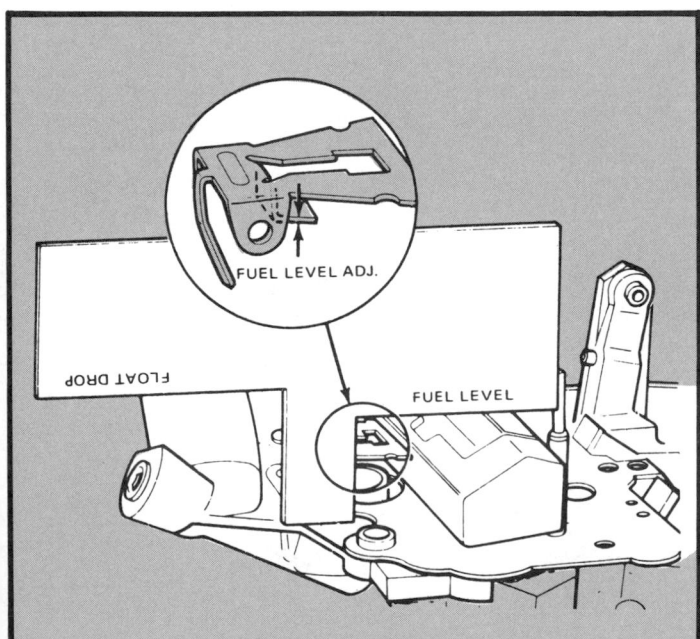
Float level adjustment—Motorcraft 2700 VV feedback carburetor

Fast idle speed adjustment—2700 VV

Fast idle cam adjustment—2700 VV

Internal vent adjustment—2700 VV

rivets will have to be drilled out: the bottom rivets will have to be driven out from the rear. New rivets must be used upon installation.

2. Place the fast idle lever in the corner of the specified step of the fast idle cam (the highest step is first) with the high speed cam positioner retracted.

3. If the adjustment is being made with the carburetor removed, hold the throttle lightly closed with a rubber band.

4. Turn the stator cap clockwise until the lever contacts the fast idle cam adjusting screw.

5. Turn the fast idle cam adjusting screw until the index mark on the cap lines up with the specified mark on the casting.

6. Remove the stator cap. Install the choke coil cap and set to the specified housing mark.

Cold Enrichment Metering Rod Adjustment

A dial indicator and the stator cap are required for this adjustment.

1. Remove the choke coil cap. See Step 1 of the "Fast Idle Cam Adjustment."

2. Attach a weight to the choke coil mechanism to seat the cold enrichment rod.

3. Install and zero a dial indicator with the tip on top of the enrichment rod. Raise and release the weight to verify zero on the dial indicator.

4. With the stator cap at the index position, the dial indicator should read the specified dimension. Turn the adjusting nut to correct.

5. Install the choke cap at the correct setting.

Internal Vent Adjustment

1978 ONLY

This adjustment is required whenever the idle speed adjustment is changed.

1. Make sure the idle speed is correct.

2. Place of 0.010 in. feeler gauge between the accelerator pump stem and the operating link.

3. Turn the nylon adjusting nut until there is a slight drag on the gauge.

Venturi Valve Limiter Adjustment

1. Remove the carburetor. Take off the venturi valve cover and the two rollers.

2. Use a center punch to loosen the expansion plug at the rear of the carburetor main body on the throttle side. Remove it.

3. Use an Allen wrench to remove the venturi valve wide open screw.

4. Hold the throttle wide open.

5. Apply a light closing pressure on the venturi valve and check the gap between the valve and the air horn wall. To adjust, move the venturi valve to the wide open position and insert an Allen

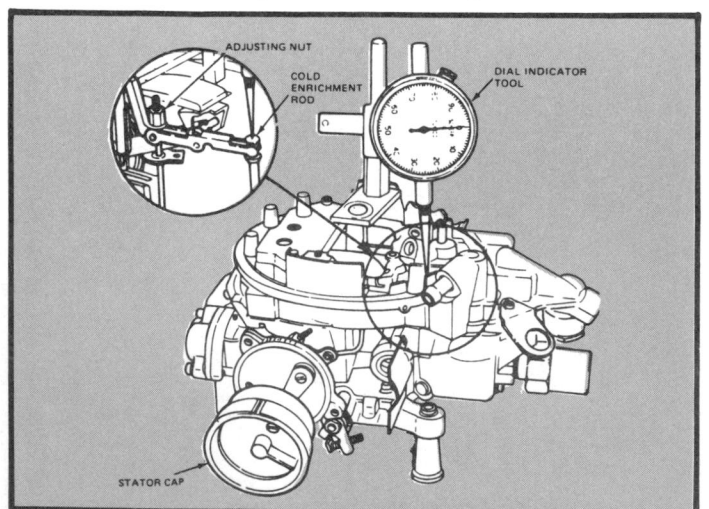

Cold enrichment metering rod adjustment—2700 VV

Venturi valve limiter adjustment—2700 VV

wrench into the stop screw hole. Turn clockwise to increase the gap. Remove the wrench and check the gap again.

6. Replace the wide open stop screw and turn it clockwise until it contacts the valve.

7. Push the venturi valve wide open and check the gap. Turn the stop screw to bring the gap to specifications.

8. Reassemble the carburetor with a new expansion plug.

Control Vacuum Regulator Adjustment

There are two systems used. The earlier system's C.V.R. rod threads directly through the arm. The revised system, introduced in late 1977, has a 3/8 in. nylon hex adjusting nut on the C.V.R. rod and a flange on the rod.

Control vacuum regulator adjustment—2700 VV

EARLY SYSTEM

1. Make sure that the cold enrichment metering rod adjustment is correct.

2. Rotate the choke coil cap half a turn clockwise from the index mark. Work the throttle to set the fast idle cam.

3. Press down lightly on the regulator rod. If there is no down travel, turn the adjusting screw counter-clockwise until some travel is felt.

4. Turn the regulator rod clockwise with an Allen wrench until the adusting nut just begins to rise.

5. Press lightly on the regulator rod. If there is any down travel, turn the adjusting screw clockwise in 1/4 turn increments until it is eliminated.

6. Return the choke coil cap to the specified setting.

REVISED SYSTEM

The cold enrichment metering rod adjustment must be checked and set before making this adjustment.

1, After adjusting the cold enrichment metering rod, leave the dial indicator in place but remove the stator cap. Do not rezero the dial indicator.

2. Press down on the C. V. R. rod until it bottoms on its seat. Measure this amount of travel with the dial indicator.

3. If the adjustment is incorrect, hold the 3/8 in. C. V. R. adjusting nut with a box wrench to prevent it from turning. Use a 3/32 in. Allen wrench to turn the C. V. R. rod; turning counter-clockwise will increase the travel, and vice versa.

High Speed Cam Positioner Adjustment

1979 ONLY

1. Place the high speed cam positioner in the corner of the specified cam step, counting the highest step as the first.

2. Place the fast idle lever in the corner of the positioner.

3. Hold the throttle firmly closed.

Idle mixture adjustment—2700 VV

4. Remove the diaphragm cover. Adjust the diaphragm assembly clockwise until it lightly bottoms. Turn it counterclockwise 1/2 to 1 1/2 turns until the vacuum port and diaphragm hole line up.

5. Replace the cover.

Motorcraft 7200 VV Carburetor

The Motorcraft model 7200 variable venturi (VV) carburetor shares most of its design features with the model 2700 VV. The major difference between the two is that the 7200 is designed to work with Ford's EEC (electronic engine control) feedback system. The feedback system precisely controls the air/fuel ratio by varying signals to the feedback control monitor located on the carburetor, which opens or closes the metering valve in response. This expands or reduces the amount of control vacuum above the fuel bowl, leaning or richening the mixture accordingly.

High speed cam positioner adjustment—2700 VV

TOP VIEW

LEFT SIDE VIEW

CENTER VIEW

BOTTOM VIEW

RIGHT SIDE VIEW

Motorcraft 7200 VV feedback carburetor

MOTORCRAFT MODEL 7200 VV SPECIFICATIONS

Year	Model	Float Level (in.)	Float Drop (in.)	Fast Idle Cam Setting (notches)	Cold Enrichment Metering Rod (in.)	Control Vacuum (in. H2O)	Venturi Valve Limiter (in.)	Choke Cap Setting (notches)
'79	D9AE-ACA	1 3/64	1 15/32	1 Rich/3rd step	.125	7.5	.73-.77 ①	Index
	D9ME-AA	1 3/64	1 15/32	1 Rich/3rd step	.125	7.5	.73-.77 ①	Index
'80	All	1 3/64	1 15/32	1 Rich/3rd step	.125	②	③	④
'81	D9AE-AZA	1.015-1.065	1.435-1.485	1 Rich/3rd step	.125	②	⑤	Index
	EIAE-LA	1.015-1.065	1.435-1.485	0.360/2nd step	⑦	②	⑥	1 Rich
	EIAE-SA	1.015-1.065	1.435-1.485	0.360/2nd step	⑦	②	⑥	1 Rich
	EIAE-KA	1.010-1.070	1.430-1.490	0.360/2nd step	⑩	②	⑭	Index
	EIDE-AA	1.010-1.070	1.430-1.490	0.360/2nd step	⑩	②	⑭	Index
	EIVE-AA	1.015-1.065	1.435-1.485	0.360/2nd step	⑦	②	③	Index
'82	E2AE-LB	1.010-1.070	1.430-1.490	0.360/2nd step	⑧	②	⑨	Index
	E2DE-NA	1.010-1.070	1.430-1.490	0.360/2nd step	⑧	②	⑨	Index
	E2AE-LC	1.010-1.070	1.430-1.490	0.360/2nd step	⑧	②	⑨	Index
	E25E-FA	1.010-1.070	1.430-1.490	0.360/2nd step	⑧	②	⑨	Index
	E25E-GB	1.010-1.070	1.430-1.490	0.360/2nd step	⑧	②	⑨	Index
	E2SE-GA	1.010-1.070	1.430-1.490	0.360/2nd step	⑧	②	⑨	Index

MOTORCRAFT MODEL 7200 VV SPECIFICATIONS

Year	Model	Float Level (in.)	Float Drop (in.)	Fast Idle Cam Setting (notches)	Cold Enrichment Metering Rod (in.)	Control Vacuum (in. H₂O)	Venturi Valve Limiter (in.)	Choke Cap Setting (notches)
'82	E2AE-RA	1.010-1.070	1.430-1.490	0.360/2nd step	⑩	②	⑨	Index
	E1AE-ACA	1.010-1.070	1.430-1.490	0.360/2nd step	⑩	②	⑨	Index
	E2SE-DB	1.010-1.070	1.430-1.490	0.360/2nd step	⑪	②	⑨	Index
	E2SE-DA	1.010-1.070	1.430-1.490	0.360/2nd step	⑪	②	⑨	Index
	E1AE-SA	1.010-1.070	1.430-1.490	0.360/2nd step	⑫	②	⑬	1 Rich
	E2AE-MA	1.010-1.070	1.430-1.490	0.360/2nd step	⑫	②	⑬	1 Rich
	E2AE-MB	1.010-1.070	1.430-1.490	0.360/2nd step	⑫	②	⑬	1 Rich
	E2AE-TA	1.010-1.070	1.430-1.490	0.360/2nd step	⑫	②	⑬	Index
	E2AE-TB	1.010-1.070	1.430-1.490	0.360/2nd step	⑫	②	⑬	Index
	E25E-AC	1.010-1.070	1.430-1.490	0.360/2nd step	⑪	②	⑨	Index
	E1AE-AGA	1.010-1.070	1.430-1.490	0.360/2nd step	⑫	②	⑨	Index
	E2AE-NA	1.010-1.070	1.430-1.490	0.360/2nd step	⑫	②	⑨	Index
'83	E2AE-NA	1.010-1.070	1.430-1.490	0.360/2nd step	⑫	②	⑨	Index
	E2AE-AJA	1.010-1.070	1.430-1.490	0.360/2nd step	⑫	②	⑨	Index
	E2AE-APA	1.010-1.070	1.430-1.490	0.360/2nd step	⑫	②	⑨	Index
'84	E2AE-AJA	1.010-1.070	1.430-1.490	0.360/2nd step	⑫	②	⑨	Index
	E2AE-APA	1.010-1.070	1.430-1.490	0.360/2nd step	⑫	②	⑨	Index

① Limiter Stop Setting: .99-1.01
② See text
③ Opening gap: 0.99-1.01
   Closing gap: 0.39-0.41
④ See underhood decal
⑤ Maximum opening: .99/1.01
   Wide open on throttle: .94/.98
⑥ Maximum opening: .99/1.01
   Wide open on throttle: .74/.76
⑦ 0°F—0.490 @ starting position
   75°F—0.475 @ starting position

⑧ 0°F—0.525 @ starting position
   75°F—0.445 @ starting position
⑨ Maximum opening: .99/1.01
   Wide open on throttle: .39/.41
⑩ 0°F—0.490 @ starting position
   75°F—0.445 @ starting position
⑪ 0°F—0.525 @ starting position
   75°F—0.475 @ starting position

⑫ 0°F—0.490 @ starting position
   75°F—0.460 @ starting position
⑬ Maximum opening: .99/1.01
   Wide open on throttle: .74/.76
⑭ Maximum opening: .99/1.01
   Wide open on throttle: .48/.52

ADJUSTMENTS

Float Level, Float Drop, Fast Idle Speed Adjustments

These adjustments are performed in the same manner as for the 2700VV. See that section for procedures.

Fast Idle Cam Adjustment

This procedure is the same as for the 2700 VV. Use the procedure in that section. The 7200 VV used on California models has a choke cover held on with rivets. The carburetor must be removed to remove the rivets. With the carburetor removed, the top two rivets can be drilled out with a ⅛ in. drill bit. Drill only through the rivet head. The bottom rivet is located in a blind hole and must be removed by lightly tapping the backside of the retainer ring with a punch. The cover must be installed with replacement rivets, Ford part no. 388575, or the equivalent.

Cold Enrichment Metering Rod Adjustment

This adjustment is made in the same manner as for the 2700 VV. See the paragraph under the Fast Idle Cam Adjustment above concerning the riveted choke used on California models.

Internal Vent, Venturi Valve Limiter Adjustments

These adjustments are the same as for the 2700 VV. See that section for details.

Control Vacuum Regulator Adjustment

Use the Revised System procedure in the 2700 VV section. Note that the control vacuum is not adjustable on any 7200 carburetor; only the regulator is adjustable.

Float level adjustment—typical

Measuring float drop—typical

High Speed Cam Positioner, Idle Mixture Adjustments

Procedures are the same as for the 2700 VV. See that section for details. Like the 2700 VV, the 7200 idle trim is preset at the factory and non-adjustable.

Holley 6520 Carburetor

ADJUSTMENTS

The model 6520 has the electronic feedback system. On the 6520 always check the condition of hoses and related wiring before making carburetor adjustments.

Float Setting and Float Drop Adjustment

1. Remove and invert the air horn.
2. Insert a 0.480 inch gauge between the air horn and float.
3. If necessary, bend the tang on the float arm to adjust.
4. Turn the air horn right side up and allow the float to hang freely. Measure the float drop from the bottom of the air horn to the bottom of the float. It should be exactly $1\frac{7}{8}$ in. Correct by bending the float tang.

Vacuum Kick Adjustment

1. Open the throttle, close the choke, then close the throttle to trap the fast idle system at the closed choke position.
2. Disconnect the vacuum hose to the carburetor and connect it to an auxiliary vacuum source.
3. Apply at least 15 inches Hg. vacuum to the unit.

Vacuum kick adjustment—typical

4. Apply sufficient force to close the choke valve without distorting the linkage.
5. Insert a gauge (see Specification Chart) between the top of the choke plate and the air horn wall.
6. Adjust by rotating the Allen screw in the center diaphragm housing.
7. Replace the vacuum hose.

Throttle Position Transducer Adjustment

1978 ONLY

1. Disconnect the wire from the transducer.
2. Loosen the locknut.
3. Place an $\frac{11}{16}$ in. gauge between the outer portion of the transducer and the mounting bracket.
4. To adjust the gap, turn the transducer.
5. Tighten the locknut.

Throttle position transducer adjustment—typical

Fast Idle Speed Adjustment

1. Remove the air cleaner, disconnect and plug the EGR line, but do not disconnect the spark control computer vacuum line. Use a jumper wire to ground the idle stop switch (through 1979). Turn the air conditioning off.
2. Disconnect the radiator fan electrical connector and use a jumper wire to complete the circuit at the fan. Do not short to ground, as this will damage the system.
3. With the parking brake set and the transmission in Neutral (engine still off), open the throttle and place the fast idle screw on the slowest step of the cam.

4. Start the engine and check the idle speed. If it continues to rise slowly, the idle stop switch is not grounded properly.

5. Adjust the fast idle with the screw, moving the screw off the cam each time to adjust. Allow the screw to fall back against the cam and the speed to stabilize between each adjustment.

Holley 6500 Carburetor

This is a Holley-Weber Unit used on 1978 and later Pinto and Bobcat California models with the 2.3L engine. It is also used on all 1981–82 models with the 2.3L engine equipped with the Feedback Electronic Engine Control System. With the exception of an externally variable fuel metering system in place of the fuel enrichment valve, it is identical to the model Motorcraft 5200.

ADJUSTMENTS

Fast Idle Cam

1978–79 MODELS

1. Insert a 5/32 in. drill between the lower edge of the choke plate and the air horn wall.

Fast idle speed adjustment—water heated choke assembly shown

Fast idle speed adjustment—typical

2. With the fast idle screw held on the second step of the fast idle cam, measure the clearance between the tang of the choke lever and the arm of the fast idle cam.

3. Bend the choke lever tang to adjust it if it is not up to specification.

1980–82

1. Place the fast idle screw on the second step of the fast idle cam against the shoulder of the top step.

2. Apply light pressure (downward) on the choke lever tang, and, using the proper size drill, measure the clearance between the lower edge of the choke plate and the air horn wall.

3. Bend the choke lever tang down to increase clearance and up to decrease the clearance.

NOTE: On 1982 and later models Ford recommends that if an adjustment is necessary, the choke lever should be replaced since the lever tang is hardened. This may also be necessary for 1980-81 models.

MODEL 6500
Ford Bobcat, Pinto, Mustang, Capri, Fairmont, Zephyr, Granada, Cougar

Year	Carb. Iden.	Dry Float Level (in.)	Pump Hole Setting	Choke Plate Pulldown (in.)	Fast Idle Cam Linkage (in.)	Dechoke (in.)	Choke Setting
'78-'79	D9EE-AFC	0.455	2	0.236	0.118	0.236	2 Rich
	D9EE-AJC, D9EE-AKC	0.460	2	0.236	0.118	0.236	1 Rich
	D9EE-AGC	0.460	2	0.236	0.118	0.236	2 Rich
'80	EOEE-NA, VA	0.460	2	0.236	0.118	0.393	①
	EOEE-NC, NV	0.460	2	0.236	0.118	0.157	①
	EOEE-ND, VD	0.460	2	0.236	0.118	0.393	①
	EOZE-AFA, SA	0.460	2	0.236	0.118	0.393	①
	EOZE-AFC, SC	0.460	—	0.236	0.118	0.393	①

MODEL 6500
Ford Bobcat, Pinto, Mustang, Capri, Fairmont, Zephyr, Granada, Cougar

Year	Carb. Iden.	Dry Float Level (in.)	Pump Hole Setting	Choke Plate Pulldown (in.)	Fast Idle Cam Linkage (In.)	Dechoke (in.)	Choke Setting
'81	EIZE-RA	0.460	3	0.240	0.120	0.400	—
	EIZE-SA	0.460	3	0.240	0.120	0.400	—
	EIDE-DA	0.460	3	0.240	0.120	0.400	—
	EIDE-EA	0.460	3	0.240	0.120	0.400	—
'82	E2ZE-ARA	.41–.51	2	0.275	0.118	0.393	—
	E2ZE-APA	.41–.51	2	0.275	0.118	0.393	—
	E2ZE-VA	.41–.51	3	0.275	0.118	0.393	—
	E2ZE-ADA	.41–.51	3	0.275	0.118	0.393	—
	E2ZE-ACA	.41–.51	3	0.275	0.118	0.393	—
	E2ZE-UA	.41–.51	3	0.275	0.118	0.393	—

① See underhood decal

Choke Plate Pulldown

THROUGH 1980

1. Remove the choke thermostatic spring cover.
2. Pull the water cover and the thermostatic spring cover assembly or the electric choke assist assembly out of the way.
3. Set the fast idle cam on the second step.
4. Push the diaphragm stem against its stop and insert the specified gauge between the lower edge of the choke valve and the air horn wall.
5. Apply sufficient pressure to the upper edge of the choke valve to take up any slack in the choke linkage.
6. Turn the adjusting screw in or out to adjust the choke plate-to-air horn clearance.

1981–82

NOTE: The following procedure requires the removal of the carburetor and also the choke cap which is retained by two rivets.

1. Remove the carburetor from the engine.
2. Remove the choke cap as follows:
   a. Check the rivets to determine if mandrel is well below the rivit head. If mandrel is within the rivit head thickness, drive it down or out with a ¹⁄₁₆ inch diameter tip punch.
   b. With a ¹⁄₈ inch diameter drill, drill into the rivet head until the rivet head comes loose from the rivet body. Use light pressure on the drill bit or the rivet will just spin in the hole.
   c. After drilling off the rivet head, drive the remaining rivet out of the hole with a ¹⁄₈ inch diameter punch.
   d. Repeat steps (a thru c) to remove the remaining rivet.
3. Remove the plastic dust cover.
4. Place the fast idle adjusting screw on the high step of the fast idle cam.
5. Attach a rubber band to remove the slack from the choke linkage. Push the diaphragm stem back against the stop screw.
6. Using the specified diameter drill check the clearance between the lower edge of the choke plate and the air horn wall.
7. If adjustment is necessary, obtain a replacement kit containing a new choke pulldown diaphragm cover, adjusting screw and cup plug.
8. After installing the adjusting screw in the cover, adjust the pulldown by turning the screw clockwise to decrease and counterclockwise to increase the setting.
9. After making the adjustment, install a new plug in the choke pulldown adjustment access opening.

10. Remove the rubber band and reinstall the choke cap using rivets (¹⁄₈ inch diameter × ¹⁄₂ inch long with a ¹⁄₄ inch diameter head).

Dechoke (Unloader) Adjustment

Dechoke clearance adjustment is controlled by the fast idle cam adjustment. The figures in the specification chart refer to choke plate clearance between the plate and the air horn wall. Clearance can be measured as follows:

1. Hold the throttle wide open. Remove any slack from the choke linkage by applying pressure to the upper edge of the choke valve.
2. Measure the distance between the lower edge of the choke plate and the air horn wall.
3. Adjust by bending the tab on the fast idle lever where it touches the cam.

Fast Idle Speed

Set the fast idle speed with the fast idle screw positioned on the second step of the fast idle cam and with the engine at operating temperature.

Remove the EGR line at the valve and plug it. If the car is equipped with a spark delay valve, remove the valve and route the distributor advance vacuum signal directly to the distributor advance diaphragm. On all manual transmission models, remove and plug the vacuum line to the distributor. If the distributor also

Adjusting float level

has a retard diaphragm, leave the hose connected to it alone. If the engine has a deceleration valve, remove this hose at the carburetor and plug it. Finally, if the car has air conditioning it must be off before adjusting the fast idle.

Float Level Adjustment

With the bowl cover held upside down and the float tang resting lightly on the spring loaded fuel inlet needle, measure the clearance between the edge of the float and the bowl cover. To adjust the level, bend the float tang up or down as required. Adjust both floats equally.

Secondary Throttle Stop Screw

1. Turn the secondary throttle stop screw counterclockwise until the secondary throttle plate seats in its bore.
2. Turn the screw clockwise until it touches the tab on the secondary throttle lever.
3. Add ¼ turn clockwise for four-cylinder engines.

Checking float level with air horn removed

GENERAL MOTORS ELECTRONIC FUEL CONTROL SYSTEM

General Information

Similar in both principle and hardware to the Ford Feedback Carburetor System, the G.M. Electronic Fuel Control System is used in 1978 and 1979 on the Pontiac 151 cubic inch (2.5 liter) four cylinder engine installed in Sunbirds, Starfires, and Monzas sold in California. It is designed to closely regulate the air/fuel ratio through electronic monitoring. A two part catalytic converter oxidizes all three pollutants, but does not have either the mixing chamber or air injection used in the Ford system. Other components in this system include an oxygen sensor which monitors the oxygen content in the exhaust, an Electronic Control Unit (ECU) which receives signals from the oxygen sensor, engine temperature switch, and vacuum input switch and sends a control signal to the vacuum modulator, the vacuum modulator which adjusts the carburetor and/fuel mixture, and a carburetor equipped with feedback diaphragms.

The ECU monitors the voltage output of the oxygen sensor. Lean mixtures reduce voltage, rich mixtures increase voltage. Adjustments of the signal sent to the vacuum modulator are made by the ECU according to the oxygen sensor output. Unlike the Ford system, there is no open loop or closed loop operation. The oxygen sensor input is a constant function. However, the ECU may limit the amount of leanness applied by the vacuum modulator according to signals received from two sources. If the temperature switch indicates that the engine is cold, the ECU allows a slightly richer mixture. If the vacuum input switch indicates low vacuum (heavy engine load), the ECU reduces the rate at which the system goes lean.

BASIC TROUBLESHOOTING

1. Before any tests are made, check the vacuum hoses for leaks, breaks, kinks, or improper connections. Inspect the wiring for breaks, shorts, or fraying. Be sure the electrical connector at the ECU is tight. Disconnect the wire from the vacuum switch (3B), and connect a test light between it and the positive battery terminal. Run the engine at 1500 rpm, with the transmission in Neutral. The test light should go on and off as the vacuum hose is removed and replaced at the switch. If not, replace the switch.
2. Turn the ignition switch to run (engine off).
3. The vacuum modulator should emit a steady clicking sound. If so, go to Step 4. If not, ground one end of a jumper wire to a ground, the other to the brown wire in the modulator connector (5B).
   a. If the modulator clicks once, check the ECU connector for tightness. If it's ok, remove the ECU connector and touch 5A with the jumper wire. If there's no click, there is an open in the brown wire. If it clicks once, replace the ECU.
   b. If the modulator does not click when the brown wire is grounded, connect a test light to a ground and the pink wire at the modulator (1D). If the test light goes on, replace the modulator. If not, there is an open in the pink wire.
4. If a clicking sound is heard, use a T-fitting to attach a vacuum gauge between the center port of the vacuum modulator and the carburetor. Start the engine, allow it to reach operating temperature, and let the engine idle. Automatic transmission should be in Drive (front wheels blocked, parking brake on), manual in Neutral.
   a. If the gauge reads above 7 in. Hg., replace the vacuum modulator.
   b. If the gauge reads 2–4 in. Hg., shift the transmission to Neutral or Park, with an automatic, and increase the engine speed to 3500 rpm. If the reading is still 2–4 in., the system is ok; either the ignition or fuel supply is faulty. If it reads below 2–4 in., the carburetor is faulty.
   c. If the guage reads below 2–4 in., shift to Neutral or Park, with automatic transmission, and increase the engine speed to 3500 rpm. If it now reads 2–4 in., adjust the idle speed to read 2–4 in. at normal idle, according to the emission sticker in the engine compartment. If the reading is still below that figure, go to the next step.
5. Remove the oxygen sensor wire (4B).
   a. If the vacuum gauge reads above 1 in. Hg., disconnect the modulator connector. If the vacuum falls below 1 in., replace the ECU. If it stays above 1 in., replace the vacuum modulator.
   b. If it reads below 1 in., connect a jumper wire from the positive battery terminal to the oxygen sensor terminal (4B). Go to the next step.
6. If the gauge reads below 4 in., go to Step 7. If it reads 4–7 in., leave the jumper connected, and disconnect the vacuum hose at the center port of the modulator. Set the fast idle screw on the high step of the cam and not the engine rpm. Reconnect the hose and note the rpm.
   a. If the engine speed drops 50 rpm or more when the hose is reconnected, replace the oxygen sensor.
   b. If it drops less than 50 rpm the problem is in the carburetor.
7. If after Step 5b the gauge still reads below 4 in., remove the jumper wire and reconnect the oxygen sensor wire. Ground the jumper wire and connect the other end to the brown wire at the modulator connector (5B).
   a. If the gauge reads 4–7 in., go to the next step.

Vacuum break adjustment—1979 and earlier models

Vacuum break adjustment—1980 and later Holley 6510C feedback carburetor

Fast idle cam adjustment—Holley 6510C models

b. If the gauge reads below 4 in., remove and plug the modulator vacuum hose from the carburetor. If the reading is still below 4 in., replace the modulator. If it is above 4 in., the problem is in the carburetor.

8. If the gauge reads 4–7 in. in Step 7a. remove the jumper wire at the modulator, and ground the engine temperature switch wire (2B).

a. If the vacuum gauge reads 4–7 in., replace the temperature switch.

b. If it reads under 4 in., go to the ECU Wiring Harness Continuity Check (diagram). If after the check the reading is still below 4 in., repair the ECU harness. If not, replace the ECU.

Holley 6510-C Carburetor

ADJUSTMENTS

NOTE: The 6510-C is used on subcompact GM cars with the 4-151 engine through 1979. In 1980 and later, it is used only on the Chevette and T-1000.

Vacuum Break Adjustment

THROUGH 1979

1. Remove the choke coil assembly.

Choke unloader adjustment—typical

2. Push the choke coil lever clockwise to close the choke valve.
3. Push the choke shaft against its stop.
4. Take the slack out of the linkage, in the open direction.
5. Insert the specified gauge between the lower edge of the choke plate and the air horn wall. Turn the adjusting screw on the diaphragm housing to adjust.

1980 AND LATER

1. Attach a hand vacuum pump to the vacuum break diaphragm. Apply vacuum until the diaphragm is seated.
2. Push the fast idle cam lever down to close the choke plate.
3. Take the slack out of the linkage in the open choke position.
4. Insert the specified gauge between the lower edge of the choke plate and the air horn wall.
5. If the clearance is incorrect, turn the screw in the end of the diaphragm to adjust.

Fast Idle Cam Adjustment

1. Set the fast idle cam so that the screw is on the second highest step of the fast idle cam.
2. Insert the specified gauge between the lower edge of the choke valve and the air horn wall.
3. Bend the tang on the arm to adjust.

Unloader Adjustment

1. Place the throttle in the wide open position.
2. Insert a 0.350 inch gauge between the lower edge of the choke valve and the air horn wall.
3. Bend the tang on the choke arm to adjust.

Choke Cap Setting

1978-79 ONLY

1. Loosen the retaining screws.
2. Make sure that the choke coil lever is located inside the coil tang.
3. Turn the cap to the specified setting.
4. Tighten the retaining screws.

Choke cap adjustment—1979 and earlier models

Float level adjustment—typical

Float drop adjustment—1979 and earlier models

Fast idle speed adjustment—typical

Secondary throttle stop screw adjustment—typical

Fast Idle Adjustment

1. With the curb idle speed correct, place the fast idle screw on the highest cam step and adjust to the specified rpm.

NOTE: The EGR line must be disconnected and plugged.

Float Level Adjustment

1. Remove and invert the air horn.
2. Place the specified gauge between the air horn and the float.
3. If necessary, bend the float arm tang to adjust.

Float Drop Setting

THROUGH 1979 ONLY

1. Hold the air horn right side up. The distance between the bottom of the air horn and the top of the float should be 1 inch.

2. If necessary, bend the tang on the side of the float arm support, to adjust.

Secondary Throttle Stop Screw Adjustment

1. Back off the screw until it does not touch the lever.
2. Turn the screw in until it touches the lever, then turn it an additional 1/4 turn.

MODEL 6510-C
General Motors Corporation

Year	Part Number	Vacuum Break Adjustment (in.)	Fast Idle Cam Adjustment (in.)	Unloader Adjustment (in.)	Fast Idle Adjustment (rpm)	Float Level Adjustment (in.)	Choke Setting
'78	10001056, 10001058	.325	.150	.350	2400	.520	1 Rich
'79	10008489, 10008490	.250	.150	.350	2400	.520	1 Rich
	10008491, 10008492	.250	.150	.350	2200	.520	2 Rich
	10009973, 10009974	.275	.150	.350	2400	.520	2 Rich

MODEL 6510-C
General Motors Corporation

Year	Part Number	Vacuum Break Adjustment (in.)	Fast Idle Cam Adjustment (In.)	Unloader Adjustment (In.)	Fast Idle Adjustment (rpm)	Float Level Adjustment (in.)	Choke Setting
'80	All w/manual	.275	.130	.350	2600	.500	Fixed
	All w/automatic	.300	.130	.350	2500	.500	Fixed
'81	14004768	.300	.130	.350	①	.500	Fixed
	14004769	.300	.130	.350	①	.500	Fixed
	14004770	.300	.130	.350	①	.500	Fixed
	14004771	.300	.130	.350	①	.500	Fixed
	14004777	.300	.130	.350	①	.500	Fixed
'82	14032364	.270	.080	.350	①	.500	Fixed
	14032365	.270	.080	.350	①	.500	Fixed
	14032366	.270	.080	.350	①	.500	Fixed
	14032367	.270	.080	.350	①	.500	Fixed
	14032368	.270	.080	.350	①	.500	Fixed
	14032369	.270	.080	.350	①	.500	Fixed
	14032370	.270	.080	.350	①	.500	Fixed
	14032371	.270	.080	.350	①	.500	Fixed
	14033392	.270	.080	.350	①	.500	Fixed
	14033393	.270	.080	.350	①	.500	Fixed
	14047072	.270	.080	.350	①	.500	Fixed
'83	14048827	.270	.080	.350	①	.500	Fixed
	14048828	.300	.080	.350	①	.500	Fixed
	14048829	.270	.080	.350	①	.500	Fixed
'84	14068690	.270	.080	.350	①	.500	Fixed
	14068691	.270	.080	.350	①	.500	Fixed
	14068692	.300	.080	.350	①	.500	Fixed

① See underhood decal

GENERAL MOTORS COMPUTER CONTROLLED CATALYTIC CONVERTER (C–4) SYSTEM, AND COMPUTER COMMAND CONTROL (CCC) SYSTEM

General Information

The GM designed Computer Controlled Catalytic Converter System (C–4) System), introduced in 1979 and used on GM cars through 1980, is a revised version of the 1978–79 Electronic Fuel Control System (although parts are not interchangeable between the systems). The C–4 System primarily maintains the ideal air/fuel ratio at which the catalytic converter is most effective. Some versions of the system also control ignition timing of the distributor.

The Computer Command Control System (CCC System), introduced on some 1980 California models and used on all 1981 and later carbureted car lines, is an expansion of the C–4 System. The CCC System monitors up to fifteen engine/vehicle operating conditions which it uses to control up to nine engine and emission control systems. In addition to maintaining the ideal air/fuel ratio for the catalytic converter and adjusting ignition timing, the CCC System also controls the Air Management System so that the catalytic converter can operate at the highest efficiency possible. The system also controls the lockup on the transmission torque converter clutch (certain automatic transmission models only), adjusts idle speed over a wide range of conditions, purges the evaporative emissions charcoal canister, controls the EGR valve operation and operates the early fuel evaporative (EFE) system. Not all engines use all of the above sub-systems.

There are two operation modes for both the C–4 System and the CCC System: closed loop and open loop fuel control. Closed loop fuel control means the oxygen sensor is controlling the carburetor's air/fuel mixture ratio. Under open loop fuel control operating conditions (wide open trottle, engine and/or oxygen sensor cold), the oxygen sensor has no effect on the air/fuel mixture.

NOTE: On some engines, the oxygen sensor will cool off while the engine is idling, putting the system into open loop operation. To restore closed loop operation, run the engine at part throttle and accelerate from idle to part throttle a few times.

COMPUTER CONTROLLED CATALYTIC CONVERTER (C–4) SYSTEM OPERATION

Major components of the system include an Electronic Control Module (ECM), an oxygen sensor, and electronically controlled variable-mixture carburetor, and a three-way oxidation-reduction catalytic converter.

The oxygen sensor generates a voltage which varies with exhaust gas oxygen content. Lean mixtures (more oxygen) reduce voltage; rich mixtures (less oxygen) increase voltage. Voltage output is sent to the ECM.

An engine temperature sensor installed in the engine coolant outlet monitors coolant temperatures. Vacuum control switches and throttle position sensors also monitor engine conditions and supply signals to the ECM.

The Electronic Control Module (ECM) monitors the voltage input the oxygen sensor along with information from other input signals. It processes these signals and generates a control signal sent to the carburetor. The control signal cycles between ON (lean command) and OFF (rich command). The amount of ON and OFF time is a function of the input voltage sent to the ECM by the oxygen sensor. The ECM has a calibration unit called a PROM (Programable Read Only Memory) which contains the specific instructions for a given engine application. In other words, the PROM unit is specifically programed or "tailor made" for the system in which it is installed. The PROM assembly is a replacable component which plugs into a socket on the ECM and requires a special tool for removal and installation.

NOTE: To prevent ECM damage on 1980 and later Cadillac C–4 and CCC equipped vehicles, the power supply feeding the ECM must not be interrupted with the ignition switch in the run, start or ACC position. The ignition switch must be placed in the *off* position when performing the following service operations:

1. Disconnecting or connecting either battery cable.

2. Removing or replacing the fuse providing continuous battery power to the ECM.

3. Disconnecting or connecting any ECM connectors.

4. **Disconnecting (unless the engine is running) or connecting jumper cables (the jumper polarity must be correct, as even a momentary reversal of cable polarity may cause ECM damage).**

5. Disconnecting or connecting a battery charger (it is recommended that the battery be charged with both battery cables disconnected using the battery side terminal adapter, AC Delco ST-1201 or equivalent).

On some 231 cu in. V6 engines, the ECM controls the Electronic Spark Timing System (EST), AIR control system, and on the Turbo-charged 231 cu in. C–4 System it controls the early fuel evaporative system (EFE) and the EGR valve control (on some models). On some 350 V8 engines, the ECM controls the electronic module retard (EMR) system, which retards the engine timing 10 degrees during certain engine operations to reduce the exhaust emissions.

NOTE: Electronic Spark Timing (EST) allows continuous spark timing adjustments to be made by the ECM. Engines with EST can easily be identified by the absence of vacuum and mechanical spark advance mechanisms on the distributor. Engines with EMR systems may be recognized by the presence of five connectors, instead of the HEI module's usual four.

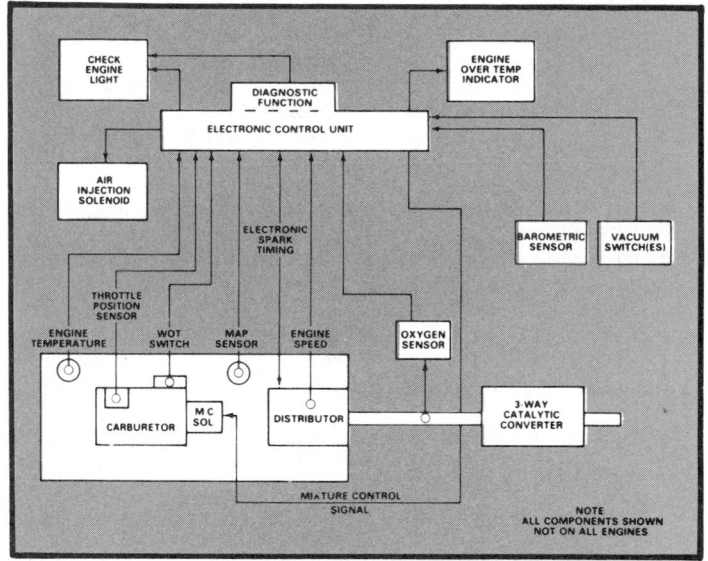

Schematic of GM Computer Controlled Catalytic Converter (C4) system

Typical 1979 C4 system wiring harness layout. Note locations of connectors, test joints and diagnostic terminal

To maintain good idle and driveability under all conditions, other input signals are used to modify the ECM output signal. Besides the sensors and switches already mentioned, these input signals include the manifold absolute pressure (MAP) or vacuum sensors and the barometric pressure (BARO) sensor. The MAP or vacuum sensors sense changes in manifold vacuum, while the BARO sensor senses changes in barometric presure. One important function of the BARO sensor is the maintenance of good engine performance at various altitudes. These sensors act as throttle position sensors on some engines. See the following paragraph for description.

A Rochester Dualjet carburetor is used with the C–4 System. It may be an E2SE, E2ME, E4MC or E4ME model, depending on engine application. An electronically operated mixture control solenoid is installed in the carburetor float bowl. The solenoid controls the air/fuel mixture metered to the idle and main metering systems. Air metering to the idle system is controlled by an idle air bleed valve. It follows the movement of the mixture solenoid to control the amount of air bled into the idle system, enriching or leaning out the mixture as appropriate. Air/fuel mixture enrichment occurs when the fuel valve is open and the air bleed is closed.

All cycling of this system, which occurs ten times per second, is controlled by the ECM. A throttle position switch informs the ECM of open or closed throttle operation. A number of different switches are used, varying with application. The four cylinder engine (151 cu. in.) uses two vacuum switches to sense open throttle and closed throttle operation. The V6 engines (except the 231 cu. in. turbo V6) use two pressure sensors–MAP (Manifold Absolute Pressure) and BARO (Barometric Pressure)–as well as a throttle-actuated wide open throttle switch mounted in a bracket on the side of the float bowl. The 231 cu in. turbo V6, and V8 engines, use a throttle position sensor mounted in the carburetor bowl cover under the accelerator pump arm. When the ECM receives a signal from the throttle switch, indicating a change of position, it immediately searches its memory for the last set of operating conditions that resulted in an ideal air/fuel ratio, and shifts to that set of conditions. The memory is continually updated during normal operation.

Some 1980 173 cu. in. V6 engines are equipped with a Pulsair control solenoid which is operated by the ECM. Likewise, many C–4 equipped engines with AIR systems (Air Injection Reaction systems) have an AIR system diverter solenoid controlled by the ECM. These systems are similar in function to the AIR Management system used in the CCC System. See below for information. Most C–4 Systems include a maintenance reminder flag connected to the odometer which becomes visible in the instrument cluster at regular intervals, signaling the need for oxygen sensor replacement.

NOTE: The 1980 Cutlass with 260 cu. in. V8 engine is equipped with a hybrid C–4 System which includes some functions of the CCC System (Air Management, EGR valve control, Idle speed control, canister purge control and transmission converter clutch).

COMPUTER COMMAND CONTROL (CCC) SYSTEM OPERATION

The CCC has many components in common with the C-4 system (although they should not be interchanged between systems. These include the Electronic Control Module (ECM), which is capable of monitoring and adjusting more sensors and components than the ECM used on the C-4 System, an oxygen sensor, an electronically controlled variable-mixture carburetor, a three way catalytic converter, throttle position and coolant sensors, a barometric pressure (BARO) sensor, a manifold absolute pressure (MAP) sensor, a "check engine" light on the instrument cluster, and an Electronic Spark Timing (EST) distributor, which on some engines (turbocharged) is equipped with an Electronic Spark Control (ESC) which retards ignition spark under some conditions (detonation, etc.).

Components of GM Computer Command Control (CCC) system

Components used almost exclusively by the CCC System include the Air Injection Reaction (AIR) Management System, charcoal canister purge solenoid, EGR valve control, vehicle speed sensor located in the instrument cluster), transmission torque converter clutch solenoid (automatic transmission models only), idle speed control, and early fuel evaporative (EFE) system.

See the operation descriptions under C-4 System for those components (except the ECM) the CCC System shares with the C-4 System.

The CCC System ECM, in addition to monitoring sensors and sending a control signal to the carburetor, also control the following components or sub-systems: charcoal canister purge, AIR Management System, idle speed control, automatic transmission converter lockup, distributor ignition timing, EGR valve control, EFE control, and the air conditioner compressor clutch operation. The CCC ECM is equipped with a PROM assembly similar to the one used in the C-4 ECM. See above for description.

The AIR Management System is an emission control which provides additional oxygen either to the catalyst or the cylinder head ports (in some cases exhaust manifold). An AIR Management System, composed of an air switching valve and/or an air control valve, controls the air pump flow and is itself controlled by the ECM. A complete description of the AIR system is given towards the front of this unit repair section. The major difference between the CCC AIR System and the systems used on other cars is that the flow of air from the air pump is controlled electrically by the ECM, rather than by vacuum signal.

The charcoal canister purge control is an electrically operated solenoid valve controlled by the ECM. When energized, the purge control solenoid blocks vacuum from reaching the canister purge valve. When the ECM de-energizes the purge control solenoid, vacuum is allowed to reach the canister and operate the purge valve. This releases the fuel vapors collected in the canister into the induction system.

The EGR valve control solenoid is activated by the ECM in similar fashion to the canister purge solenoid. When the engine is cold, the ECM energizes the solenoid, which blocks the vacuum signal to the EGR valve. When the engine is warm, the ECM de-energizes the solenoid and the vacuum signal is allowed to reach and activate the EGR valve.

The Transmission Converter Clutch (TCC) lock is controlled by the ECM through an electrical solenoid in the automatic transmission. When the vehicle speed sensor in the instrument panel signals the ECM that the vehicle has reached the correct speed, the ECM energizes the solenoid which allows the torque converter to mechanically couple the engine to the transmission. When the brake pedal is pushed or during deceleration, passing, etc., the ECM returns the transmission to fluid drive.

The idle speed control adjusts the idle speed to load conditions, and will lower the idle speed under no-load or low-load conditions to conserve gasoline.

The Early Fuel Evaporative (EFE) system is used on some engines to provide rapid heat to the engine induction system to promote smooth start-up and operation. There are two types of system: vacuum servo and electrically heated. They use different means to achieve the same end, which is to pre-heat the incoming air/fuel mixture. They are controlled by the ECM.

BASIC TROUBLESHOOTING

NOTE: The following explains how to activate the Trouble Code signal light in the instrument cluster and gives an explanation of what each code means. This is not a full C-4 or CCC System troubleshooting and isolation procedure.

Before suspecting the C-4 or CCC System or any of its components as faulty, check the ignition system including distributor, timing, spark plugs and wires. Check the engine compression, air cleaner, and emission control components not controlled by the ECM. Also check the intake manifold, vacuum hoses and hose connectors for leaks and the carburetor bolts for tightness.

Typical diagnostic test lead locations—1980 models

The following symptoms could indicate a possible problem with the C-4 or CCC System.
1. Detonation
2. Stalls or rough idle–cold
3. Stalls or rough idle–hot
4. Missing
5. Hesitation
6. Surges
7. Poor gasoline mileage
8. Sluggish or spongy performance
9. Hard starting–cold
10. Objectionable exhaust odors (that "rotten egg" smell)
12. Cuts out
13. Improper idle speed (CCC System and C-4 equipped 1980 Cutlass with 260 cu. in. engine only)

As a bulb and system check, the "Check Engine" light will come on when the ignition switch is turned to the ON position but the engine is not started.

The "Check Engine" light will also produce the trouble code or codes by a series of flashes which translate as follows. When the diagnostic test lead (C-4) or terminal (CCC) under the dash is grounded, with the ignition in the ON position and the engine not running, the "Check Engine" light will flash once, pause, then flash twice in rapid succession. This is a code 12, which indicates that the diagnostic system is working. After a longer pause, the code 12 will repeat itself two more times. The cycle will then repeat itself until the engine is started or the ignition is turned off.

NOTE: The C-4 equipped 1980 Cutlass with 260 cu in. V8 engine has a test terminal similar to the kind used on the CCC System.

When the engine is started, the "Check Engine" light will remain on for a few seconds, then turn off. If the "Check Engine" light remains on, the self-diagnostic system has detected a problem. If the test lead (C-4) or test terminal (CCC) is then grounded, the trouble code will flash three times. If more than one problem is found, each trouble code will flash three times. Trouble codes will flash in numerical order (lowest code number to highest). The trouble codes series will repeat as long as the test lead or terminal is grouned.

A trouble code indicates a problem with a given circuit. For example, trouble code 14 indicates a problem in the cooling sensor circuit. This includes the coolant sensor, its electrical harness, and the Electronic Control Module (ECM).

Since the self-diagnostic system cannot diagnose every possible fault in the system, the absence of a trouble code does not mean the system is trouble-free. To determine problems within the system which do not activate a trouble code, a system performance check must be made. This job should be left to a qualified technician.

In the case of an intermittant fault in the system, the "Check Engine" light will go out when the fault goes away, but the trouble

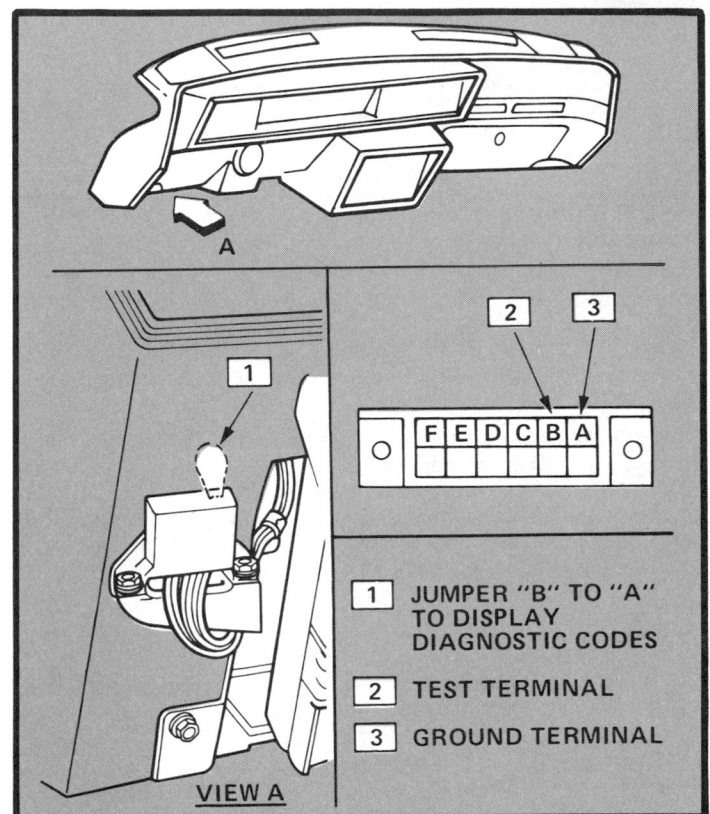

Typical 1981 and later CCC test terminal location. Ground the test terminal to activate the trouble code readout

1	JUMPER "B" TO "A" TO DISPLAY DIAGNOSTIC CODES
2	TEST TERMINAL
3	GROUND TERMINAL

Typical 1980 C4 system wiring harness layout. The location of the diagnostic test terminal depends on the position of the on-board computer (ECM) and the body style

code will remain in the memory of the ECM. Therefore, if a trouble code can be obtained even though the "Check Engine" light is not on, the trouble code must be evaluated. It must be determined if the fault is intermittant or if the engine must be at certain operating conditions (under load, etc.) before the "Check Engine" light will come on. Some trouble codes will not be recorded in the ECM until the engine has been operated at part throttle for about 5 to 18 minutes.

On the C-4 System, the ECM erases all trouble codes every time the ignition is turned off. In the case of intermittent faults, a long term memory is desirable. This can be produced by connecting the orange connector/lead from terminal "S" of the ECM directly to the battery (or to a "hot" fuse panel terminal). This terminal must

TEST LEAD

A B C D

The 1980 Oldsmobile 260 cu. in. (4.3L) V8 equipped with the C4 system uses a test terminal similar to CCC-equipped models

be disconnected after diagnosis is complete or it will drain the battery.

On the CCC System, a trouble code will be stored until terminal "R" of the ECM has been disconnected from the battery for 10 seconds.

NOTE: On 1980 Cutlass with 260 cu in. V8, the trouble code is stored in the same manner as on the CCC System. In addition, some 1980 Buicks have a long term constant memory similar to that used on the CCC System. In which case terminal S (terminal R on the 3.8 Liter V6) must be disconnected in the same manner as on the CCC System to erase the memory.

An easy way to erase the computer memory on the CCC System is to disconnect the battery terminals from the battery. If this method is used, don't forget to reset clocks and electronic preprogramable radios. Another method is to remove the fuse marked ECM in the fuse panel. Not all models have such a fuse.

Activating the Trouble Code

On the C-4 System (except 1980 Cutlass with 260 cu. in V8), activate the trouble code by grounding the trouble code test lead. Use the illustrations to locate the test lead under the instrument panel (usually a white and black wire or a wire with a green connector). Run a jumper wire from the lead to ground.

On the CCC System and the C-4 System used on the 1980 Cutlass with 260 cu. in V8, locate the test terminal under the instrument panel. Ground the test lead. On many systems, the test lead is situated side by side with a ground terminal. In addition, on some models, the partition between the test terminal and the ground terminal has a cut out section so that a spade terminal can be used to connect the two terminals.

NOTE: Ground the test lead or terminal according to the instructions given in "Basic Troubleshooting", above.

EXPLANATION OF TROUBLE CODES GM C-4 AND CCC SYSTEMS

(Ground test lead or terminal AFTER engine is running.)

Trouble Code	Applicable System	Notes	Possible Problem Area
12	C-4, CCC		No tachometer or reference signal to computer (ECM). This code will only be present while a fault exsists, and will not be stored if the problem is intermittent.
13	C-4, CCC		Oxygen sensor circuit. The engine must run for about five minutes (eighteen on C-4 equipped 231 cu in. V6) at part throttle (and under road load—CCC equipped cars) before this code will show.
13 & 14 (at same time)	C-4	Except Cadillac and 171 cu in. V6	See code 43.
13 & 43 (at same time)	C-4	Cadillac and 171 cu in. V6	See code 43.
14	C-4, CCC		Shorted coolant sensor circuit. The engine has to run 2 minutes before this code will show.
15	C-4, CCC		Open coolant sensor circuit. The engine has to operate for about five minutes (18 minutes for C-4 equipped 231 cu in. V6) at part throttle (some models) before this code will show.
21	C-4		Shorted wide open throttle switch and/or open closed-throttle switch circuit (when used).
	C-4, CCC		Throttle position sensor circuit. The engine must be run up to 10 seconds (25 seconds—CCC System) below 800 rpm before this code will show.
21 & 22 (at same time)	C-4		Grounded wide open throttle switch circuit (231 cu in. V6, 151 cu in. 4 cylinder).
22	C-4		Grounded closed throttle or wide open throttle switch circuit (231 cu in. V6, 151 cu in. 4 cylinder).
23	C-4, CCC		Open or grounded carburetor mixture control (M/C) solenoid circuit.
24	CCC		Vehicle speed sensor (VSS) circuit. The car must operate up to five minutes at road speed before this code will show.

EXPLANATION OF TROUBLE CODES GM C-4 AND CCC SYSTEMS

(Ground test lead or terminal AFTER engine is running.)

Trouble Code	Applicable System	Notes	Possible Problem Area
32	C-4, CCC		Barometric pressure sensor (BARO) circuit output low.
32 & 55 (at same time)	C-4		Grounded +8V terminal or V(REF) terminal for barometric pressure sensor (BARO), or faulty ECM computer.
34	C-4	Except 1980 260 cu in. Cutlass	Manifold absolute pressure (MAP) sensor output high (after ten seconds and below 800 rpm).
34	CCC	Including 1980 260 cu in. Cutlass	Manifold absolute pressure (MAP) sensor circuit or vacuum sensor circuit. The engine must run up to five minutes below 800 RPM before this code will set.
35	CCC		Idle speed control (ISC) switch circuit shorted (over ½ throttle for over two seconds).
41	CCC		No distributor reference pulses to the ECM at specified engine vacuum. This code will store in memory.
42	CCC		Electronic spark timing (EST) bypass circuit grounded.
43	C-4		Throttle position sensor adjustment (on some models, engine must run at part throttle up to ten seconds before this code will set).
44	C-4, CCC		Lean oxygen sensor indication. The engine must run up to five minutes in closed loop (oxygen sensor adjusting carburetor mixture), at part throttle and under road load (drive car) before this code will set.

ROCHESTER FEEDBACK CARBURETORS

Model Identification

General Motors Rochester carburetors are identified by their model number. The first number indicates the number of barrels, while one of the last letters indicates the type of choke used. These are V for the manifold mounted choke coil, C for the choke coil mounted on the carburetor, and E for electric choke, also mounted on the carburetor. Model numbers ending in A indicate an altitude-compensating carburetor.

ANGLE DEGREE TOOL

An angle degree tool is recommended by Rochester Products Division, for use to confirm adjustments to the choke valve and related linkages on their late model two and four barrel carburetors, in place of the plug type gauges.

Decimal and degree conversion charts are provided for use by technicians who have access to an angle gauge and not plug gauges. It must be remembered that the relationship between the decimal and the angle readings are not exact, due to manufacturers tolerances.

To use the angle gauge, rotate the degree scale until zero (0) is opposite the pointer. With the choke valve completely closed, place the gauge magnet squarely on top of the choke valve and rotate the bubble until it is centered. Make the necessary adjustments to have the choke valve at the specified degree angle opening as read from the degree angle tool.

NOTE: The carburetor may be off the engine for adjustments. Be sure the carburetor is held firmly during the use of the angle gauge.

PUMP CUP OR VALVE STEM SEAL

TAPE END OF COVER

TAPE HOLE IN TUBE

Plugging air bleed holes in vacuum break assemblies used on Rochester E2SE feedback carburetors

ANGLE DEGREE TO DECIMAL CONVERSION
Model M2MC, M2ME and M4MC Carburetor

Angle Degrees	Decimal Equiv. Top of Valve	Angle Degrees	Decimal Equiv. Top of Valve
5	.023	33	.203
6	.028	34	.211
7	.033	35	.220
8	.038	36	.227
9	.043	37	.234
10	.049	38	.243
11	.054	39	.251
12	.060	40	.260
13	.066	41	.269
14	.071	42	.277
15	.077	43	.287
16	.083	44	.295
17	.090	45	.304
18	.096	46	.314

ANGLE DEGREE TO DECIMAL CONVERSION
Model M2MC, M2ME and M4MC Carburetor

Angle Degrees	Decimal Equiv. Top of Valve	Angle Degrees	Decimal Equiv. Top of Valve
19	.103	47	.322
20	.110	48	.332
21	.117	49	.341
22	.123	50	.350
23	.129	51	.360
24	.136	52	.370
25	.142	53	.379
26	.149	54	.388
27	.157	55	.400
28	.164	56	.408
29	.171	57	.418
30	.179	58	.428
31	.187	59	.439
32	.195	60	.449

ANGLE DEGREE TO DECIMAL CONVERSION
Model 4MV Carburetor

Angle Degrees	Decimal Equiv. Top of Valve	Angle Degrees	Decimal Equiv. Top of Valve
5	.019	33	.158
6	.022	34	.164
7	.026	35	.171
8	.030	36	.178
9	.034	37	.184
10	.038	38	.190
11	.042	39	.197
12	.047	40	.204
13	.051	41	.211
14	.056	42	.217
15	.060	43	.225
16	.065	44	.231
17	.070	45	.239
18	.075	46	.246
19	.080	47	.253
20	.085	48	.260
21	.090	49	.268
22	.095	50	.275
23	.101	51	.283
24	.106	52	.291
25	.112	53	.299
26	.117	54	.306
27	.123	55	.314
28	.128	56	.322
29	.134	57	.329
30	.140	58	.337
31	.146	59	.345
32	.152	60	.353

Models 2SE and E2SE

The Rochester 2SE and E2SE Varajet II carburetors are two barrel, two stage down-draft units. Most carburetor components are aluminum, although a zinc choke housing is used on four cylinder engines installed in 1980 models. The E2SE is used both in conventional installations and in the Computer Controlled Catalytic Converter System. In that installation the E2SE is equipped with an electrically operated mixture control solenoid, controlled by the Electronic Control Module. The 2SE and E2SE are also used on the AMC four cylinder in 1980–83.

ADJUSTMENTS

Float Adjustment

1. Remove the air horn from the throttle body
2. Use your fingers to hold the retainer in place, and to push the float down into light contact with the needle.
3. Measure the distance from the toe of the float (furthest from the hinge) to the top of the carburetor (gasket removed).

Float level adjustment—Rochester E2SE models

4. To adjust, remove the float and gently bend the arm to specification. After adjustment, check the float alignment in the chamber.

NOTE: Some models have a float stabilizer spring. If used, remove the spring with float. Use care when removing.

Pump Adjustment

1. With the throttle closed and the fast idle screw off the steps of the fast idle cam, measure the distance from the air horn casting to the top of the pump stem.

Air valve rod adjustment—1980 GM and 1980-82 AMC models

2. To adjust, remove the retaining screw and washer and remove the pump lever. Bend the end of the lever to correct the stem height. Do not twist the lever or bend it sideways.

3. Install the lever, washer and screw and check the adjustment. When correct, open and close the throttle a few times to check the linkage movement and alignment.

NOTE: **No pump adjustment is required on 1981 and later models.**

Fast Idle Adjustment

1. Set the ignition timing and curb idle speed, and disconnect and plug hoses as directed on the emission control decal.

Fast idle adjustment—typical

Fast idle cam (choke rod) adjustment—1983 and later models

2. Place the fast idle screw on the highest step of the dam.

3. Start the engine and adjust the engine speed to specification with the fast idle screw.

Choke Coil Lever Adjustment

1. Remove the three retaining screws and remove the choke cover and coil. On models with a riveted choke cover, drill out the three rivets and remove the cover and choke coil.

Choke coil level adjustment on E2SE carburetor—typical

Accelerator pump adjustment—typical

Fast idle cam adjustment—1982 and earlier models

Rochester E2SE air valve adjustment—1981-82 4 cyl. except GM J-body

Rochester E2SE air valve adjustment—1981-82 V6 engine

NOTE: A choke stat cover retainer kit is required for reassembly.

2. Place the fast idle screw on the high step of the dam.

3. Close the choke by pushing in on the intermediate choke lever. On front wheel drive models, the intermediate choke lever is behind the choke vacuum diaphragm.

4. Insert a drill or gauge of the specified size into the hole in the choke housing. The choke lever in the housing should be up against the side of the gauge.

5. If the lever does not just touch the gauge, bend the intermediate choke rod to adjust.

Fast Idle Cam (Choke Rod) Adjustment
1980–82 MODELS

NOTE: A special angle gauge should be used.

1. Adjust the choke coil lever and fast idle first.
2. Rotate the degree scale until it is zeroed.
3. Close the choke and install the degree scale onto the choke plate. Center the leveling bubble.
4. Rotate the scale so that the specified degree is opposite the scale pointer.
5. Place the fast idle screw on the second step of the cam (against the high step). Close the choke by pushing in the intermediate lever.
6. Push on the vacuum break lever in the direction of opening choke until the lever is against the rear tang on the choke lever.
7. Bend the fast idle cam rod at the U to adjust angle to specifications.

1983–84 MODELS

Refer to the illustration for the adjustment procedure on these models.

Air Valve Rod Adjustment
1980 MODELS

1. Seat the vacuum diaphragm with an outside vacuum source. Tape over the purge bleed hole if present.
2. Close the air valve.

Rochester E2SE air valve adjustment—1982 GM J-body models

Rochester E2SE air valve adjustment—1983 and later models

3. Insert the specified gauge between the rod and the end of the slot in the plunger on fours, or between the rod and the end of the slot in the air valve on V6s.

4. Bend the rod to adjust the clearance.

1981-82 MODELS

1. Align the zero degree mark with the pointer on an angle gauge.

2. Close the air valve and place a magnet on top of it.

3. Rotate the bubble until it is centered.

4. Rotate the degree scale until the specified degree mark is aligned with the pointer.

5. Seat the vacuum diaphragm using an external vacuum source.

6. On four cylinder models plug the end cover. Unplug after adjustment.

7. Apply light pressure to the air valve shaft in the direction to open the air valve until all the slack is removed between the air link and plunger slot.

8. Bend the air valve link until the bubble is center.

1983-84 MODELS

Refer to the illustration for the adjustment procedure on these models.

Primary Side Vacuum Break Adjustment

1980 GM MODELS
1980-83 AMERICAN MOTORS

1. Follow Steps 1-4 of the "Fast Idle Cam Adjustment".

2. Seat the choke vacuum diaphragm with an outside vacuum source.

3. Push in on the intermediate choke lever to close the choke valve, and hold closed during adjustment.

4. Adjust by bending the vacuum break rod until the bubble is centered.

1981-82 GM MODELS

NOTE: Prior to adjustment, remove the vacuum break from the carburetor. Place the bracket in a vise and using the proper safety precautions, grind off the adjustment screw cap then reinstall the vacuum break.

1. Rotate the degree scale on the measuring gauge until the zero is opposite the pointer.

2. Seat the choke vacuum diaphragm by applying an external vacuum source of over 5" vacuum to the vacuum break.

NOTE: If the air valve rod is restricting the vacuum diaphragm from seating it may be necessary to bend the air valve rod slightly to gain clearance. Make an air valve rod adjustment after the vacuum break adjustment.

Primary vacuum break adjustment—1980 GM and 1980 and later AMC models with 4 cyl. engine

Primary vacuum break adjustment—1980 models

3. Read the angle gauge while lightly pushing on the intermediate choke lever so that the choke valve is toward the close position.

4. Use a 1/8 in. hex wrench and turn the screw in the rear cover until the bubble is centered. Apply a silicone sealant over the screw head to seal the setting.

1983-84 GM MODELS

Refer to the illustration for the adjustment procedure on these models.

Primary vacuum break adjustment—1981-82 GM A and X-body models with V6

Secondary vacuum break adjustment—1982 GM J-body

Secondary lockout adjustment—typical

Rochester E2SE primary vacuum break adjustment—1982 GM J-body models with 4 cyl. engine

Rochester E2SE primary vacuum break adjustment—1983 and later models

Electric Choke Setting

This procedure is only for those carburetors with choke covers retained by screws. Riveted choke covers are preset and nonadjustable.
1. Loosen the three retaining screws.
2. Place the fast idle screw on the high step of the cam.
3. Rotate the choke cover to align the cover mark with the specified housing mark.

NOTE: The specification "index" which appears in the specification table refers to the mark between "1 notch lean" and "1 notch rich".

Rochester E2SE primary vacuum break adjustment—1981-82 GM A and X-body models with 4 cyl. engine

Secondary Vacuum Break Adjustment

1980 MODELS

This procedure is for V6 installations in front wheel drive models only.
1. Follow Steps 1–4 of the "Fast Idle Cam Adjustment".
2. Seat the choke vacuum diaphragm with an outside vacuum source.
3. Push in on the intermediate choke lever to close the choke valve, and hold closed during adjustment. Make sure the plunger spring is compressed and seated, if present.
4. Bend the vacuum break rod at the U next to the diaphragm until the bubble is centered.

1981–82 GM MODELS

NOTE: Prior to adjustment, remove the vacuum break from the carburetor. Place the bracket in the vise and using the proper safety precautions, grind off the adjustment screw cap then reinstall the vacuum break. Plug the end cover using an accelerator pump plunger cup or equivalent. Remove the cup after the adjustment (A and X series only).

1. Rotate the degree scale on the measuring gauge until the zero is opposite the pointer.
2. Seat the choke vacuum diaphragm by applying an external vacuum source of over 5 in. vacuum to the vacuum break.

NOTE: If the air valve rod is restricting the vacuum diaphragm from seating it may be necessary to bend the air valve rod lightly to gain clearance. make an air valve rod adjustment after the vacuum break adjustment.

3. Read the angle gauge while lightly pushing on the intermediate choke lever so that the choke valve is toward the close position.
4. Use a 1/8 in. hex wrench and turn the screw in the rear cover until the bubble is centered. Apply a silicone sealant over the screw head to seal the setting.

Secondary vacuum break adjustment—1980 models

Secondary vacuum break adjustment—1981 and later GM A and X-body models

Rochester E2SE choke unloader adjustment—typical

Rochester E2SE choke unloader adjustment—1983 and later models

1983–84 GM MODELS

Refer to the illustration for the adjustment procedure on these models.

Choke Unloader Adjustment

THROUGH 1982

1. Follow Steps 1–4 of the "Fast Idle Cam Adjustment".
2. Install the choke cover and coil, if removed, aligning the marks on the housing and cover as specified.
3. Hold the primary throttle wide open.
4. If the engine is warm, close the choke valve by pushing in on the intermediate choke lever.
5. Bend the unloader tang until the bubble is centered.

1983–84 MODELS

Refer to the illustration for the adjustment procedure on these models.

2SE, E2SE CARBURETOR SPECIFICATIONS
American Motors

Year	Carburetor Identification	Float Level (in.)	Pump Rod (in.)	Fast Idle (rpm)	Choke Coil Lever (in.)	Fast Idle Cam (deg./in.)	Air Valve Rod (in.)	Primary Vacuum Break (deg./in.)	Choke Setting (notches)	Choke Unloader (deg./in.)	Secondary Lockout (in.)
'80	17080681	3/16	17/32	2400	.142	18/0.096	.018	20/.110	Fixed	32/.195	N.A.
	17080683	3/16	½	2400	.142	18/0.096	.018	20/.110	Fixed	32/.195	N.A.
	17080686	3/16	½	2600	.142	18/0.096	.018	20/.110	Fixed	32/.195	N.A.
	17080688	3/16	½	2600	.142	18/0.096	.018	20/.110	Fixed	32/.195	N.A.
'81	17081790	0.256	0.128	2600	0.085	25/0.142	.011	19/.103	Fixed	32/.195	0.065
	17081791	0.256	0.128	2400	0.085	25/0.142	.011	19/.103	Fixed	32/.195	0.065
	17081792	0.256	0.128	2400	0.085	25/0.142	.011	19/.103	Fixed	32/.195	0.065
	17081794	0.256	0.128	2600	0.085	25/0.142	.011	19/.103	Fixed	32/.195	0.065
	17081795	0.256	0.128	2600	0.085	25/0.142	.011	19/.103	Fixed	32/.195	0.065
	17081796	0.208	0.128	2400	0.065	25/0.142	.011	19/.103	Fixed	32/.195	0.065
	17081797	0.208	0.128	2600	0.085	25/0.142	.011	19/.103	Fixed	32/.195	0.085
	17081793	0.256	0.128	2400	0.085	25/0.142	.011	19/.103	Fixed	32/.195	0.065

2SE, E2SE CARBURETOR SPECIFICATIONS
American Motors

Year	Carburetor Identification	Float Level (in.)	Pump Rod (in.)	Fast Idle (rpm)	Choke Coil Lever (in.)	Fast Idle Cam (deg./in.)	Air Valve Rod (in.)	Primary Vacuum Break (deg./in.)	Choke Setting (notches)	Choke Unloader (deg./in.)	Secondary Lockout (in.)
'82	17082385	0.256	0.128	2400	0.085	18/.096	2①	21/.117	Fixed	34/.211	0.065
	17082383	0.256	0.128	2400	0.085	18/.096	2①	21/.117	Fixed	34/.211	0.065
	17082380	0.216	0.128	2400	0.085	18/.096	2①	21/.117	Fixed	34/.211	0.065
	17082386	0.125	0.128	2400	0.065	18/.096	2①	19/.103	Fixed	34/.211	0.065
	17082387	0.125	0.128	2600	0.085	18/.096	2①	19/.103	Fixed	34/.211	0.065
	17082388	0.125	0.128	2500	0.085	18/.096	2①	19/.103	Fixed	34/.211	0.065
	17082389	0.125	0.128	2500	0.085	18/.096	2①	19/.103	Fixed	34/.211	0.065
'83–'84	1982380	0.216②	0.128	2500③	0.085	18/.096	2①	21/.117	Fixed	34/.211	0.065
	1983384	0.138	0.128	2700	0.085	18/.096	2①	19/.103	Fixed	34/.211	0.065
	1983385	0.138	0.128	2500	0.085	18/.096	②①	19/.103	Fixed	34/.211	0.065

N.A.: Not Available
① Degrees—see procedure
② Auto. trans.—.138
③ Auto. trans.—2700

2SE, E2SE CARBURETOR SPECIFICATIONS
General Motors—U.S.A.

Year	Carburetor Identification	Float Level (in.)	Pump Rod (in.)	Fast Idle (rpm)	Choke Coil Lever (in.)	Fast Idle Cam (deg./in.)	Air Valve Rod (in.)	Primary Vacuum Break (deg./in.)	Choke Setting (notches)	Secondary Vacuum Break (deg./in.)	Choke Unloader (deg./in.)	Secondary Lockout (in.)
'79	17059674	13/64	1/2	2400	.120	18/0.096	.025	19/.103	2 Rich	—	32/.195	.030
	17059675	13/64	17/32	2200	.120	18/0.096	.025	21/.117	1 Rich	—	32/.195	.030
	17059676	13/64	1/2	2400	.120	18/0.096	.025	19/.103	2 Rich	—	32/.195	.030
	17059677	13/64	17/32	2200	.120	18/0.096	.025	21/.117	1 Rich	—	32/.195	.030
'80	17059614	3/16	1/2	2600	.085	18/.096	.025	17/.090	Fixed	—	36/.227	.120
	17059615	3/16	5/32	2600	.085	18/.096	.025	19/.103	Fixed	—	36/.227	.120
	17059616	3/16	1/2	2600	.085	18/.096	.025	17/.090	Fixed	—	36/.227	.120
	17059617	3/16	5/32	2600	.085	18/.096	.025	19/.103	Fixed	—	36/.227	.120
	17059618	3/16	1/2	2600	.085	18/.096	.025	17/.090	Fixed	—	36/.227	.120
	17059619	3/16	5/32	2600	.085	18/.096	.025	19/.103	Fixed	—	36/.227	.120
	17059620	3/16	1/2	2600	.085	18/.096	.025	17/.090	Fixed	—	36/.227	.120
	17059621	3/16	5/32	2600	.085	18/.096	.025	19/.103	Fixed	—	36/.227	.120
	17059650	3/16	3/32	2600	.085	27/.157	.025	30/.179	Fixed	38/.243	30/.179	.120
	17059651	3/16	3/32	1900	.085	27/.157	.025	22/.123	Fixed	23/.120	30/.179	.120
	17059652	3/16	3/32	2000	.085	27/.157	.025	30/.179	Fixed	38/.243	30/.179	.120
	17059653	3/16	3/32	1900	.085	27/.157	.025	22/.123	Fixed	23/.120	30/.179	.120
	17059714	11/16	5/32	2600	.085	18/.096	.025	23/.129	Fixed	—	32/.195	.120
	17059715	11/16	3/32	2200	.085	18/.096	.025	25/.142	Fixed	—	32/.195	.120

2SE, E2SE CARBURETOR SPECIFICATIONS
General Motors—U.S.A.

Year	Carburetor Identification	Float Level (in.)	Pump Rod (in.)	Fast Idle (rpm)	Choke Coil Lever (in.)	Fast Idle Cam (deg./in.)	Air Valve Rod (in.)	Primary Vacuum Break (deg./in.)	Choke Setting (notches)	Secondary Vacuum Break (deg./in.)	Choke Unloader (deg./in.)	Secondary Lockout (in.)
'80	17059716	11/16	5/32	2600	.085	18/.096	.025	23/.129	Fixed	—	32/.195	.120
	17059717	11/16	3/32	2200	.085	18/.096	.025	25/.142	Fixed	—	32/.195	.120
	17059760	1/8	5/64	2000	.085	17.5/.093	.025	20/.110	Fixed	33/.203	35/.220	.120
	17059762	1/8	5/64	2000	.085	17.5/.093	.025	20/.110	Fixed	33/.203	35/.220	.120
	17059763	1/8	5/64	2000	.085	17.5/.093	.025	20/.110	Fixed	33/.203	35/.220	.120
	17059774	5/32	1/2	①	.085	18/0.096	.018	19/.103	Fixed	—	32/.195	.012
	17059775	5/32	17/32	①	.085	18/0.096	.018	21/.117	Fixed	—	32/.195	.012
	17059776	5/32	1/2	①	.085	18/0.096	.018	19/.103	Fixed	—	32/.195	.012
	17059777	5/32	17/32	①	.085	18/0.096	.018	21/.117	Fixed	—	32/.195	.012
	17080674	3/16	1/2	①	.085	18/0.096	.018	19/.103	Fixed	—	32/.195	.012
	17080675	3/16	1/2	①	.085	18/0.096	.018	21/.117	Fixed	—	32/.195	.012
	17080676	3/16	1/2	①	.085	18/0.096	.018	19/.103	Fixed	—	32/.195	.012
	17080677	3/16	1/2	①	.085	18/0.096	.018	21/.117	Fixed	—	32/.195	.012
'81	17081650	1/4	Fixed	2600	.085	17/.090	1②	25/.142	Fixed	34/.211	35/.220	.012
	17081651	1/4	Fixed	2400	.085	17/.090	1②	29/.171	Fixed	35/.220	35/.220	.012
	17081652	1/4	Fixed	2600	.085	17/.090	1②	25/.142	Fixed	34/.211	35/.220	.012
	17081653	1/4	Fixed	2600	.085	17/.090	1②	29/.171	Fixed	35/.220	35/.220	.012
	17081670	5/32	Fixed	2600	.085	18/.096	1②	19/.103	Fixed	—	32/.195	.012
	17081671	5/32	Fixed	2600	.085	33.5/.207	1②	21/.117	Fixed	—	32/.195	.012
	17081672	5/32	Fixed	2600	.085	18/.096	1②	19/.103	Fixed	—	32/.195	.012
	17081673	5/32	Fixed	2600	.085	33.4/.207	1②	21/.117	Fixed	—	32/.195	.012
	17081740	1/4	Fixed	2400	.085	17/.090	1②	25/.142	Fixed	35/.220	35/.220	.012
	17081742	1/4	Fixed	2400	.085	17/.090	1②	25/.142	Fixed	35/.220	35/.220	.012
'82	17081600	5/16	Fixed	①	③	24/.136	1②	20/.110	Fixed	27/.157	35/.220	③
	17081601	5/16	Fixed	①	③	24/1.36	1②	20/.110	Fixed	27/.157	35/.220	③
	17081607	5/16	Fixed	①	③	24/.136	1②	20/.110	Choke	27/.157	35/.220	③
	17081700	5/16	Fixed	①	③	24/.136	1②	20/.110	Fixed	27/.157	35/.220	③
	17081701	5/16	Fixed	①	③	24/.136	1②	20/.110	Fixed	27/.157	35/.220	③
	17082196	5/16	Fixed	①	.085	18/.096	1②	21/.117	Fixed	19/.103	27/157	③
	17082316	1/4	Fixed	2600	.085	17/.090	1②	30/.179	Fixed	34/.211	45/.304	③
	17082317	1/4	Fixed	260	.085	17/.090	1②	30/.179	Fixed	35/.220	45/.304	③
	17082320	1/4	Fixed	2800	.085	25/.142	1②	30/.179	Fixed	35/.220	45/.304	③
	17082321	1/4	Fixed	2600	.085	25/.142	1②	30/.179	Fixed	35/.220	45/.304	③
	17082390	13/32	Fixed	2500	.085	17/.090	1②	26/.149	Fixed	34/.211	35/.220	.011–.040
	17082391	13/32	Fixed	2600	.085	25/.142	1②	29/.171	Fixed	35/.220	35/.220	.011–.040
	17082490	13/32	Fixed	2500	.085	17/.090	1②	26/.149	Fixed	34/.211	35/.220	.011–.040
	17082491	13/32	Fixed	2600	.085	25/.142	1②	29/.171	Fixed	35/.220	35/.220	.011–.040
	17082640	1/4	Fixed	2600	.085	17/.090	1②	30/.179	Fixed	34/.211	45/.304	③

2SE, E2SE CARBURETOR SPECIFICATIONS
General Motors—U.S.A.

Year	Carburetor Identification	Float Level (in.)	Pump Rod (in.)	Fast Idle (rpm)	Choke Coil Lever (in.)	Fast Idle Cam (deg./in.)	Air Valve Rod (in.)	Primary Vacuum Break (deg./in.)	Choke Setting (notches)	Secondary Vacuum Break (deg./in.)	Choke Unloader (deg./in.)	Secondary Lockout (in.)
'82	17082641	¼	Fixed	2400	.085	17/.090	1②	30/.179	Fixed	35/.220	45/.304	③
	17082642	¼	Fixed	2800	.085	25/.142	1②	30/.179	Fixed	35/.220	45/.304	③
'83	17083356	13/32	Fixed	①	.085	22/.123	1②	25/.142	Fixed	35/.220	30/.179	.025
	17083357	13/32	Fixed	①	.085	22/.123	1②	25/.142	Fixed	35/.220	30/.179	.025
	17083358	13/32	Fixed	①	.085	22/.123	1②	25/.142	Fixed	35/.220	30/.179	.025
	17083359	13/32	Fixed	①	.085	22/.123	1②	25/.142	Fixed	35/.220	30/.179	.025
	17083368	13/32	Fixed	①	.085	22/.123	1②	25/.142	Fixed	35/.220	30/.179	.025
	17083369	13/32	Fixed	①	.085	22/.123	1②	25/.142	Fixed	35/.220	30/.179	.025
	17083370	13/32	Fixed	①	.085	22/.123	1②	25/.142	Fixed	35/.220	30/.179	.025
	17083391	13/32	Fixed	①	.085	28/.164	1②	30/.179	Fixed	35/.220	38/.243	.025
	17083392	13/32	Fixed	①	.085	28/.164	1②	30/.179	Fixed	35/.220	38/.243	.025
	17083393	13/32	Fixed	①	.085	28/.164	1②	30/.179	Fixed	35/.220	38/.243	.025
	17083394	13/32	Fixed	①	.085	28/.164	1②	30/.179	Fixed	35/.220	38/.243	.025
	17083395	13/32	Fixed	①	.085	28/.164	1②	30/.179	Fixed	35/.220	38/.243	.025
	17083396	13/32	Fixed	①	.085	28/.164	1②	30/.179	Fixed	35/.220	38/.243	.025
	17083397	13/32	Fixed	①	.085	28/.164	1②	30/.179	Fixed	35/.220	38/.243	.025
	17083450	¼	Fixed	①	.085	28/.164	1②	27/.157	Fixed	35/.220	45/.304	.025
	17083451	¼	Fixed	①	.085	28/.164	1②	27/.157	Fixed	35/.220	45/.304	.025
	17083452	¼	Fixed	①	.085	28/.164	1②	27/.157	Fixed	35/.220	45/.304	.025
	17083453	¼	Fixed	①	.085	28/.164	1②	27/.157	Fixed	35/.220	45/.304	.025
	17083454	¼	Fixed	①	.085	28/.164	1②	27/.157	Fixed	35/.220	45/.304	.025
	17083455	¼	Fixed	①	.085	28/.164	1②	27/.157	Fixed	35/.220	45/.304	.025
	17083456	¼	Fixed	①	.085	28/.164	1②	27/.157	Fixed	35/.220	45/.304	.025
	17083630	¼	Fixed	①	.085	28/.164	1②	27/.157	Fixed	35/.220	45/.304	.025
	17083631	¼	Fixed	①	.085	28/.164	1②	27/.157	Fixed	35/.220	45/.304	.025
	17083632	¼	Fixed	①	.085	28/.164	1②	27/.157	Fixed	35/.220	45/.304	.025
	17083633	¼	Fixed	①	.085	28/.164	1②	27/.157	Fixed	35/.220	45/.304	.025
	17083634	¼	Fixed	①	.085	28/.164	1②	27/.157	Fixed	35/.220	45/.304	.025
	17083635	¼	Fixed	①	.085	28/.164	1②	27/.157	Fixed	35/.220	45/.304	.025
	17083636	¼	Fixed	①	.085	28/.164	1②	27/.157	Fixed	35/.220	45/.304	.025
'84	17072683	9/32	Fixed	①	.085	28/.164	1②	25/.142	Fixed	35/.220	45/.304	.025
	17074812	9/32	Fixed	①	.085	28/.164	1②	25/.142	Fixed	35/.220	45/.304	.025
	17084356	9/32	Fixed	①	.085	22/.123	1②	25/.142	Fixed	30/.179	30/.179	.025
	17084357	9/32	Fixed	①	.085	22/.123	1②	25/.142	Fixed	30/.179	30/.179	.025
	17084358	9/32	Fixed	①	.085	22/.123	1②	25/.142	Fixed	30/.179	30/.179	.025
	17084359	9/32	Fixed	①	.085	22/.123	1②	25/.142	Fixed	30/.179	30/.179	.025
	17084368	⅛	Fixed	①	.085	22/.123	1②	25/.142	Fixed	30/.179	30/.179	.025
	17084370	⅛	Fixed	①	.085	22/.123	1②	25/.142	Fixed	30/.179	30/.179	.025

2SE, E2SE CARBURETOR SPECIFICATIONS
General Motors—U.S.A.

Year	Carburetor Identification	Float Level (in.)	Pump Rod (in.)	Fast Idle (rpm)	Choke Coil Lever (in.)	Fast Idle Cam (deg./in.)	Air Valve Rod (in.)	Primary Vacuum Break (deg./in.)	Choke Setting (notches)	Choke Unloader (deg./in.)	Secondary Lockout (in.)
'84	17084430	$^{11}/_{32}$	Fixed	①	.085	15/.077	1②	26/.149	Fixed	30/.179	30/.179	.025
	17084431	$^{11}/_{32}$	Fixed	①	.085	15/.077	1②	26/.149	Fixed	38/.243	42/.277	.025
	17084434	$^{11}/_{32}$	Fixed	①	.085	15/.077	1②	26/.149	Fixed	38/.243	42/.277	.025
	17084435	$^{11}/_{32}$	Fixed	①	.085	15/.077	1②	26/.149	Fixed	38/.243	42/.277	.025
	17084452	$^{5}/_{32}$	Fixed	①	.085	28/.164	1②	25/.142	Fixed	38/.243	42/.277	.025
	17084453	$^{5}/_{32}$	Fixed	①	.085	28/.164	1②	25/.142	Fixed	35/.220	45/.304	.025
	17084455	$^{5}/_{32}$	Fixed	①	.085	28/.164	1②	25/.142	Fixed	35/.220	45/.304	.025
	17084456	$^{5}/_{32}$	Fixed	①	.085	28/.164	1②	25/.142	Fixed	35/.220	45/.304	.025
	17084458	$^{5}/_{32}$	Fixed	①	.085	28/.164	1②	25/.142	Fixed	35/.220	45/.304	.025
	17084532	$^{5}/_{32}$	Fixed	①	.085	28/.164	1②	25/.142	Fixed	35/.220	45/.304	.025
	17084534	$^{5}/_{32}$	Fixed	①	.085	28/.164	1②	25/.142	Fixed	35/.220	45/.304	.025
	17084535	$^{5}/_{32}$	Fixed	①	.085	28/.164	1②	25/.142	Fixed	35/.220	45/.304	.025
	17084537	$^{5}/_{32}$	Fixed	①	.085	28/.164	1②	25/.142	Fixed	35/.220	45/.304	.025
	17084538	$^{5}/_{32}$	Fixed	①	.085	28/.164	1②	25/.142	Fixed	35/.220	45/.304	.025
	17084540	$^{5}/_{32}$	Fixed	①	.085	28/.164	1②	25/.142	Fixed	35/.220	45/.304	.025
	17084542	$^{1}/_{8}$	Fixed	①	.085	28/.164	1②	25/.142	Fixed	35/.220	45/.304	.025
	17084632	$^{9}/_{32}$	Fixed	①	.085	28/.164	1②	25/.142	Fixed	35/.220	45/.304	.025
	17084633	$^{9}/_{32}$	Fixed	①	.085	28/.164	1②	25/.142	Fixed	35/.220	45/.304	.025
	17084635	$^{9}/_{32}$	Fixed	①	.085	28/.164	1②	25/.142	Fixed	35/.220	45/.304	.025
	17084636	$^{9}/_{32}$	Fixed	①	.085	28/.164	1②	25/.142	Fixed	35/.220	45/.304	.025

① See underhood decal
② Measurement in degrees
③ Not available

2SE, E2SE CARBURETOR SPECIFICATIONS
General Motors—Canada

Year	Carburetor Identification	Float Level (In.)	Pump Rod (in.)	Fast Idle (rpm)	Choke Coil Lever (in.)	Fast Idle Cam (deg./in.)	Air Valve Rod (deg.)	Primary Vacuum Break (deg./in.)	Choke Setting (notches)	Secondary Vacuum Break (deg./in.)	Choke Unloader (deg./in.)	Secondary Lockout (in.)
'81	17059660	$^{1}/_{4}$	$^{17}/_{32}$	①	.085	24/.136	1	30/.179	Fixed	32/.195	30/.179	②
	17059662	$^{1}/_{4}$	$^{17}/_{32}$	①	.085	24/.136	1	30/.179	Fixed	37/.195	30/.179	②
	17059651	$^{1}/_{4}$	$^{17}/_{32}$	①	.085	24/.136	1	30/.179	Fixed	32/.195	30/.179	②
	17059666	$^{1}/_{4}$	$^{17}/_{32}$	①	.085	24/.136	1	26/.149	Fixed	32/.195	30/.179	②
	17059667	$^{1}/_{4}$	$^{17}/_{32}$	①	.085	24/.136	1	26/.149	Fixed	32/.195	30/.179	②
	17059622	$^{5}/_{32}$	$^{17}/_{32}$	①	.085	18/.096	1	17/.090	Fixed	—	36/.227	②
	17059623	$^{5}/_{32}$	$^{17}/_{32}$	①	.085	18/.096	1	19/.103	Fixed	—	36/.227	②
	17059624	$^{5}/_{32}$	$^{17}/_{32}$	①	.085	18/.096	1	17/.090	Fixed	—	36/.227	②

2SE, E2SE CARBURETOR SPECIFICATIONS
General Motors—Canada

Year	Carburetor Identification	Float Level (In.)	Pump Rod (in.)	Fast Idle (rpm)	Choke Coil Lever (in.)	Fast Idle Cam (deg./in.)	Air Valve Rod (deg.)	Primary Vacuum Break (deg./in.)	Choke Setting (notches)	Secondary Vacuum Break (deg./in.)	Choke Unloader (deg./in.)	Secondary Lockout (in.)
'82	17082440	1/4	19/32	①	.085	24/.136	1	30/.179	Fixed	32/.195	45/.304	②
	17082441	1/4	19/32	①	.085	24/.136	1	30/.179	Fixed	32/.195	45/.304	②
	17082443	1/4	19/32	①	.085	24/.136	1	30/.179	Fixed	32/.195	45/.304	②
	17082460	1/4	19/32	①	.085	18/.096	1	21/.117	Fixed	—	36/.227	②
	17082461	1/4	19/32	①	.085	18/.096	1	21/.117	Fixed	—	36/.227	②
	17082462	1/4	19/32	①	.085	18/.096	1	21/.117	Fixed	—	36/.227	②
	17082464	1/8	19/32	①	.085	18/.096	1	21/.117	Fixed	—	36/.227	②
	17082465	1/8	19/32	①	.085	18/.096	1	21/.117	Fixed	—	36/.227	②
	17082466	1/8	19/32	①	.085	18/.096	1	21/.117	Fixed	—	36/.227	②
	17082620	7/16	19/32	①	.085	24/.136	1	30/.179	Fixed	32/.195	45/.304	②
	17082621	7/16	19/32	①	.085	24/.136	1	30/.179	Fixed	32/.195	45/.304	②
	17082622	7/16	19/32	①	.085	24/.136	1	30/.179	Fixed	32/.195	45/.304	②
	17082623	7/16	19/32	①	.085	24/.136	1	30/.179	Fixed	32/.195	45/.304	②
'83	17083311	5/16	Fixed	①	.085	24/.136	1	18/.096	Fixed	20/.110	35/.220	.025
	17083401	5/16	Fixed	①	.085	24/.136	1	18/.096	Fixed	20/.110	35/.220	.025
	17083440	1/4	19/32	①	.085	24/.136	1	28/.164	Fixed	32/.195	40/.260	.025
	17083441	1/4	19/32	①	.085	24/.136	1	28/ 164	Fixed	32/.195	40/.260	.025
	17083442	1/4	19/32	①	.085	24/.136	1	28/.164	Fixed	32/.195	40/.260	.025
	17083443	1/4	19/32	①	.085	24/.136	1	28/.164	Fixed	32/.195	40/.260	.025
	17083444	1/4	19/32	①	.085	24/.136	1	28/.164	Fixed	32/.195	40/.260	.025
	17083445	1/4	19/32	①	.085	24/.136	1	28/.164	Fixed	32/.195	40/.260	.025
	17083460	1/4	19/32	①	.085	18/.096	1	19/.103	Fixed	—	36/.227	.025
	17083461	1/4	19/32	①	.085	18/.096	1	18/.096	Fixed	—	36/.227	.025
	17083462	1/4	19/32	①	.085	18/.096	1	19/.103	Fixed	—	36/.227	.025
	17083464	1/8	19/32	①	.085	18/.096	1	19/.103	Fixed	—	36/.227	.025
	17083465	1/8	19/32	①	.085	18/.096	1	20/.110	Fixed	—	36/.227	.025
	17083466	1/8	19/32	①	.085	18/.096	1	19/.103	Fixed	—	36/.227	.025
	17083620	7/16	19/32	①	.085	24/.136	1	28/.164	Fixed	32/.195	40/.260	.025
	17083621	7/16	19/32	①	.085	24/.136	1	28/.164	Fixed	32/.195	40/.260	.025
	17083622	7/16	19/32	①	.085	24/.136	1	28/.164	Fixed	34/.195	40/.260	.025
	17083623	7/16	19/32	①	.085	24/.136	1	28/.164	Fixed	32/.195	40/.260	.025
'84	17084312	5/16	Fixed	①	.085	24/.136	1	18/.096	Fixed	20/.110	35/.220	.025
	17084314	5/16	Fixed	①	.085	29/.171	1	16/.083	Fixed	20/.110	30/.179	.025
	17084480	1/4	Fixed	①	.085	24/.136	1	28/.164	Fixed	32/.195	45/.304	.025
	17084481	1/4	Fixed	①	.085	24/.136	1	28/.164	Fixed	32/.195	45/.304	.025
	17084482	1/4	Fixed	①	.085	24/.136	1	28/.164	Fixed	32/.195	45/.304	.025
	17084483	1/4	Fixed	①	.085	24/.136	1	28/.164	Fixed	32/.195	45/.304	.025
	17084484	1/4	Fixed	①	.085	24/.136	1	28/.164	Fixed	32/.195	45/.304	.025

2SE, E2SE CARBURETOR SPECIFICATIONS
General Motors—Canada

Year	Carburetor Identification	Float Level (In.)	Pump Rod (in.)	Fast Idle (rpm)	Choke Coil Lever (in.)	Fast Idle Cam (deg./in.)	Air Valve Rod (deg.)	Primary Vacuum Break (deg./in.)	Choke Setting (notches)	Secondary Vacuum Break (deg./in.)	Choke Unloader (deg./in.)	Secondary Lockout (in.)
'84	17084485	¼	Fixed	①	.085	24/.136	1	28/.164	Fixed	32/.195	45/.304	.025
	17084486	¼	Fixed	①	.085	24/.136	1	28/.164	Fixed	32/.195	45/.304	.025
	17084487	¼	Fixed	①	.085	24/.136	1	28/.164	Fixed	32/.195	45/.304	.025
	17084620	⁷⁄₁₆	Fixed	①	.085	24/.136	1	26/.149	Fixed	32/.195	45/.304	.025
	17084621	⁷⁄₁₆	Fixed	①	.085	24/.136	1	26/.149	Fixed	32/.195	45/.304	.025
	17084622	⁷⁄₁₆	Fixed	①	.085	24/.136	1	26/.149	Fixed	32/.195	45/.304	.025
	17084623	⁷⁄₁₆	Fixed	①	.085	24/.136	1	26/.149	Fixed	32/.195	45/.304	.025

① See underhood decal
② Not available

Secondary Lockout Adjustment

1. Pull the choke wide open by pushing out on the intermediate choke lever.
2. Open the throttle until the end of the secondary actuating lever is opposite the toe of the lockout lever.
3. Gauge clearance between the lockout lever and secondary lever should be as specified.
4. To adjust, bend the lockout lever where it contacts the fast idle cam.

Model E2ME Carburetor

The Dualjet E2ME Model 210 is a variation of the M2ME, modified for use with the Electronic Fuel Control System (also called the Computer Controlled Catalytic Converter, or C-4, System). An electrically operated mixture control solenoid is mounted in the float bowl. Mixture is thus controlled by the Electronic Control Module, in response to signals from the oxygen sensor mounted in the exhaust system upstream of the catalytic converter.

ADJUSTMENTS

Float Level Adjustment

See the illustration for float level adjustment for all carburetors.

The E2ME procedure is the same except for adjustment (step 4 in the figure). For the E2ME only, if the float level is too high, hold the retainer firmly in place and push down on the center of the float to adjust.

If the float level is too low on the E2ME, lift out the metering rods. Remove the solenoid connector screws. Turn the lean mixture

Secondary vacuum break adjustment—1983 and later models

Typical float level adjustment on Rochester E2ME and M2ME models

Checking float level on the car with external float gauge

Fast idle speed adjustment—Rochester E2ME and M2ME models

Typical choke coil lever adjustment

Fast idle cam (choke rod) adjustment—typical

Rear vacuum break adjustment—1981-82 E2ME models

Front vacuum break adjustment—1981-82 models

solenoid screw in clockwise, counting the exact number of turns until the screw is lightly bottomed in the bowl. Then turn the screw out counterclockwise and remove it. Lift out the solenoid and connector. Remove the float and bend the arm up to adjust. Install the parts, installing the mixture solenoid screw in until it is lightly bottomed, the turning it out the exact number of turns counted earlier.

Fast Idle Speed

1. Place the fast idle lever on the high step of the fast idle cam.
2. Turn the fast idle screw out until the throttle valves are closed.
3. Turn the screw in to contact the lever, then turn it in the number of turns listed in the specifications. Check this preliminary setting against the sticker figure.

Fast Idle Cam (Choke Rod) Adjustment

1. Adjust the fast idle speed.
2. Place the cam follower lever on the second step of the fast idle cam, holding it firmly against the rise of the high step.
3. Close the choke valve by pushing upward on the choke coil

lever inside the choke housing, or by pushing up on the vacuum break lever tang.
4. Gauge between the upper edge of the choke valve and the inside of the air horn wall.
5. Bend the tang on the fast idle cam to adjust.

Choke Coil Lever Adjustment

1. Remove the choke cover and thermostatic coil from the choke housing. On models with a fixed choke cover, drill out the rivets and remove the cover. A stat cover kit will be required for assembly.
2. Push up on the coil tang (counterclockwise) until the choke valve is closed. The top of the choke rod should be at the bottom of the slot in the choke valve lever. Place the fast idle cam follower on the high step of the cam.
3. Insert a 0.120 in. plug gauge in the hole in the choke housing.
4. The lower edge of the choke coil lever should just contact the side of the plug gauge.
5. Bend the choke rod to adjust.

Front/Rear Vacuum Break Adjustment
1978-80 MODELS

1. Seat the front diaphragm, using an outside vacuum source. If there is an air bleed hole on the diaphragm, tape it over.
2. Remove the choke cover and coil. Rotate the inside coil lever counter-clockwise. On models with a fixed choke cover (riveted), push up on the vacuum break lever tang and hold it in position with a rubber band.
3. Check that the specified gap is present between the top of the choke valve and the air horn wall.
4. Turn the front vacuum break adjusting screw to adjust.

5. To adjust the rear vacuum break diaphragm, perform Steps 1-3 on the rear diaphragm, but make sure that the plunger bucking spring is compressed and seated in Step 2. Adjust by bending the link at the bend nearest the diaphragm.

1981-84 MODELS

On these models a choke valve measuring gauge J-26701 or equivalent is used to measure angle (degrees instead of inches). See illustration for procedure.

Unloader Adjustment

1. With the choke valve completely closed, hold the throttle valves wide open.

2. Measure between the upper edge of the choke valve and air horn wall.

3. Bend the tang on the fast idle lever to obtain the proper measurement.

Typical choke unloader adjustment

Mixture Control Solenoid Plunger Adjustments

1. Remove air horn, mixture control solenoid plunger, air horn gasket and plastic filler block, using normal service procedures.

2. Check carburetor for cause of incorrect mixture:

   a. M/C solenoid bore or plunger worn or sticking.

   b. Metering rods for incorrect part number, sticking, or rods or springs not installed properly.

   c. Foreign material in jets.

3. Remove throttle side metering rod. Install mixture control solenoid gaging tool, J-33815-1, BT-8253-A or equivalent, over the throttle side metering jet rod guide, and temporarily reinstall the solenoid plunger into the solenoid body.

4. Holding the solenoid plunger in the DOWN position, use Tool J-28696-10, BT-7928, or equivalent, to turn lean mixture (solenoid) screw counterclockwise until the plunger breaks contact with the gaging tool. Turn slowly clockwise until the plunger makes contact with the gaging tool. The adjustment is correct when the solenoid plunger is contacting BOTH the SOLENOID STOP and the GAGING TOOL

NOTE: If the total difference in adjustment required less than 3/4 turn of the lean mixture (solenoid) screw, the original setting was within the manufacturer's specifications.

5. Remove solenoid plunger and gaging tool, and reinstall metering rod and plastic filler block.

6. Invert air horn, and remove rich mixture stop screw from bottom side of air horn, using Tool J-28696-4, BT7967 A or equivalent.

7. Remove lean mixture screw plug and the rich mixture stop screw plug from air horn, using a suitable sized punch.

8. Reinstall rich mixture stop screw in air horn and bottom lightly, then back screw out 1/4 turn.

9. Reinstall air horn gasket, mixture control solenoid plunger and air horn to carburetor.

10. Adjust M/C Solenoid Plunger travel.

   a. Insert float gage down "D" shaped vent hole. Press down on gage and release, observing that the gage moves freely and does not bind. With gage released, (plunger UP position), read

① ATTACH RUBBER BAND TO GREEN TANG OF INTERMEDIATE CHOKE SHAFT

② OPEN THROTTLE TO ALLOW CHOKE VALVE TO CLOSE

③ SET UP ANGLE GAGE AND SET TO SPECIFICATION

④ RETRACT VACUUM BREAK PLUNGER USING VACUUM SOURCE, AT LEAST 18" HG. PLUG AIR BLEED HOLES WHERE APPLICABLE
ON QUADRAJETS, AIR VALVE ROD MUST NOT RESTRICT PLUNGER FROM RETRACTING FULLY. IF NECESSARY, BEND ROD (SEE ARROW) TO PERMIT FULL PLUNGER TRAVEL. FINAL ROD CLEARANCE MUST BE SET AFTER VACUUM BREAK SETTING HAS BEEN MADE.

⑤ WITH AT LEAST 18" HG STILL APPLIED, ADJUST SCREW TO CENTER BUBBLE

Front vacuum break adjustment—1983 and later E2ME models

① ATTACH RUBBER BAND TO GREEN TANG OF INTERMEDIATE CHOKE SHAFT.

② OPEN THROTTLE TO ALLOW CHOKE VALVE TO CLOSE.

③ SET UP ANGLE GAGE AND SET ANGLE TO SPECIFICATION.

④ RETRACT VACUUM BREAK PLUNGER, USING VACUUM SOURCE, AT LEAST 18" HG. PLUG AIR BLEED HOLES WHERE APPLICABLE.

④A ON QUADRAJETS, AIR VALVE ROD MUST NOT RESTRICT PLUNGER FROM RETRACTING FULLY. IF NECESSARY, BEND ROD HERE TO PERMIT FULL PLUNGER TRAVEL. WHERE APPLICABLE, PLUNGER STEM MUST BE EXTENDED FULLY TO COMPRESS PLUNGER BUCKING SPRING.

⑤ TO CENTER BUBBLE, EITHER:
A. ADJUST WITH 1/8" HEX WRENCH (VACUUM STILL APPLIED)
-OR-
B. SUPPORT AT "S" AND BEND VACUUM BREAK ROD (VACUUM STILL APPLIED)

Rear vacuum break adjustment—1983 and later E2ME models

Adjusting lean mixture solenoid screw—E2ME models

2MC, M2MC, M2ME, E2ME CARBURETOR SPECIFICATIONS
General Motors—U.S.A.

Year	Carburetor Identification ①	Flat Level (in.)	Choke Rod (in.)	Choke Unloader (in.)	Vacuum Break Lean or Front (deg./in.)	Vacuum Break Rich or Rear (deg./in.)	Pump Rod (in.)	Choke Coil Lever (in.)	Automatic Choke (notches)
'78	All Chev.	¼	.314	.314	.136	—	9/32 ②	.120	Index
	17058150, 152	3/8	.065	.203	.203	.133	¼ ②	.120	2 Rich
	17058151, 156, 158	3/8	.065	.203	.229	.133	11/32 ③	.120	2 Rich
	17058154, 155	3/8	.071	.220	.157	.260	11/32 ③	.120	2 Rich
	17058160 Buick	11/32	.133	.220	.149	.227	¼ ②	.120	2 Lean
	17058160 Pontiac	11/32	.126	.203	.142	.195	¼ ②	.120	2 Rich
	17058192	¼	.074	.350	.117	.103	9/32 ②	.120	1 Rich
	17058450	3/8	.065	.203	.146	.289	11/32 ③	.120	2 Rich
	17058496	¼	.077	.243	.136	.211	3/8 ③	.120	1 Rich
'79	17059134, 135, 136, 137	11/32	.243	.243	.157	—	9/32 ②	.120	1 Lean
	17059150, 152	3/8	.065	.203	.203	.133	¼ ②	.120	2 Rich
	17059151	3/8	.071	.220	.243	.142	11/32 ③	.120	2 Rich
	17059154	3/8	.071	.220	.157	.260	11/32 ③	.120	2 Rich
	17059160	11/32	.110	.195	.129	.187	¼ ②	.120	2 Rich
	17059180, 190, 191	11/32	.039	.243	.103	.090	¼ ②	.120	2 Rich
	17059193	5/16	.139	.243	.117	.187	Fixed	.120	Fixed
	17059194	5/16	.139	.243	.117	.179	Fixed	.120	Fixed
	17059196	5/16	.139	.243	.164	.136	Fixed	.120	Fixed
	17059430, 432	9/32	.243	.243	.157	—	¼ ②	.120	1 Lean
	17059434, 436	13/32	.243	.243	.171	—	¼ ②	.120	1 Lean
	17059492, 493	11/32	.139	.277	.129	.117	9/32 ②	.120	1 Rich
'80	17080108, 110 17080130, 131	3/8	.243	.243	.142	—	5/16 ②	.120	Fixed
	17080132, 133, 147, 148, 149	5/16	.243	.243	.142	—	5/16 ②	.120	Fixed
	17080138, 140 17080150, 152, 153	3/8 3/8	.243 .071	.243 .220	.142 .243	— .157	5/16 ② 11/32 ③	.120 .120	Fixed Fixed
	17080160	5/16	.110	.243	.168	.207	¼ ②	.120	Fixed
	17080190, 192	9/32	.074	.243	.123	.110	¼ ②	.120	Fixed
	17080191	11/32	.139	.243	.096	.096	¼ ②	.120	Fixed
	17080195, 197	9/32	.139	.243	.103	.071	¼ ②	.120	Fixed
	17080490, 492	5/16	.139	.243	.117	.203	¼ ②	.120	Fixed
	17080491	5/16	.139	.243	.117	.220	¼ ②	.120	Fixed
	17080493, 495	5/16	.139	.243	.117	.179	3/8	.120	Fixed

17080454

2MC, M2MC, M2ME, E2ME CARBURETOR SPECIFICATIONS
General Motors—U.S.A.

Year	Carburetor Identification①	Flat Level (in.)	Choke Rod (in.)	Choke Unloader (in.)	Vacuum Break Lean or Front (deg./in.)	Vacuum Break Rich or Rear (deg./in.)	Pump Rod (in.)	Choke Coil Lever (in.)	Automatic Choke (notches)
'80	17080494	5/16	.139	.243	.117	.179	1/4②	.120	Fixed
	17080496, 498	5/16	.139	.243	.117	.203	Fixed	.120	Fixed
'81	17080185, 187	9/32	.139	.243	19/.103	14/.071	1/4②	.120	Fixed
	17080191	11/32	.139	.243	18/.096	18/.096	1/4②	.120	Fixed
	17081130, 131, 132, 133	11/32	.110	.243	25/.142	—	Fixed	.120	Fixed
	17081138, 140	11/32	.110	.260	25/.142	—	Fixed	.120	Fixed
	17081150, 152	13/32	.071	.220	24/.136	36/.227	Fixed	.120	Fixed
	17081160	11/32	.074	.220	24/.136	37/.234	④	.120	Fixed
	17081196	5/16	.139	.243	28/.164	24/.136	④	.120	Fixed
	17081190, 193	5/16	.139	.243	21/.117	31/.187	Fixed	.120	Fixed
	17081191, 194	5/16	.139	.243	28/.164	24/.136	④	.120	Fixed
	17081198	3/8	.139	.243	28/.164	24/.136	④	.120	Fixed
	17081192, 197	5/16	.139	.243	21/.117	30/.179	④	.120	Fixed
	17081199	3/8	.096	.243	18/.096	24/.136	Fixed	.120	Fixed
'82	17082130, 132, 138, 140	3/8	.110	.164	27/.157	—	④	④	Fixed
	17082150	13/32	.071	.220	24/.136	38/.243⑤	④	④	Fixed
	17082182, 184	5/16	.096	.195	28/.164	24/.136	④	④	Fixed
	17082192, 194	5/16	.096	.195	28/.164	24/.136	④	④	Fixed
	17082196	5/16	.096	.157	21/.117	19/.103	④	④	Fixed
	17082497	5/16	.113	.195	28/.164	24/.136	④	.120	Fixed
'83	17082130, 132	3/8	.110	.243	27/.157	—	④	.120	Fixed
	17083190, 192	5/16	.096	.195	28/.164	24/.136	④	.120	Fixed
	17083193	5/16	.090	.157	23/.129	28/.164	④	.120	Fixed
	17083194	5/16	.090	.220	27/.157	25/.142	④	.120	Fixed
'84	17082130	3/8	.110	.243	27/.157	None	④	.120	Fixed
	17082132	3/8	.110	.243	27/.157	None	④	.120	Fixed
	17084191	5/16	.096	.195	28/.164	24/.136	④	.120	Fixed
	17084193	5/16	.090	.220	27/.157	25/.142	④	.120	Fixed
	17084194	5/16	.090	.220	27/.157	25/.142	④	.120	Fixed
	17084195	5/16	.090	.220	27/.157	25/.142	④	.120	Fixed

① The carburetor identification number is stamped on the float bowl, next to the fuel inlet nut.
② Inner hole
③ Outer hole
④ Not Adjustable
⑤ High altitude—0.206

2MC, M2MC, M2ME, E2ME CARBURETOR SPECIFICATIONS
General Motors—Canada

Year	Carburetor Identification ①	Float Level (in.)	Choke Rod (in.)	Choke Unloader (in.)	Vacuum Break Lean or Front (deg./in.)	Vacuum Break Rich or Rear (deg./in.)	Pump Rod (in.)	Choke Coil Lever (in.)	Automatic Choke (notches)
'81	17080191	11/32	.139	.243	18/.096	18/.096	1/4 ②	.120	Fixed
	17081492	9/32	.139	.243	17/.090	19/.103	1/4 ②	.120	Fixed
	17081493	9/32	.139	.243	17/.090	19/.103	1/4 ②	.120	Fixed
	17081170	13/32	.110	.243	25/.142	—	1/4 ②	.120	Fixed
	17081171	13/32	.110	.243	25/.142	—	1/4 ②	.120	Fixed
	17081174	9/32	.110	.243	25/.142	—	1/4 ②	.120	Fixed
	17081175	9/32	.110	.243	25/.142	—	1/4 ②	.120	Fixed
'82	17082174	9/32	.110	.243	25/.142	—	5/16 ②	.120	Fixed
	17082175	9/32	.110	.243	25/.142	—	5/16 ②	.120	Fixed
	17082492	9/32	.139	.243	17/.090	19/.103	1/4 ②	.120	Fixed
	17082172	9/32	.110	.243	25/.142	—	5/16 ②	.120	Fixed
	17082173	9/32	.110	.243	25/.142	—	5/16 ②	.120	Fixed
'83–'84	17083172	9/32	.139	.243	17/.090	19/.103	1/4 ②	.120	Fixed

① The carburetor identification number is stamped on the float bowl, next to the fuel inlet nut.
② Inner hole

at eye level and record the reading of the gage mark (in inches) that lines up with the top of air horn casting, (upper edge).

b. Lightly press down on gage until bottomed, (plunger DOWN position). Read and record (in inches) the reading of the gage mark that lines up with top of air horn casting.

c. Subtract gage UP position (Step 1) from gage DOWN position (Step 2), and record difference. This difference is total plunger travel. Insert external float gage in vent hole and, with Tool J-28696-10, BT-7928, or equivalent, adjust rich mixture stop screw to obtain 4/32 in. total plunger travel.

11. With solenoid plunger travel correctly set, install plugs (supplied in service kits) in the air horn, as follows:

a. Install plug, hollow end down, into the access hole to lean mixture (solenoid) screw, and use suitably sized punch to drive plug into the air horn until the top of plug is even with the lower.

Plug must be installed to retain the screw setting and to prevent fuel vapor loss.

b. Install plug, with hollow end down, over the rich mixture stop screw access hole, and drive plug into place so that the top of the plug is 1/16 in. below the surface of the air horn casting.

NOTE: Plug must be installed to retain screw setting.

12. To check the M/C solenoid dwell, first disconnect vacuum line to the canister purge valve and plug it. Ground diagnostic "test" terminal and run engine until it is at normal operation temperature (upper radiator hose hot) and in closed loop.

13. Check M/C dwell at 3000 RPM. If within 10°–50°, calibration is complete. If higher than 50°, check carburetor for cause of rich condition. If below 10°, look for cause of lean engine condition such as vacuum leaks. If none found, check for cause of lean carburetor.

Location of rich and lean mixture stop screws—E2ME models

Adjusting rich mixture stop screw—E2ME models

Idle Mixture and Speed Adjustment

A cover is in place over the idle air bleed valve, and the access holes to the idle mixture needles are sealed with hardened plugs, to seal the factory settings, during original equipment production. These items are NOT to be removed unless required for cleaning, part replacement, improper dwell readings, or if the System Performance Check indicates the carburetor is the cause of the trouble.

Remove the idle air bleed cover. A missing cover indicates that the idle air bleed valve setting has been changed from its original factory setting. With cover removed, look for presence (or absence) of a letter identification on top of idle air bleed valve.

If no identifying letter appears on top of the valve, begin Procedure A, below. If the valve is identified with a letter, begin Procedure B.

PROCEDURE A (NO LETTER ON IDLE AIR BLEED VALVE)

Carburetors WITHOUT letter identification on the idle air bleed valve are adjusted by presetting the idle air bleed valve to a gage dimension if the valve was serviced prior to on-vehicle adjustment. Install idle air bleed valve gaging Tool J-33815-2, BT-8253-B, or equivalent, in throttle side "D" shaped vent hole in the air horn casting. The upper end of the tool should be positioned over the open cavity next to the idle air bleed valve.

While holding the gaging tool down lightly, so that the solenoid plunger is against the solenoid stop, adjust the idle air bleed valve so that the gaging tool will pivot over and just contact the top of the valve. The valve is now preset for on-vehicle adjustment. Remove gaging tool.

1. Disconnect the vacuum hose from the canister purge valve and plug it.
2. Start engine and allow it to reach normal operating temperature.
3. While idling in Drive (Neutral for manual transmission), use a screwdriver to slowly turn the valve counterclockwise or clockwise, until the dwell reading varies within the 25-35° range, attempting to be as close to 30° as possible.

NOTE: Perform this step carefully. The air bleed valve is very sensitive and should be turned in 1/8 turn increments only.

4. If, after performing Steps b and c above, the dwell reading does not vary and is not with the 25-35° range, it will be necessary to remove the plugs and to adjust the idle mixture needles.

Idle Mixture Needle Plug Removal

1. Remove the carburetor from the engine, following normal service procedures, to gain access to the plugs covering the idle mixture needles.
2. Invert carburetor and drain fuel into a suitable container.

─────────────CAUTION─────────────

Take precautions to avoid the risk of fire. Do not smoke.

3. Place carburetor on a suitable holding fixture, with manifold side up. Use care to avoid damaging linkage, tubes, and parts protruding from air horn.
4. Make two parallel cuts in the throttle body, one on each side of the locator points beneath the idle mixture needle plug (manifold side), with a hacksaw.

NOTE: The cuts should reach down to the steel plug, but should not extend more than 1/8 in. beyond the locator points. The distance between the saw cuts depends on the size of the punch to be used.

5. Place a flat punch near the ends of the saw marks in the throttle body. Hold the punch at a 45° angle and drive it into the throttle body until the casting breaks away, exposing the steel plug. The hardened plug will break, rather than remaining intact. It is not necessary to remove the plug in one piece, but remove the loose pieces.

Installing lean and rich mixture stop screw plugs on E2ME models

Removing idle mixture plugs—E2ME models

6. Repeat this procedure with the other mixture needle.

Setting the Idle Mixture Needles

1. Using Tool J-29030, BT-7610B, or equivalent, turn both idle mixture needles clockwise until they are lightly seated, then turn each mixture needle counterclockwise the number of turns specified in an applicable manufacturer's specifications.
2. Reinstall carburetor on engine using a new flange mounting gasket, but do not install air cleaner and gasket at this time.
3. Readjust the idle air bleed valve to finalize correct dwell reading.
4. Start engine and run until fully warm, and repeat the idle air bleed valve adjustment.
5. If unable to set dwell to 25–35°, and the dwell is below 25°, turn both mixture needles counterclockwise an additional turn. If dwell is above 35°, turn both mixture needles clockwise an additional turn. Readjust idle air bleed valve to obtain dwell limits.
6. After adjustments are complete, seal the idle mixture needle openings in the throttle body, using silicone sealant, RTV rubber, or equivalent. The sealer is required to discourage unnecessary adjustment of the setting, and to prevent fuel vapor loss in that area.

7. On vehicles without a carburetor-mounted Idle Speed Control or Idle Load Compensator, adjust curb idle speed if necessary.

8. Check, and only if necessary adjust, fast idle speed as described on Vehicle Emission Control Information label.

PROCEDURE B (LETTER APPEARS ON IDLE AIR BLEED VALVE)

Carburetors WITH letter identification on the idle air bleed valve are adjusted by installing air bleed valve gaging tool J-33815-2, BT-8253-B, or equivalent, in throttle side "D" shaped vent hole in the air horn casting. The upper end of the tool should be positioned over the open cavity next to the idle air bleed valve. While holding the gaging tool down lightly, so that the solenoid plunger is

Correct installation of idle air bleed valve gauging tool

Positioning idle air bleed valve—E2ME models

against the solenoid stop, adjust the idle air bleed valve so that the gaging tool will pivot over and just contact the top of the valve. The valve is now set properly. No further adjustment of the valve is necessary. Remove gaging tool.

Adjusting the Idle Mixture Needles

1. Remove idle mixture needle plugs, following instructions in PROCEDURE A.

2. Using Tool J-29030-B, BT-7610-B, or equivalent, turn each idle mixture needle clockwise until lightly seated, then turn each mixture needle counterclockwise 3 turns.

3. Reinstall carburetor on engine, using a new flange mounting gasket, but do not install air cleaner or gasket at this time.

4. Disconnect vacuum hose to canister purge valve and plug it.

5. Start engine and allow it to reach normal operating temperature.

6. While idling in Drive (Neutral for manual transmission), adjust both mixture needles equally, in 1/8 turn increments, until dwell reading varies within the 25–35° range, attempting to be as close to 30° as possible.

7. If reading is too low, turn mixture needles counterclockwise. If reading is too high, turn mixture needles clockwise. Allow time for dwell reading to stabilize after each adjustment.

NOTE: After adjustments are complete, seal the idle mixture needle openings in the throttle body, using silicone sealant, RTV rubber, or equivalent. The sealer is required to discourage unnecessary readjustment of the setting, and to prevent fuel vapor loss in that area.

8. On vehicles without a carburetor-mounted Idle Speed Control or Idle Load Compensator, adjust curb idle speed if necessary.

9. Check, and if necessary, adjust fast idle speed, as described on the Vehicle Emission Control Information label.

THROTTLE POSITION SENSOR (TPS)

The plug covering the TPS adjustment screw is used to provide a tamper-resistant design and retain the factory setting during vehicle operation. Do not remove the plug unless diagnosis indicates the TPS Sensor is not adjusted correctly, or it is necessary to replace the air horn assembly, float bowl, TPS, or TPS adjustment screw. This is a critical adjustment that must be performed accurately to ensure proper vehicle performance and control of exhaust emissions. Remove TPS plug if not already removed.

TPS Plug Removal

1. Using a 5/64 in. drill, drill a 1/16 in. to 1/8 in. deep hole in aluminum plug covering TPS adjustment screw. Use care in drilling to prevent damage to adjustment screw head.

2. Start a No. 8, 1/2 in. long self-tapping screw in drilled hole

Removing throttle position sensor (TPS) adjustment plug

THROTTLE POSITION SWITCH ADJUSTMENT SPECIFICATIONS

Year	Engine	Carburetor	Throttle Position		Voltage
'80–'85	All	E2SE	Curb Idle		.26
'80–'84	8,Y,A,9	E2ME, E4ME	Curb Idle High Step of Fast Idle		.46 .77
	4,E	E2ME, E4ME	Curb Idle High Step of Fast Idle		.46 .97
	L,H	E2ME, E4ME	Curb Idle		.56
'85	All	E2ME, E2MC	Curb Idle	Automatic 3-spd Man 4-spd Man	.46 .57 .60
	All	E4ME, E4MC	Curb Idle		.41

turning screw in only enough to ensure good thread engagement in hole.

3. Placing a wide-blade screwdriver between screw head and air horn casting, pry against screw head to remove plug. Discard plug.

TPS Adjustment

NOTE: Adjustment is required if voltage is different than specifications by more than ± .05 volts.

1. Using Tool J-28696 or equivalent, remove TPS adjustment screw.

2. Connect digital voltmeter J29125-A from TPS connector center "C" to bottom terminal "C" (Jumpers for access can be made using terminals).

3. With ignition ON, engine stopped, reinstall TPS adjustment screw, and with tool J-28696, BT-7967A or equivalent, quickly adjust screw to obtain specified TPS voltage with A/C off.

4. After adjustment, install a new plug (supplied in service kits) in air horn, driving plug in place until flush with raised pump lever boss on casting.

NOTE: Plug must be installed to retain the TPS adjustment screw setting. If plug is not available, remove screw and apply GM Threadlock® Adhesive or equivalent to screw threads, then repeat adjustment.

5. Clear trouble code memory after adjustment.

Removal and Installation

1. Disconnect the M/C Solenoid and TPS electrical connector.

2. Disconnect the idle speed control or idle speed solenoid electrical connector.

3. Loosen the attaching screws and remove idle speed control or, idle speed solenoid or idle load compensator.

4. Disconnect the upper choke lever from the end of choke shaft by removing retaining screw. Rotate the upper choke lever to remove choke rod from slot in lever.

5. Remove the choke rod from lower lever inside the float bowl casting by holding lower lever outward with small screwdriver and twisting rod counterclockwise.

6. Using tool J25322 or a 2.4 mm (3/32 in.) drift punch, drive roll pin (pump lever pivot pin) inward until end of pin is against air cleaner locating boss on air horn casting. Remove pump lever and lever from pump rod.

7. Remove front vacuum break hose from tube on float bowl.

8. Remove air horn-to-bowl screws; then remove the two countersunk attaching screws located next to the venturi. Remove the air horn from float bowl by lifting it straight up.

9. Remove Solenoid-metering rod plunger by lifting straight up.

10. Remove air horn gasket by lifting it from the dowel locating pins on float bowl. DISCARD GASKET.

11. Stake the TPS in bowl as follows:

    a. Lay a flat tool or metal piece across bowl casting to protect gasket sealing surface.

    b. Use a small screwdriver to depress TPS sensor lightly and hold against spring tension.

    c. Observing safety precautions, pry upward with a small chisel or equivalent to remove bowl staking, making sure prying force is exerted against the metal piece and not against the bowl casting.

    d. Push up from bottom on electrical connector and remove TPS and connector assembly from bowl.

12. Install the TPS and connector assembly in float bowl by aligning groove in electrical connector with slot in float bowl casting. Push down on connector and sensor assembly so that connector and wires are located below bowl casting surface. Be sure green TPS actuator plunger is in place in air horn.

13. Install the air horn, holding down on pump plunger assembly against return spring tension, and aligning pump plunger stem with hole in gasket, and aligning holes in gasket over TPS plunger, solenoid plunger return spring, metering rods, solenoid attaching screw and electrical connector. Position gasket over the two dowel locating pins on the float bowl.

14. Solenoid-metering rod plunger, holding down on air horn gasket and pump plunger assembly, and aligning slot in end of plunger with solenoid attaching screw. Remove the solenoid.

15. Carefully lower air horn assembly onto float bowl while positioning the TPS Adjustment Lever over the TPS sensor, and guiding pump plunger stem through seal in air horn casting. To ease installation, insert a thin screwdriver between air horn gasket and float bowl to raise the TPS Adjustment Lever positioning it over the TPS sensor.

16. Install the air horn screws and lockwashers, and two countersunk screws (located next to the carburetor venturi area). Tighten all screws evenly and securely, following air horn screw tightening sequence.

17. Install the front vacuum break and bracket assembly on the air horn, using two attaching screws. Tighten screws securely.

18. Reconnect the upper end of pump rod to pump lever. Place lever between raised bosses on air horn casting, making sure lever engages TPS actuator plunger and the pump plunger stem. Align hole in pump lever with holes in air horn casting bosses. Using a small drift or rod the diameter of the pump lever roll pin will aid alignment. Using diagonal (sidecutter) pliers on the end of the roll pin, pry the roll pin only enough to insert a thin bladed screwdriver between the end of the pump lever roll pin and the air cleaner locating boss on air horn casting. Use screwdriver to push pump lever roll pin back through the casting until end of pin is flush with casting bosses on the air horn.

NOTE: Use care installing the roll pin to prevent damage to the pump lever bearing surface and casting bosses.

19. Install the choke rod into lower choke lever inside bowl cavity. Install choke rod in slot in upper choke lever, and position lever on end of choke shaft, making sure flats on end of shaft align with flats in lever. Install attaching screw and tighten securely. When properly installed, the lever will point to the rear of the carburetor, and the number on the lever will face outward.

20. Install the idle speed control motor.

21. Install the M/C solenoid, TPS and idle speed control or idle speed solenoid electrical connectors.

22. Clear trouble code memory after replacement.

23. Check TPS voltage and refer to TPS adjustment procedure if required.

MIXTURE CONTROL SOLENOID

Checking Plunger Travel

Mixture control solenoid plunger travel should be checked before proceeding with any carburetor adjustments or disassembly. Using Float Gage J-9789-130, BT-7720, or equivalent, (used to check float level setting externally), insert gage in the vertical "D" shaped vent hole in the air horn casting, next to the Idle Air Bleed Cover.

Checking plunger travel—E2ME models

NOTE: It may be necessary to file or grind material off the gage to allow it to enter the vent hole freely. Gage will be used to check total mixture control solenoid plunger travel.

1. Insert float gage down "D" shaped vent hole. Press down on gage and release, observing that the gage moves freely and does not bind. With gage released, (plunger UP position), read at eye level and record the reading of the gage mark (in inches) that lines up with the top of air horn casting, (upper edge).

2. Lightly press down on gage until bottomed, (plunger DOWN position). Read and record mm (inches) the reading of the gage mark that lines up with top of air horn casting.

3. Subtract gage UP position (Step 1) from gage DOWN position Step 2), and record difference. This difference is total plunger travel.

4. If total plunger travel (Step 3) is between 2.4 mm and 4.8 mm (^{2}/32 in. and ^{6}/32 in.), proceed to Idle Air Bleed Valve Adjustment. If it is less than 2.4 mm (^{2}/32 in.) or greater than 4.8mm (^{6}/32 in.) adjust mixture control solenoid plunger travel indicated below.

Adjusting Plunger Travel

1. Remove air horn, mixture control solenoid plunger, air horn gasket and plastic filler block, using normal service procedures.

2. Remove throttle side metering rod. Install mixture control

Correct installation of mixture control solenoid gauging tool

solenoid gaging tool, J-33815-1, BT-8253-A, or equivalent, over the throttle side metering jet rod guide, and temporarily reinstall the solenoid plunger into the solenoid body.

3. Holding the solenoid plunger in the DOWN position, use Tool J-28696-10, BT-7928, or equivalent, to turn lean mixture (solenoid) screw counterclockwise until the plunger breaks contact with the gaging tool. Turn slowly clockwise until the plunger just contacts the gaging tool. The adjustment is correct when the solenoid plunger is contacting both the solenoid stop and the gaging tool.

If the total difference in adjustment required less than ^{3}/4 turn of the lean mixture (solenoid) screw, the original setting was within the manufacturer's specifications.

4. Remove solenoid plunger and gaging tool, and reinstall metering rod and plastic filler block.

5. Invert air horn, and remove rich mixture stop screw from bottom side of air horn, using Tool J-28696-4, BT7967A or equivalent.

6. Remove lean mixture screw plug and the rich mixture stop screw plug from air horn, using a suitable sized punch.

7. Reinstall rich mixture stop screw in air horn and bottom lightly, then back screw out ^{1}/4 turn.

8. Reinstall air horn gasket, mixture control solenoid plunger and air horn to carburetor.

9. Insert external float gage in vent hole and, with Tool J-28696-10, BT-7928, or equivalent, adjust rich mixture stop screw to obtain ^{4}/32 in. total plunger travel.

10. With solenoid plunger travel correctly set, install plugs (supplied in service kits) in the air horn. Install plug, hollow end down, into the access hole to lean mixture (solenoid) screw, and use suitably sized punch to drive plug into the air horn until the top of the plug is even with the lower edge of hole chamfer. Plug must be installed to retain the screw setting and to prevent fuel vapor loss. Install plug, with hollow end down, over the rich mixture stop screw access hole, and drive plug into place so that the top of the plug is ^{1}/16" below the surface of the air horn casting.

NOTE: Plug must be installed to retain screw setting.

Removal and Installation

1. Disconnect the M/C solenoid and TPS electrical connector.

2. Disconnect the idle speed control electrical connector.

3. Loosen the attaching screws and remove idle speed control. Disconnect the upper choke lever from the end of the choke shaft by removing retaining screw. Rotate upper choke lever to remove choke rod from slot in lever. Disconnect the choke rod from lower lever inside the float bowl casting. Remove rod by holding lower lever outward with small screwdriver and twisting rod counterclockwise.

4. With a small drift punch of the correct size or J25322 tool drive roll pin (pump lever pivot pin) inward until end of pin is

against air cleaner locating boss on air horn casting. Remove pump lever and lever from pump rod.

5. Remove the front vacuum break hose from tube on float bowl.

6. Loosen the horn-to-bowl screws; then remove the two countersunk attaching screws located next to the venturi. Remove the air horn from float bowl by lifting it straight up.

7. Remove the solenoid-metering rod plunger by lifting straight up. Remove the air horn gasket by lifting it from the dowel locating pins on float bowl. Discard gasket.

8. Remove the plastic filler block over float bowl. Carefully lift each metering rod out of the guided metering jet, checking to be sure the return spring is removed with each metering rod.

9. Remove the lean mixture screw using tool J28696-10, BT-7928 or equivalent.

10. Remove the screw attaching solenoid connector to float bowl and lift the mixture control solenoid and connector assembly from the float bowl.

NOTE: If a service replacement Mixture Control Solenoid package is installed, the solenoid and plunger MUST be installed as a matched set.

11. Install the mixture control solenoid carefully in the float chamber, aligning pin on end of solenoid with hole in raised boss at bottom of bowl. Align solenoid connector wires to fit in slot in bowl, or plastic insert if used.

12. Install the lean mixture (solenoid) screw through hole in solenoid bracket and tension spring in bowl, engaging first six screw threads to assure proper thread engagement.

13. Install mixture control solenoid gaging Tool, J-33815-1, BT-8253-A or equivalent, over the throttle side metering jet rod guide, and temporarily install solenoid plunger.

14. Holding the solenoid plunger against the Solenoid Stop, use Tool J-28696-10, BT-7938, or equivalent, to turn the lean mixture (solenoid) screw slowly clockwise, until the solenoid plunger just contacts the gaging tool. The adjustment is correct when the solenoid plunger is contacting BOTH the Solenoid Stop and the Gaging Tool. Remove solenoid plunger and gaging tool.

15. Align solenoid wires with notch in plastic insert (if used) and connector lugs with recesses in bowl. Install connector attaching screw. Tighten screw securely.

---CAUTION---

DO NOT overtighten the screw; it could cause damage to the connector.

16. Install the plastic filler clock over float valve, pressing downward until properly seated (flush with bowl casting surface).

17. Install metering rod and spring assembly through hole in plastic filler block and gently lower the metering rod into the guided metering jet, until large end of spring seats on the recess on end of jet guide.

NOTE: Do not force metering rod down in jet. Use extreme care when handling these critical parts to avoid damage to rod and spring. If service replacement metering rods, springs and jets are installed, they must be installed in matched sets.

18. Install the air horn, holding down on pump plunger assembly against return spring tension and aligning pump plunger stem with hole in gasket, and aligning holes in gasket over TPS plunger, solenoid plunger return spring, metering rods, solenoid attaching screw and electrical connector. Position gasket over the two dowel locating pins on the float bowl.

19. Install the solenoid-metering rod plunger, holding down on aligning slot in end of plunger with solenoid attaching screw. Be sure plunger arms engage top of each metering rod.

20. Carefully lower air horn assembly onto float bowl while positioning the TPS Adjustment Lever over the TPS sensor, and guiding pump plunger stem through seal in air horn casting. To ease installation, insert a thin screwdriver between air horn gasket and float bowl to raise the TPS Adjustment Lever positioning it over the TPS sensor.

Location of solenoid metering plunger in throttle body—E2ME models

NOTE: Make sure that the tubes are positioned properly through the holes in the air horn gasket. Do not force the air horn assembly onto the bowl, but lower it lightly into place.

21. Install attaching screws and lockwashers, and two countersunk screws (located next to the carburetor venturi area). Tighten all screws evenly and securely, following air horn screw tightening sequence.

IDLE SPEED CONTROL (ISC)

On some carburetors, there is an idle speed control (ISC) to control idle engine speed with the ECM. It is mounted on the carburetor, and moves the throttle lever to open or close the throttle blades at idle. A switch in the housing closes when the throttle lever contacts the ISC plunger. When the switch is closed the ECM controls RPM of the engine. When it is open, the motor is unoperative. When the ignition is turned off, the motor extends slightly, therefore, if the ISC contacts did not close, the engine would have a high idle speed after repeated starts. When A/C is turned "on", the ECM, because of change on engine load, adjusts ISC to maintain idle speed.

On-Car Speed Adjustments

When a new Idle Speed Control (ISC) assembly is installed, a base (minimum) and extended (maximum) rpm speed check must be performed and adjustments made as required. When making a low and high speed adjustment, the low speed adjustment is always made first. DO NOT use the ISC plunger to adjust curb idle speed as the idle speed is controlled by the ECM. Before starting the engine, place transmission selector level in park or neutral, set parking brake, and block drive wheels. Prior to adjustment, check for identification letter on the ISC adjustment plunger Adjust plunger, if required, to Dimension "B".

---CAUTION---

Do not disconnect or connect ISC connector with ignition ON as damage to the ECM may occur.

1. Connect tachometer.
2. Connect a dwell meter to mixture control (M/C) solenoid dwell (green) lead. Set dwell meter on the six cylinder scale.
3. Turn A/C OFF.
4. Start engine and run until stabilized by entering "closed loop" (dwell meter needle starts to vary).
5. Turn ignition OFF.
6. Unplug connector from ISC motor.
7. Fully retract ISC plunger by applying 12 volts to terminal "C" of the ISC motor connection and ground lead to terminal "D" of the ISC motor connection. It may be necessary to install jumper

Idle speed control (ISC) plunger adjustment—typical

ENGINE	ID LETTER	PLUNGER LENGTH DIMENSION A	AFTER ADJUSTMENT (STEPS 14, 15, OR 16). DISTANCE AT DIMENSION "B" MUST NOT EXCEED
3.8L (231)	NONE	16.3 mm (41/64")	8.0mm (5/16")
3.8L (229)	A	19.3 mm (49/64")	10.8 mm (27/64")
3.0L AT-4 SPD	L	27.5 mm (1-3/32")	19.0 mm (3/4")
3.0L AT-3 SPD	J	30.0 mm (1-3/16")	21.5 mm (27/32")
4.1L	NONE	16.3 mm (41/64")	8.0 mm (5/16")

leads from the ISC motor in order to make proper connections (refer to Special Tools).

NOTE: Do not leave battery voltage applied to motor longer than necessary to retract ISC plunger. Prolonged contact will damage motor. Also, NEVER connect voltage source across terminals "A" and "B" as damage to the internal throttle contact switch will result.

Do not use the ISC plunger to set curb idle speed

8. Start engine and wait until dwell meter needle starts to vary, indicating "closed loop" operation.

9. With parking brake applied and drive wheels blocked, place transmission in DRIVE.

10. With ISC plunger fully retracted, adjust carburetor base (slow) idle stop screw if required to obtain minimum RPM idle speed.

11. Place transmission in PARK and fully extend ISC plunger by apply 12 volts to terminal "D" of the ISC motor connection and ground lead to terminal "C" is the ISC motor connection. Apply voltage only long enough to extend plunger.

NOTE: When the plunger is in the fully extended position, the plunger must be in the contact with the throttle lever to prevent possible internal damage to unit.

12. Place transmission in DRIVE.

13. With ISC plunger fully extended, check maximum rpm. Adjust ISC plunger if required using tool J29607, BT-8022 or equivalent to obtain maximum rpm speed.

14. Recheck maximum rpm adjustment with voltage applied to ISC motor. Motor will ratchet at full extension with power applied. Readjust if necessary.

15. Place transmission in Park or Neutral and turn ignition OFF. Disconnect 12 volt DC power source, jumper leads, ground lead and tachometer.

16. Reconnect 4 terminal harness connector to ISC motor.

17. Remove blocks from drive wheels.

Rochester Quadrajet Models

The Rochester Quadrajet carburetor is a two stage, four-barrel downdraft carburetor. It has been built in many variations designated as 4MC, 4MV, M4MC, M4MCA, M4ME, M4MEA, E4MC, and E4ME. See the beginning of the Rochester section for an explanation of these designations. The primary side of the carburetor is equipped with two primary bores and a triple venturi with plain tube nozzles. During off idle and part throttle operation, the fuel is metered through tapered metering rods operating in specially designed jets positioned by a manifold vacuum responsive piston. The secondary side of the carburetor contains two secondary boxes. An air valve is used on the secondary side for metering control and supplements the primary bore. The secondary air valve operates tapered metering rods which regulate the fuel in constant proportion to the air being supplied.

Fast Idle Speed Adjustment

1. Position the fast idle lever on the high step of the fast idle cam.

2. Be sure that the choke is wide open and the engine warm. Plug the EGR vacuum hose. Disconnect the vacuum hose to the front vacuum break unit, if there are two.

3. Make a preliminary adjustment by turning the fast idle screw out until the throttle valves are closed, then screwing it in the specified number of turns after it contacts the lever (see the carburetor specifications).

Quadrajet fast idle adjustment

4. Use the fast idle screw to adjust the fast idle to the speed, and under the conditions, specified on the engine compartment sticker or in the specifications chart.

Choke Rod (Fast Idle Cam) Adjustment

1. Adjust the fast idle and place the cam follower on the second step of the fast idle cam against the shoulder of the high step.

2. Close the choke valve by exerting counterclockwise pressure on the external choke lever. Remove the coil assembly from the choke housing and push upon the choke coil lever. On models with a fixed (riveted) choke cover, push up on the vacuum break lever tang and hold in position with a rubber band.

3. Insert a gauge of the proper size between the upper edge of the choke valve and the inside air horn wall.

4. To adjust, bend the tang on the fast idle cam. Be sure that the tang rests against the cam after bending.

Primary (Front) Vacuum Break Adjustment

1978–81 MODELS

1. Loosen the three retaining screws and remove the thermostatic cover and coil assembly from the choke housing through 1979.

2. Seat the front vacuum diaphragm using an outside vacuum source. If there is a diaphragm unit bleed hole, tape it over.

3. Push up on the inside choke coil lever until the tang on the vacuum break lever contacts the tang on the vacuum break plunger. On models with a fixed choke coil cover, push up on the vacuum break lever tang.

4. Place the proper size gauge between the upper edge of the choke valve and the inside of the air horn wall.

5. To adjust, turn the adjustment screw on the vacuum break plunger lever.

6. Install the vacuum hose to the vacuum break unit.

1982–84 MODELS

On these models a choke valve measuring gauge J-26701 or equivalent is used to measure angle (degrees instead of inches). See illustration for procedure.

Secondary (Rear) Vacuum Break Adjustment

1978–80 MODELS

1. Remove the thermostatic cover and coil assembly from the choke housing through 1979.

Quadrajet rear vacuum break adjustment (without adjusting screw)—1980 and earlier models

2. Tape over the bleed hole in the rear vacuum break diaphragm and seat the diaphragm using an outside vacuum source. Make sure the diaphram plunger bucking spring, if any, is compressed. On delay models (1980), plug the end cover with a pump plunger cup or equivalent and remove after adjustment.

3. Close the choke by pushing up on the choke coil lever inside the choke housing. On models with a fixed choke coil cover, push

Quadrajet choke rod (fast idle cam) adjustment—typical

Quadrajet front vacuum break adjustment—1981 and earlier

Quadrajet front vacuum break adjustment—1982 and later

up on the vacuum break lever tang and use a rubber band to hold in place.

4. With the choke rod in the bottom of the slot in the choke lever, measure between the upper edge of the choke valve and the air horn wall with a wire type gauge.

5. To adjust, bend the vacuum break rod at the first bend near the diaphragm except on 1980 models with a screw at the rear of the diaphragm; on those models, turn the screw to adjust.

6. Remove the tape covering the bleed hole of the diaphragm and connect the vacuum hose.

① REMOVE VACUUM BREAK FROM CARBURETOR. PLACE BRACKET IN A VISE AND, USING SAFETY PRECAUTIONS, GRIND OFF ADJUSTMENT SCREW CAP. RE-INSTALL VACUUM BREAK.

⑨ TO ADJUST, USING 1/8" HEX WRENCH TURN SCREW IN REAR COVER UNTIL BUBBLE IS CENTERED. APPLY SEALER (SUCH AS SILICONE SEALER RTV RUBBER OR EQUIVALENT) OVER SCREW HEAD TO SEAL SETTING.

RUBBER BAND

PLUNGER BUCKING SPRING

⑦ SEAT DIAPHRAGM USING VACUUM SOURCE (SEE NOTE 2)

⑥ SPECIFIED ANGLE (SEE SPECS.)

② DEGREE SCALE

⑤ POINTER MAGNET

④ LEVELING BUBBLE (CENTERED)

④ CHOKE VALVE CLOSED

FIGURE 1

PUMP PLUNGER CUP   FIGURE 3

FIGURE 2

⑧ LIGHTLY CLOSE CHOKE BY PUSHING UPWARD ON CHOKE COIL LEVER OR VACUUM BREAK LEVER TANG (HOLD IN POSITION WITH RUBBER BAND). MAKE SURE PLUNGER BUCKING SPRING (IF USED) IS COMPRESSED AND SEATED.

NOTE 2: ON DELAY MODELS, PLUG END COVER USING AN ACCELERATOR PUMP PLUNGER CUP - 2G TYPE (FIGURE 3) OR EQUIVALENT. SEAT VACUUM DIAPHRAGM MAKING SURE VACUUM IS ABOVE 5" Hg WHEN READING GAUGE (STEP 9). REMOVE CUP AFTER ADJUSTMENT.

NOTE 1: MAKE CHOKE COIL LEVER ADJUSTMENT AND FAST IDLE ADJUSTMENT. DO NOT REMOVE RIVETS AND CHOKE COVER TO PERFORM THIS ADJUSTMENT. USE RUBBER BAND ON VACUUM BREAK LEVER TANG TO HOLD CHOKE VALVE CLOSED (STEP 8).

Quadrajet rear vacuum break adjustment—1981-82 models

① LOOSEN THREE RETAINING SCREWS AND REMOVE THE THERMOSTATIC COVER AND COIL ASSEMBLY FROM CHOKE HOUSING

CHOKE VALVE CLOSED

⑥ BEND CHOKE ROD AT THIS POINT TO ADJUST (SEE INSET)

③ ROD AT BOTTOM OF SLOT

② PUSH UP ON THERMOSTATIC COIL TANG (COUNTERCLOCKWISE) UNTIL CHOKE VALVE IS CLOSED

④ INSERT SPECIFIED PLUG GAUGE

⑤ LOWER EDGE OF LEVER SHOULD JUST CONTACT SIDE OF PLUG GAUGE

Quadrajet choke coil lever adjustment—typical

① ATTACH RUBBER BAND TO GREEN TANG OF INTERMEDIATE CHOKE SHAFT.

② OPEN THROTTLE TO ALLOW CHOKE VALVE TO CLOSE.

③ SET UP ANGLE GAGE AND SET ANGLE TO SPECIFICATION.

④ RETRACT VACUUM BREAK PLUNGER, USING VACUUM SOURCE, AT LEAST 18" HG. PLUG AIR BLEED HOLES WHERE APPLICABLE.

④A ON QUADRAJETS, AIR VALVE ROD MUST NOT RESTRICT PLUNGER FROM RETRACTING FULLY. IF NECESSARY, BEND ROD HERE TO PERMIT FULL PLUNGER TRAVEL. WHERE APPLICABLE, PLUNGER STEM MUST BE EXTENDED FULLY TO COMPRESS PLUNGER BUCKING SPRING.

⑤ TO CENTER BUBBLE, EITHER:
A. ADJUST WITH 1/8" HEX WRENCH (VACUUM STILL APPLIED)
-OR-
B. SUPPORT AT "S" AND BEND VACUUM BREAK ROD (VACUUM STILL APPLIED)

Quadrajet rear vacuum break adjustment—1983 and later models

① OPEN PRIMARY THROTTLE UNTIL ACTUATING LINK CONTACTS TANG

② LINK SHOULD BE IN CENTER OF SLOT

③ BEND TANG TO ADJUST

Quadrajet secondary opening adjustment with two point linkage

④ GAUGE BETWEEN UPPER EDGE OF CHOKE VALVE AND AIR HORN WALL (SEE NOTE*)

③ ON WARM ENGINE, CLOSE CHOKE VALVE BY PUSHING UP ON TANG ON INTERMEDIATE CHOKE LEVER (HOLD IN POSITION WITH RUBBER BAND)

⑤ BEND TANG TO ADJUST

② HOLD THROTTLE VALVES WIDE OPEN

① INSTALL CHOKE THERMOSTATIC COVER AND COIL ASSEMBLY IN HOUSING ALIGN INDEX MARK WITH SPECIFIED POINT ON HOUSING

Quadrajet unloader adjustment—typical

① Lightly open primary throttle until link just contacts tang on secondary lever

② With link against tang there should be .070" clearance between link and tang at this point

③ Bend tang to adjust

Secondary opening adjustment with three point linkage

1981-84 MODELS

On these models a choke valve measuring gauge J-26701 or equivalent is used to measure angle (degrees instead on inches). See illustration for procedure.

Choke Unloader Adjustment

1. Push up on the vacuum break lever to close the choke valve, and fully open the throttle valves.

2. Measure the distance from the upper edge of the choke valve to the air horn wall.

3. To adjust, bend the tang on the fast idle lever.

4MV Choke Coil Rod Adjustment

1. Close the choke valve by rotating the choke coil lever counter-clockwise.

2. Disconnect the thermostatic coil rod from the upper lever.

3. Push down on the rod until it contacts the bracket of the coil.

4. The rod must fit in the notch of the upper lever.

5. If it does not, it must be bent on the curved portion just below the upper lever.

MC, ME Choke Coil Lever Adjustment

1. Remove the choke cover and thermostatic coil from the choke housing. On models with a fixed (riveted) choke cover, the rivets must be drilled out. A choke stat kit is necessary for assembly. Place the fast idle cam follower on the high step.

2. Push up on the coil tang (counter-clockwise) until the choke valve is closed. The top of the choke rod should be at the bottom of the slot in the choke valve lever.

3. Insert a 0.120 in. drill bit in the hole in the choke housing.

4. The lower edge of the choke coil lever should just contact the side of the plug gauge.

5. Bend the choke rod at the top angle to adjust.

Secondary Closing Adjustment

This adjustment assures proper closing of the secondary throttle plates.

1. Set the slow idle as per instructions in the appropriate car section. Make sure that the fast idle cam follower is not resting on the fast idle cam and the choke valve is wide open.

2. There should be 0.020 in. clearance between the secondary throttle actuating rod and the front of the slot on the secondary throttle lever with the closing tang on the throttle lever resting against the actuating lever.

3. Bend the secondary closing tang on the primary throttle actuating rod or lever to adjust.

Secondary Opening Adjustment

1. Open the primary throttle valves until the actuating link contacts the upper tang on the secondary lever.

2. With two point linkage, the bottom of the link should be in the center of the secondary lever slot.

3. With three point linkage, there should be 0.070 in. clearance between the link and the middle tang.

4. Bend the upper tang on the secondary lever to adjust as necessary.

Float Level Adjustment

With the air horn assembly removed, measure the distance from the air horn gasket surface (gasket removed) to the top of the float at the toe (3/16 in. back from the toe).

NOTE: Make sure the retaining pin is firmly held in place and that the tang of the float is lightly held against the needle and seat assembly.

Remove the float and bend the float arm to adjust except on carburetors used with the computer controlled systems (E4MC and E4ME). For those carburetors, if the float level is too high, hold the retainer firmly in place and push down on the center of the float to adjust. If the float level is too low on models with the computer controlled system, lift out the metering rods. Remove the solenoid connector screw. Turn the lean mixture solenoid screw in clockwise, counting and recording the exact number of turns until the screw is lightly bottomed in the bowl. Then turn the solenoid and connector. Remove the float and bend the arm up to adjust. Install the parts, turning the mixture solenoid screw in until it is lightly bottomed, then unscrewing it the exact number of turns counted earlier.

Air Valve Spring Adjustment

To adjust the air valve spring windup, loosen the Allen head lockscrew and turn the adjusting screw counter-clockwise to remove all spring tension. With the air valve closed, turn the adjusting screw clockwise the specified number of turns after the torsion spring contacts the pin on the shaft. Hold the adjusting screw in this position and tighten the lockscrew.

Quadrajet secondary closing adjustment

Quadrajet float level adjustment

Quadrajet air valve spring setting—typical

Quadrajet accelerator pump rod adjustment

Secondary lockout adjustment—Rochester E4ME and E4MC carburetors

557

Front air valve rod adjustment—Rochester E4ME and E4MC carburetors

Rear air valve rod adjustment—Rochester E4ME and E4MC carburetors

QUADRAJET CARBURETOR SPECIFICATIONS
Cadillac

Year	Carburetor Identification ①	Float Level (in.)	Air Valve Spring (turn)	Pump Rod (in.)	Primary Vacuum Break (in./deg.)	Secondary Vacuum Break (in./deg.)	Secondary Opening (in.)	Choke Rod (in.)	Choke Unloader (in.)	Fast Idle Speed (rpm)
'78	17058230	13/32	1/2	3/8	0.150	0.165	③	0.080	0.230	1500
	All others	13/32	1/2	3/8	0.140	0.250	③	0.080	0.230	1400
'79	17059230	13/32	1/2	9/32②	0.142	0.234	0.015	0.083	0.142	1000
	17059232	13/32	1/2	9/32②	0.142	0.234	0.015	0.083	0.142	1500
	17059530	13/32	1/2	9/32②	0.149	0.164	0.015	0.083	0.142	1500
	17059532	13/32	1/2	9/32②	0.149	0.164	0.015	0.083	0.142	1500
'80	17080230	7/16	1/2	9/32②	0.149	0.136	③	0.083	0.220	1450
	17080530	17/32	1/2	Fixed	0.142	0.400	③	0.083	0.260	1350
'81	17081248	3/8	5/8	Fixed	0.164	0.136	③	0.139	0.243	④
	17081289	13/32	5/8	Fixed	0.164	0.136	③	0.139	0.243	④
'82	17082246	3/8	5/8	Fixed	0.149/26	0.149/26	③	0.139	0.195	④
	17082247	13/32	5/8	Fixed	0.164/28	0.136/24	③	0.139	0.243	④
'83	17082266	3/8	5/8	Fixed	0.149/26	0.149/26	③	0.071	0.195	④
	17082267	3/8	5/8	Fixed	0.149/26	0.149/26	③	0.071	0.195	④

① The carburetor identification number is stamped on the float bowl, near the secondary throttle lever.
② Inner hole
③ No measurement necessary on two point linkage; see text.
④ See underhood decal.

QUADRAJET CARBURETOR SPECIFICATIONS
Buick

Year	Carburetor Identification ①	Float Level (in.)	Air Valve Spring (turn)	Pump Rod (in.)	Primary Vacuum Break (in./deg.)	Secondary Vacuum Break (in./deg.)	Secondary Opening (in.)	Choke Rod (in.)	Choke Unloader (in.)	Fast Idle Speed④ (rpm)
'78	17058240	7/32	3/4	9/32	0.117	0.117	②	0.074	0.243	⑤
	17058241	5/16	3/4	3/8	0.120	0.103	②	0.096	0.243	⑤
	17058250	13/32	1/2	9/32	0.129	0.183	②	0.096	0.220	⑤
	17058253	13/32	1/2	9/32	0.129	0.183	②	0.096	0.220	⑤
	17058254	15/32	1/2	9/32	0.136	—	②	0.103	0.220	⑤
	17058257	13/32	1/2	9/32	0.136	0.231	②	0.103	0.220	⑤
	17058258	13/32	1/2	9/32	0.136	0.231	②	0.103	0.220	⑤
	17058259	13/32	1/2	9/32	0.136	0.231	②	0.103	0.220	⑤
	17058582	15/32	7/8	9/32	0.179	—	②	0.314	0.277	⑤
	17058584	15/32	7/8	9/32	0.179	—	②	0.314	0.277	⑤
	17058282	15/32	7/8	9/32	0.157	—	②	0.314	0.277	⑤
	17058284	15/32	7/8	9/32	0.157	—	②	0.314	0.277	⑤
	17058228	15/32	1	9/32	0.179	—	②	0.314	0.277	⑤
	17058502	15/32	7/8	9/32	0.164	—	②	0.314	0.277	⑤
	17058504	15/32	7/8	9/32	0.164	—	②	0.314	0.277	⑤
	17058202	15/32	7/8	9/32	0.157	—	②	0.314	0.277	⑤
	17058204	15/32	7/8	9/32	0.157	—	②	0.314	0.277	⑤
	17058540	7/32	3/4	9/32	0.117	0.117	②	0.074	0.243	⑤
	17058550	13/32	1/2	9/32	0.136	0.231	②	0.103	0.220	⑤
	17058553	15/32	1/2	9/32	0.129	0.231	②	0.096	0.220	⑤
	17058559	15/32	1/2	9/32	0.136	—	②	0.096	0.231	⑤
'79	17059240	7/32	3/4	9/32	0.117	0.117	②	0.074	0.179	⑥
	17059243	7/32	3/4	9/32	0.117	0.117	②	0.074	0.179	⑥
	17059540	7/32	3/4	9/32	0.117	0.129	②	0.074	0.243	⑥
	17059543	7/32	3/4	9/32	0.117	0.129	②	0.074	0.243	⑥
	17059242	7/32	3/4	9/32	0.066	0. 066	②	0.074	0.179	⑥
	17059553	13/32	1/2	9/32	0.136	0.230	②	0.103	0.220	⑥
	17059555	13/32	1/2	9/32	0.149	0.230	②	0.103	0.220	⑥
	17059250	13/32	1/2	9/32	0.129	0.182	②	0.096	0.220	⑥
	17059253	13/32	1/2	9/32	0.129	0.182	②	0.096	0.220	⑥
	17059208	15/32	7/8	9/32	—	0.129	②	0.314	0.277	⑥
	17059209	15/32	7/8	9/32	—	0.129	②	0.314	0.277	⑥
	17059210	15/32	1	9/32	0.157	—	②	0.243	0.243	⑥
	17059211	15/32	1	9/32	0.157	—	②	0.243	0.243	⑥
	17059228	15/32	1	9/32	0.157	—	②	0.243	0.243	⑥
	17059241	5/16	3/4	3/8	0.120	0.113	②	0.096	0.243	⑥
	17059247	5/16	3/4	3/8	0.110	0.103	②	0.096	0.243	⑥
	17059272	15/32	5/8	3/8	0.136	0.195	②	0.074	0.220	⑥

QUADRAJET CARBURETOR SPECIFICATIONS
Buick

Year	Carburetor Identification ①	Float Level (in.)	Air Valve Spring (turn)	Pump Rod (in.)	Primary Vacuum Break (in./deg.)	Secondary Vacuum Break (in./deg.)	Secondary Opening (in.)	Choke Rod (in.)	Choke Unloader (in.)	Fast Idle Speed ④ (rpm)
'80	17080240	3/16	9/16	9/32 ③	0.083	0.083	②	0.074	0.179	⑥
	17080241	7/16	3/4	9/32 ③	0.129	0.114	②	0.096	0.243	⑥
	17080242	13/32	9/16	9/32 ③	0.077	0.096	②	0.074	0.220	⑥
	17080243	3/16	9/16	9/32 ③	0.083	0.083	②	0.074	0.179	⑥
	17080244	5/16	5/8	9/32 ③	0.096	0.071	②	0.139	0.243	⑥
	17080249	7/16	3/4	9/32 ③	0.129	0.114	②	0.096	0.243	⑥
	17080253	13/32	1/2	9/32 ③	0.149	0.211	②	0.090	0.220	⑥
	17080259	13/32	1/2	9/32 ③	0.149	0.211	②	0.090	0.220	⑥
	17080270	15/32	5/8	3/8 ⑦	0.149	0.211	②	0.074	0.220	⑥
	17080271	15/32	5/8	3/8 ⑦	0.142	0.211	②	0.110	0.203	⑥
	17080272	15/32	5/8	3/8 ⑦	0.129	0.175	②	0.074	0.203	⑥
	17080502	1/2	7/8	Fixed	0.136	0.179	②	0.110	0.243	⑥
	17080504	1/2	7/8	Fixed	0.136	0.179	②	0.110	0.243	⑥
	17080540	3/8	9/16	Fixed	0.103	0.129	②	0.074	0.243	⑥
	17080542	3/8	9/16	Fixed	0.103	0.066	②	0.074	0.243	⑥
	17080543	3/8	9/16	Fixed	0.103	0.129	②	0.074	0.243	⑥
	17080553	15/32	1/2	Fixed	0.142	0.220	②	0.090	0.220	⑥
	17080554	15/32	1/2	Fixed	0.142	0.211	②	0.090	0.220	⑥
81	17081202 204	11/32	7/8	Fixed	0.157 ⑧	—	②	0.110	0.243	⑩
	17081203 207	11/32	7/8	Fixed	0.157 ⑧	—	②	0.110	0.243	⑩
	17081216 218	11/32	7/8	Fixed	0.157 ⑧	—	②	0.110	0.243	⑩
	17081242	3/8	9/16	Fixed	0.090 ⑧	0.077 ⑨	②	0.139	0.243	⑩
	17081243	5/16	9/16	Fixed	0.103 ⑧	0.090 ⑨	②	0.139	0.243	⑩
	17081245	3/8	5/8	Fixed	0.164 ⑧	0.136 ⑨	②	0.139	0.243	⑩
	17081247	3/8	5/8	Fixed	0.164 ⑧	0.136 ⑨	②	0.139	0.243	⑩
	17081248 249	3/8	5/8	Fixed	0.164 ⑧	0.136 ⑨	②	0.139	0.243	⑩
	17081253 254	15/32	1/2	Fixed	0.142 ⑧	0.227 ⑨	②	0.071	0.220	⑩
	17081270	7/16	5/8	Fixed	0.136 ⑧	0.211 ⑨	②	0.074	0.220	⑩
	17081272	5/8	5/8	Fixed	0.136 ⑧	0.260 ⑨	②	0.074	0.220	⑩
	17081274	5/8	5/8	Fixed	0.136 ⑧	0.220 ⑨	②	0.083	0.220	⑩
	17081289	5/8	5/8	Fixed	0.164 ⑧	0.136 ⑨	②	0.139	0.243	⑩
'82	17082202	11/32	7/8	Fixed	0.110/20	—	②	0.110	0.243	⑤
	17082204	11/32	3/8	Fixed	0.110/20	—	②	0.110	0.243	⑤
	17082244	7/16	9/16	Fixed	0.117/21	0.083/16	②	0.139	0.195	⑤
	17082245	3/8	5/8	Fixed	0.149/26	0.149/26	②	0.139	0.195	⑤

QUADRAJET CARBURETOR SPECIFICATIONS
Buick

Year	Carburetor Identification ①	Float Level (in.)	Air Valve Spring (turn)	Pump Rod (in.)	Primary Vacuum Break (in./deg.)	Secondary Vacuum Break (in./deg.)	Secondary Opening (in.)	Choke Rod (in.)	Choke Unloader (in.)	Fast Idle Speed ④ (rpm)
'82	17082246	3/8	5/8	Fixed	0.149/26	0.149/26	②	0.139	0.195	⑤
	17082247	13/32	5/8	Fixed	0.164/28	0.136/24	②	0.139	0.243	⑤
	17082248	13/32	5/8	Fixed	0.164/28	0.136/24	②	0.139	0.243	⑤
	17082251	15/32	1/2	Fixed	0.142/25	0.304/45	②	0.071	0.220	⑤
	17082253	15/32	1/2	Fixed	0.142/25	0.227/36	②	0.071	0.220	⑤
	17082264	7/16	9/16	Fixed	0.117/20	0.083/16	②	0.139	0.195	⑤
	17082265	3/8	5/8	Fixed	0.149/26	0.149/26	②	0.139	0.195	⑤
	17082266	3/8	5/8	Fixed	0.149/26	0.149/26	②	0.139	0.195	⑤
	17082267	3/8	5/8	Fixed	0.164/28	0.136/24	②	0.139	0.243	⑤
	17082268	13/32	5/8	Fixed	0.164/28	0.136/24	②	0.139	0.243	⑤
'83	17082265	3/8	5/8	Fixed	0.149/26	0.149/26	②	0.139	0.195	⑪
	17082266	3/8	5/8	Fixed	0.149/26	0.149/26	②	0.139	0.195	⑪
	17082267	3/8	5/8	Fixed	0.149/26	0.149/26	②	0.096	0.195	⑪
	17082268	3/8	5/8	Fixed	0.149/26	0.149/26	②	0.096	0.195	⑪
	17083242	9/32	9/16	Fixed	0.110/20	—	②	0.139	0.243	⑪
	17083244	1/4	9/16	Fixed	0.117/21	0.083/16	②	0.139	0.195	⑪
	17083248	3/8	5/8	Fixed	0.149/26	0.149/26	②	0.139	0.195	⑪
	17083250	7/16	1/2	Fixed	0.157/27	0.271/42	②	0.071	0.220	⑪
	17083253	7/16	1/2	Fixed	0.151/27	0.269/41	②	0.071	0.220	⑪
	17083553	7/16	1/2	Fixed	0.157/27	0.269/41	②	0.071	0.220	⑪
'84	17084201	11/32	7/8	Fixed	0.157/27	—	②	0.110	0.243	⑪
	17084205	11/32	7/8	Fixed	0.157/27	—	②	0.243	0.243	⑪
	17084208	11/32	7/8	Fixed	0.157/27	—	②	0.110	0.243	⑪
	17084209	11/32	7/8	Fixed	0.157/27	—	②	0.243	0.243	⑪
	17084210	11/32	7/8	Fixed	0.157/27	—	②	0.110	0.243	⑪
	17084240	5/16	1	Fixed	0.136/24	—	②	—	0.195	⑪
	17084244	5/16	1	Fixed	0.136/24	—	②	—	0.195	⑪
	17084246	5/16	1	Fixed	0.123/22	0.136/24	②	—	0.195	⑪
	17084248	5/16	1	Fixed	0.136/24	—	②	—	0.195	⑪
	17084252	7/16	1/2	Fixed	0.157/27	0.269/41	②	—	0.220	⑪
	17084254	7/16	1/2	Fixed	0.157/27	0.269/41	②	—	0.220	⑪

① The carburetor identification number is stamped on the float bowl, near the secondary throttle lever.
② No measurement necessary on two point linkage; see text
③ Inner hole
④ On high step of cam, automatic in Park

⑤ 3 turns after contacting lever for preliminary setting
⑥ 2 turns after contacting lever for preliminary setting
⑦ Outer hole
⑧ Front
⑨ Rear

⑩ 4½ turns after contacting lever for preliminary setting
⑪ See underhood decal

QUADRAJET CARBURETOR SPECIFICATIONS
Chevrolet

Year	Carburetor Identification ①	Float Level (in.)	Air Valve Spring (turn)	Pump Rod (in.)	Primary Vacuum (deg./in.)	Secondary Vacuum (deg./in.)	Secondary Opening (in.)	Choke Rod (in.)	Choke Unloader (in.)	Fast Idle Speed ④ (rpm)
'78	17058202	15/32	7/8	9/32	0.179	—	⑤	0.314	0.277	⑥
	17058203	15/32	7/8	9/32	0.179	—	⑤	0.314	0.277	⑥
	17058204	15/32	7/8	9/32	0.179	—	⑤	0.314	0.277	⑥
	17058210	15/32	1/2	9/32	0.203	—	⑤	0.314	0.277	⑥
	17058211	15/32	1/2	9/32	0.203	—	⑤	0.314	0.277	⑥
	17058228	15/32	7/8	9/32	0.203	—	⑤	0.314	0.277	⑥
	17058502	15/32	7/8	9/32	0.187	—	⑤	0.314	0.277	⑥
	17058504	15/32	7/8	9/32	0.187	—	⑤	0.314	0.277	⑥
	17058582	15/32	7/8	9/32	0.203	—	⑤	0.314	0.277	⑥
	17058584	15/32	7/8	9/32	0.203	—	⑤	0.314	0.277	⑥
'79	17059203	15/32	7/8	1/4	0.157	—	⑤	0.243	0.243	⑦
	17059207	15/32	7/8	1/4	0.157	—	⑤	0.243	0.243	⑦
	17059216	15/32	7/8	1/4	0.157	—	⑤	0.243	0.243	⑦
	17059217	15/32	7/8	1/4	0.157	—	⑤	0.243	0.243	⑦
	17059218	15/32	7/8	1/4	0.164	—	⑤	0.243	0.243	⑦
	17059222	15/32	7/8	1/4	0.164	—	⑤	0.243	0.243	⑦
	17059502	15/32	7/8	1/4	0.164	—	⑤	0.243	0.243	⑦
	17059504	15/32	7/8	1/4	0.164	—	⑤	0.243	0.243	⑦
	17059582	15/32	7/8	11/32	0.203	—	⑤	0.243	0.314	⑦
	17059584	15/32	7/8	11/32	0.203	—	⑤	0.243	0.314	⑦
	17059210	15/32	1	9/32	0.157	—	⑤	0.243	0.243	⑦
	17059211	15/32	1	9/32	0.157	—	⑤	0.243	0.243	⑦
	17029228	15/32	1	9/32	0.157	—	⑤	0.243	0.243	⑦
'80	17080202	7/16	7/8	1/4 ⑧	0.157	—	⑤	0.110	0.243	⑩
	17080204	7/16	7/8	1/4 ⑧	0.157	—	⑤	0.110	0.243	⑩
	17080207	7/16	7/8	1/4 ⑧	0.157	—	⑤	0.110	0.243	⑩
	17080228	7/16	7/8	9/32 ⑧	0.179	—	⑤	0.110	0.243	⑩
	17080243	3/16	9/16	9/32 ⑧	0.016	0.083	⑤	0.074	0.179	⑩
	17080274	15/32	5/8	5/16 ⑨	0.110	0.164	⑤	0.083	0.203	⑩
	17080282	7/16	7/8	11/32 ⑨	0.142	—	⑤	0.110	0.243	⑩
	17080284	7/16	7/8	11/32 ⑨	0.142	—	⑤	0.110	0.243	⑩
	17080502	1/2	7/8	Fixed	0.136	0.179	⑤	0.110	0.243	⑩
	17080504	1/2	7/8	Fixed	0.136	0.179	⑤	0.110	0.243	⑩
	17080542	3/8	9/16	Fixed	0.103	0.066	⑤	0.074	0.243	⑩
	17080543	3/8	9/16	Fixed	0.103	0.129	⑤	0.074	0.243	⑩
'81	17081202	11/32	7/8	Fixed	0.149	—	⑤	0.110	0.243	⑪
	17081203	11/32	7/8	Fixed	0.149	—	⑤	0.110	0.243	⑪
	17081204	11/32	7/8	Fixed	0.149	—	⑤	0.110	0.243	⑪

QUADRAJET CARBURETOR SPECIFICATIONS
Chevrolet

Year	Carburetor Identification ①	Float Level (in.)	Air Valve Spring (turn)	Pump Rod (in.)	Primary Vacuum (deg./in.)	Secondary Vacuum (deg./in.)	Secondary Opening (in.)	Choke Rod (in.)	Choke Unloader (in.)	Fast Idle Speed ④ (rpm)
'81	17081207	11/32	7/8	Fixed	0.149	—	⑤	0.110	0.243	⑪
	17081216	11/32	7/8	Fixed	0.149	—	⑤	0.110	0.243	⑪
	17081217	11/32	7/8	Fixed	0.149	—	⑤	0.110	0.243	⑪
	17081218	11/32	7/8	Fixed	0.149	—	⑤	0.110	0.243	⑪
	17081242	5/16	9/16	Fixed	0.090	0.077	⑤	0.139	0.243	⑪
	17081243	1/4	9/16	Fixed	0.103	0.090	⑤	0.139	0.243	⑪
'82	17082202	11/32	7/8	Fixed	0.157	—	⑤	0.110	0.243	⑫
	17082204	11/32	7/8	Fixed	0.157	—	⑤	0.110	0.243	⑫
	17082203	11/32	7/8	Fixed	0.157	—	⑤	0.243	0.243	⑫
	17082207	11/32	7/8	Fixed	0.157	—	⑤	0.243	0.243	⑫
'83	17083202	11/32	7/8	Fixed	—	27/.157	⑤	0.110	0.243	⑬
	17083203	11/32	7/8	Fixed	—	27/.157	⑤	0.243	0.243	⑬
	17083204	11/32	7/8	Fixed	—	27/.157	⑤	0.110	0.243	⑬
	17083207	11/32	7/8	Fixed	—	27/157	⑤	0.243	0.243	⑬
	17083216	11/32	7/8	Fixed	—	27/.157	⑤	0.110	0.243	⑬
	17083218	11/32	7/8	Fixed	—	27/.157	⑤	0.110	0.243	⑬
	17083236	11/32	7/8	Fixed	—	27/.157	⑤	0.110	0.243	⑬
	17083506	7/16	7/8	Fixed	27/.157	36/.227	⑤	0.110	0.227	⑬
	17083508	7/16	7/8	Fixed	27/.157	36/.227	⑤	0.110	0.227	⑬
	17083524	7/16	7/8	Fixed	25/.142	36/.227	⑤	0.110	0.227	⑬
	17083526	7/16	7/8	Fixed	25/.142	36/.227	⑤	0.110	0.227	⑬
'84	17084201	11/32	7/8	Fixed	.157/27	—	⑤	0.110	0.243	⑬
	17084205	11/32	7/8	Fixed	.157/27	—	⑤	0.243	0.243	⑬
	17084208	11/32	7/8	Fixed	.157/27	—	⑤	0.110	0.243	⑬
	17084209	11/32	7/8	Fixed	.157/27	—	⑤	0.243	0.243	⑬
	17084210	11/32	7/8	Fixed	.157/27	—	⑤	0.110	0.243	⑬
	17084507	7/16	1	Fixed	.157/27	.227/36	⑤	0.110	0.227	⑬
	17084509	7/16	1	Fixed	.157/27	.227/36	⑤	0.110	0.227	⑬
	17084525	7/16	1	Fixed	.142/25	.227/36	⑤	0.110	0.227	⑬
	17084527	7/16	1	Fixed	.142/25	.227/36	⑤	0.110	0.227	⑬

① The carburetor identification number is stamped on the float bowl, near the secondary throttle lever.
② Without vacuum advance.
③ With automatic transmission; vacuum advance connected and EGR disconnected and the throttle positioned on the high step of cam.
④ With manual transmission; without vacuum advance and the throttle positioned on the high step of cam.

⑤ No measurement necessary on two point linkage; see text.
⑥ 3 turns after contacting lever for preliminary setting.
⑦ 2 turns after contacting lever for preliminary setting.
⑧ Inner hole
⑨ Outer hole

⑩ 4 turns after contacting lever for preliminary setting.
⑪ 4½ turns after contacting lever for preliminary setting
⑫ 3⅛ turns after contacting lever for preliminary setting
⑬ See underhood sticker

QUADRAJET CARBURETOR SPECIFICATIONS
Oldsmobile

Year	Carburetor Identification ①	Float Level (in.)	Air Valve Spring (turn)	Pump Rod (in.)	Primary Vacuum Break (in./deg.)	Secondary Vacuum Break (in./deg.)	Secondary Opening (in.)	Choke Rod (in.)	Choke Unloader (in.)	Fast Idle Speed ④ (rpm)
'78	17058202	15/32	7/8	9/32	0.157	—	④	0.314	0.277	⑤
	17058204	15/32	7/8	9/32	0.157	—	④	0.314	0.277	⑤
	17058250	13/32	1/2	9/32	0.129	0.183	④	0.096	0.220	⑤
	17058253	13/32	1/2	9/32	0.129	0.183	④	0.096	0.220	⑤
	17058257	13/32	1/2	9/32	0.136	0.230	④	0.103	0.220	⑤
	17058258	13/32	1/2	9/32	0.136	0.230	④	0.103	0.220	⑤
	17058259	13/32	1/2	9/32	0.136	0.183	④	0.103	0.220	⑤
	17058502	15/32	7/8	9/32	0.164	—	④	0.314	0.277	⑤
	17058504	15/32	7/8	9/32	0.164	—	④	0.314	0.277	⑤
	17058553	13/32	1/2	9/32	0.136	0.230	④	0.103	0.220	⑤
	17058555	13/32	1/2	9/32	0.136	0.230	④	0.103	0.220	⑤
	17058582	15/32	7/8	9/32	0.179	—	④	0.314	0.277	⑤
	17058584	15/32	7/8	9/32	0.179	—	④	0.314	0.277	⑤
'79	17059202	1/2	7/8	1/4	0.164	—	④	0.314	0.243	⑥
	17059207	15/32	7/8	1/4	0.157	—	④	0.243	0.243	⑥
	17059216	15/32	7/8	1/4	0.157	—	④	0.243	0.243	⑥
	17059217	15/32	7/8	1/4	0.157	—	④	0.243	0.243	⑥
	17059218	15/32	7/8	9/32	0.164	—	④	0.243	0.243	⑥
	17059222	15/32	7/8	9/32	0.164	—	④	0.243	0.243	⑥
	17059250	13/32	1/2	9/32	0.129	0.183	④	0.096	0.220	⑥
	17059251	13/32	1/2	9/32	0.129	0.183	④	0.096	0.220	⑥
	17059253	13/32	1/2	9/32	0.129	0.183	④	0.096	0.220	⑥
	17059256	13/32	1/2	9/32	0.136	0.195	④	0.103	0.220	⑥
	17059258	13/32	1/2	9/32	0.136	0.195	④	0.103	0.220	⑥
	17059502	15/32	7/8	1/4	0.164	—	④	0.243	0.243	⑥
	17059504	15/32	7/8	1/4	0.164	—	④	0.243	0.243	⑥
	17059553	13/32	1/2	9/32	0.136	0.230	④	0.103	0.220	⑥
	17059554	13/32	1/2	9/32	0.136	0.230	④	0.103	0.220	⑥
	17059582	15/32	7/8	11/32	0.203	—	④	0.243	0.314	⑥
	17059584	15/32	7/8	11/32	0.203	—	④	0.243	0.314	⑥
'80	17080202	7/16	7/8	1/4 ⑦	0.157	—	④	0.110	0.243	⑤
	17080204	7/16	7/8	1/4 ⑦	0.157	—	④	0.110	0.243	⑤
	17080250	13/32	1/2	9/32 ⑦	0.149	0.211	④	0.090	0.220	⑤
	17080251	13/32	1/2	9/32 ⑦	0.149	0.211	④	0.090	0.220	⑤
	17080252	13/32	1/2	9/32 ⑦	0.149	0.211	④	0.090	0.220	⑤
	17080253	13/32	1/2	9/32 ⑦	0.149	0.211	④	0.090	0.220	⑤
	17080259	13/32	1/2	9/32 ⑦	0.149	0.211	④	0.090	0.220	⑤
	17080260	13/32	1/2	9/32 ⑦	0.149	0.211	④	0.090	0.220	⑤

QUADRAJET CARBURETOR SPECIFICATIONS (Cont'd)
Oldsmobile

Year	Carburetor Identification ①	Float Level (in.)	Air Valve Spring (turn)	Pump Rod (in.)	Primary Vacuum Break (in./deg.)	Secondary Vacuum Break (in./deg.)	Secondary Opening (in.)	Choke Rod (in.)	Choke Unloader (in.)	Fast Idle Speed ④ (rpm)
'80	17080504	½	⅞	⑧	0.136	0.179	④	0.110	0.243	⑤
	17080553	15/32	½	⑧	0.142	0.220	④	0.090	0.220	⑤
	17080554	15/32	½	⑧	0.142	0.211	④	0.090	0.220	⑤
'81	17081250	13/32	½	9/32 ⑦	0.149⑨	0.211⑩	④	0.090	0.220	⑤
	17081253	15/32	½	⑧	0.142⑨	0.227⑩	④	0.071	0.220	⑤
	17081254	15/32	½	⑧	0.142⑨	0.227⑩	④	0.071	0.220	⑤
	17081248	⅜	—	⑧	0.164⑨	0.136⑩	④	0.139	0.243	⑤
	17081289	13/32	—	⑧	0.164⑨	0.136⑩	④	0.139	0.243	⑤
'82	17082202	11/32	⅞	Fixed	0.110/20	—	④	0.110	0.243	⑤
	17082204	11/32	⅜	Fixed	0.110/20	—	④	0.110	0.243	⑤
	17082244	7/16	9/16	Fixed	0.117/21	0.083/16	④	0.139	0.195	⑤
	17082245	⅜	⅝	Fixed	0.149/26	0.149/26	④	0.139	0.195	⑤
	17082246	⅜	⅝	Fixed	0.149/26	0.149/26	④	0.139	0.195	⑤
	17082247	13/32	⅝	Fixed	0.164/28	0.136/24	④	0.139	0.243	⑤
	17082248	13/32	⅝	Fixed	0.164/28	0.136/24	④	0.139	0.243	⑤
	17082251	15/32	½	Fixed	0.142/25	0.304/45	④	0.071	0.220	⑤
	17082253	15/32	½	Fixed	0.142/25	0.227/36	④	0.071	0.220	⑤
	17082264	7/16	9/16	Fixed	0.117/20	0.083/16	④	0.139	0.195	⑤
	17082265	⅜	⅝	Fixed	0.149/26	0.149/26	④	0.139	0.195	⑤
	17082266	⅜	⅝	Fixed	0.149/26	0.149/26	④	0.139	0.195	⑤
	17082267	⅜	⅝	Fixed	0.164/28	0.136/24	④	0.139	0.243	⑤
	17082268	13/32	⅝	Fixed	0.164/28	0.136/24	④	0.139	0.243	⑤
'83	17082265	⅜	⅝	Fixed	0.149/26	0.149/26	②	0.139	0.195	⑪
	17082266	⅜	⅝	Fixed	0.149/26	0.149/26	②	0.139	0.195	⑪
	17082267	⅜	⅝	Fixed	0.149/26	0.149/26	②	0.096	0.195	⑪
	17082268	⅜	⅝	Fixed	0.149/26	0.149/26	②	0.096	0.195	⑪
	17083242	9/32	9/16	Fixed	0.110/20	—	②	0.139	0.243	⑪
	17083244	¼	9/16	Fixed	0.117/21	0.083/16	②	0.139	0.195	⑪
	17083248	⅜	⅝	Fixed	0.149/26	0.149/26	②	0.139	0.195	⑪
	17083250	7/16	½	Fixed	0.157/27	0.271/42	②	0.071	0.220	⑪
	17083253	7/16	½	Fixed	0.157/27	0.269/41	②	0.071	0.220	⑪
	17083553	7/16	½	Fixed	0.157/27	0.269/41	②	0.071	0.220	⑪
'84	17084201	11/32	⅞	Fixed	0.157/27	—	②	0.110	0.243	⑪
	17084205	11/32	⅞	Fixed	0.157/27	—	②	0.243	0.243	⑪
	17084208	11/32	⅞	Fixed	0.157/27	—	②	0.110	0.243	⑪
	17084209	11/32	⅞	Fixed	0.157/27	—	②	0.243	0.243	⑪
	17084210	11/32	⅞	Fixed	0.157/27	—	②	0.110	0.243	⑪
	17084240	5/16	1	Fixed	0.136/24	—	②	—	0.195	⑪

QUADRAJET CARBURETOR SPECIFICATIONS
Oldsmobile

Year	Carburetor Identification①	Float Level (in.)	Air Valve Spring (turn)	Pump Rod (in.)	Primary Vacuum Break (in./deg.)	Secondary Vacuum Break (in./deg.)	Secondary Opening (in.)	Choke Rod (in.)	Choke Unloader (in.)	Fast Idle Speed ④ (rpm)
'84	17084244	5/16	1	Fixed	0.136/24	—	②	—	0.195	⑪
	17084246	5/16	1	Fixed	0.123/22	0.136/24	②	—	0.195	⑪
	17084248	5/16	1	Fixed	0.136/24	—	②	—	0.195	⑪
	17084252	7/16	½	Fixed	0.157/27	0.269/41	②	—	0.220	⑪
	17084254	7/16	½	Fixed	0.157/27	0.269/41	②	—	0.220	⑪

① The carburetor identification number is stamped on the float bowl, next to the secondary throttle lever.
② 1800 rpm on Omega and 400 cu. in. engines with the cam follower on the highest step of the fast idle cam; 900 rpm on all others with the fast idle cam follower on the lowest step of the fast idle cam.
④ No measurement necessary on two point linkage; see text.
⑤ 3 turns after contacting lever for preliminary setting.
⑥ 2 turns after contacting lever for preliminary setting.
⑦ Inner hole
⑧ Not Adjustable
⑨ Front
⑩ Rear
⑪ See underhood sticker

QUADRAJET CARBURETOR SPECIFICATIONS
Pontiac

Year	Carburetor Identification①	Float Level (in.)	Air Valve Spring (turn)	Pump Rod (in.)	Primary Vacuum Break (in./deg.)	Secondary Vacuum Break (in./deg.)	Secondary Opening (in.)	Choke Rod (in.)	Choke Unloader (in.)	Fast Idle Speed ② (rpm)
'78	17058202	15/32	—	9/32	0.157	—	④	0.314	0.277	③
	17058204	15/32	—	9/32	0.157	—	④	0.314	0.277	③
	17058241	5/16	¾	3/8	0.117	0.103	④	0.096	0.243	③
	17058250	13/32	½	9/32	0.119	0.167	④	0.088	0.203	③
	17058253	13/32	½	9/32	0.119	0.167	④	0.088	0.203	③
	17058258	13/32	½	9/32	0.126	0.212	④	0.092	0.203	③
	17058263	17/32	5/8	3/8	0.164	0.260	④	0.129	0.220	③
	17058264	17/32	½	3/8	0.149	0.260	④	0.129	0.220	③
	17058266	17/32	½	3/8	0.149	0.260	④	0.129	0.220	③
	17058272	15/32	5/8	3/8	0.126	0.195	④	0.071	0.222	③
	17058274	17/32	½	3/8	0.149	0.260	④	0.129	0.220	③
	17058276	17/32	½	3/8	0.149	0.260	④	0.129	0.220	③
	17058278	17/32	½	3/8	0.149	0.260	④	0.129	0.220	③
	17058502	15/32	—	9/32	0.164	—	④	0.314	0.277	③
	17058504	15/32	—	9/32	0.164	—	④	0.314	0.277	③
	17058553	13/32	½	9/32	0.126	0.212	④	0.092	0.203	③
	17058582	15/32	7/8	9/32	0.179	—	④	0.314	0.277	③
	17058584	15/32	7/8	9/32	0.179	—	④	0.314	0.277	③

QUADRAJET CARBURETOR SPECIFICATIONS
Pontiac

Year	Carburetor Identification①	Float Level (in.)	Air Valve Spring (turn)	Pump Rod (in.)	Primary Vacuum Break (in./deg.)	Secondary Vacuum Break (in./deg.)	Secondary Opening (in.)	Choke Rod (in.)	Choke Unloader (in.)	Fast Idle Speed② (rpm)
'79	17058263	17/32	5/8	3/8	0.164	0.243	④	0.129	0.220	⑤
	17059250,253	13/32	1/2	9/35	0.129	0.183	④	0.096	0.220	⑤
	17059241	5/16	3/4	3/8	0.120	0.113	④	0.096	0.243	⑤
	17059271	9/16	5/8	3/8	0.142	0.227	④	0.010	0.203	⑤
	17059272	15/32	5/8	3/8	0.136	0.195	④	0.074	0.220	⑤
	17059502,504	15/32	7/8	1/4	0.164	—	④	0.243	0.243	⑤
	17059553	13/32	1/2	9/32	0.136	0.230	④	0.103	0.220	⑤
	17059582,584	15/32	7/8	11/32	0.203	—	④	0.243	0.314	⑤
'80	17080249	7/16	3/4	9/32⑥	0.129	0.114	④	0.096	0.243	③
	17080270	15/32	5/8	3/8⑦	0.149	0.211	④	0.074	0.220	③
	17080272	15/32	5/8	3/8⑦	0.129	0.175	④	0.074	0.203	③
	17080274	15/32	5/8	5/16⑥	0.110	0.164	④	0.083	0.203	③
	17080502	1/2	7/8	⑧	0.136	0.179	④	0.110	0.243	③
	17080504	1/2	7/8	⑧	0.136	0.179	④	0.110	0.243	③
	17080553	15/32	1/2	⑧	0.142	0.220	④	0.090	0.220	③
'81	17081202,204	11/32	7/8	⑧	0.157⑩	—	④	0.110	0.243	⑨
	17081203,207	11/32	7/8	⑧	0.157⑩	—	④	0.110	0.243	⑨
	17081216, 17,218	11/32	7/8	⑧	0.157⑩	—	④	0.110	0.243	⑨
	17081242	3/8	9/16	⑧	0.090⑩	0.077⑪	④	0.139	0.243	⑨
	17081243	5/16	9/16	⑧	0.103⑩	0.090⑪	④	0.139	0.243	⑨
	17081245	3/8	5/8	⑧	0.164⑩	0.136⑪	④	0.139	0.243	⑨
	17081247	3/8	5/8	⑧	0.164⑩	0.136⑪	④	0.139	0.243	⑨
	17081248,249	3/8	5/8	⑧	0.164⑩	0.136⑪	④	0.139	0.243	⑨
	17081253,254	15/32	1/2	⑧	0.142⑩	0.227⑪	④	0.071	0.220	⑨
	17081270	7/16	5/8	⑧	0.136⑩	0.211⑪	④	0.074	0.220	⑨
	17081272	7/16	5/8	⑧	0.136⑩	0.260⑪	④	0.074	0.220	⑨
	17081274	7/16	5/8	⑧	0.136⑩	0.220⑪	④	0.083	0.220	⑨
	17081289	13/36	5/8	⑧	0.164⑩	0.136⑪	④	0.139	0.243	⑨
'82	17082202	11/32	7/8	Fixed	0.110/20⑭	—	④	0.110	0.243	⑫⑮
	17082204	11/32	3/8⑬	Fixed	0.110/20⑭	—	④	0.110	0.243	⑫⑮
	17082203	11/32	7/8	Fixed	0.157/27	—	④	0.243	0.243	⑮
	17082207	11/32	7/8	Fixed	0.157/27	—	④	0.243	0.243	⑮
	17082244	7/16	9/16	Fixed	0.117/21	0.083/16	④	0.139	0.195	⑫
	17082245	3/8	5/8	Fixed	0.149/26	0.149/26	④	0.139	0.195	⑫
	17082246	3/8	5/8	Fixed	0.149/26	0.149/26	④	0.139	0.195	⑫
	17082247	13/32	5/8	Fixed	0.164/28	0.136/24	④	0.139	0.243	⑫
	17082248	13/32	5/8	Fixed	0.164/28	0.136/24	④	0.139	0.243	⑫
	17082251	15/32	1/2	Fixed	0.142/25	0.304/45	④	0.071	0.220	⑫

QUADRAJET CARBURETOR SPECIFICATIONS
Pontiac

Year	Carburetor Identification ①	Float Level (in.)	Air Valve Spring (turn)	Pump Rod (in.)	Primary Vacuum Break (in./deg.)	Secondary Vacuum Break (in./deg.)	Secondary Opening (in.)	Choke Rod (in.)	Choke Unloader (in.)	Fast Idle Speed ② (rpm)
'83	17082253	15/32	1/2	Fixed	0.142/25	0.227/36	④	0.071	0.220	⑫
	17082264	7/16	9/16	Fixed	0.117/20	0.083/16	④	0.139	0.195	⑫
	17082265	3/8	5/8	Fixed	0.149/26	0.149/26	④	0.139	0.195	⑫
	17082266	3/8	5/8	Fixed	0.149/26	0.149/26	④	0.139	0.195	⑫
	17082267	3/8	5/8	Fixed	0.164/28	0.136/24	④	0.139	0.243	⑫
	17082268	13/32	5/8	Fixed	0.164/28	0.136/24	④	0.139	0.243	⑫
'83	17082265	3/8	5/8	Fixed	0.149/26	0.149/26	②	0.139	0.195	⑯
	17082266	3/8	5/8	Fixed	0.149/26	0.149.26	②	0.139	0.195	⑯
	17082267	3/8	5/8	Fixed	0.149/26	0.149/26	②	0.096	0.195	⑯
	17082268	3/8	5/8	Fixed	0.149/26	0.149/26	②	0.096	0.195	⑯
	17083242	9/32	9/16	Fixed	0.110/20	—	②	0.139	0.243	⑯
	17083244	1/4	9/16	Fixed	0.117/21	0.083/16	②	0.139	0.195	⑯
	17083248	3/8	5/8	Fixed	0.149/26	0.149/26	②	0.139	0.195	⑯
	17083250	7/16	1/2	Fixed	0.157/27	0.271/42	②	0.071	0.220	⑯
	17083253	7/16	1/2	Fixed	0.157/27	0.269/41	②	0.071	0.220	⑯
	17083553	7/16	1/2	Fixed	0.157/27	0.269/41	②	0.071	0.220	⑯
'84	17084201	11/32	7/8	Fixed	0.157/27	—	②	0.110	0.243	⑪
	17084205	11/32	7/8	Fixed	0.157/27	—	②	0.243	0.243	⑪
	17084208	11/32	7/8	Fixed	0.157/27	—	②	0.110	0.243	⑪
	17084209	11/32	7/8	Fixed	0.157/27	—	②	0.243	0.243	⑪
	17084210	11/32	7/8	Fixed	0.157/27	—	②	0.110	0.243	⑪
	17084240	5/16	1	Fixed	0.136/24	—	②	—	0.195	⑪
	17084244	5/16	1	Fixed	0.136/24	—	②	—	0.195	⑪
	170804246	5/16	1	Fixed	0.123/22	.136/24	②	—	0.195	⑪
	17084248	5/16	1	Fixed	0.136/24	—	②	—	0.195	⑪
	17084252	7/16	1/2	Fixed	0.157/27	.269/41	②	—	0.220	⑪
	17084254	7/16	1/2	Fixed	0.157/27	.269/41	②	—	0.220	⑪

① The carburetor identification number is stamped on the float bowl, near the secondary throttle lever.
② On highest step.
③ 1½ turns after contacting lever for preliminary setting
④ No measurement necessary on two point linkage; see text.
⑤ 2 turns after contacting lever for preliminary setting.
⑥ Inner hole
⑦ Outer hole
⑧ Not adjustable
⑨ 4½ turns after contacting lever for preliminary setting

⑩ Front
⑪ Rear
⑫ 3 turns after contacting lever for preliminary setting
⑬ Firebird—7/8
⑭ Firebird—0.157 in./27°
⑮ Firebird—3⅛ turns after contacting lever for preliminary setting
⑯ See underhood sticker

QUADRAJET CARBURETOR SPECIFICATIONS
All Canadian Models

Year	Carburetor Identi-fication①	Float Level (in.)	Air Valve Spring (turn)	Pump Rod (in.)	Primary Vacuum Break (deg./in.)	Secondary Vacuum Break (deg./in.)	Secondary Opening (in.)	Choke Rod (in.)	Choke Unloader (in.)	Fast Idle Speed② (rpm)
'81	17080201	15/32	7/8	9/32②	—	23/0.129	④	0.314	0.277	⑤
	17080205	15/32	7/8	9/32②	—	23/0.129	④	0.314	0.277	⑤
	17080206	15/32	7/8	9/32②	—	23/0.129	④	0.314	0.277	⑤
	17080290	15/32	7/8	9/32②	—	26/0.149	④	0.314	0.277	⑤
	17080291	15/32	7/8	9/32②	—	26/0.149	④	0.314	0.277	⑤
	17080292	15/32	7/8	9/32②	—	26/0.149	④	0.314	0.277	⑤
	17080213	3/8	1	9/32②	23/0.129	30/0.179	④	0.234	0.260	⑤
	17080215	3/8	1	9/32②	23/0.129	30/0.179	④	0.234	0.260	⑤
	17080298	3/8	1	9/32②	23/0.129	30/0.179	④	0.234	0.260	⑤
	17080507	3/8	1	9/32②	23/0.129	30/0.179	④	0.234	0.260	⑤
	17080513	3/8	1	9/32②	23/0.129	30/0.179	④	0.234	0.260	⑤
	17081250	13/32	1/2	9/32②	26/0.149	34/0.211	④	0.090	0.220	⑤
	17080260	13/32	1/2	9/32②	26/0.149	34/0.211	④	0.090	0.220	⑤
	17081276	15/32	5/8	5/16②	20/0.110	28/0.164	④	0.083	0.203	⑤
	17081286	13/32	1/2	9/32②	18/0.096	34/0.211	④	0.077	0.220	⑤
	17081287	13/32	1/2	9/32②	18/0.096	34/0.211	④	0.077	0.220	⑤
	17081282	3/8	5/8	9/32②	20/0.110	—	④	0.110	0.243	⑤
	17081283	3/8	7/8	9/32②	20/0.110	—	④	0.110	0.243	⑤
	17081284	1/2	7/8	9/32③	20/0.110	—	④	0.110	0.243	⑤
	17081285	1/2	7/8	9/32③	20/0.110	—	④	0.110	0.243	⑤
	17080243	3/16	9/16	9/32②	14.5/0.075	16/0.083	④	0.075	0.179	⑤
	17081295	13/32	9/16	9/32②	14.5/0.075	13/0.066	④	0.075	0.220	⑤
	17081294	5/16	5/8	9/32②	24.5/0.139	14/0.071	④	0.139	0.243	⑤
	17081290	13/32	7/8	9/32②	46/0.314	24/0.136	④	0.314	0.277	⑤
	17081291	13/32	7/8	9/32②	46/0.314	24/0.136	④	0.314	0.277	⑤
	17081292	13/32	7/8	9/32②	46/0.314	24/0.136	④	0.314	0.277	⑤
	17081506	13/32	7/8	9/32②	46/0.314	36/0.227	④	0.314	0.227	⑤
	17081508	13/32	7/8	9/32②	46/0.314	36/0.227	④	0.314	0.227	⑤
	17080202	7/16	7/8	1/4②	20/0.110	—	④	0.110	0.243	⑤
	17080204	7/16	7/8	1/4②	20/0.110	—	④	0.110	0.243	⑤
	17080207	7/16	7/8	1/4②	20/0.110	—	④	0.110	0.243	⑤
'82	17082280	3/8	7/8	9/32②	25/0.142	—	④	0.110	0.243	⑤
	17082281	3/8	7/8	9/32②	25/0.142	—	④	0.110	0.243	⑤
	17082282	3/8	7/8	9/32②	25/0.142	—	④	0.110	0.243	⑤
	17082283	3/8	7/8	9/32②	25/0.142	—	④	0.110	0.243	⑤
	17082286	13/32	1/2	9/32②	22/0.123	34/0.211	④	0.077	0.243	⑤
	17082287	13/32	1/2	9/32②	22/0.123	34/0.211	④	0.077	0.243	⑤
	17082288	3/8	7/8	9/32②	25/0.142	—	④	0.110	0.243	⑤

QUADRAJET CARBURETOR SPECIFICATIONS
All Canadian Models

Year	Carburetor Identi-fication ①	Float Level (in.)	Air Valve Spring (turn)	Pump Rod (in.)	Primary Vacuum Break (deg./in.)	Secondary Vacuum Break (deg./in.)	Secondary Opening (in.)	Choke Rod (in.)	Choke Unloader (in.)	Fast Idle Speed ② (rpm)
'82	17082289	⅜	⅞	9/32 ②	25/0.142	—	④	0.110	0.243	⑤
	17082296	½	⅞	9/32 ②	25/0.142	—	④	0.110	0.243	⑤
	17082297	½	⅞	9/32 ②	25/0.142	—	④	0.110	0.243	⑤
'83	17080213	⅜	1	9/32	23/.129	30/.179	④	0.234	0.260	⑤
	17082213	9/32	1	9/32	23/.129	30/.179	④	0.234	0.260	⑤
	17082282	⅜	⅞	9/32	25/.142	—	④	0.110	0.243	⑤
	17082283	⅜	⅞	9/32	25/.142	—	④	0.110	0.243	⑤
	17082286	13/32	½	9/32	23/.129	34/.211	④	0.107	0.220	⑤
	17082287	13/32	½	9/32	23/.129	34/.211	④	0.107	0.220	⑤
	17082296	½	⅞	9/32	25/.142	—	④	0.110	0.243	⑤
	17082297	½	⅞	9/32	25/.142	—	④	0.110	0.243	⑤
	17083280	⅜	⅞	9/32	25/.142	—	④	0.110	0.243	⑤
	17083281	⅜	⅞	9/32	25/.142	—	④	0.110	0.243	⑤
	17083282	⅜	⅞	9/32	25/.142	—	④	0.110	0.243	⑤
	17083283	⅜	⅞	9/32	25/.142	—	④	0.110	0.243	⑤
	17083290	13/32	⅞	9/32	—	24/.136	④	0.314	0.251	⑤
	17083292	13/32	⅞	9/32	—	24/.136	④	0.314	0.251	⑤
	17083298	⅜	1	9/32	23/.129	30/.179	④	0.234	0.260	⑤
'84	17084280	⅜	⅞	9/32 ②	23/.129	—	④	0.110	0.243	⑤
	17084281	⅜	⅞	9/32 ②	23/.129	—	④	0.110	0.243	⑤
	17084282	⅜	⅞	9/32 ②	23/.129	—	④	0.110	0.243	⑤
	17084283	⅜	⅞	9/32 ②	23/.129	—	④	0.110	0.243	⑤
	17084284	⅜	⅞	9/32 ②	23/.129	—	④	0.110	0.243	⑤
	17084285	⅜	⅞	9/32 ②	23/.129	—	④	0.110	0.243	⑤

MITSUBISHI FEEDBACK CARBURETOR

General Information

The feedback carburetor system consists of various kinds of sensors and actuators and an on-board computer. If any feedback carburetor system components fail, interruption of the fuel supply or failure to supply the proper amount of fuel for engine operating conditions will result. This usually results in symptoms that include hard starting, unstable idle or poor driveability. If any of these symptoms are noted, first perform basic engine checks for ignition system operation or obvious problems such as loose connections or vacuum hoses, etc. The Mitsubishi FBC system can only be diagnosed with a special tester and adapter. Since instructions for connecting and using the diagnostic tester is included with the unit, they will not be covered here.

NOTE: The tester used is the same one for the Mitsubishi Electronically Controlled Injection (ECI).

ADJUSTMENTS

Float Level Adjustment

1. Invert the float chamber cover assembly without a gasket.
2. Position the universal float level gauge or suitable depth gauge and measure the distance from the bottom of the float to the surface of the float chamber cover. It should be 20mm (.787 in.). If the reading is not within 1 mm (.0394 in.), the shim under the needle seat must be changed. Adding or removing a shim will change the float level by three times the thickness of the shim.

3. To remove the float, slide the pin out and remove the float and needle.

4. Unscrew the retainer and remove the needle seat used with pliers.

NOTE: When removing the needle seat, clamp the chamferred portion with the jaws of the pliers. DO NOT clamp the machined surface of the needle seat that fits in the bore.

5. Check the filter for blockage or damage and replace if necessary.

6. Install a new O-ring into the needle seat.

7. Install the shim and filter into the needle seat.

8. Insert the needle seat assembly into the float chamber cover.

Mitsubishi feedback carburetor assembly showing component locations

9. Install the needle seal retainer and tighten the screw firmly.

10. Insert the needle into the seat.

11. Install the float and insert the retaining pin.

12. Check the distance from the bottom of the float to the surface of the float chamber cover and readjust if necessary.

Carburetor Removal

1. Disconnect the battery.

2. Drain the coolant down to intake manifold level or below.

3. Remove the air cleaner.

4. Place a suitable container under the fuel inlet fitting to catch any fuel that may be trapped in the line, then disconnect the fuel line from the carburetor inlet nipple.

Mitsubishi feedback carburetor assembly showing component locations

Schematic of Mitsubishi feedback carburetor system

Measuring float level with gauge (float chamber cover inverted)

DO NOT CLAMP HERE

CLAMP PLIERS HERE

Be extremely careful where the pliers clamp the needle seat assembly during removal

CHECK WEIGHT AND BALL

ANTI-OVERFILL DEVICE

Location of check weight and ball of the anti-overfill device

5. Disconnect the vacuum hoses from the carburetor.
6. Disconnect the throttle cable from the carburetor.
7. Remove the carburetor mounting bolts and carefully remove the carburetor from the engine. Hold the carburetor level to avoid spilling fuel from the float bowl.

Disassembly

───CAUTION───

Do not remove the following parts from the feedback carburetor:
* *Choke valves*
* *Choke levers and related parts*
* *Round nut of accelerator pump link*
* *Adjusting screws except the idle speed adjusting screws, idle mixture adjusting screw and dashpot adjusting screw*
* *Throttle valves*

DECELERATION SOLENOID VALVE

Location of deceleration solenoid valve in float chamber cover

ENRICHMENT SOLENOID VALVE

Location of enrichment solenoid valve in float chamber cover

1. Pull the water hose off the nipple of the throttle body and from the nipple of the wax element portion.
2. Grind down the head of the choke cover lock screws by using a hand grinder.
3. Remove the throttle return spring and the damper spring.
4. Remove the vacuum hose from the vacuum chamber and the throttle body.
5. Remove the accelerator pump rod from the throttle lever.
6. Remove the dashpot/idle-up actuator rod (manual transaxle), or idle-up actuator rod (automatic transaxle) from the free lever.

JET MIXTURE SOLENOID VALVE

Location of jet mixture solenoid valve in float chamber cover

Remove the float chamber cover screws (B) to remove the throttle body, then float chamber cover screws (A) to remove the float chamber from the main body

Location of needle valve assembly in float bowl

7. Remove the actuator from the float chamber cover.

8. Remove the deceleration solenoid valve from the float chamber cover.

9. Remove the enrichment solenoid valve from the float chamber cover.

10. Remove the jet mixture solenoid valve from the float chamber cover.

11. Remove the depression chamber rod from the secondary throttle lever.

12. Remove the vacuum (depression) chamber. To remove the depression chamber, first remove the choke breaker cover, then remove the depression chamber attaching screws.

13. Remove the float chamber cover screws (B) and remove the throttle body.

14. Remove the remaining chamber cover screws (A) and remove the float chamber from the main body.

15. Remove the check weight and ball and the steel ball of the anti-overfill device.

16. Pull off the pin and remove the float.

17. Remove the needle valve retainer and then remove the needle valve assembley with pliers.

18. Remove the main jets from the jet blocks. When the main jet is to be removed, use a screwdriver with the proper blade for the slot in the jet.

19. Remove the pilot jet retainer and pull out the secondary pilot jet with pliers.

20. Remove the accelerator pump mounting screws and remove the pump cover-link assembly, diaphragm, spring, body and gasket from main body.

21. Remove the snap ring from the sub EGR control valve pin.

22. Remove the pin and then remove the link from the valve, then remove the little steel ball and spring from the sub EGR control valve.

23. Remove the sub EGR control valve from the throttle body.

Assembly

The carburetor is assembled in the reverse of the disassembly procedure, paying special attention to the following items:

    a. Clean all parts before assembly

    b. Check that no air or fuel passages are blocked

    c. Check for smooth operation of all throttle and choke linkage

    d. Make sure the sub EGR valve operates smoothly

    e. When replacing a main or pilot jet, the old jet and the new jet must be the same size. The jets are selected after an exact flow measurement at the factory and must not be interchanged

Installation

1. Inspect the mating surfaces of the carburetor and intake manifold and make sure both surfaces are clean, smooth and free from any gasket material. Look for nicks, burrs or other damage.

2. Place a new carburetor gasket on the intake manifold.

3. Carefully place the carburetor on the intake manifold.

4. Install the carburetor mounting bolts and tighten them alternately to compress the gasket evenly. The nuts must be drawn down tightly to prevent vacuum leakage between the carburetor and the intake manifold.

5. Connect the throttle cable, vacuum hoses and fuel hoses.

6. Check for worn or loose vacuum hose connections.

7. Check to be sure the choke plate open fully when operated.

8. Check to see that full throttle travel is obtained.

9. Install the air cleaner and replace the element, if necessary.

10. Reconnect the battery cable. Start the engine and reset the idle speed to the specifications listed on the underhood emission sticker.

---CAUTION---

Priming the carburetor by pouring gasoline into the air horn while cranking the engine should be strictly avoided. Depressing the accelerator pedal several times while cranking the engine should be adequate.

Sub EGR valve assembly showing internal components

Idle Speed and Mixture Adjustment

NOTE: The carburetor must be removed and held in a suitable fixture for this procedure. DO NOT clamp the carburetor body in a vise. Fabricate a holding plate from heavy brackets or sheet metal and bolt the carburetor mounting flange to it.

1. Remove the carburetor from the engine.
2. Mount the carburetor in a suitable holding fixture and remove the concealment plug.
3. Reinstall the carburetor on the engine.
4. Start the engine and allow it to reach normal operating temperature. Make sure all accessories are off and the transaxle is in neutral.

5. Turn the ignition OFF and disconnect the negative terminal from the battery for about three seconds, then reconnect it.
6. Disconnect the oxygen sensor.
7. Run the engine for more than five seconds at 2000-3000 rpm, then let the engine return to idle for two minutes.
8. Using a suitable meter, set the engine CO and idle speed to the specifications listed on the underhood emission control sticker by turning the idle speed and mixture adjusting screws until the correct values are obtained.
9. Reconnect the oxygen sensor.
10. Reset the engine speed to specifications by turning the idle speed adjusting screw, if necessary.
11. Install the concealment plug to seal the idle mixture screw.

Fuel Injection Systems

SECTION

INDEX

NOTE: Please refer to the Application Chart at the front of this Manual.

FUEL INJECTION

General Information

There are two basic types of fuel injection systems currently in production, Port and Throttle Body. Constant Injection Systems (CIS) are a mechanically controlled, Port type of fuel injection that uses linkage between an air flow sensor and fuel distributor to regulate the air/fuel mixture by moving a piston up and down. Air Flow Controlled (AFC) Port and Throttle Body (TBI) injection systems use an intake air flow (or air mass) sensor and an electronic control unit that monitors engine conditions and then regulates the fuel mixture by sending electrical impulses to the injector(s). By varying the length of time the solenoid-type fuel injector is open, more or less fuel is delivered. A fuel injection systems is called PORT type when the injectors are mounted in the cylinder head and spray the fuel charge directly behind the intake valve. Throttle Body Injection (TBI) uses one or two injectors mounted atop the intake manifold (much like a conventional carburetor) that spray the fuel charge down through a throttle body butterfly valve. The fuel charge is drawn into the intake manifold and distributed to the cylinders in the conventional manner.

Fuel injection combined with electronics and various engine sensors provides a precise fuel management system that meets all the demands for improved fuel economy, increased performance and lower emissions more precisely and reliably than is possible with a conventional carburetor. A fuel injected engine generally averages ten percent more power and fuel economy with lower emissions than a carbureted engine. Even "feedback" carburetors with computer controls cannot achieve the accurate fuel metering necessary to meet the lower emission levels required by upcoming Federal standards. Because of its precise control, fuel injection allows the engine to operate with a stoichiometric or optimum fuel ratio of 14.7 parts air to one part fuel throughout the entire engine rpm range, under all operating conditions. This 14.7:1 fuel mixture assures that all the carbon and hydrogen is burned in the combustion chamber during the power stroke. This produces the lowest combination of emissions from unburned hydrocarbons, carbon monoxide and oxides of nitrogen in the exhaust gases. By using an oxygen sensor to measure the oxygen content of the exhaust gases, the on-board computer (control unit) can constantly adjust and "fine tune" the fuel mixture in response to changing temperature, load and altitude conditions. In addition, this degree of fuel control allows the catalytic converter to function at peak efficiency for emission control.

It's important to identify all system components, how they work and their relationship to one another in operation before attempting any maintenance or repair procedures on any particular type of fuel injection. All fuel injection systems are delicate and vulnerable to damage from rust, dirt, water and careless handling. The shock of hitting a cement floor when dropped from about waist height can ruin a control unit, for example. Because of the close tolerances involved in fuel injector construction (25 millionths of an inch on some), any rust or dirt particles in the fuel lines can ruin machined surfaces or block the nozzle completely. Water in the fuel can do more damage than a well-placed grenade and some fuel additives or chemicals may damage fuel lines or components like the oxygen sensor. Many fuel injection components, while similar in both appearance and function, can vary from one manufacturer to another so it is very important to identify exactly which type of injection system is being used on a particular engine, and to become familiar with all related sensors and equipment. In addition, there are manufacturer's modifications within the major groups of CIS, AFC and TBI type systems that utilize different sensors and electronic control units that are similar in appearance but are not interchangeable with any other system. For example, the Bosch L-Jetronic AFC injection system has four modifications that are designated LH, LH II, LU and Motronic. Each individual system has some sensors, capabilities and characteristics unique to its own design. Although they may look pretty much the same to

the casual observer, each PROM or memory unit is programmed differently for each type of engine it is supposed to regulate. For this reason, the careful recording of part numbers or engine serial numbers and the correct identification of vehicle make, model and year is vital to insure the correct replacement parts are obtained. Always double check all numbers before installing any new component.

COMPARING CARBURETOR AND FUEL INJECTION CIRCUITS

Carburetor Component	Fuel Injection Component
Accelerator pump	Wide open throttle (WOT) switch
Fast idle cam	Auxiliary air bypass device
Choke pull-off	Thermo-time switch
Float and needle valve	Pressure regulator
Float bowl	Fuel manifold
Power valve metering rods	Manifold pressure or airflow sensor
Metering jets	Fuel injectors
Choke assembly	Cold start injector
Carburetor linkage	Throttle valve cable
Idle speed adjusting screw	Bypass air adjusting screw
Fast idle solenoid	Idle air control valve

NOTE: These are general comparisons. Some fuel injection systems may not use all of the components listed, while others incorporate additional sensors, actuators and control capabilities such as ignition timing or idle speed control systems.

COMPARING CARBURETOR CIRCUITS TO FUEL INJECTION COMPONENTS

It makes fuel injection a little easier to understand by comparing the functions of major systems and components in the carburetor to those in a typical port fuel injection system. Fuel injection is basically just a more precise way of doing the same thing—delivering the correct air/fuel mixture to the combustion chambers at the correct time under all engine operating conditions.

One major difference is that the accelerator pedal actually feeds fuel to the intake manifold when depressed (via the accelerator pump linkage) on the carburetor, even if the engine is stopped and the ignition switch is turned OFF. On a fuel injection system, the accelerator pedal merely opens or closes the butterfly-type throttle plate, allowing more air to flow into the intake system. There is no direct, mechanical linkage connection that provides fuel for the engine. The amount of fuel delivered by the port fuel injection system is regulated either by movement of the fuel distributor plunger (CIS systems), or by the electronic control unit that sets the fuel mixture according to the output signals from various sensors (AFC system). It's impossible to flood a fuel injected engine by pumping the accelerator pedal with the ignition switch off since the pedal only opens and closes an air valve. No fuel can be delivered unless the control unit is energized and sends impulses to the injectors.

To assist cold starting, modern carburetors incorporate an automatic choke assembly which consists of mechanical linkage operating a butterfly valve that reduces the amount of incoming air, thereby increasing the amount of vacuum that pulls on the main fuel discharge nozzle in the carburetor. This increased vacuum draws a larger quantity of fuel from the float bowl, providing the richer fuel mixture necessary for cold starting. The butterfly valve (choke plate) movement is controlled either manually, or by a bimetal coil spring that responds to temperature and is usually heated either by hot water from the cooling system, hot air from the exhaust manifold, or by an electric element in the choke spring housing. Because it is a mechanical system, it is vulnerable to malfunctions due to loose or sticking linkage, broken springs, and incorrect adjustment, causing hard starting or flooding problems on cold engines. All fuel injection systems incorporate a cold start system that does essentially the same thing as the carburetor choke system, but in a much more precise way with different components. Some fuel injection systems use an extra fuel injector called a "cold start valve" that is mounted in the intake manifold downstream from the throttle plate. This solenoid-type injector provides an extra fuel charge when the ignition is switched ON with the engine cold and is regulated through a temperature sensitive switch designed to cut off the signal to the cold start injector after about 12 seconds. This temperature sensitive switch, called a "thermo-time switch," is also designed to lock out the cold start system operation when the engine is warm and the enriched fuel mixture is not necessary for starting. Some computer-controlled fuel injection systems are designed to enrich the fuel mixture by providing longer signal to the injectors (increasing the amount of time the nozzle is open) without the need for a separate cold start injector. The longer the solenoid-type injectors are open, the more fuel is delivered to the combustion chambers.

NOTE: Because some cold start injectors are designed to operate when the key is switched ON, it is possible to flood a cold engine by turning the key on and off a few times. Although the effect is the same as pumping the accelerator on a carbureted engine, the cause is totally different. Some manufacturers design the cold start valve to spray only when the starter is cranking to avoid this problem.

Safety Precautions

—CAUTION—

Whenever working on or around any fuel injection system, always observe these general precautions to prevent the possibility of personal injury or damage to fuel injection components.

• Never install or remove battery cables with the key ON or the engine running. Jumper cables should be connected with the key OFF to avoid power surges that can damage electronic control units. Engines equipped with computer controlled fuel injection systems should avoid both giving and getting jump starts due to the possibility of serious damage to components due to arcing in the engine compartment.
• Always remove the battery cables before charging the battery. Never use a high-output charger on an installed battery or attempt to use any type of "hot shot" (24 volt) starting aid.
• Never remove or attach wiring harness connectors with the ignition switch ON, especially to the electronic control unit.
• When checking compression on engines with AFC injection systems, unplug the cable from the battery to the relays.
• Always depressurize the fuel system before attempting to disconnect any fuel lines.
• Always use clean rags and tools when working on an open fuel injection system and take care to prevent any dirt from entering the system. Wipe all components clean before installation and prepare a clean work area for disassembly and inspection of components. Use lint-free cloths to wipe components and avoid using any caustic cleaning solvents.
• Do not drop any components during service procedures and never apply 12 volts directly to a fuel injector unless instructed specifically to do so. Some injectors windings are designed to safely handle only 4 or 5 volts and can be destroyed in seconds if 12 volts are applied directly to the connector.
• Remove the electronic control unit if the vehicle is to be placed in an environment where temperatures exceed approximately 176 degrees F (80 degrees C), such as a paint spray booth or when arc or gas welding near the control unit location in the car.

BOSCH CONTINUOUS INJECTION SYSTEM (CIS)

K and KE-Jetronic
GENERAL INFORMATION

The Bosch CIS fuel injection system differs from the electronic AFC system in that injection takes place continuously: it is controlled through variation of the fuel flow rate through the injectors, rather than by variation of the fuel injection duration as on the AFC system. Prior to 1983, CIS used no electronic computer, and is an electro-mechanical system that will provide suitable air/fuel mixtures under all driving conditions.

Basic operation schematic of K-Jetronic fuel injection system

1. Fuel tank
2. Fuel delivery pump
3. Fuel accumulator
4. Fuel filter
5. Fuel distributor
6. System pressure regulator
7. Warming-up regulator
8. Airflow meter
9. Sensor plate
10. Throttle butterfly
11. Idle adjustment screw
12. Aux. air device
13. Electric starting valve
14. Thermo time switch
15. Injectors
16. Vacuum limiter
17. Start air valve

Typical K-Jetronic fuel injection system (without push valve)

1. Mixture–control unit
1a. Air–flow sensor
1b. Fuel distributor
1c. Idle–mixture adjusting screw
2. Fuel tank
3. Electric fuel pump
4. Fuel accumulator
5. Fuel filter
6. Primary–pressure regulator
6a. Push–up valve
7. Fuel injection valve
8. Idle speed adjusting screw
9. Battery
10. Ignition and starting switch
11. Control relay
12. Ignition distributor
13. Start valve
14. Thermo-time switch
15. Auxiliary air device
16. Warm–up regulator
16a. Full–load diaphragm

Typical K-Jetronic fuel injection system (with push valve)

The complete CIS system consists of the following components: air/fuel control unit (housing both air flow sensor and fuel distributor), electric fuel pump(s) (and fuel pressure accumulator), fuel filter, control pressure regulator, fuel injectors, auxiliary air valve, cold start injector, engine sensors and various switches and relays.

The heart of the early (non-electronic) CIS system is the air/fuel control unit. It consists of an air flow sensor and a fuel distributor. Intake air flows past the air cleaner and through the air venturi raising or lowering the counterbalanced air flow sensor plate. The plate is connected to a pivoting lever which moves the control plunger in the fuel distributor in direct proportion to the intake air flow.

NOTE: The KE type CIS system uses a new electronic actuator which replaces several mixture control components, including the push valve, frequency valve and control pressure regulator.

The fuel distributor, which controls the amount of fuel to the injectors, consists of a line pressure regulator, a control plunger, and (4, 6, or 8) pressure regulator valves (one for each injector). The line pressure regulator maintains the fuel distributor inlet pressure at a constant psi., and will recirculate fuel to the tank if pressure exceeds this value. The control plunger, which is connected to the air flow sensor plate, controls the amount of fuel available to each of the pressure regulator valves. The presure regulator valves maintain a constant-fuel pressure differential between the inlet and outlet sides of the control plunger. This is independent of the

Typical KE-Jetronic fuel injection system

amount of fuel passing through the valves, which varies according to plunger height.

The fuel distributor on the KE-Jetronic is different than the earlier K model. The system pressure regulator piston and pressure compensating valve are no longer installed and the adjusting screws and compression springs are moved to the lower chamber. An additional strainer has been installed in front of the differential pressure valve and a strainer with a permanent magnet is in the supply line to the electrohydraulic actuator to catch any rust particles in the fuel. The pressure on top of the control plunger is now equal to system pressure and there is a pressure measuring connection located in the lower chamber.

The main difference between the K and KE-Jetronic is the electrohydraulic actuator used for mixture correction. The actuator is flanged onto the fuel distributor and acts as a pressure regulator which operates as a plate valve. The place valve position can be varied, causing a differential pressure change in the actuator and lower chamber and thereby correcting the mixture. The signal for actuation comes from an electronic control unit which adjusts the mixture according to the engine operating conditions.

With the ignition ON, the control unit is connected to battery voltage. A voltage correction circuit prevents fluctuations when components are energized and controls the operating voltage to approximately 8 volts. The amount of cranking enrichment depends on coolant temperature. A timing element regulates the enrichment after one second to the warm-up plus the after-starting value. This value remains constant as long as the engine is cranked. The after-start enrichment establishes smooth running characteristics after starting: the amount of after-start enrichment also depends on coolant temperatures, as does warm-up enrichment. The lower the temperature, the higher the current rate at the actuator and the greater the fuel enrichment.

NOTE: The KE-Jetronic system also controls altitude enrichment, based on a signal from an altitude correction capsule.

The injectors themselves are spring loaded and calibrated to open at a preset pressure. They are not electrically operated as on the AFC fuel injection system.

The control pressure regulator, located on the intake manifold, acts to regulate the air/fuel mixture according to engine temperature. When the engine is cold, the control pressure regulator enriches the mixture. This is accomplished when a certain amount of fuel is bled off into a separate control pressure system. The control pressure regulator maintains this fuel at a set pressure. The regulator is connected to the upper side of the fuel distributor control plunger. When the engine temperature is below operating parameters, a bi-metal spring in the regulator senses this and reduces the fuel pressure on top of the plunger, allowing the plunger to rise further and channel more fuel to the regulator valves and injectors, thereby enriching the mixture. When the engine warms, the bi-metal spring in the regulator increases the pressure back to the preset value leaning the air/fuel mixture back to its normal operating ratio.

The auxiliary air valve provides extra air for the richer mixture during warm-up, thus raising the engine speed and improving cold driveability. The auxiliary air valve, which also has a temperature sensitive bi-metal spring, works directly with the control pressure regulator. At cold start-up, the valve is fully open. As the engine warms, an electric coil slowly closes the valve (4-8 minutes max.), blocking off the extra air and lowering the idle speed.

The cold start injector, located on the inlet duct, sprays extra fuel into the intake air stream during starter motor operation when the engine is cold.

The thermal time switch, located on the cylinder head, actuates the cold injector. The switch has a bi-metal spring which senses coolant temperature and an electric coil which limits the cold start injector spray to about 12 seconds, to prevent flooding the engine.

The fuel accumulator has a check valve which keeps residual fuel pressure from dropping below a minimum psi when the engine or fuel pump are shut off. The fuel system is always pressurized, preventing vapor lock in a hot start situation.

Add-on functions of the KE-Jetronic

Engine speed → Electronic control unit → Electro-hydraulic correcting element

Engine temperature →

Position of sensor plate →

Position of throttle idling/full-load →

Lambda →

Air pressure (altitude) →

Other input signals →

Influenced via differential pressure:

Voltage increase for starting

After-start enrichment

Warm-up

Acceleration enrichment

Full-load enrichment

Deceleration shutoff

Lambda control

Load matching of Lambda control

Altitude compensation

Schematic of KE-Jetronic operation

—CAUTION—

Because the fuel system is constantly under pressure, it is very important to follow the procedures outlined under "Relieving Fuel System Pressure" before attempting to disconnect any fuel lines.

Engine emissions are controlled by means of a catalytic converter and/or Lambda (Oxygen) Sensor system, which provides a signal to regulate the fuel mixture according to the measured oxygen content of the exhaust gases.

NOTE: On KE type CIS fuel injection systems the oxygen sensor is electrically heated for faster operation.

On-Car Service

Water in the fuel, and the resulting rust, are the number one enemies of any fuel injection system, especially CIS. Rust particles inflict more damage more often on K-Jetronic than any other Bosch injection system. Because normal operating pressure on K systems ranges from 65-85 psi, the fuel pump usually pushes any

1. Outlet
2. Nylon strainer
3. Paper element
4. Arrow showing direction of flow
5. Rubber cone
6. Inlet

Cross section of typical fuel filter

TROUBLESHOOTING—K-JETRONIC

Symptoms

Engine does not start or starts poorly when **cold**	Engine does not start or starts poorly when **warm**	Irregular idle (engine shakes) during warm-up	Irregular idle (engine shakes) with engine **warm**	Engine does not draw fuel smoothly (backfires)	Engine misfires under full load	Insufficient power	Engine runs on (diesels)	Excessive fuel consumption	Flat spot during acceleration	Idle CO value too **high**	Idle CO value too **low**	Idle speed cannot be adjusted (too high)	Engine stalls immediately after starting	Cause(s)
►	►	►	►		►			►		►				Vacuum system leaking (see *Vacuum Leaks*)
►	►		►			►	►		►	►	►			Air flow sensor plate and/or control plunger not moving smoothly (see *Air Flow Sensor Movement*)
	►					►								Air flow sensor plate stop incorrectly set (see *Air Flow Sensor Position*)
►		►												Auxiliary air valve does not open (see *Auxiliary Air Valve*)
											►			Auxiliary air valve does not close (see *Auxiliary Air Valve*)
►	►			►									►	Electric fuel pump not operating (see *Fuel Pump*)
►														Defective cold start system (see *Cold Start System*)
	►	►				►	►			►				Leaking cold start valve (see *Cold Start System*)
►		►												Incorrect cold control pressure (see *Warm-up Regulator*)
	►		►	►	►	►			►				►	Warm control pressure too high (see *Warm-up Regulator*)
			►	►		►			►	►	►		►	Warm control pressure too low (see *Warm-up Regulator*)
				►	►				►				►	Incorrect system pressure (see *System Pressure*)
	►													Fuel system pressure leakage (see *Fuel Leaks*)
	►	►	►		►			►						Injection valve(s) leaking, opening pressure too low (see *Testing Injectors*)
		►	►		►			►						Unequal fuel delivery between cylinders (see *Comparative Test*)
►	►	►	►			►	►	►		►	►			Basic idle and/or CO adjustment incorrect (see *Idle and CO Adjustment*)
					►									Throttle plate does not open completely

water right through the fuel filter. A small plastic filter in the center of the fuel distributor traps the water, which then rusts out the fuel distributor. Not only will the rust block the tiny metering slits in the fuel distributor, it can also flow into the injectors and warmup compensator. Finding rust in one part usually means there's rust in the other. When rust particles block a metering slit, the cylinder fed by that slit will either die completely or develop an intermittent misfire closely resembling the conditions created by a bad spark-plug. If the plug is known to be good, look for rust or water in the fuel. Disconnect the injector lines and spread fresh white paper towels on the workbench. Remove the entire fuel distributor and tap it gently against the bench. Shake and tap it again. If rust particles shake out of those injector line openings, replace the fuel distributor and flush the lines.

Water contamination can be prevented with regular fuel filter changes. Filters for these cars are expensive, but a rusty fuel distributor can't be fixed.

PRELIMINARY CHECKS

NOTE: Before doing any injection system testing, first check the three basics; ignition, compression and the fuel gauge.

Always make a complete ignition check first and then perform all the injection pressure tests in sequence.

The cause of many CIS complaints is a minor vacuum leak. Vacuum leaks fool the fuel metering system and affect the mixture. This gives poor gas economy and poor performance. Look for leaks at:
1. EGR valve
2. Intake manifold
3. Cold start injector
4. Air sensor boot
5. Brake booster vacuum lines
6. Air ducts

Also check vacuum limiter, evaporative canister, and A/C door actuator.

To quick test the system for leaks, disconnect the auxiliary air valve hose, block open the throttle, and apply pressure to the hose. Use a spray bottle of soapy water to hit all the fittings where leaks could occur.

RELIEVING FUEL SYSTEM PRESSURE

—CAUTION—

Fuel pressure must be relieved before attempting to disconnect any fuel lines.

1. Carefully loosen the fuel line on the control pressure regulator (large connection).
2. Wrap a clean rag around the connection while loosening to catch any fuel.

Alternate Method For Relieving Fuel Pressure

1. Disconnect the electrical plug from the cold start valve.
2. Using a jumper wire, apply 12 volts to the cold start valve terminal for 10 seconds.
3. Reconnect the cold start valve.

1. Intake side
2. Excess pressure valve
3. Roller cell pump
4. Electric motor armature
5. Non-return check valve
6. Pressure side

Typical roller cell pump

Check K-Jetronic systems for vacuum leaks at the arrows

FUEL PUMP TESTS

The electric fuel pump is a roller cell type with the electric motor permanently surrounded by fuel. An eccentrically mounted roller disc is fitted with rollers resting in notches around the circumference. These rollers are pressured against the thrust ring of the pump housing by centrifugal force. The fuel is carried in the cavities between the rollers and the pump delivers more than the maximum requirement to the engine so that fuel pressure is maintained under all operating conditions. During starting, the pump runs as long as the ignition key is turned. The pump continues to run once the engine starts, but has a safety device that will stop the pump if the ignition is turned on but the engine stops moving.

NOTE: Some models utilize a priming fuel pump, mounted in the tank, in addition to the main fuel pump.

Fuel Pump Power Check

Remove the round cover plate from the top of the fuel pump and measure the voltage between the positive and negative terminals when the pump is operating. The lowest permissible voltage is 11.5 V. Disconnect the terminals connecting the pump to the air flow sensor and the warm-up regulator if these are to be checked later. If the pump is dead, check the fuse, the ground, and try bridging the relay with a jumper wire. During winter months, water in the gas can cause the pump to freeze and then blow a fuse. K-Jetronic type pumps need 12 volts and a good ground. A relay located somewhere in the pump's power wire operates the pumps. And like L-Jetronic systems, the relay may be a hide-and-seek item. All K-Jetronic pumps are fused someplace in the car, usually right in the vehicle's fuse panel.

Fuel Pump Safety Circuit Check

The pump will only run if the starter motor is actuated or if the engine is running.
1. Remove the air filter.
2. Turn on the ignition and briefly depress the sensor plate.
3. Remove the coil wire from the distributor.
4. Connect a voltmeter to the positive fuel pump terminal and ground.
5. Actuate the starter. The voltmeter should indicate 11 volts.
6. If the fuel pump runs only when the sensor plate is depressed or only when the engine is cranked, replace the fuel pump relay. If the pump is already running when the ignition is turned ON, replace the safety switch.

Fuel Volume Test

The test point for fuel pump operation depends on the type of fuel distributor. Fuel distributors WITH push valves (most vehicles covered in this manual) have two fuel lines connecting with the warm-up regulator, the other fuel line connects to a "T" and returns to the gas tank. Determine whether the vehicle to be tested is fitted with or without a push valve before proceeding further.

1. Remove the gas cap to vent tank pressure.

2. Disconnect the return fuel line leading to the gas tank at the appropriate test point.

3. Hold the line coming from the fuel distributor in a large container (1500 cc or larger). Inflexible metal fuel lines may require a rubber hose to reach the container.

4. Remove the electric plug from the warm-up regulator and the auxiliary air valve. Bridge the electric safety circuit for 30 seconds. Delivery rate should be about one quart in 30 seconds.

5. If fuel quantity is not within specification, check for sufficient voltage supply to the fuel pump (minimum 11.5 volts) or a dirty fuel filter. If all the above are satisfactory, replace the electric fuel pump.

NOTE: Use a bridging adapter to energize the fuel pump through the relay connector on early models without push valves.

PRESSURE TESTS

Diagnose a K-Jetronic system in this order: check cold control pressure first, hot control pressure next, then primary pressure, and finally rest pressure. The gauge for testing K-Jetronic always tees into the line running between the fuel distributor and the warmup compensator. With the 3-way valve open, the gauge remains teed-in and therefore reads control pressure. Remember that control pressure is derived or fed from the primary circuit pressure so a pressure change in one circuit means a change in the other.

Closing the valve shuts off fuel flow to the warm-up compensator and forces the gauge to read only one circuit—the primary circuit.

Fuel pressure test points with push valve (top) and without push valve (bottom). Most 1978 and later K-Jetronic systems have push valves.

When you shut the engine off and leave the 3-way valve open, the teed-in gauge should show the system's holding pressure. This residual pressure is called rest pressure. The valve functions are: *valve open—control pressure; valve closed—primary pressure; valve open and engine off—rest pressure.*

Control Pressure Test-Engine Cold

1. Connect a pressure gauge between the fuel distributor and the control pressure regulator.

2. Remove the electrical connector from the regulator.

3. Idle the engine for no more than one minute.

4. Read the control pressure from the chart for cold control. If control pressure is wrong, check the control pressure (warmup) regulator for proper operation.

CIS PRESSURE TEST SPECIFICATIONS

(All measurements in psi)

Manu-facturer	Normal Fuel Pressure	Injector Opening Pressure	Rest Pressure	System Pressure
Audi (all models)	49–55	36–59	23–35	65–78 ①
BMW 320i	49–55	36–52	23–35	65–75
Mercedes-Benz (all models)	49–55	36–52	41	65–75
Peugeot 505	49–55	44–59	38	65–75
Porsche (all models)	38–55	44–59	14–25	65–75
Saab (all models)	49–55	44–59	14–22	65–75
VW (all models)	49–55	51–59	35	68–78
Volvo (all models)	49–55	37–51	25	65–75 ①

NOTE: Minimum-maximum test ranges are given. Exact pressures may vary.

① Turbo models: 75–84 psi

Control Pressure Test—Engine Warm

1. Carry out this test when poor performance has been experienced when the engine is warm. Connect gauge and 3-way valve.

2. Open the valve.

3. Connect the warm-up regulator plug.

4. Leave the ignition switched on until rest pressure is present.

5. Refer to the test values.

6. If the value should differ, replace the warm-up regulator.

NOTE: Perform primary and rest pressure tests before disconnecting the gauge and 3-way valve.

Primary Pressure Test

Close the 3-way valve. Switch on the ignition. Refer to the test values. If the line pressure should differ from the recommended values this may be due to:

• Insufficient pressure from fuel pump Blockage of the strainer in the tank

• Leakage in the fuel line

When you close the 3-way valve with the engine idling and the primary pressure reads low, there could be a fuel pump problem or a primary regulator problem. To isolate on from the other, locate

Typical fuel pressure test connection

the return line leading from the fuel distributor back to the gas tank. Now plug the return line securely at some convenient point. Have an assistant switch on the pump *just long enough* to get a pressure reading. If the pump is good, the pressure will jump almost instantly to 100 psi or higher. Should the primary pressure exceed 116 psi during this momentary test, the check valve in the intake side of the fuel pump will vent the pressure back into the gas tank.

If the fuel pump produces good pressure with the return line plugged, then the primary pressure regulator is causing a low primary pressure reading.

Rest Pressure Test

Good rest pressure enables a K-Jetronic-equipped engine to start easily when it's hot. If the K system loses rest pressure for any reason, the injector lines will vapor lock. Then the driver has to crank the engine until the pump can replenish the lines with liquid fuel.

If rest pressure drops off too quickly, start the engine and run it long enough to build the system pressure back up. Stop the engine, pull the electrical connector off the cold start injector and remove the injector from the intake manifold. If the cold start injector is dripping, replace it and re-check the rest pressure.

If the cold start valve is holding pressure, reinstall it and run the engine again to build up pressure. Stop the engine and close the 3-way valve. If the pressure reading remains steady now, the return side of the system—the warm-up compensator—is leaking. Replace the compensator.

If the rest pressure still drops rapidly after closing the 3-way valve, the leak is in the feed side of the system. This could mean a bad fuel pump, bad accumulator, or a bad primary pressure regulator.

The fuel pump's intake hose is flexible. Clamp this hose shut and recheck rest pressure. If the system holds pressure, then the check ball in the output side of the pump is leaking.

A sharp eye and ear will help isolate a bad accumulator. Watch the pressure gauge as a helper shuts off the engine. If the accumulator is good, the pressure will drop, stop for a second, and then the gauge needle will actually rise—pressure will increase for a moment—before the pressure stabilizes. If you don't see that slight upward needle movement, the accumulator is leaking rest pressure. Furthermore, a bad accumulator will cause a loud, tell-tale groaning noise at the fuel pump. If still in doubt about the accumulator, try blocking off its return line.

The same primary pressure regulator that can cause low primary pressure can also leak *rest* pressure. If you've eliminated the fuel pump and the accumulator, install a primary regulator repair kit.

Component Removal and Testing

LINE PRESSURE REGULATOR

The line pressure regulator ensures that the pressure in the circuit remains constant when the fuel pump is in operation and also controls the recirculation of fuel to the tank. When the fuel pump is switched off, the regulator will cause a rapid pressure drop to approximately 2.5 bar (kp/cm^2, 35 psi), i.e. the rest pressure, which is maintained by means of the O-ring seal and the quantity of fuel contained in the fuel accumulator. The purpose of the rest pressure is to prevent the fuel from vaporizing in the circuit when the engine is warm, which would otherwise make restarting difficult.

The line pressure regulator forms an integral unit with a shut-off valve to which the return fuel line from the control pressure regulator is connected. When the fuel pump is operating, the shut-off valve is actuated mechanically by the control pressure regulator, whereupon the return fuel from the control pressure regulator bypasses the shut-off valve to the return line.

Fuel pressure regulator on fuel pump (arrow)

When the fuel pump stops running and the line pressure regulator valve is pressed into its seating, the shut-off valve is also pressed into its seating, preventing the fuel system from emptying through the control pressure return.

Removal and Installation

The pressure regulator is removed by loosening the screw plug on the fuel distributor and removing the copper gasket, shim, spring, control piston and O-ring. On 1979 and later systems, a push valve is attached to the large screw plug. Make sure all parts are kept clean and in order for assembly. Replace the O-ring and copper gasket, especially if any fuel leakage is noted.

————————**CAUTION**————————

Relieve fuel system pressure before removing the screw plug.

NOTE: The piston in front of the shim is matched to the housing and is not replaceable.

Fuel pressure regulator without push valve

1. Mounting screw	8. O-ring
2. Seal	9. Shim (0.1-0.5mm)
3. Allen screw plug	10. Spring
4. Washer	11. Spacer
5. Push valve	12. Snap ring
6. Hex screw plug	13. O-ring
7. Washer	14. Repair kit contents

Fuel pressure regulator with push valve

Fuel Pressure Adjustment

NOTE: On some early models, the fuel pressure can be adjusted on the regulator with the adjusting screw. Adjust to 28 psi. If a slight turn of the screw shows no change of pressure, replace the regulator.

If the fuel distributor is fitted with a push valve, loosen the large screw plug with attached push valve assembly. Change the adjusting shim as required to raise or lower fuel system pressure. Each 0.1mm increase in shim thickness increases fuel pressure by 2.2 psi.

If the fuel distributor doesn't have a push valve, remove the screw plug and change the shim as required. Again, each 0.1mm increase is shim thickness will increase system pressure by 2.2 psi.

WARM-UP REGULATOR

When the engine is cold, the warm-up regulator reduces control pressure, causing the metering slits in the fuel distributor to open further. This enrichment process prevents combustion miss during the warm-up phase of engine operation and is continually reduced as temperature rises. The warm-up regulator is a spring controlled flat seat diaphragm-type valve with an electrically heated bi-metal spring. When cold, the bi-metal spring overcomes the valve spring pressure, moving the diaphragm and allowing more fuel to be diverted out of the control pressure circuit thereby lowering the

Warm-up regulator typical of California models

1. Electrical coil
2. Bimetal spring
3. Spring
4. Diaphragm valve

Warm-up regulator typical of Federal (49 States) models

1. Electrical coil
2. Bimetal spring
3. Spring
4. Diaphragm valve
5. Connection for hose to intake duct
6. Spring
7. Diaphragm

control pressure. When the bi-metal spring is heated electrically or by engine temperature the valve spring pushes the diaphragm up, allowing less fuel to be diverted thereby raising the control pressure. When the bi-metal spring lifts fully off the valve spring the warm-up enrichment is completed and control pressure is maintained at normal level by the valve spring. The warm-up regulator should be checked when testing fuel pressure.

Control pressure regulator showing connector

Testing

1. Disconnect the terminal from the warm-up regulator and connect a voltmeter across the contacts in the connector. Ensure that the ignition is switched on and that the safety circuit connection at the air flow sensor has been bypassed. The lowest permissible voltage is 11.5V.
2. Check that there are no breaks in the heater coil of the regulator by connecting a test lamp in series with the coil. If the coil is found to be damaged, the warm-up regulator should be replaced.
3. Connect an ohmmeter across the terminals in the regulator socket. Resistance must be 16–22 ohms. If the resistance is not within the specifications, the regulator will require replacement.

NOTE: The system is under considerable constant pressure. The only practical test that should be attempted is one using an ohmmeter. Be sure the engine is at normal operating temperature. There should be no loose fuel fittings or other fire hazards when the electrical connections are disengaged.

Removal and Installation

1. Disconnect the negative battery cable.
2. Unplug the electrical connector.
3. Depressurize the fuel system as previously described.

NOTE: Wrap a cloth around the connection to catch any escaping fuel.

4. Remove both of the fuel lines.
5. Remove the vacuum hose.
6. Unscrew the four mounting bolts and remove the control pressure regulator.
7. Installation is in the reverse order of removal.

FUEL ACCUMULATOR

This device maintains the fuel system pressure at a constant level under all operating conditions. The pressure regulator, incorporated into the fuel distributor housing, keeps delivery pressure at approximately 5.0 bar (73 psi). Because the fuel pump delivers more fuel than the engine can use, a plunger shifts in the regulator to open a port which returns excess fuel to the tank. When the engine is switched off and the primary pressure drops, the pressure regulator closes the return port and prevents further pressure reduction in the system.

The fuel accumulator has a check valve which keeps residual fuel pressure from dropping below a pre-determined pressure when the engine or fuel pump are shut off.

1. Inlet
2. Outlet
3. Accumulator housing
4. Diaphragm
5. Stop
6. Spring

Cross section of typical fuel accumulator

Removal and Installation

The fuel accumulator is usually mounted near or on the fuel pump bracket somewhere near the fuel tank. It may be necessary to remove the fuel pump assembly to gain access to the fuel accumulator. Loosen the hose clamps and the retaining clamp and remove the accumulator. Reverse the procedure to install.

———————CAUTION———————
Relieve fuel system pressure before disconnecting any fuel lines.

Testing

If the pump fails a volume test, raise the car and trace the fuel feed line back to the pump. Look for crimped fuel lines from a carelessly placed jack. Plug the accumulator return hose and repeat the volume test. If this yields good fuel volume, the accumulator diaphragm is ruptured. Soak a new fuel filter with clean gas and install it. Remember to wet the filter beforehand. When 80 psi of incoming fuel hits a dry filter, it can tear off some of the element and carry the paper debris into the rest of the system.

FUEL DISTRIBUTOR

K-Jetronic

The fuel distributor meters the correct amount of fuel to the individual cylinders according to the position of the air flow sensor plate. A control plunger opens or closes metering slits in the barrel, allowing more or less fuel to pass into the system. Control pressure assures that the plunger follows the movement of the sensor plate immediately. Control pressure is tapped from primary fuel pressure through a restriction bore. It acts through a damping restriction on the control plunger, eliminating any oscillations of the sensor plate due to a pulsating air flow. 1978 and later models incorporate a "push valve" in the fuel distributor to maintain pressure when the engine is switched off. The push valve is a one-way device mounted in the primary pressure regulator which is held open in normal operation by the pressure regulator plunger. Differential pressure valves in the fuel distributor hold the drop in pressure at the metering slits at a constant value.

KE-Jetronic

The internal components and operation of the KE type fuel distributor is slightly different than the K model. With the engine running, a constant system pressure of approximately 79 psi (5.4 bar) is present at the fuel inlet. The plate valve is adjusted depending on current intensity and in this manner determines the flow rate, in combination with a fixed orifice (0.3mm in diameter) at the fuel distributor outlet. The pressure change in the lower chamber causes movement of the diaphragm and regulates the fuel volume flowing to the injectors.

During cold start and warm-up, current at the electrohydraulic actuator (EHA) is approximately 8–120 milliamps. The plate valve is positioned in the direction of the intake port and the differential pressure drop in the lower chamber is approximately 6–22 psi (0.4–1.5 bar). With increasing coolant temperature, the current at the actuator drops to approximately 8 milliamps and the differential pressure drops at the same rate, down to approximately 6 psi (0.4 bar). For acceleration enrichment, the current to the actuator is determined by the coolant temperature and the amount of sensor plate deflection. The plate valve is moved closer to the intake port and the differential pressure decreases by approximately 22 psi (1.5 bar).

NOTE: Acceleration enrichment is cancelled at approximately 176°F (80°C).

The airflow sensor position indicator operates with approximately 8 volts supplied constantly. During acceleration, a voltage signal is transmitted to the control unit, depending on the position of the airflow sensor plate. The control unit provides acceleration enrichment as an impulse which increases the instantaneous current value. During acceleration enrichment, Lambda (oxygen sensor) control is influenced by the control unit.

NOTE: With the accelerator pedal at idle, the microswitch on the side of the airflow sensor is closed and no enrichment is possible.

Fuel distributor mounting screws

The throttle valve switch receives a constant 8 volt signal from the control unit. With the throttle valve fully open (switch closed), approximately 8 mA of current flows to the electrohydraulic actuator, independent of engine speed. At full load enrichment, the plate valve moves in the direction of the intake port and the differential pressure in the lower chamber of the fuel distributor is approximately 6 psi (0.4 bar) below system pressure. Under deceleration, the circuit to the control unit is closed by the microswitch. The speed at which deceleration shutoff occurs depends on coolant temperature. The lower the temperature, the higher the speed at which restart of fuel injection begins. With the microswitch closed, the current at the actuator is approximately 45 mA and the plate valve moves away from the intake port. The pressure difference between the upper and lower chamber is cancelled and system pressure is present in the lower chamber. Operational signals from the control unit will change the direction of the current flow at the actuator plate valve; the plate valve then opens. When the lower chamber pressure changes, pressure and spring force push the diaphragm against the ports to the injectors and cut off the fuel supply.

Removal and Installation

1. Release the pressure in the system by loosening the fuel line on the control pressure regulator (large connector). Use a clean rag to catch the fuel that escapes.

2. Mark the fuel lines in the top of the distributor in order to put them back in their correct positions.

NOTE: Using different colored paints is usually a good marking device. When marking each line, be sure to mark the spot where it connects to the distributor.

3. Clean the fuel lines, then remove them from the distributor. Remove the little looped wire plug (the CO adjusting screw plug). Remove the two retaining screws in the top of the distributor.

---CAUTION---

When removing the fuel distributor be sure the control plunger does not fall out from underneath. Keep all parts clean.

---

4. If the control plunger has been removed, moisten it with gasoline before installing. The small shoulder on the plunger is inserted first.

NOTE: Always use new gaskets and O-ring when removing and installing fuel distributor. Lock all retaining screws with Loctite® or its equivalent.

Identification numbers of fuel injector hexagon (A) and shaft (B)

FUEL INJECTORS

The fuel injection valves are mounted in the intake manifold at the cylinder head, and continuously inject atomized fuel upstream of the intake valves.

A spring loaded valve is contained in each injector, calibrated to open at a fuel start pressure of 47–54 psi. The valves also contain a small fuel filter.

1. Valve housing
2. Filter
3. Valve needle
4. Valve seat

Cross section of typical K-Jetronic fuel injector showing closed (a) and open (b) positions

Lifting air flow sensor plate with magnet (updraft type)

The fuel injector (one per cylinder) delivers the fuel allocated by the fuel distributor into the intake tubes directly in front of the intake valves of the cylinders. The injectors are secured in a special holder in order to insulate them from engine heat. The insulation is necessary to prevent vapor bubbles from forming in the fuel injection lines which would lead to poor starting when the engine is hot. The fuel injectors have no metering function: they open when the pressure exceeds 47–54 psi and are fitted with a valve needle that "chatters" at high frequency to atomize the fuel. When the engine is switched off, the injection valve closes tightly, forming a seal that prevents fuel from dripping into the intake tubes.

Testing

NOTE: Leave the fuel lines attached to the injectors for testing, but be careful not to crimp any metal fuel lines.

Remove the rubber intake hose leading from the mixture control unit to the throttle unit. Expose the air flow sensor plate and bypass the safety circuit with a bridging adapter. Use a small magnet to lift the sensor plate during the test.

To check spray pattern, remove the injectors, one at a time, and hold them over a beaker. Switch the ignition key on and disconnect the electrical connector at the air-flow sensor to activate the fuel pump. Move the air flow sensor plate. The injector should provide a dose of uniformly atomized fuel at about a 15–52 degree wide angle.

To check injection quantity, connect the removed injectors via hoses to equal sized beakers. Switch on the ignition. Disconnect the electrical connector at the airflow sensor to activate the fuel pump. Run the pump for approximately 30 seconds to pressurize the system, then connect the air flow sensor to stop the fuel pump. Lift or

Uneven spray

Fire hose

Off center

Correctly atomized

Fuel injector spray patterns

depress the airflow sensor plate halfway until one of the beakers fills up. Check the beakers. If injection quantity deviates more than 20% between injectors, isolate the problem by swapping the lowest and highest (in fuel quantity) injectors and repeating the test. If the same injector still injects less, clean or replace that injector and fuel supply line. If the other injector is now faulty, the fuel distributor is defective.

The check for injector leak-down (when closed) can now be conducted. Injector leakage (more than slight seepage) may be due to airflow sensor plate set to incorrect height, seizing of fuel distributor plunger, or internal leaks in the fuel distributor. Connect the airflow sensor connector to de-activate the fuel pump and switch off the ignition. Check for injector leakage at rest pressure. Depress the sensor plate to open the fuel distributor slots. Maximum permissible leakage is one drop per 15 seconds. If all injectors leak, the problem may be excessive rest pressure.

NOTE: The injectors can be replaced individually.

COLD START VALVE

The cold start valve is mounted near the throttle valve housing and is connected to the pressure line. The valve, which is operated by a solenoid coil, is actuated by a thermo-time switch which is controlled by the engine temperature.

During cold starting, part of the fuel mixture is lost due to condensation on the cold cylinder walls. To compensate for this loss, extra fuel is injected by means of a solenoid-operated cold start valve. Fuel is delivered downstream of the throttle valve. A thermo-time switch determines the injection period of the cold start valve according to either engine temperature or an electrically heated bimetal strip which de-energizes the cold start valve after approximately 8 seconds to prevent flooding. The cold start valve does not function when the engine is warm.

Typical cold start valve installation

Removal and Installation

The cold start valve is mounted in the intake manifold, downstream from the air flow sensor. The valve is usually retained with two small Allen screws and can be removed for inspection without disconnecting the fuel line. When removing the valve, take care not to damage the valve body which is usually made of plastic. Make sure the valve is clean and the sealing O-ring is seated properly and in good condition when installing. Do not overtighten the mounting screws.

──────CAUTION──────

Depressurize the fuel system before attempting to remove any fuel hoses. Use plenty of rags around fuel connections to absorb and deflect any fuel spray.

Testing

Remove the cold start injector from the intake manifold and hold over a beaker. With a cold engine (95°F or lower coolant temperature), the injector should spray during starter operation (max. 12 seconds). If not, check the voltage between the terminals of the

Testing the cold start valve

injector when the starter is on. Voltage indicates a bad cold start injector. No voltage indicates a faulty thermo-time switch or wiring. Ground one terminal and connect the second to the positive side of the coil. When you run the pump, 10–30 seconds, you should get a good, cone-shaped spray. Dry the injector, disconnect jumpers, and energize the pump again. There shouldn't be any fuel. If it drips, replace it. Check the thermo-time switch when it's below 95°F. Disconnect the cold start valve and hook up a test light across its connector. Ground the No. 1 coil terminal and run the starter. The light should glow for several seconds and then go out. If not, replace the thermo-time switch.

NOTE: Remove the fuel pump relay and attach a bridging adaptor to energize the fuel pump during testing. See the "Tools" section for specifics on adapter construction.

With the starter off, attach a test relay to operate fuel pump. Check for cold start valve leakage. Maximum allowable leakage is one drop per minute. Any excessive leakage is reason enough to replace the cold start valve. Don't forget to wipe the valve nozzle with a clean towel after every test and before installing.

THERMO-TIME SWITCH

The thermo time switch, located on the cylinder head, actuates the cold start valve. It has a bi-metal spring which senses coolant temperature and an electric coil which limits the cold start valve spray to 12 seconds. A thermo-time switch also measures water temperature and opens the cold start valve, located on the intake header, a varying amount of each time the engine is started, depending on the conditions. With a hot engine (coolant temperature over 95°F), the injector should not operate. If it does, the thermo-time switch is defective. Also, on a cold engine, the cold start valve should not inject fuel for more than 12 seconds (during starter cranking). If it does, the thermo-time switch is defective.

Testing

NOTE: To perform the following test properly, the engine must be cold with a coolant temperature below 95°F (35°C).

With the use of a test lamp, the switch can be tested at various temperatures for continuity. The operating time is eight seconds at −4°F (−20C) and declines to 0 seconds at +59°F (+15C.).

When the engine temperature is below approximately 113°F (+45°FC), current is allowed to flow for a certain period (depending on the temperature) while the starter motor is running.

Check that the switch closes when the engine is started by means of connecting a test lamp in series across the contacts of the cold start valve plug.

It is not possible to make a more accurate check of the cut-in time or temperature. If the condition of the switch is at all in doubt, it should be replaced.

1. Electrical connection
2. Threaded pin
3. Bimetal strip
4. Heating filament
5. Switching contact

INPUT   OUTPUT

Typical thermo-time switch showing construction and terminal location

1. With the engine cold, remove the harness plug from the cold start valve and connect a test light across the harness plug connections.
2. Connect a jumper wire from coil terminal No. 1 to ground.
3. Operate the starter. If the test light does not light for about 8 seconds, replace the switch. Removal of the switch requires that the engine be cold and the cooling system drained.

Removal and Installation

1. Disconnect the negative battery cable. Drain the cooling system.
2. Locate the thermo-time switch on the left side of the engine block and disconnect the electrical connection.
3. Unscrew the switch and remove it.
4. Installation is in the reverse order of the removal. Refill the cooling system.

―――――――CAUTION―――――――
The engine must be cold when removing the switch.

AIR FLOW SENSOR

This device measures the amount of air drawn in by the engine. It operates according to the suspended body principle, using a counterbalanced sensor plate that is connected to the fuel distributor

1. Air cleaner
2. Air flow sensor
3. Air bellows
4. Throttle valve housing
5. Intake manifold
6. Auxiliary air valve

Air flow through typical K-Jetronic induction system

Updraft air flow sensor plate movement

control plunger by a lever system. A small leaf spring assures that the sensor plate assumes the correct zero position when the engine is stationary.

The air flow sensor consists of an air venturi tube in which an air flow sensor plate moves. The air flowing into the venturi from the air cleaner lifts the air flow sensor plate, allowing the air to flow through. The greater the amount of air, the higher the sensor plate will be raised.

The air flow sensor plate is fitted to a lever which is compensated by a counterweight. The lever acts on the control plunger in the fuel distributor which is pressed down by the control pressure, thus counteracting the lifting force of the air flow sensor plate.

The height to which the air flow sensor plate is raised is governed by the magnitude of the air flow.

The air/fuel mixture varies with the engine load. The inclination of the venturi walls therefore varies in stages in order to provide a correct air/fuel mixture at all loads. Thus, the mixture is enriched at full load and leaned at idle.

1. Air funnel
2. Sensor plate
3. Relief cross-section
4. Idle mixture adjusting screw
5. Counterweight
6. Fulcrum
7. Main lever
8. Leaf spring

Updraft air flow sensor in zero position

The lever acts on the control plunger in the fuel distributor by means of an adjustable link with a needle bearing at the contact point. The basic fuel setting, and thus the CO setting, is adjusted by means of the adjustment screw on the link. This adjustment is made with a special tool and access to the screw can be gained through a hole in the air flow sensor between the air venturi and the fuel distributor. The CO adjustment is sealed on later models.

A rubber bellows connects the air flow sensor to the throttle valve housing.

NOTE: On KE systems, the sensor plate rest position is angled upward, not horizontal as is the K system.

Testing

The air flow sensor plate in the fuel distributor must operate smoothly in order to do a good job of measuring air. Remove the air boot and check the sensor plate movement. When released, the plate should fall freely with one or two bounces. If the plate sticks, loosen the mounting screws and retighten them uniformly. Clean the funnel and sensor plate too, as these can get dirty from PCV fumes.

Check for leakage in the inlet system between the air flow sensor and the engine Air leaking into the system may result in poor engine performance, owing to the fact that it bypasses the air flow sensor, causing a lean mixture.

Leakage can occur in the following places:

a. At the rubber bellows between the air flow sensor and the throttle valve housing.

b. At the gasket on the flange of the cold start valve.

c. At the gasket between the throttle valve housing and the inlet manifold.

d. At the gasket between the inlet manifold and the cylinder head.

e. At the hose connections on the throttle valve housing, auxiliary air valve or inlet manifold.

f. Via the crankcase ventilation hose from the oil filler cap, dip stick or valve cover gasket.

NOTE: Move the sensor plate gently with a small magnet.

The plate should not bind, and although the plate will offer some resistance when depressed (due to the control pressure), it should return to its rest position when released. Be careful not to scratch the plate or venturi.

To check the air flow sensor contact switch, depress or lift the sensor plate by hand. The fuel injectors should buzz, and the fuel pump should activate. If the pump operates, but the injectors do not buzz, check the fuel pressure. If the pump does not operate, check for a short in the air flow sensor connector.

Sensor Plate Position Adjustment

NOTE: The air flow sensor plate adjustment is critical. The distance between the sensor plate and the plate stop must be 0–0.2 in. The plate must also be centered in the venturi, and must not contact the venturi walls.

1. Remove the air cleaner assembly.

2. Using a 0.004 in. (0.10mm) feeler gauge, check the clearance around the sensor plate at four opposite points around the plate.

3. If necessary, loosen the bolt in the center of the sensor plate and center the plate. Torque the bolt to 3.6 ft. lbs. (4.9 Nm).

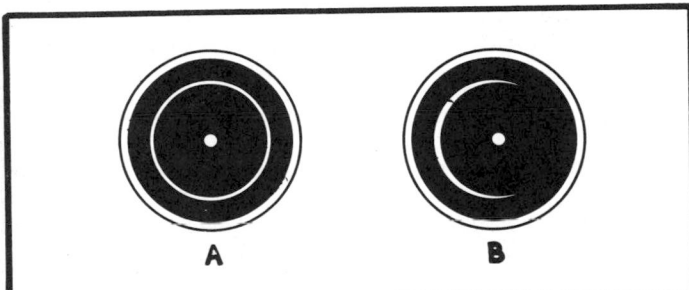

Sensor plate showing correct (A) and incorrect (B) centering in the venturi

———————CAUTION———————
Do not scratch the venturi or the plate.

Sensor Plate Height Adjustment

NOTE: The sensor plate height adjustment must be checked under fuel pressure.

1. Install a pressure gauge in the line between the fuel distributor and the control pressure regulator as previously described.

2. Remove the rubber elbow from the air flow sensor assembly.

3. Remove the fuel pump replay from the fuse panel and install a bridge adapter on pre-1979 models. Check that the fuel pressure is within specifications as previously described.

4. The sensor plate should be flush or 0.02 in. (0.5mm) below the beginning of the venturi taper. If necessary to adjust, remove the mixture control from the intermediate housing and bend the spring accordingly.

NOTE: With the sensor plate too high, the engine will run on, and with the sensor plate too low, poor cold and warm engine start-up will result. If the sensor plate movement is erratic, the control piston can be sticking.

5. Recheck the pressure reading after any adjustments.

6. Remove the pressure gauge, reconnect the fuel lines and install the fuel pump relay, if removed.

Air flow sensor used on KE-Jetronic systems showing counterbalanced sensor arm (1), fuel distributor plunger (2) and angled air sensor plate (3)

7. Reset the idle speed if necessary. See the individual car sections for details. Anytime an adjustment is made on the fuel system, or if a component is replaced, the idle CO should be reset with a CO meter.

Removal and Installation

1. Relieve the fuel system pressure as previously described.

NOTE: Wrap a cloth around the connection to catch any escaping fuel.

2. Thoroughly clean all fuel lines on the fuel distributor and then remove them.

3. Remove the rubber air intake duct.

4. Remove the air flow sensor/fuel distributor as a unit.

5. Remove the three retaining screws and remove the fuel distributor.

NOTE: When installing the air flow sensor, always replace the O-ring and gaskets. Use Loctite® on all retaining bolts.

6. Installation is in the reverse order of removal.

Correct sensor plate height in venturi. Adjust by bending spring. (A)

Cutaway of the air flow sensor assembly showing the direction of air flow and proper placement of the mixture (CO) adjusting tool. Never accelerate the engine with the tool in place

Internal components of the auxiliary air regulator showing cold (open) and warm (closed) positions

AUXILIARY AIR REGULATOR

The auxiliary air regulator allows more air/fuel mixture when the engine is cold in order to improve driveability and provide idle stabilization. The increased air volume is measured by the air flow sensor and fuel is metered accordingly. The auxiliary air regulator contains a specially shaped plate attached to a bi-metal spring. The plate changes position according to engine temperature, allowing the moist air to pass when the engine is cold. As the temperature rises, the bi-metal spring slowly closes the air passage. The bi-metal spring is also heated electrically, allowing the opening time to be limited according to engine type. The auxiliary air regulator does not function when the engine is warm.

Testing

NOTE: The engine must be cold to perform this test.

1. Disconnect the electrical terminal-plug and the two air hoses at the auxiliary air regulator.
2. Voltage must be present at the terminal plug with the ignition switch ON. Check the continuity of the heater coil by connecting a test light or ohmmeter to the terminals on the regulator.
3. Use a mirror to look through the bore of the regulator. If the air valve is not open, replace the auxiliary air regulator.
4. Connect the terminal plug and the two air hoses to the auxiliary air regulator.
5. Start the engine: the auxiliary air regulator bore should close within five minutes of engine operation by the cut-off valve.

NOTE: A quick check of the auxiliary air regulator can be made by unplugging the electrical connector with the engine cold. Start the engine and pinch the hose between the regulator and the intake manifold—the idle speed should drop. Reconnect the air regulator and allow the engine to warm up. With the engine at operating temperature, pinching the hose to the intake manifold should not affect the idle speed. If it does, replace the auxiliary air regulator.

Removal and Installation

1. Locate the auxiliary air regulator on the rear of the intake

Typical auxiliary air regulator installation

manifold. Disconnect the electrical connection and remove the air hoses.
2. Remove the mounting bolts and remove the regulator.
3. Installation is in the reverse order of removal. Make sure all hose and electrical connections are tight.

THROTTLE VALVE

The throttle valve housing is connected to the intake manifold and, in addition to the throttle valve, it contains the idling air passage and the idling adjustment screw, connections for the hoses to the auxiliary air valve, and the cold start valve and the vacuum outlet for ignition timing.

NOTE: Some later models with electronic engine controls do not use vacuum advance units on the distributor.

Adjustment

The stop screw is set by the factory and should not be moved. If for some reason it is moved, adjust as follows:

1. Turn the screw counterclockwise until a gap is visible between the stop and the screw.
2. Turn the screw until it just touches the stop.
3. Turn the screw clockwise an additional 1/2 turn.
4. Adjust the idle speed and CO and check the linkage for proper operation and free movement.

Idle Adjustments

The idle speed screw (called a bypass screw by some manufacturers) on the throttle body housing of a K-Jetronic system bleeds air into the manifold when you increase idle speed—or cuts it off to slow the engine down. When idle speed changes the idle mixture always changes to some degree, and vice-versa. Therefore, you must juggle the speed and mixture adjustments back and forth to get the specified idle speed within the right range of CO. Unlike a carburetor, changing the idle CO changes the mixture throughout the entire rpm range. Never rev the engine with the Allen wrench sitting in the mixture screw or it may damage the air sensor plate.

Engine oil temperature is the most critical factor in getting an accurate CO adjustment on any K-Jetronic system. Don't touch the mixture screw until the oil temperature is between 140–176°F (60–80°C). CO adjustment is sealed on late K and all KE systems.

Typical adjustment points on K-Jetronic systems

Lambda (Closed Loop) System

K AND KE-JETRONIC

With the advent of the 3-way catalytic converter, the K-Jetronic system has undergone two major modifications; the addition of a Lambda or Oxygen Sensor system (K-Jetronic) and the integration of an electrohydraulic actuator (KE-Jetronic). Both systems use an electronic control unit (ECU) for precise mixture (read emissions) control. Various new components have been integrated, such as an oxygen sensor, an electronic control unit (ECU), and a frequency valve, which convert K-Jet into a closed loop fuel system. In order for the 3-way converter to work effectively, the air/fuel mixture must be kept within a very precise range. Between 15 and 14 parts of air to one part of fuel, there's an ideal ratio called "stoichiometric" where HC, CO, and NO_x emissions are all at a minimum. Bosch calls this ratio (or stoichiometric point) "Lambda". Combined with an oxygen (or Lambda) sensor, mounted in the exhaust manifold, the air/fuel ratio in a fuel injected system can be controlled within a tolerance of 0.02%.

Operational schematic of K-Jetronic Lambda (Oxygen) Sensor System closed loop mode of operation

The oxygen sensor in the exhaust system monitors the oxygen content of the exhaust gases. It produces a small amount of voltage that varies depending on the amount of oxygen present in the exhaust. This voltage signal is sent to the ECU. The ECU, in turn, then signals the frequency valve to enrichen or lean the mixture. The voltage signal is approximately one volt. The frequency valve is located between the fuel distributor and the fuel return line. It does not change control pressure in the K-Jet system; it alters system pressure in the lower chamber of the fuel distributor for each cylinder's differential pressure valve.

NOTE: On the KE type CIS injection system, an electronic actuator replaces the frequency valve and conrol pressure regulator, as described under "Fuel Distributor" earlier. The control units are different for K and KE systems.

Operation

When the oxygen sensor signals a rich mixture to the ECU, it will close the frequency valve. This causes pressure in the lower chamber of the fuel distributor to increase and push the diaphragm up to reduce fuel quantity. If the air/fuel mixture is too lean, the frequency valve will be open and reduce pressure in the lower chamber. The diaphragm is then pushed down and the amount of fuel is increased. The valve opens and closes many times per second. The average pressure is determined by the ratio of valve openings and closings. A higher open-to-closed ratio would provide a richer mixture, a lower open-to-closed ratio would give a leaner mixture. This is called the duty cycle of the frequency valve.

In the KE-Jetronic system, the Lambda control is integrated into the control unit which monitors the input signals from the various engine sensors (including the oxygen sensor), amplifies these signals and then calculates the correct output signal for the electrohydraulic actuator on the fuel distributor to modify the mixture as necessary. There is not frequency valve or control pressure regulator on KE systems. In addition, the oxygen sensor has three wires; one of which supplies current to a heating element that warms the oxygen sensor up to operating temperature faster and doesn't allow it to cool off at idle. The Lambda control system on the KE-Jetronic system is designed to cut out (go to open loop mode) under the following operating conditions.

- Oxygen sensor not warmed up to operating temperature
- During deceleration (fuel shut-off)

1. Air flow sensor
2. Fuel metering distributor
3. Frequency valve
4. Oxygen sensor
5. Catalytic converter
6. Electronic control unit

Components of K-Jetronic oxygen sensor system

Cross section of a typical oxygen sensor

- At full load operation (wide open throttle)
- Whenever the engine coolant temperature is below 59°F (15°C) and until engine temperature reaches approximately 104°F (40°C)

The heating element of the oxygen sensor is usually energized from a terminal on the fuel pump relay and is heated as long as the fuel pump is running.

NOTE: Do not interchange different types of oxygen sensors (one, two, or three wire) when servicing. Do not let grease or oil contaminate the sensor tip while it's removed. Replace the oxygen sensor at 30,000 mile intervals.

Testing

Bosch makes a tester for the Lambda system that measures the open-to-closed ratio, or duty cycle. The Bosch KDJE 7453 tester (KDJ#-P600 for KE systems) reads out the duty cycle on a percentage meter. A reading of 60, for instance, would be a frequency valve pulse rate of 60%. You can also use a sensitive dwell meter that reads to at least 70° to measure duty cycle on the 4-cyl. scale. Manufacturers using K-Jet with Lambda provide a test socket, so that a duty cycle tester can easily be hooked up. Audi's test connection, for instance, is located behind the throttle valve housing. Saab and most other makers locate the test socket in the wiring harness right near the underhood relay box.

CAUTION

If connected improperly, an analog meter may damage the oxygen sensor. Read the manufacturer's instructions before any testing

The following is a general procedure for checking the duty cycle with a dwell meter on K-Jetronic systems.

1. Disconnect the thermo switch wiring. Shorting the switch will enrich the mixture to about 60% for a cold engine. The meter needle should stay steady, which indicates an "open loop." This means the system isn't being affected by the oxygen sensor. Reconnect the thermo switch.

2. Disconnect the oxygen sensor with a warm engine. The meter should register a 50% signal.

3. Reconnect the oxygen sensor. You should see a change from open to closed loop. The needle will stay steady in the middle at 50% for about a minute. When the oxygen sensor warms up, it should signal the frequency valve for closed loop operation. That will be shown by a swinging needle on the meter, when the system is working correctly.

The KE-Jetronic system requires the use of a special tester for diagnosis. Before tracing possible faults in the oxygen sensor regulating system itself, make sure that the symptoms are not caused by mechanical faults in the engine, ignition system or other components in the injection system. For example, an incorrectly adjusted exhaust valve may have a considerable effect on regulation of the system. Aside from the dwell meter test described earlier, extensive testing of the Oxygen Sensor System requires the use of a special Bosch tester or its equivalent equipment.

NOTE: Before testing Lambda system with tester KDJE-P600, or equivalent, unplug the oxygen sensor and run the engine at idle until it reaches normal operating temperature. Read and record the voltage.

1. Connect the oxygen sensor, run the engine at approximately 2000 rpm and check that the readout on the test meter stays around the recorded value (taken with the sensor disconnected) and that the reading never exceeds ± 0.8 volts above or below that value. If these test results are achieved, the Lambda system is operating properly and no further testing is necessary.

2. If the readout is higher than approximately 4.8 volts, or lower than 2.1 volts, then the Lambda control is in need of adjustment. If the readout is constant, replace the oxygen sensor or repair the open circuit between the sensor and the control unit.

3. Test the oxygen sensor with the engine running at operating temperature. Disconnect the sensor electrical lead, run the engine at approximately 2000 rpm, then check the voltage of the sensor to ground. If the voltage does not exceed 450 mV, replace the oxygen sensor. If equipped with a heating element, check the circuit by measuring the voltage at the connector with the fuel pump relay removed and the sockets bridged at the connector. It should read approximately 12 volts and have a current value of 0.5A or greater.

OXYGEN SENSOR

Removal and Installation

Before fitting the oxygen sensor, coat all threads and gaskets with an antiseize compound (e.g. Never Seize® or Molycote 1000®). Do not apply compound to the sensor body.

NOTE: The joint between the oxygen sensor and the exhaust manifold must be gas-tight. Check that the other joints between the cylinder head cover and the muffler are tight.

---CAUTION---

The oxygen sensor is highly sensitive to knocks and must be handled carefully. Torque the sensor to 15–30 ft. lbs.

ELECTRONIC CONTROL UNIT (ECU)

Unlike the early K-Jetronic's mechanical control, the later K and KE-Jetronic system control is accomplished by an electronic unit (ECU) that receives and processes signals from various engine sensors to regulate the fuel mixture and accommodate several other functions not present in the early K-Jet system. The control unit is connected to battery voltage and is provided with a voltage correction (safety) circuit to prevent harmful voltage surges. The control unit on the KE-Jetronic system measures:

- Engine speed (tachometer)
- Coolant temperature (sensor in cylinder head)
- Airflow sensor position (position sensor)
- Full load signal (throttle valve switch)
- Idle speed signal (microswitch)
- Oxygen (Lambda) sensor signal
- Signal from altitude compensator

K-JETRONIC LAMBDA SYSTEM TEST SPECIFICATIONS

Circuit Tested	Terminal Numbers	Normal Reading
Check for short circuit	2–4 ①	0 ohms-wiring OK (look for short if continuity exists)
Ground check	8-GND ②	key ON-12 volts key OFF-0 volts
Frequency valve windings	Frequency valve terminals ①	2–3 ohms
Frequency valve harness connector ②	harness (+) connector and GND ②	12 volts with key ON and ECU connected
Battery voltage from ignition switch to ECU	15–GND ②	key ON-12 volts
Relay operation (key ON)	Relay terminal 87-GND ②	12 volts-OK
	Relay terminal 87b-GND ②	12 volts-OK
	Relay terminal 30-GND ②	12 volts
	Relay terminal 86-GND ②	12 volts

NOTE: Turn ignition off between tests and when removing or installing wiring harness connector. Probe all terminals carefully from the rear; test probes can spread terminals and cause a poor connection. Make sure test equipment is compatible with Lambda system or components may be damaged.

GND-Ground
① Ohmmeter connections
② Voltmeter connections

The signals are converted into the appropriate current values and sent to the electrohydraulic actuator and idle speed air valve. The control unit provides an enrichment signal during cranking and establishes smooth running characteristics after starting.

NOTE: The amount of after-start enrichment depends on coolant temperature.

The engine speed is limited by the control unit, which actuates the EHA to shut off fuel to the injectors at a preset rpm. Fuel mixture is also adjusted according to signals from an altitude compensator.

Removal and Installation

Locate the control unit and remove any covers or fastening bolts. The ECU is mounted somewhere in the passenger compartment, usually under the dash or one of the front seats. Carefully pull the unit clear to expose the main connector. Release the clip and remove the connector. Remove the control unit. Reverse the procedure for installation. Make sure all connectors are clean.

NOTE: Some control units are mounted under the passenger seat. Move the seat all the way back to gain access.

MODULATING VALVE

Removal and Installation

NOTE: During removal and fitting of the modulating valve, prevent the rubber valve retainer from coming into contact with gasoline. The rubber is of a special grade to prevent vibrations from the valve being transmitted to the body. The rubber swells considerably if allowed to come into contact with gasoline.

1. Disconnect the electric cable.
2. Disconnect the small-bore line to the modulating valve. Grip the hexagonal nut closest to the hose (14 mm) and undo the valve nut (17 mm).
3. Disconnect the modulating valve return line from the warmup regulator, from the fuel distributor and the joint in the return line on the latter.
4. Remove and disconnect the valve and return lines.
5. Installation is the reverse of removal.

Typical modulating or frequency valve assembly

Constant Idle Speed (CIS) Control System

GENERAL INFORMATION

This electronic control system is designed to correct engine idle speed deviations very quickly; holding the idle speed constant even when loads such as power steering, air conditioning or automatic transmission are applied to the engine. Sensors on the engine read the engine speed (rpm), operating temperature and throttle position, then supply a voltage signal to a separate control unit which in turn adjusts the engine speed by feeding more or less air into the injection system by means of an idle air device. The control unit adjusts the idle speed according to pre-set (programmed) "ideal" rpm values contained in its memory.

The constant idle speed system is designed to be maintenance-free and will operate regardless of wear or changes in ignition timing. Under normal circumstances, no adjustment of the idle speed is necessary or possible. The idle air valve is located in a bypass hose which routes air around the throttle valve much the same way as the auxiliary air valve this system replaces. The idle speed control unit processes voltage signals from the various sensors on:

• Engine speed (tachometer)

Schematic of Bosch Constant Idle Speed control system

• Coolant temperature (sensor in cylinder head)
• Throttle position (microswitch)
• Shift lever position (automatic transmission)
• A/C compressor cut-in signal

With the ignition OFF, the idle air valve is opened fully by a set of return springs. With the ignition ON, the idle air valve is controlled by a specific voltage from the control unit, providing an air valve opening dependent on coolant temperature. In this manner, the idle speed is constantly controlled between approximately 1000 rpm @ −4° F (−20°C) to roughly 750 rpm @ 68°F (20°C). The control unit also receives a voltage signal when the transmission shift lever is in PARK or NEUTRAL; this voltage signal usually drops when the transmission is engaged (DRIVE) to maintain the idle speed at the factory-established specification (usually around 650–700 rpm). The same type of voltage signal is produced by the air conditioner compressor, which also drops when the compressor engages, sending another signal to the idle air valve to once again maintain engine idle speed under load.

Testing

NOTE: Testing the constant idle system (CIS) requires the use of Bosch tester KDJE-P600, or equivalent, along with the proper test cable adapter.

1. Connect test cable to idle air valve and tester. The engine should be idling at normal operating temperature.
2. Press the IR 100% button and note the reading on the tester. It should be 27–29% @ 670–770 rpm. If the reading is correct, the CIS system is operating properly.
3. If the reading on the tester is higher or lower, adjust to the correct value or test the microswitch for proper operation.
4. If the readout is 0%, test for voltage on the plug for the idle air valve. There should be 12 volts from the feed side of the pin socket to ground. If not, check for an open circuit in the idle air valve harness and repair as necessary.
5. Check the resistance of the idle air valve. It should be approximately 12 ohms between terminals 2 and 3; and the same value between terminals 2 and 1. If not, replace the idle air valve assembly.

NOTE: If the voltage signal to the idle air valve is correct (12 volts), check the ground line to the control unit. Replace the control unit if no ground connection is present. Make sure the ignition switch is OFF before disconnecting or reconnecting any CIS system components.

BOSCH AIR FLOW CONTROLLED (AFC) FUEL INJECTION

General Information

The most common type of AFC fuel injection is the Bosch L-Jetronic system. The L stands for "Luftmengenmessung" which means "air flow management." The L-Jetronic AFC injection sys-

tem is used, with various modifications, by both European and Asian manufacturers. Different versions of the basic L-Jetronic design include LH, LH II, LU, LU Digital and Motronic. Although similar in design and operation, each separate system uses slightly different components. LH-Jetronic, for example, measures the incoming air mass with a heated wire built into the air flow meter, instead of a flap valve.

Aside from different terminology, most Asian and European AFC systems are similar in both appearance and function. For this reason, it is important to accurately identify the particular type of AFC system being serviced. A small diagram of the fuel injection system is usually found under the hood on a sticker somewhere near the emission control label; it's very important to understand how the different components function and affect one another when troubleshooting any AFC fuel injection system.

AIR FLOW CONTROLLED (AFC) SYSTEMS

Type of System	Primary Control Measurement
L-Jetronic	Air flow
LH-Jetronic	Air mass
LH II-Jetronic	Air mass
LU-Jetronic	Air flow (Utilizes a hybrid ECU that converts analog signals to digital map)
LU-Digital Jetronic	Air flow (Digital ECU with inputs)
Motronic	Air flow with digital control of ignition and injection
K-Jetronic	Air flow Controlling fuel flow non-electronically
KE-Jetronic	Electronically controlled K-Jetronic
E.C.C.S. ①	Air mass
I-TEC ②	Air flow
EGI ③	Air flow

NOTE: Identification numbers are located on control unit housing. Compare replacement part numbers to original unit before installing.

ECU—Electronic Control Unit
① Nissan (Datsun) fuel injection system
② Isuzu fuel injection system
③ Mazda fuel injection system

L-JETRONIC

The Bosch L-Jetronic is an electronically controlled system that injects the fuel charge into the engine intake ports in intermittent pulses by means of electromagnetic, solenoid-type fuel injectors (one per cylinder). The quantity of fuel injected per pulse depends on the length of time the injector is open, which is determined by an electrical impulse signal from the electronic control unit (ECU) that reacts to inputs from various engine sensors. The main control sensor is the air flow meter, which measures the amount of air being inducted into the engine. Sensors for engine temperature, engine speed (rpm), intake air temperature, throttle position, exhaust gas oxygen content and barometric pressure also feed information into the control unit to help determine the fuel injection quantity (mixture) that will produce the best performance with

Typical European L-Jetronic injection system schematic

the least emissions. The L-Jetronic control unit is used in both analog and digital versions which are not interchangeable.

Fuel is supplied to the injectors under fairly constant pressure by an electric roller cell pump and a fuel pressure regulator that responds to manifold vacuum and returns excess gasoline to the tank. A set of points in the intake air sensor assures that the pump only gets current when the engine is running or being cranked. This eliminates flooding in the event that an injector springs a leak.

Three components that aren't connected to the computer assist in starting and warm-up. The cold start valve in the intake manifold injects extra fuel while the engine is being cranked. It's controlled by the thermotime switch, a thermostatic device that energizes the cold start valve for 3 to 10 seconds. Its bimetal strip is affected by both engine temperature and an electrical heating coil. The auxiliary air regulator bypasses the throttle plate to provide extra air during warm-up, which prevents stalling. A heating element inside causes it to close gradually.

Operation

The L-Jetronic system measures intake air and meters the proper fuel to obtain the correct air/fuel ratio under a wide range of driving conditions.

We can break the L-Jetronic into three basic systems: air intake; fuel supply and electronic control. Some components like the air flow meter are part of two systems. The air intake system consists of the air cleaner, air flow meter, throttle housing, connecting hoses, air valve (air regulator) and the manifold. The fuel system includes the tank, fuel pump, fuel damper, filter, fuel rail, cold start valve, fuel injectors, and connecting lines. Some European L-Jet systems don't use a fuel damper. Both Datsun/Nissan and Toyota employ dampers to reduce pulsation from pump output.

Typical Japanese L-Jetronic injection system schematic

TROUBLESHOOTING—L-JETRONIC

Condition / **Cause** / **Correction**

Cause	Correction	No maximum power	Fuel consumption too high	Engine misses when driving	Engine running	Erratic running	CO value incorrect	Idle speed incorrect	Rough or unstable idle	Engine starts but then dies	Engine cranks but does not start
Defect in ignition system	Check battery, distributor, plugs, coil and timing	●	●	●		●			●	●	●
Mechanical defect in engine	Check compression, valve adj. and oil pressure	●	●	●		●			●	●	●
Leaks in air intake system (false air)	Check all hoses and connections; eliminate leaks	●	●	●		●		●	●	●	●
Blockage in fuel system	Check fuel tank, filter and lines for free flow	●								●	●
Relay defective, wire to injector open	Test relay; check wiring harness										●
Fuel pump not operating	Check pump fuse, pump relay and pump									●	●
Fuel system pressure incorrect	Check pressure regulator	●	●					●	●	●	●
Cold start valve not operating	Test for spray; check wiring and thermo-time switch										●
Cold start valve leaking	Check valve for leakage					●		●	●	●	●
Thermo-time switch defective	Test for resistance readings vs. temperature										●
Auxiliary air valve not operating correctly	Must be open with cold engine; closed with warm							●	●	●	●
Temperature sensor defective	Test for 2-3 kΩ at 68° F.					●		●	●	●	●
Air flow meter defective	Check pump contacts; test flap for free movement	●				●		●	●	●	●
Throttle butterfly does not completely close or open	Readjust throttle stops	●				●		●	●	●	●
Throttle valve switch defective	Check with ohmmeter and adjust	●						●	●		●
Idle speed incorrectly adjusted	Adjust idle speed with bypass screw							●	●		●
Defective injection valve	Check valves individually for spray	●					●	●	●	●	●
CO concentration incorrectly set	Readjust CO with screw on air flow meter					●	●	●	●	●	●
Loose connection in wiring harness or system ground	Check and clean all connections					●		●	●	●	●
Control unit defective	Use known good unit to confirm defect	●				●		●	●	●	●

Dampers have what looks like an adjusting screw, but *don't attempt any adjustment*. The Datsun 200SX injection system doesn't use a cold start valve.

The electronic control system is made up of the electronic control unit (ECU) and several sensors. Each sensor signals measurements on engine condition to the ECU, which then computes fuel needs. Injectors are then opened and closed by ECU command to feed the needed amount of fuel. Injectors are connected in parallel. All supply fuel at the same time. They open twice for each rotation of the engine camshaft, injecting ½ the needed fuel each time.

The big sensor, and the one that gives the system its name, is the air flow sensor. This is located in the large airbox. A flap in the box opens and closes in response to air being drawn into the engine. The ECU is then signalled as to the amount of air being taken in. An air temperature sensor in the box sends that information to the ECU. Engine rpm is picked up from the negative side of the coil. A throttle valve switch tells the control unit how much the throttle is open. Engine temperature is transmitted from a coolant temperature sensor. Later model Datsuns/Nissans use a cylinder head temperature sensor instead of a coolant temperature sensor. A signal from the ignition switch tells the ECU when the engine is being started. An O_2 sensor has been added to feed exhaust gas oxygen content to the ECU.

LH AND LH II-JETRONIC

These systems are further developments of the L-Jetronic. LH is an abbreviation of "Luft-Hitzdracht" which means "hot air wire." Both the LH and LH II work on the same principle as the L system, but instead of an air flow sensor flap to measure intake air quantity, these systems use a heated platinum wire to measure the air mass. In this manner, altitude influences are eliminated from the injection systems input quantities. A very thin platinum wire is stretched across the air intake opening in the air flow meter and forms part of a bridge circuit. Air flowing over the wire draws heat from it, changing the wire's electrical resistance as the temperature changes. An electronic amplifier instantly responds to any such resistance change and regulates the current to the wire so as to maintain it at a virtually constant temperature. The current necessary to maintain the wire temperature is the measure of the air mass flowing into the induction system, and this signal is used by the ECU to determine the injector opening time to adjust the air/fuel mixture.

Operation

The LH and LH II-Jetronic fuel injection are electronic systems with the same basic components as the L-Jetronic. The systems consist of a control unit with various engine sensors that measure and monitor engine operating conditions and adjust the fuel mixture for optimum performance with minimum emissions, according to load, throttle position, temperature, etc. The control unit regulates the fuel quantity by varying the length of time the injectors are open and regulates idle speed by varying an air control valve opening. The system measures the air mass entering the engine by means of a heated platinum wire. Because dirt and impurities may accumulate on the wire surface and affect the voltage signal, the system is designed to clean the wire each time the engine is turned off to eliminate impurities and corrosion.

1. Air mass sensor	6. Oxygen sensor	11. Ignition switch	16. Fuel pump relay	21. Line pressure regulator
2. Throttle valve switch	7. Starter	12. Fuse	17. Injectors	22. Injection manifold
3. Temperature sensor	8. Control unit	13. Tank pump	18. Air control valve	23. Idle adjustment screw
4. A/C microswitch	9. System relay	14. Fuel pump	19. Lambda test point	24. Catalytic converter
5. Ignition coil	10. Battery	15. Fuel filter	20. Idle speed test point	

Schematic of LH-Jetronic injection system

The LH and LH II injection systems operate with a moderate fuel pressure which is held constant by a fuel pressure regulator. Fuel injection is by means of electrically controlled solenoid-type injectors which spray fuel directly behind the engine intake valves. The injection duration is usually measured in milliseconds and is controlled by the electronic control unit (ECU). The ECU receives signals from a set of engine sensors, the most important of which is the air mass meter that continuously measures the mass of air entering the intake manifold. When the engine stops, the wire is heated up to 1050-1920°F for less than one second to burn off any dirt, corrosion or impurities on the filament. If allowed to build up these impurities would cause false signals to be sent to the control unit and affect the air/fuel mixture. In addition to the air flow meter, the other sensors providing input to the ECU include:

- Throttle valve position sensor (switch)
- Vacuum switch (indicating part and full load idle conditions)
- Engine speed sensor (tachometer connection)
- Oxygen sensor (Lambda system)
- Coolant temperature sensor
- Cold starting control (enrichment program)

The electronic control unit receives and processes signals from the engine sensors and calculates the correct fuel mixture according to a preprogrammed memory unit contained within the ECU assembly. *The ECU and its connector should be handled with the utmost care during all testing and/or service procedures.*

NOTE: Each individual variant of the L-Jetronic injection system uses a different control unit. They are not interchangeable.

MOTRONIC

The Motronic fuel injection system combines the digital control of individual systems such as fuel injection and ignition into a single unit. The heart of the Motronic system is a microcomputer that is programmed according to dynomometer data on a specific engine's characteristics. In operation, various engine sensors deliver data on engine speed (rpm), crankshaft position and temperature (engine and ambient air). From this input, the control unit determines the ideal spark advance and fuel quantity, up to 400 times a second. In this manner, spark advance and fuel quantity is tailored exactly to the engine operating conditions such as idling, part load, full load, warmup, deceleration and transient modes. Optimal fuel injection and ignition settings improve the engine's overall performance while reducing fuel consumption and emissions. Motronic systems can be made to incorporate other features from modified L-Jetronic systems, such as the air mass sensor wire in the intake air meter and electronic control of automatic transmission. Its basic operation is very similar to the previously described L, LH and LH II injection systems, except for the automatic ignition timing control.

Service Precautions

- Make sure the ignition is switched OFF before removing or installing any component connectors, especially to the control unit.
- Do not replace any control unit without first checking all wiring and components, otherwise an existing fault could ruin a new ECU the same way the old one was damaged.
- Never check connector terminals from the front, especially the main harness connector to the ECU. Excessive force can damage connector terminals and cause other faults. The correct testing method is to remove the connector cover and check the terminals from the holes provided in the side of the connector. Terminal numbers are usually stamped on the side of the connector.
- When removing the control unit connector, release the lock tabs, then fold out the connector. Do not pull the ECU connector straight out. All electrical connectors should have some kind of lock device to keep the connectors from coming apart.
- Remove any electronic control unit before subjecting the car to any temperature in excess of 176°F (80°C), such as when baking paint in an oven.

Exploded view of air mass sensor used on LH and LH II injection systems

Schematic of Motronic fuel injection system

Release the locks, then fold out the ECU connector. Do not pull the connector straight out

• Cleanliness is extremely important when working on or around the fuel system. Do not allow dirt or grease to contaminate the fuel system. Always use new gaskets and seals during reassembly of components using them. Clean all fuel connections before removal, and prepare a clean work area.

• Disconnect the ignition system when performing compression tests. Any arcing to the injectors or injector wiring can damage the control unit. Arcing to the ignition coil low tension side can damage vehicles equipped with Hall Effect distributors.

• Never use a quick charger on the battery or attempt to use a "hot shot" 24 volt starting aid. Maximum charging current should not exceed 15 amps.

• Always depressurize the fuel system before attempting to disconnect any fuel lines or components.

• Harsh chemicals such as carburetor cleaner should not be used to find vacuum leaks. The oxygen sensor is easily contaminated and ruined by certain chemicals and fuel additives commonly used on carbureted engines.

On-Car Service

Water is one of the biggest killers of electronic fuel injection (EFI) system components, regardless of the type of system. The high pressures generated by the fuel pump can and will push water and fuel right through the fuel filter into the rest of the system.

Water problems can be minimized by changing filters regularly, using water absorbing fuel additives (especially in colder weather), and by installing a water filter.

Several companies manufacture water separation/filtration systems which electronically detect the presence of water in the fuel. They can be used in all environments under the hood, with all fuels, and packaged with all fittings, brackets and hardware for easy installation.

---CAUTION---

Read the service precautions at the beginning of this section before attempting repairs or tests.

PRELIMINARY CHECKS

Before assuming the EFI system is at fault, make the standard preliminary checks of ignition system and engine conditions before going any further. Check the battery.

Check the electrical connections; EFI electrical systems won't tolerate corrosion or sloppy connections. Clean connections with one of the electrical cleaners available and be absolutely certain that spaded terminals snap tightly into their plastic connector bodies. Carefully crimp these where necessary with needlenose pliers. Also, check the main harness connector that plugs into the ECU for dirt, corrosion, or bent or spread-out terminals.

Typical fuel pump used on L-Jetronic systems

This check alone has solved many intermittent EFI performance problems.

NOTE: Sealing electrical connections against moisture is important. Make sure all connectors snap tightly together and no bare wire protrudes from the back of the connector body. Replace any rubber protector caps removed during testing.

A bad set of ignition wires will cause the same symptoms as a bad pressure regulator, so check the ignition system first. Steady vacuum that's within specs is a must on these cars. A vacuum leak unbalances the system throughout its entire operating range. A leaky engine will start, idle, and run poorly.

NOTE: L-Jetronic systems tend to be so "mixture-sensitive" that crankcase air leaks will upset them. If the sealing ring around the oil filter cap is broken or missing, a VW for instance, with L-Jetronic just won't perform.

FUEL PUMP TESTS

Fuel is drawn from the fuel tank into the fuel pump, from which it is discharged under pressure. As it flows through the mechanical fuel damper (if so equipped), pulsation in the fuel flow is damped. Then, the fuel is filtered in the fuel filter, goes through the fuel line, and is injected into the intake port. Surplus fuel is bled through the pressure regulator and is returned to the fuel tank. The pressure regulator controls the injection pressure in such a manner that the pressure difference between the fuel pressure and the intake manifold vacuum is always approximately 36 psi.

The fuel pump is a wet type pump where the vane rollers are directly coupled to a motor which is filled with fuel. The fuel cools and lubricates the pump internal components as it flows through, so the fuel pump should never be allowed to run dry. A relief valve in the pump is designed to open when the pressure in the fuel lines rises over 43–64 psi due to a malfunction in the pressure system. A check valve prevents abrupt drop of pressure in the fuel pipe when stopping the engine.

---CAUTION---

Operating the fuel pump dry for more than a few seconds can cause pump seizure.

Relieving fuel system pressure on L-Jetronic systems

Relieving Fuel System Pressure

1. Remove the vacuum hose from the fuel pressure regulator.
2. Connect a hand vacuum pump to the regulator and pump vacuum up to 20 in. Hg.
3. Wrap a clean rag around a fuel connection to catch any fuel while carefully loosening connection. Listen for sound of venting into fuel tank.

---CAUTION---

Fire hazard. Relieve fuel system pressure before attempting to disconnect any fuel injection system components. This procedure allows the fuel system pressure to vent into the tank, it does not however, remove all fuel from the lines.

Alternate Methods for Relieving Fuel Pressure

1. Disconnect the battery ground cable.
2. Disconnect the wiring harness to the cold start valve.

CAUTION

Do not disconnect any components with the engine running on later LH, LH II, LU and Motronic systems. Removing the battery cable will clear the trouble code memory on self-diagnosing injection systems.

---

3. Using two jumper wires from the battery, energize the cold start valve for two or three seconds to relieve pressure in the fuel system. Be careful not to short the jumpers together.
4. If an early L-Jet system is used, start the engine, then remove the fuel pump relay or unplug the pump connector and allow the engine to stall.
5. Carefully loosen the fuel line as in primary method.

Fuel Pump Power Check

If an AFC equipped car doesn't start, there's a good chance it might be the fuel pump or its circuit. First, visually check all the pump and relay wiring, as it could be nothing more than a bad connection. Be sure that the pump is grounded. Corrosion can break the ground circuit. Check the pump fuse and look to see if the fusible link in the system is burned. Don't forget to clean the battery cables—the pump calls for 12 volts. If the link or fuse is burned, it could be a seized or worn out pump. Or it could be watered gas, which will freeze the pump in winter. The last item to try is bypassing the relay with a jumper wire. If it works, then the relay's bad. Some models have a convenient fuel pump check connector under the air flow meter or fuel rail. Pry the cap off and, with a jumper wire, you can run the pump without starting the engine. If you can feel fuel pressure at the cold start valve and hear fuel returning through the regulator, the pump's working.

Exercise caution with the dual relays used in L-Jetronic cars. Refer to a wiring diagram of the particular vehicle because the main relay side and the pump relay side of the dual relay are seldom labeled by the manufacturer. Make sure the correct terminals connect the jumper across the *pump relay* side of the dual relay. Remember, too, that all AFC electric fuel pumps use a separate ground wire. So don't neglect to ground check during pump troubleshooting. As is the case with the fuse, these relays could be anywhere. Datsun hides a dual relay inside the kick panel; VW may have it under the dashboard; and others may have their pump relays under the hood. Some AFC systems use a single, main relay on later models.

Fuel Pressure Check

NOTE: Use this check to determine if the fuel pump is operating properly and to check for restrictions in fuel lines.

To test the L-Jetronic systems, you must have an extremely accurate pressure gauge that reads 0–50 psi in 0.5-psi increments. Also, remember that high operating pressures mean that connections must be tight. 30–40 psi pressures won't tolerate any haphazard connections. Don't risk a fire—use a reinforced fuel line hose that'll withstand 30–40 psi and use worm gear type clamps to secure the hose. Keep an eye out for leakage in the fuel plumbing and check the braided hose used as OEM equipment.

CAUTION

The fuel system must be depressurized before disconnecting any fuel system components. The cold start valve body is plastic, use care in removing the fuel hose.

Connect the pressure gauge to the cold start injector connection on the fuel rail, or that line between the fuel rail and filter. Banjo fittings are used throughout the Toyota AFC system. An adapter with a banjo fitting at one end will be needed to hook up the gauge. Take a good look at the hoses on these cars. Hoses must be in decent shape and fittings or clamps should be tight.

Alternate method for relieving fuel pressure

COLD START VALVE

Testing the fuel pump on the L-Jetronic system. Not all models have the test connector

FUEL PUMP CHECK CONNECTOR

SERVICE WIRE

Typical L-Jetronic dual relay set, usually mounted somewhere in the engine compartment

RELAY SET

CONNECTOR

Checking the fuel pressure on L-Jetronic systems-typical

FUEL PRESSURE GAUGE

COLD START VALVE

HOSE TO COLD START VALVE

Start the engine and disconnect and plug the vacuum line to the pressure regulator. Pressure at idle should be approximately 33–38 psi (34–45 psi on later models). A bad pressure regulator is indicated by pressure that's too high. Look for kinked fuel lines, restrictive fuel filter, or a faulty pump or pump check valve, if the pressure is too low.

Connect the vacuum hose to the pressure regulator. Watch the gauge. Pressure should drop to 28 psi. A reading over 33 psi means the regulator's bad. Check pressure at full throttle. Pressure should climb to 37 psi as soon as the throttle is wide open. On all L-Jetronic systems, pressure should hold when the engine is shut off. An immediate pressure drop means an internally leaking injector(s), pressure regulator, or fuel pump.

NOTE: The pressure reading may slowly drop through the regulator valve seating or the pump non-return valve. A slow, steady drop is permissable, a rapid fall is not.

Typical fuel pressure gauge hookup on Japanese L-Jetronic systems—note the banjo fittings used for fuel connections

When taking a fuel pressure reading at idle, normal injector pulsation will cause the gauge to fluctuate. This pulsation is most pronounced on 4 cylinder engines. Watch the needle carefully and take the *average* pressure value. At idle, simply take your pressure reading as being the mid-point between the highest and lowest fluctuations of the pressure gauge needle. If fuel pressure isn't within specs at idle, you could have a clogged fuel filter or either a restricted fuel line or fuel return line. Be sure to change fuel filters at least every 7,500–10,000 miles. Make sure any additives will not damage the oxygen sensor or converter before using them in the fuel system.

After taking the idle pressure reading, shut off the engine and watch the pressure gauge. The system should hold 17–20 psi. If the pressure drops to zero, there's a leak in the system. On a car with a conventional fuel system, such a pressure loss would suggest that either the fuel pump or the carburetor inlet valve were leaking. But assuming that they're not leaking fuel *externally,* there are four places an L-Jetronic system can leak *internally:*

1. The check valve in the output side of the electric fuel pump.
2. The pressure regulator.
3. One or more injectors.
4. The cold start valve.

To begin isolating a leak, crimp the hose connecting the fuel pressure regulator to the fuel tank. Turn the ignition switch off and on to cycle the fuel pump so you build up pressure in the system again.

---CAUTION---

Do not allow fuel system pressure to exceed 85 psi.

If the system now holds pressure, then the regulator is leaking. If the pressure still drops, keep the locking pliers on the regulator hose and have someone cycle the fuel pump with the ignition switch. Then quickly crimp the hose connecting the pump to the main fuel rail. If the pressure holds steady, the check valve in the output side of the fuel pump is defective. A bad pump check valve usually causes a hard start condition on an EFI equipped engine when hot.

Volume Test

A pressure test alone won't reveal trouble with an EFI fuel pump. It's important to also perform a volume test as well as a pressure test. With 12 volts at the pump and at least half a tank of gas in the car, a typical L-Jetronic pump should deliver about a quart (almost a liter) of fuel in 30 seconds.

---CAUTION---

Take precautions to avoid fire hazard when performing pressure and volume tests.

Component Removal and Testing
FUEL PRESSURE REGULATOR

Removal and Installation

1. Relieve fuel system pressure.
2. Disengage the vacuum line connecting the regulator to the intake manifold from the pressure regulator.
3. Remove the bolt and washers securing the pressure regulator mounting bracket and carefully pull the regulator and bracket upward. Note the position of the regulator in the bracket.

Typical L-Jetronic fuel pressure regulator

Typical pressure regulator mounting on L-Jetronic systems. Bracket fasteners and fuel connections will vary

4. Unfasten the hose clamps and disconnect the pressure regulator from the fuel hose. Inspect the hose for signs of wear, cracks or fuel leaks.

NOTE: Place a clean rag under the pressure regulator to catch any spilled fuel.

5. Remove the lock nut and remove the pressure regulator.
6. Installation is the reverse of removal.

NOTE: Torque the fuel delivery union bolt to 18–25 ft. lbs. Do not overtighten.

FUEL INJECTORS

Fuel in the L-Jetronic system is not injected directly into the cylinder. Fuel in injected into the intake port, where the air/fuel mixture is drawn into the cylinder when the intake valve opens to start the intake stroke. An electrical signal from each engine sensor is introduced into the control unit for computation. The open valve time period of the injector is controlled by the duration of the pulse computed in the control unit.

The injector operates on the solenoid valve principle. When an electric signal is applied to the coil built into the injector, the plunger is pulled into the solenoid, thereby opening the needle valve for fuel injection. The quantity of injected fuel is in proportion to the duration of the pulse applied from the control unit. The longer the pulse, the more fuel is delivered.

The fuel injectors are electrically connected, in parallel, in the control unit. All injectors receive the injection signal from the control unit at the same time. Therefore, injection is made independently of the engine stroke cycle (intake, combustion, and exhaust).

A bad injection valve can cause a number of problems:
- Hot restart troubles.
- Rough idle.
- Hesitation.
- Poor power.

Hot starting complaints can come from an injector or injectors that are leaking fuel droplets when they're supposed to be completely shut. The next three problems can be caused by a bad spray pattern from one or more of the injectors. Dribble patterns, fire hose shots, and uneven sprays will produce hesitation, stumbling and general lack of power. Replace any injector with a bad spray pattern.

L-Jetronic fuel injector installation showing position of nozzle in the intake port

Cross section of a typical L-Jetronic fuel injector

TESTING THE FUEL INJECTOR

With the engine running or cranking, use an engine stethoscope to check that there is normal operating noise in proportion to engine rpm. Using a stethoscope or a screwdriver, you can listen to each injector. A regular clicking means it's working. The interval between clicks should shorten as engine speed is increased. If you don't hear an injector clicking, there may a poor electrical connection at that injector. Try switching injector wires with an adjacent good injector. If swapping wires brings the dead injector to life, look for a corroded or loose connection or a broken injector wire.

Testing the fuel injector windings with an ohmmeter

Early L-Jetronic systems apply 12 volts to the injectors, but later models usually use only 4 volts to energize the injectors. Check for voltage at the wire harness connector with a voltmeter.

NOTE: Be wary of smelling gasoline when starting a cold engine. Some EFI injectors have a bad habit of allowing fuel to gush out from the seam where the black plastic part of the injector mates with the colored plastic part. But as soon as they warm up, the leak stops.

Injector Winding Test

Use an ohmmeter to measure the resistance value of each injector by connecting the test leads to the terminals on the injector. Resistance should be 1.5–4.0 ohms. On LH II systems, connect ohmmeter between pump relay terminal 87 and control unit connector terminal 13. Resistance should be approximately 16 ohms across the injector terminals.

For continuity tests, remove the ground cable from the battery and disconnect the electrical connectors from the injectors. Check for continuity readings between the two injector terminals. If there is no indication, the injector is faulty.

---CAUTION---

Applying 12 volts directly to the fuel injector terminals can burn out the winding and ruin the injector. Do not apply battery voltage to fuel injectors under any circumstances.

Dead or Plugged Injectors

You can spot a dead or plugged injector several ways; perform a routine ignition and engine condition test on any EFI equipped

Pointer shows seam where leaks usually develop in fuel injectors

engine before digging into its fuel system. If the ignition is sound and there is little or no rpm drop when you short a cylinder, there could be a vacuum leak at the nozzle seal. Injector O-rings are a potential vacuum leak on any EFI equipment engine.

To determine if there is a leaking O-ring, use the same technique for finding standard intake manifold leaks: spritz the O-ring with some carb and choke cleaner and watch for a response on a vacuum gauge. Needle fluctuations indicate vacuum leaks.

Leaking Injectors

If the system doesn't hold pressure after crimping both the regulator and pump hoses, then an injector is leaking. Remove the entire fuel rail from the engine and switch the pump on and off again, then watch for the injector that's leaking fuel. The injector orifice may become wet, but no more than two drops should form on the valve (injector) per minute.

COLD START VALVE (INJECTOR)

NOTE: Not all AFC fuel injection systems use a cold start valve.

To assist cold starting, a separate cold start valve sprays a fine jet of fuel against the air stream entering the plenum (air intake) chamber before fuel is added to it by the main injectors. The cold start valve is energized from the engine starter motor circuit through a thermo-time switch. The purpose of the thermo-time

Sectional view of cold start valve

switch is to ensure that the cold start valve will not be energized when the engine is at normal operating temperature or when the starter motor is used for prolonged periods when the engine is below operating temperature, preventing extra fuel being supplied to the engine when it is not needed. The thermo-time switch will isolate the cold start valve after 8 to 12 seconds.

Testing

———CAUTION———
Fire hazard. Take precautions when performing all tests.

Place the cold start valve nozzle into a clear container when testing

1. Remove the screws holding the valve in the intake manifold. DO NOT disconnect the fuel lines or electrical connector.
2. Place the cold start valve in a container to catch fuel. Wrap a clean rag around the mouth of the container.
3. Operate the starter and note the injection time. Valve should spray fuel for 1–12 seconds if the coolant temperature is lower that approximately 35°C (95°F). Above this temperature, no drip or spray should be noted.
4. If the cold start valve sprays continuously or drips, replace it.
5. If the cold start valve fails to function below 35°C (95°F), replace it.

NOTE: Perform this test as quickly as possible. Avoid energizing the injector for any length of time.

Using a fabricated test light to check the voltage signal from the wiring harness connector. Pulsed injector signals will cause the light to flash

6. Disconnect the cold start valve and hook up a test light across its connector. Ground the No. 1 coil terminal and run the starter. The light should glow for several seconds and then go out. If not, replace the thermo-time switch. Measure the resistance of the cold start valve using an ohmmeter. Correct resistance is 3–5 ohms. Check continuity across the cold start valve terminals.

NOTE: No starts or poor cold starting can be caused by a malfunctioning cold start valve. Cranking a cold engine with the coil wire grounded should produce a cone-shaped spray from the cold start valve. Cranking a warm engine should produce no fuel; if the injector dribbles gas, replace it.

Removal and Installation

1. Relieve fuel system pressure as previously described.
2. Provide a container to catch any fuel, or wrap clean rags around connections. *Use care to prevent dirt from entering the fuel system, and take precautions to avoid the risk of fire.*
3. Disconnect the electrical connector from the cold start valve. Clean any dirt or grease.
4. Remove fuel line from the valve. Pull the fuel hose off of the valve. Inspect the hose condition.

———CAUTION———
The valve body is plastic. Use care in removing fuel hose.

5. Remove the two fasteners holding the cold start valve in the intake manifold, then remove the valve. Remove and discard O-ring or gasket.
6. Reinstall in reverse order, making sure the system is tight and free from leaks. Replace the rubber sealing ring, or gasket and hose clamp if questionable.

NOTE: Fuel injection systems are highly susceptible to dirt in the system. Take care that all components are clean and free from dirt before reinstalling them.

THERMO-TIME SWITCH

NOTE: Not all AFC fuel injection systems use a thermo-time switch.

The thermo-time switch contains a bimetallic switch and heater coil. The switch completes the circuit for the cold start valve. The harness is connected in series to the cold start valve from the thermo-time switch. The bi-metal contact in the thermo-time switch opens or closes depending on the cooling water temperature, and sends a signal to the cold start valve so that an additional amount of fuel can be injected for starting operation of the engine (mixture enrichment).

Schematic of an L-Jetronic air flow sensor. Note the sensor flap and idle air adjustment screw

Typical thermo-time switch showing construction and wiring connector pins

During starting, power is supplied to the heater coil which warms the bi-metallic switch. The switch opens within 15 seconds regardless of coolant temperature. The lower the temperature, the longer for the coil to warm up. When the switch opens, the cold start valve is no longer energized and stops enriching the fuel mixture. To remove the thermo-time switch, disconnect the electrical connector and unscrew the switch from its mounting. It may be necessary to drain the cooling system or replace lost coolant.

—CAUTION—

Do not attempt to remove the thermo-time switch from a hot engine.

Testing

PRIMARY TEST

1. Remove the thermo-time switch and replace it with a plug to prevent loss of coolant liquid. Perform all tests on cold engine.
2. Cool the thermo-time switch by immersing it in cold water. Use a thermometer to check water temperature.
3. Connect the test wiring to the thermo-time switch as follows:
4. Connect one terminal to one of the wires of a test lamp. Connect the other end of the lamp to the positive (+) terminal of the battery.
5. Connect the negative (−) terminal of the battery to the body of thermo-time switch with a jumper wire. The lamp should light.
6. Place the thermo-time switch in a container of water and heat up the water while monitoring its temperature with a thermometer.

NOTE: Do not immerse test connections in water; just the lower end of the thermo-time switch should be submerged.

7. The lamp should go out between 31° and 39°C (88° and 102°F).
8. The nominal values of the thermo-time switch are marked on the six sides of the body (for example: 8 sec./35°C).

SECONDARY TEST

Check the resistance values with an ohmmeter between terminals of the thermo-time switch connector and ground for temperatures lower than 30°C (86°F) and higher than 40°C (104°F). Resistance should be around 50–80 ohms on switches marked 95°F/85; and 25–40 ohms on switches marked 35°C/85.

AIR FLOW (OR AIR MASS) SENSOR

On L and LU injection systems, the air flow sensor measures the quantity of intake air, and sends a signal to the control unit so that the base pulse width (voltage signal) can be determined for correct fuel injection by the injector. The air flow sensor is provided with a flap in the air passage. As the air flows through the passage, the flap rotates and its angle of rotation electronically signals the control unit by means of a potentiometer.

The engine will draw in a certain volume of fresh air depending on the throttle valve position and engine speed. This air stream will cause the sensor plate inside the air flow sensor to move against the force of its return spring. The sensor plate is connected to the potentiometer, which sends a voltage signal to the control unit. The temperature sensor in the air flow sensor influences this signal. The

Potentiometer function on the air flow sensor. The voltage signal goes to the ECU

control unit then sends out an opening signal to the fuel injectors to make sure that the volume of injected fuel is exactly right for the volume of intake air. A damping flap in the air flow sensor eliminates unwanted movement of the sensor plate. As the sensor plate moves, the damping flap moves into its damping chamber, acting like a shock absorber for the sensor plate. A small amount of intake air volume moves around the sensor plate via a bypass port. The air/fuel mixture for idling can be adjusted by changing the amount of air flowing through the bypass port with the adjusting screw.

If the sensor plate or its attached damper should become stuck inside the air flow sensor, excessive fuel consumption, marginal performance or a no-start condition could result. LH, LH II and Motronic injection systems incorporate an air mass sensor into the air box. On these systems, the flap valve is replaced with a heated platinum wire that is used to measure air mass without altitude influences.

NOTE: Because of the sensitivity of the air flow (or air mass) meter, there cannot be any air leaks in the ducts. Even the smallest leak could unbalance the system and affect the performance of the engine. During every check, pay attention to hose connections, dipstick and oil filler cap for evidence of air leaks. Should you encounter any, take steps to correct the problem before proceeding with testing.

Removal and Installation

1. Disconnect the air duct hoses from both sides of the air box.
2. Disconnect the electrical connector from the wire harness.
3. Remove all bolts, lockwashers, washers and bushings holding the air flow sensor to the bracket. Remove the unit assembly.
4. Reinstall in reverse order.

Testing Air Flow Sensor

1. Connect an ohmmeter to any terminal on the flow meter. Touch the flow meter body with the other connector. If any continuity is indicated, the unit is defective and must be replaced.
2. Reach into the air flow meter and check the flap operation. If the flap opens and closes smoothly, without binding, the mechanical portion of the unit is working.

Checking the air flow meter insulation with an ohmmeter. Continuity indicates a problem

NOTE: If the air temperature sensor or potentiometer is malfunctioning, the entire air flow sensor must be replaced.

Testing Air Mass Sensor

NOTE: Replace the air mass sensor as an assembly if the test results indicate a malfunction in any of the following procedures.

1. Ground the main relay terminal No. 21 and make sure the relay switches ON (a slight click should be heard when grounding).
2. Peel back the rubber boot from around the air mass sensor harness connector, but leave it connected to the sensor assembly.
3. Connect a voltmeter between terminal 9 and ground. The voltmeter should read battery voltage (12 volts). Probe all terminals from the rear of the connector.
4. Connect the voltmeter between terminals 9 and 36; the reading should again be 12 volts.
5. If no voltage is present, check for an open circuit or broken wire in the power feed from the battery. If voltage is present, remove the ground connection from relay terminal 21 and proceed with testing. Leave the connector boot peeled back and probe all wire terminals from the rear of the wiring harness connector for all tests.

Typical auxiliary air regulator used on Japanese L-Jetronic systems

---

CAUTION

Harness connectors can be damaged by test leads if probed from the front, causing a poor connection problem that didn't exist before testing. Exercise caution during all electrical test procedures and never use excessive force during probing, removal or installation of wire harness connectors or components.

---

6. Connect an ohmmeter between terminals 6 and 7 on the air mass meter. Resistance should be about 4 ohms.
7. Connect the ohmmeter between terminals 6 and 14 and read the resistance value. It should be between 0–1000 ohms (resistance varies depending on CO adjustment screw positioning). If values are as described, proceed with testing.
8. Connect a voltmeter between terminal 7 (+) and terminal 6 (−) on the air mass sensor connector.
9. Start the engine and note the voltage reading.
10. The voltage should increase with engine rpm. Slowly increase and decrease engine speed while watching the voltmeter and make sure the voltage changes up and down. Specific values are not as important as the fact that the needle (or digital readout) on the voltmeter swings back and forth as the rpm changes. If the readings change as described, proceed with testing.

Operation of gate valve in auxiliary air regulator

11. Connect a voltmeter between terminals 8 (+) and 36 (−) to check the air mass sensor wire cleaning (burn-off) operation.
12. Start the engine and increase the engine speed to approximately 2500 rpm for a few seconds.
13. Switch off the engine. After about 5 seconds, the voltmeter should read approximately 1 volt for 1 second. Repeat this test a few times to verify the results.
14. If all tests are as described, remove the voltmeter and reposition the rubber boot cover around the air mass meter connector. Make sure the boot seals correctly to prevent moisture from corroding the electrical connectors.

AUXILIARY AIR REGULATOR

The auxiliary air regulator allows more air to bypass the throttle plate when the engine is cold, triggering a richer fuel mixture for better cold starting.

A rotating metal disc inside the valve contains an opening that lines up with the bypass hoses when the engine is cold. As the engine heats up, a bi-metallic spring gradually closes the opening by rotating the disc. The bi-metallic spring is heated by coolant temperature and a heater coil which is energized through the ignition circuit.

A double relay, usually located near the electronic control unit and grounded by a terminal of the control unit, controls the input to the fuel pump, the cold start valve, the injector positive feed, the control unit, and the auxiliary air regulator.

Removal and Installation

1. Disconnect the air valve hoses.
2. Disconnect the air valve connector.

Location of adjustment screw and terminal numbers on air mass sensor

3. Disconnect the water bypass hose.
4. Remove the air valve attaching bolts and air valve.
5. Installation is the reverse of removal. Use a new gasket.

Testing

With the whole assembly at a temperature of about 20°C (about 68°F) and the electrical connectors and air hoses disconnected, visually check through the inside of the air lines to make sure that the diaphragm is partly open.

1. Using an ohmmeter, measure the resistance between the air valve terminals. Normal resistance is 29–49 ohms, depending on manufacturer's specifications.
2. Connect a voltmeter across the terminals of the connector and crank the engine.
3. If there is no voltage in the connector, look for a fault in the electrical system. If voltage is present, reconnect the valve and start the engine.
4. Check the engine rpm while pinching shut the air hose. At low temperature (below 140°F) the engine rpm should drop. After warm up, the engine speed should not drop more than 50 rpm.

AIR CONTROL VALVE

On AFC systems with an air mass sensor, an air control valve is used to regulate the idle speed by bypassing air around the throttle valve. The amount of air bypassed is determined by a signal from the electronic control unit (ECU). Replacement of the air control valve is similar to the auxiliary air valve removal procedure.

Terminal locations for testing air control valves

Testing

1. Connect an ohmmeter between the fuel pump relay terminal 87 and the control unit connector terminal 10. The reading should be approximately 20 ohms.
2. Connect the ohmmeter between relay terminal 87 and the control unit connector terminal 23. The resistance value should again be about 20 ohms.
3. Remove the ohmmeter and reconnect the harness connectors, if removed. Start and warm-up the engine.
4. Check the idle speed with a tachometer and compare the test results with the idle specification listed on the underhood emission control sticker.
5. Switch on the air conditioner (if equipped) and verify that the idle speed increases when the compressor is energized. If the idle doesn't increase, check for a sticking air control valve or failure of the A/C power circuit (shorted or open wire or microswitch).
6. Switch the engine OFF, then remove the connector from the coolant temperature sensor to simulate a cold engine.
7. Start the engine and verify that the high idle specification is obtained with a tachometer. Turn the ignition OFF and reconnect the coolant temperature sensor if the high idle is correct, then restart the engine and make sure the idle speed is once again at the normal (warm) value.

NOTE: If the air control valve is suspected of malfunction, install a new valve and repeat the test procedures. Adjust idle speed, if necessary.

THROTTLE SWITCH

The throttle switch forms part of the control for the fuel injection system, providing the ECU with information on throttle operating conditions. The switch is grounded at the intake manifold.

The throttle valve switch is attached to the throttle chamber and actuates in response to accelerator pedal movement. This switch has two or three sets of contact points. One set monitors the idle position and the other set monitors full throttle position. Some use additional contacts for mid-range operation.

The idle contact closes when the throttle valve is positioned at idle and opens when it is at any other position. The idle contact compensates for after idle enrichment, and sends the fuel shut-off signal.

Typical throttle switch showing pin numbers

The full throttle contact closes only when the throttle valve is positioned at full throttle (more than 35 degree opening of the throttle valve). The contact is open while the the throttle valve is at any other position. The full contact compensates for enrichment in full throttle.

On AFC systems with a Constant Idle Speed (CIS) feature incorporated into the injection circuit, a microswitch is used in place of the throttle switch. The microswitch is mounted so as to contact the throttle linkage at idle and signal the ECU as to what throttle position is being used. Some microswitches are set to be open at idle and some are closed. Use a test light to determine which type of microswitch is being used by checking for voltage while moving the throttle lever to open and close the contact lever. The microswitch is usually adjusted when setting the idle speed.

Adjustment

NOTE: A click should be heard when the throttle valve moves and the idle contact opens

1. Make sure that the idle speed is correct. Check the underhood sticker for correct specification.
2. Disconnect the connector from the switch. The center pin is usually the 12 volt input terminal.

Checking the throttle switch adjustment with an ohmmeter

3. Connect an ohmmeter between terminals 2 and 18 of the switch.
4. Loosen the two screws holding the throttle plate switch.
5. With the engine off, rotate the switch clockwise until the ohmmeter indicates a closed circuit (idle contact closes).
6. At the exact point that the ohmmeter indicates a closed circuit, tighten the two screws holding the switch.
7. Check the adjustment.

Adjust the throttle switch by loosening the fasteners

Removal and Installation

1. Disconnect the electrical connector.
2. Remove the two screws and washers holding the switch to the intake manifold.
3. Remove the switch by slowly pulling it.
4. Reinstall in the reverse order and adjust the switch.

VACUUM SWITCH—LH-JETRONIC SYSTEM

On some applications, a vacuum switch takes the place of the throttle valve switch to indicate full load and idle (low ported vacuum signal) and part load (maximum vacuum signal) conditions to the electronic control unit. Instead of being mounted directly on the throttle shaft, the vacuum switch is usually located on the bulkhead or fender panel under the hood and is connected to a ported vacuum orifice in the throttle valve assembly by a vacuum hose.

Typical vacuum switch

Testing

To test the vacuum switch, connect a hand vacuum pump to the vacuum fitting and connect an ohmmeter across terminals 3 and 5 at the control unit harness connector. With no vacuum applied to the switch, the resistance should be zero. When approximately 4 in. Hg. is applied with the hand vacuum pump, the resistance should be infinite. A high resistance reading without vacuum indicates an open circuit and zero resistance when vacuum is applied indicates a short circuit. In either case, if incorrect resistance is noted, replace the vacuum switch and repeat the test.

DETONATION SENSOR

On some AFC installations, a detonation sensor is incorporated into the system to detect engine knock conditions. Engine knock (or ping) can be caused by using fuel with too low an octane rating or advanced timing. The detonations within the cylinder set up vibrations within the cylinder block that are detected by a piezoelectric element which converts vibrational pressure into an electrical signal (voltage impulse) which is used as an input signal to the control unit. The ECU uses the signal to measure detonation

Cross section of typical detonation sensor

and retard the timing to eliminate the problem. A detonation sensor is usually found on turbocharged engines, since serious engine damage can occur if turbocharged engines detonate under boost.

Testing

To test the detonation sensor operation first locate the sensor, remove the harness connector and check for continuity with an ohmmeter. If continuity exists, reconnect the sensor and start the engine after installing a timing light. When the engine bloc is tapped with a small hammer near the detonation sensor, the timing should change. Repeat the test several times and make sure the ignition timing changes (retards) when the block is tapped and returns to normal when the tapping stops. If no change in the timing is noted and the sensor shows continuity, the problem is in the ECU, or the wiring harness.

FUEL TEMPERATURE SENSOR

On some models, a fuel temperature sensor is built into the pressure regulator assembly to monitor fuel temperature. If the temperature rises beyond a preset value, the control unit enriches the mixture to compensate.

PRESSURE REGULATOR

FUEL TEMPERATURE SENSOR

Location of fuel temperature sensor on pressure regulator

Testing

The fuel temperature sensor is tested in the same manner as a coolant sensor. Connect an ohmmeter and check that the resistance value (ohms) changes as the temperature rises. On the Nissan ECCS system, for example, the resistance should fall as the temperature rises. If the temperature sensor checks out, perform a continuity test on the wiring harness connectors at the switch and control unit. If no problem is found, the control unit itself may be malfunctioning.

NOTE: If found to be defective, the fuel temperature sensor and fuel pressure regulator should be replaced as an assembly.

SPEED SENSOR

On some models, a speed sensor is used to provide a signal to the control unit on vehicle road speed. Two general types of sensors are used, depending on whether the instrument cluster is an analog (needle) type or digital (LED) readout type of display. In the analog speedometer, the speed sensor is usually a reed switch which transforms vehicle speed into a pulse signal. On digital type instrument clusters the speed sensor consists of an LED (light emitting diode), photo diode, shutter and wave forming circuit (signal generator) whose operation closely resembles the crank angle sensor described under "ECCS Control Unit" later in the chapter.

Testing

Regardless of instrument cluster type, the easiest method of checking the speed sensor operation is to disconnect the speedometer cable at the transmission and connect an ohmmeter between the control unit harness connector terminal from the speed sensor (e.g. terminal No. 29 on Nissan 300 ZX models) to ground. Check for continuity while slowly rotating the speedometer cable. The ohmmeter should register the pulses from the speed sensor. If no reading is obtained, check the wiring harness to the speed sensor for continuity.

NOTE: Rotate the speedometer slowly and watch for meter changes. Most speed sensors send impulses about 24 times per revolution of the speedometer cable. If found to be defective, the speed sensor is usually replaced with the speedometer assembly as a unit, although some separate sensor assemblies are used in digital instrument cluster displays. Digital cluster speed sensors are checked with the key ON.

BOOST SENSOR SWITCH

TURBOCHARGED MODELS ONLY

On some turbocharged engines, a vacuum-operated boost sensor provides a signal to the ECU for fuel enrichment or electronic wastegate control while under boost. Some manufacturers use vacuum switches to provide protection against a dangerous overboost situation by cutting off the fuel injectors above a certain boost pressure. Boost sensor switches may be located in the engine compartment, or behind the instrument cluster.

Testing

To test vacuum actuated boost pressure switches, connect a hand-pumped vaccum gauge to the switch vacuum port and an ohmmeter to the terminals of the sensor connector. Pump the vacuum gauge and check for continuity between the terminals when the vacuum is applied. There should be no continuity when the vacuum is absent, and the resistance between the terminals should vary as the vacuum level applied rises and falls. The switch can be inspected in the same manner by using a voltmeter and connecting battery voltage to one side of the switch. Voltage should vary just as resistance did, when the vacuum level changes. Look for changes rather than specific volt or ohm values to determine if the switch is functioning.

COOLANT TEMPERATURE SENSOR

NOTE: Most later models are equipped with cylinder head temperature sensors rather than water temperature sensors. However, the test is the same for both units.

The coolant temperature sensor is located near the cylinder head and provides a signal to the ECU that causes a longer injector open time when the engine is cold. The open time decreases as the engine reaches normal operating temperature. The coolant temperature sensor also completes the circuit for the extra air valve when the engine is cold. Typical resistance values at different temperatures are:

Temperature	Resistance (Ohms)
+80°C (175°F)	270–390
+20°C (68°F)	2100–2900
−10°C (14 °F)	7000–116000

Note: Exact resistance values vary with manufacturer.

The cylinder head temperature sensor, built into the cylinder head, monitors change in cylinder head temperature and transmits a signal to increase the pulse duration (fuel delivery) during the warm-up period. The temperature sensing unit employs a thermistor which is very sensitive in the low temperature range. The elec-

Typical coolant temperature sensor used on L-Jetronic systems

trical resistance of the thermistor decreases in response to the temperature rise.

Removal and Installation

—CAUTION—

Allow the engine to cool before attempting this procedure.

Partially drain the cooling system. Then, disconnect the electrical terminal plug and unscrew the coolant temperature sensor. Install in reverse order, refilling and bleeding the cooling system.

Testing

In general, coolant and cylinder head temperature sensors have a fairly high mortality rate on EFI systems. VW's, for example, use up cylinder head sensors often. On L-Jetronic systems, the intake air temperature sensor is incorporated into the air flow meter. If it fails, replace the air flow meter. It's impossible to tune or adjust an EFI equipped engine if one of its sensors is bad. Check that the temperature sensor resistance, measured with an ohmmeter, changes when the sensor is checked cold, then after the engine is warmed up. Engine should be off for all tests. Extremely high test values indicates open circuit in temperature sensor or wiring (check temperature sensor ground at intake manifold). Zero resistance indicates short circuit.

Sensor Insulation Check

This check is done on the engine.
1. Disconnect the battery ground cable.
2. Disconnect the sensor harness connector.
3. Connect an ohmmeter to one of the terminals on the sensor and touch the engine block with the other. Any indication of continuity indicates a need to replace the unit.

LAMBDA (OXYGEN) SENSOR

The Lambda or Oxygen sensor is a probe with a ceramic body in a protective housing. It measures the oxygen concentration in the exhaust system and provides a feedback signal to the control unit.

The exhaust gas sensor produces a signal depending on air/fuel mixture ratio. The signal varies directly with the density of oxygen in exhaust gases. The fuel is burned at the best theoretically determined air/fuel ratio of the mixture; the oxygen sensor signal increases when there is a richer mixture, and decreases when there is a lean mixture. The signal from the sensor allows the ECU to fine tune the fuel mixture to allow the catalytic converter to operate at its peak efficiency.

Cross section of a typical oxygen sensor

NOTE: As with the catalytic converter, the use of leaded fuel will contaminate and ruin the Lambda sensor.

The idle switch will turn off the oxygen sensor when coasting due to the excessive oxygen present in the exhaust gas. The idle contact will open when the free play in the accelerator linkage is taken up, even though the throttle valve is still closed. The full throttle contact switches off the oxygen sensor if the throttle is opened more than 30° in order to lower exhaust gas temperature and protect the sensor and the catalytic converter. The control unit will simultaneously switch to a 12% partial and full throttle enrichment.

NOTE: A service interval counter, much like the EGR and Catalytic Converter counters will light a dash warning light when the need for Oxygen Sensor replacement arises (around 30,000 miles). The service indicator must be reset after replacement of the lambda sensor.

Since the oxygen sensor doesn't function until it reaches operating temperature, late models incorporate a heater circuit to warm up the sensor for quicker response and to keep the oxygen sensor at operating temperature during prolonged idle or low speed operation. Oxygen sensors with heaters are recognized by the third wire connector on the sensor body. Do not interchange old and new type sensors.

—CAUTION—

Testing the oxygen sensor output with a powered voltmeter can damage the sensor by drawing too much current through the sensor. The average oxygen sensor puts out about one volt in operation.

Removal and Installation

1. Allow the exhaust system to cool.
2. Disconnect the cable from the oxygen sensor.
3. Remove the sensor from the exhaust manifold. It may be necessary to use penetrating oil or rust solvent.
4. Coat the threads of the sensor with anti-seize, anti-rust grease. Do not get grease on the sensor body itself.
5. Thread the sensor into the exhaust manifold and torque to 30-36 ft. lb.
6. Connect the electrical cable to the sensor and check the CO.

—CAUTION—

Do not allow grease to get on the sensor surface. This will contaminate and ruin the Lambda sensor. Exercise care when coating the threads with anti-seize compound. Check CO with suitable meter.

Use anti-seize compound when installing the oxygen sensor

Electronic Control Unit (ECU)

GENERAL INFORMATION

The electronic control unit is the brain of the AFC fuel injection system. It controls various engine operating conditions by constantly measuring specific engine parameters (e.g. temperature, rpm, air mass or volume, etc.) and making adjustments by sending out appropriate voltage signals to components. Each ECU

E.C.C.S. control unit used on Nissan models. Except for the pin connectors, all ECU units look pretty much alike

ELECTRONIC CONTROL UNIT FOR FUEL INJECTION SYSTEM

ELECTRONIC CONTROL UNIT FOR CONSTANT IDLE SPEED SYSTEM

Typical control unit installations

responds to its sensor inputs according to a specific design of its internal integrated circuits, or according to manufacturers instructions programmed into a PROM (Programmed Read Only Memory) microchip computer memory plugged into the solid state circuit board. The number and type of sensors employed by a particular ECU and the manner in which it responds to these sensor input signals is unique to each type of system and different from one manufacturer to another. For this reason, the ECU's are not interchangeable, even if the same type of injection system (L-Jetronic, for example) is used on two different models built by the same manufacturer. When replacing any ECU it is important to correctly identify not only the type of injection system and manufacturer, but also the year and model of car, engine and transmission. Carefully compare the part numbers of both old and new ECU to make sure the correct control unit is being installed or serious damage to the replacement part is likely.

Depending on the type of fuel injection system, the ECU is designed to do different things. The basic L-Jetronic system is designed to control the fuel mixture under various engine load conditions and not much else. Later modifications incorporate other functions such as ignition timing control, EGR and other emission control device operation, idle speed, etc. Some ECU's operate with analog electrical signals while others use digital signals. The manner in which the AFC injection systems measures the intake air can vary from a counterbalanced air flap (L-Jetronic) to a heated platinum wire (LH-Jetronic) and the type and number of engine sensors will vary from one manufacturer to another. Some injection systems (Motronic and the E.C.C.S. system used on the Nissan 300ZX, for example) utilize sensors that measure the crankshaft angle to precisely control ignition timing and injection according to engine dynamometer data programmed into the control unit by the manufacturer. In addition, some injection systems are designed with a self-diagnosis capability that flashes a trouble code to indicate various malfunctions detected during operation. Before attempting any service or diagnosis procedures, familiarize yourself with the specific type of injection system used, as well as the various components, to determine what may be causing a problem and therefore what is in need of testing.

There are certain similarities common to most AFC systems that should be noted when testing. The service precautions outlined at the beginning of this section should be read and carefully followed to avoid causing damage to the control unit or electrical system during service. All ECU's are installed somewhere inside the passenger compartment and all use a large, multi-pin connector to tie the ECU into the wiring harness. This ECU connector is held in place with some form of locking device that must be released before the connector can be removed.

CAUTION

Never attempt to disconnect the ECU with the key ON or the engine running. Serious damage to the ECU can occur if the electrical connectors on any components are allowed to arc or the wrong connections are made when performing tests with a volt/ohmmeter or jumper wire.

PUSH CLIP TO RELEASE CONNECTOR

Never disconnect the ECU connector with the key On or the engine running. Exercise care when handling the ECU connector so as not to damage the contact pins

The pin numbers on the ECU and its connector will vary from one model to another, so care must be taken to make sure the correct connections are being made before any test is attempted. These numbers are usually stamped on the side of the main connector. Do not probe the ECU connector terminals from the front, as test probes can damage the connectors. Probe all ECU connections from the rear of the connector, after removing the harness cover, in the test holes provided or with a thin paper clip carefully installed from the wire side to allow the use of small clips. Be careful not to damage any connector during test procedures and never use excessive force when dealing with any electrical component. The control unit should be handled with care when removed and protected from contact with any kind of solvents, water or direct contact with any electrical or magnetic devices. Never apply power directly to a control unit on the bench for any reason.

Most ECU's require special test equipment for pinpoint troubleshooting; however some simple pass/fail procedures are possible using an appropriate tach/dwell meter, volt/ohm meter and fabricating jumper wires and test bulbs with the correct terminal connections. Not all analog (meter) test equipment is compatible with all electronic control systems and a digital multimeter may be necessary for some procedures. Consult the manufacturer's instructions before connecting any powered test equipment to make sure it won't damage the ECU. When testing with an analog volt/ohm or tach/dwell remember that it is usually more important to look for needle movement (swing) than exact test values. Be sure to perform the preliminary checks on fuel, compression and ignition systems before assuming that the ECU is causing a problem. Experience usually shows that simple problems like loose or corroded connections, clogged air, fuel or emission control filters and vacuum or air leaks in the intake system cause most of the problems blamed on a faulty electronic control unit.

Because of their solid state construction and the fact that there are no moving parts, most ECU's are designed to last the life of the car in operation, and are maintenance-free. The ECU should be removed if any AFC-equipped vehicle is to be placed in a paint oven or exposed to any temperature exceeding approximately 176°F. Never attempt to disconnect any control unit with the ignition switch ON or the engine running, and inspect all connectors for damage before reconnecting the wiring harness.

ECU DIAGNOSIS

Quick Test

By fabricating a small test light with an appropriate injector harness connector, the injector signal from the ECU can be ckecked. With the key OFF, connect the test lamp to the harness side of the fuel injector connector. Crank the engine and make sure the light flashes on and off. If the test lamp flashes, it indicates the control unit is supplying a pulse voltage to the injector and chances are it is operating properly.

NOTE: Because two different transistors are used in some AFC electronic control units, it may be necessary to test both the No. 1 and No. 4 cylinder injectors to determine if the control unit is supplying pulses to all of the injectors.

Circuit Tests

Individual control circuits within the ECU can be checked by performing resistance and continuity tests according to the following charts and connector pin locations illustrated. Read the service precautions concerning the ECU before attempting any tests and make sure the test equipment used will not damage the control unit. Make absolutely sure you are probing the correct terminals before making any connections, as serious ECU damage can occur if the wrong two pins are connected in a circuit.

—CAUTION—

On the Volvo LH-Jetronic system, the test point located behind the battery is NOT to be used in fault tracing the system. Unless special test equipment is used, using this test point can cause serious ECU damage. If equipped with a Constant Idle Speed system, there may be two test points.

L-JETRONIC TEST SPECIFICATIONS

Circuit Tested	Terminal Connection	Correct Value (ohms)
OHMMETER TESTS		
Wire to coil terminal #1	1-GND	Wire grounded-0 Coil disconnected-∞
Idle circuit through throttle switch	2-18	Throttle closed-0 (Type IV only)
Full throttle enrichment through throttle switch	3-18	0 @ WOT
Ground circuit	5-GND	0
Air sensor circuit	6-9	200-400
	6-8	130-260
	8-9	70-140
	6-7	40-300
	7-8	100-500
	6-27	2800 @ 68°F

L-JETRONIC TEST SPECIFICATIONS

Circuit Tested	Terminal Connection	Correct Value (ohms)
Head sensor	13-GND	2100-2900 @ 68°F 270-390 @ 176°F
Injector wire and resistor	14-10	7
	15-10	7
	32-10	7
	33-10	7
Ground circuit	16-GND	0
	17-GND	0
Auxiliary air regulatory and wiring	34 @ ECU- 37 @ relay	30
VOLTMETER TESTS		
Signal from starter	4-GND	12v-Cranking 0v-Otherwise
Voltage to ECU	10-GND	12v-Key ON 0v-Key OFF
Fuel pump circuit	28-GND	12v-Key ON and sensor flap open

NOTE: Probe all terminals carefully from the rear. Test probes can damage terminals and cause poor connections. Make sure test meters are compatible with injection system

ECU—Electronic Control Unit   WOT—Wide Open Throttle
GND—Ground

LH-JETRONIC TEST SPECIFICATIONS

Circuit Tested	Terminal Numbers	Test Results
Battery voltage from ignition switch to ECU	20-GND ①	key ON-12 volts key OFF-0 volts
System Relay test	34-GND ③ 10-GND ①	Voltmeter should indicate 12 volts
Fuel Pump Relay	28-GND ③	Fuel pump runs
Ground Check ④	5-GND ② 16-GND ② 17-GND ②	Resistance should be 0 ohms at all points

NOTE: Test connector located behind the battery is not to be used for fault tracing. Special test equipment must be used or system will be damaged.

GND—Ground
ECU—Electronic Control Unit
① Voltmeter connections
② Ohmmeter connections
③ Jumper wire connections
④ Ground circuits can be checked with 12v test light by connecting one end to the positive battery cable and probing connectors 5, 16 and 17. Test light should come on.

LH II-JETRONIC TEST SPECIFICATIONS

Circuit Tested	Terminal Numbers	Test Results
Battery voltage from ignition switch to ECU	18-GND ①	key ON–12 volts key OFF–0 volts
Fuel Pump relay	17-GND ③	key ON–pump runs
System Relay	9-GND ① 21-GND ③	Voltmeter should read 12 volts. Relay is on
Ground Check	11-GND ② 25-GND ②	0 ohms (no resistance) for both terminals
Ignition coil connection	1-GND ①	Meter should deflect when ignition is switched ON
Air Control Valve circuit	④	20 ohms

NOTE: Terminal numbers should be marked on connectors. Turn ignition OFF when removing or installing connectors. All terminals are at ECU connector.

ECU—Electronic Control Unit   GND—Ground
① Voltmeter connections
② Ohmmeter connections
③ Jumper wire connection
④ Connect ohmmeter between pump relay terminal 87 and ECU connector terminal 10; then between pump relay terminal 87 and ECU connector terminal 23. Readings should match.

PORSCHE 928 TEST SPECIFICATIONS

Circuit Tested	Terminal Test Connections	Normal Reading
OHMMETER TESTS		
Temperature sensor ①	5-13	2–3 kΩ @ 68 deg. F 1.2–2.4 kΩ @ 83 deg. F
Idle microswitch A	2-18 ① 2-18 ②	2–3 kΩ @ 68 deg. F 1.2–2.4 kΩ @ 83 deg. F 0Ω
Full throttle microswitch B	3-18 ① 3-18 ③	0Ω 0 Ω @ 68 deg. F 0–10 Ω @ 83 deg. F
Air flow sensor ④	6-9 6-8 8-9 6-7 7-8	400–800 Ω 260–520 Ω 140–280 Ω 80–600 Ω 200–1000 Ω
Air flow temperature sensor	27-6	2–3 kΩ @ 68 deg. F 1.2–2.4 kΩ @ 83 deg. F

PORSCHE 928 TEST SPECIFICATIONS

Circuit Tested	Terminal Test Connections	Normal Reading
Fuel injectors ⑤		
1 + 5	10-15	1–1.5 Ω
4 + 8	10-14	1–1.5 Ω
3 + 7	10-32	1–1.5 Ω
2 + 6	10-33	1–1.5 Ω
Ground checks	16-GND	0Ω
	17-GND	0Ω
	35-GND	0Ω
	5-GND	0Ω
VOLTMETER TESTS		
Test conditions ⑥		
IGN ON	1-GND	1 volt
IGN ON	10-GND	12 volts
IGN ON	29-GND	12 volts
Cranking	4-GND	8 volts (minimum)
Cranking	1-GND	2.5 volts

NOTE: When conducting tests, look for a change rather than specific values. ALl voltage values are approximate.

GND–Ground   Ω–Ohms (kΩ-kilo-ohms)
① Accelerator pedal released
② Throttle linkage play eliminated
③ Throttle open more than 1/3 (30 deg.)
④ As of production month 042 or later. For earlier production sensors, divide test values in half.
⑤ 2–3 ohms when each injector is checked separately.
⑥ All voltage values are approximate.

Self-Diagnosing AFC Injection Systems

Some AFC fuel injection systems are equipped with a self-diagnosis capability to allow retrieval of stored trouble codes from the ECU memory. The number of codes stored and the meaning of the code numbers varies from one manufacturer to another. By activating the diagnostic mode and counting the number of flashes on the CHECK ENGINE or ECU lights, it is possible to ask the computer where the problem is (which circuit) and narrow down the number of pin connectors tested when diagnosing an AFC fuel injection problem.

NISSAN E.C.C.S. SYSTEM

On 1984 and later models, the E.C.C.S. control unit used on the 300ZX has a self-diagnosing capability. The E.C.C.S. control unit consists of a microcomputer, connectors for signal input and output and power supply, inspection lamps and a diagnostic mode selector. The control unit calculates basic injector pulse width (fuel delivery) by processing signals from the crank angle sensor and air flow meter. The crank angle sensor monitors engine speed and piston position and sends signals to the ECU for control of fuel injection, ignition timing, idle speed, fuel pump operation and EGR (emission control) operation.

The crank angle sensor consists of a rotor plate and wave forming circuit built into the distributor. The rotor plate has 360 slits for a 1° (engine speed) signal and 6 slits for a 120° signal (crankshaft angle). Light Emitting Diodes (LED's) and Photo Diodes are built

Crank angle sensor used on Nissan E.C.C.S. system

Terminal numbers on 16 pin connector for Nissan E.C.C.S. system

into the wave forming circuit. When the rotor plate cuts the light which is sent to the photo diode from the LED, it causes an alternate voltage which is converted into an on-off pulse by the wave forming circuit and sent to the control unit. Enrichment rates are pre-programmed into the control unit for engine speed and basic injection pulse width.

NOTE: The ECU will shut off the injectors if the engine speed exceeds 6500 rpm, or road speed exceeds 137 mph, whichever comes first. The crank angle sensor is an important component in the E.C.C.S. system and a malfunctioning sensor is sometimes accompanied by a display which shows faults in other systems. Check the crank angle sensor first.

The self-diagnostic system determines the malfunctions of signal systems such as sensors, actuators and wire harness connectors based on the status of the input signals received by the E.C.C.S. control unit. Malfunction codes are displayed by two LED's (red and green) mounted on the side of the control unit. The self-diagnosis results are retained in the memory chip of the ECU and displayed only when the diagnosis mode selector (located on the left side of the ECU) is turned fully clockwise. The self-diagnosis system on the E.C.C.S. control unit is capable of displaying malfunctions being checked, as well as trouble codes stored in the memory. In this manner, an intermittent malfunction can be detected during service procedures.

Terminal numbers on 20 pin connector for Nissan E.C.C.S. system. Test ignition signal by checking continuity between terminals 3, 5 and ground

Terminal numbers on 15 pin connector for Nissan E.C.C.S. system. Test the fuel pump circuit by checking for current (with the key ON) between terminal 108 and ground

the two together indicate a code number. The red LED is the tenth digit, and the green LED is the unit digit. For example, when the red light blinks three times and the green light blinks twice, the code displayed is 32. All malfunctions are classified by code numbers. When all service procedures are complete, erase the memory by disconnecting the battery cable or the ECU harness connector. *Removing the power to the control unit automatically erases all trouble codes from the memory. Never erase the stored memory before performing self diagnosis tests.*

Control unit for Nissan E.C.C.S. system showing location of diagnostic mode selector and readout light

---CAUTION---

Turn the diagnostic mode selector carefully with a small screwdriver. Do not press hard to turn or the selector may be damaged.

Service codes are displayed as flashes of both the red and green LED. The red LED blinks first, followed by the green LED, and

NISSAN E.C.C.S. TROUBLE CODES

Code Number	ECU Circuit	Test Point Pin Numbers	Normal Test Results
11	Crank Angle Sensor	Check harness for open circuit	Continuity

NISSAN E.C.C.S. TROUBLE CODES

Code Number	ECU Circuit	Test Point Pin Numbers	Normal Test Results
12	Air Flow Meter	Ground terminal 26 ①connect VOM @ 26–31	IGN ON—1.5–1.7 volts
		Apply 12v @ E–D ② connect VOM @ B–D	1.5–1.7 volts
		VOM @ 12–GND ③	Continuity
		VOM @ C–R ②	Continuity
13	Cylinder Head Temperature Sensor	VOM @ 23–26 ①	Above 68 deg F–2.9 kΩ Below 68 deg F–2.1 kΩ
14	Speed Sensor	VOM @ 29–GND ④	Continuity
21	Ignition Signal	VOM @ 3–GND	Continuity
		VOM @ 5–GND Check power transistor terminals to base plate	Continuity
			Continuity
22	Fuel Pump	VOM @ 108–GND ⑤ Pump connectors Pump relay: VOM @ 1–2 VOM @ 3–4 12v @ 1–2, VOM @ 3–4	IGN ON–12 volts Continuity Continuity ∞
23	Throttle Valve Switch	VOM @ 18–25 ⑥ VOM @ 18–GND VOM @ 25–GND	Continuity ∞ ∞
24	Neutral/Park Switch	VOM @ Switch terminals	Neutral-0Ω Drive-∞Ω
31	Air Conditioner	VOM @ 22–GND ①	IGN ON–12 volts
32	Start Signal	VOM @ 9–GND ③	12 volts with starter S terminal disconnected
34	Detonation Sensor	Disconnect sensor and check timing with engine running	Timing should retard 5 degrees above 2000 rpm
41	Fuel Temperature Sensor	VOM @ 15–GND ③	Above 68 deg. F–2.9 kΩ
		VOM @ Sensor terminals	Below 68 deg. F–2.1 kΩ Resistance (ohms) should decrease as temperature rises
44	Normal Operation—no further testing required		

NOTE: Make sure test equipment will not damage the control unit before testing

VOM—Volt/ohm meter
GND—Ground
Ω—Ohms (kΩ = kilo-ohms)
∞—Infinite resistance
① 16-pin harness connector
② 6-pin air flow meter connection
③ 20-pin harness connector
④ 16-pin connector at ECU
⑤ Throttle valve switch connector

ISUZU I-TEC SYSTEM

The self diagnosis system is designed to monitor the input and output signals of the sensors and actuators and to store any malfunctions in its memory as a trouble code. When the electronic control unit detects a problem, it activates a CHECK ENGINE light on the dash to alert the driver. The computer will store trouble codes indicating problems in monitored systems including:

- Air flow sensor system
- Coolant temperature sensor
- Speed sensor
- Oxygen sensor
- Detonation sensor
- Injector system
- Electronic Control Unit (ECU)

NOTE: The self diagnosis system is only capable of troubleshooting the circuits in the I-TEC system, not in the components themselves. Malfunctions in a circuit may be caused by a variety of problems, including loose connections, failed components or damage to wiring.

Activating Diagnosis Mode

Locate the diagnosis lead near the control unit and connect the two leads with the ignition ON. The trouble codes stored in the memory are displayed by the CHECK ENGINE light as flashes that indicate numbers (trouble codes). The I-TEC system ECU memory is capable of storing three different trouble codes which are displayed in numerical sequence no matter when the malfunctions occur. Each trouble code is repeated three times, then the next code is displayed. The ECU memory will display all stored trouble codes as long as the diagnosis lead is connected with the key ON. A code 12 indicates that the I-TEC system is functioning normally and that no further testing is necessary. After servicing, clear the trouble codes by disconnecting the No. 4 fuse in the fuse block.

Diagnostic lead for Isuzu I-TEC injection system

ECU terminal numbers for Isuzu I-TEC injection system

NOTE: All codes stored in the memory will be automatically cleared whenever the main harness connector is removed from the control unit.

Testing

The control unit wiring harness has three types of connectors with specifically numbered terminals. All inspection procedures refer to these numbers when describing terminal connections.

ISUZU I-TEC SYSTEM TROUBLE CODES

Trouble Code	ECU Circuit	Indicated Problem
12	Normal operation	No testing required
13	Oxygen sensor	Open or short circuit, failed sensor
44	Oxygen sensor	Low voltage signal
45	Oxygen sensor	High voltage signal
14	Coolant temperature sensor	Shorted with ground (no signal)
15	Coolant temperature sensor	Incorrect signal (too high or low)
16	Coolant temperature sensor	Excessive signal (harness open)
21	Throttle valve switch	Idle and WOT contacts closed at the same time
43	Throttle valve switch ①	Idle contact shorted
65	Throttle valve switch	Full throttle contact shorted
22	Starter signal	No signal to ECU
41	Crank angle sensor	No signal or wrong signal
61	Air flow sensor	Weak signal (harness shorted or open hot wire)
62	Air flow sensor	Excessive signal (open cold wire)
63	Speed sensor ①	No signal to ECU
66	Detonation sensor	Harness open or shorted to ground
51, 52, 55	ECU malfunction	Incorrect injection pulse or fixed timing
23	Power transistor for ignition	Output terminal shorted to ground
35	Power transistor for ignition	Open harness wire
54	Power transistor for ignition	Faulty transistor or ground
25	Vacuum switching valve	Output terminal shorted to ground or open harness
53	Vacuum switching valve	Faulty transistor or ground
33	Fuel injector	Output terminal shorted to ground or open harness wire
64	Fuel injector	Faulty transistor or ground

NOTE: Make sure test equipment will not damage ECU before making any connections. See manufacturer's instructions to verify compatibility with I-TEC System.
ECU—Electronic Control Unit
① Not diagnosed when the air flow sensor is defective

―CAUTION―

Make sure of the terminal numbers and location when making test connections, since battery power is supplied to some terminals only when the ignition is ON. Do not probe connector terminals from the front as test probes can damage the pins and connectors. Use a pin to probe connectors from the rear.

TOYOTA EFI SYSTEM

NOTE: The Toyota ECU employs a dash-mounted CHECK ENGINE light that illuminates when the control unit detects a malfunction. The memory will store the trouble codes until the system is cleared by removing the EFI fuse with the engine off.

Activating Diagnosis Mode

To activate the trouble code readout and obtain the diagnostic codes stored in the memory, first check that the battery voltage is at least 11 volts, the throttle valve is fully closed, transmission is in neutral, the engine is at normal operating temperature and all accessories are turned off.

1. Turn the ignition switch ON, but do not start the engine.
2. Locate the Check Engine Connector under the hood, near the ignition coil, and use a short jumper wire to connect the terminals together.
3. Read the diagnostic code as indicated by the number of flashes of the CHECK ENGINE light. If normal system operation is occurring (no malfunctions), the light will blink once every 3 seconds (code 1).
4. The light will blink once every second to indicate a trouble code stored in the memory, with 3 second pauses between each code number. For example, three blinks, a pause, then three blinks indicates a code 3 (air flow meter malfunction) stored in the memory.

NOTE: The diagnostic code series will be repeated as long as the CHECK ENGINE terminals are connected by the jumper wire.

5. After all trouble codes are recorded, remove the jumper wire and replace the rubber cap on the connector.

Diagnostic mode connector used on Toyota models—1984 Starlet shown

Disconnect the fusible link for 30 seconds to clear the trouble code memory on Toyota Starlet models

Disconnect the STOP fuse to clear the trouble code memory on Toyota Celica models

Diagnostic mode connector used on Toyota Celica models

6. Cancel the trouble codes in the memory after repairs by removing the STOP fuse for about 30 seconds (longer at lower ambient temperatures). If the diagnostic codes are not removed from the memory, they will be retained and reported as new problems the next time a malfunction occurs in any other system. Repair success can be verified by clearing the memory and road testing the car to see if any malfunction codes appear. Code 1 should appear when the diagnostic connector is shorted with a jumper wire.

NOTE: Cancellation can also be done by removing the battery negative (−) terminal, but in this case other memory systems (radio ETR, etc.) will also be cancelled out.

TOYOTA EFI TROUBLE CODES

Code No.	ECU Circuit	Possible Cause	Diagnosis Testing
1	Normal operation	This appears when one of the other codes are stored in the memory	EFI system operating normally. No further testing required
2	Air Flow Meter signal (V_c)	Open circuit in V_c or $V_c - V_s$ short circuited. Open circuit in V_B	Air flow meter circuit (V_c, V_s) Air flow meter EFI computer
3	Air flow meter signal (V_s)	Open circuit in V_s, or $V_s - E_2$ short ciruited. Open circuit in V_B	Air flow meter circuit (V_B, V_c, V_s) Air flow meter EFI computer
4	Water thermo sensor signal (THW)	Open circuit in coolant temperature sensor signal.	Coolant temperature sensor circuit Coolant temperature sensor EFI computer
5	O_2 sensor signal	Open or short circuit in O_2 sensor signal (only lean or rich indication)	O_2 sensor circuit O_2 sensor EFI computer
6	Ignition signal	No ignition signal	Ignition system circuit Distributor Ignition coil and igniter EFI computer
7	Throttle position sensor signal	IDL-Psw short circuited	Throttle position sensor circuit Throttle position sensor EFI computer

NOTE: 5-speed transmission models do not use code 7

TOYOTA STARLET EFI TESTING

ECU Terminal Connection	Test Meter Reading	Test Condition(s)
	VOLTMETER TESTS	
+ B-E$_1$	10–14 V	Ignition switch ON
BATT-E$_1$	10–14 V	Ignition switch OFF
IDL-E$_1$	8–14 V	Throttle valve fully closed
P$_{sw}$-E$_1$	8–14 V	Throttle valve fully open
TL-E$_1$	8–14 V	Ignition switch OFF
IG-E$_1$	Above 3 V	Cranking and engine running
STA-E$_1$	6–12 V	Cranking
No. 10-E$_1$	9–14 V	Ignition switch ON
No. 20-E$_1$	9–14 V	Ignition switch ON
+ B-E$_2$	8–14 V	Ignition switch OFF
V$_c$-E$_2$	4–9 V	Ignition switch OFF
V$_s$-E$_2$	0.5–2.5 V	Measuring plate fully closed
	5–8 V	Measuring plate fully open
	2.5–5.5 V	Idling
THA-E$_2$	2–6 V	Intake air temperature 20°C (68°F)
THW-E$_2$	0.5–2.5 V	Coolant temperature 80°C (176°F)
B/K-E$_1$	8–14 V	Stop light switch ON
	OHMMETER TESTS	
TL-IDL	0	Throttle valve fully closed
TL-IDL	∞	Throttle valve fully open
TL-P$_{sw}$	∞	Throttle valve fully closed
TL-P$_{sw}$	0	Throttle valve fully open
IDL, TL, P$_{sw}$-Ground	∞	Ignition switch OFF
THW-E$_2$	200–400 Ω	Coolant temp. 80°C (176°F)
THA-E$_2$	2–3 kΩ	Intake air temp. 20°C (68°F)
THW, THA-Ground	∞	Ignition switch OFF
+ B-E$_2$	200–400 Ω	Ignition switch OFF
V$_c$-E$_2$	100–300 Ω	Ignition switch OFF
V$_s$-E$_2$	20–100 Ω	Measuring plate fully closed
V$_s$-E$_2$	20–1,000 Ω	Measuring plate fully open
+ B, V$_c$, V$_s$-Ground	∞	Ignition switch OFF
E$_1$, E$_2$, E$_{01}$, E$_{02}$-Ground	0	Ignition switch OFF

NOTE: Make sure test equipment will not damage the control unit before testing

Ω—Ohms
V—Volts
∞—Infinity

| E$_2$ | Vs | Vc | BATT | THA | B/K | STA | | Ox | THW | IDL | VF | T | #10 | E$_{01}$ |
| IG | E$_3$ | W | +B | | SPD | | | | E$_1$ | TL | Psw | | #20 | E$_{02}$ |

ECU connector terminal numbers—1984 Toyota Starlet

TOYOTA CELICA EFI TESTING

ECU Terminal Connection	Test Meter Reading	Test Condition(s)
OHMMETER TESTS		
TL-IDL	0	Throttle valve fully closed
TL-IDL	∞	Throttle valve fully open
TL-P_{sw}	∞	Throttle valve fully closed
TL-P_{sw}	0	Throttle valve fully open
IDL, TL, P_{sw}-Ground	∞	Ignition switch OFF
THW-E_2	200–400 Ω	Coolant temp. 80°C (176°F)
THA-E_2	2–3 kΩ	Intake air temp. 20°C (68°F)
THW, THA-Ground	∞	Ignition switch OFF
V_B-E_2	200–400 Ω	Ignition switch OFF
V_C-E_2	100–300 Ω	Ignition switch OFF
V_S-E_2	20–400 Ω	Measuring plate fully closed
V_S-E_2	20–1,000 Ω	Measuring plate fully open
V_B, V_C, V_S-Ground	∞	Ignition switch OFF
E_1, E_{01}, E_{02}-Ground	0	Ignition switch OFF
VOLTMETER TESTS		
+B_E_1	10–14 V	Ignition switch ON
BAT-E_1	10–14 V	Ignition switch OFF
IDL-E_1	8–14 V	Throttle valve fully closed
P_{sw}-E_1	8–14 V	Throttle valve fully open
TL-E_1	8–14 V	Ignition switch OFF
IG-E_1	Above 3 V	Cranking and engine running
STA-E_1	6–12 V	Cranking
No. 10-E_1	9–14 V	Ignition switch ON
No. 20-E_1	9–14 V	Ignition switch ON
W-E_1	8–14 V	No trouble and engine running
MS-E_1	8–14 V	Idling
V_C-E_2	4–9 V	Ignition switch OFF
V_S-E_2	0.5–2.5 V	Measuring plate fully closed
	5–8 V	Measuring plate fully open
	2.5–5.5 V	Idling
THA-E_2	2–6 V	Intake air temperature 20°C (68°F)
THW-E_2	0.5–2.5 V	Coolant temperature 80°C (176°F)
A/C-E_1	8–14 V	Air conditioning ON

NOTE: Make sure test equipment will not damage control unit or components before testing

Ω—Ohms
V—Volts
∞—Infinity

| E_2 | Vs | Vc | BAT | THA | / | STA | A/C | O₂ | THW | IDL | VF | T | #10 | EO1 |
| IG | E_3 | W | +B | MS | / | / | / | / | E_1 | TL | Psw | / | #20 | EO2 |

ECU connector terminal numbers—1984 Toyota Celica

Idle Speed Control System

IDLE-UP SOLENOID VALVE

On the Nissan E.C.C.S. system, the idle-up solenoid valve is attached to the throttle body and responds to signals from the control unit (ECU) to stabilize the idle speed when the engine is loaded by accessories (A/C, power steering pump, electrical loads, etc.). The operation of the solenoid is part of the ECU's programmed capabilities. As with all AFC fuel injection systems, the solenoid controls an auxiliary air control valve that bypasses air around the throttle plate to raise the engine rpm. By regulating the amount of bypassed air the ECU maintains the idle at a preset rpm value for the engine load sensed.

Idle-up solenoid valve used on Nissan E.C.C.S. system

NOTE: Bosch LH and Motronic injection systems also have idle speed control as one of their programmed functions. On the LH system, an idle speed test point is provided that, when grounded, locks the air control valve in its minimum position for base idle setting.

Testing

On the E.C.C.S. system, check the voltage between terminal 2 at the control unit connector and ground when the ignition switch is turned ON. If battery voltage (12v) is not present, check the wiring harness for continuity and check the EFI relay operation. The solenoid valve itself is checked by making sure continuity exists between the connector terminals on the switch.

Bosch Constant Idle Speed (CIS) System

GENERAL INFORMATIOM

Some AFC fuel injection systems are equipped with a separate idle speed control system designed to correct engine speed deviations very quickly, regardless of wear or changes in ignition timing. In the Bosch system, sensors read engine speed, temperature and throttle position and send impulses to an electronic control unit. The control unit continuously compares the sensor inputs with the ideal engine specifications programmed into the system memory by the manufacturer after dynamometer testing and tailored to every type of engine. The system is designed to be maintenance-free for the life of the engine.

The CIS system consists of the following components:
- Coolant Temperature Sensor
- Tachometer Connection (via ignition coil)
- Throttle Switch (position sensor)

Schematic of Bosch Constant Idle Speed (CIS) system used with LH-Jetronic injection system. Note the separate electronic control unit

- Air Control Valve (bypass air controls rpm)
- Electronic Control Unit (ECU)

NOTE: The ECU for idle speed control is a separate unit from the fuel injection control system. The CIS control unit is usually mounted near the fuel injection ECU. The two are very similar in appearance and care should be taken not to confuse one with the other during testing. The same service precautions apply as previously described for the fuel injection ECU.

The CIS system controls the idle speed by regulating an air control valve to bypass more air around the throttle valve, thereby raising the idle speed in the same manner as described under "Auxiliary Air Valve." A small electric motor rotates clockwise or counterclockwise, depending on the signal from the control unit, opening or closing the valve very quickly and precisely to regulate the air flow. There are three basic air flow modes: the low flow or deceleration mode reduces the air flow when the throttle switch circuit is closed during deceleration. The high or driving mode increases the air bypass flow at normal road speeds with the accelerator depressed. The regulated or idle flow mode maintains a steady idle speed under all temperature conditions. Some newer models incorporate a fourth air flow mode which increases the idle speed when the air conditioner is turned on or other engine accessory loads are applied, providing improved cooling for both the engine and passenger compartment.

TROUBLESHOOTING

The CIS system is diagnosed in the same manner as described for the AFC fuel injection electrical system and control unit. Make all of the preliminary checks for obvious problems such as loose or corroded connectors and broken wires. Bad contacts cause many problems. On Volvo models, there are two connectors on the firewall and at the control unit. This dual wiring harness connection at the control unit differs from the standard single harness connector common to fuel injection ECU assemblies. If there is a problem with the engine idle speed on models equipped with a Bosch CIS system, check the air hoses for obstruction and the air control valve for sticking due to deposits from the PCV (positive crankcase ventilation) system. If there is a problem with periodic buildup of crankcase deposits in the air control valve, more frequent oil change intervals may be all that is necessary to correct the problem.

If the CIS system is suspected of causing a problem, most testing can be done with a good quality volt/ohmmeter and a 12V test light. The test light uses more current than a volt meter and sometimes is better at finding bad connections. The most common faults are poor or corroded contacts at the multipin connectors on the control unit, firewall and sensors.

─────CAUTION─────

Do not force the test probes directly into the wire harness connectors from the front. Test probes can spread the terminal contacts and cause a bad connection where none existed. Always test ECU connectors from the rear, using a pin to provide an accessible connection for test clips, if necessary. DO NOT pierce any wires with probes.

CIS System Testing

1. Locate the CIS system electronic control unit and remove any cover panels as necessary to gain access to the wire harness connectors.

2. Make sure the ignition switch is OFF and disconnect both connectors at the electronic control unit.

NOTE: The ignition switch must be OFF whenever disconnecting or reconnecting components to avoid the possibility of arcing which can damage the ECU. Pin numbers are for Volvo models; others may vary.

3. Switch the ignition ON and check for 12 volts at harness connector No. 1 (ECU power input) and a good ground at terminal No. 2. If no battery voltage is present, check the fuse block for a blown CIS system fuse and the ignition switch for continuity.

4. Check the throttle switch (microswitch) with an ohmmeter connected between terminal 8 and ground with the ignition OFF.

By operating the throttle and observing the resistance valve of the microswitch, correct operation can be verified. This on/off function can also be checked using a test light connected between harness terminals 1 and 8.

NOTE: It is important to determine how (open or closed) the throttle switch is indicating idle position to the control unit before any adjustment or testing is possible.

5. Check the coolant temperature sensor by connecting an ohmmeter across terminals 9 and 11 and measuring the resistance change at various engine temperatures. Look for a change rather than a specific value; if the resistance changes as the temperature rises, the sensor is operating properly.

6. Connect a tachometer between terminal 12 and ground, then start the engine and note the tach reading. The engine speed as measured by the tachometer should match the actual rpm at idle. If an obviously wrong value is indicated, or no reading at all is obtained, check the firewall connectors. There should be a tach signal from the ignition switch.

7. To check the air control valve, fabricate two appropriate jumper wires and connect one across terminals 1 and 4; and the other across terminals 2 and 5. Start the engine and note the idle speed. It should be 1600-2400 rpm. If not, the idle air control valve is malfunctioning.

VOLVO CIS THROTTLE SWITCH OPERATION

Year/ Model	Throttle Position	Resistance ohms	Test Light
1981 B21F	idle	∞	OFF
	above idle	0	ON
B28F	idle	0	ON
	above idle	∞	OFF
1982 B21F	idle	∞	OFF
	above idle	0	ON
B28F	idle	∞	OFF
	above idle	0	ON

Note: Make sure of correct microswitch operation before attempting any adjustments.

CADILLAC DIGITAL ELECTRONIC FUEL INJECTION

General Information

Digital electronic fuel injection consists of a pair of electrically actuated fuel metering valves which, when actuated, spray a calculated quantity of fuel into the engine intake manifold. These valves or injectors are mounted on the throttle body above the throttle blades with the metering tip pointed into the throttle throats. The injectors are normally actuated alternately.

Gasoline is supplied to the inlet of the injectors through the fuel lines and is maintained at a constant pressure across the injector inlets. When the solenoid-operated valves are energized, the injector ball valve moves to the full open position. Since the pressure differential across the valve is constant, the fuel quantity is changed by varying the time that the injector is held open.

The amount of air entering the engine is measured by monitoring the intake manifold absolute pressure (MAP), the intake manifold air temperature (MAT) and the engine speed (in rpm). This information allows the computer to compute the flow rate of air being inducted into the engine and, consequently, the flow rate of fuel required to achieve the desired air-fuel mixture for the particular engine operating condition.

The following abbreviations are used in this section:
TPS: throttle position sensor
ECM: electronic control module
ISC: idle speed control (includes idle speed motor and throttle switch)
HEI: high energy igition
EST: electric spark timing
MAP: manifold absolute pressure (sensor)
BARO: barometric pressure (sensor)
ECC: electronic climate control
MAT: manifold air temperature (sensor)
CTS: coolant temperature sensor
MPG: miles per gallon (display panel)
EGR: exhaust gas recirculation

1984 DIGITAL FUEL INJECTION

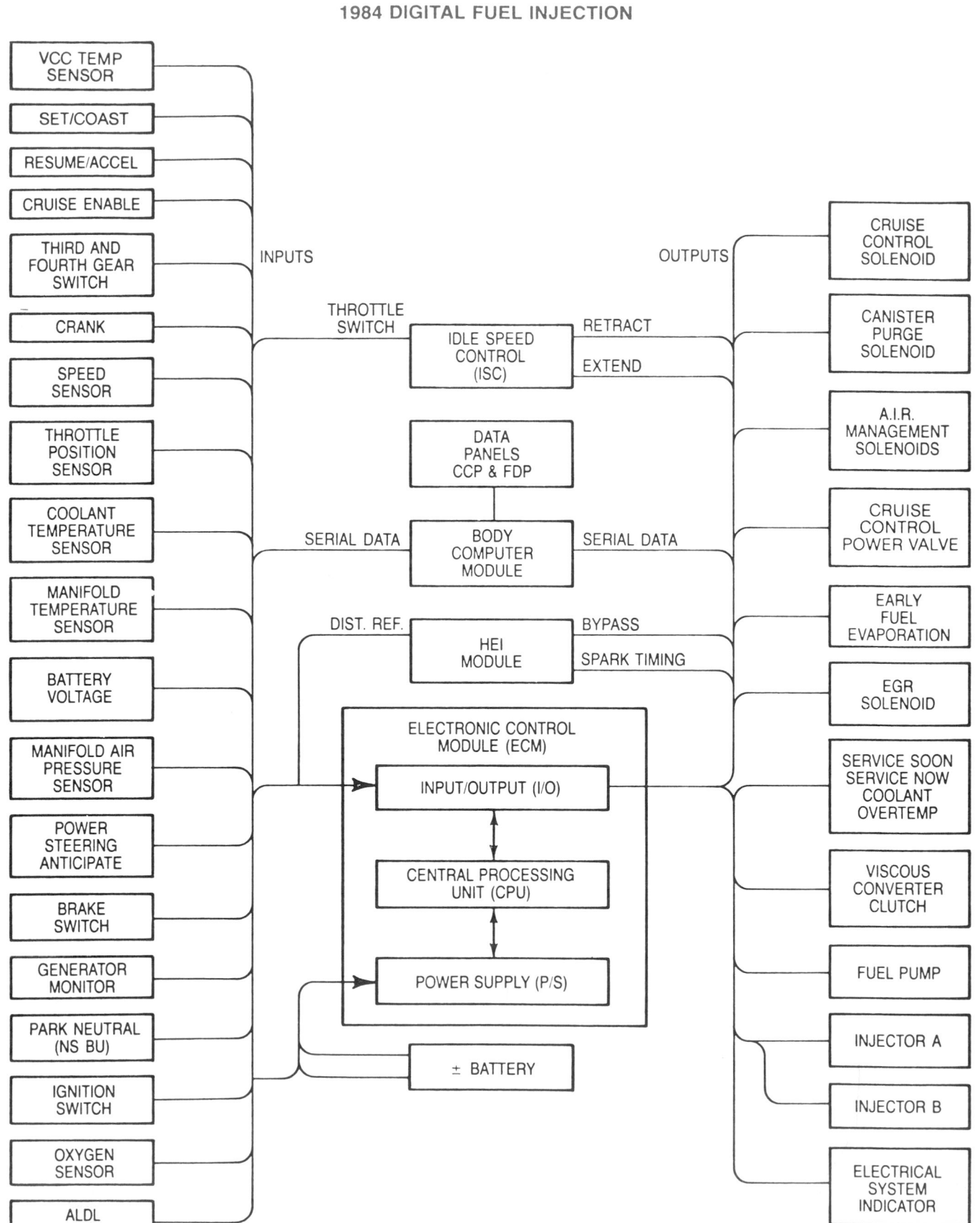

Schematic of Cadillac DFI system operation

THROTTLE BODY
- INJECTORS
- PRESSURE REGULATOR
- TPS
- ISC

MAP AND BARO SENSORS

ECM

COOLANT AND AIR TEMP SENSORS

EST DISTRIBUTOR

IN-TANK TWIN TURBINE FUEL PUMP

FUEL FILTER

Cadillac DFI system components

ELECTRICAL TERMINALS

ELECTRICAL TERMINALS

SOLENOID COIL

CORE PIECE

FUEL IN

BALL VALVE

VALVE SEAT

SPRAY PATTERN

ATOMIZER

Typical DFI fuel injector

FUEL SUPPLY SYSTEM

The fuel supply system components provide fuel at the correct pressure for metering into the throttle bores by the injectors. The pressure regulator controls fuel pressure to a nominal 10.5 psi across the injectors. The fuel supply system is made up of a fuel tank mounted electric pump, a full-flow fuel filter mounted on the vehicle frame, a fuel pressure regulator integral with the throttle body, fuel supply and fuel return lines and two fuel injectors. The timing and amount of fuel supplied is controlled by the computer.

An electric motor-driven twin turbine-type pump is integral with the fuel tank float unit. It provides fuel at a positive pressure to the throttle body and fuel pressure regulator. The pump is specific for DEFI application and is not repairable. However, the pump may be serviced separately from the fuel gauge unit.

Fuel pump operation is controlled by the fuel pump relay, located in the relay center. Operation of the relay is controlled by a signal from the computer. The fuel pump circuit is protected by a 10 amp fuse, located in the minifuse block. The computer turns the pump on with the ignition "ON" or "START." However, if the engine is not cranked within one second after the ignition is turned on, the computer signal is removed and the pump turns off.

Fuel is pumped from the fuel tank through the supply line and the filter to the throttle body and pressure regulator. The injectors supply fuel to the engine in precisely timed bursts as a result of electrical signals from the computer. Excess fuel is returned to the fuel tank through the fuel return line.

The fuel tank incorporates a reservoir directly below the sending unit-in-tank pump assembly. The "bathtub" shaped reservoir is used to ensure a constant supply of fuel for the in-tank pump even at low fuel level and severe maneuvering conditions.

On-Car Service

FUEL SYSTEM DIAGNOSIS

1. Low or no fuel pressure diagnosis should begin by trying to determine if the fuel pump is operating or not. This is most easily accomplished by turning the ignition on and listening for the one second "run" of the fuel pump and the associated relay clicks. Since this may not be possible in some shops, the best test is to probe both sides of the fuel pump fuse in the mini-fuse block with a voltmeter. Observe the meter as the ignition is turned on. It should go to battery voltage (12 volts) and then, after one second, to zero volts.

2. If the fuel pump circuit is operating properly, the computer signal and the relay are okay. The last connector in the fuel pump circuit is the six-way connector at the tail panel. The voltage actions seen at the fuse should be repeated. If not, there is an open in the circuit. Check the connectors and repair wiring as required. Individual sections of the wiring can be tested with an ohmmeter.

3. If the fuel pump signal is correct at the tail panel connector, a fuel delivery system situation exists. If the pump cannot be heard to run during the one second on period, the pump should be replaced. This observation is more easily made if helper turns the ignition on as the technician listens at the fuel tank or filler neck area. If the fuel pump can be heard to run, disconnect the fuel return line at the throttle body and install a plug in the throttle body opening. This will effectively "dead head" the fuel pump and eliminate the pressure regulator. If the pump is able to produce above 9 psi under these conditions (with the ignition on), replace the fuel pressure regulator as it is controlling at too low pressure.

4. If the fuel pressure remains below 9 psi with the return line plugged, a restriction in the fuel supply line may exist. A blocked fuel line or fuel filter can be determined by visually inspecting the filter element and the fuel line routing for kinks, damage, etc. If lines and filter are okay, replace fuel pump.

5. If the voltage at the fuel pump fuse does not go to 12 volts, first inspect the fuse. If the fuse is okay, check the contacts at terminals 1 and 3 of the fuel pump relay connecting block. The contacts close when the relay coil is energized by the computer. Remove the relay. Probe the relay center socket, which corresponds to relay terminal 4, with a voltmeter.

After ignition has been off for at least 10 seconds, turn the ignition on. If the voltage does not go to 12 volts and back to zero, inspect for opens or shorts to ground. Checking for opens can be done with an ohmmeter connected to both ends of the circuit. If continuity is indicated (0 ohms), check for a short to ground by jumping one end to ground and probing the opposite end with an ohmmeter to ground. An infinite reading indicates the wire is not grounded and the circuit is OK. Replace the computer. If a short to ground in the circuit is found the computer will be damaged. Replace the computer after repair.

6. If voltage at relay terminal 4 goes to 12 volts and then to zero, the computer is performing properly. Probe the relay center socket which corresponds to relay pin 3 with a voltmeter. Since this circuit comes directly from the battery terminal of the starter solenoid, it should be 12 volts at all times. If voltage is zero, inspect the circuit for open.

7. Twelve volts at pin 3 indicates that most of the relay's requirements are met. However, there are still two wiring circuits which could prevent proper relay operation. The computer signal has been proven okay. However, if the coil ground is open, the coil will not be energized. To check, probe the relay center socket which corresponds to relay pin 5, with an ohmmeter connected to ground. Continuity (0 ohms) indicates a good circuit. An infinite reading indicates an open. Repair wire as required.

The second circuit in which an open could occur, preventing the proper voltage at the fuse, is between the fuel pump relay terminal 1 and the mini-fuse block. This circuit can be checked by probing both ends with an ohmmeter. If the circuit has continuity as indicated by a zero ohms reading, replace fuel pump relay.

8. High fuel pressure is caused by either a malfunction of the pressure regulator or a restriction in the fuel return line. To determine which of these problems exists, disconnect the fuel return line at the throttle body and connect a suitable fitting to the throttle body to accept a length of flexible rubber fuel hose. Insert the open end of the hose into a suitable fuel container. Observe the fuel pressure as the ignition switch is turned on. If the fuel pressure remains above 12 psi, replace the pressure regulator as it is unable to regulate with no return restriction.

9. If the fuel pressure now falls into the correct pressure range of 9-12 psi, the restriction has been eliminated by bypassing the return system. A restricted fuel return line can be located by visually inspecting the line routing for kinks, damage, etc.

DIAGNOSING POOR PERFORMANCE

1. Unsatisfactory engine performance complaints which are related to the digital electronic fuel injection system are caused either by improper fuel delivery or improper ignition advance (controlled by the computer).

To isolate the problem to one of these systems, remove the air cleaner and observe the injector spray pattern of both injectors at idle. The spray pattern should be compared to a proper injector spray pattern of a known good car.

2. Improper fuel delivery which affects both injectors is most likely a fuel delivery system problem. By switching injector connectors, it can be determined if the problem is the injector assembly or the signal to the injector. If the problem remains with the original injector, it is most likely an injector problem. Replace the injector. If the problem moves with the injector connector, an improper signal circuit is indicated. The injectors are powered through the 3 amp fuses in the mini-fuse block. The fuse block receives battery voltage from the starter solenoid battery terminal when the fuel pump relay is energized by the computer during crank or run. With the relay closed, the circuits apply 12 volts to the injector. The computer provides the ground to energize the solenoid.

---CAUTION---
Do not apply direct battery voltage to the injector. 12 volts will destroy the fuel injector coil within 1/2 second.

---

3. Check the injector fuses by visually inspecting the fuse filament. If the fuses are okay there is a harness problem in the voltage feed or ground. The troubled circuit should be investigated. Check for opens with an ohmmeter. If harness checks okay, replace computer.

4. A blown injector fuse should be replaced. If it blows again, a short to ground is indicated. To check for this condition, connect ohmmeter between the red or white wire at the injector connector and ground (ignition off and computer disconnected). A low reading indicates a short circuit. Repair as required. If harness is okay, replace the computer.

5. A proper injector spray pattern indicates that improper ignition timing is the main DEFI component which can cause poor performance. Ground the "set timing" pigtail and check timing. It should be at the base (or initial) value of 10°BTDC (800 rpm or less). If not, reset to 10°.

6. Once it has been established that the ignition timing is using the proper reference signal, the system's ability to advance the spark must also be determined. Since the actual ignition advance produced is the result of other variables besides engine rpm and manifold vacuum, it is not possible to establish checkpoints. However, if the system does advance, the shape of the advance curve can be assumed to be correct, since it is determined by the electronic circuitry which was able to recognize that some advance was required and did respond to this information.

Disconnect the "set timing" jumper and check ignition timing. At normal idle, this should be approximately 20° to 30°BTDC.

7. If the ignition timing does not advance as a result of disconnecting the "set timing" jumper, a problem with the advance system is indicated. Since the computer selects and determines the spark advance curve, it is necessary to determine if the computer is operating properly or not.

During cranking, no spark advance is desired. The computer limits the advance to base timing by turning off the voltage signal. The pick-up coil pulse is used directly to turn the HEI module on. When the engine starts, the computer turns on the voltage in the circuit and the pick-up coil pulse is sent to the computer, modified by the computer and sent back to the module.

Whether the computer advances the timing or not depends upon whether it applied a voltage to the circuit or not (no voltage = base timing; voltage = electric spark timing). To check the circuit, disconnect the four-way connector at the distributor while the engine is idling. This will stop the engine. Probe the harness side pin C

STATUS LIGHT DISPLAY

	ECM OPERATING MODE	O₂ SENSOR INPUT	THROTTLE SWITCH INPUT	TCC OUTPUT	4TH GEAR INPUT	A/C CLUTCH OUTPUT
LIGHT ON	CLOSED LOOP	RICH	CLOSED THROTTLE	TCC ENABLED	IN 4TH GEAR	CLUTCH ENABLED
LIGHT OFF	OPEN LOOP	LEAN	OPEN THROTTLE	TCC DISABLED	NOT IN 4TH GEAR	CLUTCH DISABLED

Control head status light display—1982 shown

(not distributor side harness) with a voltmeter while the ignition switch remains on. If voltage is greater than 4 volts, refer to HEI diagnosis because the computer has signaled that EST should be used, but timing did not advance when checked.

8. Voltage less than 1 volt indicates that either the computer signal is not being produced or the circuit is open or shorted to the ground. To check for shorts, disconnect the black/green computer connector and probe harness pin D with an ohmmeter to ground (ignition off and distributor connector disconnected). A zero ohm reading indicates a short. Repair as required.

If the ohmmeter reads infinity, check for opens by jumping distributor connector pin C to ground. If the ohmmeter reading remains infinite, circuit is open. Repair as required. If the ohmmeter reads zero ohms, the circuit is okay.

Check MAT and coolant sensor circuits for an open between the splice and the computer. Attention should be focused on the bulk head and computer connectors. If the circuit is okay, substitute a new computer and observe performance.

9. The EGR system utilizes various controls in order to provide EGR gases only when they are needed for emission control. One of these controls is the EGR solenoid, with power feed from the ignition switch through the 20 amp fuse. Ground for the solenoid is provided by the computer. The computer provides this ground whenever the coolant temperature signal from the coolant sensor says the temperature is below 43°C (110°F). This energizes the solenoid and blocks the flow of vacuum to the EGR transducer thus preventing EGR operation at cold engine temperatures. Above 71°C (160°F), the solenoid ground is removed and the solenoid

opens, allowing vacuum to the EGR valve. This vacuum signal is a ported vacuum which exists only off idle. This means that even on a warm engine, there is no EGR vacuum signal and no EGR flow at idle.

10. If EGR operation is okay, check to make sure that throttle valves open to wide open throttle when the accelerator pedal is wide open. If this is okay, the performance problem is not related to the DEFI system. If EGR problems are found, check hoses, etc.

Electronic Control Module (ECM)

GENERAL INFORMATION

The Electronic Control Module, (ECM) or computer provides all computation and controls for the DEFI system. Sensor inputs are fed into the computer from the various sensors. They are processed to produce the appropriate pulse duration for the injectors, the correct idle speed for the particular operating condition and the proper spark advance. Analog inputs from the sensors are converted to digital signals before processing. The computer assembly is mounted under the instrument panel and consists of various printed circuit boards mounted in a protective metal box.

The computer receives power from the vehicle battery. When the ignition is set to the "ON" or "CRANK" position, the following information is received from the sensors:
1. Engine coolant temperature
2. Intake manifold air temperature
3. Intake manifold absolute pressure

Typical electronic climate control head—1982 shown

Cadillac DFI electronic control module location

4. Barometric pressure
5. Engine speed
6. Throttle position

The following commands are transmitted by the ECM:
1. Electric fuel pump activation
2. Idle speed control
3. Spark advance control
4. Injection valve activation
5. EGR solenoid activation

The desired air-fuel mixture for various driving and atmospheric conditions are programmed into the computer. As signals are received from the sensors, the computer processes the signals and computes the engine's fuel requirements. The computer issues commands to the injection valves to open for a specific time duration. The duration of the command pulses varies as the operating conditions change.

The digital electronic fuel injection system is activated when the ignition switch is turned to the "ON" position. The following events occur at this moment.

1. The computer receives the ignition "ON" signal.

2. The fuel pump is activated by the ECM. The pump will operate for approximately one second only, unless the engine is cranking or running.

3. All engine sensors are activated and begin transmitting signals to the computer.

4. The EGR solenoid is activated to block the vacuum signal to the EGR valve at coolant temperatures below 110°F.

5. The "CHECK ENGINE" and "COOLANT" lights are illuminated as a functional check of the bulb and circuit.

6. Operation of the fuel economy lamps begins.

The following events occur when the engine is started.

1. The fuel pump is activated for continuous operation.

2. The idle speed control motor will begin controlling idle speed, including fast idle speed, if the throttle switch is closed.

3. The spark advance shifts from base (bypass) timing to the computer programmed spark curve.

4. The fuel pressure regulator maintains the fuel pressure at 10.5 psi by returning excess fuel to the fuel tank.

5. The following sensor signals are continuously received and processed by the computer:
   a. Engine coolant temperature
   b. Intake manifold air temperature
   c. Barometric pressure
   d. Intake manifold absolute air pressure
   e. Engine speed
   f. Throttle position changes

6. The computer alternately grounds each injector, precisely

controlling the opening and closing time (pulse width) to deliver fuel to the engine.

Fuel Delivery System

The computer's control of fuel delivery can be considered in three basic modes: cranking, part throttle and wide open throttle.

If the engine is determined to be in the cranking mode by the presence of a voltage in the cranking signal wire from the ignition switch, the starting fuel delivery consists of one long "prime" pulse from both injectors followed by a series of "starting" pulses until the cranking mode signal is no longer present.

In addition, there is a "clear flood" condition in which smaller alternating fuel pulses are delivered if the throttle is held wide open and cranking exceeds five seconds.

Once the engine is running, injector pulse width is then adjusted to account for operating conditions such as idle, part throttle, acceleration, deceleration and altitude.

For wide open throttle conditions, which are sensed by matching the manifold absolute pressure and barometric pressure sensor inputs, additional enrichment is provided.

Electronic Spark Timing (EST)

The EST type HEI distributor receives all spark timing information from the computer when the engine is running. The computer provides spark plug firing pulses based upon the various engine operating parameters. The electronic components for the electronic spark control system are integral with the computer. The two basic operating modes are cranking (or bypass) and normal engine operation.

When the engine is in the cranking/bypass mode, ignition timing occurs at a reference setting (distributor timing set point) regardless of other engine operating parameters. Under all other normal operating conditions, basic engine ignition timing is controlled by the computer and modified or added to, depending on particular conditions such as altitude and/or engine loading.

Idle Speed Control System

The idle speed control system is controlled by the computer. The system acts to control engine idle speed in three ways; as a normal idle (rpm) control, as a fast idle device and as a "dashpot" on decelerations and throttle closing.

Electronic spark timing distributor

The normal engine idle speed is programmed into the computer and no adjustments are possible. Under normal engine operating conditions, idle speed is maintained by monitoring idle speed in a closed loop fashion. To accomplish this loop, the computer periodically senses the engine idle speed and issues commands to the idle speed control to move the throttle stop to maintain the correct speed.

For engine starting, the throttle is either held open by the idle speed control for a longer (cold) or a shorter (hot) period to provide adequate engine warm-up prior to normal operation. When the engine is shut off, the throttle is opened by fully extending the idle speed control actuator to get ready for the next start.

Signal inputs for transmission gear, air conditioning compressor clutch (engaged or not engaged) and throttle (open or closed) are used to either increase or decrease throttle angle in response to these particular engine loadings.

Vehicle idle speed is controlled by an electrically driven actuator (idle speed control) which changes the throttle angle by acting as a movable idle stop. Inputs to the ISC actuator motor come from the ECM and are determined by the idle speed required for the particular operating condition. The electronic components for the ISC system are integral with the ECM. An integral part of the ISC is the throttle switch. The position of the switch determines whether the ISC should control idle speed or not. When the switch is closed, as determined by the throttle lever resting upon the end of the ISC actuator, the ECM will issue the appropriate commands to move the idle speed control to provide the programmed idle speed. When the throttle lever moves off the idle speed control actuator from idle, the throttle switch is opened. The computer then extends the actuator and stops sending idle speed commands and the driver controls the engine speed.

Self-Diagnosis System

An amber dash-mounted digital display panel normally used for the Electronic Climate Control (ECC) system, is used to display trouble codes stored in the computer when desired. Any codes that may be stored can be called up and/or cleared by properly exercising the ECC controls.

In the event the computer detects a system malfunction, the "CHECK ENGINE" light will be activated, the corresponding trouble code stored and substitute values to replace missing data may be made available for computations by the computer. This can be thought of as a "Fail-Safe" operation. In this mode, driveability of the car may be poor under certain conditions and the diagnostic procedures should be exercised.

How to Enter Diagnostic Mode

To enter diagnostics, proceed as follows:
1. Turn ignition "ON".
2. depress "OFF" and "WARMER" buttons on the ECC panel simultaneously and hold until ".." appears. "88" will then be displayed, which indicates the beginning of the diagnostic readout.
3. Trouble codes will be displayed on the digital ECC panel beginning with the lowest numbered code. Note that the test panel does not display when the system is in the diagnostic mode.

How to Clear Trouble Codes

Trouble codes stored in the ECM's memory may be cleared (erased) by entering the diagnostic mode and then depressing the "OFF" and "HI" buttons simultaneously. Hold until "00" appears.

How to Exit Diagnostic Mode

To get out of the diagnostic mode, depress any of the ECC function keys (Auto, Econ, etc. except Rear Defog) or turn ignition switch off for 10 seconds. Trouble codes are not erased when this is done.

DIAGNOSIS PROCEDURE

Illumination of the "CHECK ENGINE" light indicates that a malfunction has occurred for which a trouble code has been stored and can be displayed on the ECC control panel. The malfunction may or may not result in abnormal engine operation. To determine which system(s) has malfunctioned, proceed as follows.
1. Turn ignition switch "ON" for 5 seconds.
2. Depress the "OFF" and "WARMER" buttons on the electronic climate control panel simultaneously and hold until ".." appears.
3. Numerals "88" should then appear. The purpose of the "88" display is to check that all segments of the display are working. Diagnosis should not be attempted unless the entire "88" appears, as this could lead to misdiagnosis (Code 31 could be Code 34 with two segments of the display inoperative, etc).
4. Trouble codes will then be displayed for approximately three seconds.
  a. The lowest numbered code will be displayed for approximately three seconds.
  b. Progressively higher codes, if present, will be displayed consecutively for three second intervals until the highest code present has been displayed.
  c. "88" is again displayed.
  d. Displays from steps a., b. and c. will be repeated a second time.
  e. Displays from steps a. and b. will be repeated a third time.
  f. Code 70 will then be displayed, which signals the beginning of the "switch tests" section.
  g. Switch tests require some action on the part of the technician. This action is analyzed by the computer for proper operation.

Switch Test Procedure

When all stored trouble codes have been displayed for the third time, the computer will automatically begin the switch tests. To perform these checks, proceed as follows:
1. Display of trouble Code 70 signals the beginning of this section. This code will continue to be displayed until the proper test action is taken. When ready to begin tests, depress service brake pedal. This begins the test sequence by displaying Code 71.
2. With Code 71 displayed, depress the service brake pedal again to test the brake light circuit. When this check is completed, the test program will automatically sequence to Code 72. If the test action is not performed within 10 seconds, the test program will automatically sequence to "72" and Code 71 will be stored in the computer memory as "not passed".
3. With Code 72 displayed, depress the throttle from idle to wide open throttle and release. This action allows the computer to analyze the operation of the throttle switch. When this check is completed, the test program will automatically sequence to Code 73. Again, if action is not taken within 10 seconds, a Code 72 will be stored as "not passed".
4. With Code 73 displayed, shift the transmission lever to Drive and then to Neutral. When this check is completed, the test program will automatically sequence to code 74. This action must be taken within 10 seconds or a Code 73 will be set.
5. With Code 74 displayed, shift the transmission lever to Reverse and then to Park. Shift transmission within 10 seconds or a Code 74 will be set. When this check is completed, the test program will automatically sequence to Code 78.
6. With code 78 displayed, depress the "AVERAGE" button on the test panel. When this check is completed, the test program will automatically sequence to Code 79. Again, this must be done within 10 seconds or a Code 78 will be set.
7. With Code 79 displayed, depress the "RESET" button on the test panel within 10 seconds to test the function of this switch. This is the end of the switch tests.
8. With the switch tests completed, the computer will now go back and display the switch test code(s) which did not test properly.

DIAGNOSTIC DISPLAY

The dash-mounted digital display panel normally used for the electronic climate control (ECC) system, is used to display trouble codes stored in the computer when desired. Any codes that may be stored can be called up and/or cleared by properly exercising the ECC controls.

- ENTER DIAGNOSTICS BY SIMULTANEOUSLY PUSHING OFF AND WARMER BUTTONS

- EXIT DIAGNOSTIC MODE BY PUSHING ANY CLIMATE CONTROL BUTTON EXCEPT REAR DEFOG

- CLEAR TROUBLE CODES, AND RETURN TO 70 BY SIMULTANEOUSLY PUSHING OFF AND HI BUTTONS ON CLIMATE CONTROL

- RESET FROM 90, 95, 96, OR 97 AND RETURN TO 70 BY SIMULTANEOUSLY PUSHING OFF AND HI BUTTONS ON ECC CLIMATE CONTROL

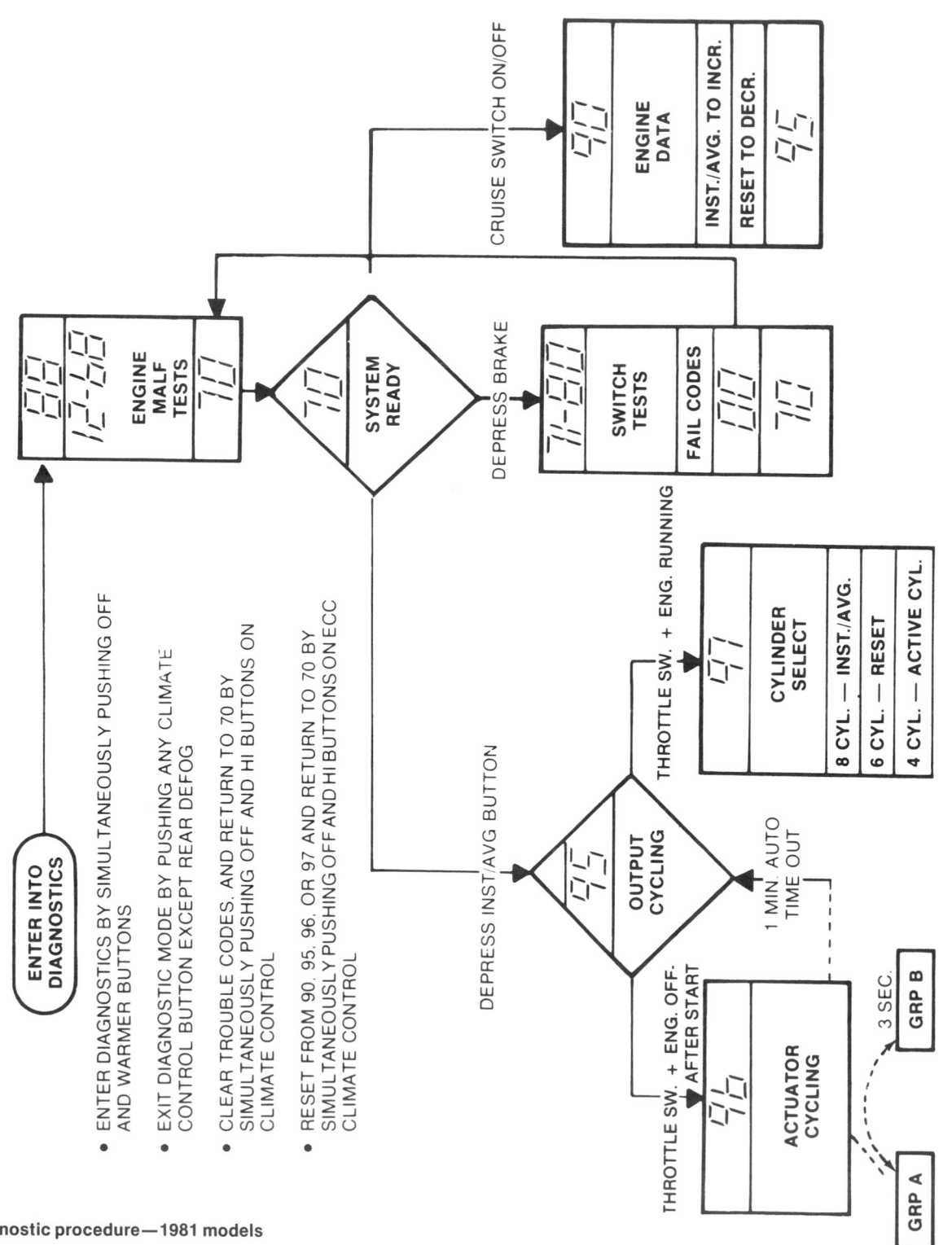

Cadillac DFI diagnostic procedure—1981 models

OPERATION WITH SYSTEM FAILURES

In the event the computer detects a system malfunction, the "CHECK ENGINE" light will be activated, the corresponding trouble code stored and substitute values to replace missing date may be made available for computations by the computer. This can be thought of as a "Fail Safe" operation. In this mode, driveability of the car may be poor under certain conditions and the diagnostic procedures should be exercised.

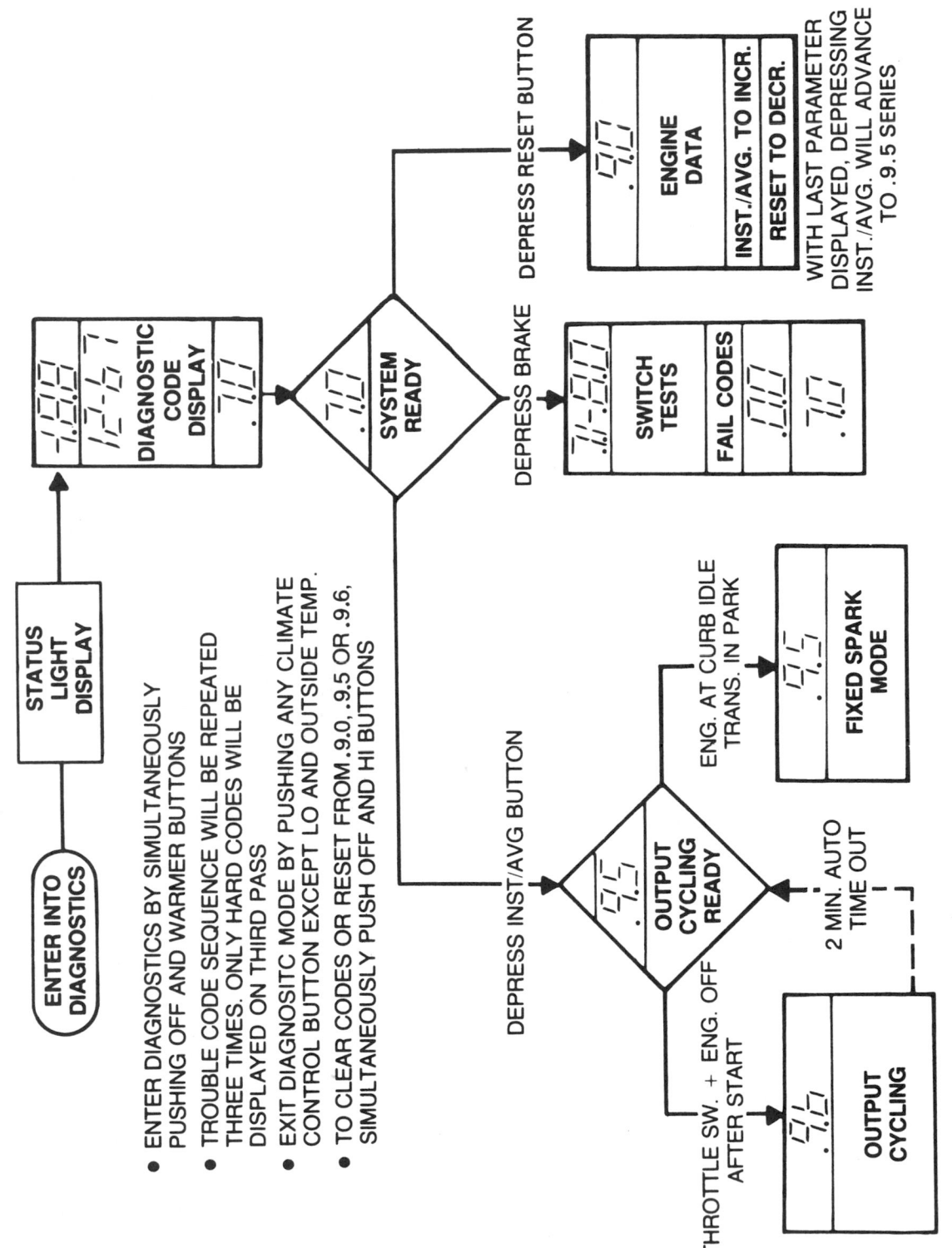

- ENTER DIAGNOSTICS BY SIMULTANEOUSLY PUSHING OFF AND WARMER BUTTONS
- TROUBLE CODE SEQUENCE WILL BE REPEATED THREE TIMES. ONLY HARD CODES WILL BE DISPLAYED ON THIRD PASS
- EXIT DIAGNOSITC MODE BY PUSHING ANY CLIMATE CONTROL BUTTON EXCEPT LO AND OUTSIDE TEMP.
- TO CLEAR CODES OR RESET FROM .9.0, .9.5 OR .9.6, SIMULTANEOUSLY PUSH OFF AND HI BUTTONS

Cadillac DFI diagnostic procedure—1982 models

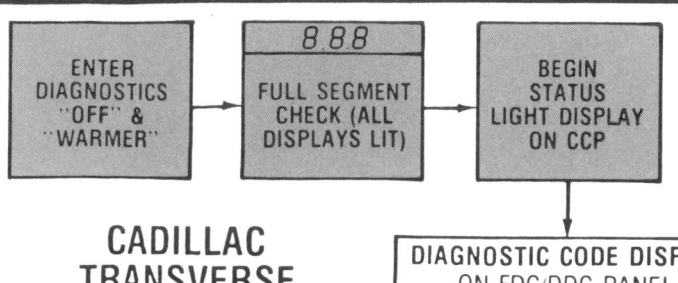

```
ENTER          8.8.8           BEGIN
DIAGNOSTICS →  FULL SEGMENT  → STATUS
"OFF" &        CHECK (ALL      LIGHT DISPLAY
"WARMER"       DISPLAYS LIT)   ON CCP
```

CADILLAC TRANSVERSE DE VILLE & FLEETWOOD VEHICLE DIAGNOSTIC SYSTEM

FIXED SPARK

EXIT DIAGNOSTICS
AND CONNECT PINS
A & B OF ALDL
TEST CONNECTOR

DIAGNOSTIC CODE DISPLAY
ON FDC/DDC PANEL

```
. .E       ECM HISTORY CODES
E12
to
E67

.E.E       ECM CURRENT CODES
E12
to
E67

. .F       BCM HISTORY CODES
F10
to
F51

.F.F       BCM CURRENT CODES
F10
to
F51
```

DIAGNOSTICS — BASIC OPERATION

- ENTER DIAGNOSTICS BY SIMULTANEOUSLY PUSHING CCP "OFF" AND "WARMER" BUTTONS UNTIL ALL DISPLAYS ARE LIT.
- MALFUNCTION CODE SEQUENCE BEGINS WITH ECM CODES FOLLOWED BY BCM CODES (DIESEL HAS BCM DIAGNOSTICS ONLY).
- TO PROCEED FROM "7.0" TO THE OTHER DIAGNOSTIC FEATURES, PRESS AND RELEASE THE INDICATED BUTTON OR PEDAL.
- RETURN TO "7.0" BY CLEARING EITHER ECM OR BCM CODES.
- EXIT DIAGNOSTICS BY PUSHING "AUTO".

FDC/DDC DISPLAY MODE CODES

DIAGNOSTIC DISPLAY	DESCRIPTION
8.8.8	FDC/DDC Display Check ("188" On CCP)
.7.0	System Ready For Further Tests
E 0.0	ECM Malfunction Codes Cleared Or Switch Tests Completed
F 0.0	BCM Malfunction Codes Cleared
E 9.0	System Ready To Display ECM Data
E 9.5	System Ready For Output Cycling
E 9.6	Output Cycling
F 8.0	System Ready To Display BCM Data. ECC Program Number On CCP
F 8.5	Cooling Fans Override

E.9.5 — ECM OUTPUT CYCLING READY

THROTTLE SWITCH / 2 MIN AUTOMATIC TIME OUT

E.9.6 — ECM OUTPUT CYCLING

CLEAR ECM CODES
"OFF" & "HI"
E.0.0
.7.0

CLEAR BCM CODES
"OFF" & "LO"
F.0.0
.7.0

"HI" WITH ENGINE OFF AFTER START

BRAKE

E.7.1 – E.7.8 ECM SWITCH TESTS
FAIL CODES
E.0.0
.7.0

.7.0 SYSTEM READY

E.7.1 — E.7.8 SWITCH TESTS

DIAGNOSTIC DISPLAY	CIRCUIT TEST
E.7.1	Cruise Control Brake
E.7.2	Throttle Switch
E.7.4	Park Neutral Switch
E.7.5	Cruise "On-Off" — Return Switch to "On" Before Testing E.7.6 & E.7.7
E.7.6	Cruise "Set Coast"
E.7.7	Cruise "Resume Accel"
E.7.8	Power Steering Pressure Switch (Engine Running)

E.9.6 OUTPUTS

Coolant Temp Fan Light
Service Electrical System Light
AIR Switch Solenoid
AIR Divert Solenoid
ISC Motor

Cruise Vacuum Solenoid & Engage Light
Cruise Power Solenoid
Canister Purge Solenoid
EGR Solenoid
VCC Solenoid
EFE Relay

"LO"
E.9.0 ECM DATA
P.0.1 HI / LO P.1.3

"ECON"
F.8.5 COOLING FANS OVERRIDE
"LO" — FANS OFF
"HI" — HI FANS
NONE — NORMAL

"OUTSIDE TEMP"
F.8.0 BCM DATA
P.2.0 HI / LO P.3.1

ECC PROGRAM NUMBER OVERRIDE
ECC PROGRAM NUMBER (0-100) IS DISPLAYED ON CCP DURING F.8.0 SEQUENCE.
0 = MAX A C
100 = MAX HEAT
TO INCREASE PROGRAM NUMBER, PUSH "WARMER"
TO DECREASE PROGRAM NUMBER, PUSH "COOLER"

Cadillac diagnostic procedure—1983 and later models with HT4100 engine

E.9.0 ENGINE DATA DISPLAY

PARAMETER NUMBER	PARAMETER	PARAMETER RANGE	DISPLAY UNITS
P.0.1	Throttle Position	-10 - 90	Degrees
P.0.2	MAP	14 - 109	kPa
P.0.3	Computed BARO	61 - 103	kPa
P.0.4	Coolant Temperature	-40 - 151	°C
P.0.5	MAT	-40 - 151	°C
P.0.6	Injector Pulse Width	0 - 99.9	ms
P.0.7	Oxygen Sensor Voltage	0 - 1.14	Volts
P.0.8	Spark Advance	0 - 52	Degrees
P.0.9	Ignition Cycle Counter	0 - 50	Key Cycles
P.1.0	Battery Voltage	0 - 25.5	Volts
P.1.1	Engine RPM	0 - 6370	RPM ÷ 10
P.1.2	Car Speed	0 - 255	MPH
P.1.3	ECM PROM I.D.	0 - 255	Code

F.8.0 BCM DATA DISPLAY

PARAMETER NUMBER	PARAMETER	PARAMETER RANGE	DISPLAY UNITS
P.2.0	Commanded Blower Voltage	-3.3 - 18.0	Volts
P.2.1	Coolant Temperature	-40 - 215	°C
P.2.2	Commanded Air Mix Door Position	0 - 100	%
P.2.3	Actual Air Mix Door Position	0 - 100	%
P.2.4	Air Delivery Mode 0 = Max A C 4 = Off 1 = A/C 5 = Normal Purge 2 = Intermediate 6 = Cold Purge 3 = Heater 7 = Front Defog	0 - 7	Code
P.2.5	In-Car Temperature	-40 - 102	°C
P.2.6	Actual Outside Temperature	-40 - 93	°C
P.2.7	High Side Temperature (Condenser Out)	-40 - 215	°C
P.2.8	Low Side Temperature (Evaporator In)	-40 - 93	°C
P.2.9	Actual Fuel Level	0 - 19.0	Gallons
P.3.0	Ignition Cycle Counter	0 - 99	Key Cycles
P.3.1	BCM PROM I.D.	0 - 255	Code

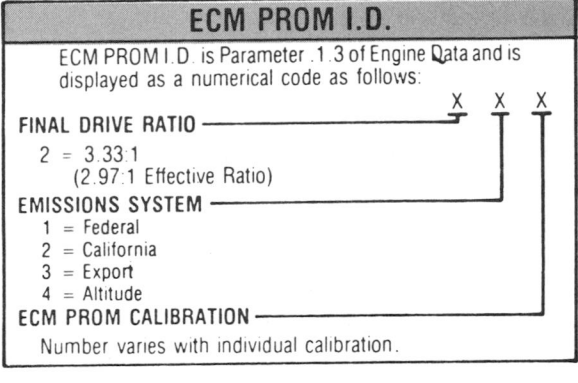

ECM PROM I.D.

ECM PROM I.D. is Parameter .1.3 of Engine Data and is displayed as a numerical code as follows:

      X X X

FINAL DRIVE RATIO
 2 = 3.33:1
  (2.97:1 Effective Ratio)

EMISSIONS SYSTEM
 1 = Federal
 2 = California
 3 = Export
 4 = Altitude

ECM PROM CALIBRATION
Number varies with individual calibration.

BCM PROM I.D.

BCM PROM I.D. is Parameter .3.1 of BCM Data and is displayed as a numerical code as follows:

      X X X

ENGINE SYSTEM
 Blank = Gas
   1 = Diesel

BCM PROM CALIBRATION
Numbers vary with individual calibration.

ECM STATUS LIGHT DISPLAY

	IN 4th GEAR	VCC ENABLED	CLOSED THROTTLE	RICH	CLOSED LOOP
LIGHT ON	IN 4th GEAR	VCC ENABLED	CLOSED THROTTLE	RICH	CLOSED LOOP
LIGHT OFF	NOT IN 4TH GEAR	VCC DISABLED	OPEN THROTTLE	LEAN	OPEN LOOP
INDICATOR	(symbol)	(symbol)	Off	Econ	Auto
FUNCTION	4TH GEAR INPUT	VCC OUTPUT	THROTTLE SWITCH INPUT	OXYGEN SENSOR INPUT	ECM OPERATING MODE

BCM STATUS LIGHT DISPLAY

FUNCTION	A/C CLUTCH OUTPUT	COMPRESSOR LOW PRESSURE SWITCH INPUT	HEATER WATER VALVE OUTPUT	A/C-DEF MODE DOOR OUTPUT	COOLING FANS STATUS	UP/DOWN MODE DOOR OUTPUT
INDICATOR	Outside Temp	°F	°C	Lo Fan	Auto Fan	Hi Fan
LIGHT ON	ENERGIZED	OPEN (LOW PRESSURE)	CLOSED (NO WATER FLOW)	A C	FANS RUNNING	UP
LIGHT OFF	DE-ENERGIZED	CLOSED	OPEN	DEF	FANS OFF	DOWN

Cadillac diagnostic procedure—1983 and later models with HT4100 engine

1981 DIAGNOSTIC CODES

(The following codes are programmed into the ECM.)

Code	Circuit Affected
12	No tach signal
13	O2 sensor not ready
14	Shorted coolant sensor
15	Open coolant sensor circuit
16	Generator voltage out of range
17	Crank signal circuit high
18	Open crank signal circuit
19	Fuel pump circuit high
20	Open fuel pump circuit
21	Shorted throttle position sensor circuit
22	Open throttle position sensor circuit
23	EST/bypass circuit shorted or open
24	Speed sensor failure
25	Modulated displacement failure
26	Shorted throttle switch circuit
27	Open throttle switch circuit
30	Idle speed control circuit
31	Short MAP sensor circuit
32	Open MAP sensor circuit
33	MAP/BARO sensor correlation
34	MAP hose
35	Shorted BARO sensor circuit
36	Open BARO sensor circuit
37	Shorted MAT sensor circuit
38	Open MAT sensor circuit
44	O2 sensor lean
45	O2 sensor rich
51	PROM insertion faulty
60	Drive (ADL) switch circuit
61	Set and resume switch circuit
62	Car speed exceeds maximum limit
63	Car and set speed tolerance exceeded
64	Car acceleration exceeds maximum limit
65	Coolant temperature exceeds maximum limit
66	Engine rpm exceeds maximum limit
68	Set and resume switch circuit
70	System ready—switch tests
71	Brake light switch
72	ISC throttle switch
73	Drive (ADL) switch
74	Back-up lamp switch
75	Cruise on/off circuit
76	Set/coast circuit
77	Resume/acceleration circuit
78	Instant/average mpg button
79	Reset mpg button
80	A/C clutch circuit
88	Display check
90	System ready to display engine data
95	System ready for actuator cycling
96	Actuator cycling
97	MD cylinder solenoid cycling
00	All diagnostic complete

1982 DIAGNOSTIC CODES

Code	Circuit Affected
12	No distributor (tach) signal
13	O$_2$ sensor not ready
14	Shorted coolant sensor circuit
15	Open coolant sensor circuit
16	Generator voltage out of range
18	Open crank signal circuit
19	Shorted fuel pump circuit
20	Open fuel pump circuit
21	Shorted throttle position sensor circuit
22	Open throttle position sensor circuit
23	EST circuit problem in run mode
24	Speed sensor circuit problem
25	EST circuit problem in bypass mode
26	Shorted throttle switch circuit
27	Open throttle switch circuit
28	Open fourth gear circuit
29	Shorted fourth gear circuit
30	ISC circuit problem
31	Short MAP sensor circuit
32	Open MAP sensor circuit
33	MAP/BARO sensor correlation
34	MAP signal too high
35	Shorted BARO sensor circuit
36	Open BARO sensor circuit
37	Shorted MAT sensor circuit
38	Open MAT sensor circuit
39	TCC engagement problem
44	Lean exhaust signal
45	Rich exhaust signal
51	PROM error indicator
52	ECM memory reset indicator
60	Transmission not in drive
63	Car and set speed tolerance exceeded
64	Car acceleration exceeds max. limit
65	Coolant temperature exceeds maximum limit
66	Engine rpm exceeds maximum limit
67	Shorted set or resume circuit
.7.0	System ready for further tests
.7.1	Cruise control brake circuit test
.7.2	Throttle switch circuit test
.7.3	Drive (ADL) circuit test
.7.4	Reverse circuit test
.7.5	Cruise on/off circuit test
.7.6	"Set/coast" circuit test
.7.7	"Resume/acceleration" circuit test
.7.8	"Instant/average" circuit test
.7.9	"Reset" circuit test
.8.0	A/C clutch circuit test
-1.8.8	Display check
.9.0	System ready to display engine data
.9.5	System ready for output cycling or in fixed spark mode
.9.6	Output cycling
.0.0	All diagnostics complete

Each code which did not pass the interrogation will be displayed beginning with the lowest number. This time through, the codes will not disappear until the tested component has been repaired and/or tested for proper operation.

9. Upon completion of the trouble code and switch test displays, the ECC panel will remain in the diagnostic mode and display "00" until an ECC mode is selected or the ignition is turned off.

10. Malfunctioning circuits should be analyzed.

"Intermittent" Codes vs. "Hard Failure" Codes

Trouble codes stored in the ECM's memory at any time can be either of the following.

1. A code for malfunctions which are occurring now ("HARD FAILURE"). This malfunction will cause illumination of the "CHECK ENGINE" light.

2. A code for any intermittent malfunctions which have occurred within the last 20 ignition switch cycles. These codes will not cause the "CHECK ENGINE" light to be on now.

Intermittent codes should be diagnosed by inspecting the connectors. During any diagnostic interrogation which displays more than one diagnostic code, it is necessary to determine which code is for the "HARD FAILURE" and which is the "INTERMITTENT." To make this determination, proceed as follows.

1. Enter diagnostics, read and record stored trouble codes.

2. Clear trouble codes.

3. Exit diagnostics by turning the ignition switch off for ten seconds.

4. Turn ignition on and wait 5 seconds, then start engine.

5. Accelerate the engine (to approximately 2000 rpm) for a few seconds.

6. Return to idle.

7. Shift transmission into Drive.

8. Shift to Park.

9. If the "CHECK ENGINE" light comes on, enter diagnostics. Read and record trouble codes. This will reveal only "HARD FAILURE" codes. If the light does not come on, then all stored codes are "INTERMITTENTS."

10. Begin diagnosis with lowest numbered code displayed.

CHART A
MULTIPLE DFI CODES STORED HARD

A-1 CONDITION: CODES 22, 32, AND 36 ALL STORED HARD.
CAUSE: LOSS OF "5 VOLT REFERENCE" VOLTAGE TO SENSORS.

CORRECTION

- VERIFY "CAUSE" BY DISCONNECTING THE MAP, BARO AND TPS SENSOR CONNECTORS AND MEASURING VOLTAGE BETWEEN CIRCUIT #474 AND GROUND ON EACH SENSOR HARNESS CONNECTOR.

| 0 VOLTS FOR ALL SENSORS | NOT 0 VOLTS FOR ALL SENSORS |

- CHECK FOR AN OPEN OR SHORT TO GROUND IN CIRCUIT #474.
- CHECK FOR A FAULTY ECM CONNECTOR OR FAULTY ECM.

- CAUSE NOT VERIFIED. FOLLOW DIAGNOSTIC PROCEDURE FOR INDIVIDUAL CODES.

A-2 CONDITION: CODE 15 STORED HARD ALONG WITH HARD CODE 21, 26 OR 33.
CAUSE: OPEN IN "SENSOR GROUND" TO SENSORS.

CORRECTION

- VERIFY "CAUSE" BY DISCONNECTING THE COOLANT TEMP., TPS AND BARO SENSOR CONNECTORS AND MEASURING THE VOLTAGE BETWEEN 12 VOLTS AND CIRCUIT #476-X ON EACH SENSOR HARNESS CONNECTOR.

| 0 VOLTS FOR ALL SENSORS | NOT 0 VOLTS FOR ALL SENSORS |

- CHECK FOR AN OPEN IN CIRCUIT #476-X.
- CHECK FOR A FAULTY ECM CONNECTOR OR FAULTY ECM.

- CAUSE NOT VERIFIED. FOLLOW DIAGNOSTIC PROCEDURE FOR INDIVIDUAL CODES.

A-3 CONDITION: CODE 38 STORED HARD ALONG WITH A HARD CODE 33, 34 OR A VERY LOW OUTSIDE TEMP DISPLAY
CAUSE: OPEN IN "SENSOR GROUND" TO SENSORS.

CORRECTION

- VERIFY "CAUSE" BY DISCONNECTING THE MAT, MAP AND OUTSIDE TEMP SENSOR CONNECTORS AND MEASURING THE VOLTAGE BETWEEN 12 VOLTS AND CIRCUIT #476-Y ON EACH SENSOR HARNESS CONNECTOR.

| 0 VOLTS FOR ALL SENSORS | NOT 0 VOLTS FOR ALL SENSORS |

- CHECK FOR AN OPEN IN CIRCUIT #476-Y.
- CHECK FOR A FAULTY ECM CONNECTOR OR FAULTY ECM.

- CAUSE NOT VERIFIED. FOLLOW DIAGNOSTIC PROCEDURE FOR INDIVIDUAL CODES.

WHEN ALL DIAGNOSIS AND REPAIRS ARE COMPLETED, CLEAR STORED CODES AND VERIFY PROPER OPERATION.

HARD DFI CODE 12
NO DISTRIBUTOR (TACH) SIGNAL

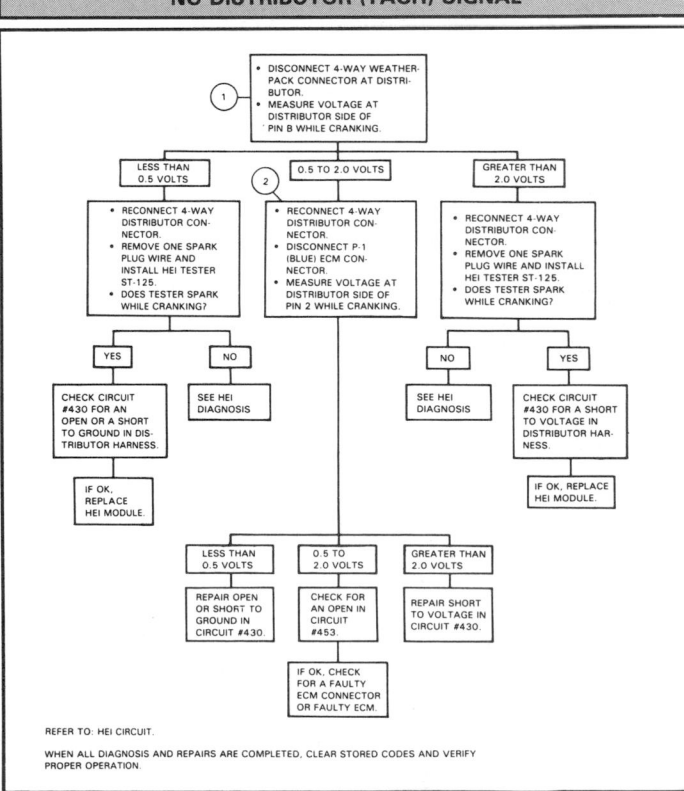

REFER TO: HEI CIRCUIT.

WHEN ALL DIAGNOSIS AND REPAIRS ARE COMPLETED, CLEAR STORED CODES AND VERIFY PROPER OPERATION.

HARD OR INTERMITTENT DFI CODE 13
OXYGEN SENSOR NOT READY

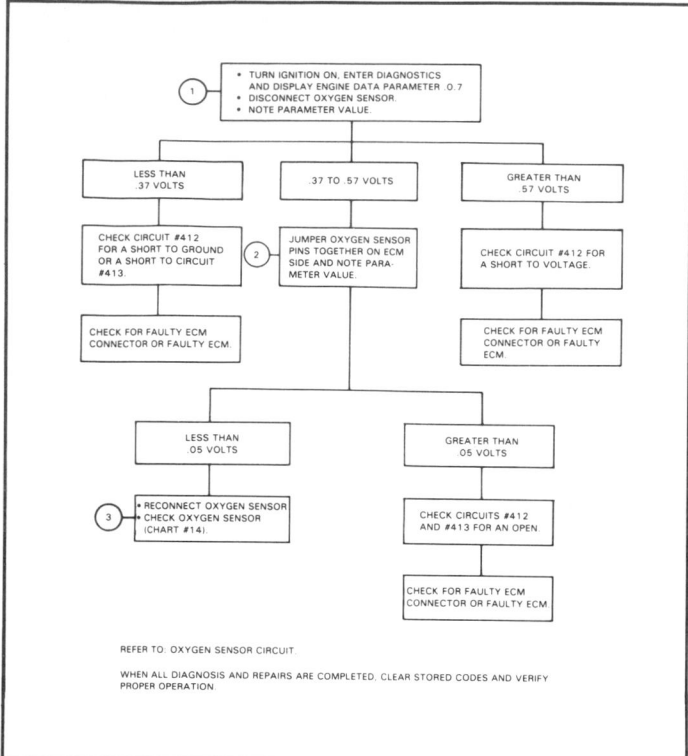

REFER TO: OXYGEN SENSOR CIRCUIT.

WHEN ALL DIAGNOSIS AND REPAIRS ARE COMPLETED, CLEAR STORED CODES AND VERIFY PROPER OPERATION.

HARD DFI CODE 14
SHORTED COOLANT SENSOR CIRCUIT

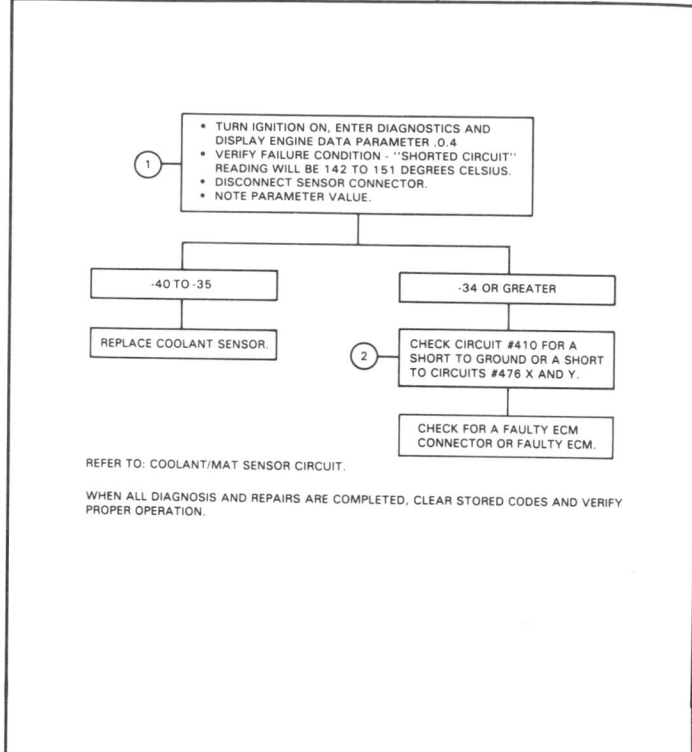

REFER TO: COOLANT/MAT SENSOR CIRCUIT.

WHEN ALL DIAGNOSIS AND REPAIRS ARE COMPLETED, CLEAR STORED CODES AND VERIFY PROPER OPERATION.

HARD DFI CODE 15
OPEN COOLANT SENSOR CIRCUIT

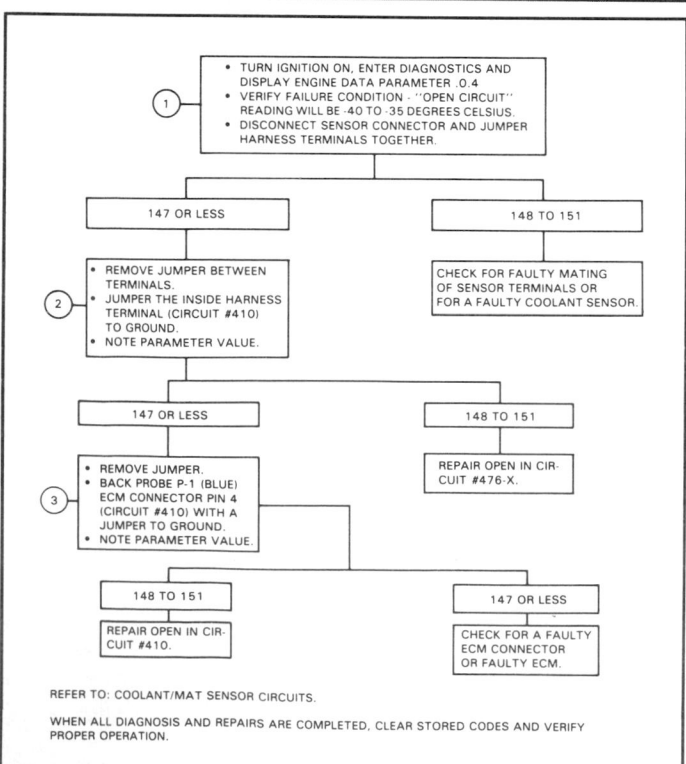

REFER TO: COOLANT/MAT SENSOR CIRCUITS.

WHEN ALL DIAGNOSIS AND REPAIRS ARE COMPLETED, CLEAR STORED CODES AND VERIFY PROPER OPERATION.

HARD DFI CODE 16
GENERATOR VOLTAGE OUT OF RANGE

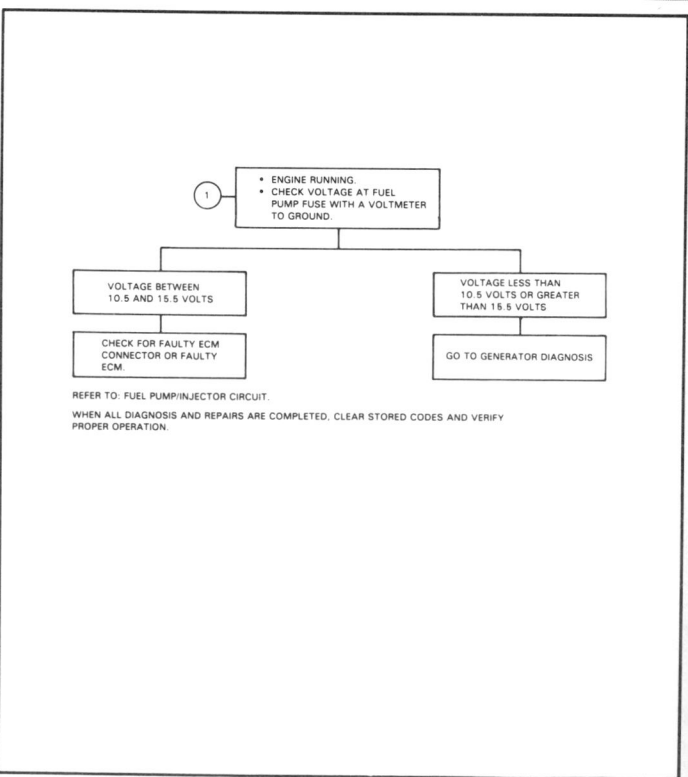

REFER TO: FUEL PUMP/INJECTOR CIRCUIT.

WHEN ALL DIAGNOSIS AND REPAIRS ARE COMPLETED, CLEAR STORED CODES AND VERIFY PROPER OPERATION.

HARD DFI CODE 18
OPEN CRANK SIGNAL CIRCUIT

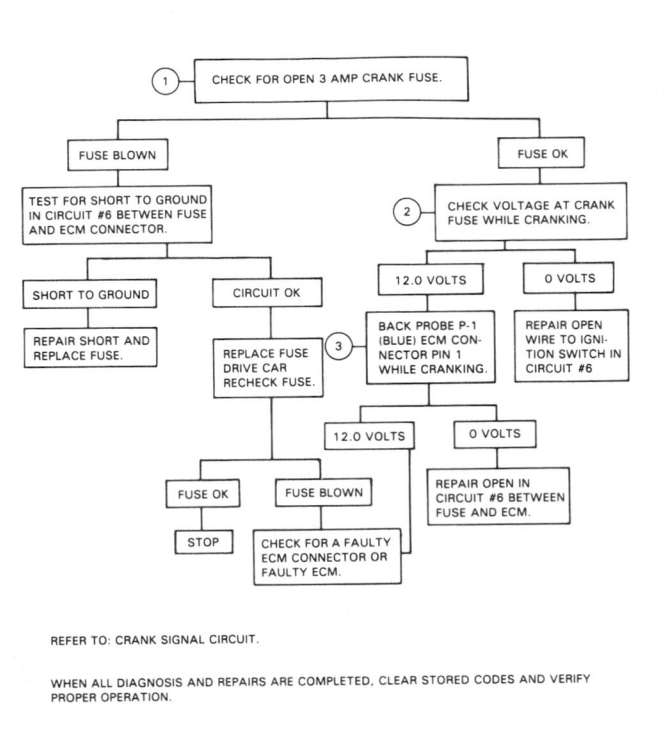

REFER TO: CRANK SIGNAL CIRCUIT.

WHEN ALL DIAGNOSIS AND REPAIRS ARE COMPLETED, CLEAR STORED CODES AND VERIFY PROPER OPERATION.

HARD DFI CODE 19
SHORTED FUEL PUMP CIRCUIT

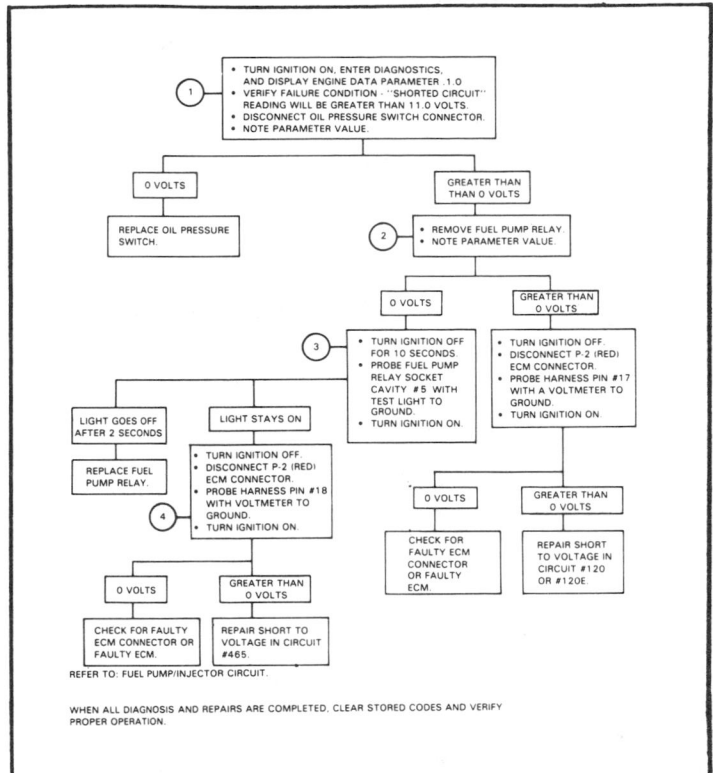

REFER TO: FUEL PUMP/INJECTOR CIRCUIT.

WHEN ALL DIAGNOSIS AND REPAIRS ARE COMPLETED, CLEAR STORED CODES AND VERIFY PROPER OPERATION.

HARD OR INTERMITTENT DFI CODE 20
OPEN FUEL PUMP CIRCUIT

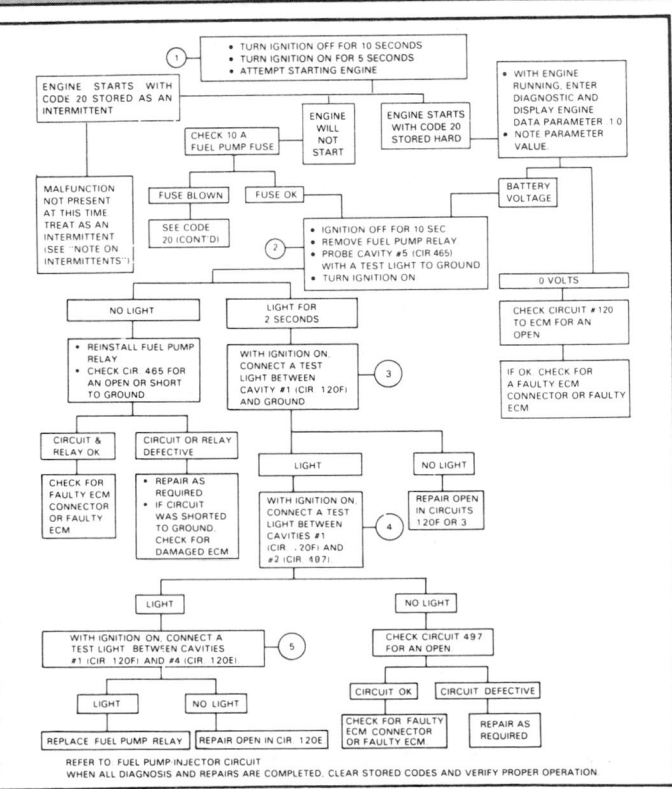

REFER TO: FUEL PUMP INJECTOR CIRCUIT.
WHEN ALL DIAGNOSIS AND REPAIRS ARE COMPLETED, CLEAR STORED CODES AND VERIFY PROPER OPERATION.

DFI CODE 20 - (CONT'D)
FUSE BLOWN

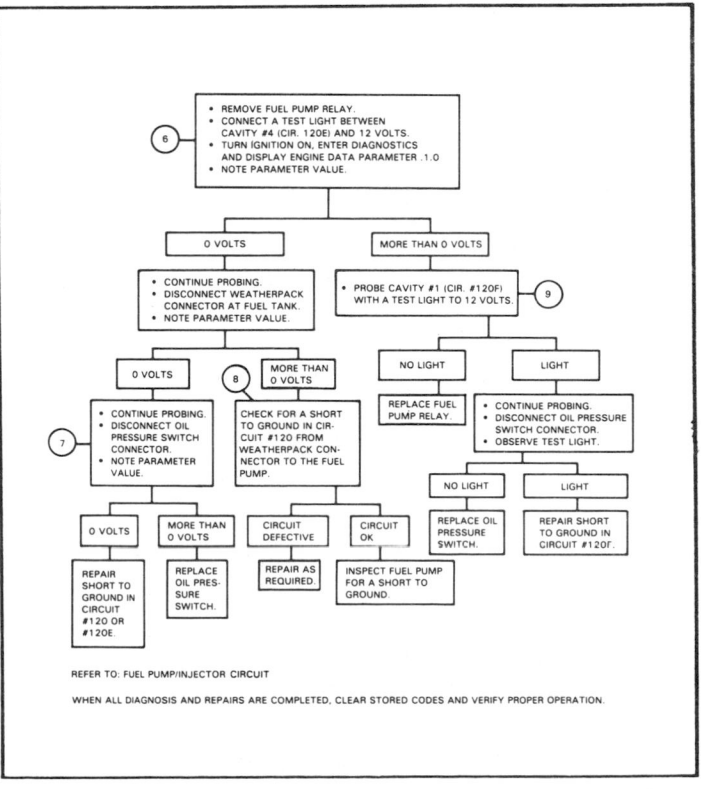

REFER TO: FUEL PUMP/INJECTOR CIRCUIT

WHEN ALL DIAGNOSIS AND REPAIRS ARE COMPLETED, CLEAR STORED CODES AND VERIFY PROPER OPERATION.

HARD DFI CODE 21
SHORTED THROTTLE POSITION SENSOR CIRCUIT

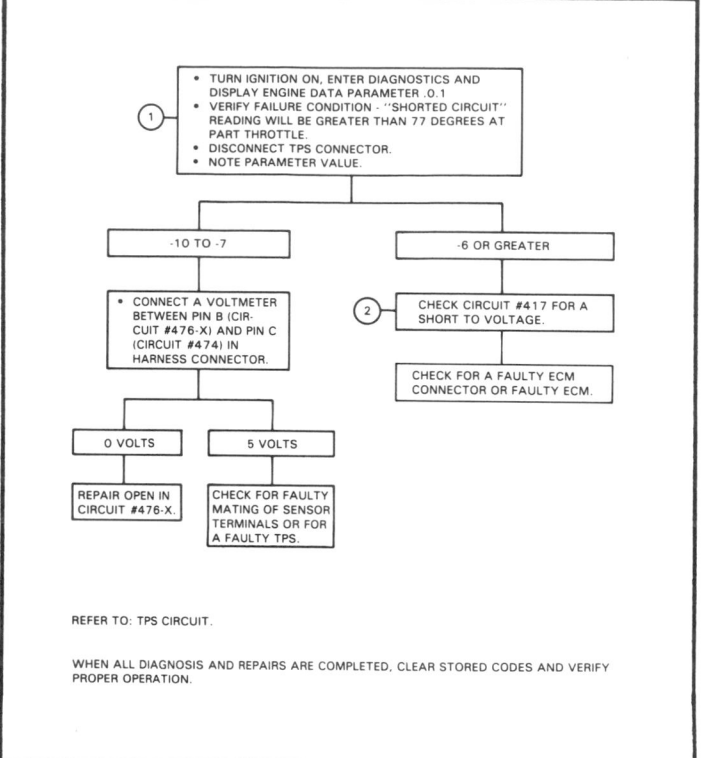

REFER TO: TPS CIRCUIT.

WHEN ALL DIAGNOSIS AND REPAIRS ARE COMPLETED, CLEAR STORED CODES AND VERIFY PROPER OPERATION.

HARD DFI CODE 22
OPEN THROTTLE POSITION SENSOR CIRCUIT

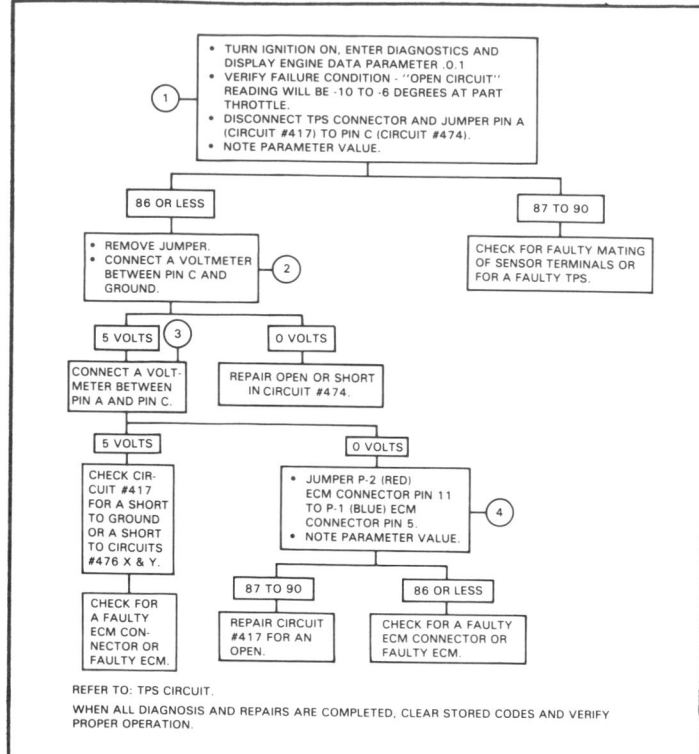

REFER TO: TPS CIRCUIT.

WHEN ALL DIAGNOSIS AND REPAIRS ARE COMPLETED, CLEAR STORED CODES AND VERIFY PROPER OPERATION.

HARD DFI CODE 23
EST CIRCUIT PROBLEM

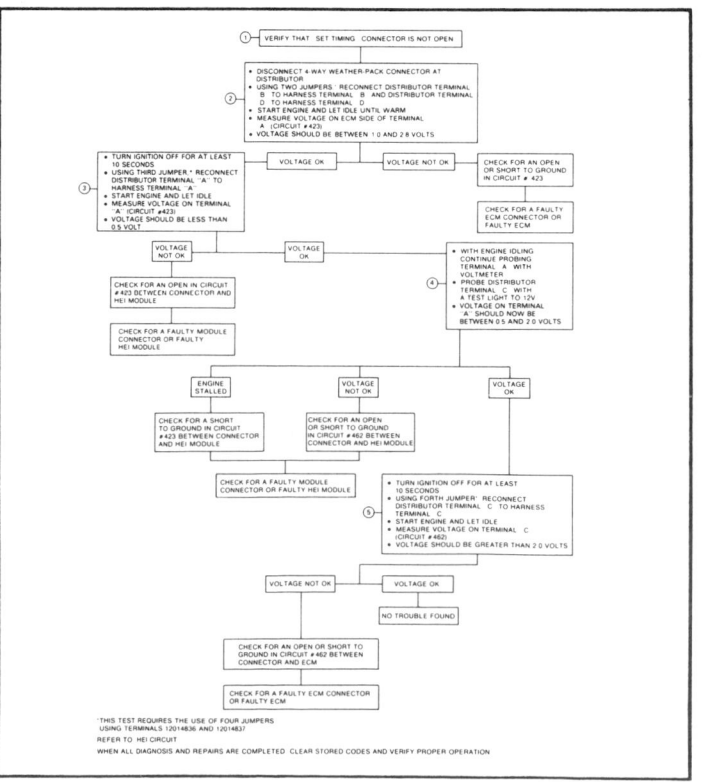

HARD DFI CODE 24(A)
SPEED SENSOR CIRCUIT PROBLEM
(FOR VEHICLES WITHOUT DIGITAL CLUSTER)

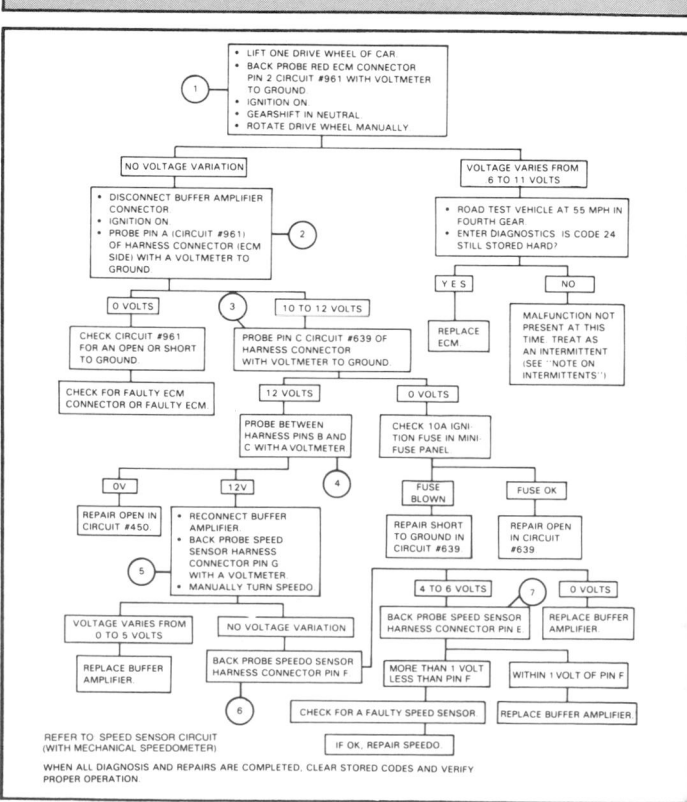

HARD DFI CODE 24(B)
SPEED SENSOR CIRCUIT PROBLEM
(FOR VEHICLES WITH DIGITAL SPEEDOMETER)

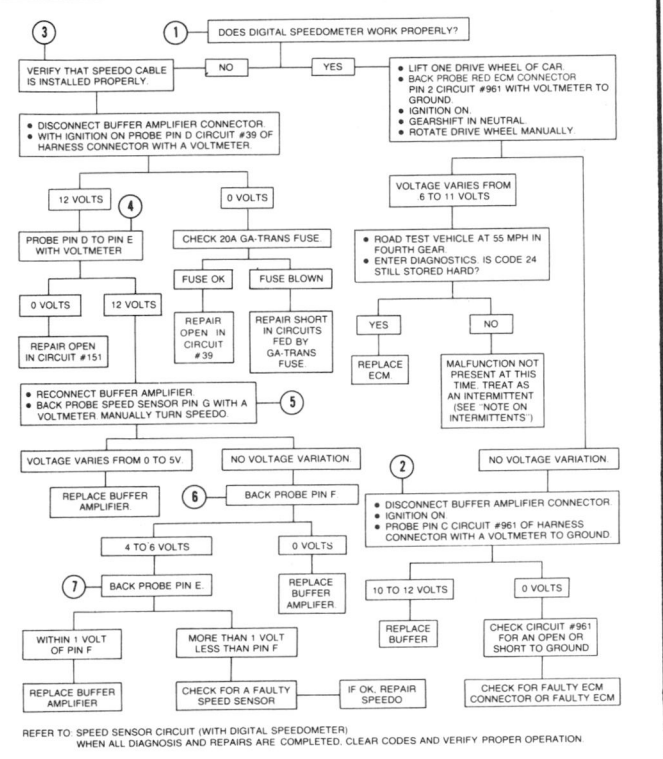

REFER TO: SPEED SENSOR CIRCUIT (WITH DIGITAL SPEEDOMETER).
WHEN ALL DIAGNOSIS AND REPAIRS ARE COMPLETED, CLEAR CODES AND VERIFY PROPER OPERATION.

HARD DFI CODE 26
SHORTED THROTTLE SWITCH CIRCUIT

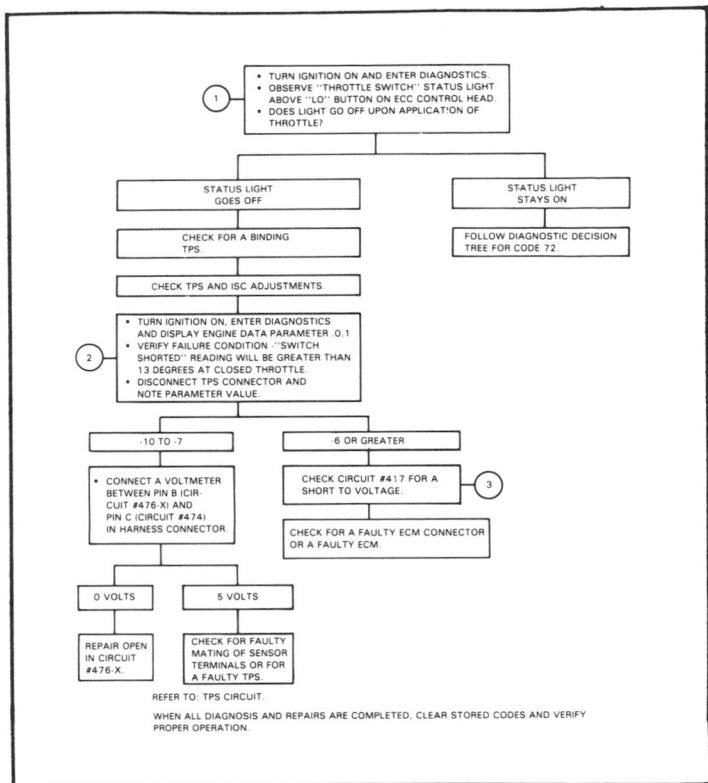

REFER TO: TPS CIRCUIT.
WHEN ALL DIAGNOSIS AND REPAIRS ARE COMPLETED, CLEAR STORED CODES AND VERIFY PROPER OPERATION.

HARD DFI CODE 27
OPEN THROTTLE SWITCH CIRCUIT

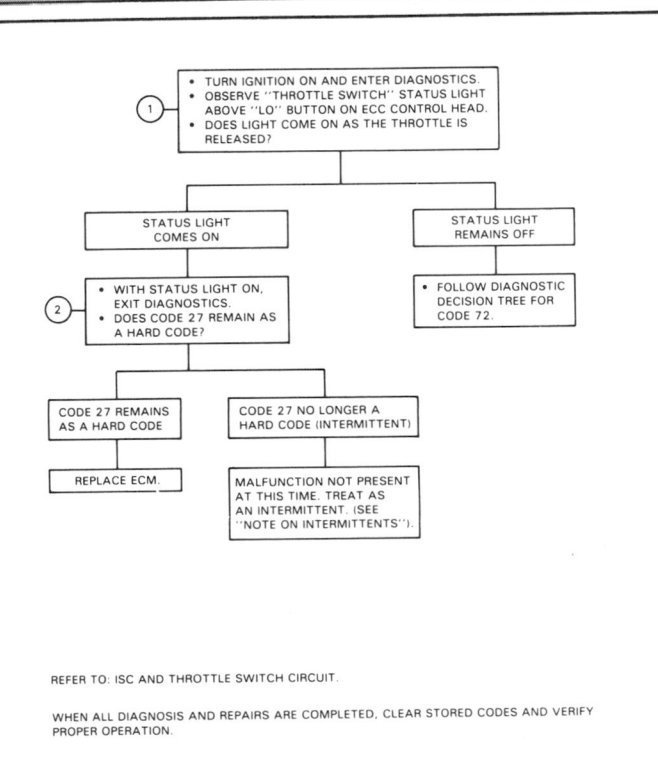

REFER TO: ISC AND THROTTLE SWITCH CIRCUIT.

WHEN ALL DIAGNOSIS AND REPAIRS ARE COMPLETED, CLEAR STORED CODES AND VERIFY
PROPER OPERATION.

HARD DFI CODE 28
OPEN 4TH GEAR CIRCUIT

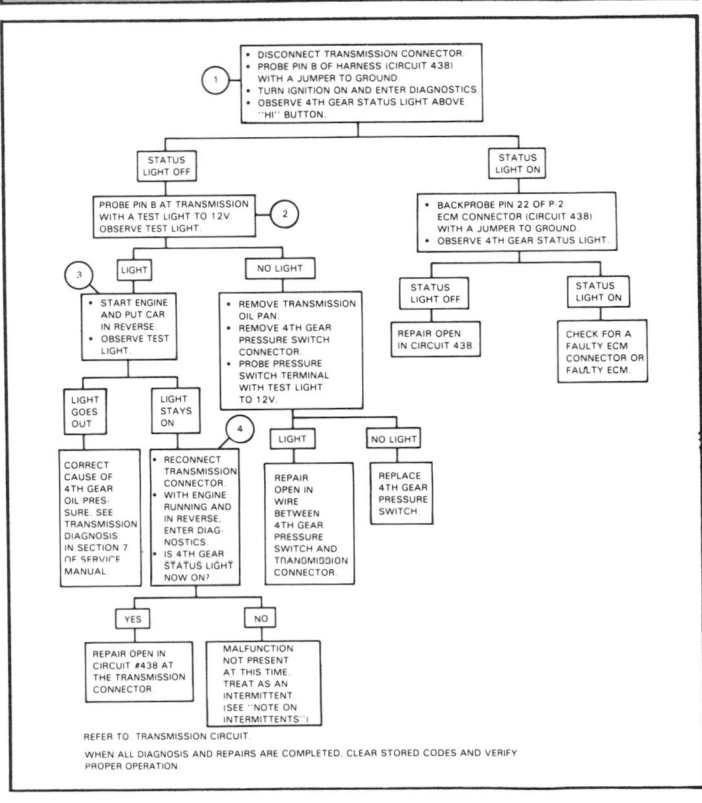

REFER TO: TRANSMISSION CIRCUIT.
WHEN ALL DIAGNOSIS AND REPAIRS ARE COMPLETED, CLEAR STORED CODES AND VERIFY
PROPER OPERATION.

HARD DFI CODE 29
SHORTED 4TH GEAR CIRCUIT

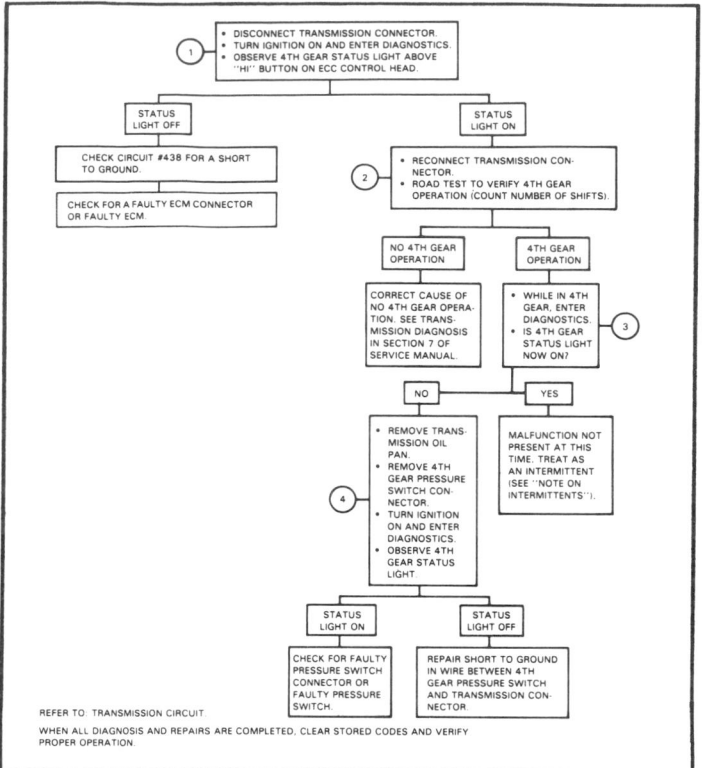

REFER TO: TRANSMISSION CIRCUIT.

WHEN ALL DIAGNOSIS AND REPAIRS ARE COMPLETED, CLEAR STORED CODES AND VERIFY PROPER OPERATION.

HARD OR INTERMITTENT DFI CODE 30
IDLE SPEED CONTROL CIRCUIT PROBLEM

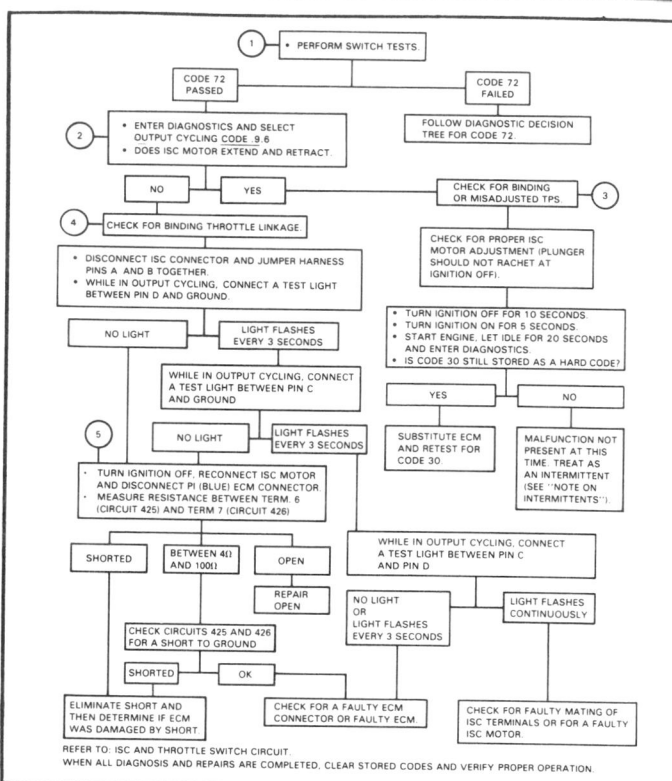

REFER TO: ISC AND THROTTLE SWITCH CIRCUIT.

WHEN ALL DIAGNOSIS AND REPAIRS ARE COMPLETED, CLEAR STORED CODES AND VERIFY PROPER OPERATION.

HARD DFI CODE 31
SHORTED MAP SENSOR CIRCUIT

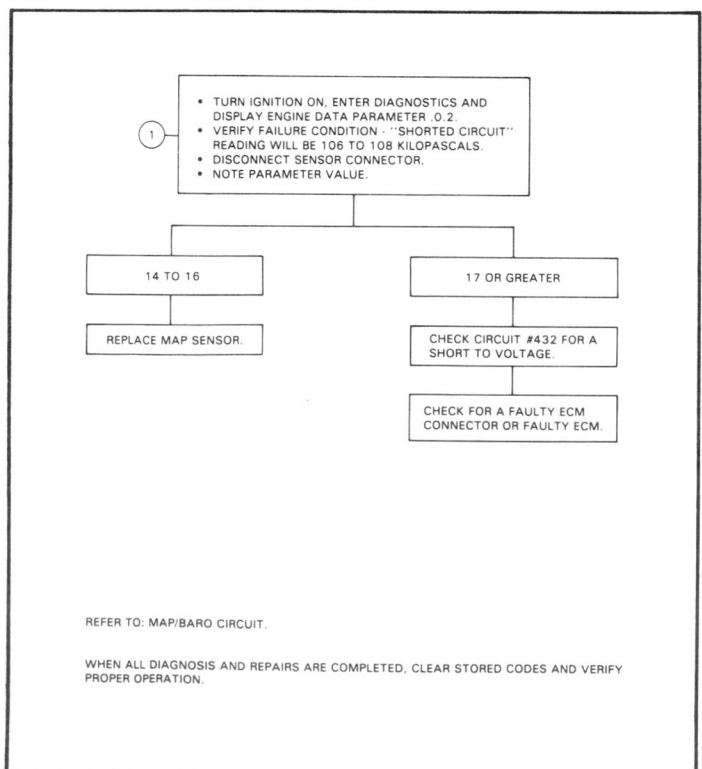

REFER TO: MAP/BARO CIRCUIT.

WHEN ALL DIAGNOSIS AND REPAIRS ARE COMPLETED, CLEAR STORED CODES AND VERIFY PROPER OPERATION.

HARD DFI CODE 32
OPEN MAP SENSOR CIRCUIT

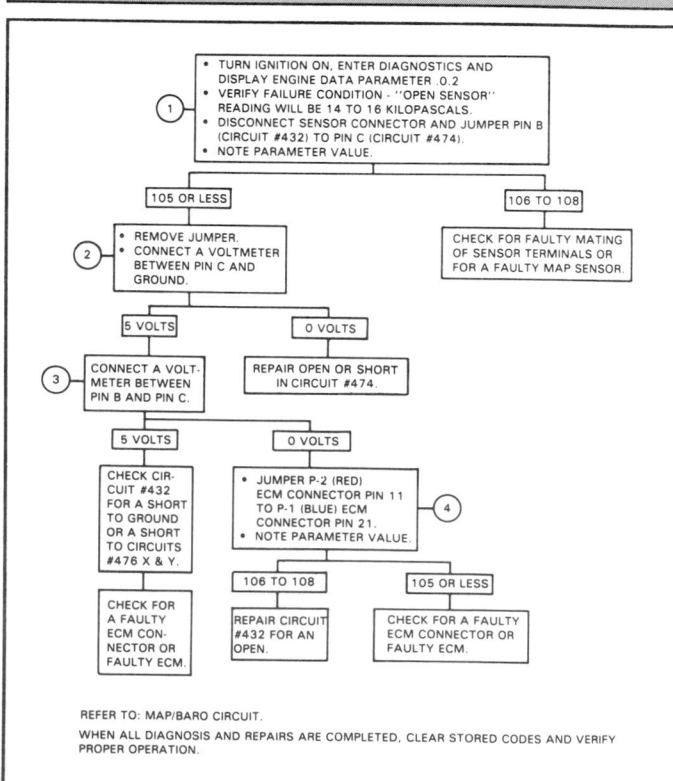

REFER TO: MAP/BARO CIRCUIT.

WHEN ALL DIAGNOSIS AND REPAIRS ARE COMPLETED, CLEAR STORED CODES AND VERIFY PROPER OPERATION.

HARD OR INTERMITTENT DFI CODE 33
MAP/BARO SENSOR CORRELATION

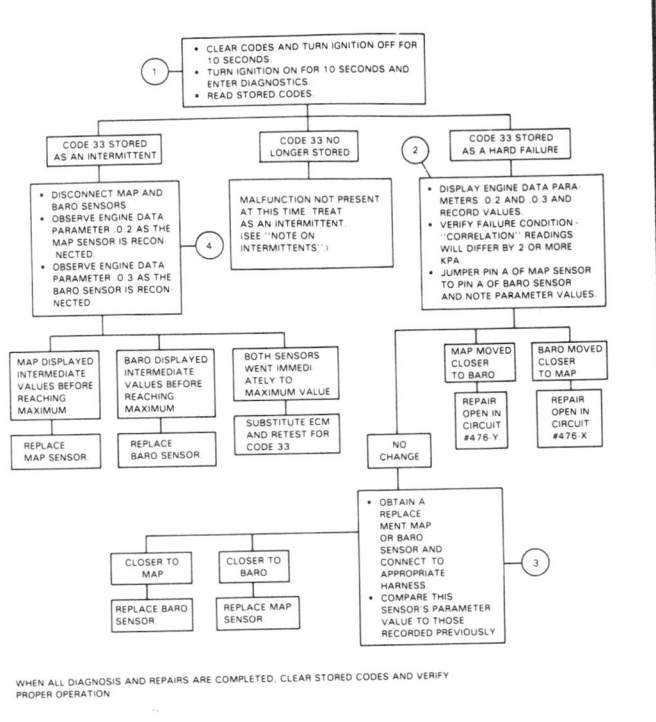

WHEN ALL DIAGNOSIS AND REPAIRS ARE COMPLETED, CLEAR STORED CODES AND VERIFY PROPER OPERATION.

HARD DFI CODE 34
MAP SIGNAL TOO HIGH

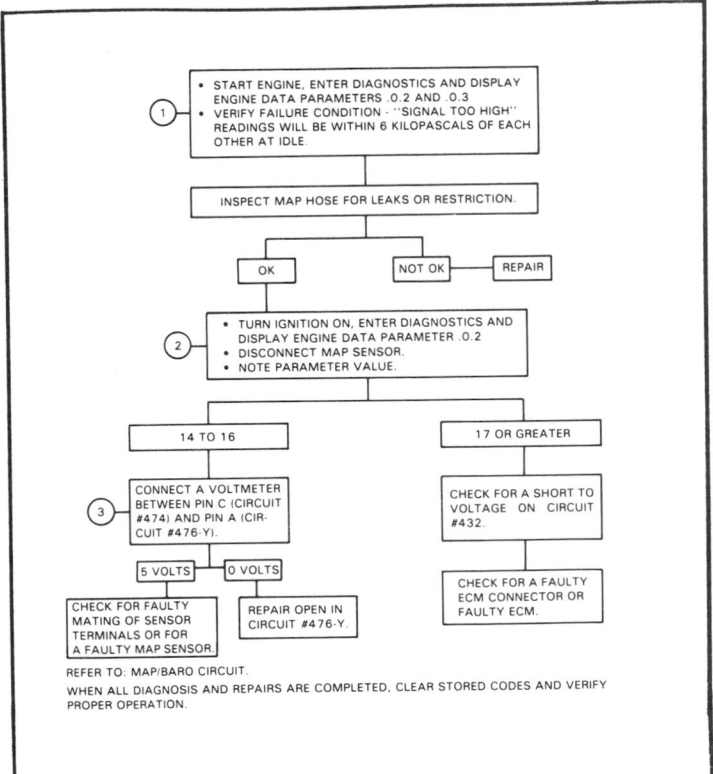

REFER TO: MAP/BARO CIRCUIT.
WHEN ALL DIAGNOSIS AND REPAIRS ARE COMPLETED, CLEAR STORED CODES AND VERIFY PROPER OPERATION.

HARD DFI CODE 35
SHORTED BARO SENSOR CIRCUIT

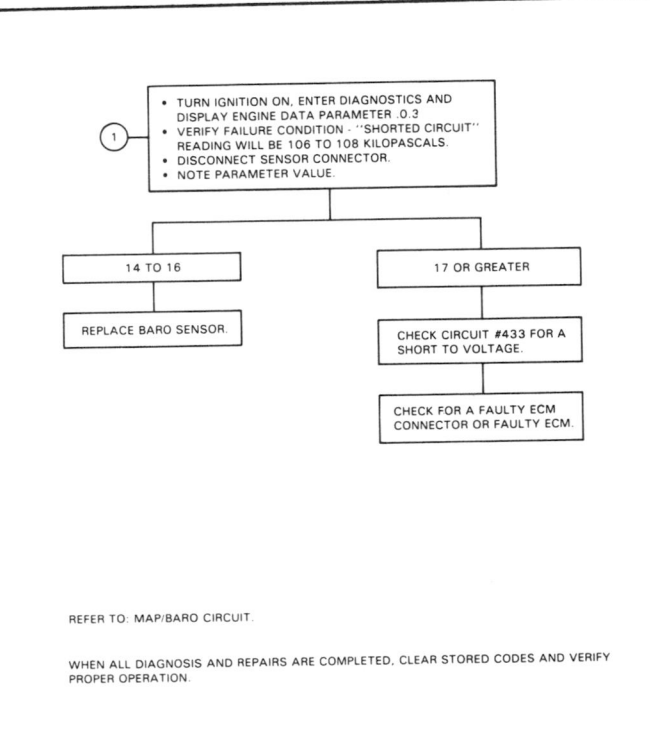

REFER TO: MAP/BARO CIRCUIT.

WHEN ALL DIAGNOSIS AND REPAIRS ARE COMPLETED, CLEAR STORED CODES AND VERIFY PROPER OPERATION.

HARD DFI CODE 36
OPEN BARO SENSOR CIRCUIT

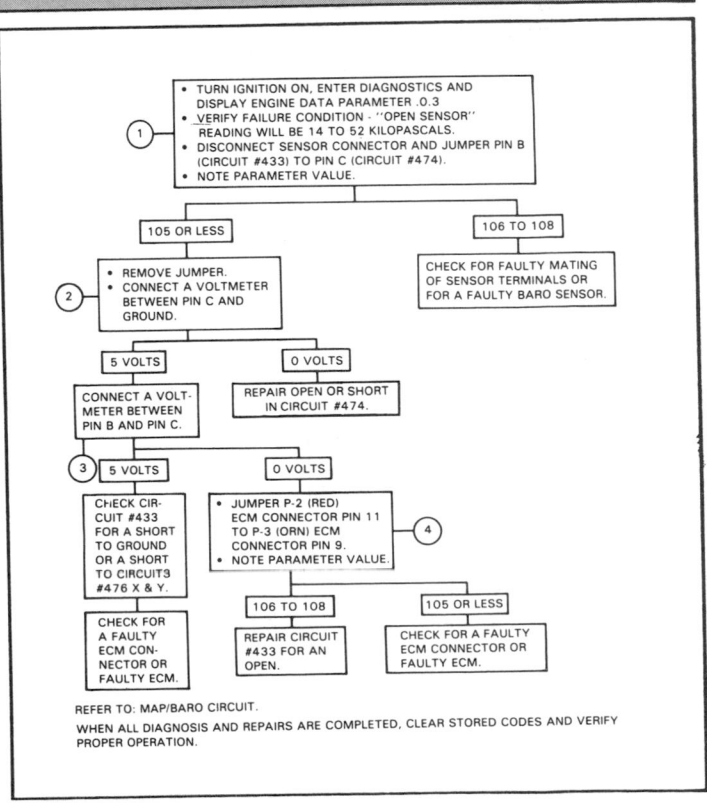

REFER TO: MAP/BARO CIRCUIT.
WHEN ALL DIAGNOSIS AND REPAIRS ARE COMPLETED, CLEAR STORED CODES AND VERIFY PROPER OPERATION.

HARD DFI CODE 37
SHORTED MAT SENSOR CIRCUIT

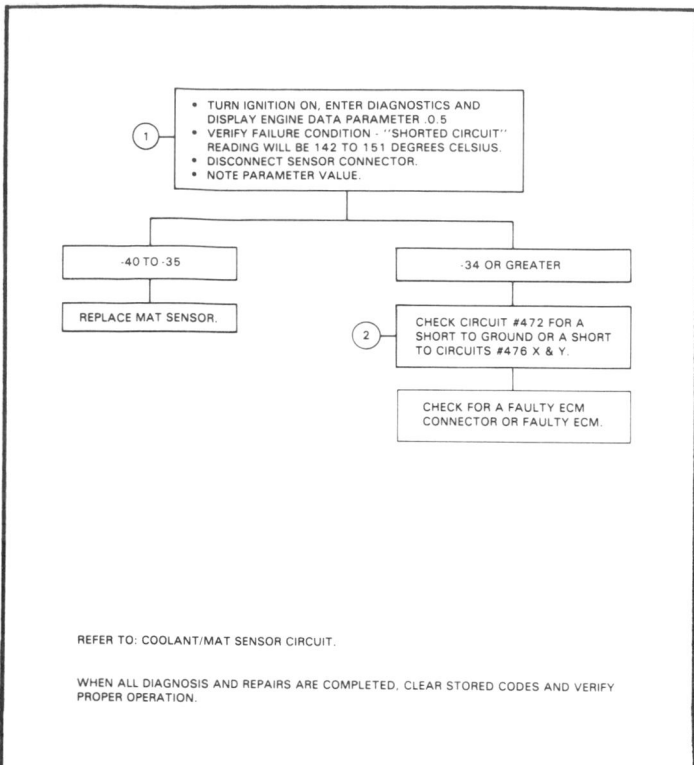

REFER TO: COOLANT/MAT SENSOR CIRCUIT.

WHEN ALL DIAGNOSIS AND REPAIRS ARE COMPLETED, CLEAR STORED CODES AND VERIFY PROPER OPERATION.

HARD DFI CODE 38
OPEN MAT SENSOR CIRCUIT

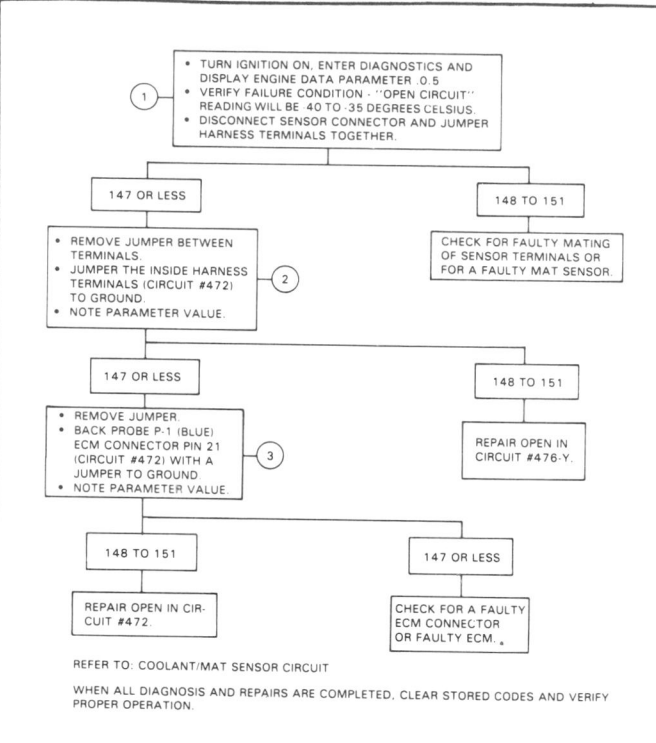

REFER TO: COOLANT/MAT SENSOR CIRCUIT

WHEN ALL DIAGNOSIS AND REPAIRS ARE COMPLETED, CLEAR STORED CODES AND VERIFY PROPER OPERATION.

HARD OR INTERMITTENT DFI
CODE 39 TCC ENGAGEMENT PROBLEM

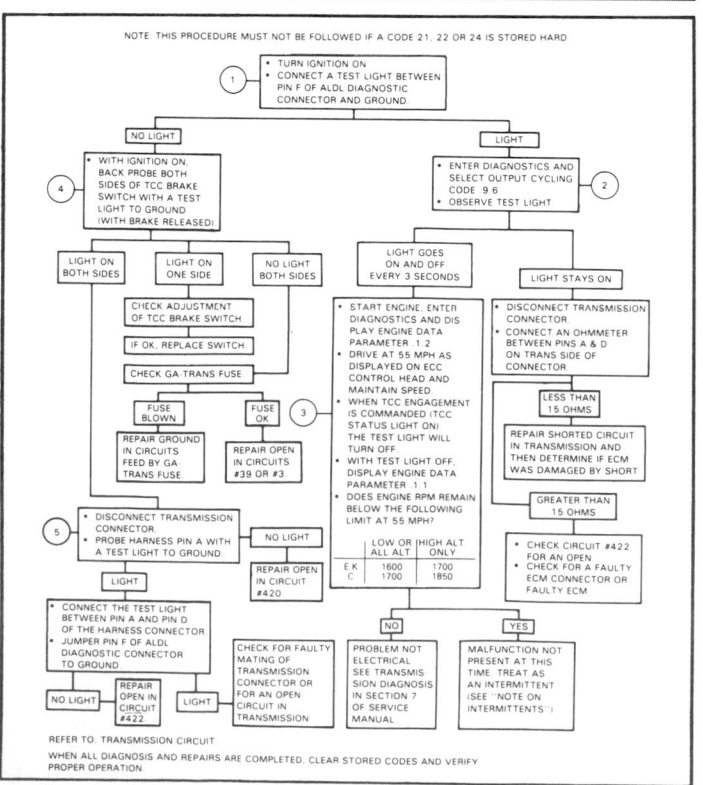

REFER TO: TRANSMISSION CIRCUIT

WHEN ALL DIAGNOSIS AND REPAIRS ARE COMPLETED. CLEAR STORED CODES AND VERIFY PROPER OPERATION.

HARD OR INTERMITTENT DFI CODE 44
LEAN EXHAUST SIGNAL

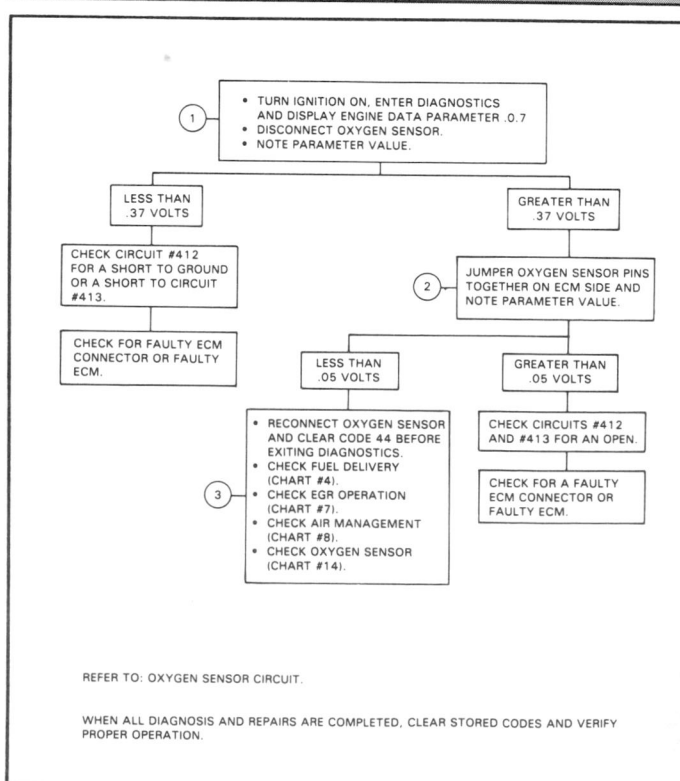

REFER TO: OXYGEN SENSOR CIRCUIT.

WHEN ALL DIAGNOSIS AND REPAIRS ARE COMPLETED, CLEAR STORED CODES AND VERIFY PROPER OPERATION.

HARD OR INTERMITTENT DFI CODE 45 RICH EXHAUST SIGNAL

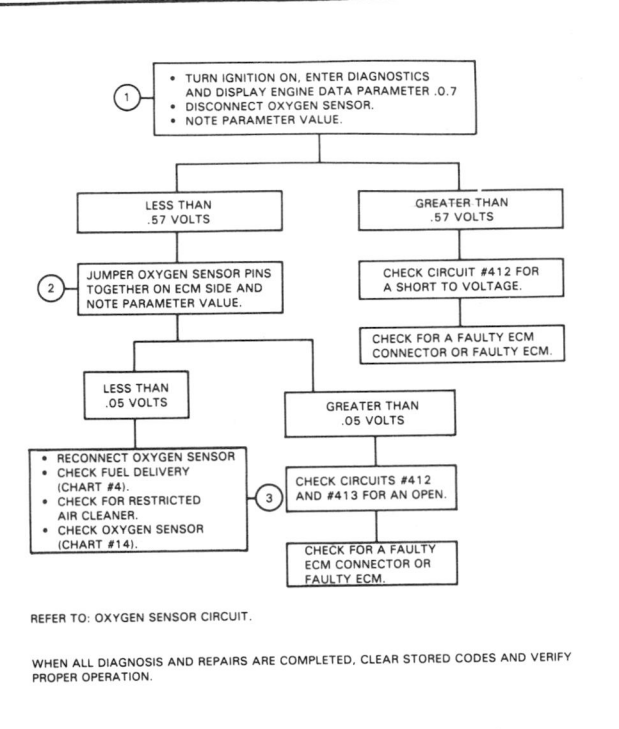

REFER TO: OXYGEN SENSOR CIRCUIT.

WHEN ALL DIAGNOSIS AND REPAIRS ARE COMPLETED, CLEAR STORED CODES AND VERIFY PROPER OPERATION.

DFI CHART #1 NO START OR STALL AFTER START

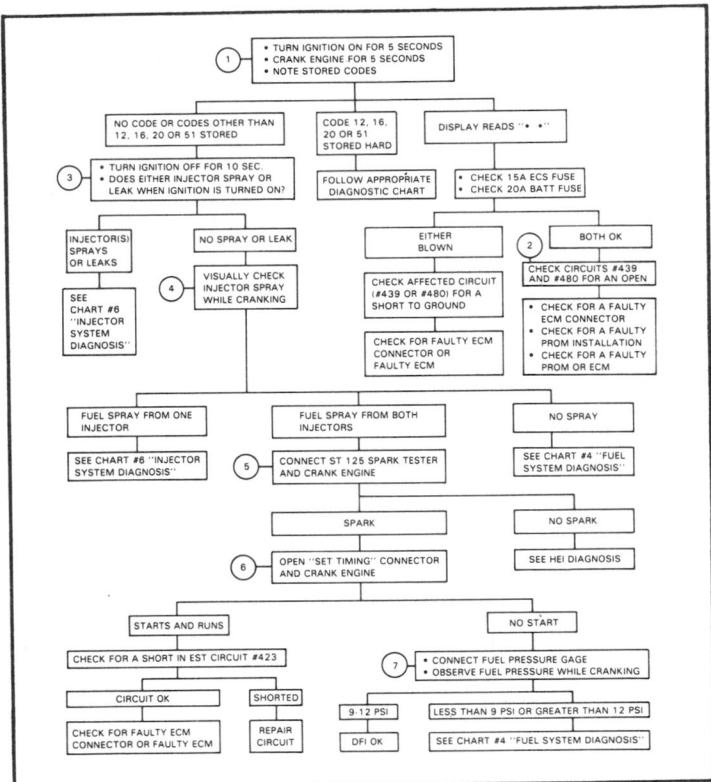

DFI CHART #2 "SERVICE NOW" AND/OR "SERVICE SOON" LIGHTS ON — NO HARD CODES

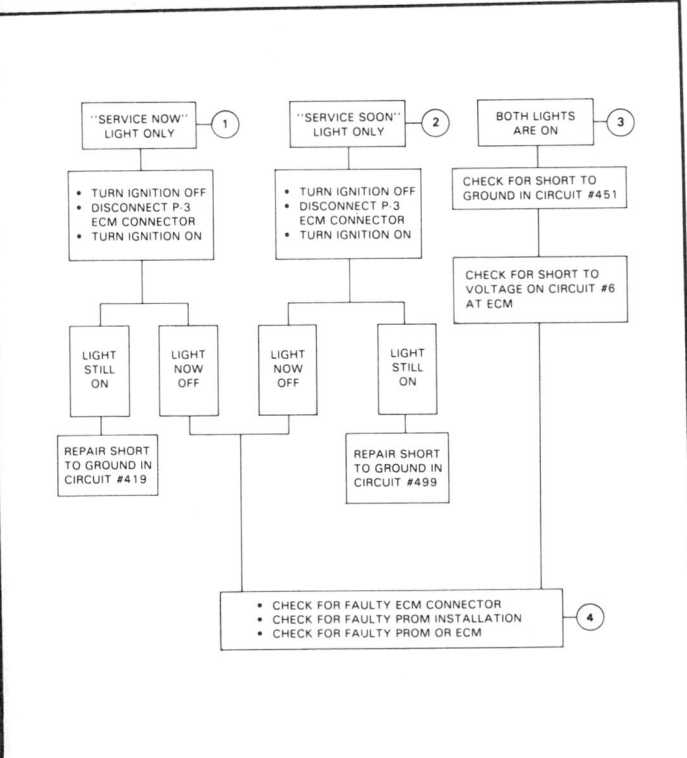

DFI CHART #3A 'SERVICE NOW' LIGHT INOPERATIVE

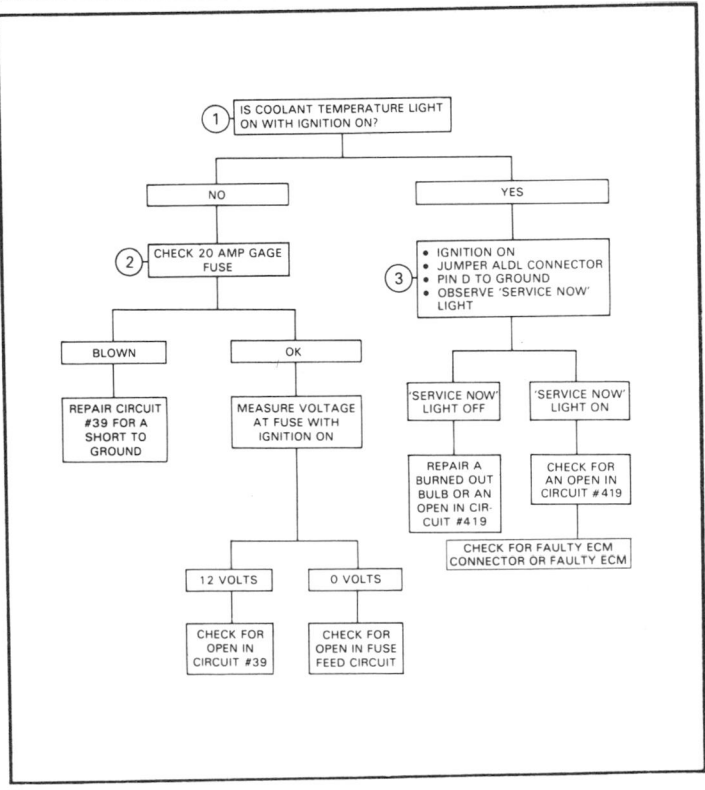

DFI CHART #3B
'SERVICE SOON' LIGHT INOPERATIVE

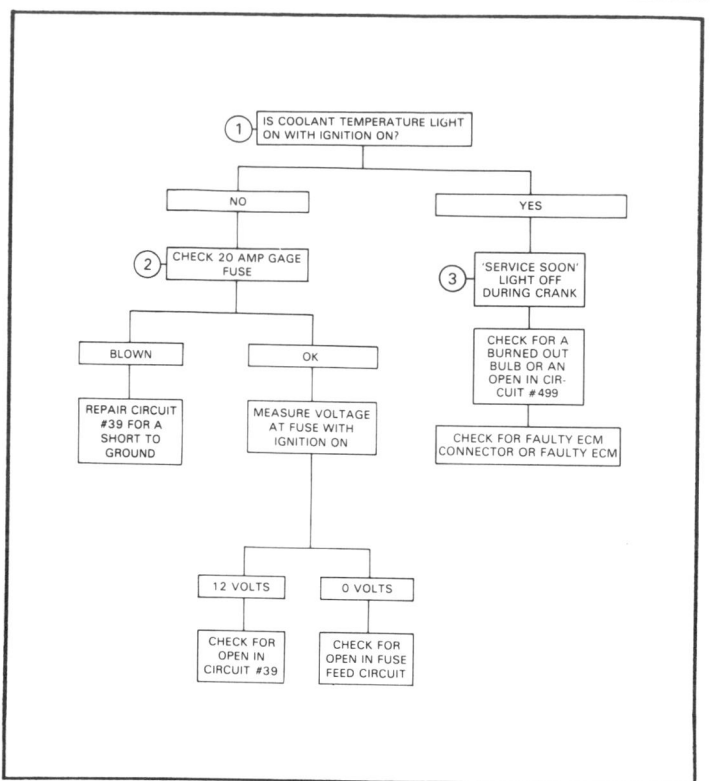

DFI CHART #4
FUEL SYSTEM DIAGNOSIS

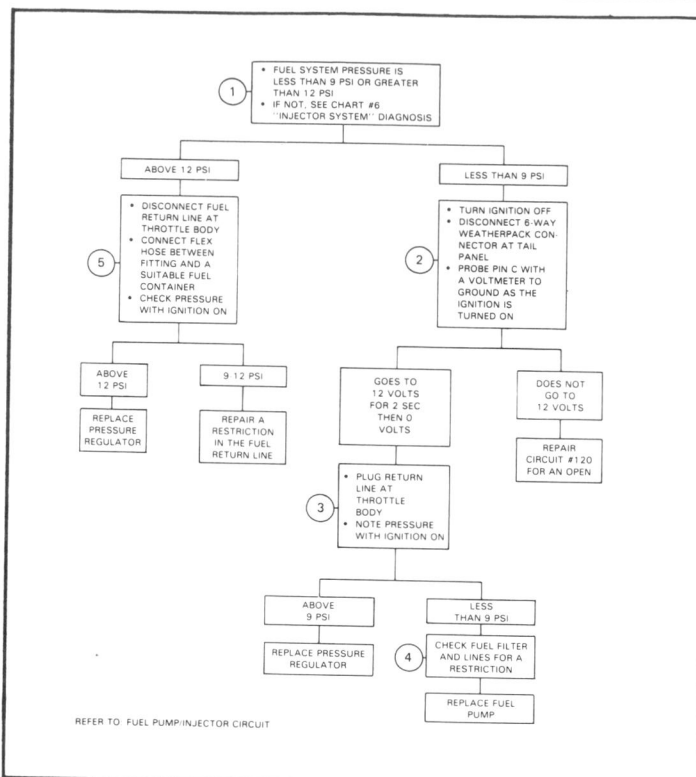

DFI CHART #5
POOR PERFORMANCE AND/OR POOR FUEL ECONOMY

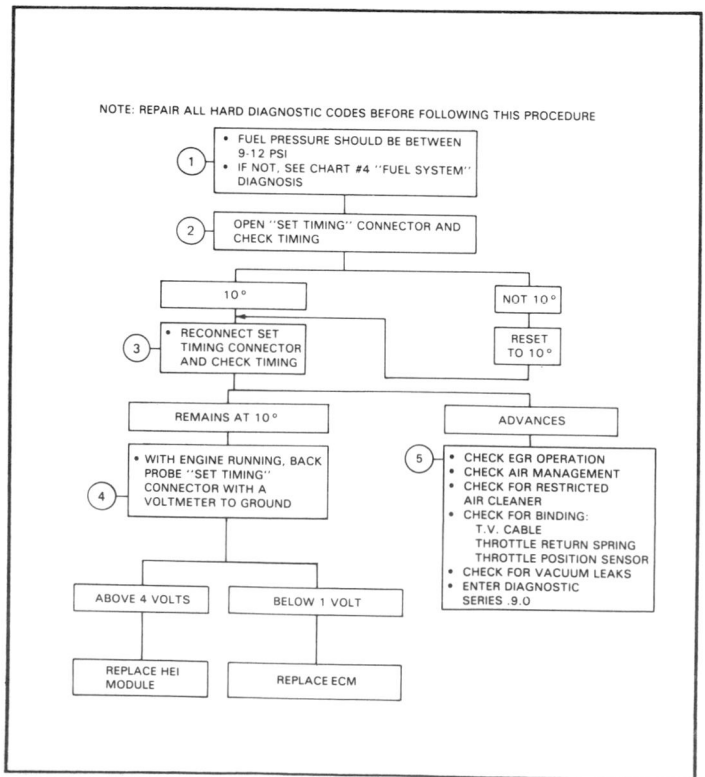

DFI CHART #6
INJECTOR SYSTEM DIAGNOSIS

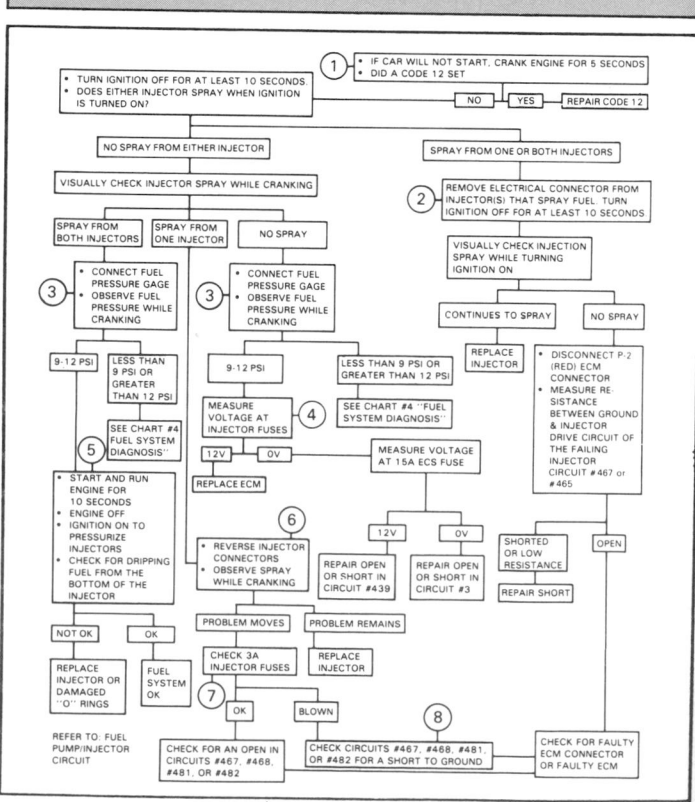

DFI CHART #7
EGR DIAGNOSIS

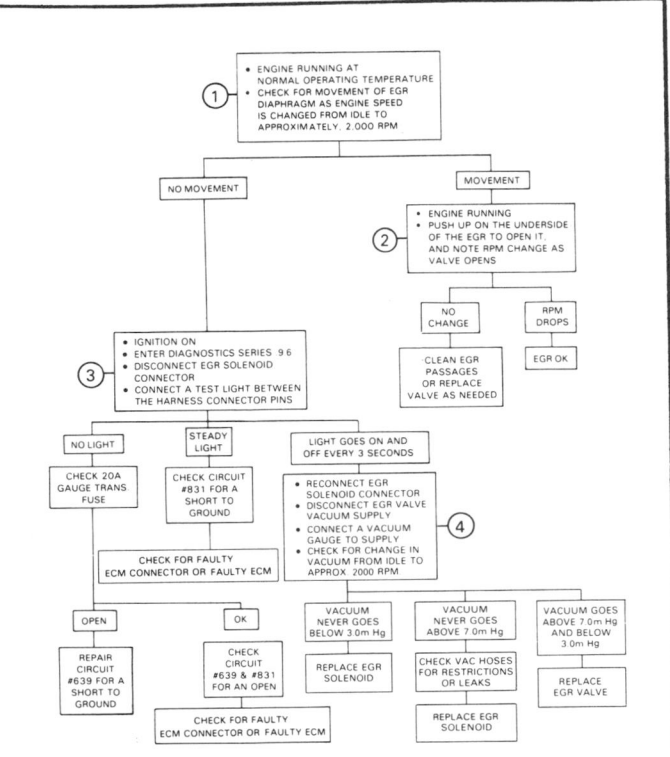

DFI CHART #8
AIR MANAGEMENT DIAGNOSIS

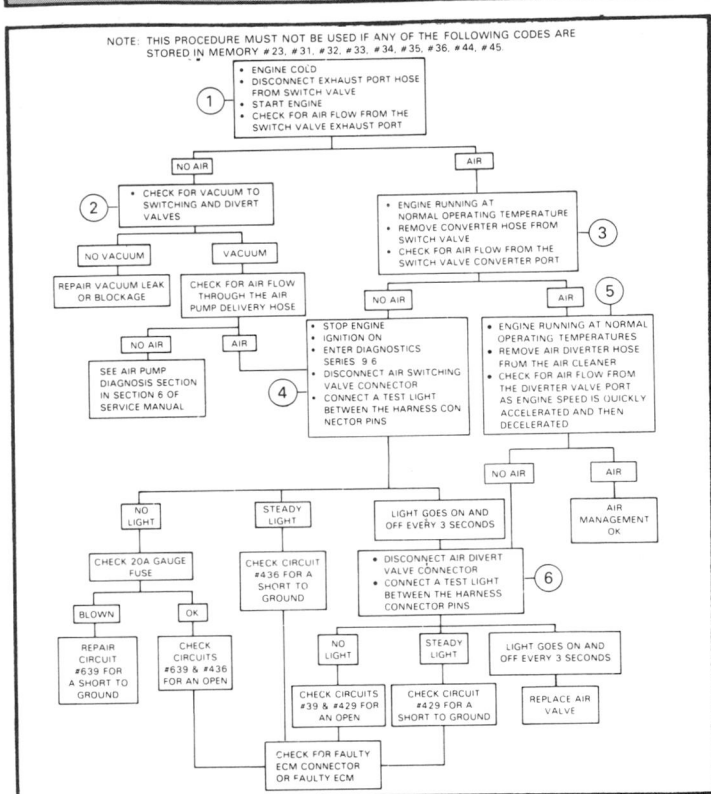

DFI CHART #9
CANISTER PURGE CONTROL DIAGNOSIS

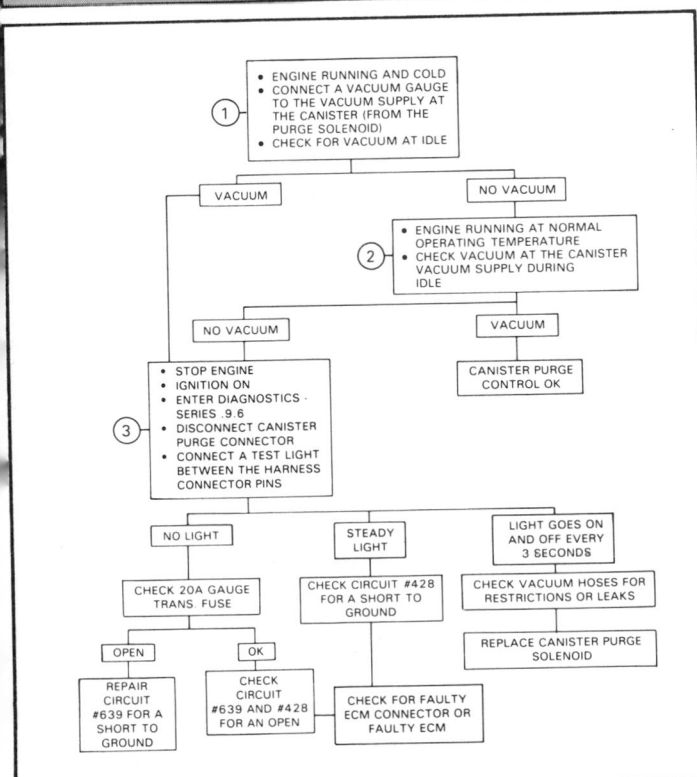

DFI CHART #10
NO CRUISE CONTROL

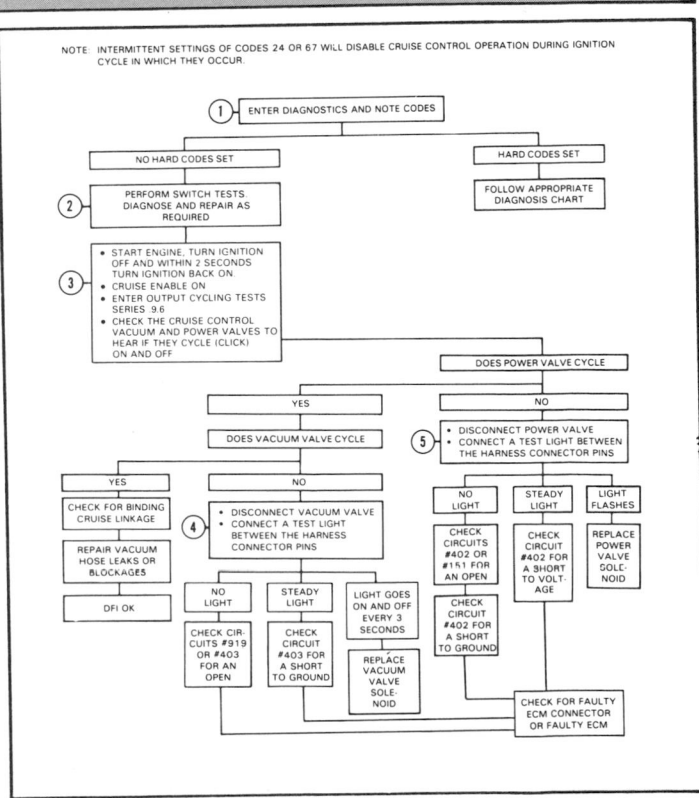

DFI CHART #11A
BLANK FUEL DATA DISPLAY
(IF NOT BLANK, FOLLOW CHART #11B)

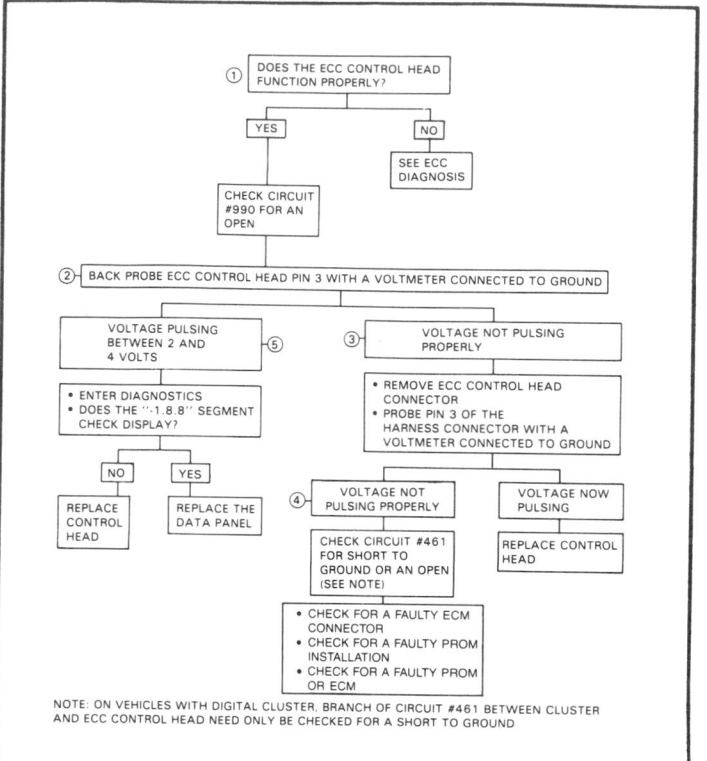

DFI CHART #11B
IMPROPER FUEL DATA DISPLAY
(IF BLANK, FOLLOW CHART #11A)

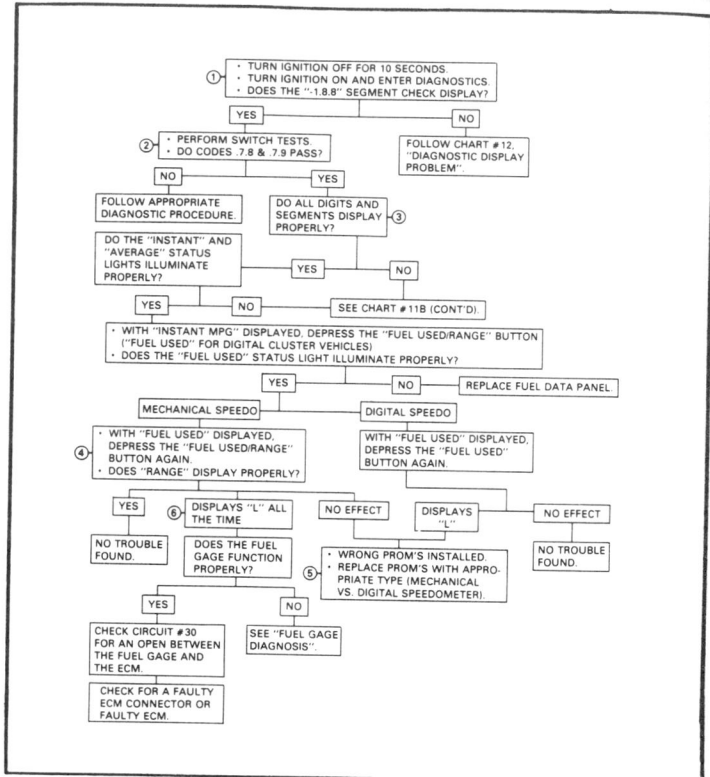

DFI CHART #12
DIAGNOSTIC DISPLAY PROBLEMS

DFI CHART #13
IMPROPER IDLE SPEED

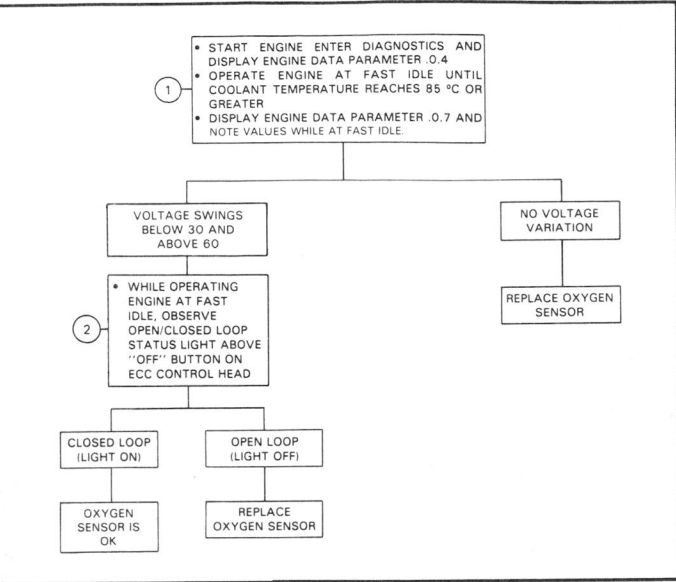

DFI CHART #14
OXYGEN SENSOR TEST

1. • START ENGINE ENTER DIAGNOSTICS AND DISPLAY ENGINE DATA PARAMETER .0.4
   • OPERATE ENGINE AT FAST IDLE UNTIL COOLANT TEMPERATURE REACHES 85 °C OR GREATER
   • DISPLAY ENGINE DATA PARAMETER .0.7 AND NOTE VALUES WHILE AT FAST IDLE.

- VOLTAGE SWINGS BELOW 30 AND ABOVE 60
- NO VOLTAGE VARIATION → REPLACE OXYGEN SENSOR

2. • WHILE OPERATING ENGINE AT FAST IDLE, OBSERVE OPEN/CLOSED LOOP STATUS LIGHT ABOVE "OFF" BUTTON ON ECC CONTROL HEAD

- CLOSED LOOP (LIGHT ON) → OXYGEN SENSOR IS OK
- OPEN LOOP (LIGHT OFF) → REPLACE OXYGEN SENSOR

DFI CHART #15
IMPROPER COOLANT LIGHT OPERATION

1. LIGHT ON WITH ENGINE RUNNING (ENG. TEMP. NORMAL)
   • DISCONNECT ORN ECM CONNECTOR
   • IGNITION ON

- LIGHT REMAINS ON → REPAIR SHORT IN CIRCUIT #35 BETWEEN ECM AND LIGHT
- LIGHT OFF → CHECK FOR FAULTY ECM CONNECTOR OR FAULTY ECM

2. NO LIGHT AT ANY TIME
   ARE THE "SERVICE SOON" AND "SERVICE NOW" LIGHTS WORKING

- YES → CHECK FAULTY BULB OR OPEN CIRCUIT #35 TO ECM
- NO → REPAIR OPEN IN 12V CIRCUIT #39

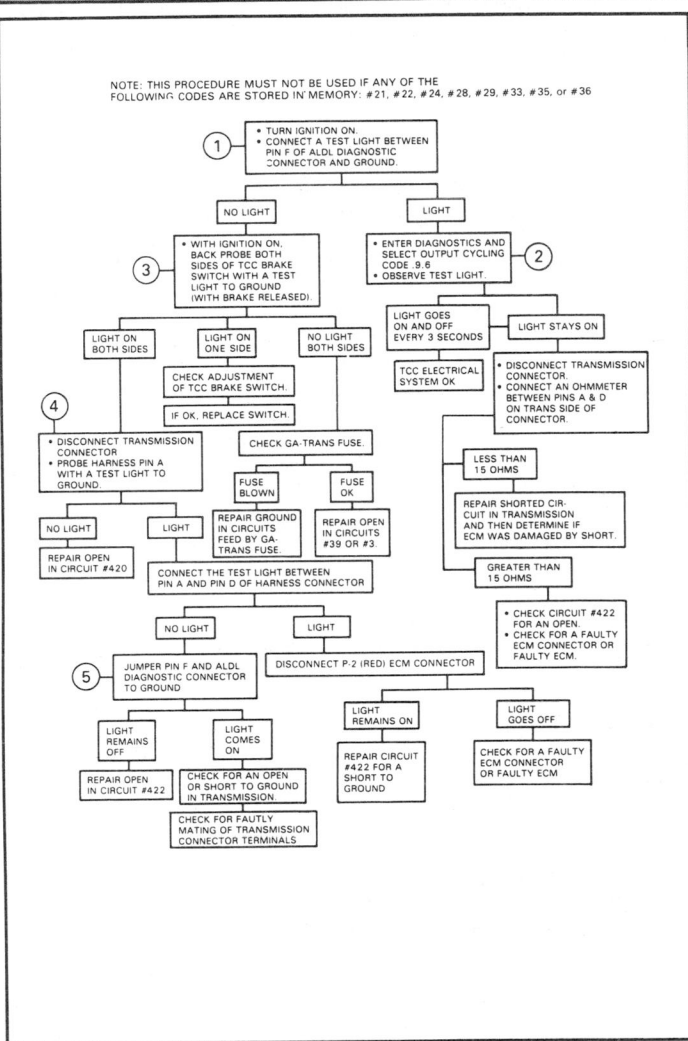

DFI CHART #16
TCC ELECTRICAL TEST

NOTE: THIS PROCEDURE MUST NOT BE USED IF ANY OF THE FOLLOWING CODES ARE STORED IN MEMORY: #21, #22, #24, #28, #29, #33, #35, or #36

1. • TURN IGNITION ON.
   • CONNECT A TEST LIGHT BETWEEN PIN F OF ALDL DIAGNOSTIC CONNECTOR AND GROUND.

- NO LIGHT
- LIGHT

3. • WITH IGNITION ON, BACK PROBE BOTH SIDES OF TCC BRAKE SWITCH WITH A TEST LIGHT TO GROUND (WITH BRAKE RELEASED).

2. • ENTER DIAGNOSTICS AND SELECT OUTPUT CYCLING CODE .9.6
   • OBSERVE TEST LIGHT.

- LIGHT ON BOTH SIDES
- LIGHT ON ONE SIDE → CHECK ADJUSTMENT OF TCC BRAKE SWITCH. IF OK, REPLACE SWITCH.
- NO LIGHT BOTH SIDES

- LIGHT GOES ON AND OFF EVERY 3 SECONDS → TCC ELECTRICAL SYSTEM OK
- LIGHT STAYS ON → • DISCONNECT TRANSMISSION CONNECTOR. CONNECT AN OHMMETER BETWEEN PINS A & D ON TRANS SIDE OF CONNECTOR.

4. • DISCONNECT TRANSMISSION CONNECTOR
   • PROBE HARNESS PIN A WITH A TEST LIGHT TO GROUND.

CHECK GA-TRANS FUSE.

- FUSE BLOWN → REPAIR GROUND IN CIRCUITS FEED BY GA-TRANS FUSE.
- FUSE OK → REPAIR OPEN IN CIRCUITS #39 OR #3.

- NO LIGHT → REPAIR OPEN IN CIRCUIT #420
- LIGHT

- LESS THAN 15 OHMS → REPAIR SHORTED CIRCUIT IN TRANSMISSION AND THEN DETERMINE IF ECM WAS DAMAGED BY SHORT.
- GREATER THAN 15 OHMS → • CHECK CIRCUIT #422 FOR AN OPEN. • CHECK FOR A FAULTY ECM CONNECTOR OR FAULTY ECM.

CONNECT THE TEST LIGHT BETWEEN PIN A AND PIN D OF HARNESS CONNECTOR

- NO LIGHT
- LIGHT → DISCONNECT P-2 (RED) ECM CONNECTOR

5. JUMPER PIN F AND ALDL DIAGNOSTIC CONNECTOR TO GROUND

- LIGHT REMAINS OFF → REPAIR OPEN IN CIRCUIT #422
- LIGHT COMES ON → CHECK FOR AN OPEN OR SHORT TO GROUND IN TRANSMISSION. CHECK FOR FAULTY MATING OF TRANSMISSION CONNECTOR TERMINALS

- LIGHT REMAINS ON → REPAIR CIRCUIT #422 FOR A SHORT TO GROUND
- LIGHT GOES OFF → CHECK FOR A FAULTY ECM CONNECTOR OR FAULTY ECM

CADILLAC ELECTRONIC FUEL INJECTION SYSTEM

General Information

Electronic Fuel Injection (EFI) precisely controlls the air/fuel mixture for combustion. This is accomplished by monitoring selected engine operating conditions, and electronically metering the fuel requirements to meet those conditions.

EFI basically involves electrically actuated fuel metering valves which, when actuated, spray a predetermined quantity of fuel into the engine.

This arrangement is commonly known as port injection. The injector opening is timed in accordance with the engine frequency so that the fuel charge is in place prior to the intake stroke for the cylinder.

Gasoline is supplied to the inlet of the injectors through the fuel rail at high enough pressure to obtain good fuel atomization and to prevent vapor formation the fuel system. When the solenoid operated valves are energized the injector metering valve (pintle) moves to the full open position and since the pressure differential across the valve is constant, the fuel quantity is changed by varying the time that the injector is held open by the computer.

The injectors could be energized all at one time (called continu-

Air induction system on Cadillac EFI system

ous injection) or one after the other in phase with the opening of each intake valve (called sequential injection) or they can be energized in groups.

The EFI System is a two-group system. In a two-group system, the eight injectors are divided into two groups of four each. Cylinders 1, 2, 7 and 8 form group 1 while group 2 consists of cylinders 3, 4, 5, and 6. All four injectors in a group are opened and closed simultaneously while the groups operate alternately.

The amount of air entering the engine is measured by monitoring the intake manifold absolute pressure, the inlet air temperature, and the engine speed (in rpm). This information, allows the electronic unit to compute the flow rate of air being inducted into the engine, and consequently, the flow rate of fuel required to achieve the desired air/fuel ratio for the particular engine operating condition. Each of the groups are activated once for every revolution of the camshaft and two revolutions of the crankshaft.

The input/output block diagram shown represents two group EFI system. In this system, the prevailing engine conditions are monitored with sensors and provide information to the Electronic Control Unit (ECU). The ECU converts the multi-variable input information into an injector pulse width which opens the injectors for the proper duration and at the proper time with respect to the cylinder firing sequence.

The object of the ECU is to calculate fuel requirements for the engine for various combinations of inputs from the sensors to determine an injector pulse width to provide accurate control of the air/fuel ratio.

Computer Input/Output Diagram

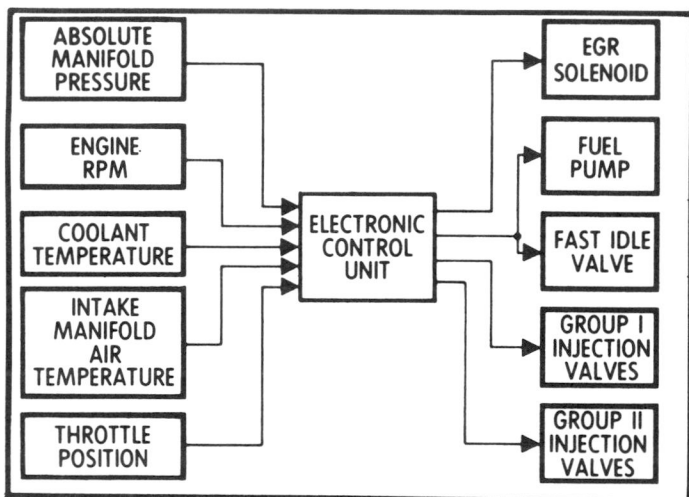

Electronic control system on Cadillac EFI system

FUEL SUPPLY SYSTEM

The fuel delivery system, includes an in-tank pump, a chassis-mounted constant-displacement fuel pump, a fuel filter, the fuel rails, one injector for each cylinder, a fuel pressure regulator, and supply and return lines. The fuel pumps are activated by the electronic control unit (ECU) when the ignition is turned on and the engine is cranking or operating. (If the engine stalls or if the starter is not engaged, the fuel pumps will deactivate in approximately one second.) Fuel is pumped from the fuel tank through the supply line and the filter to the fuel rails. The injectors supply fuel to the engine cylinders in precisely timed bursts as a result of electrical signals from the ECU. Excess fuel is returned to the fuel tank.

The fuel delivery system components are as follows:

Tank-Mounted Fuel Pump

Located inside the fuel tank and an integral part of the fuel gauge

Fuel delivery system on Cadillac EFI system

tank unit, the in-tank boost pump, used to supply fuel to the chassis mounted pump.

Chassis-Mounted Fuel Pump

The Chassis-Mounted Fuel Pump is a constant-displacement, roller-vane pump driven by a 12 volt motor. The pump incorporates a check valve to prevent backflow. This maintains fuel pressure when the pump is off. The pump has a flow rate of 33 gallons per hour under normal operating conditions (39 PSI). An internal relief valve provides over-pressure protection by opening at an excessive pressure.

Fuel Pressure Regulator

The Fuel Pressure Regulator contains an air chamber and fuel chamber separated by a spring-loaded diaphragm. The air chamber is connected by a rubber hose to the throttle body assembly. The pressure in this chamber is identical to the pressure of the intake manifold. The changing manifold pressure and the spring, control the action of the diaphragm valve, opening or closing an orifice in the fuel chamber. (Excess fuel is returned to the fuel tank.) This regulator, being connected to the fuel rail and intake manifold, maintains a constant 39 psi differential across the injectors.

ENGINE SENSORS

The sensors are electrically connected to the Electronic Control Unit and all operate independently of each other. Each sensor transmits a signal to the ECU, relating a specific engine operating condition. The ECU analyzes all the signals and transmits the appropriate commands.

Manifold Absolute Pressure Sensor

The Manifold Absolute Pressure (MAP) Sensor monitors the changes in intake manifold pressure which result from engine load, speed and barometric pressure variations. These pressure changes are supplied to the electronic control unit circuitry in the form of electrical signals. The sensor also monitors the changes in the intake manifold pressure due to changes in altitude. As intake manifold pressure increases, additional fuel is required. The MAP sensor sends this information to the ECU so that the pulse width will be increased. Conversely as manifold pressure decreases the pulse width will be shortened.

The sensor is mounted within the electronic control unit. A manifold pressure line, routed with the engine harness, connects it to the front of the throttle body.

Throttle Position switch

The Throttle Position Switch, is mounted to the throttle body and connected to the throttle valve shaft. Movements of the accelerator causes the throttle shaft to rotate (opening or closing the throttle blades). The switch senses the shaft movement and position (closed throttle, wide open throttle, or position changes), and transmits

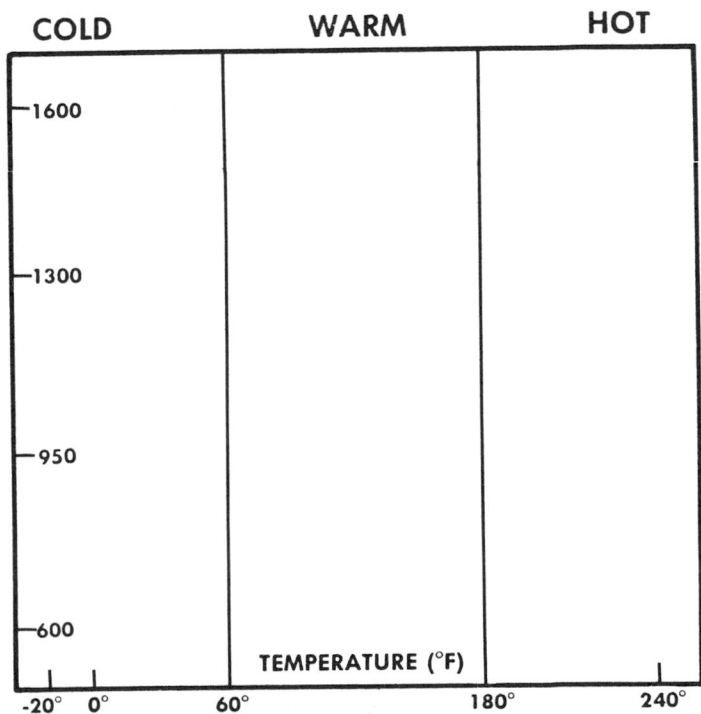

Normal fuel pressure on Cadillac EFI system

appropriate electrical signals to the electronic control unit. The electronic control unit processes these signals to determine the fuel requirements for the particular situation.

Temperature Sensors

The Temperature Sensors, (Coolant and Air) are comprised of a coil of high temperature nickel wire sealed into an epoxy case, and molded into a brass housing with two wires and a connector extending from the body. The resistance of the wire changes as a function of temperature. Low temperature provides low resistance and as temperatures increase, so does resistance. The voltage drop across each sensor is monitored by the ECU.

Speed Sensor

The Speed Sensor, is incorporated within the ignition distributor assembly (HEI). It consists of two components. The first has two reed switches mounted to a plastic housing. The housing is affixed to the distributor shaft housing. The second is a rotor with two magnets, attached to and rotating with the distributor shaft.

The rotor rotates past the reed switches causing them to open and close. This provides two types of information: synchronization of the ECU and the proper injector group with the intake valve timing (phasing); and engine rpm for fuel scheduling.

ELECTRONIC CONTROL UNIT

The Electronic Control Unit, is a pre-programmed analog computer. The ECU is electrically connected to the vehicle power supply and the other EFI components by a harness that is routed through the firewall.

The ECU receives power from the vehicle battery when the ignition is set to the ON or CRANK position. During cranking and engine operation, the following events occur.

The following information is received from the EFI sensors:
1. Engine coolant temperature
2. Intake manifold air temperature

Temperature sensor resistance characteristics on Cadillac EFI system

645

Wiring diagram showing cranking signal circuit on Cadillac EFI system

3. Intake manifold absolute pressure
4. Engine speed and firing position
5. Throttle position and change of position
The following commands are transmitted by the ECU:
1. Electric fuel pump activation
2. Fast idle valve activation
3. Injection valve activation
4. EGR solenoid activation
5. Vacuum retard solenoid activation (California Seville and Eldorado only)

The desired air/fuel ratios for various driving and atmospheric conditions are designed into the ECU. As the above signals are received from the sensors, the ECU processes the signals and computes the engines fuel requirements. The ECU issues commands to the injection valves to open for a specific time duration. The duration of the command pulses varies as the operating conditions change. All injection valves in each group open simultaneously upon command.

Removal

1. Disconnect negative battery cable.
2. Remove three climate control outlet grilles right, left and right center.
3. Working through outlet openings, remove 3 fasteners securing pad to instrument panel support.
4. Remove screws securing pad to instrument panel horizontal support.
5. Pull pad outward and disconnect electrical connector from windshield wiper switch.
6. Remove pad.

NOTE: To facilitate removal or installation, place shift lever in lo range and, on cars equipped with tilt wheel, place wheel in lowest position.

7. Remove MAP sensor hose.
8. Remove three mounting screws holding ECU in position (one in front, two at side bracket, and remove ECU.

CADILLAC ELECTRONIC FUEL INJECTION SYSTEM DIAGNOSIS

THE PROBLEM	THE CAUSE
Engine Cranks But Will Not Start/Il Not Start	(NOTE: The following problems assume that the rest of the car electrical system is functioning properly.) 1. Blown 10 amp in-line fuel pump fuse located below instrument panel near ECU connectors.* 2. Open circuit in 12 purple wire between starter solenoid and ECU. 3. Open circuit in 18 dark green wire between generator "BAT" terminal and ECU (fusible link).* 4. Poor connection at ECU jumper harness (below instrument panel) or at ECU. 5. Poor connection at fuel pump jumper harness (below instrument panel near ECU), 14 dark green wire.* 6. Poor connection at engine coolant sensor or open circuit in sensor or wiring (cold engine only).** 7. Poor connection at distributor trigger (speed sensor). 8. Distributor trigger (speed sensor) stuck closed. 9. Malfunction in chassis-mounted pump. 10. Malfunction in throttle position switch (W.O.T. section shorted). To check, disconnect switch—engine should start. 11. Fuel flow restriction.
Hard Starting	1. Open engine coolant sensor (cold or partially warm engine only—starts ok hot).** 2. Malfunction in throttle position switch (W.O.T. section shorted). To check, disconnect switch—Engine should start normally. 3. Malfunction in chassis-mounted fuel pump. (Check valves leaking back). 4. Malfunction in pressure regulator.
Poor Fuel Economy	1. Disconnected or leaking MAP sensor hose. 2. Disconnected vacuum hose at fuel pressure regulator or at throttle body. 3. Malfunction of air or coolan sensor.***
Engine Stalls After Start	1. Open circuit in 12 black/yellow ignition signal wire between fuse block and ECU or poor connection at connector (12 black/yellow wire) located below instrument panel near ECU. 2. Poor connection at engine coolant sensor or open circuit in sensor or wiring (cold or warm engine only).**
Rough Idle	1. Disconnected, leaking or pinched MAP sensor hose. If plastic harness line requires replacement, replace entire EFI engine harness. 2. Poor connection at air or coolant sensor or open circuit in sensor or wiring (cold engine only).** 3. Poor connection at injection valve(s). 4. Shorted engine coolant sensor.*** 5. Speed sensor harness located to close to secondary ignition wires.
Prolonged Fast Idle	1. Poor connection at fast idle valve or open circuit in heating element. 2. Throttle position switch misadjusted. 3. Vacuum Leak.
No Fast Idle	1. Bent fast idle valve micro switch causing heater to malfunction and drive valve section down to locked closed position.
Engine Hesitates or Stumbles on Acceleration	1. Disconnected, leaking on pinched MAP sensor hose. If plastic harness line requires replacement, replace entire EFI engine harness. 2. Throttle position switch misadjusted. 3. Malfunction in throttle position switch. 4. Intermittent malfunction in distributor trigger (speed sensor). 5. Poor connection at 6 pin connector of ECU. 6. Poor connection at EGR solenoid or open solenoid (cold engine only).
Lack of High Speed Performance	1. Misadjusted throttle position switch (W.O.T. only). 2. Malfunction in throttle position switch. 3. Malfunction of chassis-mounted fuel pump. 4. Intermittent malfunction in distributor trigger (speed sensor). 5. Fuel filter blocked or restricted. 6. Open circuit in 12 purple wire between starter solenoid and ECU.

*To check, listen for chassis-mounted fuel pump "Whine" (one second only) as key is turned to "ON" position (not to "START" position).

**To check for an "open" circuit in an EFI temperature sensor, connect an ohmmeter to the sensor connector terminals. If the sensor resistance is greater than 1600 ohms, replace the sensor.

***To check for a "closed" (short) circuit in an EFI temperature sensor, connect an ohmmeter to the sensor connector terminals. If the sensor resistance is less than 700 ohms, replace the sensor.

9. Remove electrical connectors ECU.

Installation

1. Connect electrical harness to ECU.
2. Position ECU with electrical connectors on right side of car and install three mounting screws.
3. Install MAP sensor hose.
4. Position pad to instrument panel and connect electrical connector for wiper switch.
5. Install screws securing pad to instrument panel horizontal support.
6. Working through climate control outlet openings, install 3 fasteners securing pad to instrument panel support.
7. Install air outlet grilles as described in Section 1, Note.
8. Connect negative battery cable.

Component Removal

THROTTLE BODY ASSEMBLY

Removal

1. Remove air cleaner.
2. Disconnect throttle return springs (2) from throttle lever.
3. Remove retainer and remove cruise control chain from throttle lever on cars so equipped.
4. Remove "hairpin" clip and disconnect throttle cable from throttle lever.
5. Remove left rear throttle body mounting screw and remove one screw holding throttle bracket to intake manifold.
6. Disengage downshift switch from throttle lever and position bracket, switch and linkage out of way.
7. Disconnect throttle position switch electrical connector and fast idle valve electrical connector. Slide fast idle valve wiring out of notch in throttle body.
8. Remove vacuum hoses from nipples on throttle body. Use back-up wrench when removing power brake vacuum line.
9. Remove remaining throttle body mounting screws and remove throttle body.
10. Remove gasket material from intake manifold and bottom of throttle body. Clean all foreign material from area around intake manifold throttle bores.
11. The following parts are not included in a new throttle body assembly and should be removed as necessary:
    a. Throttle position switch.
    b. Fast idle valve seat.
    c. Fast idle valve spring.
    d. Fast idle valve.
    e. Fast idle valve heater assembly.
    f. Power brake vacuum fitting.

Installation

1. Position a new throttle body gasket to intake manifold with identification tab on left.
2. Install throttle position switch to right side of throttle body, and adjust switch.
3. Position throttle body to intake manifold and loosely install both front and right rear mounting screws.
4. Move throttle linkage bracket into position over left rear mounting screw and install throttle body mounting screw.
5. Install one additional bracket mounting screw and torque screws 4–15 ft. lbs. Adjust transmission downshift.
6. Position throttle cable to throttle lever and secure with "hairpin" clip. Check for proper operation and wide-open-throttle.
7. Position cruise control chain to throttle lever and secure with clip on cars so equipped. Check for proper operation.
8. Install power brake vacuum fitting to rear of throttle body and tighten securely. Use back-up wrench.
9. Install throttle return springs (2) between throttle lever and

pressure regulator bracket with open end of spring on outside of throttle lever.
10. Install vacuum hoses to appropriate nipples on throttle body.
11. Install fast idle valve.
12. Install air cleaner.

THROTTLE POSITION SWITCH

Removal

1. Remove throttle body as described earlier in this section.
2. Remove two mounting screws and remove switch from throttle body.

Installation

1. Install throttle position switch to right side of throttle body so that tab on switch engages flat on throttle shaft.
2. Install two mounting screws and tighten screws so that switch will still move but is not loose.
3. Adjust throttle position switch.
4. Install throttle body.

Adjustment

1. Loosen two throttle position switch mounting screws to permit rotation of the switch.
2. Hold the throttle valves in the idle position while performing step 3 and 4.
3. Turn the throttle position switch carefully counterclockwise until the end-stop has been reached.
4. Tighten throttle position switch mounting screws to 11 in. lbs.
5. Check to insure that throttle valves close to the throttle stop. If not, repeat steps 2, 3 and 4.

FAST IDLE VALVE

Removal

1. Remove air cleaner and disconnect electrical connector from fast idle valve heater.
2. Remove air cleaner stud.
3. To remove fast idle valve heater, push down and twist 90° counter clockwise.
4. Remove fast idle valve, spring and seat from position in throttle body.

Installation

1. Install fast idle valve seat, spring and valve in position in throttle body.
2. Position heater on top of fast idle valve and push down to compress spring. Care should be taken to avoid damaging microswitch contact arm on bottom of heater housing.
3. Align tabs on fast idle valve heater with cut-out portion of throttle body and compress spring further.
4. Rotate heater 90° clockwise to secure in position.
5. Connect electrical connector.
6. Install air cleaner stud and air cleaner.

———————CAUTION———————

Do not loosen fittings until all precautions have been taken to relieve pressure. Fuel in system may be under high pressure which could spray out and result in a fire hazard and possible personal injury.

INJECTION VALVE

Removal

1. Remove front and rear fuel rails.
2. Remove electrical conduit from injector brackets 4 places each side.

3. Remove screws holding each injector bracket to intake manifold and remove brackets and grommets.

4. Disconnect electrical lead from all injectors on fuel rail being removed.

5. Remove fuel rail and injectors from engine as a unit. Some injectors will stick in fuel rail while others may remain in manifold.

6. Remove injectors from fuel rail and from intake manifold as required.

7. Injection valves are sealed by O-rings at both fuel rail and intake manifold. Remove and discard all used O-rings.

—CAUTION—

EFI fuel injectors can be damaged by full battery voltage (12v). Using the battery to apply test voltage will destroy the injector coil within 1/2 second.

Installation

1. Lubricate and install a new O-ring on the fuel rail end of each injector.

2. Install injectors into fuel rail with electrical connector facing inboard.

NOTE: **Fuel rails are specific for right and left sides of engine.**

3. Lubricate and install a new O-ring into each injector port in the intake manifold.

4. Install fuel rail-injector assembly to intake manifold making sure that each injector is properly installed in manifold O-ring.

5. Install rubber grommets on fuel rail (flange down) and install injector brackets in position.

6. Secure each bracket with two screws.

7. Route electrical harness along bracket and secure to brackets—4 positions.

8. Connect injector leads as follows:
Front cylinder—red/black wires
Front-center cylinder—black/white wires
Rear-center cylinder—black/white wires
Rear cylinder—red/black wires

NOTE: **Injectors may be rotated to provide proper harness routing.**

9. Repeat steps 1 thru 8 for opposite side if necessary.

10. Install front and rear fuel rails.

11. Turn ignition ON and OFF several times to build up fuel rail pressure and check for fuel leaks.

12. Start engine and check for leaks.

NOTE: **A "dry" fuel system on cars equipped with EFI may require a substantial cranking period.**

FUEL PRESSURE REGULATOR

Removal

1. Remove vacuum hose from nipple on top of pressure regulator.

2. Remove and discard clamps securing flexible fuel hose connecting regulator to fuel rail. Remove return line.

3. Remove one nut securing pressure regulator to bracket.

NOTE: **This nut has metric threads**

4. Work regulator off of flexible fuel hose and out of bracket.

Installation

1. Install new hose clamp over flexible fuel hose.

2. Position regulator to bracket and work flexible fuel hose to fuel rail over nipple on side of regulator. Secure to bracket with one nut.

NOTE: **This nut has metric threads. Use the nut supplied with each new regulator or the nut removed.**

3. Connect return line to fitting on end of regulator.

4. Tighten clamps, securing flexible fuel hose to regulator.

5. Install vacuum hose to remaining nipple on pressure regulator.

6. A "dry" fuel system on cars with EFI may require a substantial cranking period before starting.

FUEL RAIL

Front—Removal

1. Remove and discard hose clamp securing pressure regulator hose to front fuel rail.

2. Using a back-up wrench at side rail fitting, remove flare nut from each end of fuel rail.

3. Disengage front rail from pressure regulator hose and remove from vehicle.

Front—Installation

1. Install new hose clamp over flexible hose.

2. Position front rail to pressure regulator hose and force hose over nipple.

3. Move rail into position and tighten flare nut into fitting on each side rail to *Use a back-up wrench to hold side rail fittings.* Do *not* use teflon tape on flare nuts.

4. Tighten hose clamp securing pressure regulator hose to rail.

5. Turn ignition ON and OFF several times to build up fuel rail pressure and check for fuel leaks.

Rear—Removal

1. Using a back-up wrench on fuel rail remove fuel inlet line from rear rail.

2. Using a back-up wrench on fuel rail, remove nut at each side rail and remove rear fuel rail.

Rear—Installation

1. Position rear fuel rail and thread flare nuts into side rails. Do *not* use teflon tape on flare nuts.

2. Thread fuel inlet line flare nut into rear rail. Do *not* use teflon on flare nut.

3. *Using a back-up wrench on fuel rail,* tighten flare nuts.

4. Turn ignition ON and OFF several times to build up fuel rail pressure and check for fuel leaks.

NOTE: **Right or Left side fuel rail removal is the same as injector removal.**

FUEL FILTER

The fuel filter element is replaced by unscrewing the bottom cover and removing the filter element. Replace element and gasket with AC type GF 157 or equivalent. Hand tighten bottom cover.

A "Dry" fuel system on cars equipped with EFI may require a substantial cranking period before starting.

CHASSIS-MOUNTED FUEL PUMP

Removal and Installation

The chassis-mounted pump is located forward of the rear wheel along the frame side rail. The mounting nuts have metric threads. Peel back rubber boot and remove two nuts, one from each electrical terminal. Remove electrical leads. Reinstall in reverse order, making sure all connections are tight.

TANK FUEL PUMP

Removal

1. Remove fuel inlet and outlet hoses from nipples on pump.

2. Remove locknuts securing fuel gauge tank unit and fuel pump feed wires to tank unit.

3. Position fuel tank sending unit remover and installer J-24187 on cam locking ring so that tool engages three tabs on ring.

4. Install ratchet and turn counter clockwise to disengage lock ring from fuel tank. Remove tool and lift gauge-pump unit from tank.

Installation

1. Install gage-pump unit in fuel tank, using new gasket.

2. Install fuel tank sending unit remover and installer J-24187 so that it engages three tabs on cam locking ring.

3. Turn clockwise until locking rings is fully engaged in fuel tank.

4. Connect electrical leads to fuel gauge and secure with locknut.

5. Position tank near underbody and attach fuel pump lead wire (14 green) to terminal marked "pump".

6. Move tank to underbody; position fuel tank support straps under tank and loosely install screws securing straps to body.

7. Secure ground wire to rear cross member.

8. Tighten tank strap screws until bottomed. Torque to 25 ft. lbs.

9. Connect fuel line, evaporative loss control system line and return line to fittings at front of tank. Secure with new clamps.

10. Lower car.

11. With fuel filler door open, connect sending unit feed wire (tan).

12. Replace drained fuel in tank.

13. A "dry" fuel system on cars equipped with EFI may require a substantial cranking period before starting.

AIR TEMPERATURE SENSOR

Removal and Installation

1. Locate air temperature sensor at right rear of intake manifold and disconnect sensor from car harness.

2. Remove sensor from intake manifold.

3. Apply a non-hardening sealer to threads of sensor and install sensor in intake manifold.

4. Tighten sensor to 15 ft. lbs.

5. Connect air temperature sensor connector to car harness.

COOLANT TEMPERATURE SENSOR

Removal and Installation

1. Drain radiator until coolant level is below level of cylinder heads.

2. Locate water temperature sensor in heater hose outlet at rear of right hand cylinder head, and disconnect sensor from car harness.

3. Remove sensor from position in heater hose.

4. Apply a non-hardening sealer to threads of sensor and install sensor in heater hose outlet fitting.

5. Tighten sensor to 15 ft. lbs.

6. Connect coolant temperature sensor connector to car harness.

7. Fill cooling system to proper level.

Vacuum circuits on early DeVille, Fleetwood and Eldorado (Federal)

Vacuum circuits on early Seville and all California models

Vacuum circuits on late Seville models

651

Vacuum circuits on late DeVille models (Federal)

Vacuum circuits on late DeVille models (California)

MANIFOLD VACUUM

PORTED VACUUM

CANISTER PURGE

DISTRIBUTOR

CAR VACUUM HARNESS

POWER BRAKE BOOSTER

TRANSMISSION MODULATOR

THROTTLE BODY

FUEL PRESSURE REGULATOR

VENT

EGR SOLENOID

PCV VALVE

MAP SENSOR

EXHAUST PRESSURE TRANSDUCER

EGR VALVE

AIR PUMP DIVERTER VALVE

Vacuum circuits on late Eldorado models (Federal)

CANISTER PURGE

SPARK DELAY SOLENOID

DISTRIBUTOR

POWER BRAKE BOOSTER

VENT

M C
D
DISTRIBUTOR TVS (220°F)

CAR VACUUM HARNESS

THROTTLE BODY

FUEL PRESSURE REGULATOR

TRANSMISSION MODULATOR

VENT

EGR SOLENOID

PCV VALVE

MANIFOLD VACUUM

PORTED VACUUM

EGR VALVE

MAP SENSOR

EXHAUST PRESSURE TRANSDUCER

AIR PUMP DIVERTER VALVE

Vacuum circuits on late Eldorado models (California)

MANIFOLD VACUUM
PORTED VACUUM

EGR VALVE

EXHAUST BACKPRESSURE TRANSDUCER

CANISTER PURGE

BOOSTER POWER BRAKE

CAR VACUUM HARNESS

CAP

THROTTLE BODY

DISTRIBUTOR

FUEL PRESSURE REGULATOR

VENT

TRANSMISSION MODULATOR

EGR SOLENOID

PCV VALVE

MAP SENSOR

FUEL ECONOMY SWITCH

AIR PUMP DIVERTER VALVE

Vacuum circuits on late Seville models (Federal)

MANIFOLD VACUUM
PORTED VACUUM

EGR VALVE

EXHAUST PRESSURE TRANSDUCER

CAR VACUUM HARNESS

CANISTER PURGE

TRANSMISSION

ADVANCE

THROTTLE BODY

FUEL PRESSURE REGULATOR

VENT

DISTRIBUTOR TVS (220°F)

RETARD

EGR SOLENOID

PCV VALVE

D

C   MT

VENT SOLENOID

MAP SENSOR

ECONOMY SWITCH

AIR PUMP DIVERTER VALVE

Vacuum circuits on late Seville models (California)

Diagnosis and Testing

The diagnostic tree charts are designed to help solve problems on fuel injected vehicles by leading the user through closely defined conditions and tests so that only the most likely components, vacuum and electrical circuits are checked for proper operation when troubleshooting a particular malfunction. By using the trouble trees to eliminate those systems and components which normally will not cause the condition described, a problem can be isolated within one or more systems or circuits without wasting time on unnecessary testing. Experience has shown that most problems tend to be the result of a fairly simple and obvious cause, such as loose or corroded connectors or air leaks in the intake system; making careful inspection of components during testing essential to quick and accurate troubleshooting. Frequent references to the Electronic Fuel Injection Analyzer J-25400 will be found in the text and in the diagnosis charts. This device or its compatible equivalent is necessary to perform some of the more complicated test procedures listed, but many of the electronic fuel injection components can be functionally tested with the quick checks outlined in the "On-Car Service" procedures. Aftermarket testers are available from a variety of sources, as well as from the manufacturer, but care should be taken that the test equipment being used is designed to diagnose this particular system accurately without damaging the control unit (ECU) or components being tested.

NOTE: Some test procedures incorporate other engine systems in addition to the EFI, since many conditions are the result of something other than the fuel injection system itself. Electrical and vacuum circuits are at the back of this section to help identify small changes incorporated into later models that may affect the diagnosis results. Circuit numbers are given whenever possible.

Because of the specific nature of the conditions listed in the diagnosis procedures, it's important to understand exactly what the definitions of various problems are:

• STALLS—engine stops running at idle or when driving. Determine if the stalling condition is only present when the engine is either hot or cold, or if it happens consistently regardless of operating temperature.

• LOADS UP—engine misses due to excessively rich mixture. This usually occurs during cold engine operation and is characterized by black smoke from the tailpipe.

• ROUGH IDLE—engine runs unevenly at idle. This condition can range from a slight stumble or miss up to a severe shake.

• TIP IN STUMBLE—a delay or hesitation in engine response when accelerating from idle with the car at a standstill. Some slight hesitation conditions are considered normal when they only occur during cold operation and gradually vanish as the engine warms up.

• MISFIRE—rough engine operation due to a lack of combustion in one or more cylinders. Fouled spark plugs or loose ignition wires are the most common cause.

• HESITATION—a delay in engine response when accelerating from cruise or steady throttle operation at road speed. Not to be confused with the tip in stumble described above.

• SAG—engine responds initially, then flattens out or slows down before recovering. Severe sags can cause the engine to stall.

• SURGE—engine power variation under steady throttle or cruise. Engine will speed up or slow down with no change in the throttle position. Can happen at a variety of speeds.

• SLUGGISH—engine delivers limited power under load or at high speeds. Engine loses speed going up hills, doesn't accelerate as fast as normal, or has less top speed than was noted previously.

• CUTS OUT—temporary complete loss of power at sharp, irregular intervals. May occur repeatedly or intermittently, but is usually worse under heavy acceleration.

• POOR FUEL ECONOMY—significantly lower gas mileage than is considered normal for the model and drive-train in question. Always perform a careful mileage test under a variety of road conditions to determine the severity of the problem before attempting corrective measures. Fuel economy is influenced more by external conditions, such as driving habits and terrain, than by a minor malfunction in the fuel injection system that doesn't cause another problem (like rough operation).

Stall After Start—Hot or Hot Stall

Stall After Start—Cold

Hard Start—Cold

No Start

Stalls While Driving—Immediate Restart (Intermit.)

Hard Start—Hot

Tip-In Stumble

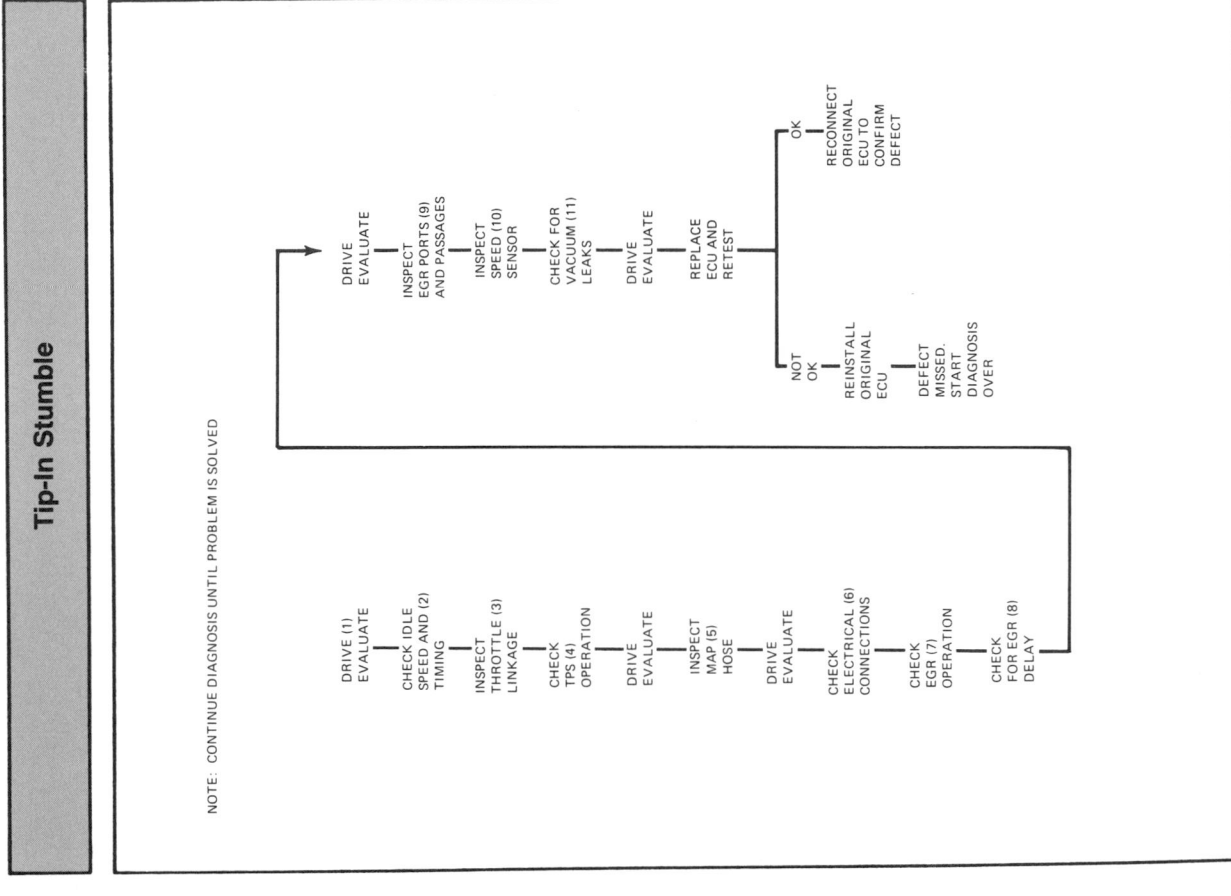

NOTE: CONTINUE DIAGNOSIS UNTIL PROBLEM IS SOLVED

DRIVE EVALUATE (1) → CHECK IDLE SPEED AND TIMING (2) → INSPECT THROTTLE LINKAGE (3) → CHECK TPS (4) OPERATION → DRIVE EVALUATE → INSPECT MAP (5) HOSE → DRIVE EVALUATE → CHECK ELECTRICAL (6) CONNECTIONS → CHECK EGR (7) OPERATION → CHECK FOR EGR (8) DELAY

DRIVE EVALUATE → INSPECT EGR PORTS (9) AND PASSAGES → INSPECT SPEED (10) SENSOR → CHECK FOR VACUUM (11) LEAKS → DRIVE EVALUATE → REPLACE ECU AND RETEST

OK → RECONNECT ORIGINAL ECU TO CONFIRM DEFECT

NOT OK → REINSTALL ORIGINAL ECU → DEFECT MISSED. START DIAGNOSIS OVER

Stalls While Driving—No Immediate Restart (Intermit.)

INSTALL ANALYZER (1) AND FUEL PRESSURE GAGE → DRIVE CAR UNTIL STALL (2) DEVELOPS

OTHER FACTORS OK → CHECK EGR (9) VALVE → CHECK FOR (11) HEI MALFUNCTIONS

FUEL (4) PRESSURE LOW

FUEL PUMP LIGHT ON → CYCLE IGNITION SWITCH (5) AND NOTE FUEL PUMP OPERATION

PUMP OPERATES → INSPECT FUEL (7) LINE → DEFECT FOUND → REPAIR AND RETEST

NO DEFECT FOUND → REPLACE IN-TANK (8) PUMP

FUEL PUMP LIGHT OFF → PERFORM ANALYZER (10) STEP 2

PUMP DOES NOT OPERATE → CHECK FOR 12V AT (6) PUMP

VOLTAGE → REPLACE CHASSIS PUMP

NO VOLTAGE → REPAIR AND RETEST

DEFECT FOUND → REPAIR AND RETEST

OK

NOT OK

OK → REPLACE ECU AND RETEST

OK → RECONNECT ORIGINAL ECU TO CONFIRM DEFECT

NOT OK → REINSTALL ORIGINAL ECU → DEFECT MISSED. START DIAGNOSIS OVER

GROUP LIGHT (3) INDICATES MALFUNCTION → REPLACE ECU AND RETEST

OK → RECONNECT ORIGINAL ECU TO CONFIRM DEFECT

NOT OK → REINSTALL ORIGINAL ECU → DEFECT MISSED. START DIAGNOSIS OVER

TRIGGER LIGHTS (3) INDICATE MALFUNCTION → REPLACE SPEED SENSOR

Rich Operation—Black Smoke From Tailpipe

Surge (Lean Operation)

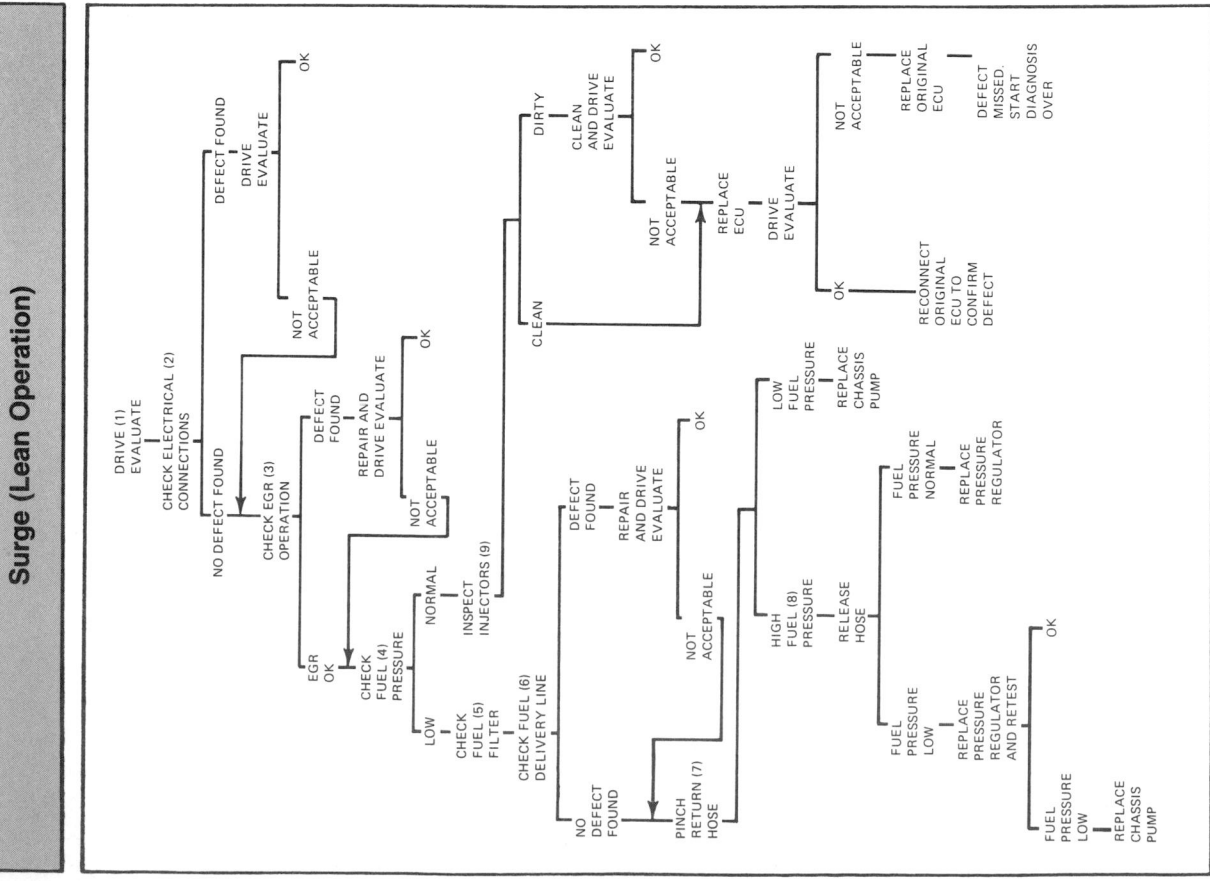

Rough Idle

Hesitation

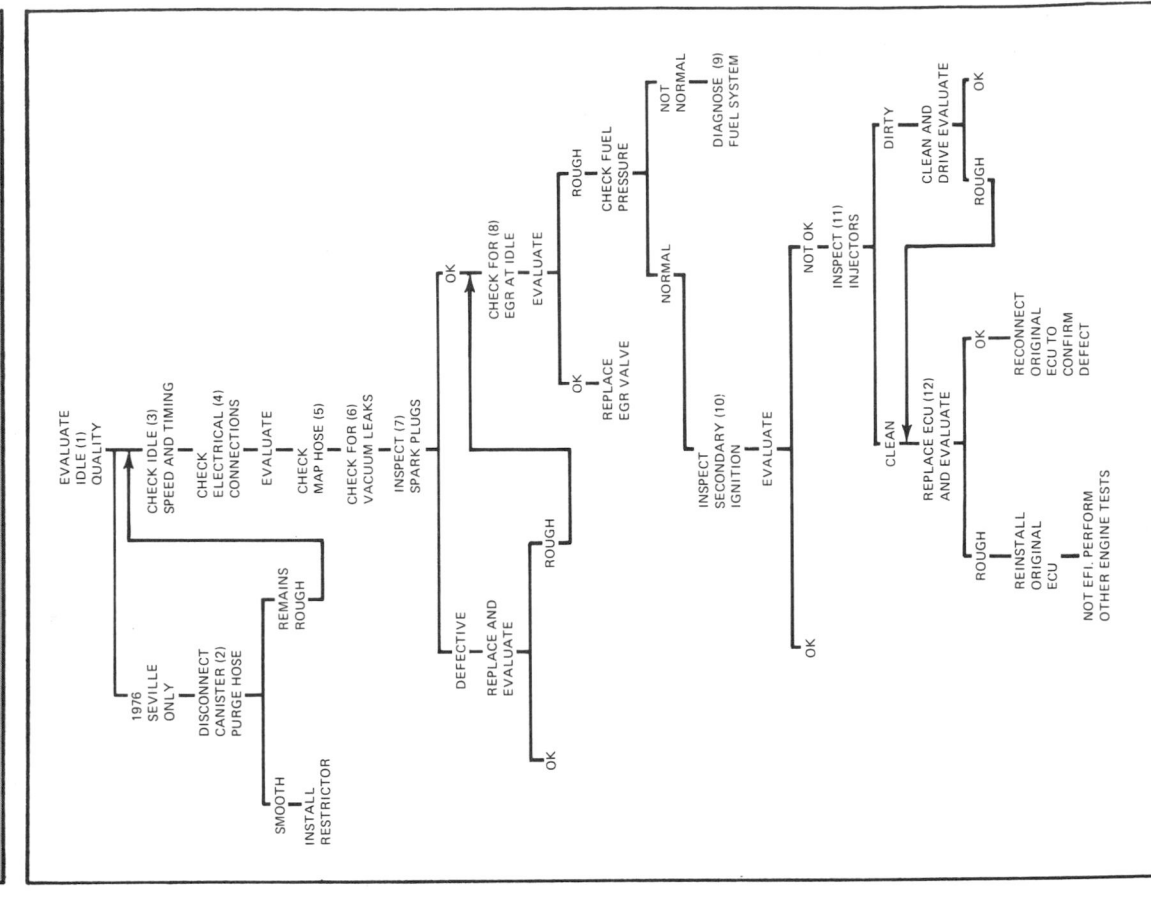

Misfire On Light Acceleration

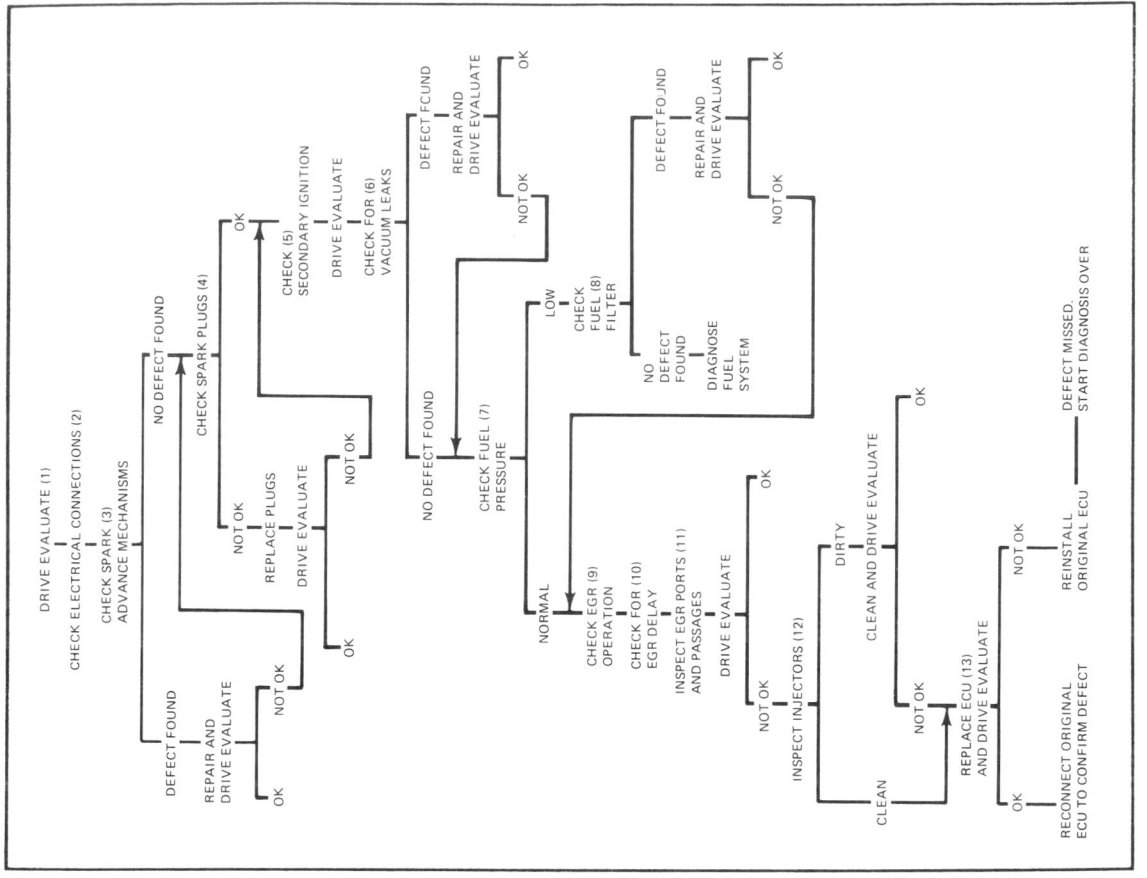

Idle Speed Change

Poor Cold Driveability

No Fast Idle

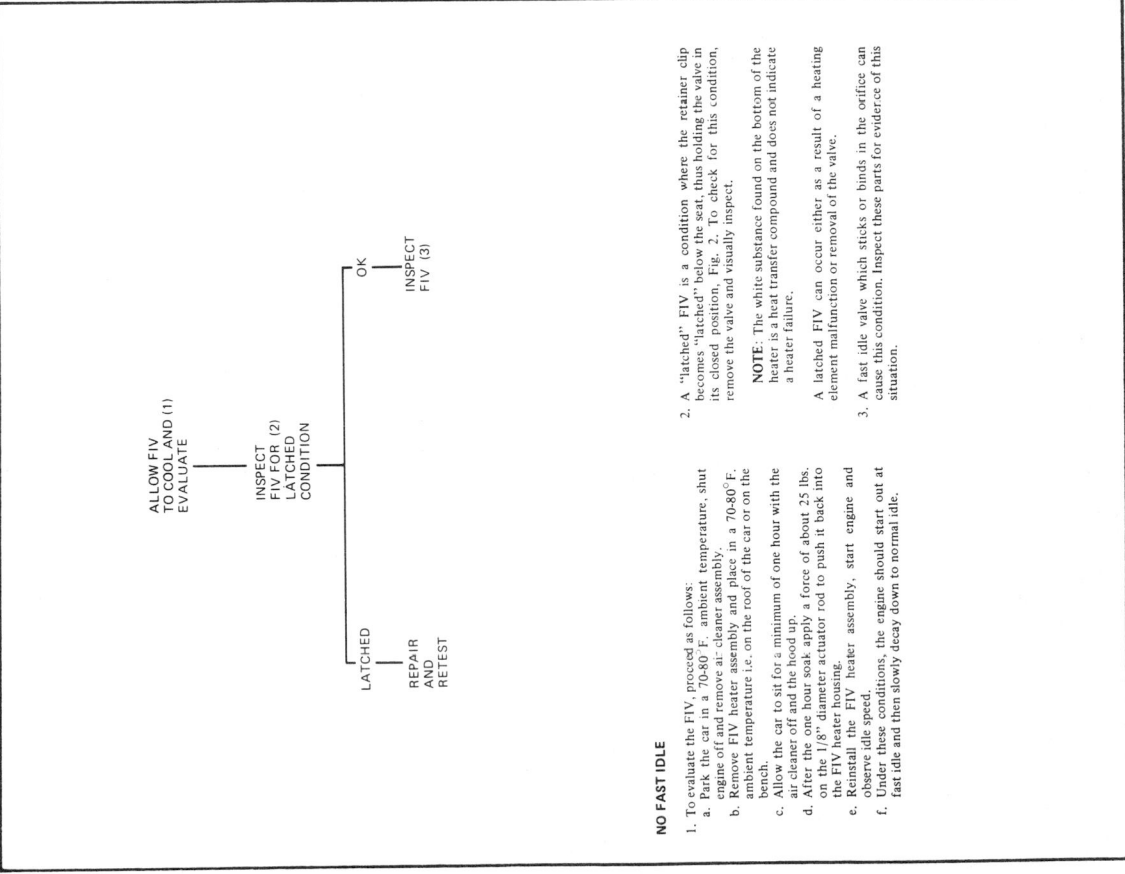

NO FAST IDLE

1. To evaluate the FIV, proceed as follows:
   a. Park the car in a 70-80° F. ambient temperature, shut engine off and remove air cleaner assembly.
   b. Remove FIV heater assembly and place in a 70-80° F. ambient temperature i.e. on the roof of the car or on the bench.
   c. Allow the car to sit for a minimum of one hour with the air cleaner off and the hood up.
   d. After the one hour soak apply a force of about 25 lbs. on the 1/8" diameter actuator rod to push it back into the FIV heater housing.
   e. Reinstall the FIV heater assembly, start engine and observe idle speed.
   f. Under these conditions, the engine should start out at fast idle and then slowly decay down to normal idle.

2. A "latched" FIV is a condition where the retainer clip becomes "latched" below the seat, thus holding the valve in its closed position, Fig. 2. To check for this condition, remove the valve and visually inspect.

   NOTE: The white substance found on the bottom of the heater is a heat transfer compound and does not indicate a heater failure.

   A latched FIV can occur either as a result of a heating element malfunction or removal of the valve.

3. A fast idle valve which sticks or binds in the orifice can cause this condition. Inspect these parts for evidence of this situation.

Cuts Out At Wide Open Throttle

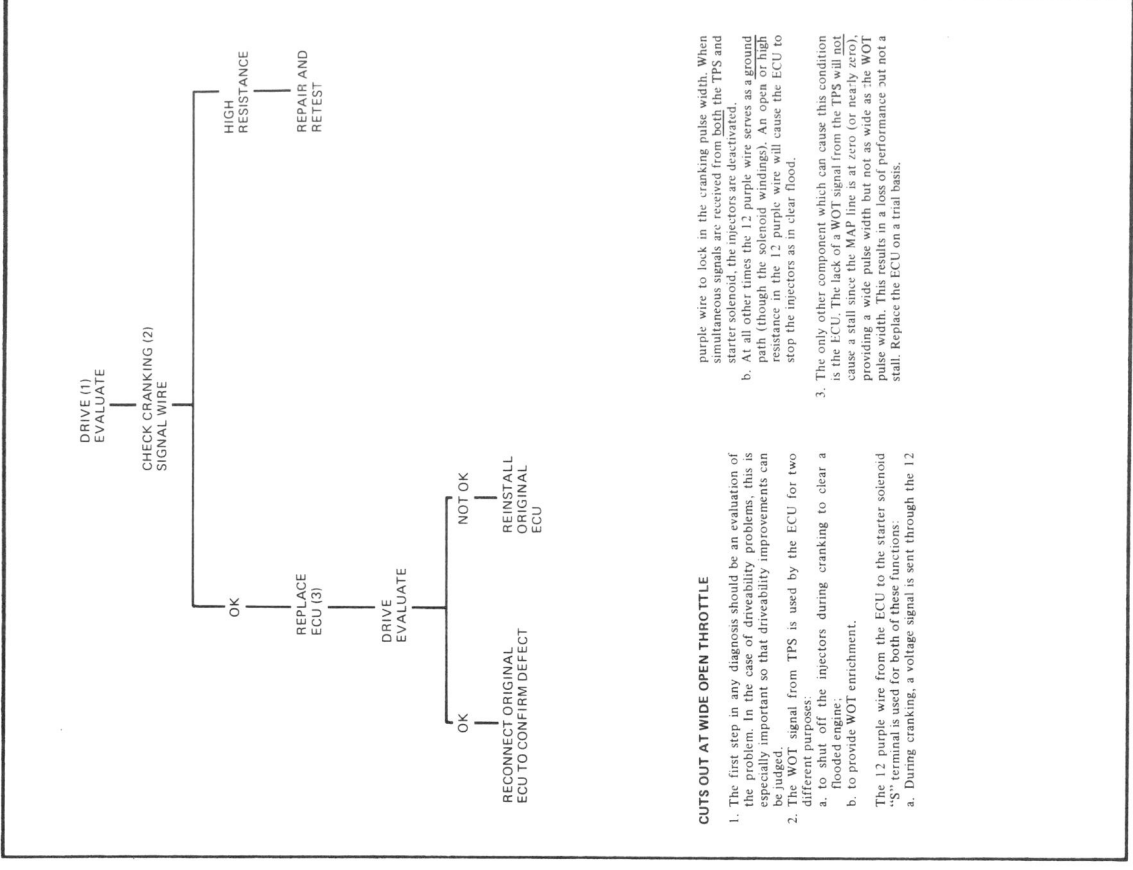

purple wire to lock in the cranking pulse width. When simultaneous signals are received from both the TPS and starter solenoid, the injectors are deactivated.

b. At all other times the 12 purple wire serves as a ground path (though the solenoid windings). An open or high resistance in the 12 purple wire will cause the ECU to stop the injectors as in clear flood.

3. The only other component which can cause this condition is the ECU. The lack of a WOT signal from the TPS will not cause a stall since the MAP line is at zero (or nearly zero), providing a wide pulse width but not as wide as the WOT pulse width. This results in a loss of performance but not a stall. Replace the ECU on a trial basis.

CUTS OUT AT WIDE OPEN THROTTLE

1. The first step in any diagnosis should be an evaluation of the problem. In the case of driveability problems, this is especially important so that driveability improvements can be judged.

2. The WOT signal from TPS is used by the ECU for two different purposes:
   a. to shut off the injectors during cranking to clear a flooded engine;
   b. to provide WOT enrichment.

The 12 purple wire from the ECU to the starter solenoid "S" terminal is used for both of these functions:
   a. During cranking, a voltage signal is sent through the 12

Poor Hot Driveability (or Sag)

Sluggish Performance

Cuts Out While Driving (No Stall) (Intermit.)

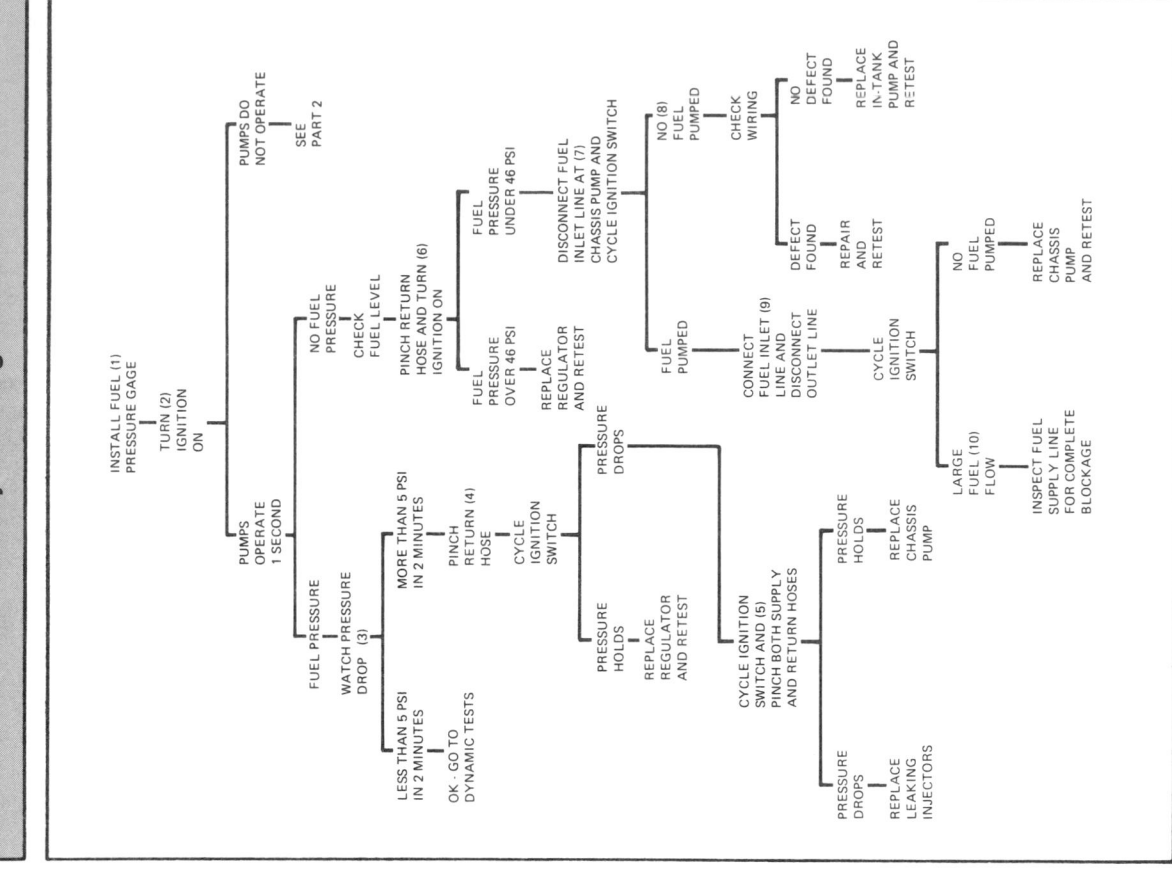

Static Fuel System Diagnosis—Part 1

Poor Fuel Economy

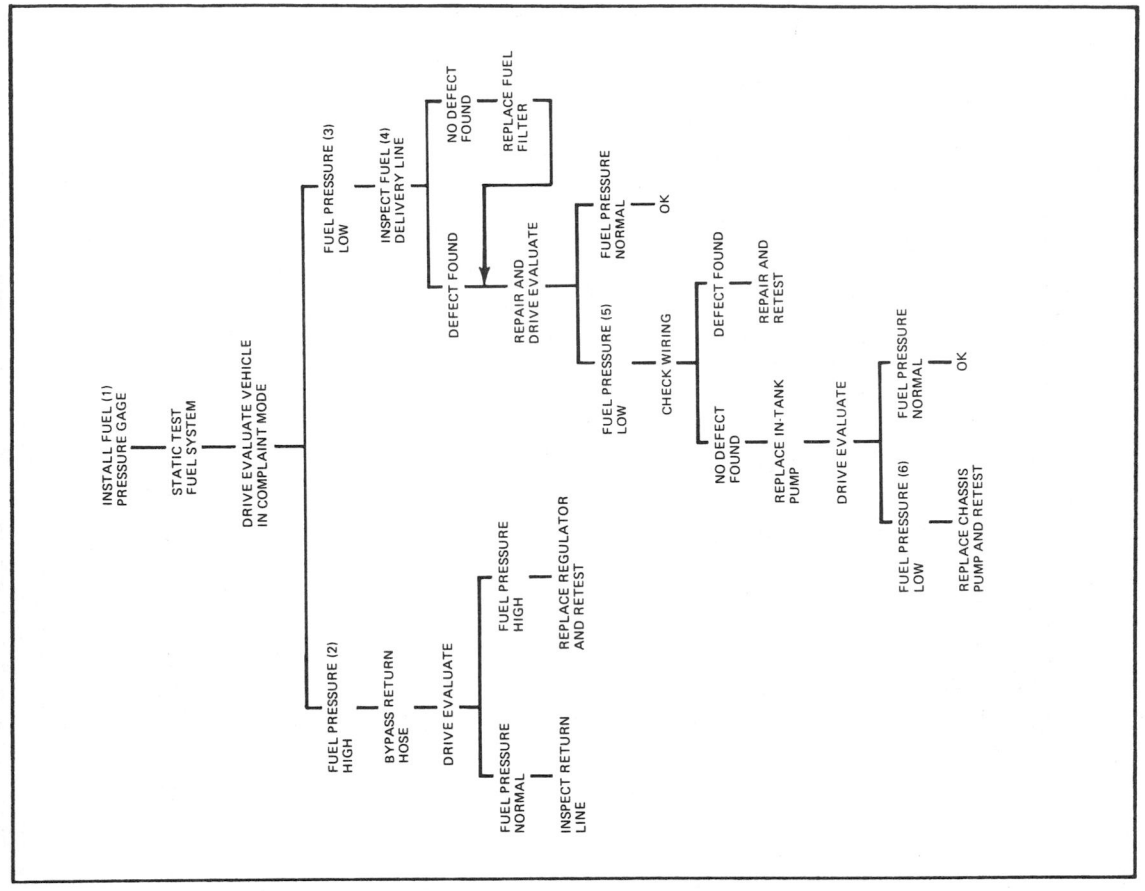

Dynamic Fuel System Diagnosis

Static Fuel System Diagnosis—Part 2

DIAGNOSIS CHART

CAUSES \ COMPLAINTS	Poor Fuel Economy	Sluggish Performance	Intermittent Cut-Out No Stall	Poor Driveability Hot or Sag	Poor Driveability Cold	No Fast Idle	Cuts Out at WOT	Misfire on Light Acceleration	Idle Speed Change	Rough Idle	Hesitation	Rich Operation	Surge - Lean Operation	Tip-in Stumble	Intermittent Stall - No Restart	Intermittent Stall - Restart	Hard Start Hot	Hard Start Cold	Stall After Start - Hot	Stall After Start - Cold	No Start
Electrical Connections			1					1		3		1	2	4		2					1
Cranking Signal Wire Open							1														7
TPS WOT Circuit																					8
TPS Adjustment and Operation			2						3		3			2							
ECU	9	6	4	11			2	10		15	4	6	6	14	5	3	8	3	7	8	9
Speed Sensor Malfunction			3												2	1	5				6
Speed Sensor Magnet And Sensor Orientation														11							
Coolant Sensor - High Resistance Cold				1														1		1	5
Coolant Sensor - Low Resistance Hot																	4				
Air Temperature Sensor				3																7	
FIV Inoperative						2															
FIV Latched				5		1														3	
Intank Pump															1		6		4		
Fuel Pressure Low Or Drops Off		3		6	2			7		10			4				2	2	3	2	2
Fuel Pressure High	5									11		3									
Fuel Pressure Low At Speed		7																			
Restricted Filter		5											1								
Damaged Fuel Lines		4		7																	
Evaporative Canister Excessive Purge									2	2									3	2	
Low Idle Speed										1				1			1		1	4	
High Idle Speed	3																				
MAP Hose Leak Or Obstruction	4		1							8	1	2		3					5	6	
Dirty or Sticking Injectors				10				9		14		5	5						6		
Injector Tip Damage								8		13											
Sticking Throttle Linkage														12							
Vacuum Leaks at Throttle Body	6							6		5			4	13							
Throttle Body Bore Contamination									1												
Restricted EGR Port In Throttle Body				5				11						10							
Restricted EGR Passage	8			4				12						9							
Wrong EGR Orifice	7			2				13						8							
EGR Solenoid Inoperative					4			14													
EGR Transducer				3				15													
EGR Operating At Idle										9									3		
No EGR								16					3	7							
EGR Delay								17						6							
HEI										12					4		7				3

CHRYSLER ELECTRONIC FUEL INJECTION

General Information

The Chrysler Electronic Fuel Injection (EFI) system is used on the 1981–82 Imperial exclusively. The system is broken down into three parts; the Fuel Hydraulic System, the Air Induction System, and the Fuel, Air and Ignition Command System.

The fuel hydraulic system includes all parts of the EFI system which are in physical contact with the fuel. Together they form the fuel flow path from the fuel tank to the fuel injection assembly and back again. The fuel hydraulic system is divided into two subsystems; the fuel supply subsystem and the fuel control subsystem.

Fuel Supply Subsystem

This system is composed of the in-tank fuel pump, the fuel delivery and return lines, a pair of parallel fuel filters, the control pump housing, the pressure regulator and bypass orifice and a pair of check valves.

In operation, the in-tank fuel pump picks up fuel from the fuel tank and delivers it forward through the fuel delivery line and pair of fuel filters until it reaches the control pump housing. The control pump housing serves as a connecting link between the fuel delivery and return lines. It also serves as a fuel reservoir for the control pump and ensures that the pump is always primed with fuel. A check valve in the control housing prevents the fuel from draining back into the lines when the engine is off (in-tank fuel pump not running).

The pressure regulator maintains the desired fuel pressure within the control pump housing by releasing excess fuel into the fuel return line, which carries it back to the fuel tank. The pressure regulator is equipped with a bypass orifice which purges fuel vapors from the control pump housing when the system is shut down. The fuel return line has a check valve which prevents fuel from running backwards out the return line in the event of an accident in which the vehicle rolls over.

Fuel Control Subsystem

The fuel control subsystem consists of the control pump, located in the control pump housing, the fuel flowmeter and temperature sensor, the fuel pressure switch and the fuel injection assembly.

The control pump is a positive displacement pump driven by a variable-speed electric motor. The control pump delivers fuel at high pressure (24–60 psi) through the fuel flowmeter, temperature sensor and fuel pressure switch to the fuel injection assembly.

The fuel flowmeter consists of a cylindrical cavity containing a free-turning vaned wheel. The fuel flowing through the flowmeter causes the wheel to spin at a rate proportionate to fuel flow. As the wheel spins, the vanes interrupt the light path between a light-emitting diode (LED) and a phototransistor. The frequency of the interruptions (pulses) is interpreted as flow rate by the fuel flowmeter module. A temperature sensor is used in conjunction with the fuel flowmeter to monitor fuel temperature. Together, these

Chrysler EFI air induction components

two sensors relay part of the information needed for precise control of the control pump motor speed.

A fuel pressure switch is located between the fuel flowmeter and the fuel injection assembly which opens when there is sufficient fuel pressure to start or run the engine, and closes when pressure is insufficient. When closed, the fuel pressure switch completes a bypass circuit which drives the control pump at full speed (with the ignition key in the start position). This pressurizes the fuel control circuit and insures quick starts. It also prevents vapor locks in the control pump. This entire pressurization process is completed within the time it takes the engine to revolve once.

Metered fuel entering the fuel injection assembly is directed to two pressure-regulating valves. Each valve feeds into its own U-shaped fuel injection bar, located over the throttle body assembly. The light load regulator valve opens when fuel pressure reaches or exceeds 21 psi and delivers fuel to the light load injector bar. Four tiny holes in the lower surface of the injector bar spray fuel onto crescent-shaped ridges at the edges of the throttle plates, where the actual fuel-air mixing occurs. Airfoil-shaped nozzles around the injector holes help refine fuel spray patterns and promote fuel

In-tank fuel pump assembly

Hydraulic support plate assembly showing components

AIR FLOW SENSOR

FUEL CONTROL PUMP

FUEL FLOW METER

SUPPLY CHECK VALVE

AIR FLOW MEASURING MODULE

FUEL PRESSURE SWITCH

FUEL RETURN REGULATOR

FUEL SUPPLY LINE

VACUUM AMPLIFIER

FUEL BARS

LOW FLOW & HIGH FLOW CONTROL VALVES

FUEL TEMPERATURE SENSOR

FUEL FILTER

COOLANT CONTROLLED EGR VALVE

THROTTLE BODY ASSY

CONTROL PUMP POWER MODULE

IN-TANK FUEL PUMP ASSEMBLY

EGR VALVE

THROTTLE POSITION POTENTIOMETER

AUTOMATIC IDLE SPEED MOTOR

INTANK PUMP BALLAST RESISTOR

FUEL RETURN LINE

INTANK PUMP RELAY

CHECK VALVE

FUEL LEVEL INDICATOR

AUTOMATIC SHUTDOWN MODULE

AIR SWITCH CANISTER PURGE TIMER

EFI COOLANT TEMPERATURE SENSOR

EXHAUST GAS OXYGEN SENSOR

AIR SWITCH CANISTER PURGE SOLENOID

DISTRIBUTOR

IGNITION — CONSTANT IDLE MOTOR BALLAST RESISTOR

ELECTRONIC FUEL CONTROL — ELECTRONIC SPARK ADVANCE COMPUTER MODULE

Chrysler EFI functional command components

DELIVERY PRESSURE
RETURN PRESSURE
METERED PRESSURE

FUEL SUPPLY SUBSYSTEM

FUEL CONTROL SUBSYSTEM

PRESSURE REGULATOR

CONTROL PUMP HOUSING

BY-PASS ORIFICE

CONTROL PUMP MOTOR

CONTROL PUMP HOUSING CHECK VALVE

CONTROL PUMP

DUAL FUEL FILTERS

RETURN LINE (1-2 PSI)

METERED FUEL (24-60 PSI)

DELIVERY LINE (11-13 PSI)

FUEL FLOWMETER & TEMPERATURE SENSOR

RETURN LINE CHECK VALVE

FUEL PRESSURE SWITCH

FUEL INJECTION ASSEMBLY

DELIVERY LINE CHECK VALVE

IN-TANK PUMP

IN-TANK FILTER

LIGHT LOAD REGULATOR VALVE (21 PSI) & INJECTOR BARS

POWER REGULATOR VALVE (34 PSI) & INJECTOR BARS

Fuel flow and control circuit for Chrysler EFI system

atomization. The light load circuit supplies all engine fuel when fuel pressure is between 21 and 34 psi, and some of the requirements beyond these pressures. At pressures above 34 psi (heavy engine loads, starting, etc.) the power regulator valve opens and allows the power fuel injection bar to add its spray pattern to the air/fuel mixing process.

Air Supply Subsystem

The air supply subsystem is comprised of the fresh/heated air mixing unit, which provides heated intake air during engine warmup, the air cleaner assembly and the airflow sensor assembly. The airflow sensor assembly is located inside the inlet duct on the air cleaner and measures engine intake airflow volume. This information is compared with fuel flowmeter information electronically and insures precise air/fuel mixture control.

Air Control Subsystem

The air control subsystem is contained in the throttle body assembly. Major parts include the throttle plate and blade subassembly, a throttle position potentiometer, a closed throttle switch and an automatic idle speed motor.

The throttle plates are similar to those used on a carburetor with the exception of a crescent-shaped ridge on the leading edge of each plate which promotes uniform air/fuel mixing.

The throttle position potentiometer senses the angle of throttle blade opening and sends this information to the combustion control computer which then adjusts the air/fuel mixture.

The closed throttle switch activates the automatic idle speed circuit and returns the ignition timing to its basic (minimum) advance timing when the throttle valves are closed (idling). In the event of malfunction, the brake signal circuit acts as a back-up circuit.

Fuel, Air and Ignition Command System

The EFI command system includes the following functions: automatic fuel flow metering to provide optimum air/fuel ratios for every engine operating mode; automatic advance or retardation of ignition timing to optimum points for every engine operating

mode; automatic throttle opening adjustment to maintain optimum idling speed for every engine condition when the driver releases the accelerator pedal; automatic fuel flow shut off if certain ignition, engine speed or time requirements are not satisfied.

The heart of the command system is the Combustion Controlled Computer (CCC) which acts in conjunction with two other modules, the power module and the automatic shutdown module. The CCC receives input signals from a wide array of sensors and uses this information to adjust fuel flow and ignition timing to the correct levels.

The CCC also controls the feedback loop oxygen sensor system which has two modes of operation, closed loop and open loop. Under closed loop operation, the CCC receives signals from the oxygen sensor (located in the exhaust gas stream) and adjusts the air/fuel mixture in accordance with that signal. The sensor measures oxygen content in the exhaust system. Under closed loop operation, engine emissions are kept to a minimum. When the system is in open loop (initial start-up, engine cold, etc), the CCC disregards the oxygen signal and substitutes a pre-programmed air/fuel mixture circuit.

Throttle body assembly

Closed loop command operation

Open loop command operation

On-Car Service

The following is a general diagnostic procedure used to identify which system (ignition, fuel, etc.) is causing the no-start condition. If this procedure fails to produce positive results, the EFI system should be fully tested using a suitable EFI tester.

Take the time to make a preliminary check of all electrical wiring and vacuum hose connections for damage or looseness. Many times, problems occur simply because a connector or hose has become disconnected.

Step 1 (Spark Test)

1. Remove a spark plug wire and insert a well insulated screwdriver into the terminal of the disconnected plug wire. During the spark test, wear a heavy glove on the hand holding the screwdriver and hold the screwdriver by its insulated handle.

2. While holding the screwdriver shaft about 3/16 in. away from a good ground (metal alternator bracket, etc.), have someone crank the engine. Make sure no clothing, etc., is in the way of moving engine parts.

3. If there is a good spark between the screwdriver and ground, perform Step 2 (Fuel Flow Test). If there is no spark, the problem is in the ignition system, not in the fuel injection system.

Step 2 (Fuel Flow Test)

1. Remove the air cleaner.

2. Remove the secondary coil wire from the distributor cap and *ground this wire.*

3. Have someone crank the engine while observing the fuel flow from the fuel injection nozzles on the hydraulic support plate.

4. If there is an adequate fuel flow from the nozzles, the fuel system is probably OK. Perform Step 3 (Spark Plug Test). If there is little or no flow from the injection nozzles, or if there seems to be too much flow from the nozzles (along with other indications of flooding) the fuel system is faulty and should be tested by a qualified technician.

Step 3 (Spark Plug Test)

1. Remove the spark plugs and check for plug fouling. Clean or replace as necessary.

2. Attempt to start the engine. If the engine still won't start, the fault could be with incorrect ignition timeing. Have the timing checked. If it is not 12° ± BTDC, have it reset to 12° BTDC and attempt to restart.

NO START/IGNITION TEST

OPERATION	PROCEDURE	TEST INDICATION	ACTION REQUIRED
2. NO START/IGNITION TEST #2. (Checking pick-up coil resistance at ESA connector.)	• Remove ESA connector from Combustion Control Computer. • Select OHM setting on EFI tester. • Connect test leads to Pins #5 and #9 of ESA connector.	Ohmmeter reads between 150 and 900 ohms.	No shorts or breaks, but possible ground in circuit. Resistance OK. • Perform NO START/IGNITION TEST #2A.
		Ohmmeter reads at or near zero ohms.	Short in circuit. • Perform NO START/IGNITION TEST #2B.
		Ohmmeter reads at or near maximum reading. (Check for good connection and repeat.)	Break in circuit. • Perform NO START/IGNITION TEST #2C.
2A. NO START/IGNITION TEST #2A. (Checking for possible ground in ESA harness.)	(Use 200 OHM scale.) • Connect test leads between ESA harness terminals #5 and ground, then #9 and ground.	Ohmmeter reads near or at maximum resistance, with either terminal.	No Fault in pick-up circuit. • Perform NO START/IGNITION TEST #3.
		Ohmmeter reads low or no resistance.	Ground in either ESA harness or pick-up coil. • Perform NO START/IGNITION TEST #2B.

NO START/IGNITION TEST

OPERATION	PROCEDURE	TEST INDICATION	ACTION REQUIRED
1. NO START/IGNITION TEST #1. (Checking for spark at secondary coil wire.)	• Remove secondary coil wire from distributor. • Hold secondary coil wire terminal near (3/16") good ground. • Crank engine.	Good spark between terminal and ground.	• Fault in distributor rotor, cap or secondary wires. • Repair or replace as required. • Attempt engine start. • If no start, go back and perform sequence starting with SPARK PLUG TEST (Step 3).
		No spark between terminal and ground.	Ignition fault not identified. • Perform NO START/IGNITION TEST #2.

NO START/IGNITION TEST

OPERATION	PROCEDURE	TEST INDICATION	ACTION REQUIRED
3. NO START/IGNITION TEST #3. (Checking Pick-Up Coil Air Gap.)	• Remove distributor cap. • Measure Pick-Up Coil Air Gap with non-magnetic feeler gauge.	Air Gap is .006".	**Air Gap OK.** • Perform NO START/IGNITION TEST #4.
		Air gap is not .006".	**Air Gap not at specification.** • Readjust air gap to .006". • Reconnect Pick-Up Coil connector at distributor. • Attempt engine start. • If no start, go back and perform sequence starting with SPARK PLUG TEST (Step 3).
4. NO START/IGNITION TEST #4. (Checking voltage at coil positive terminal.)	• Set EFI tester to voltmeter position. • Connect test leads to coil **positive terminal** and to **ground.** • Crank engine.	Voltmeter reads 9 volts or more.	**Voltage OK.** • Perform NO START/IGNITION TEST #6.
		Voltmeter reads LESS than 9 volts.	**Voltage not up to specification.** • Perform NO START/IGNITION TEST #5.

NO START/IGNITION TEST

OPERATION	PROCEDURE	TEST INDICATION	ACTION REQUIRED
2B. NO START/IGNITION TEST #2B. (Checking whether ground is in ESA harness or in Pick-Up Coil.)	• Disconnect Pick-Up Coil connector at distributor. • Select 200 OHM setting. • Connect Ohmmeter test leads to either **terminal** of pick-up coil connector on distributor and to **ground.** Repeat with other terminal.	Ohmmeter shows continuity at either or both terminals.	**Pick-Up Coil has short.** • Replace pick-up coil. • Reconnect ESA harness and pick-up coil connectors. • Attempt restart. • If no start, go back and perform sequence starting with SPARK PLUG TEST (Step 3).
		Ohmmeter does not show continuity at either terminal.	**Pick-up Coil not grounded.** • Perform NO START/IGNITION TEST #4.
2C. NO START/IGNITION TEST #2C. (Checking for break in Pick-Up Coil.)	• Disconnect Pick-Up Coil connector at distributor. • Connect Ohmmeter test leads to both terminals of Pick-Up Coil connector.	Ohmmeter reads between 150 and 900 ohms.	**ESA harness has fault.** • Repair harness. • Reconnect ESA and Pick-Up Coil connector. • Attempt restart. • If no start, go back and perform sequence starting with SPARK PLUG CHECK (Step 3).
		Ohmmeter reading not to specs.	**Harness OK.** • Replace Pick-Up Coil. • Reconnect connector. • Attempt engine start. • If no start, go back and perform sequence starting with SPARK PLUG TEST (Step 3).

NO START/IGNITION TEST

OPERATION	PROCEDURE	TEST INDICATION	ACTION REQUIRED
7. NO START/IGNITION TEST #7. (Checking that ESA Pin #10 is grounded.)	• Set tester in Ohmmeter position. • Connect test leads to ESA connector **Pin #10** and to **ground**.	Ohmmeter shows continuity.	**GROUND OK.** • Perform NO START/IGNITION TEST #8.
		Ohmmeter shows no continuity.	**Break in ground wire #10 in ESA harness.** • Repair ESA harness. • Reconnect circuit. • Attempt engine start. • If no start, go back and perform sequence starting with SPARK PLUG TEST (Step 3).
8. NO START IGNITION/TEST #8. (Checking for possible fault in ASD circuit.)	• Remove ASD connector. • Repeat Step #1 - SPARK TEST PROCEDURE.	Good spark between screwdriver and ground.	**Faulty ASD.** • Replace ASD module. • Attempt engine start. • If no start, go back and perform sequence starting with SPARK PLUG TEST (Step 3).
		No spark between screwdriver and ground.	**Faulty CCC.** • Replace CCC. • Attempt engine start. • If no start, go back and perform sequence starting with SPARK PLUG TEST (Step 3).

NO START/IGNITION TEST

OPERATION	PROCEDURE	TEST INDICATION	ACTION REQUIRED
5. NO START/IGNITION TEST #5. (Checking voltage of BAL terminal on starter relay.)	• Connect test leads to **BAL terminal** on starter relay and **ground**. • Crank engine.	Voltmeter reads 9 volts or more.	**Fault in harness to coil.** • Repair as required. • Attempt engine start. • If no start, go back and perform sequence starting with SPARK PLUG TEST (Step 3).
		Voltmeter reads less than 9 volts.	**Voltage not up to specification.** • Test starter relay per car service manual procedure and repair or replace if necessary. • Attempt engine start. • If no start, go back and perform sequence starting with SPARK PLUG TEST (Step 3).
6. NO START/IGNITION TEST #6. (Checking voltage at coil negative terminal.)	• Remove ESA connector from Combustion Control Computer. • Connect test leads to ESA Connector **pin #1** and to ground. • Crank engine.	Voltmeter reads 9 volts or more.	**Voltage OK.** • Perform NO START/IGNITION TEST #7.
		Voltmeter reads less than 9 volts.	**Voltage not to specs.** • Check harness and coil continuity. • Repair as required. • Attempt restart. • If no start, go back and perform sequence starting with SPARK PLUG TEST (Step 3).

NO START/FUEL TEST

OPERATION	PROCEDURE	TEST INDICATION	ACTION REQUIRED
2. NO START/FUEL TEST #2. (Check Power Module drive signal.)	• Repeat NO START/FUEL TEST #1 procedure, including depressing ASD button momentarily.	Power Module drive signal light OFF.	**Power Module Drive Signal OK.** • Perform NO START/FUEL TEST #3.
		Power Module drive signal test light ON.	**No Power Module Drive Signal.** • Replace CCC. • Attempt engine start. • If no start, go back and perform sequence starting with SPARK PLUG TEST (Step 3).
3. NO START/FUEL TEST #3. (Check Control Pump operation.)	• Remove Air Cleaner Cover. • Remove secondary coil wire from distributor and **ground this wire.** • Have someone observe fuel flow. • Repeat NO START/FUEL TEST #1 procedure.	Short flow of fuel from Injector Nozzles.	**Control Pump operating.** • Perform NO START/FUEL TEST #5. Note: after test replace Air Cleaner Cover.
		No fuel flow.	**Control Pump not operating.** • Perform NO START/FUEL TEST #4.

NO START/FUEL TEST

OPERATION	PROCEDURE	TEST INDICATION	ACTION REQUIRED
1. NO START/FUEL TEST #1. (Check for fault In-Tank pump and ASD circuits.)	• Connect EFI Tester to vehicle (do not connect Diagnostic Aid). • Set: - Air By-Pass switch to "OFF" setting. - Rotary switch to Volt setting. - Toggle switch to "Volt - OHM" setting. • Depress ASD By-Pass button momentarily.	Listen for sound of In-Tank Pump running; ASD light, off.	**OK** • Perform NO START/FUEL TEST #2.
		Sound of In-Tank Pump running; ASD light, on.	**Fault in ASD circuit.** • Replace ASD module. • Attempt engine start. • If no start, go back and perform sequence starting with SPARK PLUG TEST (Step 3).
		No sound of In-Tank Pump running.	**Fault in In-Tank Pump circuit.** • Check fuse (cavity #2) 20 amp. • If **OK**, perform NO START FUEL TEST #7. • If **blown**, replace fuse and correct cause (short, defective pump ballast resistor, or low voltage). • Attempt engine start. • If no start, go back and perform sequence starting with SPARK PLUG TEST (Step 3).

NO START/FUEL TEST

OPERATION	PROCEDURE	TEST INDICATION	ACTION REQUIRED
6. NO START/FUEL TEST #6. (Checking for Power Module fault.)	• Repeat NO START/FUEL TEST #1 set-up procedure. • Disconnect - air flowmeter - fuel flowmeter - throttle position potentiometer connectors. - coolant sensor • Depress ASD By-Pass button.	Power Module light ON.	**Fault in Power Module.** • Replace power module. • Attempt engine start. • If no start, reconnect components and go back and perform sequence starting with SPARK PLUG TEST (Step 3).
		Power Module light OFF.	**Fault somewhere in Power Module loads.** • Perform NO START/FUEL TEST #6A.
6A. NO START/FUEL TEST #6A. (Check for fault in Power Module loads.)	Same set-up as TEST #6. • Reconnect Air Flowmeter. • Depress ASD By-Pass button momentarily.	If light comes ON . . .	**Fault in Air Flowmeter.** • If light comes on after circuit is reconnected, locate fault in harness and repair. Otherwise, replace Air Flowmeter. • Attempt engine start. • If no start, reconnect other components and go back and perform sequence starting with SPARK PLUG TEST (Step 3).

NO START/FUEL TEST

OPERATION	PROCEDURE	TEST INDICATION	ACTION REQUIRED
4. NO START/FUEL TEST #4. (Checking Control Pump voltage.)	• Disconnect terminal at Control Pump. • Connect voltmeter leads across both terminals of Control Pump harness. • Depress ASD button momentarily.	Voltmeter reads 9.5 volts or higher.	**Fault in Hydraulic Support Plate.** • Replace Hydraulic Support Plate. • Attempt engine start. • If no start, reconnect terminals and go back and perform sequence starting with SPARK PLUG TEST (Step 3).
		Voltmeter reads less than 9.5 volts.	**Fault not located.** • Replace terminal. Perform NO START/FUEL TEST #14.
5. NO START/FUEL TEST #5. (Checking Power Module operation.)	• Repeat NO START/FUEL TEST #1 set-up procedure. • Depress ASD By-Pass button.	Power Module light OFF.	**Power Module operation OK.** • Perform NO START/FUEL TEST #13.
		Power Module light ON.	**Fault in Power Module or in Power Module loads.** • Perform NO START/FUEL TEST #6.

NO START/FUEL TEST

OPERATION	PROCEDURE	TEST INDICATION	ACTION REQUIRED
7. NO START/FUEL TEST #7. (Checking voltage at In-Tank Ballast Resistor.)	• Repeat NO START/FUEL TEST #1 set-up procedure. • Connect voltmeter leads to green wire on the In-Tank resistor and to ground. • Depress ASD button.	Voltage reads at least 10.5 volts.	**Voltage OK.** • Perform NO START/FUEL TEST #8.
		Voltage reads less than 10.5 volts.	**Voltage not to specs.** • Check for continuity, leak or ground between Point A on Ballast and at ASD terminal connector. (See wiring diagram). • Repair or replace if faulted. • If OK replace ASD. • Attempt engine start. • If no start, go back and perform sequence starting with SPARK PLUG TEST (Step 3).
8. NO START/FUEL TEST #8. (Checking resistance of In-Tank Ballast Resistor.)	• Put rotary switch to OHM position. (use 200 OHM scale.) • Connect Ohmmeter leads to points A & B of Ballast Resistor.	Ohmmeter reads .4 OHMS.	**Resistance OK.** • Perform NO START/FUEL TEST #9.
		Ohmmeter does not read .4 OHMS.	**Resistance not to specs.** • Replace In-Tank Ballast Resistor. • Attempt engine start. • If no start, go back and perform sequence starting with SPARK PLUG TEST (Step 3).

NO START/FUEL TEST

OPERATION	PROCEDURE	TEST INDICATION	ACTION REQUIRED
6A. (Continued) NO START/FUEL TEST #6A. (Check for fault in Power Module loads.)	• Reconnect Fuel Flowmeter. • Depress ASD by-pass button momentarily.	If light comes ON . . .	**Fault is in Fuel Flowmeter circuit.** • If light comes on after circuit is reconnected, locate fault in harness and repair. Otherwise, replace Fuel Flowmeter. • Attempt engine start. • If no start, reconnect other components and go back and perform sequence starting with SPARK PLUG TEST (Step 3).
	• Reconnect throttle position potentiometer and depress ASD by-pass button momentarily.	If light comes ON . . .	**Fault in Throttle Position Potentiometer.** • Check and correct possible fault in throttle pot harness. • If no fault replace throttle pot. • Recalibrate potentiometer. • Attempt restart.
	• Reconnect Coolant Sensor		**Fault is in Coolant Sensor circuit.** • If light comes on after circuit is reconnected, locate fault in harness and repair. Otherwise, replace Coolant Sensor. • Attempt engine start. • If no start, reconnect other components and go back and perform sequence starting with SPARK PLUG TEST (Step 3).

NO START/FUEL TEST

OPERATION	PROCEDURE	TEST INDICATION	ACTION REQUIRED
11. NO START/FUEL TEST #11. (Checking for fault in In-Tank Relay or in harness to Starter Relay.)	• Connect voltmeter leads to **Point C** of In-Tank Pump Relay and to ground. • Crank engine.	Voltmeter reads 9 volts.	**Voltage OK.** • Replace In-Tank Relay. • Attempt engine start. • If no start, go back and perform sequence starting with SPARK PLUG TEST (Step 3).
		Voltmeter reads less than 9 volts.	Voltage not up to specs. • Perform NO START FUEL/TEST #12.
12. NO START FUEL/TEST #12. (Checking for break in harness to Starter Relay.)	• Put rotary switch to Ohmmeter position. • Connect test leads to **Point C** and solenoid terminal of Starter Relay.	Ohmmeter shows continuity.	**Harness OK.** Possible fault in Starter Relay. • Check relay per service manual procedure and replace if necessary. • Attempt engine start. • If no start, go back and perform sequence starting with SPARK PLUG TEST (Step 3).
		Ohmmeter shows no continuity.	Break in harness. • Repair harness as required. • Attempt engine start. • If no start, go back and perform sequence starting with SPARK PLUG TEST (Step 3).

NO START/FUEL TEST

OPERATION	PROCEDURE	TEST INDICATION	ACTION REQUIRED
9. NO START/FUEL TEST #9. (Checking voltage by In-Tank Pump Relay.)	• Put rotary switch in Volt position. • Connect leads to **Point A** of In-Tank Relay and to **ground**. • Crank engine.	Voltage reads 8-10 volts.	**Voltage OK.** • Perform NO START/FUEL TEST #10.
		Voltage reads less than 8-10 volts.	**Voltage not to specs.** • Perform NO START/FUEL TEST #11.
10. NO START/FUEL TEST #10. (Checking for break in harness by-pass to In-Tank Pump.)	• Put rotary switch to Ohmmeter setting. • Connect leads to point A of In-Tank Relay at point indicated in circuit (Z1, 12" DG) and to Eight-way connector above right Rocker Cover.	Ohmmeter shows continuity.	**Harness OK.** • Perform NO START/FUEL TEST #13.
		Ohmmeter shows no continuity.	**Break in harness.** • Repair harness. • Attempt engine start. • If no start, go back and perform sequence starting with SPARK PLUG TEST (Step 3).

NO START/FUEL TEST

OPERATION	PROCEDURE	TEST INDICATION	ACTION REQUIRED
14. NO START/FUEL TEST #14. (Checking for proper EFI crank signals.)	• Remove coil secondary wire from distributor and ground wire with jumper. • Connect EFI tester to vehicle. - Toggle switch in "EFI" position. - Air By-Pass "Off" - Rotary switch in "FUEL" position. • Crank engine. • Record signals in each of the following positions: Fuel Air Fuel Temp. Throttle Pot. Vac. Sol. Water Temp.	Engine cold. Crank signals should be: Fuel - 3-25 Air - 2-25 Fuel Temp. - 16-21 Throttle Pot. - Not to exceed 13.8 Vac. Sol. - .1 - .2 Water Temp. - 8-12	Crank signals should all be to specs. If not, with: Fuel - Replace Hydraulic Support Plate. Air - Replace Air Flowmeter. Fuel Temp. - Replace Hydraulic Support Plate. Throttle Pot. - Replace and adjust as required (See recalibration procedure. Vac. Sol. - Verify circuit replace Vac. Solenoid. Water Temp. - Replace water temp. sensor. Note: Before any components are replaced verify that all connectors and harness' are properly installed and have continuity.

NO START/FUEL TEST

OPERATION	PROCEDURE	TEST INDICATION	ACTION REQUIRED
13. NO START/FUEL TEST #13. (Checking fuel supply line pressure.)	• Check battery voltage is at least 12 volts. • Connect pressure gauge to fuel supply line "tee" fitting on hydraulic support plate. (You may have to hook in "tee" fitting if not already on Hydraulic Support Plate.) • Crank engine.	Pressure at least 8 psi. Pressure is much less than 8 psi.	**Fuel Supply Line Pressure OK.** • Perform NO START/FUEL TEST #14. **Fuel Supply Line Pressure Not Up to specs.** Possible leaks, mechanical or vacuum restriction in fuel supply system. Check for the following: • frozen lines. • pinched lines. • leaks in lines or fittings. • restricted fuel tank vent lines. • blocked fuel filter. • If found, correct and retest. • When pressure is at least 8 psi — • Attempt engine start. • If no start, go to Step #14.

STARTS BUT STALLS TEST

OPERATION	PROCEDURE	TEST INDICATION	ACTION REQUIRED
1. STARTS BUT STALLS TEST #1. (Checking ignition coil ballast resistor circuit voltage.)	• Remove secondary coil wire from distributor. • Crank engine. • Hold secondary coil wire terminal near (3/16") good ground. (Refer to Spark Test Step #1.) • Connect voltmeter leads to ignition coil ballast resistor **Point A** and to **Ground**. • Turn ignition key to "RUN" position.	Voltmeter reads 6 volts or more. Voltmeter reads less than 6 volts.	**Voltage OK.** • Verify 6 volts at positive side of ignition coil. If not correct, fault in circuit. • Perform STARTS BUT STALLS TEST #3. **Voltage not to specs.** • Perform STARTS BUT STALLS TEST #2.

NO START/FUEL TEST (Cold Engine)

OPERATION	PROCEDURE	TEST INDICATION	ACTION REQUIRED
15. NO START/FUEL TEST #15. (Checking for fault in CCC or harness to Starter Relay.)	• Disconnect EFI connector from CCC. • Connect voltmeter leads to pin #8 and to **ground**. • Crank engine.	Voltmeter reads at least 9 volts. Voltmeter reads less than 9 volts.	**Voltage OK.** • Replace CCC. • Attempt engine start. • If no start, go back and perform sequence starting with SPARK PLUG TEST (Step 3). **Voltage not up to specs.** • Check harness to starter relay. (NO START/FUEL TEST #12.)

NO START/FUEL TEST (Excessive Fuel Spray)

OPERATION	PROCEDURE	TEST INDICATION	ACTION REQUIRED
16. NO START/FUEL TEST #16.	• Air Cleaner cover still removed. • Turn ignition key to "RUN" position. • If fuel is continually flowing from injection nozzle, disconnect Control Pump connector. • Recycle ignition key.	Fuel continues flowing from Injection Nozzles. No fuel flow from Injection Nozzles, or fuel flow from all Nozzles.	**Fault in Hydraulic Support Plate.** • Replace Hydraulic Support Plate. • Attempt engine start. • If no start, go back and perform sequence starting with SPARK PLUG TEST (Step 3). **Fault in CCC.** • Replace CCC. • Attempt engine start. • If no start, go back and perform sequence starting with SPARK PLUG TEST (Step 3).

STARTS BUT STALLS TEST

OPERATION	PROCEDURE	TEST INDICATION	ACTION REQUIRED
4. STARTS BUT STALLS TEST #4. (Checking Ballast Resistor resistance.)	• Reset rotary switch to Ohmmeter position. • Connect Ohmmeter leads to ballast resistor terminals C and D.	Ohmmeter reading 9-11 ohms.	**Resistance OK.** • Perform STARTS BUT STALLS TEST #5.
		Ohmmeter does not read 9-11 ohms.	**Resistance not to specs.** • Replace Ballast Resistor. • Reconnect harness connector. • Restart to verify stalling complaint corrected.
5. STARTS BUT STALLS TEST #5. (Checking Ballast Resistor resistance.)	• Reset rotary switch to Ohmmeter position. • Remove harness connector from Ballast Resistor. • Connect Ohmmeter leads to ballast resistor terminals D and E.	Ohmmeter reads 4-6 ohms.	**Ballast resistance OK.** • Perform STARTS BUT STALLS TEST #6
		Ohmmeter does not read 4-6 ohms.	**Ballast resistance not to specs.** • Replace Ballast Resistor. • Reconnect harness connector. • Restart to verify stalling complaint corrected.

STARTS BUT STALLS TEST

OPERATION	PROCEDURE	TEST INDICATION	ACTION REQUIRED
2. STARTS BUT STALLS TEST #2. (Checking voltage to Ballast Resistor.)	• Connect voltmeter to terminal B and to ground.	Voltmeter reads at least 10 volts.	**Voltage OK.** • Replace Ballast Resistor. • Restart to verify stalling complaint corrected.
		Voltmeter reads less than 10 volts.	**Voltage not to specs.** • Check circuit to ignition switch and correct fault. • Restart to verify stalling complaint corrected.
3. START BUT STALLS TEST #3. (Checking AIS motor for start position.)	• Turn ignition key to RUN position. • Visually check position of throttle arm at AIS motor. FRONT OF ENGINE — MINIMUM IDLE — NORMAL IDLE — START POSITION	Throttle arm is in START position.	**AIS motor is OK.** • Perform STARTS BUT STALLS TEST #7.
		Throttle arm not in START position.	• Perform STARTS BUT STALLS TEST #4.

STARTS BUT STALLS TEST

OPERATION	PROCEDURE	TEST INDICATION	ACTION REQUIRED
6. STARTS BUT STALLS TEST #6. (Checking circuit from CCC to AIS motor.)	• Move rotary switch to voltmeter position. • Connect voltmeter leads to Pin 6 of ESA connector and to ground.	Voltmeter reads 8 volts or more.	**Voltage OK.** • Replace CCC. • Restart to verify stalling complaint corrected.
		Voltmeter reads less than 8 volts.	**Voltage not to specs.** • Check for fault in ESA harness to AIS motor and repair if necessary. —OR— • If harness OK, replace AIS motor. • Restart to verify stalling problem corrected.
7. STARTS BUT STALLS TEST #7. (Checking ASD module.)	• Connect EFI tester to vehicle. • Put rotary switch to FUEL position. • Put air By-Pass switch ON. • Turn ignition key to RUN position while noting Air By-Pass light and ASD light.	ASD light on.	• Perform additional procedure below.
		Air By-Pass light comes on and ASD light goes out momentarily - then Air By-Pass light goes out and ASD light comes back on.	**Proper test light sequence.** • Perform STARTS BUT STALLS TEST #8.
		Above light sequence does not occur.	• Check ASD ground and retest. • If ground OK replace ASD module. • Restart and verify stalling complaint corrected.

STARTS BUT STALLS TEST

OPERATION	PROCEDURE	TEST INDICATION	ACTION REQUIRED
8. STARTS BUT STALLS TEST #8. (Checking fuel flow.)	• Remove Air Cleaner cover. • Turn ignition key to RUN position. • Have someone observe fuel flow.	Brief fuel flow from injector bars.	**Fuel flow normal.** • Perform STARTS BUT STALLS TEST #17.
		No fuel flow.	• Perform STARTS BUT STALLS TEST #9.
		Fuel flows continually from injector bars.	• Perform STARTS BUT STALLS TEST #8A.
8A. STARTS BUT STALLS TEST #8A. (Checking cause of continuous fuel flow.)	• Disconnect Control Pump connector.	Fuel flow stops.	• Replace CCC. • Replace Air Cleaner cover and reconnect connector. • Restart to verify stalling complaint corrected.
	• Recycle ignition key OFF-ON.	Fuel flow continues.	**Defective Hydraulic Support Plate.** • Replace Hydraulic Support Plate. • Replace Air Cleaner cover and reconnect connector. • Restart and verify stalling complaint corrected.

STARTS BUT STALLS TEST

OPERATION	PROCEDURE	TEST INDICATION	ACTION REQUIRED
10. STARTS BUT STALLS TEST #10. (Checking voltage at In-Tank Ballast Resistor.)	• Repeat NO START/FUEL TEST #1 set-up procedure. • Connect voltmeter leads to green wire on the In-Tank resistor and to ground. • Depress ASD button.	Voltage reads at least 10.5 volts.	**Voltage OK.** • Perform STARTS BUT STALLS TEST #12.
		Voltage reads less than 10.5 volts.	**Voltage not to specs.** • Check for continuity, leak or ground between Point A (Z1, 12, DG) and at ASD terminal connector. • Repair or replace if faulted. • If OK replace ASD. • Attempt engine start. • If no start, go back and perform sequence starting with SPARK PLUG TEST (Step 3).
11. STARTS BUT STALLS TEST #11. (Checking resistance of In-Tank Ballast Resistor.)	• Put rotary switch to OHM position. • Select 200 OHM setting. • Connect Ohmmeter leads to points A & B of ballast resistor.	Ohmmeter reads .4 ohms.	**Resistance OK.** • Perform STARTS BUT STALLS TEST #12.
		Ohmmeter does not read .4 ohms.	**Resistance not to specs.** • Replace In-Tank Ballast Resistor. • Attempt engine start. • If no start, go back and perform sequence starting with SPARK PLUG TEST (Step 3).

STARTS BUT STALLS TEST

OPERATION	PROCEDURE	TEST INDICATION	ACTION REQUIRED
9. STARTS BUT STALLS TEST #9. (Check for fault in In-Tank Pump and ASD circuits.)	• Connect EFI Tester to vehicle (do not connect Diagnostic Aid). • Set: -Air By-Pass switch to OFF setting. -Rotary switch to VOLT setting. -Toggle switch to VOLT OHM setting. • Depress ASD By-Pass button momentarily.	Sound of In-Tank Pump running; ASD light, OFF.	**OK.** • Perform NO START/FUEL TEST #2.
		Sound of In-Tank Pump running; ASD light, ON.	**Fault in ASD circuit.** • Replace ASD module. • Attempt engine start. • If no start, go back and perform sequence starting with SPARK PLUG TEST (Step 3.)
		No Sound of In-Tank Pump running.	**Fault in In-Tank Pump circuit.** • Check fuse (cavity #2) 20 amp. • If OK, perform STARTS BUT STALLS TEST #10. • If blown, replace fuse and correct cause (short, defective pump ballast resistor, or low voltage.) • Attempt engine start. • If no start, go back and perform sequence starting with SPARK PLUG TEST (Step 3).

STARTS BUT STALLS TEST

OPERATION	PROCEDURE	TEST INDICATION	ACTION REQUIRED
14. STARTS BUT STALLS TEST #14. (Checking for fault in In-Tank Relay or in harness to Starter Relay.)	• Connect voltmeter leads to **Point C** of In-Tank Pump Relay and to ground. • Crank engine.	Voltmeter reads 9 volts. Voltmeter reads less than 9 volts.	**Voltage OK.** • Replace In-Tank Relay. • Attempt engine start. • If no start, go back and perform sequence starting with SPARK PLUG TEST (Step 3). **Voltage not up to specs.** • Perform STARTS BUT STALLS TEST #15.
15. STARTS BUT STALLS TEST #15. (Checking for break in harness to Starter Relay.)	• Put rotary switch to Ohmmeter position. • Connect test leads to **Point C** and solenoid terminal of starter relay.	Ohmmeter shows continuity. Ohmmeter shows no continuity.	**Harness OK.** Possible fault in Starter Relay. • Check relay per service manual procedure and replace if necessary. • Attempt engine start. • If no start, go back and perform sequence starting with SPARK PLUG TEST (Step 3). **Break in harness.** • Repair harness as required. • Attempt engine start. • If no start, go back and perform sequence starting with SPARK PLUG TEST (Step 3).

STARTS BUT STALLS TEST

OPERATION	PROCEDURE	TEST INDICATION	ACTION REQUIRED
12. STARTS BUT STALLS TEST #12. (Checking voltage by In-Tank Pump Relay.)	• Put rotary switch in VOLT position. • Connect leads to **Point A** of In-Tank Relay and to **ground.** • Crank engine.	Voltage reads 8-10 volts. Voltage reads less than 8-10 volts.	**Voltage OK.** • Perform STARTS BUT STALLS TEST #13. **Voltage not to specs.** • Perform NO START/FUEL TEST #14.
13. STARTS BUT STALLS TEST #13. (Checking for break in harness by-pass to In-Tank Pump.)	• Put rotary switch to Ohmmeter setting. • Connect leads to **Point A** of In-Tank relay at point indicated in circuit (Z1, 12 DG) and to eight-way connector above right Rocker Cover.	Ohmmeter shows continuity. Ohmmeter shows no continuity.	**Harness OK.** • Perform STARTS BUT STALLS TEST #14. **Break in harness.** • Repair harness. • Attempt engine start. • If no start, go back and perform sequence starting with SPARK PLUG TEST (Step 3).

STARTS BUT STALLS TEST

OPERATION	PROCEDURE	TEST INDICATION	ACTION REQUIRED
17. STARTS BUT STALLS TEST #17. (Checking for proper EFI Crank signals.)	• Remove coil secondary wire from distributor and **ground wire with jumper.** • Connect EFI tester to vehicle: - Toggle switch in EFI position. - Air by-pass switch OFF - Rotary switch in FUEL position. • Crank engine. • Record signals in each of the following positions: Fuel. Air. Fuel Temp. Throttle Pot. Vac. Sol. Water Temp.	Engine cold. Crank signals should be: Fuel - 3-.25. Air - 2-.25. Fuel Temp. - 16-.21. Throttle Pot. - Not to exceed 13.8 Vac. Sol. - .1 - .2 Water Temp. - 8-12	Crank signals should all be to specs. If not, with: Fuel - Replace Hydraulic Support Plate. Air - Replace Air Flowmeter. Fuel Temp. - Replace Hydraulic Support plate. Throttle Pot. - Replace and adjust as required (see recalibration procedure). Vac. Sol. - Verify circuit replace Vac. Solenoid. Water Temp.- Replace Water Temp. Sensor. Note: Before any components are replaced verify that all connectors and harnesses are properly installed.

STARTS BUT STALLS TEST

OPERATION	PROCEDURE	TEST INDICATION	ACTION REQUIRED
16. STARTS BUT STALLS TEST #16. (Checking fuel supply line pressure.)	• Check battery voltage is at least 12 volts. • Connect pressure gauge to fuel supply line "tee" fitting on Hydraulic Support Plate. (You may have to hook in "tee" fitting if not already on Hydraulic Support Plate.) • Crank engine.	Pressure at least 8 psi. Pressure is much less than 8 psi.	**Fuel Supply Line Pressure OK.** • Perform STARTS BUT STALLS TEST #17. **Fuel Supply Line Pressure Not Up to specs.** Possible leaks, mechanical or vacuum restriction in fuel supply system. Check for the following: • pinched lines. • leaks in lines or fittings. • restricted fuel tank vent lines. • If found, correct and retest. • When pressure is at least 8 psi — • Attempt engine start. • If no start, go back and perform sequence starting with SPARK PLUG TEST (Step 3).

DRIVEABILITY TEST

OPERATION	PROCEDURE	TEST INDICATION	ACTION REQUIRED
Preliminary Check. (Idle Speed.)	• Connect EFI Tachometer to engine. • Set rotary switch to RPM position. • Turn all vehicle accessories off. • Set parking brake and block front wheels. • Place transmission in "P" position. • Start engine. • Allow engine to reach normal operating temperature. • Place transmission in "D" position.	Tachometer should read 580 RPM (±50) with smooth idle in Drive. (Disregard ASD light ON.)	• **If idle speed not to specs —** • Adjust using automatic idle speed system procedures. • **If rough idle,** check for fouled plugs, cross firing, etc. and correct. • Check basic timing. (Follow procedures.) • Shut down engine and place transmission in "P" position.
Preliminary Check. (Basic Timing.)	• Connect magnetic timing probe to tester and engine. • Ground closed throttle switch with jumper wire. • Rotary switch to TIMING position. • Start engine.	Basic timing should read 12° (±2°). (Disregard ASD light ON.)	• Adjust to specified basic timing, if necessary. • Perform DRIVEABILITY TEST #1 (engine still running).

STARTS BUT STALLS TEST

OPERATION	PROCEDURE	TEST INDICATION	ACTION REQUIRED
18. STARTS BUT STALLS TEST #18. (Checking for fault in CCC or harness to Starter Relay.)	• Disconnect EFI connector from CCC. • **Connect voltmeter leads to pin #8 and to ground.** • Crank engine.	**Voltmeter reads at least 9 volts.** **Voltmeter reads less than 9 volts.**	**Voltage OK.** • Replace CCC. • Attempt engine start. • If no start, go back and perform sequence starting with SPARK PLUG TEST (Step 3). **Voltage not up to specs.** • Reconnect connector. • Check harness to Starter Relay. (NO START/FUEL TEST #12.)

687

DRIVEABILITY TEST

OPERATION	PROCEDURE	TEST INDICATION	ACTION REQUIRED
3. DRIVEABILITY TEST #3. (Further checking of spark curve.)	• Increase engine speed to 2,000 RPM.	Timing should read: Fed: 36° ± 2° plus Basic Timing. Cal: 17° ± 2° plus Basic Timing.	**Timing OK.** • Shut down engine. • Perform DRIVEABILITY TEST #4.
		Timing not within above specifications.	• Shut down engine. • Replace CCC. • Road test to verify driveability complaint corrected.
4. DRIVEABILITY TEST #4. (Checking primary fuel flow-normal performance complaint.)	• Connect EFI tester to car: - rotary switch in FUEL position. - Air By-Pass OFF. • Start engine. • Turn Air By-Pass ON. • Remove Air Flowmeter harness connector. • Remove Air Cleaner cover. • Observer fuel spray bars.	Fuel flowing from all four primary nozzles in uniform and steady streams.	**Primary Fuel flow OK.** • Perform DRIVEABILITY TEST #5.
		Fuel not flowing from all four primary nozzles in uniform and steady streams.	• Replace Hydraulic Support Plate. • Remove tester, replace connector and Air Cleaner cover. • Road test to verify normal performance complaint corrected.

DRIVEABILITY TEST

OPERATION	PROCEDURE	TEST INDICATION	ACTION REQUIRED
1. DRIVEABILITY TEST #1. (Checking spark curve.)	• Increase engine RPM to 1,500 RPM. • Throttle switch still grounded with jumper wire.	Timing unchanged at 12° ±2°.	**Timing OK.** • Perform DRIVEABILITY TEST #2 (engine still running).
		Timing no longer at 12° ±2°.	**Timing not at specs.** • Replace CCC. • Road test to verify driveability complaint corrected.
2. DRIVEABILITY TEST #2. (Further checking of spark curve.)	• Remove ground jumper wire. • Decrease engine speed to 1,000 RPM.	Timing should read: Fed: 15° ± 3° plus Basic Timing Cal: 5° ± 2° plus Basic Timing	**Timing OK.** • Perform DRIVEABILITY TEST #3 (engine still running).
		Timing not within above specifications.	• Shut down engine. • Replace CCC. • Road test to verify driveability complaint corrected.

DRIVEABILITY TEST

OPERATION	PROCEDURE	TEST INDICATION	ACTION REQUIRED
6. DRIVEABILITY TEST #6. (Continued)			If run signals are not to specs: Fuel - Replace Hydraulic Support Plate. Air - Replace Air Flowmeter. O₂ Sensor - Perform DRIVEABILITY TEST #8. Fuel Temp. - Replace Hydraulic Support Plate. Throttle Position - Adjust or replace as required. Vac. Sol. - Perform DRIVEABILITY TEST #10. Water Temp. - Replace water sensor.
7. DRIVEABILITY TEST #7. (Checking ignition primary & secondary with ignition oscilloscope.)	• Connect suitable ignition oscilloscope to engine.	Follow equipment manufacturer's instructions in analyzing ignition system.	• If ignition system fault, repair as required. • If no ignition faults are indicated, replace CCC. • Road test to verify driveability complaint corrected.

DRIVEABILITY TEST

OPERATION	PROCEDURE	TEST INDICATION	ACTION REQUIRED
5. DRIVEABILITY TEST #5. (Checking secondary fuel flow - w.o.t. performance complaint.)	• Same procedure as in #4 except engine off. - toggle switch in EFI position.	Fuel flowing from all eight nozzles in uniform and steady streams.	**Secondary fuel flow OK.** • Perform DRIVEABILITY TEST #6.
	- remove connector from fuel pressure switch and ground connector. • Depress ASD By-Pass button momentarily. • Observe fuel spray bars.	Fuel not flowing from all eight nozzles in uniform and steady streams.	• Replace Hydraulic Support Plate. • Remove tester, replace connectors and Air Cleaner cover. • Road test to verify w.o.t. performance complaint corrected.
6. DRIVEABILITY TEST #6. (Checking EFI run signals.)	• Connect EFI tester to vehicle: - toggle switch to EFI position. - Air By-Pass OFF. - AIS Control in normal position; Rotary switch to fuel position. • Start engine. Note: Engine should be at normal operating temp. unless complaint is a cold driveability problem.	Check run signals as follows: (see table below)	If all run signals are to specs., perform DRIVEABILITY TEST #7.

	Idle N	After 70 Sec.	2,000 RPM
Fuel	3.5-6.0	3.5-6.0	10.0-15.0
Air	15-35	15-35	35-55
O₂ Sensor	—	45-70	60-75
Fuel Temp.	16-21	16-21	16-21
Throttle Pos.	3.5-4.5	3.5-4.5	4.6-6.0
Vac. Sol.	.1	13.0	13.0
Water Temp.	8-12	8-12	8-12

DRIVEABILITY TEST

OPERATION	PROCEDURE	TEST INDICATION	ACTION REQUIRED
9. DRIVEABILITY TEST #9. (Identifying whether fault in CCC or O_2 Sensor.)	• Disconnect O_2 Sensor wire at the sensor.	Tester reading changes to 90 - 100.	• If readings change as indicated, replace O_2 Sensor and repeat DRIVEABILITY TEST #8.
	• Ground harness end of wire.	Tester reading changes to 0-10.	• If readings do not change as indicated, replace CCC and repeat DRIVEABILITY TEST #8.
		Tester reading does not change to 90 - 100 range when O_2 sensor wire disconnected.	• Check for short in harness from O_2 sensor to CCC. Repair and retest. Still no change, perform DRIVEABILITY TEST #10.
9A. DRIVEABILITY TEST # 9A. Checking fuel flow meter to control pump match.	• Connect EFI Tester to engine including Diagnostic Aid. • Start engine. • Run until engine at normal operating temperature (engine must run at least 70 seconds) after warm. • Put Rotary Switch in O_2 Sensor Position.	Tester reading indicates 0 at idle and 45 to 70 at 2000 RPM.	Replace Support Plate Assembly.

DRIVEABILITY TEST

OPERATION	PROCEDURE	TEST INDICATION	ACTION REQUIRED
8. DRIVEABILITY TEST #8. (Checking O_2 Sensor circuit for performance or fuel economy complaint.)	• Connect EFI Tester to engine, including Diagnostic Aid. • Start engine. • Run until engine at normal operating temperature (engine must run at least 70 seconds) AFTER WARM. • Put rotary switch in O_2 Sensor position.	Tester reads in range from 45 to 70.	**O_2 Sensor OK.** • Perform calibration verification. • If no improvement, tune engine and road test.
		Tester reads 99-100.	**Break in O_2 harness to CCC.** • Check harness from O_2 Sensor circuit (N11 18 BK) to terminal #12 of CCC. Repair if necessary. • Retest. If still high perform DRIVEABILITY TEST #9.
		Tester reads in range from 0 to 10.	**Possible bad connection from battery feed.** • Shut down engine. • Disconnect and reconnect battery feed connector or (8 gauge red wire at battery connector). • Perform auto calibration. • Retest. If still low, perform DRIVEABILITY TEST #9.

DRIVEABILITY TEST

OPERATION	PROCEDURE	TEST INDICATION	ACTION REQUIRED
11. DRIVEABILITY TEST #11. (Verifying air switching operation after 70 seconds.)	• Note reading on tester after 70 seconds have elapsed from engine start.	After 70 seconds: • reading switches to 13.0 with air flow coming from downstream port of air switching valve.	**Air switching OK.** • Replace CCC and repeat DRIVEABILITY TEST #6.
		After 70 seconds: • reading switches to 13.0 but no air coming from downstream port of Air Switching Valve.	**Fault in air switching vacuum circuit.** • Check vacuum circuit back to tree. If fault identified, repair and retest. • If no fault in vacuum circuit, fault is in Air Switching Valve. • Replace Air Switching Valve and retest Vac. Sol. valve. • Verify complaint corrected.
		After 70 seconds: • reading is not within 1 volt of battery voltage.	**Fault in air switching electrical circuit.** • Check harness and connectors at power module and CCC. • Repair as necessary and retest. • If harness and connectors are OK: - replace timer and retest. - verify complaint corrected.

DRIVEABILITY TEST

OPERATION	PROCEDURE	TEST INDICATION	ACTION REQUIRED
10. DRIVEABILITY TEST #10. (Verifying air switching operation during first 70 seconds.)	• Engine off. • Disconnect downstream air hose from Air Switching Valve. • Put tester switch in Vac. Sol. position. • Start engine (note time of start.)	During first 70 seconds: • reading is 0.1 with no air coming from downstream port of Air Switching Valve.	**Reading OK.** • Continue timing sequence into DRIVEABILITY TEST #11.
		During first 70 seconds: • reading goes to and remains at 13.0 with air coming from downstream port of Air Switching Valve.	**Reading not within specs.** • Check harness and connectors at CCC and Timer. Correct any fault and repeat test. • If CCC and Timer harness and connectors OK, fault is in Air Switching Timer. • Replace Timer and repeat test. • Verify complaint corrected.
		During first 70 seconds: • reading is 0.1 with air coming from Air Switching Valve.	• Replace Air Switching Valve and repeat test.

CHRYSLER MULTI-PORT ELECTRONIC FUEL INJECTION

General Information

The turbocharged multi-point Electronic Fuel Injection system combines an electronic fuel and spark advance control system with a turbocharged intake system. At the center of this system is a digital pre-programmed computer known as a Logic Module that regulates ignition timing, air-fuel ratio, emission control devices and idle speed. This component has the ability to update and revise its programming to meet changing operating conditions.

Various sensors provide the input necessary for the Logic Module to correctly regulate fuel flow at the fuel injectors. These include the Manifold Absolute Pressure, Throttle Position, Oxygen Feedback, Coolant Temperature, Charge Temperature, and Vehicle Speed Sensors. In addition to the sensors, various switches also provide important information. These include the Transmission Neutral-Safety, Heated Backlite, Air Conditioning, and the Air Conditioning Clutch Switches.

Inputs to the Logic Module are converted into signals sent to the Power Module. These signals cause the Power Module to change either the fuel flow at the injector or ignition timing or both. The Logic Module tests many of its own input and output circuits. If a fault is found in a major circuit, this information is stored in the Logic Module. Information on this fault can be displayed to a technician by means of the instrument panel power loss lamp or by connecting a diagnostic readout and observing a numbered display code which directly relates to a general fault.

ELECTRONIC CONTROL SYSTEM

Power Module

The Power Module contains the circuits necessary to power the ignition coil and the fuel injector. These are high current devices and their power supply has been isolated to minimize any "electrical noise" reaching the Logic Module. The Power Module also energizes the Automatic Shut Down (ASD) Relay which activates the fuel pump, ignition coil, and the Power Module itself. The module also receives a signal from the distributor. In the event of no distributor signal, the ASD relay is not activated and power is shut off from the fuel pump and ignition coil. The Power Module

Power module on Chrysler MFI system

contains a voltage converter which reduces battery voltage to a regulated 8.0V output. This 8.0V output powers the distributor and also powers the Logic Module.

Logic Module

The logic module is a digital computer containing a microprocessor. The module receives input signals from various switches, sensors, and components. It then computes the fuel injector pulse width, spark advance, ignition coil dwell, idle speed, and purge and EGR solenoid cycles from this information. The Logic Module tests many of its own input and output circuits. If a fault is found in a major system, this information is stored in the Logic Module.

Logic module on Chrysler MFI system showing pin connector locations

Information on this fault can be displayed to a technician by means of flashing lamp on the instrument panel or by connecting a diagnostic readout tool and reading a numbered display code which relates to a general fault.

Automatic Shutdown Relay (ASD)

The Automatic Shutdown Relay (ASD) is powered and controlled through the Power Module. When the Power Module senses a distributor signal during cranking, it grounds the ASD closing its contacts. This completes the circuit for the electric fuel pump, Power Module, and ignition coil. If the distributor signal is lost for any reason the ASD interrupts this circuit in less than one second preventing fuel, spark, and engine operations.

ENGINE SENSORS

Manifold Absolute Pressure (MAP) Sensor

The Manifold Absolute Pressure (MAP) sensor is a device which monitors manifold vacuum. It is mounted in the right side passen-

692

ger compartment and is connected to a vacuum nipple on the throttle body and, electrically to the Logic Module. The sensor transmits information on manifold vacuum conditions and barometric pressure to the Logic Module. The MAP sensor data on engine load is used with data from other sensors to determine the correct air-fuel mixture.

Oxygen Sensor (O₂ Sensor)

The Oxygen Sensor (O₂ Sensor) is a device which produces an electrical voltage when exposed to the oxygen present in the exhaust gasses. The sensor is mounted in the exhaust manifold and must be heated by the exhaust gasses before producing the voltage.

Fuel injection connections

Oxygen sensory connections

Location of logic module and component connectors on Chrysler MFI system

When there is a large amount of oxygen present (lean mixture), the sensor produces a low voltage. When there is a lesser amount present (rich mixture) it produces a higher voltage. By monitoring the oxygen content and converting it to electrical voltage, the sensor acts as a rich-lean switch. The voltage is transmitted to the Logic Module. The Logic Module signals the Power Module to trigger the fuel injector. The injector changes the mixture.

Typical oxygen sensor

Charge Temperature Sensor

The Charge Temperature Sensor is a device mounted in the intake manifold which measures the temperature of the air-fuel mixture. This information is used by the Logic Module to determine engine operating temperature and engine warm-up cycles in the event of a Coolant Temperature Sensor failure.

Coolant Temperature Sensor

The Coolant Termperature Sensor is a device which monitors coolant temperature (which is the same as engine operating temperature). It is mounted in the thermostat housing. This sensor provides data on engine operating temperature to the Logic Module. This data along with data provided by the Charge Temperature Switch allows the Logic Module to demand slightly richer air-fuel mixtures and higher idle speeds until normal operating temperatures are reached. The sensor is a variable resistor with a range of —60°F to 300°F.

Coolant and charge temperature sensors—typical

SWITCHES AND SOLENOIDS

Various switches provide information to the Logic Module. These include the Neutral Safety, Air Conditioning Clutch, and Brake Light switches. If one or more of these switches is sensed as being in the on position, the Logic Module signals the Automatic Idle Speed Motor to increase idle speed to a scheduled rpm. With the air conditioning on and the throttle blade above a specific angle, the wide open throttle cut-out relay prevents the air conditioning clutch from engaging until the throttle blade is below this angle.

Power Loss Lamp

The Power Loss Lamp comes on each time the ignition key is turned on and stays on for a few seconds as a bulb test. If the Logic Module receives an incorrect signal or no signal from either the Coolant Temperature Sensor, Manifold Absolute Pressure Sensor,

EGR and canister purge solenoids

or the Throttle Position Sensor, the Power Loss Lamp on the instrument panel is illuminated. This is a warning that the Logic Module has gone into Limp in Mode in an attempt to keep the system operational. It signals an immediate need for service. The Power Loss can also be used to display fault codes. Cycle the ignition switch on, off, on, off, on within five seconds and any fault codes stored in the Logic Module will be displayed.

Limp In Mode is the attempt by the Logic Module to compensate for the failure of certain components by substituting information from other sources. If the Logic Module senses incorrect data or no data at all from the MAP Sensor, Throttle Position Sensor, Charge Temperature Sensor or Coolant Temperature Sensor, the system is placed into Limp In Mode and the Power Loss lamp on the instrument panel is activated.

Purge Solenoid

The Purge Solenoid works in the same fashion as the EGR solenoid. When engine temperature is below 61°C (145°F) the Logic Module grounds the Purge Solenoid energizing it. This prevents vacuum from reaching the charcoal canister valve. When this temperature is reached the Logic Module de-energizes the solenoid by turning the ground off. Once this occurs vacuum will flow to the canister purge valve and purge fuel vapors through the throttle body.

Exhaust Gas Recirculation Solenoid

The EGR solenoid is operated by the Logic Module. When engine temperature is below 21°C (70°F), the Logic Module energizes the solenoid by grounding it. This closes the solenoid and prevents ported vacuum from reaching the EGR valve. When the prescribed temperature is reached, the logic module will turn off the ground for the solenoid de-energizing it. Once the solenoid is de-energized, ported vacuum from the throttle body will pass through to the EGR valve. At idle and wide open throttle the solenoid is energized which prevents EGR operation.

Air Conditioning Cut Out Relay

The air conditioning cut out relay is electrically in series with the cycling clutch switch and low pressure cut out switch. This relay is in the normally closed (on) position during engine operation. When the Logic Module senses wide open throttle through the Throttle Position Sensor, it will energize the relay, open its contacts, and prevent air conditioning clutch engagement.

FUEL CONTROL SYSTEM

Throttle Body

The throttle body assembly replaces a conventional carburetor air intake system and is connected to both the turbocharger and the intake manifold. The throttle body houses the Throttle Position Sensor and the Automatic idle Speed Motor. Air flow through the throttle body is controlled by a cable operated throttle blade located in the base of the throttle body.

Fuel Supply Circuit

Fuel is pumped to the fuel rail by an electrical pump which is mounted in the fuel tank. The pump inlet is fitted with a filter to prevent water and other contaminents from entering the fuel supply circuit. Fuel pressure is controlled to a preset level above intake manifold pressure by a pressure regulator which is mounted near the fuel rail. The regulator uses intake manifold pressure at the vacuum tee as a reference.

Fuel Injectors and Fuel Rail Assembly

The four fuel injectors are retained in the fuel rail by lock rings. The rail and injector assembly is then bolted in position with the injectors inserted in the recessed holes in the intake manifold. The Fuel Injector is an electric solenoid powered by the Power Module but, controlled by the Logic Module. The Logic Module, based on ambient, mechanical, and sensor input, determines when and how long the Power Module should operate the injector. When an electric current is supplied to the injector, the armature and pintle move a short distance against a spring, opening a small orifice. Fuel is supplied to the inlet of the injector by the fuel pump, then passes through the injector, around the pintle, and out the orifice. Since the fuel is under high pressure a fine spray is developed in the shape of a hollow cone. The injector, through this spraying action, atomizes the fuel and distributes it into the air entering the combustion chamber.

Fuel Pressure Regulator

The pressure regulator is a mechanical device located downstream of the fuel injector on the throttle body. Its function is to maintain a constant 53 psi (380kPa) across the fuel injector tip. The regulator uses a spring loaded rubber diaphragm to uncover a fuel return port. When the fuel pump becomes operational, fuel flows past the injector into the regulator and is restricted from flowing any further by the blocked return port. When fuel pressure reaches 53 psi (380kPa), it pushes on the diaphragm, compressing the spring, and uncovers the fuel return port. The diaphragm and spring will constantly move from an open to closed position to keep the fuel pressure constant. An assist to the spring loaded diaphragm comes from vacuum in the throttle body above the throttle blade. As venturi vacuum increases less pressure is required to supply the same amount of fuel into the air flow. The vacuum assists in opening the fuel port during high vacuum conditions. This fine tunes the fuel pressure for all operating conditions.

Cross section of fuel pressure regulator

Typical solenoid-type fuel injector

Removing fuel pump from tank on Chrysler MFI system

Throttle body assembly on Chrysler MFI system

Fuel supply system on Chrysler MFI system

Throttle Position Sensor (TPS)

The throttle Position Sensor (TPS) is an electric resistor which is activated by the movement of the throttle shaft. It is mounted on the throttle body and senses the angle of the throttle body and senses the angle of the throttle blade opening. The voltage that the sensor produces increases or decreases according to the throttle blade opening. This voltage is transmitted to the Logic Module where it is used along with data from other sensors to adjust the air-fuel ratio to varying conditions and during acceleration, deceleration, idle, and wide open throttle operations.

Automatic Idle Speed (AIS) Motor

The Automatic Idle Speed Motor (AIS) is operated by the Logic Module. Data from the Throttle Position Sensor, Speed Sensor, Coolant Temperature Sensor, and various switch operations, (Electric Backlite, Air Conditioning, Safety/Neutral, Brake) are used by the Logic Module to adjust engine idle to an optimum during all idle conditions. The AIS adjusts the air portion of the air-fuel mixture through an air bypass on the back of the throttle body. Basic (no load) idle is determined by the minimum air flow through the throttle body. The AIS opens or closes off the air bypass as an increase or decrease is needed due to engine loads or ambient conditions. The Logic Module senses an air/fuel change and increases or decreases fuel proportionally to change engine idle. Deceleration die out is also prevented by increasing engine idle when the throttle is closed quickly after a driving (speed) condition.

Fuel Pump

The fuel pump used in this system is a positive displacement, roller vane immersible pump with a permanent magnet electric motor. The fuel is drawn in through a filter sock and pushed through the electric motor to the outlet. The pump contains two check valves. One valve is used to relieve internal fuel pump pressure and regulate maximum pump output. The other check valve, located near the pump outlet, restricts fuel movement in either direction when the pump is not operational. Voltage to operate the pump is supplied through the Auto Shutdown Relay.

Fuel Reservoir

The fuel pump is mounted within a fuel reservoir in the fuel tank. The purpose of the reservoir is to provide fuel at the pump intake furing all driving conditions, especially those when low fuel levels are present. The fuel return line directs fuel into a cup on the side of the reservoir. The stream of fuel coming into this cup creates a low pressure area and causes additional fuel from the main tank to flow into the reservoir. This combination of return fuel and fuel from the main tank keeps the reservoir full even when the fuel level is below the reservoir walls.

Exhaust Gas Recirculation (EGR)

The Exhaust Gas Recirculation system is a back pressure type and is controlled two ways. The Logic Module controls vacuum through the EGR solenoid, turning the vacuum circuit on or off. A back pressure transducer measures the amount of exhaust back pressure on the exhaust side of the EGR valve and varies the strength of the vacuum signal applied to the EGR valve. The Logic Module will prevent EGR operation by turning the EGR solenoid off at idle, wide open throttle or when engine temperature falls below 70°F (21°C). The back pressure transducer adjusts the EGR signal to provide programmed amounts of Exhaust Gas Recirculation under all other conditions.

Air Aspirator System

The air aspirator system uses exhaust pressure pulses to draw air into the exhaust system. This reduces carbon monoxide (CO) and hydrocarbon (HC) emissions. It draws fresh air from the clean side of the air cleaner past a one-way diaphragm in the aspirator valve.

The diaphragm opens to allow fresh air to mix with exhaust gasses during negative pressure pulses. If pressure pulses are positive, the diaphragm closes, which prevents exhaust gasses from entering the air cleaner. The air aspirator is most effective at idle and slightly off idle where negative pressure pulses are greatest.

On-Car Service

NOTE: Most complaints that may occur with turbocharged multi-point Electronic Fuel Injection can be traced to poor wiring or hose connections. A visual check will help spot these faults and save unnecessary test and diagnosis time.

ON BOARD DIAGNOSTICS

The Logic Module has been programmed to monitor several different circuits of the fuel injection system. This monitoring is called On Board Diagnosis. If a problem is sensed with a monitored circuit, often enough to indicate an actual problem, its Fault Code is stored in the Logic Module for eventual display to the service technician. If the problem is repaired or ceases to exist, the Logic Module cancels the Fault Code after 30 ignition key on/off cycles.

Fault Codes

When a fault code appears (either by flashes of the power loss lamp or by watching the diagnostic readout—Tool C-4805 or equivalent), it indicates that the Logic Module has recognized an abnormal signal in the system. Fault codes indicate the results of a failure do not always identify the failed component.

CODE 11 indicates a problem in the distributor circuit. This code appears if the Logic Module has not sensed a distributor signal since the battery was reconnected.

CODE 12 indicates a problem in the stand-by memory circuit. This code appears if direct memory feed to the Logic Module is interrupted.

CODE 13 indicates a problem in the MAP sensor pneumatic system. This code appears if the MAP sensor vacuum level does not change between start and start/run transfer speed (500-600 rpm).

CODE 14 indicates a problem in the MAP sensor electrical system. This code appears if the map sensor signal is either too low (below .02 volts) or too high (above 4.9 volts).

CODE 15 indicates a problem in the vehicle Speed Sensor circuit. This code appears if engine speed is at idle and speed sensor indicates less than 2 mph. This code is valid only if it is sensed while moving.

CODE 21 indicates a problem in the O_2 feedback circuit. This code appears if engine temperature is above 170°F (77°C), engine speed is above 1500 rpm, and there has been no O_2 signal for more than 5 seconds.

CODE 22 indicates a problem in the coolant temperature circuit. This code appears if the temperature sensor indicates an improbable temperature or a temperature that changes too fast to be real.

CODE 23 indicates a problem in the charge temperature circuit. This code appears if the charge temperature is an improbable temperature or a temperature that changes too fast to be real.

CODE 24 indicates a problem in the Throttle Position Sensor circuit. This code appears if the sensor signal is either below .16 volts or above 4.7 volts.

CODE 25 indicates a problem in the Automatic Idle Speed system. This code appears if the proper voltage from the AIS system is not present. An open motor or harness will not activate this code.

CODE 31 indicates a problem in the Canister Purge Solenoid circuit. This code appears when the proper voltage at the purge solenoid is not present (open or shorted).

CODE 32 indicates a problem in the Power Loss Lamp circuit. This code appears if proper voltage to the Power Loss Lamp is not present (open or shorted system).

CODE 33 indicates a problem in the Air Conditioning Wide Open Throttle Cut Out Relay circuit. This code appears if the proper voltage at the EGR Solenoid is not present (open or shorted).

CODE 34 indicates a problem in the EGR Solenoid circuit. This code appears if proper voltage at the EGR Solenoid is not present (open or shorted).

CODE 35 indicates a problem in the Fan Relay circuit. This code appears if the radiator fan is either not operating or operating at the wrong time.

CODE 41 indicates a problem in the Charging System. This code appears if battery voltage from the Automatic Shut Down Relay is below 11.75 volts.

CODE 42 indicates a problem in the Automatic Shut Down Relay (ASD) circuit. This code appears if during cranking, battery voltage from the ASD relay is not present for at least $1/3$ second after the first distributor pulse or, after engine stall, battery voltage is not off within 3 seconds after last distributor pulse.

CODE 43 indicates a problem in the interface circuit. This code appears if the anti-dwell or injector control signal is not present between the Logic Module and Power Module.

CODE 44 indicates a problem in the Logic Module. This code appears if an incorrect PROM has been installed in the Logic Module.

CODE 45 indicates a problem in the Overboost Shut Off circuit. This code appears if MAP sensor electrical signal rises above 10 psi boost.

CODE 51 indicates a problem in the closed loop fuel system. This code appears if during closed loop conditions, the O_2 signal is either low or high for more than 2 minutes.

CODE 52 indicates a problem in the Logic Module. This code appears if an internal failure exists in the Logic Module.

CODE 53 indicates a problem in the Logic Module. This code appears if an internal failure exists in the Logic Module.

CODE 54 indicates a problem in the Synchronization pick-up circuit. This code appears, if at start/run transfer speed, the reference pick-up signal is present but the synchronization pick-up signal is missing at the logic module.

CODE 55 indicates message complete. This code appears after all fault codes are displayed.

CODE 88 indicates start of message. This code appears at start of fault code messages. This code only appears on Readout Tool C-4805, or equivalent, and may also be used for switch check.

SYSTEM TESTS

Obtaining Fault Codes

1. Connect Diagnostic Readout Box Tool C-4805, or equivalent, to the diagnostic connector located in the engine compartment near the passenger side strut tower.

2. Start the engine if possible, cycle the transmission selector and the A/C switch if applicable. Shut off the engine.

3. Turn the ignition switch on, off, on, off, on. Within 5 seconds record all the diagnostic codes shown on the diagnostic readout box tool, observe the power loss lamp on the instrument panel the lamp should light for 2 seconds then go out (bulb check).

Switch Test

After all codes have been shown and has indicated Code 55 end of message, actuate the following component switches. The digital display must change its numbers when the switch is activated and released:
- Brake Pedal
- Gear Shift Selector park, reverse, park.
- A/C Switch (if applicable).
- Electric Backlite Switch (if applicable).

Actuator Test Mode (ATM)

1. Remove coil wire from cap and place $1/4$ in. from a ground.

-CAUTION-

Coil wire must be $1/4$ in. or less from ground or power module damage may result.

2. Remove air cleaner hose from throttle body.

3. Press the ATM button on the diagnostic readout box tool and observe the following:
- 3 sparks from the coil wire to ground.
- 2 AILS motor movements (1 open 1 close) you must listen carefully for AIS operation.
- With the ATM button still depressed, install a jumper wire between pins 2 and 3 of the gray distributor synch. connector. Listen for the click which indicates one set of injectors has been activated. Remove jumper wire and second set of injectors will be activated. Reconnect distributor connector.

4. The ATM capability is cancelled 5 minutes after the ignition switch is turned on. To reinstate this capability cycle the ignition on and off three times ending in the on position.

5. When the ATM button is pressed, fault Code 42 is generated because the ASD relay is by passed. Do not use this code for diagnostics after ATM operation.

6. The ATM test will check 3 categories of operation:
- When coil fires three times.
  a. Coil operational
  b. Logic Module portion operational
  c. Power Module portion operational
  d. Interface between Power Module and Logic Module is working.
- AIS is operational
- Injector fuel pulse into Throttle Body:
  a. Fuel injector operational
  b. Fuel pump operational
  c. Fuel lines intact.

7. The Electronic Fuel Injection system must be evaluated using all the information found in the systems test:
- Start/No Start
- Fault Codes
- Loss of Power Lamp on or off (limp in)
- ATM Results:
  Spark yes/no
  Fuel yes/no
  AIS movement yes/no

Once this information is found it will be easier to determine what circuit to look at for further testing.

Relieving Fuel System Pressure

The E.F.I. fuel system is under a constant pressure of approximately 53 psi (380 kPa). Before servicing the fuel tank, fuel pump, fuel lines, fuel filter, or fuel components of the throttle body the fuel pressure must be released as follows:

1. Loosen gas cap to release any in tank pressure.
2. Remove wiring harness connector from any injector.
3. Ground one injector terminal with a jumper.
4. Connect a jumper wire to second terminal and touch battery positive post for no longer than 10 seconds.
5. Remove jumper wires.
6. Continue fuel system service.

Fuel System Pressure Test

-CAUTION-

Fuel system pressure must be released each time a fuel hose is to be disconnected.

1. Remove fuel intake hose from throttle body and connect fuel system pressure testers C-3292, and C-4749, or equivalent, between fuel filter hose and throttle body.

2. Start engine. If gauge reads 380 kPa = 14, Pa (53 psi = 2 psi) pressure is correct and no further testing is required. Reinstall fuel hose using a new original equipment type clamp and torque to 10 inch lbs. (1 nm).

Location of ground wire

3. If fuel pressure is below specifications, install tester between fuel filter hose and fuel line.

4. Start engine. If pressure is now correct, replace fuel filter. If no change is observed, gently squeeze return hose. If pressure increases, replace pressure regulator. If no change is observed, problem is either a plugged pump filter sock or defective fuel pump.

5. If pressure is above specifications, remove fuel return hose from pressure regulator end. Connect a substitute hose and place other end of hose in clean container. Start engine. If pressure is now correct, check for restricted fuel return lilne. If no change is observed, replace fuel regulator.

Component Removal

Mechanical malfunctions are more difficult to diagnose with the EFI system. The Logic Module has been programmed to compensate for some mechanical malfunctions such as incorrect cam timing, vacuum leaks, etc. If engine performance problems are encountered, and no fault codes are displayed, the problem may be mechanical rather than electronic.

THROTTLE BODY

When servicing the fuel portion of the throttle body it will be necessary to bleed fuel pressure before opening any hoses. Always reassemble throttle body components with new O-rings and seals where applicable. Never use lubricants on O-rings or seals, damage may result. If assembly of components is difficult use water to aid assembly. Use care when removing fuel hoses to prevent damage to hose or hose nipple. Always use new hose clamps of the correct type when reassembling and torque hose clamps to 10 inch lbs. (1 Nm). Do not use aviation-style clamps on this system or hose damage may result.

NOTE: It is not necessary to remove the throttle body from the intake manifold to perform component disassembly. If fuel system hoses are to be replaced, only hoses marked EFI/EFM may be used.

Removal and Installation

1. Disconnect negative battery cable.

2. Remove air cleaner to throttle body screws, loosen hose clamp and remove air cleaner adaptor.

3. Remove accelerator, speed control, and transmission kickdown cables and return spring.

4. Remove throttle cable bracket from throttle body.
5. Disconnect 6 way connector.
6. Disconnect vacuum hoses from throttle body.
7. Loosen throttle body to turbocharger hose clamp.
8. Remove throttle body to intake manifold screws.
9. Remove throttle body.
10. Reverse the above procedure for installation.

THROTTLE POSITION SENSOR

Removal and Installation

1. Disconnect negative battery cable and 6-way throttle body connector.

2. Remove 2 screws mounting throttle position sensor to throttle body.

3. Unclip wiring clip from convoluted tube and remove mounting bracket.

4. Lift throttle position sensor off throttle shaft and remove O-ring.

5. Pull the 3 wires of the throttle position sensor from the convoluted tubing.

6. Look inside the 6-way throttle body connector and lift a locking tab with a small screwdriver for each T.P.S. wire blade terminal. Remove each blade from connector. (Not wiring position for reassembly.)

7. Insert each wire blade terminal into throttle body connector. Make sure wires are inserted into correct locations.

8. Insert wires from throttle position sensor into convoluted tube.

9. Install throttle position sensor and new O-ring with mounting bracket to throttle body. Torque screws to 20 inch lbs. (2 Nm).

10. Install wiring clips to convoluted tube.

11. Connect 6 way connector and battery cable.

AUTOMATIC IDLE SPEED MOTOR

Removal and Installation

1. Disconnect negative battery cable and 6-way throttle body connector.

2. Remove 2 screws that mount the A.I.S. to its adaptor. (Do not remove the clamp on the A.I.S. or damage will result.)

3. Remove wiring clips and remove the two A.I.S. wires from the 6-way throttle body connector. Lift each locking tab with a small screwdriver and remove each blade terminal. (Note wiring position for reassembly).

4. Lift A.I.S. from its adaptor.

5. Remove the 2 O-rings on the A.I.S. carefully.

6. Install 2 new O-rings on A.I.S.

7. Carefully work A.I.S. into its adaptor.

8. Install 2 mounting screws and torque to 20 inch lbs. (2 Nm).

9. Route A.I.S. wiring to 6-way connector and install each wire blade terminal into the connector. Make sure wires are inserted in correct locations.

10. Connect wiring clips, 6-way connector, and battery cable.

AUTOMATIC IDLE SPEED MOTOR ASSEMBLY

Removal and Installation

1. Disconnect negative battery cable and 6-way throttle body connector.

2. Remove 2 screws on back of throttle body from A.I.S. adaptor.

3. Remove wiring clips and remove the two A.I.S. wires from the 6-way throttle body connector. Lift each locking tab with a small screwdriver and remove each blade terminal. (Note wiring position for reassembly).

4. Carefully pull the assembly from the rear of the throttle body. The O-ring at the top and seal at the bottom may fall off adaptor.

5. Remove O-ring and seal.

6. Place a new O-ring and seal on adaptor.

7. Carefully position assembly onto back of throttle body (make sure seals stay in place) insert screws and torque to 65 inch lbs. (7 Nm).

8. Route A.I.S. wiring to 6-way connector and install each wire blade terminal into the connector. Make sure wires are inserted in correct locations.

9. Connect wiring clips, 6-way connector, and battery cable.

OXYGEN SENSOR

Removal and Installation

Removing the oxygen sensor from the exhaust manifold may be difficult if the sensor was overtorqued during installation. Use Tool C-4589, or equivalent, to remove the sensor. The threads in the exhaust manifold must be cleaned with a 18mm x 1.5 x 6E tap. If the same sensor is to be reinstalled, the threads must be coated with an anti-seize compound such as Loctite® 771-64 or equivalent. New sensors are packaged with anti-seize compound on the threads and no additional compound is required. Sensors must be torqued to 20 ft. lbs. (27 Nm).

IDLE SPEED

Adjustment

Before adjusting the idle on an electronic fuel injected vehicle the following items must be checked:

a. AIS motor has been checked for operation.

b. Engine has been checked for vacuum or EGR leaks.

c. Engine timing has been checked and set to specifications.

d. Coolant temperature sensor has been checked for operation.

1. Install a tachometer.

2. Warm up engine to normal operating temperature (accessories off).

3. Shut engine off and disconnect radiator fan.

4. Disconnect Throttle Body 6-way connector. Remove the brown with white tracer AIS wire from the connector and reconnect connector.

5. Start engine with transaxle selector in park or neutral.

6. Apply 12 volts to AIS brown with white tracer wire. This will drive the AIS fully closed and the idle should drop.

7. Disconnect then reconnect coolant temperature sensor.

8. With transaxle in neutral, idle speed should be 775 ± 25 (700 ± 25 green engine).

9. If idle is not to specifications adjust idle air bypass screw.

10. If idle will not adjust down, check for vacuum leaks, AIS motor damage, throttle body damage, or speed control cable adjustment.

IGNITION TIMING

Adjustment

1. Connect a power timing light to the number one cylinder, or a magnetic timing unit to the engine. (Use a 10° degree offset when required).

2. Connect a tachometer to the engine and turn selector to the proper cylinder position.

3. Start engine and run until operating temperature is reached.

4. Disconnect and reconnect the water temperature sensor connector on the thermostat housing. The loss of power lamp on the dash must come on and stay on. Engine rpm should be within emission label specifications.

5. Aim power timing light at timing hole in bell housing or read the magnetic timing unit.

6. Loosen distributor and adjust timing to emission label specifications if necessary.

7. Shut engine off, disconnect and reconnect positive battery quick disconnect. Start vehicle, the loss of power lamp should be off.

8. Shut engine off, then turn ignition on, off, on, off, on. Fault codes should be clear with 88-51-55 shown.

CHRYSLER THROTTLE BODY INJECTION SYSTEM

General Information

This electronic fuel injection system is a computer regulated single point fuel injection system that provides precise air/fuel ratio for all driving conditions. At the center of this system is a digital pre-programmed computer known as a logic module that regulates ignition timing, air-fuel ratio, emission control devices and idle speed. This component has the ability to update and revise its programming to meet changing operating conditions.

Various sensors provide the input necessary for the logic module to correctly regulate the fuel flow at the fuel injector. These include the manifold absolute pressure, throttle position, oxygen feedback, coolant temperature, charge temperature and vehicle speed sensors. In addition to the sensors, various switches also provide important information. These include the neutral-safety, heated back lite, air conditioning, air conditioning clutch switches, and an electronic idle switch.

All inputs to the logic module are converted into signals sent to the power module. These signals cause the power module to change either the fuel flow at the injector or ignition timing or both.

The logic module tests many of its own input and output circuits. If a fault is found in a major system this information is stored in the logic module. Information on this fault can be displayed to a technician by means of a flashing light emitting diode (LED) or by connecting a diagnostic read out and reading a numbered display code which directly relates to a specific fault.

ELECTRONIC CONTROL SYSTEM

Power Module

The power module contains the circuits necessary to power the ignition coil and the fuel injector. These are high current devices and their power supply has been isolated to minimize any "electri-

Typical power module showing harness connector terminals

Schematic of Chrysler EFI system

cal noise" reaching the logic module. The power module also energizes the automatic shut down (ASD) relay which activates the fuel pump, ignition coil, and the power module itself. The module also receives a signal from the distributor and sends this signal to the logic module. In the event of no distributor signal, the ASD relay is not activated and power is shut off from the fuel pump and ignition coil. The power module contains a voltage converter which

reduces battery voltage to a regulated 8.0V output. This 8.0V output powers the distributor and also powers the logic module.

Logic Module

The logic module is a digital computer containing a microprocessor. The module receives input signals from various switches, sensors, and components. It then computes the fuel injector pulse width, spark advance, ignition coil dwell, automatic idle speed actuation, and purge, and EGR control solenoid cycles.

The logic module tests many of its own input and output circuits.

Typical logic module showing harness connector terminals

Location of logic module, components and harness connectors

If a fault is found in a major system, this information is stored in the logic module. Information on this fault can be displayed to a technician by means of a flashing, light emitting diode (LED) or by connecting a diagnostic read out and reading a numbered display code which directly relates to a specific fault.

When the power module senses a distributor signal during cranking, it grounds the ASD closing its contacts. This completes the circuit for the electric fuel pump, power module, and ignition coil. If the distributor signal is lost for any reason the ASD interrupts this circuit in less than one second preventing fuel, spark, and engine operations. This fast shutdown serves as a safety feature in the event of an accident.

ENGINE SENSORS

Manifold Absolute Pressure (MAP) Sensor

The manifold absolute pressure (MAP) sensor is a device which monitors manifold vacuum. It is mounted in the right side passenger compartment and is connected to a vacuum nipple on the throttle body and, electrically to the logic module. The sensor transmits information on manifold vacuum conditions and barometric pressure to the logic module. The MAP sensor data on engine load is used with data from other sensors to determine the correct air-fuel mixture.

Manifold absolute pressure (MAP) sensor

Oxygen Sensor

The oxygen sensor (O_2 sensor) is a device which produces an electrical voltage when exposed to the oxygen present in the exhaust gases. The sensor is mounted in the exhaust manifold and must be heated by the exhaust gases before producing the voltage. When there is a large amount of oxygen present (lean mixture), the sensor produces a low voltage. When there is a lesser amount present (rich mixture) it produces a higher voltage. By monitoring the oxygen content and converting it to electrical voltage, the sensor acts as a rich-lean switch. The voltage is transmitted to the logic module. The logic module signals the power module to trigger the fuel injector. The injector changes the mixture.

Coolant Temperature Sensor

The coolant temperature sensor is mounted in the thermostat housing. This sensor provides data on engine operating temperature to the logic module. This data along with data provided by the charge temperature switch allows the logic module to demand slightly richer air-fuel mixtures and higher idle speeds until normal operating temperatures are reached. The coolant temperature sensor allows the logic module to act as an automatic choke.

Typical oxygen sensor

Charge Temperature sensor

The charge temperature sensor is a device mounted in the intake manifold which measures the temperature of the air-fuel mixture. This information is used by the logic module to determine engine operating temperature and engine warm-up cycles in the event of a coolant temperature sensor failure.

Switch Input

Various switches provide information to the logic module. These include the idle, neutral safety, electric backlite, air conditioning, air conditioning clutch, and brake light switches. If one or more of these switches is sensed as being in the on position, the logic module signals the automatic idle speed motor to increase idle speed to a scheduled rpm.

With the air conditioning on and the throttle blade above a specific angle, the wide open throttle cut-out relay prevents the air conditioning clutch from engaging until the throttle blade is below this angle.

Power Loss Lamp

The power loss lamp comes on each time the ignition key is turned on and stays on for a few seconds as a bulb test.

If the logic module receives an incorrect signal or no signal from either the coolant temperature sensor, manifold absolute pressure sensor, or the throttle position sensor, the power loss lamp on the instrument panel is illuminated. This is a warning that the logic module has gone into limp in mode in an attempt to keep the system operational.

Limp in mode is the attempt by the logic module to compensate for the failure of certain components by substituting information from other sources. If the logic module senses incorrect data or no data at all from the MAP sensor, throttle position sensor or coolant temperature sensor, the system is placed into Limp in Mode and the power loss lamp on the instrument panel is activated.

FUEL CONTROL SYSTEM

Throttle Body

The throttle body assembly replaces a conventional carburetor and is mounted on top of the intake manifold. The throttle body houses the fuel injector, pressure regulator, throttle position sensor, and automatic idle speed motor. Air flow through the throttle body is

Typical coolant sensor

Throttle body assembly

controlled by a cable operated throttle blade located in the base of the throttle body. The throttle body itself provides the chamber for metering atomizing and distributing fuel through out the air entering the engine.

Fuel Injector

The fuel injector is an electric solenoid powered by the power module but, controlled by the logic module. The logic module, based on ambient, mechanical, and sensor input, determines when and

Cross section of typical solenoid-type fuel injector

how long the power module should operate the injector. When an electric current is supplied to the injector, the armature and pintle move a short distance against a spring, opening a small orifice. Fuel is supplied to the inlet of the injector by the fuel pump, then passes through the injector, around the pintle, and out the orifice. Since the fuel is under high pressure a fine spray is developed in the shape of a hollow cone. The injector, through this spraying action, atomizes the fuel and distributes it into the air entering the throttle body.

Fuel Pressure Regulator

The pressure regulator is a mechanical device located downstream of the fuel injector on the throttle body. Its function is to maintain a constant 250kPa (36PSI) across the fuel injector tip. The regulator uses a spring loaded rubber diaphragm to uncover a fuel return port. When the fuel pump becomes operational, fuel flows past the injector into the regulator, and is restricted from flowing any further by the blocked return port. When fuel pressure reaches 250kPa (36PSI) it pushes on the diaphragm, compressing the spring, and uncovers the fuel return port. The diaphragm and spring will constantly move from an open to closed position to keep the fuel pressure constant. An assist to the spring loaded diaphragm comes from vacuum in the throttle body above the throttle blade. As venturi vacuum increases less pressure is required to supply the same amount of fuel into the air flow. The vacuum assists

Cross section of typical fuel pressure regulator

in opening the fuel port during high vacuum conditions. This fine tunes the fuel pressure for all operating conditions.

Throttle Position Sensor (TPS)

The throttle position sensor (TPS) is an electric resistor which is activated by the movement of the throttle shaft. It is mounted on the throttle body and senses the angle of the throttle blade opening. The voltage that the sensor produces increases or decreases according to the throttle blade opening. This voltage is transmitted to the logic module where it is used along with data from other sensors to adjust the air-fuel ratio to varying conditions and during acceleration, deceleration, idle, and wide open throttle operations.

Automatic Idle Speed (AIS) Motor

The automatic idle speed motor (AIS) is operated by the logic module. Data from the throttle position sensor, speed sensor, coolant temperature sensor, and various switch operations, (electric backlite, air conditioning, safety/neutral, brake) are used by the logic module to adjust engine idle to an optimum during all idle conditions. The AIS adjusts the air portion of the air/fuel mixture through an air bypass on the back of the throttle body. Basic (no load) idle is determined by the minimum air flow through the throttle body. The AIS opens or closes off the air bypass as an increase or decrease is needed due to engine loads or ambient conditions. The logic module senses an air/fuel change and increases or decreases fuel proportionally to change engine idle. Deceleration die out is also prevented by increasing engine idle when the throttle is closed quickly after a driving (speed) condition.

Fuel Pump

The fuel pump used in this system is a positive displacement, roller vane immersible pump with a permanent magnet electric motor.

Fuel pump assembly (in-tank)

The fuel is drawn in through a filter sock and pushed through the electric motor to the outlet. The pump contains two check valves. One valve is used to relieve internal fuel pump pressure and regulate maximum pump output. The other check valve, located near the pump outlet, restricts fuel movement in either direction when the pump is not operational. Voltage to operate the pump is supplied through the auto shutdown relay.

On-Car Service

NOTE: Experience has shown that most complaints that may occur with EFI can be traced to poor wiring or hose connections. A visual check will help spot these most common faults and save unnecessary test and diagnosis time.

ON BOARD DIAGNOSTICS

The logic module has been programmed to monitor several different circuits of the fuel injection system. This monitoring is called On Board Diagnosis. If a problem is sensed with a monitored circuit, often enough to indicate an actual problem, its fault code is stored in the logic module for eventual display to the service technician. If the problem is repaired or ceases to exist, the logic module cancels the fault code after 30 ignition key on/off cycles.

Fault Codes

When a fault code appears (either by flashes of the light emitting diode or by watching the diagnostic readout—Tool C-4805 or equivalent, it indicates that the logic module has recognized an abnormal signal in the system. Fault codes indicate the results of a failure but do not always identify the failed component.

CODE 11 means a problem in the distributor circuit. This code appears when the logic module has not seen a distributor signal since the battery was reconnected.
CODE 12 indicates a problem in the stand-by memory circuit. This code appears if direct battery feed to the logic module is interrupted.
CODE 13 means a problem exists in the MAP sensor pneumatic system. This code appears if the MAP sensor vacuum level does not change between start and start/run transfer speed (500–600 rpm).
CODE 14 means a problem exists in the MAP sensor electrical system. This code appears if the MAP sensor signal is either too low (below .02 volts) or too high (above 4.9 volts).
CODE 15 means a problem exists in the vehicle Speed Sensor ciruit. This code appears if engine speed is above 1468 rpm and speed sensor indicates less than 2 mph. This code is valid only if it is sensed while vehicle is moving.
CODE 21 indicates a problem in the O_2 sensor circuit. This code appears if there has been no O_2 signal for more than 5 seconds.
CODE 22 means a problem exists in the coolant temperature sensor circuit. This code appears if the temperature sensor circuit indicates an incorrect temperature or a temperature that changes too fast to be real.
CODE 24 means a problem exists in the throttle position sensor circuit. This code appears if the sensor signal is either below 0.16 vcolts or above 4.7 volts.
CODE 25 means a problem in the automatic idle speed (AIS) control circuit. This code appears if the proper voltage from the AIS system is not present. An open harness or motor will not activate code.
CODE 31 means a problem in the canister purge solenoid circuit. This code appears when the proper voltage at the purge solenoid is not present (open or shorted system).
CODE 32 means a problem in the power loss lamp circuit. This code appears when proper voltage to the power loss lamp circuit is not present (open or shorted system).
CODE 33 means a problem in the air conditioning wide open throttle cut out relay circuit. This code appears if the proper volt-

age at the air conditioning wide open throttle relay circuit is not present (open or shorted).

CODE 34 means a problem in the EGR solenoid circuit. This code appears if proper voltage at the EGR solenoid circuit is not present (open or shorted system).

CODE 35 indicates a problem in the fan relay circuit. This code appears if the radiator fan is either not operating or operating at wrong time.

CODE 41 means a problem in the charging system. This code appears if battery voltage from the automatic shut down relay is below 11.75 volts.

CODE 42 means a problem in the automatic shut down relay (ASD) circuit. This code appears if during cranking, battery voltage from ASD relay is not present for at least 1/3 second after first distributor pulse or after engine stall, battery voltage is not off within 3 seconds after last distributor pulse.

CODE 43 means a problem in the interface circuit. This code appears if the anti-dwell or injector control signal is not present between the logic module and power module.

CODE 44 means a problem in the logic module. This code appears if an internal failure exists in the logic module.

CODE 51 indicates a problem in the closed loop fuel system. This code appears if during closed loop conditions, the O_2 signal is either low or high for more than 2 minutes.

CODE 52 means a problem in the logic module. This code appears if an internal failure exists in the logic module.

CODE 53 means a problem in the logic module. This code appears if an internal failure exists in the logic module.

CODE 54 means a problem in the logic module. This code appears if an internal failure exists in the logic module.

CODE 55 means "end of message". This code appears as the final code after all other fault codes have been displayed and means "end of message".

CODE 88 means start of message. This code only appears on the diagnostic readout Tool C-4805 or equivalent, and means start of message.

SYSTEMS TEST

Obtaining Fault Codes

1. Connect diagnostic readout box tool C-4805 or equivalent, to the diagnostic connector located in the engine compartment near the passenger side strut tower.

2. Start the engine if possible, cycle the transmission selector and the A/C switch if applicable. Shut off the engine.

3. Turn the ignition switch on, off, on, off, on. Within 5 seconds record all the diagnostic codes shown on the diagnostic readout box tool, observe the power loss lamp on the instrument panel the lamp should light for 2 seconds then go out (bulb check).

Switch Test

After all codes have been shown and has indicated Code 55 end of message, actuate the following component switches. The digital display must change its numbers when the switch is activated and released:

- Brake pedal
- Gear shift selector park, reverse, park.
- A/C switch (if applicable).
- Electric backlite switch (if applicable).

Actuator Test Mode (ATM)

1. Remove coil wire from cap and place 1/4 in. from a ground.

---CAUTION---

Coil wire must be 1/4 in. or less from ground or power module damage may result.

---

2. Remove air cleaner hose from throttle body.

3. Press the ATM button on the diagnostic readout box tool and observe the following:
- 3 sparks from the coil wire to ground.
- 2 AIS motor movements (1 open, 1 close) you must listen carefully for AIS operation.
- 1 fuel pulse from the injector into the throttle body.

4. The ATM capability is cancelled 5 minutes after the ignition switch is turned on. To reinstate this capability cycle the ignition ON and OFF three times ending in the ON position.

5. When the ATM button is pressed, fault Code 42 is generated because the ASD relay is bypassed. Do not use this code for diagnostics after ATM operation.

6. The ATM test will check 3 categories of operation:
- When coil fires three times:
    a. Coil operational
    b. Logic module portion operational
    c. Power module portion operational
    d. Interface between power module and logic module is working.
- AIS is operational
- Injector fuel pulse into Throttle Body:
    a. Fuel injector operational
    b. Fuel pump operational
    c. Fuel lines intact

7. The electronic fuel injection system must be evaluated using all the information found in the systems test:
- Start/no start
- Fault codes
- Loss of power lamp on or off (limp in)
- ATM results:
    a. Spark yes/no
    b. Fuel yes/no
    c. AIS movement yes/no

Once this information is found, it will be easier to determine what circuit to look at for further testing.

Ignition Timing Adjustment

1. Connect a power timing light to the number one cylinder, or a magnetic timing unit to the engine. (Use a 10° degree offset when required).

2. Connect a tachometer to the engine and turn selector to the proper cylinder position.

3. Start engine and run until operating temperature is reached.

4. Disconnect and reconnect the water temperature sensor connector on the thermostat housing. The loss of power lamp on the dash must come on and stay on. Engine rpm should be within emission label specifications.

5. Aim power timing light at timing hole in bell housing or read the magnetic timing unit.

6. Loosen distributor and adjust timing to emission label specifications if necessary.

7. Shut engine off, disconnect and reconnect positive battery quick disconnect. Start vehicle, the loss of power lamp should be off.

8. Shut engine off, then turn ignition on, off, on, off, on. Fault codes should be clear with 88-51-55 shown.

9. Increase engine to 2000 rpm.

10. Read timing it should be approximately 40 degrees.

11. If timing advance does not reach specifications, replace logic module.

Idle Speed Adjustment

1. Before adjusting the idle on an electronic fuel injected vehicle the following items must be checked.
    a. AIS motor has been checked for operation.
    b. Engine has been checked for vacuum or EGR leaks.
    c. Engine timing has been checked and set to specifications.
    d. Coolant temperature sensor has been checked for operation.

2. Connect a tachometer and timing light to engine.

3. Disconnect throttle body 6-way connector. Remove brown with white tracer AIS wire from connector and rejoin connector.

4. Connect one end of a jumper wire to AIS wire and other end to battery positive post for 5 seconds.

5. Connect a jumper to radiator fan so that it will run continuously.

6. Start and run engine for 3 minutes to allow speed to stabilize.

7. Using tool C-4804 or equivalent, turn idle speed adjusting screw to obtain 800 ± 10 rpm (Manual) 725 ± 10 rpm (Automatic) with transaxle in neutral.

NOTE: If idle will not adjust down, check for binding linkage, speed control servo cable adjustments, or throttle shaft binding.

8. Check that timing is 18 ± 2° BTDC (Manual) 12 ± 2° BTDC (Automatic).

9. If timing is not to above specifications turn idle speed adjusting screw until correct idle speed and ignition timing are obtained.

10. Turn off engine, disconnect tachometer and timing light, reinstall AIS wire and remove jumper wire.

Relieving Fuel System Pressure

The E.F.I. fuel system is under a constant pressure of approximately 36 psi (250 kPa). Before servicing the fuel tank, fuel pump, fuel lines, fuel filter, or fuel components of the throttle body the fuel pressure must be released as follows.

1. Loosen gas cap to release any in tank pressure.
2. Remove wiring harness connector from injector.
3. Ground one injector terminal with a jumper.
4. Connect a jumper wire to second terminal and touch battery positive post for no longer than 10 seconds.
5. Remove jumper wires.
6. Continue fuel system service.

Fuel System Pressure Test

-CAUTION-

Fuel system pressure must be released each time a fuel hose is to be disconnected.

1. Remove fuel intake hose from throttle body and connect fuel system pressure testers C-3292, and C-4749 or equivalent, between fuel filter hose and throttle body.

2. Start engine. If gauge reads 250 kPa ± 14 kPa (36 psi ± 2 psi) pressure is correct and no further testing is required. Reinstall fuel hose using a new original equipment type clamp and torque to 10 inch lbs. (1 Nm).

3. If fuel pressure is below specifications, install tester between fuel filter hose and fuel line.

4. Start engine. If pressure is now correct, replace fuel filter. If no change is observed, gently squeeze return hose. If pressure increases, replace pressure regulator. If no change is observed, problem is either a plugged pump filter sock or defective fuel pump.

5. If pressure is above specifications, remove fuel return hose from throttle body. Connect a substitute hose and place other end of hose in clean container. Start engine. If pressure is now correct, check for restricted fuel return line. If no change is observed, replace fuel regulator.

Component Removal

Mechanical malfunctions are more difficult to diagnose with the EFI system. The logic module has been programmed to compensate for some mechanical malfunctions such as incorrect cam timing, vacuum leaks, etc. If engine performance problems are encountered, and no fault codes are displayed, the problem may be mechanical rather than electronic.

THROTTLE BODY

Removal and Installation

1. Release fuel system pressure.
2. Disconnect negative battery terminal.
3. Disconnect fuel injector wiring connector and throttle body 6-way connector.
4. Remove electrical ground wire from 6-way wiring connector.
5. Remove air cleaner hose.
6. Remove throttle cable and if so equipped, the speed control and transmission kickdown cables.
7. Remove return spring.
8. Remove vacuum hoses.
9. Loosen fuel intake and return hose clamps. Wrap a shop towel around each hose, twist and pull off each hose.
10. Remove throttle body mounting screws and lift throttle body from vehicle.
11. Installation is the reverse of removal. Using a new gasket, with tabs facing forward, install throttle body and torque mounting screws to 17 ft. lbs. (23 Nm).

Disassembly

When servicing the fuel portion of the throttle body it will be necessary to bleed fuel pressure before opening any hoses. Always reassemble throttle body components with new O-rings and seals where applicable. Never use lubricants on O-rings or seals, damage may result. If assembly of components is difficult use water to aid assembly. Use care when removing fuel hoses to prevent damage to hose or hose nipple. Always use new hose clamps of the correct type when reassembling and torque hose clamps to 10 inch lbs. (1 Nm). Do not use aviation-style clamps.

Exploded view of throttle body

NOTE: It is not necessary to remove the throttle body from the intake manifold to perform component disassembly. If fuel system hoses are to be replaced, only hoses marked EFI/EFM may be used.

Injector Removal

1. Perform fuel system pressure release.
2. Disconnect negative battery cable.
3. Remove 4 Torx® screws holding fuel inlet chamber to throttle body.
4. Remove vacuum tube from pressure regulator to throttle body.

---CAUTION---

Place a shop towel around fuel inlet chamber to contain any fuel left in system.

---

5. Lift fuel inlet chamber and injector off throttle body.
6. Pull injector from fuel inlet chamber.
7. Remove upper and lower O-ring from fuel injector by peeling them off.
8. Remove snap ring that retains seal and washer on injector and remove seal and washer.
9. Installation is the reverse of removal. Place new O-ring washer, and seal on injector and install snap ring.
10. Place assembly into throttle body, install 4 Torx® screws and torque these screws to 35 inch lbs. (4 Nm).

PRESSURE REGULATOR

Removal and Installation

1. Perform fuel system pressure release.
2. Disconnect negative battery cable.
3. Remove 3 Torx® screws mounting pressure regulator to fuel inlet chamber.

---CAUTION---

Place a shop towel around fuel inlet chamber to contain any fuel left in system.

---

4. Remove vacuum tube from pressure regulator to throttle body.
5. Pull pressure regulator from throttle body.
6. Carefully peel O-ring off pressure regulator and remove flat seal.
7. Place new seal on pressure regulator and new O-ring.
8. Position pressure regulator on throttle body, press into place, install 3 Torx® screws and torque to 40 inch lbs. (5 Nm).
9. Install vacuum tube from pressure regulator to throttle body.
10. Connect battery, start vehicle, and check for any fuel leaks.

THROTTLE POSITION SENSOR

Removal and Installation

1. Disconnect negative battery cable and 6-way throttle body connector.
2. Remove 2 screws mounting throttle position sensor to throttle body.
3. Unclip wiring clip from convoluted tube and remove mounting bracket.

4. Lift throttle position sensor off throttle shaft and remove O-ring.
5. Pull the 3 wires of the throttle position sensor from the convoluted tubing.
6. Look inside the 6-way throttle body connector and lift a locking tab with a small screwdriver for each T.P.S. wire blade terminal. Removal each blade from connector. (Note wiring position for reassembly.)
7. Insert each wire blade terminal into throttle body connector. Make sure wires are inserted into correct locations.
8. Insert wires from throttle position sensor into convoluted tube.
9. Install throttle position sensor and new O-ring with mounting bracket to throttle body. Torque screws to 20 inch lbs. (2 Nm).
10. Install wiring clips to convoluted tube.
11. Connect 6-way connector and battery cable.

AUTOMATIC IDLE SPEED MOTOR

Removal and Installation

1. Disconnect negative battery cable and 6-way throttle body connector.
2. Remove screws that mount the A.I.S. to its adaptor. (Do not remove the clamp on the A.I.S. or damage will result.)
3. Remove wiring clips and remove the two A.I.S. wires from the 6-way throttle body connector. Lift each locking tab with a small screwdriver and remove each blade terminal. (Note wiring position for reassembly).
4. Lift A.I.S. from its adaptor.
5. Remove the O-rings on the A.I.S. carefully.
6. Install new O-rings on A.I.S.
7. Carefully work A.I.S. into its adaptor.
8. Install 2 mounting screws and torque to 20 inch lbs. (2 Nm).
9. Route A.I.S. wiring to 6-way connector and install each wire blade terminal into the connector. Make sure wires are inserted in correct locations.
10. Connect wiring clip, 6-way connector, and battery cable.

AUTOMATIC IDLE SPEED MOTOR ASSEMBLY

Removal and Installation

1. Disconnect negative battery cable and 6-way throttle body connector.
2. Remove 2 screws on back of throttle body from A.I.S. adaptor.
3. Remove wiring clips and remove the two A.I.S. wires from the 6-way throttle body connector. Lift each locking tab with a small screwdriver and remove each blade terminal. (Note wiring position for reassembly).
4. Carefully pull the assembly from the rear of the throttle body. The O-ring at the top and seal at the bottom may fall off adaptor.
5. Remove O-ring and seal.
6. Place a new O-ring and seal on adaptor.
7. Carefully position assembly onto back of throttle body (make sure seals stay in place) insert screws and torque to 65 inch lbs. (20 Nm).
8. Route A.I.S. wiring to 6-way connector and install each wire blade terminal into the connector. Make sure wires are inserted in correct locations.
9. Connect wiring clips, 6-way connector, and battery cable.

FORD EFI-EEC IV PORT FUEL INJECTION SYSTEM

General Information

The EFI-EEC IV System combines an electronic engine control module with a port fuel injection system to provide a more precise control over the air/fuel ratio, spark timing, deceleration fuel shut-off, EGR, curb and fast idle speed, evaporative emission control, and cold engine enrichment. The EFI-EEC IV system can be divided into three basic subsystems—Fuel, Air and Electronic Engine Control. This section will deal with the Fuel and Air systems only; for all service information on the Electronic Engine

Control system, please see the "Engine Controls" Unit Repair section.

NOTE: For wiring diagrams and diagnosis charts on the EEC IV System, see the "Engine Controls" section.

EFI-EEC IV Fuel System
COMPONENTS AND OPERATION

The fuel subsystem includes a high pressure electric fuel pump, fuel charging manifold, pressure regulator, fuel filter and both solid and flexible fuel lines. The fuel charging manifold includes four electronically controlled fuel injectors, each mounted directly above an intake port in the lower intake manifold. All injectors are energized simultaneously and spray once every crankshaft revolution, delivering a predetermined quantity of fuel into the intake airstream.

The fuel pressure regulator maintains a constant pressure drop across the injector nozzles. The regulator is referenced to intake manifold vacuum and is connected parallel to the fuel injectors and positioned on the far end of the fuel rail. Any excess fuel supplied by the pump passes through the regulator and is returned to the fuel tank via a return line.

NOTE: The pressure regulator reduces fuel pressure to 39–40 psi under normal operating conditions. At idle or high manifold vacuum condition, fuel pressure is reduced to about 30 psi.

Location of fuel pump on 1.6L engine

The fuel pressure regulator is a diaphragm operated relief valve in which one side of the diaphragm senses fuel pressure and the other side senses manifold vacuum. Normal fuel pressure is established by a spring preload applied to the diaphragm. Control of the fuel system is maintained through the EEC power relay and the EEC IV control unit, although electrical power is routed through the fuel pump relay and an inertia switch. The fuel pump relay is normally located on a bracket somewhere above the Electronic Control Assembly (ECA) and the Inertia Switch is located in the left rear kick panel. The fuel pump is usually mounted on a bracket at the fuel tank.

The inertia switch opens the power circuit to the fuel pump in the event of a collision. Once tripped, the switch must be reset manually by pushing the reset button on the assembly. Check that the inertia switch is reset before diagnosing power supply problems.

FUEL INJECTORS

The fuel injectors used with the EFI-EEC IV system are electro-mechanical (solenoid) type designed to meter and atomize fuel delivered to the intake ports of the engine. The injectors are mounted in the lower intake manifold and positioned so that their spray nozzles direct the fuel charge in front of the intake valves.

Location of components on 1.6L EFI-EEC IV engine—front view

Location of components on 1.6L EFI-EEC IV engine—rear view

Location of fuel pumps on 2.3L engine

TURBO WARNING
SWITCH

EGR
SOLENOID

TURBO OIL
SUPPLY LINE

FUEL
PRESSURE
REGULATOR

VACUUM SYSTEM
(VACUUM TREE)

TURBOCHARGER

AIR CLEANER

EGR VALVE

INTAKE
MANIFOLD

KNOCK SENSOR

ENGINE OIL
COOLER

OIL FILTER

EXHAUST
MANIFOLD

TO FUEL
TANK

CANISTER

UNIVERSAL
DISTRIBUTOR
WITH TFI
MODULE

Location of components on 2.3L EFI—EEC IV turbocharged engine

The injector body consists of a solenoid actuated pintle and needle valve assembly. The control unit sends an electrical impulse that activates the solenoid, causing the pintle to move inward off the seat and allow the fuel to flow. The amount of fuel delivered is controlled by the length of time the injector is energized since the fuel flow orifice is fixed and the fuel pressure drop across the injector tip is constant. Correct atomization is achieved by contouring the pintle at the point where the fuel enters the pintle chamber.

NOTE: Exercise care when handling fuel injectors during service. Be careful not to lose the pintle cap and replace damaged O-rings to assure a tight seal. Never apply direct battery voltage to test an EFI fuel injector.

The injectors receive high pressure fuel from the fuel manifold (fuel rail) assembly. The complete assembly includes a single, preformed tube with four injector connectors, mounting flange for the pressure regulator, mounting attachments to locate the manifold and provide the fuel injector retainers and Schrader® quick disconnect fitting used to perform fuel pressure tests.

NOTE: The fuel manifold is normally removed with fuel injectors and pressure regulator attached. Fuel injector electrical connectors are plastic and have locking tabs that must be released when disconnecting.

EFI-EEC IV Air System

COMPONENTS AND OPERATION

The EFI-EEC IV air subsystem components include the air cleaner assembly, air flow (vane) meter, throttle air bypass valve and air ducts that connect the air system to the throttle body assembly. The throttle body regulates the air flow to the engine through a single butterfly-type throttle plate controlled by conventional accelerator linkage. The throttle body has an idle adjustment screw (throttle air bypass valve) to set the throttle plate position, a PCV fresh air source upstream of the throttle plate, individual vacuum taps for PCV and control signals and a throttle position sensor that provides a voltage signal for the EEC IV control unit.

FUEL RAIL
O-RING SEAL

INTEGRAL FILTER

ELECTRICAL
CONNECTOR

COIL

ARMATURE

STAINLESS
STEEL BODY

MANIFOLD
O-RING SEAL

STAINLESS
STEEL NEEDLE

PINTLE

PINTLE PROTECTION
CASE

Cross section of typical solenoid—type fuel injector

Air flow meter installation on 1.6L engine

Typical vane air temperature sensor located in air flow meter

NOTE: For information on diagnosis and testing of all EFI-EEC IV system sensors, see the "Engine Controls" section.

The hot air intake system uses a thermostatic flap valve assembly whose components and operation are similar to previous hot air intake systems. Intake air volume and temperature are measured by the vane meter assembly which is mounted between the air cleaner and throttle body. The vane meter consists of two separate devices; the vane airflow sensor (VAF) uses a counterbalanced L-shaped flap valve mounted on a pivot pin and connected to a variable resistor (potentiometer). The control unit measures the amount of deflection of the flap vane by measuring the voltage signal from the potentiometer mounted on top of the meter body; larger air volume moves the vane further and produces a higher voltage signal. The vane air temperature (VAT) sensor is mounted in the middle of the air stream just before the flap valve. Since the mass (weight) of a specific volume of air varies with pressure and temperature, the control unit uses the voltage signal from the air temperature sensor to compensate for these variables and provide a more exact measurement of actual air mass that is necessary to calculate the fuel required to obtain the optimum air/fuel ratio under a wide range of operating conditions. On the EEC IV system, the VAT sensor affects spark timing as a function of air temperature.

NOTE: Make sure all air intake connections are tight before testing. Air leaking into the engine through a loose bellows connection can result in abnormal engine operation and affect the air/fuel mixture ratio.

Air flow meter installation on 2.3L engine

THROTTLE AIR BYPASS VALVE

The throttle air bypass valve is an electro-mechanical (solenoid) device whose operation is controlled by the EEC IV control unit. A variable air metering valve controls both cold and warm idle airflow in response to commands from the control unit. The valve operates by bypassing a regulated amount of air around the throttle plate; the higher the voltage signal from the control unit, the more air is bypassed through the valve. In this manner, additional air can be added to the fuel mixture without moving the throttle plate. At curb idle, the valve provides smooth idle for various engine coolant temperatures, compensates for A/C load and compensates for transaxle load and no-load conditions. The valve also provides fast idle for start-up, replacing the fast idle cam, throttle kicker and anti-dieseling solenoid common to previous models.

NOTE: Curb and fast idle speeds are proportional to engine coolant temperature and controlled through the EEC IV control unit. Fast idle kick-down will occur when the throttle is depressed, or after approximately 15–25 seconds after coolant temperature reaches 160°F.

EXHAUST GAS OXYGEN (EGO) SENSOR

The oxygen sensor used on the EFI-EEC IV system is a new design, located between the two downstream tubes in the header in its own mounting boss. The sensor works between zero and one volt output

Typical throttle air bypass valve

Typical oxygen sensor

depending on the amount of oxygen in the exhaust gas. A voltage reading above 0.6 volt indicates a rich fuel mixture, while a reading below 0.4 volt indicates a lean fuel mixture. Operation of the oxygen sensor is the same as similar systems used on other EEC and MCU models. A new type oxygen sensor can be identified by the metal cap that replaces the rubber protective cover on earlier designs.

CAUTION

Applying direct battery voltage to the oxygen sensor will destroy the sensor's calibration. Even the use of an ohmmeter could cause damage. Before connecting and using a voltmeter, make sure it has a high-input impedence (at least 10 megohms) and is set on the correct voltage range.

On-Car Service

The EFI-EEC IV system has a self-diagnostic capability to aid the technician in locating faults and troubleshooting components. All information on testing procedures is contained in the EEC IV Engine Controls Unity Repair Section. Before removing any fuel lines or fuel system components, first relieve the fuel system pressure by using the same Schrader adapter and fitting that is used to check fuel pressure at the fuel rail.

CAUTION

Exercise care to avoid the chance of fire whenever removing or installing fuel system components.

NOTE: The 2.3L system is similar to the 1.6L, with the addition of a "keep alive" memory in the ECA that retains any intermittent trouble codes stored within the last 20 engine starts. With this system, the memory is not erased when the ignition is switched OFF. In addition, the 2.3L EEC IV system incorporates a knock sensor to detect engine detonation (mounted in the lower intake manifold at the rear of the engine), and a barometric pressure sensor to compensate for altitude variations. The barometric pressure sensor is mounted on the right fender apron.

EEC IV TESTING

As in any service procedure, a routine inspection of the system for loose connections, broken wires or obvious damage is the best way to start. Perform the system Quick Test outlined below before going any further. Check all vacuum connections and secondary ignition wiring before assuming that the problem lies with the EEC IV system. A self-diagnosis capability is built in to the EEC IV system to aid in troubleshooting. The primary tool necessary to read the trouble codes stored in the system is an analog voltmeter or special Self Test Automatic Readout (STAR) tester (Motorcraft No. 007-0M004, or equivalent). While the self-test is not conclusive by itself, when activated it checks the EEC IV system by testing its memory integrity and processing capability. The self-test also verifies that all sensors and actuators are connected and working properly.

When a service code is displayed on an analog voltmeter, each code number is represented by pulses or sweeps of the meter needle. A code 3, for example, will be read as three needle pulses followed by a six-second delay. If a two digit code is stored, there will

1 NEEDLE PULSE (SWEEP) **+** 1 NEEDLE PULSE (SWEEP) **=** 2 NEEDLE PULSES (SWEEPS) FOR 1ST DIGIT

2-SECOND PAUSE BETWEEN DIGITS

SERVICE CODE

1 NEEDLE PULSE (SWEEP) FOR 1/2 SECOND **+** 1/2 SECOND PAUSE 1 NEEDLE PULSE (SWEEP) FOR 1/2 SECOND **+** 1/2 SECOND PAUSE 1 NEEDLE PULSE (SWEEP) FOR 1/2 SECOND **=** 3 NEEDLE PULSES (SWEEPS) FOR 2ND DIGIT

4-SECOND PAUSE BETWEEN SERVICE CODES, WHEN MORE THAN ONE CODE IS INDICATED

Reading service codes with analog voltmeter

INPUTS

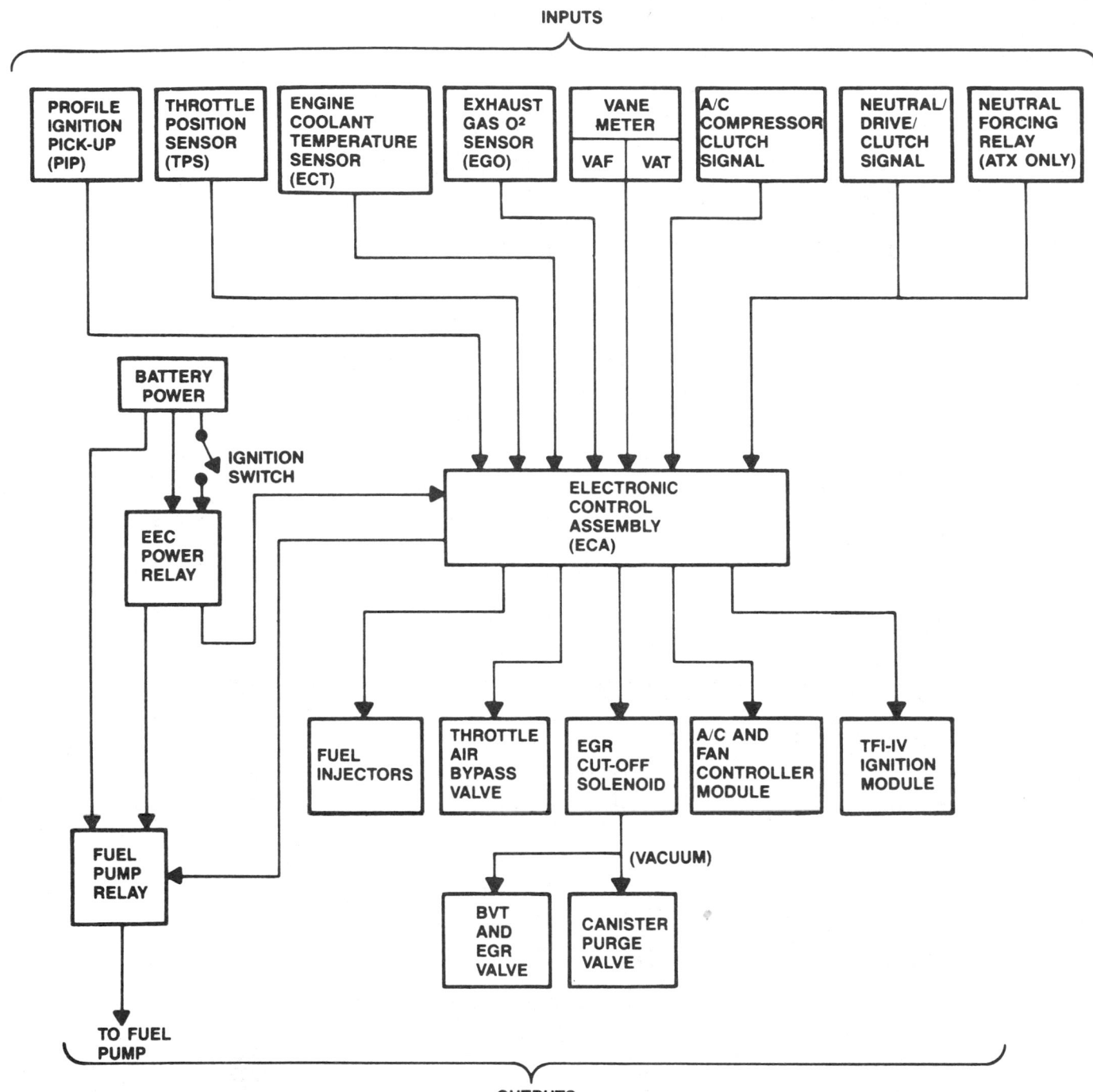

OUTPUTS

Schematic of EFI-EEC IV system operation—1.6L engine shown

be a two second delay between the pulses for each digit of the number. Code 23, for example, will be displayed as two needle pulses, a two second pause, then three more pulses followed by a four second pause. All testing is complete when the codes have been repeated once. The pulse format in ½ second ON-time for each digit, 2 seconds OFF-time between digits, 4 seconds OFF-time between codes and either 6 seconds (1.6L) or 10 seconds (2.3L) OFF-time before and after the half-second separator pulse.

NOTE: If using the STAR tester, or equivalent, consult the manufacturers instructions included with the unit for correct hookup and trouble code interpretation.

In addition to the service codes, two other types of coded information are outputted during the self-test; engine identification and fast codes. Engine ID codes are one digit numbers equal to one-half the number of engine cylinders (e.g. 4 cylinder is code 2, 8 cylinder is code 4, etc.). Fast codes are simply the service codes transmitted at 100 times the normal rate in a short burst of information. Some meters may detect these codes and register a slight meter deflection just before the trouble codes are flashed. Both the ID and fast codes serve no purpose in the field and this meter deflection should be ignored.

Activating Self-Test Mode on EEC IV

Turn the ignition key OFF. On the 2.3L engine, connect a jumper wire from the self-test input (STI) to pin 2 (signal return) on the self-test connector. On the 1.6L engine, connect a jumper wire from

STAR HOOKUP (WITH ADAPTER CABLE ASSEMBLY

VEHICLE SELF-TEST CONNECTORS

STAR SERVICE CONNECTORS

LED LIGHT

JUMPER/VOLTMETER HOOKUP

JUMPER (PIN 2)

TO VEHICLE HARNESS

TRIGGER (SELF-TEST INPUT)

OUTPUT (PIN 4)

VEHICLE BATTERY

Analog voltmeter hookup—2.3L engine

JUMPER/VOLTMETER HOOKUP

JUMPER (PIN 2)

TRIGGER (PIN 5)

OUTPUT (PIN 4)

VEHICLE BATTERY

STAR DEVICE HOOKUP (WITHOUT ADAPTER CABLE ASSEMBLY)

WHITE TO TRIGGER (PIN 5)

RED TO OUTPUT (PIN 4)

BLACK TO SIGNAL RETURN (PIN 2)

STAR HOOKUP (WITH ADAPTER CABLE ASSEMBLY)

SELF-TEST CONNECTOR

SERVICE CONNECTOR

LED LIGHT

WHITE TO TRIGGER (PIN 5)

RED TO OUTPUT (PIN 4)

BLACK TO SIGNAL RETURN (PIN 2)

Analog voltmeter hookup—1.6L engine

pin 5 self-test input to pin 2 (signal return) on the self-test connector. Set the analog voltmeter on a DC voltage range to read from 0–15 volts, then connect the voltmeter from the battery positive (+) terminal to pin 4 self-test output in the self-test connector. Turn the ignition switch ON (engine off) and read the trouble codes on the meter needle as previously described. A code 11 means that the EEC IV system is operating properly and no faults are detected by the computer.

NOTE: This test will only detect "hard" failures that are present when the self-test is activated. For intermittent problems, remove the voltmeter clip from the self-test trigger terminal and wiggle the wiring harness. With the voltmeter still attached to the self-test output, watch for a needle deflection that signals an intermittent condition has occurred. The meter will deflect each time the fault is induced and a trouble code will be stored. Reconnect the self-test trigger terminal to the voltmeter to retrieve the code.

Output Cycling Test

2.3L ENGINE ONLY

This test is performed with the key ON and the engine OFF after the self-test codes have been sent and recorded. Without disconnecting the voltmeter or turning the key OFF, momentarily depress the accelerator pedal to the floor and then release it. All auxiliary EEC IV codes (including the self-test) will be activated and can be read on the voltmeter as before. Another pedal depresssion will turn them off. This cycle may be repeated as necessary, but if activated for more that 10 minutes, the cycle will automatically cancel. This feature forces the processor to activate these outputs for additional diagnosis.

EEC IV System Quick Test

Correct test results for the quick test are dependent on the correct operation of related non-EEC components, such as ignition wires, battery, etc. It may be necessary to correct defects in these areas before the EEC IV system will pass the quick test. Before connecting any test equipment to check the EEC system, make the following checks:

1. Check the air cleaner and intake ducts for leaks or restrictions. Replace the air cleaner if excessive amounts of dust or dirt are found.

2. Check all engine vacuum hoses for proper routing according to the vacuum schematic on the underhood sticker.

Check for proper connections and repair any broken, cracked or pinched hoses or fittings.

3. Check the EEC system wiring harness connectors for tight fit, loose or detached terminals, corrosion, broken or frayed wires, short circuits to metal in the engine compartment or melted insulation exposing bare wire.

NOTE: It may be necessary to disconnect or disassemble the connector to check for terminal damage or corrosion and perform some of the inspections. Note the location of each pin in the connector before disassembly. When doing continuity checks to make sure there are no breaks in the wire, shake or wiggle the harness and connector during testing to check for looseness or intermittent contact.

4. Check the control module, sensors and actuators for obvious physical damage.

5. Turn off all electrical loads when testing and make sure the doors are closed whenever readings are made. DO NOT disconnect any electrical connector with the key ON. Turn the key off to disconnect or reconnect the wiring harness to any sensor or the control unit.

6. Make sure the engine coolant and oil are at the proper level.

7. Check for leaks around the exhaust manifold, oxygen sensor and vacuum hoses connections with the engine idling at normal operating temperature.

8. Only after all the above checks have been performed should the voltmeter be connected to read the trouble codes. If not, the self-diagnosis system may indicate a failed component when all that is wrong is a loose or broken connection.

CKT. 359 BK/W (SIG RTN)

PIN 3   PIN 1

2   1

PIN 12   J-2

PIN 18

20   19

CKT. 57 BLK (PWR GRD.)
CKT. 57 BLK (PWR. GRD.)
CKT. 361 RED (V. PWR.)
CKT. 361 RED (V. PWR.)

PIN 11

TO IGN. SW

PWR RELAY

VEH. BATT.

PIGTAIL CONNECTOR

CONNECTOR AS VIEWED FROM THE REAR (WIRE SIDE)

PIN 5

2   1

J-1

20   19

PIN 12

PIN 13

CKT. 201 T/R D, (STO)

CKT. 89 O (EGO GND.)

EGO GRD.

CKT. 100 W/R D (STI)

STI — SELF-TEST IN   STO — SELF-TEST OUT

2   1

J-2

20   19

J-1 & J-2 CONNECTORS AS VIEWED FROM THE REAR (WIRE SIDE)

PIN 9

PIN 11

2   1

J-1

20   19

PIN 12

CKT. 355 DG/LG (TP)
CKT. 351 O/W (V REF.)
CKT. 359 BK/W (SIG RTN)

TP SENSOR

2   1

J-2

20   19

PIN 15

CKT. 69 (A/C CUT OFF)

J-1 & J-2 CONNECTOR AS VIEWED FROM THE REAR (WIRE SIDE)

14
10
7

AC CLUTCH

A/C-FAN ELECTRICAL CONTROLLER

CYCLIC PRESSURE SW

A/C DEMAND SWITCH

GEAR SW

CLUTCH SW

MTX ONLY

PIN 1

2   1

J-1

PIN 12   20

PIN 2

CKT. 614 GY/O (N-D SW)
CKT. 347 BK/Y H (ACC)
CKT. 359 BK/W (SIG. RTN)

V BATT IGN START SW (3)

N/D SWITCH

ATX ONLY

STARTER RELAY

TO CKT. 347 (ACC)

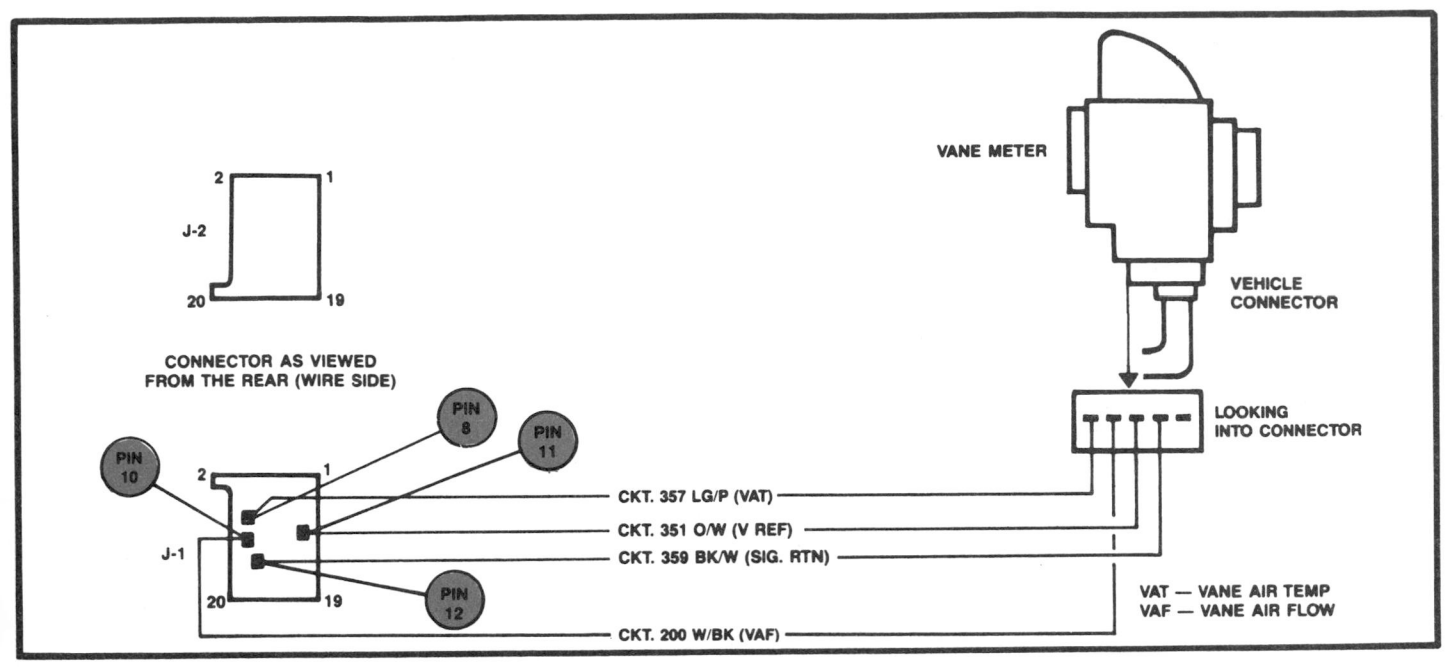

CONNECTOR AS VIEWED
FROM THE REAR (WIRE SIDE)

VANE METER

VEHICLE CONNECTOR

LOOKING INTO CONNECTOR

CKT. 357 LG/P (VAT)
CKT. 351 O/W (V REF)
CKT. 359 BK/W (SIG. RTN)

CKT. 200 W/BK (VAF)

VAT — VANE AIR TEMP
VAF — VANE AIR FLOW

PIN 10
PIN 8
PIN 11
PIN 12

QUICK TEST

Procedure	Result		Action	
Voltage Check Turn all accessories off. Check that open circuit battery voltage is greater than 12.4 volts. If engine runs, operate at 2000 rpm for 2 minutes and verify battery voltage of 14.2–14.7 volts with engine running.	a.	Battery OK	a.	Go to next step
	b.	Battery not within specs	b.	Recharge battery, check charging system
Key ON/Engine OFF Self-Test Transmission in Neutral or Park, A/C off and key ON. Observe and record trouble codes. When more than one code is present, always start with the first code received.	a.	Code 11	a.	Go to next step. For no-starts go to pinpoint step A1.
	b.	No Codes	b.	Go to pinpoint test A
	c.	Meter always high	c.	Go to pinpoint test step
	d.	Code 15	d.	Replace processor and retest
	e.	Code 21	e.	Go to pinpoint test B
	f.	Code 23	f.	Go to pinpoint test C
	g.	Code 24	g.	Go to pinpoint test D
	h.	Code 26	h.	Go to pinpoint test E
	i.	Code 67	i.	Go to pinpoint test F
Check Timing Verify self-test trigger is installed and check timing while system is in self-test mode	a.	Timing is 27–33° BTDC	a.	Go to next step
	b.	Timing out of spec	b.	Reset timing

QUICK TEST

Procedure	Result		Action	
Engine Running Test Disconnect self-test trigger, start and run engine at 2000 rpm for 2 minutes. Turn engine off and reconnect self-test trigger. Restart engine and idle. Observe and record trouble codes.	a.	No code or meter reads above 10 volts	a.	Go to pinpoint test A
	b.	Code 11	b.	System OK. Go to continuous testing to check intermittent failure
	c.	Code 12	c.	Check idle speed control (isc) circuit
	d.	Code 13	d.	Check idle speed control (isc) circuit
	e.	Code 21	e.	Go to pinpoint test B
	f.	Code 23	f.	Go to pinpoint test C
	g.	Code 24	g.	Go to pinpoint test D
	h.	Code 26	h.	Go to pinpoint test E
	i.	Code 41	i.	Adjust fuel mixture (CO)
	j.	Code 42	j.	Adjust fuel mixture (CO)

Continuous Testing
This test is used to detect intermittent failures at the moment the interrupt occurs. It will store the service code until the key is turned off. To begin the test, turn the key off and disconnect the self-trigger. Connect an analog voltmeter negative (−) lead to the self-test out pin and the positive (+) lead to the positive battery post. Turn the key on or start the engine, but do not turn the key off if the engine stalls or the stored service codes will be lost. Monitor the voltmeter reading while wiggling or moving the wiring harness, tap the sensors and connectors and look for any meter deflection that will indicate a short or failure. If any deflection is noted on the voltmeter, initiate the self-test before turning the key off and record the trouble codes stored. The vehicle can also be driven if necessary while in the continuous testing mode to isolate a drive complaint.

PINPOINT TEST

Procedure	Result		Action	
No-Start Problem Check for fuel leaks and correct fuel pressure. Check for spark at plug wire and check plugs for fouling or damage.	a.	Fuel leaks	a.	Correct as necessary
	b.	Fouled spark plugs	b.	Clean or replace plugs
	c.	No spark at plug	c.	Go to next step
Ignition Module Signal (IMS) or Spark Output Check. Voltmeter on 20 volt range, probe J2 pin 14 to chassis ground. Crank engine and record reading.	a.	Reading is 3-6 volts	a.	EEC OK, check cap, rotor and wires
	b.	Any other voltage reading	b.	Go to next step
Harness Check (IMS Circuit) Key OFF, J2 disconnected. Check circuit 324, J2 pin 14 for shorts to ground.	a.	Reading above 2000 ohms	a.	Go to next step
	b.	Reading below 2000 ohms	b.	Repair short in circuit

PINPOINT TEST

Procedure	Result		Action	
Distributor Signal Check Voltmeter on 20 volt range, disconnect J1 and J2. Connect voltmeter to J1 pin 14 (circuit 349) and J2 pin 14 (circuit 60). Crank engine and record reading.	a.	Reading is 3-6 volts	a.	Inspect processor connectors for bent, damaged or corroded terminals. If OK, replace processor
	b.	Any other voltage reading	b.	Go to next step
Harness Check (Circuit 349) Disconnect vehicle harness from TFI at the distributor and J1 from the processor. Check distributor signal J1 pin 14 (circuit 349) for opens or shorts.	a.	No shorts or opens	a.	Go to next step
	b.	Short or open indicated	b.	Repair wire harness as necessary
Harness Check (Circuit 60) Check ignition ground J2 pin 5 (circuit 60) to TFI connector pin 6 for opens.	a.	No open indicated	a.	Check Thick Film Ignition (TFI) module. Replace if necessary
	b.	Open circuit	b.	Repair as necessary
Pinpoint Test A Key ON/Engine OFF, processor connected. Voltmeter on 20v range, take voltage measurement at J1 pin 11 to J2 pin 12.	a.	Reading 6 volts or more	a.	Check for short to battery voltage or processor power. Replace processor if necessary
	b.	Reading 4 volts or less	b.	Check battery power circuit. Check for shorted throttle position sensor
	c.	Reading between 4 and 6 volts	c.	Check battery connections
Pinpoint Test B Voltmeter on 20v range, processor connected. Key ON/Engine OFF, take voltage reading from J1 pin 11 to J1 pin 12.	a.	Reading 4-6 volts	a.	Check coolant temperature sensor and harness for short or open
	b.	Any other reading	b.	Check battery power cicuit for shorts to processor power or shorted throttle position sensor, vane air meter or harness
Pinpoint Test C Disconnect idle speed control solenoid and verify curb idle per emission decal. Adjust if necessary. Connect voltmeter to J1 pin 9 and J1 pin 12 and rerun self test while monitoring meter.	a.	Reading is .5-1.3 volts during test	a.	Disconnect J1 and J2 and inspect for damage or corrosion. If none is present, replace processor
	b.	Any other reading	b.	Check throttle position sensor circuit for shorts or opens. Check for short to battery voltage
Pinpoint Test D Check heated air inlet system. Ambient air temperature must exceed 40°F for this test. Disconnect J1 from the processor and measure resistance from J1 pin 8 to J1 pin 12.	a.	Volt-ohmmeter reading between 100-4000 ohms	a.	Check vane air temperature sensor for shorts or opens
	b.	Reading under 100 or over 4000 ohms	b.	Check circuits 357 and 359 for shorts or opens and service as required. If no problem is found, replace vane air flow meter

PINPOINT TEST

Procedure	Result		Action	
Pinpoint Test E Connect voltmeter to J1 pin 10 and J1 pin 12. Rerun self-test while monitoring meter.	a.	Reading .2-.5 volts with Key ON/Engine OFF or 1.4-2.7 volts with engine running	a.	Disconnect J1 and J2 and inspect for damage or corrosion. If no problem is found, replace processor
	b.	Any other reading	b.	Check circuits 200, 351 and 359 for opens or shorts to ground (sensor and processor must be disconnected). If no problem is found, replace vane air flow meter
Pinpoint Test F Manual Transaxle A/C OFF, shifter in neutral. With key OFF, disconnect J1 and measure resistance from J1 pin 1 and J1 pin 12.	a.	Reading less than 5 ohms	a.	Take voltage measurement at J1 pin 2 (circuit 347). If reading is above 1 volt, correct short. If reading is below 1 volt, replace processor
	b.	Reading above 5 ohms	b.	Correct open in circuit or replace gear/clutch switch
Automatic Transaxle Heater controls OFF, shifter in neutral or park. Key ON/Engine OFF. Set voltmeter on 20v range and take measurement from connected J1 pin 1 (circuit 150) to chassis ground.	a.	Reading below .5 volts	a.	Take voltage measurement at J1 pin 2 (circuit 347). If reading is above 1 volt, correct short. If reading is below 1 volt, replace processor
	b.	Reading above .5 volts	b.	Correct open in circuit 150 harness or replace N/D switch

Wiring diagram for 1.6L engine—manual transmission

Wiring diagram for 1.6L engine—automatic transmission

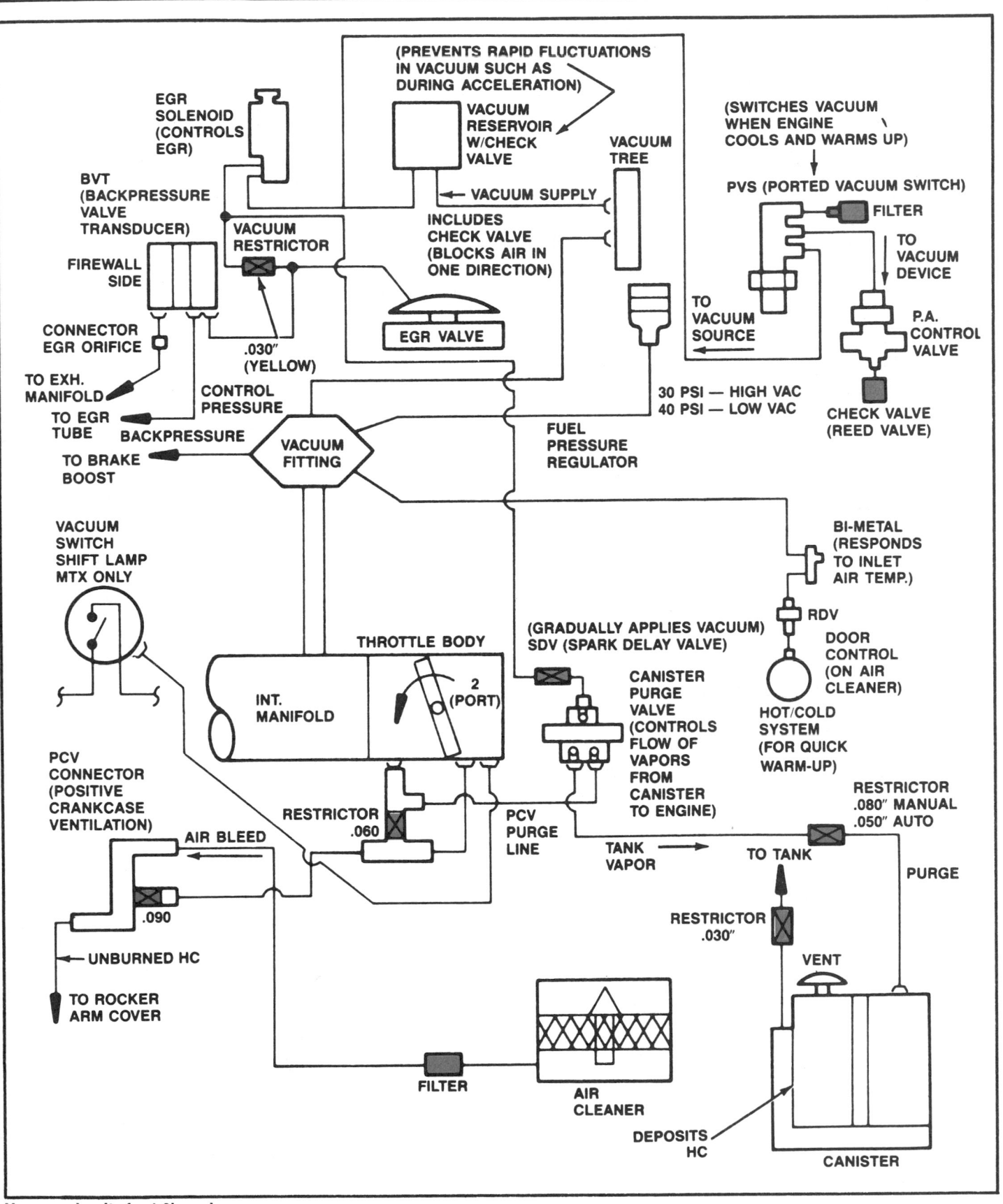

(PREVENTS RAPID FLUCTUATIONS IN VACUUM SUCH AS DURING ACCELERATION)

EGR SOLENOID (CONTROLS EGR)

VACUUM RESERVOIR W/CHECK VALVE

VACUUM TREE

(SWITCHES VACUUM WHEN ENGINE COOLS AND WARMS UP)

BVT (BACKPRESSURE VALVE TRANSDUCER)

VACUUM SUPPLY

PVS (PORTED VACUUM SWITCH)

FILTER

VACUUM RESTRICTOR

INCLUDES CHECK VALVE (BLOCKS AIR IN ONE DIRECTION)

TO VACUUM DEVICE

FIREWALL SIDE

EGR VALVE

P.A. CONTROL VALVE

CONNECTOR EGR ORIFICE

.030" (YELLOW)

TO VACUUM SOURCE

CHECK VALVE (REED VALVE)

TO EXH. MANIFOLD

CONTROL PRESSURE

30 PSI — HIGH VAC
40 PSI — LOW VAC

TO EGR TUBE

BACKPRESSURE

VACUUM FITTING

FUEL PRESSURE REGULATOR

TO BRAKE BOOST

BI-METAL (RESPONDS TO INLET AIR TEMP.)

VACUUM SWITCH SHIFT LAMP MTX ONLY

RDV

(GRADUALLY APPLIES VACUUM) SDV (SPARK DELAY VALVE)

DOOR CONTROL (ON AIR CLEANER)

THROTTLE BODY

2 (PORT)

CANISTER PURGE VALVE (CONTROLS FLOW OF VAPORS FROM CANISTER TO ENGINE)

HOT/COLD SYSTEM (FOR QUICK WARM-UP)

INT. MANIFOLD

RESTRICTOR .080" MANUAL .050" AUTO

PCV CONNECTOR (POSITIVE CRANKCASE VENTILATION)

AIR BLEED

RESTRICTOR .060

PCV PURGE LINE

TANK VAPOR

TO TANK

PURGE

.090

RESTRICTOR .030"

UNBURNED HC

VENT

TO ROCKER ARM COVER

FILTER

AIR CLEANER

DEPOSITS HC

CANISTER

Vacuum circuits for 1.6L engine

Wiring diagram for 2.3L engine

KNOCK SENSOR
EGO SENSOR GROUND
EXHAUST GAS OXYGEN SENSOR
ENGINE COOLANT TEMPERATURE
THROTTLE POSITION SENSOR
VANE METER VAT/VAF
VIP CONNECTOR
BAROMETRIC PRESSURE SENSOR

23	KS
26	VREF
46	SIG RET
49	EGO GND (1)
29	EGO
7	ECT
47	TPS
25	VAT
43	VAF
17	STO
48	STI
45	BP
56	PIP (4)
36	SPOUT
16	

TFI-IV

IGNITION GROUND → TO PIN 20

22 FP

FUEL PUMP RELAY

TO VBATT

58	INJ A
59	INJ B
21	ISC
41	ISC LOS

INJ B   INJ A

INERTIA SWITCH

FUEL PUMP

IN-TANK PUMP

1 OHM

35	EGR S/O
20	CASE GND (2)
1	KEEP ALIVE POWER

EGR S/O SOLENOID

(10W)

10

(3)

THROTTLE AIR BYPASS VALVE

EEC POWER RELAY

| 37 | |
| 57 | VPWR |

BATTERY

| 40 | BAT GND |
| 60 | BAT GND (5) |

| 10 | ACC |

(3) AC CLUTCH

CYCLIC PRESSURE SW

A/C DEMAND SWITCH

MAN VAC

TURBO WARN SWITCH

V CK V

EGR

SOL V

V REST

Vacuum circuits for 2.3L turbocharged engine

FORD CENTRAL FUEL INJECTION (CFI) SYSTEM

General Information

The Ford Central Fuel Injection (CFI) System is a single point, pulse time modulated injection system. Fuel is metered into the air intake stream according to engine demands by two solenoid injection valves, mounted in a throttle body on the intake manifold. Fuel is supplied from the fuel tank by a high pressure, electric fuel pump, either by itself or in addition to a low-pressure pump. The fuel is filtered, and sent to the air throttle body where a regulator keeps the fuel delivery pressure at a constant 39 psi (269 kPa). Two injector nozzles are mounted vertically above the throttle plates and connected in parallel with the fuel pressure regulator. Excess fuel supplied by the pump but not needed by the engine, is returned to the fuel tank by a steel fuel return line.

The electronic fuel injection system has several distinct advantages over conventional carburetion. It has improved fuel distribution, capability of fine tuning for altitude and temperature variations, fuel vapor formation and vapor lock largely eliminated due to high pressure in fuel system and reduced evaporative losses due to elimination of the fuel bowl. It also has eliminated engine run-on, since fuel flow immediately stops electrically with engine shut down and elimination of fuel starvation during hard driving maneuvers provided by constant high pressure injection. It provides the precise air-fuel control required for efficient three-way catalyst operation.

FUEL DELIVERY SYSTEM

Fuel Charging Assembly

The fuel charging assembly controls air-fuel ratio. It consists of a typical carburetor throttle body. It has two bores without venturis. The throttle shaft and valves control engine air flow based on driver demand. The throttle body attaches to the intake manifold mounting pad.

A throttle position sensor is attached to the throttle shaft. It includes a potentiometer (or rheostat) that electrically senses throttle opening. A throttle kicker solenoid fastens opposite the throttle position sensor. During air conditioning operation, the solenoid extends to slightly increase engine idle speed.

Typical EEC III system—V-8 engine shown

Cold engine speed is controlled by an automatic kick-down vacuum motor. There is also an all-electric, bi-metal coil spring which controls cold idle speed. The bi-metal electric coil operates like a conventional carburetor choke coil, but the electronic fuel injection system uses no choke. Fuel enrichment for cold starts is controlled by the computer and injectors.

Fuel Pressure Regulator

The fuel pressure regulator controls critical injector fuel pressure. The regulator receives high pressure fuel from the electric fuel pump. It then adjusts the fuel to the desired pressure for uniform fuel injection. The regulator sets fuel pressure at 39 psi.

Central Fuel Injection (CFI) fuel charging assembly (left side view)

Central Fuel Injection (CFI) fuel charging assembly (right side view)

Fuel Rail

The fuel rail evenly distributes fuel to each injector. Its main purpose is to equalize the fuel flow. One end of the fuel rail contains a relief valve for testing fuel pressure during operation.

Fuel Injectors

The two identical fuel injectors are electro-mechanical devices. The electrical solenoid operates a pintle valve which always travels the same distance from closed to open to closed. Injection is controlled by varying the length of time the pintle valve is open.

The delivery end of the injector is a precisely ground nozzle. The manufacturing and handling of this component is very important for proper operation. When closed, the valve must seal tightly to shut off fuel flow completely. It must seat itself repeatedly with the same precision. Any dirt particles from contaminated fuel can prevent the valve from seating. The shape of the pintle valve and nozzle also determines the fuel spray pattern during injection. Since the injectors are atomizing fuel into droplets, this fuel mist pattern is important to fast vaporization and good combustion.

Cross section of typical solenoid-type fuel injector

Electric fuel pump inertia switch

The computer, based on voltage inputs from the crank position sensor, operates the injector solenoids four (two per injector) times per engine revolution. When the injector pintle valve unseats, fuel is sprayed in a fine mist into the intake manifold. The computer varies fuel enrichment based on voltage inputs from the exhaust gas oxygen sensor, barometric pressure sensor, manifold absolute pressure sensor, etc., by calculating how long to hold the injectors open. The longer the injectors remain open, the richer the mixture.

Fuel Pump

The fuel delivery system includes an in-line or in-tank high pressure fuel pump, an in-tank low pressure fuel pump (on some 1983–84 models when in-line high pressure pump is used), a primary fuel filter, a secondary fuel filter, fuel supply and return lines, fuel injectors and a fuel pressure regulator. It is a recirculating system that delivers fuel to a pressure regulating valve in the throttle body and returns excess fuel from the throttle body regulator back to the fuel tank. The electrical system has two control relays, one controlled by a vacuum switch and the other controlled by an electronic engine control module. These provide for power to the fuel pump under various operating conditions.

---CAUTION---

Fuel supply lines on vehicles equipped with fuel injected engine will remain pressurized for long periods of time after engine shutdown. The pressure must be relieved before servicing the fuel system.

An inertia switch is used as a safety device in the fuel system. The inertia switch is located in the trunk, near the left rear wheel well. It is designed to open the fuel pump power circuit in the event of a collision. The switch is reset by pushing each of 2 buttons on the switch simultaneously (some models use switches with only 1 reset button). The inertia switch should not be reset until the fuel system has been inspected for damage or leaks.

With the ignition switch off, the vacuum switch controlled relay is closed and the EEC controlled relay is open. When the ignition switch is first turned to ignition "ON" position, the vacuum switch controlled relay remains closed and the EEC controlled relay also closes. This provides power to the fuel pump to pre-pressurize the fuel system. If the ignition switch is not turned to the "CRANK" position, the EEC module will open its relay after approximately two seconds and shut off power to the pump. When the ignition switch is turned to the "CRANK" position, both the vacuum switch controlled relay and the EEC controlled relay are closed. This provides full battery power to the pump. When the engine starts, manifold vacuum increases and causes the vacuum switch to close and the vacuum controlled relay to open. This provides reduced normal operating voltage to the fuel pump through the resistor which by-passes the vacuum controlled relay. Under heavy engine load conditions, manifold vacuum will reduce, causing the vacuum switch to open. This causes the vacuum controlled relay to close, thus providing the return of full battery power to the pump. The EEC module senses engine speed and shuts off the pump by opening the EEC controlled relay when the engine stops.

ELECTRONIC CONTROL SYSTEM

Electronic Control Assembly (ECA)

The Electronic Control Assembly (ECA) is a solid-state microcomputer consisting of a processor assembly and a calibration assembly. It is located under the instrument panel or passenger's seat and is usually covered by a kick panel. 1981–82 models use an EEC III engine control system, while 1983 and later models use the EEC IV. Although the two systems are similar in appearance and operation, the ECA units are not interchangeable. A multipin connector links the ECA with all system components. The processor assembly is housed in an aluminum case. It contains circuits designed to continuously sample input signals from the engine sensors. It then calculates and sends out proper control signals to adjust air/fuel ratio, spark timing and emission system operation. The processor also provides a continuous reference voltage to the B/MAP, EVP and TPS sensors. EEC III reference voltage is 8–10 volts, while EEC IV systems use a 5 volt reference signal. The calibration assembly is contained in a black plastic housing which plugs into the top of the processor assembly. It contains the memory and programming information used by the processor to determine optimum operating conditions. Different calibration information is used in different vehicle applications, such as California or Federal models. For this reason, careful identification of the engine, year, model and type of electronic control system is essential to insure correct component replacement.

ENGINE SENSORS

Air Charge Temperature Sensor (ACT)

The ACT is threaded into the intake manifold air runner. It is located behind the distributor on V6 engines and directly below the accelerator linkage on V8 engines. The ACT monitors air/fuel charge temperature and sends an appropriate signal to the ECA. This information is used to correct fuel enrichment for variations in intake air density due to temperature changes.

Barometric & Manifold Absolute Pressure Sensors (B/MAP)

The B/MAP sensor on V8 engines is located on the right fender panel in the engine compartment. The MAP sensor used on V6 engines is separate from the barometric sensor and is located on the left fender panel in the engine compartment. The barometric sensor signals the ECA of changes in atmospheric pressure and density to regulate calculated air flow into the engine. The MAP sensor monitors and signals the ECA of changes in intake manifold pressure which result from engine load, speed and atmospheric pressure changes.

Crankshaft Position (CP) Sensor

The CP sensor is mounted on the right front of 1982–83 and some California 1984 5.0L V8 engines. Its purpose is to provide the ECA with an accurate ignition timing reference (when the piston reaches 10° BTDC) and injector operation information (twice each crankshaft revolution). The crankshaft vibration damper is fitted with a 4 lobe "pulse ring". As the crankshaft rotates, the pulse ring lobes interrupt the magnetic field at the tip of the CP sensor.

EGR Valve Position Sensor (EVP)

This sensor, mounted on EGR valve, signals the computer of EGR opening so that it may subtract EGR flow from total air flow into the manifold. In this way, EGR flow is excluded from air flow information used to determine mixture requirements.

Engine Coolant Temperature Sensor (ECT)

The ECT is threaded into the intake manifold water jacket directly above the water pump by-pass hose. The ECT monitors coolant temperature and signals the ECA, which then uses these signals for mixture enrichment (during cool operation), ignition timing and EGR operation. The resistance value of the ECT increases with temperature, causing a voltage signal drop as the engine warms up.

Exhaust Gas Oxygen Sensor (EGO)

The EGO is mounted in the right side exhaust manifold on V8 engines, in the left and right side exhaust manifolds on V6 models. The EGO monitors oxygen content of exhaust gases and sends a constantly changing voltage signal to the ECA. The ECA analyzes this signal and adjusts the air/fuel mixture to obtain the optimum (stoichiometric) ratio.

Knock Sensor (KS)

This sensor is used on 1984 Mustangs and Capris equipped with the

3.8L V6 engine, only. It is attached to the intake manifold in front of the ACT sensor. The KS detects engine vibrations caused by pre-ignition or detonation and provides information to the ECA, which then retards the timing to eliminate detonation.

Thick Film Integrated Module sensor (TFI)

The TFI module sensor plugs into the distributor just below the distributor cap on 3.8L V6 engines and replaces the CP sensor for some 1984 5.0L V8 engines. Its function is to provide the ECA with ignition timing information, similar to what the CP sensor provides.

Throttle Position Sensor (TPS)

The TPS is mounted on the right side of the throttle body, directly connected to the throttle shaft. The TPS senses throttle movement and position and transmits an appropriate electrical signal to the ECA. These signals are used by the ECA to adjust the air/fuel mixture, spark timing and EGR operation according to engine load at idle, part throttle, or full throttle. The TPS is non-adjustable.

On-Car Service

NOTE: For all diagnosis and test procedures on the EEC III and EEC IV electronic control systems, see the "Engine Controls" section.

FUEL PRESSURE TESTS

The diagnostic pressure valve (Schrader type) is located at the top of the Fuel charging main body. This valve provides a convenient point for service personnel to monitor fuel pressure, bleed down the system pressure prior to maintenance, and to bleed out air which may become trapped in the system during filter replacement. A pressure gauge with an adapter is required to perform pressure tests.

Cross section of CFI fuel charging assembly

—CAUTION—

Under no circumstances should compressed air be forced into the fuel system using the diagnostic valve. Depressing the pin in the diagnostic valve will relieve system pressure by expelling fuel into the throttle body.

System Pressure Test

Testing fuel pressure requires the use of a special pressure gauge (T80L-9974-A or equivalent) that attaches to the diagnostic pressure tap on the fuel charging assembly. Depressurize the fuel system before disconnecting any lines.

1. Disconnect fuel return line at throttle body (in-tank high pressure pump) or at fuel rail (in-line high pressure and in-tank low pressure pumps) and connect the hose to a one-quart calibrated container. Connect pressure gauge.

2. Disconnect the electrical connector to the fuel pump. The connector is located ahead of fuel tank (in-tank high pressure pump) or just forward of pump outlet (in-line high pressure pump). Connect auxiliary wiring harness to connector of fuel pump. Energize the pump for 10 seconds by applying 12 volts to the auxiliary harness connector, allowing the fuel to drain into the calibrated container. Note the fuel volume and pressure gauge reading.

3. Correct fuel pressure should be 35–45 psi (241–310 kPa). Fuel volume should be 10 ozs. in 10 seconds (minimum) and fuel pressure should maintain minimum 30 psi (206 kPa) immediately after pump cut-off.

If pressure condition is met, but fuel flow is not, check for blocked filter(s) and fuel supply lines. After correcting problem, repeat test procedure. If fuel flow is still inadequate, replace high pressure pump. If flow specification is met but pressure is not, check for worn or damaged pressure regulator valve on throttle body. If both pressure and fuel flow specifications are met, but pressure drops excessively after de-energization, check for leaking injector valve(s) and/or pressure regulator valve. If injector valves and pressure regulator valve are okay, replace high pressure pump. If no pressure or flow is seen in fuel system, check for blocked filters and fuel lines. If no trouble is found, replace in-line fuel pump, in-tank fuel pump and the fuel filter inside the tank.

Electric fuel pump wiring and fuel lines routing schematic

Fuel Injector Pressure Test

1. Connect pressure gauge T80L-9974-A, or equivalent, to fuel pressure test fitting. Disconnect coil connector from coil. Disconnect electrical lead from one injector and pressurize fuel system. Disable fuel pump by disconnecting inertia switch or fuel pump relay and observe pressure gauge reading.

2. Crank engine for 2 seconds. Turn ignition OFF and wait 5 seconds, then observe pressure drop. If pressure drop is 2-16 psi (14–110 kPa), the injector is operating properly. Reconnect injector, activate fuel pump, then repeat the procedure for other injector.

3. If pressure drop is less than 2 psi (14 kPa) or more than 16 psi (110 kPa), switch electrical connectors on injectors and repeat test. If pressure drop is still incorrect, replace disconnected injector with one of the same color code, then reconnect both injectors properly and repeat test.

4. Disconnect and plug vacuum hose to EGR valve. It may be necessary to disconnect the idle speed control (3.8L V6) or throttle kicker solenoid (5.0L V8) and use the throttle body stop screw to set engine speed. Start and run the engine at 1800 RPM (2000 rpm on 1984 and later models). Disconnect left injector electrical connector. Note rpm after engine stabilizes (around 1200 rpm). Reconnect injector and allow engine to return to high idle.

5. Perform same procedure for right injector. Note difference between rpm readings of left and right injectors. If difference is 100 rpm or less, check the oxygen sensor. If difference is more than 100 rpm, replace both injectors.

CFI COMPONENT TESTS

NOTE: Note: Complete CFI system diagnosis requires the use of a special tester. See the "Engine Controls" section for details.

Before beginning any component testing, always check the following:
- Check ignition and fuel systems to ensure there is fuel and spark.
- Remove air cleaner assembly and inspect all vacuum and pressure hoses for proper connection to fittings. Check for damaged or pinched hoses.
- Inspect all sub-system wiring harnesses for proper connections to the EGR solenoid valves, injectors, sensors, etc.
- Check for loose or detached connectors and broken or detached wires. Check that all terminals are seated firmly and are not corroded. Look for partially broken or frayed wires or any shorting between wires.
- Inspect sensors for physical damage. Inspect vehicle electrical system. Check battery for full charge and cable connections for tightness.
- Inspect the relay connector and make sure the ECA power relay is securely attached and making a good ground connection.

Fuel Pump Circuit Test

HIGH PRESSURE IN-TANK PUMP

Disconnect electrical connector just forward of the fuel tank. Connect voltmeter to body wiring harness connector. Turn key ON while watching voltmeter. Voltage should rise to battery voltage, then return to zero after about 1 second. Momentarily turn key to START position. Voltage should rise to about 8 volts while cranking. If voltage is not as specified, check electrical system.

HIGH PRESSURE IN-LINE & LOW PRESSURE IN-TANK PUMPS

Disconnect electrical connector at fuel pumps. Connect voltmeter to body wiring harness connector. Turn key ON while watching voltmeter. Voltage should rise to battery voltage, then return to zero after about 1 second. If voltage is not as specified, check inertia switch and electrical system. Connect ohmmeter to in-line pump wiring harness connector. If no continuity is present, check continuity directly at in-line pump terminals. If no continuity at in-line

EXHAUST GAS OXYGEN (EGO)

SHELL GROUNDED

ENG. BLOCK GROUND

DS111

IGNITION MODULE

BLACK
ORANGE
GREEN

IGNITION COIL "TACH" TERMINAL

EGOR

EGO 94

MANIFOLD CHARGING TEMPERATURE (MCT)

MCT 357

THROTTLE POSITION (TP)

TP 355

ENGINE COOLANT TEMPERATURE (ECT)

ECT 354

EGR VALVE POSITION (EVP)

EVP 352

BAROMETRIC MANIFOLD ABSOLUTE PRESSURE (BMAP)

MAP 358

SRTN 359

VREF 351

BP 356

CRANKSHAFT POSITION SENSOR (CP)

CP SHIELD

350 349

BATTERY

57

175

RUN/ START PWR. 37

20

POWER RELAY

361

89

TO STARTER MOTOR RELAY COIL "S" TERMINAL

97

32

CANISTER PURGE SOLENOID (CANP)

101

THER- MACTOR AIR DIVERTER SOLENOID (TAD)

99 TAD

THER- MACTOR AIR BYPASS SOLENOID (TAB)

TAB 100

EGRC 362

EGR CONTROL SOLENOID (EGRC)

EGRV 360

EGR VENT SOLENOID (EGRV)

FUEL PUMP RELAY

24

FUEL PUMP

INERTIA SWITCH

95

RT

INJECTORS

96

LT

347 A/C CLUTCH

2 18 19 3 20 22 4 21 5 6 23 8 24 17 7 9 29 26 13 1 11 12 28 10 31

HARNESS CONNECTOR

32

17

1

16

1. RED/LIGHT BLUE
2. GRAY
3. ORANGE/WHITE
4. BROWN/LIGHT GREEN
5. DARK GREEN/LIGHT GREEN
6. VACANT
7. BLACK
8. BLACK (SYSTEM GROUND)
9. LIGHT GREEN/BLACK DOT
10. GRAY/YELLOW HASH
11. TAN/LIGHT GREEN DOT

12. TAN/RED DOT
13. DARK GREEN
14. VACANT
15. VACANT
16. VACANT
17. ORANGE/YELLOW HASH
18. DARK BLUE
19. BLACK/WHITE
20. LIGHT GREEN/BLACK
21. LIGHT GREEN/YELLOW
22. DARK BLUE/LIGHT GREEN

23. DARK GREEN/PURPLE HASH
24. RED (SYSTEM POWER)
25. RED/LIGHT GREEN
26. WHITE/RED DOT
27. TAN/LIGHT BLUE DOT
28. TAN/ORANGE DOT
29. YELLOW
30. VACANT
31. BLACK/YELLOW HASH
32. VACANT

Ford CFI wiring diagram

pump terminals, replace in-line pump. If continuity is present, service or replace wiring harness.

Connect ohmmeter across body wiring harness connector. If continuity is present (about 5 ohms), low pressure pump circuit is OK. If no continuity is present, remove fuel tank and check for continuity at in-tank pump flange terminals on top of tank. If continuity is absent at in-tank pump flange terminals, replace assembly. If continuity is present at in-tank pump but not in harness connector, service or replace wiring harness to in-tank pump.

Solenoid and Sensor Resistance Tests

All CFI components must be disconnected from the circuit before testing resistance with a suitable ohmmeter. Repace any component whose measured resistance does not agree with the specifications chart. Shorting the wiring harness across a solenoid valve can burn out the circuitry in the ECA that controls the solenoid valve actuator. Exercise caution when testing solenoid valves to avoid accidental damage to ECA.

CFI RESISTANCE SPECIFICATIONS

Component	Resistance (Ohms)
Air Charge Temp (ACT)	
1981–83	1700–60,000
1984	1100–58,000
Coolant (ECT) Sensor	
1981–83	1100–8000
1984—Engine Off	1300–7700
1984—Engine On	1500–4550
Crank Position Sensor	100–640
FGB Control Solenoid	30–70
EGR Vent Solenoid	30–70
Fuel Pump Relay	50–100
Throttle Kicker Solenoid	50–100
Throttle Position Sensor	
1981–83 Closed Throttle	3000–5000
1984 Closed Throttle	550–1100
Wide Open Throttle	More than 2100
TAB Solenoid	50–100
TAD Solenoid	50–100

Component Removal

IN-TANK FUEL PUMP

CAUTION

The fuel supply lines will remain pressurized for long periods of time after the engine is turned off. A valve is provided on the throttle body for this purpose. Remove the air cleaner and relieve system pressure by depressing the pin in the relief valve cautiously. Fuel will be expelled into the throttle body.

Removal

1. It is necessary to remove the fuel tank.
2. Depressurize the fuel system.
3. Remove fuel from the fuel tank by pumping out through the filter tube.
4. Disconnect the supply and return line fittings and the vent line.
5. Disconnect and remove the fuel filler tube.

Electric fuel pump installation

6. Disconnect the electrical connections to both the fuel sender and the fuel pump wiring harness.
7. Remove the fuel tank support straps and remove the fuel tank.
8. Turn the fuel pump locking ring counter-clockwise with the necessary tool and remove the locking ring.
9. Remove the fuel pump and bracket assembly.
10. Remove the seal gasket and discard.
11. Remove any dirt that has accumulated around the fuel pump attaching flange, to prevent it from entering the tank during removal and installation.

Installation

1. Put a light coating of heavy grease on a new seal ring to hold it in place during assembly. Install it in fuel tank ring groove.
2. Install the tank in the vehicle.
3. Install the electrical connector.
4. Install the fuel line fittings and tighten to 40-54 N·m (30-40 ft. lbs.).
5. Install a minimum of 10 gallons of fuel and inspect for leaks.
6. Install pressure gauge on valve on throttle body and turn ignition to "ON" position for 3 seconds. Turn ignition key off and back on for 3 seconds repeatedly, 5 to 10 times, until pressure gauge shows at least 35 psi. Reinspect for leaks at fittings.
7. Remove pressure gauge. Start engine and reinspect for leaks.

FUEL CHARGING ASSEMBLY

Removal and Installation

1. Remove the air cleaner.
2. Release pressure from the fuel system at the diagnostic valve on the fuel charging assembly by carefully depressing the pin and discharging fuel into the throttle body.
3. Disconnect the throttle cable and transmission throttle valve lever.

4. Disconnect fuel, vacuum and electrical connections.

NOTE: Either the multi or single ten pin connectors may be used on the system. To disconnect electrical ten pin connectors, push in or squeeze on the right side lower locking tab while pulling up on the connection. Multi connectors disconnect by pulling apart. The ISC connector tab must be moved out while pulling apart.

5. Remove fuel charging assembly retaining nuts, then, remove fuel charging assembly.

6. Remove mounting gasket from intake manifold. Always use a new gasket for installation.

7. Clean gasket mounting surfaces of spacer and fuel charging assembly.

8. Place spacer between two new gaskets and place spacer and gaskets on the intake manifold. Position the charging assembly on the spacer and gasket.

9. Secure fuel charging assembly with attaching nuts. Tighten to 10 ft. lbs (14Nm). To prevent leakage, distortion or damage to the fuel charging assembly body flange, snug the nuts; then, alternately tighten each nut in a criss cross pattern. Tighten to specifications.

10. Connect the fuel line, electrical connectors, throttle cable and all emission lines.

11. Start the engine, check for leaks. Adjust engine idle speed if necessary. Refer to Engine/Emission Control Decal for idle speed specifications.

Disassembly

To prevent damage to the throttle plates, the fuel charging assembly should be placed on a work stand during disassembly and assembly procedures. If a proper stand is not available, use four bolts $5/16 \times 2^1/2$ inches as legs. Install nuts on the bolts above and below the throttle body. The following is a step-by-step sequence of operations for completely overhauling the fuel charging assembly. Most components may be serviced without a complete disassembly of the fuel charging assembly. To replace individual components follow only the applicable steps.

NOTE: Use a separate container for the component parts of each sub-assembly to insure proper assembly. The automatic transmission throttle valve lever must be adjusted whenever the fuel charging assembly is removed for service or replacement.

1. Remove the air cleaner stud. The air cleaner stud must be removed to separate the upper body from the throttle body.

2. Turn the fuel charging assembly over and remove four screws from the bottom of the throttle body.

3. Separate throttle body from main body. Set throttle body aside.

4. Carefully remove and discard gasket. Note if scraping is necessary, be careful not to damage gasket surfaces of main and throttle screws.

5. Remove three pressure regulator retaining screws.

6. Remove pressure regulator. Inspect condition of gasket and O-ring.

7. Disconnect electrical connectors at each injector. Pull the connectors outward.

NOTE: Pull the connector, not the wire. Tape Identify the connectors. They must be installed on same injector as removed.

8. Loosen, DO NOT REMOVE, wiring harness retaining screw with multi connector; with single ten-pin connector loosen the two retaining screws.

9. Push in on tabs on harness to remove from upper body.

10. Remove fuel injector retainer screw.

11. Remove the injector retainer.

12. One at a time, pull injectors out of upper body. Identify each injector as "choke" or "throttle" side.

NOTE: Each injector has a small O-ring at its top. If the O-ring does not come out with the injector, carefully pick the O-ring out of the cavity in the throttle body.

13. Remove fuel diagnostic valve assembly.

14. Note the position of index mark on choke cap housing.

15. Remove three retaining ring screws.

16. Remove choke cap retaining ring, choke cap, and gasket, if so equipped.

17. Remove thermostat lever screw, and lever, if so equipped.

18. Remove fast idle cam assembly, if so equipped.

19. Remove fast idle control rod positioner, if so equipped.

20. Hold control diaphragm cover tightly in position, while removing two retaining screws, if so equipped.

21. Carefully, remove cover, spring, and pulldown control diaphragm, if so equipped.

22. Remove fast idle retaining nut, if so equipped.

23. Remove fast idle cam adjuster lever, fast idle lever, spring and E-clip, if so equipped.

24. Remove throttle position sensor connector bracket retaining screw.

25. Remove throttle position sensor retaining screws and slide throttle position sensor off the throttle shaft.

26. If CFI assembly is equipped with a throttle positioner, remove the throttle positioner retaining screw, and remove the throttle positioner. If the CFI assembly is equipped with an ISC DC Motor, remove the motor.

Idle speed control actuator—3.8L engine only

Assembly

1. Install fuel pressure diagnostic valve and cap. Tighten valve to 48–84 inch lbs. (5–9 Nm). Tighten cap to 5–10 inch lbs. (0.6–2 Nm).

2. Lubricate new O-rings and install on each injector (use a light grade oil).

3. Identify injectors and install them in their appropriate locations (choke or throttle side). Use a light twisting, pushing motion to install the injectors.

4. With injectors installed, install injector retainer into position.

5. Install injector retainer screw, and tighten to 36–60 inch lbs. (4–7 Nm).

6. Install injector wiring harness in upper body. Snap harness into position.

7. Tighten injector wiring harness retaining screw, (two screws if equipped with a single ten pin connector), to 8–10 inch lbs. (1 Nm).

8. Snap electrical connectors into position on injectors.

9. Lubricate new fuel pressure regulator O-ring with light oil. Install O-ring and new gasket on regulator.

10. Install pressure regulator in upper body. Tighten retaining screws to 27–40 inch lbs. (3–4 Nm).

11. Depending upon CFI assembly, install either the throttle positioner, or the ISC DC Motor.

Legend:

1. PLUG – FUEL PRESSURE REGULATOR ADJUSTING SCREW
2. REGULATOR ASSEMBLY – FUEL PRESSURE
3. SEAL – 5/16 x .070 "O" RING
4. GASKET – FUEL PRESSURE REGULATOR
5. CONNECTOR – 1/4 PIPE TO 1/2-20
6. CONNECTOR – 1/8 PIPE TO 9/16-16
7. BODY – FUEL CHARGING MAIN
8. PLUG – 1/16 27 HEADLESS HEX
9. INJECTOR ASSEMBLY – FUEL
10. SEAL – 5/8 x .103 "O" RING
11. SCREW – FUEL INJECTOR RETAINING
12. GASKET – FUEL CHARGING BODY
13. RETAINER – FUEL INJECTOR
14. SCREW M5.0 x 20.0 PAN HEAD
15. VALVE ASSEMBLY – DIAGNOSTIC VALVE
16. CAP – FUEL PRESSURE RELIEF VALVE
17. WIRING ASSEMBLY – FUEL CHARGING
18. SCREW – M3.5 x 1.27 x 12.7 PAN HEAD
19. SCREW & WASHER – M4 x 7.0 20.00
20. BALL – LEAD SHOT .26 - .24 DIA.
21. COVER ASSEMBLY – CONTROL DIAPHRAGM
22. SPRING – CONTROL MODULATOR
23. RETAINER – PULLDOWN DIAPHRAGM

24. DIAPHRAGM – PULLDOWN CONTROL
25. ADJUSTER – PULLDOWN CONTROL
26. ROD – FAST IDLE CONTROL
27. CAM – FAST IDLE
28. SHAFT – CHOKE HOUSING
29. POSITIONER – FAST IDLE CONTROL ROD
30. BUSHING – CHOKE HOUSING
31. GASKET – THERMOSTAT HOUSING
32. SCREW & WASHER – M3.5 x 0.6 x 6 PAN HEAD
33. LEVER – CHOKE THERMOSTAT
34. HOUSING ASSEMBLY – THERMOSTAT
35. RETAINER – HOUSING ASSEMBLY
36. SCREW
37. NUT & WASHER ASSEMBLY – .7-6H HEX
38. LEVER – FAST IDLE CAM ADJUSTER
39. SCREW – NO. 10 - 32 x .50 SET SLOTTED HEAD
39a. FAST IDLE PICK-UP LEVER RETURN SPRING
40. LEVER – FAST IDLE
41. SCREW & WASHER – M4.07 x 22.0 PAN HEAD
42. THROTTLE POSITION SENSOR
43. SCREW – M4 x .7 x 14.0 HEX WASHER TAP
44. SCREW – M5 x .7 x 55.0
45. BODY – FUEL CHARGING – THROTTLE

46. SCREW – M3 x 0.5 x 7.4 HEX WASHER HEAD
47. PLATE – THROTTLE
48. BEARING – THROTTLE CONTROL LINKAGE
49. "E" RING – 7/32 RETAINING
50. PIN – SPRING COILED
51. SHAFT – THROTTLE
52. "C" RING – THROTTLE SHAFT BUSHING
53. BEARING – THROTTLE CONTROL LINKAGE
54. SPRING – THROTTLE RETURN
55. BUSHING – ACCELERATOR PUMP OVER TRAVEL SPRING
56. LEVER – TRANSMISSION LINKAGE
57. SCREW – M4 x 0.7 x 7.6
58. PIN – TRANSMISSION LINKAGE LEVER
59. SPACER – THROTTLE SHAFT
60. BALL – THROTTLE LEVER
61. LEVER – THROTTLE
62. POSITIONER ASSEMBLY – THROTTLE
63. SCREW – 1/4 - 28 x 2.53 HEX HEAD ADJUSTING
64. SPRING – THROTTLE POSITIONER RETAINING
65. "E" RING – RETAINING
66. BRACKET – THROTTLE POSITIONER
67. SCREW – M5 x 8 x 14.0 HEX WASHER TAP

Exploded view of 5.0L CFI assembly—3.8L CFI similar

12. Hold throttle position sensor so wire faces up.

13. Slide throttle position sensor on throttle shaft.

14. Rotate throttle position sensor clockwise until aligned with screw holes on throttle body. Install retaining screws and tighten to 11–16 inch lbs. (1–2 Nm).

15. Install throttle position wiring harness bracket retaining screw. Tighten screw to 18–22 inch lbs. (2–3 Nm).

16. Install E-clip, fast idle lever and spring, fast idle adjustment lever and fast idle retaining nut, if so equipped.

17. Tighten fast idle retaining nut to 16–20 inch lbs. (1–2 Nm), if so equipped.

18. Install pull down control diaphragm, control modulator spring and cover, if so equipped. Hold cover in position and install two retaining screws, and tighten to 13–19 inch lbs. (1–2 Nm).

19. Install fast idle control rod positions, if so equipped.

20. Install fast idle cam, if so equipped.

21. Install thermostat lever and retaining screws, if so equipped. Tighten to 13–19 inch lbs. (1–2 Nm).

22. Install choke cap gasket, choke cap, and retaining ring, if so equipped.

NOTE: Be sure the choke cap bimetal spring is properly inserted between the fingers of the thermostat lever and choke cap index mark is properly aligned.

23. Install choke cap retaining screws, tighten to 13–18 inch lbs. (1–2 Nm).

24. Install fuel charging gasket on upper body. Be sure gasket is positioned over bosses. Place throttle body in position on upper body.

3.8L CFI with 10 pin connector

25. Install four upper body to throttle body retaining screws. Tighten to specifications.

26. Install air cleaner stud. Tighten stud to 70–95 inch lbs. (8–11 Nm).

Wiring and Vacuum Diagrams

CFI vacuum schematic

Wiring and Vacuum Diagrams

EEC III wiring diagram showing harness connector pin numbers

No Start Problem — Pinpoint Test — A (EFI)

TEST STEP	RESULT ▶	ACTION TO TAKE
A1 CHECK FOR FUEL LEAKS	Fuel not leaking ▶	GO to A2
NO LIGHTED TOBACCO NEARBY • Remove air cleaner • Inspect and service any: — Loose connections — Corrosion — Water or other foreign matter in fuel — Fuel Leaks • Watch for leaks* as you pressurize fuel system (Turn key ON and OFF five times with one second periods ON before switching OFF) • Key OFF *WARNING: If fuel starts leaking or injectors discharge, IMMEDIATELY turn key OFF. No Smoking. NOTE: This step requires two technicians	Fuel being injected ▶	CHECK for short to ground in circuits 95 and 96* in harness or processor. If none found, replace injectors.
	Fuel is leaking elsewhere than from injectors ▶	REPLACE leaking component* *If no short or leaking found, GO to A34
A2 TRY TO START ENGINE	Engine cranks, but does not start or stalls out ▶	GO to A3
	Engine does not crank ▶	REFER to the Shop Manual. If battery were discharged and you suspect the EEC-III system, charge the battery, and perform the QUICK TEST

No Start Problem — Pinpoint Test — A (EFI)

TEST STEP	RESULT ▶	ACTION TO TAKE
A7 ENGINE COOLANT TEMPERATURE SENSOR (ECT) — ENGINE AT NORMAL OPERATING TEMPERATURE	DVOM Reading:	
• Tester to A-5	Between 0.83V-7.4V ▶	GO to A8
	Under 0.83V ▶	GO to E3
	More than 7.4V ▶	GO to E5
A8 AIR CHARGE TEMPERATURE SENSOR (ACT)	DVOM Reading:	
• Tester to A-6	Between 0.83V-6.9V ▶	GO to A9
	Under 0.83 or more than 6.9V ▶	GO to S1
A9 MANIFOLD ABSOLUTE PRESSURE SENSOR (MAP)	ELEVATION (FT.)	
• Tester to A-7	LIMITS DVOM Reading: 0-1500 7.6-8.4 1501-2500 7.2-8.1 2501-3500 6.9-7.8 3501-4500 6.7-7.3 4501-5500 6.6-7.2 5501-6500 6.3-7.0 6501-7500 6.1-6.7 7501-8500 5.8-6.5 8501-9500 5.6-6.3 9501-10500 5.4-6.0 ▶	GO to A10
• Fill in appropriate limits for your local elevation. (For future reference.)	DVOM Reading does not correspond to your local elevation. ▶	GO to F1

No Start Problem — Pinpoint Test — A (EFI)

TEST STEP	RESULT ▶	ACTION TO TAKE
A3 CHECK EEC-III SYSTEM	DVOM Reading:	
• Turn key to OFF • Connect Tester • Tester to A1 • Disconnect injectors electrically • DVOM switch to Tester • Turn key to RUN — engine OFF	10.50V or more ▶	GO to A4
	Less than 10.50V ▶	GO to B1
A4 SENSOR REFERENCE VOLTAGE (VREF)	DVOM Reading:	
• Tester to A-3	Between 8-10V ▶	GO to A5
	Under 8V or more than 10V ▶	GO to C1
A5 THROTTLE POSITION SENSOR (TP)	DVOM Reading:	
• Tester to A-4	Between 1.8-2.8V ▶	GO to A6
	Under 1.8 or more than 2.8V ▶	GO to D1
A6 THROTTLE POSITION SENSOR MOVEMENT CHECK	DVOM Reading:	
• Tester to A-4	6V or more ▶	GO to A7
• Depress accelerator pedal	Under 6V ▶	GO to D2

No Start Problem — Pinpoint Test — A (EFI)

TEST STEP	RESULT ▶	ACTION TO TAKE
A10 CHECK MANIFOLD VACUUM ON ENGINE CRANK	DIFFERENCE IN READINGS:	
• Tester to A-7	0.4V or more ▶	GO to A11
• Key to RUN, and observe initial DVOM reading	Under 0.4V ▶	GO to F1
• Crank engine, and note reading NOTE: Do not depress gas pedal during test.		
A11 CHECK BMAP SENSOR	DIFFERENCE BETWEEN THE TWO READINGS:	
• Tester to A-8		
• Compare reading with MAP reading A19	0.75V or less ▶	GO to A12
	More than 0.75V ▶	GO to F1
A12 CHECK EGR VALVE POSITION SENSOR AND EGR LIGHTS	DVOM Reading:	
• Tester to A-9	1.4 to 2.45 ▶	GO to A12a
	Under 1.4 or over 2.45 ▶	GO to G1
ON EGRV OFF ON EGRC OFF	If lights are not as shown ▶	GO to G6

| No Start Problem | | Pinpoint Test | A (EFI) |

TEST STEP	RESULT	ACTION TO TAKE
A12a CHECK FOR FULL EGR • Disconnect EGR valve vacuum hose at EGR solenoid assembly • Attempt to start engine	Engine does not start or stalls when starting Engine starts	GO to A13 GO to G12
A13 CRANKING SIGNAL VOLTAGE • Tester to A-2	DVOM Reading: 1V or less Over 1V	GO to A14 GO to R1
A14 CHECK CP AND IMS SIGNALS AND POWER TO STARTER VOLTAGE • Tester connected • Tester to A-2 • Observe DVOM reading and Tester CP and IMS lights while cranking engine for 5 seconds	WHILE CRANKING DVOM Reading: Under 6.5V on A-2 6.5V or more on A-2 AND TESTER LIGHTS	GO to R1 GO to A15 GO to A17 GO to A20 GO to A20

| No Start Problem | | Pinpoint Test | A (EFI) |

TEST STEP	RESULT	ACTION TO TAKE
A17 CHECK IGNITION MODULE • Disconnect Ignition Module • Crank engine for 5 seconds, and observe CP and IMS light after 3 seconds of cranking	TESTER LIGHTS: IMS CP IMS CP	GO to A18 RECONNECT Ignition Module REFER to Ignition System in Part 29-02
A18 CHECK WIRING HARNESS TO IGNITION MODULE • Disconnect processor assembly from vehicle harness • Tester to B-11 • Turn key to RUN — engine OFF • Turn key to OFF	DVOM Reading: 0.5V or less More than 0.5V	GO to A19 SERVICE short to voltage source in wire 144 (orange/yellow hash) RECONNECT Ignition Module
A19 CHECK HARNESS • Turn key to OFF • Tester to 3-11 • Depress and hold Ohms button • Reconnect Ignition Module	DVOM Reading: 1000 ohms or more Under 1000 ohms	REPLACE Processor Assembly SERVICE short-to-ground in wire 144 (orange/yellow hash)
A20 CHECK CP SENSOR • Turn key to OFF • Tester to A-10 • Depress and hold Ohms button	DVOM Reading: Between 100 and 640 ohms Under 100 or more than 640 ohms	GO to A21 GO to A24

| No Start Problem | | Pinpoint Test | A (EFI) |

TEST STEP	RESULT	ACTION TO TAKE
A15 CHECK FOR SPARK • Reconnect coil harness clip • Disconnect the Spark Plug wire to cylinder No. 2 or No. 4 • Connect spark tester between spark plug wire and engine ground • Crank engine • Reconnect the spark plug wire to the spark plug	Spark No spark	CHECK rotor, CP ring, and damper for proper alignment. If OK, go to A29 GO to A16
A16 CHECK IGNITION MODULE • Disconnect Ignition Module harness. Install Rotunda Test Adapter T79P-12-127A. • Turn key to RUN • Connect the spark tester between the cap end of the ignition coil wire and engine ground • Repeatedly touch battery terminal with the orange diagnosis test lead, and check for ignition sparks (at coil) when the lead is touched to battery positive • Turn key to OFF • Remove test adapter, and reconnect the ignition module • Reconnect the coil wire to the distributor cap	No Spark Spark at coil	REFER to Ignition System CHECK for open in Circuit 144 from EEC harness to Ignition Module. If OK, replace processor

| No Start Problem | | Pinpoint Test | A (EFI) |

TEST STEP	RESULT	ACTION TO TAKE
A21 CHECK FOR PHYSICAL DAMAGE • Check CP Sensor and pulse ring for damage, such as missing lobes, sensor cracks, damaged wiring, etc. • Check for proper CP Sensor seating	No damage and seating is proper Damage or improper seating	GO to A22 SERVICE as required
A22 CHECK PROCESSOR ASSEMBLY • Disconnect processor assembly from vehicle harness • Crank engine for 5 seconds, and observe CP light after 6 seconds of cranking	TESTER LIGHT: CP CP	GO to A23 REPLACE Processor Assembly
A23 CHECK CP HARNESS FOR CONTINUITY • Turn key to OFF • Tester to A-10 • Disconnect CP Sensor from vehicle harness • Jumper a wire between CP + (349) and CP − (350) in CP harness • Depress and hold Ohms button	DVOM Reading: 5 ohms or more Under 5 ohms	SERVICE wire 350 (gray) or wire 349 (dark blue) for open circuit or high resistance REPLACE CP Sensor

Top Left

No Start Problem	Pinpoint Test	A (EFI)

TEST STEP	RESULT	ACTION TO TAKE
A24 CHECK CP SENSOR RESISTANCE • Disconnect CP sensor from vehicle harness	DVOM Reading: Between 100-640 ohms Under 100 or more than 640 ohms	GO to A25 REPLACE CP Sensor
A25 CHECK CP+ TO GROUND SHEATH RESISTANCE • Measure resistance from CP+ in sensor to both CP shield connectors (sensor and harness) for shorts	No short Short	GO to A26 REPLACE CP Sensor
A26 CHECK CP SENSOR HARNESS FOR SHORT • Turn key to OFF • Tester to A-10 • Disconnect Processor Assembly from Tester • DVOM switch to Tester • Depress and hold Ohms button	DVOM Reading: +1 (overrange, no shorts) Under 1999 ohms (Short)	GO to A27 SERVICE short in harness between circuits 350 and 349

Top Right

No Start Problem	Pinpoint Test	A (EFI)

TEST STEP	RESULT	ACTION TO TAKE
A29 FUEL PUMP CHECK NO SMOKING NEARBY • Disconnect ignition coil connector • Disconnect both fuel injector electrical connections at the injectors • Connect pressure gauge to Schraeder valve on Throttle Body injector bar • Note initial pressure reading • Observe pressure gauge as you pressurize fuel system (turn key to RUN for 1 second, then turn key to OFF. Repeat 5 times) • Turn key to OFF WARNING: If fuel starts leaking or injectors discharging, turn key OFF immediately. No smoking. Reconnect ignition coil connector. GO to A1	PRESSURE GAUGE READING: Increase Did not increase	GO to A31 TURN key OFF, reconnect ignition coil connector, and go to A30

Bottom Left

No Start Problem	Pinpoint Test	A (EFI)

TEST STEP	RESULT	ACTION TO TAKE
A27 CHECK CP HARNESS FOR CONTINUITY • Turn key to OFF • Tester to A-10 • Disconnect CP Sensor from vehicle harness • Jumper a wire between CP+ and CP− in harness • Depress and hold Ohms button	DVOM Reading: 5 ohms or less More than 5 ohms	GO to A28 SERVICE circuits 350 (gray) or 349 (dark blue) for open circuit or high resistance
A28 CHECK CP SENSOR HARNESS FOR SHORTS FROM CP+ TO GROUND (CIRCUIT 60)	DVOM Reading: 5 ohms or more Under 5 ohms	REPLACE Processor Assembly SERVICE short in Harness

Bottom Right

No Start Problem	Pinpoint Test	A (EFI)

TEST STEP	RESULT	ACTION TO TAKE
A30 CHECK INERTIA SWITCH • Locate inertia switch (in trunk) • Push the button of Inertia switch to turn it on • Watch pressure gauge as you attempt to pressurize fuel system NOTE: If switch will not turn "ON", replace it.	PRESSURE GAUGE READING: Increases Did not increase	GO to QUICK TEST GO to Q2
A31 CHECK FUEL DELIVERY • Pressurize fuel system • Turn key to OFF • Wait for pressure to become steady • Read pressure gauge	PRESSURE GAUGE READING: Between 35 and 45 psi Over 45 psi or under 35 psi	GO to A32 RECONNECT ignition coil. REFER to Part 24-29 of the Shop Manual
A32 CHECK FOR LEAK DOWN • Wait 2 minutes after pressure gauge reading of test Step A31 then note drop in gauge reading	PRESSURE DROP: 4 psi drop or less in 2 min. More than 4 psi drop in 2 min.	GO to A33 RECONNECT ignition coil.

No Start Problem		Pinpoint Test	A (EFI)

TEST STEP	RESULT ▶	ACTION TO TAKE
A33 CHECK FOR FUEL DISCHARGE WITH INJECTORS DISCONNECTED		
• Crank engine for 3 seconds	Pressure does not drop, AND Injectors do not discharge ▶	GO to A34
• Watch pressure gauge and injectors	Pressure drops, AND Injectors discharge ▶	TURN key OFF immediately CHECK for hydraulic lockup or fuel fouled spark plugs RECONNECT ignition coil REPLACE leaking injector(s) with the same color code
A34 CHECK SIGNAL AT DRIVER SIDE INJECTOR	TEST LIGHT:	
• Reconnect injectors	Off ▶	GO to A35
• Connect a 12 V Test Light across 2 pins on the driver side of Throttle Body connector	On ▶	REMOVE Test Light GO to A41
• Turn key to RUN		

No Start Problem		Pinpoint Test	A (EFI)

TEST STEP	RESULT ▶	ACTION TO TAKE
A38 CHECK ONE INJECTOR'S PRESSURE	PRESSURE DROP:	
• Disconnect one injector electrically (leave other one connected)	Between 2 and 16 psi drop (1 to 8 psi drop per second of cranking) ▶	GO to A39
• Pressurize fuel system		
• Disable fuel pump by disconnecting Inertia Switch or disconnecting Fuel Pump Relay	Less than 2 or more than 16 psi drop (less than 1 or more than 8 psi drop per second of cranking) ▶	GO to A40
• Observe pressure gauge reading		
• Crank engine for 2 seconds		
• Turn key to OFF		
• Wait 5 seconds then observe pressure gauge reading drop		
A39 CHECK OTHER INJECTOR'S PRESSURE	PRESSURE DROP:	
• Reactive fuel pump	Between 2 and 16 psi drop (1 to 8 psi drop per second of cranking) ▶	RECONNECT ignition coil Spark plug and fuel is present. Check to make sure plugs are not fouled and all plugs are firing and the rotor is turning. Be sure there is no mechanical problem like distributor cross-fire, flooding, or improper fuel.
• Reconnect injector, and disconnect the other one		
• Repeat A38 for this injector		
	Less than 2 or more than 16 psi drop (less than 1 or more than 8 psi drop per second of cranking) ▶	GO to A40

No Start Problem		Pinpoint Test	A (EFI)

TEST STEP	RESULT ▶	ACTION TO TAKE
A35 CHECK PROCESSOR OUTPUT TO DRIVER SIDE INJECTOR	TEST LIGHT:	
• Crank engine	Flickers ▶	GO to A36
• Leave test light connected as in A34	Does not flicker ▶	DISCONNECT Test Light GO to A41
A36 CHECK SIGNAL AT PASSENGER SIDE INJECTOR	TEST LIGHT:	
• Connect the 12V Test Light across 2 pins on the passenger side of Throttle Body right connector	Off ▶	GO to A37
• Turn key to RUN	On ▶	DISCONNECT Test Light GO to A41
A37 CHECK PROCESSOR OUTPUT TO PASSENGER SIDE INJECTOR	TEST LIGHT:	
• Crank engine	Flickers ▶	GO to A38
• Leave test light connected as in A36	Does not flicker ▶	DISCONNECT Test Light GO to A41

No Start Problem		Pinpoint Test	A (EFI)

TEST STEP	RESULT ▶	ACTION TO TAKE
A40 ISOLATE IMPROPER FUEL DELIVERY	PRESSURE DROP:	
• Remove the connected electrical connector from the injector, and connect it to the other injector	Between 2 and 16 psi (1 to 8 psi per second of cranking) ▶	REPLACE the Disconnected injector with same color code RECONNECT both injectors correctly RETEST.
	Less than 2 or more than 16 psi (less than 1 or more than 8 psi per second of cranking) ▶	GO to A41
• Reactivate fuel pump		
• Pressurize fuel system		
• Disable fuel pump by turning off Inertia Switch or disconnecting Fuel Pump Relay		
• Observe pressure gauge reading		
• Crank engine for 2 seconds		
• Turn key to OFF		
• Wait 5 seconds then observe pressure gauge reading drop		

Panel A41–A43

No Start Problem		Pinpoint Test	A (EFI)

TEST STEP	RESULT	▶	ACTION TO TAKE
A41 CHECK FOR INJECTOR SHORT-TO-GROUND • Turn key to OFF • Reconnect ignition coil connector • Reconnect injectors properly • Check each pin on Throttle Body connector for short-to-ground 200 OHMS →	No short at any pin Short at one or more pins	▶ ▶	GO to A45 GO to A42
A42 CHECK FOR PROCESSOR SHORT-TO-GROUND • Turn key to OFF • Disconnect harness from Processor Assembly • Check each pin of Throttle Body for short-to-ground (See A41)	No short any pin Short at one or more pins	▶ ▶	REPLACE Processor Assembly GO to A43
A43 CHECK FOR SHORT-TO-GROUND IN DRIVER SIDE INJECTOR (Processor disconnected) • Disconnect driver side injector • Check each pin of Throttle Body connector for short-to-ground (See A41)	No short at any pin Short at one or more pins	▶ ▶	REPLACE driver side injector GO to A44

Panel A47–A48

No Start Problem		Pinpoint Test	A (EFI)

TEST STEP	RESULT	▶	ACTION TO TAKE
A47 CHECK FOR SHORT BETWEEN INJECTOR LINES • Disconnect harness from Processor Assembly • Using DVOM Test Leads, measure resistance between pins: — 12 and 28 — 24 and 28 (left injector) — 24 and 12 (right injector) on Harness connector 200 OHMS →	DVOM Reading: 2 or more ohms for each pair of pins Under 2 ohms for one or more pair of pins	▶ ▶	GO to A49 NOTE which lines, GO to A48
A48 ISOLATE OBSERVED SHORT TO INJECTORS OR HARNESS • Disconnect both injectors electrically • Using DVOM Test Leads, measure resistance (200 x 1000 scale) between pins: — 12 and 28 — 24 and 28 (left injector) — 24 and 12 (right injector) on Harness connector	DVOM Reading: 10,000 ohms or more for each pair of pins Under 10,000 ohms for one or more pair of pins	▶ ▶	REPLACE injector(s) connected to the pin(s) that were shorted in A47 (replace with the same color code) SERVICE short in harness

Panel A44–A46

No Start Problem		Pinpoint Test	A (EFI)

TEST STEP	RESULT	▶	ACTION TO TAKE
A44 CHECK FOR SHORT-TO-GROUND IN PASSENGER SIDE INJECTOR (Left injector disconnected) • Disconnect passenger side injector • Check each pin on Throttle Body connector again for short-to-ground	No short at any pin Short at one or more pins	▶ ▶	REPLACE passenger side injector SERVICE short circuit
A45 CHECK INJECTOR CIRCUITS TO BATTERY VOLTAGE • Using DVOM Test Leads, measure voltage between battery negative and each injector signal line	DVOM Reading: 1V or less for both lines Over 1V for either line	▶ ▶	GO to A46 SERVICE short in circuit 95 or 96 between battery positive and circuit(s) out of limits
A46 CHECK RESISTANCE OF INJECTORS HARNESS AND PROCESSOR CONNECTION • Using DVOM Test Leads, measure resistance from 361 to 95 and from 361 to 96 200 OHMS 96 361 361 95	DVOM Reading: Under 2 ohms 2 or more ohms	▶ ▶	GO to A47 GO to A49

Panel A49–A50

No Start Problem		Pinpoint Test	A (EFI)

TEST STEP	RESULT	▶	ACTION TO TAKE
A49 CHECK FOR OPENS IN LINES TO INJECTORS • Using DVOM Test Leads, measure resistance (200 Ohms Scale) between pins: — 24 and 28 (driver side injector) — 24 and 12 (passenger side injector) on Harness connector 200 OHMS 24 28 EEC HARNESS CONNECTOR	DVOM Reading: 4 or less ohms for each line Over 4 ohms between 24 and 28 Over 4 ohms between 24 and 12 Over 4 ohms on both	▶ ▶ ▶ ▶	REPLACE Processor Assembly GO to A50 GO to A51 SERVICE open in Circuit 361
A50 CHECK FOR OPEN IN DRIVER SIDE INJECTOR HARNESS • Disconnect driver side injector electrically • Connect jumper wire across injector harness pins • Using DVOM Test Leads, measure resistance between pins 24 and 28 on Harness connector	DVOM Reading: 5 or less ohms Over 5 ohms	▶ ▶	REPLACE driver side injector SERVICE open in circuit 96 or 361 to injector

No Start Problem		Pinpoint Test	A (EFI)

TEST STEP	RESULT ▶	ACTION TO TAKE
A57 CHECK FOR OPEN IN PASSENGER SIDE INJECTOR HARNESS • Disconnect passenger side injector electrically • Connect jumper wire across injector harness pins • Using DVOM Test Leads measure resistance between pins 24 and 12 of Harness connector	DVOM Reading: 5 or less ohms ▶ Over 5 ohms ▶	REPLACE passenger side injector SERVICE open in circuit 95 or 361 to injector

Fuel Pump Relays		Pinpoint Test	Q (EFI)

TEST STEP	RESULT ▶	ACTION TO TAKE
Q2 CHECK IF FUEL PUMP RUNS • Turn key to RUN, but keep engine OFF • Listen* for fuel pump to run briefly when key is first turned on *You may want to open gas filler cap to hear the pump. No smoking	Pump runs briefly ▶ Pump does not run ▶	GO to Q11 GO to Q3
Q3 RECHECK IF FUEL PUMP RUNS • Tester hooked up • Press tester LOS button to "ON" (green flag), and leave LOS button "ON" during entire PINPOINT TEST • Turn key to RUN, but keep engine OFF • Listen closely for fuel pump; it should run constantly	Pump runs ▶ Pump does not run ▶	REPLACE Calibration Assembly. Retest. If not OK, replace Processor GO to Q4
Q4 CHECK VOLTAGE ON WIRE TO PROCESSOR • Tester to C-4 (the processor grounds this lead to turn on the fuel pump) • LOS button ON	DVOM Reading: Under 2.0V ▶ 2.0V or more ▶	GO to Q5 GO to Q14

Fuel Pump Relays		Pinpoint Test	Q (EFI)

This Test Checks
Cause of Low/No Fuel Pressure

TEST STEP	RESULT ▶	ACTION TO TAKE
Q1 INERTIA SWITCH CHECK • Locate Inertia Switch • Check connections on switch • Push top button to turn on Inertia Switch • Pressurize fuel system (turn key to RUN for 1 second, then turn OFF) repeat 5 times • Observe fuel pressure gauge	PRESSURE INCREASES TO: More than 35 psi ▶ 35 psi or less ▶	RUN QUICK TEST (page 5) GO to Q2

Fuel Pump Relays		Pinpoint Test	Q (EFI)

TEST STEP	RESULT ▶	ACTION TO TAKE
Q5 CHECK FOR POWER TO FUEL PUMP • Use DVOM Test Leads to measure voltage on circuit 787 at the Inertia Switch to fuel pump • LOS button ON	DVOM Reading: Under 6V ▶ 6V or more ▶	GO to Q6 GO to Q17
Q6 CHECK FOR POWER TO INERTIA SWITCH • Use DVOM to measure voltage on circuit 787 at Inertia Switch to fuel pump relay • LOS button ON	DVOM Reading: 6V or more ▶ Under 6V ▶	REPLACE Inertia Switch GO to Q7

Fuel Pump Relays		Pinpoint Test	Q (EFI)

TEST STEP	RESULT ▶	ACTION TO TAKE
Q7 CHECK FOR VOLTAGE OUT OF FUEL PUMP RELAY • Use DVOM Test Leads to measure voltage on circuit 787 at Fuel Pump Relay • LOS button ON	DVOM Reading: Under 6V ▶ 6V or more ▶	GO to Q8 SERVICE open in circuit 787 from fuel pump relay to inertia switch
Q8 CHECK FOR VOLTAGE INTO FUEL PUMP RELAY • Use DVOM Test Leads to measure voltage on circuit 787A at the Ballast Bypass Relay	DVOM Reading: Under 6V ▶ 6V or more ▶	GO to Q9 GO to Q19

Fuel Pump Relays		Pinpoint Test	Q (EFI)

TEST STEP	RESULT ▶	ACTION TO TAKE
Q10 CHECK OUTPUT OF BALLAST BYPASS RELAY • Use DVOM Test Leads to measure voltage on circuit 787A at the Ballast Bypass Relay	DVOM Reading: 6V or more ▶ Under 6V ▶	SERVICE open in circuit 787A between bypass relay and fuel pump relay, circuit 787A. If reading were between 6V and 10V, GO to Q11. Relay is open or energized or contacts opened SERVICE open in circuit 37A ballast resistor. Also, ballast bypass relay is energized or contacts open, GO to Q11

Fuel Pump Relays		Pinpoint Test	Q (EFI)

TEST STEP	RESULT ▶	ACTION TO TAKE
Q9 CHECK FOR VOLTAGE INTO BALLAST BYPASS RELAY • Use DVOM Test Leads to measure voltage on circuit 37B at the Ballast Bypass Relay	DVOM Reading: More than 10V ▶ Less than 10V ▶	GO to Q10 SERVICE open or bad connection in circuit 37B to power. If fuse link is blown, service short to ground in 787, 787A, 787B, 37, or the fuel pump itself; this must be serviced prior to fixing the fuse link

Fuel Pump Relays		Pinpoint Test	Q (EFI)

TEST STEP	RESULT ▶	ACTION TO TAKE
Q11 CHECK FOR VOLTAGE DROP ACROSS FUEL PUMP BALLAST BYPASS RELAY • Use DVOM Test Leads to measure voltage from circuit 37 to circuit 787A at Ballast Bypass Relay	DVOM Reading: More than 1V ▶ 1V or less ▶	GO to Q12 GO to Part 24-29 in the Shop Manual, and check for clogged fuel line, filter, or defective Throttle Body
Q12 CHECK FOR RELAY ENERGIZED • Use DVOM Test Leads to measure voltage on circuit 57A at Ballast Bypass Relay	DVOM Reading: Under 10V ▶ 10V or more ▶	GO to Q13 REPLACE Ballast Bypass Relay

Fuel Pump Relays	Pinpoint Test	Q (EFI)

TEST STEP	RESULT ▶	ACTION TO TAKE
Q13 CHECK VACUUM SWITCH • Disconnect Vacuum Swich from vehicle harness • Use DVOM Test Leads to check for short-to-ground in circuit 57A	DVOM Reading: More than 10V 10V or less ▶	REPLACE Vacuum Switch SERVICE short in circuit 57A
Q14 ISOLATE REASON FOR HIGH VOLTAGE (AT TESTER C-4) • Turn key to off • Disconnect fuel pump relay • Disconnect Adapter Harness from processor assembly • Turn key to RUN, but keep engine off • Tester to C-4	DVOM Reading: Under 1V ▶ 1V or more ▶	GO to Q15 SERVICE short to power in circuit 97 or fuel pump relay

Fuel Pump Relays	Pinpoint Test	Q (EFI)

TEST STEP	RESULT ▶	ACTION TO TAKE
Q18 CHECK WIRES TO FUEL PUMP • Use DVOM to measure voltage on each of the two pins of the fuel pump. Measure voltage between one of the pins and ground, then between the other pin and ground • Do not disconnect connector from fuel tank	DVOM Reading: Under 6V on both pins ▶ 6V or more for both ▶ One reads more than 7V and other reads under 7V	SERVICE open in circuit 787 between Inertia Switch and Fuel Tank SERVICE open in circuit 57 ground wire REPLACE Fuel Pump Assembly
CAUTION: Fuel supply lines will remain pressurized for long periods of time after key is turned OFF. This pressure must be relieved before servicing of the fuel system has begun. A valve is provided on the throttle body for this purpose. Remove air cleaner, and relieve system pressure by depressing pin in relief valve CAUTIOUSLY; fuel will be expelled into throttle body		

Fuel Pump Relays	Pinpoint Test	Q (EFI)

TEST STEP	RESULT ▶	ACTION TO TAKE
Q15 CHECK FOR SHORTED FUEL PUMP RELAY COIL • Measure resistance of fuel pump relay coil	More than 40 ohms ▶ Less than 40 ohms ▶	GO to Q15 REPLACE Relay
Q16 CHECK FOR SHORT TO 787A IN RELAY COIL	No short ▶ Short ▶	REPLACE Processor Assembly, and RUN QUICK TEST. If still not OK, replace Calibration Assembly using original Processor Assembly REPLACE fuel pump relay
Q17 CHECK WIRES TO FUEL PUMP • Visually check wires to fuel Pump for bad connections or opens	Problem identified as bad wiring ▶ Problem not seen in wiring ▶	SERVICE as needed GO to Q18

Fuel Pump Relays	Pinpoint Test	Q (EFI)

TEST STEP	RESULT ▶	ACTION TO TAKE
Q19 CHECK FOR VOLTAGE TO RELAY COIL • Use DVOM Test Leads to measure voltage on circuit 361 at the Fuel Pump Relay	DVOM Reading: More than 10V ▶ 10V or less ▶	GO to Q20 SERVICE open in circuit 361 between Power Relay and Fuel Pump Relay
Q20 CHECK PROCESSOR SIDE OF RELAY COIL • Use DVOM test leads to measure voltage on circuit 97 at the fuel pump relay	More than 2V ▶ 2V or less ▶	SERVICE open in circuit 97 REPLACE Fuel Pump Relay

Fuel Pump Relays		Pinpoint Test		Q (EFI)

TEST STEP	RESULT	▶	ACTION TO TAKE
Q21 CHECK FUEL PUMP RELAY			
NOTE: This check is made if Fuel Pump is always ON	Fuel Pump OFF ▶		GO to Q22
• Turn key to OFF	Fuel Pump RUNS ▶		SERVICE short to power in circuit 787 between Fuel Pump Relay and Fuel Pump
• Disconnect Fuel Pump Relay			
• Listen for Fuel Pump			
Q22 CHECK CIRCUIT 97 FOR SHORT-TO-GROUND IN HARNESS	DVOM Reading:		
• Using DVOM, check for a short between circuit 97 and ground at fuel pump relay harness connector	Short ▶		GO to Q23
• Check at the relay connector with relay disconnected	No short ▶		REPLACE Fuel Pump Relay
Q23 CHECK CIRCUIT 97 FOR SHORT-TO-GROUND WITH ECA DISCONNECTED	DVOM Reading:		
• Disconnect harness from Processor Assembly	150 ohms or less ▶		SERVICE short-to-ground in wire 97
• Tester to C-4			
• Press Ohms button DVOM	More than 150 ohms ▶		REPLACE Processor Assembly. If still not OK, replace calibration assembly using original processor

Fuel Pump Relays		Pinpoint Test		Q (EFI)

TEST STEP	RESULT	▶	ACTION TO TAKE
Q26 CHECK IF BALLAST BYPASS RELAY IS ENERGIZED	DVOM Reading:		
• Measure voltage on Circuit 57A at the relay	10V or more ▶		GO to Q27
	Under 10V ▶		GO to Q29
Q27 CHECK HOSE TO VACUUM SWITCH			
• Check hose from manifold to Vacuum Switch for good connections, leaks, cracks, blockage, etc.	Hose good ▶		GO to Q28
	Hose faulty ▶		SERVICE hose
Q28 CHECK VACUUM SWITCH VOLTAGE	DVOM Reading:		
• Use DVOM Test Leads to measure voltage from each Vacuum Switch connector pin to ground (leave switch connected) with vehicle at idle	Both readings 10V or more ▶		SERVICE open in ground wire 57B
	Both readings under 10V ▶		SERVICE open or bad connection in circuit 57A between Ballast Bypass Relay and vacuum switch (57A)
	One reading 10V or more and other reading under 10V ▶		REPLACE vacuum switch

Fuel Pump Relays		Pinpoint Test		Q (EFI)

TEST STEP	RESULT	▶	ACTION TO TAKE
Q24 CHECK FUEL PUMP VOLTAGE			
NOTE: This check is made if Fuel Pump is always noisy	DVOM Reading:		
• Engine at idle	Under 10V ▶		CHECK Fuel Pump mechanically if noise is excessive
• Measure Fuel Pump voltage at Inertia Switch	10V or more ▶		GO to Q25
Q25 CHECK VOLTAGE ON CIRCUIT 361 AT THE BALLAST BYPASS RELAY	DVOM Reading:		
• Use DVOM Test Leads to measure voltage on circuit 361 at the ballast bypass relay	10V or more ▶		GO to Q26
	Under 10V ▶		SERVICE open circuit in 361

Fuel Pump Relay		Pinpoint Test		Q (EFI)

TEST STEP	RESULT	▶	ACTION TO TAKE
Q29 CHECK "FUEL PUMP BALLAST BYPASS" RELAY	DVOM Reading:		
• Disconnect ballast bypass relay from the harness	10V or more ▶		SERVICE short to power in circuit 787 between Ballast Bypass Relay and Fuel Pump Relay
• Use DVOM Test Lead to measure voltage on circuit 787A at relay connector			
	Under 10V ▶		REPLACE the Ballast Bypass Relay
Q30 FUEL PUMP BALLAST WIRE CHECK			
NOTE: This check is made if vehicle starts but quickly stalls	DVOM Reading:		
• Turn key to OFF	3 ohms or less ▶		GO to A1
• Disconnect Ballast Bypass Relay from harness	Over 3 ohms ▶		SERVICE open circuit or bad connection in Ballast wire circuit 37A
• Use DVOM Test Leads to measure resistance of Ballast wire			

Cranking Signal	Pinpoint Test	R (EFI)

This Test Checks

Crank Signal Circuit

TEST STEP	RESULT ▶	ACTION TO TAKE
R1 CHECK CRANKING SIGNAL WITH KEY ON		
• Turn key to RUN, but keep engine OFF	DVOM Reads:	
• Tester to A-2 (Cranking Signal)	Under 1V ▶	GO to R3
	1V or more ▶	GO to R2
R2 CHECK FOR SHORT TO POWER		
• Turn key to OFF		
• Disconnect harness from Tester	No short ▶	CHECK for proper chassis ground to engine and engine ground to battery If OK, RUN QUICK TEST
• Using DVOM Test Leads measure resistance (200 x 1000 ohms range) between: — Pins 1 and 24 (circuit 361) — Pins 1 and 3 (circuit 351)	Shorted ▶	SERVICE short

Air Charge Temperature	Pinpoint Test	S (EFI)

This Test Checks

• Air Charge Temperature (ACT)

• Sensor and Harness

AIR CHARGE TEMPERATURE SENSOR

TEST STEP	RESULT ▶	ACTION TO TAKE
S1 CHECK ENGINE TEMPERATURE		
• What does the operating temperature of the engine appear to be by observation (ignoring tester readings)	ENGINE TEMPERATURE:	
	Overheated ▶	GO to Part 29 Routine 217
	Below normal ▶	GO to Part 29 Routine 216
	At normal operating	GO to S2
S2 ATTEMPT TO BRING AIR CHARGE TEMPERATURE WITHIN LIMITS		
• Tester to A-6 (ACT)	DVOM Reading:	
• Start engine, increase RPM and hold for 5 to 10 minutes	Between 1.0V and 5.6V ▶	RUN QUICK TEST
• Observe DVOM	Under 1.0V ▶	GO to S3
	More than 5.6V ▶	GO to S5

Cranking Signal	Pinpoint Test	R (EFI)

TEST STEP	RESULT ▶	ACTION TO TAKE
R3 CHECK FOR OPENS		
• Disconnect wire from Starter Relay "S" terminal	DVOM Reading:	
• Tester at A-2	More than 6.5V ▶	RUN QUICK TEST
• Turn key to START	6.5V or less ▶	GO to R4
R4 CONTINUE CHECK FOR OPENS		
• Key OFF	DVOM Reading:	
• Disconnect Tester from EEC harness	Under 5 ohms ▶	GO to R5
• Using DVOM Test Leads, measure resistance (200 ohm range) between: — Pin 1 to Starter Relay "S" wire (circuit 32) — Pin 8 to Battery Negative (circuit 57)	5 or more ohms ▶	SERVICE open circuit RECONNECT "S" terminal RUN QUICK TEST
R5 CHECK FOR CRANK SHORT-TO- GROUND		
• Using DVOM Test Leads, measure resistance between: — Pin 1 to Battery Negative	DVOM Reading:	
	More than 10,000 ohms ▶	RECONNECT Tester RECONNECT Starter "S" terminal RUN QUICK TEST
	Under 10,000 ohms ▶	SERVICE short-to-ground in circuit 32 RECONNECT Tester RECONNECT Starter "S" terminal RUN QUICK TEST

PIN 1

200X1000 OHMS

Air Charge Temperature	Pinpoint Test	S (EFI)

TEST STEP	RESULT ▶	ACTION TO TAKE
S3 CHECK ACT SENSOR RESISTANCE	DVOM Reading:	
• Disconnect harness from ACT sensor	Less than 8.00 ▶	GO to S4
• Switch tester to A-6	More than 8.00 ▶	CHECK engine for overtemperate, and let cool down. If this fails to correct problem, replace ACT sensor, and retest
• Read DVOM		
S4 CHECK ACT SENSOR HARNESS FOR SHORTS		
• Turn key to OFF	DVOM Reading:	
• Use DVOM Test Leads to check for short from pin 6 (ACT) to all remaining 31 connector pins	More than 10,000 ohms ▶	REPLACE ACT SENSOR, and run QUICK TEST. If problem still exists, REPLACE Processor Assembly
	10,000 or less ohms ▶	SERVICE short(s) in EEC harness
200 x 1000 OHMS		
S5 CHECK FOR ACT SHORT TO POWER		
• Disconnect EEC Harness from Tester	DVOM Reading:	
• Turn key to RUN, but keep engine OFF	Under 0.2V on both pins ▶	GO to S6
• Use DVOM Test Leads to measure voltage from each Sensor harness pin to chassis ground	0.2V or more on either pin ▶	SERVICE harness short to power

Air Charge Temperature		Pinpoint Test	S (EFI)

TEST STEP		RESULT ▶	ACTION TO TAKE
S6 CHECK ACT SENSOR HARNESS CONTINUITY • Turn key to OFF • Use DVOM Test Leads to check continuity from Sensor connector to the ECA harness connector pins 19 and 6		DVOM Reading: Under 5.0 ohms ▶ 5.0 or more ohms ▶	GO to S6a SERVICE open or bad harness connection
S6a CHECK ACT SENSOR RESISTANCE • Turn key to OFF • Disconnect harness from ACT Sensor • Use DVOM Test Leads to measure resistance across sensor pins		DVOM Reading: 1,700-60,000 ohms ▶ Under 1,700 or over 60,000 ohms ▶	REPLACE processor REPLACE ACT sensor
S7 LOCATE CAUSE OF CODE 24 (ECA has interpreted air temperature to be outside the 40-240°F range) • Engine at idle • Tester to A-6 (ACT) • While observing DVOM, wiggle ACT Sensor and harness, checking for bad connections		DVOM Reading: Remains Under 1.0V or more than 5.6V ▶ Jumps to under 1.0V or more than 5.6V ▶ Remains between 1.0-5.6V ▶	GO to S1 SERVICE connection REPLACE Processor Assembly

GENERAL MOTORS MULTI-PORT (MFI) AND SEQUENTIAL (SFI) FUEL INJECTION SYSTEMS

General Information

On 1984 and later non-turbocharged models, a new multi-port fuel injection (MFI) system is available. The MFI system is controlled by an electronic control module (ECM) which monitors engine operations and generates output signals to provide the correct air/fuel mixture, ignition timing and engine idle speed control. Input to the control unit is provided by an oxygen sensor, coolant temperature sensor, detonation sensor, hot film air mass sensor and throttle position sensor. The ECM also receives information concerning engine rpm, road speed, transmission gear position, power steering and air conditioning.

On turbocharged models, a sequential port fuel injection system (SFI) is used for more precise fuel control. With SFI, metered fuel is timed and injected sequentially through six Bosch injectors into individual cylinder ports. Each cylinder receives one injeection per working cycle (every two revolutions), just prior to the opening of the intake valve. The main difference between the two types of fuel injection systems is the manner in which fuel is injected. In the multiport system, all injectors work simultaneously, injecting half the fuel charge each engine revolution. The control units are different for SFI and MFI systems, but most other components are similar. In addition, the SFI system incorporates a new Computer Controlled Coil Ignition system that uses an electronic coil module that replaces the conventional distributor and coil used on most engines. An electronic spark control (ESC) is used to adjust the spark timing.

Both systems use Bosch injectors, one at each intake port, rather than the single injector found on the earlier throttle body system.

The injectors are mounted on a fuel rail and are activated by a signal from the electronic control module. The injector is a solenoid-operated valve which remains open depending on the width of the electronic pulses (length of the signal) from the ECM; the longer the open time, the more fuel is injected. In this manner, the air/fuel mixture can be precisely controlled for maximum performance with minimum emissions.

Fuel is pumped from the tank by a high pressure fuel pump, located inside the fuel tank. It is a positive displacement roller vane pump. The impeller serves as a vapor separator and pre-charges the high pressure assembly. A pressure regulator maintains 28-36 psi (28-50 psi on turbocharged engines) in the fuel line to the injectors and the excess fuel is fed back to the tank. On MFI systems, a fuel accumulator is used to dampen the hydraulic line hammer in the system created when all injectors open simultaneously.

The Mass Air Flow Sensor is used to measure the mass of air that is drawn into the engine cylinders. It is located just ahead of the air throttle in the intake system and consists of a heated film which measures the mass of air, rather than just the volume. A resistor is used to measure the temperature of the incoming air and the air mass sensor maintains the temperature of the film at 75 degrees above ambient temperature. As the ambient (outside) air temperature rises, more energy is required to maintain the heated film at the higher temperature and the control unit uses this difference in required energy to calculate the mass of the incoming air. The control unit uses this information to determine the duration of fuel injection pulse, timing and EGR.

The throttle body incorporates an idle air control (IAC) that provides for a bypass channel through which air can flow. It consists

OPERATING CONDITIONS SENSED

- A/C "On" or "Off"
- Engine Coolant Temperature
- Engine Crank (1.8L)
- Exhaust Oxygen (0₂)
- Cruise Control "On" or "Off" (3.8L)
- Distributor Reference
  - Crankshaft Position
  - Engine Speed (RPM)
- Manifold Absolute Pressure (MAP) (1.8L)
- Park/Neutral Switch (P/N) Position
- System Voltage (1.8L)
- Throttle Position (TPS)
- Transmission Gear Position
- Vehicle Speed (VSS)
- Mass Air Flow (MAF) (3.8L)
- Manifold Air Temperature (MAT) (1.8L)
- EGR Vacuum

ELECTRONIC CONTROL MODULE (ECM)

SYSTEMS CONTROLLED

- Canister Purge (3.8L)
- Turbo Wastegate
- Exhaust Gas Recirc. (EGR) (3.8L)
- Electronic Spark Timing (EST)
- Fuel Control (Injector)
- Idle Air Control (IAC)
- Transmission Converter Clutch (TCC)
- Electric Fuel Pump
- Air Conditioning
- Engine Cooling Fan
- Diagnostics
  - "Check Engine" Light
  - Diagnostic "Test" Terminal (ALCL)
  - Data Output (ALCL)

Operation schematic of GM MFI and SFI systems. Not all systems are used on all engines

of an orifice and pintle which is controlled by the ECM through a stepper motor. The IAC provides air flow for idle and allows additional air during cold start until the engine reaches operating temperature. As the engine temperature rises, the opening through which air passes is slowly closed.

The throttle position sensor (TPS) provides the control unit with information on throttle position, in order to determine injector pulse width and hence correct mixture. The TPS is connected to the throttle shaft on the throttle body and consists of a potentiometer with one end connected to a 5 volt source from the ECM and the other to ground. A third wire is connected to the ECM to measure the voltage output from the TPS which changes as the throttle

valve angle is changed (accelerator pedal moves). At the closed throttle position, the output is low (approximately .4 volts); as the throttle valve opens, the ouput increases to a maximum 5 volts at wide open throttle (WOT). The TPS can be misadjusted open, shorted, or loose and if it is out of adjustment, the idle quality or WOT performance may be poor. A loose TPS can cause intermittent bursts of fuel from the injectors and an unstable idle because the ECM thinks the throttle is moving. This should cause a trouble code to be set. Once a trouble code is set, the ECM will use a preset value for TPS and some vehicle performance may return. A small amount of engine coolant is routed through the throttle assembly to prevent freezing inside the throttle bore during cold operation.

1. Electronic control module (ECM)
2. Speed sensor buffer
3. Speed sensor pulse generator
4. Oil pressure and fuel pump relay (digital instruments only)
5. Fuel pump relay (analog instrument panel)
6. Low speed fan control relay
7. Temperature sending unit
8. A/C control relay
9. Electronic spark control (ESC) module
10. Oxygen sensor
11. Computer control harness
12. Fuel injector
13. CHECK ENGINE light
14. Idle air control (IAC) valve
15. ALCL connector
16. Fuse panel
17. High speed fan control relay
18. Canister purge solenoid valve
19. Vapor charcoal canister
20. Electronic spark timing connector
21. System ground
22. Coolant sensor
23. Coolant temperature override switch
24. EGR valve
25. ESC detonation (knock) sensor
26. Throttle position sensor (TPS)
27. Mass air flow sensor
28. Transmission converter clutch (TCC) connector
29. Fuel pump test lead
30. 12 volt power supply

GM MFI component locations on 3.8L V6 engine

Mass air flow sensor assembly-type

Assembly line communication link (ALCL) connector—typical

On-Car Service

CHECK ENGINE LIGHTS

The "check engine" light on the instrument panel is used as a warning lamp to tell the driver that a problem has occured in the electronic engine control system. When the self-diagnosis mode is activated by grounding the test terminal of the diagnostic connector, the check engine light will flash stored trouble codes to help isolate

Location of PROM and CALPAK in the ECM

Electronic control module (ECM) used on GM MFI and SFI systems

system problems. The electronic control module (ECM) has a memory that knows what certain engine sensors should be under certain conditions. If a sensor reading is not what the ECM thinks it should be, the control unit will illuminate the check engine light and store a trouble code in its memory. The trouble code indicates what circuit the problem is in, each circuit consisting of a sensor, the wiring harness and connectors to it and the ECM.

The Assembly Line Communications Link (ALCL) is a diagnostic connector located in the passenger compartment, usually under the left side of the instrument panel. It has terminals which are used in the assembly plant to check that the engine is operating properly before shipment. Terminal B is the diagnostic test terminal and Terminal A is the ground. By connecting the two terminals together with a jumper wire, the diagnostic mode is activated and the control unit will begin to flash trouble codes using the check engine light.

NOTE: Some models have a "Service Engine Soon" light instead of a "Check Engine" display.

When the test terminal is grounded with the key ON and the engine stopped, the ECM will display code 12 to show that the system is working. The ECM will usually display code 12 three times, then start to display any stored trouble codes. If no trouble codes are stored, the ECM will continue to display code 12 until the test terminal is disconnected. Each trouble code will be flashed three times, then code 12 will display again. The ECM will also energize all controlled relays and solenoids when in the diagnostic mode to check function.

When the test terminal is grounded with the engine running, it will cause the ECM to enter the Field Service Mode. In this mode, the service engine soon light will indicate whether the system is in Open or Closed loop operation. In open loop, the light will flash 2½ times per second; in closed loop, the light will flash once per second. In closed loop, the light will stay out most of the time if the system is too lean and will stay on most of the time if the system is too rich.

NOTE: The vehicle may be driven in the Field Service mode and system evaluated at any steady road speed. This mode is useful in diagnosing driveability problems where the system is rich or lean too long.

Trouble codes should be cleared after service is completed. To clear the trouble code memory, disconnect the battery for at least 10 seconds. This may be accomplished by disconnecting the ECM harness from the positive battery pigtail or by removing the ECM fuse.

---CAUTION---

The ignition switch must be OFF when disconnecting or reconnecting power to the ECM. The vehicle should be driven after the ECM memory is cleared to allow the system to readjust itself. The vehicle should be driven at part throttle under moderate acceleration with the engine at normal operating temperature. A change in performance should be noted initially, but normal performance should return quickly.

GM PORT INJECTION TROUBLE CODES

Trouble Code	Circuit
12	Normal operation
13	Oxygen sensor
14	Coolant sensor (low voltage)
15	Coolant sensor (high voltage)
21	Throttle position sensor (high voltage)
22	Throttle position sensor (low voltage)
24	Speed sensor
32	EGR vacuum control
33	Mass air flow sensor
34	Mass air flow sensor
42	Electronic spark timing
43	Electronic spark control
44	Lean exhaust
45	Rich exhaust
51	PROM failure
52	CALPAK
55	ECM failure

FUEL SYSTEM PRESSURE TEST

When the ignition switch is turned ON, the in-tank fuel pump is energized for as long as the engine is cranking or running and the control unit is receiving signals from the HEI distributor. If there are no reference pulses, the control unit will shut off the fuel pump within two seconds. The pump will deliver fuel to the fuel rail and injectors, then the pressure regulator where the system pressure is controlled to maintain 26-46 psi.

1. Connect pressure gauge J-34370-1, or equivalent, to fuel pressure test point on the fuel rail. Wrap a rag around the pressure tap to absorb any leakage that may occur when installing the gauge.

2. Turn the ignition ON and check that pump pressure is 34-40 psi. This pressure is controlled by spring pressure within the regulator assembly.

3. Start the engine and allow it to idle. The fuel pressure should drop to 28-32 psi due to the lower manifold pressure.

NOTE: The idle pressure will vary somewhat depending on barometric pressure. Check for a drop in pressure indicating regulator control, rather than specific values.

4. On turbocharged models, use a low pressure air pump to apply air pressure to the regulator to simulate turbocharger boost pressure. Boost pressure should increase fuel pressure one pound for every pound of boost. Again, look for changes rather than specific pressures. The maximum fuel pressure should not exceed 46 psi.

5. If the fuel pressure drops, check the operation of the check valve, the pump coupling connection, fuel pressure regulator valve and the injectors. A restricted fuel line or filter may also cause a pressure drop. To check the fuel pump output, restrict the fuel return line and run 12 volts to the pump. The fuel pressure should rise to approximately 75 psi with the return line restricted.

1. Fuel inlet connection
2. Fuel rail assembly
3. Fuel pressure test point
4. Fuel pressure regulator
5. Fuel return connection
6. Fuel injector

Fuel rail assembly

CAUTION

Before attempting to remove or service any fuel system component, it is necessary to relieve the fuel system pressure.

Relieving Fuel System Pressure

1. Remove the fuel pump fuse from the fuse block.
2. Start the engine. It should run and then stall when the fuel in the lines is exhausted. When the engine stops, crank the starter for about three seconds to make sure all pressure in the fuel lines is released.
3. Replace the fuel pump fuse.

Component Removal

FUEL INJECTORS

Removal and Installation

Use care in removing the fuel injectors to prevent damage to the electrical connector pins on the injector and the nozzle. The fuel injector is serviced as a complete assembly only and should not be immersed in any kind of cleaner.

Fuel rail and injectors—3.8L turbocharged engine

1. Fuel rail assembly
2. Fuel injector
3. Intake manifold
4. Injector housing assembly
5. Injector retaining clip
6. Injector assembly retaining groove
7. Injector cup flange
8. Injector control harness assembly
9. Pressure regulator assembly
10. Fuel pressure gauge test point

Fuel rail and injector assembly on 4 cyl. engine

Fuel rail and injectors—3.8L V6 engine

1. Oil pressure and fuel pump relay (digital instruments only)
2. Fuel pump relay (analog instrument panel)
3. Low speed fan control relay
4. A/C control relay
5. Electronic spark control (ESC) module

GM MFI and SFI relay assembly

1. Relieve fuel system pressure.
2. Remove the injector electrical connections.
3. Remove the fuel rail.
4. Separate the injector from the fuel rail.
5. Installation is the reverse of removal. Replace the O-rings when installing injectors into intake manifold.

FUEL PRESSURE REGULATOR

Removal and Installation

1. Relieve fuel system pressure.
2. Remove pressure regulator from fuel rail. Place a rag around the base of the regulator to catch any spilled fuel.
3. Installation is the reverse of removal.

IDLE AIR CONTROL VALVE

Removal and Installation

1. Remove electrical connector from idle air control valve.
2. Remove the idle air control valve using a suitable wrench.
3. Installation is the reverse of removal. Before installing the idle air control valve, measure the distance that the valve is extended. Measurement should be made from the motor housing to the end of the cone. The distance should not exceed $1^{1}/_{8}$ inches, or damage to the valve may occur when installed. Use a new gasket and turn the ignition on then off again to allow the ECM to reset the idle air control valve.

Idle air control valve installation

Engine sensors on GM MFI and SFI systems—3.8L engine shown

NOTE: Identify replacement IAC valve as being either Type 1 (with collar at electric terminal end) or Type 2 (without collar). If measuring distance is greater than specified above, proceed as follows:

Type 1: Press on valve firmly to retract it

Type 2: Compress retaining spring from valve while turning valve in with a clockwise motion. Return spring to original position with straight portion of spring end aligned with flat surface of valve.

THROTTLE POSITION SENSOR

Removal and Installation

1. Disconnect the electrical connector from the sensor.
2. Remove the attaching screws, lockwashers and retainers.
3. Remove the throttle position sensor. If necessary, remove the screw holding the actuator to the end of the throttle shaft.
4. With the throttle valve in the normal closed idle position, install the throttle position sensor on the throttle body assembly, making sure the sensor pickup lever is located above the tang on the throttle actuator lever.
5. Install the retainers, screws and lockwashers using a thread locking compound. DO NOT tighten the screws until the throttle position switch is adjusted.

Typical port fuel injector installation

Cross section of typical fuel pressure regulator

1. Fuel inlet
2. Fuel return outlet
3. Valve
4. Valve holder
5. Diaphragm
6. Compression spring
7. Vacuum connection

6. Install three jumper wires between the throttle position switch and the harness connector.
7. With the ignition switch ON, use a digital voltmeter connected to terminals B and C and adjust the switch to obtain 0.35-0.45 volts.
8. Tighten the mounting screws, then recheck the reading to insure that the adjustment hasn't changed.
9. Turn ignition OFF, remove jumper wires, then reconnect harness to throttle position switch.

OXYGEN SENSOR

Removal and Installation

NOTE: The oxygen sensor uses a permanently attached pigtail and connector. This pigtail should not be removed from the oxygen sensor. Damage or removal of the pigtail or connector could affect proper operation of the oxygen sensor.

The oxygen sensor is installed in the exhaust manifold and is removed in the same manner as a spark plug. The sensor may be

Typical oxygen sensor

difficult to remove when the engine temperature is below 120 deg. F (48 deg. C) and excessive force may damage threads in the exhaust manifold or exhaust pipe. Exercise care when handling the oxygen sensor; the electrical connector and louvered end must be kept free of grease, dirt, or other contaminants. Avoid using cleaning solvents of any kind and don't drop or roughly handle the sensor. A special anti-seize compound is used on the oxygen sensor threads when installing and care should be used NOT to get compound on the sensor itself. Disconnect the negative battery cable when servicing the oxygen sensor and torque to 30 ft. lbs. (41 Nm) when installing.

ELECTRONIC CONTROL MODULE (ECM)

The electronic control module (ECM) is located under the instrument panel. To allow one model of ECM to be used on different models, a device called a calibrator or PRCM (Programmable Read Only Memory) is installed inside the ECM which contains information on the vehicle weight, engine, transmission, axle ratio,

Location of PROM and CALPAK microprocessors in the control unit

Remove the PROM using the special removal tool

etc. The PROM is specific to the exact model and replacement part numbers must be checked carefully to make sure the correct PROM is being installed during service. Replacement ECM units (called Controllers) are supplied WITHOUT a PROM. The PROM from the old ECM must be carefully removed and installed in the replacement unit during service. Another device called a CALPAK

is used to allow fuel delivery if other parts of the ECM are damaged (the "limp home" mode). The CALPAK is similiar in appearance to the PROM and is located in the same place in the ECM, under an access cover. Like the PROM, the CALPAK must be removed and transferred to the new ECM unit being installed.

NOTE: If the diagnosis indicates a faulty ECM unit, the PROM should be checked to see if they are the correct parts. Trouble code 51 indicates that the PROM is installed incorrectly. When replacing the production ECM with a new part, it is important to transfer the Broadcast code and production ECM number to the new part label. Do not record on the ECM cover.

-CAUTION-

The ignition must be OFF whenever disconnecting or connecting the ECM electrical harness. It is possible to install a PROM backwards during service. Exercise care when replacing the PROM that it is installed correctly, or the PROM will be destroyed when the ignition is switched ON.

Removal and Installation

To remove the ECM, first disconnect the battery. Remove the wiring harness and mounting hardware, then remove the ECM from the passenger compartment. The PROM and CALPAK are located under the access cover on the top of the control unit. Using the rocker type PROM removal tool, or equivalent, engage one end of the PROM carrier with the hook end of the tool. Press on the vertical bar end of the tool and rock the engaged end of the PROM carrier up as far as possible. Engage the opposite end of the PROM carrier in the same manner and rock this end up as far as possible. Repeat this process until the PROM carrier and PROM are free of the socket. The PROM carrier should only be removed with the removal tool or damage to the PROM or PROM socket may occur.

Note the position of the reference notch when installing the PROM

When installing the PROM carrier in the PROM socket, the small notch of the carrier should be aligned with the small notch in the socket. Press on the PROM carrier until it is firmly seated in the socket. DO NOT press on the PROM; only the carrier. To check the PROM installation, reinstall the ECM and turn the ignition switch ON. Activate the diagnostic mode as previously described and check that a code 12 is displayed. Code 12 indicates that the PROM is installed correctly and is functioning normally. If trouble code 51 is displayed, or the "service engine soon" light is on steadily with no codes, the PROM is not fully seated, installed backwards, has bent pins, or is defective. Bent pins may be straightened and the PROM can be seated properly with a gentle push, but a PROM that has been installed backwards should be replaced. Any time the PROM is installed backwards and the ignition is switched ON, the PROM is destroyed.

ECM Connector ID

FUEL INJECTION ECM CONNECTOR IDENTIFICATION

THIS ECM VOLTAGE CHART IS FOR USE WITH A DIGITAL VOLTMETER TO FURTHER AID IN DIAGNOSIS. THE VOLTAGES YOU GET MAY VARY DUE TO LOW BATTERY CHARGE OR OTHER REASONS, BUT THEY SHOULD BE VERY CLOSE.

THE FOLLOWING CONDITIONS MUST BE MET BEFORE TESTING.

● ENGINE AT OPERATING TEMPERATURE ● ENGINE IDLING IN CLOSED LOOP (FOR "ENGINE RUN" COLUMN) ●
● TEST TERMINAL NOT GROUNDED ● ALCL TOOL NOT INSTALLED ●

24 PIN A-B CONNECTOR

PIN	CIRCUIT	KEY "ON" RUN	ENG. RUN	OPEN CRT.
A1	FUEL PUMP RELAY ④	.13	13.48	0
A2	A/C CLUTCH CONTROL	12.46 on.1 off13.8	12.21	12.21
A3	CANISTER PURGE CONTROL	12.45	13.8	12.21
A4	EGR CONTROL	12.45	13.8	12.21
A5	"CHECK ENGINE" CONTROL (ALCL)	.14	13.77	12.19
A6	IGN—ECM FUSE	12.34	13.6	12.15
A7	TCC CONTROL ALCL	12.40	13.78	12.20
A8	SERIAL DATA ALCL ③	4.30	2.5 4.5	.03
A9	DIAG. TERM. ALCL	4.95	4.95	.02
A10	SPEED SENSOR SIGNAL ①	.49	.49	.55
A11	CAM HI ⑤	.11 10.75	11.3	.01 11.40
A12	GRN'D	.07	.07	0

PIN	CIRCUIT	KEY "ON" RUN	ENG. RUN	OPEN CRT.
B1	NOT USED			
B2	NOT USED			
B3	CRANK REF LO	.14	.14	0
B4	EST CONTROL	.08	1.10	0
B5	CRANK REF HI	.09 10.02	5.56 10.43	.03
B6	MASS AIRFLOW SENSOR SIGNAL	2.50	2.48	.01
B7	ESC SIGNAL	8.71	8.75	9.60
B8	A/C SIGNAL	ON 11.97 OFF .02	13.34 .02	12.2 .01
B9	NOT USED	.06	.07	.04
B10	PARK/NEUTRAL SW SIGNAL			
B11	NOT USED			
B12	INJ. 5	12.06	13.2	12.17

32 PIN C-D CONNECTOR

PIN	CIRCUIT	KEY "ON" RUN	ENG. RUN	OPEN CRT.
C1	NOT USED			
C2	NOT USED			
C3	IAC-B-LO	.82	.83	.83
C4	IAC-B-HI	10.59	12.35	12.16
C5	IAC-A-LOW	.82	.83	.83
C6	IAC-A-HI	10.59	12.35	12.16
C7	3RD GEAR SIGNAL	.13	.13	.13
C8	4TH GEAR SIGNAL	.13	.14	.14
C9			13.5	
C10	COOLANT TEMP SIGNAL ②	2.04	2.18	.02
C11	NOT USED			
C12	INJ. 6	11.99	13.15	12.16
C13	TPS SIGNAL	.43	.42	.03
C14	TPS 5V REF	4.96	4.95	.02
C15	INJ. 2	11.98	13.15	12.15
C16	BATT. 12 VOLTS	11.89	13.73	12.16

PIN	CIRCUIT	KEY "ON" RUN	ENG. RUN	OPEN CRT.
D1	GRN'D	.0	.01	.04
D2	NOT USED			
D3	WASTEGATE CONTROL	11.94	13.70	12.14
D4	NOT USED			
D5	EST-BYPASS	4.56	4.55	0
D6	GRN'D (O2)	.14	.14	0
D7	O2 SENSOR SIGNAL ③	.26	.51	0
D8	NOT USED			
D9	EGR DIAG	11.77	13.38	0
D10	GRN'D	.07	.07	.07
D11	NOT USED			
D12	TPS/CTS GRN'D	.02	.03	.20
D13	NOT USED			
D14	INJ. 1	11.90	13.15	12.12
D15	INJ. 3	11.90	13.15	12.12
D16	INJ. 4	11.90	13.15	12.12

ENGINE: 3.8L TURBO
CARLINE: G & E

A-B table footnotes:
① Varies from .45 to battery voltage depending on position of drive wheels.
② Normal operating temperature.
③ Varies.
④ 12V first two seconds.

C-D table footnotes:
① Depends on position of vane in relation to "hall effect" switch. Voltage will be low when vane or vanes is passing through switch.
② Engine running voltage will be high or low depending whether A/C is on or off.

SR 84 6E 0985

Schematic

SR 84 6E 0162

Schematic

Diagnostic Circuit Check—3.8L

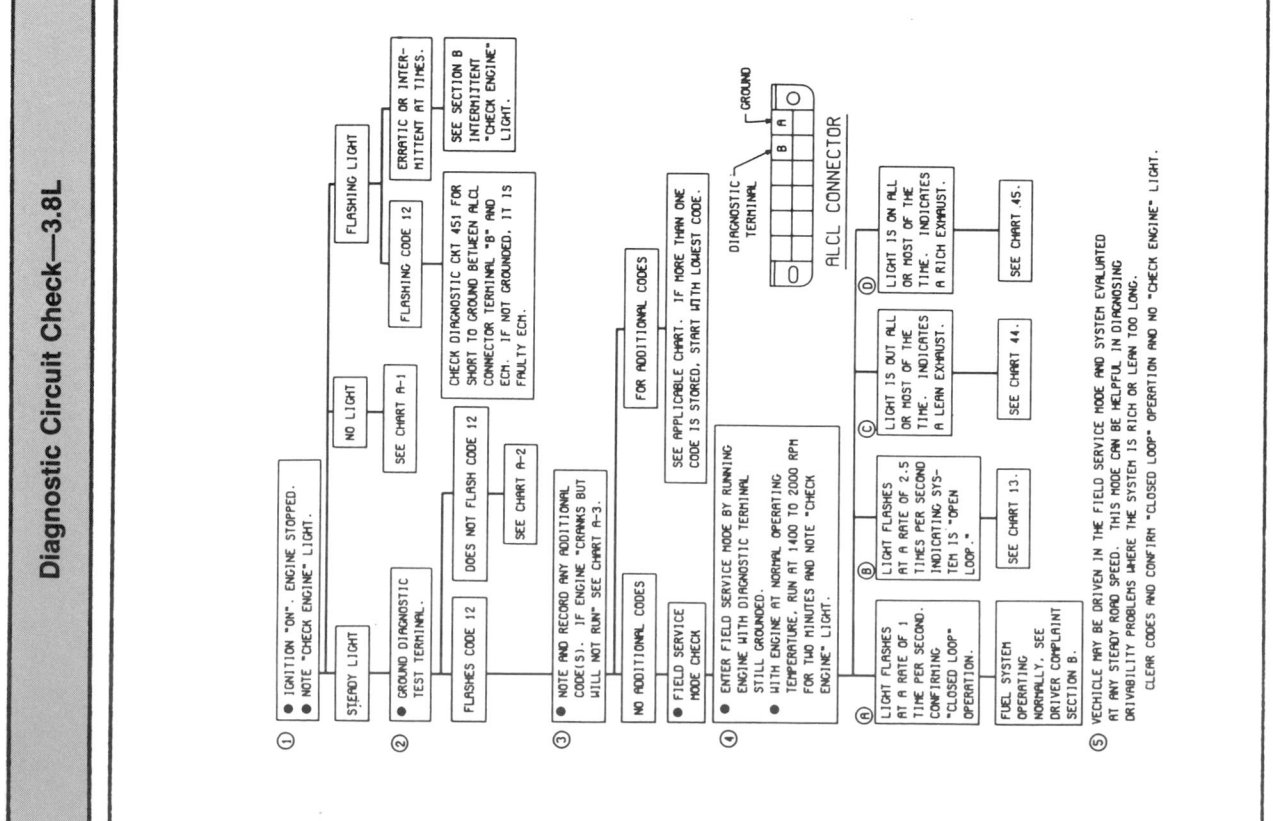

CHART A-1
No "Check Engine" Light—3.8L

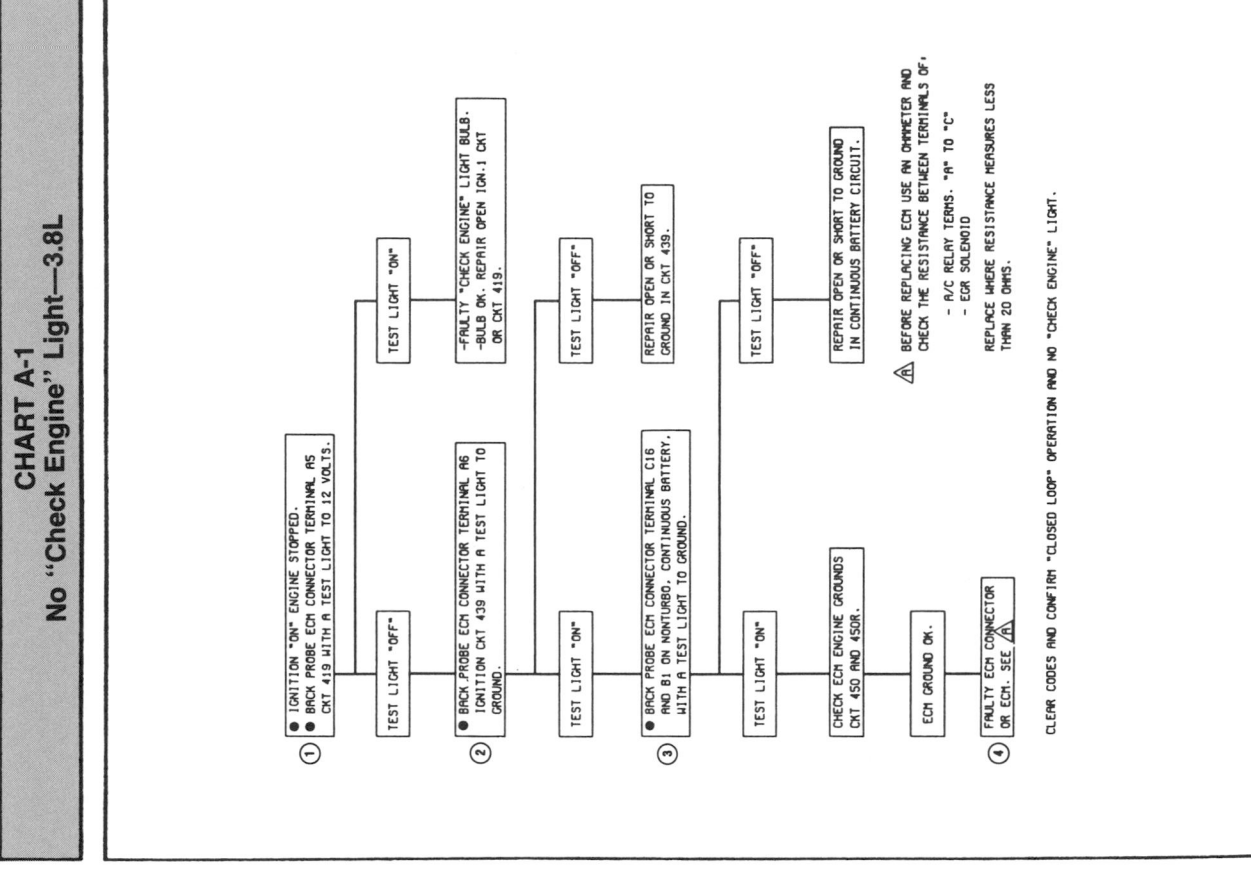

① • IGNITION "ON" ENGINE STOPPED.
• BACK PROBE ECM CONNECTOR TERMINAL A5 CKT 419 WITH A TEST LIGHT TO 12 VOLTS.

TEST LIGHT "OFF" — TEST LIGHT "ON"

② • BACK PROBE ECM CONNECTOR TERMINAL A6 IGNITION CKT 439 WITH A TEST LIGHT TO GROUND.

TEST LIGHT "ON" — TEST LIGHT "ON"
-FAULTY "CHECK ENGINE" LIGHT BULB.
-BULB OK. REPAIR OPEN IGN-1 CKT OR CKT 419.

TEST LIGHT "OFF"
REPAIR OPEN OR SHORT TO GROUND IN CKT 439.

③ • BACK PROBE ECM CONNECTOR TERMINAL C16 AND B1 ON NONTURBO. CONTINUOUS BATTERY. WITH A TEST LIGHT TO GROUND.

TEST LIGHT "OFF"
REPAIR OPEN OR SHORT TO GROUND IN CONTINUOUS BATTERY CIRCUIT.

TEST LIGHT "ON"
CHECK ECM ENGINE GROUNDS CKT 450 AND 450R.

ECM GROUND OK.

④ FAULTY ECM CONNECTOR OR ECM. SEE ⚠

⚠ BEFORE REPLACING ECM USE AN OHMMETER AND CHECK THE RESISTANCE BETWEEN TERMINALS OF:
- A/C RELAY TERMS. "A" TO "C"
- EGR SOLENOID
REPLACE WHERE RESISTANCE MEASURES LESS THAN 20 OHMS.

CLEAR CODES AND CONFIRM "CLOSED LOOP" OPERATION AND NO "CHECK ENGINE" LIGHT.

CHART A-2
Won't Flash Code 12—3.8L

① • IGNITION "OFF."
• DISCONNECT BOTH ECM CONNECTORS.
• IGNITION "ON."

LIGHT "OFF" — LIGHT "ON"
REPAIR SHORT TO GROUND IN CKT 419.

② • IGNITION "OFF."
• RECONNECT ECM.
• IGNITION ON. ENGINE STOPPED.
• DIAGNOSTIC TERMINAL NOT GROUNDED.
• BACK PROBE ECM CONNECTOR TERMINAL A-9. CKT 451. WITH A TEST LIGHT TO GROUND.

NO CODE 12 — CODE 12
CHECK FOR OPEN IN ALCL DIAGNOSTIC CKT 451. TERM. "B" TO ECM. IF OK. CHECK FOR OPEN IN ALCL TERM. "A" TO GROUND.

③ • DIAGNOSTIC TERMINAL NOT GROUNDED.
• IGNITION "OFF." ENGINE STOPPED.
• REMOVE PROM.
• IGNITION "ON."
• GROUND DIAGNOSTIC TERM.
• NOTE CODE.

CODE 51
CHECK FOR PROPER PROM INSTALLATION. IF OK. INSTALL NEW PROM AND RECHECK FOR CODE 12.

CODE 12
SYSTEM OK.

NO CODE — NO CODE
④ FAULTY ECM
BEFORE REPLACING ECM USE OHMMETER AND CHECK RESISTANCE BETWEEN TERMINALS OF:
- A/C RELAY TERMS. "A" TO "C"
- EGR SOLENOID
REPLACE WHERE RESISTANCE MEASURES LESS THAN 20 OHMS.

CLEAR CODES AND CONFIRM "CLOSED LOOP" OPERATION AND "CHECK ENGINE" LIGHT.

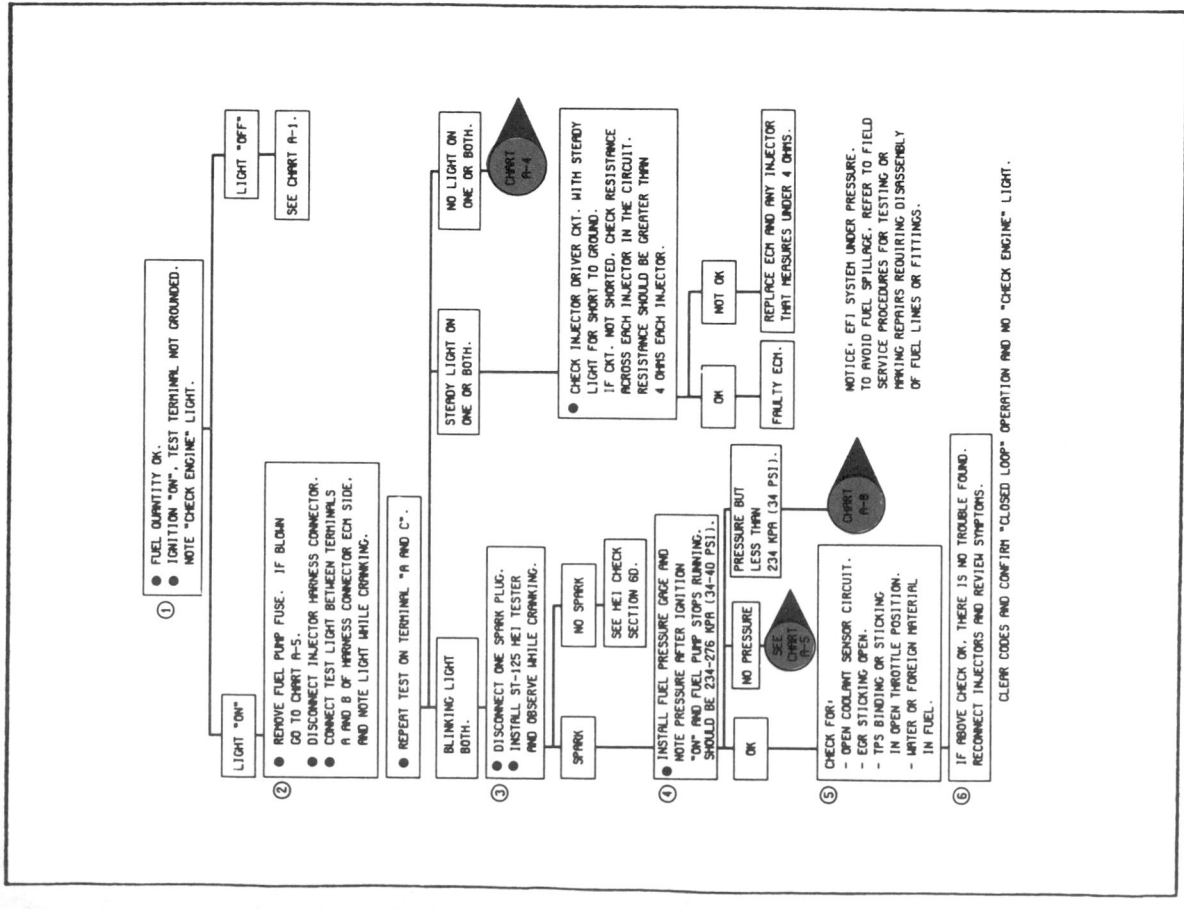

CHART A-4
Engine Cranks, But Will Not Run—3.8L

FROM CHART A-3

NO LIGHT

⑦
- IGNITION "ON".
- PROBE TERM. "A" OF INJECTOR HARNESS CONNECTOR, ECM SIDE, WITH A TEST LIGHT TO GROUND.

NO LIGHT → OPEN IGNITION CKT 439.

LIGHT

⑧
- RECONNECT INJECTORS.
- IGNITION "OFF".
- DISCONNECT "A-B" & "C-D" CONNECTORS.
- IGNITION "ON".
- PROBE ECM HARNESS CONNECTOR TERMS. D14 AND D15 WITH A TEST LIGHT TO GROUND. LIGHT SHOULD BE ON BOTH AT BOTH TERMS.

NOT OK → OPEN CKT 841 OR 844.

OK

⑨
- RECONNECT ECM.
- VOLTMETER SELECTOR SWITCH IN THE "AC VOLTS" POSITION.
- BACK PROBE ECM TERM. B5 WITH A VOLTMETER TO GROUND AND NOTE VOLTAGE WHILE CRANKING.

.9 VOLTS AC OR MORE. → FAULTY ECM CONNECTOR TERM B5 OR ECM.

LESS THAN .9 VOLTS AC.

⑩
- CHECK FOR AN OPEN OR SHORT TO GROUND OR BAT.+ IN CKT 430. IF CKT 430 NOT OPEN OR SHORTED.
- DISCONNECT ONE SPARK PLUG , INSTALL ST-125 HEI TESTER AND OBSERVE WHILE CRANKING ENGINE.

SPARK → IT IS FAULTY IGNITION MODULE CONNECTOR TERM. "R" OR MODULE.

NO SPARK → SEE HEI CHECK SECTION 6D.

CLEAR CODES AND CONFIRM "CLOSED LOOP" OPERATION AND NO "CHECK ENGINE" LIGHT.

CHART A-3
Engine Cranks, But Will Not Run—1984 3.8L

①
- FUEL QUANTITY OK.
- IGNITION "ON", TEST TERMINAL NOT GROUNDED.
- NOTE "CHECK ENGINE" LIGHT.

LIGHT "ON"

LIGHT "OFF" → SEE CHART A-1.

②
- REMOVE FUEL PUMP FUSE. IF BLOWN GO TO CHART A-5.
- DISCONNECT INJECTOR HARNESS CONNECTOR.
- CONNECT TEST LIGHT BETWEEN TERMINALS A AND B OF HARNESS CONNECTOR ECM SIDE, AND NOTE LIGHT WHILE CRANKING.
- REPEAT TEST ON TERMINAL "A AND C".

BLINKING LIGHT BOTH.

STEADY LIGHT ON ONE OR BOTH.

NO LIGHT ON ONE OR BOTH. → CHART A-4

- CHECK INJECTOR DRIVER CKT. WITH STEADY LIGHT FOR SHORT TO GROUND. IF CKT. NOT SHORTED, CHECK RESISTANCE ACROSS EACH INJECTOR IN THE CIRCUIT. RESISTANCE SHOULD BE GREATER THAN 4 OHMS EACH INJECTOR.

OK → FAULTY ECM.

NOT OK → REPLACE ECM AND ANY INJECTOR THAT MEASURES UNDER 4 OHMS.

③
- DISCONNECT ONE SPARK PLUG.
- INSTALL ST-125 HEI TESTER AND OBSERVE WHILE CRANKING.

SPARK

NO SPARK → SEE HEI CHECK SECTION 6D.

④
- INSTALL FUEL PRESSURE GAGE AND NOTE PRESSURE AFTER IGNITION "ON" AND FUEL PUMP STOPS RUNNING. SHOULD BE 234-276 KPA (34-40 PSI).

OK

NO PRESSURE → SEE CHART A-5

PRESSURE BUT LESS THAN 234 KPA (34 PSI). → CHART A-5

⑤
- CHECK FOR:
  - OPEN COOLANT SENSOR CIRCUIT.
  - EGR STICKING OPEN.
  - TPS BINDING OR STICKING IN OPEN THROTTLE POSITION.
  - WATER OR FOREIGN MATERIAL IN FUEL.

⑥
- IF ABOVE CHECK OK. THERE IS NO TROUBLE FOUND. RECONNECT INJECTORS AND REVIEW SYMPTOMS.

CLEAR CODES AND CONFIRM "CLOSED LOOP" OPERATION AND NO "CHECK ENGINE" LIGHT.

NOTICE: EFI SYSTEM UNDER PRESSURE. TO AVOID FUEL SPILLAGE. REFER TO FIELD SERVICE PROCEDURES FOR TESTING OR MAKING REPAIRS REQUIRING DISASSEMBLY OF FUEL LINES AND FITTINGS.

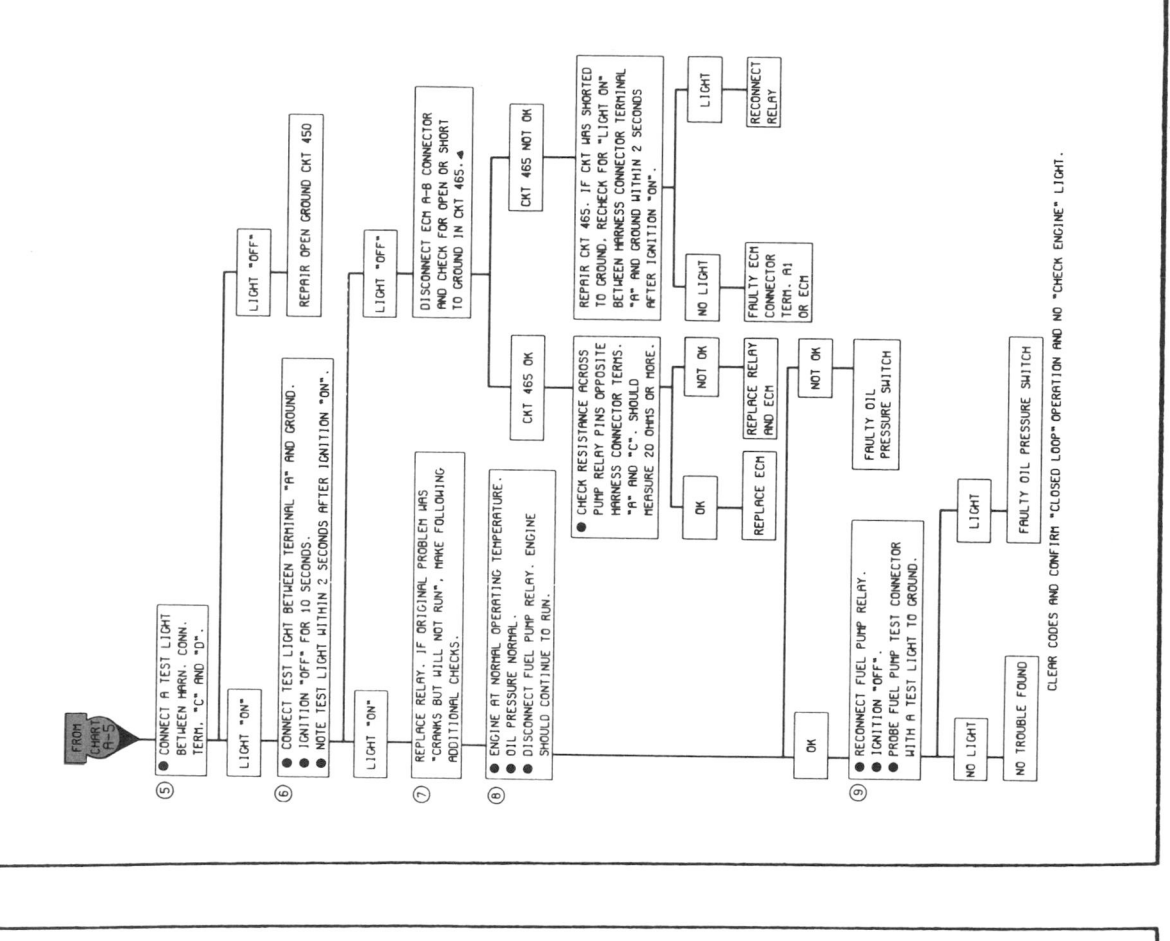

CHART A-6
Engine Cranks, But Will Not Run—3.8L

FROM CHART A-5

⑤ • CONNECT A TEST LIGHT BETWEEN HARN. CONN. TERM. "C" AND "D".

LIGHT "ON" → LIGHT "OFF" → REPAIR OPEN GROUND CKT 450

⑥ • CONNECT TEST LIGHT BETWEEN TERMINAL "A" AND GROUND.
• IGNITION "OFF." FOR 10 SECONDS.
• NOTE TEST LIGHT WITHIN 2 SECONDS AFTER IGNITION "ON".

LIGHT "ON" → LIGHT "OFF" → DISCONNECT ECM A-B CONNECTOR AND CHECK FOR OPEN OR SHORT TO GROUND IN CKT 465.◄

CKT 465 OK / CKT 465 NOT OK

REPAIR CKT 465. IF CKT WAS SHORTED TO GROUND, RECHECK FOR "LIGHT ON" BETWEEN HARNESS CONNECTOR TERMINAL "A" AND GROUND WITHIN 2 SECONDS AFTER IGNITION "ON".

NO LIGHT → LIGHT → RECONNECT RELAY

FAULTY ECM CONNECTOR. TERM. A1 OR ECM

⑦ • REPLACE RELAY. IF ORIGINAL PROBLEM WAS "CRANKS BUT WILL NOT RUN", MAKE FOLLOWING ADDITIONAL CHECKS.

⑧ • ENGINE AT NORMAL OPERATING TEMPERATURE.
• OIL PRESSURE NORMAL.
• DISCONNECT FUEL PUMP RELAY. ENGINE SHOULD CONTINUE TO RUN.

• CHECK RESISTANCE ACROSS PUMP RELAY PINS OPPOSITE HARNESS CONNECTOR TERMS. "A" AND "C". SHOULD MEASURE 20 OHMS OR MORE.

OK / NOT OK → REPLACE RELAY AND ECM

REPLACE ECM

NOT OK → FAULTY OIL PRESSURE SWITCH

OK

⑨ • RECONNECT FUEL PUMP RELAY.
• IGNITION "OFF."
• PROBE FUEL PUMP TEST CONNECTOR WITH A TEST LIGHT TO GROUND.

LIGHT → FAULTY OIL PRESSURE SWITCH

NO LIGHT → NO TROUBLE FOUND

CLEAR CODES AND CONFIRM "CLOSED LOOP" OPERATION AND NO "CHECK ENGINE" LIGHT.

CHART A-5
Engine Cranks, But Will Not Run—3.8L

FROM CHART A-3

NO PRESSURE

• CHECK FUEL PUMP FUSE.

OK / NOT OK

TEST POINT ONE FROM SECTION B

① • DISCONNECT FUEL PUMP AT REAR BODY CONNECTOR.
• IGNITION "OFF.".
• PROBE FUEL PUMP TEST CONNECTOR CKT 120. WITH A TEST LIGHT TO 12 VOLTS.

LIGHT "ON" → REPAIR SHORT TO GROUND IN CKT 12C.

LIGHT "OFF" → • RECONNECT FUEL PUMP.
• REPLACE FUSE.
• IGNITION "ON."
• RECHECK FUSE.

OK / NOT OK

② • PROBE FUEL PUMP TEST CONNECTOR WITH A TEST LIGHT TO GROUND.
• IGNITION "OFF." FOR 10 SECONDS.
• NOTE LIGHT WITHIN 2 SECONDS AFTER IGNITION "ON."

LIGHT "ON" → LIGHT "OFF" → DEFECTIVE FUSE OR INTERMITTENT SHORT TO GROUND IN CKT 120.

IN TANK FUEL PUMP OR PUMP HARNESS SHORTED TO GROUND.

LIGHT "OFF" / LIGHT "ON" → REPAIR OPEN CKT 839 OR 939.

CHART A-6

③ • APPLY BATTERY VOLTAGE TO PUMP TEST CONNECTOR.
• LISTEN FOR PUMP RUNNING AT FUEL TANK.

PUMP RUNS / PUMP NOT RUNNING

④ • DISCONNECT PUMP RELAY.
• IGNITION "ON." ENGINE STOPPED.
• PROBE RELAY HARNESS CONNECTOR TERMINAL "D" WITH A TEST LIGHT TO GROUND.

CHECK FOR:
- PLUGGED IN-LINE FILTER.
- PLUGGED PUMP INLET FILTER.
- RESTRICTED FUEL LINE.

IF OK → REPLACE IN-TANK FUEL PUMP

CHECK FOR:
- OPEN WIRE IN CKT 120.
- OPEN PUMP GROUND WIRE CKT 150.

IF OK

CLEAR CODES AND CONFIRM "CLOSED LOOP" OPERATION AND NO "CHECK ENGINE" LIGHT.

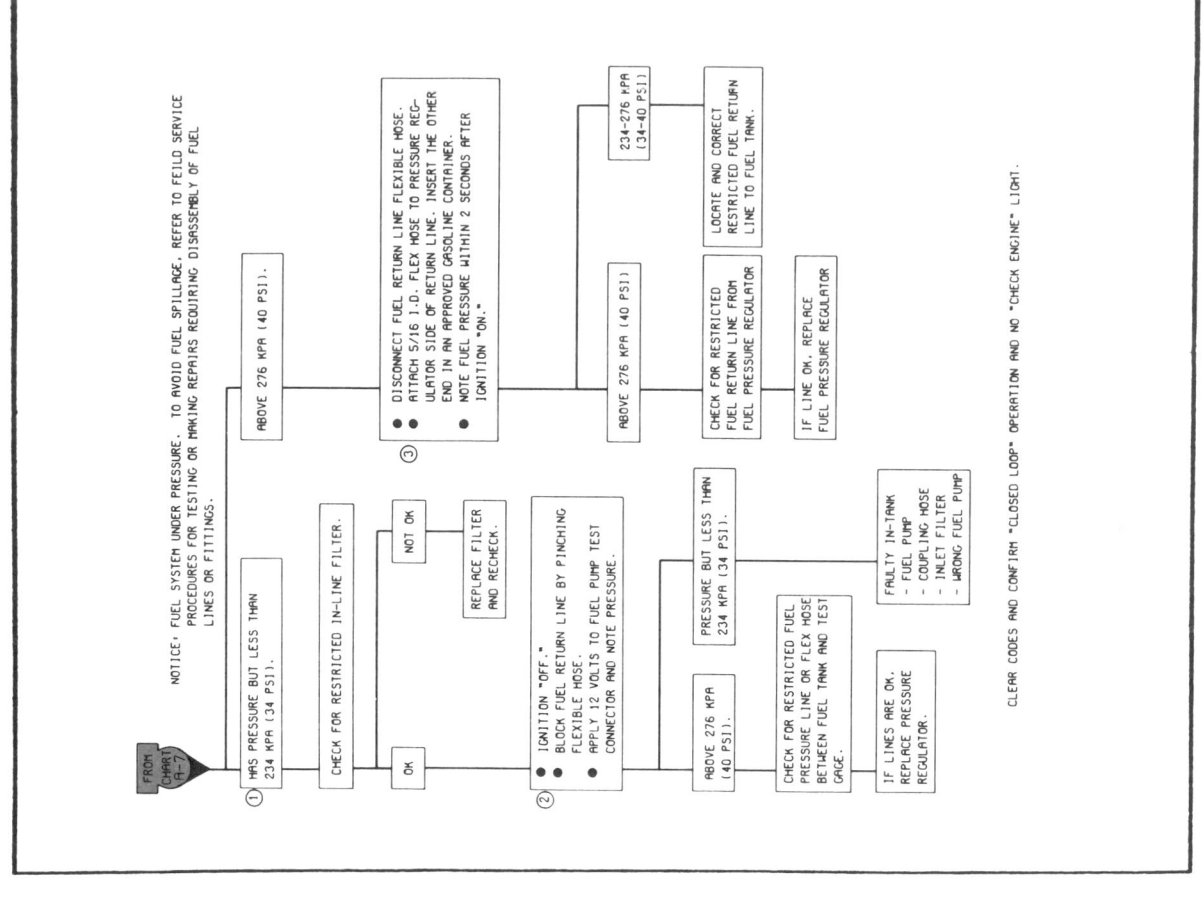

CHART A-8
Fuel System Diagnosis (2 of 2)

NOTICE: FUEL SYSTEM UNDER PRESSURE. TO AVOID FUEL SPILLAGE. REFER TO FEILD SERVICE PROCEDURES FOR TESTING OR MAKING REPAIRS REQUIRING DISASSEMBLY OF FUEL LINES OR FITTINGS.

① HAS PRESSURE BUT LESS THAN 234 KPA (34 PSI).

CHECK FOR RESTRICTED IN-LINE FILTER.

ABOVE 276 KPA (40 PSI).

NOT OK — REPLACE FILTER AND RECHECK.

OK

② IGNITION "OFF."
• BLOCK FUEL RETURN LINE BY PINCHING FLEXIBLE HOSE.
• APPLY 12 VOLTS TO FUEL PUMP TEST CONNECTOR AND NOTE PRESSURE.

ABOVE 276 KPA (40 PSI).

CHECK FOR RESTRICTED FUEL PRESSURE LINE OR FLEX HOSE BETWEEN FUEL TANK AND TEST GAGE.

IF LINES ARE OK. REPLACE PRESSURE REGULATOR.

PRESSURE BUT LESS THAN 234 KPA (34 PSI).

FAULTY IN-TANK
– FUEL PUMP
– COUPLING HOSE
– INLET FILTER
– WRONG FUEL PUMP

③ • DISCONNECT FUEL RETURN LINE FLEXIBLE HOSE. ATTACH 5/16 I.D. FLEX HOSE TO PRESSURE REGULATOR SIDE OF RETURN LINE. INSERT THE OTHER END IN AN APPROVED GASOLINE CONTAINER.
• NOTE FUEL PRESSURE WITHIN 2 SECONDS AFTER IGNITION "ON."

234-276 KPA (34-40 PSI).

LOCATE AND CORRECT RESTRICTED FUEL RETURN LINE TO FUEL TANK.

ABOVE 276 KPA (40 PSI).

CHECK FOR RESTRICTED FUEL RETURN LINE FROM FUEL PRESSURE REGULATOR.

IF LINE OK. REPLACE FUEL PRESSURE REGULATOR.

CLEAR CODES AND CONFIRM "CLOSED LOOP" OPERATION AND NO "CHECK ENGINE" LIGHT.

FROM CHART A-7

CHART A-7
Fuel System Diagnosis (1 of 2)

NOTICE: FUEL SYSTEM UNDER PRESSURE. TO AVOID SPILLAGE, REFER TO FIELD SERVICE PROCEDURES FOR TESTING OR MAKING REPAIRS REQUIRING DISASSEMBLY OF FUEL LINES OR FITTINGS.

① • INSTALL FUEL PRESSURE GAGES. J-34730-1 OR EQUIVALENT.
• IGNITION "OFF" FOR 10 SECONDS. A/C "OFF".
• IGNITION "ON". FUEL PUMP WILL RUN FOR ABOUT 2 SECONDS.
• NOTE FUEL PRESSURE AFTER PUMP STOPS. SHOULD BE 234-276 KPA (34-40 PSI) AND HOLD STEADY.

OK

② START AND IDLE ENGINE AT NORMAL OPERATING TEMP.
• PRESSURE SHOULD BE LOWER BY 34-62 KPA (5-9 PSI).

OK

NO TROUBLE FOUND. REVIEW SYMPTOMS SECTION B.

NOT OK

PRESSURE BUT NOT HOLDING 234-276 KPA (34-40 PSI).

PRESSURE BUT LESS THAN 234 KPA (34 PSI).

ABOVE 276 KPA (40 PSI).

SEE CHART A8

• BLOCK FUEL PRESSURE LINE BY PINCHING FLEX HOSE.
• IGNITION "OFF" FOR 10 SECONDS.
• IGNITION "ON". PRESSURE SHOULD HOLD.

NOT HOLDING.

• BLOCK FUEL RETURN LINE BY PINCHING HOSE.
• RECHECK PRESSURE.

HOLDS

FAULTY FUEL PRESSURE REGULATOR.

HOLDS

CHECK
– LEAKING PUMP COUPLING HOSE
– FAULTY IN-TANK PUMP.

NOT HOLDING.

LOCATE AND CORRECT LEAKING INJECTOR. REMOVE SPARK PLUGS TO LOCATE FLOODING CYLINDERS.

CLEAR CODES AND CONFIRM "CLOSED" OPERATION AND NO "CHECK ENGINE" LIGHT.

CODE 14
Coolant Sensor Circuit—Signal Voltage Low

CODE 13
Open Oxygen Sensor Circuit—3.8L

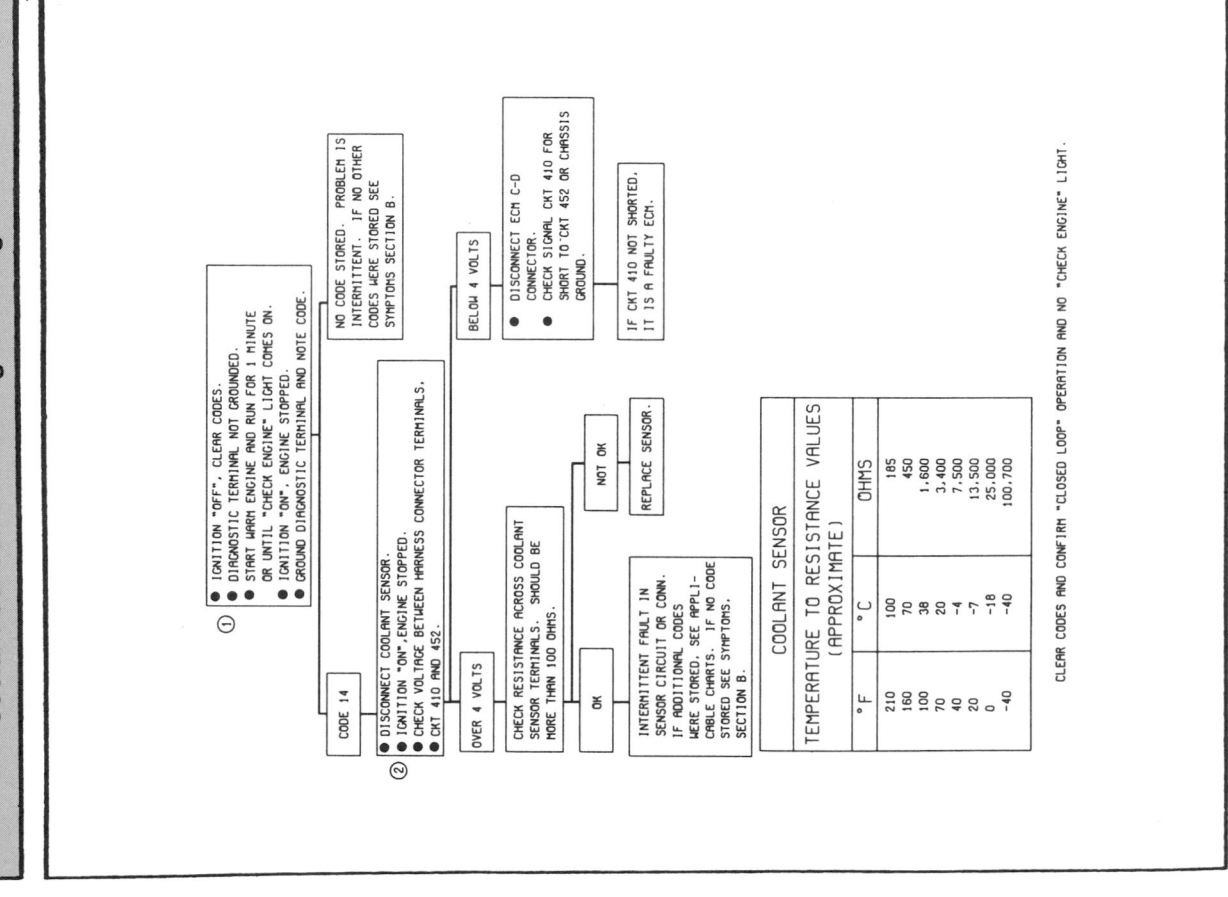

CODE 14

① ● IGNITION "OFF", CLEAR CODES.
● DIAGNOSTIC TERMINAL NOT GROUNDED.
● START WARM ENGINE AND RUN FOR 1 MINUTE OR UNTIL "CHECK ENGINE" LIGHT COMES ON.
● IGNITION "ON", ENGINE STOPPED.
● GROUND DIAGNOSTIC TERMINAL AND NOTE CODE.

NO CODE STORED. PROBLEM IS INTERMITTENT. IF NO OTHER CODES WERE STORED SEE SYMPTOMS SECTION B.

② ● DISCONNECT COOLANT SENSOR.
● IGNITION "ON", ENGINE STOPPED.
● CHECK VOLTAGE BETWEEN HARNESS CONNECTOR TERMINALS. CKT 410 AND 452.

OVER 4 VOLTS

BELOW 4 VOLTS

DISCONNECT ECH C-D CONNECTOR.
● CHECK SIGNAL CKT 410 FOR SHORT TO CKT 452 OR CHASSIS GROUND.

IF CKT 410 NOT SHORTED, IT IS A FAULTY ECM.

CHECK RESISTANCE ACROSS COOLANT SENSOR TERMINALS. SHOULD BE MORE THAN 100 OHMS.

OK

NOT OK

REPLACE SENSOR.

INTERMITTENT FAULT IN SENSOR CIRCUIT OR CONN. IF ADDITIONAL CODES WERE STORED. SEE APPLI- CABLE CHARTS. IF NO CODE STORED SEE SYMPTOMS, SECTION B.

COOLANT SENSOR
TEMPERATURE TO RESISTANCE VALUES
(APPROXIMATE)

°F	°C	OHMS
210	100	185
160	70	450
100	38	1,600
70	20	3,400
40	-4	7,500
20	-7	13,500
0	-18	25,000
-40	-40	100,700

CLEAR CODES AND CONFIRM "CLOSED LOOP" OPERATION AND NO "CHECK ENGINE" LIGHT.

CODE 13

① ● CLEAR CODES
● ENGINE AT NORMAL OPERATING TEMPERATURE.
● GROUND DIAGNOSTIC TERMINAL.
● RUN ENGINE ABOVE 1200 RPM FOR TWO MINUTES AND NOTE "CHECK ENGINE" LIGHT.

FLASHING "OPEN LOOP"

FLASHING "CLOSED LOOP"

③ ● IGNITION "OFF".
● DIAGNOSTIC TERMINAL GROUNDED.
● DISCONNECT OXYGEN SENSOR AND JUMPER HARNESS CONNECTOR CKT 412 TO GROUND.
● START ENGINE AND IMMEDIATELY NOTE "CHECK ENGINE" LIGHT.

② ● UNGROUND DIAGNOSTIC TERMINAL.
● RUN ENGINE FOR TWO MORE MINUTES OR UNTIL "CHECK ENGINE" LIGHT COMES ON.

LIGHT ON

● IGNITION ON.
● GROUND DIAGNOSTIC TERMINAL.
● NOTE CODE AND REFER TO APPLICABLE CHART.

LIGHT OFF

CODE 13 IS INTERMITTENT. IF NO OTHER CODE STORED REFER TO SYMPTOMS IN SECTION B.

"CHECK ENGINE" LIGHT WENT OFF FOR AT LEAST 15 SECONDS.

"CHECK ENGINE" LIGHT FLASHING OPEN LOOP.

CHECK FOR OPEN OXYGEN SENSOR SIGNAL CKT 412 OR CKT 413. IF CKT 412 OR 413 OK, IT IS FAULTY CONNECTION AT ECM TERMS. D6 OR D7 OR ECM.

FAULTY OXYGEN SENSOR CONNECTOR OR SENSOR.

CLEAR CODES AND CONFIRM "CLOSED LOOP" OPERATION AND NO "CHECK ENGINE" LIGHT.

CODE 21
Throttle Position Sensor—Signal Voltage High

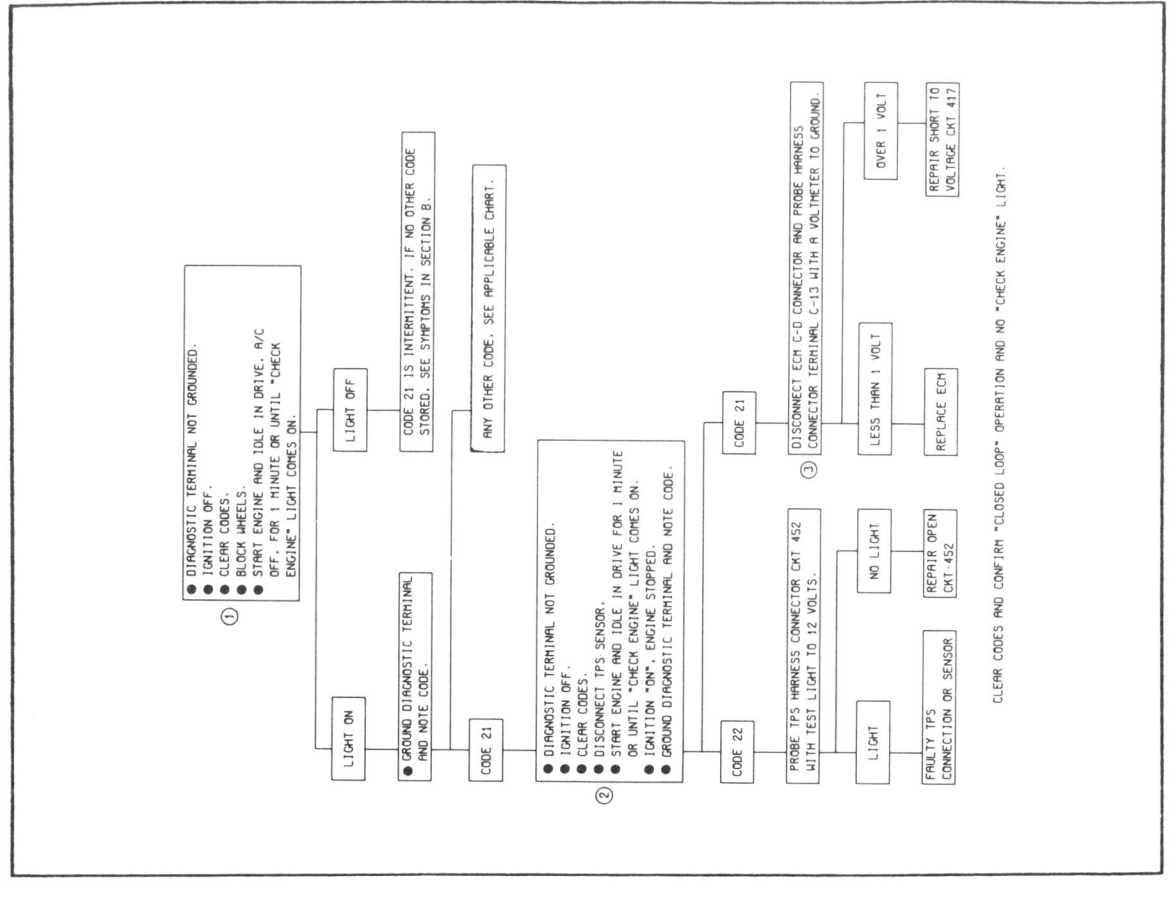

① • DIAGNOSTIC TERMINAL NOT GROUNDED.
• IGNITION OFF.
• CLEAR CODES.
• BLOCK WHEELS.
• START ENGINE AND IDLE IN DRIVE, A/C OFF, FOR 1 MINUTE OR UNTIL "CHECK ENGINE" LIGHT COMES ON.

LIGHT ON
• GROUND DIAGNOSTIC TERMINAL AND NOTE CODE.

LIGHT OFF
CODE 21 IS INTERMITTENT. IF NO OTHER CODE STORED. SEE SYMPTOMS IN SECTION B.

ANY OTHER CODE. SEE APPLICABLE CHART.

CODE 21

CODE 22

② • DIAGNOSTIC TERMINAL NOT GROUNDED.
• IGNITION OFF.
• CLEAR CODES.
• DISCONNECT TPS SENSOR.
• START ENGINE AND IDLE IN DRIVE FOR 1 MINUTE OR UNTIL "CHECK ENGINE" LIGHT COMES ON.
• IGNITION "ON", ENGINE STOPPED.
• GROUND DIAGNOSTIC TERMINAL AND NOTE CODE.

CODE 22
PROBE TPS HARNESS CONNECTOR CKT 452 WITH TEST LIGHT TO 12 VOLTS.

LIGHT → FAULTY TPS CONNECTION OR SENSOR

NO LIGHT → REPAIR OPEN CKT 452

③ CODE 21
DISCONNECT ECM C-D CONNECTOR AND PROBE HARNESS CONNECTOR TERMINAL C-13 WITH A VOLTMETER TO GROUND.

OVER 1 VOLT → REPAIR SHORT TO VOLTAGE CKT 417

LESS THAN 1 VOLT → REPLACE ECM

CLEAR CODES AND CONFIRM "CLOSED LOOP" OPERATION AND NO "CHECK ENGINE" LIGHT.

CODE 15
Coolant Sensor Circuit—Signal Voltage High

① • IGNITION "OFF", CLEAR CODES.
• DIAGNOSTIC TERMINAL NOT GROUNDED.
• START ENGINE IN HOT (CLEAR FLOOD) AND RUN FOR 1 MINUTE OR UNTIL "CHECK ENGINE" LIGHT COMES ON.

CODE 15

NO CODE STORED → PROBLEM IS INTERMITTENT. IF NO OTHER CODES WERE STORED SEE SYMPTOMS. SECTION B.

② • ENGINE AT NORMAL OPERATING TEMPERATURE.
• DISCONNECT COOLANT SENSOR.
• IGNITION "ON" ENGINE STOPPED.
• CHECK VOLTAGE BETWEEN HARNESS CONNECTOR TERMINALS. CKT 410 AND 452.

OVER 4 VOLTS → CHECK RESISTANCE ACROSS COOLANT SENSOR TERMINALS. SHOULD BE LESS THAN 1000 OHMS.

OK → INTERMITTENT FAULT IN SENSOR CIRCUIT OR CONN. IF ADDITIONAL CODES WERE STORED. SEE APPLICABLE CHARTS. IF NO CODE STORED SEE SYMPTOMS. SECTION B.

NOT OK → REPLACE SENSOR.

BELOW 4 VOLTS → CHECK FOR OPEN IN CKTS 410 OR 452.

IF CKTS 410 AND 452 NOT OPEN, IT IS FAULTY ECM CONNECTOR TERMS. C10 OR D12 OR ECM.

COOLANT SENSOR
TEMPERATURE TO RESISTANCE VALUES
(APPROXIMATE)

°F	°C	OHMS
210	100	185
160	70	450
100	38	1,600
70	20	3,400
40	-4	7,500
20	-7	13,500
0	-18	25,000
-40	-40	100,700

CLEAR CODES AND CONFIRM "CLOSED LOOP" OPERATION AND NO "CHECK ENGINE" LIGHT.

CODE 24
Vehicle Speed Sensor (VSS)—3.8L 'C' Series

CODE 22
Throttle Position Sensor—Signal Voltage Low

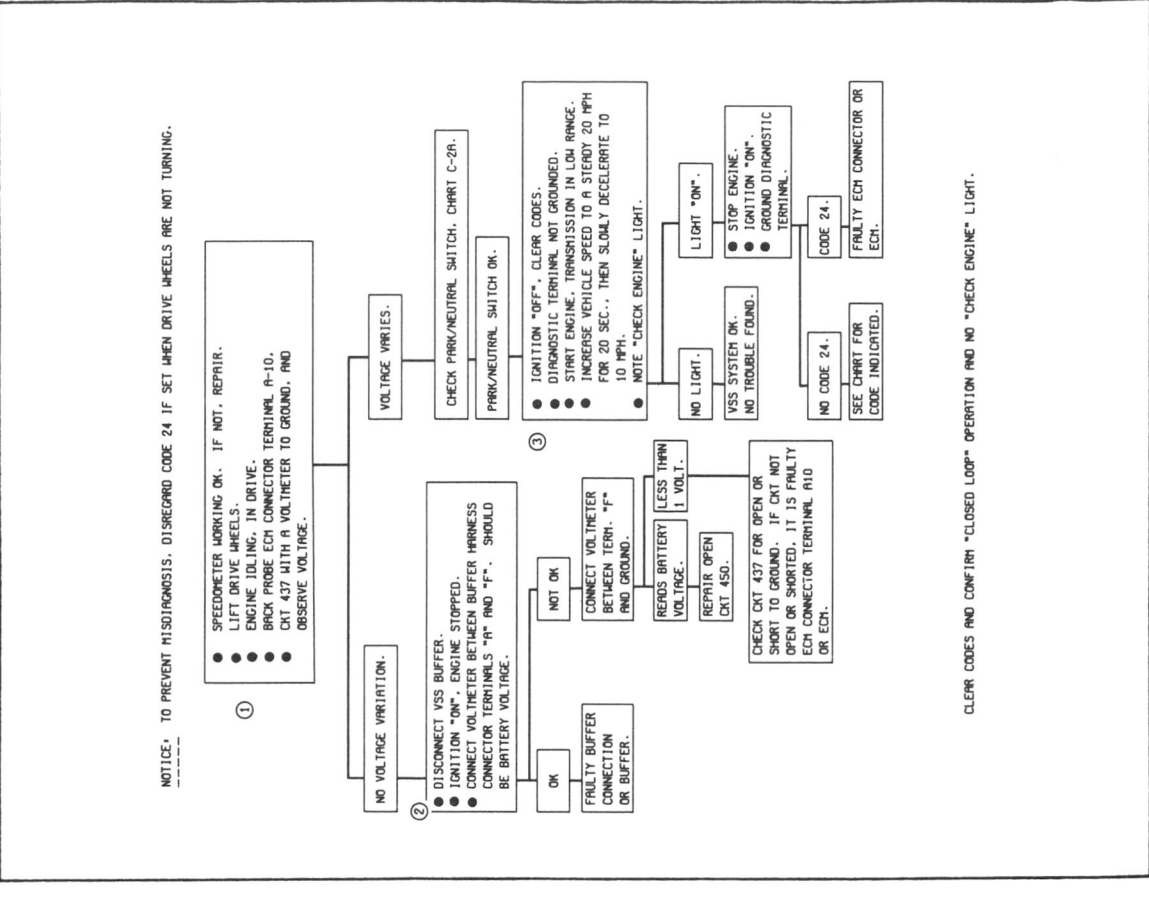

NOTICE: TO PREVENT MISDIAGNOSIS, DISREGARD CODE 24 IF SET WHEN DRIVE WHEELS ARE NOT TURNING.

①
- SPEEDOMETER WORKING OK. IF NOT, REPAIR.
- LIFT DRIVE WHEELS.
- ENGINE IDLING, IN DRIVE.
- BACK PROBE ECM CONNECTOR TERMINAL A-10, CKT 437 WITH A VOLTMETER TO GROUND, AND OBSERVE VOLTAGE.

VOLTAGE VARIES.
NO VOLTAGE VARIATION.

CHECK PARK/NEUTRAL SWITCH, CHART C-2A.
PARK/NEUTRAL SWITCH OK.

③
- IGNITION "OFF", CLEAR CODES.
- DIAGNOSTIC TERMINAL NOT GROUNDED.
- START ENGINE, TRANSMISSION IN LOW RANGE. INCREASE VEHICLE SPEED TO A STEADY 20 MPH FOR 20 SEC., THEN SLOWLY DECELERATE TO 10 MPH.
- NOTE "CHECK ENGINE" LIGHT.

NO LIGHT.
LIGHT "ON".

VSS SYSTEM OK.
NO TROUBLE FOUND.

- STOP ENGINE.
- IGNITION "ON".
- GROUND DIAGNOSTIC TERMINAL.

NO CODE 24.
CODE 24.

SEE CHART FOR CODE INDICATED.
FAULTY ECM CONNECTOR OR ECM.

②
- DISCONNECT VSS BUFFER.
- IGNITION "ON", ENGINE STOPPED.
- CONNECT VOLTMETER BETWEEN BUFFER HARNESS CONNECTOR TERMINALS "A" AND "F". SHOULD BE BATTERY VOLTAGE.

OK
NOT OK

FAULTY BUFFER CONNECTION OR BUFFER.

CONNECT VOLTMETER BETWEEN TERM. "F" AND GROUND.

READS BATTERY VOLTAGE.
LESS THAN 1 VOLT.

REPAIR OPEN CKT 450.

CHECK CKT 437 FOR OPEN OR SHORT TO GROUND. IF CKT NOT OPEN OR SHORTED, IT IS FAULTY ECM CONNECTOR TERMINAL A10 OR ECM.

CLEAR CODES AND CONFIRM "CLOSED LOOP" OPERATION AND NO "CHECK ENGINE" LIGHT.

---

①
- DIAGNOSTIC TERMINAL NOT GROUNDED.
- IGNITION "OFF", CLEAR CODES.
- BLOCK WHEELS.
- START ENGINE AND IDLE IN DRIVE, A/C OFF, FOR 1 MINUTE OR UNTIL "CHECK ENGINE" LIGHT COMES ON.

LIGHT ON.
LIGHT OFF.

- IGNITION "ON", ENGINE STOPPED. GROUND DIAGNOSTIC TERMINAL AND NOTE CODE.

CODE 22 IS INTERMITTENT. IF NO OTHER CODE STORED SEE SYMPTOMS SECTION B.

CODE 22
ANY OTHER CODE. SEE APPLICABLE CHART.

②
- DIAGNOSTIC TERMINAL NOT GROUNDED.
- IGNITION "OFF", CLEAR CODES.
- DISCONNECT TPS AND JUMPER CKTS 416 TO 417.
- BLOCK WHEELS.
- START ENGINE AND IDLE IN DRIVE FOR 1 MINUTE OR UNTIL "CHECK ENGINE" LIGHT COMES ON.
- IGNITION "ON", ENGINE STOPPED. GROUND DIAGNOSTIC TERMINAL AND NOTE CODE.

CODE 21
CODE 22

CHECK TPS ADJUSTMENT. IF ADJUSTMENT OK, REPLACE TPS.

③
- REMOVE JUMPER FROM 416 AND 417.
- CHECK VOLTAGE BETWEEN HARNESS CONN. TERMINALS A AND C USING DIGITAL VOLTMETER (J-29125).

4 - 6 VOLTS
BELOW 4 VOLTS

DISCONNECT ECM C-D CONNECTOR AND CHECK FOR OPEN OR SHORT TO GROUND IN CKT 417. IF CKT 417 OK, IT IS FAULTY ECM CONNECTOR TERMINAL C-13 OR ECM.

DISCONNECT ECM C-D CONNECTOR. CHECK FOR OPEN OR SHORT TO GROUND IN CKT 416. IF CKT 416 OK, IT IS FAULTY ECM CONNECTOR TERMINAL C-14 OR ECM.

CLEAR CODES AND CONFIRM "CLOSED LOOP" OPERATION AND NO "CHECK ENGINE" LIGHT.

CODE 33
Mass Air Flow Sensor (MAF)—Signal Frequency High

CODE 32
EGR Vacuum Control—3.8L

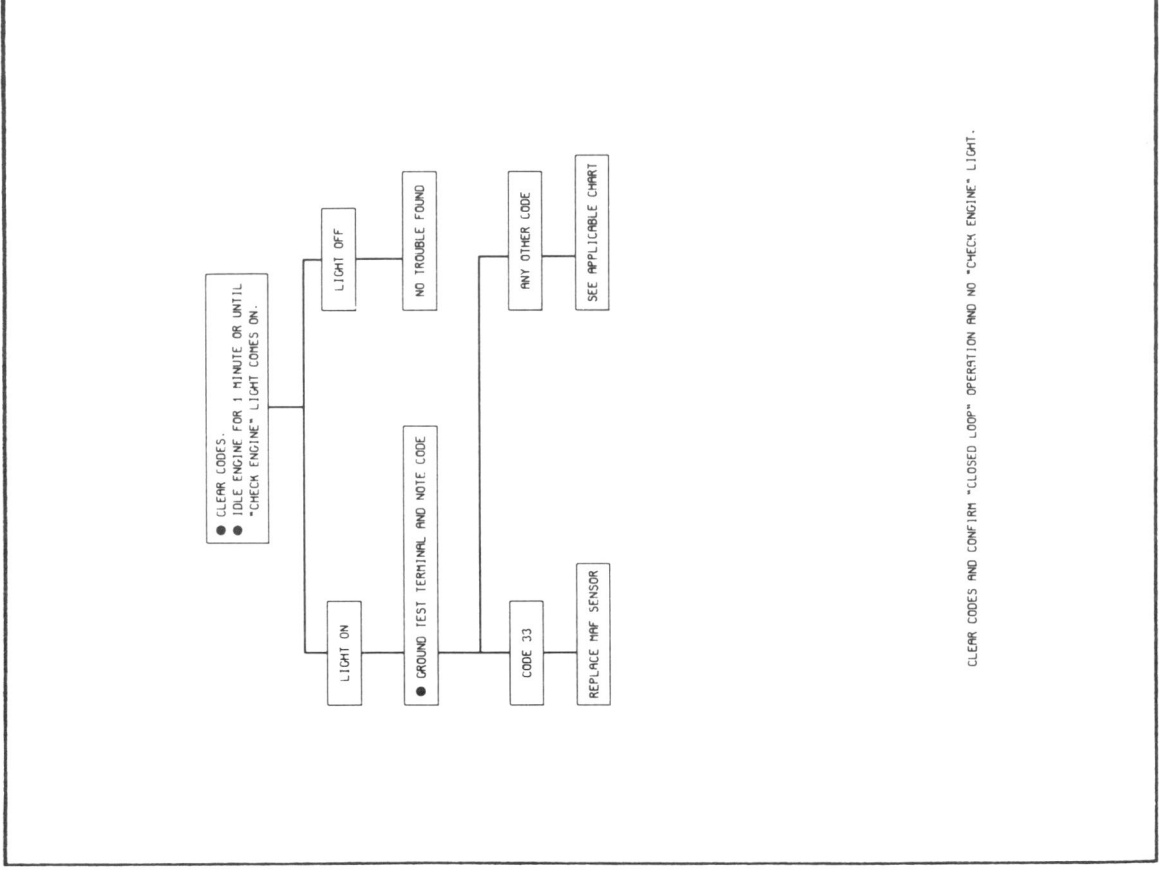

CODE 42
Electronic Spark Timing (EST)—3.8L

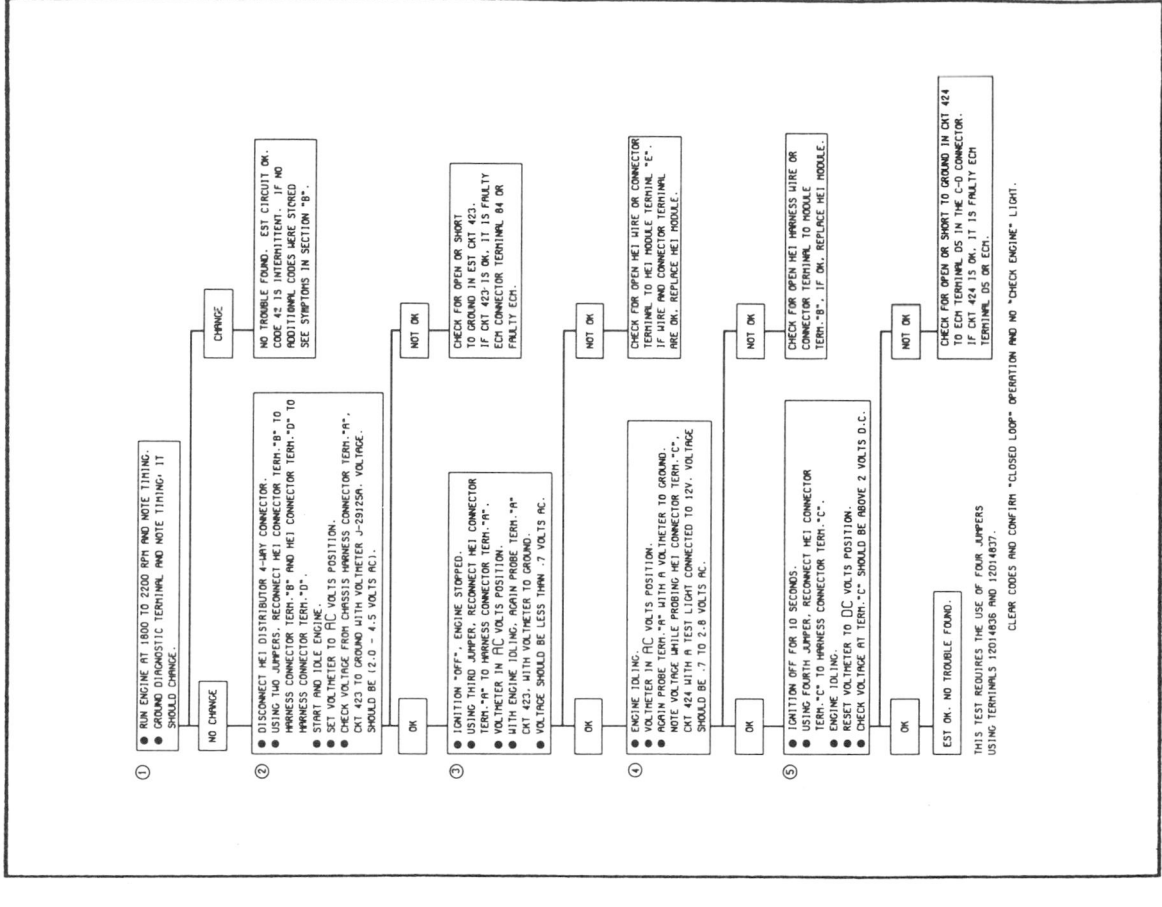

① • RUN ENGINE AT 1800 TO 2200 RPM AND NOTE TIMING.
• GROUND DIAGNOSTIC TERMINAL AND NOTE TIMING. IT SHOULD CHANGE.

NO CHANGE | CHANGE

CHANGE: NO TROUBLE FOUND. EST CIRCUIT OK. IF CODE 42 IS INTERMITTENT. IF NO ADDITIONAL CODES WERE STORED SEE SYMPTOMS IN SECTION "B".

② • DISCONNECT HEI DISTRIBUTOR 4-WAY CONNECTOR.
• USING TWO JUMPERS, RECONNECT HEI CONNECTOR TERM."B" TO HARNESS CONNECTOR TERM."B" AND HEI CONNECTOR TERM."D" TO HARNESS CONNECTOR TERM."D".
• START AND IDLE ENGINE.
• SET VOLTMETER TO AC VOLTS POSITION.
• CHECK VOLTAGE FROM CHASSIS HARNESS CONNECTOR TERM."A". CKT 423 TO GROUND WITH VOLTMETER J-29125A. VOLTAGE SHOULD BE (2.0 - 4.5 VOLTS AC).

OK | NOT OK

NOT OK: CHECK FOR OPEN OR SHORT TO GROUND IN EST CKT 423. IF CKT 423 IS OK. IT IS FAULTY ECM CONNECTOR TERMINAL B4 OR FAULTY ECM.

③ • IGNITION "OFF". ENGINE STOPPED.
• USING THIRD JUMPER, RECONNECT HEI CONNECTOR TERM."A" TO HARNESS CONNECTOR TERM."A".
• VOLTMETER IN AC VOLTS POSITION.
• WITH ENGINE IDLING. AGAIN PROBE TERM."A". CKT 423. WITH VOLTMETER TO GROUND.
• VOLTAGE SHOULD BE LESS THAN .7 VOLTS AC.

OK | NOT OK

NOT OK: CHECK FOR OPEN HEI WIRE OR CONNECTOR TERMINAL TO HEI MODULE TERMINAL. "C". IF WIRE AND CONNECTOR TERMINAL ARE OK. REPLACE HEI MODULE.

④ • ENGINE IDLING.
• VOLTMETER IN AC VOLTS POSITION.
• AGAIN PROBE TERM."A" WITH A VOLTMETER TO GROUND. NOTE VOLTAGE WHILE PROBING HEI CONNECTOR TERM."C". CKT 424 WITH A TEST LIGHT CONNECTED TO 12V. VOLTAGE SHOULD BE .7 TO 2.8 VOLTS AC.

OK | NOT OK

NOT OK: CHECK FOR OPEN HEI HARNESS WIRE OR CONNECTOR TERMINAL TO MODULE TERM."B". IF OK. REPLACE HEI MODULE.

⑤ • IGNITION OFF FOR 10 SECONDS.
• USING FOURTH JUMPER, RECONNECT HEI CONNECTOR TERM."C" TO HARNESS CONNECTOR TERM."C".
• ENGINE IDLING.
• RESET VOLTMETER TO DC VOLTS POSITION.
• CHECK VOLTAGE AT TERM."C" SHOULD BE ABOVE 2 VOLTS D.C.

OK | NOT OK

NOT OK: CHECK FOR OPEN OR SHORT TO GROUND IN CKT 424 TO ECM TERMINAL D5 IN THE C-D CONNECTOR. IF CKT 424 IS OK. IT IS FAULTY ECM TERMINAL. OR NO "CHECK ENGINE" LIGHT.

OK: EST OK. NO TROUBLE FOUND.

THIS TEST REQUIRES THE USE OF FOUR JUMPERS USING TERMINALS 12014836 AND 12014837.

CLEAR CODES AND CONFIRM "CLOSED LOOP" OPERATION AND NO "CHECK ENGINE" LIGHT.

CODE 34
Mass Air Flow Sensor (MAF)—Signal Frequency Low

① CHECK FOR LOOSE OR DAMAGED AIR DUCT BETWEEN MAF SENSOR AND THROTTLE VALVE ASSEMBLY

② START ENGINE AND IDLE FOR 2 MINUTES OR UNTIL "CHECK ENGINE" LIGHT COMES ON.

LIGHT ON | LIGHT OFF

LIGHT OFF: NO TROUBLE FOUND. CHECK FOR LOOSE WIRING CONNECTIONS AT MAF SENSOR AND ECM.

LIGHT ON: • GROUND DIAGNOSTIC TEST TERMINAL AND NOTE CODE.

CODE 34 | ANY OTHER CODE

ANY OTHER CODE: SEE APPLICABLE CHART.

③ • IGN. OFF.
• DISCONNECT MAF SENSOR ELECTRICAL CONNECTOR.
• IGN. ON. ENGINE STOPPED.
• CONNECT VOLTMETER BETWEEN HARNESS CONNECTOR TERMINAL "B" AND GROUND.

OVER 4 VOLTS | LESS THAN 1 VOLT

LESS THAN 1 VOLT: • DISCONNECT ECM A-B CONNECTOR.
• CHECK CKT 492 FOR OPEN OR SHORT TO GROUND. IF NOT OPEN OR SHORTED. IT IS FAULTY ECM CONNECTOR TERMINAL B6 OR ECM.

④ CONNECT TEST LIGHT BETWEEN HARNESS CONNECTOR TERMINALS "A" AND "C".

NO LIGHT | LIGHT

LIGHT: FAULTY MAF SENSOR CONNECTION OR SENSOR.

⑤ CONNECT TEST LIGHT BETWEEN HARNESS CONNECTOR TERMINAL "A" AND CHASSIS GROUND.

NO LIGHT | LIGHT

LIGHT: REPAIR OPEN IN GROUND CKT TO MAF SENSOR.

NO LIGHT: REPAIR OPEN CKT 639 TO IGNITION.

CLEAR CODES AND CONFIRM "CLOSED LOOP" OPERATION AND NO "CHECK ENGINE" LIGHT.

CODE 44
Lean Exhaust Indication—3.8L

A CODE 33 OR 34 MAY CAUSE A CODE 44. THEREFORE, IF EITHER OF THESE CODES IS PRESENT, SEE THAT CODE CHART FIRST.

① ● GROUND DIAGNOSTIC TERMINAL.
   ● RUN WARM ENGINE AT APPROX. 1200 TO 1800 RPM FOR 2 MINUTES AND NOTE LIGHT.

LIGHT STAYING "OFF" MORE THAN "ON" OR FLASHING "OPEN LOOP" AT EITHER RPM.

FLASHING "CLOSED LOOP"

CODE IS INTERMITTENT. IF NO ADDITIONAL CODES WERE STORED, REFER TO SYMPTOMS IN SECTION B.

② ⊗ IGNITION "OFF".
   ● DIAGNOSTIC TERMINAL GROUNDED.
   ● DISCONNECT OXYGEN SENSOR.
   ● START ENGINE AND IMMEDIATELY NOTE "CHECK ENGINE" LIGHT.

"CHECK ENGINE" LIGHT FLASHING OPEN LOOP.

"CHECK ENGINE" LIGHT WENT OFF FOR AT LEAST 15 SECONDS.

CHECK SIGNAL CKT 412 FOR SHORT TO GROUND.

CKT 412 OK

IT IS A FAULTY ECM

③ ● CHECK FOR OPEN GROUND CIRCUIT 413. IF NOT OPEN CHECK -
   - FOR GROUND IN WIRE FROM CONNECTOR TO SENSOR.
   - FOR INTAKE AIR LEAKS.
   - EGR. SEE CHART C-7.
   - FOR LOW FUEL PRESSURE. SHOULD BE 166-288 KPA (24-42 PSI).
   - FOR EXHAUST MANIFOLD LEAKS AHEAD OF SENSOR.

ALL CHECKS OK

FAULTY OXYGEN SENSOR

CLEAR CODES AND CONFIRM "CLOSED LOOP" OPERATION AND NO "CHECK ENGINE" LIGHT.

CODE 43
Electronic Spark Control (ESC)—3.8L

① ● IGNITION OFF. CLEAR CODES.
   ● IDLE ENGINE FOR 1 MINUTE OR UNTIL "CHECK ENGINE" LIGHT COMES ON.
   ● GROUND DIAGNOSTIC TERMINAL AND NOTE CODE.

NO CODE

PROBLEM IS INTERMITTENT. IF NO OTHER CODES WERE STORED, SEE SYMPTOMS SECTION B.

CODE 43

② WITH ENGINE IDLING, BACK PROBE ECM A-B CONNECTOR TERM. B7 WITH A VOLTMETER TO GROUND AND NOTE VOLTAGE.

UNDER 6 VOLTS

OVER 6 VOLTS

IT IS FAULTY CONNECTION AT ECM A-B CONNECTOR TERMINAL B7 OR ECM.

③ ● IGNITION "ON". ENGINE STOPPED.
   ● RECHECK VOLTAGE AT ECM TERM. B7.

UNDER 6 VOLTS

OVER 6 VOLTS

IT IS MOST LIKELY FAULTY ESC MODULE CONNECTION AT TERMINAL "C" OR ESC MODULE. BUT COULD BE A KNOCK SENSOR.

④ DISCONNECT ECM A-B CONNECTOR AND RECHECK VOLTAGE AT TERMINAL B7 IN CONNECTOR.

UNDER 6 VOLTS

OVER 6 VOLTS

REPLACE ECM

⑤ DISCONNECT ESC CONTROLLER. CHECK VOLTS FROM ESC CONNECTOR TERM. B TO GROUND.

OVER 9 VOLTS

UNDER 9 VOLTS

REPAIR CIRCUIT FROM ESC TERM. "B" TO IGNITION CKT 639.

CHECK FOR OPEN OR GROUNDED WIRE TO ECM TERM. B7, CKT 457. IF NOT OPEN OR GROUNDED. IT IS FAULTY ESC CONNECTION OR ESC CONTROLLER.

CLEAR CODES AND CONFIRM "CLOSED LOOP" OPERATION AND NO "CHECK ENGINE" LIGHT.

Port Fuel Injection—3.8L

CODE 51

CHECK THAT ALL PINS ARE FULLY INSERTED IN THE SOCKET. IF OK, REPLACE PROM, CLEAR MEMORY, AND RECHECK. IF CODE 51 REAPPEARS, REPLACE ECM.

CODE 52
FUEL CALPAC MISSING

● ENGINE IDLING.
● NOTE "CHECK ENGINE" LIGHT AFTER 10 SECONDS.

LIGHT ON — ● IGNITION ON, ENGINE STOPPED.
          ● GROUND TEST TERMINAL AND NOTE CODE.

  CODE 52 — INSTALL CALPAC PROM IN ECM.

  OTHER CODES — REFER TO APPLICABLE CHARTS

LIGHT OFF — NO TROUBLE FOUND. CHECK CALPAC PROM TO INSURE PROPER INSTALLATION.

CODE 55

REPLACE ELECTRONIC CONTROL MODULE (ECM).

CLEAR CODES AND CONFIRM "CLOSED LOOP" OPERATION AND NO "CHECK ENGINE" LIGHT.

CODE 45
Rich Exhaust Indication—3.8L

A CODE 33 OR 34 MAY CAUSE A CODE 45. THEREFORE, IF EITHER OF THESE CODES IS PRESENT, SEE THAT CODE CHART FIRST.

① ● GROUND DIAGNOSTIC TERMINAL.
  ● RUN WARM ENGINE AT APPROX. 1200 TO 1800 RPM FOR 2 MINUTES
  ● AND NOTE "CHECK ENGINE" LIGHT.

LIGHT STAYING "ON" MORE THAN "OFF", OR FLASHING "OPEN LOOP" AT EITHER RPM.

FLASHING "CLOSED LOOP".

CODE IS INTERMITTENT. IF NO ADDITIONAL CODES WERE STORED, SEE SYMPTOMS IN SECTION B.

② ● IGNITION "OFF".
  ● DIAGNOSTIC TERMINAL GROUNDED.
  ● DISCONNECT OXYGEN SENSOR AND JUMPER HARNESS CONNECTOR SIGNAL CKT 412 TO GROUND.
  ● START ENGINE AND IMMEDIATELY NOTE "CHECK ENGINE" LIGHT.

"CHECK ENGINE" LIGHT WENT OFF FOR AT LEAST 15 SECONDS.

SYSTEM RICH

STEADY LIGHT

FAULTY ECM

③ CHECK:
  - FOR HIGH FUEL PRESSURE. SHOULD BE 166-288 KPA (24-42 PSI).
  - INJECTOR(S) FOR LEAKAGE.
  - HEI SHIELD CKT 453 FOR OPEN CIRCUIT.
  - CANISTER PURGE. CHART C-3.
  - COOLANT SENSOR FOR INTERMITTENT OPEN CIRCUIT.

FIELD SERVICE MODE:
ENGINE RUNNING, DIAGNOSTIC TERMINAL GROUNDED.
OPEN - LOOP: "CHECK ENGINE" LIGHT FLASHES AT A RATE OF 2 TIMES PER SECOND.
CLOSED LOOP: "CHECK ENGINE" LIGHT FLASHES AT A RATE OF 1 TIME PER SECOND.

CLEAR CODES AND CONFIRM "CLOSED LOOP" OPERATION AND NO "CHECK ENGINE" LIGHT.

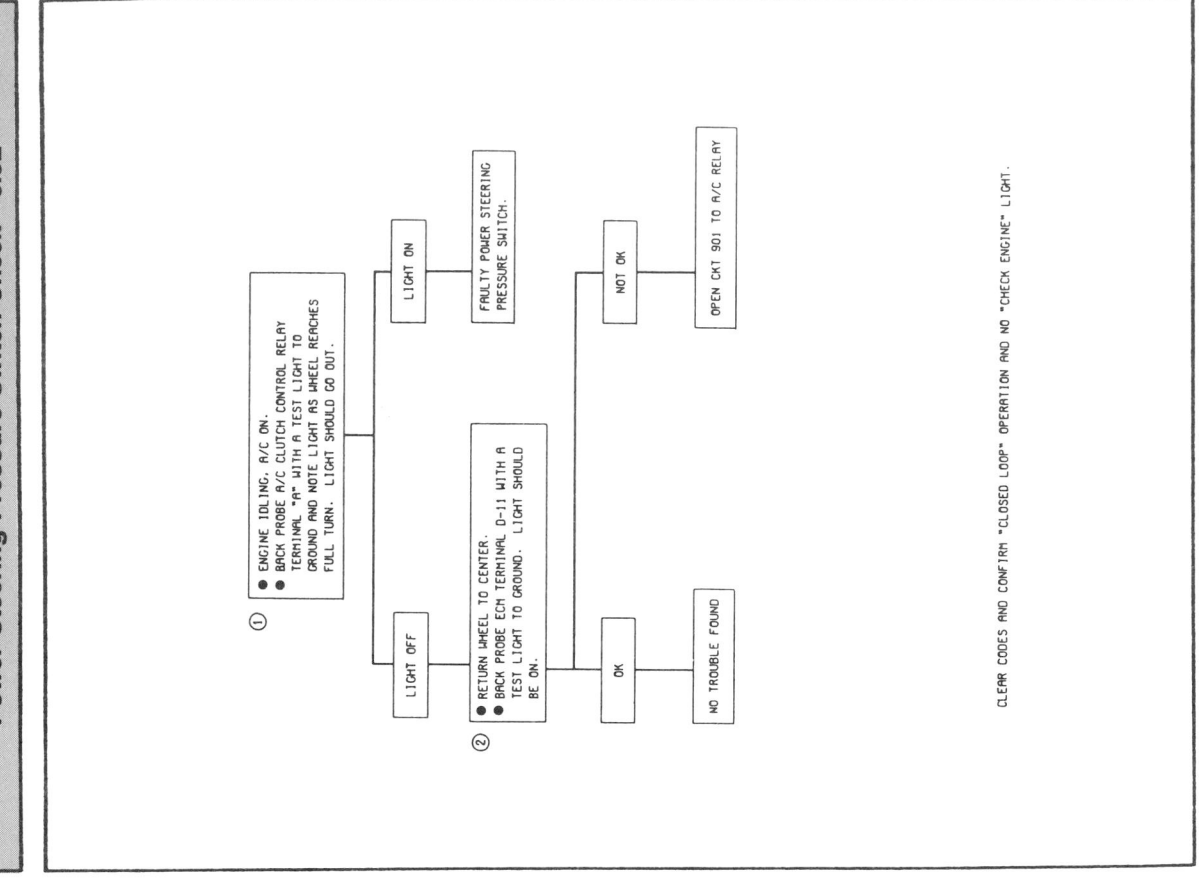

CHART C-1E
Power Steering Pressure Switch Check—3.8L

① • ENGINE IDLING. A/C ON.
   • BACK PROBE A/C CLUTCH CONTROL RELAY TERMINAL "A" WITH A TEST LIGHT TO GROUND AND NOTE LIGHT AS WHEEL REACHES FULL TURN. LIGHT SHOULD GO OUT.

LIGHT OFF

LIGHT ON

② • RETURN WHEEL TO CENTER.
   • BACK PROBE ECM TERMINAL D-11 WITH A TEST LIGHT TO GROUND. LIGHT SHOULD BE ON.

FAULTY POWER STEERING PRESSURE SWITCH.

OK

NOT OK

NO TROUBLE FOUND

OPEN CKT 901 TO A/C RELAY

CLEAR CODES AND CONFIRM "CLOSED LOOP" OPERATION AND NO "CHECK ENGINE" LIGHT.

CHART C-1A
Park/Neutral Switch—3.8L

① • IGNITION "ON", ENGINE STOPPED.
   • TRANSMISSION IN "PARK."
   • CONNECT VOLTMETER J29125 TO CIRCUIT 434 (ORN/BLK WIRE) OF P/N SWITCH TO GROUND. DO NOT USE TEST LIGHT.

LESS THAN 1 VOLT

9 - 12 VOLTS

② • MOVE TRANSMISSION SELECTOR INTO "DRIVE" AND NOTE VOLTAGE.

CHECK FOR OPEN IN GROUND CKT 450 FROM P/N SWITCH TO ENGINE GROUND.

LESS THAN 1 VOLT

9 - 12 VOLTS

CKT 450 OK

③ • DISCONNECT P/N SWITCH.
   • RECHECK VOLTAGE CKT 434 (ORN/BLK WIRE).

NO TROUBLE FOUND

CHECK SWITCH ADJUSTMENT. IF OK, REPLACE SWITCH.

LESS THAN 1 VOLT

9 - 12 VOLTS

CHECK FOR OPEN OR SHORT TO GROUND IN CKT 434. IF CKT 434 IS NOT OPEN OR SHORTED, IT IS A FAULTY ECM CONNECTOR TERMINAL B-10 OR ECM.

CHECK ADJUSTMENT. IF OK. REPLACE SWITCH.

CLEAR CODES AND CONFIRM "CLOSED LOOP" OPERATION AND NO "CHECK ENGINE" LIGHT.

CHART C-2C
Idle Air Control—3.8L

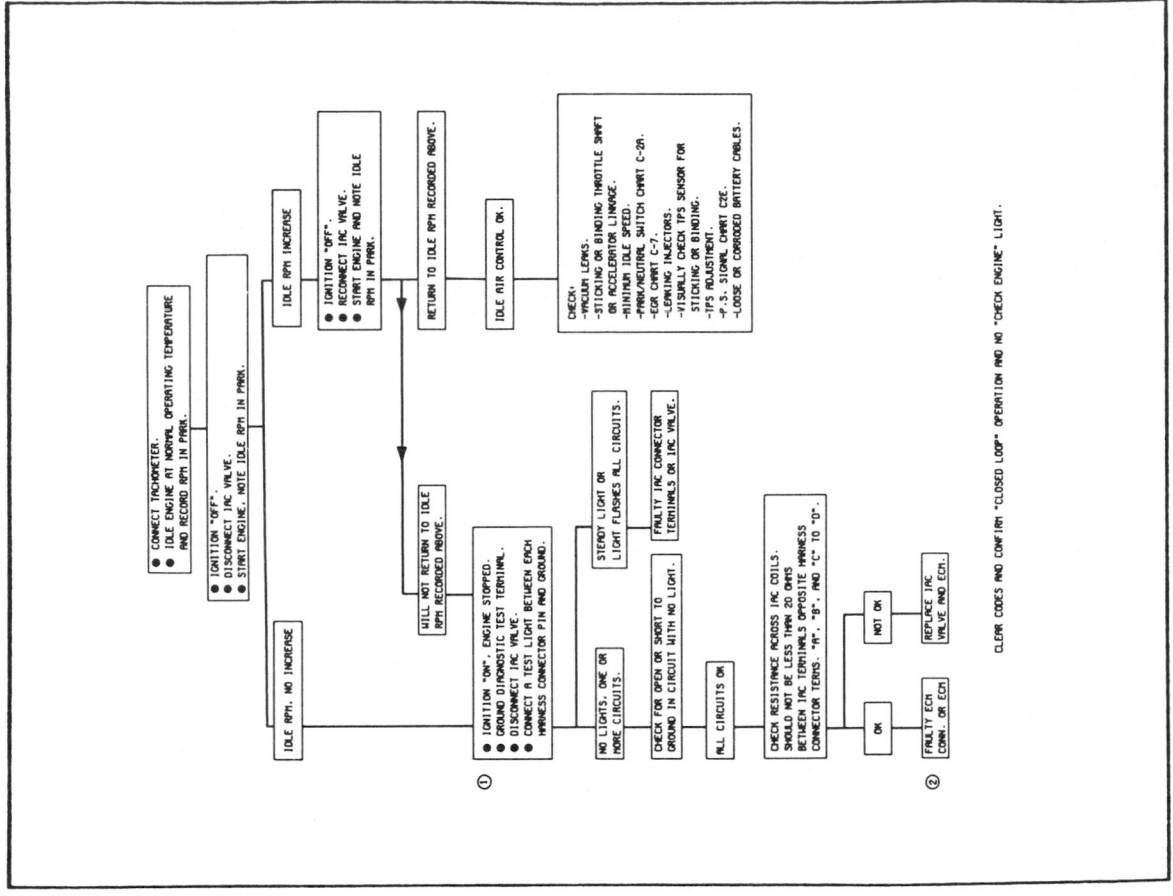

CHART C-2A
Injector Balance Test

CHART C-4A
Ignition System Check—3.8L Turbo

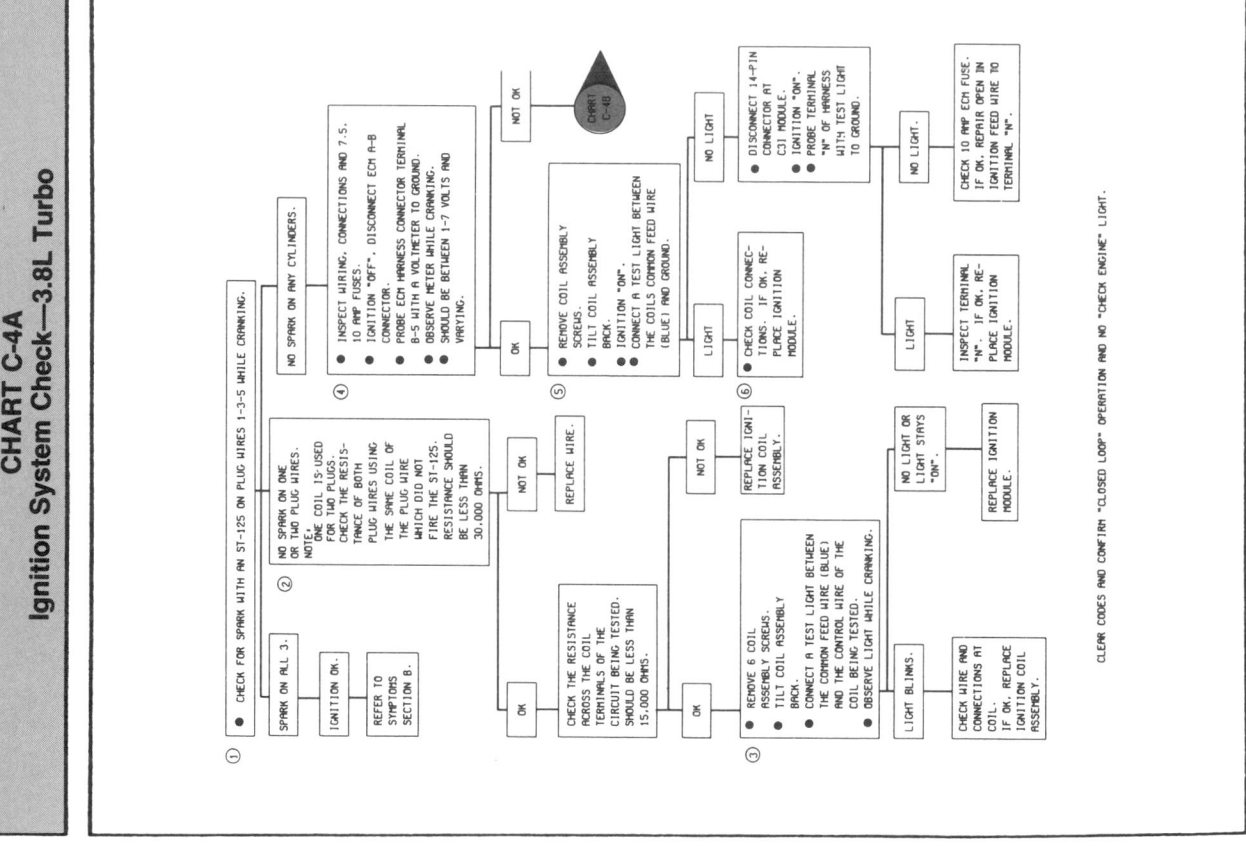

① CHECK FOR SPARK WITH AN ST-125 ON PLUG WIRES 1-3-5 WHILE CRANKING.

- SPARK ON ALL 3.
  - IGNITION OK.
  - REFER TO SYMPTOMS SECTION B.

- ② NO SPARK ON ONE OR TWO PLUG WIRES. NOTE: ONE COIL IS USED FOR TWO PLUGS. CHECK THE RESISTANCE OF BOTH PLUG WIRES USING THE SAME COIL OF THE PLUG WIRE WHICH DID NOT FIRE THE ST-125. RESISTANCE SHOULD BE LESS THAN 30,000 OHMS.
  - OK → CHECK THE RESISTANCE ACROSS THE COIL TERMINALS OF THE CIRCUIT BEING TESTED. SHOULD BE LESS THAN 15,000 OHMS.
    - OK → ⑦ REMOVE 6 COIL ASSEMBLY SCREWS. TILT COIL ASSEMBLY BACK. CONNECT A TEST LIGHT BETWEEN THE COMMON FEED WIRE (BLUE) AND THE CONTROL WIRE OF THE COIL BEING TESTED. OBSERVE LIGHT WHILE CRANKING.
      - LIGHT BLINKS → CHECK WIRE AND CONNECTIONS AT COIL. IF OK, REPLACE IGNITION COIL ASSEMBLY.
      - NO LIGHT OR LIGHT STAYS "ON". → REPLACE IGNITION MODULE.
    - NOT OK → REPLACE IGNITION COIL ASSEMBLY.
  - NOT OK → REPLACE WIRE.

- NO SPARK ON ANY CYLINDERS. ④ INSPECT WIRING, CONNECTIONS AND 7.5, 10 AMP FUSES. IGNITION "OFF". DISCONNECT ECM A-B CONNECTOR. PROBE ECM HARNESS CONNECTOR TERMINAL B-5 WITH A VOLTMETER TO GROUND. OBSERVE METER WHILE CRANKING. SHOULD BE BETWEEN 1-7 VOLTS AND VARYING.
  - NOT OK → CHART C-4B
  - OK → ⑤ REMOVE COIL ASSEMBLY SCREWS. TILT COIL ASSEMBLY BACK. IGNITION "ON". CONNECT A TEST LIGHT BETWEEN THE COIL'S COMMON FEED WIRE (BLUE) AND GROUND.
    - NO LIGHT → DISCONNECT 14-PIN CONNECTOR AT C3I MODULE. IGNITION "ON". PROBE TERMINAL "N" OF HARNESS WITH TEST LIGHT TO GROUND.
      - NO LIGHT → CHECK 10 AMP ECM FUSE. IF OK, REPAIR OPEN IN IGNITION FEED WIRE TO TERMINAL "N".
      - LIGHT → INSPECT TERMINAL "N". IF OK, REPLACE IGNITION MODULE.
    - LIGHT → ⑥ CHECK COIL CONNECTIONS. IF OK, REPLACE IGNITION MODULE.

CLEAR CODES AND CONFIRM "CLOSED LOOP" OPERATION AND NO "CHECK ENGINE" LIGHT.

CHART C-3
Canister Purge Valve—3.8L

① IGNITION "ON". ENGINE STOPPED. AT THE SOLENOID, APPLY 10" VACUUM TO THROTTLE BODY SIDE OF PURGE SOLENOID.

- ABLE TO GET 10" VACUUM → ② GROUND DIAGNOSTIC TEST TERMINAL AND NOTE VACUUM.
  - NO DROP → ③ PROBE EACH HARNESS CONNECTOR TERMINAL WITH A TEST LIGHT TO GROUND.
    - LIGHT ON ONE TERMINAL → CONNECT A TEST LIGHT BETWEEN HARNESS TERMINALS A AND B.
      - NO LIGHT → CHECK FOR OPEN CKT 428. IF CKT 428 NOT OPEN, CHECK RESISTANCE ACROSS SOLENOID TERMINALS. SHOULD BE 20 OHMS OR MORE.
        - NOT OK → REPLACE BOTH SOLENOID AND ECM
        - OK → FAULTY ECM CONNECTOR TERMINAL A3 OR ECM
      - LIGHT → FAULTY SOLENOID
    - NO LIGHT → REPAIR OPEN CKT 639 OR 339.
  - DROPS → DISCONNECT SOLENOID.
- NO TROUBLE FOUND

- UNABLE TO GET 10" VACUUM → ④ DISCONNECT PURGE SOLENOID. CONNECT TEST LIGHT BETWEEN HARNESS CONNECTOR TERMINALS.
  - NO LIGHT → FAULTY SOLENOID
  - LIGHT → CHECK CKT 428 FOR SHORT TO GROUND. IF CKT 428 NOT SHORTED TO GROUND, IT IS FAULTY ECM. SEE ⚠
    - NO LIGHT → REPAIR OPEN CKT 639 OR 339.
    - LIGHT BOTH TERMINALS → REPAIR SHORT TO VOLTAGE IN CKT 428.

⚠ BEFORE REPLACING ECM, USE AN OHMMETER AND CHECK THE RESISTANCE BETWEEN SOLENOID TERMINALS OF: -PURGE SOLENOID -COOLANT FAN RELAY -WASTEGATE SOLENOID. REPLACE SOLENOID OR RELAY IF RESISTANCE MEASURES LESS THAN 20 OHMS.

CLEAR CODES AND CONFIRM "CLOSED LOOP" OPERATION AND NO "CHECK ENGINE" LIGHT.

CHART C-5
Electronic Spark Control (ESC)—3.8L

CHART C-4B
Ignition System Check—3.8L Turbo

CHART C-8A
Transmission Converter Clutch (TCC)—3.8L W/440- T4

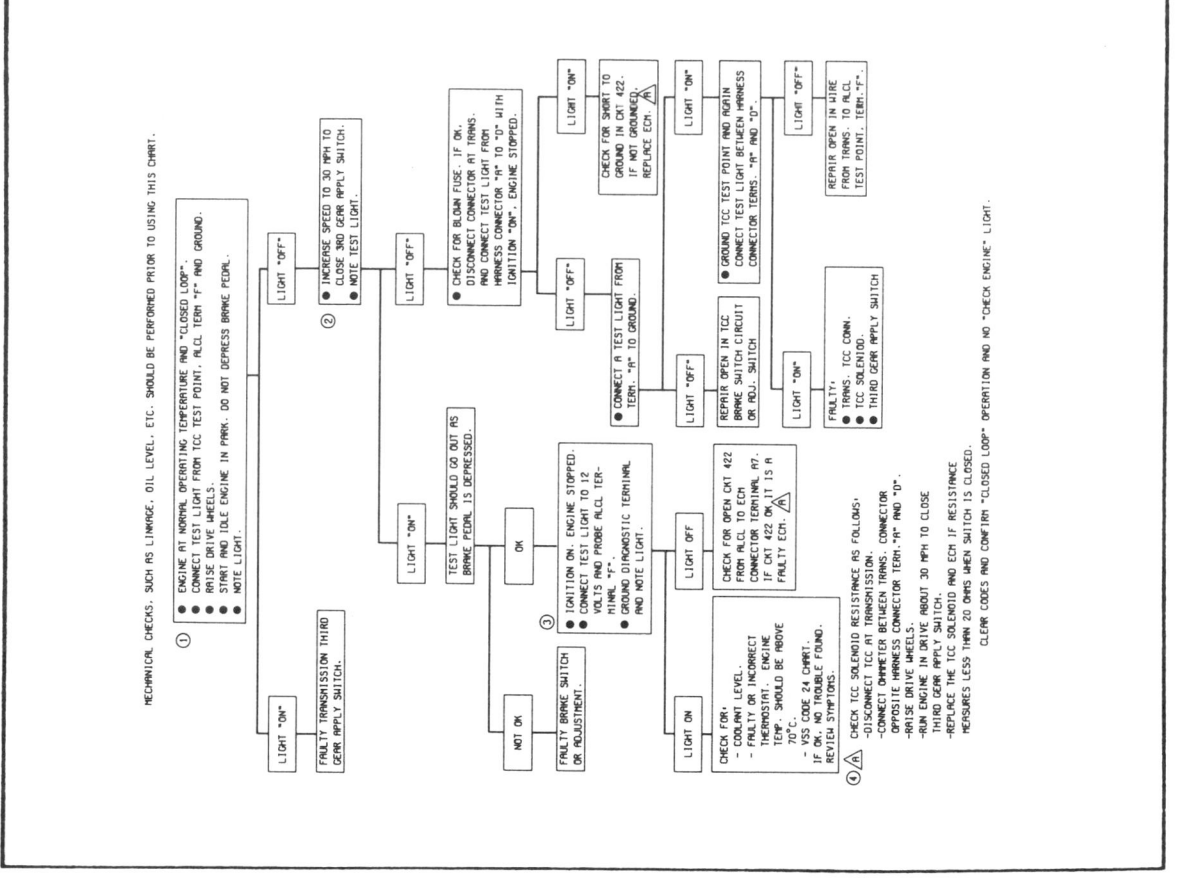

MECHANICAL CHECKS, SUCH AS LINKAGE, OIL LEVEL, ETC. SHOULD BE PERFORMED PRIOR TO USING THIS CHART.

① • ENGINE AT NORMAL OPERATING TEMPERATURE AND "CLOSED LOOP".
   • CONNECT TEST LIGHT FROM TCC TEST POINT, ALCL TERM "F" AND GROUND.
   • RAISE DRIVE WHEELS.
   • START AND IDLE ENGINE IN PARK. DO NOT DEPRESS BRAKE PEDAL.
   • NOTE LIGHT.

LIGHT "ON"

LIGHT "OFF"

② INCREASE SPEED TO 30 MPH TO CLOSE 3RD GEAR APPLY SWITCH. NOTE TEST LIGHT.

LIGHT "ON"

LIGHT "OFF"

FAULTY TRANSMISSION THIRD GEAR APPLY SWITCH.

LIGHT "ON"

TEST LIGHT SHOULD GO OUT AS BRAKE PEDAL IS DEPRESSED.

OK

NOT OK

FAULTY BRAKE SWITCH OR ADJUSTMENT.

③ • IGNITION ON, ENGINE STOPPED.
   • CONNECT TEST LIGHT TO 12 VOLTS AND PROBE ALCL TERMINAL "T".
   • GROUND DIAGNOSTIC TERMINAL AND NOTE LIGHT.

LIGHT ON

LIGHT OFF

CHECK FOR OPEN CKT 422 FROM ALCL TO ECH CONNECTOR TERMINAL A7. IF CKT 422 OK, IT IS A FAULTY ECH. △

CHECK FOR:
- COOLANT LEVEL.
- FAULTY OR INCORRECT THERMOSTAT. ENGINE TEMP. SHOULD BE ABOVE 70°C.
- VSS CODE 24 CHART.
IF OK, NO TROUBLE FOUND. REVIEW SYMPTOMS.

④ △ CHECK TCC SOLENOID RESISTANCE AS FOLLOWS:
- DISCONNECT TCC AT TRANSMISSION.
- CONNECT OHMMETER BETWEEN TRANS. CONNECTOR OPPOSITE HARNESS CONNECTOR TERM. "A" AND "D".
- RAISE DRIVE WHEELS.
- RUN ENGINE IN DRIVE ABOUT 30 MPH TO CLOSE THIRD GEAR APPLY SWITCH.
- REPLACE THE TCC SOLENOID AND ECH IF RESISTANCE MEASURES LESS THAN 20 OHMS WHEN SWITCH IS CLOSED.

CHECK FOR BLOWN FUSE. IF ON, DISCONNECT CONNECTOR AT TRANS. AND CONNECT TEST LIGHT FROM HARNESS CONNECTOR "A" TO "D" WITH IGNITION "ON". ENGINE STOPPED.

LIGHT "OFF"

LIGHT "ON"

CONNECT A TEST LIGHT FROM TERM. "A" TO GROUND.

LIGHT "OFF"

LIGHT "ON"

REPAIR OPEN IN TCC BRAKE SWITCH CIRCUIT OR ADJ. SWITCH

FAULTY:
• TRANS. TCC CONN.
• TCC SOLENOID.
• THIRD GEAR APPLY SWITCH

CHECK FOR SHORT TO GROUND IN CKT 422. IF NOT GROUNDED, REPLACE ECH. △

LIGHT "ON"

GROUND TCC TEST POINT AND AGAIN CONNECT TEST LIGHT BETWEEN HARNESS CONNECTOR TERMS. "A" AND "D".

LIGHT "ON"

LIGHT "OFF"

REPAIR OPEN IN WIRE FROM TRANS. TO ALCL TEST POINT, TERM. "F".

CLEAR CODES AND CONFIRM "CLOSED LOOP" OPERATION AND NO "CHECK ENGINE" LIGHT.

CHART C-7
EGR Check—3.8L

ASSUMES NO CODE 32 IS STORED FOR EGR VALVE.
MAKE PHYSICAL INSPECTION OF EGR VACUUM HOSE FOR RESTRICTIONS.

① • IGNITION "OFF".
   • PUSH UP ON UNDERSIDE OF EGR DIAPHRAGM THEN RELEASE AND WATCH FOR A FIRM CLOSING OF THE VALVE.

CLOSES OK

STICKING OPEN

CLEAN OR REPLACE EGR VALVE AS NECESSARY.

② • ENGINE IDLING.
   • PUSH UP ON UNDERSIDE OF EGR DIAPHRAGM AND NOTE ANY CHANGE IN IDLE SMOOTHNESS.

IDLE ROUGHENS

NO CHANGE

CLEAN EGR PASSAGES OR REPLACE VALVE AS NECESSARY.

EGR VALVE OK, NO PROBLEM FOUND.

CLEAR CODES AND CONFIRM "CLOSED LOOP" OPERATION AND NO "CHECK ENGINE" LIGHT.

CHART C-10A
A/C Clutch Control (1 of 2)—3.8L

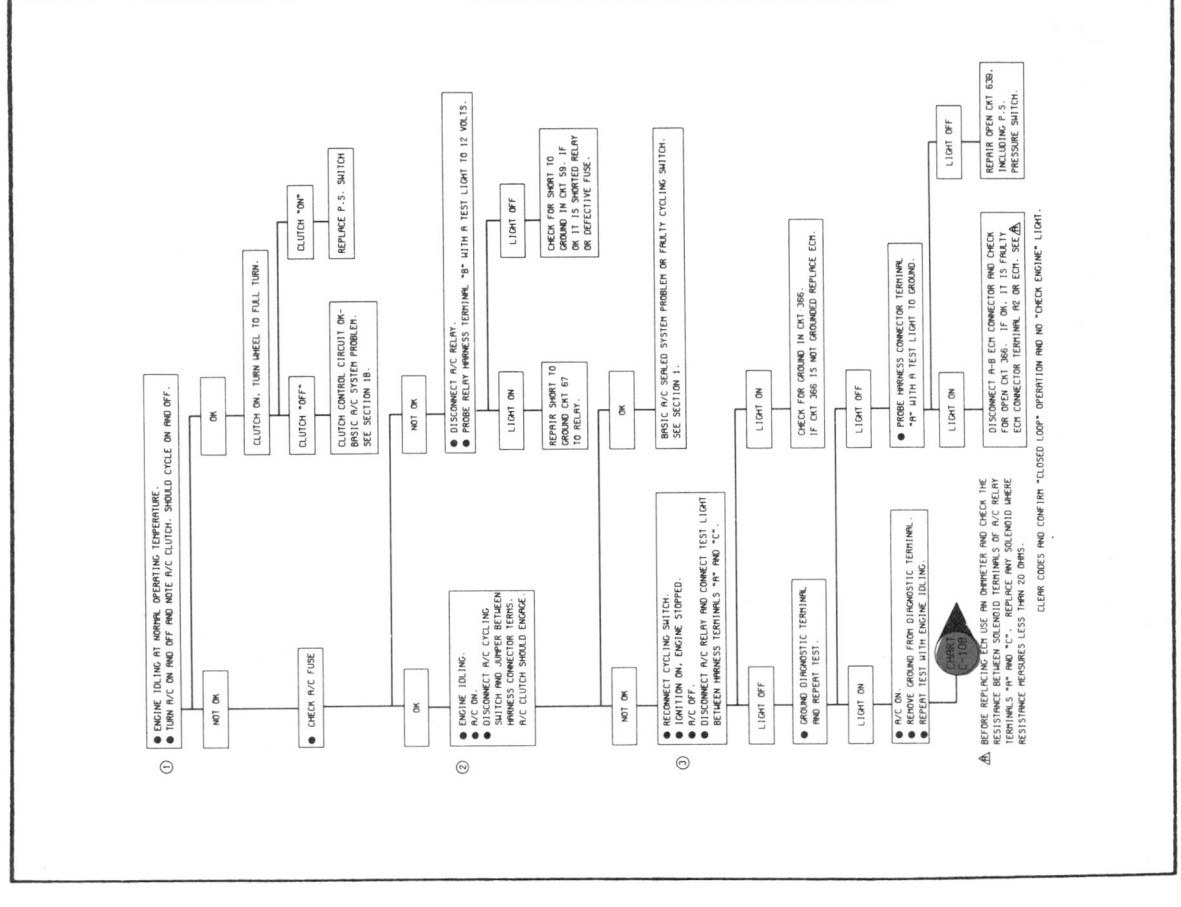

① • ENGINE IDLING AT NORMAL OPERATING TEMPERATURE.
• TURN A/C ON AND OFF AND NOTE A/C CLUTCH. SHOULD CYCLE ON AND OFF.

— OK → CLUTCH ON. TURN WHEEL TO FULL TURN.
  — CLUTCH "ON" → REPLACE P.S. SWITCH
  — CLUTCH "OFF" → CLUTCH CONTROL CIRCUIT OK- BASIC A/C SYSTEM PROBLEM. SEE SECTION 1B.

— NOT OK → CHECK A/C FUSE.

② • ENGINE IDLING.
• A/C ON.
• DISCONNECT A/C CYCLING SWITCH AND JUMPER BETWEEN HARNESS CONNECTOR TERMS. A/C CLUTCH SHOULD ENGAGE

— OK → • DISCONNECT A/C RELAY. • PROBE RELAY HARNESS TERMINAL "B" WITH A TEST LIGHT 12 VOLTS.
  — LIGHT OFF → CHECK FOR SHORT TO GROUND IN CKT 59. IF OK IT IS SHORTED RELAY OR DEFECTIVE FUSE.
  — LIGHT ON → REPAIR SHORT TO GROUND CKT 67 TO RELAY.

— NOT OK → BASIC A/C SEALED SYSTEM PROBLEM OR FAULTY CYCLING SWITCH. SEE SECTION 1.

③ • RECONNECT CYCLING SWITCH. • IGNITION ON, ENGINE STOPPED. • A/C OFF. • DISCONNECT A/C RELAY AND CONNECT TEST LIGHT BETWEEN HARNESS TERMINALS "A" AND "C".

— LIGHT ON → • A/C ON. • REMOVE GROUND FROM DIAGNOSTIC TERMINAL. • REPEAT TEST WITH ENGINE IDLING. (CHART C-10B)

— LIGHT OFF → GROUND DIAGNOSTIC TERMINAL AND REPEAT TEST.
  — LIGHT ON → CHECK FOR GROUND IN CKT 366. IF CKT 366 IS NOT GROUNDED REPLACE ECM.
  — LIGHT OFF → • PROBE HARNESS CONNECTOR TERMINAL "A" WITH A TEST LIGHT TO GROUND.
    — LIGHT ON → DISCONNECT A+B ECM CONNECTOR AND CHECK FOR OPEN CKT 366. IF OK, IT IS FAULTY ECM CONNECTOR TERMINAL, R2 OR ECM. SEE ⚠
    — LIGHT OFF → REPAIR OPEN CKT 639, INCLUDING P.S. PRESSURE SWITCH.

⚠ BEFORE REPLACING ECM USE AN OHMMETER AND CHECK THE RESISTANCE BETWEEN SOLENOID TERMINALS OF A/C RELAY TERMINALS "A" AND "C". REPLACE ANY SOLENOID WHERE RESISTANCE MEASURES LESS THAN 20 OHMS.

CLEAR CODES AND CONFIRM "CLOSED LOOP" OPERATION AND NO "CHECK ENGINE" LIGHT.

CHART C-8B
Transmission Converter Clutch (TCC)—3.8L W/400- T4

CHECKS MADE ON THIS PAGE WILL NOT PREVENT THE TCC FROM WORKING, BUT MAY AFFECT ENGAGE OR DISENGAGE SPEEDS

① • RAISE DRIVE WHEELS.
• IGNITION "ON", ENGINE STOPPED.
• BACK PROBE ECM CONNECTOR TERMINAL "C-9" WITH A VOLTMETER TO GROUND.

— OVER 6 VOLTS
— UNDER 6 VOLTS

② • CHECK VOLTAGE FROM ECM TERMINAL "C-8" TO GROUND.

— UNDER 6 VOLTS → CHECK CKT 494 TO CRUISE MODULE FOR SHORT TO GROUND. IF CKT NOT SHORTED, DISCONNECT CRUISE MODULE AND RECHECK VOLTAGE AT ECM TERMINAL "C-9".
  — OVER 6 VOLTS → FAULTY CRUISE MODULE
  — UNDER 6 VOLTS → FAULTY ECM CONNECTOR TERMINAL "C-9" OR ECM.

③ • START ENGINE AND WITH TRANSMISSION IN "D" INCREASE SPEED TO 50-55 MPH AND NOTE VOLTAGE READING.

— OVER 6 VOLTS → CHECK FOR OPEN IN WIRE FROM ECM TERMINAL "B" TO TRANSMISSION CONNECTOR TERMINAL "B". IF NOT OPEN, IT IS FAULTY CONNECTOR AT TRANSMISSION OR OPEN IN TRANSMISSION 4TH GEAR SWITCH.
— UNDER 6 VOLTS → NO ELECTRICAL TROUBLE FOUND

④ • IGNITION "ON", ENGINE STOPPED. DISCONNECT TRANSMISSION CONNECTOR. CHECK VOLTAGE FROM HARNESS CONNECTOR TERMINAL "B" TO GROUND.

— OVER 6 VOLTS → TRANSMISSION 4TH GEAR SWITCH OR WIRE IS GROUNDED OR SWITCH NOT OPENING.
— UNDER 6 VOLTS → CHECK FOR GROUNDED WIRE TO ECM TERMINAL "C-8". IF NOT GROUNDED, IT IS FAULTY ECM CONNECTOR TERMINAL "C-8" OR ECM.

CLEAR CODES AND CONFIRM "CLOSED LOOP" OPERATION AND NO "CHECK ENGINE" LIGHT.

CHART C-12A
Coolant Fan Functional Check—3.8L

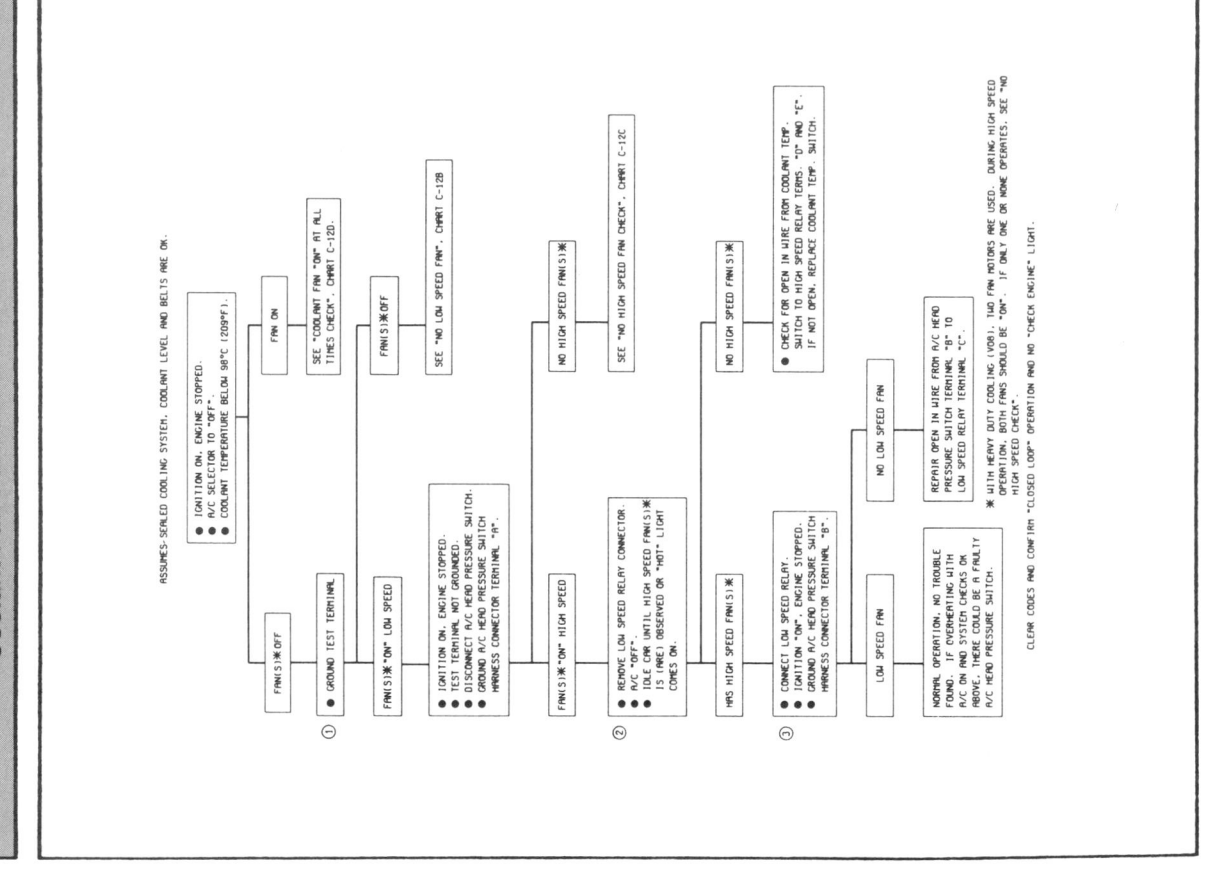

ASSUMES: SEALED COOLING SYSTEM. COOLANT LEVEL AND BELTS ARE OK.

- IGNITION ON, ENGINE STOPPED.
- A/C SELECTOR TO "OFF".
- COOLANT TEMPERATURE BELOW 98°C (209°F).

① GROUND TEST TERMINAL

- FAN(S)❋ OFF
- FAN(S)❋ LOW SPEED

FAN ON → SEE "COOLANT FAN "ON" AT ALL TIMES CHECK". CHART C-12D.

FAN(S)❋ OFF → SEE "NO LOW SPEED FAN". CHART C-12B

- IGNITION ON, ENGINE STOPPED.
- TEST TERMINAL NOT GROUNDED.
- DISCONNECT A/C HEAD PRESSURE SWITCH.
- GROUND A/C HEAD PRESSURE SWITCH HARNESS CONNECTOR TERMINAL "A".

FAN(S)❋ "ON" HIGH SPEED

② REMOVE LOW SPEED RELAY CONNECTOR.
- A/C "OFF".
- IDLE CAR UNTIL HIGH SPEED FAN(S) IS (ARE) OBSERVED OR "HOT" LIGHT COMES ON.

NO HIGH SPEED FAN(S)❋ → SEE "NO HIGH SPEED FAN CHECK". CHART C-12C

HAS HIGH SPEED FAN(S)❋
NO HIGH SPEED FAN(S)❋

③ CONNECT LOW SPEED RELAY.
- IGNITION "ON", ENGINE STOPPED.
- GROUND A/C HEAD PRESSURE SWITCH HARNESS CONNECTOR TERMINAL "B".

- CHECK FOR OPEN IN WIRE FROM COOLANT TEMP. SWITCH TO HIGH SPEED RELAY TERMS. "D" AND "E". IF NOT OPEN, REPLACE COOLANT TEMP. SWITCH.

LOW SPEED FAN
NO LOW SPEED FAN

NORMAL OPERATION. NO TROUBLE FOUND. IF OVERHEATING WITH A/C ON AND SYSTEM CHECKS OK ABOVE, THERE COULD BE A FAULTY A/C HEAD PRESSURE SWITCH.

REPAIR OPEN IN WIRE FROM A/C HEAD PRESSURE SWITCH TERMINAL "B" TO LOW SPEED RELAY TERMINAL "C".

❋ WITH HEAVY DUTY COOLING (V08), TWO FAN MOTORS ARE USED. DURING HIGH SPEED OPERATION, BOTH FANS SHOULD BE "ON". IF ONLY ONE OR NONE OPERATES, SEE "NO HIGH SPEED CHECK".

CLEAR CODES AND CONFIRM "CLOSED LOOP" OPERATION AND NO "CHECK ENGINE" LIGHT.

CHART C-10B
A/C Clutch Control (2 of 2)—3.8L

FROM CHART C-10A

LIGHT OFF
LIGHT ON

① - PROBE HARNESS CONNECTOR TERMINAL "B" WITH A TEST LIGHT TO GROUND.

② - JUMPER BETWEEN HARNESS TERMINALS "B" & "D". A/C CLUTCH SHOULD ENGAGE.

OK → FAULTY A/C RELAY CONNECTION OR RELAY.

NOT OK → CHECK:
- OPEN CKT 59 TO CLUTCH.
- OPEN CLUTCH COIL.
- OPEN HIGH PRESSURE SWITCH.
- FAULTY GROUND.

③ - DISCONNECT A/C PRESSURE CYCLING SWITCH.
- PROBE BOTH HARNESS TERMINALS WITH A TEST LIGHT TO GROUND.

LIGHT OFF
LIGHT ON

LIGHT ON ONE TERMINAL → REPAIR OPEN CKT 67 TO A/C RELAY.

④ - DISCONNECT ECM A-B CONNECTOR.
- PROBE TERMINAL B8 WITH A TEST LIGHT TO GROUND.

LIGHT ON → REPAIR OPEN CKT 67 TO CYCLING SWITCH.

LIGHT OFF → FAULTY TERMINAL B8 OR ECM.

NO LIGHT EITHER TERMINAL → CHECK FOR OPEN CKT 67 TO A/C CONTROL SWITCH OR FAULTY A/C SWITCH.

CLEAR CODES AND CONFIRM "CLOSED LOOP" OPERATION AND NO "CHECK ENGINE" LIGHT.

CHART C-12C
No High Speed Fan—3.8L

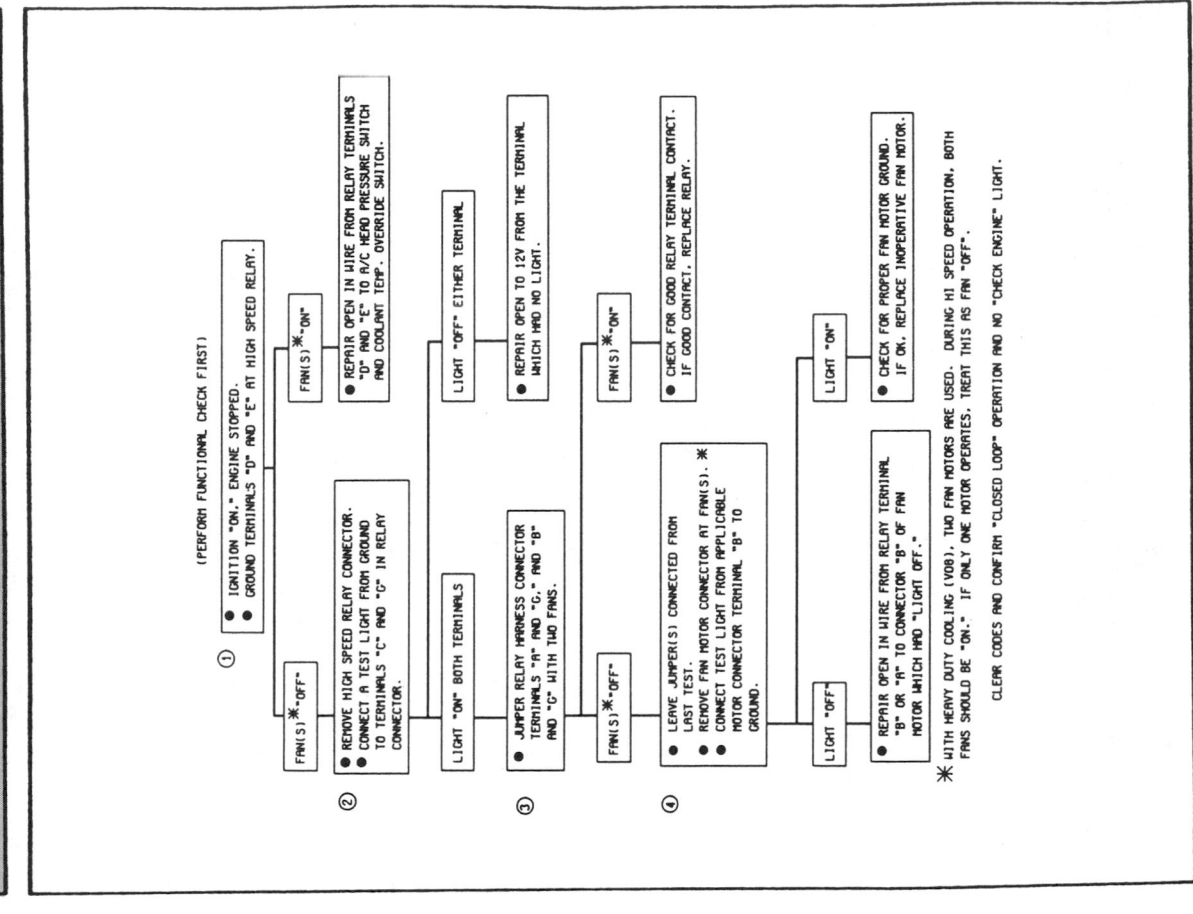

(PERFORM FUNCTIONAL CHECK FIRST)

① • IGNITION "ON." ENGINE STOPPED.
   • GROUND TERMINALS "D" AND "E" AT HIGH SPEED RELAY.

FAN(S) "OFF"

② • REMOVE HIGH SPEED RELAY CONNECTOR.
   • CONNECT A TEST LIGHT FROM GROUND TO TERMINALS "C" AND "G" IN RELAY CONNECTOR.

FAN(S) *"ON"

• REPAIR OPEN IN WIRE FROM RELAY TERMINALS "D" AND "E" TO A/C HEAD PRESSURE SWITCH AND COOLANT TEMP. OVERRIDE SWITCH.

LIGHT "ON" BOTH TERMINALS

LIGHT "OFF" EITHER TERMINAL

• REPAIR OPEN TO 12V FROM THE TERMINAL WHICH HAD NO LIGHT.

③ • JUMPER RELAY HARNESS CONNECTOR TERMINALS "A" AND "G," AND "B" AND "G" WITH TWO FANS.

FAN(S) *"ON"

• CHECK FOR GOOD RELAY TERMINAL CONTACT. IF GOOD CONTACT, REPLACE RELAY.

FAN(S) "OFF"

④ • LEAVE JUMPER(S) CONNECTED FROM LAST TEST.
   • REMOVE FAN MOTOR CONNECTOR AT FAN(S).
   • CONNECT TEST LIGHT FROM APPLICABLE MOTOR CONNECTOR TERMINAL "B" TO GROUND.

LIGHT "ON"

• CHECK FOR PROPER FAN MOTOR GROUND. IF OK, REPLACE INOPERATIVE FAN MOTOR.

LIGHT "OFF"

• REPAIR OPEN IN WIRE FROM RELAY TERMINAL "B" OR "A" TO CONNECTOR "B" OF FAN MOTOR WHICH HAD "LIGHT OFF."

* WITH HEAVY DUTY COOLING (VO8), TWO FAN MOTORS ARE USED. DURING HI SPEED OPERATION, BOTH FANS SHOULD BE "ON." IF ONLY ONE MOTOR OPERATES, TREAT THIS AS FAN "OFF."

CLEAR CODES AND CONFIRM "CLOSED LOOP" OPERATION AND NO "CHECK ENGINE" LIGHT.

CHART C-12B
No Low Speed Fan—3.8L

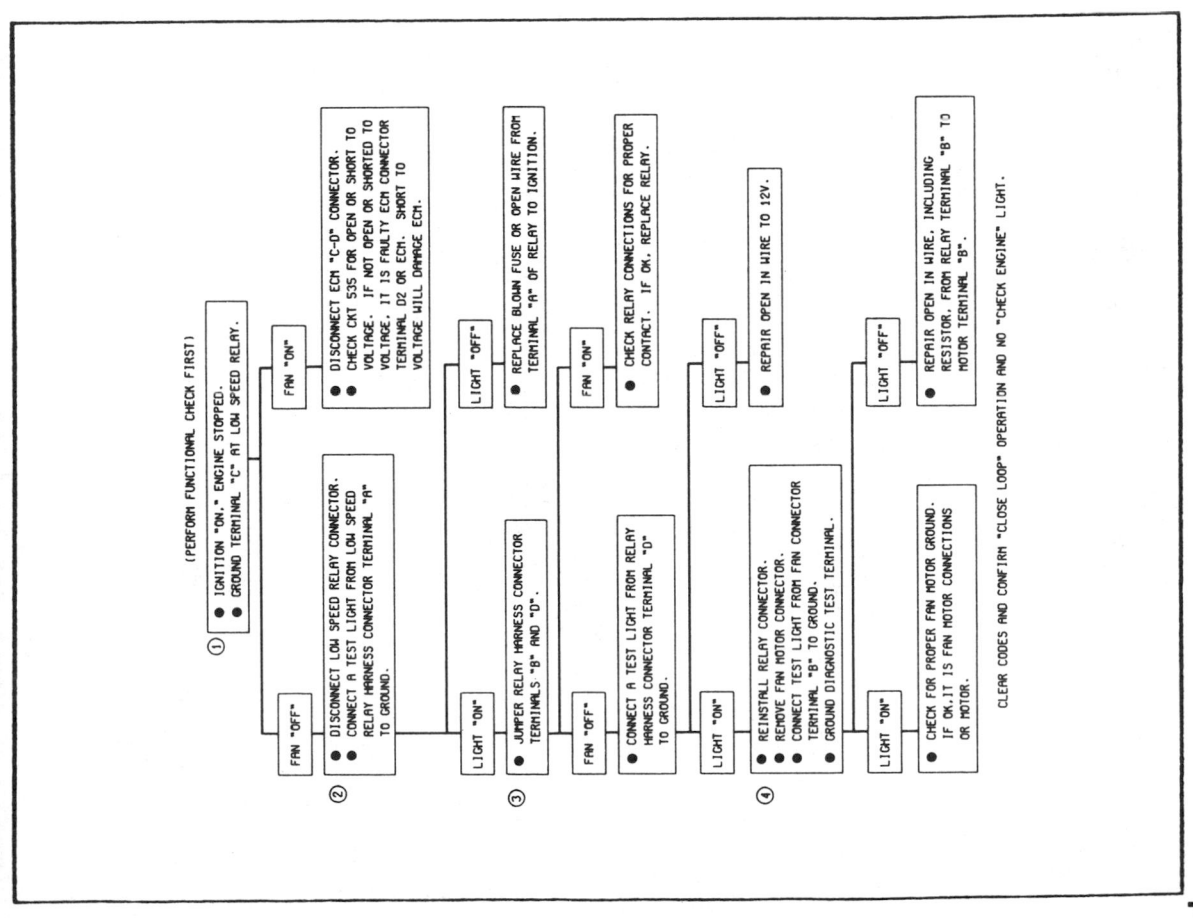

(PERFORM FUNCTIONAL CHECK FIRST)

① • IGNITION "ON," ENGINE STOPPED.
   • GROUND TERMINAL "C" AT LOW SPEED RELAY.

FAN "ON"

• DISCONNECT ECM "C-D" CONNECTOR.
   • CHECK CKT 535 FOR OPEN OR SHORT TO VOLTAGE. IF NOT OPEN OR SHORTED TO VOLTAGE, IT IS FAULTY ECM CONNECTOR TERMINAL D2 OR ECM. SHORT TO VOLTAGE WILL DAMAGE ECM.

FAN "OFF"

② • DISCONNECT LOW SPEED RELAY CONNECTOR.
   • CONNECT A TEST LIGHT FROM LOW SPEED RELAY HARNESS CONNECTOR TERMINAL "A" TO GROUND.

LIGHT "ON"

• REPLACE BLOWN FUSE OR OPEN WIRE FROM TERMINAL "A" OF RELAY TO IGNITION.

LIGHT "OFF"

③ • JUMPER RELAY HARNESS CONNECTOR TERMINALS "B" AND "D".

FAN "OFF"

• CONNECT A TEST LIGHT FROM RELAY HARNESS CONNECTOR TERMINAL "D" TO GROUND.

FAN "ON"

• CHECK RELAY CONNECTIONS FOR PROPER CONTACT. IF OK, REPLACE RELAY.

LIGHT "ON"

• REPAIR OPEN IN WIRE TO 12V.

LIGHT "OFF"

④ • REINSTALL RELAY CONNECTOR.
   • REMOVE FAN MOTOR CONNECTOR.
   • CONNECT TEST LIGHT FROM FAN CONNECTOR TERMINAL "B" TO GROUND.
   • GROUND DIAGNOSTIC TEST TERMINAL.

LIGHT "ON"

• CHECK FOR PROPER FAN MOTOR GROUND. IF OK, IT IS FAN MOTOR CONNECTIONS OR MOTOR.

LIGHT "OFF"

• REPAIR OPEN IN WIRE, INCLUDING RESISTOR, FROM RELAY TERMINAL "B" TO MOTOR TERMINAL "B".

CLEAR CODES AND CONFIRM "CLOSE LOOP" OPERATION AND NO "CHECK ENGINE" LIGHT.

ECM Connector ID—1.8L

PORT FUEL INJECTION ECM CONNECTOR IDENTIFICATION

THIS ECM VOLTAGE CHART IS FOR USE WITH A DIGITAL VOLTMETER TO FURTHER AID IN DIAGNOSIS. THE VOLTAGES YOU GET MAY VARY DUE TO LOW BATTERY CHARGE OR OTHER REASONS, BUT THEY SHOULD BE VERY CLOSE.
THE FOLLOWING CONDITIONS MUST BE MET BEFORE TESTING:
• ENGINE AT OPERATING TEMPERATURE • ENGINE IDLING IN CLOSED LOOP (FOR "ENGINE RUN" COLUMN) •
• TEST TERMINAL NOT GROUNDED • ALCL TOOL NOT INSTALLED •

24 PIN A-B CONNECTOR

VOLTAGE KEY "ON"	ENG RUN	OPEN CRT	PIN	CIRCUIT	PIN	CIRCUIT	KEY "ON"	ENG RUN	OPEN CRT
0	13.4		A1	FUEL PUMP RELAY	B1	BATTERY	12.5	13.4	
			A2		B2				
			A3		B3	DIST. GRD.	0		
12.5	.5		A4	WASTEGATE	B4				
			A5		B5	DIST. REF.	0	.7	
0	13.4		A6	"CHECK ENGINE" LIGHT	B6				
12.5	13.6		A7	IGNITION	B7	ESC	9.2	9.2	
0	13.1		A8	TCC OR SHIFT LIGHT	B8	A/C CLUTCH SIG.	0	0	
	2.5 (varies)		A9	SERIAL DATA	B9				
5.1	5.1		A10	DIAGNOSTICS	B10	PARK/NEUTRAL	0	0	
.4	.4		A11	VEHICLE SPEED SENSOR	B11				
0	0		A12	MAP/MAT GROUND / GROUND	B12				

32 PIN C-D CONNECTOR

VOLTAGE KEY "ON"	ENG RUN	OPEN CRT	PIN	CIRCUIT	PIN	CIRCUIT	KEY "ON"	ENG RUN	OPEN CRT
0	0		C1	COOLANT FAN	D1	GROUND	0	0	
0	0		C2	A/C RELAY	D2	TPS & COOLANT GROUND	0	0	
NOT USEABLE			C3	IAC "B" LO	D3				
NOT USEABLE			C4	IAC "B" HI	D4	EST	0	1.0	
NOT USEABLE			C5	IAC "A" HI	D5	EST BYPASS	0	4.6	
NOT USEABLE			C6	IAC "A" LO	D6	O2 GROUND	0		
			C7		D7	O2 SIGNAL	0	1.8 (varies)	
12.4	13.4		C8	P/S PRESS. SIG.	D8				
0	0		C9	CRANK SIG.	D9				
1.44	.8		C10	COOLANT SIG.	D10				
2.41	1.07		C11	MAP SIG	D11				
2.46	2.09		C12	MAT SIG.	D12				
.46	.46		C13	TPS SIG.	D13				
5.1	5.1		C14	5V REG.	D14	INJ. 3 & 4	12.5	13.4	
			C15	BATTERY...	D15				
12.5	13.4		C16	BATTERY	D16	INJ. 1 & 2	12.5	13.4	

① ENGINE RUNNING IN PARK, AT IDLE, NORMAL OPERATING TEMPERATURE, IN CLOSED LOOP
② ALL VOLTAGES SHOWN AS "0" SHOULD READ LESS THAN 1.0 VOLT WITH A DIGITAL VOLT-OHM METER SUCH AS J-29125.
③ READS BATTERY VOLTAGE IN GEAR
④ A.C. OFF
⑤ VOLTAGE DEPENDS ON ENGINE TEMPERATURE

ENGINE 1.8 TURBO
CARLINE J

CHART C-12D Fan 'On' At All Times—3.8L

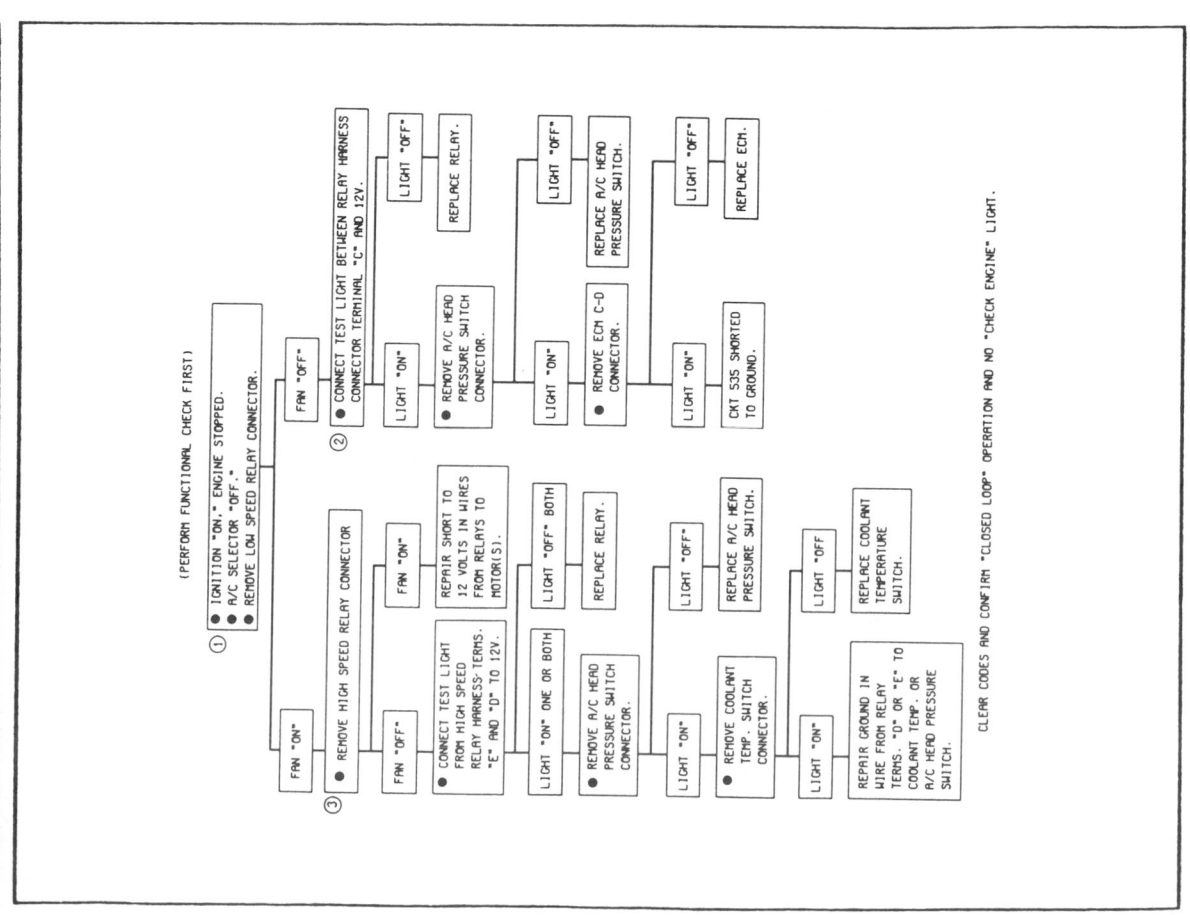

(PERFORM FUNCTIONAL CHECK FIRST)

① • IGNITION "ON", ENGINE STOPPED.
• A/C SELECTOR "OFF".
• REMOVE LOW SPEED RELAY CONNECTOR.

CLEAR CODES AND CONFIRM "CLOSED LOOP" OPERATION AND NO "CHECK ENGINE" LIGHT.

ECM Schematic—1.8L

ECM Schematic—1.8L

CHART A-8
Fuel System Diagnosis (2 of 2)—1.8L

NOTICE: EFI SYSTEM UNDER PRESSURE. TO AVOID FUEL SPILLAGE, REFER TO FIELD SERVICE PROCEDURES FOR TESTING OR MAKING REPAIRS REQUIRING DISASSEMBLY OF FUEL LINES OR FITTINGS.

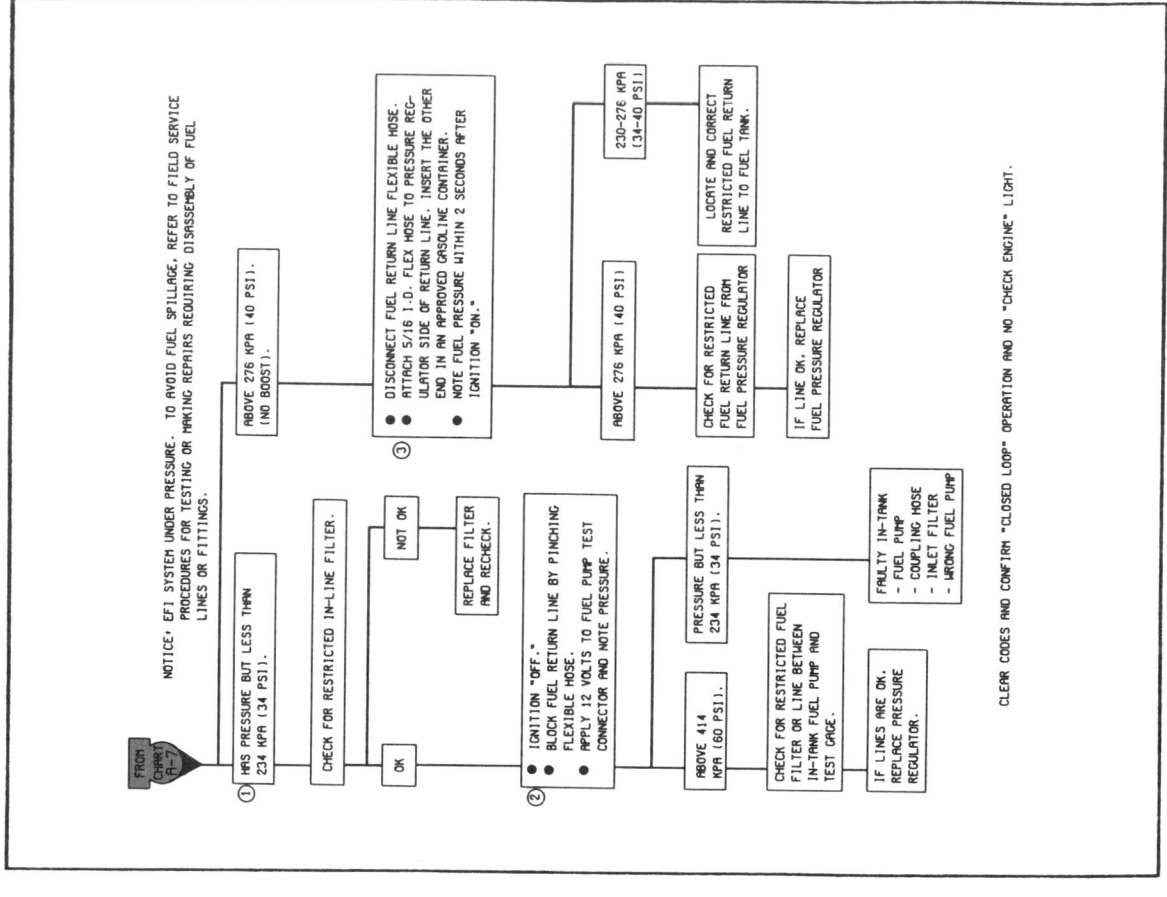

FROM CHART A-7

① HAS PRESSURE BUT LESS THAN 234 KPA (34 PSI).

CHECK FOR RESTRICTED IN-LINE FILTER.

NOT OK → REPLACE FILTER AND RECHECK.

OK

② • IGNITION "OFF."
• BLOCK FUEL RETURN LINE BY PINCHING FLEXIBLE HOSE.
• APPLY 12 VOLTS TO FUEL PUMP TEST CONNECTOR AND NOTE PRESSURE.

ABOVE 414 KPA (60 PSI).

CHECK FOR RESTRICTED FUEL FILTER OR LINE BETWEEN IN-TANK FUEL PUMP AND TEST GAGE.

IF LINES ARE OK, REPLACE FUEL PRESSURE REGULATOR.

PRESSURE BUT LESS THAN 234 KPA (34 PSI).

FAULTY IN-TANK
- FUEL PUMP
- COUPLING HOSE
- INLET FILTER
- WRONG FUEL PUMP

ABOVE 276 KPA (40 PSI). (NO BOOST).

③ • DISCONNECT FUEL RETURN LINE FLEXIBLE HOSE.
• ATTACH 5/16 I.D. FLEX HOSE TO PRESSURE REGULATOR SIDE OF RETURN LINE. INSERT THE OTHER END IN AN APPROVED GASOLINE CONTAINER.
• NOTE FUEL PRESSURE WITHIN 2 SECONDS AFTER IGNITION "ON."

230-276 KPA (34-40 PSI)

LOCATE AND CORRECT RESTRICTED FUEL RETURN LINE TO FUEL TANK.

ABOVE 276 KPA (40 PSI).

CHECK FOR RESTRICTED FUEL RETURN LINE FROM FUEL PRESSURE REGULATOR.

IF LINE OK, REPLACE FUEL PRESSURE REGULATOR.

CLEAR CODES AND CONFIRM "CLOSED LOOP" OPERATION AND NO "CHECK ENGINE" LIGHT.

CHART A-7
Fuel System Diagnosis (1 of 2)—1.8L

NOTICE: FUEL SYSTEM UNDER PRESSURE. TO AVOID FUEL SPILLAGE, REFER TO FIELD SERVICE PROCEDURES FOR TESTING OR MAKING REPAIRS REQUIRING DISASSEMBLY OF FUEL LINES OR FITTINGS.

① • INSTALL FUEL PRESSURE GAGE J-34730-1 OR EQUIVALENT.
• IGNITION "OFF" FOR 10 SECONDS. A/C "OFF".
• IGNITION "ON". FUEL PUMP WILL RUN FOR ABOUT 2 SECONDS.
• NOTE FUEL PRESSURE AFTER PUMP STOPS. SHOULD BE 234-276 KPA (34-40 PSI) AND HOLD STEADY.

OK

② • START AND IDLE ENGINE AT NORMAL OPERATING TEMPERATURE.
• PRESSURE SHOULD BE LOWER, 64 KPA (5-9 PSI) LESS.

OK

NO TROUBLE FOUND. REVIEW SYMPTOMS SECTION B.

③ PRESSURE BUT NOT HOLDING 234-276 KPA (34-40 PSI).

• IGNITION "OFF" FOR 10 SECONDS.
• IGNITION "ON".
• BLOCK FUEL PRESSURE LINE BY PINCHING FLEX HOSE. PRESSURE SHOULD HOLD.

NOT HOLDING

• BLOCK FUEL RETURN LINE BY PINCHING HOSE. RECHECK PRESSURE.

HOLDS

FAULTY FUEL PRESSURE REGULATOR.

NOT OK

PRESSURE BUT LESS THAN 234 KPA (34 PSI).

ABOVE 276 KPA (40 PSI).

HOLDS

CHECK:
- LEAKING PUMP COUPLING HOSE.
- FAULTY IN-TANK PUMP.

NOT HOLDING

LOCATE AND CORRECT LEAKING INJECTOR. REMOVE SPARK PLUGS TO LOCATE FLOODING CYLINDERS.

CHART A-8

CLEAR CODES AND CONFIRM "CLOSED LOOP" OPERATION AND NO "CHECK ENGINE" LIGHT.

GM THROTTLE BODY INJECTION

General Information

All 1982 and later USA cars equipped with the Pontiac 4-151, the 1.8L OHC or the 2.0L OHV engine use a single bore, throttle body fuel injection unit. All Canadian 4-151s retain the 2 bbl carburetors. The 1982 and later Corvette equipped with the V8 350 and the 1982 and later Camaro and Firebird equipped with the V8 305 engine use a pair of single bore throttle body injection units.

In this throttle body system, a single fuel injector mounted at the top of the throttle body sprays fuel down through the throttle valve and into the intake manifold. The throttle body resembles a carburetor in appearance but does away with much of the carburetor's complexity (choke system and linkage, power valves, accelerator pump, jets, fuel circuits, etc.), replacing these with the electrically operated fuel injector.

The injector is actually a solenoid which when activated lifts a pintle valve off its seat, allowing the pressurized (10 psi) fuel behind the valve to spray out. The nozzle of the injector is designed to atomize the fuel for complete air/fuel mixture.

The activating signal for the injector originates with the Electronic Control Module (ECM), which monitors engine temperature, throttle position, vehicle speed and several other engine-related conditions then continuously updates injector opening times in relation to the information given by these sensors.

The throttle body is also equipped with an idle air control motor. The idle air control motor operates a pintle valve at the side of the throttle body. When the valve opens it allows air to bypass the throttle, which provides the additional air required to idle at elevated speed when the engine is cold. The idle air control motor also compensates for accessory loads and changing engine friction during break-in. The idle speed control motor is controlled by the ECM.

Fuel pressure for the system is provided by an in-tank fuel pump. The pump is a two-stage turbine design powered by a DC motor. It is designed for smooth, quiet operation, high flow and fast priming. The design of the fuel inlet reduces the possibility of vapor lock under hot fuel conditions. The pump sends fuel forward through the fuel line to a stainless steel high-flow fuel filter mounted on the engine. From the filter the fuel moves to the throttle body. The fuel pump inlet is located in a reservoir in the fuel tank which insures a constant supply of fuel to the pump during hard cornering and on steep inclines. The fuel pump is controlled by a fuel pump relay, which in turn receives its signal from the ECM. A fuel pressure regulator inside the throttle body maintains fuel pressure at 10 psi and routes unused fuel back to the fuel tank through a fuel return line. On the dual throttle body system, a fuel pressure compensator is used on the second throttle body assembly to compensate for a momentary fuel pressure drop between the two units. This constant circulation of fuel through the throttle body prevents component overheating and vapor lock.

The electronic control module (ECM), also called a microcomputer, is the brain of the fuel injection system. After receiving inputs from various sensing elements in the system. The ECM commands the fuel injector, idle air control motor, EST distributor, torque converter clutch and other engine actuators to operate in a pre-programmed manner to improve driveability and fuel economy while controlling emissions. The sensing elements update the computer every tenth of a second for general information and every 12.5 milli-seconds for critical emissions and driveability information.

The ECM has limited system diagnostic capability. If certain system malfunctions occur, the diagnostic "check engine" light in the instrument panel will light, alerting the driver to the need for service.

Since both idle speed and mixture are controlled by the ECM on this system, no adjustments are possible or necessary.

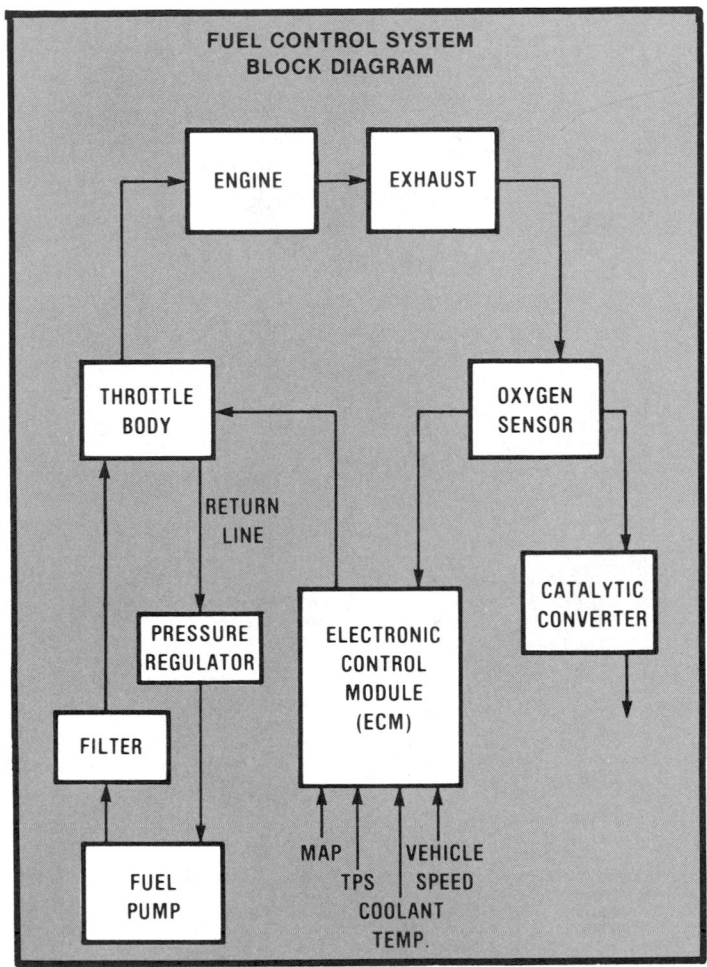

Schematic of fuel control system on GM TBI system

1. Fuel inlet
2. Fuel return
3. Fuel pressure regulator
4. Idle air control (IAC) valve
5. Fuel injector
6. Fuel injector connector terminals
7. Ported vacuum sources (may vary)
8. Manifold vacuum source (may vary)
9. Throttle valve

Throttle body unit operation

NECESSARY TOOLS

DIGITAL VOLTMETER (10 MEGOHM INPUT IMPEDANCE, MINIMUM) J-29125-A

TACH METER

VACUUM PUMP (20 IN. HG MINIMUM)

1.7MM (.07 IN.)

1.2MM (.05 IN.)

J-28742

CONNECTOR PIN EXTRACTION TOOLS

OXYGEN SENSOR WRENCH J-29533

IAC ADJUSTMENT WRENCH J-33631 or 1 1/4" 33 MM OPENING

CLIP TYPE JUMPER WIRE

IDLE AIR PLUGS (TO BLOCK AIR PASSAGE) J-33047

TEST LIGHT

SIX JUMPER WIRES—APPROX. 6" LONG:
1 — FEMALE BOTH ENDS
1 — MALE BOTH ENDS
4 — MALE-FEMALE ON OPPOSITE ENDS
(TERMINAL NOS. 12014836 AND 12014837 MAKE JUMPERS UP WITH #16, 18 OR 20 WIRE.)

Special tools used to service the GM TBI system

FUEL INJECTOR

FUEL METER BODY

FUEL METER COVER

IDLE AIR CONTROL VALVE (IACV)

THROTTLE POSITION SENSOR

FUEL RETURN NUT (TO TANK SUPPLY)

FUEL INLET NUT (FROM FUEL PUMP AND TANK SUPPLY)

Typical GM throttle body unit assembly

On-Car Service

The system does not require special tools for diagnosis. A tachometer, test light, ohmmeter, digital voltmeter with 10 megohms impedance, vacuum pump, vacuum gauge and jumper wires are required for diagnosis. A test light or voltmeter must be used when specified in the procedures.

FUEL SYSTEM PRESSURE TEST

—CAUTION—

To reduce the risk of fire and personal injury, it is necessary to relieve the fuel system pressure before servicing fuel system components.

1. Remove the fuel pump fuse from the fuse block.
2. Crank the engine. The engine will run until it runs out of fuel. Crank the engine again for 3 seconds making sure it is out of fuel.
3. Turn the ignition off and replace the fuse.
4. Remove the air cleaner. Plug the thermal vacuum port on the throttle body.
5. Remove the fuel line between the throttle body and filter.
6. Install a fuel pressure gauge between the throttle body and fuel filter. The gauge should be able to register at least 15 psi.
7. Start the car. Observe the fuel pressure reading. It should be 9–13 psi.

NOTE: Before removing the fuel pressure gauge the fuel system must be depressurized.

8. Reinstall the parts in the reverse order of removal.

1. Front TBI assembly
2. Rear TBI assembly
3. Fuel inlet
4. Fuel return
5. Idle air control (IAC) valve
6. Throttle position sensor (TPS)
7. Fuel injector
8. Cross-Fire intake manifold
9. Fuel line
10. Throttle synchronizing screw collar

5.7L V8 Cross Fire throttle body units

MINIMUM AIR RATE ADJUSTMENT (2.5L)

This adjustment should be performed only when the throttle body parts have been replaced or required to do so by the T.P.S. adjustment. Engine should be at normal operating temperature before making adjustment.

1. Remove air cleaner and air cleaner to TBI gasket. Plug vacuum port on TBI unit for THERMAC.

NOTE: On vehicles equipped with a tamper resistant plug covering the minimum air adjustment screw, the throttle body unit must be removed from the engine to remove the plug.

2. Remove T.V. cable from throttle control bracket to allow access to minimum air adjustment screw.

3. Connect a tachometer to engine.

4. Start engine, transmission in Park (Neutral on manual transmission) and allow engine rpm to stabilize.

5. Install tool J-33047, or its equal, and idle air passage of throttle body. Be certain that tool seats fully in passage and no air leaks exist.

6. Using appropriate screwdriver, turn minimum air screw until engine rpm is 500 ± 25 in neutral with automatic transaxle, and 775 ± 25 in neutral with manual transaxle.

7. Stop engine and remove tool J-33047 from throttle body.

8. Reinstall T.V. cable into throttle control bracket.

9. Use silicone sealant or equivalent to cover minimum air adjustment screw.

10. Install air cleaner gasket and air cleaner to engine.

CURB IDLE AIR RATE (5.0L CROSSFIRE INJECTION SYSTEM)

The throttle position of each throttle body must be balanced so that the throttle plates are synchronized to open simultaneously. This is a checking and adjustment procedure; adjustment should be performed only when a throttle body has been replaced or when checking procedure indicates an adjustment is required.

1. Remove air cleaner and air cleaner to TBI unit for THERMAC.

2. Start engine and allow engine rpm to stabilize.

3. Plug idle air passages of each throttle body with plugs J-33047, or their equal. Be certain plugs are fully seated in passages and no air leaks exist. Engine rpm should decrease to curb idle air rate. If engine rpm does not decrease, check for vacuum leak.

4. Remove cap from ported tube on rear TBI unit and connect the vacuum gauge.

5. Observe the gauge, reading should be approximately 0.45 in. Hg. If adjustment is required proceed as follows:

    a. Remove tamper resistant screw covering the minimum air adjustment screw if required.

    b. Adjust minimum air adjustment screw to obtain approximately 0.45 in. Hg.

    c. After adjustment, proceed to front TBI unit.

6. Remove gauge from rear TBI unit and re-install cap on ported tube.

7. Remove cap from ported tube on front TBI unit and connect vacuum gauge. Reading should also be approximately 0.45 in. Hg. If adjustment is required proceed as follows:

    a. Locate split lever screw on throttle linkage. If screw is welded for tamper resistance, break weld and install new screw with thread locking compound applied.

    b. Adjust split lever screw to obtain approximately 0.45 in. Hg.

1. TBI assembly
2. Canister purge ported vacuum
3. Air cleaner port
4. Crankcase vent port
5. EGR valve port
6. MAP sensor port

TBI port and manifold vacuum sources

Installing idle air passage blocking tool

Blocking throttle lever

8. Remove gauge from front TBI unit and re-install cap on ported tube.

9. If both readings are approximately 0.45 in. Hg., no adjustment is required; throttle plates are synchronized.

10. Stop engine and remove idle air passage plugs.

11. Check T.P.S. voltage and adjust if required.

12. Install air cleaner gaskets, connect vacuum line to TBI unit and install air cleaner.

THROTTLE POSITION SENSOR

Testing

Throttle position sensor adjustment should be checked after minimum air adjustment is completed.

1. Remove air cleaner.

Adjusting throttle position switch (1) using digital volt-ohmmeter (2) with 10 mega-ohm impedance

2. Disconnect T.P.S. harness from T.P.S.

3. Using three jumper wires connect T.P.S. harness to T.P.S.

4. With ignition "ON," engine stopped, used a digital voltmeter to measure voltage between terminals B and C.

5. Voltage should read .525 ± .075 volts. 5.0L engine and .820 + .250 volts 2.5L engine.

6. Adjust T.P.S. if required.

7. With ignition "OFF," remove jumpers and connect T.P.S. harness to T.P.S.

8. Install air cleaner.

Adjustment

1. After installing TPS to throttle body, install throttle body unit to engine.

2. Remove EGR valve and heat shield from engine.

3. Using three six inch jumpers, connect TPS harness to TPS

4. With ignition "ON," engine stopped, use a digital voltmeter to measure voltage between TPS terminals B and C.

5. Loosen two TPS attaching screws and rotate throttle position sensor to obtain a voltage reading of .525 ± .075 volts 5.0L engine and .820 ± .250 volts 2.5L engine.

6. With ignition "OFF," remove jumpers and reconnect TPS harness to TPS

7. Install EGR valve and heat shield to engine, using new gasket as necessary.

8. Install air cleaner gasket and air cleaner to throttle body unit.

NOTE: Throttle position sensors are not adjustable on 1983–85 2.5L and 1982–85 1.8L engines with TBI.

Removal

The throttle position sensor (TPS) is an electrical unit and must not be immersed in any type of liquid solvent or cleaner. The TPS is factory adjusted and the retaining screws are spot welded in place to retain the critical setting. With these considerations, it is possible to clean the throttle body assembly without removing the TPS if care is used. Should TPS replacement be required however, proceed using the following steps:

1. Invert throttle body and place on a clean, flat surface.

1. Mounting screw
2. Lockwasher
3. Retainer
4. TPS pickup lever
5. Throttle actuator lever
6. TPS overhaul kit

Throttle position switch (TPS) attaching screws. Note lever position when removing the TPS

2. Using a 5/16 in. drill bit, drill completely through two (2) TPS screw access holes in base of throttle body to be sure of removing the spot welds holding TPS screws in place.

3. Remove the two TPS attaching screws, lockwashers, and retainers. Then, remove TPS sensor from throttle body. DISCARD SCREWS. New screws are supplied in service kits.

4. If necessary, remove screw holding throttle position sensor actuator lever to end of throttle shaft.

5. Remove the idle air control assembly and gasket from the throttle body.

NOTE: DO NOT immerse the idle air control motor in any type of cleaner and it should always be removed before throttle body cleaning. Immersion in cleaner will damage the IAC assembly. It is replaced only as a complete assembly.

Further disassembly of the throttle body is not required for cleaning purposes. The throttle valve screws are permanently staked in place and should not be removed. The throttle body is serviced as a complete assembly.

Installation

1. Place throttle body assembly on holding fixture to avoid damaging throttle valve.

2. Using a new sealing gasket, install idle air control motor in throttle body. Tighten motor securely.

NOTE: DO NOT overtighten to prevent damage to valve.

3. If removed, install throttle position sensor actuator lever by aligning flats on lever with flats on end of shaft. Install retaining screw and tighten securely.

NOTE: Install throttle position sensor after completion of assembly of the throttle body unit. Use thread locking compound supplied in service kit on attaching screws.

Component Removal

FUEL INJECTOR

Removal and Installation

1. Remove the air cleaner.

2. Disconnect injector electrical connector by squeezing two tabs together and pulling straight up.

NOTE: Use care in removing to prevent damage to the electrical connector pins on top of the injector, injector fuel filter and nozzle. The fuel injector is only serviced as a complete assembly. Do not immerse it in any type of cleaner.

3. Remove the fuel meter cover.

4. Using a small awl, gently pry up on the injector evenly and carefully remove it.

Removing fuel injector

5. Installation is the reverse of removal, with the following recommendations.

Use Dextron®II transmission fluid to lubricate all O-rings. Install the steel backup washer in the recess of the fuel meter body. Then, install the O-ring directly above backup washer, pressing the O-ring into the recess.

NOTE: Do not attempt to reverse this procedure and install backup washer and O-ring after injector is located in the cavity. To do so will prevent seating of the O-ring in the recess.

Installing fuel injector

Fuel injector components

IDLE AIR CONTROL ASSEMBLY

Removal and Installation

1. Remove the air cleaner.
2. Disconnect the electrical connection from the idle air control assembly.
3. Using a 1¼ in. wrench, remove the idle air control assembly from the throttle body.

NOTE: Before installing a new assembly, measure the distance that the conical valve is extended. This measurement should be made from motor housing to end of cone. It should be greater than 1.259 in. If the cone is extended too far damage to the motor may result.

On cars with manual transmissions, idle speed will be controlled when operating temperature is reached. For automatic transmission cars, engage the transmission in drive after operating temperature is reached. This will allow the ECM to control idle speed.

FUEL PRESSURE REGULATOR/ COMPENSATOR

Removal and Installation

1. Remove air cleaner.
2. Disconnect electrical connector to injector by squeezing on two tabs and pulling straight up.
3. Remove five screws securing fuel meter cover to fuel meter body. Notice location of two short screws during removal.

Idle air control (IAC) valve designs

1. Idle air control (IAC) valve
2. Less than 1⅛ in. (28mm)
3. Type 1 (with collar)
4. Type 2 (without collar)
5. Gasket

Idle air control valve installation

Installing fuel meter cover

---CAUTION---

Do not remove the four screws securing the pressure regulator to the fuel meter cover. The fuel pressure regulator includes a large spring under heavy tension which, if accidentally released, could cause personal injury. The fuel meter cover is only serviced as a complete assembly and includes the fuel pressure regulator preset and plugged at the factory.

NOTE: DO NOT immerse the fuel meter cover (with pressure regulator) in any type of cleaner. Immersion in cleaner will damage the internal fuel pressure regulator diaphragms and gaskets.

4. Installation is the reverse of removal.

Fuel meter cover removal

FUEL METER COVER

Removal and Installation

1. Remove the five fuel meter cover screws and lockwashers holding the cover on the fuel meter body.
2. Lift off fuel meter cover (with fuel pressure regulator assembly).
3. Remove the fuel meter cover gaskets.

---CAUTION---

Do not remove the four screws securing the pressure regulator to the fuel meter cover. The fuel pressure regulator includes a large spring under heavy tension, which, if accidentally released, could cause personal injury. The fuel meter cover is only serviced as a complete assembly and includes the fuel pressure regulator preset and plugged at the factory.

NOTE: Do not immerse the fuel meter cover (with pressure regulator) in any type of cleaner. Immersion in cleaner will damage the internal fuel pressure regulator diaphragms and gaskets.

4. Remove the sealing ring (dust seal from the fuel meter body).
5. Installation is the reverse of removal.

FUEL METER BODY

Removal and Installation

1. Remove the fuel inlet and outlet nuts and gaskets from fuel meter body.
2. Remove three screws and lockwashers. Remove fuel meter body from throttle body assembly.

NOTE: The air cleaner stud must have been removed previously.

3. Remove fuel meter body insulator gasket.
4. Installation is the reverse of removal.

THROTTLE BODY

Removal and Installation

SINGLE UNIT—FOUR CYLINDER ENGINE

Refer to the "Rear Unit-V8 Engine" procedure which follows. Disregard Steps 6 and 7 of that procedure, instead, just disconnect the fuel feed and return lines.

FRONT UNIT—V8 ENGINE

1. Disconnect the battery cables at the battery.
2. Remove the air cleaner assembly, noting the connection points of the vacuum lines.
3. disconnect the electrical connectors at the injector and the idle air control motor.
4. Disconnect the vacuum line from the TBI unit, noting the connection points. During installation, refer to the underhood emission control information decal for vacuum line routing information.
5. Disconnect the transmission detent cable from the TBI unit.
6. Disconnect the fuel inlet (feed) and fuel balance line connections at the front TBI unit.
7. Disconnect the throttle control rod between the two TBI units.
8. Unbolt and remove the TBI unit.
9. Installation is the reverse of the previous steps. Torque the TBI bolts to 120-168 inch lbs. during installation.

REAR UNIT—V8 ENGINE

1. Disconnect the battery cables at the battery.
2. Remove the air cleaner assembly, noting the connection points of the vacuum lines.
3. Disconnect the electrical connectors at the injector, idle air control motor, and throttle position sensor.
4. Disconnect the vacuum lines from the TBI unit, noting the connection points. During installation, refer to the underhood emission control information decal for vacuum line routing information.
5. Disconnect the throttle and cruise control (if so equipped) cables at the TBI unit.
6. Disconnect the fuel return and balance line connections from the rear TBI unit.
7. Disconnect the throttle control rod between the two units.
8. Unbolt and remove the TBI unit.
9. Installation is the reverse of the previous steps. Torque the TBI bolts to 120-168 inch lbs. during installation.

Throttle Body Disassembly

When servicing the single TBI unit on four cylinder engines, follow all steps except those specified "front unit." "Rear Unit" steps DO apply.

---CAUTION---

Use extreme care when handling the TBI unit to avoid damage to the swirl plates located beneath the throttle valve.

NOTE: If both TBI units are to be disassembled, DO NOT mix parts between either unit.

1. Remove the fuel meter cover assembly (five screws). Remove the gaskets after the cover has been removed. The fuel meter cover assembly is serviced only as a unit. If necessary, the entire unit must be replaced.

---CAUTION---

DO NOT remove the four screws which retain the pressure regulator (rear unit) or pressure compensator (front unit). There is a spring beneath the cover which is under great pressure. If the cover is accidentally released, personal injury could result.

Do not immerse the fuel meter cover in any type of cleaning solvent.

Exploded view of Cross Fire TBI units

1. Fuel meter cover and pressure regulator assembly
2. Long screw and washer (3)
3. Short screw and washer (2)
4. Fuel meter cover gasket
5. Fuel meter outlet gasket
6. Pressure regulator dust seal
7. Fuel injector
8. Fuel injector filter
9. Small O-ring
10. Large O-ring

11. Injector back-up washer
12. Fuel line
13. Fuel inlet nut
14. Fuel nut gasket (2)
15. Fuel return nut
16. Fuel return nut
17. Fuel inlet nut
18. Fuel meter body assembly
19. Attaching screw and washer
20. Fuel meter body gasket
21. Throttle rod retaining clip

22. Throttle rod and bearing assembly
23. Throttle body assembly
24. TBI mounting bolt (short)
25. TBI mounting bolt (long)
26. Air cleaner mounting stud
27. TBI mounting gasket
28. Tube cap
29. Throttle position sensor (TPS)
30. TPS mounting screw
31. Washer
32. TPS retainer
33. TPS lever attaching screw

34. TPS lever
35. Idle air control (IAC) assembly
36. IAC gasket
37. Throttle stop screw
38. Throttle stop screw spring
39. Throttle synchronizing screw
40. Throttle synchronizing screw collar
41. Intake manifold cover
42. Intake manifold cover gasket
43. Manifold cover throttle bore tube (swirl plate)

2. Remove the foam dust seal from the meter body of the rear unit.

3. Remove the fuel injector using a pair of small pliers as follows:

a. Grasp the injector collar, between the electrical terminals.

b. Carefully pull the injector upward, in a twisting motion.

c. If the injectors are to be removed from both TBI units, mark them so that they may be installed in their original units.

4. Remove the filter from the base of the injector by rotating it back and forth.

5. Remove the O-ring and the steel washer from the top of the fuel meter body, then remove the small O-ring from the bottom of the injector cavity.

6. Remove the fuel inlet and outlet nuts (and gaskets) from the fuel meter body.

7. Remove the fuel meter body assembly and gasket from the throttle body assembly (three screws).

8. For the rear TBI unit only: Remove the throttle position sensor (TPS) from the throttle body (two screws). If necessary, remove the screw which holds the TPS actuator lever to the end of the throttle shaft.

9. Remove the idle air control motor from the throttle body.

───────────CAUTION───────────

Because the TPS and idle air control motors are electrical units, they must not be immersed in any type of cleaning solvent.

Throttle Body Assembly

NOTE: During assembly, replace the gaskets, injector washer, O-rings, and pressure regulator dust seal with new parts.

1. Install the idle air control motor in the throttle body, using a new gasket. Torque the retaining screws to 13 ft. lbs.

NOTE: DO NOT overtighten the screws.

2. For the rear TBI unit only: If removed, install the TPS actuator lever by aligning the flats of the lever and the shaft. Install and tighten the retaining screw.

3. Install the fuel meter body on the throttle body, using a new gasket. Also, apply thread locking compound to the three fuel meter body screws according to the chemical manufacturers instructions. Torque the screws to 35 inch lbs.

4. Install the fuel inlet and outlet nuts, using new gaskets. Torque the nuts to 260 inch lbs.

5. Carefully twist the fuel filter onto the injector base.

6. Lubricate the new O-rings with Dexron®II transmission fluid.

7. Install the small O-ring onto the injector, pressing it up against the fuel filter.

8. Install the steel washer into the injector cavity recess of the fuel meter body. Install the large O-ring above the steel washer, in the cavity recess. The O-ring must be flush with the fuel meter body surface.

9. Using a pushing/twisting motion, carefully install the injector. Center the nozzle O-ring in the bottom of the injector cavity and align the raised lug on the injector base with the notch in the fuel meter body cavity. Make sure the injector is seated fully in the cavity. The electrical connections should be parallel to the throttle shaft of the throttle body.

10. For the rear TBI unit only: Install the new pressure regulator dust seal into the fuel meter body recess.

11. Install the new fuel meter cover and fuel outlet passage gaskets on the fuel meter cover.

12. Install the fuel meter cover assembly, using thread locking compound on the five retaining screws. Torque the screws to 28 inch lbs. Note that the two short screws must be installed alongside the fuel injector (one screw each side).

13. For the rear TBI unit only: With the throttle valve in the closed (idle) position, install the TPS but do not tighten the attaching screws. The TPS lever must be located ABOVE the tang on the throttle acutator lever.

14. Install the TBI unit(s) as previously outlined and adjust the throttle position sensor.

Cleaning and Inspection

The throttle body injection parts, except as noted below, should be cleaned in a cold immersion-type cleaner such as Carbon X (X-55) or its equivalent.

NOTE: The throttle position sensor, idle air control motor, fuel meter cover (with pressure regulator), fuel injector, fuel filter, rubber parts, diaphragms, etc., should NOT be immersed in cleaner as they will swell, harden or distort.

1. Thoroughly clean all metal parts and blow dry with shop air. Make sure all fuel passages are free of burrs and dirt.

2. Inspect casting mating surfaces for damage that could affect gasket sealing.

3. Check, repair or replace parts as required, if the following problems are encountered:

  a. Flooding

  (1) Inspect large and small fuel injector O-rings for damage such as cuts, distortion, etc. check that the steel backup washer is located beneath the large (upper) O-ring. Use new O-rings when reinstalling injector.

  (2) Inspect fuel injector fuel filter for damage, cleanliness, etc. Clean or replace as necessary.

  (3) If the fuel injector continues to supply fuel with injector electrical connections removed, replace injector as required.

  b. Hesitation

  (1) Inspect fuel injector fuel filter for being plugged, dirty, etc. Clean or replace as necessary.

  (2) If improper fuel inlet and outlet pressure readings, are noted check for restricted passages or inoperative fuel pressure regulator. Repair or replace as required.

───────────CAUTION───────────

DO NOT remove the four screws securing the fuel pressure regulator to the fuel meter cover. The fuel pressure regulator includes a large spring under heavy tension, which if accidentally released, could cause personal injury. The fuel meter cover is only serviced as a complete assembly and includes the fuel pressure regulator preset and plugged at the factory.

  c. Hard Starting - Poor Cold Operation (See items listed under "Hesitation," above.)

  d. Rough Idle

  (1) Inspect large and small fuel injector O-rings for damage such as cuts, distortion, etc. check that the steel backup washer is located beneath the large (upper) O-ring. Use new O-rings when reinstalling injector.

  (2) Inspect fuel injector fuel filter for damage, cleanliness, etc. Clean or replace as necessary.

  (3) If the fuel injector continues to supply fuel with injector electrical connections removed, replace injector as required.

Diagnostic Circuit Check

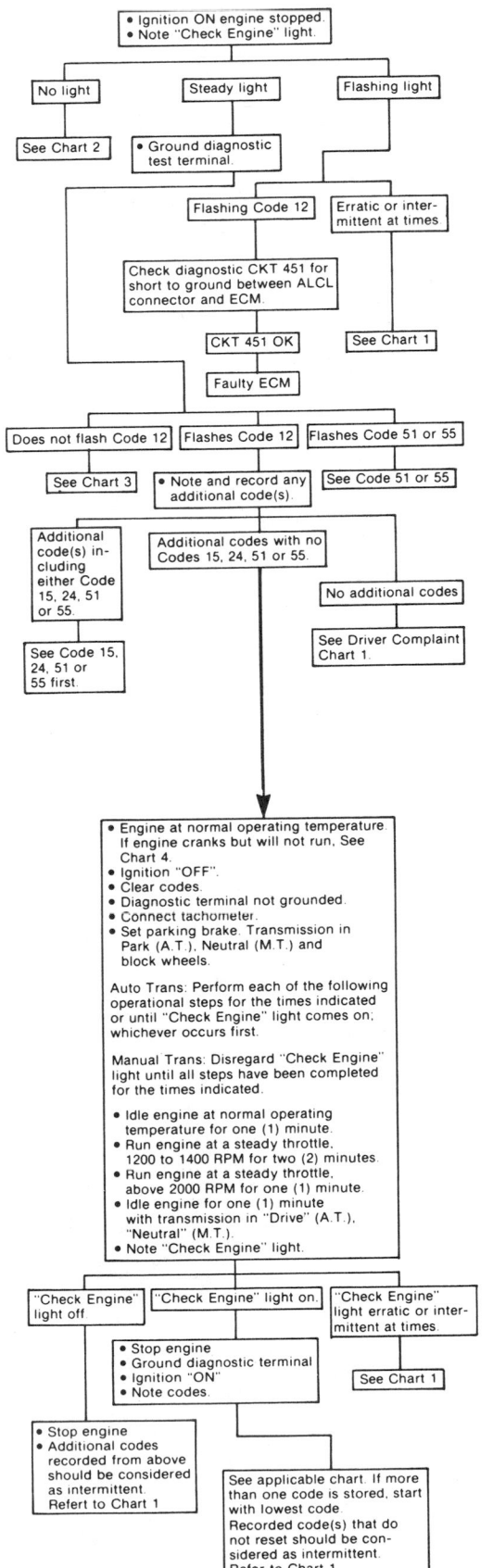

- Ignition ON engine stopped.
- Note "Check Engine" light.

No light → See Chart 2

Steady light
- Ground diagnostic test terminal.

Flashing light

Flashing Code 12 / Erratic or intermittent at times

Check diagnostic CKT 451 for short to ground between ALCL connector and ECM.

CKT 451 OK / See Chart 1

Faulty ECM

Does not flash Code 12 → See Chart 3

Flashes Code 12 → Note and record any additional code(s).

Flashes Code 51 or 55 → See Code 51 or 55

Additional code(s) including either Code 15, 24, 51 or 55.

Additional codes with no Codes 15, 24, 51 or 55.

See Code 15, 24, 51 or 55 first.

No additional codes → See Driver Complaint Chart 1.

- Engine at normal operating temperature. If engine cranks but will not run, See Chart 4.
- Ignition "OFF".
- Clear codes.
- Diagnostic terminal not grounded.
- Connect tachometer.
- Set parking brake. Transmission in Park (A.T.), Neutral (M.T.) and block wheels.

Auto Trans: Perform each of the following operational steps for the times indicated or until "Check Engine" light comes on; whichever occurs first.

Manual Trans: Disregard "Check Engine" light until all steps have been completed for the times indicated.

- Idle engine at normal operating temperature for one (1) minute.
- Run engine at a steady throttle, 1200 to 1400 RPM for two (2) minutes.
- Run engine at a steady throttle, above 2000 RPM for one (1) minute.
- Idle engine for one (1) minute with transmission in "Drive" (A.T.), "Neutral" (M.T.).
- Note "Check Engine" light.

"Check Engine" light off.
- Stop engine
- Additional codes recorded from above should be considered as intermittent. Refer to Chart 1.

"Check Engine" light on.
- Stop engine
- Ground diagnostic terminal
- Ignition "ON"
- Note codes.

See applicable chart. If more than one code is stored, start with lowest code. Recorded code(s) that do not reset should be considered as intermittent. Refer to Chart 1.

"Check Engine" light erratic or intermittent at times.
See Chart 1

Chart 2

No "Check Engine" Light

- Ignition "on", engine stopped.
- Back probe white ECM connector Pin 20, CKT 419, with test light to 12 volts.

Test light on.
Faulty "Check Engine" light bulb. Bulb OK. Repair open IGN 1 CKT or CKT 419.

Test light off. → Repair open or short to ground in CKT 439.

Test light off. → Repair open or short to ground in continuous battery circuit.

Test light off.
- Back probe white ECM connector, Pin 16, with a test light to ground.

Test light on.
- Back probe white connector Pins 10 or 15, with a test light to ground.

Test light on.
Check engine ground CKTS 450 and 450R.

ECM ground OK. → Faulty ECM connector or ECM.

"Check Engine" Light / White Connector

IGN 1 —10A— PNK/BLK — 419 — 20 Lamp Driver
Fusible Link A,F,X. 20 A Fuse Y. — ORN — 10 / 15
IGN 1 —10A— PNK/BLK — 439 — 16
— 451 — 3 Diagnostic's

B A — ALCL Connector — ECM

Clear codes and confirm "Closed Loop" operation and no "Check Engine" light. (Perform Diagnostic Circuit Check)

Chart 3

Won't Flash Code 12

- Ignition "off".
- Disconnect White ECM connector.
- Ignition "on".

Light off
- Ignition off.
- Reconnect ECM.
- Ignition on, engine stopped.
- Back probe white ECM connector Pin 3 CKT 451, with a test light to ground.

Light on → Repair short to ground in CKT 419.

Code 12 → Repair open in diagnostic CKT 451.

No Code 12
- Ignition off, engine stopped.
- Remove PROM.
- Ignition on.
- Ground diagnostic term.
- Note code.

Code 51 → Check for proper PROM installation. If OK, install new PROM and recheck for Code 12.

No code. → Faulty ECM connector or ECM.

No Code 12 / Code 12

Replace ECM   System OK

Gage fuse
10A
IGN 1 —o\\o— PNK/BLK ——— 419
Fusible Link A,F,X ——o\\o—— ORN
20 A Fuse Y
10A
IGN 1 —o\\o— PNK/BLK ——— 439
ECM fuse ———————————— 451

"Check Engine" Light

White Connector

20 Lamp Driver
10
15
16
3   Diagnostic's

B A
ALCL Connector   ECM

Clear codes and confirm "Closed Loop" operation and no "Check Engine" light. (Perform Diagnostic Circuit Check)

Chart 4

2.5 ℓ

— Engine cranks but will not run.

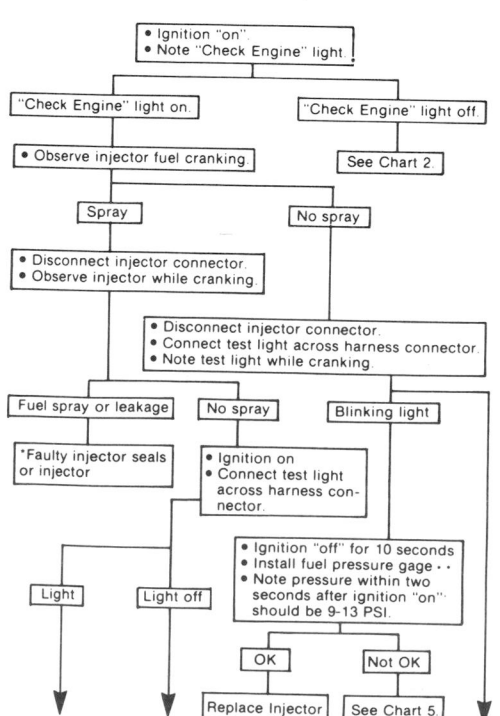

- Ignition "on".
- Note "Check Engine" light.

"Check Engine" light on. | "Check Engine" light off.

- Observe injector fuel cranking. | See Chart 2.

Spray | No spray

- Disconnect injector connector.
- Observe injector while cranking.

- Disconnect injector connector.
- Connect test light across harness connector.
- Note test light while cranking.

Fuel spray or leakage | No spray | Blinking light

*Faulty injector seals or injector

- Ignition on
- Connect test light across harness connector.

- Ignition "off" for 10 seconds
- Install fuel pressure gage ••
- Note pressure within two seconds after ignition "on" should be 9-13 PSI.

Light | Light off

OK | Not OK

Replace Injector | See Chart 5.

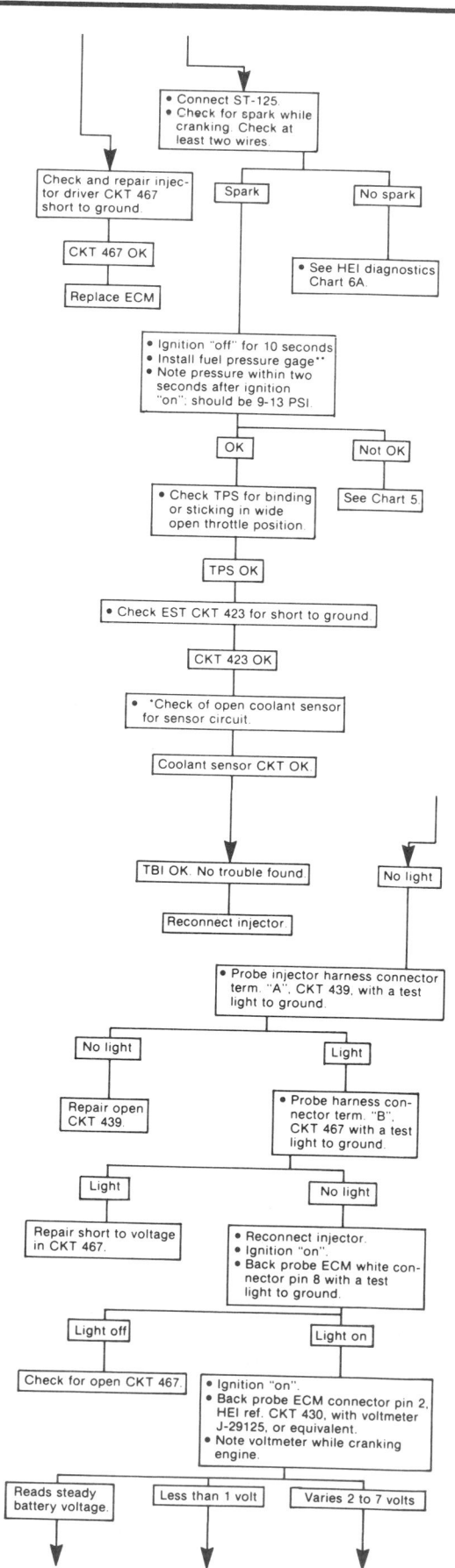

- Connect ST-125.
- Check for spark while cranking. Check at least two wires.

Check and repair injector driver CKT 467 short to ground. | Spark | No spark

CKT 467 OK | | • See HEI diagnostics Chart 6A.

Replace ECM

- Ignition "off" for 10 seconds
- Install fuel pressure gage••
- Note pressure within two seconds after ignition "on"; should be 9-13 PSI.

OK | Not OK

| See Chart 5.

- Check TPS for binding or sticking in wide open throttle position.

TPS OK

• Check EST CKT 423 for short to ground.

CKT 423 OK

• *Check of open coolant sensor for sensor circuit.

Coolant sensor CKT OK

TBI OK. No trouble found. | No light

Reconnect injector.

- Probe injector harness connector term. "A", CKT 439, with a test light to ground.

No light | Light

Repair open CKT 439. | • Probe harness connector term. "B", CKT 467 with a test light to ground.

Light | No light

Repair short to voltage in CKT 467. | • Reconnect injector.
• Ignition "on".
• Back probe ECM white connector pin 8 with a test light to ground.

Light off | Light on

Check for open CKT 467. | • Ignition "on".
• Back probe ECM connector pin 2, HEI ref. CKT 430, with voltmeter J-29125, or equivalent.
• Note voltmeter while cranking engine.

Reads steady battery voltage. | Less than 1 volt | Varies 2 to 7 volts

Chart 4A

5.0L and 5.7L

— Engine cranks but will not run.

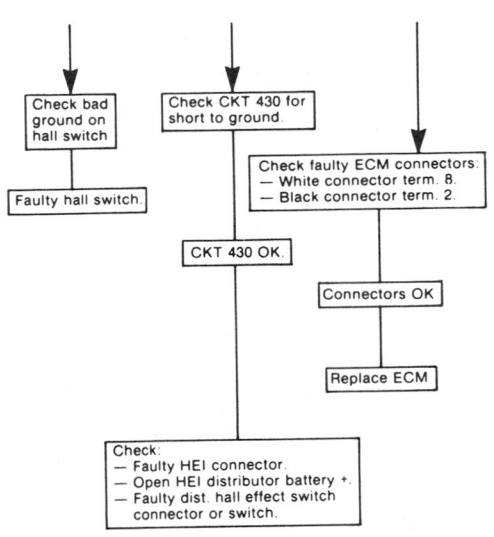

Left column (flow chart continuation):

- Check bad ground on hall switch → Faulty hall switch.

- Check CKT 430 for short to ground. → CKT 430 OK.

- Check faulty ECM connectors:
  — White connector term. 8.
  — Black connector term. 2. → Connectors OK → Replace ECM

Check:
— Faulty HEI connector.
— Open HEI distributor battery +.
— Faulty dist. hall effect switch connector or switch.

*May require spark plug cleaning to start engine.

**EFI fuel system under pressure. To avoid fuel spillage, refer to field service procedure for testing or making repairs requiring the disassembly of fuel line or fittings.

SCHEMATIC CHARTS
4 and 5 (2.5L)

RELAY HARNESS CONNECTOR

RELAY END VIEW

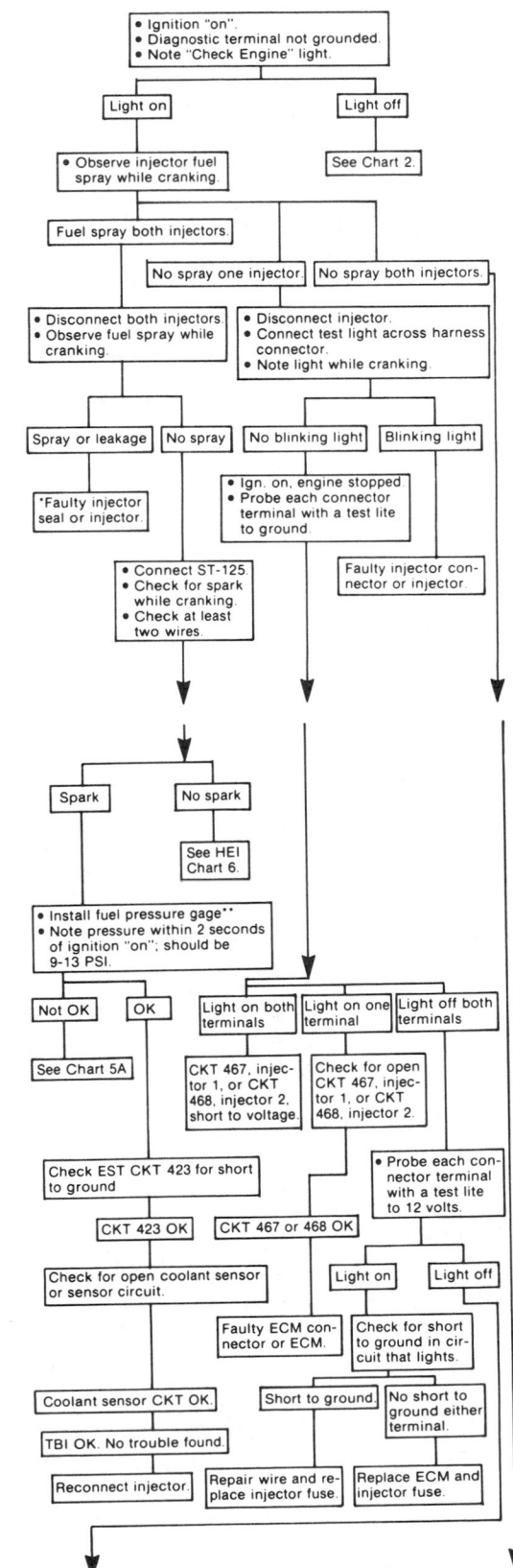

Right column (Chart 4A flow):

- Ignition "on".
- Diagnostic terminal not grounded.
- Note "Check Engine" light.

→ Light on / Light off

Light off → See Chart 2.

Light on → • Observe injector fuel spray while cranking.

→ Fuel spray both injectors. / No spray one injector. / No spray both injectors.

No spray one injector → • Disconnect both injectors. • Observe fuel spray while cranking.
→ Spray or leakage / No spray

Spray or leakage → *Faulty injector seal or injector.

No spray both injectors → • Disconnect injector. • Connect test light across harness connector. • Note light while cranking.
→ No blinking light / Blinking light

No blinking light → • Ign. on, engine stopped. • Probe each connector terminal with a test lite to ground. → Faulty injector connector or injector.

No spray → • Connect ST-125. • Check for spark while cranking. • Check at least two wires.

→ Spark / No spark

No spark → See HEI Chart 6.

Spark → • Install fuel pressure gage** • Note pressure within 2 seconds of ignition "on"; should be 9-13 PSI.

→ Not OK / OK

Not OK → See Chart 5A

OK → TBI OK. No trouble found.

Light on both terminals → CKT 467, injector 1, or CKT 468, injector 2, short to voltage. → Check EST CKT 423 for short to ground → CKT 423 OK → Check for open coolant sensor or sensor circuit. → Coolant sensor CKT OK. → Reconnect injector.

Light on one terminal → Check for open CKT 467, injector 1, or CKT 468, injector 2. → CKT 467 or 468 OK → Faulty ECM connector or ECM. → Repair wire and replace injector fuse.

Light off both terminals → • Probe each connector terminal with a test lite to 12 volts. → Light on / Light off

Light on → Check for short to ground in circuit that lights. → Short to ground → Repair wire and replace injector fuse.

Light off → No short to ground either terminal. → Replace ECM and injector fuse.

783

- Ignition on 10 seconds.
- Note fuel pressure within 10 seconds after ignition on. Should be 9-13 PSI

| Not OK | OK |

See Chart 5.

- Ignition "on".
- Back probe ECM connector Pin 2 HEI ref. CKT 430 with voltmeter J-29125A.
- Note voltage while cranking engine.

| Reads steady battery voltage. | Less than 1 volt. | 1 to 2 volts and varying |

Faulty HEI module.

Check CKT 430 for open or short to ground.

CKT 430 OK

Faulty ECM connector or ECM.

Check:
— Faulty HEI connector.
— Open HEI distributor battery connector or wire.
— Faulty HEI module connector or module.

- Check 3 AMP injector fuse

| Fuse OK | Fuse not OK |

Repair open wire CKT 481, inj. #1, CKT 482, inj. #2 or ignition CKT 39.

Check for intermittent short to ground in the indicated injector circuit.

*May require spark plug cleaning to start engine.

**EFI fuel system under pressure. To avoid fuel spillage, refer to field service procedure for testing or making repairs requiring the disassembly of fuel line or fittings.

SCHEMATIC CHARTS
4A and 5A (5.0L and 5.7L)

Chart 5

2.5 ℓ Fuel System Diagnosis
Schematic See Page 33

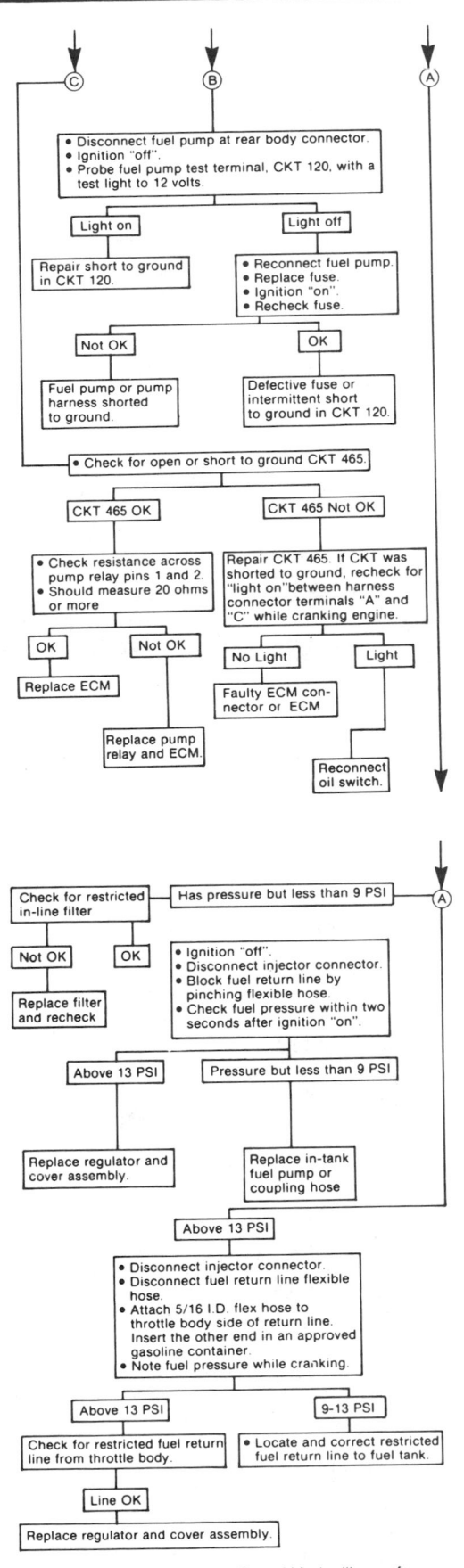

- Disconnect fuel pump at rear body connector.
- Ignition "off".
- Probe fuel pump test terminal, CKT 120, with a test light to 12 volts.

Light on	Light off

Light on:
Repair short to ground in CKT 120.

Not OK

Fuel pump or pump harness shorted to ground.

Light off:
- Reconnect fuel pump.
- Replace fuse.
- Ignition "on".
- Recheck fuse.

OK

Defective fuse or intermittent short to ground in CKT 120.

- Check for open or short to ground CKT 465.

CKT 465 OK	CKT 465 Not OK

CKT 465 OK:
- Check resistance across pump relay pins 1 and 2.
- Should measure 20 ohms or more

OK	Not OK

Replace ECM

Replace pump relay and ECM.

CKT 465 Not OK:
Repair CKT 465. If CKT was shorted to ground, recheck for "light on" between harness connector terminals "A" and "C" while cranking engine.

No Light	Light

Faulty ECM connector or ECM

Reconnect oil switch.

Check for restricted in-line filter | Has pressure but less than 9 PSI

Not OK	OK

Replace filter and recheck

- Ignition "off".
- Disconnect injector connector.
- Block fuel return line by pinching flexible hose.
- Check fuel pressure within two seconds after ignition "on".

Above 13 PSI	Pressure but less than 9 PSI

Replace regulator and cover assembly.

Replace in-tank fuel pump or coupling hose

Above 13 PSI

- Disconnect injector connector.
- Disconnect fuel return line flexible hose.
- Attach 5/16 I.D. flex hose to throttle body side of return line. Insert the other end in an approved gasoline container.
- Note fuel pressure while cranking.

Above 13 PSI	9-13 PSI

Check for restricted fuel return line from throttle body.

- Locate and correct restricted fuel return line to fuel tank.

Line OK

Replace regulator and cover assembly.

*EFI fuel system under pressure. To avoid fuel spillage, refer to field service procedure for testing or making repairs requiring the disassembly of fuel line or fittings.

Chart 5A

Fuel System Diagnosis 5.0ℓ - 5.7ℓ

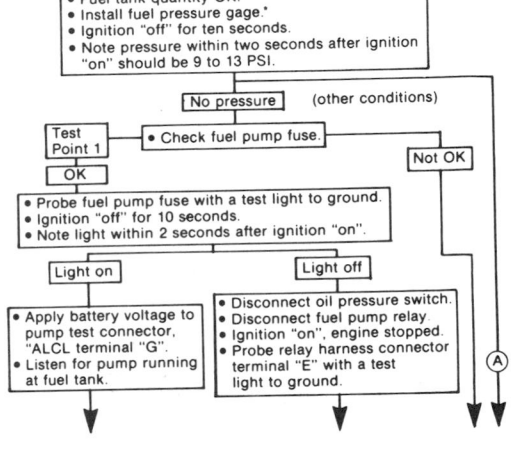

- Fuel tank quantity OK.
- Install fuel pressure gage.*
- Ignition "off" for ten seconds.
- Note pressure within two seconds after ignition "on" should be 9 to 13 PSI.

No pressure	(other conditions)

Test Point 1
- Check fuel pump fuse.

OK		Not OK

- Probe fuel pump fuse with a test light to ground.
- Ignition "off" for 10 seconds.
- Note light within 2 seconds after ignition "on".

Light on	Light off

Light on:
- Apply battery voltage to pump test connector, "ALCL terminal "G".
- Listen for pump running at fuel tank.

Light off:
- Disconnect oil pressure switch.
- Disconnect fuel pump relay.
- Ignition "on", engine stopped.
- Probe relay harness connector terminal "E" with a test light to ground.

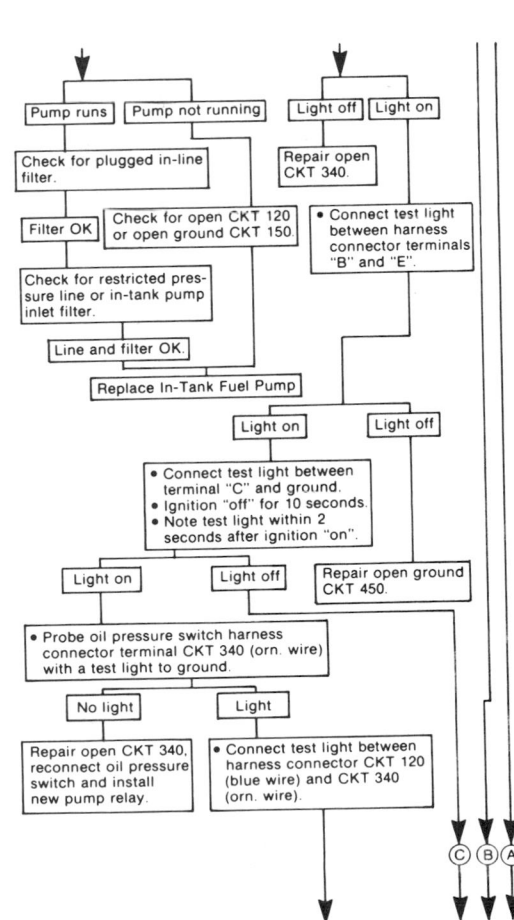

Pump runs	Pump not running	Light off	Light on

Pump runs:
Check for plugged in-line filter.

Filter OK	Check for open CKT 120 or open ground CKT 150.

Check for restricted pressure line or in-tank pump inlet filter.

Line and filter OK.

Replace In-Tank Fuel Pump

Light off / Light on (right branch):
Repair open CKT 340.

- Connect test light between harness connector terminals "B" and "E".

Light on	Light off

- Connect test light between terminal "C" and ground.
- Ignition "off" for 10 seconds.
- Note test light within 2 seconds after ignition "on".

Light on	Light off	Repair open ground CKT 450.

- Probe oil pressure switch harness connector terminal CKT 340 (orn. wire) with a test light to ground.

No light	Light

Repair open CKT 340, reconnect oil pressure switch and install new pump relay.

- Connect test light between harness connector CKT 120 (blue wire) and CKT 340 (orn. wire).

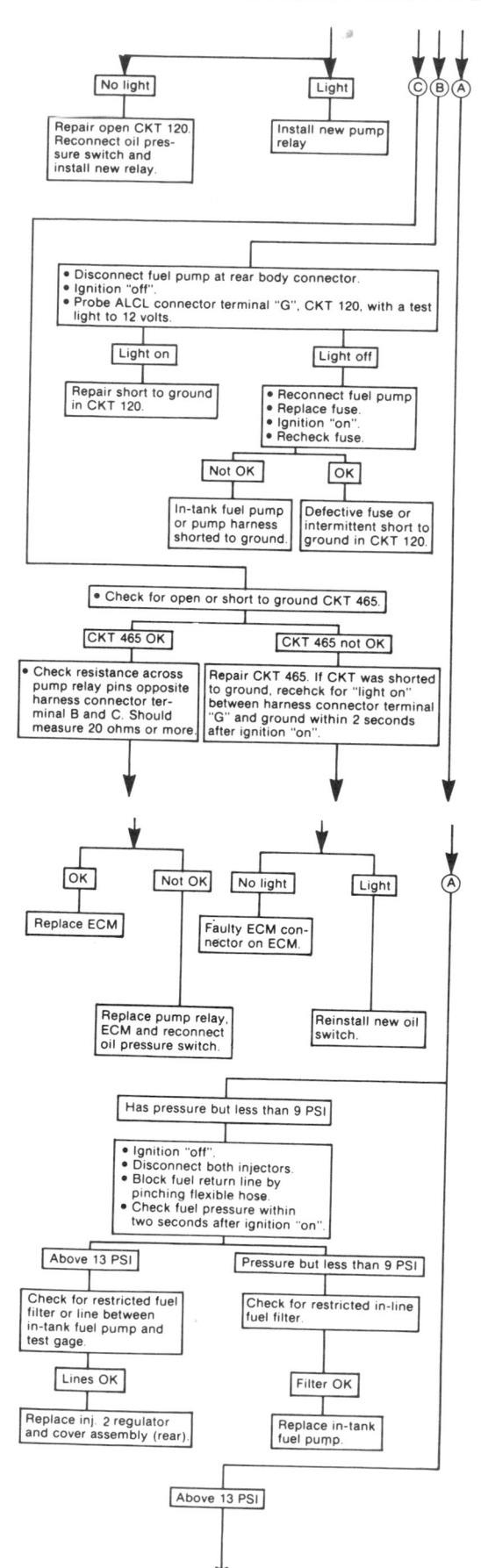

No light → Repair open CKT 120. Reconnect oil pressure switch and install new relay.

Light → Install new pump relay.

© B A

- Disconnect fuel pump at rear body connector.
- Ignition "off".
- Probe ALCL connector terminal "G", CKT 120, with a test light to 12 volts.

Light on → Repair short to ground in CKT 120.

Light off →
- Reconnect fuel pump.
- Replace fuse.
- Ignition "on".
- Recheck fuse.

Not OK → In-tank fuel pump or pump harness shorted to ground.

OK → Defective fuse or intermittent short to ground in CKT 120.

- Check for open or short to ground CKT 465.

CKT 465 OK →
- Check resistance across pump relay pins opposite harness connector terminal B and C. Should measure 20 ohms or more.

CKT 465 not OK → Repair CKT 465. If CKT was shorted to ground, recehck for "light on" between harness connector terminal "G" and ground within 2 seconds after ignition "on".

OK → Replace ECM

Not OK → Faulty ECM connector on ECM.

No light

Light → (A)

Replace pump relay, ECM and reconnect oil pressure switch.

Reinstall new oil switch.

Has pressure but less than 9 PSI

- Ignition "off".
- Disconnect both injectors.
- Block fuel return line by pinching flexible hose.
- Check fuel pressure within two seconds after ignition "on".

Above 13 PSI →
Check for restricted fuel filter or line between in-tank fuel pump and test gage.

Lines OK → Replace inj. 2 regulator and cover assembly (rear).

Pressure but less than 9 PSI →
Check for restricted in-line fuel filter.

Filter OK → Replace in-tank fuel pump.

Above 13 PSI

- Disconnect injector connector.
- Disconnect fuel return line flexible hose.
- Attach 5/16 I.D. flex hose to throttle body side of return line. Insert the other end in an approved gasoline container.
- Note fuel pressure within 2 seconds after ignition "on".

Above 13 PSI → Check for restricted fuel return line from throttle body.

9-13 PSI → Locate and correct restricted fuel return line to fuel tank.

Line OK → Replace inj. 2 regulator and cover assembly (rear).

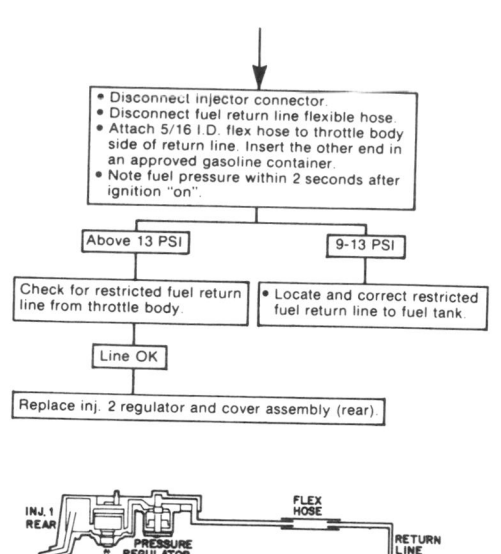

*EFI fuel system under pressure. To avoid fuel spillage, refer to field service procedure for testing or making repairs requiring the disassembly of fuel line or fittings.

Chart 6

HEI Distributor

(With Integral Ignition Coil)

NOTE: If a tachometer is connected to the tachometer terminal, disconnect it before proceeding with the test.

1. No spark.

2. Check voltage at distributor "bat." terminal while cranking.

7 volts or more → 3. With ignition "on" check "tach" terminal voltage.

Under 7 volts → Repair primary circuit to ignition switch.

Under 1 volt → It is faulty ign. coil connection or coil.

10 volts or more

1 to 10 volts → Replace module and check for spark from coil as in Step 6.

4. Check for spark at coil output terminal with ST-125 while cranking

Spark →
- Check color match of pick-up coil connector and ign. coil lead.
- Inspect cap for water, cracks, etc. If OK, replace rotor.

No spark

Spark

No spark

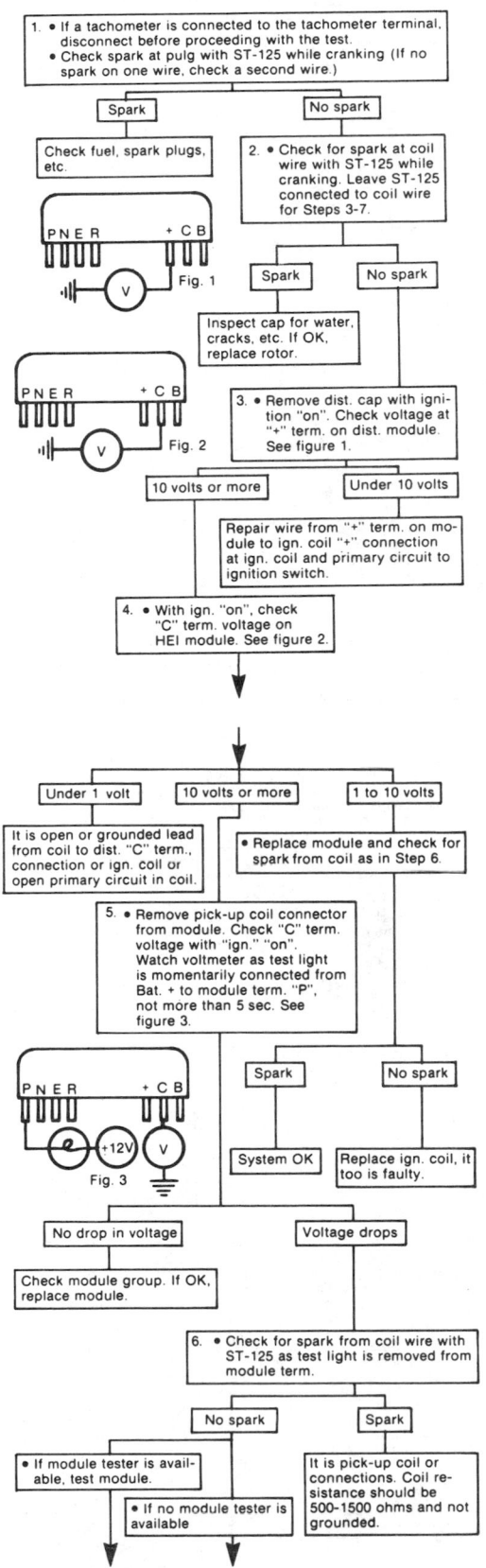

Chart 6A

HEI Distributor

(With Remote Coil)

5. Remove pick-up coil leads from module. Check tach. term. voltage with "ign." "on". Watch voltmeter as test light is momentarily connected from bat. + to module term. P. (View B) not more than 5 seconds.

System OK

Replace ign. coil. It too is faulty.

REMOVE GREEN AND WHITE LEADS FROM MODULE

(TO BAT +)

No drop in voltage

Voltage drops

CONNECT VOLTMETER "TACH" TERMINAL TO GROUND

Check module grnd. and for open in wires from cap to distributor. If OK, replace mod.

6. Check for spark from coil with ST-125 as test light is removed from module terminal.

No spark

Spark

If module tester is available, test mod.

If no module tester is available.

It is pick-up coil or connec- tions. Coil re- sistance should be 500-1500 ohms and not grounded.

OK

Bad

7. Check ign. coil ground circuit. If OK, replace ign. coil and repeat Step 6.

Replace mod.

Check ign. coil ground. If OK, replace ign. coil.

Spark

No spark

System OK

Coil removed is OK, reinstall original coil and replace module.

1. • If a tachometer is connected to the tachometer terminal, disconnect before proceeding with the test.
   • Check spark at pulg with ST-125 while cranking (If no spark on one wire, check a second wire.)

Spark

No spark

Check fuel, spark plugs, etc.

2. • Check for spark at coil wire with ST-125 while cranking. Leave ST-125 connected to coil wire for Steps 3-7.

P N E R   + C B

V   Fig. 1

Spark

No spark

Inspect cap for water, cracks, etc. If OK, replace rotor.

P N E R   + C B

V   Fig. 2

3. • Remove dist. cap with igni- tion "on". Check voltage at "+" term. on dist. module. See figure 1.

10 volts or more

Under 10 volts

Repair wire from "+" term. on mo- dule to ign. coil "+" connection at ign. coil and primary circuit to ignition switch.

4. • With ign. "on", check "C" term. voltage on HEI module. See figure 2.

Under 1 volt

10 volts or more

1 to 10 volts

It is open or grounded lead from coil to dist. "C" term., connection or ign. coil or open primary circuit in coil.

• Replace module and check for spark from coil as in Step 6.

5. • Remove pick-up coil connector from module. Check "C" term. voltage with "ign." "on". Watch voltmeter as test light is momentarily connected from Bat. + to module term. "P", not more than 5 sec. See figure 3.

P N E R   + C B

+12V   V

Fig. 3

Spark

No spark

System OK

Replace ign. coil, it too is faulty.

No drop in voltage

Voltage drops

Check module group. If OK, replace module.

6. • Check for spark from coil wire with ST-125 as test light is removed from module term.

No spark

Spark

• If module tester is avail- able, test module.

• If no module tester is available

It is pick-up coil or connections. Coil re- sistance should be 500-1500 ohms and not grounded.

OK | Bad

• Replace HEI module and repeat Step 6.

Replace mod.

Check coil wire from cap to coil. If OK, replace coil.

Spark | No spark

System OK

Module removed is OK, reinstall module. Check coil wire from cap to coil. If OK, replace coil.

Chart 8

EGR Check 5.0 ℓ and 5.7 ℓ

Make physical inspection of hoses and electrical connections.

• Install tachometer.
• Engine at normal operating temperature.
• Start engine; do not ground "test" term.
• With engine idling, RPM should drop as EGR valve is opened by pushing up on underside of EGR diaphragm.

No change | RPM drops

Clean EGR passages or replace valve as needed.

• Check for movement of EGR diaphragm as RPM is increased to 1200 RPM and returned to idle.

No movement | Movement

• Connect vac. gage in place of EGR valve and check vac. at 1200 RPM.

System OK. No trouble found.

Over 3" | Under 3"

Replace EGR valve.

Check vac. at engine side of EGR sol. at 1200 RPM.

Under 3" | Over 3"

Repair hose or connections.

• Check EGR sol. elec. circuit as follows:

Chart 7

(No Stored Code)

These conditions, related to EFI, are in addition to those listed under "Engine Performance Diagnosis" at the front of Section 6 of Chassis Repair Manual.

Poor Performance

Hesitates, sluggish, sags, or poor mileage. | Cuts out or stalls | Surge | Hard starting hot or cold

Check:
— Intermittent open or short to ground in circuits:
  • 416, 5 Volt reference.
  • 430, HEI reference.
  • 120, Fuel pump Circuit.
  • 467 & 468, Injector drive circuit.
  • 441, 442, 443 or 444 IAC drive CKTS.
— Restricted fuel filter.
— Fuel pressure; should be 9-13 PSI all speed ranges.

Check:
— MAP Hose; visually for leaks or restriction.
— TPS Sensor; visually for sticking or binding.
— Fuel pressure; should be 9-13 PSI all speed ranges.
— Base Timing; see Field Service Adjustments.
— TBI Injector(s); with injector harness connector disconnected, check for fuel leakage while cranking.
— TBI Balance Adjustment on 5.0 ℓ and 5.7 ℓ. See Field Adjustments.
— Fan Control Circuit, Chart 8A, 2.5 ℓ A/cond. only.
— A/Cond. Compressor Control; see Chart 9.
— TCC Chart 8D
— Check for open HEI Ground CKT 453

Check:
— Intermittent open or short to ground in circuits:
  • 420 & 422 Trans. Convertor Clutch.
  • 424, HEI Bypass
  • 423, EST
— EGR Chart 8, 5.0 ℓ and 5.7 ℓ.

— Crank CKT Chart 9B.
— High resistance in coolant sensor circuit.
— Fuel Pump Relay. Disconnect oil pressure switch. If engine cranks but won't start, see Chart 5.
— TBI Injector(s); with injector harness connector(s) disconnected, check for fuel leakage while cranking.
— TPS Sensor; visually check for sticking or binding.
— Fuel pressure should be 9-13 PSI all speed ranges. Fuel pressure leak down should be gradual after ignition "OFF" on 2.5 ℓ. An instant drop in pressure indicates a leaking in tank pump coupling hose or check valve.

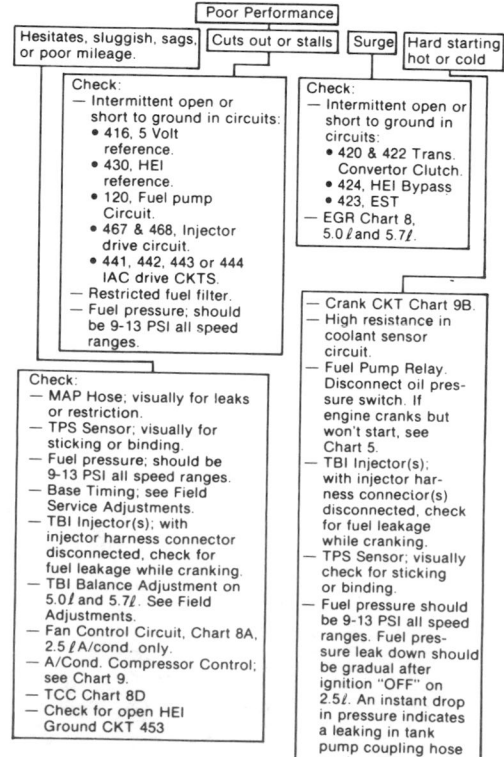

Manifold Vacuum

EGR Solenoid

Black Connector

435 — 22

EGR Signal

ECM

To EGR

Ign 1

• Ignition "on", engine stopped.
• Disconnect sol. and connect test light across harness connector terminals and note light.

On | Off

Check for grounded wire from sol. to ECM. If not grounded, replace ECM.

• Ground diagnostic terminal and note light.

Off | On

• Connect test light from each harness connector terminal to ground and note light.

Faulty EGR sol. connector or sol.

Light on one Terminal | Light on both Terminals | No light

Check for open in wire from sol. to ECM. If not open, check resistance of sol. If under 20 ohms, replace sol. and ECM. If sol. OK, replace ECM.

Repair short between bat + and wire from sol. to ECM and recheck. ECM may be damaged.

Repair open circuit between sol. and ignition switch.

FUEL INJECTION 7
SYSTEMS

Chart 8A

Coolant Fan Control Circuit

2.5ℓ With Air Conditioning

- Disconnect cooling fan temperature switch.
- Engine idling.
- Turn A/cond. "on" and "off".
- Note cooling fan.

| Turns "on" and "off" | Fan does not turn "on" and "off" |

Turns "on" and "off":
- Raise drive wheels.
- Idle engine with transmission in "Drive".
- A/cond. "on".
- Probe temp. switch harness connector with a test light to 12 volts.
- Increase wheel speed to 35 MPH and note light.

Fan does not turn "on" and "off":
- Disconnect fan control relay.
- Engine idling.
- A/conditioning "on".
- Probe fan temp. switch harness connector with a test light to 12 volts.

| Light goes out | Light remains "on" |

| Light off | Light on |

Light goes out:
ECM fan control circuit OK, no trouble found.

Light remains "on":
- Ignition "on", engine stopped.
- Back probe white ECM connector terminal 2, CKT 437, with a voltmeter to ground.
- Manually rotate drive wheel and note voltage. Be sure opposite wheel does not turn.

Light on:
Check for faulty A/cond. mode switch or open CKT 409 to ECM.

A/cond. switch and CKT 409 OK.

Faulty ECM connector or ECM.

- A/cond. "off".
- Reconnect fan relay.
- Probe fan temp. switch harness connector with a test light to ground.

| Light off | Light on |

No Voltage Variation

Voltage varies from under 3 to over 9 volts. Faulty ECM.

See Code 24

See fan control relay diagnostics.

Check for short to ground in CKT 409 to fan relay.

CKT 409 OK

ECM fan control CKT OK. No trouble found.

Chart 8B

Air Management Check 5.0ℓ 5.7ℓ

With Electric Divert And Electric

Switching Valve (ED/ES)

Check vacuum hose condition and connection. Repair as necessary. On some applications, some air may divert above 2000 RPM.

- "Test" term. ungrounded.
- Start engine, running at part throttle, below 2000 RPM, air should be felt at outlet to exhaust ports during Open Loop operation (from 6 seconds to 3 minutes on warm engine depending on application) and switch to converter when system goes Closed Loop.

| OK | Constant Air Divert | Constant Converter Air | Constant Port Air |

Constant Air Divert:
- Check air control valve Ckt. 429 as follows:

Constant Converter Air:
- Check air switching valve Ckt. 436 as follows:

- Disconnect HEI bypass.
- Air should divert as soon as "check engine" lite comes on.

| OK | No Divert |

OK: No trouble found. Clear memory.

No Divert:
- Ign. "on", engine stopped.
- Disconnect Air Control solenoid electrical connector and connect test lite between harness connector term. Note lite.

- Ign. "on", engine stopped.
- Ground "test" term.
- Disconnect applicable sol. electrical connector and connect test light between harness conn. term and note lite.

| On | Off |

Off: Connect test lite from both wire term. to ground.

| On | Off |

On: Check for short to groun Ckt. 429.

Off: Replace air control valve.

CKT. 429 OK

With engine idling, check for at least 10" of vac. at valve. If OK, it is faulty valve conn. or valve.

Check resistance between solenoid terms. Should be more than 20 ohms.

- Ign. "on", engine stopped.
- "Test" term. not grounded.
- Disconnect air switching valve sol electrical conn. and connect test lite between harness conn. term. and note lite.

| Not OK | OK |

Not OK: Replace control solenoid and ECM.

OK: Faulty ECM.

| No lite | Lite on both term. | Lite on one term. |

| On | Off |

No lite: Repair open in Ckt. 39 to ign. switch.

Lite on both term.: Repair short to 12 volts in Ckt. to ECM. Recheck.

Lite on one term.: Check for open in wire from applicable sol. to ECM term. 16 for air control or term. 14 for air switching. If not open, check resistance of applicable sol. If under 20 ohms, replace sol. and ECM. If not, it is faulty ECM connection or ECM.

789

Chart 8C

Canister Purge Valve

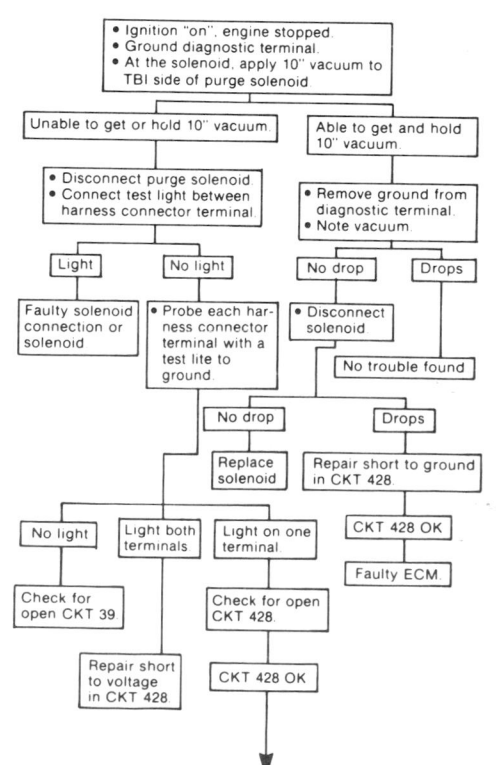

Chart 8D

Torque Converter Clutch (TCC)

Electrical Diagnosis

Mechanical checks such as linkage, oil level, etc., should be performed prior to using this chart.

OK

Replace Hood Louvre
Solenoid

Chart 9

Air Conditioning Control 2.5 ℓ

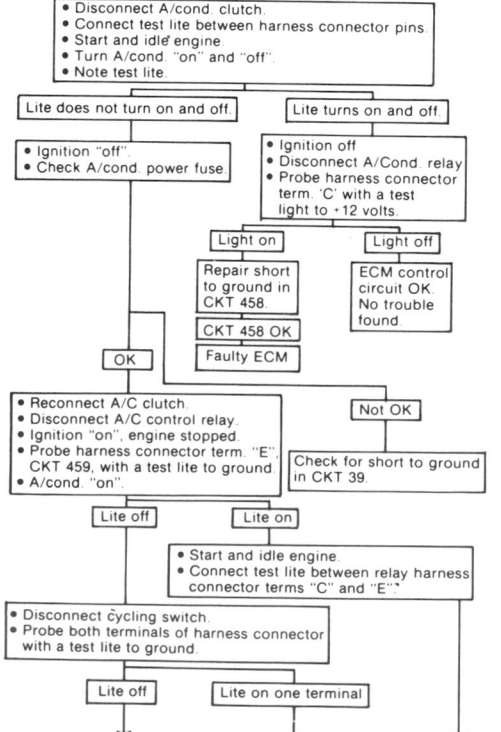

- Disconnect A/cond. clutch.
- Connect test lite between harness connector pins.
- Start and idle engine.
- Turn A/cond. "on" and "off".
- Note test lite.

Lite does not turn on and off.

Lite turns on and off.

- Ignition "off".
- Check A/cond. power fuse.

- Ignition off.
- Disconnect A/Cond. relay.
- Probe harness connector term. 'C' with a test light to +12 volts.

Light on

Light off

Repair short to ground in CKT 458.

ECM control circuit OK. No trouble found.

CKT 458 OK

Faulty ECM

OK

- Reconnect A/C clutch.
- Disconnect A/C control relay.
- Ignition "on", engine stopped.
- Probe harness connector term. "E", CKT 459, with a test lite to ground.
- A/cond. "on".

Not OK

Check for short to ground in CKT 39.

Lite off

Lite on

- Start and idle engine.
- Connect test lite between relay harness connector terms "C" and "E".

- Disconnect cycling switch.
- Probe both terminals of harness connector with a test lite to ground.

Lite off

Lite on one terminal

Check for open wire from A/C mode to cycling switch.

Wire OK

Check battery feed to A/cond. mode switch.

OK

Faulty A/C mode switch

No lite

- Reconnect cycling switch.
- Disconnect power steering pressure switch.
- Probe both terminals of harness connector with a test lite to ground.

Lite on one terminal

Check for open wire between A/C cycling and power steering switch.

Wire OK

Replace cycling switch.

Check for open wire between power steering switch and A/C control relay term "B".

Wire OK

Replace power steering pressure switch.

Lite off

Lite on

- Connect test lite between relay connector terms. "A" and "C".

- Ignition "on", engine stopped.
- Back probe ECM white connector term. 21, CKT 459, with a test lite to ground.
- A/cond. mode switch "on".

Lite off

Lite on

Repair open CKT 459.

Repair open or short to ground in CKT 458.

CKT 458 OK.

- Connect jumper wire between harness connector terms. "B" and "E".
- Note A/C clutch.

- Check resistance across A/C control relay pins "1" and "3". Shoud measure 20 ohms or more.

OK

Not OK

Replace A/cond. control relay and ECM.

Faulty ECM connector or ECM.

Lite off

Lite on

Repair CKt 39.

Not OK

OK

Repair open CKT 59

Faulty A/Cond control relay

Chart 9A

Park/Neutral Switch

2.5ℓ and 5.0ℓ

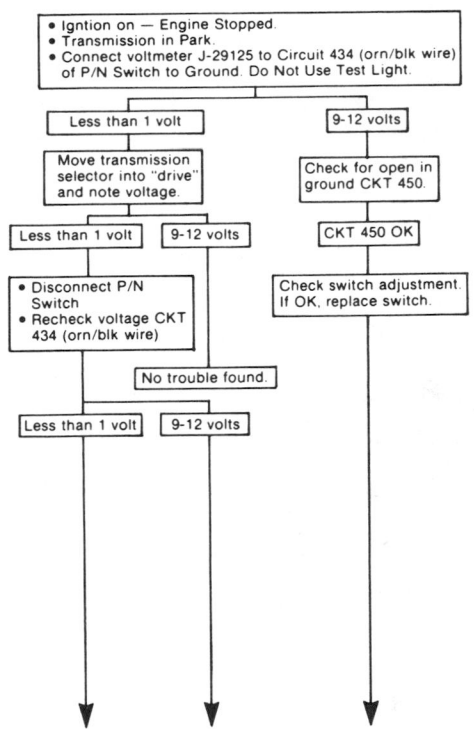

- Ignition on — Engine Stopped.
- Transmission in Park.
- Connect voltmeter J-29125 to Circuit 434 (orn/blk wire) of P/N Switch to Ground. Do Not Use Test Light.

| Less than 1 volt | 9-12 volts |

Less than 1 volt → Move transmission selector into "drive" and note voltage.

9-12 volts → Check for open in ground CKT 450.

| Less than 1 volt | 9-12 volts | CKT 450 OK |

- Disconnect P/N Switch
- Recheck voltage CKT 434 (orn/blk wire)

Check switch adjustment. If OK, replace switch.

| Less than 1 volt | 9-12 volts | No trouble found. |

Check for open CKT 434.

CKT 434 OK

Faulty ECM connector on ECM

Check adjustment. If OK, replace switch.

Chart 9B

Crank Signal

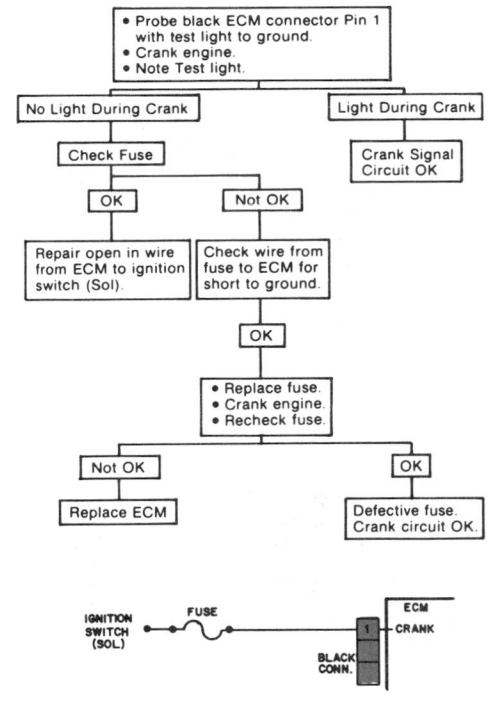

- Probe black ECM connector Pin 1 with test light to ground.
- Crank engine.
- Note Test light.

| No Light During Crank | Light During Crank |

No Light During Crank → Check Fuse

Light During Crank → Crank Signal Circuit OK

| OK | Not OK |

OK → Repair open in wire from ECM to ignition switch (Sol).

Not OK → Check wire from fuse to ECM for short to ground.

OK

- Replace fuse.
- Crank engine.
- Recheck fuse.

| Not OK | OK |

Not OK → Replace ECM

OK → Defective fuse. Crank circuit OK.

Chart 9C

Park/Neutral Relay

1982 Corvette

Be sure park/neutral switch is OK and properly adjusted before using chart.

- Ignition on. Engine stopped.
- Trans. selector in park or neutral.
- Using voltmeter J-29125 or equivalent, back brobe white ECM connector between CKTS 434, Term. 5, CKT 450, Term. 12.
- Voltage should be less than 1 volt in both park and neutral positions.

| OK | Not OK |

Not OK →
- Disconnect park/neutral relay.
- Check voltage at harness connector. Ign. 1. CKT (PPL wire), should be 9-12 volts.

OK →
- Place trans. selector in "drive".
- Voltmeter should read battery voltage.

| Reads battery voltage | Does not read battery voltage |

Reads battery voltage → No trouble found

Does not read battery voltage → Not OK / OK

Not OK → Repair open Ign. 1 CKT.

- Disconnect park/neutral relay
- Check voltage between harness connector CKT 434, (Orn/Blk) and DKT 450, (Blk/Wht).

- Check voltage between harness connector ign. 1 CKT (PPL) and CKT 450, (Blk/Wht). Should be 9-12 volts.

| Reads Battery Voltage | Does not read battery voltage |

Reads Battery Voltage → Faulty P/N relay.

Does not read battery voltage → Check CKT 434 for short to ground.

| CKT 434 OK | Not OK | OK |

Repair open CKT 450.

Faulty ECM connector or ECM.

• Check voltage between harness connector CKT 450 (Blk/Wht) and CKT 434 (orn/blk). Should be 9-12 volts.

| Not OK | OK |

Check for open CKT 434 to ECM

Faulty park/neutral relay or connector

CKT 434 OK

Faulty ECM connector or ECM

| Open CKT 486 | | Most likely a faulty ESC controller, but could be knock sensor. |

Repair and recheck | CKT 486 OK

• Disconnect knock sensor and check resistance of sensor. Should be 175 to 375 ohms.

| Below 2 volts | Over 2 volts |

| Not OK | OK |

Replace ECM

Replace knock sensor.

Check and repair CKT 485 if shorted to 12 volts.

Repair faulty connector, open or short to ground in sensor signal CKT 496.

Clear codes and confirm "Closed Loop" operation and no "Check Engine" light. (Perform Diagnostic Circuit Check)

Chart 10

Electronic Spark Control (ESC)

System Check

Engine Knock — No Code 43

This chart should only be used after all other causes of Spark Knock have been checked, i.e., Base Timing, EGR, Engine Temperature, or Excessive Engine Noise.

• Diagnostic terminal not grounded.
• Connect tachometer.
• Engine running at steady part throttle (1200 to 1500 RPM).
• Transmission in park or neutral and engine at normal operating temperature.
• Tap Engine Block in area of knock sensor and check for RPM drop.

| RPM drop | No RPM drop |

System OK

• Disconnect ESC.
• Check for RPM change.

| RPM drops | No RPM change |

• Ignition off.
• Using J-29125 meter, check resistance between ESC harness connector pins B and K, CKTS 496 and 486. Should be 175 to 375 ohms.

| Not OK | OK |

Faulty ESC connector or ESC Controller.

Note "Check Engine" light.

| Off | On |

Check for open in ESC grd. CKT 486, ESC connector Pin K.

• Ignition "on" engine stopped.
• Check voltage between ESC harness connector Pins J and K, CKTS 485 and 486.

Chart 11

Idle Air Control

• Connect tachometer.
• Idle engine at normal operating termperature and record RPM in park or neutral.

• Ignition "off".
• Disconnect IAC motor. Rear IAC motor on 5.0ℓ and 5.7ℓ.
• Start engine, note idle RPM in neutral.

| Idle RPM, no increase | Idle RPM increase |

• Ignition "off".
• Reconnect IAC.
• Start engine and note RPM in neutral.

Will not return to idle RPM recorded above.

Return to idle RPM noted above.

• 5.0ℓ and 5.7ℓ; return to beginning of chart and repeat test with front IAC motor.

• Ignition "OFF".
• Jumper fuel pump test terminal to 12 volts.
• Ignition "on", engine stopped.
• Ground diagnostic test terminal.
• Disconnect IAC. Disconnect both front and rear IAC motors on 5.0ℓ and 5.7ℓ.
• Connect a test light between each harness connector terminal and ground.

Idle air control OK

No light, one or more circuits.

Repair open or short to ground in circuits with no light.

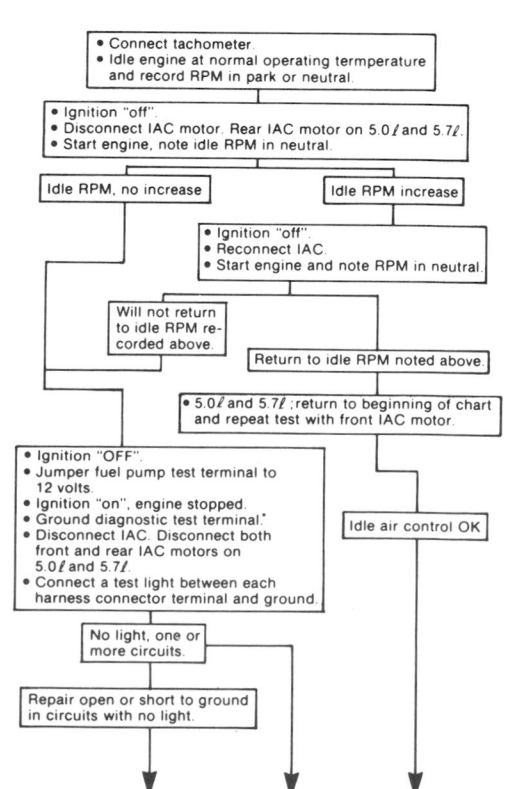

Chart 14

Coolant Sensor Circuit
(Signal Voltage Low)

If the "Engine Hot" light is "on", check for overheating condition before making following test:

- Engine stopped, ignition "off".
- Diagnostic terminal ungrounded.
- Disconnect coolant sensor.
- Jumper harness connector signal CKT 410 to CKT 452.
- Start engine and idle at normal operating temperature for 1 minute or until "Check Engine" light comes on.
- While engine is idling, remove jumper from harness connector and run engine for 1 more minute.
- Stop engine, enter diagnostics and note code(s).

| Code 14 only | Both Codes 14 and 15 |

Disconnect black ECM Connector. Check signal CKT 410 for short to CKT 452 or chassis ground.

Replace coolant sensor.

CKT 410 OK.

Replace ECM.

Clear codes and confirm "Closed Loop" operation and no "Check Engine" light. (Perform Diagnostic Circuit Check)

All circuits OK.

CHECK:
— TBI idle air rate balance, 5.0ℓ & 57ℓ
— Vacuum leaks.
— Sticking or binding throttle shaft or accelerator linkage.
— Base idle air rate.
— Park/Neutral Switch, Chart 9A.
— A/Cond. Clutch Signal, Chart 9.
— EGR Chart 8, 5.0ℓ and 5.7ℓ
— Leaking injector(s)

- Check voltage at white ECM connector term. 17. Should be about 8 volts.

| OK | Not OK |

Faulty ECM connector or ECM

Repair open CKT 120

Light flashes all circuits.

| Two circuits On/Off and Two circuits Dim/Bright. | Three circuits Dim/Bright, one circuit On/Off or Three circuits On/Off, one circuit Dim/Bright. |

Replace IAC

Faulty ECM.

*"F" and "Y" ALCL connector terminal "G" "A" and "X" engine compartment left side.

Clear codes and confirm "Closed Loop" operation and no "Check Engine" light. (Perform Diagnostic Circuit Check)

Chart 13

Oxygen Sensor Circuit

- Ignition "off".
- Diagnostic terminal grounded.
- Disconnect oxygen sensor and jumper harness connector CKT 412 to ground.
- Start engine and note "Check Engine" light.

| "Check Engine" light went "off" for at least 15 sec. | "Check Engine" light flashing *Open Loop. |

Faulty oxygen sensor connector or sensor.

Check for open oxygen sensor CKT 412.

Signal CKT 412 OK.

Faulty ECM connector or ECM.

Field Service Mode:
- Engine running — diagnostic terminal grounded.
  — Open Loop; "Check Engine" light flashes at the rate of 2 times per second.
  — Closed Loop; "Check Engine" light flashes at a rate of 1 time per second.

Clear codes and confirm "Closed Loop" operation and no "Check Engine" light. (Perform Diagnostic Circuit Check)

Chart 15

Coolant Sensor Circuit
(Signal Voltage High)

- Engine at normal operating temperature.
- Disconnect coolant sensor.
- Ignition "on", engine stopped.
- Check voltage between harness connector terminals, CKT's 410 and 452.

| Over 4 volts | Below 4 volts |

*Check resistance across coolant sensor terminals. Should be less than 1000 ohms.

Check for open in CKT's 410 or 452.

CKT's 410 and 452 OK.

Faulty ECM connector or ECM.

| OK | Not OK |

Intermittent fault in sensor connector or circuit. If additional codes were stored, return to "Diagnostic Circuit Check."

Replace sensor.

*Sensor check may require use of wire and connector assembly. Part No. 12026621.

Clear codes and confirm "Closed Loop" operation and no "Check Engine" light. (Perform Diagnostic Circuit Check)

Code 21

Throttle Position Sensor

- Diagnostic terminal not grounded.
- Clear codes.
- Disconnect TPS.
- Start engine idle for 1 minute or until "Check Engine" light comes on.
- Ignition "on", engine stopped.
- Ground diagnostic terminal and note code.

Code 22	Code 21
Probe TPS harness connector CKT 452 with test light to 12 volts.	Disconnect black ECM connector and probe harness connector Pin 5 with a test light to ground.

Code 22 branch:
- Light → Replace TPS Sensor.
- No light → Repair open CKT 452.

Code 21 branch:
- No light → Replace ECM.
- Light → Repair short to voltage in signal CKT 417.

Clear codes and confirm "Closed Loop" operation and no "Check Engine" light. (Perform Diagnostic Circuit Check)

Code 22

Throttle Position Sensor (Signal Voltage Low)

- Diagnostic terminal not grounded.
- Clear codes.
- Disconnect TPS and jumper CKTS 416 and 417.
- Start engine and idle for 1 minute or until "Check Engine" light comes on.
- Ignition on. Engine stopped. Ground diagnostic terminal and note code.

Code 21 branch:
- Check TPS adjustment
- Adjustment OK → Replace TPS

Code 22 branch:
- Remove jumper from CKT's 416 and 417.
- Check voltage between harness connector Pins A and C using voltmeter J-29125.

4-6 volts → Check for open or short to ground in signal CKT 417. → CKT 417 OK. Faulty ECM connector or ECM.

Below 4 volts → Disconnect white ECM connector. Check for open or short to ground in CKT 416. → CKT 416 OK. Faulty ECM connector or ECM.

Clear codes and confirm "Closed Loop" operation and no "Check Engine" light. (Perform Diagnostic Circuit Check)

Codes 24

Vehicle Speed Sensor (VSS)

NOTICE: A false Code 24 and "Check Engine" light may be set if engine is run above 1200 RPM in neutral on vehicles equipped with manual transmissions. To prevent misdiagnosis, disregard Code 24 if set under these circumstances.

See chart for code indicated.

Faulty ECM connector or ECM.

Clear codes and confirm "Closed Loop" operation and no "Check Engine" light. (Perform Diagnostic Circuit Check)

Code 34

MAP Sensor

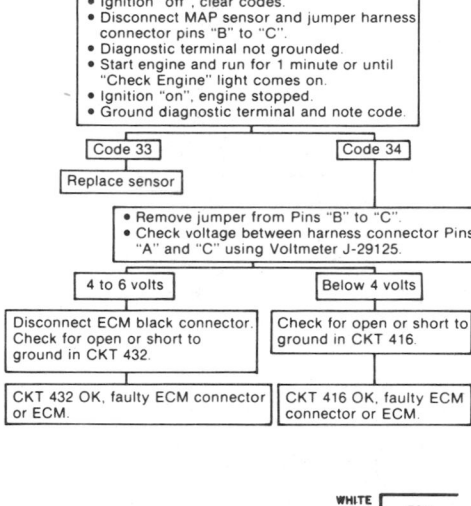

- Ignition "off", clear codes.
- Disconnect MAP sensor and jumper harness connector pins "B" to "C".
- Diagnostic terminal not grounded.
- Start engine and run for 1 minute or until "Check Engine" light comes on.
- Ignition "on", engine stopped.
- Ground diagnostic terminal and note code.

| Code 33 | Code 34 |

Replace sensor

- Remove jumper from Pins "B" to "C".
- Check voltage between harness connector Pins "A" and "C" using Voltmeter J-29125.

| 4 to 6 volts | Below 4 volts |

Disconnect ECM black connector. Check for open or short to ground in CKT 432.

Check for open or short to ground in CKT 416.

CKT 432 OK, faulty ECM connector or ECM.

CKT 416 OK, faulty ECM connector or ECM.

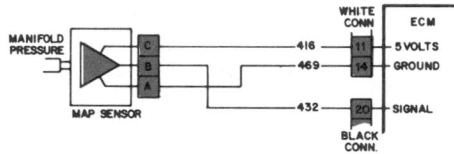

Clear codes and confirm "Closed Loop" operation and no "Check Engine" light. (Perform Diagnostic Circuit Check)

Code 33

MAP Sensor

- Ignition "off", clear codes.
- Disconnect MAP sensor connector.
- Diagnostic terminal not grounded.
- Start engine and run for 1 minute or until "Check Engine" light comes on.
- Ignition "on", engine stopped.
- Ground diagnostic terminal and note code.

| Code 33 |

Check for open in ground CKT 469

CKT 469

Check for short to voltage CKT 432.

CKT 432 OK

Replace ECM

| Code 34 |

Check for plugged or leaking sensor vacuum line.

Vacuum line OK

Replace Sensor

Clear codes and confirm "Closed Loop" operation and no "Check Engine" light. (Perform Diagnostic Circuit Check)

Code 42

Electronic Spark Timing (EST)

- Run engine at 1800 to 2200 RPM and note timing.
- Ground diagnostic terminal and note timing, it should change.

| No Change | Change |

- Disconnect HEI distributor 4-way connector.
- Using two jumpers*, reconnect HEI connector term. "B" to harness connector term. "B" and HEI connector term. "D" to harness connect term. "D".
- Start and idle engine.
- Probe chassis harness connector term. "A", CKT 423, with voltmeter J-29125. Voltage should vary 2.0 to 2.8.

No trouble found. Infrequently a rare set of circumstances during engine crank could result in a "Check Engine" light after engine starts. The light will stay on until ignition "off" for 10 seconds and a normal restart. EST circuits 430 and 423 should be physically checked for proper harness routing, connectors and wiring for intermittent open or short to ground. If OK, no further repair should be made.

| OK | Not OK |

Check for open or short to ground in EST CKT 423.

CKT 423 OK

Faulty ECM connector or ECM.

- Ignition "off", engine stopped.
- Using third jumper, reconnect HEI connector term. "A" to harness connector term. "A".
- With engine idling, probe term. "A", CKT 423, with voltmeter to ground.
- Voltage should be less than 1 volt.

| Not OK | | OK |

Not OK:
Faulty wire or connector to HEI term. "E"

Wire and connector OK.

Replace HEI module.

OK:
- Engine idling.
- Again probe term. "A" with a voltmeter to ground. Note voltage while probing HEI harness connector term. "C", CKT 424, with a test light connected to 12 volts. Voltage should be 1.0 to 2.8.

| Not OK | | OK |

Not OK:
Faulty HEI harness wire or connector to module term. "B". If OK, replace module.

OK:
- Stop engine, ignition off for 10 seconds.
- Using fourth jumper, reconnect HEI harness connector term. "C" to harness connector term. "C".
- Engine idling.
- Check voltage at term. "C"; should be above 2 volts.

| Not OK | | OK |

Not OK:
Check for open or short to ground in CKT 424 to ECM.

CKT 424 OK

Faulty ECM connector or ECM.

OK:
EST OK. No trouble found.

Clear codes and confirm "Closed Loop" operation and no "Check Engine" light. (Perform Diagnostic Circuit Check)

*This test requires the use of four jumpers using terminals 12014836 and 12014837.

Code 43

Electronic Spark Control (ESC)

5.0ℓ and 5.7ℓ

- Engine idling at normal operating temperature
- Using voltmeter J-29125 back probe ECM white connector Pin 4, signal CKT 485.

| Less than 6 volts | Over 6 volts |

Less than 6 volts:
- Ign. "on", engine stopped.
- Recheck voltage at ECM Pin 4.

Over 6 volts:
Faulty ECM connector or ECM.

| Less than 6 volts | Over 6 volts |

Less than 6 volts:
- Ignition "on", engine stopped.
- Disconnect ECM white connector.
- Recheck voltage at harness connector Pin 4, CKT 485.

Over 6 volts:
Disconnect controller. Check and repair sensor shield CKT 454 if open or shorted to grnd.

Shield CKT 454 OK

Most likely a faulty controller but could be knock sensor.

| Over 6 volts | Less than 6 volts |

Over 6 volts:
Replace ECM

Less than 6 volts:
Back probe ESC connector Pin J, CKT 485, with voltmeter to ground.

| Less than 6 volts | Over 6 volts |

Less than 6 volts:
Back probe between ESC connector Pins F, CKT 439 and Pin K, CKT 486.

Over 6 volts:
Repair open in signal CKT 485, between ESC and ECM.

| Above 9 volts | Less than 9 volts |

Above 9 volts:
Check and repair signal CKT 485 if shorted to ground.

CKT 485 OK

Faulty ESC connector or controller.

Less than 9 volts:
Repair open in ignition CKT 439.

Clear codes and confirm "Closed Loop" operation and no "Check Engine" light. (Perform Diagnostic Circuit Check)

Code 44

Lean Exhaust Indication

- Ignition "off".
- Diagnostic terminal grounded
- Disconnect oxygen sensor.
- Start engine and note "Check Engine" light.

| "Check Engine" light went off for at least 15 sec. | "Check Engine" light flashing *Open Loop. |

- Measure voltage at oxygen sensor harness connector CKT 412 using J-29125 volt meter or equivalent.
- Voltage should be .36 to .54 volts.

| Not OK | OK |

Check signal CKT 412 for short to ground.

- Check for ground in wire from connector to sensor.
- Check for intake air leaks including air management.
- Check for imbalance of TBI units on 5.0 *l* and 5.7*l*
- Check EGR, See Service Manual Section 6E or Chart 8 for 5.0L and 5.7L.
- Check fuel pressure. Should be 9-13 PSI.

Check for open oxygen sensor ground CKT 413.

All checks OK

| CKT 412 OK | CKT 413 OK |

Faulty oxygen sensor

Faulty ECM connector or ECM

Field Service Mode:
Engine running — diagnostic terminal grounded.
*— Open Loop; "Check Engine" light flashes at the rate of 2 times per second.
— Closed Loop; "Check Engine" light flashes at a rate of 1 time per second.

Clear codes and confirm "Closed Loop" operation and no "Check Engine" light. (Perform Diagnostic Circuit Check)

Code 45

Rich Exhaust Indication

- Ignition "off".
- Diagnostic terminal grounded.
- Disconnect oxygen sensor and jumper harness connector signal CKT 412 to ground.
- Start engine and note "Check Engine" light.

| "Check Engine" light went off for at least 15 sec. | Steady light |

Check oxygen sensor signal CKT 412 for short to voltage.

CKT 412 OK

Replace ECM

System rich, check:
— Fuel pressure 9-13 PSI.
— Injector(s) for leakage or sticking.
— HEI shield CKT 453 for open circuit.
— Check for leakage or restriction in MAP hose.
— Check CCP Chart 8C.

*Field Service Mode:
Engine running — diagnostic terminal grounded.
— Open Loop; "Check Engine" light flashes at the rate of 2 times per second.
— Closed Loop; "Check Engine" light flashes at a rate of 1 time per second.

Clear codes and confirm "Closed Loop" operation and no "Check Engine" light. (Perform Diagnostic Circuit Check)

Code 51

Check that all pins are fully inserted in the socket. If OK, replace PROM, clear memory, and recheck. If code 51 reappears, replace ECM.

Code 55

Replace Electronic Control Module (ECM)

Clear codes and confirm "Closed Loop" operation and no "Check Engine" light. (Perform Diagnostic Circuit Check)

MAZDA ELECTRONIC GASOLINE INJECTION (EGI) SYSTEM

General Information

The Mazda Electronic Gasoline Injection (EGI) system is a computer controlled, port-type fuel injection system used on 1984 RX-7 models equipped with the 13B rotary engine. Fuel is metered to the engine by two solenoid-type injectors that open and close in response to signals from the elctronic control unit (ECU). By varying the amount of time the injectors remain open, the ECU precisely controls the fuel mixture according to data on engine operating conditions provided by various engine sensors. The EGI fuel injection system can be divided into three main subsystems; the electronic control system, the air induction system and the fuel supply system.

ELECTRONIC CONTROL SYSTEM

The heart of the EGI system is a micro-processor called the electronic control unit (ECU). The ECU receives data from the engine sensors and, based on the information received and the instructions programmed into the ECU memory, generates output signals to control fuel delivery, idle speed and various solenoid valves to control engine emissions and allow the most efficient operation of the three-way catalytic converter by controlling the secondary air supply system and air switching valve to divert air from the air pump to either the air cleaner or catalytic converter. The ECU receives data on engine speed (rpm), engine and coolant temperature, throttle position, manifold vacuum, intake air volume, intake air temperature, atmospheric pressure, and the amount of oxygen in the exhaust gasses. In addition, the ECU is provided with signals for starter operation (cranking), A/C operation and in-gear operation (neutral/clutch switch). The ECU is located under the floor pan on the right (passenger) side of the vehicle.

AIR INDUCTION SYSTEM

The EGI air induction system consists of the air cleaner assembly and ducting, an air flow meter with a sensor flap that measures the amount of intake air entering the system, a throttle chamber and dynamic chamber or air plenum which is attached to the intake manifold. A throttle position sensor is mounted on the throttle valve assembly to provide the ECU with information on the throttle opening angle. A By-Pass Air Control (BAC) valve controls idle speed under various engine conditions and loads by allowing a regulated amount of air to bypass the throttle plates. The BAC valve is controlled by the vent solenoid valve and the vacuum solenoid valve in response to signals from the ECU. The air temperature

Adjusting idle speed

sensor (thermistor) is mounted in the dynamic chamber and provides a signal to the ECU to allow "fine tuning" of the mixture to compensate for air density changes due to temperature. The ECU also uses the air temperature signal to control the BAC valve operation and to shut the vacuum passage between the dynamic chamber and the fuel pressure regulator control valve when the intake air temperature is above 122 degrees F (50 degrees C).

FUEL SUPPLY SYSTEM

The EGI fuel supply system consists of the fuel tank and lines, fuel filter, electric fuel pump, pulsation damper, fuel pressure regulator, fuel delivery manifold and two solenoid-type fuel injectors. A check and cut valve releases excessive pressure or vacuum in the fuel tank to the atmosphere and prevents the loss of fuel if the vehicle overturns. The fuel system is constantly under pressure, which is regulated to 37 psi.

The fuel pump provides more fuel than the injection system needs for normal operation, with excess fuel being returned to the tank via the fuel return line. The fuel pump is a roller cell type which is capable of providing 49–71 psi of pressure as measured at the pump outlet. The pump is located near the fuel tank, under a protective shield on the underbody of the vehicle. The pump connector is located under the storage compartment located behind the driver's seat. The pressure regulator and pulsation damper are mounted on the fuel delivery manifold, located under the dynamic chamber just above the injectors. The operation of the fuel delivery system is controlled through the main relay mounted in the engine compartment next to the master cylinder, with power feeding through a fusible link located near the battery.

On-Car Service

IDLE SPEED

Adjustment

Before checking or adjusting the idle speed, switch off all accessories, remove the fuel filler cap and connect a suitable tachometer. The throttle sensor should also be checked for proper adjustment.

1. Start the engine and allow it to reach normal operating temperature.

2. Disconnect the vent and vacuum solenoid valve connector.

3. Remove the blind cap and adjust the idle speed to 800 rpm by turning the air adjust screw. Raise the engine speed, then allow it to return to idle and recheck rpm with the tachometer.

4. After idle speed adjustment is complete, reinstall the blind cap onto the air adjust screw.

IDLE MIXTURE

Adjustment

The idle mixture is preset at the factor, and should not normally require adjustment unless the variable resistor is replaced. Disconnect the variable resistor connector and connect an ohmmeter to the resistor terminals. If continuity does not exist, or if the resistance value is not within 0.5–4.5 kilo-ohms, replace the variable resistor. Before adjusting the idle mixture, switch off all accessories, remove the fuel filler cap and connect a suitable tachometer to the engine. The throttle sensor adjustment should also be checked.

1. Start the engine and allow it to reach normal operating temperature.

2. Disconnect the vent and vacuum solenoid valve connector.

3. Remove the blind cap and adjust the idle speed as previously described.

4. Turn the variable resistor adjusting screw until the highest idle

Schematic of Mazda EGI fuel injection system

Adjusting idle mixture with variable resistor

Variable resistor used to adjust idle speed on Mazda EGI system. See text for details

Checking resistance for idle mixture adjustment. Note the terminal identification

is obtained, then reset the idle speed to 800 rpm by turning the idle adjustment screw.

5. Turn the variable resistor adjusting screw counterclockwise until the idle speed reaches 780 rpm, then turn clockwise until the idle is again 800 rpm.

6. Connect the vent and vacuum solenoid connector.

7. Install the blind cap onto the idle adjustment screw and fill the head of the variable resistor adjustment screw with epoxy cement.

PRESSURE TESTS

Fuel Pump Pressure Test

1. Disconnect the negative battery terminal.
2. Disconnect the main fuel hose from the fuel pipe and connect a suitable pressure gauge.

---CAUTION---

Fuel system is under pressure. Wrap a clean cloth around the fuel connection when loosening to catch the fuel spray and take precautions to avoid the risk of fire.

---

3. Reconnect the negative battery terminal.
4. Turn the ignition switch ON and use a jumper to energize the fuel pump through the shortcircuit terminal.
5. Read the fuel pump pressure on the pressure gauge. It should be between 49–71 psi. If not, replace the fuel pump.

Testing fuel pump pressure with gauge connected to fuel feed line

Install a jumper wire into the fuel pump short circuit terminal to energize the fuel pump during test procedures

System Pressure Test

1. Disconnect the negative battery terminal.
2. Disconnect the fuel main hose from the fuel pipe and connect pressure gauge using a three-way joint.

———————CAUTION———————

Fuel system is under pressure. Wrap a clean cloth around the fuel connection when loosening to catch any fuel spray and take precautions to avoid the risk of fire.

3. Connect the negative battery cable and start the engine.
4. Disconnect the vacuum hose to the pressure regulator control valve.
5. Measure the fuel system pressure at idle. It should be about 37 psi.
6. Connect the vacuum hose to the pressure regulator control valve and again measure the fuel system pressure. It should drop to about 28 psi.
7. Replace the fuel pressure regulator if any other results are obtained.

Testing Fuel Injector Operation

Use a mechanic's stethescope to check for operation noise from the injectors at idle and under acceleration. The injectors should buzz as the pintle opens and closes rapidly. If the injectors are not operating, check that continuity is present in the wire from the trailing coil negative (−) coil to terminal U in the control unit connector. Check the EGI main fusible link and turn the ignition on and off and make sure the relays click. If clicking is not heard in the main relay when the ignition is switched on, check for 12 volts at main relay connector No. 2 terminal.

BYPASS AIR CONTROL (BAC) SYSTEM

Testing

Start the engine and allow it to reach normal operating temperature. With the engine idling, turn the headlight switch ON and disconnect the vent and vacuum solenoid valve connector. The engine speed should decrease. Reconnect the vent and vacuum solenoid valve connector and make sure the engine speed increases back up to 800 rpm. If the test results are not as described, perform the following tests to isolate which solenoid is malfunctioning.

VENT SOLENOID VALVE

Testing

1. Disconnect the vacuum line from the control solenoid to the vent solenoid valve.
2. Disconnect the vent solenoid connector.
3. Blow through the vent solenoid valve vacuum line and make sure that air does not pass.
4. Apply 12 volts to the vent solenoid valve connector and again blow through the vacuum line. Air should now pass through.
5. If the test results are not as described, replace the vent solenoid valve and retest.

VACUUM SOLENOID VALVE

Testing

1. Disconnect the vacuum line from the control solenoid to the vacuum solenoid valve.
2. Disconnect the vacuum solenoid connector.
3. Blow through the vacuum solenoid line and make sure that air passes.
4. Apply 12 volts to the vacuum solenoid connector and again blow through the disconnected line. Air should not pass through.
5. If the test results are not as described, replace the vacuum solenoid valve and retest.

Testing fuel pressure regulator with tee adapter. Make sure all connections are tight

Testing vent solenoid valve. See text for details

Test connections for checking vacuum solenoid operation.

AIR SUPPLY VALVE

Testing

1. Start the engine and allow it to idle at normal operating temperature.
2. Turn the A/C switch ON and make sure the engine speed does not decrease.
3. Disconnect the air supply valve connector. The engine speed should drop.

Disconnect the air supply valve when testing

Location of throttle sensor adjusting screw.

4. Reconnect the air supply valve connector and make sure the engine returns to normal idle speed (800 rpm).

5. Turn the steering wheel to the right and left and make sure the magnetic clutch of the compressor turns off.

6. If the test results are not as described, connect a tachometer to the engine.

7. Disconnect the vent and and vacuum solenoid valve connector.

8. Check and adjust the idle speed, if necessary.

9. Disconnect the air supply valve connector and apply 12 volts to the connector. The engine speed should be within 1000–1070 rpm.

10. If the engine speed is not as specified, remove the blind cap and adjust the engine speed with the adjusting screw on the air supply valve.

11. Install the blind cap after adjustment and repeat the test.

THROTTLE SENSOR

Testing

1. Start the engine and allow it to reach normal operating temperature, then turn the ignition OFF.

2. Connect two voltmeters to the test connector.

3. Turn the ignition ON and check that current flows to only one voltmeter.

4. If both voltmeters show current flow, remove the cap and turn the adjusting screw counterclockwise until only one voltmeter shows current.

5. If no current is registered by either voltmeter, turn the adjusting screw clockwise until only one voltmeter shows current.

6. Install the cap on the adjusting screw and disconnect the throttle sensor connector. Connect an ohmmeter to the throttle sensor terminals.

7. Open the throttle valve and check the resistance reading from

Testing throttle sensor resistance. It should be about 1kΩ @ idle and 5kΩ @ full throttle

the throttle sensor. At idle, the throttle sensor should show about 1 kilo-ohm resistance. At wide open throttle, the sensor should show about 5 kilo-ohms resistance.

8. Any results other than these, replace the throttle sensor and retest.

NOTE: During deceleration above a certain engine speed, fuel is not injected to reduce emissions. Check this fuel cut operation by holding the engine at 2000 rpm in neutral and making sure the engine speed varies when the throttle sensor is pushed in with a finger.

DASH POT

Testing

1. Make sure the dash pot rod does not prevent the throttle lever from returning to the idle stop.

2. Open the throttle lever fully and make sure the dash pot lever extends quickly. Release the throttle lever and make sure it returns slowly to the idle position after touching the dash pot rod.

3. Connect a suitable tachometer to the engine.

Adjusting the throttle sensor on Mazda EGI system requires the use of two ohmmeters

Loosen the locknut to adjust the dash pot

4. Start the engine and allow it to reach normal operating temperature. Check the idle speed and adjust if necessary.

5. Operate the throttle lever until it is away from the dash pot rod, then slowly decrease the engine speed and note the rpm at which the throttle lever just touches the dash pot rod. It should contact the rod at between 2350–2650 rpm.

6. If the engine speed is not within the range specified when the throttle lever contacts the dash pot rod, loosen the lock nut and adjust the contact point by turning the dash pot diaphragm. Tighten the lock nut and retest after all adjustments are complete.

ANTI-BACKFIRE VALVE

Testing

Start the engine and allow it to reach normal operating temperature. With the engine at idle, disconnect the hose from the air control valve to the air pump at the air pump. Place a finger over the air hose and make sure no vacuum is present at idle. Increase the engine speed to 3000 rpm, then allow the engine to return to idle rapidly. Vacuum should be present at the air hose for a few seconds while decelerating. If no air is being drawn into the air hose during deceleration, or if air is drawn in at idle, replace the air control valve and retest.

Test the vacuum control solenoid valve by disconnecting the hoses and making sure air passes from port B to the air cleaner.

VACUUM CONTROL SOLENOID VALVE

Testing

1. Start the engine and allow it to reach normal operating temperature.
2. Connect a suitable tachometer to the engine.
3. Disconnect the vacuum line at the solenoid and place a finger over the solenoid connection. Make sure no vacuum is present through the solenoid valve at idle.
4. Gradually increase the engine speed to about 1200 rpm and make sure vacuum is now present at the solenoid valve connection.
5. Decrease engine speed rapidly from 4000 rpm and make sure no vacuum is present at the solenoid connection while decelerating.
6. Turn the A/C switch ON and make sure vacuum is present at the solenoid valve connection at idle.
7. Disconnect the vacuum sensing lines from the solenoid valve and blow through the valve from port B. Make sure air passes through the valve and comes out the filter (C).
8. Disconnect the connector from the vacuum control solenoid valve and apply 12 volts to the connector terminals at the valve.
9. Blow through the valve at port B and make sure air passes through the valve and comes out port A.
10. If any other test results are obtained, replace the vacuum control solenoid valve and retest.

When testing, air should pass from port B to port A with battery voltage applied to terminals

PRESSURE REGULATOR CONTROL SOLENOID

Valve Test

Disconnect the vacuum lines from the solenoid valve and blow through the solenoid valve at port B. Air should pass through the valve and come out port A at the air filter. Disconnect the solenoid valve connector and apply 12 volts to the terminals of the valve. Blow through the valve from port B and make sure air passes and comes out port C. If any other results are obtained, replace the pressure regulator control solenoid valve and retest.

Testing pressure regulator control solenoid valve. Air should pass from port B to port C with battery voltage applied to terminals

INTAKE AIR TEMPERATURE SENSOR

Testing

Remove the intake air temperature sensor from the dynamic air chamber and connect an ohmmeter to the sensor terminals. Check the sensor calibration by reading the resistance values at various temperatures. If the resistance is out of range or fails to vary at different temperatures, replace the sensor.

AIR TEMPERATURE SENSOR TEST

Temperature	Resistance
20°C (68°F)	41.5 ± 4.15 kΩ
50°C (122°F)	11.85 ± 1.19 kΩ
85°C (185°F)	3.5 ± 0.35 kΩ

Testing atmospheric pressure sensor. See text for details

ATMOSPHERIC PRESSURE SENSOR

Testing

Connect the voltmeter to atmospheric pressure sensor terminal D, turn the ignition switch ON and take a voltage reading. It should read 3.5–4.5 volts at sea level and 2.5–3.5 volts at high altitude (areas above 8500 ft. in elevation.)

ELECTRONIC CONTROL UNIT

Testing

Connect a voltmeter to the control unit by probing the main harness connector carefully from the rear and grounding the other voltmeter probe. All control unit testing is limited to simple voltage checks with the ignition ON and the engine OFF at normal operating temperature. If the voltage is not as specified in the test specifications chart, first check all wiring, connections and components before assuming that the control unit is defective. The Mazda System Checker 83 (40 G040 920) is necessary to troubleshoot the electronic control system with the OEM test connector located next to the ECU harness connectors at the control unit. With the tester the on-board diagnosis system will read out trouble codes (1 through 6) to indicate problems in different circuits within the fuel injection system. Follow the manufacturer's instructions included with the tester for all wiring and sensor checks using the special tester.

——————CAUTION——————

Do not attempt to disconnect or reconnect the control unit main harness connector with the ignition switch ON, or the ECU can be damaged or destroyed.

MAZDA ECU TEST SPECIFICATIONS

Terminal	Connection to	Voltage with ignition ON (when functioning properly)
A	Main relay	approx. 12V
B	Ground	0V
C	Water thermo sensor	1 ~ 2V (warm engine)
D	Ground	0V
E	Air flow meter	4 ~ 6V . . . at 20°C 1.5 ~ 3.5V . . . at 50°C
F	Injector (#20)	approx. 12V
G	Throttle sensor & Atmospheric pressure sensor	4.5 ~ 5.5V
H	Injector (#10)	approx. 12V
I	Throttle sensor	approx. 1V
J	Vacuum switch	approx. 12V
L	Variable resistor (V/R)	0 ~ 12V (Varies according to the V/R adjustment)
M	Ignition switch "START" terminal	below 1.5V
N	O₂ sensor	0V
O	Air flow meter	approx. 12V
P	Atmospheric pressure sensor	approx. 4V
Q	Air flow meter	approx. 2V
R	Air flow meter	approx. 7.5V
S	Ground	0V
T	Ground	0V
U	Ignition coil (T) – terminal	approx. 12V
V	Main relay	approx. 12V
a	Switching solenoid valve	approx. 12V
b	Relief solenoid valve control unit	approx. 12V
c	Checking connector	0V
d	Vacuum control solenoid valve (T/L)	approx. 12V
e	Pressure regulator control valve	below 1.5V
f	Checking connector	0V
h	Vent solenoid valve	below 1.5V (throttle sensor is adjusted properly)
i	Clutch switch	below 1.5V . . . pedal released approx. 12V . . . pedal depressed
j	Neutral switch	below 1.5V . . . in neutral approx. 12V . . . in gear
k	Water temperature switch	below 1.5V . . . above 15°C
l	Intake air temperature sensor	8.5 ~ 10.5V . . . at 20°C 5 ~ 7V . . . at 50°C
m	Air-con. switch	below 1.5V . . . air-con. switch OFF
n	Vacuum control valve	approx. 12V (throttle sensor is adjusted properly)

Component Removal and Testing

FUEL PUMP

Removal and Installation

—CAUTION—

Fuel system is under pressure. Wrap a clean cloth around the fuel connection when loosening to catch any fuel spray and take precautions to avoid the risk of fire.

1. Remove the storage compartment located behind the driver's seat and disconnect the fuel pump connector.
2. Raise the vehicle and support it safely.
3. Remove the pump bracket clamp bolt.
4. Disconnect the inlet and outlet hoses from the fuel pump and plug the lines.
5. Remove the fuel pump from the bracket.
6. Installation is the reverse of removal.

FUEL PRESSURE REGULATOR

Removal and Installation

1. Remove the dynamic chamber as detailed later in this section.
2. Disconnect the vacuum hose.
3. Disconnect the fuel return hose after covering the starter to prevent fuel from splashing on it. Wrap a clean cloth around all fuel connections when disconnecting to catch any fuel spray from the pressurized system.
4. Remove the pressure regulator mounting nut and remove the pressure regulator.
5. Installation is the reverse of removal. Check for fuel leaks with fuel pressure applied before installing the dynamic chamber.

FUEL INJECTOR

Removal and Installation

1. Remove the dynamic chamber as detailed later in this section.
2. Remove the fuel feed and return lines from the fuel manifold and damper. Wrap a clean cloth around the fuel connections to catch any fuel spray from the pressurized system.
3. Remove the vacuum line from the fuel pressure regulator.
4. Remove the fuel injector harness connector.
5. Remove the fuel manifold by attaching bolts and remove the fuel manifold with the damper and pressure regulator attached.
6. Remove the injector(s) from the intermediate casing, making sure the insulator comes out with the injector.

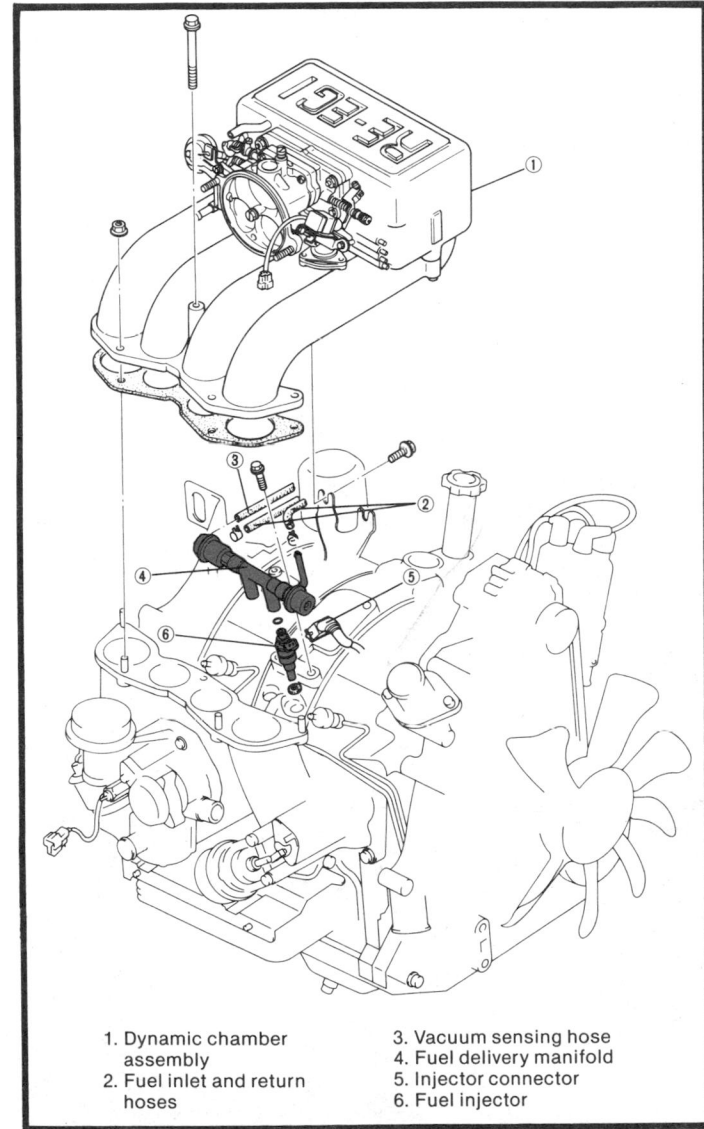

1. Dynamic chamber assembly
2. Fuel inlet and return hoses
3. Vacuum sensing hose
4. Fuel delivery manifold
5. Injector connector
6. Fuel injector

Exploded view of injector mounting and dynamic chamber assembly

Injector fuel leak test. Wire the injectors to the fuel rail as shown to prevent fuel pressure from blowing off hose connections.

7. Installation is the reverse of removal. Replace the O-ring and insulator. Lubricate the O-ring with clean gasoline when installing on the injector tip. Check for fuel leaks with fuel pressure applied before installing dynamic chamber.

Injector Winding Test

Measure the resistance of the injector with an ohmmeter across the injector terminals. It should be 1.5–3 ohms. If no resistance is measured or if the resistance exceeds 3 ohms, replace the fuel injector.

Injector Fuel Leak Test

Install the fuel injectors onto the fuel manifold and connect all fuel lines, vacuum lines and harness connectors. Use mechanic's wire to secure the injectors to the fuel manifold so that no movement is possible. If the injectors are not securely attached to the fuel manifold, they may blow off when fuel pressure is applied. Install a jumper wire on the fuel pump short circuit terminal and turn the ignition ON to pressurize the fuel system. Check for leaks from the fuel injector nozzles. After 5 minutes, a very slight amount of fuel leakage is acceptable. If the injectors drip continuously or more than a very slight amount of fuel leaks, replace the fuel injectors and retest.

Testing the air flow meter with an ohmmeter

NOTE: Injectors may be replaced individually if only one is found to be defective. Use a clean cloth to catch any fuel during testing.

Injector Volume Test

With the injectors still attached to the fuel manifold as described above, connect Injector Tester 49 9200 040, or equivalent, to the injector to be tested. Install a suitable fuel hose from the end of the test injector to a graduated container. Short the fuel pump test terminal and apply 12 volts to the injector tester. The fuel injector is good if 149–197 cc of fuel is delivered within 15 seconds.

CAUTION

Do not apply 12 volts directly to the injector or the windings will be destroyed.

AIR FLOW METER

Removal and Installation

Remove the air cleaner element, then loosen the air flow meter attaching bolts and remove the air cleaner. Loosen the air funnel (duct) band and remove the air flow meter assembly. Installation is the reverse of removal.

Air flow meter terminal locations. See the specifications chart for test connections and resistance values

Testing

Check the air flow meter body for cracks and check the resistance of each terminal using an ohmmeter. Compare the resistance measurements with the specification chart and replace the air flow meter if there is no reading or the reading is out of range. Press on the measuring plate and measure the resistance between the terminals as detailed in the chart to check vane meter operation. Replace the air flow meter if no change is noted when the sensor plate is moved.

AIR FLOW METER SPECIFICATIONS

Terminal	Resistance (ohms)
E_2–V_s	20–400
E_2–V_c	100–300
E_2–V_b	200–400
E_2–THA (Intake air temperature sensor)	− 4 F—10k–20k 32 F—4k–7k 68 F—2k–3k 104 F—900–1300 140 F—400–700

AIR FLOW METER SPECIFICATIONS

Terminal	Resistance (ohms)
E_1–F_c	Infinity (plate closed) Zero (plate open)
E_2–V_s	20–400 (plate closed) 20–1000 (plate open)

k—one thousand

THROTTLE CHAMBER

Removal and Installation

1. Remove the air funnel (duct) from the throttle chamber.
2. Disconnect the accelerator cable.
3. Disconnect the throttle sensor harness connector.
4. Disconnect the metering oil pump connecting rod.
5. Disconnect the water hoses.
6. Loosen and remove the mounting bolts and remove the throttle chamber.

7. Installation is the reverse of removal.

DYNAMIC CHAMBER

Removal and Installation

1. Disconnect the air funnel (duct) to the throttle chamber.
2. Disconnect the accelerator cable.
3. Disconnect the throttle sensor harness connector.
4. Disconnect the metering oil pump connecting rod.
5. Disconnect the water hoses.
6. Disconnect the negative battery cable.
7. Remove the terminal cover.
8. Disconnect the vacuum sensing lines.
9. Disconnect the air supply valve harness connector.
10. Disconnect the intake air temperature sensor connector.
11. Loosen the mounting bolts holding the dynamic chamber to the intake manifold ports and lift off the dynamic chamber.
12. Installation is the reverse of removal. Use a new gasket when installing the dynamic chamber.

NOTE: Cover the intake manifold ports with a clean cloth when the dynamic chamber is removed to prevent debris from entering the engine during service and testing procedures.

MITSUBISHI ELECTRONICALLY CONTROLLED INJECTION (ECI) SYSTEM

Mitsubishi throttle body system schematic

General Information

The Mitsubishi Electronically Controlled Injection (ECI) system is basically a standard throttle body system with some variations in operation and components. The fuel control system consists of an electronic control unit (ECU), two solenoid-type fuel injectors, an air flow sensor and several engine sensors. The ECU receives voltage signals from the engine sensors on operating conditions, then sends out impulses to the injectors to constantly adjust the fuel mixture. In addition, the ECU controls starting enrichment, warm-up enrichment, fast idle, deceleration fuel cut-off and overboost fuel cut-off on turbocharged models.

One of the primary components is the air flow sensor with its device for generating Karman vortexes. Ultrasonic waves are transmitted across the air flow containing the Karman vortexes, which are generated in proportion to the air flow rate. The greater the number of vortexes, the more the frequency of the ultrasonic waves are changed (modulated). These modulated ultrasonic waves are picked up by the receiver in the air flow sensor and converted into a voltage signal for the ECU. The ECU uses this signal to measure air flow and control fuel delivery and secondary air management. An intake air temperature sensor is used to provide a signal so that air density changes due to temperature can be calculated.

Other components in the system are common to all throttle body systems. During closed loop operation, the ECU monitors the oxygen sensor to determine the correct fuel mixture according to the oxygen content of the exhaust gases. In the open loop mode, fuel mixture is preprogrammed into the control unit memory.

When the ECI system is activated by the ignition switch, the fuel pump is energized by the ECU. The pump will only operate for about one second unless the engine is running or the starter is cranking. When the engine starts, the fuel pump relay switches to continuous operation and all engine sensors are activated and begin providing input for the ECU. The ISC motor will control idle speed (including fast idle) if the throttle position switch is in the idle position, and the ignition advance shifts from base timing to the pre-programmed ignition advance curve. The fuel pressure regulator maintains system pressure at approximately 14.5 psi (1 bar) by returning excess fuel provided by the fuel pump to the tank.

The ECU provides a ground for the injectors to precisely control the open and closing time (pulse width) to deliver exact amounts of fuel to the engine, continuously adjusting the air/fuel mixture while monitoring signals from the various engine sensors including:

- Engine coolant temperature
- Intake manifold air temperature and volume
- Barometric pressure
- Intake manifold absolute pressure
- Engine speed (rpm)
- Idle speed
- Detonation
- Boost pressure (turbo models only)
- Throttle position
- Exhaust gas content (oxygen level)

On-Car Service
SELF-DIAGNOSIS SYSTEM

The Mitsubishi self-diagnosis system monitors the various input signals from the engine sensors and enters a trouble code in the on-board computer memory if a problem is detected. There are nine monitored items, including the "normal operation" code which can be read by using a special ECI tester and adapter. The adapter connects the ECI tester to the diagnosis connector located on the right cowl, next to the control unit. Because the computer memory draws its power directly from the battery, the trouble codes are not erased when the ignition is switched OFF. The memory can only be cleared (trouble codes erased) if a battery cable is disconnected or the main ECU wiring harness connector is disconnected from the computer module.

NOTE: The trouble codes will not be erased if the battery cable or harness connector is reconnected within 10 seconds.

If two or more trouble codes are stored in the memory, the computer will read out the codes in order beginning with the lowest number. The needle of the ECI tester will sing back and forth between 0 and 12 volts to indicate the trouble code stored. There is no memory for code No. 1 (oxygen sensor) once the ignition is switched OFF, so it is necessary to perform this diagnosis with the

MITSUBISHI ECI TROUBLE CODES

Trouble Code	ECU Circuit	Indicated Problem
1	Oxygen sensor	Open circuit in wire harness, faulty oxygen sensor or connector
2	Ignition signal	Open or shorted wire harness, faulty igniter
3	Air flow sensor	Open or shorted wire harness, loose connector, defective air flow sensor
4	Boost pressure sensor	Defective boost sensor, open or shorted wire harness or connector
5	Throttle position sensor	Sensor contacts shorted, open or shorted wire harness or connector
6	ISC motor position sensor	Defective throttle sensor open or shorted wire harness or connector defective ISC servo
7	Coolant temperature sensor	Defective sensor, open or shorted wire harness or connector
8	Speed sensor	Malfunction in speed sensor circuit, open or shorted wire harness or connector

ISC—Idle Speed Control

engine running. The oxygen sensor should be allowed to warm up for testing (engine at normal operating temperature) and the trouble code should be read before the ignition is switched OFF. All other codes will be read out with the engine ON or OFF. If there are no trouble codes stored in the computer (system is operating normally), the ECI tester will indicate a constant 12 volts on the meter. Consult the instructions supplied with the test equipment to insure proper connections for diagnosis and testing of all components.

If there is a problem stored, the meter needle will swing back and forth every 0.4 seconds. Trouble codes are read by counting the pulses, with a two second pause between different codes. If the battery voltage is low, the self-diagnosis system will not operate properly, so the battery condition and state of charge should be checked before attempting any self-diagnosis inspection procedures. After completing service procedures, the computer trouble code memory should be erased by disconnecting the battery cable or main harness connector to the control unit for at least 10 seconds.

Connecting ECI tester to control unit harness

NOTE: Installation of CB or other two-way radio equipment may affect the operation of the electronic control unit. Antennas and other radio equipment should be installed as far away from the ECU as possible.

IDLE SPEED CONTROL (ISC) SERVO AND THROTTLE POSITION SENSOR

Adjustment

If the ISC Servo, throttle position sensor, throttle body or injectors have been removed or replaced, the following adjustments should be made. These adjustments are important to driveability.
1. Start the engine and allow it to reach operating temperature.
2. Stop the engine.

3. Loosen the throttle position sensor mounting screws and turn the throttle position sensor clockwise as far as it will go, then temporarily tighten the screws.
4. Set the ISC Servo position by turning the ignition ON for 15 seconds, then turn the ignition OFF.
5. Disconnect the ISC servo harness connector.
6. Start the engine and check the idle speed. Adjust to specifications as listed on the underhood emission control sticker, if necessary, by turning the adjusting screw clockwise to increase rpm or counterclockwise to decrease rpm.

Mitsubishi fuel injection tester

Idle speed adjustment

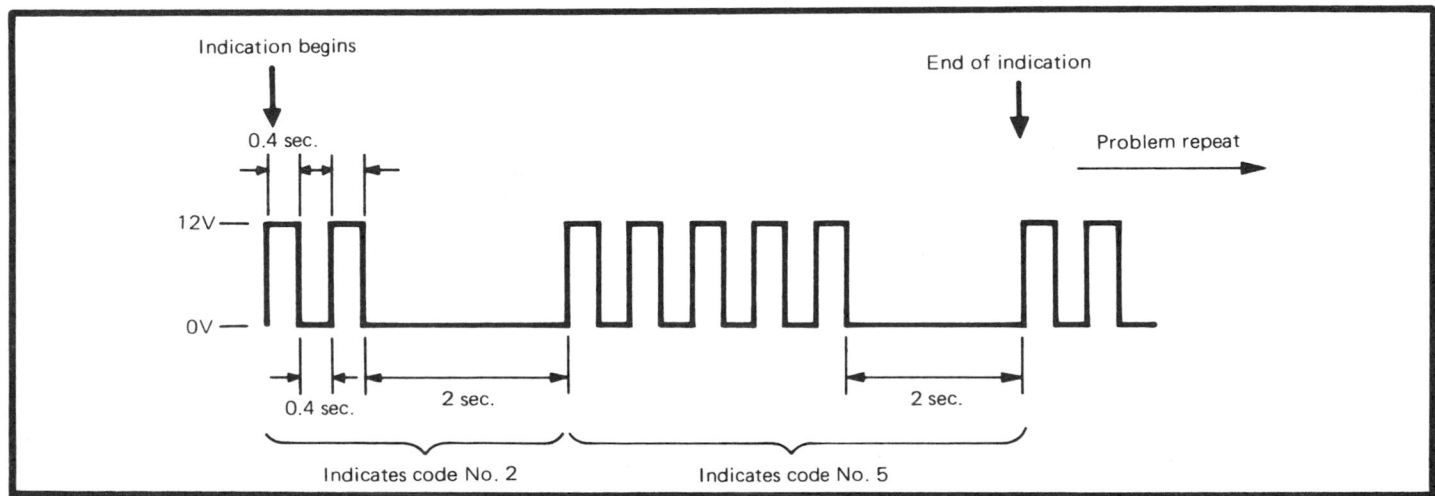
Reading Mitsubishi trouble codes. Note the time between pulses

ECI SYSTEM DIAGNOSIS

NOTE
When ECI system is checked, make sure that the connector is connected securely. Use special care in checking for loose connectors since they can cause every one of the problems.

Pin numbers on throttle position switch connectors

Component Removal and Testing

AIR FLOW SENSOR

Testing

Check the air cleaner element for contamination and damage and replace if necessary. Check the air cleaner case and cover for cracks and damage that could allow air leaks in the system. Check the

Air flow sensor location on Mitsubishi ECI system

7. Stop the engine and disconnect the throttle position sensor harness connector.

8. Connect adapter and digital voltmeter between the throttle position sensor connector.

9. Turn the ignition switch ON but do not start the engine.

10. Read the throttle position sensor output voltage on the digital voltmeter. If the voltage is not 0.45–0.51 volts, loosen the throttle position sensor mounting screws and turn the sensor until the reading is within the specified range, then tighten the mounting screws.

11. Open the throttle fully and confirm that the output voltage is correct when the throttle valve is returned to the idle position.

12. Remove the digital voltmeter connections and recheck idle speed.

Using adapter to connect digital voltmeter to throttle position sensor

Terminal pin numbers on air flow sensor connector

resistance of the air intake temperature sensor between terminals 1 and 4 of the connector. Resistance should be approximately 2.5 ohms at 68 degrees F (20 degrees C).

Removal and Installation

1. Disconnect the air flow sensor connector. The connector must be disconnected before removing the air cleaner cover and air cleaner body.
2. Unsnap the finger clip and remove the air cleaner cover.
3. Remove the filter element from the air cleaner body.
4. Remove the air flow sensor.
5. Installation is the reverse of removal. Make sure the connector is correctly fastened.

FUEL INJECTORS AND THROTTLE BODY

Removal and Installation

1. Disconnect the battery ground cable.
2. Drain the engine coolant down to the intake manifold level or below.
3. Disconnect the air intake hose from the throttle body assembly.

1. Pulsation damper cover
2. O-ring
3. Spring
4. Pulsation damper
5. O-ring (2)
6. Fuel pressure regulator
7. Mixing body
8. Hose
9. Seal ring
10. Throttle body assembly
11. Throttle position sensor
12. Joint
13. Connector bracket
14. Return spring
15. Throttle lever
16. Ring
17. Free lever
18. Kickdown lever
19. Adjusting screw
20. Spring
21. Seal ring (2)
22. Injector (2)
23. Collar (2)
24. O-ring (2)
25. Injector holder
26. ISC servo assembly
27. Damper spring
28. Return spring

Exploded view of throttle body assembly for Mitsubishi ECI system

Throttle body components, fuel and coolant connections

4. Disconnect the throttle cable from the throttle lever.
5. Disconnect the fuel inlet pipe and fuel return hose from the assembly.
6. Disconnect the harness connectors from the injectors.
7. Disconnect the ISC servo and throttle position sensor connectors.
8. Disconnect the vacuum hose from the throttle body.
9. Remove the four mounting bolts and remove the throttle body and injectors as an assembly.
10. Installation is the reverse of removal. Adjust the ISC servo and throttle position sensor as previously described. Check for fuel leaks.

Overhaul

1. Clamp the throttle body assembly in a soft-jawed vise, being careful not to damage the housing.
2. Disconnect the rubber hose from the fuel pressure regulator and throttle body.
3. Remove the injector retainer tightening screws and remove the retainer.
4. Remove the pressure regulator from the retainer.
5. Remove the pulsation damper cover from the retainer and take out the spring and diaphragm.
6. Pull the injectors from the throttle body. Do not use pliers to remove the injectors. Remove the gaskets from the throttle body.
7. Remove the throttle return spring and the damper spring.
8. Remove the connector bracket.
9. Remove the ISC servo mounting bracket with the servo attached. Do not remove the ISC servo from the bracket unless it is being replaced.

Throttle body component locations

10. Remove the two screws, then remove the mixing body and seal ring from the throttle body.

11. Remove the throttle position sensor only if it is being replaced.

---CAUTION---

Do not immerse parts in cleaning solvent. Immersing the ISC servo, throttle position sensor and injector will damage the insulation. Wipe all parts clean with a dry cloth. Clean vacuum and fuel ports with compressed air.

---

12. Reassemble throttle body and injectors in reverse order of removal. Adjust the throttle position sensor, if removed, and make sure the resistance value changes when the throttle lever is moved. Install new seal rings in the throttle body and mixing body and replace O-rings on injectors. Press the injectors into the throttle body cavities firmly using finger pressure only. Install the pulsation damper diaphragm as illustrated and replace the O-rings on the fuel pressure regulator. Check the filters in the retainer for clogging or damage and replace if necessary. Tighten the retainer screws alternately, but do not overtighten.

Connector and vacuum port locations

Installing pulsation damper diaphragm

Removing pulsation damper cover

Location of O-rings on fuel pressure regulator

Throttle position sensor connector terminal numbers

Location of filters in injector retainer

Install sealing ring with the flat side up

Control relay on Mitsubishi ECI system showing pin numbers

ECU used on Mitsubishi ECI system showing harness connector pin numbers

ECI RESISTOR

Testing

The resistor is mounted on the left side of the firewall. To test, disconnect the resistor harness connector and measure the resistance across terminals 1 and 2, then across terminals 1 and 3. Resistance should be about 6 ohms. If the resistance measures zero or infinity, replace the resistor. If resistance is as specified, make sure the connector terminals are tight and free from corrosion.

COOLANT TEMPERATURE SENSOR

Testing

Remove the coolant temperature sensor from the intake manifold and immerse the sensor probe in water. Do not immerse the electrical connections, just the sensor itself. Heat the water and check

Resistor used on Mitsubishi ECI system showing terminal numbers

that the resistance changes from approximately 16 kilo-ohms at −4 degrees F (−20 degrees C) to 296 ohms at 176 degrees F (80 degrees C). At room temperature, the sensor should read about 2.45 kilo-ohms. If the resistance is as described, apply sealant to the threaded portion of the sensor and install into the intake manifold. If not, replace the sensor. Make sure all harness connections are fastened securely. Torque the sensor to 21 ft. lbs. (30 Nm).

ECI CONTROL RELAY

Testing

The control relay is mounted on top of the ECU, under the air duct of the instrument panel. Test for continuity between terminals 1 and 7, then between terminals 3 and 7. If there is no continuity, the relay is good; if continuity exists, replace the relay. Apply 12 volts across terminals 8 and 4 while testing continuity between terminals 3 and 7; if continuity exists, the relay is good. Apply 12 volts across terminals 6 and 4 while testing continuity between terminals 1 and 7; again, if continuity exists, the relay is good.

MITSUBISHI ECI TEST SPECIFICATIONS

Circuit Tested	ECU Terminal Location	Normal Reading
Power supply	B-1	Key OFF-0 volts Key ON- 11–13 volts
Secondary air control valve	A-10	Reading should change from 0.2–15 volts within 30 seconds at warm idle
Throttle position switch	A-1	Key ON- 0.4–1.5 volts (4.5–5.0 volts @ WOT)
Coolant temperature sensor	A-3	3.5 volts @ 32 deg. F 0.5 volts @ 176 deg. F
Air temperature sensor	A-4	3.5 volts @ 32 deg. F 0.6 volts @ 176 deg. F
Idle position switch	A-5	Key ON- 0–0.4 volts @ idle 11–13 volts @ WOT
ISC motor position	A-14	Key ON- 11–13 volts ①
EGR control valve solenoid	B-4	0–0.5 volts above 3000 rpm 13–15 volts @ idle ②
Speed sensor	A-15	0.2–5 volts with transmission in gear and slowly accelerating
Cranking signal	A-13	Over 8 volts
Control relay	B-5	0–1 volts @ idle

MITSUBISHI ECI TEST SPECIFICATIONS

Circuit Tested	ECU Terminal Location	Normal Reading
Ignition pulse signal	A-8	12–15 volts @ idle 11–13 volts @ 3000 rpm
Air flow sensor signal	A-7	2.7–3.2 volts between idle and 3000 rpm
Injector No. 1	B-9	13–15 volts @ idle 12–13 volts @ 3000 rpm
Injector No. 2	B-10	13–15 volts @ idle 12–13 volts @ 3000 rpm
Oxygen sensor	A-6	0–2.7 volts ③
Pressure sensor	A-17	1.5–2.6 volts

NOTE: Turn ignition OFF between tests when making connections. All testing done with ignition ON unless noted otherwise. Make sure test equipment is compatible with injection system before making any voltage checks.

WOT = Wide Open Throttle

① If ignition switch is turned on for 15 seconds or more, the reading drops to 1 volt or less momentarily, then returns to 6–13 volts

② Engine warmed up to operating temperature

③ Do not use a power voltmeter to test oxygen sensor. The sensor can be damaged by the voltage draw

RENAULT ELECTRONIC FUEL INJECTION

1. Injector	5. Solenoid-to-EGR valve	8. O₂-sensor	14. Solenoid-to-EVAP canister control	18. Ignition control module	22. Closed–throttle (idle) switch
2. Throttle position sensor	6. EGR valve	9. Speed sensor	15. Starter motor relay	19. In-line fuel filter	23. Wide open throttle (WOT) switch
3. Pressure regulator	7. Manifold air/fuel temperature sensor	10. Ignition switch	16. Fuel pump relay	20. Air conditioner on	24. Temperature sensor (coolant)
4. Idle speed control motor		11. Power relay	17. Fuel pump	21. Transaxle neutral/park switch	
		12. Map sensor			
		13. Electronic control unit (ECU)			

Throttle body fuel injection system used on Renault Alliance

General Information

The Throttle Body Fuel Injection (TBI) system is a "pulse time" system that injects fuel into the throttle body above the throttle blade. Fuel is metered to the engine by one or more electronically controlled fuel injector(s). The Electronic Control Unit (ECU) controls injection according to input provided from sensors that detect exhaust gas oxygen content, coolant temperature, manifold absolute pressure, crankshaft position and throttle position. The sensors provide an electronic signal usually modulated by varying resistance within the sensor itself.

TBI fuel injection has two main sub-systems. The fuel system consists of an electric fuel pump (in tank), a fuel filter, a pressure regulator and a fuel injector. The control system consists of a manifold air/fuel mixture temperature (MAT) sensor, a coolant temperature sensor (CTS), a manifold absolute pressure (MAP) sensor, a wide open throttle (WOT) switch, a closed throttle (idle) switch, an exhaust oxygen (O_2) sensor, an electronic control unit (ECU), a gear position indicator (automatic transmission models only), a throttle position sensor and an idle speed control (ISC) motor. There may be more than one fuel injector used.

TBI TROUBLE DIAGNOSIS

Condition or Trouble Code	Possible Cause	Correction
CODE 1 (poor low air temp. engine performance).	Manifold air/fuel temperature (MAT) sensor resistance is not less than 1000 ohms (HOT) or more than 100 kohms (VERY COLD).	Replace MAT sensor if not within specifications. Refer to MAT sensor test procedure.
CODE 2 (poor warm temp. engine performance-engine lacks power).	Coolant temperature sensor resistance is less than 300 ohms or more than 300 kohms (10 kohms at room temp.).	Replace coolant temperature sensor. Test MAT sensor. Refer to coolant temp. sensor test and MAT sensor test procedures.
CODE 3 (poor fuel economy, hard cold engine starting, stalling, and rough idle).	Defective wide open throttle (WOT) switch or closed (idle) throttle switch or both, and/or associated wire harness.	Test WOT switch operation and associated circuit. Refer to WOT switch test procedure. Test closed throttle switch operation and associated circuit. Refer to closed throttle switch test procedure.
CODE 4 (poor engine acceleration, sluggish performance, poor fuel economy).	Simultaneous closed throttle switch and manifold absolute pressure (MAP) sensor failure.	Test closed throttle switch and repair/replace as necessary. Refer to closed throttle switch test procedure. Test MAP sensor and associated hoses and wire harness. Repair or replace as necessary. Refer to MAP sensor test procedure.
CODE 5 (poor acceleration, sluggish performance).	Simultaneous WOT switch and manifold absolute pressure (MAP) sensor failure.	Test WOT switch and repair or replace as necessary. Refer to WOT switch test procedure. Test MAP sensor and associated hoses and wire harness. Repair or replace as necessary. Refer to MAP sensor test procedure.
CODE 6 (poor fuel economy, bad driveability, poor idle, black smoke from tailpipe).	Inoperative oxygen sensor.	Test oxygen sensor operation and replace if necessary. Test the fuel system for correct pressure. Test the EGR solenoid control. Test canister purge. Test secondary ignition circuit. Test PCV circuit. Refer to individual component test procedure.
No test bulb flash.	No battery voltage at ECU (J1-A with key on). No ground at ECU (J1-F). Simultaneous WOT and CTS switch contact (Ground at both D2 Pin 6 and D2 Pin 13). No battery voltage at test bulb (D2 Pin 4). Defective test bulb. Battery voltage low (less than 11.5V).	Repair or replace wire harness, connectors or relays. Repair or replace WOT switch, CTS switch, harness or connectors. Repair wire harness or connector. Replace test bulb. Charge or replace battery, repair vehicle wire harness.

On-Car Service
PRELIMINARY CHECKS

The Throttle Body Fuel Injection (TBI) System should be considered as a possible source of trouble for engine performance, fuel economy and exhaust emission complaints only after normal tests and inspections of other engine components have been performed. An integral self-diagnostic system within the ECU detects common malfunctions that are most likely to occur.

On Renault models the self-diagnostic system will illuminate a test bulb if a malfunction exists. When the trouble code terminal (at the diagnostic connector in the engine compartment) is connected to a test bulb the system will flash a trouble code if a malfunction has been detected.

CONNECTOR D2   CONNECTOR D1

1. Battery (memory)
2. Trouble code
3. Park/Neutral Switch
4. B+ (power relay)
5. AC on
6. WOT switch
7. Sensor ground
8. Air temp. sensor
9. EGR solenoid
10. Canister purge solenoid
11. ISC motor forward
12. Coolant temp. sensor
13. Closed throttle switch
14. ISC motor reverse
15. Auto trans potentiometer

1. Tach (rpm) voltage
2. Ignition
3. Ground
4. Starter motor relay
5. Battery
6. Fuel pump

Diagnostic connector terminal identification. Make sure the correct terminals are connected during testing

Before performing any test, make sure that the malfunction is not caused by a component other than the fuel injection system (e.g., spark plugs, distributor, advance timing, etc.); that no air is entering the intake and exhaust system above the catalytic converter and, finally, that fuel is actually reaching the injector (test the pressure in the circuit).

TBI SERVICE PRECAUTIONS

1. Never connect or disconnect any electrical component without turning off the ignition switch.
2. With the engine stopped and the ignition on, the fuel pump should not be operative. The fuel pump is controlled by the electronic control unit (ECU).
3. Disconnect the battery cables before charging.
4. If the temperature is likely to exceed 80°C (176°F), as in a paint shop bake oven, remove the electronic control unit (ECU).
5. Misconnections should be carefully avoided because even momentary contact may cause serious ECU or system damage.

1983–84 Renault TBI
---CAUTION---
Be extremely careful when making any test connections. Never apply more than 12 volts to any point or component in the TBI system.

DIAGNOSIS PROCEDURE

The self-diagnostic feature of the electronic control unit (ECU) provides support for diagnosing system problems by recording six possible failures should they be encountered during normal engine

operation. Additional tests should allow specific tracing of a failure to a single-component source. Multiple disassociated failures must be diagnosed separately. It is possible that the test procedures can cause false interpretations of certain irregularities and consider them as ECU failures.

NOTE: In the following procedures, no specialized service equipment is necessary. It is necessary, however, to have available a volt/ohmmeter, a 12V test lamp, and an assortment of jumper wires and probes.

Trouble Code Test Lamp

Poor fuel economy, erratic idle speed, power surging and excessive engine stalling are typical symptoms when the fuel system has a component failure. If the ECU is functional, service diagnostic codes can be obtained by connecting a No. 158 test bulb (or equivalent) to pins D2-2 and D2-4 of the large diagnostic connector. With the test bulb installed, push the WOT switch lever on the throttle body and with the ISC motor plunger (closed throttle switch) also closed, have a helper turn on the ignition switch while observing the test bulb.

NOTE: If the ECU if functioning normally, the test bulb should light for a moment then go out. This will always occur regardless of the failure condition, and serves as an indication that the ECU is functional.

After the initial illumination the ECU will cycle through and flash a single digit code if any system malfunctions have been detected by the ECU during engine operation.

The ECU is capable of storing various trouble codes in memory. The initial trouble detected will be flashed first and then, followed by a short pause, the second trouble detected will be flashed. There will be a somewhat longer pause between the second code and the repeat cycle of the first code again. This provides distinction between codes 3 – 6 and 6 – 3. While both codes indicate the same two failures, the first digit indicates the initial trouble while the last digit indicates the most recent failure.

CONNECTOR D2   CONNECTOR D1   FRONT OF CAR
FENDER

Trouble code test lamp connections

RENAULT TBI TROUBLE CODES

In a given situation where further testing indicates no apparent cause for the failure indicated by the ECU self-diagnostic system, an intermittent failure, except that marginal components must be more closely examined. If the trouble code is erased and quickly returns with no other symptoms, the ECU should be suspected. However, in the absence of other negative symptoms, replacement of the ECU can be suspected. Again, because of the cost involved and the relative reliability of the ECU, the ECU should never be replaced without testing with dealer test equipment. If the ECU is determined to be defective, it must be replaced. There are no dealer serviceable parts in the ECU. No repairs should be attempted.

Relay block connector and bracket

It is important to note that the trouble memory is erased if the ECU power is interrupted by disconnecting either battery cable terminal, or allowing the engine to remain unstarted in excess of five days.

It is equally important to erase the trouble memory when a defective component is replaced. This can be done by any one of the actions listed above.

Component Removal and Testing

The fuel pump is a roller type with a permanent magnet electric motor that is immersed in fuel. The check valve is designed to maintain the fuel pressure after the engine has stopped. The pump has two electric wire terminals marked + and − to ensure that it rotates in the correct direction.

The ECU controls the fuel pump, which is usually located inside the fuel tank and is attached to the fuel gauge sending unit assembly. Fuel pump power is supplied through two relays, located in the engine compartment.

PRESSURE REGULATOR

The fuel pressure regulator (overflow-type) is integral with the throttle body. The valve is a diaphragm-operated relief valve in which one side of the valve is exposed to fuel pressure and the other side is exposed to air horn pressure. Nominal pressure is established by a calibrated spring.

The pressure regulator has a spring chamber that is vented to the same pressure as the tip of the injector. Because the differential pressure between the injector nozzle and the spring chamber is the same, the volume of fuel injected is dependent only on the length of time the injector is energized. The pump delivers fuel in excess of the maximum required by the engine and the excess fuel flows back to the fuel tank from the pressure regulator via the fuel return hose.

Adjustment

Adjustment of the fuel pressure regulator is necessary only to establish the correct pressure after a replacement has been installed.

1. Remove the air filter.
2. Connect a tachometer to the diagnostic connector terminals D1-1 and D1-3.
3. Connect an accurate fuel pressure gauge to the fuel body pressure test fitting. Exercise caution when removing fuel lines.
4. Start the engine and accelerate to approximately 2000 rpm.
5. Turn the allen head adjustment screw on the bottom of the regulator to obtain 1 bar (14.5 psi) of pressure.

NOTE: Turning the screw inward increases the pressure and turning the screw outward decreases the pressure.

6. Install a lead seal ball to cover the regulator adjustment screw after adjusting the pressure to specification.
7. Turn the ignition off, then disconnect the tachometer.
8. Disconnect the fuel pressure gauge and install the cap on the test fitting. Install the air filter.

Removal and Installation

1. Remove the three retaining screws that secure the pressure regulator to the throttle body.
2. Remove the pressure regulator assembly. Note the location of the components for assembly reference.
3. Discard the gasket.
4. Position the pressure regulator assembly with a replacement gasket.
5. Install the three retaining screws to secure the pressure regulator to the throttle body.
6. Start the engine and inspect for leaks.

Exploded view of pressure regulator assembly

FUEL INJECTOR

The injector body contains a solenoid with a plunger or core piece that is pulled upward by the solenoid armature allowing the spring loaded ball valve to come off the valve seat. This allows fuel to pass through to the atomizer/spray nozzle. During engine operation, the fuel injector is energized by the ECU and serves to meter and direct atomized fuel into the throttle bore above the throttle blade. During engine start-up the injector is energized to deliver a predetermined volume of fuel to aid starting.

NOTE: More than one injector may be used.

TBI fuel injector installation

Removal and Installation

1. Remove the air filter.
2. Remove the injector wire connector.
3. Remove the injector retainer clip screws.
4. Remove the injector retainer clip.
5. Using a small pair of pliers, gently grasp the center collar of the injector (between electrical terminals) and carefully remove the injector with a lifting/twisting motion.
6. Discard the upper and lower O-rings. Note that the back-up ring fits over the upper O-ring.
7. To install the injector, proceed as follows: Lubricate with light oil and install a replacement lower O-ring in the housing bore.
8. Lubricate with light oil and install a replacement upper O-ring into housing bore.
9. Install the back-up ring over the upper O-ring.
10. Position the replacement injector in the throttle body and center the nozzle in the lower housing bore. Seat the injector using a pushing/twisting motion.
11. Align the wire terminals.
12. Install the retainer clip and screws.
13. Install the injector wire connector.
14. Install the air filter.

THROTTLE BODY

Removal

1. Remove the throttle cable and return spring.
2. Disconnect the wire harness connector from the injector.

Throttle body assembly. Note testing and adjustment points for fuel pressure

3. Disconnect the wire harness connector from the wide open throttle (WOT) switch.
4. Disconnect the wire harness connector from the ISC motor.
5. Disconnect the fuel supply pipe from the throttle body.
6. Disconnect the fuel return pipe from the throttle body.
7. Disconnect the vacuum hoses from the throttle body assembly. Identify and tag the hoses for installation reference.
8. Remove the throttle body-to-manifold retaining nuts from the studs.
9. Remove the throttle body assembly from the intake manifold.

NOTE: If the throttle body assembly is being replaced, transfer the following components to the replacement throttle body; idle speed control (ISC) motor/WOT switch and bracket assembly.

Installation

1. Install the replacement throttle body assembly on the intake manifold. Use a replacement gasket between the components.
2. Install the throttle body-to-manifold retaining nuts on the studs.
3. Connect the vacuum hoses.
4. Connect the fuel return pipe to the throttle body.
5. Connect the fuel supply pipe to the throttle body.
6. Connect the wire harness connector to the injector.
7. Connect the wire harness connector to the WOT switch.
8. Connect the wire harness connector to the ISC motor.
9. Install the throttle cable and return spring.

Removing the throttle body assembly

MAT SENSOR

Location of the manifold air/fuel temperature (MAT) sensor

CTS CONNECTOR

Coolant temperature sensor (CTS) installation

4. Test the resistance of the wire harness between the ECU harness connector J2-13 and the sensor connector, and J2-11 to sensor connector. Repair as necessary if the resistance is greater than 1 ohm.

NOTE: J2-13 and J2-11 are at ECU harness conductor.

FUEL BODY ASSEMBLY

Removal and Installation

1. Remove the throttle body assembly from the intake manifold.
2. Remove the three Torx® screws that retain the fuel body to the throttle body.
3. Remove the original gasket and discard it.
4. Install the replacement fuel body on the throttle body using a replacement gasket.
5. Install the three fuel body-to-throttle body retaining Torx® head screws and tighten securely.
6. Install the throttle body assembly on the intake manifold.

MANIFOLD AIR/FUEL TEMPERATURE (MAT) SENSOR

The manifold air/fuel temperature (MAT) sensor is installed in the intake manifold in front of an intake port. This sensor reacts to the temperature of the air/fuel mixture (charge) in the intake manifold and provides an analog voltage for the ECU.

Testing

1. Disconnect the wire harness connector from the MAT sensor.
2. Test the resistance of the sensor with a high input impedance (digital) ohmmeter. Resistance ranges from 300 ohms to 300K ohms (10K ohms at room temperature).
3. Replace the sensor if it is not within the range of resistance specified above.

Removal and Installation

1. Disconnect the wire harness connector from the MAT sensor.
2. Remove the MAT sensor from the intake manifold.
3. Clean the threads in the manifold.
4. Install the replacement MAT sensor in the intake manifold.
5. Connect the wire harness connector to the MAT sensor.

COOLANT TEMPERATURE SENSOR (CTS)

The coolant temperature sensor is installed in the engine water jacket. This sensor provides an analog voltage for the ECU. The ECU will enrich the fuel mixture delivered by the injector as long as the engine is cold.

Testing

1. Disconnect the harness from the coolant temperature sensor.
2. Disconnect the wire harness connector.
3. Test the resistance of the sensor with a high input impedance (digital) ohmmeter. The resistance ranges from 300 ohms to more than 300K ohms (10K ohms at room temperature).
4. Replace the sensor if not within the range of resistance specified above.
5. Test the resistance of the wire harness between J2-14 and the sensor connector, and J2-11 to the sensor connector. Find and repair open wire in harness, if indicated.

NOTE: J2-14 and J2-11 are at the ECU connector.

Removal and Installation

1. Remove the wire harness connector from the coolant temperature sensor (CTS).
2. Remove the CTS from the cylinder head and rapidly plug the hole to prevent loss of coolant. Installation is the reverse of removal.

—CAUTION—
DO NOT remove the CTS with the cooling system hot and under pressure. Serious burns from coolant can result.

MANIFOLD ABSOLUTE PRESSURE (MAP) SENSOR

The MAP sensor reacts to absolute pressure in the intake manifold and provides an analog voltage for the ECU. Manifold pressure is used to supply mixture density information and ambient barometric pressure information to the ECU. The sensor is remote mounted and a tube from the throttle body provides its input pressure.

1. Ground
2. Output voltage
3. 5 volts

Manifold absolute pressure (MAP) sensor

Testing

1. Inspect the MAP sensor vacuum hose connections at the throttle body and sensor. Repair as necessary.
2. Test the MAP sensor output voltage at the MAP sensor connector pin B (as marked on the sensor body) with the ignition switch ON and the engine OFF. Output voltage should be 4–5 volts.

NOTE: The voltage should drop 0.5–1.5 volts with a hot neutral idle speed condition.

3. Test ECU pin J2-12 for the same voltage described above to verify the wire harness condition. Repair as necessary.
4. Test the MAP sensor supply voltage at the sensor connector pin C with the ignition ON. The voltage should be 5 volts (± 0.5V). The voltage should also be at pin J2-2 of the ECU wire harness connector. Repair or replace the wire harness as necessary.
5. Test the MAP sensor ground at sensor connector pin A and ECU connector pin J2-13. Repair the wire harness if necessary.
6. Test the sensor ground at the ECU connector between pin J2-13 and J1-F with an ohmmeter. If the ohmmeter indicates an open circuit, inspect for a good sensor ground on the flywheel housing near the starter motor. If the ground is good, replace the ECU. If J2-13 is shorted to 12 volts, correct this condition before replacing the ECU.

Removal and Installation

1. Disconnect the electrical connector.
2. Disconnect the vacuum hose.
3. Remove the retaining nuts.
4. Remove the MAP sensor from the cowl panel.
5. Installation is the reverse of removal.

WIDE OPEN THROTTLE (WOT) SWITCH

The WOT switch is mounted on the side of the throttle body. This switch provides a digital voltage for the ECU, which in turn enriches the fuel mixture delivered by the injector that is necessary for the increased air flow.

Testing

1. Disconnect the wire harness from the WOT switch.
2. Test the operation of the WOT switch with a high input impedance ohmmeter. Open and close the switch manually.
3. Resistance should be infinite when the throttle is closed. A low resistance should be indicated at the WOT position. Test the switch operation several times.
4. Replace the WOT switch if defective. Connect the wire harness connector.
5. With the ignition switch ON, test the WOT switch voltage at the diagnostic connector (D2-6 to ground, D2-7). Voltage should be zero (0) at the WOT position; greater than 2 volts if not at WOT position.
6. If the voltage is always zero, test for a short circuit to ground in the wire harness or switch. Check for an open circuit between J2-19 (ECU) and the switch connector. Repair or replace the wire harness as necessary.
7. If the voltage is always greater than 2 volts, test for an open wire or connector between the switch and ground. Repair as necessary.

Adjustment

NOTE: Adjustment of the WOT switch is necessary only to establish the initial position of the switch after it has been replaced.

1. With the throttle body assembly removed from the engine, loosen the two retaining screws that attach the WOT switch to the bracket.
2. Open the throttle to wide open position.
3. Attach the alignment gauge J-26701 or equivalent on the flat surface of the throttle lever.
4. Rotate the degree scale of the gauge until the 15 degree mark is aligned with the pointer.

Replacement of the pressure sensor assembly—typical

Wide open throttle (WOT) switch mounted on throttle body

Wide open throttle switch adjustment

5. Adjust the bubble until it is centered.

6. Rotate the degree scale to align zero degrees with the pointer.

7. Close the throttle slightly to center the bubble on the gauge. The throttle is now at 15 degrees before WOT position.

8. Position the WOT switch lever on the throttle cam so that the switch plunger is just closed at 15 degrees before WOT position.

9. Tighten the WOT switch retaining screws.

10. Remove the alignment bubble gauge.

Removal and Installation

1. Remove the air filter.

2. Disconnect the throttle return spring.

3. Disconnect the throttle cable.

4. Remove the ISC motor bracket-to-throttle body screws.

5. Disconnect the wire connectors from the WOT switch and ISC motor.

6. Remove the bracket, ISC motor and WOT switch assembly from the throttle body.

7. Remove the ISC motor.

8. Remove the two WOT switch-to-bracket screws.

9. Remove the WOT switch.

10. Installation is the reverse of removal.

IDLE SPEED CONTROL (ISC) MOTOR

Engine idle speed and engine deceleration throttle stop angle are controlled by an electric motor driven actuator that changes the throttle stop angle by being a movable idle stop. The ECU controls the ISC motor actuator by providing the appropriate voltage outputs to produce the idle speed or throttle stop angle required for the particular engine operating condition. The electronic components that control the ISC motor are integral with the ECU.

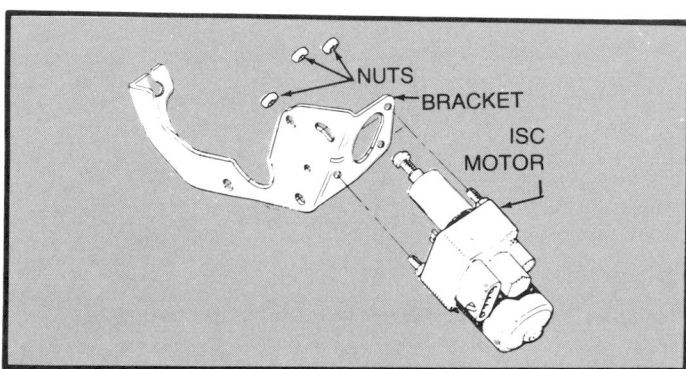

Idle speed control (ISC) motor replacement

The system controls engine idle speed or throttle stop angle as would a dashpot for deceleration, as would a fast idle device for cold engine operation, and as would a normal idle speed device for warm engine operation. The inputs from the air conditioner compressor (ON/OFF), transaxle (PARK, NEUTRAL), and throttle extremities (OPEN/CLOSED) are used to increase or decrease the throttle stop angle in response to particular engine operating conditions.

For engine starting, the throttle is either held open for a longer period (COLD) or a short time (HOT) to provide adequate engine warm-up prior to normal engine operation. With normal engine idle speed operation, the idle speed is maintained at a programmed rpm and varies slightly according to engine operating conditions. Additionally, with certain engine deceleration conditions, the throttle is held slightly open.

Adjustment

NOTE: Adjustment is necessary only to establish the initial position of the plunger after the ISC motor has been replaced.

1. Remove the air cleaner.

2. Start the engine and allow it to reach normal operating temperature. Make sure that the air conditioning is turned off.

3. Connect a tachometer to terminal D1-1 and D1-3 of the diagnostic connector.

4. Turn the ignition off. The ISC motor plunger should move to the fully extended position.

5. Disconnect the ISC motor wire and start the engine. The engine idle should be 3300–3700 rpm. If not, turn the hex screw on the end of the plunger to achieve a 3500 rpm reading.

6. Fully retract the plunger by holding the closed throttle switch plunger in while the throttle is open. If the closed throttle switch plunger touches the throttle lever when the throttle is closed, check the throttle linkage for binding or damage and correct as required.

7. Connect the ISC motor wire.

8. Turn the ignition off for 10 seconds. The ISC plunger should fully extend.

9. Start the engine. The idle should be 3500 rpm for a short period, then gradually reduce to the specified idle speed.

10. Turn off the ignition and disconnect the tachometer.

NOTE: Holding the closed throttle switch plunger as described above may activate an intermittant trouble code in the ECU memory. To erase the code, disconnect the battery for at least 10 seconds.

Closed Throttle Switch Test

NOTE: It is important that all testing be done with the idle speed control motor plunger in the fully extended position, as it would be after a normal engine shut down. If it is necessary to extend the motor plunger to test the switch an ISC motor failure can be suspected. Refer to ISC motor test if necessary.

1. With the ignition switch ON, test the switch voltage at the diagnostic connector (D2-13 and D2-7, ground). Voltage should be close to zero at closed throttle and greater than 2 volts off the closed throttle position.

2. If the voltage is always zero, test for a short circuit to ground in the wire harness or switch. Test for an open circuit between J2-20 (ECU connector) and the switch.

3. If voltage is always more than 2 volts, test for an open circuit in the wire harness between the ECU and the switch connector, and between the switch connector, and ground. Repair or replace the wire harness as necessary.

Removal and Installation

NOTE: The closed throttle (idle) switch is integral with the motor.

1. Disconnect the throttle return spring.

2. Disconnect the wire connector from the motor.

3. Remove the motor-to-bracket retaining nuts.

4. Remove the motor from its bracket.

5. Installation is the reverse of removal.

OXYGEN (O₂) SENSOR

The oxygen sensor is located in the exhaust pipe adaptor. The analog voltage output from this sensor, which varies with the oxygen content of the exhaust gas, is supplied to the ECU. The ECU utilizes it as a reference voltage.

Testing

1. Test the continuity of the harness between the O_2 sensor connector and J2-9 on the ECU wire harness connector with an ohmmeter. Ensure that the wire harness is not shorted to ground. Repair or replace the wire harness as necessary.

2. Test the continuity between the sensor ground (exhaust manifold) and Pin J2-13 on the ECU wire harness connector. Repair wire harness if necessary.

3. Test the fuel system for the correct pressure. Pressure should be approximately 1 bar (14–15 psi) with the engine at idle speed.

Schematic of typical oxygen sensor

Use anti-seize compound when installing the oxygen sensor

Refer to the fuel system pressure test. Repair the fuel system if necessary.

4. Check the sensor operation by driving the vehicle with a test lamp (No. 158 bulb) connected between the diagnostic connector D2-2 and D2-4.

5. Bulb lighted at start is normal operation for test circuit. If the bulb does not light after warm up, the O_2 sensor is functioning normally. If the bulb stays lit or lights after the engine warms up, replace the O_2 sensor.

NOTE: Additional testing may be required to locate the cause of an oxygen sensor failure. Other system failures that could cause an O_2 failure include EGR solenoid control, canister purge control, PCV system, secondary ignition circuit and fuel delivery system.

Removal and Installation

1. Disconnect the wire connector from the O_2 sensor.
2. Remove the O_2 sensor from the exhaust pipe adaptor.
3. Clean the threads in the adaptor.
4. Apply anti-seize sealer to the threads on the O_2 sensor.

————CAUTION————

Apply anti-seize sealer only to the threads and not to any other part of the sensor.

5. Hand thread the sensor into the exhaust pipe adaptor.
6. Tighten the sensor with 20–25 ft. lbs. (27–34 Nm) torque.
7. Connect the wire connector.

————CAUTION————

Make sure that the wire terminal ends are properly seated in the connector prior to joining the connectors. Do not push the rubber boot down on the sensor body beyond 13 mm (0.5 in.) above the base. Also, the Oxygen Sensor pigtail wires cannot be spliced or soldered. If broken, replace the sensor.

ELECTRONIC CONTROL UNIT (ECU)

The Electronic Control Unit (ECU) is located below the glove box adjacent to the fuse panel. The ECU controls the injector fuel delivery time and changes the injected flow according to inputs received from sensors that react to exhaust gas oxygen, air temperature, coolant temperature, manifold absolute pressure, and crankshaft and throttle positions. The ECU is powered by the vehi-

Location of test pins on the ECU and wiring harness on Renault models

cle battery and, when the ignition is turned to the ON or START position, the voltage inputs are received from the sensors and switches. The desired air/fuel mixtures for various driving and atmospheric conditions are programmed into the ECU. As inputs are received from the sensors and switches, the ECU processes the inputs and computes the engine fuel requirements. The ECU energizes the injector for a specific time duration. The duration of pulse varies as engine operating conditions change.

Testing

The only accurate and safe way to test the ECU is by using the self-diagnosis feature described earlier.

Removal and Installation

1. Remove the retaining screws and bracket that support the ECU below the glove box.
2. Remove the ECU.
3. Disconnect the wire harness connectors from the ECU.
4. Installation is the reverse of removal.

NOTE: It should be understood that the ECU is extremely reliable and must be the final component to be replaced if a doubt exists concerning the cause of an injection system failure.

GM TURBOCHARGERS

General Description

A turbocharger is used to increase power on a demand basis, thus allowing a smaller, more economical engine to perform the job of a larger engine. As load on the engine is increased and the throttle is opened, more air-fuel mixture flows into the combustion chambers. As this increased flow is burned, a larger volume of higher energy exhaust gas enters the engine exhaust system and is directed through the turbocharger turbine housing. Some of this energy is used to increase the speed of the turbine wheel. The turbine wheel is connected by a shaft to the compressor wheel. The increased speed of the compressor wheel allows it to compress the air-fuel mixture it receives from the carburetor and delivers it to the intake manifold. The resulting higher pressure in the intake manifold allows a denser charge to enter the combustion chambers. The denser charge can develop more power during the combustion cycle.

The intake manifold pressure (boost) is controlled to a correct maximum value by an exhaust bypass valve (wastegate). The valve allows a portion of the exhaust gas to bypass the turbine wheel, thus not increasing turbine speed. The wastegate is operated by a spring loaded diaphragm device (actuator assembly) that senses the pressure differential across the compressor. When boost reaches a set value about ambient pressure, the wastegate beings to bypass exhaust gas.

NOTE: Any alteration to the air intake or exhaust system which upsets the air flow balance may result in serious damage to the turbocharged engine.

Operation

ELECTRONIC SPARK CONTROL

Turbocharged engines use a modified HEI system which is called Electronic Spark Control (ESC). The ESC system is used to control engine detonation by automatically retarding ignition timing during periods of engine operation when detonation occurs.

The intake manifold transmits the vibrations caused by detonation to the sensor mounting location. The sensor detects the presence and intensity of detonation and feeds this information to the controller. The controller, which is mounted on the fan shroud, evaluates the sensor signal and sends a command signal to the distributor to adjust timing.

The HEI distributor has a modified electronic module which responds to signals from the controller. Electronic spark control is continually monitoring engine operation for detonation and retarding ignition timing up to 18 to 20° (V-6) or 13 to 17° (V-8) to minimize detonation levels, as necessary.

ENRICHMENT VACUUM REGULATOR

The Power Enrichment Vacuum Regulator (PEVR) is designed to control vacuum flow to the carburetor power piston on turbocharged engines. The PEVR regulates vacuum to the remote power enrichment port on the carburetor based on the manifold vacuum/pressure signal.

The PEVR has an input port and an output port. The vacuum input port is in the center of the PEVR. The vacuum output port is located on the perimeter of the PEVR. The manifold signal port extends into the intake manifold.

TURBOCHARGER OIL SUPPLY

An adequate supply of clean engine oil is essential to the proper operation of the turbocharger. The rotating assembly (turbine wheel, connecting shaft and compressor wheel) can attain speeds of 130,000 to 140,000 rpm during boost. Interruption or contamination of the oil supply to the support bearings in the center housing rotating assembly

Turbine housing removal

Turbocharger components

(CHRA) can result in major turbocharger damage.

When changing the oil and oil filter on a turbocharged engine or performing any operation which results in oil drainage or loss, use the following procedures before starting the engine:

1. Disconnect ignition switch connector (pink wire) from the HEI distributor.

2. Crank engine several times (not to exceed 30 seconds for each cranking interval) until oil light goes out.

3. Reconnect pink wire to the distributor. This procedure will aid the filling of the oil system.

NOTE: Any time a basic engine bearing (main bearing, connecting rod bearing and camshaft bearing) has been damaged in a turbocharged engine, the oil and oil filter should be changed as a part of the repair procedure. In addition, the turbocharger should be flushed with clean engine oil to reduce the possibility of contamination.

Any time a center housing rotating assembly, or any part of a turbocharger which includes the center housing rotating assembly, is being replaced, the oil and oil filter should be changed as a part of the repair procedure.

Test Procedures

GENERAL PRECAUTIONS

Before starting any turbocharger unit repair procedure, several general precautions should be considered.

1. Clean area around turbocharger with non-caustic solution before removal of assembly.

2. When removing turbocharger assembly, take special care not to bend, nick or in any way damage compressor or turbine wheel blades. Any damage may result in rotating assembly imbalance, failure of center housing rotating assembly (CHRA) and failure of compressor and/or turbine housings.

3. Before disconnecting center housing rotating assembly from either compressor housing or turbine housing, scribe the components in order that they may be reassembled in the same relative position.

4. If silastic sealer, or equivalent, is found at any point in turbocharger disassembly (such as between center housing rotating assembly backplate and compressor housing), the area should be cleaned and sealed with an equivalent sealer during reassembly.

WASTEGATE/BOOST PRESSURE

1. Visually inspect wastegate-actuator mechanical linkage for damage.

2. Check hose from compressor housing to actuator assembly and return tubing from actuator to PCV tee.

3. Attach hand operated vacuum/pressure pump J-23738 in series with compound gauge J-28474 to actuator assembly. Replace compressor housing to actuator assembly hose.

4. Apply pressure to actuator assembly. At approximately 9 psi (8.5 to 9.5 psi), the actuator rod end should move .015 inch, actuating the wastegate linkage. If not, replace the actuator assembly and check that opening calibration pressure is 9 psi. Crimp threads on actuator rod to maintain correct calibration.

5. Remove test equipment and reconnect compressor housing to actuator assembly hose.

6. An alternative method of checking wastegate operation is to perform a road test which measures boost pressure.

POWER ENRICHMENT VACUUM REGULATOR (PEVR)

1. Visually check the PEVR and attaching hoses for deterioration, cracking or other damage.

2. Tee one hose from manometer J-23951 between the yellow-striped input hose and the input port. Connect the other manometer hose directly to the output port of the PEVR.

3. Start the engine and let it idle. There should be no more than a 1.0 in. Hg difference. If there is, replace the PEVR.

4. If the PEVR passes the preceding test and is still considered to be a possible problem source, remove the PEVR from the intake manifold.

5. Plug the intake manifold and connect the input and output hoses to the PEVR.

6. Tee compound gauge J-28474 into the output hose of the PEVR.

7. Start the engine and let it idle. The compound gauge reading from the output port should be 7.0 to 9.0 in. Hg. (V-6), or 8.0 to 10.0 in. Hg. (V-8).

8. Apply 3 psi to the manifold signal port of the PEVR. The vacuum reading from the output port should be 1.4 to 2.6 in. Hg. If there is difficulty in measuring this low level of vacuum output, an additional requirement can be used. Apply a minimum of 5 psi to the manifold signal port of the PEVR. There should be no vacuum output from the PEVR.

9. If the PEVR does not meet requirements 7 and 8, replace it.

TURBOCHARGER INTERNAL INSPECTION

1. Remove turbocharger exhaust outlet pipe from the elbow assembly. Using a mirrow, observe movement of wastegate while manually operating actuator linkage. Replace elbow assembly if wastegate fails to open or close. Inspect wastegate poppet valve for deterioration and warpage. Replace elbow assembly if poppet valve is damaged.

2. Remove turbocharger assembly from engine.

3. Check for loose backplate to CHRA bolts and missing gasket or O-ring. Tighten or replace as necessary.

4. Gently spin compressor wheel. If rotating assembly binds, replace CHRA.

5. Remove oil drain from CHRA. Check CHRA for sludging in oil drain area. Clean, if minor. Replace CHRA if severely sludged or coked.

6. Inspect compressor wheel area for oil leakage from CHRA. If leakage is present, replace CHRA.

7. If compressor wheel is damaged or severely cocked, replace CHRA.

8. If CHRA is being replaced, pre-lubricate with clean engine oil and proceed to step 9. If CHRA is not being replaced, proceed to step 10.

9. Inspect compressor housing (still attached to engine) and turbine housing. Replace either housing if gouged, nicked or distorted.

10. If CHRA is not being replaced, remove turbine housing from CHRA.

11. Check the journal bearings for radial clearance as follows.

a. Attach a dial indicator with a two inch long, 3/4 to 1 inch offset extension rod to the center housing such that the indicator

Thrust bearing clearance measurement

plunger extends through the oil outlet port and contacts the shaft of the rotating assembly.

b. Manually apply pressure equally and at the same time to both the compressor and turbine wheels as required to move the shaft away from the dial indicator plunger as far as it will go.

c. Set the dial indicator to zero.

d. Manually apply pressure equally and at the same time to both the compressor and turbine wheels to move the shaft toward the dial indicator plunger as far as it will go. Move the maximum value on the indicator dial.

NOTE: Make sure that the dial indicator reading noted is the maximum reading obtainable, which can be verified by rolling the wheels slightly in both directions while applying pressure.

e. Manually apply pressure equally and at the same time to the compressor and turbine wheels as required to move the shaft away from the dial indicator plunger as far as it will go. Note that the indicator pointer returns exactly to zero.

f. Repeat steps a. through f. as required to make sure that the maximum clearance between the center housing bores and the shaft bearing diameters, as indicated by the maximum shaft travel, has been obtained.

g. If the maximum bearing radial clearance is less than 0.003 inch or greater than 0.006 inch, replace CHRA and inspect housings as indicated in step 9.

NOTE: Continued operation of a turbocharger having improper bearing radial clearance will result in severe damage to the compressor wheel and housing or to the turbine wheel and housing.

12. Check for thrust bearing axial clearance as follows.

a. Mount a dial indicator at the turbine end of the turbocharger such that the dial indicator tip rests on the end of the turbine wheel.

b. Manually move the compressor wheel and turbine wheel assembly alternately toward and away from the dial indicator plunger. Note the travel of the shaft in each direction, as shown on the dial indicator.

c. Repeat step b. as required to make sure that the maximum clearance between the thrust bearing components has been obtained.

d. If the maximum thrust bearing axial clearance is less than 0.001 inch or greater than 0.003 inch, replace CHRA and inspect housings as indicated in step 9.

NOTE: Continued operation of a turbocharger having an improper amount of thrust bearing axial clearance will result in severe damage to the compressor wheel and housing or to the turbine wheel and housing.

13. Install oil drain adapter and tube on CHRA.

Journal bearing clearance measurement

Wastegate actuator attachment

14. Install turbocharger assembly to engine.

NOTE: **Before connecting turbocharger exhaust outlet pipe to elbow assembly, gently spin the turbine wheel to be certain that the rotating assembly (turbine wheel, connecting shaft and compressor wheel) does not bind.**

ROAD TEST

V-6

1. Tee compound gauge J-28474 into tubing between compressor housing and boost gauge switches with sufficient length of hose to place gauge in passenger compartment.

—— CAUTION ——
Determine that hose and compound gauge are in proper operating condition to avoid possible leakage of air-fuel mixture into passenger compartment during road test.

2. Conditions and speed limits permitting, perform a zero to 40 to 50 mph wide open throttle acceleration. Boost pressure, as measured by the compound gauge during road testing, should reach 9-10 psi. If not, replace actuator assembly and check for proper calibration. Actuator rod end should move .015 in. at approximately 9 psi.

V-8

1. Remove 1/4 in. pipe plug or vacuum switch located in the power enrichment adapter. Install a straight vacuum fitting and compound gauge tubing J-28474 into the power enrichment adapter, with sufficient length of hose to place gauge in passenger compartment.

—— CAUTION ——
Determine that the hose and compound gauge are in proper operating condition to avoid possible leakage of air-fuel mixture into the passenger compartment during road test.

2. Conditions and speed limits permitting, perform a zero to 40 or 50 mph wide open throttle acceleration. Boost pressure, as measured by the compound gauge during road testing, should reach 9-10 psi. If not, replace actuator assembly and check for proper calibration. Actuator rod end should move .015 in. at approximately 9 psi, as detailed in the wastegate test procedure.

Component Service

WASTEGATE ACTUATOR

V-6

1. Disconnect hoses. Remove the clip attaching wastegate linkage to actuator rod and remove mounting bolts.
2. Installation is the reverse of removal.

V-8

1. Disconnect hose clamp and two hoses from actuator assembly.
2. Remove retainer attaching wastegate linkage to actuator rod.
3. Remove two bolts attaching actuator assembly to compressor housing.
4. Installation is the reverse of removal.

ELECTRONIC SPARK CONTROL (ESC) DETONATION SENSOR

V-6 and V-8

1. Squeeze sides of metal connector crosswise to wire from controller and gently pull straight up to remove connector. Do not pull up on the wire.
2. Remove detonation sensor.
3. When installing, torque detonation sensor to 19 N·m (14 ft. lb.).

NOTE: Do not over-torque. Proper sensor torque is critical to the sensor performance. Do not use impact tool. Do not apply a side load to the detonation sensor. Do not attempt to repair tapped hole in intake manifold for detonation sensor.

4. Squeeze sides of metal connector crosswise to wire from controller and start straight down over detonation sensor terminal. Release sides of metal connector and push down until connector snaps into place.

ELBOW ASSEMBLY

V-6

1. Loosen turbocharger exhaust outlet pipe at the catalytic converter and disconnect it from the elbow assembly.
2. Remove the clip attaching wastegate linkage to actuator rod. Remove the bolts which mount the elbow to the turbine housing.
3. Installation is the reverse of removal.

V-8

NOTE: Whenever the elbow assembly is replaced, the wastegate actuator assembly must also be replaced with the adjustable type. Adjust as described in wastegate test procedure.

1. Detach turbocharger exhaust outlet pipe and catalytic converter at the intermediate pipe.
2. Disconnect turbocharger exhaust outlet pipe from elbow assembly.
3. Disconnect turbocharger inlet pipe at elbow assembly. Loosen at exhaust manifold and swing out of the way.
4. Remove retainer attaching wastegate linkage to actuator rod.
5. Remove elbow assembly support bracket bolts at elbow. Loosen bracket bolts at intake manifold and swing out of the way.
6. Remove six bolts attaching elbow assembly to turbine housing.
7. Installation is the reverse of removal.

BOLT (3)

ELBOW ASSEMBLY

GASKET

COMPRESSOR HOUSING, TURBINE HOUSING, AND CENTER HOUSING ROTATING ASSEMBLY

Elbow assembly removal

BOLT
19.5 N·m (15 lb. ft.)

LOCKPLATE

CLAMP

TURBINE HOUSING

CENTER HOUSING AND ROTATING ASSEMBLY

Center housing rotating assembly

TURBINE HOUSING AND ELBOW ASSEMBLY/CENTER HOUSING ROTATING ASSEMBLY

V-6

1. Disconnect turbocharger exhaust outlet pipe from the catalytic converter and the elbow assemply.
2. Disconnect turbocharger exhaust inlet pipe from the turbine housing and the exhaust manifold.
3. Remove bolts attaching turbine housing to bracket on intake manifold.
4. Disconnect oil feed pipe from center housing rotating assembly and remove oil drain hose from oil drain pipe.
5. Remove clip attaching wastegate linkage to actuator rod.
6. Remove bolts and clamps attaching CHRA backplate to compressor housing.
7. Remove bolts, clamps, etc. attaching turbine housing to CHRA.
8. Installation is the reverse of removal.

CENTER HOUSING ROTATING ASSEMBLY

V-8

1. Remove elbow assembly.
2. Remove oil feed and return lines from housing.
3. Remove six bolts and three lockplates attaching turbine housing to CHRA.

4. Installation is the reverse of removal.

COMPRESSOR HOUSING

V-6

1. Disconnect turbocharger exhaust outlet pipe from the catalytic converter and the elbow assembly.
2. Disconnect turbocharger exhaust inlet pipe from the turbine housing and the exhaust manifold.
3. Remove bolts attaching turbine housing to bracket on intake manifold.
4. Disconnect oil feed pipe from center housing rotating assembly and remove oil drain hose from oil drain pipe.
5. Remove clip attaching wastegate linkage to actuator rod.
6. Remove bolts and clamps attaching CHRA backplate to compressor housing.
7. Remove bolts attaching compressor housing to plenum.
8. Disconnect boost gauge hose from housing connector.
9. Remove bolts attaching compressor housing to intake manifold.
10. Installation is the reverse of removal.

V-8

1. Remove turbo elbow assembly and CHRA.
2. Remove air cleaner.
3. Remove EGR valve and heat shield.
4. Remove six bolts attaching compressor housing to plenum.
5. Remove three bolts attaching compressor housing to intake manifold.
6. Installation is the reverse of removal.

CLAMP

BOLT
17.5 N·m (13 lb. ft.)

GASKET

COMPRESSOR HOUSING

TURBINE HOUSING AND CENTER HOUSING AND ROTATING ASSEMBLY

Compressor housing

Glossary 8 SECTION

ACT Air Charge Temperature sensor.

AIR GAP the distance or space between the reluctor tooth and pick-up coil.

AFC Air Flow Controlled fuel injection.

AMMETER an electrical meter used to measure current flow (amperes) in an electrical circuit. Ammeter should be connected in series and current flowing in the circuit to be checked.

AMPERE (AMP) the unit current flow is measured in. Amperage equals the voltage divided by the resistance.

ARMATURE another name for reluctor used by Ford. See Reluctor for definition.

BALLAST RESISTOR is a resistor used in the ignition primary circuit between the ignition switch and coil to limit the current flow to the coil when the primary circuit is closed. Can also be used in the form of a resistance wire.

BID Breakerless Inductive Discharge ignition system.

BP Barometric Pressure sensor.

BYPASS system used to bypass ballast resistor during engine cranking to increase voltage supplied to the coil.

CALIBRATION ASSEMBLY memory module that plugs into an on-board computer that contains instructions for engine operation.

CANP Canister Purge solenoid that opens the fuel vapor canister line to the intake manifold when energized.

CAPACITOR a device which stores an electrical charge.

CCC Computer Command Control system used on GM models.

C3I Computer Controlled Coil Ignition used on GM models.

C4 Computer Controlled Catalytic Converter system used on GM and some AMC models.

CFI Central Fuel Injection system used on Ford models.

CIS Constant Injection System or Constant Idle Speed system manufactured by Bosch.

CP Crankshaft Position sensor.

CONDUCTOR any material through which an electrical current can be transmitted easily.

CONTINUITY continuous or complete circuit. Can be checked with an ohmmeter.

DIELECTRIC SILICONE COMPOUND non-conductive silicone grease applied to spark plug wire boots, rotors and connectors to prevent arcing and moisture from entering a connector.

DIODE an electrical device that will allow current to flow in one direction only.

DURA SPARK SYSTEM Ford electronic ignition system that followed the SSI system.

EEC Ford electronic engine control system uses an electronic control assembly (ECA) micro computer to control engine timing, air/fuel ratio and emission control devices.

EFI Electronic Fuel Injection.

EGI Electronic Gasoline Injection system used on Mazda models.

EGO Exhaust Gas Oxygen sensor.

EGR Exhaust Gas Recirculation.

EIS Electronic Ignition System which uses a reluctor and a pick up coil along with a module to replace the ignition points and condenser.

ELECTRONIC CONTROL UNIT (ECU) ignition module, module, amplifier or igniter. See Module for definition.

ESA Chrysler electronic spark advance system uses a spark control computer (SCC) to control ignition timing based on sensor inputs. Also called Electronic Lean Burn (ELB) and Electronic Spark Control (ESC).

EVP EGR valve position sensor.

FBC Feedback Carburetor.

GND Ground or negative (−).

HALL EFFECT PICK-UP ASSEMBLY used to input a signal to the electronic control unit. The system operates on the Hall Effect principle whereby a magnetic field is blocked from the pick-up by a rotating shutter assembly. Used by Chrysler, Bosch and General Motors.

IAT Intake Air Temperature sensor.

IGNITER term used by the Japanese automotive and ignition manufacturers for the electronic control unit or module.

IGNITION COIL a step-up transformer consisting of a primary and a secondary winding with an iron core. As the current flow in the primary winding stops, the magnetic field collapses across the secondary winding inducing the high secondary voltage. The coil may be oil filled or an epoxy design.

INDUCTION a means of transferring electrical energy in the form of a magnetic field. Principle used in the ignition coil to increase voltage.

INFINITY an ohmmeter reading which indicates an open circuit in which no current will flow.

INJECTOR a solenoid or pressure-operated fuel delivery valve used of fuel injection systems.

INTEGRATED CIRCUIT (IC) electronic micro-circuit consisting of a semi-conductor components or elements made using thick-film or thin-film technology. Elements are located on a small chip made of a semi-conducting material, greatly reducing the size of the electronic control unit and allowing it to be incorporated within the distributor.

ISC Idle speed control device.

MAP Manifold absolute pressure sensor.

MCT Manifold charge temperature sensor.

MCU Microprocessor Control Unit used on Ford models.

MFI Multiport Fuel Injection used on GM models.

MICROPROCESSORS a miniature computer on a silicone chip.

MODULE Electronic control unit, amplifier or igniter of solid state or integrated design which controls the current flow in the ignition primary circuit based on input from the pick-up coil. When the module opens the primary circuit, the high secondary voltage is induced in the coil.

OHM the electrical unit of resistance to current flow.

OHMMETER the electrical meter used to measure the resistance in ohms. Self-powered and must be connected to an electrically open circuit or damage to the ohmmeter will result.

OXYGEN SENSOR used with the feedback system to sense the presence of oxygen in the exhaust gas and signal the computer which can reference the voltage signal to an air/fuel ratio.

PICK-UP COIL inputs signal to the electronic control unit to open the primary circuit. Consists of a fine wire coil mounted around a permanent magnet. As the reluctor's ferrous tooth passes through the magnetic field an alternating current is produced, signalling the electronic control unit. Can operate on the principle of metal detecting, magnetic induction or Hall Effect. Is also referred to as a stator or sensor.

POTENTIOMETER a variable resistor used to change a voltage signal.

PRIMARY CIRCUIT is the low voltage side of the ignition system which consists of the ignition switch, ballast resistor or resistance wire, bypass, coil, electronic control unit and pick-up coil as well as the connecting wires and harnesses.

PULSE GENERATOR also called a pulse signal generator. Term used by Japanese and German automotive and ignition manufacturers to describe the pick-up and reluctor assembly. Generates an electrical pulse which triggers the electronic control unit or igniter.

RELUCTOR also called an armature or trigger wheel. Ferrous metal piece attached to the distributor shaft. Made up of teeth of which the number are the same as the number of engine cylinders. As the reluctor teeth pass through the pick-up magnetic field an alternating current is generated in the pick-up coil. The reluctor in effect references the position of the pistons on their compression strokes to the pick-up coil.

RESISTANCE the opposition to the flow of current through a circuit or electrical device, and is measured in ohms. Resistance is equal to the voltage divided by the amperage.

SECONDARY the high voltage side of the ignition system, usually above 20,000 volts. The secondary includes the ignition coil, coil wire, distributor cap and rotor, spark plug wires and spark plugs.

SENSOR also called the pick-up coil or stator. See pick-up coil for definition.

SFI Sequential Fuel Injection system used on GM models.

SHUTTER also called the vane. Used in a Hall Effect distributor to block the magnetic field from the Hall Effect pick-up. It is attached to the rotor and is grounded to the distributor shaft.

SPARK DURATION the length of time measured in milliseconds (1/1000th second) the spark is established across the spark plug gap.

SSI Solid State Ignition used on some Ford and American Motors vehicles.

STATOR another name for a pick-up coil. See pick-up coil for definition.

SWITCHING TRANSISTOR used in some electronic ignition systems, it acts as a switch for high current in response to a low voltage signal applied to the base terminal.

TAB Thermactor air bypass solenoid.

TAD Thermactor air diverter solenoid.

THERMISTOR a device that changes its resistance with temperature.

THICK FILM INTEGRATED (TFI) used by Ford to describe their integrated ignition module electronic ignition system.

TK or TKS throttle kicker solenoid. An actuator moves the throttle linkage to increase idle rpm.

TPS Throttle Position Sensor.

TRANSDUCER a device used to change a force into an electrical signal. Used in the Chrysler electronic spark advance system as the vacuum transducer, throttle position transducer to input a voltage to the spark command computer relating the engine vacuum and throttle position.

TRANSISTOR a semi-conductor component which can be actuated by a small voltage to perform an electrical switching function.

TRIGGER WHEEL see Reluctor for definition.

VOLT the unit of electrical pressure or electromotive force.

VOLTAGE DROP the difference in voltage between one point in a circuit and another, usually across a resistance. Voltage drop is measured in parallel with current flowing in the circuit.

VOLTMETER electrical meter used to measure voltage in a circuit. Voltmeters must be connected in parallel across the load or circuit.

VREF The reference voltage or power supplied by the computer control unit to some sensors regulated at a specific voltage.